3RD EDITION

FINANCIAL ACCOUNTING
IN AN ECONOMIC CONTEXT

JAMIE PRATT
Professor of Accounting
Price Waterhouse Fellow
Indiana University, Bloomington

SOUTH-WESTERN College Publishing

An International Thomson Publishing Company

Accounting Team Director: Mary H. Draper
Sponsoring Editor: David L. Shaut
Marketing Manager: Sharon Oblinger
Developmental Editor: Mignon D. Worman
Production Editor: Mark D. Sears
Production House: Litten Editing and Production with The Beacon Group
Cover and Internal Designer: Craig LaGesse Ramsdell
Photo Researcher: Ruth Kimmel
Cover photo acknowledgments:
    Man presenting: © Frank Herholdt/ Tony Stone Worldwide
    New York Stock Exchange: © W. Baeuerle/PhotoPaq
    Exxon shareholders meeting: © Arthur Grace/Stock Boston
    Office building: © NationsBank
    Women discussing: © Frank Herholdt/Tony Stone Worldwide
Internal photo acknowledgments: © Arthur Grace/Stock Boston (page 1); © Yvonne Hemsey/Liaison (page 75);
    © Neil Selkirk/Tony Stone Images (page 257); © E. A. McGee/FPG International (page 473);
    © Brad Market/Liaison (page 641).

I ⓣ P

International Thomson Publishing
South-Western Publishing Co. is an ITP Company.
The ITP trademark is used under license.

Library of Congress Cataloging-in-Publication Data

Pratt, Jamie.
    Financial accounting : in an economic context / Jamie Pratt. -- 3rd ed.
      p.   cm.
    Includes index.
    ISBN 0-538-85584-3
    1. Accounting.   I. Title.
HF5635.P916   1996
657--dc20
                                               96-20344
                                               CIP

3 4 5 6 7 8 D 3 2 1 0 9 8

Printed in the United States of America

PREFACE

From the very first edition published in 1989, this text has personified the concepts, perspectives, and recommendations of the Accounting Education Change Commission (AECC). Largely for this reason, the first and second editions have become an important part of the curricula at a large and impressive group of forward-thinking schools. The third edition is even better. It builds upon the strengths of previous editions while introducing new ideas and perspectives that better communicate its economic decision-making theme. Many texts claim to reflect the philosophy of the AECC, but only this one has done so for three editions. *Financial Accounting in an Economic Context* has truly played a pioneering role in the evolution of accounting education throughout the world.

THE APPROACH REMAINS THE SAME

The first two editions took a decision-making perspective and balanced the coverage of three important themes: economic factors, measurement issues, and mechanics. The third edition maintains and improves upon this approach.

ECONOMIC FACTORS

Financial accounting is meaningless without an understanding of the economic environment in which it exists. Each chapter in the third edition, therefore, includes frequent references to actual events and companies; quotes from well-known business publications and corporate annual reports; information about industry practices, debt covenants, compensation arrangements, and debt and equity markets; and in-depth discussions of legal liability, ethical issues, and management's incentives and influence on financial reports. The annual report of MCI, which is the subject of short case questions at the end of each chapter, is also provided at the end of the text. Further, ratio analysis and international issues are introduced early and integrated throughout the text, and the coverage still reflects a strong user orientation with a distinct "quality and persistence of earnings" flavor. The important role of the economic environment in this text makes it more than simply a study of financial accounting. It is a study of modern business management as seen through the financial accounting process.

MEASUREMENT ISSUES

Students, as future managers and users, must understand the measurement issues underlying the financial statements before they can interpret and meaningfully use them. The third edition devotes considerable attention to the conceptual and theoretical foundation of financial accounting measurement, with special emphasis on how the financial statements provide useful measures of solvency and earning power. Cash and accrual statements are treated as equally important, with the statement of cash flows being covered from the very beginning. Chapter 4 provides a framework for accounting measurement that is used throughout the remainder of the text.

MECHANICS

Using financial statements without understanding the underlying mechanics is like trying to interpret a foreign language without knowing the vocabulary. Consequently, the third edition provides a strong mechanical foundation and stresses mechanics early and throughout the text. Journal entries and T-accounts play an important role, but they are never treated as a goal. Rather, they are characterized as an efficient way to communicate how economic events are reflected on the financial statements. A special coding is used throughout the text to link the form of each entry to the basic accounting equation and financial statements. Thorough mechanical coverage is especially important in a text that takes a user orientation, because effective users must be able to infer transactions from the financial statements. This mechanical skill, referred to as *reverse T-account analysis*, is covered several times in the text, and many exercises and problems are designed to test it.

DECISION-MAKING PERSPECTIVE

This text presents financial accounting in a way that helps managers make decisions—a decision-making perspective. At a fundamental level, managers make two kinds of decisions: attracting capital and investing capital. Simply put, managers must attract capital from debt and equity investors and then invest it in operations, producing assets, and investment securities. As depicted in Figure P–1, these two kinds of decisions can be matched with the three themes discussed above (mechanics, measurement issues, and economic factors) to produce six basic questions that must be answered by managers who use financial accounting information when making decisions.

A decision-making perspective

	Management Decisions	
	Attract Capital	**Invest Capital**
Mechanics	**1** How do the transactions affect the financial statements?	**4** How are financial ratios computed and how can transactions be inferred from the financial statements?
Measurement Theory	**2** How do these financial statement effects influence outside perceptions of the company's earning power and solvency?	**5** How do the financial statements and ratios indicate a firm's solvency and earning power?
Economics	**3** How do these financial statement effects influence decisions of outsiders as well as debt and compensation contracts?	**6** What action should be taken (invest, extend credit, adjust loan terms)?

In their effort to attract capital, managers must address three questions when considering whether to enter into certain transactions: How do the transactions affect the financial statements? (cell 1) How do these financial statement effects influence outside perceptions of the company's earning power and solvency? (cell 2) and How do these financial statement effects influence the decisions of outsiders as well as debt and compensation contracts? (cell 3) These questions must be answered if management is to understand the economic consequences of the transactions under consideration.

In their effort to invest capital, managers must address three different questions: How are financial ratios computed and how can transactions be inferred from the financial statements? (cell 4) How do the financial statements and ratios indicate a firm's solvency and earning power? (cell 5) and What action should be taken (e.g., invest, extend credit, adjust loan terms)? (cell 6) These questions must be answered if management is to understand how to use financial accounting information properly.

The decision-making perspective simply means that all six questions are addressed in this text. These are the areas where management decision-making intersects with financial accounting information or, in other words, this is what managers need to know about financial accounting. It is this perspective that makes *Financial Accounting in an Economic Context* different from all other texts.

CHANGING THE WAY STUDENTS LEARN: NEW TO THIS EDITION

The changes to this edition were guided by an impressive and creative group of instructors at over thirty business schools. Overwhelmingly and not surprisingly, these instructors confirmed the approach but also offered excellent insight regarding the topic coverage and end-of-chapter materials that would aid them in teaching the first course in accounting. In response, not only was the text restructured but new problems, exercises, cases, and other features were created to support a stronger decision-making perspective.

TEXT REORGANIZATION: EMPHASIS ON DECISION MAKING AND FLEXIBILITY

No consensus exists as to the proper ordering of topics for the first course in financial accounting. The reorganization, therefore, is designed to bolster the decision-making perspective and allow instructors to implement it in a way that matches their preferences, teaching styles, and views.

Using Financial Information. Both using financial statement information (Chapter 15 in the previous edition) and the appendix covering analyzing financial statements (Appendix C in the previous edition) now make up Chapter 3. This change more efficiently covers this material and establishes a strong decision-making perspective early in the text.

Measurement. Measurement fundamentals of financial accounting (Chapter 5 in the previous edition) are now covered in Chapter 4, and the appendix covering the time value of money (Appendix A in the previous edition) is now Appendix 4A. This change brings together present value concepts and the chapter on measurement fundamentals, where present value is first used. It also ensures that students understand present value, an important management decision-making concept, early in the course.

Mechanics. The mechanics of financial accounting (Chapters 3 and 4 in the previous edition) is now covered in Chapter 5. Detailed coverage of the accounting cycle is included as Appendix 5A. The material is covered more efficiently, and the instructor can now more easily choose whether to cover the accounting cycle. A section covering reverse T-account analysis, an important user skill, has also been added as Appendix 5B.

Accruals and Cash Flows. Converting accruals to cash flows (Appendix 4A in the previous edition) is now Appendix A at the end of the text. This change allows instructors to cover this material, which includes the indirect method of presenting the statement of cash flows, at any time during the course.

Flexible Modules. Chapters 3 (Using Financial Statement Information), 4 (The Measurement Fundamentals of Financial Accounting), and 5 (The Mechanics of Financial Accounting) have been written so that they can be covered in any order. This modular structure adds an important dimension of flexibility to the text.

INNOVATIVE PEDAGOGY AND SUPPORTING END-OF-CHAPTER MATERIALS

Reverse T-account Analysis. New to this edition is a user-oriented, analytical skill called reverse T-account analysis. It is first covered in Appendix 5B, but it is also discussed and illustrated in Appendix A at the end of the text and Chapter 14. This material shows students how to derive transactions from the financial statements by analyzing changes in the balance sheet T-accounts. Much of the end-of-chapter material is devoted to developing this skill, enabling students to become more astute users of financial statements.

Ratio Analysis. As indicated above, Chapter 3 is now a stand-alone chapter covering ratio analysis and the use of financial information. This puts the decision-making perspective of the text right up front, and as in the previous edition, ratios are integrated throughout the text starting with Chapter 1.

Ethics Vignettes. Each chapter closes with a short business scenario that introduces an ethical issue related to the material covered in the chapter. Several questions follow each scenario designed to encourage meaningful discussion between students and instructors. While this coverage does not resolve major ethical dilemmas, it works in conjunction with the ethical discussion already in the text to highlight ethical accounting issues that must be faced by managers. These vignettes also address our social responsibility to encourage ethical behavior in students—helping them to recognize and respond to ethical questions raised in future business situations.

Spreadsheet Exercise. Appendix B at the end of the text contains a case that requires students to build a financial accounting simulation model using a spreadsheet program. The case includes ten cumulative exercises that can be assigned at different time periods throughout the course. The students are first shown how to program a simple model that links environmental factors, management decisions, and accounting choices to financial statements projected over a two-year period. They are then asked to use the model to answer a few simple "what if" questions. Subsequent exercises require students to add different features to the program, using the enhanced model to assess the effects of various economic factors, management decisions, and accounting methods on future earnings and cash flows. Gradually, the exercises increase the realism and usefulness of the model, and by the tenth exercise the students have built a reasonably complete simulation program. This exercise has been successfully class-tested in a number of different settings and represents an excellent way to meaningfully integrate the computer into a financial accounting course. It provides a modern, creative, and useful way to drill students on the mechanics of the financial accounting process.

"Quality of Earnings" Cases. Placed after Chapters 8 and 14 are quality of earnings cases that require students to analyze a complete set of financial statements and footnotes. In each case management has used its discretion in a variety of ways to "slant" the reports, and the students must discover how it was done and how the reported dollar amounts should be adjusted to better represent the company's financial performance and condition. These cases have been class-tested in many settings and provide an excellent vehicle for covering the use of financial information in a way that involves more than simply computing financial ratios. Not only must the ratios be calculated, but they must be interpreted in terms of how they relate to each other as well as to the footnotes.

End-of-Chapter Materials. The end-of-chapter materials (questions, exercises, problems, and cases) in the third edition differ from the second in three ways: (1) many have been revised to more closely reflect the decision-making perspective, (2) the quantity has been increased, especially the exercises and cases, and (3) a much larger number of exercises and problems require the student to perform reverse T-account analysis.

Reduced Length. The length of the overall text has been reduced considerably, tightening the organization and streamlining the presentation. The repetition and much of the technical bookkeeping detail was eliminated by restructuring certain chapters and appendices. The total number of chapters is now fourteen, instead of fifteen.

SECOND EDITION FEATURES RETAINED

INTERNATIONAL COVERAGE

In the first edition, international issues were covered in a separate chapter. In the second edition, international issues were incorporated into all chapters of the text, consistent with my belief that they are not independent but should be integrated into all areas of financial accounting. The third edition updated these end-of-chapter discussions of timely, relevant, and important international issues. These sections encourage students to think more broadly about global business issues and how they relate to accounting.

REAL-WORLD FEATURES

The economic perspective followed in this text requires that the material be up to date and reflect important contemporary economic issues. Several text features were meaningfully designed for this purpose. The third edition contains updated journal references to these issues.

INDUSTRY DATA

Many of the chapters contain tables that compare accounting practices and show students the importance of accounting numbers and ratios across different industries and well-known companies. Updated in the third edition, these tables illustrate that the financial accounting issues faced by retailers, manufacturers, service enterprises, and financial institutions are quite different. A brief explanation of the operations of companies in different industries and how these operations give rise to different financial accounting concerns follows each table.

EXCERPTS FROM BUSINESS PUBLICATIONS AND PROFESSIONAL JOURNALS

Over 10,000 references from various business publications (*The Wall Street Journal, Forbes*, and other professional and academic journals) are integrated throughout the text. Updated to reflect the most recent developments, these references document and clarify important chapter concepts and introduce students to information sources that will be useful to them in their business careers.

MCI COMMUNICATIONS, INC., ANNUAL REPORT

The 1994 annual report of MCI Communications, Inc., appears in Appendix C at the end of the text. In addition to being referenced periodically throughout the text, each chapter contains an end-of-chapter case that requires students to relate the report to accounting issues covered in the chapter.

COMPANY INDEX

An index of actual companies has been provided to facilitate referencing specific companies. Over 900 references, current and data-based, are made throughout the text to real companies. These references help students tie in accounting concepts with readily recognizable companies.

END-OF-CHAPTER MATERIALS

Learning Objectives and Chapter Summaries. Each chapter is preceded by a list of learning objectives designed to highlight the important issues in the chapter. In the third edition, learning objectives are highlighted in the margins next to the relevant chapter discussions. The chapter summary restates the learning objectives and includes a summary answer of each, providing both a concise statement of the basic issues addressed by each objective and an efficient summary of the chapter material.

Key Terms and Glossary. An important objective of this course is to establish an understanding of the relevant terminology. The important terms in each chapter are printed in bold-face type when they are first defined in the text. A list of these terms appears at the end of each chapter, and a glossary of key terms is provided in the back of the text.

Questions, Exercises, Problems, and Cases. The review material at the end of each chapter is comprehensive and complete. An average of twenty-five questions, which follow the order of topics covered in the text to provide a systematic review of the chapter material, are provided at the end of each chapter.

Chapters typically contain fifteen to twenty exercises and fifteen to twenty problems. The exercises are relatively simple and require fewer and less complicated computations than do the problems. Each chapter is also followed by at least five cases. As mentioned earlier, Chapters 8 and 14 are followed by a set of comprehensive review cases designed to prepare students for mid-terms and finals.

SUPPLEMENTS

STUDENT LEARNING AIDS—PRINTWARE

Study Guide. Prepared by Joseph H. Anthony, Michigan State University, and Robin Clement, Tulane University. Designed to have a conceptual flavor that complements the text, this invaluable study aid includes for each chapter: (1) a review of key concepts and (2) a set of practice questions and exercises to enhance learning. This approach highlights important concepts and relations introduced in the text.

STUDENT LEARNING AIDS—MULTIMEDIA

Financial Accounting Simulation Analysis. Developed by Jamie Pratt and Mike Groomer to be used on either Lotus 1-2-3 or Excel, this flexible simulation provides the students with the ultimate form of role playing. Step-by-step instructions allow the student to build a set of financial statements and assess the effects of a variety of managerial, operating, investing, financing, and reporting decisions on these statements and related financial ratios over a three-year period. The decisions include (1) issuing stock and long-term debt under various terms, (2) purchasing and selling marketable securities, inventory, land, and equipment at various prices, (3) selling goods at various prices, (4) declaring cash and stock dividends, (5) employing different collection and payment strategies, and (6) choosing from among different methods of accounting for uncollectibles, inventory, depreciation, and amortizing debt premiums and discounts. This unique simulation will bring to life the economic consequences of financial accounting.

Rama: Introduction to the Accounting Cycle (A Computer-Aided Instruction). This self-directed tutorial gives students additional instruction on the intricacies of the accounting cycle.

SUPPLEMENTS FOR THE INSTRUCTOR—PRINTWARE

Instructor's Manual. Prepared by Donald Loster, University of California-Santa Barbara. This instructor's resource includes suggested syllabi for courses for various lengths and approaches. New to this edition is an AECC chart which correlates selected end-of-chapter materials to a skill development recommended by the AECC. Each chapter includes a synopsis that highlights general chapter topics; chapter learning objectives; a list of key terms; a text/lecture outline that summarizes the chapter in detail; lecture tips for areas in which students commonly have difficulty; an annotated bibliography relevant to chapter topics; answers to chapter questions; and an assignment classification table on relating chapter learning objectives for each exercise and problem. The manual also contains a checklist of key figures.

Test Bank. Prepared by Steven Reimer, University of Iowa. Because many of you want a microcomputer version, the Third Edition will include an expanded Test Bank in both printed and microcomputer versions. More than 1,700 questions are categorized by learning objectives and by question orientation (i.e., whether the questions test procedures, measurement concepts, or economic concepts). In the Third Edition, AECC-oriented questions are highlighted throughout the Test Bank.

Solutions Manual. Developed by Parveen Gupta, Lehigh University. This supplement provides complete solutions to all exercises, problems, and cases in the text.

Solutions Transparencies. This package includes 250 acetates that illustrate the solutions to all exercises, problems, and cases in the text.

SUPPLEMENTS FOR THE INSTRUCTOR—MULTIMEDIA AIDS

PowerPoint Presentation Slides. Developed by Glenn Owen, University of California-Santa Barbara. Over 250 lecture slides were prepared exclusively for this text using MicroSoft PowerPoint version 3.0. The major concepts of each chapter are highlighted and supported where appropriate by spreadsheet examples. The instructor may print out transparencies from the diskette for use on overhead projectors as well.

MicroExam 4. MicroExam is a microcomputer test-generation package that consists of test banks on disks and the software necessary to create instructor-customized examinations as well as instructor-created test questions. MicroExam is compatible with IBM PC and other compatible computers.

Interactive CD-ROM Simulation. Developed by Jamie Pratt, Krishnamoorthy Ramesh, and David Foster. Available in Spring 1997. The instructor can assign this set of three cases of progressive difficulty throughout the course. The student simulates the decision-making process of a lender by analyzing industry data, available financial records, and other information provided. Based upon the analysis, the student then recommends whether or not to lend to the requesting company and can print out their recommendations for grading purposes. Instructors are provided with security codes to control the solutions, as desired. Unlike any product on the market, this technology allows the student to immediately apply financial accounting information in a real world context.

ACCOMPANIMENTS TO THE TEXT

Writing, Ethics, and Group Projects for Financial Accounting. Prepared by Bruce Stuart and Iris Stuart, Concordia College. This casebook is designed to accompany the introductory accounting course. Each chapter, topically oriented, provides ethics problems, writing assignments, and group exercises as well as preparer-oriented materials to illustrate distinctive features of business circumstances and professional standards that call for accounting judgments—both technical and moral. This is an excellent supplement for professors desiring a focus on the unique role that accountants play in the business world.

Cases in Financial Accounting. Prepared by John S. Hughes, Duke University. Ideally suited for the introductory-level course in financial accounting, undergraduate or MBA, this book contains 80 brief cases based on excerpts from annual reports of actual companies. Case requirements are both procedural and conceptual. Procedural requirements require working backwards from financial statements to analyses of transactions. Conceptual requirements involve analysis of the rationale and consequences of an accounting treatment.

CUSTOMER SERVICE

Instructors using our products have several options to communicate with South-Western concerning our products and services:

- **E-mail the Author.** The author and South-Western Publishing Company would like your input regarding the features of the third edition. E-mail Jamie Pratt at review@swpco.com.
- **Telephone the Preferred Accounting Customer (PAC) Hotline.** Special benefits and services to assist instructors in course preparation are available through the PAC Hotline. 1-800-342-8798
- **Visit South-Western's World Wide Web Site.** Find out the latest information on South-Western texts, software, multimedia, and other resources, participate in

instructor/author discussions or simply browse our Internet site. To access: http://www.thomson.com/swcp.html

ACKNOWLEDGMENTS

Throughout the development and production of this book, accuracy has been a primary concern. The manuscript was extensively reviewed by accounting faculty from various universities and was also class tested. All exercises, problems, and cases were solved completely by independent reviewers. Alice B. Sineath was especially instrumental in providing a thorough solutions verification. This text benefited significantly from the constructive and insightful comments provided by the individuals listed below. Their painstaking review of the text resulted in suggestions that helped to focus and integrate the ideas presented:

Joseph H. Anthony
Michigan State University

Mary Nisbet
University of California-Santa Barbara

Deborah F. Beard
Southeast Missouri State University

Glenn Owen
University of California-Santa Barbara

Ervin L. Black
University of Washington

Martha Pointer
Eastern Tennessee State University

John J. Cheh
St. Cloud State University

Steven C. Reimer
University of Iowa

Robin C. Clement
Tulane University

Rachel Schwartz
Washington University

David Fetyko
Kent State University

Brian Shapiro
Arizona University

Parveen P. Gupta
Lehigh University

Paul Simko
Emory University

Eric Hirst
University of Texas-Austin

Alice B. Sineath
Forsyth Technical Community College

Richard L. Hodges
Western Michigan University

Karen Smith
Arizona State University

Donald Loster
University of California-Santa Barbara

Donn W. Vickrey
University of San Diego

Mary Lea McAnally
University of Texas-Austin

Stephen D. Willits
Bucknell University

Many other people deserve thanks and recognition for the contributions they have made to this text. I appreciate the efforts of all those who prepared ancillary material.

The editorial, design, and marketing staffs, including Mark Hubble, Mary Draper, Elizabeth Bowers, Mignon Worman, Sharon Oblinger, Mark Sears, Malvine Litten, and Craig Ramsdell, represent a first-rate group of professionals. Their high-quality work helped to ensure that the manuscript was comprehensive, coherent, and completed in a timely and orderly fashion.

Special thanks go to my wife, Kathy, and children, Jason, Ryan, and Dylan. Their support and understanding were consistent throughout the seemingly endless development and production processes. Now that the Third Edition is complete, it will be nice to turn more attention to being a husband and father.

Jamie Pratt

BRIEF CONTENTS

CONTENTS

PART 3
ASSETS: A CLOSER LOOK

PART 4
LIABILITIES AND STOCKHOLDERS' EQUITY: A CLOSER LOOK

AN OVERVIEW OF FINANCIAL ACCOUNTING

CHAPTER 1
FINANCIAL ACCOUNTING AND ITS
ECONOMIC CONTEXT

CHAPTER 2
THE FINANCIAL STATEMENTS

FINANCIAL ACCOUNTING AND ITS ECONOMIC CONTEXT

L E A R N I N G   O B J E C T I V E S

LO 1 Explain the economic role of financial accounting statements and why managers must have both an economic consequence perspective and a user orientation.

LO 2 Briefly describe the contents of the standard audit report, the management letter, and the footnotes to the financial statements.

LO 3 Name the four financial statements, and briefly explain the kind of financial information that each provides.

LO 4 Describe the two basic forms of investment, and explain how the information on the financial statements relates to them.

LO 5 Explain why ethics is important in the accounting process.

LO 6 Describe the Securities and Exchange Commission and the Financial Accounting Standards Board and their respective roles in the development of generally accepted accounting principles.

LO 7 Describe the current status of international accounting practices and standards.

This text covers the **financial accounting** process, which consists of four basic components. Each component is briefly introduced below.

1. **Profit-Seeking Companies**—The financial accounting process is initiated when managers of profit-seeking companies prepare reports containing financial information for the owners of these companies. In addition to other information, these reports contain four basic financial statements: the balance sheet, the income statement, the statement of retained earnings, and the statement of cash flows.

2. **Owners and Other Interested Parties (Users)**—Although prepared primarily for the owners, these financial reports are available to the public and are read by other interested parties, who use them to assess the financial condition and performance of the company as well as the performance of its managers. Such interested parties, called users in this text, include potential investors, bankers, government agencies, and the company's customers and suppliers.

3. **User Decisions**—Users obtain information from the financial reports that helps assess the company's past performance, predict its future performance, and control the activities of its managers. Financial reports, therefore, help users to make better decisions. Investors, for example, use financial reports to choose companies in which to invest their funds; bankers use them to decide where to loan their funds and what interest rates to charge.

4. **Effects of User Decisions**—User decisions affect the financial condition and performance of the company and the economic well-being of its managers. For example, a banker may use the information contained in a financial report to decide not to loan a certain company much-needed funds. Such a decision may cause the company to fail and cost its managers their jobs.

Figure 1–1 illustrates the four basic components of the financial accounting process. Note in particular the dynamic nature of the process: the financial information provided by managers of a profit-seeking company is used by interested parties to make decisions which, in turn, affect a company's financial condition and the

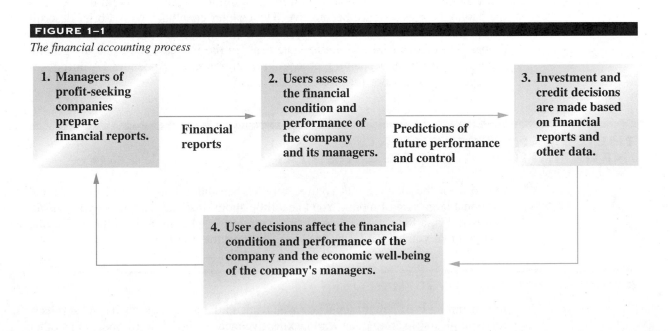

FIGURE 1–1

The financial accounting process

1. Managers of profit-seeking companies prepare financial reports.

Financial reports

2. Users assess the financial condition and performance of the company and its managers.

Predictions of future performance and control

3. Investment and credit decisions are made based on financial reports and other data.

4. User decisions affect the financial condition and performance of the company and the economic well-being of the company's managers.

economic well-being of its managers. Managers need to understand the process depicted in Figure 1–1 from two separate, but related, perspectives:

1. economic consequence perspective, and
2. user orientation.

LO 1 **ECONOMIC CONSEQUENCE PERSPECTIVE.** To run a company effectively, management must be able to attract capital from outsiders who use financial statements to evaluate the company's performance and financial health. Managers apply for loans from bankers, for example, who use the financial statements to determine whether to grant the loan and, if so, what interest rate to charge. Since using financial statements by outsiders leads to economic consequences for managers and the companies they operate (e.g., higher interest rates), it is important that they know how economic events (e.g., business decisions) affect the financial statements. Consider a case where management is deciding to either purchase or rent equipment. When making such a decision, an astute manager would consider how the choice affects the financial statements because it could influence the way in which the company is viewed by outsiders. Considering and understanding how such events affect the financial statements is referred to in this text as an **economic consequence perspective.**

USER ORIENTATION. Managers are also users of financial statements, where they are often called upon to assess the performance and financial health of other companies. Questions like—Should we purchase a company? Should we use a company as a supplier? Should we extend credit or loan funds to a company?—are often answered by analyzing financial statements provided by those companies. Accordingly, managers also need to know how to read, evaluate, and analyze financial statements. We call this perspective a **user orientation**.

The next section adopts a user orientation in that it develops a scenario designed to highlight issues that are particularly important to users of financial statements. That same scenario serves as the basis for further discussion of the environment of financial accounting, followed by a section focusing on management's point-of-view and the economic consequence perspective. The chapter concludes with a brief description of generally accepted accounting principles (GAAP), the standards that guide the preparation of financial accounting statements in the United States, and the general state of the financial accounting process in other countries. Appendix 1A introduces managerial, tax, and not-for-profit accounting.

THE DEMAND FOR FINANCIAL INFORMATION: A USER'S ORIENTATION

Suppose for the moment that you recently learned that a long-lost relative died and left you a large sum of money. You know little about financial matters, so you consult Mary Jordan, a financial advisor, to help you decide what to do with the funds. She tells you that you have two choices: you can consume it or you can invest it.

CONSUMPTION AND INVESTMENT

In consuming your new fortune, you would spend the money on goods and services; for example, a trip around the world, expensive meals, a lavish wardrobe, or any other expenses that bring about immediate gratification. Consumption expenditures, by definition, are enjoyed immediately and have no future value.

In investing the fortune, you would spend the money on items that provide little in the way of immediate gratification. Rather, they generate returns of additional money at later dates. In essence, investments trade off current consumption for more consumption at a later date. Examples include investing in stocks and bonds, real estate, rare art objects, or simply placing the money in the bank.

WHERE TO INVEST?

You decide to invest the money, and with a little direction from Mary, you begin to explore investment alternatives. You find that investments come in a number of different forms, however, and you quickly become overwhelmed, confused, and frustrated. Just as you are about to give up your search and put all your money in the bank, a man by the name of Martin Wagner knocks at your door. Through a mutual friend, Martin has heard of your recent windfall and states that he has an interesting offer for you.

Martin claims that he manages a very successful research company, called Microline, owned by a group of European investors. In its short, two-year history the company has earned a reputation for innovation in software development. As Martin describes it, Microline's research staff is on the verge of designing a voice-activated word-processing system that will revolutionize word-processing in the future.

Martin has come to you for capital, $1 million to be exact. The company's research and development efforts have run short of funds, and money is still needed to complete the design. With your money, Martin asserts that the software system can be completed and sold, producing millions of dollars of income, some of which will provide you with a handsome return on your investment. Without your capital, on the other hand, Martin believes that the project may have to be abandoned.

THE DEMAND FOR DOCUMENTATION

You have listened to Martin's story and now must decide what to do. Your first thought is that you cannot simply accept his word without some documented evidence. How do you really know that he has successfully managed this business for the past two years and that $1 million will enable the company to turn this design into a fortune in the future?

After careful consideration, you decide that you need to see some proof before making a final decision. You ask specifically for documents to show that Microline has been run successfully for the past two years, is presently in reasonably good financial condition, and has the potential to generate income of the magnitude Martin suggests. He agrees to provide you with such documentation because he knows that if he does not, you will invest your money elsewhere, and both he and Microline will suffer.

Several days later Martin returns with a set of financial statements prepared by Microline's accountants. He explains the meanings of the numbers on the statements and further claims that the records at his office can be used to verify them. Taken at face value, the figures look promising, but somehow Martin's explanation is not convincing. It occurs to you that Martin might fabricate or at least bias the figures. After all, Microline needs money, and who would blame Martin for showing you only the figures that make Microline's situation look attractive to a potential investor?

THE DEMAND FOR AN INDEPENDENT AUDIT

You require that Martin go one step further: he must return again with financial statements that have been checked and verified by an independent outsider who is an expert in such matters. You insist that the person not be employed by Microline or have any interest whatsoever in the company and have the appropriate credentials to perform such a task. In essence, you demand that Martin hire a **certified public accountant (CPA)** to verify Microline's financial statements. You require, in other words, that Microline subject itself to an **independent audit**. Martin agrees because, once again, if he does not, you will take your money and invest it elsewhere. At the same time, however, Martin is somewhat troubled. He knows that hiring and working with a CPA can be very costly and time-consuming.

MARTIN AND THE CPA: DIFFERENT PERSPECTIVES

Time passes and you become concerned that Martin has taken too long to return with the financial statements. You have thought of several questions since Martin's last visit and decide to call on him in person. You arrive at Microline's office and are seated by Martin's secretary. While you are waiting, you hear Martin's voice through the partly open door to his office. He seems to be discussing Microline's financial statements with the CPA. While you cannot understand exactly what is being said, it is clear that they are not in complete agreement and that they are both strong in their convictions.

You wonder why Martin and the CPA might view the financial statements from different perspectives and speculate that perhaps the CPA recommended presenting Microline's financial condition in a way that was unsatisfactory to Martin. You reason that Martin should probably follow the CPA's recommendation because, after all, the CPA is the expert in financial reporting. You realize, however, that Martin wants the statements to be as attractive as possible and that he may have some influence over the CPA. Indeed, Martin did hire the CPA and does pay the CPA's fee.

Before long, the CPA leaves and Martin invites you into his office. During your short discussion, you mention nothing of what you think you have heard. Martin answers your questions confidently and assures you that the statements will be ready within the week. Satisfied, you return home.

THE AUDITOR'S REPORT, THE MANAGEMENT LETTER, AND THE FINANCIAL STATEMENTS

L O 2 Martin arrives at your home with seven official-looking documents: (1) an **auditor's report**, a short letter written by the auditor that describes the activities of the audit and comments on the financial position and operations of Microline, (2) a **management letter**, signed by Martin, which accepts responsibility for the figures on the statements, (3) a balance sheet, (4) an income statement, (5) a statement of retained earnings, (6) a statement of cash flows, and

(7) a comprehensive set of footnotes, which more fully explain certain items on the four statements listed above. You briefly review the documents and tell Martin that you will have a decision for him soon.

THE AUDITOR'S REPORT

You begin your examination by reviewing the auditor's report, from which you hope to learn how credible the financial statements actually are (see Figure 1–2).

Overall, you are reassured by the auditor's report. It indicates that the auditor reviewed Microline's records thoroughly and concluded that the statements (1) were prepared in conformity with generally accepted accounting principles and (2) present fairly Microline's financial condition and operations. You suspect that the auditor could have rendered a much less favorable report, such as that the statements were not prepared in conformance with generally accepted accounting principles, or that no opinion could be reached because Microline's accounting system was so poorly designed, or that Microline was in danger of failure. You also realize, however, that you know very little about either generally accepted auditing standards or generally accepted accounting principles, and that Microline's management made a number of significant estimates when preparing the statements. This discovery is somewhat troubling because, even with the audit, it seems that Microline's management may have had some subjective influence on the financial statements.

FIGURE 1–2	
The standard audit report	**To the Board of Directors and Shareholders of Microline:** **We have audited the accompanying balance sheet of Microline as of December 31, 1996 and 1995, and the related statements of income, retained earnings, and cash flows for the years then ended. These financial statements are the responsibility of the Company's management. Our responsibility is to express an opinion on these financial statements based on our audit.** **We conducted our audit in accordance with generally accepted auditing standards. Those standards require that we plan and perform the audit to obtain reasonable assurance about whether the financial statements are free of material misstatement. An audit includes examining, on a test basis, evidence supporting the amounts and disclosures in the financial statements. An audit also includes assessing the accounting principles used and significant estimates made by management, as well as evaluating the overall financial statement presentation. We believe that our audit provides a reasonable basis for our opinion.** **In our opinion, the financial statements referred to above present fairly, in all material respects, the financial position of Microline as of December 31, 1996 and 1995, and the results of its operations and its cash flows for the years then ended, in conformity with generally accepted accounting principles.** *Arthur Price* **Arthur Price, Certified Public Accountant** **March 12, 1997**

THE MANAGEMENT LETTER

You next move to the management letter, hoping to learn more about how the financial statements were prepared and audited (see Figure 1–3).

Once again, you are both reassured and troubled. It is comforting to know that Microline's management is accepting responsibility for the integrity of the statements,

FIGURE 1–3	**Management's Responsibilities:**
Management's letter	Management is responsible for the preparation and integrity of the financial statements and the financial comments appearing in this financial report. The financial statements were prepared in accordance with generally accepted accounting principles and include certain amounts based on management's best estimates and judgments. Other financial information presented in this financial report is consistent with the financial statements.

The Company maintains a system of internal controls designed to provide reasonable assurance that the assets are safeguarded and that transactions are executed as authorized and are recorded and reported properly. The system of controls is based upon written policies and procedures, appropriate division of responsibility and authority, careful selection and training of personnel, and a comprehensive internal audit program. The Company's policies and procedures prescribe that the Company and all employees are to maintain the highest ethical standards and that its business practices are to be conducted in a manner which is above reproach.

Arthur Price, an independent certified public accountant, has examined the Company's financial statements, and the audit report is present herein. The Board of Directors has an Audit Committee composed entirely of outside directors. Arthur Price has direct access to the Audit Committee and meets with the committee to discuss accounting, auditing, and financial reporting matters.

Martin Wagner

Martin Wagner, Chief Executive Officer
March 12, 1997

which have been prepared in conformance with generally accepted accounting principles, and that the company has an **internal control system** that safeguards the assets and reasonably ensures that transactions are properly recorded and reported. It is also nice to know that Microline's policies prescribe that its employees maintain high ethical standards. However, you still do not understand generally accepted accounting principles, are still concerned that the statements reflect management's estimates and judgments, and have very little idea about the function of Microline's Board of Directors and Audit Committee.

THE FINANCIAL STATEMENTS

You briefly review the four financial statements (see Figure 1–4) and note first that dollar amounts are listed for both 1996 and 1995. This discovery is somewhat discouraging because only information about the past is included on the statements and subject to the auditor's report and management letter. Nothing about Microline's future prospects is included in the financial statements—but the future is what interests you most. Whether Microline is able to provide an acceptable return on your $1 million investment depends primarily on what happens in the future. The past is often a poor indicator of the future.

You also observe that each statement emphasizes a different aspect of Microline's financial condition and performance. The balance sheet, for example, lists the company's assets, liabilities, and stockholders' equity. On the income statement, expenses are subtracted from revenues to produce a number called net income. The statement of retained earnings includes (1) the beginning and ending retained earnings balance, which can be found on the 1995 and 1996 balance sheets, (2) net income, which is the bottom line on the income statement, and (3) dividends. The statement of cash flows

FIGURE 1–4	MICROLINE FINANCIAL STATEMENTS FOR THE YEARS ENDED DECEMBER 31, 1996 AND 1995		
Financial statements for Microline		**1996**	**1995**
	BALANCE SHEET		
	ASSETS		
	Cash	$ 100,000	$ 60,000
	Accounts receivable	80,000	90,000
	Equipment	330,000	300,000
	Land	500,000	500,000
	Total assets	$1,010,000	$ 950,000
	LIABILITIES AND STOCKHOLDERS' EQUITY		
	Short-term payables	$ 50,000	$ 30,000
	Long-term payables	420,000	450,000
	Common stock	400,000	400,000
	Retained earnings	140,000	70,000
	Total liabilities and stockholders' equity	$1,010,000	$ 950,000
	INCOME STATEMENT		
	Revenues	$1,650,000	$1,500,000
	Expenses	1,450,000	1,350,000
	Net income	$ 200,000	$ 150,000
	STATEMENT OF RETAINED EARNINGS		
	Beginning retained earnings balance	$ 70,000	$ 0
	Plus: Net income	200,000	150,000
	Less: Dividends	130,000	80,000
	Ending retained earnings balance	$ 140,000	$ 70,000
	STATEMENT OF CASH FLOWS		
	Net cash flow from operating activities	$ 250,000	$ 120,000
	Net cash flow from investing activities	(50,000)	(340,000)
	Net cash flow from financing activities	(160,000)	280,000
	Net increase (decrease) in cash	$ 40,000	$ 60,000
	Beginning cash balance	60,000	0
	Ending cash balance	$ 100,000	$ 60,000

includes the beginning and ending balance of cash, which can be found on the 1995 and 1996 balance sheets, and net cash flows from operating, investing, and financing activities. It becomes clear quite quickly that you do not understand these terms, that you know very little about the information conveyed by these statements and, therefore, cannot begin to assess whether Microline would be a good company in which to invest.

THE FOOTNOTES

At this point you decide to examine the **footnotes**, hoping that they will clear up some of your uncertainty about the financial statements (Figure 1–5). They state that many of the numbers on the statements are the result of assumptions and estimates made by Microline's management, which does not surprise you because similar statements were made in both the audit report and the management letter. It is also clear from

Cash. Cash consists of cash on hand and cash in a bank checking account.

Accounts Receivable. The balance in accounts receivable has been adjusted for an estimate of future uncollectibles.

Equipment. Equipment is carried at a cost and includes expenditures for new additions and those which substantially increase its useful life. The cost of the equipment is depreciated using the straight-line method over an estimated useful life of ten years.

Land. Land is carried at cost.

Short-Term Payables. Short-term payables consist of wages payable, short-term borrowings, interest payable, taxes payable, and an estimate of future warranty costs.

Long-Term Payables. Long-term payables consist primarily of notes that must be paid back after one year.

Common Stock. Common stock represents the contributions of the company's stockholders.

Revenue Recognition. Revenues from sales are reflected in the income statement when products are shipped. Revenues from services are estimated in proportion to the completion of the service.

Expenses. Expenses include selling and administrative expenses and estimates of uncollectible receivables and depreciation on the equipment.

the footnotes that Microline was able to choose from a number of different acceptable accounting methods. While you know little about generally accepted accounting principles, you confidently conclude that they do not ensure exact and unbiased statements. Alternative accounting methods as well as assumptions and estimates by Microline's management are very evident.

After your initial examination you decide that Microline may be a reasonable investment, but your lack of knowledge renders you incapable of making a confident choice. You decide to return to Mary Jordan, your financial advisor, for help. Perhaps she can explain the nature of the financial statements and improve your understanding of the decision that faces you.

THE FINANCIAL STATEMENTS: DEFINITIONS AND PRELIMINARY ANALYSIS

 Mary begins by defining some of the fundamental terms used on the financial statements.

BALANCE SHEET

The **balance sheet**, which lists Microline's assets, liabilities, and stockholders' equity, is a statement of the company's financial position as of a certain date. **Assets** include Microline's cash balance, the dollar amounts due from Microline's customers (accounts receivable), and the original cost of the equipment and land purchased by the company. **Liabilities** consist of the amounts presently owed by Microline to its **creditors**. Satisfying these liabilities will generally require cash payments in the future. Common stock and retained earnings comprise the **stockholders' equity** section. **Common stock** represents the initial investments by Microline's owners, and

retained earnings is a measure of Microline's past profits that have been retained in the business.

INCOME STATEMENT

The **income statement** is divided into two components: **revenues**, a measure of the assets generated from the products and services sold, and **expenses**, a measure of the asset outflows (costs) associated with selling these products and services. The difference between these two amounts is a number called **net income (profit)**, which measures the success of Microline's operations over a particular period of time.

STATEMENT OF RETAINED EARNINGS

The **statement of retained earnings** describes the increases and decreases to retained earnings, which is a measure of Microline's past profits. The net income or profit amount from the income statement is first added to the beginning balance of retained earnings. **Dividends**, the assets paid to Microline's owners as a return for their initial investment, are then subtracted from this amount to compute ending retained earnings. The ending retained earnings amount appears on the balance sheet and becomes the beginning balance of the following period.

STATEMENT OF CASH FLOWS

The **statement of cash flows** summarizes the increases and decreases in cash over a period of time. The beginning cash balance is adjusted for the *net cash flows* (cash inflows less cash outflows) associated with Microline's operating, investing, and financing activities. **Operating activities** are associated with the actual products and services provided by Microline for its customers. **Investing activities** include the purchase and sale of assets, such as equipment and land. **Financing activities** refers to the cash collections and payments related to Microline's *capital sources*. Examples include cash borrowings and loan payments as well as collections from owners' contributions and the payment of dividends.

After defining the terms on the financial statements, Mary notes that Microline appears to be in reasonably strong financial shape. She focuses first on the statement of cash flows, pointing out that the company's cash position has been increasing and that operating activities have contributed $120,000 and $250,000 in cash in the last two years. She also notes that Microline has invested heavily in new assets since its inception and that $160,000 was paid during 1996 for dividends and to reduce outstanding debts. In short, Microline has demonstrated the ability to generate cash. Mary believes this is very important, because in order to remain solvent, the company must be able to generate enough cash to meet its debts as they come due. She comments that **solvency** is a requirement for financial health.

Mary then moves to the income statement and statement of retained earnings, noting that Microline has shown profits of $150,000 and $200,000 over the past two years and, at the same time, has paid significant dividends to its owners, specifically $80,000 in 1995 and $130,000 in 1996. These numbers show that Microline has demonstrated **earning power**, the ability to grow and provide a substantial return to its owners. Mary also notes that the balance sheets indicate Microline's assets have increased during the past year from $950,000 to $1,010,000, while its liabilities (payables) have decreased from $480,000 to $470,000. She indicates that such a trend is promising.

To further support Microline's financial strength Mary computes a few ratios using the dollar values on the income statement and balance sheet. She points out that net income as a percentage of revenues increased from 10 percent ($150,000/$1,500,000) in 1995 to over 12 percent ($200,000/$1,650,000) in 1996; total payables as a percent of total assets decreased from over 50 percent ($480,000/$950,000) in 1995 to less than 47 percent ($470,000/ $1,010,000) in 1996; and dividends as a percent of net income increased substantially over the two-year period—to 65 percent. After consulting some statistics covering the industry in which Microline is a member, Mary reports that Microline's financial ratios, in general, are stronger than those of many other similar firms.

WHAT FORM OF INVESTMENT: DEBT OR EQUITY?

LO 4 The definitions and analysis provided by Mary are encouraging, and you decide that Microline is a good investment. However, Mary states that now you must decide what form your investment should take. Should it be in the form of a loan, or should you purchase ownership (equity) in Microline? She explains that the risks you face and the potential returns associated with these two forms of investment are really quite different. Moreover, the relative importance to you of the different kinds of information disclosed on the financial statements depends on the kind of investment you make.

A DEBT INVESTMENT

You would make a **debt investment** if you loaned the $1 million to Microline. You would then become one of the company's creditors and would require that Microline's management sign a **loan contract**, specifying (1) the *maturity date*, the date when the loan is to be paid back; (2) the **annual interest** payment, the amount of interest to be paid each year; (3) *collateral*, assets to be passed to you in case the principal or the interest on the loan is in *default* (not paid back); and (4) any other **debt restrictions** you feel you should impose on Microline to protect your investment. The contract might specify, for example, that Microline maintain a certain cash balance throughout the period of the loan or that dividends during that period be limited.

As one of Microline's creditors, your first concern would be Microline's ability to meet the loan's interest and principal payments as they come due. Since such payments are made in cash, you would be especially interested in Microline's cash management record and its ability to generate cash over the period of the loan. Thus, the information in the statement of cash flows would be very relevant. You would also be interested in the selling prices of assets that could be used as collateral and in the amounts of the loans and other liabilities owed by Microline to other creditors. The balance sheet, therefore, which lists Microline's assets and liabilities, would also contain some useful information.

Mary reminds you, however, that many of Microline's assets are valued on the balance sheet at **historical cost**, the dollar amount paid when the assets were acquired, which, in many cases, was two years ago. This discovery is worrisome, because the historical cost of an asset is rarely the same as its current selling price, the relevant amount if an asset is to be considered as collateral for the loan.

AN EQUITY INVESTMENT

Rather than loaning Microline the $1 million, you may wish to purchase **equity** in the company. As an equity investor you would become one of the owners, or **stockholders**, of Microline.

Equity investments give rise to considerations that are somewhat different from those of debt investments. As a stockholder, for example, your return would be primarily in the form of dividends, which would tend to be large if Microline performed well and small, or nonexistent, if the company performed poorly. Unlike a loan investment, for which interest and principal payments are specified by contract, dividend payments are at the discretion of Microline's **board of directors**, which is elected annually by the stockholders to represent their interests. Such representation involves quarterly meetings where company policies are set, dividends are declared, and the performance and compensation of the company's upper management is reviewed. The board of directors has the power to hire and fire upper management as well as determine the form and amount of their compensation.

As a stockholder who could vote in the election of the board of directors, your primary concern would be the performance of Microline's management—specifically, its ability to generate and maintain earnings in the future. To achieve such an objective, management must both ensure that cash is available to meet debts as they come due and invest in assets that produce a satisfactory return in the long run. Consequently, stockholders are interested in the information contained in all four of the financial statements: the balance sheet because it indicates Microline's assets and liabilities, the income statement and statement of retained earnings because they indicate Microline's earning power and dividend payments, and the statement of cash flows because it provides a report of Microline's past cash management policies. As a stockholder, however, you would be especially interested in the income statement, since the board of directors often sets dividends as a percentage of income, which is generally considered to be the overall measure of management's performance and the company's earning power.

You would also be interested in the methods used to compensate Microline's upper management. You may wish, for example, to encourage the board of directors to institute a system of compensation that paid upper management on the basis of its performance. One way to implement such a system would be to set compensation levels at amounts expressed as percentages of net income. This would motivate Microline's management to increase net income and, accordingly, their compensation. Such a result should also mean increased earning power and greater dividend payments in the future.

A DECISION IS MADE BUT IMPORTANT QUESTIONS STILL REMAIN

After a lengthy discussion with Mary, you decide to invest in the equity of Microline. From the information contained in the audit report, the management letter, the financial statements, and the footnotes, you have concluded that Microline is a legitimate operation that is solvent, has shown significant earning power, and has provided a reasonable return to its stockholders. You reason further that if Martin is correct in his prediction that their new voice-activated word-processing system will revolutionize the industry, there is a distinct possibility of large returns in the future. Stockholders would receive such returns in the form of larger dividends, while payments to creditors would be limited to the contractual interest and principal payments.

You thank Mary for her advice and feel satisfied with your decision. You realize, however, that the future is uncertain and that your investment involves risks.

THE ENVIRONMENT OF
FINANCIAL ACCOUNTING

Figure 1–6 depicts the financial accounting process in terms of the relationships among providers of capital, managers, and auditors. It is designed to illustrate the main points introduced in the previous scenario where you acted as the capital provider, Martin Wagner and Microline represented the company [manager], and Arthur Price was the auditor. The figure shows that providers of capital, in the form of debt and equity investors, invest in companies operated by managers with the expectation of receiving interest, principal, and dividend payments in the future. As a condition of these investments, they require that managers provide audited financial information and enter into debt and/or compensation contracts. Financial accounting information helps investors and creditors to evaluate and predict the ability of managers to generate investment returns. It also provides numbers that are used in the debt and compensation contracts, which serve to protect the providers of capital by enabling them to exert control over the manager's activities. Note also that managers and auditors are guided by their professional reputations and ethics (the use of their specialized skill for the benefit of others) as well as the threat of legal liability. At the same time, auditors are in the ironic position of having a reporting responsibility to capital providers while their fees are paid by managers whose financial statements are being audited. Such conflicting goals create a tension that is part of everyday auditing. In the remainder of this section we provide more complete descriptions for each of the components in Figure 1–6.

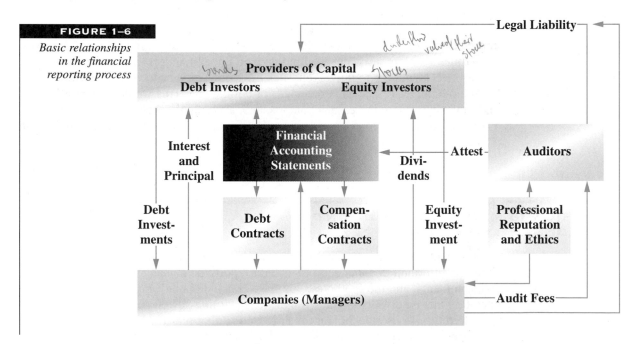

FIGURE 1–6

Basic relationships in the financial reporting process

FINANCIAL ACCOUNTING INFORMATION: MORE
THAN THE FINANCIAL STATEMENTS

Financial accounting information extends beyond that which is contained in the four financial statements, the accompanying footnotes, the auditor's report, and the management letter. For example, **annual reports**, which are published each year by major U.S. companies, and the *Form 10-K*, which must be completed and filed annually with a government agency by companies whose securities are traded on the major U.S. stock exchanges, contain a wealth of information beyond what is contained in the financial statements alone.

ANNUAL REPORTS

Generally accepted accounting principles, for example, require that annual reports furnished to stockholders include audited balance sheets for the two most recent years and audited statements of income, retained earnings, and cash flows for the three most recent years. GAAP also require the following:

- Selected quarterly information.
- Summaries of selected financial information for the last five years.
- Descriptions of business activities.
- Separate information about each of a company's major segments.
- A listing of the members of the board of directors and the executive officers.
- Market prices of a company's stock for each quarterly period for the two most recent years.
- Management's discussion and analysis of the company's financial condition and results of operations.

The 1994 annual report of MCI is provided in Appendix C at the end of this text. Take a few minutes now to review it, especially the sections mentioned in the preceding paragraph. We refer to this report frequently throughout the remainder of the text.

A VARIETY OF USERS

In addition to a company's stockholders, annual reports are also available to the general public and can be obtained by virtually anyone interested in a company's financial condition and performance. Recall, for example, that management often uses the financial statements of other firms to assess whether to enter into business relationships with these firms. As you probably noticed when you reviewed the MCI annual report, however, financial accounting information can be complex and confusing. Consequently, many interested parties delegate the task of analyzing financial statement information to more knowledgeable representatives. *Financial and security analysts* use financial information to evaluate equity and debt investments for individuals, companies, and other institutions. *Stockbrokers* use it to buy and sell securities for their clients. *Bank loan officers* and *credit analysts* use it when deciding whether to loan money to individuals or businesses.

While investors, creditors, management, and their representatives are the largest group of financial information users, there are many others. Government bodies, like the Federal Trade Commission, often base regulatory decisions on information disclosed in annual reports, and public utilities normally base their rates (the prices they charge their customers) on financial accounting numbers such as net income. Labor unions often use accounting numbers to argue for more wages or other benefits, and companies often use their own financial statements to determine dividend payments, set company policies, and in general to help guide operating business decisions. Indeed, financial accounting reports provide information to a variety of users, each with specific needs.

PROVIDERS OF CAPITAL: INVESTORS AND CREDITORS

Providers of capital represent people or organizations who have cash beyond what they need for current consumption. They seek ways to invest their extra funds so that they can increase their future levels of wealth and consumption. This group includes both current and potential equity and debt investors: individuals and entities who provide companies with the capital they need to conduct operations. Equity investors (often referred to simply as investors) purchase shares of stock, which represent ownership interests in a corporation, with the expectation of receiving dividends in the future; debt investors (creditors) loan funds in exchange for interest and principal payments.[1]

WHO HOLDS EQUITY AND DEBT INVESTMENTS?

Equity and debt investments are held by both individuals and entities. Over 51 million people in the United States, for example, hold shares of stock in large U.S. corporations which, in turn, hold shares of stock in each other. The equity securities of General Electric, for example, are held by almost 500,000 individual stockholders, while General Electric as an entity holds 100% of the equity securities of the National Broadcasting Company (NBC). Debt securities are held primarily by banks, who loan billions of dollars to individuals and corporations each year. For example, the balance sheet of Citicorp, a major U.S. bank, indicates that the company holds debt investments in the form of outstanding loans valued at almost $100 billion. In addition, many debt securities in the form of bonds issued by large corporations are also held by individuals and institutions.

WHERE ARE EQUITY AND DEBT SECURITIES BOUGHT AND SOLD?

Stock markets, such as the New York Stock Exchange, the American Stock Exchange, the Over-the-Counter market, and the Tokyo, London, and Zurich exchanges provide forums for the buying and selling of equity interests issued by major U.S. and foreign companies. Active domestic and international bond markets provide forums for the buying and selling of debt securities issued by these same companies.

COMPANIES (MANAGERS)

Companies, operated by **managers**, provide goods and services that are consumed by individuals and other entities. They compete with each other for capital, attempting to convince investors and creditors that they offer the best potential return at the lowest level of risk. In 1994, for example, General Electric collected over $23 billion from creditors, much of which was used to finance expansion which, in turn, enabled the company to produce cash that was used to meet debt payments and pay dividends.

INDUSTRIES

Companies are often grouped into **industries** based on the nature of their operations. While there are many industry classifications, they can be summarized into three basic categories: manufacturing, retailing, and services (general and financial). Manufacturing firms like General Motors, IBM, and PepsiCo acquire raw materials and convert them into goods that are sold either to consumers, usually through retailers,

---

1. Owners of equity securities also hope that the market prices of their stocks increase, but note that these increases occur because future dividends are expected to increase.

or to other manufacturers who use them as raw materials. Retail firms like Wal-Mart, K mart, Toys "R" Us, and J.C. Penney purchase goods from manufacturers and sell them to consumers. The service industry includes firms like Ameritech, MCI, Federal Express, and H&R Block, who provide general services, as well as firms like Citicorp, American Express, and Prudential Insurance, who provide financial services. We frequently refer to these firms and industry classifications throughout the remainder of the text.

ECONOMIC ENTITIES: DIFFERENT KINDS

Financial accounting statements refer to a specific and definable *economic entity*. In this text we call this entity a *company* or *business* and limit our coverage to entities established primarily to generate profits. Such profit-seeking entities may be subdivided into segments and subsidiaries, each of which provides its own financial statements. For example, in the annual report of PepsiCo, Inc., the financial statements are referred to as **consolidated financial statements**, which means that the total dollar amounts in the accounts on PepsiCo's financial statements include those of other companies, such as Kentucky Fried Chicken, Pizza Hut, and Taco Bell, which PepsiCo owns. These companies, called *subsidiaries*, publish their own separate financial statements. Furthermore, PepsiCo is divided into three segments: beverages, snack foods, and restaurants, and financial reports on each of these segments can be compiled.

Accounting reports are also prepared for entities that are not established to make profits. Counties, cities, school districts, and other municipalities as well as charitable organizations and foundations are examples of **nonprofit entities**.

CONTRACTS

Capital providers require that managers, and the entities they manage, enter into contracts so that legal influence can be exerted over management's activities which, in turn, protects the interests of the capital providers. Debt (loan) and management **compensation contracts** are common examples. To illustrate, the annual reports of both Boeing and Owens-Corning Fiberglas Corporation indicate that their long-term debt contracts require that both companies limit future dividends, capital expenditures, and borrowings. Violating these terms (i.e., defaulting on the contract) would give the debtholder the right to demand that the entire debt be paid immediately. DuPont's annual report discloses that the compensation of the company's executives is based, in part, on whether the company achieves certain net income goals. In both cases financial accounting numbers can be found in the contracts, thereby playing a critical role in shaping the behavior of corporate management.

INDEPENDENT AUDITORS

Major U.S. companies incur considerable costs to have their financial statements audited by independent public accounting firms. Such audits lend credibility to the financial statements and are required by law for companies whose ownership shares are traded on the public stock exchanges. Six public accounting firms, known as the **"Big 6,"** audit most of the large companies. These firms and a selection of their major clients are listed in Figure 1–7. There are also many regional and local public accounting firms located throughout the United States. Their audit clients comprise the thousands of middle-sized and small companies who, for various reasons, wish to have their financial statements audited.

FIGURE 1–7	ACCOUNTING FIRM	MAJOR CLIENT
"Big 6" accounting firms and major clients	Arthur Andersen & Co.	Ameritech, Federal Express, Owens-Corning
	Coopers & Lybrand	Wendy's, American Brands, Alcoa
	Deloitte & Touche	General Motors, Boeing, Sears Roebuck & Co.
	Ernst & Young	Time Warner, BankAmerica, Wal-Mart
	KPMG Peat Marwick	Citicorp, General Electric, J.C. Penney
	Price Waterhouse	DuPont, Walt Disney, Kmart

RELATIONSHIPS AMONG CAPITAL PROVIDERS, MANAGEMENT, AND THE INDEPENDENT AUDITOR

Since investors and creditors demand the independent audit, it seems reasonable that they would choose the auditor and make sure that the audit was conducted in an independent manner. Such a solution is often impractical, however, because stockholders and creditors are often too widely separated and removed from the business to agree on an auditor and monitor the audit. As Figure 1–8 shows, in all major U.S. companies the stockholders elect a board of directors, which appoints a subcommittee of outside directors, called the **audit committee**. This committee, which is part of the board of directors and therefore represents the interests of the stockholders, works with management to choose an auditor. The committee monitors the audit to make sure that it is thorough, objective, and independent.

In spite of these controls, management still pays the audit fee and has considerable influence over whether the auditing firm is hired again. Such influence can threaten the auditor's independence. *Forbes* magazine reports that "there is little doubt that the pursuit of ever-increasing revenues and profits [by company management] puts continuing pressure on auditors to be sympathetic, if not malleable."[2] Some managers have been known to "shop around" for favorable audit opinions. For example, when Broadview Financial Corporation, a large company in Ohio, switched auditors, it was revealed later that the switch was due to disagreements about proper methods of accounting.

LEGAL LIABILITY

While pressure from management can threaten an auditor's independence, it is important to realize that there are federal regulations against "opinion shopping" and that auditors have a responsibility to the public to conduct a thorough and independent audit. Such responsibility gives rise to **legal liability**, which provides an economic incentive for auditors to conduct their work in a diligent and ethical manner.

Suppose in the Microline scenario that the company was not a legitimate operation and, for whatever reason, the auditor conducted an incomplete and careless audit and was influenced by Martin to write a favorable audit report. Trusting the report and the financial statements, you decide to invest your $1 million. In a short time the company fails, you lose your investment, and it is revealed later that the statements were

2. Richard Greene, "If I Don't Cross the t . . . ," Forbes, February 11, 1985, pp. 134–135.

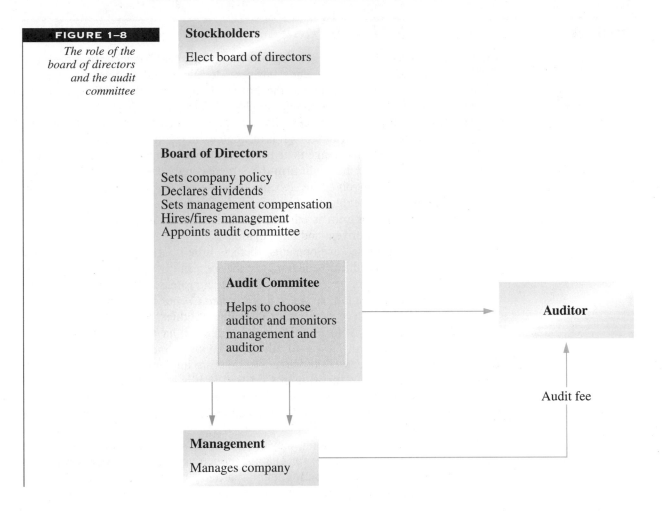

FIGURE 1–8

The role of the board of directors and the audit committee

Stockholders

Elect board of directors

Board of Directors

Sets company policy
Declares dividends
Sets management compensation
Hires/fires management
Appoints audit committee

Audit Commitee

Helps to choose auditor and monitors management and auditor

Auditor

Audit fee

Management

Manages company

in error as of the time of the audit. In such a situation you would have a strong case for suits against both Martin and the auditor. Such suits can be very costly in the United States, and the auditor's legal liability seems to be increasing with each passing year. Recently, for example, the seventh largest accounting firm in the United States, Laventhol & Horwath, declared bankruptcy largely due to the costs of defending itself against lawsuits. Over several years prior to the failure the firm paid approximately $50 million in claims to owners and creditors of clients who accused it of shoddy audit work. In addition, failures in the Savings & Loan industry, which cost taxpayers billions of dollars in the early 1990s, led S&L regulators to file suits against major accounting firms, seeking well over $1 billion in damages for fraud, negligence, and misconduct. *Time* (April 13, 1992) reported that "All told, U.S. accountants now face 4,000 liability suits—double the number in 1985—and more than $15 billion in damages."

Consequently, auditors have strong economic incentives to maintain their independence and not allow themselves to be influenced by pressures from managers. Similarly, the legal liability faced by managers encourages them to refrain from pressuring auditors too strongly.

ETHICS AND PROFESSIONAL REPUTATION

LO 5 Financial accounting statements are one of several mechanisms designed to control management's business decisions and protect the interests of the shareholders. Others include the board of directors, the audit committee, regulations against "opinion shopping," and legal liability.

All these control devices suggest that a large amount of mistrust exists among shareholders, managers, and auditors. It is difficult to question such a conjecture when you realize that cases of management fraud and embezzlement have risen significantly in recent years and that audit firms have increasingly been found guilty of misconduct. Companies involved in recent well-known frauds include Phar-Mor, Miniscribe, Leslie Fay, Regina, and Crazy Eddie's. Some have even suggested that the United States is suffering from an ethics crisis. Indeed, business people in general are often viewed as greedy, driven, and unscrupulous.

Notwithstanding these developments, there is little doubt that **ethics** is a major business asset and that ethical behavior is in the long-run best interest of managers, shareholders, and auditors. Indeed, Clifford Smith, a professor of finance at the University of Rochester, stated in the *Journal of Applied Corporate Finance* that "ethical behavior is profitable." In recognition of the value of ethics, major U.S. companies, such as Boeing, General Mills, and Johnson & Johnson, have instituted special programs designed specifically to instill ethical behavior in their employees. Harvard Business School and other well-known universities are implementing courses in business ethics. The **American Institute of Certified Public Accountants (AICPA)**, the professional organization of CPAs, has recently rewritten and strengthened its professional code of ethics, largely to instill higher ethical standards in the members of the accounting profession.

Such efforts are not only moral, they are driven by sound economic logic. Companies like IBM with reputations for quality, service, and ethical business practices are valued highly by investors and creditors partially because their financial statements can be trusted. Such companies and their managers are sued less frequently. As noted in *The Wall Street Journal*,

There can be little doubt that most corporate chief executives place a high value on the reputations of their companies and employees. Aside from the general market benefits, a good reputation makes companies less vulnerable to the legal and political attacks launched against business by "public interest" groups and the like in this contentious and litigious age. Also, a code of conduct may help discourage an unscrupulous employee from trying to take advantage of the company.[3]

Auditors also benefit from ethical behavior and strong reputations. Independent and respectable auditors face fewer liability suits and can generally charge client companies higher fees, primarily because their audit reports are trusted by the public. Consequently, it is important to realize that while the financial accounting process is a system of control, and manager and auditor fraud will continue to occur, it is best to be ethical, from both a moral and an economic standpoint. Not surprisingly, the most successful companies and audit firms enjoy the best reputations for high ethical standards.

---

3. George Melloan, "Business Ethics and the Competitive Urge," *The Wall Street Journal*, August 9, 1988, p. 27.

ECONOMIC CONSEQUENCES: MANAGEMENT'S PERSPECTIVE

Capital providers need financial information to evaluate and control management's activities, and management responds to this demand by providing the financial statements. You might wonder why managers are willing to (1) incur the costs of preparing the statements, (2) pay to have them audited, and (3) enter into contracts that restrict and/or direct their behavior. The simple answer is that managers need equity and debt capital to operate their businesses, and in a competitive capital market they can only attract it at reasonable rates if they convince capital providers that their firms offer high potential returns at low levels of risk.

Capital providers use the financial statements to assess potential returns and levels of risk, and financial statement numbers are used in debt covenants and management compensation contracts. Consequently, there are important economic consequences to managers associated with the financial statements they provide. Real-world examples are provided below.

- "More than $7 billion of IBM's stock market value evaporated in a matter of minutes Tuesday morning after it said it would earn half what investors expected in the first quarter." (*USA Today*, March 21, 1991).
- "Moody's Investor's Service lowered its credit rating on General Host Corp. . . . citing the company's weak financial condition. It raised its rating of Scott Paper Co. . . . citing a dramatic improvement in the company's balance sheet." (*Wall Street Journal*, November 11, 1994).
- "Citicorp may have to raise as much as $800 million in additional equity capital because of an accounting rule change on securities it has sold on Wall Street." (*Wall Street Journal*, August 30, 1991).
- "Riddell Sports Inc. said a federal court rendered an $8 million verdict against it in a product liability action . . . The company [states that reducing net income by that amount] would put it in default under certain debt covenants in its bank loan agreement with Detroit-based NBD Bancorp." (*Wall Street Journal*, November 3, 1994).
- "Harold Poling, the chairman of Ford Motor Company, and other Ford executives did not receive bonuses because the No. 2 automaker's net income fell 78% to $860 million." (*USA Today*, April 9, 1991).

In each of these cases the reporting of financial statement numbers led to an economic consequence to the firm and its management. Astute managers should be aware of these consequences and attempt to anticipate them when making business decisions. Thus, managers should understand how their business decisions affect the financial statements and how the financial statements are used by capital providers and other outsiders.

These economic consequences can be quite large and in some cases create strong incentives for management to manipulate the financial statements. *Forbes* (May 1988) reports that "many young companies use accounting rules to maximize income and minimize expenses where they can," while *The Wall Street Journal* (December 17, 1990) noted that "finding out what companies' earnings really are . . . may be more difficult than ever because . . . companies are coming under greater pressure to spruce up reported earnings with cosmetic fixes, for example, understating costs and overstating revenue."

It even happens that management sometimes goes beyond ethical boundaries in its attempt to make the financial statements appear as attractive as possible. *The Wall Street Journal* (September 27, 1993) reported, for example, that Leslie Fay, a well-known women's dress manufacturer, "disclosed that [it] falsified company books to inflate profits . . . reporting a profit of $23.4 million in the first three quarters of 1992 [when] those familiar with the situation say Leslie Fay's combined losses for 1991 and 1992 . . . may be as large as $100 million." Unfortunately, such cases are not unusual and financial statement users must be savvy to the possibility that management has influence over the reported statements. But rarely does falsifying the financial records lead to benefits in the long run for management. Indeed, recent academic research in accounting has shown that firms that use conservative accounting methods are valued more highly by the stock market and, as mentioned earlier, ethics is viewed by many as a prime business asset. Not surprisingly, Leslie Fay sought bankruptcy protection in April 1993.

GENERALLY ACCEPTED ACCOUNTING PRINCIPLES

Generally accepted accounting principles (GAAP) play a critical role in the financial accounting process. They define the standards for external reporting, which produces greater uniformity in the accounting methods used by the variety of profit-seeking entities in the economy. Defining general reporting practices by a single set of standards facilitates meaningful comparisons of the financial performance of different companies. In addition, the level of credibility in the financial statements is largely determined by the extent to which their preparation follows GAAP. For example, if neither Exxon nor Amoco, two major oil companies, followed GAAP in the preparation of their financial statements, not only would it be virtually impossible to compare their levels of performance, because their measures of profit would be computed in different ways, but neither measure of profit would be very credible.

While the development of financial accounting and the need for reporting standards can be traced back to the beginning of record keeping, perhaps the most important single event occurred in 1929 when the U.S. capital markets collapsed, and the Great Depression followed. Many factors contributed to this dramatic economic downturn, and the lack of both credibility and uniformity in the financial accounting information available to investors and creditors did little to help the situation.

THE SECURITIES AND EXCHANGE COMMISSION

L O 6 In response to demands from the investing community for uniform and credible financial accounting information, in 1934 the U.S. Congress created the **Securities and Exchange Commission (SEC)**. An agency of the federal government, the SEC was commissioned to implement and enforce the Securities Act of 1933 and the Securities Exchange Act of 1934. The Securities Act of 1933 requires that companies issuing securities on the public security markets file a registration statement (Form S-1) with the SEC prior to the issuance. The SEC Act of 1934 states that, among other requirements, companies with securities listed on the public security markets *(listed companies)* must (1) annually file audited financial reports with the

SEC (Form 10-K), (2) file quarterly financial statements with the SEC (Form 10-Q), and (3) provide audited financial reports annually to the stockholders.

THE ROLE OF THE ACCOUNTING PROFESSION

The SEC was given broad powers by Congress to prescribe the accounting practices and standards to be used by companies within its jurisdiction. However, it has chosen not to assume this responsibility. Instead, it has allowed and encouraged the American Institute of Certified Public Accountants (AICPA), a nongovernment body, to take an active role. The AICPA has responded by establishing several standard-setting bodies since 1939: the Committee on Accounting Procedures (1939-59), the Accounting Principles Board (1959-71), and the Financial Accounting Standards Board (1973-present).

THE FINANCIAL ACCOUNTING STANDARDS BOARD

The **Financial Accounting Standards Board (FASB)** consists of seven, well-compensated, full-time individuals who have severed all ties from previous employers and represent many business backgrounds. Since 1973 this private-sector body has issued well over 100 **statements of financial accounting standards** covering a wide variety of topics. In addition, the FASB has improved the standard-setting process in two important ways. First, it developed a **conceptual framework** which consists of a number of essays that provide a structure for a comprehensive and coherent set of interrelated goals and fundamentals for financial accounting. General subject areas such as the objectives of financial reporting, the desirable characteristics of accounting information, and the exact definitions of essential accounting terms have been addressed by this project. Using this framework as a kind of constitution, the FASB is better able to consider accounting and reporting issues in an organized and consistent manner.

A second improvement brought about by the FASB is the opening of its deliberations to the public and the initiation of a number of procedural changes that specifically invite public participation. The process of establishing accounting standards now includes several points at which letters and personal presentations from the public are encouraged. Indeed, generally accepted accounting principles are the result of a joint effort among specialized experts, industry interests, government representatives, report users, auditors, academics, and the FASB.

ACCOUNTING STANDARD SETTING: A POLITICAL PROCESS

Even though the FASB is a private body, standard setting is very much a political process. Figure 1–9 illustrates its political nature. Policymakers, represented by the SEC and the FASB, are influenced in their deliberations by public input from Congress, the White House, government agencies, public hearings, and letters from interested parties. The result is Generally Accepted Accounting Principles which, in turn, lead to Actual Accounting Practices, the methods used by companies to

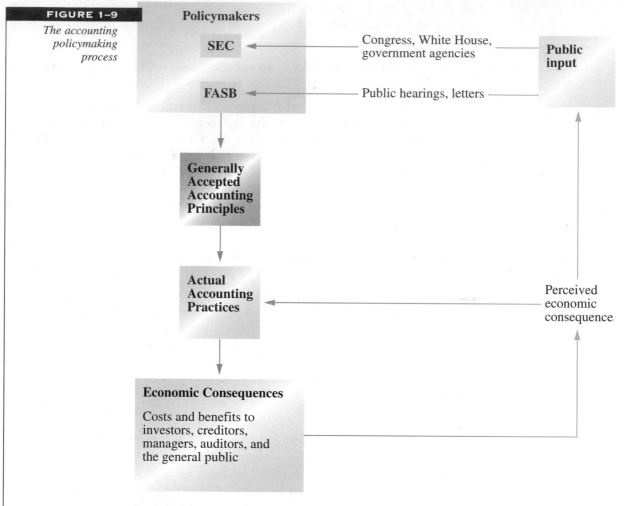

FIGURE 1–9

The accounting policymaking process

Source: Jamie Pratt, "The Economics of External Reporting: Three Frameworks for the Classroom," *Journal of Accounting Education* (1987), p. 182.

account for their business activities. These methods, in turn, bring about **economic consequences**, the costs and benefits to investors, creditors, managers, auditors, and the general public associated with reported financial accounting information. Such costs and benefits play a special role in the political process because they create incentives for interested parties to provide public input to policymakers.

REACTIONS TO ECONOMIC CONSEQUENCES: LOBBYING ACCOUNTING NUMBERS

Economic consequences, like the examples listed earlier, encourage interested parties, especially corporate management, to lobby the SEC and FASB in an attempt to influence generally accepted accounting principles. Corporations in the United States spend millions of dollars each year on such lobbying efforts by contacting Congressmen, appearing at public FASB hearings, and sending letters to the FASB and SEC.

These efforts are often successful. The November 16, 1994 issue of *The Wall Street Journal* recently reported:

"The FASB is moving toward modifying its stock-option proposal in ways that may soften the impact on corporate earnings . . . following a storm of protest from industry."

This quote followed another article in *The Wall Street Journal* (March 7, 1994) on this same issue which was entitled: "FASB's Stock-Option Plan Threatens Pay Packages; Lobbying Gets Intense."

INTERNATIONAL PERSPECTIVE: ACCOUNTING PRACTICES AND STANDARDS THROUGHOUT THE WORLD

LO 7 The financial accounting process existing in the U.S. has evolved within a capitalistic system where markets are relatively free. Full disclosure is advocated and the decision needs of investors, creditors and other outsiders are first priority. Financial accounting practices and standards used in other countries, however, are quite diverse. Just as nations have different histories, economies, cultures, and political systems, they also have different systems of financial accounting. Indeed, accounting systems have evolved in response to the demands of the business environment, and the business environments faced by companies in different parts of the world are vastly dissimilar.

At a very general level, four basic kinds of accounting systems have been identified: (1) the British-American-Dutch model, (2) the Continental model, (3) the South American model, and (4) the Communist model.[4] The countries in each of these four categories tend to have certain environmental characteristics in common. Such characteristics include the nature and development of the domestic capital market, political and economic ties with other countries in the category, the legal system, annual rates of inflation, the size and complexity of the companies operating within the country, the sophistication of management and the financial community, and the general level of education.

BRITISH-AMERICAN-DUTCH MODEL

The **British-American-Dutch model**, which is based primarily on the generally accepted accounting principles of the United States, is used largely by countries in North America, Australia, and India. These accounting systems tend to be oriented toward the decision needs of investors and are designed to measure the effectiveness of management. The countries in this category tend to have large, well-developed securities markets, high levels of education, and a number of multinational corporations. A consumer orientation and a legal system that encourages litigation also tend to be more prevalent in these countries.

---

4. For a discussion of the different accounting systems used throughout the world, see Gerhard Mueller, H. Gernon, and G. Meek, *Accounting: An International Perspective*, Richard D. Irwin, Homewood, Ill., 1987, and note that other ways to classify accounting systems have also been proposed.

CONTINENTAL MODEL

The **Continental model** includes Japan and most of the countries in Europe. The accounting methods used in these countries are not oriented toward the needs of investors. Rather, they provide information that is used to satisfy government requirements, such as computing income taxes. Banks are very important providers of capital in these economies, and financial accounting practices tend to be largely at the discretion of management and highly conservative, sometimes withholding relevant information from the shareholders.

SOUTH AMERICAN MODEL

The **South American model** includes most of the countries in South America. These countries, with the exception of Brazil which uses Portuguese, share Spanish as their common language as well as a rich cultural heritage. In general, their accounting methods are oriented toward the needs of government planners, and uniform rules are imposed on virtually all business entities. The most distinguishing feature about this system is that it includes periodic adjustments for inflation, a phenomenon that has plagued South America for many years.

COMMUNIST MODEL

The **Communist model** was used by countries formerly included in the communist bloc. Since there was limited private ownership in these countries, accounting rules were rigid and oriented to government planners. Financial statements were not prepared for outside investors and creditors. Instead, they were submitted to agency administrators who implemented the tight central economic controls of the communist system. The recent shift toward democracy and capitalism in these countries has encouraged greater economic exchange, less restricted markets, and more openness, resulting in greater levels of disclosure for investors and creditors.

INTERNATIONAL ACCOUNTING STANDARD SETTING

The fact that so much diversity exists in world-wide accounting standards and practice makes it difficult for investors and creditors to compare the performances of companies operating in different countries. Comparing the performance of a South American textile mill to one from Australia, for example, is almost impossible because their financial reports are prepared using different accounting methods. Such differences can lead to a loss of credibility in the financial statements and investment decisions based on misunderstanding. It is also costly and time-consuming for financial statement users to educate themselves about the different accounting practices followed internationally.

Many efforts have been made to achieve greater international understanding and uniformity of accounting practices. In Europe, for example, the European Economic Community (EEC) has its 4th and 7th Directives, which govern the format and content of financial statements for countries in the European Common Market. Perhaps the most active is the **International Accounting Standards Committee (IASC)**, which was formed in 1973 to develop worldwide accounting practices. This private-sector body, which represents approximately 100 professional accounting bodies in nearly seventy countries, could be viewed as the international counterpart of the FASB. It has issued a number of international accounting standards, each of which can be viewed as an effort to harmonize the world's accounting practices by eliminating differences that cannot be explained by the environment. Nonetheless, the environmental and cultural differences across countries are great, and the progress toward harmony has been, and will probably continue to be, slow.

ETHICS IN THE REAL WORLD

Most companies have established formal policies and procedures, including codes of conduct and ethics, designed to ensure that employees adhere to the highest standards of personal and professional integrity. There are good reasons for such policies. For example, two recent *Wall Street Journal* articles state: "In employee surveys conducted by academics and other specialists, as many as 30% of workers interviewed admitted stealing from their employers" (October 5, 1992), and "KnowledgeWare, a fast-growing software maker, played fast and loose with generally accepted accounting principles . . . [but the company] didn't do anything illegal . . . they [were simply] guilty of very weak or nonexistent financial controls" (September 7, 1994).

Further, many companies believe that ethical business practices lead to better reputations, which in turn lead to higher company value. Clifford W. Smith, University of Rochester, has written in the *Journal of Applied Corporate Finance:* "Markets impose potentially significant costs on individuals and firms that engage in unethical behavior . . . [in other words] ethical behavior is profitable." In addition, *The Wall Street Journal* (August 9, 1988) reports that the Business Roundtable, an influential group of the nation's largest companies, sees ethics "not only as a priority, but also as a prime business asset."

It is no wonder that companies attempt to encourage ethical behavior in their employees, but the definition of ethical behavior is often unclear, especially across different countries, and sometimes making the right choice is difficult. Consider, for example, an employee who works in a foreign location for a multi-national company, like IBM or DuPont, that has a formal code of conduct. Assume that the employee is bidding for a sale against a competitor who is well known in the region. It is a common and acceptable practice in this country to make small side payments (cash, gifts, etc.) to the buyer's representative in an effort to obtain the sale, and the competitor has already done so. It is highly likely that the competitor will gain the sale if no such payments are made by the employee, yet the company's code of conduct does not allow such behavior. On the other hand, the employee is paid by the company on a commission—that is, compensation is a function of sales made.

ETHICAL ISSUE

Is it ethical for the employee to make side payments to the buyer's representative in an attempt to win the sale, even when such side payments are inconsistent with the company's stated code of conduct?

SUMMARY OF LEARNING OBJECTIVES

LO 1 *Explain the economic role of financial accounting statements and why managers must have both an economic consequence perspective and a user orientation.*

Investors and creditors demand that management provide financial accounting information for two fundamental economic reasons. First, they need financial numbers to monitor and enforce the debt and compensation contracts written with management. Second, they need financial information to decide where to invest their funds. Companies incur the costs of providing the statements and having them audited because they need to attract capital from investors and creditors, and managers want to maintain their levels of compensation. Management hires auditors who must act independently because they face high levels of legal liability and must follow professional ethical standards.

Managers must have a user orientation because they often use financial statements to assess the financial condition and performance of other companies. They need an economic consequence perspective because they must understand how their business decisions affect the financial statements and how the financial statements are used by capital providers and other outsiders to evaluate and control their actions. Astute managers should be aware of these consequences and attempt to anticipate them when making business decisions.

 Briefly describe the contents of the standard audit report, the management letter, and the footnotes to the financial statements.

The auditor's report is divided into three paragraphs. The first states that the financial statements are the responsibility of management, have been audited, and that the auditor's responsibility is to express an opinion on them. The second indicates that the examination of the company's records was made in accordance with generally accepted auditing standards and that the auditor has obtained reasonable assurance that the financial statements are free of material misstatement. The final paragraph states that the financial statements present fairly the financial position of the company, the results of operations, and its cash flows in conformity with generally accepted accounting principles.

The management letter normally states that the company's management is responsible for the preparation and integrity of the statements, that the statements were prepared in accordance with generally accepted accounting principles, and that certain amounts were based on management's best estimates and judgments. It further indicates that the company maintains a system of internal controls designed to safeguard its assets and ensure that all transactions are recorded and reported properly. The footnotes provide additional information about the dollar amounts on the financial statements. They indicate which accounting methods were used and where the numbers on the statements are the result of assumptions and estimates made by management.

 Name the four financial statements, and briefly explain the kind of financial information that each provides.

The four basic financial statements are (1) the balance sheet, (2) the income statement, (3) the statement of retained earnings, and (4) the statement of cash flows. The balance sheet lists the assets, liabilities, and stockholders' equity of a company at a given point in time. The income statement contains the revenues earned and expenses incurred by a company over a period of time. Revenues less expenses equal net income. The statement of retained earnings reconciles the retained earnings amount from one period to the next. Beginning retained earnings, plus net income, less dividends, equal ending retained earnings. The statement of cash flows reconciles the cash amount from one period to the next. It lists net cash flows from operating activities, investing activities, and financing activities.

L O 4 *Describe the two basic forms of investment, and explain how the information on the financial statements relates to them.*

There are two basic forms of investment: debt and equity. A debt investment is a loan, and debt investors are called *creditors*. When debt investments are made, management is normally required to sign a loan contract. Creditors are primarily concerned that the interest and principal payments are met on a timely basis. Since such payments are made in cash, creditors are interested in financial information that helps them to predict future cash flows over the period of the loan.

Equity investments involve purchasing ownership interests in a company. Equity owners of corporations are called stockholders. Their returns come in the form of dividends (or *stock price appreciation*), which tend to be large if the company performs well and small, or nonexistent, if it performs poorly. The primary concern of stockholders is the performance of the company's management—specifically, its ability to generate and maintain earning power in the future. To achieve this objective, management must ensure that cash is available to meet debts as they come due and also invest in assets that produce satisfactory returns in the long run. Consequently, stockholders are interested in the information contained in all four of the financial statements.

L O 5 *Explain why ethics is important in the accounting process.*

The financial statements, debt and compensation contracts, the board of directors, auditors, and the audit committee all represent methods of controlling the business decisions of management in an effort to protect the investments of stockholders and creditors. While management and auditors have incentives to misrepresent the financial statements or exploit the system, there are compelling moral and economic reasons to act ethically. Ethical managers and auditors face less legal liability and are able to charge higher fees for their services than those whose behavior has been questioned. Accordingly, companies, universities, and the accounting profession have recently pursued efforts to enhance the ethical behavior of business people.

L O 6 *Describe the Securities and Exchange Commission and the Financial Accounting Standards Board and their respective roles in the development of generally accepted accounting principles.*

The SEC Act of 1934 established the Securities and Exchange Commission as the governmental body responsible for ensuring that listed companies prepare and file registration statements before they issue new securities, submit the annual Form 10-K, and prepare quarterly and annual reports for stockholders. The SEC also has broad powers to prescribe the accounting practices and standards to be employed by companies within its jurisdiction.

The SEC has allowed and encouraged the accounting profession to take an active role in setting standards. In 1973 the Financial Accounting Standards Board was established by a committee of the AICPA to assume responsibility for developing financial accounting standards. Since that time, the FASB, the third private body to develop standards of financial accounting, has issued over 100 standards and has received the full support of the SEC.

L O 7 *Describe the current status of international accounting practices and standards.*

Financial accounting practices and standards used in countries throughout the world are quite diverse due to different histories, cultures, economies, and political systems. There are four basic models: British-American-Dutch, Continental, South American, and Communist (which is disappearing). Each model represents a different orientation toward financial accounting measurement and disclosure, based primarily on the economic, political, and social characteristics of the constituent countries. Recent efforts by the International Accounting Standards Committee have attempted to bring greater uniformity to worldwide accounting practice, but due to environmental and cultural differences, progress has been slow.

APPENDIX 1A

THREE OTHER KINDS OF ACCOUNTING

This text is devoted almost exclusively to financial accounting. However, you should be aware of the three other kinds of accounting usually covered in other accounting courses: not-for-profit accounting, managerial accounting, and tax accounting.

NOT-FOR-PROFIT ACCOUNTING

Many economic entities do not have profit as an objective. Municipalities, such as cities, simply receive money from taxes, service fees, and debt investors and allocate it to address public needs. For example, a city allocates funds to a police department to ensure public safety. The process of recording these fund inflows and outflows and reporting them to the public is quite logically called *not-for-profit accounting*.

MANAGERIAL ACCOUNTING

Managers need *internal information systems* to generate timely and accurate information that helps them plan and operate efficiently on a day-to-day basis. To guide their decisions, managers rely to some extent on the information produced by the financial accounting system. However, more important to such decisions is information that is not available to the public and is produced strictly for management's own use. Such information is referred to as *managerial accounting information*, and managerial accounting is usually covered in a separate course.

TAX ACCOUNTING

The area of accounting devoted to understanding and applying the tax law is known as *tax accounting*. Our complicated and constantly changing tax structure requires that thousands of accountants specialize in this area. Furthermore, tax law is extremely detailed and complicated; even a moderate coverage of tax accounting requires a number of separate accounting or law courses.

An important distinction should be made between the income number resulting from applying income tax laws (called *taxable income*) and the income number which results from financial accounting (called net income). The *Internal Revenue Code* specifies the rules to be followed to calculate taxable income. An entity's tax obligation is then computed as a percentage of this taxable income. Financial accounting income, or *net income*, is determined by applying financial accounting principles and procedures, which differ in many ways from the tax laws stated in the Internal Revenue Code. As a result, net income is not necessarily equal to taxable income. Tax laws are enacted for purposes quite different from those which drive the development of financial accounting principles. Accounting students often confuse these two sets of rules.

COMPARING THE FOUR KINDS OF ACCOUNTING

Figure 1A–1 compares not-for-profit, managerial, and tax accounting to financial accounting. The top of the chart depicts a sequential process in which the managers of an economic entity follow certain accounting processes that convert financial facts about the entity into a set of financial statements. Interested parties then use this information for a variety of business decisions.

FIGURE 1A–1

Four kinds of accounting

Economic Entity	Managers	System	Financial Information	Recipients	Decisions

FINANCIAL ACCOUNTING

| Profit-making companies | Finance or accounting department | Generally accepted accounting principles | Income statement
Balance sheet
Statement of retained earnings
Statement of cash flows
Other disclosures
Auditor report | *External*
Investors
Creditors
Suppliers
Employees
Managers
Goverment
General public | Equity and debt investments
Contract negotiations
Regulation
Dividend payments |

NOT-FOR-PROFIT ACCOUNTING

| Nonprofit entities | Finance or accounting department | Fund accounting principles | Balance sheet
Funds flow statements | *External*
Creditors
Government
General public | Debt investments
Budget allocations |

MANAGERIAL ACCOUNTING

| All entities | Internal accounting department | Company information system | Manager reports
Production costs
Performance evaluation, etc. | *Internal*
Managers | Operating decisions |

TAX ACCOUNTING

| All entities | Finance or accounting department | Internal Revenue Code | Official tax forms:
1040 for individuals
1020 for corporations | *External*
Internal Revenue Service | Collection of government revenues |

KEY TERMS

Note: Definitions for these terms are provided in the glossary at the end of the text.

American Institute of Certified Public
    Accountants (AICPA) (p. 20)
Annual interest (p. 12)
Annual reports (p. 15)
Assets (p. 10)
Audit committee (p. 18)
Auditor's report (p. 6)
Balance sheet (p. 10)
Big 6 (p. 17)
Board of directors (p. 13)
British-American-Dutch model (p. 25)
Certified public accountant (CPA) (p. 6)
Common stock (p. 10)
Communist model (p. 26)
Compensation contracts (p. 17)
Conceptual framework (p. 23)
Consolidated financial statements (p. 17)
Continental model (p. 26)
Creditors (p. 10)
Debt investment (p. 12)
Debt restrictions (p. 12)
Dividends (p. 11)
Earning power (p. 11)
Economic consequence perspective (p. 4)
Economic consequences (p. 24)
Equity (p. 12)
Ethics (p. 20)
Expenses (p. 11)
Financial accounting (p. 3)
Financial Accounting Standards Board
    (FASB) (p. 23)
Financing activities (p. 11)
Footnotes (p. 9)

Generally accepted accounting
    principles (GAAP) (p. 22)
Historical cost (p. 12)
Income statement (p. 11)
Independent audit (p. 6)
Industries (p. 16)
Internal control system (p. 8)
International Accounting Standards
    Committee (IASC) (p. 26)
Investing activities (p. 11)
Legal liability (p. 18)
Liabilities (p. 10)
Loan contract (p. 12)
Management letter (p. 6)
Managers (p. 16)
Net income (p. 11)
Nonprofit entities (p. 17)
Operating activities (p. 11)
Profit (p. 11)
Retained earnings (p. 11)
Revenues (p. 11)
Securities and Exchange Commission
    (SEC) (p. 22)
Solvency (p. 11)
South American model (p. 26)
Statement of cash flows (p. 11)
Statement of retained earnings (p. 11)
Statements of financial accounting
    standards (p. 23)
Stock markets (p. 16)
Stockholders (p. 12)
Stockholders' equity (p. 10)
User orientation (p. 4)

QUESTIONS FOR DISCUSSION AND REVIEW

1. Define the accounting process, and briefly explain how it is a dynamic phenomenon.
2. What is a user orientation, what is an economic perspective, and why must astute managers adopt both? Provide several examples of each.
3. Capital providers include both equity and debt investors. Purchasing 100 shares of IBM common stock is an example of an equity investment. Bank loans and extensions of credit represent debt investments.
    a. What are the basic differences between equity and debt investments? Which kind of investment entails greater risk? Which has the potential for greater returns? Why?
    b. What kind of financial information would you consider when deciding whether or not to purchase IBM common stock? Would you consider the same kind of information if you were a banker considering a loan to IBM?

4. Financial accounting statements are used by many parties. Describe how each of the parties listed below might use them.
   a. Security analysts and stockbrokers
   b. Bank loan officers
   c. A company's customers or suppliers
   d. Public utilities
   e. Labor unions
   f. A company's managers

5. What does it mean to be solvent? What kind of financial information would be useful in assessing solvency? Would debt or equity investors be more likely to take a greater interest in assessing a company's solvency position? Why?

6. W.T. Grant, a large department store chain, reported profits on its income statement almost all the way up to its financial collapse. How could this happen? What kind of information could have provided an earlier warning signal than profits? How is it that profitable companies sometimes go bankrupt?

7. What is the purpose of the audit and the auditor's report? What benefits do audits provide for managers and investors? Under what conditions might managers choose not to have audited financial statements?

8. What is meant by independent when describing auditors? Why is it important that they be independent? What incentives do they have to be independent? Are there pressures on auditors not to be independent? If so, from where?

9. A major accounting firm commissioned an extensive poll to find out how people understand various business terms. According to the study, 34 percent of the shareholders questioned thought that the phrase *unqualified opinion*, which is used to describe an auditor's report, meant that every number on the financial statements was "totally accurate." Do you agree with 34 percent of the shareholders? Why?

10. Recently, a major accounting firm conducted and published an extensive survey on ethics in American business. The results indicate that intense concentration on short-term profits is a major threat to American business ethics. Briefly explain how this could be so.

11. The same study referred to in Question 10 also discovered that ethical standards are perceived by business people to strengthen a company's competitive position. Briefly explain how this could be so.

12. Consider the following scenario. Tony Howard, a CPA, has completed the audit of Galaxy Enterprise and has signed an opinion letter stating that Galaxy's books have been prepared "in conformance with generally accepted accounting principles" and "present fairly" the company's financial position and the results of its operations. The financial statements look good to a group of twenty investors, and relying on Tony's opinion letter, they decide to invest $50,000 each in the equity (i.e., purchase common stock) of Galaxy. Soon thereafter, Galaxy is forced to declare bankruptcy; all twenty investors lose their entire investments. It is later revealed that Galaxy's financial statements were in error at the time of the audit.
   a. What recourse do the investors have to recover their investments?
   b. What arguments would you expect Tony to make in an effort to defend himself in court?
   c. Would you expect Tony to carry liability insurance to protect himself in the event of a lawsuit?

13. A number of recent articles in publications like *The Wall Street Journal*, *Forbes*, and *Time* have noted that auditors are facing increasing levels of legal liability. At the same time, some business professionals advocate that future-oriented information (e.g., future earnings projections) be included in the financial statements and subject to the auditor's report. Comment on the problems that could arise in view of these seemingly opposing trends.

14. We have stated that financial statements must contain objective and verifiable numbers if they are to be useful. Yet, we have also pointed out that many estimates and subjective assumptions are required for the preparation of these reports. Can you reconcile these apparently inconsistent statements?

15. What incentives might managers have to manipulate the numbers on the financial statements by choosing various estimates, assumptions, and accounting methods? Are generally accepted accounting principles broad enough to allow for such manipulation? How does this present problems for financial statement users?

16. This chapter mentioned that investors require managers to provide financial information so that they can (1) assess the levels of risk and potential returns offered by alternative investments and (2) control the actions of managers through the creation of contracts. Refer to the list below and explain how each of the following items relates to this statement.

   a. The managers of many U.S. companies receive bonuses at the end of each year that are determined by a percentage of that year's net income.

   b. The profits of XYZ company over the past five years have far exceeded the average profit of the companies in the industry in which XYZ is a member.

   c. Leverage, Inc., has recently borrowed $1 million from First National Bank. The loan contract states that the dividends Leverage pays to its shareholders in any one year cannot exceed 50 percent of that year's net income. It also specifies that Leverage's ratio of total liabilities to total assets cannot exceed .75 at any time during the period of the loan. Net income, total liabilities, and total assets must be measured in conformance with generally accepted accounting principles.

   d. Tarpley and Sons has doubled its outstanding debt in the past year.

   e. Dun and Bradstreet, a financial rating service, determines GE's credit rating to be AAA.

17. Why might an equity investor insist that a manager be paid a bonus expressed as a percentage of income? Suppose that Elmer Smith is a manager of a company in its first year of operations who will be paid a bonus at year end that is equal to 1 percent of the company's net income for that year. The bonus contract states that net income for the purposes of the bonus must be audited and measured in conformance with generally accepted accounting principles. Suppose that either of two accounting methods for reporting inventory values are allowed under generally accepted accounting principles. One of the methods, FIFO, gives rise to net income equal to $100,000. The other method, LIFO, results in a $70,000 net income. Based on the bonus contract, which inventory method would Elmer be likely to choose? What other considerations might Elmer make in the choice of inventory accounting methods?

18. Why would a debt investor (e.g., a bank) insist on a loan contract specifying that total liabilities divided by total assets cannot exceed a certain percentage or that dividends paid to stockholders cannot exceed a certain percentage of net income? Suppose that Acme Custom Design is in danger of violating a loan contract stating that total liabilities divided by total assets (as measured by generally accepted accounting principles) cannot exceed 50 percent. If FIFO, an acceptable method for valuing inventory assets, results in a higher asset valuation than LIFO, another acceptable method, which of the two methods would Acme's management be likely to prefer?

19. According to generally accepted accounting principles, many of the assets on the balance sheet are valued at historical cost: the cost incurred when the assets were originally purchased.

   a. How useful are historical costs to equity and debt investors in their efforts to assess the solvency position and long-run earning power of a company?

   b. How useful are historical costs in providing numbers that can be objectively verified and therefore used in the legal contracts that exist between capital providers and managers?

   c. How might the fact that auditors and managers face high levels of legal liability lead to financial statements that rely heavily on historical costs?

20. In preparing financial statements to accompany a loan application for a local bank, Mary Jones was unsure about the proper reporting of a piece of land purchased by the company ten years ago. The land was purchased for $10,000, but recently, similar parcels of land in the area sold for between $25,000 and $40,000.

    a. If you were a CPA auditing Mary's books, what amount would you insist that she disclose for the land value?

    b. What amount would Mary probably prefer?

    c. What amount would the bank find to be most useful?

21. The AICPA's list of red flags, alerting auditors to possible management fraud, includes "a domineering management coupled with a weak board of directors." Briefly explain the role of the board of directors and how such a situation could indicate management fraud. Why are auditors concerned with management fraud?

22. Explain the function of the audit committee and describe why it is important that it consist of outside (nonmanagement) directors.

23. What government agency was formed shortly after the Great Depression to regulate the flow of information in the public security markets? Explain why information in the public security markets needs to be regulated.

24. What body sets financial accounting standards today? Is it a private body, a government body, or some combination of the two?

25. Each of the following quotes was taken from a well-known business publication. In each case comment on how the quote indicates an economic consequence.

    a. "Profits of public companies have the greatest and most immediate effect on a company's stock . . . As the company's profits grow, so will the stock price." (*USA Today*, October 23, 1990).

    b. "Laventhol [a major public accounting firm] says it plans to file for Chapter 11 [bankruptcy]." (*The Wall Street Journal*, November 20, 1990).

    c. "Critics say that [high-tech companies] are often tempted to inflate sales in order to keep their stocks buoyant and creditors at bay." (*The Wall Street Journal*, September 7, 1994).

    d. "Some 70 witnesses plan to address the FASB in five days of public hearings that begin today [in response to a new accounting proposal] . . . One reason for the high anxiety: So many executives have so much at stake." (*The Wall Street Journal*, March 7, 1994).

    e. "The basic drives of man are few: to get enough food, to find shelter and to keep debt off the balance sheet." (*Forbes*, November 20, 1980).

26. The AICPA considered and passed a proposal that would bar accountants from borrowing from banks that their firms audit. Briefly explain why the AICPA would pass such a proposal.

27. Why should investors, creditors, managers, and consumers be concerned if auditors must charge higher fees due to increasing levels of legal liability and increasing liability insurance rates?

28. Suppose an accounting standard, which requires companies to report projections of earnings two years in the future, is presently being considered by the FASB. The FASB is now receiving letters from interested parties. What kind of comments would you expect the FASB to receive from auditing firms? Do you believe that auditors would be willing to audit such projections? Why?

29. For years many individuals have claimed that public accounting firms should not be allowed to offer management advisory services to the same companies they audit. What is the rationale behind such claims?

30. Moody's Investors Service, Standard & Poor's Corporation, and Dun & Bradstreet are well-known services that use publicly available financial information to provide ratings on the outstanding debt securities of many U.S. companies. High ratings indicate less risky debt than low ratings. DuPont, for example has the highest AAA rating. Briefly explain why a company would desire a high debt rating and how such a desire may encourage management to manipulate the financial statements.

31. Chuck Enis, a financial analyst, is studying firms in the pharmaceutical industry, hoping to find a solid investment. He is having difficulty comparing the performance levels of companies that are based in different countries. Explain why this trouble exists.

32. Critique the following statement: Generally accepted accounting principles represent a precise and narrowly defined set of laws that are set by a council of accounting experts who insulate themselves from political pressures. Failure to follow these laws can result in heavy fines and sometimes jail sentences for managers.

33. What body is currently involved in setting international accounting standards and why might its progress be slow?

34. Refer to the MCI annual report in Appendix C and answer the following questions.
    a. Briefly describe the operations of MCI and indicate whether the company is a manufacturer, retailer, or service enterprise.
    b. Which public accounting firm audited the MCI financial statements? Briefly explain the contents of the audit report.
    c. What dollar amount for net income was reported for 1994 and how does it compare to the amounts reported in 1993 and 1992?
    d. How much long-term debt did MCI owe as of December 31, 1994, and how does this amount compare to the December 31, 1993 amount? Compute the net increase in "Senior notes and other debt" during 1994.
    e. How much cash was provided by operating activities during 1994, 1993, and 1992?
    f. Provide the name and position of the individuals who signed the MCI management letter and briefly describe what it says.
    g. Review the list of MCI's Board of Directors. How many are MCI officers? Why aren't all board members MCI officers?

35. (Appendix 1A) E. W. Hauser and Associates showed $38,000 of net income on this past year's income statement. Yet the tax form filed with the Internal Revenue Service indicated only $25,000 of taxable income. Can you suggest several reasons and cite several examples that might explain this difference?

36. (Appendix 1A) Distinguish management accounting from financial accounting, and describe how the information provided by the two systems is used differently.

THE FINANCIAL STATEMENTS

LEARNING OBJECTIVES

LO 1
Identify and describe the three basic activities of a business, and explain how each activity is reflected in the financial statements.

LO 2
Describe the contents of the balance sheet, income statement, statement of retained earnings, and statement of cash flows, and how this information is useful to external users.

This chapter focuses on the information contained in and relationships among the four basic financial statements: the balance sheet, the income statement, the statement of retained earnings, and the statement of cash flows.[1] It describes in detail the nature of each statement and how the information they contain is related.

As you read this chapter, consider the following questions. How do a manager's operating, investing, and financing decisions affect the dollar amounts reported on the financial statements? What information on the financial statements can be used to assess a company's solvency position and earning power? How might investors and creditors use the dollar values shown on the financial statements to control and monitor the business decisions of managers? How can management influence the preparation of these statements so that they depict its solvency position and earning power as attractively as possible? Such questions give economic meaning to financial statements and must be addressed by managers who adopt both a user orientation and an economic consequence perspective.

BUSINESSES ARE LIKE FRUIT TREES

In this section we discuss how businesses operate. As depicted in Figure 2–1, businesses are a lot like fruit trees.

FIGURE 2–1

Businesses are like fruit trees

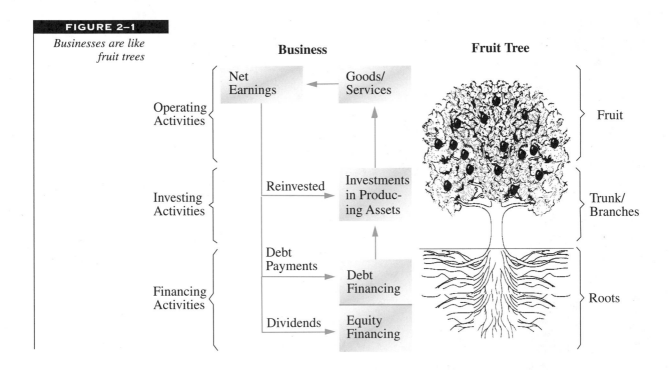

1. Major U.S. corporations are also required to prepare a statement of stockholder's equity that includes information in addition to that in the statement of retained earnings. Due to its complexity, we do not cover the statement of stockholder's equity until Chapter 12. The earlier chapters refer only to the statement of retained earnings.

FRUIT TREES

Refer first to the illustration of the fruit tree, and note that it is comprised of three parts: roots, trunk/branches, and fruit. The roots provide necessary nutrients to the trunk and branches which, in turn, bear fruit. A strong root system provides the required nourishment for a solid trunk and branching system which can lead to plump, juicy, delicious fruit. Note that the primary function of the root and trunk/branch systems is to produce and support the fruit, which can be consumed by the tree's owner or sold. Proceeds from fruit sales can be reinvested in the tree by hiring someone to prune and care for the trunk and branch system, and by purchasing and applying fertilizer to strengthen the roots.[2]

BUSINESSES

Business operations are conducted in a similar way. To start a business, an **entrepreneur** must attract capital in the form of equity or debt financing. Owners contribute cash and receive equity shares in return. Creditors loan cash in return for the promise of interest and principal payments. Note how equity and debt financing correspond to the root system of the fruit tree in that they provide the nutrients necessary to support the entire process.

Once the capital (cash) is collected, it is then invested in producing assets, such as buildings, equipment, machinery, and vehicles, which produce and support the goods and services provided by the business. Note how the producing assets correspond to the trunk and branch system of the fruit tree in that they lead directly to the final product.

In a business the final product is a good or service, which is sold to customers. The net earnings from these sales can be used in three ways: (1) reinvested in the producing assets, (2) returned to the creditors in the form of debt payments, and (3) returned to the owners in the form of dividends. Note how the goods and services provided by a business are similar to the fruit, which can be sold and (1) reinvested in the trunk and branches, (2) used to strengthen the roots or (3) consumed by the owners.

THREE ACTIVITIES OF A BUSINESS

L O 1 The comparison between businesses and fruit trees highlights three basic activities involved in conducting a business: (1) financing activities, (2) investing activities, and (3) operating activities. **Financing activities** involve the collection of capital through equity or debt issuances and any associated payments such as dividends and debt payments. These activities are the "roots" of the business. **Investing activities** involve the acquisition and sale of producing assets, the assets used to produce and support the goods and services provided. These activities are the "trunk and branches" of the business. **Operating activities** involve the sale of the goods and services and, thereby, are the "fruit" of the business. These activities produce additional capital which can be reinvested in the producing assets, used to service debt payments, and distributed to the owners in the form of dividends.

2. Interestingly, throughout its 1993 annual report PepsiCo, Inc. uses a similar tree analogy to illustrate its variety of products.

The remainder of the chapter is devoted to describing and interpreting the financial statements. As you study them keep in mind that they are designed to measure different aspects of businesses and fruit trees as depicted in Figure 2–1. The balance sheet includes assets (goods and producing assets) and financing sources (equity, debt, and reinvestments from net earnings) as of a point in time. It therefore represents a picture of the tree, including its fruit and root system. The income statement is a measure of operations, the activities involved in selling the goods and services, the "fruit" of the business. The statement of retained earnings measures the extent to which the business reinvests its net earnings and pays dividends (i.e., Is the fruit reinvested in the tree or consumed?). The statement of cash flows reports the cash inflows and outflows associated with the operating (fruit sales), investing (trunk and branches), and financing (roots) activities of the business.

From a user's orientation, managers must be able to appreciate the link between the financial statements and the company's true financial condition and performance. From an economic consequence perspective, managers must know how their operating, investing, and financing decisions are reflected on the statements.

THE CLASSIFIED BALANCE SHEET

LO 2 We now turn to more in-depth discussions of the four financial statements. The balance sheet is discussed first. We discuss the income statement, the statement of retained earnings, and the statement of cash flows after the balance sheet because all three explain the activity in one or more of the balance sheet accounts.

Figure 2–2 shows the balance sheet for Harbour Island Company as of December 31, 1996. It is entitled a **classified balance sheet** because the asset and liability accounts are grouped into classifications: current assets; long-term investments; property, plant, and equipment; intangible assets; current liabilities; and long-term liabilities.

A PHOTOGRAPH OF FINANCIAL CONDITION

Think of the balance sheet as a photograph of the business at a specific point in time. The title includes a specific date (December 31, 1996). As of this date, the balance sheet measures the financial condition of Harbour Island Company. In fact, some companies refer to the balance sheet as the *statement of financial condition*. This "photograph" of financial condition shows that as of December 31, 1996, Harbour Island has $220 in cash, total assets of $18,615, contributed capital of $9,550, retained earnings of $1,385, and total liabilities plus stockholders' equity of $18,615.

The balance sheet lists Harbour Island's assets and their sources as of December 31, 1996. The company's total assets (valued at $18,615) came from three separate sources: (1) $7,680 (41 percent) came from various forms of borrowing (total liabilities) and must be repaid in the future, (2) $9,550 (51 percent) came from investments by stockholders (contributed capital), who expect some form of return in the future, and (3) $1,385 (8 percent), the dollar amount in the Retained Earnings account, was generated through the company's operating activities and not returned to the stockholders in the form of dividends.

FIGURE 2–2	HARBOUR ISLAND COMPANY
Classified balance sheet for Harbour Island Company	CLASSIFIED BALANCE SHEET DECEMBER 31, 1996

ASSETS

Current assets:		
Cash		$ 220
Short-term investments		150
Accounts receivable	$ 350	
Less: Uncollectibles	5	345
Inventory		600
Prepaid expenses		100
Total current assets		$ 1,415
Long-term investments:		
Long-term notes receivable		$1,000
Land		500
Securities		2,500
Total long-term investments		4,000
Property, plant, and equipment:		
Property		$6,000
Plant	$4,000	
Less: Accumulated depreciation	1,100	2,900
Equipment	$3,500	
Less: Accumulated depreciation	900	2,600
Total property, plant, & equip.		11,500
Intangible assets:		
Goodwill		$ 800
Patent		200
Trademark		700
Total intangible assets		1,700
Total assets		$18,615

LIABILITIES AND STOCKHOLDERS' EQUITY

Current liabilities:		
Accounts payable		$ 250
Wages payable		25
Interest payable		155
Short-term notes payable		75
Current maturities of long-term debts		60
Deferred revenues		75
Other payables		100
Total current liabilities		$ 740
Long-term liabilities:		
Long-term notes payable		$1,500
Bonds payable		3,500
Mortgage payable		1,940
Total long-term liabilities		6,940
Stockholders' equity:		
Contributed capital		$9,550
Retained earnings		1,385
Total stockholders' equity		10,935
Total liabilities and stockholders' equity		$18,615

BALANCE SHEET CLASSIFICATIONS

Assets are divided into current assets ($1,415), long-term investments ($4,000); property, plant, and equipment ($11,500); and intangible assets ($1,700). These categories and the order of the accounts within them are listed in order of **liquidity**. The assets listed near the top of the balance sheet (e.g., current assets) are expected to be converted into cash within a shorter time period than those listed at or near the bottom. They are, therefore, considered to be more liquid. The assets in the current asset category are also listed in order of liquidity. Cash, the most liquid of all assets, is understandably listed at the top.

Liabilities are divided into current liabilities ($740) and long-term liabilities ($6,940). These two categories, and the accounts within them, are also listed in order of liquidity. Those near the top of the balance sheet (e.g., current liabilities) are expected to require the payment of cash within a shorter time period than those at or near the bottom. Study these categories and the order of the accounts contained within them. This is the general format required under generally accepted accounting principles, and it is important that you be familiar with it.

ASSETS

We now discuss the individual balance sheet accounts. This section reviews current assets; long-term investments; property, plant, and equipment; and intangible assets.

CURRENT ASSETS

Assets categorized as current are expected to be realized or, in most cases, converted into cash in the near future, usually within one year. They are grouped into a separate category because they are considered to be highly liquid. The amount of highly liquid assets held by a company can be an indication of its ability to meet debt payments as they come due. Consequently, the current asset category is often reviewed by financial statement users who are interested in assessing a company's solvency position. **Current assets** include cash, short-term investments, accounts receivable, inventory, and prepaid expenses, and they often represent a significant portion of a company's total assets. For example, current assets of Kmart, a major retailer, represents over 50% of total assets.

CASH. Cash represents the currency a company has access to as of the balance sheet date. It may be in a bank savings account, a checking account, or perhaps on the company premises in the form of petty cash. Cash amounts that a company can use immediately should be separated on the balance sheet from cash that is restricted. As a condition of granting a loan, for example, banks often require that the borrowing company maintain a certain cash balance with the bank while the loan is outstanding. Cash amounts of this nature, called *compensating balances*, are normally described in the footnotes to the financial statements so that readers can draw a distinction between available cash and restricted cash. Such a distinction can be useful when assessing how much cash is available to meet an outstanding debt. A recent financial report of Atlantic Richfield, for example, noted that "the company maintains compensating balances for some of its various banking services and products."

SHORT-TERM INVESTMENTS. **Short-term investments** include stocks (equity investments in other companies), bonds (debt investments in the government or other companies), and similar investments. These securities are both *readily marketable* (i.e., able to be sold immediately) and intended by management to be sold within a short period of time, usually less than one year. A company often purchases these kinds of securities to earn income with cash that would otherwise be idle for a short time. The dollar value of this account is the total selling price (market value) of securities held by a company as of the balance sheet date. For purposes of solvency assessment, this dollar amount is normally viewed to be the same as available cash.

Many companies invest in short-term equity and debt securities, but this account is especially important for financial institutions like banks and insurance companies. In recent years, for example, Safeco Insurance Company has reported approximately $5 billion in marketable debt and equity securities on its balance sheet, which represented almost 70 percent of the company's total assets.

ACCOUNTS RECEIVABLE. The **Accounts Receivable** account represents the amount of money a company expects to collect from its customers. Such receivables arise from sales of products or services for which customers have not yet paid. These sales are often referred to as *credit sales* or *sales on account*. The dollar amount appearing on the balance sheet for this account is computed by taking the total dollar amount of the receivables owed and subtracting an estimate for *uncollectibles*, those accounts not expected to be received. The uncollectibles estimate is highly subjective and users must be careful not to conclude that all reported receivables will necessarily lead to cash receipts.

The dollar value of accounts receivable is very significant for large retailing companies, such as Sears and J.C. Penney, whose sales are primarily on a credit basis. J.C. Penney, for example, recently reported net accounts receivable of approximately $4 billion, which was about 60 percent of current assets and 40 percent of total assets.

INVENTORY. Inventory represents items or products on hand that a company intends to sell to its customers. It is often called **merchandise inventory**. The dollar value in this account is very important because a company's success often depends on its ability to sell these items. Users are very interested in the sales' value of a company's inventory, but unfortunately the balance-sheet value of inventory is the cost of acquiring (purchasing or producing) it or the cost of replacing it as of the balance sheet date, whichever is lower.

Major retailers and manufacturers carry significant inventory balances on their balance sheets, while financial institutions and companies in the service industry carry very little. For example, on a recent balance sheet McDonnell Douglas, a major aircraft manufacturer, reported inventories of over $6 billion, which equaled 42 percent of total assets. That same year the American Express Company and H&R Block reported no inventories.

A second kind of inventory account is called *supplies inventory*. It represents items used to support a company's operations: office supplies and spare parts are two common examples. The dollar amount of this account on the balance sheet is usually the cost of acquiring the items. Major manufacturers often carry a substantial inventory of spare parts. Recently McDonnell Douglas reported materials and spare parts inventories of approximately $15 billion.

PREPAID EXPENSES. Prepaid expenses are exactly what the name suggests: expenses that have been paid by a company before the corresponding service or right is actually used. Insurance premiums, for example, are normally paid prior to the period of coverage. Similarly, rent is usually paid before the rental period. A prepaid expense, therefore, is considered an asset because it represents a benefit to be enjoyed by the company in the future. Prepaid expenses are originally recorded on the balance sheet at the cost of acquiring them. For most companies, prepaid expenses are a very small, often insignificant, part of total assets. Also, prepaid expenses do not create future cash inflows, a fact that users must recognize when assessing a company's solvency position.

LONG-TERM INVESTMENTS

Long-term investments are acquired by companies to provide benefits for periods of time usually extending beyond one year. Examples include long-term notes receivable and investments in land, debt and equity securities, life insurance, and special funds for specific purposes.

The Notes Receivable account includes company receivables that are evidenced by promissory notes. *Promissory notes* are contracts (formal, legally enforceable documents) that state the face value of the receivable, the date when the face value is due, and the periodic interest payments to be made while the note is outstanding. The date when the receivable is due, called the *maturity date*, is often beyond one year, so this account is often listed in the long-term investment section of the balance sheet. However, if the maturity date of a note receivable is within one year, it should be disclosed as a current asset.

Notes receivable often arise because companies receive notes in exchange for the sale of expensive items. For example, the Boeing Company, a major aircraft manufacturer, often receives notes in payment for sold aircraft. As of December 31, 1994, it reported $1.189 billion in long-term notes receivable. Alternatively, such notes can result from direct company loans to employees and others. It also happens that customers with large, overdue accounts are asked to sign promissory notes. Like accounts receivable, an estimate—often subjective—for uncollectibles must be provided for notes receivable.

In addition to notes receivable, the long-term investment section of the balance sheet can include a number of other investments. Land, for example, may be purchased and held as a long-term investment. Investments in debt and equity securities that are not intended to be sold in the near future represent other common examples. Most major U.S. companies have made significant investments in the equity securities of other, usually smaller, companies, intending to exert long-term influence over their management. As of the end of 1994, for example, Scott Paper Company reported an investment of $53 million in companies which own a pulp mill, forestland, and a tree plantation in Chile in the long-term investment section of its balance sheet. Users should learn as much as possible about such investments, usually by reading the footnotes, because they signal areas where management has chosen to devote considerable attention.

The *cash value of life insurance*, the amount for which ordinary insurance policies held on the lives of company officers can be cashed in, and the assets of investment funds designed to finance future events, like plant expansions and debt payments, also appear in this section of the balance sheet. The dollar amounts in these accounts, which are relatively small for most major U.S. companies, normally equal the costs of acquiring them.

PROPERTY, PLANT, AND EQUIPMENT

The property, plant, and equipment section of the balance sheet includes assets acquired for use in the day-to-day operations of the business. For many companies, especially manufacturers, this is the largest asset category on the balance sheet. For example, the property, plant, and equipment account for Texaco, a major oil company, is valued at almost $14 billion, which represents approximately 53 percent of its total assets. This account often contains the results of management's major investing activities, an important concern of financial statement users.

The **Property** account represents the land on which the company conducts its operations. It is carried on the balance sheet at the original price for the land, which is not adjusted as the value of the property appreciates (i.e., increases). Be sure not to confuse this account with land in the long-term investment section. The property referred to in this account is used in the operations of the business, while land is held for investment purposes only.

Plant and equipment represent the physical structures owned by a company that are involved in its operations. The Plant account, for example, includes the value of factory and office buildings and warehouses, while the Equipment account includes machinery, vehicles, furniture, and similar items. The dollar amount in these accounts on the balance sheet is the original cost at the time the assets were purchased, reduced by an amount that loosely approximates the asset's lost usefulness or deterioration over time. This dollar amount is called *accumulated depreciation*. Subtracting accumulated depreciation from the acquisition cost results in the *net value* or **net book value** of the assets. The excerpt below, which illustrates the methods used to disclose property, plant, and equipment, was taken from the 1994 annual report of General Mills (dollars in millions).

IN MILLIONS	MAY 29, 1994	MAY 30, 1993
Land, Buildings and Equipment:		
Land	$ 360.9	$ 302.3
Buildings	1,655.6	1,452.6
Equipment	2,373.8	2,048.1
Construction in progress	299.5	436.5
Total land, buildings and equipment	$ 4,689.8	$ 4,239.5
Less accumulated depreciation	(1,597.2)	(1,379.9)
Net land, buildings and equipment	$ 3,092.6	$ 2,859.6

INTANGIBLE ASSETS

Intangible assets are so named because they have no physical substance. In most cases they represent legal rights to the use or sale of valuable names, items, processes, or information. Many companies, such as Coca Cola, have patents on certain formulas that grant them the sole legal right to produce and sell certain products. When NBC paid over $1 billion to acquire exclusive rights to broadcast the Olympics, it recognized an intangible asset on its balance sheet. In a similar way, a company's trademark (e.g., the golden arches of McDonald's) or its name (e.g., Goodyear Tire & Rubber) can also be valuable. Perhaps the most common intangible asset, called *goodwill*, represents the cost of purchasing another company over and above the total market price of that company's individual assets and liabilities. The Goodwill account is prominent on the balance sheets of many major U.S. companies because they often purchase other companies, called *subsidiaries*. For example, when Time, Inc. purchased Warner Communications, it recognized almost $9 billion of goodwill on the transaction. Similar to property, plant, and equipment, users are interested in intangibles because they often represent the results of a company's major investing activities.

Intangible assets are carried on the balance sheet at net book value, which is equal to the cost of acquiring an intangible asset reduced by a dollar amount, called *accumulated amortization*, which loosely approximates the asset's reduction in usefulness over time. However, unlike accumulated depreciation on plant and equipment, accumulated amortization is usually not disclosed in a special account on the balance sheet; only the net book value of the intangible asset is disclosed. The excerpt below, which illustrates a method of disclosing intangible assets, was taken from the 1994 financial report of General Electric Company (dollars in millions).

	1994	1993
Goodwill	$5,605	$5,713
Other intangibles	731	753
Total	$6,336	$6,466

LIABILITIES

This section covers current and long-term liabilities. The dollar amounts disclosed in these sections of the balance sheet are very important to users who are interested in the timing of a company's future cash obligations, which is important when assessing if a company can meet its debts when they come due. Total liabilities, as a percentage of total assets, varies significantly across companies in different industries. For example, the Boeing Company, a manufacturer, carries liabilities of about 55% of total assets, while the liabilities of BankAmerica represent over 90% of total assets.

CURRENT LIABILITIES

Current liabilities are obligations that are expected to be paid (or services expected to be performed) with the use of assets that are listed in the current asset section of the balance sheet. Examples include Accounts Payable, Wages Payable, Interest Payable, Short-Term Notes Payable, Income Taxes Payable, Current Maturities on Long-Term Debts, and Deferred Revenues.

Accounts Payable are usually obligations to a company's suppliers for merchandise purchases made on account. Wages Payable are obligations to a company's employees for earned but unpaid wages as of the balance sheet date. Interest Payable and Short-Term Notes Payable are dollar amounts owed to creditors, often banks and other financial institutions. Income Taxes Payable are amounts owed to the government for taxes assessed on a company's income. **Current Maturities of Long-Term Debts** are portions of long-term liabilities that are due in the current period. They often arise when the principal amounts of long-term liabilities are due in installments over time. Deferred Revenues represent services yet to be performed by a company for which cash payments have already been collected.

Financial statement users often closely examine a company's current liabilities as they assess a company's solvency position because most current liabilities require cash payments in the short-term future. For many companies, current liabilities represent the largest source of debt financing. For example, the 1990 dollar balance in current liabilities for Boeing was $6.8 billion, which represented almost 32 percent of the company's total assets, while long-term liabilities represented only 22 percent of total assets.

LONG-TERM LIABILITIES

Long-term liabilities are obligations expected to require payment over a period of time beyond the current year. These obligations are usually evidenced by formal contracts that state their principal amounts, the periodic interest payments, and maturity dates. The form of these debt contracts, however, can vary widely. Common examples include accounts like Long-Term Notes Payable, Bonds Payable, and Mortgage Payable.

Long-Term **Notes Payable** refer to obligations on loans that are normally due more than one year beyond the balance sheet date. They usually involve either direct borrowings from financial institutions or arrangements to finance the purchase of assets. **Bonds Payable** represent notes that have been issued for cash to a large number of debt investors (called *bondholders*). Issuing bonds is a common form of financing for many major U.S. companies, which often use the funds to expand operations. During 1994, for example, May Department Stores Company, which operates a large number of well-known clothing retailers, issued $200 million in bonds. The proceeds were used primarily to finance capital expenditures and reduce other debts. **Mortgage Payables** are obligations that are secured by real estate and are usually owed to financial institutions. The contractual terms (e.g., interest notes and covenant restrictions) associated with long-term debts are particularly important to financial statement users because they identify short-term cash outflows and constraints that may inhibit management's future activities.

STOCKHOLDERS' EQUITY

The **stockholders' equity** section of the balance sheet is basically divided into two parts: contributed capital and retained earnings. Note in Figure 2–2 that the total amount of stockholders' equity ($10,935) is equal to total assets ($18,615) less total liabilities ($7,680). This dollar amount is called the *net book value* of the company.

CONTRIBUTED CAPITAL

Contributed capital is a measure of the assets that have been contributed to a company by its owners. Such contributions are made by purchasing the equity securities issued by the company, contributing cash or other noncash assets, or providing services. Whatever the form, the investor's contribution is exchanged for ownership interests (e.g., shares of stock) in the company. Such interests usually carry with them the right to have a voice in the management of the company (e.g., vote for the board of directors) as well as the right to receive assets (e.g., dividends), if they are distributed. In many cases these ownership interests can be purchased and sold freely (e.g., through public stock markets), but such transactions have no effects on the company's balance sheet.

Issuing stock is a common method used by major U.S. companies to raise capital for expansion. Recently, for example, United Airlines Corporation issued over

1.5 million shares of stock, collecting approximately $225 million dollars. These funds were used primarily to finance the acquisition of certain operations from Pan Am and Eastern Airlines.

RETAINED EARNINGS

Retained earnings is a measure of the assets that have been generated through a company's operating activities but not paid out to stockholders in the form of dividends. This account is particularly troublesome to accounting students who tend to visualize it as a tangible pool of cash. Nothing could be further from the truth. The $1,385 in Harbour Island's retained earnings account in Figure 2–2 is not in the form of cash in the company treasurer's office or in the bank. In fact, it is not associated with any specific asset or group of assets. It is simply a measure of the amount of the assets appearing on the balance sheet that have been provided by profitable operations. All we know from the balance sheet in Figure 2–2 is that $1,385 of the $18,615 total in the asset account has been provided by the company's profitable operations.

The relative size of retained earnings on the balance sheets of major U.S. companies varies significantly across industries. BankAmerica, for example, normally reports retained earnings of only 2 percent of total assets, while Microsoft, a fast-growing computer software developer, is currently reporting retained earnings of over 60 percent of total assets. Users normally consider a large balance in retained earnings to be a positive sign because it indicates that the company has been profitable in the past and has chosen to reinvest those profits.

ORGANIZATIONAL FORM AND THE EQUITY SECTION

A business entity in the United States can be legally organized in either of two basic ways: as a corporation or as a partnership (called a *proprietorship* if there is only one owner). A *corporation* is a legal entity that is separate and distinct from its owners. It can be taxed or sued, and the owners, called *stockholders* or *shareholders*, are legally liable only for the amount of their original contributions to the corporation. Stockholders acquire ownership interests by purchasing shares of stock in the corporation, and their interests give them the right to vote for its board of directors at annual stockholders' meetings as well as the right to receive dividends, which are distributed on a per-share basis, if declared by the board.

A *partnership*, or *proprietorship*, on the other hand, is not a legal entity. It can neither be taxed nor sued, and the legal liability of the owners, called *partners* or *proprietors,* is not limited to their original contributions. Asset distributions to partners are called *withdrawals*.

The differences between corporations and partnerships are reflected in differences in the equity sections of their balance sheets. The stockholders' equity section of a corporate balance sheet, as illustrated in Figure 2–2, draws a distinction between contributed capital, the measure of the assets contributed by the stockholders, and retained earnings, the assets generated through the company's operating activities and not returned to stockholders in the form of dividends.

On the other hand, the equity section on a partnership's balance sheet, called **owners' equity**, makes no distinction between contributed capital and retained earnings. Instead, it consists of separate accounts for each partner, which show the status of each partner's personal capital balance, reflecting all contributions and withdrawals. Figure 2–3 illustrates the differences between the stockholders' equity section of a corporation and the owners' equity section of a partnership with two partners.

FIGURE 2–3	CORPORATION		PARTNERSHIP	
Owners' equity: corporation vs. partnership	**Stockholders' equity:**		**Owners' equity:**	
	Contributed capital	$20,000	Capital account, Ms. A	$12,000
	Retained earnings	14,000	Capital account, Mr. B	15,000
	Total stockholders' equity	$34,000	Total owners' equity	$27,000

Throughout most of the text, the discussions and illustrations assume the corporate form of organization.

THE INCOME STATEMENT

The income statement measures operating performance over a particular period—the activities associated with the acquisition and sale of the company's inventories or services (i.e., "fruit"). An example, for the Harbour Island Company covering the year ended December 31, 1996, is illustrated in Figure 2–4. Note that it consists of two categories: revenues ($5,880) and expenses ($4,795). Subtracting expenses from revenues yields a number called *net income* or *loss*, *net earnings*, or *profits* ($1,085). Net income is a very common and useful measure of operating performance. Indeed, many business people agree that net income is the most important number disclosed on the financial statements.

REVENUES

Revenues represent the inflow of assets (or decrease in liabilities) due to a company's operating activities over a period of time. Examples include sales, fees earned, and a number of other miscellaneous revenues. The ability to generate revenues is often viewed as one of the important keys to success for a company. Indeed, the top performance plan objective for the Goodyear Tire & Rubber Company for 1995 was to "increase sales (revenue) 4.5 percent to 5 percent annually."

SALES AND FEES EARNED

Sales is perhaps the most common revenue account. It represents a measure of asset increases (usually in the form of cash or accounts receivable) due to selling a company's products or inventories. If a company provides a service (e.g., a law firm or accounting firm) instead of selling a product, the revenue account reflecting such activity is called **Fees Earned** or **Service Revenue**. For example, H&R Block, Inc., which provides tax preparation services, reported service revenues of over $1 billion in 1994.

OTHER REVENUES

The category called *Other Revenues* can include a number of items. It usually contains revenues generated from activities that are not central to a company's operations; therefore, the dollar amount of this category is usually comparatively small. This sec-

FIGURE 2-4

Income statement for Harbour Island Company

HARBOUR ISLAND COMPANY
INCOME STATEMENT
FOR THE YEAR ENDED DECEMBER 31, 1996

Revenues:			
Sales		$4,000	
Fees earned		1,000	
Other revenues		880	
Total revenues			$5,880
Expenses:			
Cost of goods sold		$1,500	
Operating expenses:			
Wage expense	$1,000		
Rent expense	295		
Selling expense	300		
Depreciation expense	500		
Amortization expense	300		
Total operating expenses		2,395	
Other expenses		900	
Total expenses			4,795
Net income			$1,085

tion often includes interest income on bank savings accounts, rent collected on the rental of excess warehouse space, and book gains recognized when assets other than inventory are sold for amounts that exceed their original costs. In its 1994 annual report, Nike, Inc., reported $19 million of interest income, which represented 6 percent of the company's profits and only 5 percent of revenues.

It is very important that users appreciate the difference between revenues generated by core business activities and revenues created by "one-shot" transactions. Presumably, core revenues can be expected to reoccur, while "one-shot" revenues cannot.

EXPENSES

Expenses represent the outflow of assets (or creation of liabilities) required to generate revenues. Examples include cost of goods sold, operating expenses, and other miscellaneous expenses. As important as generating revenues, controlling expenses is also a barometer of a company's success. To reduce its downward spiral, Kmart's management team noted in the 1994 annual report that a top priority is to "find $600 million in cost reductions for 1995."

COST OF GOODS SOLD

The **Cost of Goods Sold** account represents the original cost of the inventory items (purchase price or cost of manufacturing) that are sold to generate sales revenue. For retail and manufacturing companies, this *inventory expense* is normally separated from other operating expenses because it is comparatively large, and it is often expressed as a percentage of sales revenue to indicate the relationship between the selling price of the inventory and its cost. Users pay close attention to this percentage because it indicates by how much the sales price exceeds the cost of a good. Cost of

Goods Sold as a percentage of sales for J.C. Penney, a large retailer, and Monsanto, a large manufacturer, are normally around 65 percent. On the other hand, H&R Block, a service firm, reports no Cost of Goods Sold on its income statement.

OPERATING EXPENSES

Operating expenses are those periodic and usual expenses that a company incurs attempting to generate revenues. For retailing companies, which simply purchase finished goods and then sell them (e.g., Wal-Mart), this expense category contains accounts reflecting the decrease in assets (or creation of liabilities) due to such items as commissions to salespersons, salaries, wages, insurance, advertising, rentals, utilities, property taxes, equipment maintenance, depreciation of plant and equipment, and amortization of intangible assets. Manufacturing companies, on the other hand (e.g., General Motors), typically include only selling and administrative expenses in this category. Note from the expenses listed on the income statement in Figure 2–4 that Harbour Island is a retailer.

OTHER EXPENSES

Like the category Other Revenues, *Other Expenses* can include a number of items. It usually contains expenses incurred from activities that are not central to a company's operations, therefore, the dollar amount of this category is also usually small. Interest expense on outstanding loans and book losses recognized when assets other than inventory are sold for amounts that are less than their original costs are often found in this section of the income statement. Similar to revenues, it is also important for users to appreciate the difference between core expenses and "one-shot" expenses.

THE STATEMENT OF RETAINED EARNINGS

The statement of retained earnings, which is illustrated for Harbour Island in Figure 2–5, describes the activity in the Retained Earnings account over a period of time. Note that the beginning dollar balance in Retained Earnings, which comes from the December 31, 1995 balance sheet, is increased (decreased) by net income (loss), which comes from the 1996 income statement, and reduced by 1996 dividends, leading to the ending dollar balance, which can be found on the December 31, 1996 balance sheet. Thus, the balance in the Retained Earnings account at any point in time simply consists of past net income (earnings) amounts that have been retained in the business (i.e., not paid out in the form of dividends).

Companies retain profits to finance operations and capital expenditures and to pay off debts. The remaining profits are often returned to the shareholders in the form of

FIGURE 2–5	HARBOUR ISLAND COMPANY	
Statement of retained earnings for Harbour Island Company	STATEMENT OF RETAINED EARNINGS FOR THE YEAR ENDED DECEMBER 31, 1996	
	Beginning retained earnings balance (December 31, 1995)	$ 500
	Plus: Net income	1,085
	Less: Dividends	(200)
	Ending retained earnings balance (December 31, 1996)	$1,385

dividends. Users are interested in the statement of retained earnings because it provides information about the company's dividend policy, specifically how dividends compare to reported profits.

It is important to realize that retained earnings is nothing in and of itself, but rather a measure of something else. It is not cash, nor is it an asset that can be touched or used. Instead, it is similar to an inch, a gallon, or a pound, all of which are measures of something tangible. An inch reflects a length of rope, the width of a table, or the height of a person, while retained earnings represents a measure of the assets, all of which are listed on the asset side of the balance sheet, that have been generated through profitable operations and retained in the business. Recall that assets can come from three sources: borrowings, contributions from owners, and profitable operations. Retained earnings is a measure of the third source.

THE STATEMENT OF CASH FLOWS

The statement of cash flows is a summary of the activity in a company's cash account over a period of time. Preparing a statement of cash flows is simply a matter of recognizing that certain transactions entered into by a company during a given period increase the Cash account, while others decrease it. The statement summarizes these transactions and, in the process, explains how the cash balance at the beginning of the period came to be the cash balance at the end of the period. The statement of cash flows for Harbour Island Company for the year ended December 31, 1996, appears in Figure 2–6.[3]

The statement of cash flows is divided into three basic categories: (1) operating activities, (2) investing activities, and (3) financing activities—the same categories of business activities introduced in the "tree analogy" earlier in the chapter. The transactions summarized within each of these three categories either increased or (decreased) cash during the period, and the net result of the three totals explains the change in a company's overall cash balance. For example, on Harbour Island's cash flow statement, operating activities increased cash by $1,470, investment activities decreased cash by $4,100, and financing activities increased cash by $2,750. The net result is $120 (1,470 − 4,100 + 2,750), the increase in the cash balance during 1996.

The statement of cash flows provides important information to investors and creditors, especially those who are interested in assessing a company's solvency position. A recent survey reported in *Management Accounting* (July 1992) noted that "a majority of investors report that the statement of cash flows is a useful source of information . . . [and that] investors use the statement of cash flows more, and the income statement less, than previously."

CASH FLOWS FROM OPERATING ACTIVITIES

Cash flows from operating activities include those cash inflows and outflows associated with the acquisition and sale of a company's products and services. The items found in this section are closely related to those found on the income statement

---

3. The operating section of this statement of cash flows can be presented under either the direct or indirect method. The statement in Figure 2–6 uses the direct form of presentation. Most major U.S. companies use the indirect form of presentation, which is described in detail in both Chapter 14 and Appendix A at the end of the text.

FIGURE 2–6	HARBOUR ISLAND COMPANY
Statement of cash flows for Harbour Island Company	STATEMENT OF CASH FLOWS FOR THE YEAR ENDED DECEMBER 31, 1996

Operating activities:			
Cash collections from sales	$ 4,800		
Cash collections from rent	800		
Cash collections from interest	10		
Cash provided by operating activities		$5,610	
Cash paid to suppliers	$(1,800)		
Cash paid to employees	(1,050)		
Cash paid for rent	(290)		
Cash paid for selling activities	(300)		
Cash paid for interest and taxes	(700)		
Cash disbursed for operating activities		(4,140)	
Net cash increase (decrease) from operating activities			$1,470
Investing activities:			
Purchase of investment securities	$ (100)		
Purchase of property	(4,500)		
Proceeds from sale of investment securities	500		
Net cash increase (decrease) from investing activities			(4,100)
Financing activities:			
Proceeds from issuing equity	$ 3,000		
Principle payments on short-term notes	(100)		
Principle payments on long-term debt	(50)		
Cash dividends to stockholders	(100)		
Net cash increase (decrease) from financing activities			2,750
Increase (decrease) in cash balance			$ 120
Beginning cash balance (December 31, 1995)			100
Ending cash balance (December 31, 1996)			$ 220

because both measure operating inflows and outflows. However, the dollar amounts of these items on the statement of cash flows do not necessarily agree with the dollar amounts appearing for these items on the income statement. The statement of cash flows records only *cash* inflows and outflows; the income statement consists of revenues and expenses, which reflect more general *asset* and *liability* inflows and outflows. Cash is just one of a company's many assets.

Consider, for example, the sale of a service in exchange for a receivable. This transaction produces no cash; therefore, it has no effect on the statement of cash flows. It does, however, appear as a revenue on the income statement because an asset in the form of a receivable has been created. Consequently, net cash flow from operating activities on the statement of cash flows is rarely equal to net income on the income statement. In the case of Harbour Island, for example, net cash flow from operating activities in Figure 2–6 is equal to $1,470, while net income for the same period (see Figures 2–4 and 2–5) is equal to $1,085.

For many major U.S. companies, net cash flow from operating activities is the primary source of cash. In its 1994 annual report, for example, The Quaker Oats

Company noted that "The ability to generate funds internally remains one of the company's significant financial strengths." In support of this statement, the company reported $451 million of cash inflow from operating activities on its statement of cash flows. This amount exceeded net income for the year by $220 million. Users are very interested in net cash from operating activities because they represent the company's main source of cash for its investing activities.

CASH FLOWS FROM INVESTING ACTIVITIES

Cash flows from investing activities include the cash inflows and outflows associated with the purchase and sale of a company's noncurrent assets. Cash effects from the purchase or sale of a company's investments or property, plant, and equipment are common examples. Note in Figure 2–6 that Harbour Island used $100 and $4,500 to purchase long-term investment securities and property, respectively. It also generated $500 in cash by selling long-term investments. These transactions in total reduced Harbour Island's cash balance by $4,100.

Net cash flow from investing activities is normally a negative number because, as companies grow, they typically purchase more long-term assets than they sell. In 1994, for example, The Quaker Oats Company spent $175 million in cash for additional property, plant, and equipment, and, in total, the company's investing activities used over $263 million in cash. Net cash flow from investing activities tells users in general how much the company has grown over the current period.

CASH FLOWS FROM FINANCING ACTIVITIES

Cash flows from financing activities include the cash inflows and outflows associated with a company's two sources of outside capital: liabilities and contributed capital. Cash proceeds from and cash principal payments on short- and long-term liabilities are reflected in this section of the statement of cash flows. As indicated in Figure 2–6, while Harbour Island borrowed no additional funds during 1996, it made cash principal payments on both short-term notes ($100) and long-term debt ($50). Cash proceeds from stockholder contributions, or equity issuances, and cash dividends to stockholders are also included in this section. Note that Harbour Island collected $3,000 in cash from issuing equity and paid cash dividends of $100.

The main financing cash outflows of The Quaker Oats Company during 1994 consisted of payments to repurchase its own stock in the amount of $215 million, principal payments on long-term debt of $101 million, and cash dividends of $145 million. Cash collections from financing activities included long-term borrowings of $222 million. Users focus on this section of the statement to learn to what extent the company is relying on external debt and equity to finance its growth.

RELATIONSHIPS AMONG THE FINANCIAL STATEMENTS

We now illustrate and discuss the relationships among the financial statements. Figure 2–7 presents a general overview of the four basic financial accounting statements and shows how they relate to each other. Take some time to study it.

FIGURE 2–7

Relationships among the financial statements

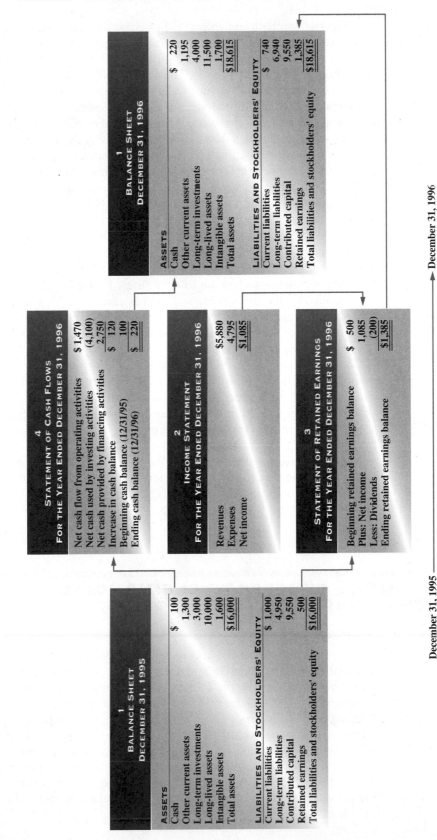

Note the four basic statements indicated by the numbers: (1) balance sheet, (2) income statement, (3) statement of retained earnings, and (4) statement of cash flows. Note also that an additional balance sheet, prepared at the end of the period, is included on the right side of the figure. The account balances on this balance sheet are different from those on the balance sheet on the left. To explain how the balance sheet accounts changed during the year, examine the other three financial statements: the statement of cash flows, the statement of retained earnings, and the income statement.

The statement of cash flows explains the activity during the year in the company's Cash account. At the beginning of 1996 the balance in the Cash account was $100. During the year, operating, investing, and financing transactions affected the cash balance, and the end result was $220. Note how the statement of cash flows ties into the Cash accounts listed on the balance sheet at the beginning and end of 1996.

The statement of retained earnings, like the statement of cash flows, also explains the activity in a balance sheet account during 1996—the Retained Earnings account, which appears in the stockholders' equity section of each balance sheet. Note how the beginning and ending balances of Retained Earnings tie directly into the Retained Earnings accounts listed on the balance sheets for the beginning and end of 1996.

The income statement contains revenues and expenses, which are reflected in the statement of retained earnings through the net income number. The income statement connects directly to the statement of retained earnings, which in turn connects directly to the two balance sheets.

As a result of these interrelationships, every transaction affecting the income statement affects the balance sheet in at least two places. Revenues and expenses are components of retained earnings and increase or decrease the Retained Earnings balance accordingly. In addition, each account on the income statement has a related account in either the asset or liability section of the balance sheet. Recognizing a sale, for example, can affect Cash and Accounts Receivable. Recognizing an expense, such as wage expense, can affect Cash and Wages Payable. Thus, the balance sheet and the income statement are inextricably related. As you work through this text, it is important that you understand these relationships well.

INTERNATIONAL PERSPECTIVE: FINANCIAL STATEMENTS AND ANALYSES IN OTHER COUNTRIES

We commented in Chapter 1 that cultural, political, and economic differences cause financial accounting standards and practices to vary substantially across different countries. Consequently, the formats and contents of the financial statements differ significantly as well. German, Swiss, and Japanese accounting standards, for example, encourage managers to intentionally understate the reported values of assets and overstate the reported values of liabilities, giving rise to special "reserve" accounts on the financial statements. In South America the financial statements are routinely adjusted for inflation, while Japanese accounting standards do not require a statement of cash flows. These differences make it extremely difficult for an investor or creditor, who is unfamiliar with such practices, to conduct meaningful evaluations of earning power and solvency.

The 1994 balance sheet of Nissan Motor Company, Japan's second largest auto-maker, is provided below. Show Ota & Co., an Ernst & Young international affiliate, rendered an unqualified opinion on this statement, stating that it has been prepared "in conformity with accounting principles generally accepted in Japan."

While the balance sheet closely resembles those of major U.S. corporations, there are several interesting differences. First, it is expressed in Japanese yen and U.S. dollar amounts are provided solely for the convenience of the reader. Second, translation adjustments of over $3 billion are added to the assets. This account reflects adjustments that are recorded when the financial statements of subsidiaries operating outside of Japan are converted to Japanese yen for purposes of consolidation. U.S. balance sheets are adjusted in a similar manner, but the translation adjustment is reflected in the stockholders' equity section.

Perhaps the most interesting difference can be found in the shareholders' equity section under the account name "legal reserve." As described in the footnotes, "in accordance with the provisions of the Commercial Code of Japan, the company has provided a legal reserve . . . [that] may be used to reduce a deficit." In other words, after the completion of a profitable year, Nissan can set aside a portion of retained earnings that can be used in the future to reduce net losses. To date, the company has set aside over $460 million of such reserves. This practice, which is not allowed in the U.S., gives Nissan's management much discretion, enabling them to "smooth" reported earnings over time.

NISSAN MOTOR CO., LTD. AND CONSOLIDATED SUBSIDIARIES
CONSOLIDATED BALANCE SHEETS
MARCH 31, 1994 AND 1993

	MILLIONS OF YEN		THOUSANDS OF U.S. DOLLARS (NOTE 2)
ASSETS	1994	1993	1994
Current assets:			
Cash (Note 6)	¥ 169,545	¥ 102,947	$ 1,646,068
Short-term investments (Note 6)	638,226	820,308	6,196,369
Notes and accounts receivable, less allowance for doubtful receivables (Notes 3 and 6)	781,717	811,453	7,589,485
Inventories (Note 4)	835,653	824,090	8,113,136
Other current assets	700,310	769,245	6,799,126
Total current assets	3,125,451	3,328,043	30,344,184
Investments and advances (Note 6):			
Unconsolidated subsidiaries and affiliates	506,343	521,750	4,915,951
Other	284,105	296,311	2,758,301
Total investments and advances	790,448	818,061	7,674,252
Property, plant and equipment, at cost (Notes 5 and 6)	5,772,570	5,164,331	56,044,369
Less accumulated depreciation	(2,678,322)	(2,350,034)	(26,003,126)
Property, plant and equipment, net	3,094,248	2,814,297	30,041,243
Translation adjustments	318,004	225,449	3,087,418
Total assets	¥7,328,151	¥7,185,850	$71,147,097

See Notes to Consolidated Financial Statements.

continued

| | MILLIONS OF YEN | | THOUSANDS OF U.S. DOLLARS (NOTE 2) |
LIABILITIES AND SHAREHOLDERS' EQUITY	1994	1993	1994
Current liabilities:			
Short-term borrowings and current portion of long-term debt (Note 6)	¥1,668,858	¥1,784,201	$16,202,505
Notes and accounts payable (Note 7)	1,060,975	1,043,468	10,300,728
Accrued income taxes	13,600	17,184	132,039
Other current liabilities	346,172	302,189	3,360,893
Total current liabilities	3,089,605	3,147,042	29,996,165
Long-term debt (Note 6)	2,367,708	2,008,876	22,987,456
Accrued retirement allowance (Note 8)	92,068	92,881	893,864
Other long-term liabilities	156,514	161,148	1,519,554
Minority interests in consolidated subsidiaries	42,463	54,591	412,262
Shareholders' equity:			
Common stock, ¥50 par value; authorized— 6,000,000,000 shares; issued—2,512,110,463 shares in 1994 and 2,512,003,908 shares in 1993	203,431	203,392	1,975,058
Capital surplus	397,068	397,029	3,855,029
Legal reserve (Note 11)	47,583	45,783	461,971
Retained earnings (Note 16)	931,711	1,075,108	9,045,738
	1,579,793	1,721,312	15,337,796
Less:			
Treasury common stock, at cost; 402 shares in 1994 and 622 shares in 1993	—	—	—
Total shareholders' equity	1,579,793	1,721,312	15,337,796
Contingent liabilities (Note 13)			
Total liabilities and shareholders' equity	¥7,328,151	¥ 7,185,850	$71,147,097

Large U.S. corporations have often been criticized for publishing annual reports that are heavy on glitz, skimpy on facts, and often bend over backwards to camouflage bad news. As stated in *Business Week* (April 25, 1994):

ETHICS IN THE REAL WORLD

"All too often, the medium masks the message. Take H. J. Heinz Co. Its report has an attractive cover, and Chief Executive Anthony J. F. O'Reilly pens a pretty mean shareholder statement. Too bad it's a little thin on facts. Sure, sales increased 7.9% in 1993, to $7.1 billion. But you'll have to dig through the book's nether regions to learn that net income of $396 million is its lowest in five years."

ETHICAL ISSUE

Are corporations acting ethically when they publish annual reports that are factually correct, but are packaged to camouflage bad news with glitzy layouts, and upbeat, slanted letters to the public and shareholders?

REVIEW PROBLEM

The following information was taken from the 1994 annual report of Sprint. Review the income statement, balance sheet, and statement of cash flows for 1994 and 1993, and briefly comment on Sprint's earning power and solvency positions. All dollar values are in millions.

SPRINT
INCOME STATEMENT
FOR THE YEARS ENDED DECEMBER 31, 1994 AND 1993

	1994	1993
Net operating revenues	$12,662	$11,368
Operating expenses:		
Costs of services and products	$ 6,361	$ 5,736
Selling, general and administrative	3,035	2,730
Depreciation and amortization	1,478	1,359
Other	—	293
Total operating expenses	$10,874	$10,118
Operating income	$ 1,788	$ 1,250
Other expenses:		
Interest expense	(398)	(452)
Other expenses	(8)	(22)
Income before taxes	$ 1,382	$ 776
Income tax provision	498	295
Net income	$ 884	$ 481

SPRINT
BALANCE SHEET
DECEMBER 31, 1994 AND 1993

	1994	1993
ASSETS		
Current assets:		
Cash and equivalents	$ 123	$ 77
Accounts receivable (net)	1,470	1,231
Investments in equity securities	—	130
Inventories	216	182
Other	380	358
Total current assets	$ 2,189	$ 1,978
Investments in equity securities	$ 178	$ 173
Property, plant, and equipment	$19,201	$17,722
Less: Accumulated depreciation	8,322	7,408
Net property, plant, and equipment	$10,879	$10,314
Other assets	$ 1,692	$ 1,683
Total assets	$14,938	$14,148

	1994	1993
LIABILITIES AND STOCKHOLDERS' EQUITY		
Current liabilities:		
Current maturities by long-term debt	$ 332	$ 523
Accounts payable	1,072	875
Accrued interconnection costs	528	538
Accrued taxes	269	307
Advance billings	168	151
Others	686	675
Total current liabilities	$ 3,055	$ 3,069
Long-term debt	4,605	4,571
Other liabilities	2,715	2,552
Preferred stock	37	39
Common stock	1,814	1,686
Retained earnings	2,731	2,184
Other	(22)	47
Total liabilities and stockholders equity	$14,935	$14,148

SPRINT
STATEMENT OF CASH FLOWS
FOR THE YEARS ENDED DECEMBER 31, 1994 AND 1993

	1994	1993
Net cash provided by operating activities	$ 2,472	$ 2,112
Investing activities:		
Capital expenditures	$ (2,016)	$ (1,595)
Proceeds from sale of equity investments	118	—
Equity investments	(49)	9
Other	(35)	17
Net cash used by investing activities	$ (1,982)	$ (1,569)
Financing activities:		
Proceeds from long-term debt	$ 108	$ 840
Retirements of long-term debt	(597)	(1,589)
Net increase in notes payable	322	394
Proceeds from stock issued	43	71
Proceeds from employee stock purchases	33	28
Dividends paid	(349)	(347)
Other	(2)	7
Net cash used by financing activities	$ (442)	$ (596)
Increase (decrease) in cash and equivalents	$ 48	$ (53)
Cash and equivalents at beginning of year	75	130
Cash and equivalents at end of year	$ 123	$ 77

SOLUTION:

Sprint appears to have demonstrated improved earning power during 1994. Net income almost doubled—increasing by $403 million, due to an 11% increase in sales, a 43% increase in operating income, and a $54 million decrease in interest expense. It seems, however, that in 1993 "other expenses" included a $293 charge that was not repeated in 1994. It would be useful to learn why that charge was not repeated. The balance sheet indicates that Sprint's current liabilities exceed its current assets. Long-term debt and other liabilities are also relatively large, and total liabilities account for almost 70% of the company's assets. During 1994, however, the company reduced its reliance on debt—total liabilities accounted for over 72% of total assets in 1993. A review of the statement of cash flows shows that operating activities produced sufficient cash to cover Sprint's capital expenditures and dividends, which equaled almost 40% of 1994's earnings, and the company's debts were reduced in each year. Overall, Sprint appears to be growing and profitable, but somewhat reliant on debt financing.

SUMMARY OF LEARNING OBJECTIVES

 Identify and describe the three basic activities of a business, and explain how each activity is reflected in the financial statements.

Business must first attract capital and then invest it in productive assets that can be used to produce saleable goods and/or services. These actions represent the three basic activities involved in conducting a business: (1) financing activities, (2) investing activities, and (3) operating activities. Financing activities involve the collection of capital through equity or debt issuances and any associated payments, such as dividends and debt payments. Investing activities involve the acquisitions and sale of producing assets, the assets used to produce and support the goods and services provided. Operating activities involve the sale of the goods and services. Operating activities produce additional capital which can be reinvested in the producing assets, used to service debt payments, and distributed to the owners in the form of dividends.

   The balance sheet lists assets (goods and producing assets) and financing sources (equity, debt, and reinvestments from net earnings) at a particular point in time. The income statement is a measure of operations, the activities (revenues and expenses) involved in selling the goods and services. The statement of retained earnings measures the extent to which the business reinvests its net earnings and pays dividends. The statement of cash flows contains the cash inflows and outflows associated with the operating, investing, and financing activities of the business.

LO 2 *Describe the contents of the balance sheet, income statement, statement of retained earnings, and statement of cash flows, and how this information is useful to external users.*

The asset accounts reported on the balance sheet are listed in order of liquidity and are divided into four categories: (1) current assets, which include cash, short-term investments, accounts receivable, inventory, and prepaid expenses, (2) long-term investments, which include long-term notes receivable, land, securities, the cash value of life insurance, and special investment funds, (3) property, plant, and equipment and (4) intangible assets, which include patents, trademarks, and other intangibles, such as goodwill.

Liabilities are divided into two categories: (1) current liabilities, which primarily include short-term payables, and (2) long-term liabilities, which include items such as long-term notes, bonds, and mortgages payable. The stockholders' equity section for a corporation contains contributed capital and retained earnings; the owners' equity section for a partnership contains an account for each partner that records the cumulative balance of the partner's contributions less withdrawals.

The income statement consists of two basic categories: revenues and expenses. Revenues, which represent asset inflows (or liability decreases) associated with operating transactions during a given period, include sales, fees earned, service revenues, and other revenues (e.g., interest, book gains). Expenses, which represent the asset outflows (or liability increases) required to generate the revenues, include cost of goods sold, operating expenses (e.g., wages, rent), and other expenses (e.g., interest, book losses). Revenues less expenses equal net income.

The statement of retained earnings has four components: (1) the balance in Retained Earnings at the beginning of the period, (2) net income (or loss), (3) distributions to stockholders, and (4) the balance in Retained Earnings at the end of the period. The statement of cash flows contains three categories: (1) cash flows from operating activities, (2) cash flows from investing activities, and (3) cash flows from financing activities.

This information enables external users to assess the earning power and solvency position of the company. Assets generate cash through their use and sale, and liabilities represent cash requirements. The income statement indicates how profitable the company's operations have been, and the statement of cash flows shows how the company's cash is managed. The statement of retained earnings provides information about individual payments relative to net income.

KEY TERMS

Note: Definitions for these terms are provided in the glossary at the end of the text.

Accounts payable (p. 46)
Accounts receivable (p. 43)
Bonds payable (p. 47)
Classified balance sheet (p. 40)
Contributed capital (p. 47)
Cost of goods sold (p. 50)
Current assets (p. 42)
Current liabilities (p. 46)
Current maturities of long-term debts (p. 46)
Entrepreneur (p. 39)
Fees earned (p. 49)

Financing activities (p. 39)
Intangible assets (p. 45)
Investing activities (p. 39)
Liquidity (p. 42)
Long-term investments (p. 44)
Merchandise inventory (p. 43)
Mortgage payables (p. 47)
Net book value (p. 45)
Notes payable (p. 47)
Operating activities (p. 39)
Operating expenses (p. 51)

Owners' equity (p. 48)   Sales (p. 49)
Plant and equipment (p. 45)   Service revenue (p. 49)
Prepaid expenses (p. 44)   Short-term investments (p. 43)
Property (p. 45)   Stockholders' equity (p. 47)
Retained earnings (p. 48)

QUESTIONS FOR DISCUSSION AND REVIEW

1. In the chapter businesses are compared to fruit trees. Briefly describe how the root system, trunk, and branches of a fruit tree lead to the production of fruit and how this process is similar to the activities of a business.
2. List and define the three basic activities of a business.
3. Where are operating activities reflected on the financial statements?
4. Where are investing activities reflected on the financial statements?
5. Where are financing activities reflected on the financial statements?
6. What are the differences between debt and equity investments? What are the characteristics of each? Give three examples of debt investments. What kind of financial information would interest a debt investor (creditor)? How does it differ from the information that would interest an equity investor?
7. If financial statements are to encourage the exchange of capital among investors, creditors, and managers, of what two general concepts must they provide measures? Explain the similarities and differences between these two concepts.
8. The balance sheet is associated with a specific date. The income statement, statement of retained earnings, and statement of cash flows are each associated with a period of time. What does this mean in terms of the kind of information each statement provides, and how is each statement related to the accounting equation?
9. What is an asset? List the asset accounts on the balance sheet. In what order are they listed? Why?
10. Suppose a manager is choosing between debt and equity as a means for financing a large investment. Describe the financial statement effects of these two forms of financing and/or any associated economic consequences.
11. From what three sources do a company's assets come? Define each source, and explain how the right side of the balance sheet provides a summary of them.
12. What asset accounts are usually considered to be current? Why is the current description helpful to users?
13. What is a prepaid expense and what liability account represents the reverse of a prepaid expense? Do these accounts represent cash inflows and outflows, respectively?
14. What is a revenue? How are revenues related to assets, liabilities, and retained earnings? What is a "core" revenue, and why are users interested in "core" revenues?
15. What is an expense? How are expenses related to assets, liabilities, and retained earnings? What is a "core" expense, and why are users interested in "core" expenses?
16. Retained Earnings is an account that appears in the stockholders' equity section of the balance sheet, yet it consists primarily of revenues and expenses, which are both found on the income statement. How can this be? What does the retained earnings balance signal to users?
17. What two statements explain the changes in balance sheet accounts during a period of time? How are the formats of these two statements similar?
18. The statement of cash flows is divided into three different categories. Name them and describe what transactions are contained within them.

19. Are all balance sheet accounts valued in the same way? Provide several examples.
20. What is the difference between short-term investments, listed in the asset section of the balance sheet, and capital stock, which can be found in the contributed capital portion of the balance sheet?
21. What income statement account is closely related to plant and equipment on the balance sheet?
22. What two asset accounts are closely related to the income statement account Sales? Can you name a liability account that relates to Sales? Go down the income statement and relate each income statement account to one or more balance sheet accounts.
23. "Net cash flow from operating activities" is listed on the statement of cash flows. This number is similar to, yet different from, net income, which appears on the income statement. Explain the similarities and differences between these two numbers. How do these two measures of operations relate to earning power and solvency?
24. What specific accounts and numbers on the financial statements would be particularly useful in assessing a company's solvency position and earning power? Why?
25. How are the numbers in the financial statements used to control the business decisions of managers? Why is this necessary?
26. Suppose you are a manager who has signed a debt contract (covenant) requiring that the current ratio (current assets divided by current liabilities) be kept above 2:1. How might this affect the methods you choose to account for certain transactions? Provide several other examples of contracts between investors, creditors, and managers that might influence the accounting methods chosen by managers.
27. Explain how cultural and environmental differences across countries make it difficult for investors and creditors who use financial statement information to make decisions.

EXERCISES

E2–1

(Identifying financing, investing, and operating transactions)

Listed below are eight transactions. In each case identify whether the transaction is an example of financing, investing, or operating activities, and which of the financial statements it would affect.
1. Common stock is issued for $500,000 in cash.
2. Twenty units of inventory are sold for $50 each.
3. Employee wages are paid.
4. A new warehouse facility is purchased.
5. Principal payments on outstanding debt are paid.
6. Dividends are paid to the shareholders.
7. A 4-year-old vehicle, used as a delivery truck, is sold for $9,000.
8. A utility bill for March is paid.

E2–2

(Identifying financing, investing, and operating transactions)

Listed below are eight transactions. In each case identify whether the transaction is an example of financing, investing, or operating activities, and which of the financial statements it would affect.
1. Company borrows $50,000 in cash, signing a 10-year note payable.
2. Twenty units of inventory are purchased from suppliers on account for $12,000.
3. The utility bill is paid at the end of the month, $5,200.
4. Services are performed and customers are billed for $13,000.
5. Five parcels of real estate are purchased for a total of $55,000 in cash.
6. A long-term investment in an equity security is sold for $4,500 cash.

7.   Principal payments are made on outstanding debts.
8.   Cash is received from customers for services completed in a previous period.

E2-3

(Balance sheet or income statement account?)

Listed below are accounts that may appear on either the balance sheet or the income statement.

a.	Equipment	j.	Prepaid Expense
b.	Fees Earned	k.	Gain on Sale of Short-Term Investments
c.	Retained Earnings	l.	Rent Revenue
d.	Wage Expense	m.	Supplies Inventory
e.	Patent	n.	Accounts Receivable
f.	Cost of Goods Sold	o.	Land
g.	Common Stock	p.	Insurance Expense
h.	Dividend Payable	q.	Interest Payable
i.	Accumulated Depreciation	r.	Deferred Revenue

REQUIRED:

For each account, indicate whether a company would ordinarily disclose the account on the balance sheet or the income statement.

E2-4

(Relationships between retained earnings and revenues and expenses across time)

Berne Incorporated, began operations in 1994. At the end of 1996 the company had a balance in its retained earnings account of $230. Compute the missing amounts in the following table, and comment on the company's performance. Specifically, analyze the company's sales growth, profits, profits as a percentage of sales, and dividends declared as a percentage of net income.

	1996	1995	1994
Beginning retained earnings	$?	$ 48	$ 0
Revenues for the period	700	575	500
Expenses for the period	565	?	440
Dividends declared	15	13	?

E2-5

(Relationships between retained earnings and revenues and expenses across time)

Merrytown Services began operations in 1994. At the end of 1996 the company had a balance in its retained earnings account of $606. Compute the missing amounts in the following table, and comment on the company's performance. Specifically, analyze the company's sales growth, profits, profits as a percentage of sales, and dividends declared as a percentage of net income.

	1996	1995	1994
Beginning retained earnings	$366	$ 150	$ 0
Revenues for the period	?	1,200	900
Expenses for the period	900	840	?
Dividends declared	160	?	100

E2-6

(The statement of cash flows across time)

Miller and Company began operations on January 1, 1994. As of the end of 1996 Miller had a cash balance of $5,000. Compute the missing amounts in the following table. Describe and evaluate the company's cash management activities in each of the three years.

	1996	1995	1994
Beginning cash balance	$2,000	$?	$ 0
Net cash flow from operating activities	4,000	?	3,000
Net cash flow from investing activities	(4,000)	1,000	?
Net cash flow from financing activities	?	(4,000)	14,000
Ending cash balance	$5,000	$2,000	$ 9,000

E2–7

(The statement of cash flows across time)

Technic began operations on January 1, 1992. As of the end of 1996 Technic had a cash balance of $10,000. Compute the missing amounts in the following table. Describe and evaluate the company's cash management activities in each of the three years.

	1996	1995	1994
Beginning cash balance	$?	$13,000	$?
Net cash flow from operating activities	23,000	16,000	24,000
Net cash flow from investing activities	?	(7,000)	(27,000)
Net cash flow from financing activities	6,000	?	1,000
Ending cash balance	$10,000	$11,000	$?

E2–8

(Using working capital to assess solvency)

A retail company's recent balance sheets showed the following information. Accounts payable is the only current liability.

	12/31/96	12/31/95
Cash	$ 4,500	$ 7,000
Accounts receivable	6,000	9,000
Inventory	14,000	10,000
Total current assets	$24,500	$26,000
Accounts payable	12,000	11,000
Current assets minus current liabilities	$12,500	$15,000

REQUIRED:

Define solvency and discuss how this information might be useful in assessing the company's solvency position. What drawbacks are associated with using this information in this way?

E2–9

(The effects of different forms of financing on financial statement numbers and debt covenants)

Suppose the retail company in E2–8 signed a debt covenant specifying that current assets must be maintained at an amount twice the size of current liabilities. Assume further that in early January of 1997 the company plans to purchase $5,000 worth of inventory and has three possible methods of paying for it: (1) cash, (2) accounts payable, or (3) long-term note payable. Compute the effect of each of the three alternatives on the ratio of current assets to current liabilities, and discuss which method seems to be the most feasible.

E2–10

(Using working capital to assess solvency)

A manufacturing company's recent balance sheets showed the following information. Accounts payable is the only current liability.

	12/31/96	12/31/95
Cash	$ 8,500	$ 9,000
Accounts receivable	15,000	12,000
Inventory	17,000	15,000
Total current assets	$40,500	$36,000
Accounts payable	26,000	20,000
Current assets minus current liabilities	$14,500	$16,000

REQUIRED:

Define solvency and discuss how this information might be useful in assessing the company's solvency position. What drawbacks are associated with using this information in this way?

E2-11

(The effects of different forms of financing on financial statement numbers and debt covenants)

Suppose the manufacturing company in E2–10 signed a debt covenant specifying that current assets must exceed current liabilities by $12,000. Assume further that in early January of 1997 the company plans to purchase a $5,000 piece of machinery and has three possible methods of paying for it: (1) cash, (2) short-term note payable, or (3) long-term note payable. Compute the effect of each of the three alternatives on the difference between current assets and current liabilities, and discuss which method seems to be the most feasible.

E2-12

(Preparing a statement of cash flows)

From the following transactions prepare a statement of cash flows for Lana and Sons in the proper form. The company began the year with a cash balance of $13,000. Describe and evaluate the company's cash management activities during the year.
1. The stockholders contributed $7,000 in cash.
2. Performed services for $5,000, receiving $4,000 in cash and a $1,000 receivable.
3. Incurred expenses of $4,000; paid $3,000 in cash and $1,000 are still payable.
4. Purchased machinery for $10,000; paid $3,000 in cash and signed a long-term note payable for the remainder.
5. Paid the stockholders a $1,500 dividend.

E2-13

(Preparing a statement of cash flows)

From the following transactions prepare a statement of cash flows for Emory Inc. in the proper form. The company began the year with a cash balance of $25,000. Describe and evaluate the company's cash management activities during the year.
1. Borrowed $30,000 from a bank, signing a long-term note.
2. Performed services for $45,000, receiving $40,000 in cash and a $5,000 receivable.
3. Incurred expenses of $34,000; paid $23,000 in cash and $11,000 are still payable.
4. Purchased equipment for $28,000; paid $23,000 in cash and signed a long-term note payable for the remainder.
5. Paid the stockholders a dividend in an amount that ensured an ending cash balance of $25,000.

E2-14

(Preparing financial statements from simple transactions)

George began a business. After collecting $6,000 from an equity investor and borrowing $5,000 from a bank, he purchased a piece of land for $8,000. During the year he leased the land to Sheila and received $3,000 in cash. He paid $2,500 cash for expenses during the year and paid an $800 dividend to the equity investor.

REQUIRED:
Prepare an income statement, a statement of retained earnings, a balance sheet, and statement of cash flows for the period. What did George do that may have concerned the bank? Why?

E2-15

(Preparing financial statements from simple transactions)

Mary began a business. After collecting $30,000 from an equity investor and borrowing $15,000 from a bank, she purchased a piece of land for $40,000. During the year she leased the land to Karl and received $12,000 in cash, paying $14,000 cash for expenses. She paid a $1,000 dividend to the equity investor at year end.

REQUIRED:
Prepare an income statement, a statement of retained earnings, a balance sheet, and statement of cash flows for the period. Evaluate Mary's decision to pay the $1,000 dividend.

E2-16

(Analyzing financial

Excerpts from the financial statements of Jones and Williams are provided on the next page.

REQUIRED:
Review this information, calculate any ratios that you believe may be useful in assessing this company's financial health and performance, and explain why this company appears to be a good or poor investment.

	1997	1996
BALANCE SHEET		
Current assets	$14,000	$12,000
Long-term assets	98,000	66,000
Current liabilities	14,000	8,000
Long-term debt	30,000	10,000
Stockholders' equity	68,000	60,000
INCOME STATEMENT		
Net income	$18,000	$16,000

E2–17

(Analyzing financial statements)

Excerpts from the financial statements of Waters and Wheel are provided below.

	1997	1996
BALANCE SHEET		
Current assets	$20,000	$22,000
Long-term assets	43,000	45,000
Current liabilities	15,000	15,000
Long-term debt	25,000	20,000
Stockholders' equity	23,000	32,000
INCOME STATEMENT		
Net income	$ 9,000	$26,000

REQUIRED:

Review this information, calculate any ratios that you believe may be useful in assessing this company's financial health and performance, and explain why this company appears to be a good or poor investment.

PROBLEMS

P2–1

(Classifying balance sheet accounts)

Presented below are the main section headings of the balance sheet:

a. Current assets
b. Long-term investments
c. Property, plant and equipment
d. Intangible assets
e. Current liabilities
f. Long-term liabilities
g. Contributed capital
h. Retained earnings

REQUIRED:

Classify the following accounts under the appropriate headings, and prepare a balance sheet in proper form without account balances.

1. Dividend Payable
2. Payments Received in Advance
3. Allowance for Uncollectible Accounts
4. Inventories
5. Capital Stock
6. Accumulated Depreciation— Building
7. Bonds Payable
8. Machinery and Equipment
9. Accounts Receivable
10. Short-term investments
11. Buildings
12. Patents
13. Property
14. Investment Fund for Plant Expansion
15. Wages Payable
16. Cash
17. Accumulated Depreciation— Equipment
18. Prepaid Rent
19. Trademarks
20. Land Held for Investment
21. Current Portion Due of Long-Term Debt
22. Accounts Payable
23. Short-Term Notes Payable

P2–2

(Classifying income statement accounts)

Presented below are the main section headings of the income statement:

a. Sales   d. Cost of goods sold
b. Fees earned   e. Operating expenses
c. Other revenues   f. Other expenses

REQUIRED:

Classify the following descriptions under the appropriate headings and prepare an income statement in proper form without account balances.

1. Office salary expense
2. Sales of services provided
3. Insurance expense
4. Sales of inventories
5. Salesmen commission expense
6. Depreciation expense
7. Office supplies expense
8. Loss on sale of equipment
9. Income from interest on savings account
10. Income from dividends on investments
11. Advertising expense
12. Loss on sale of building
13. Interest expense on outstanding loans
14. Cost of sold inventories
15. Gain on sale of short-term investments

P2–3

(Preparing a balance sheet in proper form)

The following information is available relating to the activities of Johnson Co. as of December 31, 1996.

Cash balance on 12/31/96 is $8,000.

Short-term investments with a fair market value on 12/31/96 of $40,000.

Accounts Receivable balance of $125,000 on 12/31/96 includes $2,400 that are not likely to be collected.

Inventory costing $165,000 has a replacement cost (market value) on 12/31/96 of $161,000.

Buildings having a fair market value of $68,500 were purchased for $35,000 and have accumulated depreciation of $8,000.

Accounts Payable at year end total $110,000.

Taxes Payable at year end total $29,400.

Balance in the Long-Term Notes Payable account at the end of the period is $79,100.

Fair market value of the Johnson Co. stock on 12/31/96 is $10 per share. When originally issued, 12,500 shares were sold for $8 per share.

The total amount of net income earned by Johnson Co. since its inception several years ago is $65,000. Over that same period, Johnson Co. has paid $24,900 in dividends.

REQUIRED:

Prepare a balance sheet as of 12/31/96 in proper form for Johnson Co. Would you invest in this company? Why or why not?

P2–4

(Balance sheet and income statement relationships across five years)

Compute the missing values for the chart below and analyze the financial performance and position of this company. The first year of operations is 1993.

	1996	1995	1994	1993
Assets:				
Cash	$500	$200	$300	$300
Accounts receivable	700	?	300	200
Inventory	400	400	?	500
Land	400	400	200	100
Property, plant, and equipment (net)	800	700	600	700

	1996	1995	1994	1993
Liabilities and stockholders' equity:				
Accounts payable	?	500	300	200
Bonds payable	700	800	600	500
Contributed capital	600	600	400	?
Retained earnings	600	300	800	400
Sales	?	700	1,100	1,000
Expenses	(600)	?	?	(400)
Net income	?	(100)	400	?
Dividends	200	?	?	?

P2–5

(Using financial statements to assess solvency and earning power)

Excerpts from the financial statements for Spartan Unlimited are provided below. The first year of operations was 1995.

	1997	1996	1995
Cash	$ 500	$ 400	$ 300
Accounts receivable	800	500	600
Inventory	900	500	800
Land	3,200	3,500	3,000
Property, plant, and equipment	9,600	9,000	9,000
Accounts payable	1,500	1,000	2,400
Other short-term debts	1,200	1,600	1,000
Bonds payable	4,000	2,000	2,000
Contributed capital	6,800	6,800	6,800
Retained earnings	1,500	2,500	1,500
Sales	13,000	11,000	9,000
Expenses	11,000	8,000	7,000
Dividends	3,000	2,000	500

REQUIRED:
Organize these numbers into financial statements (excluding the statement of cash flows), and comment on Spartan's solvency and earning power positions.

P2–6

(Analyzing financial statements)

The chief executive officer of Romney Heights has included the following information from the financial statements in a loan application submitted to Acme Bank. The company intends to acquire additional equipment and wishes to finance the purchase with a long-term note.

	1997	1996
BALANCE SHEET		
Current assets	$14,000	$12,000
Long-term assets	50,000	43,000
Current liabilities	7,000	6,000
Long-term liabilities	26,000	21,000
Contributed capital	25,000	25,000
Retained earnings	6,000	3,000
INCOME STATEMENT		
Revenues	$35,000	$32,000
Expenses	23,000	26,000
STATEMENT OF CASH FLOWS		
Net cash flow from operating activities	$15,000	$ 9,000
Net cash flow from investing activities	(14,000)	(12,000)
Net cash flow from financing activities	7,000	5,000
Change in cash balance	$ 8,000	$ 2,000
Beginning cash balance	3,000	1,000
Ending cash balance	$11,000	$ 3,000

REQUIRED:

Assume that you, a bank loan officer, review the financial statements and recommend whether Romney Heights should be considered for a loan. Support your recommendation with calculations.

P2–7

(Analyzing financial statements)

Ted Tooney has operated a small service company for several years. The following information is from the financial statements prepared by Ted's accountant.

	1997	1996
BALANCE SHEET		
Current assets	$ 9,000	$ 8,000
Long-term assets	18,000	15,000
Current liabilities	7,000	4,000
Long-term liabilities	9,000	7,000
Contributed capital	9,000	9,000
Retained earnings	2,000	3,000
INCOME STATEMENT		
Revenues	$92,000	$ 89,000
Expenses	78,000	72,000
STATEMENT OF CASH FLOWS		
Net cash flow from operating activities	$12,000	$ 15,000
Net cash flow from investing activities	(8,000)	(5,000)
Net cash flow from financing activities	(5,000)	(8,000)
Change in cash balance	$(1,000)	$ 2,000
Beginning cash balance	5,000	3,000
Ending cash balance	$ 4,000	$ 5,000

REQUIRED:

Assume that you have some capital to invest, and that Ted asked you to consider making an equity investment in his company. Review the financial statements and describe how you would respond to Ted's request. Support your recommendation with calculations.

P2–8

(Balance sheet value and the fair market values of the assets)

Because of consistent losses in the past several years, Eat and Run, a fast-food franchise, is in danger of bankruptcy. Its most current balance sheet follows.

ASSETS		LIABILITIES AND STOCKHOLDERS' EQUITY	
Cash	$ 25,000	Accounts payable	$ 42,000
Short-term investments	15,000	Wages payable	20,000
Accounts receivable	35,000	Other short-term payables	34,000
Inventory	42,000	Long-term notes	75,000
Prepaid insurance	10,000	Mortgage payable	25,000
Property, plant, & equip.	82,000	Contributed capital	50,000
Other assets	50,000	Retained earnings	13,000
		Total liabilities and	
Total assets	$259,000	stockholders' equity	$259,000

ADDITIONAL INFORMATION:

The fair market value of the marketable securities is $19,000.

The sale of the accounts receivable to a local bank would produce about $25,000 cash.

A portion of the inventory originally costing $21,000 is now obsolete and can be sold for $3,000 scrap value. The remaining inventory is worth approximately $30,000.

Prepaid insurance is nonrefundable.

In the event of bankruptcy, the property, plant, and equipment owned by Eat and Run would be divided up and sold separately. It has been estimated that these sales would bring approximately $100,000 cash.

Other assets (primarily organizational costs) cannot be recovered.

REQUIRED:

a. The book value (balance sheet assets less liabilities) of Eat and Run is $63,000. Comment on why this balance sheet value may not be a good indication of the value of the company in the case of bankruptcy.
b. If Eat and Run goes bankrupt, what would you consider the value of the company to be?
c. When a company goes bankrupt, the creditors are usually paid off first with the existing assets, and then, if assets remain, the stockholders are paid. If Eat and Run goes bankrupt, would the stockholders receive anything? If so, how much?

P2–9

(Debt covenants can limit investments and dividends)

A summary of the December 31, 1996, balance sheet of Ellington Industries follows:

	1996
ASSETS	
Current assets	$12,000
Land investments	55,000
Total assets	$67,000
LIABILITIES AND STOCKHOLDERS' EQUITY	
Accounts payable	$ 9,000
Long-term liabilities	30,000
Stockholders' equity	28,000
Total liabilities and stockholders' equity	$67,000

On January 1, 1997, the company borrowed $40,000 (long-term debt) to purchase additional land. The debt covenant states that Ellington must maintain a current asset balance at least twice as large as its current liability balance over the period of the loan.

REQUIRED:

a. As of January 1, 1997, how much of the $40,000 can Ellington invest in land without violating the debt covenant?
b. Assume that Ellington invested the maximum allowable in land. Prepare Ellington's balance sheet as of January 1, 1997. Compute the following ratios—current assets/current liabilities and total liabilities/total assets.
c. Assume that Ellington invested the maximum allowable in land, and that during 1997 it generated $150,000 in revenues (all cash), paid off the accounts payable outstanding as of December 31, 1996, and incurred $130,000 in expenses, of which $123,000 was paid in cash. The company neither purchased nor sold any of its long-term land investments, made no principal payments on the long-term debt, and issued no equity during 1997. Prepare a balance sheet as of the end of 1997, and compute how large a dividend the company can pay without violating the debt covenant. Compute total liabilities/total assets if the company declares the maximum allowable dividend.

CASES

C2-1
(Debt contract restrictions)

The following excerpt was taken from a recent financial report of Cummins Engine Company, a manufacturer of heavy-duty truck engines.

Loan agreements contain covenants which impose restrictions on the payment of dividends and distributions of stock, require maintenance of a 1.25:1 current ratio, and limit the amount of future borrowings. Under the most restrictive covenants, retained earnings of approximately $351 million were available for payment of dividends.

REQUIRED:
a. Briefly explain the meaning of the above excerpt.
b. Why would a bank or other creditor impose such restrictions on a borrowing company?
c. Explain the role of financial accounting numbers in the restrictions described above.

C2-2
(Negative cash flows, positive net income, and dividends)

For over a year, Center Energy Corporation, a utility company in Ohio, had negative cash flow from operating activities caused primarily by the escalating costs of one of its nuclear plants outside Cleveland. Yet, the company reported positive earnings and paid a dividend to its stockholders of $2.56 per share.

REQUIRED:
a. Briefly explain how a company could have negative cash flow from operating activities, positive net income, and still pay dividends.
b. Could a company continue such a strategy over an extended period of time? Why or why not?

C2-3
(Debt covenant restrictions and the financial statements)

Condensed statements of income and balance sheets for Deere & Co. are provided below (in millions)

STATEMENT OF CONSOLIDATED INCOME

	1994	1993	1992
Total sales and revenues	$ 9,029.8	$ 7,753.5	$ 6,960.7
Costs and expenses	7,805.9	7,112.1	6,503.8
Earnings before interest, taxes, and other charges	$ 1,223.9	$ 641.4	$ 456.9
Interest expense	303.0	369.1	413.4
Earnings before taxes and other charges	$ 920.9	$ 272.3	$ 43.5
Income tax expense	(332.2)	(97.2)	(14.7)
Other additions (deductions)	14.9	(1,096.0)	8.6
Net income (loss)	$ 603.6	$ (920.9)	$ 37.4

CONSOLIDATED BALANCE SHEET

	1994	1993
Total assets	$12,781.2	$11,467.2
Current liabilities	$ 5,798.1	$ 4,463.6
Long-term debt	4,425.2	4,918.2
Stockholders' equity	2,557.9	2,085.4
Total liabilities and stockholders' equity	$12,781.2	$11,467.2

The following restrictions, pertaining to the company's outstanding debt, were described in the footnotes.

"Certain credit agreements have various requirements of John Deere, including the maintenance of earnings before interest charges/interest charges of not less than 1.05 to 1. In addition, the ratio of long-term debt to stockholders' equity may not be more than 8 to 1. The credit agreements also contain provisions requiring Deere & Co. to maintain consolidated net worth (book value) of $1.6 billion, as measured by U.S. generally accepted accounting principles as of October 31, 1992."

REQUIRED:

a. How close is Deere & Co. to violating its debt covenants? What kind of activities would cause the company to move closer to violation?
b. Analyze the company's reported earnings numbers over the past three years. Comment on the distinction between "core" earnings and "one-shot" items. What appears to have happened in 1993?
c. Assume that in 1993 the FASB issued an accounting standard that Deere & Co. was required to adopt. The adoption led to a large special charge that reduced the company's net income and net worth (book value) to $1.5 billion. Would the company have violated its debt covenant? Why or why not?

C2–4

(Investing and financing transactions)

The Wall Street Journal (June 12, 1995) reported that Westinghouse reached an agreement to sell all of its real estate operations for about $550 million, which is estimated to be approximately book value. The assets of this operation are valued at $718 million, and the proceeds from the sale were "expected to be used to reduce debt at Westinghouse."

REQUIRED:

a. Explain how the transaction would affect the balance sheet and income statement and be reported in the statement of cash flows.
b. How much debt was associated with the real estate operations?
c. In that same issue of *The Wall Street Journal,* American Telecasting Inc. was reportedly raising $100 million through an equity issuance, "which would be used to . . . build . . . wireless cable systems." How would these transactions be reported in the statement of cash flows?

C2–5

(The annual report of MCI)

Review the annual report of MCI and answer the following questions.
a. Compute current assets, total communications systems (net), current liabilities, long-term debt, and stockholders' equity as a percentage of total assets for 1994 and 1993, and comment on how these proportions have changed.
b. Compute operating expenses, interest expense, taxes on income, and net income as a percentage of revenues for 1994, 1993, and 1992, and comment on how these proportions have changed.
c. Compute the current ratio, working capital, the debt (total liabilities)/equity ratio, earnings per share, return on equity, and the price/earnings ratio, and comment on the company's solvency and earning power position.
d. Over the past three years, from what sources has the company generated most of its cash, and in what ways has the cash been used?

PART 2

USE, MEASUREMENT, AND MECHANICS OF FINANCIAL STATEMENTS

CHAPTER 3
USING FINANCIAL STATEMENT INFORMATION

CHAPTER 4
THE MEASUREMENT FUNDAMENTALS OF FINANCIAL ACCOUNTING

CHAPTER 5
THE MECHANICS OF FINANCIAL ACCOUNTING

USING FINANCIAL STATEMENT INFORMATION

LEARNING OBJECTIVES

LO 1 Explain how financial statement information is used to predict future cash flows and influence management decisions.

LO 2 Explain the concepts of earnings persistence and quality of earnings.

LO 3 List and briefly describe the basic steps involved in assessing the earning power and solvency position of a company.

LO 4 Define operating performance, financial flexibility, and liquidity, and explain how they relate to solvency.

LO 5 Identify and describe the major limitations of financial accounting information.

LO 6 Describe why it is difficult to use annual report information to identify undervalued securities.

The information that appears in the financial statements is used in many ways by a variety of individuals and entities. Investors and creditors use it to evaluate company performance and to predict the amount and timing of the future cash flows (e.g., dividends and interest) associated with their investments. They also use financial information to influence and monitor the activities of management. As representatives of the stockholders, the boards of directors of many companies base executive compensation on various measures of income, while creditors protect their loan investments by writing debt covenants in terms of financial statement numbers. Public utilities use financial accounting numbers to set customer rates, and labor unions use such information to negotiate with management for higher wages and better working conditions. Credit-rating agencies, such as Standard & Poor's, Moody's, and Dun & Bradstreet, use financial statement information to determine credit ratings. Indeed, financial accounting information plays an important role in a number of different kinds of business decisions.

It is also true, however, that financial accounting information is only one of several alternative sources of information and in many ways is quite limited. Financial reports, for example, are typically published several months after the balance sheet date, enabling many other media to provide more timely financial information. Moreover, generally accepted accounting principles are the result of a political process that gives rise to a wide variety of acceptable accounting methods. Financial statements, as a result, (1) are significantly influenced by the subjective judgments and incentives of the managers who prepare them, (2) are based on historical information, (3) are not adjusted for inflation, and (4) generally do not reflect market values. Consequently, while financial accounting information is useful, it must be used in both the appropriate situation and the appropriate manner. Understanding how and in what situations to use financial accounting information is the subject of this chapter.

PREDICTION AND CONTROL

L O **1**   There are two fundamental ways in which financial accounting numbers are useful: (1) they help to predict a company's future cash flows by providing an indication of its earning power and solvency position, and (2) they help investors and creditors to influence and monitor the business decisions of a company's managers.

FINANCIAL ACCOUNTING NUMBERS
AS PREDICTION AIDS

L O **2**   Financial accounting numbers report on past events. In and of themselves they are neither predictions nor forecasts. However, to the extent that past events are indicative of the future, financial accounting numbers can be used to make predictions about a company's future cash flows. Financial statement numbers, for example, have been used in statistical models to predict bankruptcy with reasonable accuracy, and such models are often used by auditors to predict whether potential clients will remain in business. Indeed, the main objective of financial reporting, as stated by the Financial Accounting Standards Board, is "to help present and potential investors and creditors and other users in assessing the amount, timing, and uncertainty of *future* cash flows."[1]

Earning power and solvency are important indicators of a company's future cash flows. **Earning power** refers to a company's ability to increase its wealth through operations and generate cash in the future. **Solvency** refers to a company's ability to meet its obligations as they come due; specifically, it refers to how well the timing of a company's cash inflows matches the timing of its cash obligations. Earning power, which essentially refers to future cash flows, is distinct from solvency, which is concerned primarily with day-to-day cash inflows and outflows. Yet these two concepts are not independent, and one can hardly exist without the other. A company must meet its short-run obligations, for example, to maintain its earning power; by the same token, operations—the source of a company's earning power—provide much of the cash used to meet short-run obligations.

An important concept receiving increasing attention when using financial statement numbers as prediction aids is called **earnings persistence**, which refers to the extent to which an income number reported in the current period can be expected to reflect future income levels. An income number with high persistence would be expected to relate closely to future income amounts and be useful for predicting them, while low persistence earnings are normally associated with "one time, nonrecurring" events.

Paramount Communications, for example, recently reported sharply higher net income of $1.23 billion in its fourth quarter, but the higher earnings was due to a "one time" $1.2 billion gain from the sale of its consumer finance segment. Several years ago G.E. reported an $801 million net loss. However, the loss occurred because the company changed its method of accounting for retiree health benefits, which produced a $1.8 billion "one time" charge against earnings. In both cases the reported net income numbers would be considered to have low persistence; they would not be expected to relate closely to future income levels, and their usefulness for predictive purposes would be limited. Financial statements users often ignore (or at least discount) such items when evaluating a firm's performance. Instead, they focus on revenue and expenses that are part of the company's "core" operations and are expected to re-occur in the future.

FINANCIAL ACCOUNTING NUMBERS AND MANAGEMENT CONTROL

Financial accounting numbers can also be used to influence the business decisions of managers. Investors and creditors, who provide a company with its capital, can direct and monitor the actions of its managers by requiring that their contracts be written in terms of financial accounting numbers.

Stockholders have incentives to encourage management to act in ways that maximize the present value of future dividend payments and stock price appreciation. Since such returns depend on a company's earning power and long-run profitability, stockholders want management to make business decisions that maintain high levels of earning power. A common method used to attain such a goal is to base a significant portion of management's compensation on reported profits. Such compensation schemes, which are set by a company's board of directors, can lead to payments either

---

1. Financial Accounting Standards Board, "Objectives of Financial Reporting by Business Enterprises," *Statement of Financial Accounting Concepts No. 1* (Stamford, Conn.: FASB, November 1978).

in the form of cash or shares of stock. Exxon Corporation, for example, has implemented a management incentive program that pays eligible employees a percentage of the company's earnings if net income in a given year exceeds 6 percent of invested capital (as defined in the bonus plan). These bonuses have been paid in both cash and shares of Exxon common stock.[2]

Creditors are also interested in protecting their investments by influencing the business decisions of management. They are concerned that companies may not be able to meet their loan obligations because company assets may have been (1) paid to the shareholders in the form of dividends or purchases of outstanding stock, (2) pledged to other creditors, or (3) mismanaged. To reduce the probability of such events, a creditor may restrict certain business decisions of managers as a condition of the loan. Such restrictions are written into the loan contract and expressed in terms of financial accounting numbers.

For example, Alcoa recently entered into an eight-year, $600 million revolving credit agreement with a group of banks. The agreement requires that during the period of the loan (1) the current ratio not be less than 1:1 and (2) a minimum working capital of $500 million be maintained. In other debt covenants, The Pillsbury Company is restricted with respect to paying dividends and purchasing its own common stock, and Lockheed Corporation may be required to redeem certain outstanding notes payable if the company's credit rating declines below a specified level.

ASSESSING EARNING POWER AND SOLVENCY

LO 3 Assessing earning power and solvency involves analyzing different kinds of information, including: reviewing the auditor's report, assessing the nature and importance of significant transactions, evaluating a company's credit rating, analyzing the financial statements, and considering such concepts as operating performances, financial flexibility, and liquidity.

THE AUDIT REPORT

From a user's perspective, perhaps the most important section of the financial statements is the audit report, written and signed by the external auditor. This report serves as the accounting profession's "seal of approval," stating whether, and to what extent, the information in the financial statements fairly reflects the financial position and operations of the company.

After reviewing the financial records of a company, the auditor usually renders a **standard audit report** stating that the financial statements fairly reflect the financial position and operations of the company. Such a report also states that all necessary tests were conducted in concluding that a company's financial statements conform to generally accepted accounting principles.[3] In such cases the reader can be reasonably

---

2. It is unclear whether basing management compensation on accounting measures of profit serves to maximize the long-run earning power of major companies in the United States. Some contend that such compensation schemes encourage management to manipulate reported profits and to make operating, investing, and financing decisions that increase profits in the short run, at the expense of long-run profitability. See, for example, "Managing Our Way to Economic Decline" by Robert H. Hayes and William J. Abernathy, which appeared in the *Harvard Business Review* (July–August 1980), pp. 67–77.

3. Examples of standard audit reports can be found in Chapter 1 of this text and in Appendix C, where the annual report of MCI is located.

assured that the information in the statements is credible and that the company in question is in reasonable financial health.

Accounting Trends and Techniques (New York: AICPA, 1994) reports that, of the 600 major U.S. companies surveyed, over 70 percent received a standard report in 1993. The remainder of these companies received something other than a standard report. Auditors depart from the standard report for one or more of the following reasons:

1. The scope of the auditor's examination is affected by conditions that preclude the application of one or more auditing procedures considered necessary.
2. The auditor's opinion is based in part on the report of another auditor.
3. The financial statements are affected by a departure from generally accepted accounting principles.
4. Major accounting principles/methods have been changed.
5. The financial statements are affected by uncertainties concerning future events, the outcome of which cannot be estimated as of the date of the auditor's report.
6. There is a question about whether the company can continue as a going concern in the future.

If the auditor departs from the standard report for any of the reasons listed above, the financial statement users should proceed cautiously. Departures due to scope limitations, departures from generally accepted accounting principles, material uncertainties, and going concern questions can be serious and may raise doubts about a company as a potential investment. Departures due to relying on other auditors and accounting principle/method changes, on the other hand, are usually less worrisome. Figure 3–1 provides excerpts from several recent audit reports, each of which describes a different reason for departing from the standard report.

The audit report can generally be relied upon because auditors have significant economic incentives to maintain high levels of competence and independence. Legal liability, reputation, and professional standards of quality and ethics all play important roles in encouraging an auditor to conduct a thorough investigation and to report in an independent manner. Keep in mind, however, that management controls the audit fee and has the power to change auditors. Such influence has been used, on occasion, to compromise the quality and integrity of an auditor's work.

Be aware also that not all companies are audited by certified public accountants. Only those companies whose equity securities are traded on public stock exchanges are legally required to do so. Such publicly traded companies tend to be the largest in the United States (in terms of annual sales or total assets), yet they represent only a small portion of the total number of United States companies. These other companies may or may not choose to have their statements audited. Many are required to do so as a condition for private equity issuances or bank loans, but most are not audited at all. A comprehensive audit by a public accounting firm can be very time-consuming and costly, and for many small companies, especially those that do not rely on outside sources of capital, the benefit from the audit simply does not justify the costs. In such cases the financial statement user must proceed with extreme caution.

SIGNIFICANT TRANSACTIONS

Assessing earning power and solvency also involves reviewing significant transactions entered into by a company or significant recent events that might affect a company's performance. Such items can have an important effect on the future direction

FIGURE 3–1

Examples of non-standard audit reports

Reference to Other Auditors

To the Stockholders and Board of Directors of Valhi, Inc.:
We have audited the accompanying consolidated (financial statements) of Valhi, Inc.
and Subsidiaries. . . . We did not audit the financial statements of certain
subsidiaries constituting approximately 36% . . . of consolidated net sales for the
year. . . . These statements were audited by other auditors whose reports thereon
have been furnished to us, and our opinion, insofar as it relates to amounts included
for such subsidiaries, is based solely upon their reports.

Litigation Uncertainty

To the Board of Directors and Shareholders of Dravo Corporation:
. . . As discussed in Note 9 to the consolidated financial statements, certain lawsuits,
claims and assertions have been brought against the company for environmental
costs, contract and claim disputes, and other matters, the outcome of which
presently cannot be determined.

Going Concern Uncertainty

To the Board of Directors and Shareholders of Interco Incorporated:
. . . The accompanying consolidated financial statements have been prepared
assuming that the company will continue as a going concern. As discussed in Note 2
of the consolidated financial statements, the company has a substantial portion of its
debt due contractually within the next fiscal year and expects not to be in
compliance with certain financial covenants contained in certain of its credit
agreements, which will permit its lenders to accelerate the due dates on its debt. The
company's inability to meet its liquidity needs raises substantial doubt about the
company's ability to continue as a going concern. The financial statements do not
include any adjustments that might result from the outcome of this uncertainty . . .

Lack of Consistency Due to Change in Accounting Method

To the Board of Directors and Stockholders of Phillips Petroleum Company
. . . As discussed in Note 1 to the financial statements, the company adopted
Statement of Financial Accounting Standards No. 96, "Accounting for Income
Taxes."

of a company and may distort the financial statements, making it more difficult to assess a company's financial position and operations. Examples include major acquisitions, the discontinuance or disposal of a business segment, unresolved litigation, major write-downs of receivables or inventories, offers to purchase outstanding shares (tender offers), extraordinary gains or losses, and changes of accounting methods. Such transactions or events are usually discussed in the footnotes of the annual report, and normally the financial effects are prominently disclosed on the income statement and/or statement of cash flows.

THE CREDIT RATING

Information about a company's credit rating is also of interest to investors, creditors, and others in their evaluations of earning power and solvency. Credit-rating agencies, such as Moody's Investor Service, Dun & Bradstreet, and Standard & Poor's, provide extensive analyses of the operations and financial positions of many companies as well as ratings of the riskiness of their outstanding debts. Such ratings have a direct bearing on a company's ability to issue debt in the future and on the terms of that debt.

The Wall Street Journal (October 3, 1990), for example, reported that "Moody's Investor Service downgraded its rating on Unisys Corp.'s debt to below investment-grade, putting the company in a liquidity crunch and sending its stock and bond prices tumbling."

Procter & Gamble Company reported in a recent annual report: "The Company maintained its strong financial position. Indicative of its strength are cash and securities on hand of $741 million, and an excellent credit rating." That same year Abbott Laboratories reported: "The Company has maintained its favorable bond rating (AA+ by Standard & Poor's Corporation and Aa1 by Moody's Investor Service) and continues to have readily available financial resources, including unused lines of credit of $200 million."

ANALYZING THE FINANCIAL STATEMENTS

An important step in the assessment of a company's earning power and solvency position is the analysis of the company's financial statements. When conducting such analysis, keep in mind that accounting numbers are not very meaningful in and of themselves. They become useful only when they are compared to other numbers. For example, suppose that you read in The Wall Street Journal that MCI reported net income of $794 million for 1994. Would you interpret that announcement as favorable or unfavorable news? This question is difficult to answer in the absence of a basis for comparison. Income of $794 million is neither large nor small in an absolute sense. It depends on such factors as the amount of net income reported by MCI in previous years, the amount of net income reported by other companies similar to MCI, normally in the same industry, and the size of MCI operations and capital base. Thus, financial accounting numbers are only meaningful when compared to other relevant numbers, and such comparisons can be made in three basic ways: (1) across time, (2) across different companies within the same industry, and (3) within the financial statements of the company at a given point in time.

COMPARISONS ACROSS TIME

Financial accounting numbers can be made more meaningful if they are compared across time. At a minimum, generally accepted accounting principles require that the financial statements of the current and the preceding years be disclosed side by side in published financial reports. While this is helpful for identifying changes from one year to the next, many companies provide comparisons of selected items, accounting and non-accounting, across five- or ten-year periods. Such disclosures can often be used to identify important trends and turning points.

J.C. Penney Company, for example, provides a five-year comparison of most income statement items, selected per-share and balance sheet items, and the number of its employees. Delta Air Lines provides a ten-year comparison of most income statement items, selected per-share and balance sheet items, and such non-accounting information as available seat miles, revenue passenger miles, and passenger load factor. Wendy's International provides a ten-year comparison of selected information about operations, financial position, per-share data, financial ratios (e.g., gross margin, current ratio, and debt/equity ratio), restaurant data (e.g., number of U.S. and international restaurants), and other data, including the numbers of shareholders and employees.

Turn to the financial statements of MCI, and note that page 4 contains Selected Financial Information, a summary of MCI's activities across the five-year period, 1990–1994. Revenues have grown consistently over the time period, from $8,454 in 1990 to $13,338 in 1994. Net income has also increased, but at a somewhat less consistent rate—a large increase from 1990 to 1991, a dip in 1993, and a rebound in 1994—and cash dividends have been at a consistent .05/share rate. The balance sheet shows that total assets have almost doubled since 1990; long-term debt dropped off in 1993 and increased in 1994; and cash and stockholders' equity took a big jump in 1994. While this information is very general, it does provide a sense of MCI's growth and performance over the last five years, and raises some questions that may be worth exploring with closer analyses.

By comparing financial statement numbers across time, a user can develop a "feel" for a company's activities and its general financial condition and, at the same time, can identify certain trends and turning points. However, users must view such comparisons cautiously. First, there is no assurance that historical trends will continue into the future. Current changes in the nature of the company, the industry in which it operates, or the business environment in general must also be considered. Users must also be aware of the accounting methods used by a company over the period of the comparison. The financial effect of an accounting method change can be significant and when such changes are disclosed, the numbers reported on the statements should be adjusted to achieve a common basis for comparison across the analysis periods.

COMPARISON WITHIN THE INDUSTRY

A second type of comparison that can enhance the meaningfulness of financial accounting numbers is to compare them to those of similar companies. Similar companies are usually found in the same industry; thus, industry-wide statistics are often a useful basis for comparison. Information concerning industry averages is reported by such sources as (1) *Dun & Bradstreet's Key Business Ratios*, (2) *Robert Morris Associates' Annual Statement Studies*, (3) *Moody's Investor Service*, and (4) *Standard & Poor's Industry Surveys*.

Differences in what are considered normal accounting numbers across industries can be very significant. For example, the Hobby, Toy and Games industry, on average, current assets account for 80 percent of total assets, while in the Telephone Communications industry, (which includes MCI) the average percentage is only 31. Consequently, it is very important that the accounting numbers of a given company in a given industry be evaluated in terms of the norms established in that industry.

Like comparisons across time, however, comparisons across an industry must be prepared and interpreted with caution. Companies do not always fall neatly into industry classifications; as a result, it is not always easy to find either the appropriate industry averages or other companies in exactly the same industry. Even when the companies compared are classified in the same industry, they do not necessarily face the same business environment.

Sometimes it is more appropriate to compare companies within an industry. The financial performance of MCI, for example, may be compared to that of Sprint. In this way the user can gain a sense of the relative performance of the comparison companies. An example is provided at the end of this chapter where we compare Albertsons and Safeway, two large grocery chains.

COMPARISONS WITHIN THE FINANCIAL STATEMENTS: COMMON-SIZE STATEMENTS AND RATIO ANALYSIS

A third way to analyze financial statement numbers is to compare them to other numbers on the financial statements of the company at a particular point in time. Such comparisons can take two forms: (1) common-size financial statements and (2) ratio analysis.

COMMON-SIZE FINANCIAL STATEMENTS. Financial statement numbers can be expressed as percentages of other numbers on the same statements. On the income statement, expense items and net income arc often expressed as percentages of net sales. On the balance sheet, assets and liabilities can be expressed as percentages of total assets (or liabilities plus stockholders' equity). Presenting such information gives rise to **common-size financial statements**. Common-size income statements and balance sheets for MCI are contained in Figure 3–2.

Common-size financial statements can help to indicate why changes occur in a company's performance and financial condition. Note that MCI's revenues and net income both increased from 1993 to 1994, while net income as a percent of revenues increased by 1 percent. This increase occured because the percent decreases in telecommunications and other expenses exceeded the increase in depreciation by 1 percent. The annual report reveals, however, that in 1993 MCI recognized a $45 million extraordinary loss, which is unlikely to reoccur.[4] Consequently, 1993 net income may be understated, which in turn overstates the increase in MCI's profits from 1993 to 1994.

FIGURE 3–2		1994	%	1993	%
Common-size financial statements—MCI, Inc.	**INCOME STATEMENT**				
	Revenues	**$13,338***	**100**	**$11,921**	**100**
	Operating expenses:				
	Telecommunications	(6,916)	52	(6,373)	53
	Sales, operations, and general	(3,790)	28	(3,310)	28
	Depreciation	(1,176)	9	(970)	8
	Other expenses, net	(661)	5	(686)	6
	Net income	$ 795	6	$ 582	5
	BALANCE SHEET				
	Current assets	$ 4,888	30	$ 2,601	23
	Total communications system, net	9,059	55	7,321	65
	Other assets	2,419	15	1,354	12
	Total	$16,366	100	$11,276	100
	Current liabilities	$ 3,137	19	$ 3,201	28
	Noncurrent liabilities	4,225	26	3,362	30
	Stockholders' equity	9,004	55	4,713	42
	Total	$16,366	100	$11,276	100

*Dollars are in millions.

4. "Extraordinary" is a term used to describe losses or gains that are both unusual and infrequent. They are often ignored when analyzing financial statements across time. They are discussed in Chapter 13 of this text.

The mix of MCI's balance sheet accounts also shifted during 1994. MCI's assets appeared to shift in favor of current and other assets and away from the communications systems. In addition, MCI reduced both its current and noncurrent liabilities, as stockholders' equity experienced a major increase. Overall, MCI appears to be more solvent, with higher current assets and less reliance on debt.

RATIO ANALYSIS. Preparing common-size financial statements is simply a matter of computing ratios in which income statement or balance sheet items act as numerators and sales or total assets serve as denominators. Computing additional ratios using two or more financial statement numbers is also a common and useful practice generally known as **ratio analysis**.

Two general points are particularly important when computing ratios. First, with only a few exceptions, there are no hard and fast rules for the computation of ratios. The ratios discussed here are merely representative of ratios that are widely used. Users can adjust them to fit different situations, and certainly other ratios might be equally or more relevant to a given decision.

Second, in the computation of many ratios, income statement numbers are compared to balance sheet numbers. Since the income statement refers to a period of time and the balance sheet refers to a specific point in time, in calculating these ratios it is usually best to compute an average for the balance sheet number. One way to compute such an average is to add the account balance at the beginning of the period to the account balance at the end of the period, and divide the result by 2. This method provides a simple average for the balance sheet dollar amount.[5] The following discussion divides the ratios into five categories: (1) profitability, (2) solvency, (3) activity, (4) capitalization, and (5) market ratios.

Profitability Ratios. Net income, or profit, is the primary measure of the overall success of a company. This number is often compared to other measures of financial activity or condition (e.g., sales, assets, stockholders' equity) to assess performance as a percent of some level of activity or investment. These comparisons are referred to as **profitability ratios** and are designed to measure earning power.

Return on Equity. Return on equity compares the profits generated by a company to the investment made by the company's stockholders.

Net Income/Average Stockholders' Equity

Net income, which appears in the numerator, is viewed as the return to the company's owners, while the balance sheet value of stockholders' equity, which appears in the denominator, represents the amount of resources invested by the stockholders.

This ratio is considered a measure of the efficiency with which the stockholders' investment is being managed. As the ratio increases, management tends to be viewed as more efficient from the owner's perspective. Stockholders often compare this ratio against the returns of other potential investments available to them to determine whether their investment in a company is performing satisfactorily.

Return on equity for MCI appears in Figure 3–3. This ratio decreased substantially during 1994. Even though net income increased by $168 million, the increase in stockholders' equity was much greater. The annual report discloses that MCI issued

---

5. A weighted average, which is covered in advanced texts, may be more appropriate in certain cases.

| FIGURE 3-3 | 1993: | $627*/[($4,713 + $3,150)/2] | = | .16 |
| Return on equity for MCI | 1994: | $795/[($9,004 + $4,713)/2] | = | .12 |

*Excluding the $45 million extraordinary loss.

stock during 1994 in the amount of $3.5 billion, which accounted for most of the increase in stockholders' equity.

Return on Assets. Another measure of return on investment is return on assets. This measure is somewhat broader than return on equity because it compares the returns to both stockholders and creditors to total assets, the total resources provided by stockholders and creditors.

(Net Income + Interest Expense)/Average Total Assets

Accordingly, the numerator includes both the return to the stockholders (net income) and the return to the creditors (interest expense), while the denominator consists of the balance sheet value of total assets, which is equivalent to the investments of both the stockholders (stockholders' equity) and the creditors (total liabilities).

Return on assets for MCI appears in Figure 3–4. This ratio also decreased during 1994, again largely due to the stock issuance which increased MCI's total assets. In addition, the return to the debt holders, interest expense, also went down.

| FIGURE 3-4 | 1993: | $627* + $178/[($11,276 + $9,678)/2] | = | .08 |
| Return on assets for MCI | 1994: | $795 + $153/[($16,366 + $11,276)/2] | = | .07 |

*Excluding the $45 million extraordinary loss.

Earnings per Share. Earnings per share is perhaps the best known of all the ratios, largely because it is often treated by the financial press as the primary measure of a company's performance. It measures profitability strictly from the standpoint of the common stockholders. Unlike return on equity or return on assets, which assess profitability relative to a measure of capital investment, this ratio assesses profitability relative to the number of common shares outstanding.[6] According to generally accepted accounting principles, earnings per share must appear on the face of the income statement and be calculated in accordance with an elaborate set of complex rules that are beyond the scope of this book. The basic formula is provided below:

Net Income/Average Number of Common Shares Outstanding

Earnings per share for MCI appears in Figure 3–5. This ratio increased substantially during 1994. Net income increased at a faster pace (27%) than did the average common shares outstanding (8%).

There is considerable variation in the earnings per share amounts reported across companies in different industries. In 1994, for example, Ford Motor Company reported earnings per share of almost $5, while $3.96, $1.88, and $.63 were reported by NIKE, H & R Block and Kmart, respectively. RJR Nabisco reported a $.15 loss that year.

6. The ownership of a corporation is divided into units called common shares or common stock. Stockholders have the right to vote for the corporation's board of directors and receive dividends when declared by the corporation.

FIGURE 3–5	1993:	$627*/560 million shares**	=	$1.12
Return on assets for MCI	1994:	$795/602 million shares**	=	$1.32

*Excluding the $45 million extraordinary loss.
**Average common shares outstanding

Return on Sales, or Profit Margin. Return on sales, or profit margin is simply computed by dividing a measure of profit by net sales.

Net Income/Net Sales

This ratio provides an indication of a company's ability to generate and market profitable products and control its costs, while taking advantage of increases in sales due to increasing prices or increasing the number of units sold.

Return on sales for MCI appears in Figure 3–6. This ratio increased slightly during 1994. Apparently, MCI was able to better control its expenses during 1994.

FIGURE 3–6	1993:	$627*/$11,921	=	.05
Return on sales for MCI	1994:	$795/$13,338	=	.06

*Excluding the $45 million extraordinary loss.

Times-Interest-Earned Ratio. The times-interest-earned ratio measures the extent to which a company's annual profits cover its annual interest expense. While this ratio reflects earning power, it is also of interest to creditors who are concerned about a company's ability to meet its future interest payments. This ratio provides an example of the significant overlap between earning power and solvency.

Net Income Before Taxes/Interest Expense

The profit number in the numerator should reflect the primary, recurring business operations of the company, and should be calculated before income taxes because interest is deductible for tax purposes. The denominator, interest expense, can usually be found on the income statement.

Times-interest-earned for MCI appears in Figure 3–7. This ratio increased substantially during 1994. MCI's net income increase coupled with the drop in interest expense accounted for the change. The company is reducing its reliance on debt financing in favor of equity, so its profits appear to be more than adequate to cover its interest costs.

FIGURE 3–7	1993:	$1,045*/$178	=	5.87
Times-interest-earned for MCI	1994:	$1,280/$153	=	8.37

*Excluding the $45 million extraordinary loss.

Solvency Ratios. Solvency refers to a company's ability to meet its debts as they come due. Two ratios are often used to measure this ability: (1) the current ratio and (2) the quick ratio. Both ratios use balance sheet numbers only, comparing measures of current assets to current liabilities.

Two important points should be made about these ratios. First, the current ratio and the quick ratio are often called *liquidity ratios*, but many believe that this description is inappropriate and confusing. *Liquidity* typically refers to how quickly assets can be converted into cash, while *solvency* refers to whether cash can be produced to meet debts as they come due. Liquidity and solvency may be related, in that liquid assets are helpful in meeting debts, but the two concepts are certainly not the same. A company may have a number of liquid assets but still be unable to meet its debts if, for example, the debts all come due at the same time. Similarly, a company with few liquid assets may be able to meet its debts if the debts are all long-term. The current ratio and the quick ratio provide a measure of a company's ability to meet current obligations with current assets, which is more directly a measure of solvency than of liquidity.

The second point of interest is that neither ratio provides a very valid measure of solvency. Solvency is a complex phenomenon that is primarily related to the timing of a company's future cash inflows and outflows. Comparing current assets and current liabilities at a particular point in time is rarely a reliable measure of such a dynamic notion.

Current Ratio. The current ratio compares current assets to current liabilities as of the balance sheet date:

Current Assets/Current Liabilities

Average current ratios across industries vary from less than 1.0 (e.g., motion picture theaters) to between 3.0 and 4.0 (e.g., department stores and hardware stores).

Current ratios for MCI are contained in Figure 3–8. Note first that MCI's current ratio in 1993 is below 1.0, which is not uncommon for capital intensive companies, like MCI, where most of their investments are in long-term property, plant, and equipment. Note also that the current ratio jumped significantly in 1994—due primarily to the big jump in the company's cash and marketable securities. Recall that MCI issued stock in 1994, which had an immediate impact on its cash balance.

FIGURE 3–8	1993:	$2,601/$3,201	=	.81
Current ratios for MCI	1994:	$4,888/$3,137	=	1.56

Quick Ratio. The quick ratio is similar to the current ratio, except that it provides a more stringent test of a company's solvency position. Current assets like inventories and prepaid expenses, which are not immediately convertible to cash, are excluded from the numerator.

(Cash + Marketable Securities[7] + Accounts Receivable)/Current Liabilities

Most major U.S. companies have quick ratios that are quite low. GTE Corporation, J.C. Penney, Nordstrom, and Colgate-Palmolive, for example, all have quick ratios that are less than .05.

---

7. The account titles "marketable securities" and "short-term investments" are used interchangably.

Quick ratios for MCI are contained in Figure 3–9. Again we see a big jump from 1993 to 1994, which supports the conclusion that the large increase in current ratio was due to additional cash and marketable securities. MCI has virtually no inventory, so the difference between the current and quick ratios is very small.

FIGURE 3–9		
Quick ratios for MCI	1993: $2,296/$3,201 = .72	
	1994: $4,534/$3,137 = 1.45	

Activity Ratios. Activity ratios measure the speed with which assets move through operations. They involve the calculation of a number called *turnover*, which indicates the number of times during a given period that assets are acquired, disposed of, and replaced. Dividing 365 by the turnover number produces the average number of days during the year that the assets were carried on the balance sheet. Turnover is commonly calculated for accounts receivable and inventory but is also sometimes computed for long-lived assets and total assets.

Receivables Turnover. Receivables turnover reflects the number of times the trade receivables were recorded, collected, and recorded again during the period.

Net Credit Sales/Average Accounts Receivable

It measures the effectiveness of the credit-granting and collection activities of a company. High receivables turnover often suggests effective credit-granting and collection activities, while low turnover can indicate late payments and bad debts, probably due to credit being granted to poor-risk customers and/or to ineffective collection efforts. A very high turnover, however, is not always desirable; it may indicate overly stringent credit terms, leading to missed sales and lost profits. Note also that this ratio often can be converted to a time-basis expression (Average Days Outstanding) by dividing it into 365 days.

The average number of days outstanding for receivables varies significantly across industries, usually depending on the extent to which a particular industry relies on credit sales. Grocery stores, for example, average approximately three days because most of their customers pay immediately. Department stores, which rely heavily on credit sales, average approximately thirty days. Professional services, which normally bill their clients after a service is provided, receive payment, on average, in sixty days.

Receivables turnover ratios for MCI are contained in Figure 3–10. MCI's receivables turned over more quickly in 1994—from every 64 days to every 59 days. Quicker turnover is normally considered a positive sign, but in this case such an interpretation should be approached cautiously. First, the numerator is total revenues and there is no way of knowing what portion of these revenues are credit sales. Also, the 1992 receivables balance was not disclosed in the 1994 annual report, so we assumed that it was equal to the 1993 balance. Finally, turnover ratios are broad averages unable to identify individual slow-moving accounts, some of which could be quite large.

FIGURE 3-10	Times per year:
Receivables turnover for MCI	1993: $11,921/[($2,131 + $2,131*)/2] = 5.59
	1994: $13,338/[($2,266 + $2,131)/2] = 6.07
	Days outstanding:
	1993: 360 days/5.59 = 64 days
	1994: 360 days/6.06 = 59 days

*Assumes that 1992 receivables balance was $2,131.

Inventory Turnover. Inventory turnover ratio measures the speed with which inventories move through operations.

Cost of Goods Sold/Average Inventory

It compares the amount of inventory carried by a company to the volume of goods sold during the period, reflecting how quickly, in general, inventories are sold. Because profit (and often cash) is usually realized each time inventory is sold and substantial costs are often associated with carrying inventories, an increase in the inventory turnover ratio is normally desirable. However, high inventory turnovers can indicate that inventory levels are too low, giving rise to lost sales and profits due to items being out of stock. Like receivables turnover, this ratio is often converted to a time-basis expression by dividing it into 365 days.

The average number of days it takes companies to turn over their inventories varies across industries. Grocery stores and restaurants, which carry perishable foods, turn their inventories over every week or two. Department stores, new and used car dealers, and many manufacturing operations turn their inventories, on average, every 60–70 days. Seasonal operations, like retail sporting goods and clothing stores, replace their inventories every season, or every 90–100 days.

MCI is in the telecommunications industry and provides a wide variety of services to its customers. It does not, however, sell tangible goods, so it carries no inventories. Consequently, inventory turnover is not relevant.

Capitalization Ratios. **Capitalization ratios** help users to evaluate the capital structure of a company or, in general, the composition of the liability and stockholders' equity side of the balance sheet. Ratios like financial leverage and debt/equity address questions such as: What are the relative returns to creditors and stockholders, and from what sources does a company finance its operations? The debt/equity ratio provides an indication of a company's future cash requirements and, accordingly, its solvency position. Financial leverage is more a measure of earning power.

Financial Leverage. Financial leverage involves borrowing funds and investing them in assets that provide returns in excess of the tax-deductible cost of the borrowings. One way to measure this concept is to compare two previously discussed ratios: return on equity and return on assets.

Return on Equity − Return on Assets

Earlier we noted that return on equity reflects only the return to the stockholders, while return on assets reflects the overall return to both stockholders and creditors. To the extent that return on equity exceeds return on assets, the return to stockholders will exceed the return to creditors. In such cases a company is managing its debt effectively and is thereby reaping the benefits of financial leverage for its stockholders. However, leverage can work to the detriment of the stockholders if the cost of debt exceeds the return generated from the borrowed funds.

The financial leverage ratios of major industries vary from approximately 3 percent to around 15 percent. Life insurance and many heavy manufacturing companies experience financial leverage of about 3–4 percent, while hotels operate at approximately 6 percent, new and used car dealerships at 11 percent, and professional services at 14 percent.

Financial leverage ratios for MCI are contained in Figure 3–11. MCI's financial leverage dropped considerably during 1994, from .08 to .05. The decrease occurred primarily because the company's return on equity ratio declined. Once again, the stock issuance in 1994 increased the shareholders' investment by more than it increased net income. Recall that MCI's cash and marketable securities balance grew considerably during 1994, and these assets do not generate high returns.

FIGURE 3–11	
Financial leverage ratios for MCI	1993: .16 − .08 = .08 1994: .12 − .07 = .05

Debt/Equity Ratio. The debt/equity ratio relates the capital provided by creditors to that supplied by stockholders:

Total Liabilities/Total Stockholders' Equity

While there are a number of different ways to calculate this ratio, we have chosen what is probably the most common form: total liabilities (both current and non-current) divided by the balance of all stockholders' equity accounts.

The debt/equity ratio indicates the extent to which a company can sustain losses without jeopardizing the interests of its creditors. Recall that creditors have priority claims over stockholders; in case of liquidation, the creditors have first right to a company's assets. From an individual creditor's standpoint, therefore, the amount of equity in the company's capital structure can be viewed as a buffer, helping to ensure that there are sufficient assets to cover individual claims. A high debt/equity ratio may concern an individual creditor because it indicates that the claims of the other creditors are large relative to the available assets, increasing the chance that certain creditor claims may not be completely satisfied in the event of liquidation. In general, a high debt/equity ratio also suggests a risky and highly leveraged position, requiring large future cash outflows (interest and principal payments). This in turn raises questions about a company's ability to remain solvent.

Normal debt/equity ratios of major U.S. companies, with the exception of financial institutions, range from approximately .40 to about 2.5. Wendy's International, for example, carries a debt/equity ratio of about .40–.50. Polaroid Corporation and IBM carry debt/equity ratios of .50–.70. J.C. Penney, Chevron, General Motors, and the Boeing Company maintain ratios above 1.0 but usually below 1.5. The debt/equity ratio of McDonnell Douglas borders around 2.0. Financial institutions, such as

American Express Company and BankAmerica Corporation, can have debt/equity ratios of as much as 25–30 to 1.

Debt/equity ratios for MCI are contained in Figure 3–12. MCI's debt/equity ratio dropped during 1994, from 1.39 to .82. Note that both total liabilities and shareholders' equity increased, which indicates that the company is in a growth mode (total assets increased by over $5 billion), and using outside capital to finance it. However, the increase in stockholders' equity was much greater than the increase in liabilities. By issuing common stock in 1994, MCI dramatically shifted its capital structure away from a relatively heavy reliance on debt.

FIGURE 3–12				
Debt/equity ratios for MCI	1993:	$6,563/$4,713	=	1.39
	1994:	$7,362/$9,004	=	.82

Market Ratios. **Market ratios** measure returns to common stockholders that are due to changes in the market price of the common stock and the receipt of dividends. Three such ratios are discussed below: the price/earnings ratio, dividend yield, and return on investments.

Price/Earnings Ratio. The price/earnings ratio is used by many financial statement analysts to assess the investment potential of common stocks.

Market Price per Share/Earnings per Share

Specifically, by relating the price of a company's common stock to its earnings, this ratio provides a measure of how the stock price reacts to changes in net income. The higher the price/earnings ratio, the more sensitive the stock price. For example, a 10:1 price/earnings ratio suggests that a $1 per share increase in earnings would bring about a $10 increase in the stock price. A 20:1 ratio suggests that a $1 per share earnings increase would generate a $20 increase in stock price.

Price/earnings ratios vary widely from one company to the next. They can even change significantly from one year to the next for a single company. The price/earnings ratio of McDonnell Douglas, for example, recently went from approximately 13:1 to about 5:1 in a single year. Normally, such ratios range between 10:1 and 25:1. However, some companies have price/earnings ratios as low as 4:1, and others can be as high as 60 or 70:1.

Price/earnings ratios for MCI are contained in Figure 3–13. The ratios are calculated using the high and low stock prices during 1993 and 1994. In general, MCI's price/earnings ratio appears to have decreased over the two-year period. While earnings per share has increased, the stock price has fallen slightly.

FIGURE 3–13				
Price/earnings ratios for MCI	1993:	High: $29.87/$1.12*	=	26.7
		Low: $18.81/$1.12*	=	16.8
	1994:	High: $29.00/$1.32	=	22.0
		Low: $17.25/$1.32	=	13.1

*Excludes the $45 million extraordinary loss.

Dividend Yield Ratio. The dividend yield ratio relates the dividends paid on the share of common stock to its market price. It indicates the cash return on the stockholder's investment:

Dividends per Share/Market Price per Share

The dividend yields of most major U.S. companies are below .05. Recent yields of The Boeing Company, Goodyear Tire & Rubber, McDonald's Corporation, and General Electric, for example, all ranged from .01 to .05.

Dividend yield ratios for MCI are contained in Figure 3–14. The ratios are calculated using the high and low stock prices during 1993 and 1994. MCI's dividend yield is low and relatively consistent. The company pays dividends each year of .05/share, and share prices have generally been in the $20 to $25 range. MCI is a growing company and has chosen not to pay large dividends, preferring instead to reinvest earnings in the business. Dividends as a percent of net income consistently have been less than 5 percent.

FIGURE 3–14	1993:	High: $.05/$29.87	=	.002
Dividend yield ratios for MCI		Low: $.05/$18.81	=	.003
	1994:	High: $.05/$29.00	=	.002
		Low: $.05/$17.25	=	.003

Annual Return on Investment. The annual return on investment provided by a share of common stock is computed by subtracting the market price at the beginning of the year (Market Price$_0$) from the market price at the end of the year (Market Price$_1$), adding the dividends per share paid during the year, and dividing the result by the market price at the beginning of the year:

(Market Price$_1$ − Market Price$_0$ + Dividends)/Market Price$_0$

The numerator reflects the pretax return to the stockholder, and the denominator reflects the amount of the stockholder's investment. This ratio provides a measure of the pretax performance of an investment in a share of common stock. Returns on common stock investments vary significantly among companies and across time. Over the past few years, in general, returns of 10 to 20 percent could be considered reasonable.

Annual returns on investments in MCI stock are contained in Figure 3–15. The maximum return assumes that an investor purchased MCI stock at the lowest 1993 price and sold it at the highest 1994 price; the minimum return assumes that stock was purchased at the highest 1993 price and sold at the lowest 1994 price. Note the large difference between the maximum and minimum returns, indicating that the price of MCI stock was not stable over the two-year period.

FIGURE 3–15	Maximum:	($29.00 − $18.81 + .05)/$18.81	=	.54
Annual return on investment ratios for MCI	Minimum:	($17.25 − $29.88 + .05)/$29.88	=	−.42

SUMMARY AND OVERVIEW OF FINANCIAL RATIOS. Figure 3–16 shows all of the ratios discussed in this section and provides the formula and a brief description for each ratio.

FIGURE 3–16

Financial accounting ratios

RATIO	FORMULA	DESCRIPTION
PROFITABILITY RATIOS		
Return on equity	Net Income ÷ Average Stockholders' Equity	Effectiveness at managing capital provided by owners.
Return on assets	(Net Income + Interest Expense) ÷ Average Total Assets	Effectiveness at managing capital provided by all investors.
Earnings per share	Net Income ÷ Average Number of Common Shares Outstanding	Profits generated per share of common stock.
Return on sales	Net Income ÷ Net Sales	Ability to create profits from operating activities.
Times interest earned	Net Income Before Taxes ÷ Interest Expense	Ability to meet fixed interest charges with profits from operations.
SOLVENCY RATIOS		
Current ratio	Current Assets ÷ Current Liabilities	Ability to cover current debts with current assets.
Quick ratio	(Cash + Short-Term Investments + Accounts Receivable) ÷ Current Liabilities	Ability to cover current debts with cash-like assets.
ACTIVITY RATIOS		
Receivables turnover	Net Credit Sales ÷ Average Accounts Receivable	Number of times receivables are collected each year.
Inventory turnover	Cost of Goods Sold ÷ Average Inventory	Number of times inventories are replaced each year.
CAPITALIZATION RATIOS		
Financial leverage	Return on Equity − Return on Assets	Use of debt to produce returns for owners.
Debt/equity	Total Liabilities ÷ Total Stockholders' Equity	Relative importance of debt and equity in the capital structure.

FIGURE 3–16 (CONCLUDED)

RATIO	FORMULA	DESCRIPTION
MARKET RATIOS		
Price/earnings	Market Price per Share ÷ Earnings per Share	Sensitivity of stock price to changes in earnings.
Dividend yield	Dividends per Share ÷ Market Price per Share	Cash return on stockholders' investment.
Return on investment	$(\text{Market Price}_1 - \text{Market Price}_0 + \text{Dividends}) \div \text{Market Price}_0$	Annual rate of return on common shares for period (1).

SOLVENCY ASSESSMENT

LO 4 In recent years the investment community has become increasingly concerned with the assessment of solvency, concluding that it is not sufficient simply to analyze balance sheet ratios. In large part this concern has stemmed from company failures, leading to huge investor, creditor, and auditor losses that may have been averted if better information about solvency had been available. For example, famous bankruptcies involving such companies as W.T. Grant, Sambo's Restaurants, Penn Central, AM International, and Wickes Lumber encouraged the FASB in 1981 to require the statement of changes in financial position, a predecessor to the statement of cash flows. Further, economic recession in the late 1980s brought down such corporate giants as Campeau Corporation, including Bloomingdales and Abraham Straus and Circle K convenience stores, R.H. Macy, and several major airlines.

Assessing solvency involves estimating future cash flows and determining whether the future inflows are timed so that adequate cash is available to cover future cash obligations. Three basic factors should be considered in this assessment: (1) operating performance, (2) financial flexibility, and (3) liquidity. Figure 3–17 depicts how these factors relate to solvency.

Operating performance represents a company's ability to grow (increase its net assets) through operations. Since operations is perhaps the most important source of cash to a firm, this concept is very important for solvency assessment. The operating section of the statement of cash flows is especially useful here, as are the profitability and activity ratios discussed earlier.

Financial flexibility refers to a company's ability to produce cash through means other than operations: issuing debt, issuing equity, selling assets. Companies capable of generating cash through a number of these options are considered financially flexible. Referring to the financial statement footnotes can be useful here because a company's ability to borrow and the condition of outstanding equity issuances are normally described in some detail. The balance sheet lists the assets of the company, but users must be cautious here because the assets are not carried at market value. The statement of cash flows may be helpful in assessing financial flexibility because it describes recent debt and equity issues and payments, and recent asset acquisitions and sales.

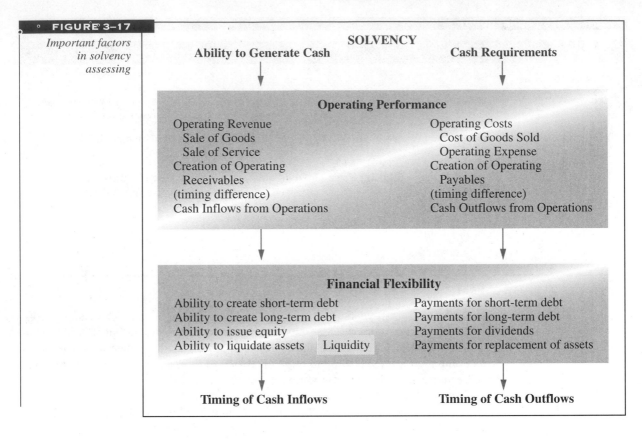

FIGURE 3–17

Important factors in solvency assessing

Liquidity is part of financial flexibility. It represents the ability of a company to covert its existing assets to cash. Highly liquid assets increase a company's solvency position because they represent quick access to cash and can be used to secure outstanding loans. Liquidity can be assessed by reviewing the order of the assets listed on the balance sheet. A large percentage of current assets relative to total assets can indicate high liquidity. Also, the receivables and inventory turnover ratios reflect liquidity—high turnover normally indicates high liquidity.

LIMITATIONS OF FINANCIAL ACCOUNTING INFORMATION

LO 5 Investors and creditors use financial information to assess company earning power and solvency in an effort to determine a company's true value. Unfortunately, reported financial statements provide an imperfect measure of true value. The balance sheet, for example, discloses book value (assets − liabilities), which is a far cry from the company's market value. There are two basic reasons why reported book value and true value are different, and these two reasons represent the fundamental limitations of financial accounting information. First, generally accepted accounting principles, even if applied in a completely objective and appropriate manner, are inherently limited because they ignore much relevant information and do not produce timely financial statements. Second, the application of generally accepted accounting principles is influenced by the judgments and biases of management, which can further distort the correspondence between reported book value and true value. The second limitation can be further divided into two categories: (1) legitimate, which refers to the use of management's allowable discretion within the scope of generally accepted accounting principles and (2) fraudulent, which refers to financial statement manipulation and reporting that is outside the scope of acceptable accounting practice.

In Figure 3–18 the difference between a company's true value and its reported book value is depicted as being comprised of two elements: (1) Inherent GAAP Limitation and (2) Management Bias. In other words, the value of a company as reported on its balance sheet does not reflect its true value because GAAP is inherently limited, and management can use its discretion in preparing the financial statements.

In terms of Figure 3–18, financial statement analysis, as discussed so far in this chapter, involves using the reported financial statements to assess earning power and solvency without considering either of these two limitations. At best, such a strategy, which accepts the reported numbers at face value, can produce an estimate of a company's true value that is no better than its reported value. Consequently, financial statement analysis can be improved, or a more accurate estimate of true value can be derived, by assessing and adjusting for both management biases and inherent GAAP limitations.

FIGURE 3–18

Limitations of financial accounting information

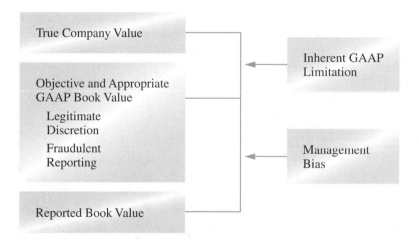

MANAGEMENT BIASES

Managers are not inherently unethical, and they do not attempt at every opportunity to exploit the investors and creditors who provide the company's capital. Indeed, it is in the manager's long-run best interest to report truthfully. However, it is well-known that managers choose those accounting methods and estimates that report the results of their actions in ways that protect and further their own interests. They are fully aware that the financial statements are used by outsiders to evaluate and influence their actions and that their future levels of wealth are often directly tied to the financial accounting numbers. To the extent that they are able, therefore, they will manage those numbers. Such influence may come in the form of a choice of a particular accounting method, the estimates used to apply the chosen accounting methods, or any of a number of other subjective operating, investing, financing, and reporting decisions that can influence important accounting numbers.

The fact that managers can influence reported accounting numbers introduces an important concept, called **quality of earnings**, that financial statement users should well understand. As defined in *The Wall Street Journal* (September 18, 1990), "Quality of earnings measures how much the profits companies publicly report diverge from true operating earnings."[8] Low quality means that management has used much of its discretionary influence to report the dollar amounts on the financial statements in a way that serves its interests, while high quality means that management has exercised little or no such influence. Four strategies used by managers to "manage" reported accounting numbers are well known. Each is discussed below.

OVERSTATING FINANCIAL CONDITION AND OPERATING PERFORMANCE

In certain situations managers will simply attempt to devise a more favorable picture by **overstating the financial condition** and operating performance of the company. This is often achieved by accelerating the recognition of revenues or deferring the recognition of expenses. Young, fast-growing, aggressive companies sometimes use this reporting strategy to help them attract much-needed capital, and it is also common in situations where companies face financial difficulties. The quotes below provide real-world evidence of this strategy.

". . . in a faltering economy, companies come under greater pressure to spruce up reported earnings with cosmetic fixes; for example, understating costs or overstating revenue at the expense of future performance." (The Wall Street Journal, December 17, 1990).

"Critics say that small [fast-growing] high-tech companies are often tempted to inflate sales in order to keep their stocks buoyant." (The Wall Street Journal, September 7, 1994)

TAKING A BATH

When a company experiences an extremely poor year it sometimes chooses very conservative accounting methods, estimates, or judgments (e.g., recognize an accounting loss) that, in turn, further reduce the company's reported financial condition and operating performance in that year. This strategy, called **taking a bath**, enables companies to recognize losses in years that are already very poor in hopes that these losses may be less obvious. Furthermore, by recognizing losses in the current year management will not have to recognize them in future years which, in turn, may improve future financial statements. Several years ago, IBM had one of its worst years in recent history. The company chose to make an accounting change that led to the recognition of a multibillion dollar loss in that year even though the recognition of the loss was not required until two years later.

CREATING HIDDEN RESERVES

Very conservative accounting methods, estimates, and judgments may also be used by management in years of extremely good performance. In such years the recognition of accounting losses may help management to "smooth" reported earnings over time. Recognizing accounting losses in the current period ensures that reported earnings in

8. The concept of quality of earnings normally refers to the extent to which management has used its discretion in preparing financial reports, but some writers interpret it to also include what Figure 3–18 refers to as an Inherent GAAP Limitation.

that period are not too high and, in addition, guarantees that the loss will not have to be recognized in future periods when reported earnings may be less impressive. This strategy, called **creating hidden reserves**, was practiced several years ago by the oil industry in response to the 1991 Gulf War. The following quote, taken from the *Bloomington Herald Tribune* (September 16, 1990), describes the situation.

Fearful of public and congressional outcry over the large profits that many oil companies are likely to report for the fiscal quarter due to the war in the Gulf, industry executives are trying to find ways to hold down those profits. A strategy for reducing those profits is to [recognize accounting losses in the current period] for future environmental expenses, for refinery and chemical plant maintenance programs, and for potential legal claims. Such a step is commonplace in the industry and conforms with accounting standards.

EMPLOYING OFF-BALANCE-SHEET FINANCING

Managers have been known to structure financing transactions and choose certain accounting methods so that debt need not be reported on the balance sheet. By avoiding the recognition of debt, such activities, called **off-balance-sheet financing**, may produce more favorable values for the current ratio and the debt/equity ratio. As noted in *Forbes* (November 20, 1980), "The basic drives of man are few: to get enough food, to find shelter and to keep debt off the balance sheet."

Given such strategies, financial statement users must not only analyze the statements, but must also attempt to assess the extent to which management has had discretionary influence over the statements. To do so, users must examine the footnotes closely to identify the accounting methods that have been chosen, while being particularly aware of those areas in the statements that are most sensitive to the subjective estimates and judgmental reporting decisions of management. Users should also learn as much as possible about the situation faced by management or, in other words, put "themselves in management's shoes" by investigating incentive compensation contracts, debt covenants, and the general economic environment in which the company itself and its industry exist. With such information users can better understand the economic incentives that may have determined the reporting strategies chosen by management.

Assessing the quality of a company's reported numbers is useful because it enables users to adjust the statements so that more meaningful comparisons are possible—comparisons across time and among similar companies. It also allows users to make a more accurate assessment of the "true" economic performance and condition of a particular company. In terms of Figure 3–18, it would provide an estimate of Objective and Appropriate Book Value. Indeed, Baruch Lev, a well-known accounting professor from New York University, commented: "We have found that quality-adjusted earnings are much more closely related to the behavior of stock prices over time than are reported earnings. A deterioration in quality of earnings would suggest a deterioration in stock prices in the future." (*The Wall Street Journal*, September 18, 1992).

INHERENT GAAP LIMITATIONS

Financial statements are inherently limited because they ignore much information that is relevant to assessing a company's true value. Astute financial statement users should consider such information in their assessments of a company's true value, making their own adjustments to the financial statements to reflect such facts. For example, macroeconomic information, such as the general rate of inflation, the rate of unemployment, and movements in the rate of interest, affects the financial situation of a company and, therefore, should be relevant to an investment decision. Yet, such information is not included in financial statements. Investors and creditors must rely on other sources for this information.

In addition, much relevant microeconomic (company-specific) information is absent from the financial statements. Several examples follow.

NO HUMAN RESOURCES

Estimates of the value of a company's human resources are not included on the balance sheet. For many companies, especially those in the fast-growing service sector, **human capital** is the most important "asset." How can one assess the value of a professional basketball team, for example, without considering the value of its players, or the value of a law or public accounting firm without considering the value of the professional staff? Certainly, estimating the value of human capital is difficult and subjective, and it is not surprising that such valuations do not fall within the scope of generally accepted accounting principles. Nonetheless, there is little doubt that human capital is an important part of successful operations for many companies.

NO VALUE AS A WORKING UNIT

The value of a company as a working unit—the way a company's assets interact to produce a product or service that has been used and relied upon, often for years, by customers or clients—is another important asset that is not recognized on the financial statements. Consider, for example, the reputation for service and quality that a company like DuPont has built up over the past years. This intangible factor is an important part of future sales, customer, supplier, and employee relationships and, in general, DuPont's overall future success. Like human resources, estimating the value of this intangible asset is difficult and subjective and is not covered within the framework of generally accepted accounting principles. However, it can be an important part of a company's value and should not be ignored by anyone interested in a company's financial condition and future.

FEW MARKET VALUES

The selling prices (market values) of assets like inventory may be relevant to the decisions of investors and creditors, yet because market values are difficult to measure objectively, such prices are disclosed on the financial statements in only a few cases. For the most part, historical costs are found on the balance sheet, and there is some question about the usefulness of historical cost for decision-making purposes. Individuals who are interested in assessing a company's financial condition and performance should consider estimating and incorporating into the financial statements the market values of the company's assets.

NO INFLATION ADJUSTMENTS

Inflation is ignored when the financial statements are prepared. Because different assets, liabilities, revenues, and expenses are recognized at different times, the dollar values attached to these accounts reflect different levels of purchasing power. It is questionable whether comparing these numbers, or adding and subtracting them, gives rise to meaningful amounts. Total assets and net income, for example, are the results of adding and/or subtracting numbers that are expressed in dollars of different purchasing power. Individuals interested in assessing the financial performance of a company should adjust the financial statements for the effects of inflation.

LACK OF TIMELINESS: ANNUAL REPORT
INFORMATION AND PREDICTING STOCK PRICES

L O 6 It is well known that stock prices react to the disclosure of accounting information. Indeed, *USA Today* (October 23, 1990) reports in an article entitled "Economic Health Tied to Profits" that "profits of public companies have the greatest and most immediate effect on the company's stock price," and in a number of accounting and finance research studies, stock prices of companies traded on the U.S. stock markets have been shown to react almost instantaneously to the disclosure of accounting information. It is important to understand, at the same time, that published annual reports are not available to the public until several months after the balance sheet date, and important numbers, such as net income, are announced quarterly and are available to the public almost as soon as they are determined. Thus, it is difficult, if not impossible, for investors to use the information contained in an annual report to identify undervalued stocks traded on the public security markets. Such information is not timely enough because the market price has already reacted to important accounting numbers that were released at an earlier date.

Consider, for example, an investor who is deciding whether to purchase General Electric (GE) common stock using the information in the company's 1995 annual report. Assume that the investor reads the annual report when it arrives on March 15, 1996, and notes that the company's net income is the highest in the company's history. On that basis the investor concludes that GE stock, which is presently trading at $80, is actually worth $100. Believing that the stock is worth more than the $80 market price, the investor chooses to purchase GE shares, expecting the price to rise as the other investors in the stock market learn of the undervaluation. Unfortunately, this strategy would probably not be very productive in today's U.S. stock markets because GE's stock price would have reacted to the company's net income announcement when it was released sometime in January of 1996. By the time the annual reports were available, the information was already reflected in the market price.

While annual report information in and of itself may not be particularly helpful in identifying undervalued publicly traded securities, this certainly does not mean that it is useless. There is some evidence, for example, that annual report information, if analyzed in a superior fashion, can lead to better-than-average returns in the stock market. Such analysis may also help an investor to better understand the expected risk and return levels associated with certain investments, to ascertain whether those levels are consistent with the investor's preferences. In addition, banks use financial statement analysis to guide loan decisions and to determine the terms of the loans they grant, and financial ratios have been used successfully by bankers and auditors to predict business failures. Financial statement analysis can also be useful when deciding whether to purchase equity or debt securities in companies that are not publicly traded. And finally, recall that financial statement numbers are used in contracts to influence the actions of managers.

INTERNATIONAL PERSPECTIVE:
FINANCIAL STATEMENT ANALYSIS
IN AN INTERNATIONAL SETTING

Recently, U.S. investors have shown increasing interest in foreign securities traded on foreign markets. Such securities often provide returns that exceed those available in U.S. markets, and holding foreign stocks can help reduce an investor's risk by diversifying the investment portfolio to include securities of companies from more than one country. In most cases the choice to buy or sell a foreign security is based on financial information provided by the investee company which, in turn, presents the investor with the difficult challenge of analyzing and interpreting financial statements prepared according to foreign accounting and business norms.

In an earlier chapter we briefly discussed variations in the quality and extent of available accounting information across companies from different countries. We also mentioned and illustrated significant differences in the accounting practices of different countries. Clearly, an investor who uses accounting information to guide trading in foreign securities should attempt to reconcile these differences if meaningful comparisons are to be made among the almost limitless selection of foreign investments. One method of reconciliation would be to adjust the foreign statements to reflect U.S. accounting principles. Unfortunately, adjusting foreign financial statements to a common basis (e.g., U.S. GAAP) by itself may not be sufficient to achieve meaningful comparisons. Since the accounting system in a particular country is a product of the social, economic, legal, and cultural environment, it follows that differences across environments would further complicate the interpretation of the adjusted financial statements. In other words, not only must the financial statements of a foreign-based company be adjusted, but the resulting numbers can only be interpreted through an understanding of the foreign environment.

In an interesting study, Professor Frederick Choi and a number of colleagues from Japan, Korea, and the United States showed that understanding the institutional, legal, and cultural aspects of an environment is as important as adjusting the foreign financial statements for differences in accounting principles.[9] The authors found that the Japanese and Korean firms, in general, were much more highly leveraged (higher debt/equity ratios) and less profitable (lower net income/sales) than their U.S. counterparts, but they noted further that important environmental and cultural characteristics explained these differences. For example, raising capital through equity issuances in Japan and Korea is relatively unusual for a number of reasons, one of which is that the local banks and government play a particularly important role in providing debt capital. The authors also reported that Japanese managers are much less concerned with short-run profits than U.S. managers because, unlike the United States, employment security for Japanese managers is virtually guaranteed. Japanese managers, therefore, are more likely to make investments that maximize long-run profitability, often at the expense of profits in the current period. As a result, Japanese and Korean firms may appear on the surface to be more highly leveraged and less profitable than U.S. firms, but in substance they may not be. They are simply products of a different business environment.

ANALYZING THE FINANCIAL STATEMENTS OF ALBERTSONS AND SAFEWAY

In this section we analyze the financial ratios of Albertsons and Safeway. Figure 3–19 compares the two companies for 1994 and 1993, using the formulas provided in Figure 3–16.

Both Albertsons and Safeway are national food retail chains that operate primarily in the West and Midwest U.S. Albertsons' total assets ($3.6 billion) and sales

---

9. F. Choi, H. Hino, S. Min, S. Nam, J. Ujiie, and A. Stonehill, "Analyzing Foreign Financial Statements: The Use and Misuse of International Ratio Analysis," *Journal of International Business Studies* (Spring–Summer 1983), pp. 113–131.

FIGURE 3–19		ALBERTSONS		SAFEWAY	
		1994	1993	1994	1993
1994 and 1993 financial ratios for Albertsons and Safeway	**PROFITABILITY RATIOS**				
	Return on equity	.26	.26	.47	.39
	Return on assets	.12	.11	.09	.08
	Earnings per share ($)	1.58	1.34	1.94	1.00
	Return on sales	.04	.03	.02	.01
	Times interest earned	10.9	10.8	1.9	.81
	SOLVENCY RATIOS				
	Current ratio	1.08	1.13	.79	.87
	Quick ratio	.15	.18	.11	.14
	ACTIVITY RATIOS				
	Receivables turnover (days)	106	111	117	121
	Inventory turnover (days)	9.8	10	10	9.6
	CAPITALIZATION RATIOS				
	Financial leverage	.14	.15	.38	.31
	Debt/equity	1.14	1.37	6.8	12.25
	MARKET RATIOS				
	Price/earnings (avg.)	18	19	15	20
	Dividend yield (avg.)	.02	.01	0	0
	Return on investment (avg.)	.09	.25	.50	.29

($11.9 billion) are less than the total assets ($5.0 billion) and sales ($15.6 billion) of Safeway, but Albertsons' net worth ($1.7 billion) is larger than that of Safeway ($644 million). Their principle accounting policies are virtually the same; both received standard, unqualified audit opinions in 1994, and both companies have strong credit ratings. Neither company entered into any large and unusual transactions during the past two years, but Safeway bears an unusually large amount of debt. Several years ago Safeway's management borrowed a large sum and used the proceeds to buy Safeway stock from the public. Since that time the company has reissued stock to the public, and has gradually reduced its total outstanding debt. From 1990 to 1994, for example, the company reduced its debt by $1 billion.

Examine the ratios of Safeway first, and note that return on equity is particularly high and increased from 1993 to 1994.The large difference between return on equity and return on assets is due primarily to the large amount of debt carried by Safeway. The company seems to be using leverage very effectively—earning returns on borrowed funds that far exceed the interest cost associated with the borrowings. The high leverage ratio supports this interpretation. The activity ratios and return on sales seem to be in line with those of Albertsons as well as those of the industry in general. Safeway appears to have considerable earning power.

However, Safeway does have a substantial amount of debt outstanding, 1994 total liabilities of $4.4 billion. The debt/equity ratio is relatively high; the times interest earned ratio shows that interest costs are substantial; and current liabilities exceed current assets. The footnotes describe significant restrictions imposed by debt covenants, but the company seems to be managing its debt effectively. The statement of cash flows shows that net cash flow from operations has provided enough funds to finance the company's capital expenditures as well as reduce its debt in each of the last three years. In addition, the stock market has reacted favorably. Return on investment has been relatively high, even though the company has chosen to pay no dividends.

Albertsons appears to be a solid and stable company. Return on equity is much lower than that of Safeway, but the company need not manage the same level of outstanding debt. The activity ratios are comparable to those of Safeway, and return on assets, earnings per share, and return on sales all show that Albertsons has earning power equal to, or better than, Safeway. The ratios involving outstanding liabilities and interest costs (current ratio, quick ratio, times interest earned, and debt/equity) suggest that Albertsons is presently a solvent company, and can probably use debt financing in the future more readily than can Safeway. Albertsons appears to have greater financial flexibility.

The statement of cash flows indicates that Albertsons' net cash provided by operations has been sufficient to cover its capital expenditures, reduce debts, and finance dividend payments during the last two years. In 1992 the company required debt financing for a major capital investment—the purchase of Osco Drugs for approximately $430 million. Also, the market price of the company's stock has risen consistently and, in addition to dividends, has provided a reasonable return to the shareholders.

A WORD OF CAUTION

This illustration shows that both Safeway and Albertsons appear to be strong and healthy companies. However, we accepted the financial ratios at face value, conducting no quality of earnings or earnings persistence analyses. A closer look at the footnotes, and other more current sources of information, could change our conclusions. Further, these ratios tell us little about either company as a potential investment. Their stock prices already reflect the analysis we just conducted, and it is naive to believe that ratio analysis can identify undervalued securities.

An article published by *The Wall Street Journal* (April 7, 1993) notes that the early 1990s represented a very difficult time for IBM. The company recognized almost $5 billion in losses in 1992, and its stock value dropped by more than $70 billion from 1987 to 1992. The article further states that "considerable evidence suggests that IBM may have been able to delay its day of reckoning with some surprisingly aggressive accounting moves, none of which violated accounting standards and some of which were fully disclosed to the public." The aggressive accounting moves involved (1) booking revenues when products were shipped, even in some cases to its own warehouses, (2) maneuvers that enabled IBM to book immediately revenues from long-term lease arrangements, (3) spreading the costs of factories and other major investments over longer-than-normal time periods, and (4) revising estimates that reduced the reported costs of its retirement plans.

ETHICS IN THE REAL WORLD

IBM's external auditor wrote a blistering letter to management that severely criticized the company's accounting practices, stating for example that "the company was reporting revenue that it might never get." However, IBM received unqualified audit reports through the entire time period, and described the letter as "part of the normal give and take between a company and an auditor with a flair for peppery language."

ETHICAL ISSUE

Is it ethical for a company to use accounting methods that technically may not violate generally accepted accounting principles, but clearly are very aggressive, and then pressure its auditors for an unqualified audit report? Is it ethical for an auditor to retain a client as large and important as IBM and to render an unqualified audit report in a case where there is strong opposition to the accounting methods used by the client?

SUMMARY OF LEARNING OBJECTIVES

Explain how financial statement information is used to predict future cash flows and influence management decisions.

Financial accounting numbers can be used in two fundamental ways: (1) they help to predict a company's future cash flows by providing an indication of its earning power and solvency position, and (2) they help investors, creditors, and other interested parties influence the business decisions of a company's managers.

Financial accounting numbers report on past events, and to the extent that past events are indicative of the future, financial accounting numbers can be used in making predictions about a company's future cash flows. Earning power and solvency are important indicators of a company's future cash flows. Income statement numbers are designed to provide information about earning power. Balance sheet numbers, which reflect short-run cash flows, and the statement of cash flows are particularly relevant in the assessment of solvency.

Investors and creditors can use financial accounting numbers to influence the actions of managers by requiring that they enter into contracts that are written in terms of financial accounting numbers. Stockholders can encourage management to act in their interests by basing management's compensation on profits. Creditors can constrain the actions of managers and protect their own interests by writing restrictions, expressed in terms of financial accounting numbers, into loan contracts.

Explain the concepts of earnings persistence and quality of earnings.

Earnings persistence refers to the extent to which an income number reported in the current period can be expected to reflect future income amounts and be useful in predicting them. Net income amounts that exclude "one-shot" events are considered to have relatively high persistence because such events have a temporary effect on income in any given period. Quality of earnings refers to the extent to which management has used its reporting discretion in preparing the financial statement dollar amounts. To the extent that management uses such discretionary reporting strategies as overstating financial condition, "taking a bath," building "hidden reserves," or practicing off-balance-sheet financing, earnings quality would be considered low. Low quality earnings is often thought to be a poor measure of "true earnings."

List and briefly describe the basic steps involved in assessing the earning power and solvency position of a company.

When assessing earning power and solvency, a financial statement user should (1) review the audit report, (2) look for significant transactions, (3) review the company's credit rating, and (4) analyze the financial statements.

The audit report states whether, and to what extent, the information in the financial statements conforms to generally accepted accounting principles. In most cases an auditor renders an unqualified opinion, but occasionally an auditor departs from the standard report for any of a number of reasons, some of which can be quite serious. Most small companies do not have their financial statements audited.

Users should also look for significant transactions entered into by a company or significant events that might have taken place recently. Such items can have an important effect on the future direction of a company and may distort the financial statements, making it more difficult to assess a company's financial health.

Information about a company's credit rating is also of interest to users. Credit-rating agencies, such as Moody's Investor Service, Dun & Bradstreet, and Standard & Poor's, provide extensive analyses of the operations and financial positions of many companies as well as ratings of the riskiness of their outstanding debts. Such ratings have a direct bearing on a company's ability to issue debt in the future and on the terms of that debt.

Users should also perform ratio and solvency analyses on the financial statements. Such examinations involve computing a number of financial ratios and comparing them to other relevant numbers. These comparisons can be made in three basic ways: (1) across time, (2) across different companies within the same industry, and (3) within the financial statements of the company at a given point in time. A solvency analysis involves assessing the operating performance and financial flexibility of a company as well as the liquidity of its assets.

 Define operating performance, financial flexibility, and liquidity, and explain how they relate to solvency.

Operating performance represents a company's ability to increase its net assets through operations. It provides perhaps the most important, and definitely the most consistent, source of a company's cash inflows and outflows. Financial flexibility refers to a company's ability to produce cash through means other than operations, such as short- and long-term debt, equity issuances, and asset sales. These activities also represent an important source of a company's cash inflows and outflows. Liquidity represents the ability of a company to convert existing assets to cash, which may be used to cover debt payments. Since solvency refers to a company's ability to meet debt payments as they come due, all three of these concepts are important to its assessment because each involves cash inflows and outflows.

 Identify and describe the major limitations of financial accounting information.

There are two basic reasons why reported book value and true value are different, and these two reasons represent the fundamental limitations of financial accounting information. First, generally accepted accounting principles, even if applied in a completely objective and appropriate manner, are inherently limited because they ignore much relevant information and do not produce timely financial statements. Second, the application of generally accepted accounting principles is influenced by the judgments and biases of management.

The first limitation indicates that financial reports are not particularly timely and that they exclude macroeconomic information, estimates of the value of a company's human resources, goodwill, and a number of relevant market values (replacement cost and fair market value). Also, the information in the financial statements is not adjusted for the effect of inflation. The second limitation indicates that financial reports are prepared by managers who have an economic stake in what the statements report and often use their discretion to bias the reported numbers. Financial statement users can improve their analyses by considering these two limitations and adjusting the reported numbers accordingly.

L O 6 *Describe why it is difficult to use annual report information to identify undervalued securities.*

It is difficult to use annual report information to identify undervalued securities because annual reports are typically not available until several months after the date of the balance sheet. Important financial information, such as net income, is normally released to the public long before the annual report is published, and market prices react almost instantaneously to such news releases. Consequently, stock prices already reflect much of the annual report information by the time it is available.

KEY TERMS

Note: Definitions for these terms are provided in the glossary at the end of the text.

Activity ratios (p. 89)
Capitalization ratios (p. 90)
Common-size financial statements (p. 84)
Creating hidden reserves (p. 99)
Earning power (p. 78)
Earnings persistence (p. 78)
Financial flexibility (p. 95)
Human capital (p. 100)
Liquidity (p. 96)

Market ratios (p. 92)
Operating performance (p. 95)
Overstating the financial condition (p. 98)
Profitability ratios (p. 85)
Quality of earnings (p. 98)
Ratio analysis (p. 85)
Solvency (p. 78)
Standard audit report (p. 79)
Taking a bath (p. 98)

QUESTIONS FOR DISCUSSION AND REVIEW

1. In what two fundamental ways are financial accounting numbers used? Provide three examples of each.
2. Discuss the concept of earning power, and differentiate it from the concept of solvency. How are they related? How can financial accounting numbers be used to assess each?
3. What are the basic differences between equity and debt investments, and why would equity and debt investors be interested in both earning power and solvency? Would equity investors tend to be more interested in both earning power or solvency? Would debt investors tend to be more interested in earning power or solvency? Why?
4. Why might a company's stockholders want its managers to be paid bonuses in the form of cash or shares of stock instead of a straight salary? How might such a compensation scheme be implemented?
5. Why do debt covenants often restrict the borrowing company to a certain minimum ratio of current assets to current liabilities? Why might the same covenant contain a provision that limits the annual payment of dividends to a percentage of net income?
6. Describe how audit reports may deviate from "clean" opinions. Explain why financial statement users should review them closely.
7. Do most U.S. companies have their financial statements audited? Why or why not? If you were the manager of a small business, under what conditions would you have your financial statements audited?
8. Why are comparisons of financial statement numbers important to financial statement analysis? In what three ways can such comparisons be made?

9. Why is it helpful to compare financial accounting numbers across time? Why must such comparisons be viewed cautiously?

10. Where can industry-wide statistics be found? Of what use are they to the financial statement analyst, and how can they be misleading?

11. Define the concept of earnings persistence, and explain how it is useful to financial statement users. What kind of income statement items tend to have the most persistence?

12. Provide five examples of significant transactions, and in each case, explain how knowledge of that transaction might influence the way you analyze the financial information of a given company.

13. Where can you find credit-rating information, why is it important, and in general how is it established?

14. What is solvency, and what three factors must be considered in its assessment? Define these factors, and explain how they are related.

15. Assume that ABC Company raised $4 million with an equity issuance and used the proceeds to acquire additional property, plant, and equipment. Provide a plausible explanation for how these transactions would affect ABC's earning power, financial flexibility, and liquidity. How would ABC's earning power, financial flexibility, and liquidity be affected if the company used the proceeds to reduce outstanding debts?

16. Identify and briefly describe the limitations of financial accounting numbers described in this chapter. What kind of relevant information is ignored on financial accounting statements? Why is it ignored?

17. Name five ways in which managers can bias financial statements and still remain within the guidelines of generally accepted accounting principles.

18. Write a short paragraph to define the concept of quality of earnings, and explain why a company's stock price may be more responsive to announcements of high quality earnings than to announcements of low quality earnings.

19. Why can't financial accounting numbers be used to identify undervalued securities that are traded on the major U.S. exchanges? In what other ways and situations can financial accounting numbers be used?

20. Explain some of the major difficulties involved when analyzing financial statements provided by companies from foreign countries.

EXERCISES

E3–1

(Analyzing financial statements)

Excerpts from the financial statements of Marley and Thomas are provided below.

	1997	1996	1995
BALANCE SHEET			
Current assets	$14,000	$13,000	$ 9,000
Long-term assets	98,000	62,000	52,000
Current liabilities	14,000	12,000	7,000
Long-term debt	30,000	20,000	15,000
Stockholders' equity	68,000	43,000	39,000
INCOME STATEMENT			
Sales	$97,000	$86,000	$82,000
Net income	18,000	16,000	25,000

REQUIRED:

Review this information, calculate relevant ratios from Figure 3–16, and explain why Marley and Thomas appears to be a good or poor investment.

E3–2

(Analyzing financial statements)

Excerpts from the financial statements of Mayberry are provided below.

	1997	1996	1995
BALANCE SHEET			
Current assets	$40,000	$44,000	$47,000
Long-term assets	86,000	90,000	95,000
Current liabilities	30,000	30,000	25,000
Long-term debt	50,000	40,000	30,000
Stockholders' equity	46,000	64,000	87,000
INCOME STATEMENT			
Sales	$79,000	$95,000	$94,000
Net income	18,000	26,000	27,000

REQUIRED:

Review this information, calculate relevant ratios from Figure 3–16, and explain why Mayberry appears to be a good or poor investment.

E3–3

(Analyzing financial statements)

The chief executive officer of Ginny's Fashions has included the following financial statements in a loan application submitted to Priority Bank. The company intends to acquire additional equipment and wishes to finance the purchase with a long-term note.

	1997	1996
BALANCE SHEET		
Current assets	$21,000	$14,000
Long-term assets	52,000	50,000
Current liabilities	9,000	7,000
Long-term liabilities	24,000	26,000
Contributed capital	25,000	25,000
Retained earnings	15,000	6,000
INCOME STATEMENT		
Revenues	$74,000	$70,000
Expenses	56,000	53,000
STATEMENT OF CASH FLOWS		
Net cash from operating activities	$ 9,000	$15,000
Net cash from investing activities	(12,000)	(14,000)
Net cash from financing activities	5,000	7,000
Change in cash balance	$ 2,000	$ 8,000
Beginning cash balance	9,000	1,000
Ending cash balance	$11,000	$ 9,000

REQUIRED:

Assume that you, a bank loan officer, review the financial statements, and recommend whether Ginny's Fashions should be considered for a loan. Support your recommendation with financial ratios.

E3–4

(Computing ratios and preparing common-size financial statements)

The 1996 and 1997 financial statements of Ken's Sportswear follow.

BALANCE SHEET	1997	1996
ASSETS		
Cash	$ 9,000	$ 7,000
Accounts receivable	12,000	9,000
Inventory	18,000	15,000
Long-lived assets (net)	60,000	50,000
Total assets	$99,000	$81,000
LIABILITIES AND STOCKHOLDERS' EQUITY		
Accounts payable	$16,500	$12,000
Long-term liabilities	46,000	40,000
Common stock	20,000	20,000
Additional paid-in capital	5,000	5,000
Retained earnings	11,500	4,000
Total liabilities and stockholders' equity	$99,000	$81,000

INCOME STATEMENT	1997	1996
Sales (all on credit)	$72,000	
Less: Cost of goods sold	30,000	
Gross profit	$42,000	
Operating expenses	12,000	
Net income from operations	$30,000	
Interest expense	5,000	
Net income from continuing operations before tax	$25,000	
Income taxes	8,500	
Net income	$16,500	
Dividends	$ 9,000	
Per-share market price	$ 36	$ 30
Outstanding common shares	2,000	2,000

REQUIRED:

a. Compute all ratios described in Figure 3–16 for 1997.
b. Prepare common-size financial statements.
c. Evaluate the company's financial performance and condition.

E3–5

(Solvency and the role of the activity ratios)

Financial information from the records of Blanchard Masonry follows. The company began operations in 1994. Assume that the year-end 1994 balances are the average balances during 1994.

	1997	1996	1995	1994
Cash	$ 7,000	$ 7,000	$ 5,000	$ 5,000
Accounts receivable	20,000	14,000	8,000	7,000
Inventory	15,000	14,000	12,000	12,000
Total current assets	$42,000	$35,000	$25,000	$24,000

	1997	1996	1995	1994
Current liabilities	$14,000	$12,000	$10,000	$10,000
Sales (all on credit)	$50,000	$45,000	$40,000	$35,000
Less: Cost of goods sold	28,000	25,000	22,000	20,000
Gross profit	$22,000	$20,000	$18,000	$15,000

REQUIRED:

a. Compute the current ratio for each year.
b. Compute gross profit as a percent of sales for each year.
c. Compute inventory turnover and average days supply of inventory.
d. Compute receivables turnover and average number of days outstanding.
e. Comment on the company's solvency position over the four-year period.

E3–6

(Solvency and the statement of cash flows)

Beecham Limited began operations in early 1995. Summaries of the statements of cash flows for 1995, 1996, and 1997 follow.

	1997	1996	1995
Net cash provided (used) by operating activities	$?	$(252)	$?
Net cash provided (used) by investing activities	150	?	(400)
Net cash provided (used) by financing activities	(200)	400	800
Net increase (decrease) in cash balance	$?	$ (2)	$ 78
Beginning cash balance	76	?	0
Ending cash balance	$156	$ 76	$?

REQUIRED:

a. Compute the missing dollar amounts, and briefly comment on the company's cash management policies during the three-year period.
b. Does the company appear to have faced any solvency problems during the period? Explain your answer.

E3–7

(Using solvency and activity ratios together)

The following information was extracted from the 1997 financial report of the Generic Clothing Company.

	1997	1996
Current assets:		
Cash	$ 15,000	$ 30,000
Short-term marketable securities	225,000	10,000
Accounts receivable (net)	90,000	95,000
Inventory	50,000	225,000
Prepaid insurance	20,000	25,000
Total current assets	$400,000	$385,000
Current liabilities:		
Accounts payable	$ 75,000	$ 60,000
Wages payable	10,000	10,000
Current portion of long-term debt	375,000	100,000
Total current liabilities	$460,000	$170,000

REQUIRED:

a. Based upon the above data, compute the following for Generic Clothing Company for both 1996 and 1997.
   (1) The current ratio
   (2) The quick ratio
b. Assume that net credit sales for the years ended December 31, 1996 and 1997, were $780,000 and $800,000, respectively, and that the balance of Accounts Receivable as of January 1, 1996, was $100,000. Compute the receivables turnover for both years. Also compute the number of days outstanding.
c. Does it appear that the solvency position of the company improved or worsened from 1996 to 1997? Explain.

E3–8

(Explaining return on equity with inventory turnover)

PLP Corporation began operations on January 1, 1994. The initial investment by the owners was $100,000. The following information was extracted from the company's records.

	NET INCOME	DECEMBER 31 STOCKHOLDERS' EQUITY	DECEMBER 31 INVENTORY	COST OF GOODS SOLD
1994	$510,000	$100,000	$200,000	$ 1,200,000
1995	490,000	290,000	255,000	1,350,000
1996	515,000	315,000	320,000	1,395,000
1997	505,000	510,000	365,000	1,400,000

REQUIRED:

a. Compute the return on equity for each year. Has the company been effective at managing the capital provided by the equity owners?
b. Does the information about inventory and the cost of goods sold indicate any reason for the trend in return on equity? Support your answer with any relevant ratios.

E3–9

(Using ratios and the statement of cash flows to assess solvency and earning power)

The financial information below was taken from the records of Lotechnic Enterprises. The company pays no dividends.

	1997	1996	1995	1994
Current assets	$ 35,000	$ 31,000	$24,000	$20,000
Noncurrent assets	93,000	86,000	64,000	33,000
Total assets	$128,000	$117,000	$88,000	$53,000
Current liabilities	$ 30,000	$ 25,000	$13,000	$ 8,000
Long-term liabilities	40,000	40,000	35,000	15,000
Capital stock	20,000	20,000	20,000	20,000
Retained earnings	38,000	32,000	20,000	10,000
Total liabilities and stockholders' equity	$128,000	$117,000	$88,000	$53,000
Net cash provided (used) by operating activities	$ (2,000)	$ 3,000	$ 6,000	$ 7,000
Net cash provided (used) by investing activities	(10,000)	(20,000)	(31,000)	(12,000)
Net cash provided (used) by financing activities	15,000	15,000	25,000	8,000
Net increase (decrease) in cash	$ 3,000	$ (2,000)	0	$ 3,000
Interest expense	$ 5,000	$ 5,000	$ 4,000	$ 2,000
Net income	24,000	21,000	14,000	13,000

REQUIRED:

a. Compute the current ratio, the debt/equity ratio, and return on assets for each of the four years. Assume that the year-end balances in 1994 reflect the average balances during the year.

b. Prepare a common-size balance sheet for each of the four years.

c. Use the statement of cash flows, and analyze the earning power and solvency positions of Lotechnic.

E3–10

(The effects of transactions on financial ratios)

Conlon Travel Supplies entered into the following transactions during 1996.

1. Purchased inventory on account.
2. Purchased plant machinery by issuing long-term debt.
3. Made a principal payment on long-term debt.
4. Paid wages.
5. Sold inventory on account for 20 percent over cost.
6. Issued stock for cash.

REQUIRED:

Fill in a chart like the one below by indicating whether each transaction would increase ($+$), decrease ($-$), or have no effect (NE) on the quick ratio, current ratio, and debt/equity ratio. Treat each transaction independently, and assume that prior to each transaction, the company's balance sheet appeared as follows.

ASSETS		LIABILITIES AND STOCKHOLDERS' EQUITY	
Cash and marketable securities	$100	Current liabilities	$ 60
Other current assets	100	Long-term liabilities	190
Long-lived assets	150	Stockholders' equity	100
		Total liabilities and	
Total assets	$350	stockholders' equity	$350

TRANSACTION	QUICK RATIO	CURRENT RATIO	DEBT/EQUITY RATIO
1.			
2.			
3.			
4.			
5.			
6.			

E3–11

(Debt covenants can limit additional debt and dividend payments)

At the end of 1996, Montvale Associates borrowed $120,000 from the Bayliner Bank. The debt covenant specified that Montvale's debt/equity ratio could not exceed 1.5:1 during the period of the loan. A summary of Montvale's balance sheet after the loan follows.

	1996
ASSETS	
Current assets	$ 130,000
Noncurrent assets	350,000
Total assets	$ 480,000

continued

1996

LIABILITIES AND STOCKHOLDERS' EQUITY

Current liabilities	$130,000
Long-term liabilities	150,000
Stockholders' equity	200,000
Total liabilities and stockholders' equity	$480,000

REQUIRED:

a. Compute Montvale's debt/equity ratio immediately after the loan.
b. How much additional debt can the company incur without violating the debt covenant?
c. How large a dividend can the company declare and pay at the end of 1996 without violating the debt covenant?
d. If Montvale had declared, but not yet paid, a $20,000 dividend before it took out the loan, could the company pay the dividend afterwards without violating the debt covenant? Why or why not?

E3–12

(Examining market ratios over time)

The information below refers to the financial records of Morrissey Brothers over a five-year period.

	1997	1996	1995	1994	1993
Net income	$60,000	$50,000	$40,000	$24,000	$20,000
Dividends declared	$24,000	$15,000	$16,000	$10,000	$12,000
Closing per-share price	$ 42	$ 37	$ 30	$ 35	$ 30
Number of shares outstanding	18,000[b]	20,000	20,000[a]	10,000	10,000

[a]The additional stock was issued on January 1, 1995.
[b]The company repurchased 2,000 shares of its common stock on January 1, 1997.

REQUIRED:

a. Compute dividends declared as a percentage of net income during each of the five years.
b. Compute the price-earnings ratio, dividend yield, and return on investment for 1994, 1995, 1996, and 1997.
c. Comment on the performance of an investment in Morrissey Brothers stock from 1994 to 1997.

E3–13

(Computing ratios and the effect of transactions on return on equity)

Kinney Conglomerate generated $1,585,000 in net income for the year ended December 31, 1997.

1. The company declared and paid $1,500,000 in dividends on December 31, 1997.
2. Kinney Conglomerate stock was selling for $30 per share on January 1, 1997, and for $35 per share on December 31, 1997.
3. As of January 1, 1997, the company had 100,000 shares of common stock outstanding. During 1997 the company issued 50,000 additional shares. Assume that the additional shares were issued evenly throughout the year.

REQUIRED:

a. Compute the following ratios:
    (1) Earnings per share
    (2) Price/earnings
    (3) Dividend yield
    (4) Return on investment
b. What effect (increase, decrease, or no effect) did each of the items listed under additional information above have on Kinney's return on equity ratio?

PROBLEMS

P3–1

(Computing ratios and the role of market values)

Avery Corporation reported the following selected items as part of its 1997 financial report.

Cash	$ 15,000
Short-term marketable securities (at cost)	150,000
Accounts receivable	100,000
Inventory	100,000
Total assets	970,000
Accounts payable	95,000
Interest payable	50,000
Mortgage payable*	300,000
Common stock (at par value of $10 per share)	200,000
Additional paid-in capital	125,000
Retained earnings	200,000
Net sales	2,000,000
Cost of goods sold	900,000
Interest expense	100,000
Net income before taxes	757,575
Net income	500,000

*$50,000 of the mortgage payable is due within the next year.

REQUIRED:

Compute the following ratios. Where necessary, assume that the year-end balances are equal to average balances during the year.

1. Current ratio
2. Quick ratio
3. Earnings per share
4. Times-interest-earned ratio
5. Return on assets
6. Inventory turnover
7. Return on equity

P3–2

(Borrow or issue equity: effects on financial ratios)

Edgemont Repairs began operations on January 1, 1995. The 1995, 1996, and 1997 financial statements follow.

	1997	1996	1995
ASSETS			
Current assets	$ 30,000	$10,000	$ 8,000
Noncurrent assets	83,000	45,000	41,000
Total assets	$113,000	$55,000	$49,000
LIABILITIES AND STOCKHOLDERS' EQUITY			
Current liabilities	$ 12,000	$ 7,000	$ 5,000
Long-term liabilities	50,000	10,000	10,000
Stockholders' equity	51,000	38,000	34,000
Total liabilities and stockholders' equity	$113,000	$55,000	$49,000

continued

	1997	1996	1995
Revenues	$ 70,000	$45,000	$ 37,000
Operating expenses	27,000	24,000	24,000
Interest expense	5,000	1,000	1,000
Income taxes	13,000	6,000	6,000
Net income	$ 25,000	$14,000	$ 6,000
Dividends	$ 12,000	$10,000	$ 2,000
Number of shares outstanding	10,000	10,000	10,000

On January 1, 1997, the company expanded operations by taking out a $40,000 long-term loan at a 10 percent annual interest rate.

REQUIRED:

a. Compute return on equity, return on assets, return on sales, the times-interest-earned ratio, financial leverage, and the debt/equity ratio for 1996 and 1997.
b. On January 1, 1997, the company's common stock was selling for $20 per share. Assume that Edgemont issued 2,000 shares of stock, instead of borrowing the $40,000, to raise the cash needed to pay for the January 1 expansion. Recompute the ratios in (a) for 1997. Ignore any tax effects.
c. Should the company have issued the equity instead of borrowing the funds? Explain.

P3–3

(Percentage changes and common-size financial statements)

You are considering investing in Gidley Electronics. As part of your investigation of Gidley Electronics, you obtained the following balance sheets for the years ended December 31, 1996 and 1997.

	1997	1996
ASSETS		
Current assets:		
Cash	$ 110,000	$ 115,000
Short-term marketable securities	175,000	220,000
Accounts receivable	350,000	400,000
Inventory	290,000	240,000
Prepaid expenses	55,000	35,000
Total current assets	$ 980,000	$1,010,000
Property, plant, and equipment	650,000	590,000
Less: Accumulated depreciation	(165,000)	(130,000)
Total assets	$1,465,000	$1,470,000
LIABILITIES AND STOCKHOLDERS' EQUITY		
Current liabilities:		
Accounts payable	$ 60,000	$ 50,000
Wages payable	15,000	20,000
Unearned revenue	50,000	35,000
Income taxes payable	55,000	35,000
Current portion of long-term debt	110,000	135,000
Total current liabilities	$ 290,000	$ 275,000
Bonds payable	380,000	440,000
Common stock ($10 par value)	220,000	170,000
Additional paid-in capital	145,000	115,000
Retained earnings	430,000	470,000
Total liabilities and stockholders' equity	$1,465,000	$1,470,000

REQUIRED:

a. Compute the dollar change in each account from 1996 to 1997. Also compute the percentage change in each account from 1996 to 1997.
b. Convert the balance sheets to common-size balance sheets. Also compute the percentage change in the common-size numbers of each account from 1996 to 1997.
c. Does the information provided in (b) provide any additional information to that contained in (a)? Explain.

P3-4

(Comprehensive ratio analysis)

(This problem relates to P3–3). You have just been hired as a stock analyst for a large stock brokerage company. Your first assignment is to analyze the performance of Gidley Electronics. Presented below are the company's income statement and statement of retained earnings for the years ended December 31, 1996 and 1997. The company's balance sheet for these years is presented as part of P3–3.

	1997	1996
INCOME STATEMENT		
Revenue:		
Net cash sales	$1,405,000	$1,255,000
Net credit sales	2,450,000	3,010,000
Total revenue	$3,855,000	$4,265,000
Cost of goods sold:		
Beginning inventory	$ 240,000	$ 300,000
Net purchases	1,755,000	2,005,000
Cost of goods available for sale	$1,995,000	$2,305,000
Less: ending inventory	290,000	240,000
Cost of goods sold	$1,705,000	$2,065,000
Gross profit	$2,150,000	$2,200,000
Selling and administrative expenses:		
Depreciation expense	(95,000)	(100,000)
General selling expenses	(470,000)	(450,000)
General administrative expenses	(580,000)	(620,000)
Net operating income	$1,005,000	$1,030,000
Interest expense	150,000	165,000
Net income from continuing operations before taxes	$ 855,000	$ 865,000
Income taxes	345,000	350,000
Net income	$ 510,000	$ 515,000
STATEMENT OF RETAINED EARNINGS		
Beginning retained earnings balance	$ 470,000	$ 165,000
Plus: Net income	510,000	515,000
Less: Dividends	(550,000)	(210,000)
Ending retained earnings balance	$ 430,000	$ 470,000

The market prices of the company's stock as of January 1, 1996, December 31, 1996, and December 31, 1997, were $65, $69, and $54 per share, respectively. The January 1, 1996, balance in stockholders' equity was $450,000, there were no changes in the number of common shares outstanding or in accounts receivable during 1996, and the income tax rate was 40 percent for 1996 and 1997. Total assets as of January 1, 1996 were $1,450,000.

REQUIRED:

Answer the following questions (including any relevant ratios in your answers) for both 1996 and 1997. Unless the December 31, 1995, balance is provided, assume that the December 31, 1996, balance reflects the average balance during 1996.

1. How effective is the company at managing investments made by the equity owners?
2. Is the company using debt to the best interests of the equity owners?
3. Will the company be able to meet its current obligations using current assets? using cash-like assets?
4. How sensitive are stock prices to changes in earnings?
5. How many days is the average account receivable outstanding? Are the days outstanding increasing or decreasing?

P3–5

(Analyzing financial statements)

Marcia Smithson has operated a small service company for several years, and the following financial statements were prepared by her accountant.

	1997	1996	1995
BALANCE SHEET			
Current assets	$ 18,000	$ 16,000	$14,000
Long-term assets	36,000	30,000	28,000
Current liabilities	14,000	8,000	2,000
Long-term liabilities	18,000	14,000	13,000
Contributed capital	18,000	18,000	10,000
Retained earnings	4,000	6,000	17,000
INCOME STATEMENT			
Revenues	$123,000	$109,000	$86,000
Expenses	91,000	76,000	92,000
STATEMENT OF CASH FLOWS			
Net cash from operating activities	$ 24,000	$ 30,000	$ (5,000)
Net cash from investing activities	(16,000)	(10,000)	6,000
Net cash from financing activities	(10,000)	(16,000)	9,000
Change in cash balance	$ (2,000)	$ 4,000	$10,000
Beginning cash balance	8,000	14,000	4,000
Ending cash balance	$ 6,000	$ 18,000	$14,000

REQUIRED:

Assume that you have some capital to invest, and that Marcia asked you to consider making an equity investment in her company. Review the financial statements and describe how you would respond to Marcia's request. Support your recommendation with financial ratios.

P3–6

(Comparing companies on earning power)

The following information was obtained from the 1997 financial reports of Hathaway Toy Company and Yakima Manufacturing.

	HATHAWAY TOY	YAKIMA MFG.
Interest expense	—	$ 195,000
Net income	$ 875,000	$ 755,000
Current liabilities	$ 240,000	$ 25,000
Mortgage payable	—	1,850,000
Common stock ($10 par value)	800,000	350,000
Additional paid-in capital	915,000	150,000
Retained earnings	745,000	325,000
Total liabilities and stockholders' equity	$2,700,000	$2,700,000

Assume that the only change to stockholders' equity during 1997 is due to net income earned in 1997.

REQUIRED:
a.   Which company is more effective at managing the capital provided by the owners?
b.   Which company is more effective at managing capital provided by all investors?
c.   Compute the earnings per share for each company.
d.   Is Yakima Manufacturing using its debt effectively for the equity owners?

P3-7

(Unusual items and financial ratios)

The following selected financial information was obtained from the 1997 financial reports of Robotronics, Inc., and Technology, Limited.

	ROBOTRONICS, INC.	TECHNOLOGY, LTD.
Interest expense	$ 100,000	$ 175,000
Unusual gain (net of taxes of $320,000)	—	$1,300,000
Net income (including unusual items)	$ 610,000	$1,675,000
Current liabilities	$ 140,000	$ 25,000
Bonds payable	725,000	0
Mortgage payable	1,490,000	405,000
Common stock	500,000	600,000
Additional paid-in capital	215,000	325,000
Retained earnings	290,000	515,000
Total liabilities and stockholders' equity	$3,360,000	$1,870,000

Assume that total assets, total liabilities, and total stockholders' equity were constant throughout 1997.

REQUIRED:
a.   Assume that you are considering purchasing the common stock of one of these companies. Which company has a higher return on equity? Would your conclusion be different if the impact of the unusual item had not been included in net income? Should unusual items be considered? Why or why not?
b.   Which company uses leverage more effectively? Does your answer change if you do not consider the impact of the unusual item on net income?

P3-8

(Preparing the financial statements from financial ratios)

Tumwater Canyon Campsites began operations on January 1, 1997. The following information is available at year end. Assume that all sales were on credit.

Net income	$25,000
Receivables turnover	8
Inventory turnover	5
Return on sales	8%
Gross margin	40%
Quick ratio	50%
Accounts payable	$200,000

REQUIRED:
Prepare an income statement and the current asset and current liability portions of the balance sheet for 1997. Current assets consist of cash, accounts receivable, and inventory. Accounts payable is Tumwater's only current liability. (*Hint:* Begin by using return on sales to compute net sales.)

P3–9

(Common-size financial statements)

Bob Cleary, the controller of Mountain-Pacific Railroad, has prepared the following financial statements for 1996 and 1997. The market prices of the company's stock as of January 1, 1996, December 31, 1996, and December 31, 1997, were $50, $45, and $70 per share, respectively. Assume an income tax rate of 34 percent and assume that interest expense was incurred only on long-term debt (including the current maturities of long-term debt).

BALANCE SHEET	1997	1996
ASSETS		
Current assets:		
Cash	$ 10,000	$ 312,000
Short-term marketable securities	125,000	120,000
Accounts receivable	500,000	150,000
Inventory	200,000	210,000
Prepaid expenses	50,000	75,000
Total current assets	$ 885,000	$ 867,000
Long-term investments	225,000	225,000
Property, plant, and equipment	430,000	540,000
Less: Accumulated depreciation	(65,000)	(100,000)
Total assets	$1,475,000	$1,532,000
LIABILITIES AND STOCKHOLDERS' EQUITY		
Current liabilities:		
Accounts payable	$ 10,000	$ 50,000
Wages payable	5,000	2,000
Dividends payable	125,000	5,000
Income taxes payable	50,000	35,000
Current portion of long-term debt	100,000	175,000
Total current liabilities	$ 290,000	$ 267,000
Mortgage payable	350,000	450,000
Common stock ($10 par value)	200,000	110,000
Additional paid-in capital	135,000	95,000
Retained earnings	500,000	610,000
Total liabilities and stockholders' equity	$1,475,000	$1,532,000

INCOME STATEMENT	1997		1996	
Revenue:				
Net cash sales	$1,955,000		$2,775,000	
Net credit sales	4,150,000		1,410,000	
Total revenue		$6,105,000		$4,185,000
Cost of goods sold:				
Beginning inventory	$ 210,000		$ 300,000	
Net purchases	4,005,000		2,475,000	
Cost of goods available for sale	$4,215,000		$2,775,000	
Less: Ending inventory	200,000		210,000	
Cost of goods sold		4,015,000		2,565,000
Gross profit		$2,090,000		$1,620,000

continued

INCOME STATEMENT	1997		1996	
Gross profit (brought fwd.)		$2,090,000		$1,620,000
Selling and administrative expenses:				
Depreciation expense	$ 75,000		$ 90,000	
General selling expenses	575,000		600,000	
General administrative expenses	480,000	1,130,000	420,000	1,110,000
Net operating income		$ 960,000		$ 510,000
Interest expense		50,000		65,000
Net income from continuing operations before taxes		$ 910,000		$ 445,000
Income taxes		310,000		151,000
Net income before unusual items		$ 600,000		$ 294,000
Unusual loss—net of tax benefit of $60,000		115,000		—
Net income		$ 485,000		$ 294,000

STATEMENT OF RETAINED EARNINGS	1997	1996
Beginning retained earnings balance	$ 610,000	$ 326,000
Plus: Net income	485,000	294,000
Less: Dividends	595,000	10,000
Ending retained earnings balance	$ 500,000	$ 610,000

REQUIRED:

a. Prepare common-size balance sheets and income statements for 1996 and 1997 and analyze the results.

b. Which income statement account experienced the largest shift from 1996 to 1997? Did this shift appear to have any impact on the balance sheet? Explain.

c. What benefits do common-size financial statements provide over standard financial statements?

P3–10

(Comparing ratios to industry averages)

(This problem is related to P3–9.) Mountain-Pacific Railroad is interested in comparing itself to the rest of the industry. Bob Cleary, the controller, has obtained the following industry averages from a trade journal. (The industry averages were the same for 1996 and 1997.)

Return on equity	.50
Current ratio	3.10
Quick ratio	1.85
Return on assets	.30
Receivables turnover	8.15
Earnings per share ($)	41.15
Price/earnings ratio	.451
Debt/equity ratio	.77
Return on sales	.072
Financial leverage	.20
Dividend yield	.375
Return on investment	.102
Times-interest-earned ratio	9.89
Inventory turnover	21.7

REQUIRED:

a. Compute these ratios for Mountain-Pacific Railroad for both 1996 (using year-end balances) and 1997 (using average balances where appropriate). Identify significant trends. Could the company experience solvency problems? Explain.

b. Compare the ratios of Mountain-Pacific Railroad to the industry averages. Do you think that Mountain-Pacific Railroad is doing better, worse, or the same as the industry? Explain your answer, and be as specific as possible.

P3–11

(Assessing the loan risk of a potential bank customer)

You have just been hired as a loan officer for Washington Mutual Savings. Selig Equipment and Mountain Bike, Inc., have both applied for $125,000 nine-month loans to acquire additional plant equipment. Neither company offered any security for the loans. It is the strict policy of the bank to have only $1,350,000 outstanding in unsecured loans at any point in time. Since the bank currently has $1,210,000 in unsecured loans outstanding, it will be unable to grant loans to both companies. The bank president has given you the following selected information from the companies' loan applications.

	SELIG EQUIPMENT	MOUNTAIN BIKE, INC.
Cash	$ 15,000	$ 160,000
Accounts receivable	215,000	470,000
Inventory	305,000	195,000
Prepaid expenses	180,000	10,000
Total current assets	$ 715,000	$ 835,000
Noncurrent assets	1,455,000	1,875,000
Total assets	$2,170,000	$2,710,000
Current liabilities	$ 285,000	$ 325,000
Long-term liabilities	950,000	875,000
Contributed capital	790,000	910,000
Retained earnings	145,000	600,000
Total liabilities and stockholders' equity	$2,170,000	$2,710,000
Net credit sales	$1,005,000	$1,625,000
Cost of goods sold	755,000	960,000

REQUIRED:

Assume that all account balances on the balance sheet are representative of the entire year. Based upon this limited information, which company would you recommend to the bank president as the better risk for an unsecured loan? Support your answer with any relevant analysis.

P3–12

(Issuing debt or equity: effects on ratios and owners)

Watson Metal Products is planning to expand its operations to France in response to increased demand from the French for quality metal products to use in production processes. Ben Watson, president of Watson Metal Products, and his consultants have estimated that the expansion will require an investment of $5 million. They have also estimated that this expansion will cause net income before interest expense to increase by $1,500,000. The company is considering financing the expansion through one of the following alternatives.

Alternative 1:	Issue 200,000 shares of common stock for $25 per share.
Alternative 2:	Issue long-term debt at an annual interest cost of 15 percent. The principal would be payable in ten years.
Alternative 3:	Issue 100,000 shares of common stock for $25 per share and finance the remainder by issuing long-term debt at an annual interest rate of 15 percent. The principal would be payable in ten years.

The income statement for the year ended December 31, 1997, of Watson Metal Products was as follows:

Sales	$ 150,000,000
Cost of goods sold	90,000,000
Other expenses	45,000,000
Income from operations	$ 15,000,000
Interest expense	4,000,000
Net income before taxes	$ 11,000,000
Income taxes	4,400,000
Net income	$ 6,600,000
Earnings per share	$3.30

Prior to the expansion, the total debt of Watson Metal Products was $35 million, and total stockholders' equity was $45 million. There were no changes in total debt and total stockholders' equity other than those due to net income and the expansion project. Federal and state income tax rates total 40%.

REQUIRED:

a.   Assume that the company's net income from non-French operations in 1998 equals the income earned in 1997 and that the estimated income from operations on the expansion is realized in 1998. Compute earnings per share, return on equity, return on assets, financial leverage, and the debt/equity ratios as of December 31, 1998, if the company finances the expansion through the following:
   (1) Alternative 1
   (2) Alternative 2
   (3) Alternative 3
   Assume that the December 31, 1998, balances equal average balances during 1998.
b.   Assume that you are currently a stockholder in Watson Metal Products. Which expansion alternative would you prefer? Explain your answer.
c.   What amount of net income would Watson Metal Products have to generate from the expansion project so that earnings per share would be the same before and after the expansion under each alternative?

P3–13

(Preparing financial statement data from financial ratios)

The following relationships were obtained for Boulder Mineral Company for 1997.

Current ratio	3:1
Inventory turnover (average days supply)	12.167
Quick ratio	2:1
Debt/equity	.4:1
Return on equity	.75:1
Return on assets	.65:1
Return on sales	.2:1
Receivables turnover	25
Earnings per share	$16.00

ADDITIONAL INFORMATION:

1.   Boulder Mineral Company generated $450,000 in net income during 1997.
2.   Credit sales comprise 80 percent of net sales.
3.   Cost of goods sold is 55 percent of net sales.
4.   Current liabilities are 35 percent of total liabilities.
5.   The balance in the Cash account is $68,000.
6.   The income tax rate was 34 percent.

Use year-end balances to compute all ratios.

REQUIRED:

Using the above information, compute the following items.

a. Stockholders' equity
b. Total liabilities
c. Total assets
d. Interest expense
e. Net income before taxes
f. Net sales
g. Credit sales
h. Accounts receivable
i. Cost of goods sold
j. Inventory turnover
k. Inventory
l. Current liabilities
m. Current assets
n. Marketable securities
o. Noncurrent assets
p. The number of shares of common stock outstanding

CASES

C3–1

(Financial performance objectives in terms of earning power and solvency)

The following quote was taken from a recent annual report of The Quaker Oats Company:

> *Any review of Quaker's financial performance over the last six years must be seen in the context of the financial objectives we have set. The financial objectives, which commit us to achieving a balance of returns and growth and thus measure our success in providing value to the stockholders, are to:*
>
> *1. achieve a return on equity at 20 percent or above.*
> *2. achieve "real" earnings per share growth averaging 5 percent or better.*
> *3. increase Quaker's dividend, consistent with "real" earnings growth, and*
> *4. maintain a strong financial position, as represented by Quaker's current bond and commercial paper ratings.*

REQUIRED:

a. Define return on equity and explain why Quaker Oats might express a financial objective in terms of it.
b. Objectives 2 and 3 above refer to "real" earnings per share and "real" earnings growth. Normally, designating a performance measure as "real" indicates that the effect of inflation has been removed from it. Why would Quaker Oats want to remove the effect of inflation from reported earnings numbers in its statement of objectives?
c. Which objectives above refer to measures of earning power and which refer to measures of solvency? Define and differentiate between these two concepts, and explain how each objective above relates to either earning power or solvency.

C3–2

(A going concern qualification)

Several years ago, the auditor's report for Allegheny International, Inc., an airline company, contained the following excerpt:

> *As described in Note 6 to the consolidated financial statements, the Company has received waivers from lending institutions suspending the applicability of certain debt covenants*

while it arranges to keep its current financing in place to the consummation of the merger described in Note 2. The Company's ability to continue as a going concern is contingent upon its ability to maintain adequate financing and attain profitable operations. The consolidated financial statements do not include any adjustments relating to the recoverability or classification of recorded asset amounts or the amounts and classification of liabilities that might be necessary should the Company be unable to continue as a going concern.

REQUIRED:

a. Explain the meaning of this excerpt and why the auditors would include such a statement in the auditor's report.
b. Briefly describe how such a report would affect the way in which an investor, creditor, or other interested party would analyze Allegheny's financial statements.

C3–3

(Human capital and the financial statements)

In *The Accounting Review* (January 1971) Baruch Lev and Aba Schwartz noted that "The dichotomy in accounting between human capital and nonhuman capital is fundamental; the latter is recognized as an asset and therefore is recorded in the books and reported on the financial statements, whereas the former is totally ignored by accountants." Most economists, on the other hand, have a different view on this issue. Milton Freidman, for example, states: "From the broadest and most general point of view, total wealth includes all sources of 'income' of consumable services. One such source is the productive capacity of human beings, and accordingly this is one form in which wealth can be held."

REQUIRED:

a. Explain why human capital is treated differently by accountants and economists.
b. From the auditor's perspective explain why human resources are not accounted for on the balance sheet.
c. Because human resources are ignored, the financial statements of what kinds of companies (i.e., manufacturers, retailers, services, or financial institutions) tend to be misstated by the greatest amount? Why?
d. Briefly explain some of the other major items of information that are ignored by financial accounting statements.

C3–4

(Financial accounting information in an efficient market)

In an article published in the *Journal of Accountancy* (February 1984), James Deitrick and Walter Harrison noted that the major markets for common stocks (e.g., the New York Stock Exchange, the American Stock Exchange) have been found to be efficient. That is, "common stock prices behave as if they fully incorporate all existing information quickly and without bias. This implies that information, old and new, has been impounded into security prices as a result of the analysis and collective wisdom of investors and their advisors." This finding has encouraged many accountants to contend that the information contained in financial reports cannot be used to identify undervalued common stocks in an efficient market.

REQUIRED:

a. Provide the rationale for why the information contained in financial reports cannot be used to identify undervalued securities.
b. Explain how financial accounting information can be useful even though it may not be helpful in identifying undervalued securities that are traded in efficient markets.

C3–5

(Recent trends in earnings quality)

Like the takeover-giddy 1980s, investors are again showing respect for hard numbers like quarterly earnings. But those reported earnings numbers are becoming less and less trustworthy, analysts say. The "quality" of reported profits is falling, which means those earnings are really weaker than they look. "One can make the statement unequivocally that the quality of earnings has been declining since 1986–87," says the co-chairman of investment policy at Goldman Sachs & Co. This has troubling implications for investors, he says, "because the stock market hasn't accommodated this deterioration yet." (*The Wall Street Journal*, September 18, 1990).

REQUIRED:

a. Define quality of earnings, and explain why earnings of low quality are less trustworthy.
b. Provide several reasons why the general quality of earnings fell for companies that, after takeovers, were heavily debt laden and were heading into an economic recession.
c. Why would falling earnings quality have "troubling implications for investors?"

C3–6

(Leverage, stock prices, and earning power)

Merger mania in the 1980s increased the leverage levels of many major U.S. corporations. The vice president and financial economist of Kemper Financial Services commented in *The Wall Street Journal* (September 18, 1990): "More leverage on the balance sheet suggests more volatile, and therefore riskier, earnings." That same article noted that the stock market seems to have punished some of the highly leveraged firms, such as Bally Manufacturing, Beverly Enterprises, Marriott, Harcourt Brace Jovanovich, and Time Warner, but other companies that made special efforts to reduce debts, like Shoney's and TW Holdings, hurt their profit levels. "Deleveraging is a trend that's destined to continue and which will drag corporate profitability," says the chief portfolio strategist at First Boston Corp.

REQUIRED:

a. Explain why leverage would give rise to more volatile and riskier earnings.
b. In terms of solvency, earning power, financial flexibility, and liquidity, explain why the stock market might punish highly leveraged firms, and why deleveraging could drag corporate profitability.

C3–7

(Earnings persistence and quality, and reporting strategies)

In 1990 General Motors recorded a $2.1 billion special charge to cover plant closings. In fact, the company's chief financial officer commented in *The Wall Street Journal* (November 11, 1990) that the "huge write-off covers all foreseeable circumstances, including plant closings that won't actually occur for two or three years."

REQUIRED:

a. Comment on the persistence of the earnings number GM reported in 1990.
b. Comment on the quality of GM's 1990 earnings.
c. Suggest why GM would record a write-off for plant closings that hadn't yet occurred. What reporting strategy might have given rise to such a decision, and would you expect the external auditors to object? Why or why not?

C3–8

(Financial reporting strategies)

In 1991 IBM, GM, and GE all experienced very poor years—slow sales, costly reorganizations, and low profits. During that year each company decided to adopt an accounting standard that required the companies to recognize a huge expense (associated with employee retirement health care benefits) that historically had been deferred. Interestingly, the companies were not required by the FASB to adopt the standard until 1993.

REQUIRED:

a. Identify which financial reporting strategy the companies appear to have practiced, and provide several plausible reasons why they may have done so.
b. That same year a number of the major oil companies experienced particularly high profits due in large part to the events surrounding the war in the Persian Gulf and Operation

Desert Storm. These companies chose to recognize expenses in 1991 that normally would not have been recognized until later years. Which reporting strategy did the oil companies appear to practice, and what are several plausible reasons for why they may have done so?

C3–9

(Financial ratios, earning power, solvency, and stock prices)

An accounting professor at the University of California at Berkley was quoted in *The Wall Street Journal* (December 17, 1990) as saying, "The most important items on the financial statements are trends in inventory, accounts receivable, and order backlogs. These are the strongest indicators and are more closely related to stock returns than reported earnings. In particular, investors should look at how companies' inventories of finished goods track their sales. If inventories are rising faster than sales, its a bad signal. . . . For similar reasons it pays to watch accounts receivable. . . . If these are rising faster than sales, not only can this signal trouble with sales but may show vulnerability to customer defaults."

REQUIRED:
a. Which of the financial ratios best captures the indicators suggested by the Berkeley professor.
b. Explain how these ratios provide information about solvency and earning power, and why they might be more closely related to stock prices than earnings.

C3–10

(Stock price reactions to earnings announcements)

In the first quarter of 1991 Compaq Computer reported a net profit of $971 million, a 24 percent increase above the previous year's first quarter. Unfortunately, the company's stock price tumbled by over $9 when the news reached the market. In the third quarter of that same year Chrysler reported an $82 million loss, yet on the day of the announcement the company's stock price jumped by 15 percent.

REQUIRED:
Explain why the stock market reacted negatively to Compaq's news and positively to Chrysler's news.

C3–11

(International ratio analysis)

A major conclusion in a study reported in *Frontiers of International Accounting: An Anthology* is that "accounting measurements reflected in corporate financial reports represent, in one sense, merely 'numbers' that have limited meaning and significance in and of themselves. Meaning and significance come from and depend upon an understanding of the environmental context from which the numbers are drawn as well as the relationship between the numbers and the underlying economic phenomena that are the real items of interest."

REQUIRED:
a. Briefly paraphrase the quote above and discuss the implications for financial ratio analysis.
b. In the same anthology, Professor Jill McKinnon, of Macquarie University in Australia, commented that the concept of consolidation in Japan is actually much different from that in the United States, concluding that the methods of accounting for consolidation under GAAP fail to adequately reflect the nature of Japanese corporate groups. Discuss how such information might affect an individual who invests in large Japanese and American companies.

C3–12

(Analyzing the financial statements of Federal Express Corporation)

Consolidated balance sheets and statements of income and cash flows, taken from the 1994 annual report of Federal Express Corporation, are provided on the following pages. Analyze the statements by assessing the company's earning power and solvency position, and provide support for your assessment. In addition, list other kinds of information that would be useful for the analysis, and in each case, briefly explain why.

Federal Express Corporation and Subsidiaries
Consolidated Statements of Operations

Years ended May 31

In thousands, except per share amounts	1994	1993	1992
REVENUES	$ 8,479,456	$7,808,043	$7,550,060
OPERATING EXPENSES:			
Salaries and employee benefits (Notes 8 and 9)	4,104,800	3,807,493	3,637,080
Rentals and landing fees (Note 4)	703,028	658,138	672,341
Depreciation and amortization	599,357	579,896	577,157
Fuel	472,786	495,384	508,386
Maintenance and repairs	464,557	404,639	404,311
Restructuring charge (Note 13)	—	(12,500)	254,000
Other	1,604,296	1,497,820	1,473,818
	7,948,824	7,430,870	7,527,093
OPERATING INCOME	530,632	377,173	22,967
OTHER INCOME (EXPENSE):			
Interest, net (Note 1)	(142,392)	(160,923)	(164,315)
Other, net	(9,778)	(12,674)	(5,480)
	(152,170)	(173,597)	(169,795)
INCOME (LOSS) BEFORE INCOME TAXES AND CUMULATIVE EFFECT OF CHANGE IN ACCOUNTING PRINCIPLE	378,462	203,576	(146,828)
PROVISION (CREDIT) FOR INCOME TAXES (Note 7)	174,092	93,767	(33,046)
INCOME (LOSS) BEFORE CUMULATIVE EFFECT OF CHANGE IN ACCOUNTING PRINCIPLE	204,370	109,809	(113,782)
CUMULATIVE EFFECT OF CHANGE IN ACCOUNTING PRINCIPLE, NET OF TAX BENEFIT OF $34,287 (Note 9)	—	(55,943)	—
NET INCOME (LOSS)	$ 204,370	$ 53,866	$ (113,782)
EARNINGS (LOSS) PER SHARE (Note 6):			
Before cumulative effect of change in accounting principle	$ 3.65	$ 2.01	$ (2.11)
Cumulative effect of change in accounting principle (Note 9)	—	(1.03)	—
	$ 3.65	$ .98	$ (2.11)
AVERAGE SHARES OUTSTANDING (Note 6)	56,012	54,719	53,961

The accompanying Notes to Consolidated Financial Statements are an integral part of these statements.

Federal Express Corporation and Subsidiaries
Consolidated Balance Sheets

May 31

In thousands	1994	1993
ASSETS		
CURRENT ASSETS:		
Cash and cash equivalents	$ 392,923	$ 155,456
Receivables, less allowance for doubtful accounts of $33,933 and $31,308	1,020,511	922,727
Spare parts, supplies and fuel	173,993	164,087
Deferred income taxes (Note 7)	113,035	133,875
Prepaid expenses and other	61,234	63,573
Total current assets	1,761,696	1,439,718
PROPERTY AND EQUIPMENT, AT COST (Notes 1, 3, 4, and 11):		
Flight equipment	2,828,021	2,843,253
Package handling and ground support equipment	1,583,428	1,413,793
Computer and electronic equipment	966,906	947,913
Other	1,511,870	1,501,250
	6,890,225	6,706,209
Less accumulated depreciation and amortization	3,441,132	3,229,941
Net property and equipment	3,449,093	3,476,268
OTHER ASSETS:		
Goodwill (Note 1)	415,178	432,215
Equipment deposits and other assets (Note 11)	366,531	444,863
Total other assets	781,709	877,078
	$5,992,498	$5,793,064
LIABILITIES AND STOCKHOLDERS' INVESTMENT		
CURRENT LIABILITIES:		
Current portion of long-term debt (Note 3)	$ 198,180	$ 133,797
Accounts payable	518,849	554,111
Accrued expenses (Note 2)	819,399	761,357
Total current liabilities	1,536,428	1,449,265
LONG-TERM DEBT, LESS CURRENT PORTION (Note 3)	1,632,202	1,882,279
DEFERRED INCOME TAXES (Note 7)	3,563	72,479
OTHER LIABILITIES (Note 1)	895,600	717,660
COMMITMENTS AND CONTINGENCIES (Notes 11 and 12)		
COMMON STOCKHOLDERS' INVESTMENT (Notes 6)		
Common Stock, $.10 par value; 100,000 shares authorized; 55,885 and 54,743 shares issued	5,589	5,474
Additional paid-in capital	759,229	699,385
Retained earnings	1,162,160	969,515
	1,926,978	1,674,374
Less treasury stock and deferred compensation stock plans	2,273	2,993
Total common stockholders' investment	1,924,705	1,671,381
	$5,992,498	$5,793,064

The accompanying Notes to Consolidated Financial Statements are an integral part of these balance sheets.

Federal Express Corporation and Subsidiaries
Consolidated Statements of Cash Flows

Years ended May 31

In thousands	1994	1993	1992
OPERATING ACTIVITIES			
Net income (loss)	$ 204,370	$ 53,866	$ (113,782)
Adjustments to reconcile income (loss) to net cash provided by operating activities:			
Depreciation and amortization	599,357	579,896	577,157
Provision for uncollectible accounts	45,763	33,552	31,670
Provision (credit) for deferred income taxes and other	3,810	19,910	(75,219)
(Gain) loss from disposals of property and equipment	(11,897)	(5,648)	1,810
Cumulative effect of accounting change	—	55,943	—
Changes in assets and liabilities, net of effects from purchases and dispositions of businesses:			
(Increase) in receivables	(173,902)	(41,535)	(727)
(Increase) decrease in other current assets	(7,826)	(5,813)	61,749
Increase in accounts payable, accrued expenses and other liabilities	110,508	13,651	33,620
Other, net	(2,905)	21,259	4,543
Net cash provided by operating activities	767,278	725,081	520,821
INVESTING ACTIVITIES			
Purchases of property and equipment, including deposits on aircraft of $112,138, $177,564, and $212,291	(1,087,708)	(1,023,723)	(915,878)
Proceeds from disposition of property and equipment:			
Sale-leaseback transactions	581,400	216,444	400,433
Reimbursements of A300 deposits	38,794	—	—
Other dispositions	46,148	5,984	12,851
Other, net	27,843	1,992	621
Net cash used in investing activities	(393,523)	(799,303)	(501,973)
FINANCING ACTIVITIES			
Proceeds from debt issuances	10,777	878,499	437,709
Principal payments on debt	(198,243)	(737,334)	(507,283)
Proceeds from stock issuances	53,759	24,512	19,272
Other, net	(2,581)	(14,176)	(8,061)
Net cash provided by (used in) financing activities	(136,288)	151,501	(58,363)
Net increase (decrease) in cash and cash equivalents	237,467	77,279	(39,515)
Cash and cash equivalents at beginning of period	155,456	78,177	117,692
Cash and cash equivalents at end of period	$ 392,923	$ 155,456	$ 78,177
SUPPLEMENTAL DISCLOSURE OF CASH FLOW INFORMATION			
Cash paid for:			
Interest (net of capitalized interest)	$ 158,149	$ 162,648	$ 178,943
Income taxes	167,209	188,943	89,729

Non-cash investing and financing activities:

In November 1992, approximately $73,000,000 of secured debt related to a portion of the purchase price of one MD-11 aircraft acquired by the Company was assumed by a third party in a sale-leaseback of the aircraft.

The accompanying Notes to Consolidated Financial Statements are an integral part of these statements.

THE MEASUREMENT FUNDAMENTALS OF FINANCIAL ACCOUNTING

LEARNING OBJECTIVES

LO 1 Identify and define the four basic assumptions of financial accounting.

LO 2 Identify the two markets in which business entities operate, express the four alternative valuation bases in terms of these two markets, and briefly describe how the valuation bases are used on the balance sheet.

LO 3 Define the principle of objectivity, and explain how it determines the dollar values that appear on the financial statements.

LO 4 Explain how the principles of matching and revenue recognition relate to the measure of performance.

LO 5 Identify and describe two exceptions to the principles of financial accounting measurement, and explain the economic rationale behind them.

This chapter covers the measurement fundamentals of financial accounting which consist of the basic assumptions, valuation issues, principles, and exceptions underlying the financial statements. You have already seen that investors, creditors, and other interested parties require information about a company's performance and financial position. To maintain its market value and ability to attract equity and debt capital, management responds to this demand by hiring auditors and providing audited financial statements, which contain measures like net income, net cash flows from operating activities, the current ratio, and the debt/equity ratio. Managers of publicly traded companies must also follow the requirements of the Securities and Exchange Commission to provide such measures of performance, which help interested parties assess the company's ability (1) to meet its debts as they come due (solvency) and (2) to generate assets in the future (earning power). In addition, these measures appear in management compensation contracts and debt covenants, where they help to control and direct management decisions. The assumptions, valuation issues, principles, and exceptions of financial accounting all play an important role in determining the nature and economic function of these measures of performance and financial position. Understanding the concept of the time value of money is helpful in understanding the measurement fundamentals of financial accounting. It also pervades a number of accounting issues that are discussed in the remainder of the text. Accordingly, the time value of money is discussed and illustrated in Appendix 4A.

ASSUMPTIONS OF FINANCIAL ACCOUNTING

LO 1 There are four basic assumptions of financial accounting: (1) economic entity, (2) fiscal period, (3) going concern, and (4) stable dollar. Some of these assumptions are reasonable representations of the real world and others are not. As each assumption is discussed, try to understand why it has evolved, and be especially aware of those that fail to capture the world as it really is. These relatively unrealistic assumptions define important limitations that are inherent in the financial statement measures of performance and financial position. Investors, creditors, managers, and auditors must thoroughly understand these limitations if they are to use financial statements appropriately.

ECONOMIC ENTITY ASSUMPTION

The most fundamental assumption of financial accounting involves the object of the performance measure. Should the accounting system provide performance information about countries, states, cities, industries, individual companies, or segments of individual companies? While it is important that each of these entities operate efficiently, financial accounting has evolved in response to a demand for company-specific measures of performance and financial position. Consequently, financial accounting reports provide information about individual, profit-seeking companies.

The process of providing information about profit-seeking entities implicitly assumes that they can be identified and measured. Individual companies must be entities in and of themselves, separate and distinct from both their owners and all other entities. This statement represents the **economic entity assumption**, the first basic assumption of financial accounting. Although this assumption may appear obvious on the surface, it nonetheless provides an important foundation upon which the financial accounting system is built. Moreover, in certain situations this assumption plays a critical role in determining the scope of financial statements.

For example, after Walt Disney acquired the common stock of Capital Cities/ABC, Inc., a major broadcasting company, it included all of ABC's assets and liabilities on its consolidated balance sheet. For financial reporting purposes, therefore, ABC, which publishes its own separate financial statements, is included within the economic entity referred to as the Walt Disney Company. In fact, the consolidated balance sheet of Disney includes the assets and liabilities of many other companies, called *subsidiaries*, each of which prepares its own financial statements. NBC, another major broadcasting company, is a subsidiary of General Electric and, as of late 1995, CBS was being acquired by Westinghouse.

FISCAL PERIOD ASSUMPTION

Once the object of measurement has been identified (i.e., the economic entity), we must recognize that to be useful, measures of performance and financial position must be available on a timely basis. Investors, creditors, and other users of financial information need periodic feedback if they are to monitor the performance of management as well as control and direct its decisions.

The need for timely performance measures underlies the **fiscal period assumption**, which states that the operating life of an economic entity can be divided into time periods over which such measures can be developed and applied. Most corporations, for example, prepare annual financial statements, providing yearly feedback and performance measures to their stockholders. The Securities and Exchange Commission requires that publicly traded companies provide financial statements (called *Form 10-Q*) to their stockholders on a quarterly basis.

TIMELY VS. OBJECTIVE FINANCIAL INFORMATION

It is important to realize that the fiscal period assumption introduces a trade-off between the timeliness of accounting information and its objectivity. Users need timely information, and thus they generally prefer fiscal periods that are relatively short. However, as the fiscal period becomes shorter, the applications of certain accounting methods become more arbitrary and subjective. The quarterly accounting reports published by major U.S. corporations, for example, are not audited and are generally more subjective than the audited annual reports. To illustrate, the unaudited Form 10-Q report published by BankAmerica Corporation for the first quarter of 1995 contained the following statement:

This document serves . . . as the quarterly report on Form 10-Q of BankAmerica Corporation to the Securities and Exchange Commission, which has taken no action to approve or disapprove the report or to pass upon its accuracy or adequacy.

A CALENDAR OR FISCAL YEAR?

Another consequence of the fiscal period assumption is that companies must choose the dates of their reporting cycles. Most major U.S. corporations report on the calendar year. That is, they publish an annual report each year as of December 31, and their quarterly statements cover periods ending March 31, June 30, September 30, and December 31. However, a number of companies report on twelve-month periods, called **fiscal years**, that end on dates other than December 31.[1] In most cases a company chooses a fiscal reporting cycle because its operations are seasonal, and the financial statements are more meaningful if the reporting period includes the entire season.

Large retailers, like Federated Department Stores, Kmart, and Toys "R" Us, for example, often end their fiscal years on January 31, after the completion of the Christmas season. Many companies in the food industry, such as Pillsbury, General Mills, and Quaker Oats, prepare annual financial statements in May or June, just after the winter grain crops are harvested. Companies in the automobile and farm machinery industries, such as Firestone and Deere & Co., close their books in September or October, following the summer season when sales are heaviest. Universal Leaf Tobacco, a major processor in the tobacco industry, ends its fiscal year on June 30, immediately after the previous year's tobacco crop has been cured.

GOING CONCERN ASSUMPTION

The **going concern assumption** follows logically from the fiscal period assumption. If we assume that an entity's life can be divided into fiscal periods, we must further assume that its life extends beyond the current period. In other words, we assume the entity will not discontinue operations at the end of the current period over which its performance is being measured. Taken to the extreme, this assumption states that the life of the entity will continue indefinitely.

The role of the going concern assumption in financial accounting is as fundamental as the definition of an asset. Recall that assets are defined to have *future* economic benefit; that is, benefits that extend beyond the current period. The cost of equipment, for example, is placed on the balance sheet because the equipment is expected to provide benefits in the future. The Financial Accounting Standards Board invoked the going concern assumption when, in Statement of Financial Concepts No. 3, it defined assets as "probable *future* economic benefits obtained or controlled by a particular entity as a result of past transactions or events."[2]

STABLE DOLLAR ASSUMPTION

To measure the dimensions, quantity, or capacity of anything requires a unit of measurement. Height and distance, for example, can be measured in terms of inches, feet, centimeters, or meters; volume can be measured in gallons or liters; and weight can be measured in pounds or kilograms. Mathematical operations, such as addition or subtraction, on any such measure require that the unit of measurement maintain a constant definition.

To illustrate, suppose you weighed yourself at the beginning of the year and found that your weight was 120 pounds. At the end of the year you weighed yourself again and noted that your weight was 128 pounds. You conclude that you gained 8 pounds during the year, but implicit in this conclusion is the assumption that the definition of a pound was the same at the beginning and the end of the year. Had a pound at the

---

1. According to a survey conducted by the American Institute of Certified Public Accountants, 37 percent of the merchandising and industrial companies in the United States close their books on dates other than December 31. (Christopher Power, "Let's Get Fiscal," *Forbes*, April 30, 1984, pp. 102, 104.)

2. Financial Accounting Standards Board, "Elements of Financial Statements of Business Enterprises," *Statement of Financial Concepts No. 3* (Stamford, Conn.: FASB, December 1980), xi and xii.

beginning of the year equaled 16 ounces but 15 ounces at the end of the year, for example, you would actually have gained no weight at all. You would have weighed 1,920 ounces at both points in time.

The logical unit of measurement for the financial performance and condition of a company is the monetary unit used in the economic transactions entered into by that company. In the United States, for example, the monetary unit is the dollar. Consequently, the financial statements of U.S. companies are expressed in terms of dollars.

The measures of financial performance and position on the financial statements all involve the addition, subtraction, or division of dollar amounts. Total assets on the balance sheet, for example, represent the addition of the dollar values of all the individual assets held by a company at a particular point in time. The current ratio and the debt/equity ratio involve dividing certain balance sheet dollar amounts by other balance sheet dollar amounts. As with the measures discussed previously, valid use of these mathematical operations requires that the definition of the dollar be constant. Thus, a **stable dollar assumption** is implicit in the measures of performance and financial condition used to evaluate and control management's decisions.

INFLATION: THE DOLLAR'S CHANGING PURCHASING POWER

A dollar's value is defined in terms of its **purchasing power**, the amount of goods and services it can buy at a given point in time. During inflation, which has come to be a fact of life, the purchasing power of the dollar decreases steadily. Therefore, financial statements, which are based on the assumption that the purchasing power of the dollar is constant (i.e., no inflation), can be seriously misstated.

Suppose, for example, that on January 1 you have $1,000, and at that time the cost of rice is $1 per bag. You could purchase 1,000 bags of rice, but you decide instead to use the money to purchase (invest in) a small tract of land. During the year the inflation rate is 10 percent, and at year end the price of the rice is $1.10 per bag, and the value of the land is $1,100. You decide to sell the land, and on your income statement you recognize a gain on the sale of $100 ($1,100 − $1,000). You read your income statement and count the cash in your hand and conclude that your economic wealth has increased by $100. However, you use the $1,100 to buy rice and you are surprised to learn that it buys only 1,000 bags, the exact amount you could have purchased at the beginning of the year. Consequently, your wealth is not increased at all, even though your income statement indicates otherwise.

A LIMITATION IN THE FINANCIAL STATEMENTS

The stable dollar assumption is one instance in which the financial statements are based on an unrealistic assumption. Financial accounting standard-setting bodies have recognized this problem for many years and have attempted to solve it many times. The most recent effort occurred in 1979, when the FASB required certain large U.S. companies to provide information about the effects of inflation in their annual reports. However, this requirement was subsequently rescinded. Companies complained that the disclosures were costly, and financial statement users showed little interest in them, probably because they believed them to be unreliable. It is important that financial statement users at least recognize that this limitation exists and in some cases learn how to adjust financial statements for the effects of inflation.

Our discussion of the basic assumptions of financial accounting is now complete. In summary, we have assumed the existence of a separate, measurable business entity (economic entity), whose infinite life (going concern) can be broken down into fiscal periods (fiscal period), and whose transactions can be measured in stable dollars (stable dollar). Each of these assumptions is briefly defined in Figure 4–1.

FIGURE 4–1	ASSUMPTION	DEFINITION
The basic assumptions of financial accounting	Economic entity	Profit-seeking entities, which are separate and distinct from their owners and other entities, can be identified and measured.
	Fiscal period	The life of the economic entity can be divided into fiscal periods, and the performance and financial position of the entity can be measured during each of those periods.
	Going concern	The life of the economic entity will extend beyond the current fiscal period.
	Stable dollar	The performance and financial position of the entity can be measured in terms of a monetary unit that maintains constant purchasing power across fiscal periods.

Now that the basic assumptions of financial accounting have been established, we can explain how dollar amounts are attached to the assets, liabilities, equities, revenues, expenses, and dividends of economic entities. In the course of this explanation we consider (1) valuations on the balance sheet and (2) the principles of financial accounting measurement.

VALUATIONS ON THE BALANCE SHEET

LO 2 The dollar values attached to the accounts on a company's balance sheet are largely determined by the markets in which the company operates. To understand these markets, it is helpful to view a business entity in the following way.

INPUTS ⟶ ENTITY OPERATIONS ⟶ OUTPUTS
(Purchase Prices)   (Sales Prices)

A business entity operates in two general markets: an **input market**, where it purchases inputs (materials, labor, overhead) for its operations, and an **output market**, where it sells its outputs (services or inventories). Input market values (prices) are normally less than output market values (prices). For example, local automobile dealers purchase automobiles from manufacturers, such as General Motors, Chrysler Corporation, and Ford Motor Company, and sell them to consumers. The prices paid for automobiles by dealers in their input market are generally less than the prices paid by consumers in the output market. A new Chevrolet, for example, may cost a dealer $15,000 in the input market and sell to you, a customer, for $17,000 in the output market.

Moreover, input and output markets are defined in terms of specific entities: one entity's output market may be another entity's input market. DuPont, for example, supplies complete front and back assemblies for the General Motors cars produced at a GM plant near Kansas City, Mo. When GM purchases these assemblies, the transaction takes place in the output market of DuPont and the input market of GM.

Viewing a business entity in terms of both its input and output markets introduces a number of different ways to value the accounts on the balance sheet. Should assets, for example, be valued in terms of prices from the input market, or prices from the output market—or is there a way to reflect both input and output prices in their valuations? For example, should the value of the Chevrolet on the dealer's balance sheet be expressed in terms of the dealer's input cost ($15,000) or the selling price in the output market ($17,000)?

FOUR ALTERNATIVE VALUATION BASES

Four different **valuation bases** are used to determine the dollar amounts attached to the accounts on the balance sheet. They are: (1) present value, (2) fair market value, (3) replacement cost, and (4) original cost. **Present value**, the computation of which is discussed and illustrated in Appendix 4A, represents the discounted future cash flows associated with a particular financial statement item. The present value of a note receivable, for example, is calculated by determining the amount and timing of its future cash inflows and then adjusting the dollar amounts for the time value of money. **Fair market value (FMV)**, or sales price, represents the value of goods and services in the output market. **Replacement cost**, or current cost, is the current price paid in the input market. **Original cost** represents the input price paid when originally purchased. Figure 4–2 depicts these four valuation bases in terms of an entity's input and output markets.

To illustrate, assume that on January 1 Watson Land Developers purchased an apartment building for $100,000, which an outsider recently (on November 1) offered to buy for $140,000. Watson estimates that if it continues to manage the apartment, it would produce net cash flows for the next ten years at a rate of $25,000 per year. The company also recently investigated replacing the apartment building with a comparable structure and learned that it would cost $175,000. The present value, fair market value, replacement cost, and original cost of the apartment building are provided below. In other words, Watson purchased an apartment building for $100,000 that could now be sold for $140,000 and/or replaced for $175,000. Continuing to manage the apartment would produce cash flows of $25,000 per year, which is equivalent to a present value of $153,614.

Present value   = **$153,614 ($25,000 × 6.14457*)**
Fair market value = **$140,000**
Replacement cost = **$175,000**
Original cost   = **$100,000**

*Present value factor (ten-year ordinary annuity, 10 percent discount rate)

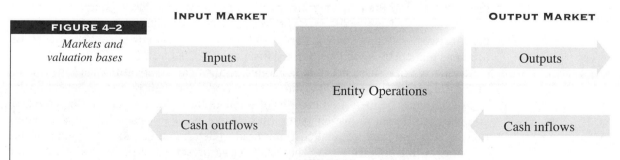

INPUT MARKET		OUTPUT MARKET

FIGURE 4–2

Markets and valuation bases

Inputs → Entity Operations → Outputs

Cash outflows ← Entity Operations ← Cash inflows

VALUATION BASES
1. Present Value—discounted future cash inflows and outflows
2. Fair market value—current cash inflow (output market)
3. Replacement cost—current cash outflow (input market)
4. Original cost—past cash outflow (input market)

VALUATION BASES USED ON THE BALANCE SHEET

All four of the valuation bases described in the previous section are contained in balance sheets prepared under generally accepted accounting principles. This point is illustrated in Figure 4–3, which provides a balance sheet with the valuation base for each account indicated in parenthesis. The code for each valuation base is located below the balance sheet.

Cash and all current liabilities are valued at **face value**. This valuation reflects the cash expected to be received or paid in the near future. For these current accounts, face value is essentially equivalent to fair market value or present value because the time period until cash receipt or payment is very short (usually less than one year). The statement of cash flows, which explains changes in the cash account, is completely expressed in terms of face value.

Short-term investments are valued at fair market value. Accounts receivable are valued at **net realizable value**, the amount of cash expected to be collected from the outstanding accounts. This dollar amount closely approximates fair market value and present value because the time period until collection is normally quite short (thirty to sixty days).

Inventories are valued at original cost or replacement cost, whichever is lower. This example of the conservative **lower-of-cost-or-market rule**, which ensures that the dollar value of this account is not overstated, illustrates that under certain circumstances replacement costs are found on the balance sheet.

Land, securities held as long-term investments,[3] and property used in a company's operations are all valued at original cost, unadjusted for amortization or depreciation. Prepaid expenses, plant and equipment, and all intangible assets are carried on the balance sheet at their original costs, reduced by accumulated amortization or depreciation. This adjusted cost dollar value is often referred to as *net book value*. Also, the expression **historical cost** is often used to describe the valuation base for land, long-term investments, property, prepaid expenses, plant and equipment, and intangible assets.

Long-term notes receivable and long-term liabilities are valued at present value. The dollar amount attached to each of these accounts is calculated by determining the amount and timing of the future cash flows associated with the account and adjusting the dollar amounts for the time value of money.

Technically, the stockholders' equity section of the balance sheet is not valued in terms of any valuation base. It represents the residual interests of the stockholders or the book value of the company. In other words, the stockholders' equity section can simply be viewed as the difference between the total balance sheet value of the company's assets and the total balance sheet value of the company's liabilities. The accounts that compose this section are discussed in Chapter 12.

So far we have assumed that economic entities can be identified and measured, their infinite lives can be divided into fiscal periods, and their performance and financial position can be measured in terms of stable dollars. We have also observed that a number of different valuation bases (face value, present value, fair market value, replacement cost, and original cost) are used to determine the dollar amounts of the accounts on the balance sheet. The next section presents the principles of financial

---

3. A special method, called the equity method, is used to value certain long-term equity investments on the balance sheet. This method is based on the original cost of the investment, but certain additional adjustments to original cost are made periodically. The method is discussed and illustrated in Chapter 8, which covers long-term investments.

accounting measurement, which explain why particular valuation bases are used for some accounts and not for others, and how the valuation bases are used to measure net income.

FIGURE 4–3	HARBOUR ISLAND COMPANY
Valuation bases on the balance sheet	BALANCE SHEET DECEMBER 31, 1996

ASSETS

Current assets:		
Cash	$ 220 (FV)	
Short-term investments	150 (FMV)	
Accounts receivable	345 (NRV)	
Inventory	600 (LCM)	
Prepaid expenses	100 (NBV)	
Total current assets		$ 1,415
Long-term investments:		
Long-term notes receivable	$ 1,000 (PV)	
Land	500 (OC)	
Securities	2,500 (OC)	
Total long-term investments		4,000
Property, plant, and equipment:		
Property	$ 6,000 (OC)	
Plant	2,900 (NBV)	
Equipment	2,600 (NBV)	
Total property, plant, and equipment		11,500
Intangible assets:		
Patent	$ 1,000 (NBV)	
Trademark	700 (NBV)	
Total intangible assets		1,700
Total assets		$18,615

LIABILITIES AND STOCKHOLDERS' EQUITY

Current liabilities:		
Accounts payable	$ 200 (FV)	
Wages payable	150 (FV)	
Interest payable	30 (FV)	
Short-term notes payable	200 (FV)	
Other payables	60 (FV)	
Unearned revenues	30 (FV)	
Dividends payable	70 (FV)	
Total current liabilities		$ 740
Long-term liabilities:		
Long-term notes payable	$ 1,500 (PV)	
Bonds payable	3,500 (PV)	
Mortgage payable	1,940 (PV)	
Total long-term liabilities		6,940
Stockholders' equity		10,935
Total liabilities and stockholders' equity		$18,615

Valuation base code: FV = face value; FMV = fair market value; LCM = lower of cost or market; NRV = net realizable value;

THE PRINCIPLES OF FINANCIAL ACCOUNTING MEASUREMENT

There are four basic principles of financial accounting measurement: (1) objectivity, (2) matching, (3) revenue recognition, and (4) consistency.

THE PRINCIPLE OF OBJECTIVITY

LO 3 Financial accounting information provides useful measures of performance and financial position. To do so, financial accounting statements must provide information about value: the value of entire companies, the value of company assets and liabilities, and the value of the specific transactions entered into by companies.

The economic value of an entity, an asset, or a liability is its present value, which reflects both the future cash flows associated with the entity, asset, or liability and the time value of money.[4] Since financial accounting systems are concerned with measuring such value, the implicit objective of financial reporting is to provide information that allows all interested parties to construct performance measures that reflect the present value of the company, its assets, and its liabilities.

There is, however, one critical problem with the present value calculation: it assumes that future interest rates and future cash flows are perfectly predictable. This assumption presents no problems in theory, but users of accounting measures of performance and financial position need reliable measures that can be audited at reasonable costs.

In 1994, for example, Scott Paper Company invested over $375 million in plant assets and timber resources. Reporting this investment on the company's balance sheet at present value would require an estimate of the net future cash flows generated by the new facilities and woodlands as well as an estimate of future interest rates. Such estimates, which would be the responsibility of the company's management, are simply too subjective for the financial statements. Auditors would be unwilling and unable to verify these subjective judgments, and the legal liability faced by both managers and auditors would make such verification potentially very costly. In sum, it is not economical for financial information users to base transactions on measures that rely on highly subjective, uncertain, and unreliable predictions.

The principle of **objectivity**, which is perhaps the most important and pervasive principle of accounting measurement, states that financial accounting information must be verifiable and reliable. It requires that the values of transactions and of the assets and liabilities created by them be objectively determined and backed by documented evidence. Although it ensures that the dollar amounts disclosed on the financial statements are reasonably reliable, the principle of objectivity also precludes much relevant and useful information from ever appearing on the financial statements.

PRESENT VALUE AND THE FINANCIAL STATEMENTS

The principle of objectivity ensures that present value cannot be used as the valuation base for all assets and liabilities. In some cases, however, the future cash flows associated with certain assets and liabilities are predictable enough to allow for suffi-

---

4. The following discussion assumes that you understand the present value calculation. If not, refer to Appendix 4A.

ciently objective present value calculations. Suppose, for example, that on December 31 The Boeing Company received payment from United Airlines for an order of jumbo jets in the form of a note receivable. The note states that United will pay Boeing $1 million at the end of each year for the next two years. Certainly, this note should appear as an asset (receivable) on Boeing's December 31 balance sheet and as a payable on the balance sheet of United, but at what dollar amount should they be reported?

If we assume a discount rate of 10 percent and realize that the note is actually a two-period $1 million cash flow, we can use the present value calculation to place a value on the note ($1.735 million = $1 million × 1.735 [Table 5: *n = 2, i = 10%*]). Further, the auditors of Boeing and United would be willing to attest to this valuation because the future cash flows are objectively determined in a legal contract, entered into and signed by both Boeing and United in an *arm's-length transaction*. The auditors for the most part are protected from legal liability because the responsibility to provide the contractual payments rests with United. The result is that a $1.735 million note receivable would appear on Boeing's balance sheet and a $1.735 million note payable would appear on United's balance sheet. In this case present value would be used to provide a balance sheet value for both an asset and a liability.

In general, present value is used on the financial statements only in those cases where future cash flows can be objectively determined. As illustrated, contractual agreements like notes receivable and payable represent cases that meet this criterion. Mortgages, bonds, leases, and pensions are other examples of contracts that underlie cash flows and remove much of the subjectivity associated with cash flow prediction.

Refer again to the balance sheet in Figure 4–3, and note that present value is used as the valuation base for long-term notes receivable, long-term notes payable, bonds payable, and mortgages payable. Recall also that all the accounts valued at face value (i.e., cash and current liabilities) are essentially equivalent to present value.

MARKET VALUE AND THE FINANCIAL STATEMENTS

Using market value (i.e., fair market value or replacement cost) as a valuation base for the accounts on the financial statements can be attractive because in many cases market value represents the best estimate of present value. If, for example, buyers and sellers in a given market use their individual estimates of present value when bidding on an asset, the resulting market price of the asset should approximate its actual present value. In addition, fair market value is often more objective than present value. Market prices for the equity securities of major U.S. companies, for example, are listed on public stock exchanges and can therefore be objectively verified. The market price of a share of DuPont common stock, for example, as of the end of trading on June 18, 1995, was exactly $66.63.[5]

Market values, however, suffer from two important deficiencies. While they are sometimes objectively determinable, in most situations they are not objective enough for use in the financial statements. For example, the market values of securities that are not traded on the major stock exchanges, most inventories, long-term investments, property, plant, and equipment, and intangible assets are not easily determined. The market values of such items may be very informative, but they fail to meet the principle of objectivity.

5. *The Wall Street Journal,* June 19, 1995.

Second, valuing an entity, or one of its assets, at fair market value (output market price) assumes that the entity or the asset is being sold. This assumption is inconsistent with the going concern assumption, which states that an entity will exist beyond the current accounting period. Indeed, many of a company's assets are not intended for sale. Property, plant, and equipment, for example, are acquired for use in operations. To value these kinds of assets on the balance sheet at fair market value could give rise to irrelevant performance measures.

Refer again to the balance sheet in Figure 4–3, and note that market values are used in the valuation of relatively few accounts. Short-term investments are valued at fair market value, accounts receivable are valued at net realizable value, which approximates fair market value, and inventories are valued at original cost or market value, whichever is lower.

ORIGINAL COST AND THE FINANCIAL STATEMENTS

Note also in Figure 4–3 that the remaining accounts on the balance sheet (Prepaid Expenses, Land, Securities, Property, Plant, and Equipment, and Intangible Assets) are valued at original cost, the price paid when the asset was originally acquired, or net book value, which is original cost adjusted for depreciation or amortization. Original costs can be objectively verified and supported by documented evidence; they are reliable, can be audited at reasonable cost, and do not violate the principle of objectivity. However, original costs are not particularly useful for the decisions made by users of financial information because they reflect values that are no longer current.

Objectivity is the most pervasive principle of financial accounting. It affects all areas of measurement, including operating performance, which is the focus of the principles discussed in the next section: matching and revenue recognition.

THE PRINCIPLES OF MATCHING AND REVENUE RECOGNITION

LO 4 The **matching** principle, which states that the efforts of a given period should be matched against the benefits that result from them, underlies the financial accounting measures of operating performance. It is initiated when a company incurs a cost (e.g., pays wages, purchases equipment, invests in a security) to generate benefits, normally in the form of revenues.[6] If the revenues are generated immediately, the cost is treated as an expense, appearing on the income statement of the current period. If the revenues are expected to be realized in future periods, the cost is considered an asset and appears on the balance sheet. In future periods, as the revenues are realized, the assets are converted to expenses appearing on the income statements of the future periods. Thus, costs incurred to generate revenues are matched against those revenues in the time periods when the revenues are realized. This process produces a periodic measure of net income, or company performance.

The most critical question in the matching process, as described in Figure 4–4, occurs at Step 2: In what time period will the revenue be realized? The cost incurred in Step 1 cannot be treated as an expense, and the matching principle cannot be applied until this question is answered. The answer, unfortunately, is not always obvious because there are many possibilities. The principle of **revenue recognition** provides the guidelines for answering this question.

---

6. Benefits can also be in the form of cost savings.

FIGURE 4–4

The matching process

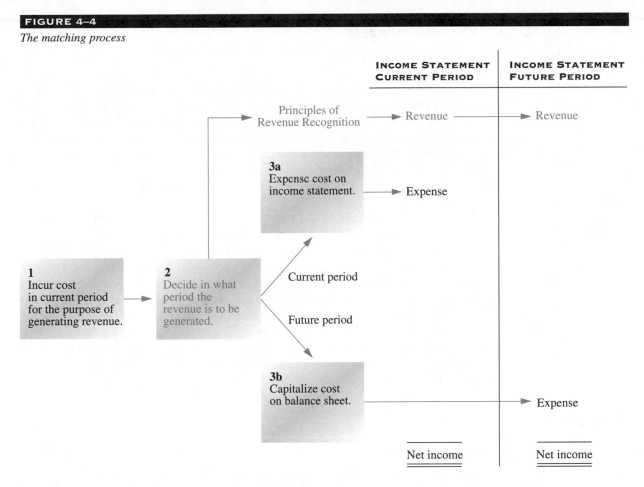

To understand the principle of revenue recognition, it is helpful to view the selling of a good or a service as involving the four steps illustrated in Figure 4–5. A good or service is (1) ordered, (2) produced, (3) transferred to the buyer, and then (4) paid for by the buyer. These four steps make a complete production/sales cycle.

FIGURE 4–5

The production sales cycle

| 1 Order | → | 2 Production | → | 3 Transfer | → | 4 Payment |

The principle of revenue recognition helps to determine at which of these four points the revenue from the sale of a good or service should be recognized on the income statement. The most common point of revenue recognition is Step 3, when the good or service is transferred to the buyer. At this point a company has normally completed the earning process and is entitled to recognize the revenue. Yet, there are times when each of the other steps may be the point at which revenue should be recognized. The principle of revenue recognition states that four criteria must be met before revenue can be included in the income statement:

1. The company must have completed a significant portion of the production and sales effort.
2. The amount of revenue can be objectively measured.

3. The major portion of the costs has been incurred, and the remaining costs can be reasonably estimated.
4. The eventual collection of the cash is reasonably assured.

While these guidelines are helpful, defining the point in time when all four criteria are met still requires much judgment and can be very important because it often dramatically affects the dollar amounts on the financial statements. In a story reported in *The Wall Street Journal*, for example, the SEC charged three former officers of Matrix Science Corporation with significantly inflating the company's earnings. The charges alleged that the officers were able to grossly overstate net income by recording revenues on products "that haven't been shipped, or in some cases, haven't even been assembled."[7]

IBM, who has for years enjoyed a reputation as the epitome of financial conservatism, was recently cited "for booking revenue when its products were shipped to dealers who could return them and sometimes even to its own warehouses."[8] *Forbes* recently reported that many struggling young companies maximize income by *front-ending* revenues. For example, Continuum, a recently organized computer software company, was estimated to have "front-ended some $15 million in revenues" from 1985 to 1988, by recording revenue on products that were only 60 percent to 70 percent complete.[9] Many other famous accounting frauds (e.g., Regina Vacuum Cleaners, Phar-Mor, MiniScribe, and Knowledge Ware) were based on exaggerating revenue and profit numbers by creating fictitious sales. Blockbuster Video has also been cited for aggressive revenue recognition practices.

THE PRINCIPLE OF CONSISTENCY

The measurement principles of objectivity, matching, and revenue recognition are very general and, as such, can be applied to a variety of companies in a variety of business environments. These general principles, however, must be implemented through accounting methods, which are considerably more specific. These relatively specific methods are applicable to a much smaller set of situations.

To illustrate, the matching principle states that costs should be matched against the revenues they generate. While this principle designates that the cost of acquiring a fixed asset should be included on the balance sheet and depreciated, it provides little guidance on how the amount of depreciation should be calculated each period. An accounting method, such as straight-line depreciation, must be chosen to apply the matching principle. Straight-line depreciation, which recognizes a constant amount of depreciation each period, however, is not an appropriate application of the matching principle for all fixed assets in all situations. In certain cases a method of depreciation that recognizes large amounts of depreciation in early periods and smaller amounts later may be a better way to match revenues and expenses.

---

7. Thomas R. Ricks, "Former Officers of Electronics Company Charged by SEC with Inflating Profit," *The Wall Street Journal*, November 2, 1988.

8. Michael W. Miller and Lee Berton, "As IBM's Woes Grew, Its Accounting Tactics Got Less Conservative," *The Wall Street Journal*, April 7, 1993.

9. Gretchen Morgenson, "They Won't Wait Forever," *Forbes*, May 16, 1988, pp. 66, 68.

Generally accepted accounting principles, therefore, allow for a number of different, acceptable methods that can be used to account for the assets, liabilities, revenues, expenses, and dividends on the financial statements. For example, several acceptable methods may be used to account for each of the following assets: accounts receivable, inventories, long-term investments, and fixed assets. Such variety exists for two related reasons: (1) no method is general enough to apply to all companies in all situations, and (2) generally accepted accounting principles are the result of a political process in which interested parties who face widely different situations are allowed and encouraged to provide input.

The principle of **consistency** states that, although there is considerable choice among methods, companies should choose a set of methods and use them from one period to the next. Its primary economic rationale is that consistency helps investors, creditors, and other interested parties to compare measures of performance and financial position across time periods. Presumably, if a company does not change its accounting methods, outside parties can more easily identify trends across time. In addition, management rarely wishes to change accounting methods; it had reasons for choosing the existing methods in the first place, and changing from one method to another could be viewed by outsiders as an attempt to manipulate the financial statements, reducing their credibility.

While consistency is important, it does not mean that companies never change accounting methods. If management can convince the independent auditor that the environment facing the company has changed to the point that an alternative accounting method is appropriate, the company is allowed to switch. However, such changes are not easily granted, and, when approved, the effects of the change on the financial statements are clearly disclosed. The change is usually described in the footnotes and mentioned in the auditor's report, and its effect on income is disclosed in a separate category on the income statement.

In a recent annual report, for example, General Motors reported a change in its method of accounting for inventory. The change was mentioned in the audit report, and the increase in net income of $224 million was disclosed as a separate item on the income statement. The following excerpt describing the change was taken from the footnotes of General Motors' financial report:

. . . accounting procedures were changed to include in inventory certain manufacturing overhead costs previously charged directly to expense. The effect of this change on earnings was a favorable adjustment of $0.35 per share. . .

Some accountants believe that all companies should be required to use the same accounting methods. Such **uniformity**, they argue, would enable financial statement users to compare measures of performance and financial position more easily across different companies. As noted before, however, the situations faced by the variety of companies operating in the economy are so different that accounting methods that are meaningful in some circumstances are not relevant in others. Entire industries are sometimes so unique that completely new accounting methods need to be devised to capture the economics of the situations they face. Financial Accounting Standard No. 73, for example, covers specifically how railroad companies should report a change in accounting for railroad track structures. Consequently, uniformity is not a principle of accounting. It is, therefore, particularly important that financial statement users be aware of the available accounting alternatives and be able to make the adjustments required to meaningfully compare companies that use different accounting methods.

TWO EXCEPTIONS TO THE BASIC PRINCIPLES: MATERIALITY AND CONSERVATISM

LO 5 Under certain circumstances the costs of applying the principles of accounting exceed the benefits. In these situations management is allowed (and, in some cases, required) to depart from the principles. All rules have exceptions, even the measurement principles of financial accounting. Two common and important exceptions are materiality and conservatism.

MATERIALITY

Materiality states that only those transactions dealing with dollar amounts large enough to make a difference to financial statements users need be accounted for in a manner consistent with the principles of financial accounting. The dollar amounts of some transactions are so small that the method of accounting has virtually no impact on the financial statements and, thus, no effect on the related evaluations and control decisions. In such cases the least costly method of reporting is chosen, regardless of the method suggested by the principles of accounting measurement. The dollar amounts of these transactions are referred to as immaterial, and management is allowed to account for them as expediently as possible.

For example, the matching principle indicates that the cost of a wastebasket should be included on the balance sheet and depreciated over future periods because its usefulness is expected to extend beyond the current period. However, the cost of an individual wastebasket is probably immaterial, and it is costly in terms of management's time and effort to carry such items on the books. For practical reasons, therefore, the purchase price is immediately treated as an expense. Granted, such treatment misstates income for both the current period and the future periods of the wastebasket's useful life. This misstatement, however, is extremely small (i.e., immaterial) and would have no bearing on the decisions of those who use the financial statements. In this case the costs of capitalizing and depreciating the purchase price of the wastebasket simply exceeds the benefits it would provide.

While materiality is practical, it represents a major problem area in accounting because it requires judgments that can differ considerably among investors, creditors, managers, auditors, and others. The U.S. Supreme Court has provided one of the few guidelines, defining a material item as one to which "there is substantial likelihood that a reasonable investor would attach importance in determining whether to purchase a security."[10]

In determining materiality, the size of an item is always considered, but whether it would affect the decisions of an investor or creditor is often unclear. A dollar amount that is too small to make a difference in a large company may be very significant in a small company, and not only must the size of an item be considered, but its nature can also be important. A small adjustment to the inventory account, for example, may be far more significant to financial statement users than a large adjustment to an account in the stockholders' equity section of the balance sheet. Finally, the user must be considered. A creditor's definition of materiality, for example, may be very different from that of an investor.

10. Laura Sanders, "Too Little Is Not Enough," *Forbes*, November 7, 1983, p. 106.

In summary, materiality is an important and practical exception to the principles of financial accounting measurement. Indeed, the standard unqualified auditor's report states that "the financial statements are free of material misstatement." Materiality is, nonetheless, very ambiguous. As stated in *Forbes*, "Too often, investors miss important information because companies deem it 'immaterial.' What does this mean? Nobody knows—and that's a big problem." The article goes on to report that Rockwell International, a multibillion-dollar conglomerate, chose not to disclose a loss that could have been as large as $220 million because it was considered immaterial.[11]

CONSERVATISM

Another important exception to the principles of financial accounting measurement is conservatism. Like materiality, conservatism is practical and has evolved overtime in response to cost/benefit considerations. In its simplest form, **conservatism** states that, *when in doubt*, financial statements should understate assets, overstate liabilities, accelerate the recognition of losses, and delay the recognition of gains.

Conservatism does not suggest, however, that the financial statements should be intentionally understated. When given objective and verifiable evidence about a material transaction, the principles of accounting measurement should be followed, and no attempt should be made to intentionally understate assets or overstate liabilities. Only when there is significant uncertainty about the value of a transaction should the most conservative alternative be chosen.

You may wonder why financial statements are prepared on a conservative basis. Stated another way, in the face of uncertainty why not overstate, instead of understate, assets? One could argue, for example, that such overstatement would be in the best interest of a manager who is being evaluated and controlled by the financial accounting information. However, as illustrated below, when the interests of all parties (managers, investors, creditors, and auditors) are considered, conservatism represents a far more practical solution.

THE NATURE AND COST OF LEGAL LIABILITY

Managers hire auditors to lend credibility to the financial statements. Auditors gather evidence and state opinions on whether the financial statements fairly present the financial condition of a company and whether generally accepted accounting principles have been followed in the preparation of the financial statements. Auditors are responsible for the opinions they render, and if the financial statements are later found to be in error, company management and its auditors can be held legally liable for any damages these errors may have caused. In present-day society, where professionals (e.g., doctors, lawyers, accountants) are increasingly being held responsible for their work, such liability can result in very costly lawsuits. Recall from Chapter 1, for example, that thousands of liability suits, asking for billions of dollars in damages, face public accounting firms. Such costs give rise to lower profits for auditors and managers, higher audit fees, higher prices for the goods and services provided by managers, and lower dividends for investors. In other words, the costs of legal liability are shared by all interested parties.

11. Ibid.

A SITUATION INVOLVING CONSERVATISM

Keeping the significant costs of legal liability in mind, consider the following situation. Suppose that an auditor, Ginny Hall, has been hired to audit Technic Incorporated, a company in strong financial condition except for one potential problem: Technic is presently being sued for a very large amount of money. At the time of the audit the outcome of the suit is uncertain. As far as Ginny can ascertain, there is an 80 percent chance that Technic will successfully defend itself. Technic's chief financial officer, Lew Hudson, arguing that the probability of losing the suit is low, has chosen not to disclose the lawsuit in the financial report. Technic is planning to raise capital by selling common stock in the near future and Lew feels that such a disclosure would reduce the market price of the shares. What should Ginny do, act conservatively and mention the suit in the audit report, or act as Lew wishes and provide a clean opinion?

AN ERROR OF OVERSTATEMENT. Assume for the moment that Ginny does not act conservatively and makes no mention of the suit, providing a clean, unqualified audit report. A number of investors buy the shares issued by Technic at a fairly high price because, as far as they can determine, Technic is in strong financial condition. Several months later, however, Technic loses the suit and ultimately must declare bankruptcy. The investors lose their entire investments, and it is revealed at that time that both Ginny and Lew chose not to disclose the suit, even though they were aware of it when the financial statements were made public.

In this case Ginny and Lew have each made an **error of overstatement** because the investors were led to believe that Technic was in better financial condition than it actually was. The investors, who have incurred great losses, have a substantial claim against both Ginny and Lew and the company. With the help of a lawyer, the injured investors could join together and file a **class-action lawsuit**, naming Ginny and Lew as defendants. Such lawsuits are often settled for millions of dollars. For example, a recent class-action lawsuit filed against Coopers & Lybrand, a major accounting firm, was settled for $200 million and involved thousands of investors and creditors.[12] Clearly, the cost of an error of overstatement to auditors and managers, in terms of both the dollar amount of the settlement and damage to professional reputations, can be very high.

AN ERROR OF UNDERSTATEMENT. Now assume that Ginny acts conservatively and chooses to disclose the suit in the audit report that accompanies the financial statements. This decision is difficult for her because it is against Lew's wishes and can jeopardize Ginny's future as Technic's auditor. Further, mentioning the suit will probably lower the selling price of the shares about to be issued by Technic.

Now suppose that the company successfully defends itself in the litigation that was pending at the time the financial statements were released. In this case, Ginny has made an **error of understatement**. Because she mentioned the suit, the investors were led to believe that Technic was in worse financial condition than it actually was. However, even though Ginny made an error, there are no injured stockholders and, thus, no class-action suits are filed against her or Lew.

THE RELATIVE COSTS OF ERRORS:
OVERSTATEMENT AND UNDERSTATEMENT

Refer now to Figure 4–6, which depicts the decision faced by Ginny and Lew in the preceding story. They could have chosen either to disclose or not to disclose the suit, and later the suit would either have been won or lost, giving rise to four possible com-

12. Thomas McCarroll, "Who's Counting?" *Time*, April 13, 1992.

FIGURE 4–6

Errors of understatement and overstatement

Outcome of Lawsuit

		Win	Lose
Manager/Auditor Decision	**Disclose**	**1** Error of understatement	**2** Correct decision
	Do not disclose	**3** Correct decision	**4** Error of overstatement

binations: (1) disclose/win, (2) disclose/lose, (3) do not disclose/win, and (4) do not disclose/lose.

In terms of Figure 4–6, the main point of the story is that, on average, errors of overstatement (Cell 4) are much more costly than errors of understatement (Cell 1). Since these costs are shared by auditors, managers, stockholders, and others, it makes economic sense to structure the financial accounting system so that errors of overstatement are minimized. One way to achieve such an objective is to encourage conservative financial reporting.

There are many examples of conservatism in the financial statements. The lower-of-cost-or-market rule, which is used to value short-term investments and inventories, has already been mentioned in this chapter and is perhaps the most evident example. Others are discussed as they arise later in the text. The following quote illustrates the economic rationale behind conservative reporting.

Virtually every time an accountant records expenditures, he or she runs the risk that a later development might, with the aid of hindsight, show that the recording was "wrong." . . . The obvious solution for avoiding this sort of situation and resulting criticisms is to [treat as expenses] all costs associated with the acquisition of assets where there is some significant probability that the asset will turn out to be worth less than its cost. . . . Lawsuits may force the adoption of such conservative practices.[13]

INTERNATIONAL PERSPECTIVE: AN EXTREME FORM OF CONSERVATISM THAT ENCOURAGES INCOME MANIPULATION

In Japan and most of western Europe most of the capital is provided by a few, very large banks, who satisfy their needs for information in a direct way—through personal contracts and visits. National governments require some public disclosure, so companies prepare financial reports, but the required disclosures are limited and heavily oriented towards the needs of creditors. One relatively unique aspect of these reports is that they appear to be extremely conservative, containing intentional asset

13. Harold Bierman and Roland Dukes, "Accounting for Research and Development Costs," *The Journal of Accountancy,* April 1975, pp. 48–55.

understatements and liability overstatements to reduce the chance that banks will grant loans that eventually are unpaid. By understating net income in certain years, this conservative reporting can also reduce the demand from shareholders for dividends.

In Switzerland, for example, federal law not only sets maximum limits for the values on the balance sheet at original cost, but expressly encourages management to (1) carry assets at less than original cost, and (2) set up "hidden reserves" through excessive depreciation or liability write-ups. Presumably, such discretion enables managers to ensure the continued prosperity of the enterprise through income smoothing—recording conservative adjustments in good years and ignoring them in poor years.

Such conservatism can encourage income manipulation by allowing managers to create and use up their "hidden reserves" at will. *Forbes* (June 20, 1994) notes:

"Yes, there are hidden reserves in Switzerland, Germany, and Sweden. But that doesn't mean that there is more to these companies than meets the eye. Loosey-goosey reserves cut both ways. They could mean that a company's book value is understated. But they could also mean that a company's earnings are overstated. Reserves tucked away in earlier years could have been used to paper over last year's losses."

The accounting profession is under intense public scrutiny and has incurred staggeringly expensive litigation over its role in financial disasters. *Time* (April 13, 1992) reported that accounting firms faced over 4,000 liability suits, asking for more than $15 billion in damages.

"The problem is that many investors think [that an audit opinion is like a 'Good Housekeeping Seal of Approval' and] if something goes wrong [with a company], they tend to blame the auditor. The common assumption is that auditors should be among the first to know whether a company is failing or even defrauding investors. To be sure, accountants can be found negligent and held liable if their own work is sloppy . . . Responsibility for spotting outright [management fraud], though, is another matter . . . In the strictest sense auditors are not required to look for fraud—but controversy rages about what they should do when they stumble upon it. Rather than inform on clients, auditors usually prefer to drop the client quietly." Indeed, a recent article in Business Week noted that Big 6 firms are increasingly "firing" their clients. Democratic Congressman Ron Wyden recently introduced legislation, defeated in the Senate, that would have required auditors to report to the SEC any client found engaging in fraud. The accounting profession opposed this legislation, claiming that requiring auditors to report fraud would expose accountants to even more legal liability.

ETHICS IN THE REAL WORLD

ETHICAL ISSUE

Are auditors acting ethically if they discover that management is defrauding the shareholders and choose to simply drop the client instead of reporting the fraud to the proper authorities?

SUMMARY OF LEARNING OBJECTIVES

LO 1 *Identify and define the four basic assumptions of financial accounting.*

The four basic assumptions of financial accounting are (1) the economic entity assumption, (2) the fiscal period assumption, (3) the going concern assumption, and (4) the stable dollar assumption. The economic entity assumption states that a company is a separate economic entity that can be identified and measured. The fiscal period assumption states that the life of an economic entity can be broken down into fiscal periods. The going concern assumption states that the life of an economic entity is indefinite. The stable dollar assumption states that the value of the monetary unit used to measure an economic entity's financial performance and position is stable across time.

 Identify the two markets in which business entities operate, express the four alternative valuation bases in terms of these two markets, and briefly describe how the valuation bases are used on the balance sheet.

A business entity operates in two general markets: an input market, where it purchases inputs for its operations, and an output market, where it sells the outputs that result from its operations. The four valuation bases (present value, fair market value, replacement cost, and original cost) can be defined in terms of these two markets.

The present value of an asset or liability represents the discounted future cash flows associated with the asset or liability. Fair market value represents the sales price in the output market. Replacement costs (or current costs) are the current prices paid in the input market. Original costs are the input prices paid when the input was originally purchased.

The financial statements contain a wide variety of valuation bases. Face value is used to value cash and short-term liabilities. Short-term investments are carried at fair market value, and inventories are valued at the lower of cost or market. Accounts receivable are valued at net realizable value, a form of market value. Notes receivable, notes payable, and most long-term liabilities are valued at present value. Prepaid expenses, fixed assets, and intangible assets are valued at original cost less an adjustment for depreciation or amortization.

 Define the principle of objectivity, and explain how it determines the dollar values that appear on the financial statements.

The principle of objectivity requires that the values of transactions and the assets and liabilities created by them be verifiable and backed by documentation. It ensures that present value is reported on the financial statements only in cases, such as contracts, where future cash flows can be objectively determined. It also ensures that market values such as fair market value and replacement costs, which are often difficult to objectively determine, are rarely reported on the financial statements (e.g., the lower-of-cost-or-market rule applied to marketable securities and inventories). Objectivity also ensures that many accounts on the financial statements are valued at original costs and that goodwill is only recognized in situations where it is purchased in an arm's-length transaction.

L O 4 *Explain how the principles of matching and revenue recognition relate to the measure of performance.*

The matching principle states that the efforts of a given period should be matched against the benefits they generate. In determining net income, benefits are usually represented as revenues, and efforts are represented by expenses, which cannot be matched against revenues until the revenues have been recognized. The principle of revenue recognition determines when revenues can be recognized. In short, the principle of revenue recognition triggers the matching principle, which in turn is necessary for determining the measure of performance.

LO 5 *Identify and describe two exceptions to the principles of financial accounting measurement, and explain the economic rationale behind them.*

Two important exceptions to the principles of financial accounting measurement are materiality and conservatism. Materiality suggests that the principles of financial accounting measurement can be violated, if the dollar amount involved in a particular transaction is so small that it would not affect the decisions of financial statements users. Conservatism guides accountants, when in doubt, to understate assets, overstate liabilities, accelerate the recognition of losses, and delay the recognition of gains. These two exceptions guide departures from the principles of financial accounting measurement when the costs of following them exceed the benefits. Conservatism, in particular, makes economic sense because the legal liability facing auditors and managers imposes a high potential cost on errors due to overstating assets or understating liabilities. An extreme form of conservatism, which encourages the manipulation of income, is also practiced in Japan and many Western European countries.

APPENDIX 4A

THE TIME VALUE OF MONEY

Financial accounting information is useful because it provides investors, creditors, and other interested parties with measures of solvency and earning power. In developing these measures, the valuation of the transactions in which the company participates and ultimately the valuation of a company's assets and liabilities as well as the company itself are very important. It is essential, therefore, that investors, creditors, managers, auditors, and others understand the concepts of valuation.

The economic value of an asset or liability is its present value. In computing present value, the future cash inflows and outflows associated with an asset or liability are predicted and then adjusted in a way that reflects the **time value of money** (i.e., a dollar in the future is worth less than a dollar at present). Financial accounting statements rely extensively on the concept of present value; in theory, providing measures of present value is the ultimate goal of financial accounting.

This appendix covers the time value of money and, specifically, the concept of present value. We first point out that money has a price (interest). The price of money gives it a time value; it ensures that money held today has a greater value than money received tomorrow. We then introduce the notion of compound interest and proceed to work a number of examples that equate future cash flows to present values. We conclude by discussing how present value fits into the financial accounting system.

INTEREST: THE PRICE OF MONEY

Money, like any other scarce resource, has a price. Individuals wishing to borrow money must pay this price, and those who lend it receive this price. The price of money is called *interest* and is usually expressed as a percentage rate over a certain time period (usually per year, but sometimes per month). The dollar amount of interest is the result of multiplying the percentage rate by the amount of money borrowed or lent (*principal*). For example, a 10 percent interest rate per year on a principal of $100 will produce $10 (10% × $100) of interest after one year.

TIME VALUE

In an environment that charges interest for the use of money, would you rather have one dollar now or would you rather receive one dollar one year from now? If you choose to receive the dollar immediately, you could lend it, and it would grow to some amount greater than one dollar after a year has passed. Someone, perhaps a bank, would be willing to pay you interest for the use of that dollar. Therefore, in a world where money has a price, a dollar today is worth more than a dollar at some time in the future. The difference between the value of a dollar today and the value of a dollar in the future is called the time value of money. For example, if the interest rate is 10%, $1 placed in a bank today will grow to $1.10 ($1 × 1.10) in one year. In this example the time value of a dollar is $.10.

SIZE OF TIME VALUE

Let's go one step further and explore the factors that determine the size of the time value of money. That is, what factors determine whether the time value of money is large or small? The first factor is obviously the price of money, or the interest rate. If there were no interest rate, the time value of money would be zero. Accordingly, as the interest rate gets larger, so does the difference between the value of a dollar today and the value of a dollar in the future. The higher the interest rate, the greater the time value of money. In the example above, a 20 percent interest rate would give rise to a time value of money equal to $.20.

The second factor determining the magnitude of the time value of money is the length of the time period. Which do you think is larger, the difference in value between a dollar today and a dollar tomorrow or the difference in value between a dollar today and a dollar one year from now? Clearly, a dollar will grow much more in one year than it will in one day. Thus, the longer the time period, the greater the time value of money.

INFLATION

One additional important point should also be noted. We have assumed in the discussion so far that interest is simply the price of money. You might view this price as a rental fee for the use of money. Just as you pay rent for the use of someone else's apartment, you must also pay rent for the use of someone else's money.

However, in addition to the rental price of money, there is another reason why someone would prefer a dollar today to a dollar in the future. In times of rising prices (inflation), for example, one would definitely prefer a dollar today to a dollar in the future because today's dollar will buy more goods than the future dollar. In inflation, the prices of today's goods are less than the prices for the same goods in the future. Thus, in an inflationary environment there are actually two reasons why one would prefer a dollar today to a dollar in the future: (1) the rental price charged for using the dollar (time value) and (2) the erosion of the purchasing power of the dollar in the future (inflation).

In the real world, interest rates are set so that they reflect both factors. A 10% interest rate, for example, might be viewed as 6% rental fee and 4% inflation factor. Unfortunately, when using an interest rate to compute the time value of money, it is quite difficult to clearly separate the rental factor from the inflation factor. As a practical matter, there is little one can do other than to realize that both factors exist and that they are nearly impossible to separate accurately. As indicated previously in this chapter, financial accounting ignores this problem by assuming that inflation does not exist.

TIME VALUE COMPUTATIONS

Computations involving the time value of money can be viewed from either of two perspectives: (1) the future value of a sum of money received today or (2) the present value of a sum of money received in the future. The following sections discuss these two perspectives.

FUTURE VALUE

In our discussion of the time value of money, we stated that $1 invested at a given interest rate for a period of time will grow to an amount greater than $1. This dollar amount is called the **future value**.

SIMPLE INTEREST

As in the example above, $1 invested at a 10% per year interest rate will grow to $1.10 ($1 × 1.10) at the end of one year. This $1.10 is referred to as the future value in one year of $1, given a 10% interest rate. In such a situation an individual would be indifferent between receiving $1 now or $1.10 in one year. A simple interest calculation for one year is illustrated below.

Now ⎯⎯⎯⎯⎯▶ 1 year
$1 ⎯⎯⎯⎯⎯▶ $1.10

COMPOUND INTEREST

If we wish to compute the future value of $1 at the end of more than one period (say, two years), given a 10 percent interest rate, we use the notion of **compound interest**. That is, in the second year the 10 percent interest rate is applied to both the original $1 principal and the $.10 interest earned in the first year. Here, the future value of $1 at the end of two years, given a 10 percent interest rate compounded annually, is equal to $1.21. An individual would be indifferent between receiving $1 now, $1.10 in one year, or $1.21 in two years, given a 10 percent interest rate compounded annually. The computation is depicted below.

Now ⎯⎯⎯⎯⎯▶ 1 year ⎯⎯⎯⎯⎯▶ 2 years
$1 ⎯⎯⎯⎯⎯▶ $1.10 ⎯⎯⎯⎯⎯▶ $1.21

TABLE FACTORS

This same basic procedure could be used to calculate the future value of $1 for any number of periods in the future. After very many periods, though, this computation becomes quite time-consuming. Try, for example, to compute the future value of $1 in forty years, given an 8 percent interest rate compounded annually. Fortunately, tables have been developed that expedite these calculations considerably. Turn now to the time value of money tables—specifically Table 1, located on the inside cover of this text. (The factors in this table and in Tables 2, 3, 4, 5, and 6 are carried out to five digits beyond the decimal point. In our discussions, however, we round the factors to two or three digits beyond the decimal point to simplify calculations.) This is a future value table. It enables you to quickly compute the future value of any amount for any number of periods in the future. To compute a future value, first find the intersection of the interest rate and the number of periods. This amount is called the **table factor**. Then, simply multiply this table factor times the dollar amount. For example, find the table factor for a 10 percent interest rate and two periods. It equals 1.21. Multiplying this factor times $1 gives you the future value in two years of $1 invested at a 10 percent annual interest rate. Multiplying this factor times $20 gives you the future value in two years of $20 invested at a 10 percent annual interest rate.

Note that the table factor in this example (1.21) is equal to 1.10×1.10 or $(1.10)^2$. In general, the formula for the future value calculation is as follows:

Future Value = A $(1 + i)^n$
where   A = money amount
** i = annual interest rate**
** n = number of periods**

Figure 4A–1 illustrates the future value calculation of $100 invested at 8 percent, 10 percent, and 12 percent for one, two, and three periods.

The chart demonstrates three important points. First, it shows that the factors found on the future value table are nothing more than an individual interest factor $(1 + i)$ multiplied by itself for the number of periods $(1 + i)^n$. For example, the table factor for $n = 3$, $i = 12\%$ is 1.40 ($1.12 \times 1.12 \times 1.12$). Can you find the table factor for three periods and an 8 percent interest rate on the future value table? Can you derive it?

FIGURE 4A–1

Future value

Note also in Figure 4A–1 that in each of the three time periods, as the interest rate gets higher, the time value of money is larger. In Period 3, for example, the time value of money at an 8 percent interest rate is $26 (126 − $100). At 10 percent, it is $33 ($133 − $100) and at 12%, it is $40 ($140 − $100). And finally, as the time period becomes longer, the time value of money becomes greater. These last two points illustrate the idea mentioned earlier that the magnitude of the time value of money is determined by two factors: (1) the size of the interest rate and (2) the length of the time period.

FUTURE VALUE OF ORDINARY ANNUITIES

It often happens in business transactions that cash payments of equal amounts are made periodically throughout a period of time. Installment payments on loans, for example, are typically set up in this manner. A flow of cash payments of equal amounts paid at periodic intervals is called an **annuity**. If these payments are made at the end of each period, the flow of payments is called an **ordinary annuity**, or an *annuity in arrears*. An ordinary annuity is illustrated below. This five-year ordinary annuity shows $100 payments made at the end of each year for five years.

Now ⟶	1 ⟶	2 ⟶	3 ⟶	4 ⟶	5
	$100	$100	$100	$100	$100

How would one go about computing the future value of this entire ordinary annuity? What would an ordinary five-year annuity of $100 grow to at the end of five years, given a 10 percent interest rate compounded annually? There are basically three ways to approach this problem, and they are illustrated in Figure 4A–2: (1) you can view each payment separately and compute its growth over each individual time period, (2) you can view each payment separately and use the table for future value (Table 1), or (3) you can use the table for future value of an ordinary annuity (Table 2). Both tables appear on the inside covers of this text.

As is evident from the illustration, all three methods bring you to the correct solution ($610). However, method (3), the use of Table 2 requires by far the fewest computations. The table factor for five periods and a 10 percent interest rate (6.10) is simply multiplied by the amount of the periodic annuity payment ($100). Note that this table factor is simply the addition of all the individual table factors used in method (2) (6.10 = 1.46 + 1.33 + 1.21 + 1.10 + 1.00). Thus, the factor in Table 2 for a given time period is simply the summation of the individual time period factors in Table 1. Table 2 is merely a shortcut that makes it easier to compute the future values for ordinary annuities.

Think for a moment now about the simple interest factor $(1 + i)$. As we have discussed, the factors in Table 1 are the simple interest factors compounded, or $(1 + i)^n$. A given factor in Table 2 for a specified length of time is the result of adding together the compound factors for each component time period. Thus, the simple interest calculation underlies the factors in both Table 1 and Table 2. In each we have built upon the very fundamental notion of simple interest.

FUTURE VALUE OF AN ANNUITY DUE

Annuities are often paid at the beginning of each period rather than at the end. Such a series of equal cash payments is referred to as an **annuity due** and is frequently observed when, for example, lease agreements require payments in advance. Calculating the future value of an annuity due follows the same concepts as those for an ordinary annuity. The only difference comes from the obvious fact that annuity due payments come one period earlier and thus earn one period more of interest than ordinary annuities. Table 3 provides table factors for future value of an annuity due calculations.

FIGURE 4A–2

Future value of ordinary annuities

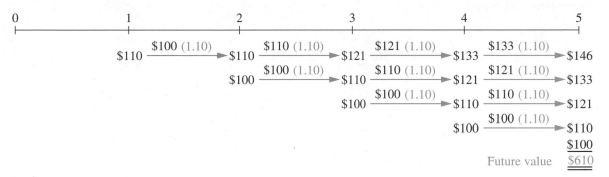

Each payment, table for future value of a fixed sum (Table 1)

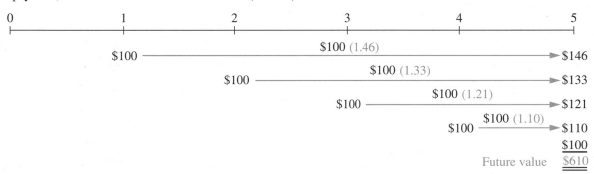

Table for future value of an ordinary annuity (Table 2)

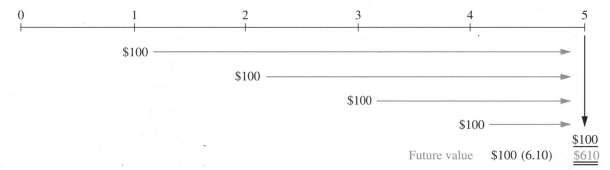

In the same manner that Figure 4A–2 illustrated the future value of an ordinary annuity calculation, Figure 4A–3 illustrates three approaches to computing the future value of a five-year annuity due, given a 10 percent interest rate compounded annually. Again, while all three methods come to the correct solution, method 3, which uses the factor found on Table 3 (6.71), is by far the easiest.

Compare the computations on this chart to those illustrating the future value of an ordinary annuity on Figure 4A–2. The future value here is $61 ($671 − $610) greater than the ordinary annuity future value. Why? This difference occurs because each annuity due payment comes one period earlier than each ordinary annuity payment and thus earns more interest over the annuity's life. The fifth $100 payment earns an extra $10 over one period, the fourth payment an extra $11 over two periods, the third

FIGURE 4A–3

Future value of an annuity due

Each payment, each period

Each payment, table for future value of a fixed sum (Table 1)

Table for future value of an annuity due (Table 3)

an extra $12 over three periods, the second an extra $13 over four periods, and the first an extra $15 over five periods (61 = 10 + 11 + 12 + 13 + 15).

PRESENT VALUE

Now that we have covered the concept of future value, it should be relatively easy to look at the "other side of the coin." Rather than asking about the future value of a current payment, we now focus on the question, "What is the present value of a future payment?"

In the original example, we stated that $1 would grow to $1.10 after one year, given a 10 percent interest rate. This relationship can just as easily be stated in the opposite way. That is, $1 is the present value of $1.10 received one year in the future, given a 10 percent interest rate. As investors, we would be indifferent between $1 now (the present value) or $1.10 (future value) one year in the future.

The computation of present value is exactly the reciprocal of the future value computation. Recall that the simple interest factor for the future value in one period at 10 percent interest is $(1 + i)$. The simple interest factor for present value is the reciprocal, $1 \div (1 + i)$. In the future value example presented earlier $1 \times (1 + .10)$ equaled $1.10, the future value. To compute the present value, we simply multiply $1.10 by $1 \div (1 + .10)$ to arrive at $1. The present value computation is illustrated as follows.

Now ◀───────── 1 year
$1 ◀───────── $1.10

If the present value computation involves more than one period, just as in the future value case, the notion of compounding must be considered. The present value factor, once again, is simply the reciprocal of the future value factor, $1 \div (1 + i)^n$. A two-period, 10 percent interest rate example follows.

Now ◀───────── 1   ◀───────── 2
$1 ◀───────── $1.10 ◀───────── $1.21
$1 ◀───────────────────────── $1.21

This example demonstrates that the present values of both $1.21 in two years and $1.10 in one year are equal to $1, given a 10 percent interest rate compounded annually. In such a case, an investor would be indifferent among having $1 now, receiving $1.10 in one year, or receiving $1.21 in two years. The example also shows that the present value of a future payment can be calculated in several different ways.

As for future values, there are tables (Tables 4, 5, and 6) designed to expedite the computations required to calculate present values. The factors contained in these tables are the reciprocals of the corresponding factors in the future value tables. Table 4 contains the table factors for the present values of single payments in the future. In the illustration above, one could use the table by multiplying $1.21 by .826 (Table 4, $n = 2$, $i = 10\%$) to arrive at the $1 present value. Obviously, as the number of time periods increases, the time savings from using the tables also increases.

Present values for ordinary annuities and annuities due must also be computed from time to time, and Table 5 (ordinary annuity) and Table 6 (annuity due) are designed for that purpose. As with future values, there are basically three ways to compute the present value of ordinary annuity and annuity due payment streams; they are depicted in Figures 4A–4 (ordinary annuity) and 4A–5 (annuity due). In both cases a $100, five-year annuity at a 10 percent interest rate is illustrated.

Again compare the two charts, and note that the present value of an annuity due is $38 ($417 − $379) greater than the present value of the ordinary annuity. The fact that each of the five payments in the annuity due is one period earlier than the corresponding ordinary annuity payment accounts for this difference.

AN ILLUSTRATION

Students often quickly grasp the general concepts of future and present value yet still have difficulty making the appropriate computations for a specific problem. We have designed the following example to demonstrate how straightforward future and pre-

FIGURE 4A–4

Present value of an ordinary annuity

Each payment, each period

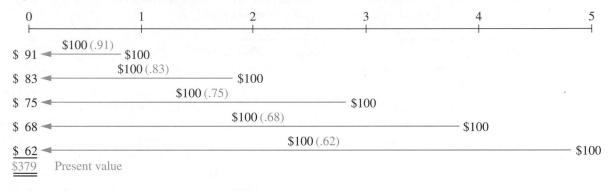

Each payment, table for present value of a fixed sum (Table 4)

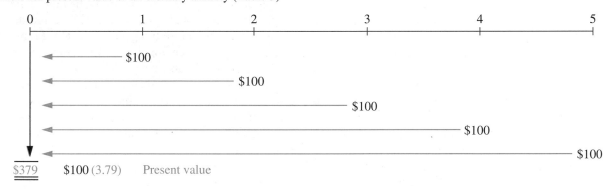

Table for present value of an ordinary annuity (Table 5)

sent value computations can be and also how many different ways one can approach the same problem. We also introduce a concept we call **equivalent value**. It can be useful in understanding the notion of time value.

Assume a $500, five-year, ordinary annuity at a 12 percent interest rate compounded annually. The cash flows are illustrated below. Let's see how many different ways we can compute the future and present value of this payment stream. Five such examples are shown in Figure 4A–6.

0	1	2	3	4	5
	$500	$500	$500	$500	$500

FIGURE 4A–5

Present value of an annuity due

Each payment, each period

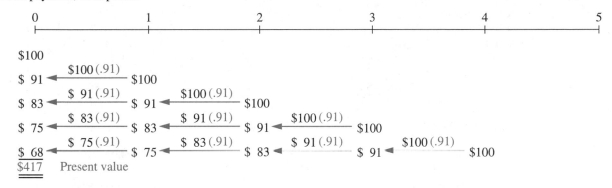

Each payment, table for present value of a fixed sum (Table 4)

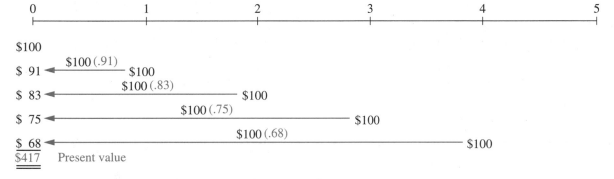

Table for present value of an annuity due (Table 6)

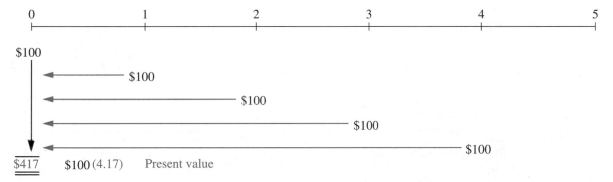

Can you follow each of the five methods shown? Note that each method brings you to a future value of $3,176 and a present value of $1,804. No matter how many different ways one tackles this problem, the same future and present values emerge.

EQUIVALENT VALUE

To understand the concept of equivalent value, view the $500 annuity payments, the present value, and the future value as being indifference amounts. That is, in this example an investor would be indifferent among a five-year, $500 ordinary annuity, $1,804 now, or $3,176 five years from now. These three payments are, in other words, equivalent in value.

FIGURE 4A–6

Example calculations

FUTURE VALUE

1. Each payment, each period

$$\begin{aligned}
\$500\ (1.12)\ (1.12)\ (1.12)\ (1.12) &= \$\ \ 787 \\
\$500\ (1.12)\ (1.12)\ (1.12) &= \ \ \ 702 \\
\$500\ (1.12)\ (1.12) &= \ \ \ 627 \\
\$500\ (1.12) &= \ \ \ 560 \\
\$500 &= \ \ \ 500 \\
\text{Future value} &\ \underline{\underline{\$3,176}}
\end{aligned}$$

2. Each payment individually

$$\begin{aligned}
\$500\ (1.574) &= \$\ \ 787 \\
500\ (1.405) &= \ \ \ 702 \\
500\ (1.254) &= \ \ \ 627 \\
500\ (1.120) &= \ \ \ 560 \\
500\ (1.000) &= \ \ \ 500 \\
\text{Future value} &\ \underline{\underline{\$3,176}}
\end{aligned}$$

3. Ordinary annuity table

Future value $\$500\ (6.353) = \underline{\underline{\$3,176}}$

4. Compute present value, and then compute future value of present value

A. Present value
$$\$500\ (3.604) = \$1,802$$

B. Future value
$$\$1,802\ (1.7623) \qquad = \underline{\underline{\$3,176}}$$

5. Compute equivalent value at Period 3, and then compute future value of that number

A. Value at Period 3

$$\begin{aligned}
\$\ 500\ (1.254) &= \$\ \ 627 \\
500\ (1.120) &= \ \ \ 560 \\
500\ (1.000) &= \ \ \ 500 \\
500\ \ (.893) &= \ \ \ 447 \\
500\ \ (.797) &= \ \ \ \underline{399} \\
&\ \ \ \underline{\$2,533}
\end{aligned}$$

B. Future value
$$\$2,533\ (1.254) = \underline{\underline{\$3,176}}$$

PRESENT VALUE

Each payment, each period

$$\begin{aligned}
\$500\ (.893)\ (.893)\ (.893)\ (.893)\ (.893) &= \$\ \ 284 \\
\$500\ (.893)\ (.893)\ (.893)\ (.893) &= \ \ \ 318 \\
\$500\ (.893)\ (.893)\ (.893) &= \ \ \ 356 \\
\$500\ (.893)\ (.893) &= \ \ \ 399 \\
\$500\ (.893) &= \ \ \ 447 \\
\text{Present value} &\ \underline{\underline{\$1,804}}
\end{aligned}$$

Each payment individually

$$\begin{aligned}
\$500\ (.567) &= \$\ \ 284 \\
500\ (.636) &= \ \ \ 318 \\
500\ (.712) &= \ \ \ 356 \\
500\ (.797) &= \ \ \ 399 \\
500\ (.893) &= \ \ \ 447 \\
\text{Present value} &\ \underline{\underline{\$1,804}}
\end{aligned}$$

Ordinary annuity table

Present value $\$500\ (3.604) = \underline{\underline{\$1,802}}*$

Compute future value, and then compute present value of future value

A. Future value
$$\$500\ (6.353) = \$3,176$$

B. Present value
$$\$3,176\ (.5674) \qquad = \underline{\underline{\$1,802}}*$$

Compute equivalent value at Period 3, and then compute present value of that number

A. Value at Period 3

$$\begin{aligned}
\$500\ (1.12)\ (1.12) &= \$\ \ 627 \\
\$500\ (1.12) &= \ \ \ 560 \\
500\ (1.00) &= \ \ \ 500 \\
500\ (.893) &= \ \ \ 447 \\
500\ (.893)\ (.893) &= \ \ \ \underline{399} \\
&\ \ \ \underline{\$2,533}
\end{aligned}$$

B. Present value
$$\$2,533\ (.712) = \underline{\underline{\$1,804}}$$

*Rounding difference

The idea of equivalent value is further illustrated in the fifth computation in Figure 4A–6. It involves two steps. We first compute the amount that would be equivalent to the five-year ordinary annuity if one lump sum were received at the end of Period 3 ($2,533). This amount is the equivalent value of this particular annuity at the end of Period 3. We then adjust this amount to present or future value by multiplying it by the appropriate table factor. Figure 4A–7 illustrates the equivalent values of the five-year ordinary annuity if lump-sum payments were made at the end of each of the five periods.

Figure 4A–7 demonstrates that given a 12 percent interest rate compounded annually, an investor would be indifferent among the following seven payments. Can you derive these amounts?

1. a five-year, $500 ordinary annuity
2. $1,804 now (present value)
3. $2,021 at the end of one year
4. $2,262 at the end of two years
5. $2,533 at the end of three years
6. $2,839 at the end of four years
7. $3,176 at the end of five years (future value)

FIGURE 4A–7

Equivalent values

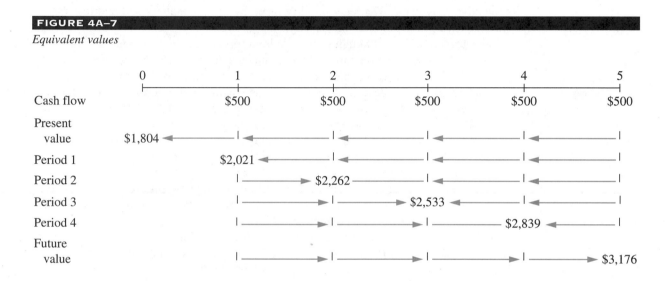

PRESENT VALUE AND FINANCIAL ACCOUNTING

We stated earlier that present value is the economic form of valuation. Investors, creditors, and managers use it to compare the values of alternative investments. Bankers, lawyers, and other business decision makers use it to derive the terms of contracts like mortgages, leases, pensions, and life insurance. Virtually any transaction that can be broken down into periodic cash flows utilizes the time value of money concept and can be reduced to present value, future value, and other equivalent values. The time value of money is covered in finance, economics, accounting, and other business courses. You may have already studied present value in previous courses, and you will probably see it again in the future. The uses of present value in business decision making are almost limitless.

The study of financial accounting and its reliance on the time value of money concept is no exception. As you already know, financial accounting information is useful because it helps investors, creditors, and other interested parties evaluate and control the business decisions of management. Such evaluation and control requires that financial accounting information be used to assess value: the value of entire companies, the value of individual assets and liabilities, and the value of specific transactions. Since present value is the economic form of valuation, financial accounting information must reflect present value if it is to be useful.

However, a critical problem is associated with using present value on the financial statements. The present value calculation requires that both future cash flows and future interest rates be predicted. In the vast majority of cases, predicting the future cash flows associated with a particular asset or liability with a reasonable degree of confidence is almost impossible. For example, how would one go about predicting the future cash inflows and outflows associated with the purchase of a specific piece of equipment like an automobile? Moreover, accurately predicting interest rates has for years eluded even the best economists. The predictions that management must make to apply present value are simply too subjective for financial statements that are to be used by those outside the company. Auditors are unwilling and unable to verify such subjective judgments. The legal liability faced by both managers and auditors makes such verification potentially very costly.

For these reasons, although present value remains the goal of financial measurement, most of the valuation bases on the financial statements represent surrogate (substitute) measures of present value. Historical cost, fair market value, replacement cost, and net realizable value can all be viewed as surrogate measures of present value. These valuation bases are used primarily because present value is simply too subjective and unreliable for a system that requires auditors to verify financial statements prepared by management for stockholders and other outside interested parties. Present value calculations, in general, violate the principle of objectivity.

In some cases, however, the future cash flows associated with an asset or a liability are predictable enough to allow for sufficiently objective present value calculations. As discussed in Chapter 4, contractual agreements like notes receivable and payable meet the criterion of objectivity. Mortgages, bonds, leases, and pensions are other examples of contracts that underlie cash flows and thus remove much of the subjectivity associated with cash flow prediction. In these cases the present value calculation is used in the preparation of the financial statements.

In summary, there are two reasons why accounting students must understand present value. First, present value is the economic form of valuation and is therefore the ultimate goal of accounting measurement. It is the standard against which all financial accounting measurements must be compared and evaluated. Second, in those cases where cash flow prediction is sufficiently objective (e.g., contracts), present value methods are used, and present values are actually incorporated into the financial statements. The balance sheet valuation of the assets and liabilities arising from such contracts results from the present value calculation.

KEY TERMS

Note: Definitions for these terms are provided in the glossary at the end of the text.

Class-action lawsuit (p. 148)
Conservatism (p. 147)
Consistency (p. 145)
Economic entity assumption (p. 132)
Error of overstatement (p. 148)

Error of understatement (p. 148)
Face value (p. 138)
Fair market value (FMV) (p. 137)
Fiscal period assumption (p. 133)
Fiscal years (p. 134)

Going concern assumption (p. 134)
Historical cost (p. 138)
Input market (p. 136)
Lower-of-cost-or-market rule (p. 138)
Matching (p. 142)
Materiality (p. 146)
Net realizable value (p. 138)
Objectivity (p. 140)
Original cost (p. 137)

Output market (p. 136)
Present value (p. 137)
Purchasing power (p. 135)
Replacement cost (p. 137)
Revenue recognition (p. 142)
Stable dollar assumption (p. 135)
Uniformity (p. 145)
Valuation bases (p. 137)

QUESTIONS FOR DISCUSSION AND REVIEW

1. List the basic assumptions, principles, and exceptions underlying the preparation of financial accounting statements. What is the difference between an assumption and a principle, an assumption and an exception, and a principle and an exception?

2. If the financial statements of two legally separate companies are combined to produce a set of consolidated financial statements, the entity for accounting purposes is different from the entity for legal purposes. In such a case, what basic accounting assumption is being invoked? State this assumption clearly.

3. A given balance sheet contains dollar amounts resulting from transactions that occurred in several different time periods. Accountants add these dollar amounts in the computation of such numbers as current assets and total assets, even though the amount of goods and services a dollar could purchase has varied widely across these time periods. What basic assumption allows accountants to make these additions? Is this assumption realistic? How are accounting reports misstated because they are based on this assumption?

4. What basic assumption allows the preparation of financial reports on a timely basis? What important trade-off is introduced because this assumption is necessary? In general, which dollar amount is more reliable: net income for a month or net income for a five-year period? Which of the two net income amounts is more timely?

5. What is a fiscal year? Why do some companies prepare financial statements on a fiscal year basis?

6. What basic assumption underlies the definition of an asset and the process of capitalizing and amortizing? Is this assumption realistic?

7. The principles of accounting measurement determine the valuation bases used on the balance sheet. The chapter describes four valuation bases. Name them.

8. Differentiate an individual company's input market from its output market. Why are these two markets relevant to financial accounting measurements? Describe each of the four valuation bases in terms of the input and output markets.

9. Name the accounts on the balance sheet, and indicate the valuation base used for each.

10. Which principle of accounting measurement is the most pervasive? Define it and describe how it determines which valuation bases are used for which balance sheet accounts.

11. Which valuation base is considered to reflect economic value? Why is this base not used to value all assets and liabilities? Under what circumstances is it used?

12. In what two ways are market values limited as valuation bases for assets and liabilities?

13. What basic principle underlies the measure of performance? State this principle, and explain how it is applied to the methods used to account for inventories and fixed assets.

14. What principle triggers the matching process? That is, what principle must be applied before the matching principle can be implemented?

15. What criteria must be met before revenue can be recognized, and how does revenue recognition, in general, relate to the matching principle? As an example, explain how inventories are accounted for in terms of revenue recognition and the matching principle.

16. What basic principle of financial accounting measurement favors the use of historical costs on the balance sheet?

17. Consider a piece of machinery that was purchased two years ago for $3,000, can be replaced for $4,500, and can be sold for $5,000. If the machinery is kept in operation, it will produce 500 widgets per year for five years. The widgets can be sold at the end of each year at a profit of $4 each. Given a 10 percent interest rate, should the machinery be kept in operation, sold, or sold and replaced? Which of the values above (original cost, replacement cost, FMV, or present value) was important in arriving at your decision? Which of these values would appear on the balance sheet?

18. Critique the following statement: "The financial statements are prepared on the basis of historical costs."

19. Differentiate uniformity from consistency. Which is a principle of financial accounting measurement? Why?

20. What is materiality? Why is it considered a departure from the principles of financial accounting measurement? Is there an economic reason that explains why it is followed? What factors are important in determining that which is material and that which is not?

21. What is conservatism? Why is it considered a departure from the principles of financial accounting measurement? Explain how the legal liability faced by managers and auditors might encourage conservatism in the financial statements. In general, would it be more costly to overstate or understate the value of an asset?

22. From the valuation bases used on the balance sheet, provide an example of conservatism.

23. Briefly characterize the accounting systems used in countries from the Continental group. What role does conservatism play in these systems, and how is that role different from that in the United States?

24. (Appendix 4A) Briefly explain why a dollar received today is worth more than a dollar received in the future? What two factors determine the size of the time value of money?

25. (Appendix 4A) In the real world interest rates are set to reflect two factors. Describe these two factors and how they are treated in the financial statements.

26. (Appendix 4A) What is the difference between simple and compound interest?

27. (Appendix 4A) Would you rather receive a 10-year ordinary annuity or a 10-year annuity due? Why? Which form of payment is more common in business? Provide several examples.

28. (Appendix 4A) What role does simple interest play in the formula for present value?

29. (Appendix 4A) What is the difference between future and present value? Explain the concept of equivalent value.

30. (Appendix 4A) An individual recently won a $10 million lottery where the prize involved receiving $1 million each year for 10 years. Do you believe that the lottery winnings were actually worth $10 million? Why? How would these winnings be valued on a balance sheet? Explain.

31. (Appendix 4A) When computing the present value of a series of future cash inflows, how is the risk that the cash payments may not be received treated? Discuss.

32. (Appendix 4A) Why are fixed assets on the balance sheet not valued at present value?

33. (Appendix 4A) The concept of present value plays what two roles in financial accounting? Provide several examples. Why would a manager need to know how present value is used in financial accounting—from both a management perspective and a financial statement user's perspective.

EXERCISES

Note to Students: Chapter 4 describes the basic assumptions, principles, and exceptions of financial accounting. The following exercises, problems, and cases present numerical examples of the concepts we covered.

E4–1

(The effects of inflation on holding cash)

Assume that a corporation holds cash of $50,000 throughout a period of time in which the general price level increases by 6 percent. Does the corporation have more or less than $50,000 of purchasing power at the end of the period? By how much? Would such a gain or loss be reflected in the corporation's financial accounting statements? Why or why not?

E4–2

(The effects of inflation on holding land)

Palomar Paper Products purchased land in 1981 for $15,000 cash. The company has held the land since that time. In 1996 Palomar purchased another tract of land for $15,000 cash. Assume that prices in general increased by 60 percent from 1981 to 1996.

REQUIRED:

a. Assuming that Palomar made only these two land purchases, what dollar amount would appear in the Land account on Palomar's balance sheet as of December 31, 1996?
b. Palomar used $15,000 cash to make each land purchase. Would $15,000 in 1981 buy the same amount of goods and services as $15,000 in 1996? If not, how much more or less, and why?
c. Explain how one could adjust the dollar amount reported in the Land account as of December 31, 1996 if the stable dollar assumption were dropped.

E4–3

(Valuation bases on the balance sheet)

Name the valuation base(s) that are used for each of the asset and liability accounts shown here. Some assets and liabilities can use more than one valuation base.

	ORIGINAL COST	FAIR MARKET VALUE (FMV)	PRESENT VALUE	REPLACEMENT COST
Cash				
Short-Term Investments				
Inventories				
Prepaid Expenses				
Long-Term Investments				
Notes Receivable				
Machinery				
Equipment				
Land				
Intangible Assets				
Short-Term Payables				
Long-Term Payables				

E4–4

(Revenue recognition)

Cascades Enterprises ordered 4,000 brackets from McKey and Company on December 1, 1996 for a contracted price of $40,000. McKey completed manufacturing the brackets on January 17 of the next year and delivered them to Cascades on February 9. McKey received a check for $40,000 from Cascades on March 14.

REQUIRED:

a. Assume that McKey and Company prepares monthly income statements. In which month should McKey recognize the $40,000 revenue from the sale?
b. Justify your answer in (a) in terms of the four criteria of revenue recognition.
c. Are there conditions under which the revenue could be recognized in a different month than the month you chose in (a)?
d. Provide several reasons why McKey's management might be interested in the timing of the recognition of revenue.

E4–5

(The effects on income of different methods of revenue recognition)

Lahmont Bridge Builders built a bridge for the state of Maryland over a two-year period. The contracted price for the bridge was $600,000. The costs incurred by Lahmont and the payments from the State of Maryland over the two-year period follow.

	PERIOD 1	PERIOD 2	TOTAL
Costs incurred by Lahmont	$300,000	$100,000	$400,000
Payments from Maryland	$400,000	$200,000	$600,000

REQUIRED:

a. Prepare income statements for Lahmont for the two periods under the following assumptions:
   (1) Revenue is recognized at the end of the project.
   (2) Revenue is recognized in proportion to the costs incurred by Lahmont.
   (3) Revenue is recognized when the payments are received.
b. Calculate the total net income over the two-year period under each assumption.

E4–6

(Assets and depreciation—which assumption and principle?)

RDP and Brothers purchased a panel truck for $25,000 on January 1, 1996. They estimated the life of the truck to be five years, and they planned to depreciate an equal amount in each of the five years.

REQUIRED:

a. In line with generally accepted accounting principles, determine the amounts required here.

	1996	1997	1998	1999	2000
Original cost					
Depreciation expense					
Accumulated depreciation					
Net book value					

b. Why did you decide to initially recognize the cost as an asset rather than treat it as an expense? What basic assumption of financial accounting are you relying upon in this decision?
c. Why did you allocate a portion of the cost to each of the five years? What basic principle of financial accounting measurement are you relying upon in this decision?

E4–7

(The concept of materiality)

Megaton, Inc., is a multimillion dollar operation that expenses all costs under $6,000. After reviewing the company's financial records, you note that many of these expenditures are for assets, items that are useful to the company beyond the period in which they were purchased.

REQUIRED:

a. Explain the proper accounting treatment for expenditures for items that are expected to generate benefits in the future.
b. Explain why it might make economic sense to expense some of these items. Upon what exception to the principles of financial accounting would such a decision be based?

E4–8

(Changing accounting methods and net income)

The net income amounts for Hauser and Bradley over the four-year period beginning in 1994 follow.

1994	1995	1996	1997
$21,000	$24,000	$23,000	$29,000

After further examination of the financial report, you note that Hauser and Bradley made accounting method changes in 1995 and 1997, which affected net income in those periods. In 1995 the company changed depreciation methods. This change increased the book value of its fixed assets in each subsequent year by $5,000. In 1997 the company adopted a new inventory method that increased the book value of the inventory by $9,000.

REQUIRED:

a. Calculate the effect of each of these changes on net income in the year of the change.
b. Prepare a chart that compares net income across the four-year period, assuming no accounting changes were made by Hauser and Bradley. How would your assessment of the company's performance change after you learned of the accounting method changes?

c.   What principle of financial accounting makes it difficult to make such changes? Describe the conditions under which Hauser and Bradley would be allowed to make changes in their accounting methods.

E4–9

(Appendix 4A: Future value/single sum)

If $150 were invested today, how large a sum could be withdrawn at the end of the following time periods at the following compound interest rates. Complete the following table.

	TIME PERIODS (YEARS)		
COMPOUND INTEREST RATES	5	10	15
5%			
10%			
15%			

E4–10

(Appendix 4A: Present value/single sum)

Compute the present value of $10,000 received at the end of the following time periods at the following discount rates. Complete the following table.

	TIME PERIODS (YEARS)		
COMPOUND INTEREST RATES	5	10	15
5%			
10%			
15%			

E4–11

(Appendix 4A: Future value/ordinary annuity)

If $150 were invested at the end of each year over the following time periods at the following interest rates, how large a sum could be withdrawn at the end of the final time period? Complete the following table.

	TIME PERIODS (YEARS)		
COMPOUND INTEREST RATES	5	10	15
5%			
10%			
15%			

E4–12

(Appendix 4A: Future value/annuity due)

If $150 were invested at the beginning of each year over the following time periods at the following interest rates, how large a sum could be withdrawn at the end of the final time period? Complete the following table.

	TIME PERIODS (YEARS)		
COMPOUND INTEREST RATES	5	10	15
5%			
10%			
15%			

E4–13

(Appendix 4A: Present value/ordinary annuity)

Compute the present value of $10,000 received at the end of each year over the following time periods at the following discount rates. Complete the following table.

	TIME PERIODS (YEARS)		
COMPOUND INTEREST RATES	5	10	15
5%			
10%			
15%			

E4–14

(Appendix 4A: Present value/annuity due)

Compute the present value of $10,000 received at the beginning of each year over the following time periods at the following discount rates. Complete the following table.

| | TIME PERIODS (YEARS) | | |
COMPOUND INTEREST RATES	5	10	15
5%			
10%			
15%			

E4–15

(Appendix 4A: Present value of different payment patterns)

Compute the present value of the payment patterns provided below, given an 8 percent discount rate.
a. $50 at the end of year 2; $100 at the end of year 5; $80 at the end of year 8.
b. $100 at the end of years 1, 2, 3, 4; $100 at the end of year 8.
c. $60 at the end of years 5, 6, 7, 8; $100 at the end of year 10.
d. $90 at the end of years 7, 8, 9.

E4–16

(Appendix 4A: Present value of different payment patterns)

Compute the present value of the payment patterns provided below, given an 8 percent discount rate.
a. $50 at the end of year 2; $100 at the end of year 5; $80 at the beginning of year 8.
b. $100 at the beginning of years 1, 2, 3, 4; $100 at the beginning of year 8.
c. $60 at the beginning of years 5, 6, 7, 8; $100 at the beginning of year 10.
d. $90 at the beginning of years 7, 8, 9.

E4–17

(Appendix 4A: Future and present values)

Ben Watson found $25,000 lying on the sidewalk and decided to invest the money. He believes that he can earn a 10 percent rate (compounded annually) on his investment for the first four years, 12 percent for the following three years, and 15 percent for the following five years.

REQUIRED:
a. How much money will Ben have at the end of 4 years, 7 years, and 12 years?
b. If someone offered to pay him $36,000 at the end of 4 years for the $25,000, should he accept? Why or why not?

E4–18

(Appendix 4A: Present value of future bond payments—ordinary annuity and annuity due)

Rudnicki Corporation raises money by issuing bonds. The bond agreement states that Rudnicki must make interest payments in the amount of $40,000 at the end of each year for ten years and make a $500,000 payment at the end of the tenth year. Assume that the discount rate is 10 percent.

REQUIRED:
a. What amount, as a lump sum, would the company have to invest today to meet the $40,000 annual interest payments and the $500,000 principal payment at the end of the tenth year?
b. What amount would have to be invested if the bond agreement stated that the interest payments were to be made at the beginning of each of the ten years and the $500,000 payment was still at the end of the tenth year?

E4–19

(Appendix 4A: The highest present value)

Congratulations! You have just won the lottery. The lottery board offers you three different options for collecting your winnings:
1. You will receive payments of $500,000 at the end of each year for twenty years.
2. You will receive a lump-sum payment of $4,500,000 today.
3. You will receive a lump-sum payment of $1 million today and payments of $2,100,000 at the end of Years 5, 6 and 7.
    Assume that all earnings can be invested at a 10 percent annual rate.

REQUIRED:
Which option should you choose and why?

E4–20

(Appendix 4A: Comparing ordinary annuities and annuities due)

Consider a three-year $700 ordinary annuity (the first payment is one year from now) and a three-year $700 annuity due (the first payment is now). Assume a discount rate of 10 percent.

REQUIRED:
For each of the two annuities, compute the equivalent value as of the following points in time.
a. Now
b. The end of Period 1
c. The end of Period 2
d. The end of Period 3
e. Which of the above is referred to as the present value?
f. Which of the above is referred to as the future value?
g. Which of the two annuities is most valuable and by how much?

E4–21

(Appendix 4A: Different terms of financing)

Dunn Drafting Company is considering expanding its business by purchasing new equipment. Because of constraints on how much the company can spend for new equipment, the president wants to make sure that the company enters into the best possible deal. Dunn Drafting has four options for paying for the new equipment.
1. Make a lump-sum payment of $240,000 today.
2. Make a lump-sum payment of $500,000 eight years from now.
3. Make a lump-sum payment of $600,000 ten years from now.
4. Make payments of $50,000 at the beginning of each year for six years. The first payment is due now.

REQUIRED:
a. Compute the present value of each option. Assume the relevant interest rate is 12 percent.
b. If you were the president of Dunn Drafting Company, which option would you select?
c. Would your answer to (b) change if the annual interest rate was 8 percent? If so, which option would you now prefer?

E4–22

(Appendix 4A: Saving for a college education—future value)

The Croziers have a three-year-old son named Ryan, and they want to provide for Ryan's college education. They estimate that it will cost $40,000 per year for four years when Ryan enters college fifteen years from now. Assume that all investments can earn a 10 percent annual interest rate, and that the four annual payments will be made at the beginning of each year.

REQUIRED:
a. How much would the Croziers have to invest today to meet Ryan's college expenses?
b. How much would the Croziers have to invest at the end of each year for fourteen years to meet Ryan's college expenses?
c. Answer questions (a) and (b) above, assuming an 8 percent annual interest rate.

E4–23

(Appendix 4A: Saving for a college education—future value)

The Smithsons have a nine-year-old daughter named Emily, and they wish to provide for her college education. They estimate that it will cost $30,000 per year for four years when Emily enters college ten years from now. Assume that all investments can earn an 8 percent annual interest rate, and that the four annual payments will be made at the beginning of each year.

REQUIRED:
a. How much would the Smithsons have to invest today to meet Emily's college expenses?
b. How much would the Smithsons have to invest at the end of each year for nine years to meet Emily's college expenses?
c. Answer questions (a) and (b) above, assuming a 6 percent annual interest rate.

PROBLEMS

P4–1

(The effects of inflation on reported profits)

On January 1, 1996, you purchased a piece of property for $10,000. On December 31 of that year you sold the property for $20,000. Assume that the general rate of inflation for 1996 was 10 percent.

REQUIRED:

a. According to generally accepted accounting principles, how much gain would be recorded in the income statement due to the sale of the property?
b. The $10,000 you used to purchase the property on January 1 could have been used to purchase any number of goods and services on January 1. Would the $20,000 you received at the end of the period enable you to purchase twice as many goods and services? Why or why not?
c. How much of the accounting gain computed in (a) could be attributed to inflation, and how much could be attributed to the fact that the property rose in value? Do generally accepted accounting principles make such a distinction? Why or why not?

P4–2

(Inflation and bank loans)

Assume that on January 1, Bush Enterprises borrowed $4,760 from Banking Corporation, promising to pay $5,000 at the end of one year. The effective rate of interest on the loan is approximately 5 percent ([$5,000 − $4,760]/ $4,760). Suppose that the general rate of inflation for that year was 10 percent.

REQUIRED:

a. How much interest revenue did Banking Corporation recognize for the year? (*Hint:* The difference between the cash payment and the face value of the note receivable is interest revenue that Banking Corporation will earn over the life of the note.)
b. Do you think that Banking Corporation is better off at the end of the year by the amount of the interest revenue? Did Banking Corporation have more or less purchasing power at the end of the year? How much?
c. Which of the two parties, Bush Enterprises or Banking Corporation, seems to have ended up with the better deal? Could one determine this from a careful examination of the financial statements prepared on the basis of generally accepted accounting principles? Why or why not?

P4–3

(The irrelevance of original cost)

Three years ago Yeagley and Sons purchased the three assets listed in the following table. The chief financial officer, Kathy Dillon, is presently trying to decide what to do with each asset. She has three choices for each of the assets: (1) she can sell it, (2) she can sell it and replace it with an equivalent asset, or (3) she can simply keep it. The following information is provided to aid her decision.

ASSET	ORIGINAL COST	REPLACEMENT COST	FAIR MARKET VALUE	PRESENT VALUE OF FUTURE CASH FLOWS PRODUCED BY OLD ASSET	PRESENT VALUE OF FUTURE CASH FLOWS OF EQUIVALENT ASSET
A	$4,000	$1,000	$1,500	$2,500	$5,000
B	1,500	2,000	500	2,500	3,500
C	2,000	3,500	3,000	2,500	5,000

REQUIRED:

a. Assuming that Kathy chooses to keep Asset A and Asset B and sell and replace Asset C, evaluate her decisions. What decisions should she have made? Support your choices.

b. How useful was the original cost of each asset in the evaluation of the officer's decisions?

c. Assume that Kathy proceeds with her decisions. According to generally accepted accounting principles, at what dollar amount would each asset be carried on Yeagley's balance sheet? What principles of financial accounting would be involved?

P4–4

(The stable dollar assumption and sales growth)

Sales data for 1995, 1996, and 1997 for Easy Growth Inc. follow.

	1995	1996	1997
Sales	$80,000	$120,000	$160,000

After reviewing the growth in sales, Milton Smarts, the company president, commented that according to the financial statements, sales doubled from 1995 to 1997. Assume that the general inflation rate as well as the price increase of Easy Growth's products for the period of 1995 to 1997 was 10 percent.

REQUIRED:

a. Considering price increases, did sales actually double from 1995 to 1997? By how much did the company's sales actually grow from 1995 to 1997? By what percentage did sales increase?

b. If prices had increased 15 percent from 1995 to 1997, by what percentage would sales have grown?

c. Describe how the stable dollar assumption could have misled Milton Smarts.

P4–5

(The economic value of a company vs. its book value)

The December 31 balance sheet and the income statement for the period ending December 31 for Buyable Goods follow. (This problem requires knowledge of present value. Refer to Appendix 4A.)

BALANCE SHEET

				INCOME STATEMENT	
Current assets	$10,000	Liabilities	$12,000	Sales	$30,000
Long-lived assets	20,000	Common stock	8,000	Expenses	(24,000)
		Retained earnings	10,000	Net income	$ 6,000
		Total liabilities and			
Total assets	$30,000	stockholders' equity	$30,000		

Mr. Black is interested in purchasing Buyable Goods. He has analyzed the future prospects of the company and estimates that it should be able to maintain at least its current earnings amount for the next ten years, at which time the assets would be worthless. He also estimates that the discount rate over that time period will be 12 percent.

REQUIRED:

a. Assuming that net income is equal to cash inflows, how much should Mr. Black be willing to pay for Buyable Goods?

b. What is the book value of Buyable Goods?

c. Explain why there is a difference between the book value of Buyable Goods and the amount Mr. Black is willing to pay for it. What assumptions and/or principles of financial accounting are important here?

P4–6

(Economic value and income vs. book value and income)

On January 1, 1996 Barry Smith established a company by donating $90,000 and used all of the cash to purchase an apartment house. At the time he estimated that cash inflows due to rentals would be $65,000 per year, while annual cash outflows to manage and maintain it would be $45,000. He felt that the apartment house had a ten-year life and could be sold at the end of that time for $40,000. He also estimated that the effective interest rate during the ten-year period would be 10 percent. (This problem requires knowledge of present value. Refer to Appendix 4A.)

REQUIRED:

a. What is the book value of the building as of January 1, 1996? Assuming that Barry's estimates are correct, what is the economic value of the building? In your opinion, did Barry make a wise investment?

b. On December 31, 1996 Barry prepares financial statements and observes that his estimates were exactly correct. Assuming that cash inflows equal revenues, cash outflows equal expenses, and the net cost of the apartment, $50,000 ($90,000 − $40,000), is depreciated evenly over the ten-year period, prepare the income statement and balance sheet for Barry's apartment house.

c. Calculate the economic income of the apartment building for 1996. Economic income equals the difference between the present value at the beginning of the year and the present value at the end of the year plus any cash received during the year. Why is there a difference between accounting income and economic income?

d. What is the value on Barry's books of the apartment building at the end of 1996? What is the present value of the apartment building at that time?

P4–7

(The differences between present value, book value, and liquidation value)

The December 31, 1996 balance sheet of Myers and Myers, prepared under generally accepted accounting principles, follows. (This problem requires knowledge of present value calculations. Refer to Appendix 4A.)

ASSETS		LIABILITIES AND STOCKHOLDERS' EQUITY	
Cash	$ 10,000	Current liabilities	$ 8,000
Short-term investments	14,000	Long-term liabilities	20,000
Land	20,000	Common stock	80,000
Buildings and machinery	80,000	Retained earnings	16,000
		Total liabilities and	
Total assets	$124,000	stockholders' equity	$124,000

An investor believes that Myers and Myers can generate $20,000 cash per year for ten years, at which time it could be sold for $80,000. The FMVs of each asset as of December 31, 1996 follow.

Cash	$ 10,000
Short-term investments	14,000
Land	60,000
Buildings and machinery	40,000
Total FMV	$124,000

REQUIRED:

a. What is the book value of Myers and Myers of December 31, 1996?

b. What is the value of Myers and Myers as a going concern (i.e., present value of the net future cash inflows) as of December 31, 1996? Assume a discount rate of 10 percent.

c. What is the liquidation value of Myers and Myers (i.e., how much cash would Myers and Myers be able to generate if each asset were sold separately and each liability were paid off on December 31, 1996)?

d. Discuss the differences among the book value of the company, the present value, and the liquidation value. Calculate goodwill, and explain it in terms of these three valuation bases.

P4–8

(Three different measures of income)

This problem is designed to follow **P4–7**. Suppose that Myers and Myers paid no dividends during 1997, and the December 31, 1997 balance sheet is listed below. (This problem requires knowledge of present value calculations. Refer to Appendix 4A.)

ASSETS		LIABILITIES AND STOCKHOLDERS' EQUITY	
Cash	$ 30,000	Current liabilities	$ 6,000
Short-term investments	20,000	Long-term liabilities	20,000
Land	20,000	Common stock	80,000
Buildings and machinery	76,000	Retained earnings	40,000
		Total liabilities and	
Total assets	$146,000	stockholders' equity	$146,000

Assume that the investor in **P4–7** was correct (i.e., the company produced $20,000 cash during 1997) and that the investor's expectations at the end of 1997 are unchanged. Assume further that an objective appraisal of the company's assets revealed the following FMVs as of December 31, 1997.

Cash	$ 30,000
Short-term investments	20,000
Land	66,000
Buildings and machinery	32,000
Total FMVs	$148,000

REQUIRED:

a. What dollar amount did Myers and Myers report in 1997 for net income under generally accepted accounting principles?
b. Calculate net income during 1997 using fair market values as the asset and liability valuation bases (i.e., $\$FMV_{1997} - \$FMV_{1996}$).
c. Calculate economic income for 1997 (i.e., cash received during 1997 plus the change in present value). The discount rate is still 10 percent.
d. Discuss the differences among these three measures of income. Discuss some of the strengths and weaknesses of each measure.

P4–9

(Different methods of recognizing revenue)

The Maple Construction Company agreed to construct twelve monuments for the city of Elderton. The total contract price was $2.4 million, and total estimated costs were $1,140,000. The construction took place over a four-year period, and the following schedule indicates the monuments completed, costs incurred, and cash collected for each period.

YEAR	1	2	3	4	TOTAL
Monuments completed	2	6	3	1	12
Costs incurred	$380,000	$380,000	$285,000	$ 95,000	$1,140,000
Cash collected	$600,000	$900,000	$300,000	$600,000	$2,400,000

REQUIRED:

a. How much revenue should Maple recognize in each of the four periods under the three following assumptions?
   (1) Revenues are recognized each year in proportion to the monuments completed.
   (2) Revenues are recognized each year in proportion to the percentage of costs incurred.
   (3) Revenues are recognized each year in proportion to the cash collected each year.
b. For each of the three assumptions, match the appropriate amount of cost against the recognized revenue. Determine net income for each period under the three assumptions.
c. Compare the total revenue, total cost, and total net income that result from each of the three assumptions. Note that although the timing of the recognition differs across the three assumptions, the total amount of income recognized is the same.

P4–10

(Revenue recognition and net income)

Hydra Aire, Inc., sells appliances to Seasons Department Store. A recent order requires Hydra Aire to manufacture and deliver 500 toasters at a price of $100 per unit. Hydra Aire's manufacturing costs are approximately $40 per unit. The following schedule summarizes the production and delivery record of Hydra.

YEAR	1	2	3	TOTAL
Toasters produced	200	200	100	500
Costs incurred	$ 8,000	$ 8,000	$ 4,000	$20,000
Toasters delivered	150	200	150	500
Cash received	$10,000	$15,000	$20,000	$45,000

REQUIRED:

a. Assuming that Hydra recognizes revenue when the toasters are produced, how much revenue should be recognized in each of the three years.

b. Assuming that Hydra Aire recognizes revenue at delivery, how much revenue should be recognized in each of the three years.

c. Calculate net income for the three periods under each of the two assumptions above.

d. If Hydra's management is paid in income-based bonus, which of the two assumptions would be preferred?

P4–11

(Comparing companies using different accounting methods)

The net income and working capital accounts for two companies in the same industry, ABC Company and XYZ Company, follow.

	ABC	XYZ
1/1—12/31 Net income	$10,000	$24,000
12/31 Working capital	$16,000	$30,000

After reviewing the complete financial statements of the two companies, you note that ABC and XYZ use different inventory valuation and depreciation methods. ABC uses method A to value its inventory while XYZ uses method B. Had ABC used B and XYZ used A, their inventory accounts would have been $10,000 greater and $10,000 smaller, respectively. Similarly, ABC uses method X depreciation, while XYZ uses method Y. Had XYZ used X and ABC used Y, their depreciation expenses for the year would have been $8,000 higher and $8,000 lower, respectively.

REQUIRED:

a. Calculate net income and working capital for the two companies under the following assumptions.

INVENTORY METHOD	DEPRECIATION METHOD	ABC INCOME/ WORKING CAPITAL	XYZ INCOME/ WORKING CAPITAL
B	Y		
B	X		
A	Y		
A	X		

b. Given this information, which combination of inventory and depreciation methods gives rise to the highest income and working capital numbers? Can you think of reasons why a manager would choose one method over another? Would managers always choose the method which results in the highest income? Why or why not?

c. If you were an investor, attempting to decide in which company to invest, how would you treat the fact that the two companies used different methods to account for inventory and fixed assets? Is there a principle of accounting that covers this situation? Why or why not?

P4–12

(The economics of conservatism)

Joe McGuire is a CPA who has recently completed the audit of Nelson Repairs, Inc. The audited balance sheet and income statement follow.

BALANCE SHEET				INCOME STATEMENT	
Current assets	$ 60,000	Liabilities	$ 80,000	Sales	$160,000
Long-term assets	140,000	Stockholders' equity	120,000	Expenses	(130,000)
		Total liabilities and			
Total assets	$200,000	stockholders' equity	$200,000	Net income	$ 30,000

During his examination Joe learned that a lawsuit is soon to be filed against Nelson. The lawsuit accuses Nelson of negligence and asks for damages over and above insurance of $60,000. If Nelson were to lose the lawsuit, the future of the business would be in jeopardy. However, as the lawyers described it to Joe, the probability that Nelson will lose the lawsuit is very low, approximately 20 percent.

Joe is unsure about whether he should require Nelson to disclose the lawsuit on the financial statements. The president of Nelson does not want it disclosed because he believes that the disclosure would cause undue concern among the company's shareholders. Joe does not want to ignore the president's request because Nelson is his most important client. On the other hand, Joe knows that if he does not require disclosure, and Nelson loses the lawsuit, he may be legally liable for the losses of the stockholders. Joe constructed the following framework to help him make his decision.

	LAWSUIT OUTCOME	
DECISION	WIN (80%)	LOSE (20%)
Require disclosure	Error 1	Correct decision
Do not require disclosure	Correct decision	Error 2

REQUIRED:

a. Study Joe's framework, and note that he can choose to require or not to require disclosure. Requiring disclosure and winning the lawsuit gives rise to Error 1. Not requiring disclosure and losing the lawsuit gives rise to Error 2. Comment on the costs that Joe would incur from each of these two errors. Which of the two errors would be more costly? Which of the two outcomes (winning or losing the suit) is more likely to occur?

b. Suppose that Joe estimates that the cost of Error 1 is $10,000 and the cost of Error 2 is $50,000. Ignoring the costs and benefits of correct decisions, should Joe choose to require disclosure?

c. Explain the concept of conservatism in terms of Joe's framework.

P4–13

(Appendix 4A: The value of common stock)

Christie Bauer is contemplating investing in South Bend Ironworks. She estimates that the company will pay the following dividends per share at the end of the next four years, and that the current price of the company's common stock ($100) will remain unchanged.

YEAR 1	YEAR 2	YEAR 3	YEAR 4
$5	$6	$7	$8

Christie wants to earn 12 percent on her investment.

REQUIRED:

Assume that Christie plans to sell the investment at the end of the fourth year. How much would she be willing to pay for one share of common stock in South Bend Ironworks?

P4–14

(Appendix 4A: Computing future value, present value, and equivalent value)

Wharton Company is planning to make the following investments.

1. $1,000 at the end of each year for five years at a 10 percent annual rate. Wharton Company will leave the accumulated principal and earnings in the bank for another five years at a 12 percent annual rate.

2. $3,000 at the end of each year for seven years at a 15 percent annual rate. Wharton will not make the first $3,000 payment until 4 years from now.

REQUIRED:

a. How much money will Wharton have at the end of ten years?
b. How much would Wharton have to invest in a lump sum today to have an equivalent amount at the end of ten years, given a 12 percent annual rate of return?

P4–15

(Appendix 4A: Computing present value and equivalent value of contract cash flows)

The terms of three different contracts follow.

1. $8,000 received at the beginning of each year for ten years, compounded at a 6 percent annual rate.
2. $8,000 received today and $20,000 received ten years from today. The relevant interest rate is 12 percent.
3. $8,000 received at the end of Years 4, 5, and 6. The relevant annual interest rate is 10 percent.

REQUIRED:

a. Compute the present value of each contract.
b. Compute the equivalent value of each contract at the end of Years 5 and 10.

P4–16

(Appendix 4A: The highest present value?)

J. Hartney, president of Doyle Industries, has a choice of three bonus contracts. The first option is to receive an immediate cash payment of $25,000. The second option is a deferred payment of $60,000, to be received in eight years. The final option is to receive an immediate cash payment of $5,000, a deferred payment of $27,000 to be received in three years, and a deferred payment of $20,000 to be received in twenty years. Assume that the relevant interest rate is 9 percent. Which bonus option should Hartney accept and why?

P4–17

(Appendix 4A: Computing equivalent values)

Boulder Wilderness Adventures purchased rafting and kayaking equipment by issuing a note to Recreational Co-op, the seller of the equipment. The note required a down payment of $5,000, annual payments of $10,000 at the end of each year for five years (the first payment to be one year from now), and a final payment of $15,000 at the end of the fifth year (this payment is in addition to the $10,000 annual payments). Assume that 10 percent is the relevant annual interest rate.

REQUIRED:

Recreational Co-op is indifferent between receiving the cash flows described above or any other cash flow that represents an equivalent value. Compute equivalent values as of the following points in time.

a. Today
b. At the end of two years
c. At the end of four years
d. At the end of five years

P4–18

(Appendix 4A: Present and future values)

Assume an annual interest rate of 8 percent for each of the following independent cases. Compute the value at time 0 and the value at the end of the investment period for all the cash flows described.

a. $10,000 is invested and held for four years.
b. $2,000 is invested at the end of each year for eight years.
c. $5,000 is invested at the beginning of each year for three years.
d. $3,000 is invested at the end of each year for five years. The balance is left to accumulate interest for an additional five years.
e. A company will receive $25,000 at the end of seven years.
f. A company will receive $3,000 at the end of each year for two years.
g. A company will receive $4,000 at the beginning of each year for three years.

P4–19

(Appendix 4A: Present value of a note receivable and inferring the effective interest rate)

Joy Don Corp. sells a building to Trifle and Life in exchange for a note. The note specifies a lump-sum payment of $300,000 ten years in the future and annual payments (beginning today) of $2,000 at the beginning of each year for ten years. Assume an annual interest rate of 10 percent.

REQUIRED:

a. Would Joy Don be wise to accept $110,000 now instead of the note? Why or why not?
b. At what interest rate would Joy Don be wise to accept the $110,000 instead of the note? (*Hint:* Use a trial and error approach. The answer is an integer.)

CASES

C4–1

(Revenue recognition and matching)

Most airlines offer promotional programs in which passengers accumulate miles over time; when they have earned enough miles, they receive free tickets. Currently, airlines do not make any accounting entries for these free tickets. The free rider merely uses available seats or, on occasion, displaces a ticketed passenger.

A panel of the American Institute of CPAs has recommended that the FASB adopt a new method of accounting for tickets issued under these programs. They propose that a portion of the fare paid when a passenger in such a program pays for a ticket be deferred until the free ride is used. For example, if a passenger purchases a $200 ticket, a portion, say $20, would not appear as revenue to the airline until the free trip is taken. It would be considered unearned revenue until then.

REQUIRED:

Evaluate the proposed accounting standard in terms of the principle of revenue recognition and matching. List the criteria of revenue recognition, and suggest when it would be appropriate to recognize the revenue from a ticket sale. Given your suggestion, how should the related costs be accounted for?

C4–2

(Revenue recognition)

A recent report on Blockbuster Video commented that Blockbuster seems to have unusual success in opening new franchises during the Christmas season. It appears that during each of the past few years product sales to new franchises have increased significantly in the fourth quarter. The report also noted, however, that Blockbuster recognizes revenue when products are shipped and there is no indication that the new franchises receiving the merchandise were actually open for business.

REQUIRED:

a. How could the policy of recognizing revenue when products are shipped enable a company like Blockbuster, who operates through franchises, to "manage" earnings?
b. Is recognizing revenue when products are shipped necessarily a violation of GAAP? Explain.

C4–3

(The matching principle)

When a television network buys the rights to show a series for film, the cost of the rights are treated as assets on the balance sheet as "program rights." Several years ago ABC's practice was to "expense" 80% of the cost in the period when the show first appears on the air. Subsequently, ABC reduced the first period expense to 75%. A financial analyst who follows the TV industry commented that the change could increase profits for ABC by as much as $50 million, which could turn a loss into a profit and boost earnings thereafter.

REQUIRED:

a. Briefly state the matching principle, and explain how, in general, it should be applied in cases like the one described above.
b. Consider the positions of ABC's stockholders, creditors, management, and auditors, and discuss how the matching principle may be very difficult to apply.

C4–4

(Consistency and uniformity)

In 1993, Procter & Gamble Company made an accounting method change that decreased 1993 net income by a total of $925 million. The net income dollar amounts reported by the company for 1992, 1993, and 1994 follow (dollars in millions).

1992	**$1,872**
1993	**$ (656)**
1994	**$2,211**

REQUIRED:

a.   Recalculate net income for 1993 assuming that the accounting changes had not been made. Which is the more appropriate comparison, the reported amounts or the recalculated amounts? Why?

b.   In what three places in Procter & Gamble's financial report would an investor be able to find a reference to this accounting change?

c.   In 1993, Procter & Gamble also chose to make a discretionary $2.7 billion write-down. Comment on the reporting strategy apparently being used by Procter & Gamble in 1993.

d.   General Electric (GE) depreciates its fixed assets using a method that recognizes a relatively large portion of depreciation in the early years of an asset's useful life. IBM, on the other hand, uses the straight-line method. Briefly describe the adjustments an investor would have to make when comparing GE's performance and financial position to that of IBM.

e.   Explain the difference between consistency and uniformity in terms of the accounting changes made by Procter & Gamble and the methods of accounting for fixed assets used by GE and IBM.

C4–5

(Errors of overstatement and conservatism)

On March 3, 1993 the common stock price of Leslie Fay, the nation's second largest maker of women's apparel, dropped from 12 3/8 to 5 1/4, when it was discovered that reported profits of $23.9 million were actually losses of $13.7 million. Hundreds of angry shareholders immediately filed suit against both the company's management, headed by CEO John Pomerantz, and the external auditor—Arthur Andersen and Co.

REQUIRED:

a.   In the context of this case explain the economic rationale behind conservatism.

b.   We noted in the chapter that certain foreign countries encourage conservative accounting practices in an effort to protect creditors. How could Leslie Fay's shareholders have been protected if the company had used conservative accounting practices?

c.   Explain why it may have been difficult for Arthur Andersen to insist that Leslie Fay report conservatively.

C4–6

(Conservative reporting?)

Forbes (June 20, 1994) reports: "Yes, there are hidden reserves in Switzerland, Germany and Sweden. But that doesn't mean that there is more to these companies than meets the eye. Loosey-goosey reserves cut both ways. They could mean that a company's book value is understated. But they could also mean that the company's earnings are overstated. Reserves tucked away in earlier years could have been used to paper over last year's losses."

REQUIRED:

Explain the meaning of this quote, and provide several examples of how "conservative" reporting in a previous year may allow for "liberal" reporting in a future year. When viewed in this way "conservative reporting" is actually part of a more general reporting strategy. Name that strategy.

C4–7

(Assumptions, principles, and exceptions)

The chapter listed and defined four basic assumptions, four principles of measurement, and two exceptions. Review the annual report of MCI, and find at least one example of each of these ten concepts. Also, indicate the accounts on MCI's balance sheet that use present value as a valuation base.

C4–8

(Appendix 4A: Present value and long-term debt)

The balance sheet of Kmart Corporation as of January 25, 1995 included a long-term debt with a principal amount of $100 million. The annual interest rate on the debt was 12.5%, and the principal amount was due in ten years (2005). The $100 million amount on the balance sheet was equal to the present value of the debt's future cash payments, discounted at 12.5%. This debt was in the form of bonds that were traded freely on the open bond market, and the 1995 annual report noted that the fair market value (January 25, 1995 market price) of the bonds was somewhat greater than the $100 million disclosed on the balance sheet.

REQUIRED:

a. Explain how the market price of the bonds on the open market could be greater than the $100 million disclosed on Kmart's balance sheet. (Hint: The price an investor is willing to pay for a bond is equal to the present value of the bond's future cash flows, discounted at the current market interest rate.)

b. Provide a plausible explanation if the market price of the bonds was less than the $100 million disclosed on Kmart's balance sheet.

CHAPTER 5

THE MECHANICS OF FINANCIAL ACCOUNTING

LEARNING OBJECTIVES

LO 1 State and describe the two criteria necessary for economic events to be reflected in the financial statements.

LO 2 State the accounting equation and describe how it relates to the balance sheet, income statement, statement of retained earnings, and statement of cash flows.

LO 3 Describe how journal entries (and T-accounts) express the effect of economic events on the basic accounting equation and the financial statements.

LO 4 Explain why managers need to understand how economic events affect the financial statements.

LO 5 Explain why the financial statements are adjusted periodically to reflect economic events that are not represented by transactions.

This chapter covers the mechanics underlying the preparation of financial statements. It begins by introducing economic events and discussing the criteria that must be met before such events can be reflected in the financial statements. The fundamental accounting equation is then described, and we show how economic events are reflected in the financial statements through their effects on this equation. Journal entries and T-accounts are then introduced and characterized as an efficient way to express the effects of economic events on the accounting equation and the financial statements. We also describe how and why the financial statements are adjusted periodically to reflect economic events that are not represented by transactions. After completing this chapter, students should be able to construct financial statements from economic events. Those interested in additional coverage of accounting procedures should refer to Appendix 5A, which contains a complete description (and comprehensive example) of the accounting cycle, and how it leads to the preparation of the financial statements.

Understanding the mechanics underlying the preparation of financial statements is crucial for effective management. Managers often choose among transactions, and such choices should not be made without considering the financial statement effects and the associated economic consequences. Consequently, managers must understand the mechanics that link transactions to the financial statements.

Managers must also understand how to read, interpret, and analyze financial statements. To do so effectively, it is useful to be able to infer from the financial statements events and transactions that occurred during the accounting period. A mechanical process, called T-account analysis, can enable users to make such inferences. This process is covered in Appendix 5B, entitled "Mechanics: A User's Perspective."

ECONOMIC EVENTS

L O 1 **Economic events** that are reflected in the financial statements must be both relevant to the financial condition of a company and objectively measurable in monetary terms.

RELEVANT EVENTS

Relevant events have economic significance to a particular company and include any occurrence that affects its financial condition. Events of general economic significance, like the election of a new U.S. president, the passage of federal legislation, or the outbreak of war, could be considered relevant. Events that are more company-specific, like the signing of a new labor agreement, the hiring of a new chief executive officer, the sale of an item of inventory, or simply the payment of monthly wages, are also relevant. Each of these events could have a significant impact on the financial resources of a particular company. Anyone interested in the company's financial status (stockholders, investors, creditors, managers, auditors, and other interested parties) wants to be able to assess the financial impact of all such events.

OBJECTIVITY

Unfortunately, only a small percentage of all relevant events are reflected on the financial statements. The dollar values assigned to the accounts on the financial statements must be determined in an objective manner.

In general, a dollar value is considered objective if it results from an exchange in which two parties with differing incentives reach agreement. To illustrate, several years ago PepsiCo, Inc., offered to purchase Kentucky Fried Chicken (KFC) from RJR Nabisco. PepsiCo and Nabisco had differing incentives because PepsiCo wanted to pay as little as possible, while Nabisco wanted to receive as much as possible. When they reached agreement on the value of KFC, a transaction took place. KFC passed to PepsiCo for a price of $841 million. The price represented an objective valuation of KFC because two parties with differing incentives reached agreement on it. The transaction was accompanied by documented evidence (e.g., receipts, canceled checks, vouchers, a bill of sale) that could be used to verify its entry into PepsiCo's financial records, and after the purchase an investment of $841 million was reflected on PepsiCo's balance sheet.

Unfortunately, the most relevant information is not always the most objective. King World Productions Inc., for example, is a television syndicator with the rights to *Jeopardy, Wheel of Fortune,* and *Oprah Winfrey*, which were expected to generate over $700 million in licensing fees. Yet, these rights were valued on the balance sheet at their purchase costs, less accumulated amortization, which totaled less than $3 million (the rights to *Wheel of Fortune* were valued at zero). Similarly, a partner at Coopers & Lybrand, a major accounting firm, noted: "Coca-Cola is one of the best-recognized trademarks in the world, but it is not on their books. It got that recognition through advertising, but you don't book advertising as an asset, because you don't know if it will have future value."[1] In the next section we introduce the fundamental accounting equation, followed by a section that demonstrates how transactions (relevant and measurable economic events) affect this equation and the financial statements.

THE FUNDAMENTAL ACCOUNTING EQUATION

LO 2   The four financial statements are all based on a mathematical equation which states that the dollar value of a company's assets equals the dollar value of its liabilities plus the dollar value of its stockholders' equity. In fact, the balance sheet is a statement of this equation.

$Assets = $Liabilities + $Stockholders' Equity

The mechanics of accounting are structured so that this equality is always maintained. If the two sides of this equation are unequal, the books do not balance, and an error has been made. However, maintaining this equality does not ensure that the financial statements are correct; errors can exist even if the **accounting equation** balances.

ASSETS

Assets are items and rights that a company acquires through objectively measurable transactions that can be used in the future to generate economic benefits (i.e., more assets). Such acquisitions are usually made by purchase: the asset is received in exchange for another asset (often cash) or a payable. Assets include cash, securities, receivables from customers, land, buildings, machinery, equipment, and rights such as

1. Richard Greene, "Inequitable Equity," *Forbes,* July 11, 1988, p. 83.

patents, copyrights, and trademarks. Simply, the left side of the accounting equation represents the dollar values of the items and rights that have been acquired by a company and are expected to benefit the company in the future.

Assets come from three sources: (1) they are borrowed, (2) they are contributed by stockholders (owners), and (3) they are generated by a company's operating activities. The right side of the equation, liabilities and stockholders' equity, represents the dollar values attached to these three sources. For each dollar amount on the asset side of the equation, a corresponding dollar amount is reflected on the liability and stockholders' equity side.

LIABILITIES

Liabilities consist primarily of a company's debts or payables. They are existing obligations for which assets must be used in the future. The dollar amount of the total liabilities on the balance sheet represents the portion of the assets that a company has borrowed and must repay.

STOCKHOLDERS' EQUITY

Stockholders' equity consists of two components: (1) contributed capital, the dollar value of the assets contributed by stockholders, and (2) retained earnings, the dollar value of the assets generated by operating activities and retained in the business (i.e., not paid to the stockholders in the form of dividends). Operating activities are those transactions directly associated with the acquisition and sale of a company's products or services. Dividing stockholders' equity into its components, the fundamental accounting equation appears as follows:

$Assets = $Liabilities + $Contributed Capital + $Retained Earnings

That is, the dollar value of the assets is equal to the sum of the dollar amounts owed, the dollar amount of stockholders' contributions, and the dollar amount retained from profitable operations.

BUSINESS TRANSACTIONS, THE ACCOUNTING EQUATION, AND THE FINANCIAL STATEMENTS

Companies conduct operations by exchanging assets and liabilities with other entities (e.g., individuals and businesses). These economic events are referred to as **business transactions**. Exchanging cash for a piece of equipment, for example, is a transaction that represents the purchase of equipment. Borrowing money is a transaction in which a promise to pay in the future (i.e., note payable) is exchanged for cash. The sale of a service on account is a transaction in which the service is exchanged for a receivable. In each of these exchanges, and in all business transactions, something is received and something is given up. These receipts and disbursements affect the financial condition of a company in a way that always maintains the equality of the fundamental accounting equation. That is, each business transaction is recorded in the books so that the dollar values of a company's assets always equal the dollar values of its liabilities and stockholders' equity.

TRANSACTIONS AND THE ACCOUNTING EQUATION

The six transactions below were entered into by Joe's Landscaping Service during 1997, its first year of operations. Figure 5–1 shows how each transaction affects the accounting equation. Study it carefully and read the following discussion of each transaction.

TRANSACTION (1). Joe, the owner of the company, contributes $10,000. This dollar amount increases the company's cash balance, an asset, by $10,000 and is also recorded on the right side of the accounting equation under contributed capital. Note that both sides of the accounting equation are increased by $10,000, so its equality is maintained.

TRANSACTION (2). $3,000 is borrowed from a bank. The dollar amount of this exchange also increases the company's cash balance, but in this case liabilities are also increased: the company now owes $3,000 to the bank.

TRANSACTION (3). The company purchases equipment for $5,000 cash. This exchange both increases and decreases the company's assets. It now has an asset called *equipment*, and its cash balance is reduced by $5,000. Still, the equality of the accounting equation is maintained because the asset side was both increased and decreased by $5,000.

TRANSACTION (4). The company performs a service for $12,000. This transaction increases the company's cash balance by $8,000 and creates a receivable of $4,000. Thus, total assets increase by $12,000. The corresponding $12,000 adjustment on the right side of the equation, which maintains its equality, is reflected in Retained Earnings because the company generated this $12,000 through its own operations.

TRANSACTION (5). The company pays $9,000 for expenses—wages, interest, and maintenance. This transaction decreases the company's cash balance by $9,000 and maintains the equality of the equation by decreasing Retained Earnings in the amount of $9,000. Retained Earnings is decreased because, as in Transaction 4, these expenses are associated with the company's operating activities.

FIGURE 5–1

Business transactions and the accounting equation

TRANSACTION	ASSETS	=	LIABILITIES	+	CONTRIBUTED CAPITAL	+	RETAINED EARNINGS
(1)	+10,000	=			+10,000		
(2)	+ 3,000	=	+3,000				
(3)	+ 5,000	=					
	− 5,000						
(4)	+ 8,000						
	+ 4,000	=					+12,000
(5)	− 9,000	=					− 9,000
(6)	− 1,000	=					− 1,000
End-of-year balance	15,000	=	3,000	+	10,000	+	2,000

TRANSACTION (6). Joe pays himself a $1,000 dividend as a return on his original investment. The dollar amount of the dividend reduces the company's cash balance by $1,000 and is also reflected on the right side of the equation by a $1,000 reduction in Retained Earnings. Retained Earnings is reduced because the fundamental objective of the company's operating activities is to provide a return for the owner, and Retained Earnings is the measure of the assets that have been accumulated through operations.

THE ACCOUNTING EQUATION AND THE FINANCIAL STATEMENTS

This section introduces and defines the concept of an account and describes the preparation of simplified versions of the balance sheet, statement of cash flows, income statement, and statement of retained earnings for Joe's Landscaping Service.

ACCOUNTS AND THE ACCOUNTING EQUATION

For purposes of recording transactions and preparing financial statements, the main components of the accounting equation (assets, liabilities, and stockholders' equity) can be further subdivided into separate categories called accounts. The general category of assets is normally divided into a number of accounts including, for example, a cash account, a receivables account, and an equipment account. Liabilities normally consist of various payable accounts, and as mentioned earlier, stockholders' equity can be divided into a contributed capital account and a retained earnings account. Accounts serve as "storage units," where the dollar values of business transactions are initially recorded and later compiled into the financial statements.

In Figure 5–2 the main components of the accounting equation are divided into separate accounts for the purpose of recording the six transactions entered into by Joe's Landscaping Service. Note that Figure 5–2 is very similar to Figure 5–1. It differs only in that it records the transactions in more specific categories, which represent the accounts that eventually appear on the financial statements.

Note that total assets ($15,000 = $6,000 + $4,000 + $5,000) equal total assets in Figure 5–1 as well as total liabilities plus stockholders' equity ($15,000 = $3,000 + $10,000 + $2,000). The components of the accounting equation have simply been divided into more specific "storage units." In the next sections the information contained in Figure 5–2 is used to prepare the financial statements.

FIGURE 5–2

Accounts and the accounting equation

	ASSETS			= LIABILITIES	+ STOCKHOLDERS' EQUITY	
TRANSACTION	CASH	+ RECEIVABLES	+ EQUIPMENT	= LOAN PAYABLE	+ CONTRIBUTED CAPITAL	+ RETAINED EARNINGS
(1)	+10,000			=	+10,000	
(2)	+ 3,000			= +3,000		
(3)	− 5,000		+5,000	=		
(4)	+ 8,000	+4,000		=		+12,000
(5)	− 9,000			=		− 9,000
(6)	− 1,000			=		− 1,000
Total	6,000 +	4,000	+ 5,000	= 3,000	+ 10,000	+ 2,000

THE BALANCE SHEET

The balance sheet is the statement of the basic accounting equation as of a particular date: in this case, the end of 1997. It is called a balance sheet because assets are always in balance with liabilities plus stockholders' equity. That is, there is a source for each asset the company has acquired. Figure 5–3 shows the balance sheet for Joe's Landscaping Service at the end of its first year of operations. This balance sheet was prepared by simply listing and grouping the totals of the individual asset, liability, and stockholders' equity accounts, which appear at the bottom of Figure 5–2.

FIGURE 5–3

Balance sheet for Joe's Landscaping

JOE'S LANDSCAPING SERVICE
BALANCE SHEET
DECEMBER 31, 1997

ASSETS		LIABILITIES AND STOCKHOLDERS' EQUITY	
Cash	$ 6,000	Loan payable	$ 3,000
Receivables	4,000	Contributed capital	10,000
Equipment	5,000	Retained earnings	2,000
		Total liabilities and	
Total assets	$15,000	stockholders' equity	$15,000

STATEMENT OF CASH FLOWS

The statement of cash flows in Figure 5–4 was prepared directly from the activity recorded in the cash account in Figure 5–2. Each dollar value on the statement of cash flows corresponds to an increase or decrease in the cash account indicated in Figure 5–2. Note also that the ending cash balance of $6,000 on the statement of cash flows equals the balance in the Cash account on the balance sheet. The statement of cash flows is nothing more than a summary of the activity in the company's cash account, divided into three sections—operating, investing, and financing activities.

FIGURE 5–4

Statement of cash flows for Joe's Landscaping

JOE'S LANDSCAPING SERVICE
STATEMENT OF CASH FLOWS
FOR THE YEAR ENDED DECEMBER 31, 1997

Operating activities:		
Sale of a service (4)	$ 8,000	
Payments for expenses (5)	(9,000)	
Net cash from operating activities		$ (1,000)
Investing activities:		
Purchase of equipment (3)	$ (5,000)	
Net cash from investing activities		(5,000)
Financing activities:		
Borrowings (2)	$ 3,000	
Owner contributions (1)	10,000	
Payment of dividends (6)	(1,000)	
Net cash from financing activities		12,000
Increase in cash balance		$ 6,000
Cash balance at beginning of year		0
Cash balance at end of year		$ 6,000

INCOME STATEMENT

The income statement is a measure of the assets generated from the company's operating activities during a period of time. It compares *revenues*, the asset inflows due to operating activities, to *expenses*, the asset outflows required to generate the revenues. The difference between revenues and expenses is called *net income* or *net loss*. If revenues exceed expenses, there is net income or profit; if expenses exceed revenues, there is a net loss.

In terms of the accounting equation, revenues, expenses, and dividends are reflected in the retained earnings account. Like the general categories of assets, liabilities, and stockholders' equity, retained earnings can be further subdivided into revenue accounts, expense accounts, and dividend accounts. Recording a transaction in a revenue account increases retained earnings; recording a transaction in an expense or dividend account decreases retained earnings.

In the example of Joe's Landscaping Service, revenues in the form of cash and a receivable were generated in Transaction (4), the sale of landscaping services for $12,000. Expenses were recognized in Transaction (5), which reflects payments made for wages, interest, and equipment maintenance. The dollar amounts of these two transactions are recorded in the Retained Earnings account in Figure 5–2, but in practice they would be recorded in separate revenue and expense accounts, which are components of retained earnings. An income statement can be prepared by disclosing Revenues and Expenses in the manner shown in Figure 5–5.

FIGURE 5–5	JOE'S LANDSCAPING SERVICE
Income statement for Joe's Landscaping	INCOME STATEMENT FOR THE YEAR ENDED DECEMBER 31, 1997

Revenues: Fees earned for service	$12,000
Expenses: Wages, interest, maintenance	9,000
Net income	$ 3,000

STATEMENT OF RETAINED EARNINGS

The statement of retained earnings is similar to the statement of cash flows in that it is a record of the activity in a single balance sheet account over a period of time. Rather than explaining the activity in the Cash account, however, it explains the activity in the Retained Earnings account. The statement of retained earnings in Figure 5–6 was prepared directly from the activity in the Retained Earnings account in Figure 5–2.

FIGURE 5–6	JOE'S LANDSCAPING SERVICE
Statement of retained earnings	STATEMENT OF RETAINED EARNINGS FOR THE YEAR ENDED DECEMBER 31, 1997

Beginning retained earnings balance	$ 0
Plus: Net income	3,000
Less: Dividend to stockholder	1,000
Ending retained earnings balance	$2,000

As indicated earlier, revenues, expenses, and dividends are reflected in the Retained Earnings account. On the statement of retained earnings, the dollar amount of revenues less expenses (i.e., net income) and the dollar amount of dividends are disclosed separately. Note that net income is also reported on the income statement and that the ending balance of retained earnings in Figure 5–6 is equal to the balance in the Retained Earnings account on the balance sheet in Figure 5–3.

THE JOURNAL ENTRY

LO 3 In the previous section we demonstrated how economic events affect the accounting equation and, ultimately, the financial statements. **Journal entries** provide a more efficient way to represent such effects. They are used to represent relevant and measurable economic events, and their content and structure indicate how such events affect the accounting equation. The form of a typical journal entry follows.

	DEBIT	CREDIT
Equipment	5,000	
Cash		5,000

Purchased equipment for cash.

The affected accounts in this entry are Equipment and Cash, and the dollar amount of the transaction is $5,000. Placing the $5,000 assigned to Equipment on the left side of the entry indicates that the Equipment account has been increased by $5,000. That account is said to have been *debited*. In the terminology of financial accounting, to **debit** an account simply means to place the dollar amount assigned to it on the left side of the journal entry.

Placing the $5,000 assigned to the Cash account on the right side of the entry, or *crediting* it, indicates that the Cash account has been decreased by $5,000. To **credit** an account means to place it on the right side of the journal entry. The sample entry indicates that equipment was purchased for $5,000 cash.

Compound journal entries are treated in exactly the same way, but they involve more than two accounts. For example, if equipment is purchased for $5,000 cash and a $10,000 note payable, we would record the following compound journal entry.

	DEBIT	CREDIT
Equipment	15,000	
Cash		5,000
Notes Payable		10,000

Purchased equipment for cash and a note payable.

THE DOUBLE ENTRY SYSTEM

Note in the preceding journal entries that the total dollar value on the debit side is always equal to the total dollar value on the credit side and that at least two different accounts were affected. Both characteristics are true of all journal entries and illustrate the **double entry system,** which is the cornerstone of financial accounting. The equality of the debit and credit sides maintains the equality of the accounting equation, and the fact that at least two different accounts are affected indicates that in all exchange transactions, something is received and something is given up.

THE JOURNAL ENTRY BOX

A useful way to learn journal entries is to view them as shown in Figure 5–7. We call this a *journal entry box*. It provides a systematic way of converting exchange transactions to journal entries.

The top of the box is an expression of the accounting equation and each cell contains a **T** that is associated with a group of accounts and has a left and a right side. All journal entries have three components: (1) the accounts affected, (2) the direction of the effect, and (3) the dollar value of the transaction.

Increases in asset accounts (Cell 1) and decreases in liability and stockholders' equity accounts (Cell 4) are always represented on the debit (left) side of the journal entry. Decreases in asset accounts (Cell 3) and increases in liability and stockholders' equity accounts (Cell 2) are always recorded on the credit (right) side of the journal entry. It is important to recall that revenue, expense, and dividend accounts are all part of the stockholders' equity account Retained Earnings. Thus, revenues, which increase Retained Earnings, are recorded on the credit side of the journal entry. Expenses and dividends, which decrease Retained Earnings, are recorded on the debit side of the journal entry.

The accounting equation at the top axis of the journal entry box shows that journal entries have been devised so that transactions are recorded in the journal in a way that always maintains the equality of the accounting equation. Debits always equal credits and, accordingly, assets always equal liabilities plus stockholders' equity.

FIGURE 5–7

The journal entry box

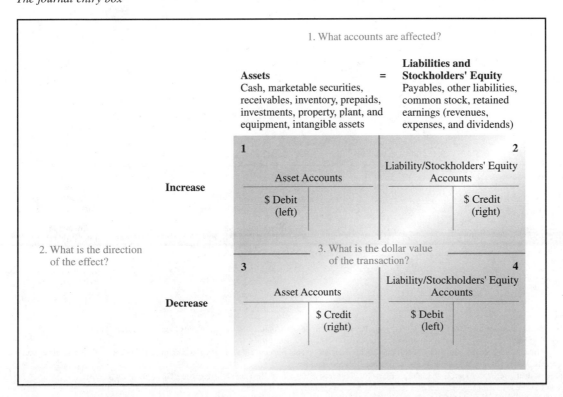

JOURNAL ENTRIES AND THE ACCOUNTING EQUATION: EXAMPLES

In Figure 5–8 seven different transactions give rise to seven different journal entries, affecting the accounting equation in seven different ways. The equality of the accounting equation is always maintained, and the debit side of each journal entry is exactly equal to the credit side. Note especially Transactions 5, 6 and 7, where the equality of the accounting equation is maintained through the effect of a revenue, an expense, and a dividend on retained earnings. The explanations on the right side of the chart indicate how the journal entry box was used to construct each journal entry.

FIGURE 5–8

Journal entries and the accounting equation

Transaction	Assets (Accounting Equation)		= Liabilities and Stockholders' Equity		Journal Entry	Debit	Credit	Explanation*
1. Company receives $100 cash in payment from a customer on account.	Cash Accts. Rec. 0 =	+100 −100		0	Cash (+A)** Accts. Rec. (−A)	100	100	Cash, an asset, is increased. Accts. Rec., an asset, is decreased.
2. Company borrows $500 from a bank in exchange for a short-term note pay.	Cash +500 =	+500	Notes Pay. +500	+500	Cash (+A) Notes. Pay. (+L)	500	500	Cash, an asset, is increased. Notes Pay., a liability, is increased.
3. Company pays $300 cash in payment of an account pay.	Cash −300 =	−300	Accts. Pay. −300	−300	Accts. Pay. (−L) Cash (−A)	300	300	Cash, an asset, is decreased. Accts. Pay., a liability, is decreased.
4. Company issues com. stk. in exchange for an outstanding note pay.	0 =		Notes Pay. Com. Stk. 0	−1,000 +1000	Notes. Pay. (−L) Com. Stk. (+SE)	1,000	1,000	Notes Pay., a liability, is decreased. Com. Stk., an equity, is increased.
5. Company provides a service for which it bills its clients $2,000.	Accts. Rec. +2,000 =	+2,000	Ret. Earn. via Fees Earned +2,000	+2,000	Accts. Rec. (+A) Fees Earned (R, +SE)	2,000	2,000	Accts. Rec., an asset, is increased. Fees Earned, a revenue, increases Retained Earnings.
6. Company pays $500 in salaries to its employees.	Cash −500 =	−500	Ret. Earn. via Salary Expense −500	−500	Salary Exp. (E, −SE) Cash (−A)	500	500	Cash, an asset, is decreased. Salary Exp. decreases Retained Earnings·
7. Company declares an $800 dividend to be paid later to its owners.	0 =		Dividends Pay. Ret. Earn. via Dividends 0	+800 −800	Dividends (−SE) Dividends Pay. (+L)	800	800	Dividends Pay., a liability, is increased. Dividends decreases Retained Earnings.

*See journal entry box in Figure 5–7.

Note: Accts. Rec. = Accounts Receivable; Accts. Pay. = Accounts Payable; Com. Stk. = Common Stock; Dividends Pay. = Dividends Payable; Notes Pay. = Notes Payable; Ret. Earn. = Retained Earnings; Salary Exp. = Salary Expense.

**Note: Typically, journal entries would not include the information in parentheses. This learning aid will help you determine the effect of the economic event on the financial statements. Most subsequent journal entries will include this information:

+ = increase and − = decrease; A = Asset; L = Liability; SE = Stockholders' Equity; R = Revenue; E = Expense; Ga = Gain; Lo = Loss;

Balance Sheet (A = L + SE)

Income Statement (R + Ga − E − Lo = NI)

The account names in each journal entry contained in Figure 5–8 are followed by parenthetical notations designed to indicate how the entry affects the fundamental accounting equation. We use this notation throughout the remainder of the text because it emphasizes the important relationship between the economic event represented by the journal entry and the accounting equation and, ultimately, the financial statements.

T-ACCOUNTS

When analyzing the effects of many economic events on the financial statements, it is useful to keep running tallies of the balances for each asset, liability, stockholders' equity, revenue, expense, and dividend account. This can be achieved by creating a T-account for each of the financial statement accounts. **T-accounts** are so named because they are in the form of a **T**—the left side of the T represents the debit side of the entry, and the right side corresponds to the credit side; for example, Figure 5–7 contains a T-account in each cell. Since journal entries also have a debit and credit side, the debited and credited dollar amounts are easily transferred (posted) to their respective T-accounts. The following example demonstrates how financial statements can be prepared from a group of economic events (transactions), each of which is represented by a journal entry, and the balances are maintained in T-accounts.

AN EXAMPLE. The December 31, 1996 balance sheet of Maple Services Company appears in Figure 5–9. The journal entries and associated T-accounts for ten transactions, entered into during 1997, are provided in Figure 5–10. Note first that the account balances from the balance sheet are the beginning balances in the T-accounts. Note also that the journal entries, numbered 1–10, are posted in the T-accounts. Review each journal entry and trace the dollar amounts of the debits and credits to the T-accounts. The financial statements, which appear in Figure 5–11, can be prepared directly from the T-accounts.

FIGURE 5–9	MAPLE SERVICES COMPANY BALANCE SHEET DECEMBER 31, 1996			
Maple Services balance sheet				
	ASSETS		**LIABILITIES AND STOCKHOLDERS' EQUITY**	
	Cash	$12,000	Salaries payable	$ 4,000
	Accounts receivable	9,000	Notes payable	6,000
	Land	15,000	Common stock	21,000
			Retained earnings	5,000
			Total liabilities and	
	Total assets	$36,000	stockholders' equity	$36,000

INCOME STATEMENT. The income statement for the period ending December 31, 1997 is prepared by subtracting the balances in the expense T-accounts (salary expense, rent expense, insurance expense, and interest expense) from the balances in the revenue T-accounts (service revenue), resulting in net income.

STATEMENT OF RETAINED EARNINGS. The statement of retained earnings for that same period consists of adding net income (or subtracting a net loss), which is taken from the income statement, to the beginning balance in the retained earnings

FIGURE 5-10

Maple Services Company

JOURNAL ENTRIES

(1)	Cash (+A)	5,000		(6)	Rent Expense (E, −SE)	500
	Common Stock (+SE)		5,000		Cash (−A)		500
	Issued common stock.				*Paid rent.*	
(2)	Land (+A)	7,000		(7)	Insurance Expense (E, −SE)	100
	Cash (−A)		7,000		Cash (−A)		100
	Purchased land.				*Paid for insurance coverage.*	
(3)	Salaries Payable (−L)	4,000		(8)	Salary Expense (E, −SE)	3,000
	Cash (−A)		4,000		Cash (−A)		3,000
	Paid salaries owed at the end of 1996.				*Paid salaries.*	
				(9)	Interest Expense (E, −SE)	500
(4)	Cash (+A)	6,000			Notes Payable (−L)	2,000
	Accounts Receivable (−A)		6,000		Cash (−A)		2,500
	Received cash on outstanding accounts receivable.				*Paid interest and principal on an outstanding loan.*	
(5)	Cash (+A)	7,000		(10)	Dividends (−SE)	1,000
	Service Revenue (R, +SE)		7,000		Cash (−A)		1,000
	Received cash for services provided.				*Paid cash dividend.*	

T-ACCOUNTS

CASH

	12,000			
(1)	5,000	(2)	7,000	
(4)	6,000	(3)	4,000	
(5)	7,000	(6)	500	
		(7)	100	
		(8)	3,000	
		(9)	2,500	
		(10)	1,000	
	11,900			

ACCOUNTS RECEIVABLE

9,000		(4)	6,000
3,000			

LAND

15,000		
(2)	7,000	
22,000		

SALARIES PAYABLE

		4,000	
(3)	4,000		
		0	

NOTES PAYABLE

		6,000	
(9)	2,000		
		4,000	

COMMON STOCK

	21,000	
	(1)	5,000
	26,000	

RETAINED EARNINGS

	5,000

SERVICE REVENUE

	(5) 7,000

SALARY EXPENSE

(8)	3,000

RENT EXPENSE

(6)	500

INSURANCE EXPENSE

(7)	100

INTEREST EXPENSE

(9)	500

DIVIDENDS

(10)	1,000

INCOME STATEMENT
FOR THE YEAR ENDED DECEMBER 31, 1997

Service revenue		$7,000
Expenses:		
Salaries	$3,000	
Rent	500	
Insurance	100	
Interest	500	
Total expenses		4,100
Net income		$2,900

STATEMENT OF RETAINED EARNINGS
FOR THE YEAR ENDED DECEMBER 31, 1997

Beginning retained earnings balance	$5,000
Plus: Net income	2,900
Less: Dividends	1,000
Ending retained earnings balance	$6,900

BALANCE SHEET
DECEMBER 31, 1997

ASSETS		LIABILITIES AND STOCKHOLDERS' EQUITY	
Cash	$11,900	Notes payable	$ 4,000
Accounts receivable	3,000	Common stock	26,000
Land	22,000	Retained earnings	6,900
		Total liabilities and	
Total assets	$36,900	stockholders' equity	$36,900

STATEMENT OF CASH FLOWS
DECEMBER 31, 1997

Operating activities:		
Cash receipts for services	$ 7,000	
Cash receipts from accounts receivable	6,000	
Cash payments for salaries	(7,000)	
Cash payments for rent	(500)	
Cash payments for insurance	(100)	
Cash payments for interest	(500)	
Cash increase (decrease) due to operating activities		$ 4,900
Investing activities:		
Cash payment for purchase of land	$(7,000)	
Cash increase (decrease) due to investing activities		(7,000)
Financing activities:		
Cash receipt from issuing stock	$ 5,000	
Cash payment for loan principal	(2,000)	
Cash payment for dividends	(1,000)	
Cash increase (decrease) due to financing activities		2,000
Increase (decrease) in cash balance		$ (100)
Beginning cash balance		12,000
Ending cash balance		$11,900

T-account ($5,000), and then subtracting the balance in the dividends T-account ($1,000), which represents the amount declared during the period. The result ($6,900) is the ending (December 31, 1997) balance in retained earnings.

BALANCE SHEET. The December 31, 1997 balance sheet consists of the balances in the asset (cash, accounts receivable, land), liability (notes payable), and stockholders' equity (common stock and retained earnings) T-accounts. Note that the ending balance in retained earnings ($6,900), which was computed on the statement of retained earnings, appears on the balance sheet.

The dollar amounts on the balance sheet represent the beginning balances for asset, liability, and stockholders' equity T-accounts for the next period (1998). Since the dollar amounts in the revenue, expense, and dividend accounts are reflected in the ending balance of retained earnings, the revenue, expense, and dividend T-accounts begin the next period (1998) with zero balances. The balance sheet accounts are described as *permanent* because their balances accumulate from one period to the next. The income statement and dividend accounts are described as *temporary* because their balances begin each new period at zero.[2]

STATEMENT OF CASH FLOWS. The statement of cash flows is prepared from the cash T-account. Each cash inflow and outflow is classified as operating, investing, or financing and then placed on the statement. This statement reconciles the change in the cash balance during the period, expressing it in terms of cash increases (decreases) due to operating, investing, and financing activities.

LO 4 After you review how the financial statements were prepared, take a moment to study how each journal entry affected each financial statement. As stated before, it is important that managers understand the mechanical process linking transactions, which are represented by journal entries, to the financial statements.

RECOGNIZING GAINS AND LOSSES

Companies often sell investments and noncurrent assets, receiving dollar amounts that do not match the amounts at which the investments are carried on the balance sheet. In such cases a gain or loss must be recognized in the amount of the difference between the proceeds and the carrying amount. Several years ago, for example, McDonnell Douglas sold its North American Field Service business for $100 million. Since this investment was carried on the company's balance sheet at $71 million, McDonnell Douglas recognized a $29 million gain on the transaction. Assuming that the business was acquired for $71 million, the following journal entries were used to record these events. (Dollar amounts are in millions.)

Investment (+A)	71	
Cash (−A)		71

Acquired North American Field Service for cash.

Cash (+A)	100	
Investment (−A)		71
Gain on sale (Ga, +SE)		29

Sold North American Field Service for gain.

2. In actual accounting systems the year-end balances in the revenue, expense, and dividend accounts are formally transferred to retained earnings through a series of journal entries. This closing process zeroes out the balances in the temporary accounts so that they begin at zero the next period. The closing process is part of the accounting cycle, which is covered in Appendix 5A.

If McDonnell Douglas would have sold the business for an amount less than the $71 million carrying amount, $55 million for example, a loss would have been recognized in the following manner.

Cash (+A)	**55**	
Loss on sale (Lo, −SE)	**16**	
Investment (−A)		**71**

Sold North American Field Service for loss.

Note that the gain or loss serves two purposes in the entry to record the sale: (1) it measures the profit or loss on the transaction in the amount of the difference between the proceeds and the balance sheet value of the investment, and (2) it acts as a "plug" number which makes the dollar amount debited in the journal entry equal the dollar amount credited. Note also that the gain or loss is a temporary account, which appears on the income statement. In addition, the cash proceeds from the investment would appear on the statement of cash flows under cash flows from investing activities.

PERIODIC ADJUSTMENTS

LO 5   Up to now the discussion has focused on the financial statement effects of exchange transactions—transactions backed by documented evidence, in which assets and/or liabilities are transferred between parties. Assets and liabilities, however, are often created or discharged without the occurrence of a visible, documentable exchange transaction. They sometimes build up or expire as time passes. Interest, for example, is earned continually on bank savings accounts, and machinery depreciates as it is used in a company's operations. Such phenomena are not evidenced by exchange transactions, but can be very important to a company's performance and financial condition.

Net income for a particular period is measured by (1) recognizing revenues when the earning process is complete and (2) matching against those revenues the expenses incurred to generate them. Under this view of performance, called the **accrual system of accounting,** revenues are booked when assets are created (or liabilities are discharged) and expenses are recorded when liabilities arise (or assets are reduced). In other words, revenues and expenses can be recognized either before or after the related cash is received or paid. The accrual system requires that periodic adjustments be made to the financial statements so that net income for a given period of time will be the result of a proper matching of the revenues and expenses within that period.

Periodic adjustments take one of three forms: (1) accruals, (2) cost expirations, and (3) revaluations. The first two are covered in this chapter; revaluation adjustments are covered in subsequent chapters as they arise.

ACCRUALS

Accruals refer to amounts in asset and liability accounts that build up over time. The term *accrue* simply means to build up gradually.[3] Two very common examples are accrued wages and accrued interest.

---

3. Note that the term accrual refers to a system of accounting, which recognizes revenues and expenses as assets and liabilities are created or discharged, as well as one of two kinds of adjusting entries. The double meaning of this term can be a source of confusion, and it is important that you be aware of the context in which it is used.

ACCRUED WAGES

Suppose that employees of Taylor Motor are paid at the end of each week. The total weekly payroll is $10,000, which is earned at a rate of $2,000 per day for each of the five working days. Assume that December 31 falls on a Tuesday, and the financial statements are prepared as of that day. Figure 5–12 illustrates these facts and the journal entries that would be recorded under accrual accounting.

FIGURE 5-12

Accrued wages

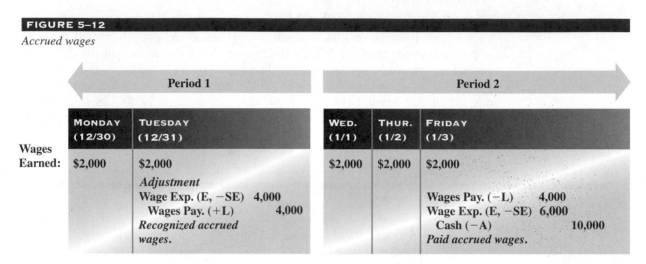

In applying the accrual system, it must be recognized that although no cash has been paid as of December 31, a liability has been created. The company owes its employees two days' worth of wages, or $4,000. This liability is recognized with an adjusting journal entry of the form indicated in Figure 5–12. Wage Expense of $4,000 is reflected on the income statement of the period ending on December 31 (Period 1). Wages Payable of $4,000 appears in the liability section of the December 31 balance sheet, and the amount is carried into Period 2. Note that on Friday, when the $10,000 cash payment for wages is made, $4,000 serves to remove the Wages Payable (the liability is discharged), and $6,000 is charged to Wage Expense of Period 2 and thus will appear on the income statement of Period 2.

The adjustment in this example achieves matching, in that it matches the cost of the effort expended by the employees in Period 1 with the revenues generated in Period 1. Wage expense of $4,000 is subtracted from Period 1 revenues in the computation of Period 1 net income. Similarly, the cost of the effort expended by the employees in Period 2 ($6,000) is matched against Period 2 revenues on the Period 2 income statement.

It is also important to realize that Taylor would prepare statements of cash flows for Periods 1 and 2 and the entire $10,000 cash payment would be reflected in the operating section of that statement in the second period only. None of it would appear on the statement of cash flows of Period 1. As Figure 5–13 indicates, the total resource expenditure recognized under the accrual system is the same as that recognized under the cash system. The difference lies in the timing of the recognition. Due to the adjustment, the accrual system recognizes $4,000 in Period 1 and $6,000 in Period 2.

FIGURE 5-13	ACCOUNTING SYSTEM/FINANCIAL STATEMENT	PERIOD 1	PERIOD 2	PERIOD 3
Expenditure recognition	Accrual/Income statement	$4,000	$ 6,000	$10,000
	Cash/Statement of cash flows	0	10,000	10,000

ACCRUED INTEREST

Suppose that on December 1, BankAmerica Corporation loans $12,000 to Exxon Oil Company at an annual interest rate of 10 percent. Assume that the accounting period ends on December 31 and that Exxon pays BankAmerica in full (principal and interest) on January 31 of the next year. Figure 5–14 illustrates these facts and the journal entries that would be recorded under accrual accounting.

FIGURE 5–14

Accrued interest revenue

Period 1

DECEMBER 1

Note Rec. (+A)	12,000	
Cash (−A)		12,000
Received note for cash.		

DECEMBER 31

Adjustment

Interest Rec. (+A)	100	
Interest Rev. (R, +SE)		100
Recognized accrued interest received.		

Period 2

JANUARY 31

Cash (+A)	12,200	
Interest Rec. (−A)		100
Interest Rev. (R, +SE)		100
Note Rec. (−A)		12,000
Received cash on outstanding note.		

BankAmerica records an adjustment on December 31, to reflect the fact that an asset, Interest Receivable, has been created. The company has earned $100 [($12,000 × 10%)/12 months] in interest during the month of December. Interest Receivable in that amount is recognized (debited), and Interest Revenue is credited. When the $12,200 cash payment is received on January 31, $12,000 serves to reduce the outstanding note receivable, $100 is charged against the Interest Receivable account, and the remaining $100 is recognized as Interest Revenue.

As in the example of accrued wages, the adjustment here helps to achieve a matching of revenues and expenses in the appropriate time period. It does so by dividing the total interest earned on the loan ($200) into two components, based on the periods in which it was earned and the time when the asset, Interest Receivable, was created. Half of the $200 interest payment was earned in Period 1 and therefore should appear as a revenue on the income statement of Period 1. The remaining $100 should appear as a revenue on the income statement of Period 2 because the loan was outstanding during one month of Period 2.

Consider again the effect of these transactions on the statements of cash flows for Periods 1 and 2. No cash inflow is recorded in Period 1, and therefore nothing would be reflected on the statement of cash flows for that period. Instead, all $200 would appear on the statement of cash flows in Period 2, when the cash is actually received. Once again, the total interest recognized across the two periods under the cash system ($200) is the same as that recognized under the accrual system, but the timing of the recognition is different. The adjusting journal entry prepared under the accrual system ensures that $100 is recognized on the income statement of Period 1, with the remaining $100 appearing on the income statement of Period 2.

Figure 5–15, using the same facts as Figure 5–14, considers the borrower's (Exxon's) point of view. Examine the journal entries, and note especially how the adjusting journal entry matches revenues and expenses in the appropriate time period and gives rise to expense recognition in a time period when no cash payment is made.

FIGURE 5-15

Accrued interest expense

Period 1		Period 2
DECEMBER 1	**DECEMBER 31**	**JANUARY 31**

Cash (+A)   12,000
    Note Pay. (+L)   12,000
Borrowed cash and
issued note payable.
	Adjustment
	Interest Exp. (E, −SE) 100
	    Interest Pay. (+L) 100
	Recognized accrued
	interest payable.
		Note Pay. (−L) 12,000
		Interest Pay. (−L) 100
		Interest Exp. (E, −SE) 100
		    Cash (−A) 12,200
		Paid interest and
		outstanding note.

COST EXPIRATIONS

The second type of adjustment is called a **cost expiration**. Like accruals, these adjusting entries (1) are recorded in the books at the end of an accounting period to achieve an appropriate matching of revenues and expenses and (2) do not reflect cash exchanges. However, rather than building up an account over time, as is done with an accrual, these adjusting entries serve to *write down* an already-established account. In a sense, cost expirations represent the "flip side" of accruals.

ASSET CAPITALIZATION AND THE MATCHING PRINCIPLE

Before studying cost expirations, you should understand one very important concept in financial accounting measurement—*asset capitalization* and how it relates to the matching principle. The **matching principle** involves a four-step process: (1) a cost is incurred in the current period for the purpose of generating revenue, (2) the revenue recognition principle determines the period in which the revenue is recognized, (3) if the revenue is recognized in the current period, the cost is **expensed** (appearing on the income statement as an expense); if the revenue is expected to be recognized in a future period, the cost is **capitalized** (appearing on the balance sheet as an asset), and (4) capitalized costs are converted to expenses (by recording cost expiration adjusting journal entries) in those future periods when revenue is recognized. Assets, by definition, are expected to generate economic benefits in the form of future revenues and, according to the matching principle, the costs of acquiring assets should be matched against those benefits when they are recognized. The accrual system of accounting accomplishes this matching by initially capitalizing the costs of assets and then converting them to expenses (through periodic adjustments) as their usefulness expires and their benefits are realized.

EXPENSE OR CAPITALIZE EXAMPLES

Figure 5–16 illustrates the basic procedures used to account for expenses and capitalized costs. It is divided into two sections. The upper section depicts the matching process. The lower section consists of nine different transactions, each carried through the four steps involved in applying the matching principle.

FIGURE 5–16

Expense or capitalize?

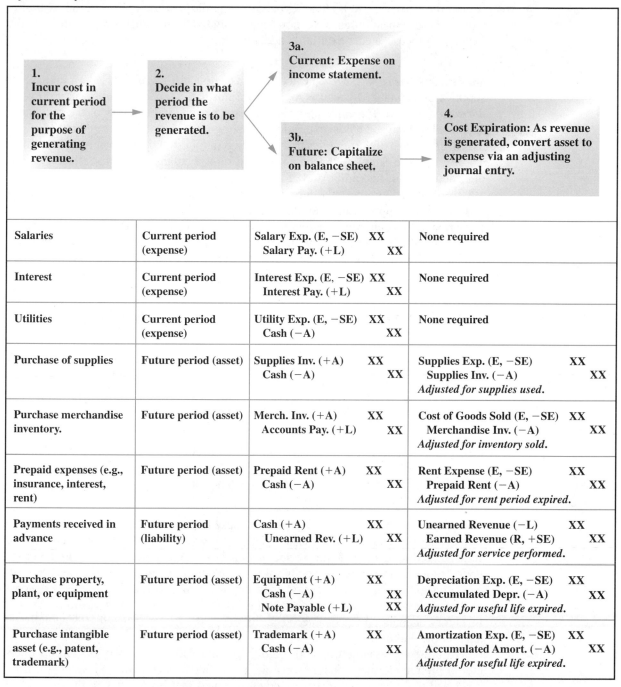

Salaries	Current period (expense)	Salary Exp. (E, −SE) XX Salary Pay. (+L) XX	None required
Interest	Current period (expense)	Interest Exp. (E, −SE) XX Interest Pay. (+L) XX	None required
Utilities	Current period (expense)	Utility Exp. (E, −SE) XX Cash (−A) XX	None required

Purchase of supplies	Future period (asset)	Supplies Inv. (+A) XX
		    Cash (−A) XX
			Supplies Exp. (E, −SE) XX
			    Supplies Inv. (−A) XX
			Adjusted for supplies used.

Purchase merchandise inventory.	Future period (asset)	Merch. Inv. (+A) XX
		    Accounts Pay. (+L) XX
			Cost of Goods Sold (E, −SE) XX
			    Merchandise Inv. (−A) XX
			Adjusted for inventory sold.

Prepaid expenses (e.g., insurance, interest, rent)	Future period (asset)	Prepaid Rent (+A) XX
		    Cash (−A) XX
			Rent Expense (E, −SE) XX
			    Prepaid Rent (−A) XX
			Adjusted for rent period expired.

Payments received in advance	Future period (liability)	Cash (+A) XX
		    Unearned Rev. (+L) XX
			Unearned Revenue (−L) XX
			    Earned Revenue (R, +SE) XX
			Adjusted for service performed.

Purchase property, plant, or equipment	Future period (asset)	Equipment (+A) XX
		    Cash (−A) XX
		    Note Payable (+L) XX
			Depreciation Exp. (E, −SE) XX
			    Accumulated Depr. (−A) XX
			Adjusted for useful life expired.

Purchase intangible asset (e.g., patent, trademark)	Future period (asset)	Trademark (+A) XX
		    Cash (−A) XX
			Amortization Exp. (E, −SE) XX
			    Accumulated Amort. (−A) XX
			Adjusted for useful life expired.

CURRENT EXPENSES. The first three transactions (salaries, interest, and utilities) represent resource expenditures, either through the creation of a liability or the payment of cash, for which the benefit is assumed to be realized in the current period. Salaries and interest in this case are accrued at the end of the current period with an accrual adjusting journal entry, and the associated cash payments expected to follow in a future period. The utility expense is both recognized and paid in the current period. Since the benefit from each of these three expenditures is assumed to be realized in the current period, all are expensed, regardless of the timing of the cash payment. These expenditures have not been capitalized and, therefore, Step 4 in the matching process, a cost expiration adjusting journal entry, is not necessary.

SUPPLIES INVENTORY. The fourth transaction in Figure 5–16, the purchase of supplies, is capitalized because supplies are normally expected to be useful beyond the current period. Typically, at the end of each period, an inventory of the remaining supplies is taken, and a cost expiration adjusting journal entry is entered in the books to reflect the cost of the supplies that were used (expired) during the period. This entry also restates the Supplies Inventory account on the balance sheet to reflect the supplies actually on hand at the end of the period.

To illustrate, assume that during 1994 Deere and Company purchased materials and supplies to support the manufacture of farm machinery at a total cost of $700. On December 31 a count revealed that supplies in the amount of $300 remained on hand. If the company began the year with $500 in the Supplies account, the cost of the supplies used during 1994 would be computed as shown below, and the following journal entries would have been recorded to reflect these facts.

Supplies Used = Beginning Inventory + Purchases − Ending Inventory
$$\$900 \quad = \quad \$500 \quad + \quad \$700 \quad - \quad \$300$$

1994: PURCHASE OF SUPPLIES		**DEC. 31: COST EXPIRATION ADJUSTING ENTRY**	
Supplies Inventory (+A)	700	Supplies Expense (E, −SE)	900
Cash (−A)	700	Supplies Inventory (−A)	900
Purchased supplies.		*Recognized use of supplies.*	

In this situation, supplies in the amount of $300 would be reported on the company's December 31 balance sheet. In reality, Deere and Company reported $206 million of materials and supplies on its 1994 balance sheet.

MERCHANDISE INVENTORY. The purchase of merchandise inventory is capitalized because inventories are expected to generate revenues in the future when they are sold. According to the matching principle, the cost of the merchandise should be converted to an expense, cost of goods sold, in the period when the inventories are sold. As with supplies, the end-of-period expiration adjusting journal entry reflects the cost of the inventories that were used (sold) during the period. It also serves to restate the Inventory account on the balance sheet to reflect the merchandise that is actually on hand at the end of the period.[4]

To illustrate, assume that Federated Department Stores, the world's largest operator of premier department stores, purchased $5,000 of merchandise inventory during 1994 and that a year-end inventory count revealed that inventories in the amount of $3,000 remained on hand. Assuming that the company began the year with inventories valued at $2,000, cost of goods sold would be computed as follows and the following journal entries would be recorded to reflect these facts.

---

4. This chapter assumes that Cost of Goods Sold is determined at the end of the year with a cost expiration adjusting journal entry. This procedure describes the periodic inventory method. The perpetual inventory method, which recognizes Cost of Goods Sold each time inventory is sold, is discussed in Chapter 7, which covers inventories more completely.

Cost of Goods Sold = Beginning Inventory + Purchases − Ending Inventory
      $4,000   = $2,000   + $5,000   − $3,000

1994: PURCHASE OF MERCHANDISE		DEC. 31: COST EXPIRATION ADJUSTING ENTRY	
Merchandise Inv. (+A) 5,000		Cost of Goods Sold (E, −SE) 4,000	
Cash (−A)	5,000	Merchandise Inv. (−A)	4,000
Purchased merchandise.		*Adjusted for inventory sold.*	

In this example, Federated would report merchandise inventory of $3,000 on its 1994 balance sheet and cost of goods sold of $4,000 on its income statement. Actually, the company reported merchandise inventories of $2.4 billion and cost of goods sold (sales) of $5.1 billion on its 1994 financial statements.

PREPAID EXPENSES. Prepaid expenses represent costs like insurance, interest, and rent that are paid in advance, before the associated benefit is realized. Insurance premiums, for example, are paid in advance and usually cover an entire year or more. Similarly, interest on loans is sometimes paid before the borrowed funds are used. In applying the matching principle, such prepayments are capitalized and then converted to expenses as the time period expires and benefits are realized. This periodic conversion is achieved through cost expiration adjusting journal entries.

To illustrate, assume that on January 1, 1994 Sprint purchased a $1,000 insurance premium for a two-year period. The following journal entries would be made on the books of Sprint over the life of the insurance coverage.

JAN. 1, 1994: PURCHASE OF INSURANCE		DEC. 31, 1994 AND 1995: COST EXPIRATION ADJUSTING ENTRY	
Prepaid Insurance (+A) 1,000		Insurance Expense (E, −SE) 500	
Cash (−A)	1,000	Prepaid Insurance (−A)	500
Paid insurance in advance.		*Adjusted for expiration of insurance.*	

In this example Sprint would report in the current asset section of its 1994 balance sheet $500 of prepaid (unexpired) insurance, which would be converted to an expense at the end of 1995. Sprint's actual 1994 balance sheet showed prepaid expenses of $144 million, which represented approximately 1 percent of total assets.

UNEARNED (DEFERRED) REVENUES. Unearned revenues are the reverse of prepaid expenses. For every entity that prepays an expense before the associated benefit is realized, another entity receives a payment before it performs the required service. When applying the revenue recognition principle to the entity that receives payment and has yet to provide the service, a liability account, called **Unearned Revenues**, is credited when the cash is initially collected. This account is then converted to a revenue as the service is performed with an end-of-period adjusting journal entry.[5]

To illustrate, suppose that Time Warner, the publisher of *Time, Sports Illustrated,* and other well-known magazines, received $5,000 during 1994 for magazine sub-

---

5. Technically, an unearned revenue does not represent a capitalized cost because it is not an asset, and therefore, the adjusting journal entry to convert it to a revenue is not a cost expiration adjusting journal entry. However, we have chosen to categorize it as such because the concept of deferring the recognition of a revenue until the service is performed is the same as deferring the recognition of an expense until the associated benefit is realized. Both are essential to implementing the matching principle.

scriptions to be fulfilled during 1994 and 1995. Time Warner's Cash account would immediately increase by $5,000, but the company would not recognize revenue at that time because it had not yet performed the contracted service. Instead, Time Warner would recognize a $5,000 liability, indicating that it owed services in the form of magazines to its subscribers. Assume that as of the end of 1994 Time Warner had fulfilled 60 percent of the subscriptions. At that time, therefore, an adjusting journal entry would be recorded to remove 60 percent of the liability from the company's balance sheet and, at the same time, recognize 60 percent of the revenue. The following journal entries reflect these facts.

RECEIPT OF ADVANCE PAYMENT		COST EXPIRATION ADJUSTING ENTRY	
Cash (+A)	5,000	Unearned Revenue (−L)	3,000
Unearned Revenue (+L)	5,000	Fees Earned (R, +SE)	3,000
Received cash prior to providing		*Recognized revenue from providing*	
service.		*service.*	

This sequence of journal entries would leave a liability for Unearned Revenues on Time Warner's 1994 balance sheet of $2,000, representing subscriptions that Time Warner still had to fulfill. In 1994 Time Warner actually reported unearned revenues of $631 million in the liability section of its balance sheet.

PROPERTY, PLANT, AND EQUIPMENT. Transaction 8 in Figure 5–16 considers the costs of purchasing property, plant, and equipment. Since these assets are expected to help generate revenues beyond the current time period, the matching principle specifies that the acquisition costs be capitalized and systematically converted to an expense (**amortized**) over the estimated useful lives of the assets. At the end of each period of the estimated useful life, a cost expiration adjusting journal entry is recorded to amortize a portion of the capitalized cost. The process of amortizing the cost of property, plant, and equipment is called **depreciation**.

To illustrate, assume that The Boeing Company, the world's largest airplane manufacturer, invested $10,000 in equipment on January 1, 1994. At the time of the purchase, Boeing management subjectively estimated that the equipment would have a useful life of ten years and chose to depreciate an equal amount of the capitalized cost ($1,000 = $10,000/10 years) at the end of each of the ten one-year periods. The following journal entries would have been recorded in Boeing's books.

JAN. 1, 1994: PURCHASE OF EQUIPMENT		DEC. 31, 1994, 1995 . . . , 2003: COST EXPIRATION ADJUSTING ENTRY	
Equipment (+A)	10,000	Depr. Exp. (E, −SE)	1,000
Cash (−A)	10,000	Accumulated Depr. (−A)	1,000
Purchased equipment.		*Adjusted for depreciation on*	
		equipment.	

Note that the cost expiration adjusting journal entry involves a debit to Depreciation Expense that appears on the income statement for each of the ten years. It also involves a credit to an account called Accumulated Depreciation, instead of a credit to the Equipment account itself. Accumulated Depreciation is a special permanent account that appears on the asset side of the balance sheet. It offsets the asset account to which it applies (i.e., Equipment), maintaining an accumulated balance of the amount of depreciation taken on the asset up to the date of the balance sheet. Balance sheet accounts like Accumulated Depreciation, which are used to offset other balance sheet accounts, are called **contra accounts**. Subtracting the balance in the Accumulated Depreciation account from the original cost of the equipment on the balance sheet gives rise to a number referred to as **net book value**.

Using the same information as in the preceding example, at the end of the second year (December 31, 1995) the Equipment account would appear on Boeing's balance sheet as follows. The original cost of the equipment is $10,000, the accumulated depreciation is $2,000, and the net book value is $8,000.

Equipment	$10,000	
Less: Accumulated depreciation	2,000	$8,000

In reality, Boeing purchased over $795 million of plant and equipment in 1994, recognized over $1 billion in depreciation, and the related portion of the company's 1994 balance sheet appeared as follows (dollars in billions).

Property, plant, and equipment (at cost)	$13,588	
Less: Accumulated depreciation	6,786	$6,802

Estimating the useful life of property, plant, and equipment and choosing a method of allocating the capitalized cost to future periods is a subjective and difficult task for management. These choices can also have a significant effect on the amount of net income recognized each year because they have a direct bearing on the amount of depreciation expense that appears on the income statement. To illustrate the importance of such estimates, several years ago Delta Airlines decided to change the useful life estimate of its flight equipment from ten years to fifteen years. The company disclosed in its financial report that the change decreased depreciation expense of that year by $130 million.

INTANGIBLE ASSETS. The final transaction in Figure 5–16 is the purchase of an intangible asset, such as a patent, trademark, or goodwill. The cost of this purchase is, once again, capitalized because the benefit of the purchase is expected to extend beyond the current period. Many intangibles have definable lives (often determined by law) over which the capitalized cost is typically amortized. The cost expiration adjusting journal entry consists of a debit to Amortization Expense and a credit to the contra account, Accumulated Amortization.

To illustrate, assume that Johnson & Johnson, a leading manufacturer of consumer health care products, purchased a patent for $34,000, which was determined by law to have a seventeen-year life. The following journal entries would be recorded by Johnson & Johnson over the patent's legal life.

PURCHASE OF PATENT		END OF EACH OF 17 SUBSEQUENT YEARS: COST EXPIRATION ADJUSTING ENTRY	
Patent (+A)	34,000	Amortization Exp. (E, −SE)	2,000
Cash (−A)	34,000	Accumulated Amort. (−A)	2,000
Acquired patent.		*Adjusted for amortization of patent.*	

In its 1994 annual report Johnson & Johnson actually reported intangible assets in the manner illustrated below. The disclosure indicated that these assets, which are amortized evenly over their useful lives, consist primarily of patents, trademarks, and goodwill. The useful life of a patent is normally seventeen years, and goodwill is amortized over a 40-year period.

	1994*	1993*
Intangible assets	$2,667	$1,255
Less: Accumulated amortization	264	330
Net book value	$2,403	$ 925

*Dollars in millions

CAPITALIZING AND MATCHING: EXAMPLES

Figure 5–17 contains several examples where cost expiration adjusting journal entries are used to apply the matching principle. Such entries are designed to convert capitalized costs to expenses in future time periods as the benefits (revenues) from the initial expenditures are recognized. The transactions illustrated in Figure 5–17 consider supplies, merchandise inventory, prepaid insurance, unearned revenue, equipment, and a patent.

The $100 capitalized cost of supplies is converted to supplies expense as the supplies are used. The $600 capitalized cost of inventory is converted to cost of goods sold as the inventories are sold. The capitalized costs of prepaid insurance, equipment, and the patent are amortized over the determinable, estimated, or legal life of each of these assets. These costs are allocated to future time periods by converting them to insurance expense, depreciation expense, and amortization expense, respectively, as their useful lives expire. The $240 received in advance is recorded as unearned revenue (a liability) and converted to fees earned (a revenue) as the contracted service is performed.

Note in Figure 5–17 that equal amounts of the cost of the equipment and the patent are depreciated, or amortized, in each of the three time periods. For example, the $9,000 equipment cost is depreciated at a rate of $3,000 per period. This method is referred to as **straight-line depreciation**. It is almost always used to amortize intangible assets, but it is only one of several methods that can be used to depreciate the capitalized costs of property, plant, and equipment.

As you study Figure 5–17, note that the cost expiration adjusting journal entries display the same features that characterize accrual adjustments: (1) they achieve matching by allocating the cost of the asset to the period in which the benefit is realized and (2) they do not reflect cash exchanges.

REVALUATION ADJUSTMENTS

At various points in the remainder of this text, we cover adjustments that do not fall into the categories of accruals or cost expirations. Such adjustments serve to restate certain accounts to keep their reported values in line with existing facts. For example, the balance sheet dollar amounts of short-term investments, accounts receivable, and inventories are sometimes adjusted when the market values of these assets change. The entries required in such situations are called **revaluation adjustments.**

FIGURE 5-17

Capitalize and match

CAPITALIZE →	ADJUSTING ENTRIES DURING COST EXPIRATION PERIOD →			EXPLANATION
	1	2	3	

Supplies (+A)   100
  Cash (−A)   100
Purchased supplies.
	Sup. Exp. (E, −SE) 30
	  Supplies (−A) 30
	Supplies costing $70 on hand.
		Sup. Exp. (E, −SE) 50
		  Supplies (−A) 50
		Supplies costing $20 on hand.
			Sup. Exp. (E, −SE) 20
			  Supplies (−A) 20
			No supplies on hand.
				The cost of supplies is converted to expense as the supplies are used up.

Inventory (+A) 600
  Accts. Pay. (−L)   600
Purchased 6 items at $100 per item.
	COGS (E, −SE) 100
	  Inventory (−A) 100
	One item sold.
		COGS (E, −SE) 200
		  Inventory (−A) 200
		Two items sold.
			COGS (E, −SE) 300
			  Inventory (−A) 300
			Three items sold.
				The cost of inventory is converted to expense (Cost of Goods Sold) as the inventory is sold.

Pre. Ins. (+A)   300
  Cash (−A)   300
Paid 3 years of insurance coverage in advance.
	Ins. Exp. (E, −SE) 100
	  Prepaid Ins. (−A) 100
	The first year of insurance coverage expires.
		Ins. Exp. (E, −SE) 100
		  Prepaid Ins. (−A) 100
		The second year of insurance coverage expires.
			Ins. Exp. (E, −SE) 100
			  Prepaid Ins. (−A) 100
			The third year of insurance coverage expires.
				The cost of prepaid insurance is converted to expense as the insurance coverage expires.

Cash (+A)   240
  Un. Rev. (+L)   240
Received $240 for services to be performed later.
	Un. Rev. (−L) 120
	  Fees Earned (R, +SE) 120
	Half of the service is performed.
		Un. Rev. (−L) 60
		  Fees Earned (R, +SE) 60
		One quarter of the service is performed.
			Un. Rev. (−L) 60
			  Fees Earned (R, +SE) 60
			One quarter of the service is performed.
				Revenue is recognized as the service is completed.

Equip. (+A)   9,000
  Notes Pay. (+L)   9,000
Purchased machinery with an estimated 3-year life and no salvage value.
	Depr. Exp. (E, −SE) 3,000
	  Accum. Depr. (−A) 3,000
	First year passes assuming straight-line depreciation rate.
		Depr. Exp. (E, −SE) 3,000
		  Accum. Depr. (−A) 3,000
		Second year passes.
			Depr. Exp. (E, −SE) 3,000
			  Accum. Depr. (−A) 3,000
			Third year passes.
				The cost of machinery is converted to expense (Depreciation Expense) as the estimated useful life passes.

Patent (+A)   900
  Cash (−A)   900
Acquired patent with 3-year legal life.
	Amort. Exp. (E, −SE) 300
	  Accum. Amort. (−A) 300
	First year passes assuming straight-line amortization rate.
		Amort. Exp. (E, −SE) 300
		  Accum. Amort. (−A) 300
		Second year passes.
			Amort. Exp. (E, −SE) 300
			  Accum. Amort. (−A) 300
			Third year passes.
				The cost of obtaining the patent is converted to an expense (Amortization Expense) as the legal life passes.

FINANCIAL STATEMENT PRESENTATION IN A MULTINATIONAL ENVIRONMENT

In this chapter we have covered the mechanics of preparing financial statements, measured in U.S. dollars, written in the English language, and using U.S. accounting principles. We now briefly discuss how **multinationals**, corporations that have their home in one country but operate and live under the laws of other countries as well, report to stockholders, creditors, and other interested parties who transact in different currencies, speak different languages, and are familiar with different accounting principles. There are five basic approaches: (1) do nothing, (2) translate the language only, (3) translate the language, and express monetary amounts in the foreign currency, (4) translate the language, express monetary amounts in the foreign currency, and restate accounting principles, and (5) prepare financial statements based on "world" accounting principles.

The first approach is followed by most of the multinational companies based in the United States. These companies choose not to adjust their statements because they raise most of their capital in the United States, and the English language, the dollar, and U.S. accounting principles are well known throughout the world. The second and third approaches are popular for multinationals based in Europe, whose capital providers reside in any of a number of countries that use different languages and foreign currencies. These companies, such as the German-based Volkswagen Group, typically prepare English, French, German, and Spanish versions, expecting that any reader will understand at least one.

Complete restatements, approach (4), are prepared by a number of Japanese multinationals, like Honda and Mitsubishi. Many of these companies list their common stock shares on the New York and American Stock Exchanges, which require that all registrants follow U.S. generally accepted accounting principles. A small number of companies, like the oil giant Royal/Dutch Shell, prepare financial statements that attempt to synthesize the "best" accounting practices of all countries. Such statements, which are intended to satisfy all user needs on a global basis, are often based

In the late 1980s and early 1990s many corporations recorded large "restructuring" expenses on their income statements. An article appearing in *The Wall Street Journal* (November 2, 1994) stated:

"It's a big issue involving a lot of bucks on the bottom line for companies . . . it involves large write-offs and big numbers. So big that some investors call such charges 'the big bath.' The routine is familiar: Behemoth Co. announces heavy layoffs and plant closings, and a big charge against earnings to make up for its mistakes. To the uninitiated, it may seem odd when the stock [price] jumps in response. But investors love restructurings because, following a jumbo charge against earnings, a company's profit nearly always improves sharply. That's because lots of companies write off certain expenses all at once that would otherwise be a drag to earnings over a longer period. 'This is guaranteed to make future earnings look better—guaranteed,' says

Robert Willens, an account analyst at Lehman Brothers."

The FASB is considering changing the rules in this area because many of these restructuring costs involve the premature accrual of future costs, often involving the recognition of costs that have not yet been incurred. For example, some companies have been known to accrue an estimate of the future costs of developing software that will be used to make the company more efficient after the restructuring.

ETHICS IN THE REAL WORLD

ETHICAL ISSUE

Is it ethical for a company to recognize a large restructuring expense, including the accrual of costs that have not yet been incurred, in a case where management believes that the practice represents conservative reporting and will help to bolster future profits as well as the price of the company's stock?

on the accounting principles established by the International Accounting Standards Committee (IASC).

The *Wall Street Journal* (August 29, 1995) recently reported that the IASC has just agreed to develop accounting standards by mid-1999 for companies seeking stock lists in global markets to raise cross-border capital. Both the SEC and the New York Stock Exchange have expressed support for such standards because it would encourage more non-U.S. companies to list their securities in the U.S. exchanges. However, some analysts fear that these standards will encourage lower quality reporting and introduce comparability problems, making it more difficult for investors.

REVIEW PROBLEM

Consider the balance sheet of a small retail company, Kelly Supply, as of December 31, 1996 (Figure 5–18). Exchange transactions that occurred during 1997 are recorded in Figure 5–19 and posted to T-accounts in Figure 5–20. The financial statements are contained in Figures 5–21 and 5–22.

The December 31, 1996 balance sheet accounts are reflected in the T-accounts as beginning balances. The exchange transactions are numbered (1)–(11) and each is described and has been posted in the T-accounts.

At year end, the adjusting journal entries are recorded and posted to the T-accounts. Adjusting entries are numbered (12)–(19). Entries (14), (17), and (18) are accruals, and entries (12), (13), (15), (16) and (19) are cost expirations.

The income statement contains revenues and expenses; the statement of retained earnings explains the change in the retained earnings balance; and the balance sheet consists of the ending balances in the asset, liability, and stockholders' equity accounts. The statement of cash flows was prepared directly from the entries in the Cash T-account.

FIGURE 5–18	KELLY SUPPLY BALANCE SHEET DECEMBER 31, 1996

Balance sheet for Kelly Supply

ASSETS			LIABILITIES AND STOCKHOLDERS' EQUITY	
Cash		$12,000	Accounts payable	$ 8,000
Accounts receivable		15,000	Wages payable	3,000
Merchandise inventory		12,000	Interest payable	1,000
Prepaid rent		3,000	Dividends payable	2,000
Machinery	$25,000		Unearned revenue	3,000
Less: Accum. depr.	5,000	20,000	Short-term notes pay.	5,000
Patent		5,000	Long-term notes pay.	10,000
			Common stock	30,000
			Retained earnings	5,000
			Total liabilities and	
Total assets		$67,000	stockholders' equity	$67,000

FIGURE 5–19

General journal for Kelly Supply

DAILY JOURNAL ENTRIES			ADJUSTING JOURNAL ENTRIES		

DAILY JOURNAL ENTRIES

(1) Cash (+A)   10,000
    Accounts Receivable (+A)   15,000
      Sales (R, +SE)   25,000
*Sold merchandise for cash and
on account.*

(2) Cash (+A)   8,000
    Accounts Receivable (−A)   8,000
Received cash on account.

(3) Merchandise Inventory (+A) 10,000
    Cash (−A)   3,000
    Accounts Payable (+L)   7,000
*Purchased merchandise inventory
for cash and on account.*

(4) Accounts Payable (−L)   10,000
    Cash (−A)   10,000
Paid cash on account.

(5) Wages Payable (−L)   3,000
    Wage Expense (E, −SE)   7,000
    Cash (−A)   10,000
Paid accrued wages.

(6) Interest Payable (−L)   1,000
    Interest Expense (E, −SE)   1,000
    Cash (−A)   2,000
Paid accrued interest.

(7) Short-Term Notes Pay. (−L)   2,500
    Cash (−A)   2,500
Paid short-term note.

(8) Cash (+A)   10,000
    Long-Term Notes Pay. (+L)   10,000
Issued long-term note for cash.

(9) Dividends Payable (−L)   2,000
    Cash (−A)   2,000
Paid cash dividend.

(10) Machinery (+A)   1,000
    Cash (−A)   1,000
Acquired machinery for cash.

Dividends (−SE)   1,000
    Dividends Payable (+L)   1,000
·lared dividends.

ADJUSTING JOURNAL ENTRIES

(12) Cost of Goods Sold (E, −SE)   9,000
    Merchandise Inventory (−A)   9,000
*Recognized $13,000 of inventory
on hand.*

(13) Unearned Revenue (−L)   2,000
    Sales (R, +SE)   2,000
Recognized 2/3 of goods delivered.

(14) Interest Receivable (+A)   50
    Interest Revenue (R, +SE)   50
*Recognized accrued interest on
savings account.*

(15) Depreciation Expense (E, −SE) 3,000
    Accumulated Depr. (−A)   3,000
*Recognized depreciation on
machinery.*

(16) Amortization Expense (E, −SE)   500
    Patent (−A)   500
Recognized amortization of patent.

(17) Wage Expense (E, −SE)   1,000
    Wages Payable (+L)   1,000
Recognized accrued wages.

(18) Interest Expense (E, −SE)   2,000
    Interest Payable (+L)   2,000
*Recognized accrued interest on
long-term note.*

(19) Rent Expense (E, −SE)   1,000
    Prepaid Rent (−A)   1,000
*Recognized 1/3 of rent
period expired.*

FIGURE 5–20

T-accounts for Kelly Supply

CASH		ACCOUNTS RECEIVABLE		INTEREST RECEIVABLE		MERCHANDISE INVENTORY	
12,000		15,000		(14) 50		12,000	
(1) 10,000		(1) 15,000				(3) 10,000	
(2) 8,000							
	(3) 3,000		(2) 8,000				(12) 9,000
	(4) 10,000						
	(5) 10,000						
	(6) 2,000						
	(7) 2,500						
(8) 10,000	(9) 2,000						
	(10) 1,000						
9,500		22,000		50		13,000	

PREPAID RENT		MACHINERY		ACCUMULATED DEPRECIATION		PATENT	
3,000	(19) 1,000	25,000			5,000	5,000	(16) 500
		(10) 1,000			(15) 3,000		
2,000		26,000			8,000	4,500	

ACCOUNTS PAYABLE		WAGES PAYABLE		INTEREST PAYABLE		DIVIDENDS PAYABLE	
	8,000		3,000		1,000		2,000
	(3) 7,000	(5) 3,000	(17) 1,000	(6) 1,000	(18) 2,000	(9) 2,000	(11) 1,000
(4) 10,000							
	5,000		1,000		2,000		1,000

UNEARNED REVENUE		SHORT-TERM NOTE PAYABLE		LONG-TERM NOTE PAYABLE		COMMON STOCK	
	3,000		5,000		10,000		30,000
(13) 2,000		(7) 2,500			(8) 10,000		
	1,000		2,500		20,000		30,000

RETAINED EARNINGS		SALES		INTEREST REVENUE	
	5,000		(1) 25,000		(14) 50
			(13) 2,000		

COST OF GOODS SOLD		WAGE EXPENSE		RENT EXPENSE		INTEREST EXPENSE	
(12) 9,000		(5) 7,000		(19) 1,000		(6) 1,000	
		(17) 1,000				(18) 2,000	

DEPRECIATION EXPENSE		AMORTIZATION EXPENSE		DIVIDENDS	
(15) 3,000		(16) 500		(11) 1,000	

FIGURE 5–21

Financial statements for Kelly Supply

KELLY SUPPLY
INCOME STATEMENT
FOR THE YEAR ENDED DECEMBER 31, 1997

Revenues:		
Sales	$27,000	
Interest revenue	50	
Total revenues		$27,050
Expenses:		
Cost of goods sold	$ 9,000	
Wage expense	8,000	
Rent expense	1,000	
Interest expense	3,000	
Depreciation expense	3,000	
Amortization expense	500	
Total expenses		24,500
Net income		$ 2,550

KELLY SUPPLY
STATEMENT OF RETAINED EARNINGS
FOR THE YEAR ENDED DECEMBER 31, 1997

Beginning balance	$5,000
Plus: Net income	2,550
Less: Dividends	(1,000)
Ending balance	$6,550

KELLY SUPPLY
BALANCE SHEET
DECEMBER 31, 1997

ASSETS			LIABILITIES AND STOCKHOLDERS' EQUITY	
Cash		$ 9,500	Accounts payable	$ 5,000
Accounts receivable		22,000	Wages payable	1,000
Interest receivable		50	Interest payable	2,000
Merchandise inventory		13,000	Dividends payable	1,000
Prepaid rent		2,000	Unearned revenue	1,000
Machinery	$26,000		Short-term notes pay.	2,500
Less: Accumulated			Long-term notes pay.	20,000
depreciation	8,000	18,000	Common stock	30,000
Patent		4,500	Retained earnings	6,550
			Total liabilities and	
Total assets		$69,050	stockholders' equity	$69,050

FIGURE 5–22	KELLY SUPPLY
Statement of cash flows for Kelly Supply	STATEMENT OF CASH FLOWS FOR THE YEAR ENDED DECEMBER 31, 1997

Operating activities:

Collections from sales	$10,000	
Collections of accounts receivable	8,000	
Payments for inventory purchases	(3,000)	
Payments on accounts payable	(10,000)	
Payments for wages	(10,000)	
Payments for interest	(2,000)	
Net cash increase (decrease) from operating activities		$ (7,000)
Investing activities:		
Purchase of machinery	$ (1,000)	
Net cash increase (decrease) from investing activities		(1,000)
Financing activities:		
Issuance of long-term notes payable	$10,000	
Payment of dividend	(2,000)	
Principal payments on short-term notes payable	(2,500)	
Net cash increase (decrease) from financing activities		5,500
Net cash increase (decrease) during 1997		$ (2,500)
Beginning cash balance (December 31, 1996)		12,000
Ending cash balance (December 31, 1997)		$ 9,500

SUMMARY OF LEARNING OBJECTIVES

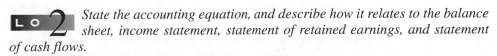

LO 1 *State and describe the criteria necessary for economic events to be reflected in the financial statements.*

Economic events must be both relevant and objectively measurable in monetary terms if they are to be reflected on the financial statements. Relevant events have economic significance to the company. Objectively measurable events must be backed by documented evidence. Economic events must be relevant so that they can be used to evaluate the financial condition of the company; they must be objectively measurable so that they can be audited and viewed as credible by users.

LO 2 *State the accounting equation, and describe how it relates to the balance sheet, income statement, statement of retained earnings, and statement of cash flows.*

The accounting equation states that assets equal liabilities plus stockholders' equity. The main components of the accounting equation (assets, liabilities, and stockholders' equity) are divided into subcategories, called *accounts*, in which transactions are recorded and from which the financial statements are compiled. When a business transaction occurs, two or more accounts are increased or decreased in such a way as to maintain the equality of the equation.

The balance sheet contains the balances as of a given point in time of all the asset, liability, and stockholders' equity accounts. It is a statement of the accounting equation.

The income statement contains a summary of the operating transactions, measured on an accrual basis, entered into by a company during a period of time. Operating transactions affect asset or liability accounts and always either increase or decrease retained earnings in the stockholders' equity section of the accounting equation.

The statement of retained earnings and the statement of cash flows summarize the transactions that affect the Retained Earnings and Cash accounts, respectively. The statement of retained earnings includes the net effect of the operating transactions as well as asset distributions to stockholders (dividends). The statement of cash flows is composed of cash inflows and outflows and explains the change in the Cash account during the period.

 Describe how journal entries (and T-accounts) express the effect of economic events on the basic accounting equation and the financial statements.

Journal entries (and T-accounts) are structured to indicate three aspects about economic events: (1) the accounts affected, (2) the direction of the effect, and (3) the dollar amount of the effect. Increases (decreases) in asset accounts and decreases (increases) in liability and equity accounts are placed on the left (right) side of the entry. Recognized revenues (expenses) are always placed on the right (left) side of the entry because they are always accompanied by increases (decreases) in assets or (increases) decreases in equities, which are indicated on the left (right) side. Following these rules ensures that economic events will be recorded in a way that maintains the equality of the accounting equation, and understanding these rules enables one to efficiently communicate the effects of any economic event on the financial statements.

 Explain why managers need to understand how economic events affect the financial statements.

Managers often face situations where they must chose whether to enter into certain transactions or how to structure transactions. Such choices should not be made without considering their economic consequences. The financial statement effects of transactions can lead to important economic consequences because outsiders use financial statement numbers to control and evaluate the firm and its management. Therefore, astute managers must understand in advance how transactions and other economic events affect the financial statements.

 Explain why the financial statements are adjusted periodically to reflect economic events that are not represented by transactions.

A large number of economic events are not represented by exchange transactions (e.g., depreciation of productive assets, and accruals of salaries, interest and rent), yet they meet the criteria (relevant and objective) for inclusion on the financial statements. These events require that adjustments be made to the financial statements periodically. Normally such adjustments are made to apply the principles of revenue recognition and matching. Revenue recognition states that revenues should be recognized when the earning process is substantially complete, not necessarily when cash is received. Matching states that expenses should be recognized in those periods when the associated benefit (revenue) is realized, not necessarily when cash is paid. These principles are fundamental to an accrual accounting system.

APPENDIX 5A

THE ACCOUNTING CYCLE: AN OVERVIEW

Figure 5A–1 illustrates the complete accounting cycle. It consists of sixteen steps that lead from (1) the recognition of an economic event (i.e., a relevant and objectively measurable exchange transaction) to (13) the preparation of the income statement, (14) statement of retained earnings, (15) balance sheet, and (16) statement of cash flows.

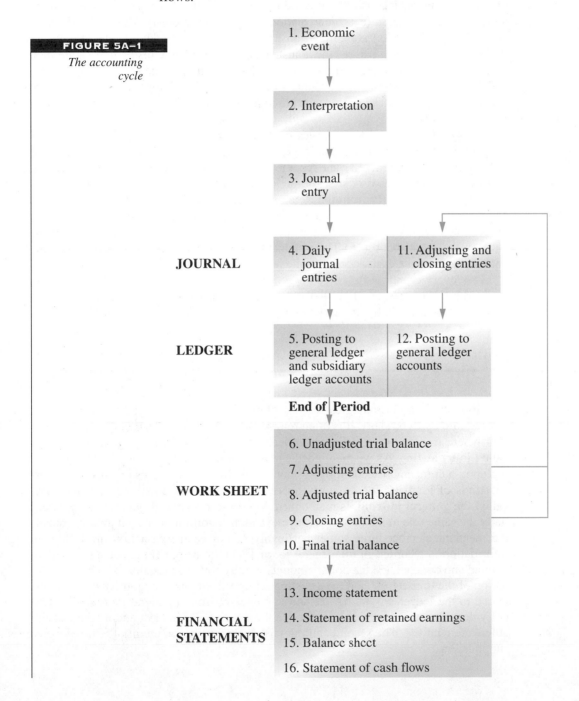

FIGURE 5A–1

The accounting cycle

1. Economic event

2. Interpretation

3. Journal entry

JOURNAL
4. Daily journal entries
11. Adjusting and closing entries

LEDGER
5. Posting to general ledger and subsidiary ledger accounts
12. Posting to general ledger accounts

End of Period

WORK SHEET
6. Unadjusted trial balance
7. Adjusting entries
8. Adjusted trial balance
9. Closing entries
10. Final trial balance

FINANCIAL STATEMENTS
13. Income statement
14. Statement of retained earnings
15. Balance sheet
16. Statement of cash flows

The accounting cycle begins when a relevant and measurable (1) economic event is (2) interpreted and (3) converted to a journal entry. Journal entries, the fundamental units of the accounting system, are recorded in the original book of record, (4) the journal, and are then posted in (5) the ledger. The process of recording journal entries and posting them to the ledger continues until it is time to prepare financial statements (monthly, quarterly, or annually).

At this time, denoted by *End of Period* in Figure 5A–1, a work sheet is prepared. Completing the work sheet encompasses Steps 6 through 10 in the accounting cycle. First, the account balances in the ledger are transferred to the work sheet. The list of the account balances on the work sheet is called (6) the unadjusted trial balance. The unadjusted trial balance is then adjusted for certain events that are not captured in the daily recording process (e.g., depreciation and earning interest). These (7) adjusting entries (or adjustments) are entered on the work sheet and added to the unadjusted trial balance, giving rise to (8) the adjusted trial balance. (9) Closing entries are then entered on the work sheet to transfer the balances in the income statement (Revenue and Expense) and Dividend accounts to the Retained Earnings account. They are added to the adjusted trial balance, resulting in (10) the final trial balance, which completes the work sheet.

The adjusting and closing entries from the work sheet are now (11) recorded in the journal and (12) posted to the ledger. At the completion of Step 12, the financial statements are prepared. (13) The income statement can be prepared from the closing entries from either the work sheet or the journal. (14) The statement of retained earnings is prepared directly from the Retained Earnings account in the ledger. (15) The balance sheet is a collection of the final balances in the asset, liability, and stockholders' equity accounts in the ledger and can simply be taken from the final trial balance on the work sheet. (16) The statement of cash flows can be prepared from the entries listed on the cash account in the ledger.

This overview should give you a general feeling for the process. The following sections present each step thoroughly. As you read through the discussion, refer often to Figure 5A–1, so that you will know where each step fits into the process.

THE JOURNAL

The **journal** is a chronological record of the transactions, in journal entry form, entered into by a company. It is often referred to as the *book of original entry* because it is where transactions are first recorded. The process of recording transactions is called **journalizing**. As we mentioned earlier, journals can take many forms, depending upon a company's accounting system. While many companies use several different kinds of journals, for the purposes of this Appendix we assume that only one, called the **general journal**, is maintained. We do so because all journals play essentially the same role in the accounting cycle, and the addition of special journals makes the mechanical procedures somewhat involved. For each transaction the following information is recorded in the general journal: (1) the date, (2) the accounts that are debited and credited, (3) the dollar amounts of the debits and credits, (4) a brief explanation of the transaction, and (5) a posting reference, so that each journal entry can be traced to the ledger. Figure 5A–2 shows an excerpt from a general journal. The first entry describes the provision of a service for which $300 in cash and a $500 receivable were received. The second entry describes the buying on credit of $200 of office supplies.

FIGURE 5A–2		GENERAL JOURNAL				PAGE 1
The general journal				POST. REF.		
	DATE		DESCRIPTION		DEBIT	CREDIT
	1997 Feb.	8	Cash (+A)		300	
			Accounts Recievable (+A)		500	
			Fees Earned (R, +SE)			800
			Provided service for cash and on account.			
		10	Supplies (I A)		200	
			Accounts Payable (+L)			200
			Bought supplies on account.			

THE LEDGER

Immediately after the transactions are recorded in the journal, they are posted in the **ledger**, where a running balance for each asset, liability, stockholders' equity, revenue, expense, and dividend account is maintained. The ledger can be viewed, therefore, as a "scoreboard" that keeps track of the "score" in each account during the period.

It is useful to think of the ledger as containing a T-account for each account on the financial statements. T-accounts are so named because they are in the form of a **T**. The left side of the **T** represents the debit side of the entry, and the right side corresponds to the credit side. Since journal entries also have a debit and a credit side, the debited and credited dollar amounts are easily transferred (posted) to their respective T-accounts. Figure 5A–3 shows how the debits and credits in two journal entries are posted to their respective T-accounts.

In the first entry a service was exchanged for $200 cash and a $300 accounts receivable. Note that in the ledger the Cash T-account is increased (debited) by $200, the Accounts Receivable T-account is increased (debited) by $300, and the Fees Earned T-account is increased (credited) by $500. In the second entry $100 cash is received on an outstanding account receivable. Accordingly, the Cash balance in the ledger is increased (debited) by $100, and the Accounts Receivable balance is decreased (credited) by that amount. Note how the final balances in each account in the ledger have been computed.

If every journal entry is immediately entered in the ledger, at any point in time the balance for a given account can be computed directly from its T-account. The balance is simply equal to the difference between the total dollar amount debited to the T-account and the total dollar amount credited. Having a convenient way to compute the account balances is particularly useful when it comes time to prepare the financial statements at the end of the accounting period. Without an up-to-date ledger, computing the account balances and preparing the financial statements would involve tracing back through the journal to find each transaction that affected each account. For most companies this would be time-consuming and tedious and could give rise to a number of recording errors.

THE GENERAL LEDGER AND SUBSIDIARY LEDGERS

We have described the ledger as containing one T-account for each account on the financial statements, which is actually a description of the **general ledger**. Companies

FIGURE 5A–3

Posting journal entries

GENERAL JOURNAL   PAGE 18

DATE		DESCRIPTION	POST. REF.	DEBIT	CREDIT
1997 March	6	Cash (+A)	102	200	
		Accounts Receivable (+A)	104	300	
		Fees Earned (R, +SE)	112		500
		Provided service for cash			
		and on account.			
	8	Cash (+A)	102	100	
		Accounts Receivable (–A)	104		100
		Paid on account.			

GENERAL LEDGER

CASH	102	ACCOUNTS RECEIVABLE	104	FEES EARNED	112
200		300	100		500
100					
300		200			500

also commonly use **subsidiary ledgers**, which contain T-accounts that relate to certain specific accounts in the general ledger. A $110 balance in an accounts receivable general ledger T-account, for example, may comprise a number of accounts associated with individual customers. Cindy Jones may owe $35 to the company, Jason Smith may owe $50, and Heather Johnson, $25. T-accounts for each individual would be kept in a subsidiary ledger, which is tied directly to the $110 (35 + 50 + 25) Accounts Receivable balance in the general ledger.[1]

THE WORK SHEET

The process of recording journal entries and posting them to the appropriate ledger accounts continues throughout the **accounting period**, the time between the preparation of financial statements, which is usually a month, a quarter (three months), or a year. At the end of the accounting period, when the time comes to summarize the accounts and prepare financial statements, a work sheet is often prepared. A **work sheet** (see Figure 5A–4) is simply a piece of paper divided into a number of columns. It is used to transfer the account balances in the general ledger to the income statement, statement of retained earnings, and balance sheet in a systematic fashion.

A work sheet is certainly useful in preparing these three financial statements, but it is not necessary. The financial statements can be prepared without it. Nevertheless, work sheets of many kinds are important in the everyday practice of accounting.

---

1. For simplicity and to avoid getting into the specifics of bookkeeping, we have shown ledger accounts in the form of a **T**. While this is true in concept, manual bookkeeping systems in practice use ledgers that contain much greater detail.

FIGURE 5A–4

Unadjusted trial balance for Kimberly Company (incomplete work sheet)

KIMBERLY COMPANY
WORK SHEET
FOR THE YEAR ENDED DECEMBER 31, 1997

ACCOUNTS	UNADJUSTED TRIAL BALANCE DR.	CR.	ADJUSTING ENTRIES DR.	CR.	ADJUSTED TRIAL BALANCE DR.	CR.	CLOSING ENTRIES DR.	CR.	FINAL TRIAL BALANCE DR.	CR.
ASSETS										
Cash	11,900									
Accounts Receivable	3,000									
Prepaid Rent	500									
Land	22,300									
LIABILITIES										
Salaries Payable										
Notes Payable		4,000								
STOCKHOLDERS' EQUITY										
Common Stock		26,000								
Retained Earnings		5,000								
Dividends	1,000									
REVENUES										
Service Revenue		7,000								
EXPENSES										
Salary Expense	2,700									
Rent Expense										
Insurance Expense	100									
Interest Expense	500									
Total	42,000	42,000								

UNADJUSTED TRIAL BALANCE

Transferring the ledger account balances to the financial statements begins by simply copying the general ledger account names in the column at the far left of the work sheet. Asset account names are usually listed first, followed by liability and stockholders' equity accounts, dividend accounts, revenue accounts, and expense accounts, in that order. The account balances from the ledger are then copied next to the account names in the adjoining two columns: debit balances on the left and credit balances on the right. The result (Step 6 in the accounting cycle) is called the **unadjusted trial balance**. Figure 5A–4 shows the unadjusted trial balance for Kimberly Company on an incomplete work sheet.

Note the order of the accounts in the unadjusted trial balance and that asset, dividend, and expense accounts have debit balances, while liability, stockholders' equity, and revenue accounts have credit balances. Keep in mind that these balances reflect the activities of Kimberly Company up to December 31, 1997, which have been journalized and posted in the ledger accounts. Note also that total debits ($42,000) on the unadjusted trial balance are equal to total credits ($42,000). If they are not equal, an error has occurred somewhere in the cycle.

ADJUSTING ENTRIES

In Step 7 of the accounting cycle the unadjusted trial balance is adjusted to capture certain relevant economic events that are not normally recorded as they occur during the accounting period. Examples include year end accruals and cost expirations.

Assume that Kimberly Company recorded one of each on December 31, 1997—$400 of prepaid rent was expired during 1997, and $300 of salaries were payable as of December 31, 1997. The journal entries, which would be recorded in the journal and posted in the ledger, are provided below.

a. Rent Expense (E, −SE)   400
      Prepaid Rent (−A)   400
      Expired prepaid rent.

b. Salary Expense (E, −SE)   300
      Salaries Payable (+L)   300
      Accrued salaries payable.

These entries would be recorded on the worksheet under "Adjusting Entries" in the manner illustrated in Figure 5A–5.

FIGURE 5A–5

Adjusted trial balance for Kimberly Company (incomplete work sheet)

KIMBERLY COMPANY
WORK SHEET
FOR THE YEAR ENDED DECEMBER 31, 1997

ACCOUNTS	UNADJUSTED TRIAL BALANCE DR.	CR.	ADJUSTING ENTRIES DR.	CR.	ADJUSTED TRIAL BALANCE DR.	CR.	CLOSING ENTRIES DR.	CR.	FINAL TRIAL BALANCE DR.	CR.
ASSETS										
Cash	11,900				11,900					
Accounts Receivable	3,000				3,000					
Prepaid Rent	500			(a) 400	100					
Land	22,300				22,300					
LIABILITIES										
Salaries Payable				(b) 300		300				
Notes Payable		4,000				4,000				
STOCKHOLDERS' EQUITY										
Common Stock		26,000				26,000				
Retained Earnings		5,000				5,000				
Dividends	1,000				1,000					
REVENUES										
Service Revenue		7,000				7,000				
EXPENSES										
Salary Expense	2,700		(b) 300		3,000					
Rent Expense			(a) 400		400					
Insurance Expense	100				100					
Interest Expense	500				500					
Total	42,000	42,000	700	700	42,300	42,300				

ADJUSTED TRIAL BALANCE

After entering the adjusting entries on the work sheet, the **adjusted trial balance** (Step 8) can be prepared. These columns simply result from adding the debits and credits from the adjusting entries to the debit and credit balances from the unadjusted trial balance. The resulting balance for each account is carried over to the two columns to the right of the adjusting entries. Once again, the total dollar amount in the debit column equals the total dollar amount in the credit column. Figure 5A–5 shows the adjusted trial balance for Kimberly Company.

CLOSING ENTRIES AND THE CLOSING PROCESS

In the closing process (Step 9) the dollar balances in the Revenue, Expense, and Dividend accounts are transferred, or *closed*, to the Retained Earnings account. Since this process is often difficult for students to understand, we first explain why closing is necessary, then distinguish permanent from temporary accounts, and finally describe and illustrate the actual procedures involved.

WHY IS CLOSING NECESSARY? Assume that Jenotech, Inc., (1) sold services for $500 cash, (2) paid $300 cash for miscellaneous expenses, and (3) paid a $100 cash dividend. These transactions would be recorded in the journal as follows.

1. Cash (+A)   500
        Fees Earned (R, +SE)   500
    Received cash for services provided.

2. Miscellaneous Expenses (E, −SE)   300
        Cash (−A)   300
    Paid cash for expenses.

3. Dividend (−SE)   100
        Cash (−A)   100
    Paid cash dividend.

Consider how these transactions affect the balance sheet and the accounting equation: assets = liabilities + stockholders' equity. Each involves cash and, accordingly, either increases or decreases assets. The accounts named *Fees Earned, Miscellaneous Expenses*, and *Dividends*, however, do not appear on the balance sheet. How are they handled so that the equality of the balance sheet and the accounting equation are maintained?

Until now we have answered this question by simply stating that retained earnings, which is part of stockholders' equity, is the net accumulation of past revenues, expenses, and dividends and is therefore adjusted when revenues, expenses, and dividends are recognized: revenues increase retained earnings, while expenses and dividends decrease retained earnings. These three transactions, therefore, would affect the accounting equation and the balance sheet as shown in Figure 5A–6.

FIGURE 5A–6	ASSETS	=	LIABILITIES	+	COMMON STOCK	+	RETAINED EARNINGS
Revenues,							
expenses,	(1) +500	=					+500
dividends, and the	(2) −300	=					−300
accounting	(3) −100	=					−100
equation							

From a procedural standpoint, if revenues, expenses, and dividends are to be reflected on the balance sheet and, in the process, maintain the equality of the accounting equation, we need a method of transferring the end-of-period balances in the Revenue, Expense, and Dividend accounts to the Retained Earnings account. This method is known as the *closing process*.

PERMANENT AND TEMPORARY ACCOUNTS. The need to transfer revenues, expenses, and dividends to retained earnings introduces an important distinction among the accounts on the financial statements. The balance sheet accounts (assets, liabilities, and stockholders' equities) are called *permanent accounts*; the income statement and dividend accounts (revenues, expenses, and dividends) are called *temporary accounts*. **Permanent accounts** have balances that accumulate from one accounting period to the next. The balance sheet, which consists of permanent accounts, reflects transactions that have occurred since a company's inception. It is a statement of a company's accumulated financial condition as of a particular point in time.

Temporary accounts accumulate only throughout a single period. At the end of that period their balances are reduced to zero, where they begin the next accounting period. For example, the income statement, which consists of temporary accounts, reflects transactions from only a single period.

The distinction between permanent and temporary accounts is at the heart of the closing process, in which a series of journal entries transfers the balances in the Revenue, Expense, and Dividend accounts to the Retained Earnings account. The balances in the temporary accounts are zeroed out and transferred to a permanent balance sheet account, where they are accumulated.

THE PROCEDURES OF THE CLOSING PROCESS. The closing process consists of four basic steps:

1. *Create an Income Summary Account.* A ledger T-account, called **Income Summary**, is created solely to execute the closing process.
2. *Close the Revenue and Expense accounts to Income Summary.* A series of **closing entries** transfers the balances in the Revenue and Expense accounts to the Income Summary account and sets the new balances in the Revenue and Expense accounts to zero.
3. *Close the Income Summary account to Retained Earnings.* A single journal entry closes the Income Summary account to Retained Earnings. As in the previous step, this entry simply transfers the balance in the Income Summary account to the Retained Earnings account and brings the Income Summary balance to zero.
4. *Close the Dividends account to Retained Earnings.* A single entry closes the Dividends account directly to Retained Earnings. Once again, the entry sets the Dividends account to zero by transferring its balance to the Retained Earnings account.

Figure 5A–7 shows the procedures to close the Revenue, Expense, and Dividend accounts for Kimberly Company at the end of 1997. The balances in the Revenue, Expense, Dividend, and Retained Earnings accounts from the adjusted trial balance are indicated by *italics*. In Step 1 an Income Summary account is created. In Step 2 closing journal entry (1) debits service revenue for $7,000 and credits each expense account (Salary, Rent, Insurance, and Interest) for the amount of expense recognized during the year. When this entry is posted in the ledger, it brings the balances in the revenue and expense accounts to zero. In addition, this entry requires a credit of $3,000 to make the total credits equal the $7,000 debit. This amount is recorded in the Income Summary account and represents the dollar amount of the difference between the revenues and expenses recognized during the year, which incidentally is Kimberly's net income for 1997.

In Step 3, closing journal entry (2) is prepared, which, when posted to the ledger, brings the balance in the Income Summary account to zero and transfers $3,000 to Retained Earnings. Thus, it transfers the net amount of revenues and expenses (net income) to the Retained Earnings account. In Step 4, closing journal entry (3) is prepared which, when posted, brings the balance in the Dividend account to zero and

FIGURE 5A–7	
Kimberly Company: The closing process	

Step 1: Create Income Summary account.

Step 2: Close Revenue and Expense accounts to Income Summary account.

Journal entry: (1)

Service Revenue	7,000	
Salary Expense		3,000
Rent Expense		400
Insurance Expense		100
Interest Expense		500
Income Summary (plug)		3,000

Closed revenues and expenses to Income Summary.

Step 3: Close Income Summary account to Retained Earnings account.

Journal entry: (2)

Income Summary	3,000	
Retained Earnings		3,000

Closed Income Summary to Retained Earnings.

Step 4: Close Dividends account to Retained Earnings account.

Journal entry: (3)

Retained Earnings	1,000	
Dividends		1,000

Closed Dividends to Retained Earnings.

GENERAL LEDGER

SERVICE REVENUE		SALARY EXPENSE		RENT EXPENSE		INSURANCE EXPENSE	
(1) 7,000	7,000	3,000	(1) 3,000	400	(1) 400	100	(1) 100
	0	0		0		0	

INTEREST EXPENSE		INCOME SUMMARY		DIVIDENDS		RETAINED EARNINGS	
500	(1) 500	(2) 3,000	(1) 3,000	1,000	(3) 1,000		5,000
0			0	0		(3) 1,000	(2) 3,000
							7,000

reduces Retained Earnings by $1,000. Note that the ending balance in the Retained Earnings T-account ($7,000) is computed by adding net income ($3,000) to the beginning balance of Retained Earnings ($5,000) and subtracting the dividend ($1,000). This computation is exactly what appears on the statement of retained earnings.

Figure 5A–7 shows only the closing entries recorded in the journal and ledger. However, as the accounting cycle in Figure 5A–8 indicates, these entries are recorded first on the work sheet in the debit and credit columns to the right of the adjusted trial balance. When the work sheet is complete, these entries are recorded in the journal and posted to the ledger. The completed work sheet for Kimberly appears in Figure 5A–8.

THE FINAL TRIAL BALANCE

After the closing entries have been recorded on the work sheet and all the temporary accounts have zero balances, the only remaining balances are in the permanent asset, liability, and stockholders' equity accounts. In Figure 5A–8 these balances are carried to the **final trial balance** (Step 10). Asset accounts typically carry debit balances in

FIGURE 5A–8

Completed work sheet for Kimberly Company

KIMBERLY COMPANY
WORK SHEET
FOR THE YEAR ENDED DECEMBER 31, 1997

ACCOUNT	UNADJUSTED TRIAL BALANCE DR.	CR.	ADJUSTING ENTRIES DR.	CR.	ADJUSTED TRIAL BALANCE DR.	CR.	CLOSING ENTRIES DR.	CR.	FINAL TRIAL BALANCE DR.	CR.
ASSETS										
Cash	11,900				11,900				11,900	
Accounts Receivable	3,000				3,000				3,000	
Prepaid Rent	500			(a) 400	100				100	
Land	22,300				22,300				22,300	
LIABILITIES										
Salaries Payable				(b) 300		300				300
Notes Payable		4,000				4,000				4,000
STOCKHOLDERS' EQUITY										
Common Stock		26,000				26,000				26,000
Retained Earnings		5,000				5,000	(3) 1,000	(2) 3,000		7,000
Dividends	1,000				1,000			(3) 1,000	0	
REVENUES										
Service Revenue		7,000				7,000	(1) 7,000			0
EXPENSES										
Salary Expense	2,700		(b) 300		3,000			(1) 3,000	0	
Rent Expense			(a) 400		400			(1) 400	0	
Insurance Expense	100				100			(1) 100	0	
Interest Expense	500				500			(1) 500	0	
Income Summary							(2) 3,000	(1) 3,000	0	
Total	42,000	42,000	700	700	42,300	42,300	11,000	11,000	37,300	37,300

the final trial balance, while liability and stockholders' equity accounts normally carry credit balances. Total debits ($37,300) will equal total credits ($37,300) if the entries have been recorded correctly.

PREPARATION OF THE FINANCIAL STATEMENTS

Preparing the income statement, statement of retained earnings, balance sheet, and statement of cash flows (Steps 13 to 16) at this point is a very straightforward procedure. Each statement comes directly from a segment of the accounting cycle.

THE INCOME STATEMENT

The income statement can be prepared directly from either the journal entry that closes the Revenue and Expense accounts (Fig. 5A–7, journal entry [1]) or the closing entries on the completed work sheet (Fig. 5A–8). These entries correspond to those on the income statement. The dollar amount initially recorded in the Income Summary account is equal to net income. Figure 5A–9 presents the income statement of Kimberly Company.

FIGURE 5A–9	KIMBERLY COMPANY INCOME STATEMENT FOR THE YEAR ENDED DECEMBER 31, 1997	
Income statement *for Kimberly* *Company*		

Service revenue		$7,000
Expenses:		
Salaries	$3,000	
Rent	400	
Insurance	100	
Interest	500	
Total expenses		4,000
Net income		$3,000

THE STATEMENT OF RETAINED EARNINGS

The statement of retained earnings can be prepared directly from the Retained Earnings T-account in the General Ledger. Recall the reconciliation format of this statement: beginning balance, plus (minus) net income (net loss), less dividends, equals ending balance. The beginning balance of Retained Earnings for the current period is the dollar amount of retained earnings that appears on the previous balance sheet ($5,000). The entry to close the Income Summary to Retained Earnings represents the adjustment for net income ($3,000). The entry to close the Dividends account to Retained Earnings reduces Retained Earnings in the amount of the dividend ($1,000). The ending balance in the Retained Earnings T-account, which also appears in the end-of-period balance sheet, is the net result of these adjustments. The statement of retained earnings for Kimberly Company appears in Figure 5A–10.

FIGURE 5A–10	KIMBERLY COMPANY STATEMENT OF RETAINED EARNINGS FOR THE YEAR ENDED DECEMBER 31, 1997	
Statement of *retained earnings* *for Kimberly* *Company*		

Beginning retained earnings balance	$5,000
Plus: Net income	3,000
Less: Dividends	1,000
Ending retained earnings balance	$7,000

THE BALANCE SHEET

The balance sheet is prepared from the ending balances in the permanent asset, liability, and stockholders' equity accounts. These balances appear in the ledger and in the final trial balance on the work sheet. Figure 5A–11 shows the balance sheet of Kimberly Company.

THE STATEMENT OF CASH FLOWS

The statement of cash flows can be prepared from the Cash account in the ledger. Entries on the left of the Cash T-account (debits) indicate cash inflows; entries on the right (credits) indicate cash outflows. Recall that the statement of cash flows is organized into three categories: cash flows from operating activities, from investing activities, and from financing activities. To prepare the statement, each of the cash inflows and outflows in the ledger must be placed in one of these three categories.

KIMBERLY COMPANY
BALANCE SHEET
DECEMBER 31, 1997

ASSETS		LIABILITIES AND STOCKHOLDERS' EQUITY	
Cash	$11,900	Salaries payable	$ 300
Accounts receivable	3,000	Notes payable	4,000
Prepaid rent	100	Common stock	26,000
Land	22,300	Retained earnings	7,000
		Total liabilities and	
Total assets	$37,300	stockholders' equity	$37,300

A statement of cash flows is not prepared for Kimberly Company because we do not provide the Cash T-account. However, the next section provides a comprehensive example of the accounting cycle, including the preparation of the statement of cash flows.

A COMPREHENSIVE EXAMPLE OF THE ACCOUNTING CYCLE

In this comprehensive example of the entire accounting cycle, Figure 5A–12 represents the journal, containing eleven entries recorded during the accounting period (1997) and three closing entries recorded at the end of 1997. Figure 5A–13 represents the ledger, which contains a T-account for each financial statement account. Figure 5A–14 shows the work sheet, income statement, statement of retained earnings, balance sheet, and statement of cash flows.

FIGURE 5A–12

Comprehensive example: General journal entries

ENTRY	DATE	JOURNAL ENTRY			DESCRIPTION OF TRANSACTION
(1)	1/4/97	Accounts Receivable (+A)	300		*Provided services on account.*
		Service Revenue (R, +SE)		300	
(2)	1/7/97	Misc. Payable (−L)	50		*Paid misc. payable.*
		Cash (−A)		50	
(3)	1/8/97	Cash (+A)	500		*Provided service for cash.*
		Service Revenue (R, +SE)		500	
(4)	1/18/97	Cash (+A)	200		*Received payment on*
		Accounts Receivable (−A)		200	*outstanding receivable.*
(5)	1/20/97	Notes Payable (−L)	100		*Paid outstanding notes payable.*
		Cash (−A)		100	
(6)	1/22/97	Land (+A)	700		*Purchased two parcels of land*
		Cash (−A)		300	*for cash and signed a note*
		Notes Payable (+L)		400	*payable for balance.*

ENTRY	DATE	JOURNAL ENTRY			DESCRIPTION OF TRANSACTION
(7)	1/26/97	Interest Expense (E, −SE)	40		*Paid interest on notes payable.*
		Cash (−A)		40	
(8)	1/27/97	Cash (+A)	1,000		*Issued stock for cash.*
		Common Stock (+SE)		1,000	
(9)	1/29/97	Salary Expense (E, −SE)	350		*Paid salaries and other*
		Other Expenses (E, −SE)	200		*expenses.*
		Cash (−A)		550	
(10)	1/29/97	Cash (+A)	420		*Sold one parcel of land which*
		Land (−A)		350	*cost $350.*
		Gain on Sale (Ga, +SE)		70	
(11)	1/30/97	Dividends (−SE)	100		*Declared dividends to be paid*
		Dividends Payable (+L)		100	*in February.*
		Closing Entries			
(12)	1/31/97	Service Revenue	800		*Closed revenues and expenses to*
		Gain on Sale	70		*Income Summary.*
		Interest Expense		40	
		Salary Expense		350	
		Other Expenses		200	
		Income Summary		280	
(13)	1/31/97	Income Summary	280		*Closed Income Summary to*
		Retained Earnings		280	*Retained Earnings.*
(14)	1/31/97	Retained Earnings	100		*Closed Dividends to Retained*
		Dividends		100	*Earnings.*

The ledger indicates that ABC company began operations in 1997 with beginning balances in its asset, liability, and stockholders' equity accounts. For example, $600 was in the Cash account, $300 in Accounts Receivable, and a $400 (credit) balance in Retained Earnings. The beginning balances in the Revenue, Expense, and Dividend accounts are zero because they were closed at the end of the previous accounting period (1996).

The journal entries numbered (1)–(11) represent the exchange transactions entered into by ABC during the month of January. Note that each entry has been posted in the ledger and is coded by an entry number. At the end of January the ledger balances are totaled and transferred to the work sheet in the form of an unadjusted trial balance. We assume no adjustments, so the adjusted trial balance is the same as the unadjusted trial balance.

The journal entries to close the temporary accounts (Revenues, Expenses, and Dividends) are numbered (12), (13), and (14) in the journal. These entries have been posted to the ledger and are also indicated on the work sheet. In entry (12) the Revenue and Expense accounts are closed to Income Summary. Entry (13) closes Income Summary to Retained Earnings, and entry (14) closes Dividends to Retained Earnings.

The income statement comes directly from journal entry (12), where the Revenue and Expense accounts are closed to Income Summary. The statement of retained earnings is simply a statement of the Retained Earnings T-account, and the final trial

FIGURE 5A–13

Comprehensive example: General ledger

ASSET ACCOUNTS

CASH				ACCOUNTS RECEIVABLE				LAND			
	600				300				1,500		
(3)	500	(2)	50	(1)	300	(4)	200	(6)	700	(10)	350
(4)	200	(5)	100		400				1,850		
		(6)	300								
		(7)	40								
(8)	1,000	(9)	550								
(10)	420										
	1,680										

LIABILITY AND STOCKHOLDERS' EQUITY ACCOUNTS

MISCELLANEOUS PAYABLE			DIVIDENDS PAYABLE			NOTES PAYABLE				COMMON STOCK		
		100		(11)	100				400			1,500
(2)	50					(5)	100	(6)	400		(8)	1,000
		50			100				700			2,500

RETAINED EARNINGS		
		400
	(13)	280
(14)	100	
		580

TEMPORARY ACCOUNTS

SERVICE REVENUE				INTEREST EXPENSE				SALARY EXPENSE			
		(1)	300	(7)	40			(9)	350		
		(3)	500			(12)	40			(12)	350
(12)	800										
			0		0				0		

OTHER EXPENSES				GAIN ON SALE				DIVIDENDS				INCOME SUMMARY			
(9)	200					(10)	70	(11)	100					(12)	280
		(12)	200	(12)	70					(14)	100	(13)	280		
	0						0		0				0		

balance on the work sheet provides the data needed for the balance sheet. The statement of cash flows was prepared by categorizing the entries to the Cash T-account as operating, investing, and financing. It may be helpful at this point to return to Figure 5A–1, the accounting cycle, and attempt to trace each of the sixteen steps in this comprehensive example. Also, make doubly sure that you are comfortable with the construction of journal entries. As this example illustrates, an error in a journal entry carries through the entire accounting cycle and is reflected in the financial statements.

FIGURE 5A–14

Comprehensive example: Work sheet and financial statements

ABC COMPANY
WORK SHEET
FOR THE PERIOD ENDED JANUARY 31, 1997

ACCOUNT	UNADJUSTED TRIAL BALANCE DR.	CR.	ADJUSTING ENTRIES DR.	CR.	ADJUSTED TRIAL BALANCE DR.	CR.	CLOSING ENTRIES DR.	CR.	FINAL TRIAL BALANCE DR.	CR.
ASSETS										
Cash	1,680				1,680				1,680	
Accounts Receivable	400				400				400	
Land	1,850				1,850				1,850	
LIABILITIES										
Misc. Payable		50				50				50
Dividends Payable		100				100				100
Notes Payable		700				700				700
STOCKHOLDERS' EQUITY										
Common Stock		2,500				2,500				2,500
Retained Earnings		400				400	(14) 100	(13) 280		580
Dividends	100				100			(14) 100		
REVENUES										
Service Revenue		800				800	(12) 800			
Gain on Sale		70				70	(12) 70			
EXPENSES										
Interest Expense	40				40			(12) 40		
Salary Expense	350				350			(12) 350		
Other Expense	200				200			(12) 200		
Income Summary							(13) 280	(12) 280		
Total	4,620	4,620	0	0	4,620	4,620	1,250	1,250	3,930	3,930

ABC COMPANY
INCOME STATEMENT
FOR THE PERIOD ENDED JANUARY 31, 1997

Service revenue	$800
Gain on sale	70
Interest expense	(40)
Salary expense	(350)
Other expenses	(200)
Net income	$280

See closing entry (12).

ABC COMPANY
STATEMENT OF RETAINED EARNINGS
FOR THE PERIOD ENDED JANUARY 31, 1997

Beginning retained earnings balance	$400
Plus: Net income	280
Less: Dividends	(100)
Ending retained earnings balance	$580

See Retained Earnings T-account.

ABC COMPANY
BALANCE SHEET
JANUARY 31, 1997

ASSETS		LIABILITIES AND STOCKHOLDERS' EQUITY	
Cash	$1,680	Miscellaneous payable	$ 50
Accounts receivable	400	Dividends payable	100
Land	1,850	Notes payable	700
		Common stock	2,500
		Retained earnings	580
Total assets	$3,930	Total liabilities and stockholders' equity	$3,930

See final balances in asset, liability, and stockholders' equity accounts and final trial balance.

FIGURE 5A–14
(Concluded)

ABC COMPANY
STATEMENT OF CASH FLOWS
FOR THE PERIOD ENDED JANUARY 31, 1997

Operating activities:		
Cash collections from services	$ 500	
Cash from receivables	200	
Cash payments on misc. payables	(50)	
Cash payments for interest	(40)	
Cash payments for salaries	(350)	
Cash payments for other expenses	(200)	
Net cash increase (decrease) from operating activities		$ 60
Investing activities:		
Cash payments for land	$ (300)	
Cash proceeds from sale of land	420	
Net cash increase (decrease) from investing activities		120
Financing activities:		
Cash collections from issuing stock	$1,000	
Cash payments on notes payable	(100)	
Net cash increase (decrease) from financing activities		900
Net increase (decrease) in cash balance		$1,080
Beginning cash balance		600
Ending cash balance		$1,680

See Cash T-account.

APPENDIX 5B

MECHANICS: A USER'S PERSPECTIVE

Chapter 5 and Appendix 5A covered accounting mechanics from an economic consequence perspective. That is, we have discussed and illustrated how economic events affect the financial statements. Managers need such understanding to assess in advance the financial statement effects, and associated economic consequences, of transactions under their consideration. To be astute financial statement users, managers need an additional skill—one that involves working backward from the financial statements to identify underlying economic events. When evaluating solvency, earning power, and the quality of a company's management, it is often useful to be able to infer information that is not directly disclosed.

T-account analysis is employed by many financial statement users to infer economic events from the financial statements. It is a mechanical process that involves examining the activity in a given T-account to acquire information that is not directly disclosed on the financial statements or footnotes. Consider, for example, a situation where a financial statement user is analyzing the financial statements of Wildcat Industries, which are provided in Figure 5B–1.

FIGURE 5B–1	WILDCAT INDUSTRIES ABBREVIATED FINANCIAL STATEMENTS FOR THE YEARS ENDED DECEMBER 31, 1997 AND 1996		
Financial statements for Wildcat Industries		**1997**	**1996**

BALANCE SHEET

ASSETS

	1997	1996
Cash	$ 4,000	$ 7,000
Accounts receivable	15,000	12,000
Inventory	18,000	15,000
Prepaid rent	5,000	3,000
Equipment	50,000	40,000
Less: Accumulated depreciation	(10,000)	(5,000)
Total assets	$82,000	$72,000

LIABILITIES AND STOCKHOLDERS' EQUITY

	1997	1996
Accounts payable	$ 8,000	$ 4,000
Salaries payable	9,000	7,000
Dividends payable	2,000	3,000
Unearned revenue	5,000	8,000
Long-term debt	35,000	30,000
Common stock	15,000	15,000
Retained earnings	8,000	5,000
Total liabilities and stockholders' equity	$82,000	$72,000

INCOME STATEMENT

Revenues	$52,000
Less:	
Cost of goods sold	(30,000)
Salaries expense	(4,000)
Rent expense	(6,000)
Depreciation expense	(6,000)
Loss on sale of equipment	(1,000)
Net income	$ 5,000

STATEMENT OF RETAINED EARNINGS

Beginning retained earnings balance (12/31/96)	$ 5,000
Plus: Net income	5,000
Less: Dividends	(2,000)
Ending retained earnings balance (12/31/97)	$ 8,000

STATEMENT OF CASH FLOWS

Net cash provided by operating activities	$ 7,000
Net cash used by investing activities	(7,000)
Net cash used by financing activities	(3,000)
Change in cash balance	$ (3,000)
Beginning cash balance (12/31/96)	7,000
Ending cash balance (12/31/97)	$ 4,000

Assume that the user is interested in the amount of cash paid during 1997 for salaries, information that is not disclosed anywhere on the financial statements. T-account analysis, as illustrated in Figure 5B–2, involves constructing a T-account for Salaries Payable and analyzing the activity in that account during 1997. Note first that the beginning and ending balances are $7,000 and $9,000, respectively, amounts that appear on the 1996 and 1997 balance sheets. Since salaries are accrued, the dollar amount for Salary Expense on the income statement indicates that during 1997 the Salaries Payable account must have been increased by $4,000. The entry to the left side of the T-account, therefore, must have been $2,000, the amount of cash paid for salaries during 1997. This $2,000 is disclosed nowhere on the financial statements (it is buried inside net cash provided by operating activities), yet it may be useful in assessing solvency and earning power.

FIGURE 5B–2

T-account analysis of Salaries Payable account

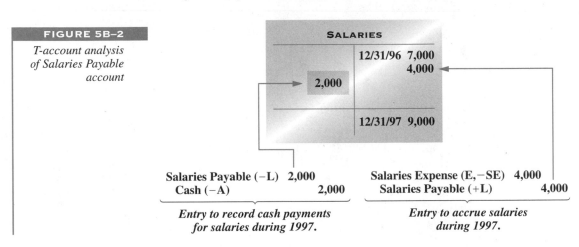

In a second example, assume that the user is interested in the dollar amount of inventory purchased during 1997, additional information—not disclosed directly on the financial statements—that may be useful in assessing solvency and earning power. In this case T-account analysis involves analyzing the activity in the Inventory account, as shown in Figure 5B–3. Once again, the beginning and ending balances ($15,000 and $18,000, respectively) come directly from the 1996 and 1997 balance sheets. Since Cost of Goods Sold on the income statement represents the outflow of sold inventory, the inventory account must have been reduced by $30,000 during 1997. Inventory purchases, therefore, must have been $33,000.

FIGURE 5B–3

T-account analysis of Inventory account

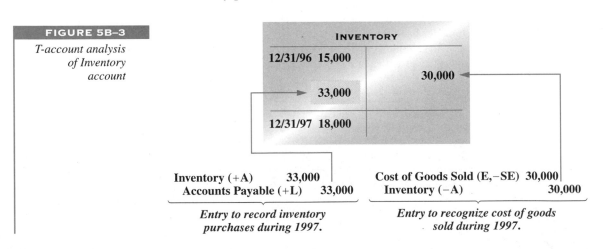

In the final example, assume that a user noticed on the income statement that Wildcat incurred a $1,000 loss on the sale of equipment, and was interested in reconstructing the transaction that produced that loss. Assume also that the footnotes indicate that Wildcat acquired equipment at a cost of $15,000 during 1997. In this case T-account analysis involves analyzing both the Equipment and the Accumulated Depreciation accounts, as illustrated in Figure 5B–4.

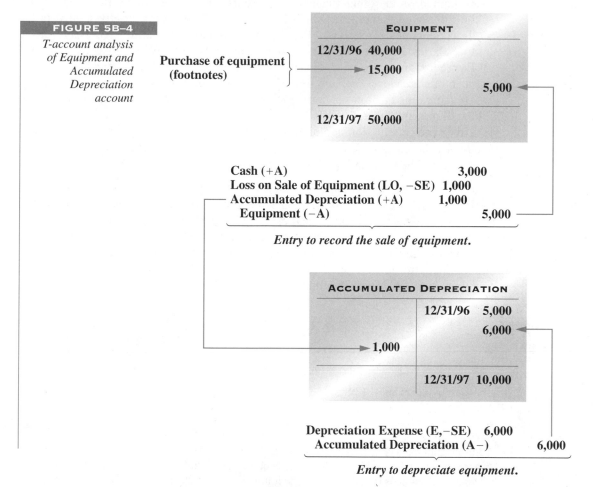

FIGURE 5B–4

T-account analysis of Equipment and Accumulated Depreciation account

Purchase of equipment (footnotes)

EQUIPMENT

12/31/96 40,000
15,000

5,000

12/31/97 50,000

Cash (+A)   3,000
Loss on Sale of Equipment (LO, −SE) 1,000
Accumulated Depreciation (+A)   1,000
    Equipment (−A)   5,000

Entry to record the sale of equipment.

ACCUMULATED DEPRECIATION

12/31/96   5,000
6,000

1,000

12/31/97 10,000

Depreciation Expense (E,−SE)   6,000
    Accumulated Depreciation (A−)   6,000

Entry to depreciate equipment.

As in the previous examples, the beginning and ending balances in the Equipment and Accumulated Depreciation T-accounts come directly from the 1996 and 1997 balance sheets. The footnotes indicate that Wildcat acquired equipment at a cost of $15,000, which explains the $15,000 entry to the left (debit) side of the Equipment account. Therefore, Wildcat must have sold equipment with a cost of $5,000 during 1997. The income statement shows depreciation expense of $6,000, which means that the Accumulated Depreciation T-account must have been credited by $6,000 during 1997. To make this account balance it must have been reduced by $1,000, the amount of accumulated depreciation associated with the equipment that was sold during 1997. Finally, the loss on the sale of equipment comes from the income statement, and to make the journal entry balance, cash of $3,000 must have been received in the exchange.

In each of the three examples above information not directly disclosed on the financial statements was derived through a technique called T-account analysis, which normally includes the following 4 steps.

1. One or more balance sheet accounts are identified for analysis depending on what the user wishes to learn.
2. T-accounts are created for each account and the beginning and ending balances are taken directly from the balance sheets.

3. Additional information from various sources is used to recreate the activity (increases or decreases) that explains the change in the T-account balance. Sometimes the information can be found in the footnotes and sometimes it is contained on the other financial statements. Often, the information is disclosed on the income statement, which includes certain accounts closely related to the T-accounts under analysis. For example, Salaries Expense is closely related to Salaries Payable; Cost of Goods Sold is closely related to Inventory; and Depreciation Expense is closely related to Accumulated Depreciation. These accounts are closely related because they often appear in the same journal entry. By recreating this journal entry, the user can determine a portion of the activity in the T-account under analysis.

4. Given the information compiled in steps 1–3, the missing part of the activity in the T-account can be inferred because it represents the dollar amount needed to complete the explanation of the change in the T-account balance.

In this section we have only introduced T-account analysis and shown how it can be used to produce useful information in three relatively simple cases. It can involve highly sophisticated procedures, and for most accounting students it is a difficult concept that requires time, effort, practice, and experience before it can be mastered. The remainder of this textbook provides a number of opportunities to learn more about, and practice, this technique because it can significantly improve your ability to learn as much as possible from the financial statements.

KEY TERMS

Note: Definitions for these terms are provided in the glossary at the end of the text.

Accounting equation (p. 184)
Accounting period (p. 218)
Accrual accounting (p. 197)
Accruals (p. 197)
Adjusted trial balance (p. 220)
Amortized (p. 204)
Business transactions (p. 185)
Capitalized (p. 200)
Closing entries (p. 222)
Compound journal entries (p. 190)
Contra accounts (p. 205)
Cost expiration (p. 200)
Credit (p. 190)
Debit (p. 190)
Depreciation (p. 204)
Double entry system (p. 190)
Economic events (p. 183)
Expensed (p. 200)
Final trial balance (p. 223)
General journal (p. 216)

General ledger (p. 217)
Income summary (p. 222)
Journal (p. 216)
Journal entries (p. 190)
Journalizing (p. 216)
Matching principle (p. 200)
Multinationals (p. 208)
Net book value (p. 205)
Permanent accounts (p. 222)
Relevant events (p. 183)
Revaluation adjustments (p. 206)
Straight-line depreciation (p. 206)
Subsidiary ledgers (p. 218)
T-account (p. 193)
T-account analysis (p. 230)
Temporary accounts (p. 222)
Unadjusted trial balance (p. 219)
Unearned revenues (p. 203)
Work sheet (p. 218)

QUESTIONS FOR DISCUSSION AND REVIEW

1. State the fundamental accounting equation. What financial statement is a statement of this equation?

2. What characterizes business transactions and how are they reported in the financial records of a company so that the equality of the accounting equation is maintained? Choose five different transactions, and explain how proper accounting for them maintains the equality of the accounting equation.

3. Explain each of the four financial statements in terms of the fundamental accounting equation.

4. Consider the following transactions and explain how recording each in journal entry form maintains the equality of the fundamental accounting equation.

   a. Issue stock for cash.

   b. Provide a service in exchange for a receivable.

   c. Pay cash for an expense.

   d. Purchase equipment for cash.

   e. Purchase equipment and sign a note payable.

5. What is an economic event? What two criteria must be met before an economic event can be recorded? Why?

6. Define objectivity as it is defined in the chapter. What kind of economic events meet this definition of objectivity? What economic forces combine to ensure that accounting statements reflect only objective information?

7. Assume that a company purchases a piece of equipment for $5,000. What accounts are affected? What is the direction of the effect? What is the dollar value of the transaction? How do the answers to these three questions provide the information necessary for a journal entry? Convert this transaction to a journal entry.

8. Refer to Figure 5–7, the journal entry box, and prepare journal entries for the following transactions: (1) purchase of machinery for $5,000 cash, (2) payment of $500 cash for an outstanding account payable, (3) completion of a service billed for $300, and (4) payment of $800 cash wages.

9. Show how each of the four transactions in (8) above affect the basic accounting equation. What stockholders' equity account does the completion of a service and the payment of cash wages affect? How do these four transactions affect the income statement and balance sheet?

10. Why are T-accounts useful?

11. Distinguish temporary accounts from permanent accounts. There are six basic categories of accounts: assets, liabilities, stockholders' equities, revenues, expenses, and dividends. Which are temporary and which are permanent? Of what use is such a distinction?

12. Is it possible for the Retained Earnings account to have a negative (debit) balance? What conditions could give rise to such a result?

13. In general terms, describe how the balance sheet is related to the income statement. Give several journal entries to illustrate this relationship. What is the role of the Retained Earnings account in this relationship?

14. Under what situations are book gains and losses recognized on the financial statements? Explain how such transactions affect the statements.

15. Briefly describe accrual accounting. Construct an example to show that the primary difference between accrual and cash accounting is the timing of the performance recognition.

16. Which of the two systems, accrual or cash accounting, provides the most useful information? What kind of investors (equity or debt) tend to be most interested in accrual-based accounting numbers and why? What kind of investors tend to be most interested in cash accounting numbers and why?

17. Define the matching principle, and explain how it relates to the accrual system of measuring performance.

18. What are adjusting journal entries, and how do they relate to the accrual system of accounting? Why are they recorded in the books?

19. Differentiate a cost expiration from an accrual.

20. Explain the difference between *capitalizing* a cost and *expensing* it. How do these two accounting treatments affect the balance sheet and income statement? Which of the two treatments has the more negative effect on net income of the current period? Which of the two treatments recognizes the greatest amount of total expense?

21. Explain how the choice of capitalizing or expensing a given cost relates to the matching principle, and discuss how this decision reflects the distinction between a capital transaction and an operating transaction.

22. Explain how a cost expiration adjusting journal entry helps to apply the matching principle appropriately. Provide three examples of cost expiration adjusting journal entries.

23. When is the cost of purchasing inventory matched against the benefit the inventory produces for a company? How and why is this done on the books? Provide an example.

24. When is the cost of paying salaries matched against the benefit it produces for a company? How and why is this done on the books? Provide an example.

25. When a cash payment is received before a service is provided, how is this accounted for in the books? How is this accounting treatment an application of the revenue recognition principle? Compare this treatment to the methods used to account for a prepaid expense.

26. Suppose that Mr. Gizmo, chief executive officer of Galaxy Enterprises, purchased a piece of machinery at the beginning of 1997 and wants net income on the income statement of that year to be as high as possible. He has the choice of depreciating the machinery over five or ten years. Which of the two choices will he take? Is it clear which of the two choices is a better application of the matching principle? Why or why not?

27. Explain how a prepayment for a three-year insurance policy is treated on the books, and compare this treatment to the method used to account for the purchase of a piece of equipment. You will note that both treatments involve capitalizing and amortizing. Which of the two is a more straightforward application of the matching principle? Why? Which of the two involves more uncertain estimates, giving the manager greater discretion over the presentation of the financial statements?

28. What is a multinational company, and how do such companies report to stockholders, creditors, and other interested parties who transact in different currencies, speak different languages, and are familiar with different accounting principles? Discuss some of the issues associated with developing a single set of global accounting standards.

29. *(Appendix 5A)* List the sixteen steps of the accounting cycle. Why is it so important that journal entries be recorded correctly?

30. *(Appendix 5A)* Distinguish the journal from the ledger. Why is the ledger referred to as a *scoreboard*?

31. *(Appendix 5A)* Explain why ledgers contain accounts in the form of a T. How do T-accounts relate to journal entries? Why are T-accounts useful? Many of the general ledger accounts are comprised of subsidiary ledgers. Provide an example.

32. *(Appendix 5A)* Explain the function of a work sheet. Is it an official book of record like the journal? Why or why not?

33. *(Appendix 5A)* What is placed in the first two columns of the work sheet following the account names? From where do these balances come?

34. *(Appendix 5A)* Where do adjusting journal entries come in the accounting cycle? Adding the adjusting entries to the unadjusted trial balance gives rise to what?

35. *(Appendix 5A)* Describe the closing process and list its four basic steps.

36. *(Appendix 5A)* Is Income Summary a temporary or permanent account? What role does it play in the closing process?

37. *(Appendix 5A)* Why is the Dividend account closed directly to the Retained Earnings account instead of through the Income Summary account?

38. *(Appendix 5A)* In terms of the accounting cycle, where can one find the numbers to be placed on the income statement, the statement of retained earnings, the balance sheet, and the statement of cash flows?

39. *(Appendix 5B)* What is T-account analysis and why is it useful to managers?

40. *(Appendix 5B)* Describe the steps involved in T-account analysis.

41. *(Appendix 5B)* Assume that Prepaid Rent on the 1996 and 1997 balance sheets of Taylor Company were $5,600 and $4,700, respectively, and that the company's 1997 income statement indicated Rent Expense of $8,000. Assume further that the statement of cash flows disclosed that cash payments from operating activities totaled $37,500. How much of that cash payment was due to rent?

EXERCISES

E5–1

(Effects of transactions on the accounting equation)

On a separate piece of paper, complete the following chart to show the effect of each transaction on the accounting equation.

TRANSACTION	ASSETS = LIABILITIES + STOCKHOLDERS' EQUITY
1. Owners contributed $30,000 cash.	
2. Purchased land for $20,000 cash.	
3. Borrowed $9,000 cash from bank.	
4. Provided services for $8,000 on account.	
5. Paid $5,500 cash for expenses.	
6. Paid $500 cash dividend to owners.	

E5–2

(Effects of transactions on accounts)

Consider the same transactions as in E5–1, but this time complete the following chart, using a separate sheet of paper.

	ASSETS			= LIABILITIES	+ STOCKHOLDERS' EQUITY	
TRANS.	CASH	ACCOUNTS RECEIVABLE	LAND =	NOTES PAYABLE +	CONTRIBUTED CAPITAL	RETAINED EARNINGS
1.						
2.						
3.						
4.						
5.						
6.						

E5–3

(Preparing the financial statements from the accounts)

Total each asset, liability, and stockholders' equity account in E5–2, and prepare an income statement, a statement of retained earnings, a balance sheet, and a statement of cash flows. Assume that the current year is the company's first year of operations.

E5–4

(Preparing the financial statements)

Assume that Cathedral Enterprises, which is in its first year of operations, entered into the following transactions. Show how the five transactions affect the accounting equation, and prepare an income statement, statement of retained earnings, a balance sheet, and a statement of cash flows.
1. Stockholders contributed $10,000 cash.
2. Performed services for $8,000, receiving $6,000 in cash and a $2,000 receivable.
3. Incurred expenses of $6,000. Paid $3,000 in cash, and $3,000 are still payable.
4. Purchased land for $12,000. Paid $2,000 in cash and signed a long-term note for the remainder.
5. Paid the stockholders $400 in the form of a dividend.
6. Sold one-half of the land purchased in (4) for $7,000 cash.

E5–5

(Which economic events are relevant and objectively measurable?)

The Brown Corporation experienced the following financial events on October 10, 1997.
1. The company entered into a new contract with the employees' union that calls for a $2.00 hour increase in wages, a longer lunch break, and cost-of-living adjustments, effective January 1, 1998.
2. The company issued $200,000 in bonds that mature on October 10, 2007. The terms of the bond issuance stipulate that interest is to be paid semiannually at an annual rate of 10 percent.

3. The company president retired and was replaced by the vice-president of finance.
4. The company received $10,000 from a customer in settlement of an open account receivable.
5. The company paid $1,000 interest on an outstanding loan. The interest is applicable to September 1997 and is included on the books as a liability "Accrued Interest Payable."
6. The market value of all the company's long-lived assets is $275,000. They are currently reported on the balance sheet at $250,000.
7. The company purchased a fire insurance policy for $1,500 that will pay the Brown Corporation $1,000,000 if its primary production plant is destroyed. The policy insures the company from November 1, 1997 through October 31, 1998.
8. The company placed an order to have $10,000 of inventory shipped on October 17, 1997.

REQUIRED:

Indicate whether each of these economic events has accounting significance (i.e., would the company prepare a journal entry for the event?). In each case explain why or why not.

E5–6

(Trial balance and the financial statements)

The following accounts and balances were taken from the ledger of Pratt Printing Company.

Equipment	$ 35,000	Accounts Payable	$ 15,000
Fees Earned	40,000	Common Stock	23,000
Retained Earnings	10,000	Advertising Expense	13,000
Notes Payable	25,000	Other Revenues	8,000
Interest Expense	3,000	Short-Term Investments	10,000
Accounts Receivable	32,000	Miscellaneous Expenses	13,000
Dividends	4,000	Loss on Sale of Investment	2,000
Prepaid Expenses	9,000		

REQUIRED:

Prepare an income statement, statement of retained earnings, and balance sheet.

E5–7

(Preparing a statement of cash flows from the cash ledger)

The following Cash T-account summarizes all the transactions affecting cash during 1997 for Miller Manufacturing.

CASH

Beginning balance	9,000	Equipment purchases	24,000
Sales of services	45,000	Rent payable payments	7,000
Receivables collections	50,000	Bank loan principal	12,000
Sale of land	7,500	Loan interest	3,000
Issuance of common stock	15,000	Salaries	26,500
Long-term borrowings	16,000	Dividend payments	4,000
		Miscellaneous expenses	13,000
		Long-term investment purchase	10,000

REQUIRED:

a. Compute the ending cash balance.
b. Prepare a statement of cash flows.

E5–8

(Preparing a statement of cash flows from journal entries)

Small and Associates, a small manufacturing firm, entered into the following cash transactions during January of 1997.

1. Issued 600 shares of stock for $25 each.
2. Sold services for $4,000.
3. Paid wages of $1,600.
4. Purchased land as a long-term investment for $9,000 cash.
5. Paid a $2,000 dividend.

6. Sold land with a book value of $3,000 for $3,500 cash.
7. Paid $1,500 to the bank: $900 to reduce the principal on an outstanding loan and $600 as an interest payment.
8. Paid miscellaneous expenses of $1,800.

REQUIRED:
a. Prepare journal entries for each transaction.
b. Prepare a cash T-account, and compute Small's cash balance as of the end of January. Assume a beginning balance of $5,000.
c. Prepare a statement of cash flows for the month of January.

E5–9

(Preparing statements from transactions)

The following transactions were entered into by Ed's Lawn Service during 1997, its first year of operations.
1. Collected $12,000 in cash from stockholders.
2. Borrowed $5,000 from a bank.
3. Purchased two parcels of land for a total of $10,000.
4. Paid $5,000 to rent lawn equipment for the remainder of the year.
5. Provided lawn services, receiving $10,000 in cash and $4,000 in receivables.
6. Paid miscellaneous expenses of $4,000.
7. Sold one parcel of land with a cost of $3,000 for $2,800.
8. Paid a $2,200 dividend to the stockholders.

REQUIRED:
a. In a manner similar to Figure 5–2, show how each transaction affected the fundamental accounting equation and prepare an income statement, statement of retained earnings, a year-end balance sheet and statement of cash flows for 1997.
b. Journalize each transaction and post it in the appropriate T-accounts. From this information, prepare a year-end balance sheet and an income statement, statement of retained earnings, and statement of cash flows for 1997.

E5–10

(Preparing the statement of cash flows from the cash T-account)

The following cash T-account summarizes all the transactions affecting cash during 1997 for Miller Manufacturing.

CASH

Beginning balance	8,000	Inventory purchases	27,000
Sales of inventories	34,000	Accounts payable payments	7,000
Receivable collections	40,000	Bank loan principal payments	10,000
Sales of long-term investments	12,500	Loan interest	3,000
Issuance of common stock	14,000	Wages	16,000
Long-term borrowings	9,000	Dividend payments	4,000
		Administrative expenses	12,000
		Equipment purchases	11,000

REQUIRED:
a. Compute the ending cash balance.
b. Prepare a statement of cash flows (direct method).

E5–11

(Classifying adjusting journal entries)

Eaton Enterprises made the following adjusting journal entries on December 31, 1996.

A 1. Rent Expense 1,200
     Rent Payable   1,200
C 2. Insurance Expense 5,000
     Prepaid Insurance   5,000
A 3. Depreciation Expense 20,000
     Accum. Depr.   20,000

4. Interest Receivable 1,500
     Interest Revenue   1,500
5. Unearned Revenue 200
     Fees Earned   200

REQUIRED:

a. Give a brief explanation for each of the above entries.
b. Classify each of the above entries as either a cost expiration adjusting entry or an accrual adjusting entry.

E5–12

(Classifying transactions)

Hog Heaven Rib Joint made the following journal entries on December 31, 1996.

1.	Wage Expense	6,000		7.	Equipment	9,000	
	Wages Payable		6,000		Cash		9,000
2.	Interest Expense	1,000		8.	Supplies Expense	12,000	
	Cash		1,000		Supplies Inventory		12,000
3.	Cash	10,500		9.	Accounts Payable	8,000	
	Note Payable		10,500		Cash		8,000
4.	Rent Expense	1,500		10.	Depreciation Expense	13,000	
	Prepaid Rent		1,500		Accum. Deprec.		13,000
5.	Insurance Expense	2,800		11.	Advertising Expense	8,000	
	Prepaid Insurance		2,800		Cash		8,000
6.	Cash	2,000		12.	Advertising Expense	3,000	
	Unearned Revenues		2,000		Prepaid Advertising		3,000

REQUIRED:
Place each of the transactions above in one of the following five categories: 1. operating cash flow, 2. investing cash flow, 3. financing cash flow, 4. accrual adjusting journal entry, 5. cost expiration adjusting journal entry.

E5–13

(Recognizing accrued wages)

The Hurst Corporation pays its employees every Friday for the 5-day week just ended. On January 2, 1998 the company paid its employees $70,000 for the week beginning Monday, December 29.

REQUIRED:

a. Assuming that the employees earned wages evenly throughout the week, prepare any adjusting journal entries that were necessary on December 31, 1997.
b. Prepare the journal entry that would be recorded on Friday, January 2 when the wages are paid.
c. Complete a chart like the following.

	1997	1998	TOTAL
Wage expense			
Cash outflow associated with wages			

d. What is the purpose of the adjusting journal entry on December 31?

E5–14

(Depreciating a fixed asset)

Valentine Manufacturing purchased a printing press on January 1, 1997 for $24,000 cash. Using the straight-line method, the company depreciated the press over a three-year useful life.

REQUIRED:

a. Compute the book value of the printing press at the end of each of the three years.
b. Complete a chart like the following.

	1997	1998	1999	TOTAL
Depreciation expense				
Cash outflow associated with the purchase of the press				

c. What is the purpose of the adjustments at the end of each period?

E5–15

(The difference between accrual and cash accounting)

Washington Forest Products began operations on January 1, 1996. On December 31, 1996 the company's accountant ascertains that the following amounts should be reported as expenses on the income statement.

Insurance expense	**$20,000**
Supplies expense	**11,000**
Rent expense	**14,000**

A review of the company's cash disbursements indicates that the company made related cash payments during 1996 as follows.

Insurance	**$29,000**
Supplies	**27,000**
Rent	**8,000**

REQUIRED:

a. Explain why the amounts shown as expenses do not equal the cash paid.
b. For each expense account, compute the amount that should be in the related balance sheet account as of December 31, 1996. *Hint*: Note that Forest Products began operations on January 1, 1996.

E5–16

(The difference between net income and net cash flow from operations)

The following journal entries were recorded by Lauren Retailing during the month of July.

1.	**Cash**	**5,000**	4.	**Accounts Payable**	**2,800**
	Accounts Receivable	**3,000**		**Cash**	**2,800**
	Sales	**8,000**			
2.	**Cash**	**2,000**	5.	**Cost of Goods Sold**	**3,700**
	Accounts Receivable	**2,000**		**Inventory**	**3,700**
3.	**Inventory**	**5,800**	6.	**Accrued Expenses**	**2,500**
	Accounts Payable	**5,800**		**Accrued Payables**	**2,500**

REQUIRED:

a. Prepare an income statement and the operating section of a statement of cash flows.
b. Explain why net income is not equal to net cash flow from operations, and reconcile the two numbers.

E5–17

(Preparing a statement of cash flows from original transactions)

Rahal and Watson, a small manufacturing company, entered into the following cash transactions during January of 1997.

1. Issued 800 shares of common stock for $30 each.
2. Collected $3,900 on outstanding accounts receivable.
3. Paid wages for the month of January of $1,530.
4. Purchased land as a long-term investment for $12,000 cash.
5. Paid a $6,000 dividend.
6. Sold a piece of equipment with a book value of $5,000 for $7,000 cash.
7. Paid $2,000 to the bank; $900 to reduce the principal on an outstanding loan, and $1,100 as an interest payment.
8. Paid miscellaneous expenses of $5,000.

REQUIRED:

a. Prepare a journal entry for each transaction. Indicate classification and effect on the accounting equation.
b. Prepare a cash T-account, and compute the company's cash balance as of the end of January. Assume a beginning balance of $4,000.
c. Prepare a statement of cash flows (direct method) for the month of January.

E5–18

(Cash and accrual accounting: comparison of performance measures)

Peters Company was in business for two years, during which it entered into the following transactions.

YEAR 1

1. The owners contributed $24,000 cash.
2. At the beginning of the year, rented a warehouse for two years with a prepaid rent payment of $12,000.
3. Purchased $10,000 of inventory on account.
4. Sold half the inventory for $24,000, receiving $20,000 in cash and an account receivable of $4,000.
5. Paid wages of $6,000 and also accrued wages payable of $4,000.

YEAR 2

1. Paid the outstanding balance for the inventory purchased in Year 1.
2. Paid the outstanding wages payable balance.
3. Sold the remaining inventory for $30,000 cash.
4. Received full payment on the outstanding accounts receivable.
5. Incurred and paid wages of $12,000.
6. Returned the cash balance to the owners and shut down operations.

REQUIRED:

a. Prepare an income statement and a statement of cash flows (direct method) for both Year 1 and Year 2.
b. Complete a chart like the following.

PERFORMANCE MEASURE	YEAR 1	YEAR 2	TOTAL
Net income			
Net cash flow from operating activities			

E5–19

(Assessing economic consequences)

Condensed balance sheets for 1996 and 1997, and the 1997 income statement for Melvin International is provided below.

	1997	1996
Current assets	$22,000	$18,500
Long-term assets	56,000	50,000
Total assets	$78,000	$68,500
Current liabilities	$18,000	$15,000
Long-term liabilities	37,000	45,000
Stockholders' equity	23,000	8,500
Total liabilities and stockholders' equity	$78,000	$68,500
Revenues	$58,000	
Expenses	(34,000)	
Net income	$24,000	

REQUIRED:

a. Early in 1998 the company is considering the following transactions. Treat each separately and compute how it would affect the company's current ratio and debt/equity ratio.
   1. Purchase $5,000 in inventory on account.
   2. Issue common stock for $30,000 cash.
   3. Refinance a $2,000 short-term liability with a $2,000 long-term liability.
   4. Purchase equipment in exchange for a $15,000 long-term note payable.
   5. Pay a $6,000 short-term debt with cash.
b. Assume that the terms of Melvin's long-term debt require the company to maintain a current ratio of 1.2. Is this covenant restriction relevant to whether the company should enter into any of the above transactions? Explain.

c. How much cash could Melvin pay for a long-term investment and still be in compliance with the covenant?

E5–20

(Appendix 5A: Complete a work sheet)

Balmer and Associates has operated for one year. Its unadjusted trial balance follows.

	UNADJUSTED TRIAL BALANCE	
ACCOUNT	DEBIT	CREDIT
Cash	4,200	
Accounts Receivable	14,800	
Rent Receivable	0	
Inventory	19,000	
Prepaid Insurance	1,200	
Office Equipment	42,500	
Accumulated Depreciation		0
Accounts Payable		8,500
Wages Payable		0
Bonds Payable		25,000
Common Stock		35,000
Retained Earnings		0
Sales		30,600
Rent Revenue		1,100
Cost of Goods Sold	11,000	
Wage Expense	7,500	
Depreciation Expense	0	
Insurance Expense	0	
Income Summary		
	100,200	100,200

The following adjusting journal entries were recorded on December 31, 1997. Journal entry explanations have been omitted.

1.	Rent Receivable	600		3.	Wage Expense	1,200	
	Rent Revenue		600		Wages Payable		1,200
2.	Insurance Expense	400		4.	Depreciation Expense	2,000	
	Prepaid Insurance		400		Accum. Depr.		2,000

REQUIRED:

a. Create a work sheet, and transfer the adjusting journal entries to the work sheet.
b. Complete the work sheet and prepare the income statement, statement of retained earnings, balance sheet, and a statement of cash flows using the indirect approach.

E5–21

(Appendix 5B: T-account analysis)

Excerpts from the financial statements of Dunbar Manufacturing are provided below.

WAGES

Cash payments for wages during 1997	$35,000
Wages payable as of December 31, 1997	17,000
Wage expense on the 1997 income statement	39,000

RENT

Prepaid rent as of December 31, 1996	$12,000
Prepaid rent as of December 31, 1997	15,000
Rent expense on the 1997 income statement	21,000

ACCOUNTS RECEIVABLE

Cash collected from customers during 1997	$38,000
Accounts receivable as of December 31, 1996	14,000
Sales revenue on the 1997 income statement	45,000

REQUIRED:
a.   Compute the wages payable as of December 31, 1996.
b.   Compute the cash payments for rent during 1997.
c.   Compute the accounts receivable as of December 31, 1997.

PROBLEMS

P5–1

(Journal entries and the accounting equation)

Below are several transactions entered into by Vulcan Metal Corporation during 1997. Unless otherwise noted, all transactions involve cash.
1.   Purchased equipment for $150,000.
2.   Paid employees $30,000 in wages.
3.   Collected $15,000 from customers as payments on open accounts.
4.   Provided services for $24,000: $16,000 received in cash and the remainder on open account.
5.   Paid $50,000 on an outstanding note payable: $10,000 for interest and $40,000 to reduce the principal.
6.   Purchased a one-month ad in the local newspaper for $5,000.
7.   Purchased a building valued at $250,000 in exchange for $130,000 cash and a long-term note payable.
8.   Sold investments with a cost of $20,000 for $35,000.

REQUIRED:
Prepare journal entries for each transaction and explain how each affects the accounting equation.

P5–2

(T-accounts and the accounting equation)

The following T-accounts reflect seven different transactions that Rodman Container Company entered into during 1997. For each transaction, describe what occurred and how it affected the accounting equation.

CASH		ACCOUNTS RECEIVABLE		EQUIPMENT
(a) 7,000	(c) 2,000	(a) 21,000	(f) 5,000	(d) 50,000
(f) 5,000	(d) 20,000			
(g) 25,000	(e) 1,200			

INVENTORY	ACCOUNTS PAYABLE		NOTES PAYABLE
(b) 6,000	(c) 2,000	(b) 6,000	(d) 30,000

COMMON STOCK	SALES REVENUE	RENT EXPENSE
(g) 25,000	(a) 28,000	(e) 1,200

P5–3

(Journal entries and preparing the four financial statements)

Ryan Hope, controller of Hope, Inc., provides you with the following information concerning Hope during 1997. (Hope, Inc., began operations on January 1, 1997.)
1.   Issued 1,000 shares of common stock at $95 per share.
2.   Paid $2,600 per month to rent office and warehouse space. The rent was paid on the last day of each month.
3.   Made total sales for services of $190,000: $65,000 for cash and $125,000 on account.
4.   Purchased land for $32,000.
5.   Borrowed $75,000 on December 31. The note payable matures in two years.
6.   Salaries totaling $80,000 were paid during the year.
7.   Other expenses totaling $40,000 were paid during the year.

8. $56,000 was received from customers as payment on account.
9. Declared and paid a dividend of $26,000.

REQUIRED:

a. Prepare journal entries for these transactions.
b. Establish T-accounts for each account, and post the journal entries to those T-accounts.
c. Prepare an income statement, statement of retained earnings, a December 31, 1997 balance sheet, and statement of cash flows for 1997.

P5–4

(Preparing the four financial statements)

The December 31, 1996 balance sheet for Morrison Home Services is summarized below.

ASSETS		LIABILITIES AND STOCKHOLDERS' EQUITY	
Cash	**$10,000**	**Liabilities**	**$ 6,000**
Receivables	**4,000**	**Common stock**	**10,000**
Long-term assets	**10,000**	**Retained earnings**	**8,000**
		Total liabilities and	
Total assets	**$24,000**	**stockholders' equity**	**$ 24,000**

During January of 1997 the following transactions were entered into:

1. Services were performed for $7,000 cash.
2. $3,000 cash was received from customers on outstanding accounts receivable.
3. $3,000 cash was paid for outstanding liabilities.
4. Long-term assets were purchased in exchange for a $6,000 note payable.
5. Expenses of $4,000 were paid in cash.
6. A dividend of $800 was issued to the owners.

REQUIRED:

a. Provide a journal entry for each transaction.
b. Treat each transaction independently and describe how each would affect Morrison's current ratio, return on equity, and debt/equity ratio.
c. Prepare the income statement, statement of retained earnings, the January 31 balance sheet, and statement of cash flows for January.

P5–5

(Effects of transactions on the income statement and statement of cash flows)

Ten transactions are listed below. For each one, indicate what specific accounts are affected as well as the direction (increase or decrease) of the effect. Also indicate whether the transaction would increase or decrease both net income (revenues minus expenses) on the income statement and net cash flow from operations (operating cash inflows minus operating cash outflows) on the statement of cash flows. Use the following key: increase (+), decrease (−), and no effect (NE). The first one has been completed for you.

TRANSACTION	ACCOUNTS	DIRECTION	NET INCOME	NET OPERATING CASH FLOW
1. Issued ownership securities for cash.	Cash	+		
	Contributed			
	Capital	+	NE	NE
2. Purchased inventory on account.				
3. Sold a service on account.				
4. Received cash payments from customers on previously recorded sales.				
5. Purchased equipment for cash.				
6. Paid cash to reduce the Wages Payable account.				
7. Sold a service for cash.				
8. Paid off a long-term loan.				
9. Made a cash interest payment.				
10. Sold land for an amount greater than its cost.				

P5-6

(The effects of adjusting journal entries on the accounting equation)

Beta Alloys made the following adjusting journal entries on December 31, 1996. Journal entry explanations have been omitted.

1.	Wage Expense	10,000		5.	Depreciation Expense	20,000	
	Wages Payable		10,000		Accum. Depr.		20,000
2.	Insurance Expense	5,000		6.	Supplies Expense	8,000	
	Prepaid Insurance		5,000		Supplies Inventory		8,000
3.	Interest Receivable	1,000		7.	Unearned Subsc. Rev.	2,000	
	Interest Revenue		1,000		Subscription Revenue		2,000
4.	Unearned Rent Rev.	6,000					
	Rent Revenue		6,000				

REQUIRED:

Classify each adjusting entry as either an accrual adjustment (A) or a cost expiration adjustment (C), and indicate whether each entry increases (+), decreases (−) or has no effect (NE) on assets, liabilities, stockholders' equity, revenues, and expenses. Organize your answer in the following way. The first journal entry has been done for you.

ENTRY	CLASSIFICATION	ASSETS	LIABILITIES	STOCKHOLDERS' EQUITY	REVENUES	EXPENSES
(1)	A	NE	+	−	NE	+

P5-7

(Preparing adjusting journal entries)

The following information is available for M&M Johnson, Inc. Prepare the adjusting journal entries necessary on December 31, 1996.

a.　The December 31, 1996 Supplies Inventory balance is $85,000. A count of supplies reveals that the company actually has $30,000 of supplies on hand.

b.　As of December 31, 1996 Johnson, Inc. had not paid the rent for December. The monthly rent is $2,400.

c.　On December 20, 1996 Johnson collected $18,000 in customer advances for the subsequent performance of a service. Johnson recorded the $18,000 as unearned revenue, and as of December 31 two-thirds of the service had been performed.

d.　The total cost of Johnson's fixed assets is $500,000. Johnson estimates that the assets have a useful life of ten years and uses the straight-line method of depreciation.

e.　Johnson borrowed $10,000 at an annual rate of 12 percent on July 1, 1996. The first interest payment will be made on January 1, 1997.

f.　Johnson placed several ads in local newspapers during December. On December 31 the company received a $28,000 bill for the ads, which was not recorded at that time.

g.　On July 1, 1996 Johnson paid the premium for a one-year life insurance policy. The $350 cost of the premium was capitalized when paid.

P5-8

(Inferring adjusting journal entries from changes in T-account balances)

The following information is available for Derrick Company. Prepare the adjusting journal entries that gave rise to the changes indicated.

ACCOUNT	T-ACCOUNT BALANCE BEFORE ADJUSTMENTS	T-ACCOUNT BALANCE AFTER ADJUSTMENTS
Prepaid Rent	14,500	11,800
Prepaid Insurance	8,500	7,800
Accumulated Depreciation	36,000	38,400
Salaries Payable	1,300	2,500
Unearned Revenues	800	600
Fees Earned	87,600	87,800
Rent Expense	6,500	9,200
Insurance Expense	5,500	6,200
Depreciation Expense	0	2,400
Salary Expense	3,500	4,700

P5–9

(Reconciling accrual and cash flow dollar amounts)

Burkholder Corporation borrowed $28,000 from its bank on January 1, 1996, at an annual interest rate of 10 percent. The $28,000 principal is to be paid as a lump sum at the end of the period of the loan, which is after December 31, 1997. This is the only interest-bearing debt held by Burkholder.

REQUIRED:

The chart below contains six independent cases, each related to the Burkholder Corporation. Compute the missing amount in each case, assuming that the loan described is Burkholder's only outstanding loan.

	CASE 1	CASE 2	CASE 3	CASE 4	CASE 5	CASE 6
12/31/96 interest payable balance	400	800	400	?	200	?
Cash interest payments—1997	3,000	?	2,300	2,600	?	2,500
12/31/97 interest payable balance	?	300	?	200	400	0

P5–10

(Revenue recognition, cost expiration, and cash flows)

Prustate Insurance Company collected $240,000 from Jacobs Printing Corporation for a two-year fire insurance policy on May 31, 1996. The policy is in effect from June 1, 1996 to May 31, 1998.

REQUIRED:

a. Assume that Prustate Insurance Company recorded the $240,000 cash collection as a liability on May 31, 1996.
   1. Prepare the entry to record the cash collection.
   2. Prepare the adjusting entry necessary on December 31, 1996.
   3. What was the purpose of the adjusting journal entry on December 31, 1996?
   4. Complete a chart like the following.

	1996	1997	1998	TOTAL
Insurance revenue				
Cash receipts associated with insurance				

b. Assume that Jacobs' Printing Corporation recorded the $240,000 cash payment as an asset on May 31, 1996.
   1. Prepare the entry to record the cash payment.
   2. Prepare the adjusting entry necessary on December 31, 1996.
   3. What was the purpose of the adjusting journal entry on December 31, 1996?
   4. Complete a chart like the following.

	1996	1997	1998	TOTAL
Insurance expense				
Cash payments associated with insurance				

P5–11

(The effects of transactions on financial ratios)

The balance sheet of Dawn and Company as of December 31, 1996 appears as follows:

ASSETS			LIABILITIES AND STOCKHOLDERS' EQUITY	
Cash		$ 6,000	Accounts payable	$ 11,000
Accounts receivable		7,000	Wages payable	2,000
Inventory		20,000	Long-term notes payable	20,000
Equipment	$45,000		Contributed capital	15,000
Less: Accum. depr.	(10,000)	35,000	Retained earnings	20,000
			Total liabilities and	
Total assets		$68,000	stockholders' equity	$68,000

REQUIRED:

Eight transactions that occurred during 1997 follow. Indicate the effect of each transaction on net income (revenues minus expenses), the current ratio (current assets divided by current liabilities), working capital (current assets minus current liabilities), and the debt/equity ratio (total debt divided by total stockholders' equity) of Dawn and Company. Use the following key: increase (+), decrease (−), no effect (NE). Treat each transaction independently.

TRANSACTION	NET INCOME	CURRENT RATIO	WORKING CAPITAL	DEBT/EQUITY RATIO
1. Issued ownership shares for $12,000 cash.				
2. Purchased equipment costing $8,000 for cash.				
3. Paid off a $700 long-term note payable.				
4. Sold inventory for $10,000 cash.				
5. Declared a $1,000 dividend but not paid.				
6. Paid $2,000 in wages payable.				
7. Received $5,000 from customers on account.				
8. Incurred and paid $1,800 in interest on notes payable.				

P5–12

(Effects of different forms of financing on the financial statements)

The following condensed balance sheet for December 31, 1997 comes from the records of Buzz and Associates.

ASSETS		LIABILITIES AND STOCKHOLDERS' EQUITY	
Cash	$ 10,000	Current liabilities	$ 20,000
Other current asset	40,000	Long-term notes payable	20,000
Property, plant, and equipment	70,000	Contributed capital	30,000
		Retained earnings	50,000
Total assets	$120,000	Total liabilities and stockholders' equity	$120,000

Buzz and Associates is considering the purchase of a new piece of equipment for $30,000. They do not have enough cash to purchase it outright, so they are considering alternative ways of financing. As management sees it, they basically have three options: (1) issue 3,000 ownership shares for $10 per share, (2) take out a long-term loan (12 percent annual interest) for $30,000 from the bank, or (3) purchase the equipment on open account (must be paid in full in thirty days). Presently Buzz has 12,000 ownership shares outstanding.

REQUIRED:

a. Compute the present current ratio, the debt/equity ratio, and the book value of Buzz's outstanding ownership shares: (assets minus liabilities) divided by number of shares outstanding.

b. Compute the current ratio, debt/equity ratio, and book value per share under each of the three financing alternatives, and express your answers in the following format.

FINANCING ALTERNATIVE	CURRENT RATIO	DEBT/EQUITY RATIO	BOOK VALUE PER SHARE
1. Stock issuance			
2. Long-term note			
3. Open account			

c. Discuss some of the pros and cons associated with each of the three financing options.

d. The chairman of the board of directors stated at a recent board meeting that with $50,000 in Retained Earnings, the company should be able to purchase the $30,000 piece of equipment. Comment on the chairman's statement.

P5–13

(Effects of events on financial ratios)

The following balances were taken from the December 31, 1996 balance sheet of Wellington Boating.

Current assets	$23,000
Long-term assets	57,000
Current liabilities	15,000
Long-term liabilities	40,000
Stockholders' equity	25,000

Early in 1997 Wellington is considering the financial effects of the five events listed below. Indicate how each event would affect the financial ratios listed below by completing the following chart. Assume that financial statements are prepared immediately after each event. Treat each event independently, and use the following key: Increase (+), Decrease (−), and No Effect (NE).

	RETURN ON EQUITY	CURRENT RATIO	DEBT/ EQUITY
1. Purchase inventory on account.			
2. Sell land for cash at a gain.			
3. Provide services to customers, receiving cash in return.			
4. Make a principal payment on an outstanding long-term liability.			
5. Issue common stock for cash.			

P5–14

(Effects of events on financial ratios)

The following balances were taken from the December 31, 1996 balance sheet of Morris Homes.

Current assets	$ 87,000
Long-term assets	109,000
Current liabilities	37,000
Long-term liabilities	90,000
Stockholders' equity	69,000

Early in 1997 Morris is considering the financial effects of the five events listed below. Indicate how each event would affect the financial ratios listed below by completing the following chart. Assume that financial statements are prepared immediately after each event. Treat each event independently, and use the following key: Increase (+), Decrease (−), and No Effect (NE).

	RETURN ON SALES	QUICK RATIO	DEBT/ EQUITY
1. Purchase equipment for cash.			
2. Purchase machinery in exchange for a long-term note payable.			
3. Pay salaries, which have not been accrued, to employees.			
4. Declare a dividend.			
5. Issue common stock to satisfy a current obligation.			

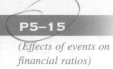

P5–15

(Effects of events on financial ratios)

The following balances were taken from the December 31, 1996 balance sheet of Mariner Enterprises.

Current assets	$15,000
Long-term assets	60,000
Current liabilities	18,000
Long-term liabilities	45,000
Stockholders' equity	12,000

Early in 1997 Mariner is considering the financial effects of the five events listed below. Indicate how each event would affect the financial ratios listed below by completing the following chart. Assume that financial statements are prepared immediately after each event. Treat each event independently, and use the following key: Increase (+), Decrease (−), and No Effect (NE).

	RETURN ON ASSETS	CURRENT RATIO	INVENTORY TURNOVER (TIMES)
1. **Purchase inventory on account.**			
2. **Sell inventory for an amount greater than its cost.**			
3. **Sell equipment for an amount less than its book value.**			
4. **Pay wages that were accrued in a previous period.**			
5. **Provide a service for which cash was collected in a previous period.**			

P5–16

(Appendix 5A: Completing the work sheet and preparing the financial statements)

The following unadjusted trial balance is presented for J. Feeney, Inc., as of December 31, 1997.

	UNADJUSTED TRIAL BALANCE	
ACCOUNT	DEBIT	CREDIT
Cash	88,000	
Accounts Receivable	178,000	
Merchandise Inventory	250,000	
Prepaid Rent	18,000	
Supplies Inventory	75,000	
Plant and Equipment	500,000	
Accumulated Depreciation		149,000
Accounts Payable		104,000
Notes Payable		50,000
Common Stock		325,000
Retained Earnings		501,000
Sales		875,000
Cost of Goods Sold	650,000	
Advertising Expense	30,000	
Insurance Expense	49,000	
Wage Expense	146,000	
Dividends	20,000	
	2,004,000	2,004,000

J. Feeney used the following information to prepare adjusting journal entries on December 31, 1997.
1. Depreciation expense in the amount of $60,000 is recorded each year.
2. A physical count of the merchandise inventory indicates that $130,000 is on hand at the end of the year.

3. The company made an $18,000 rent payment on July 1, which covers the subsequent twelve-month period.
4. A physical count on December 31, 1997 indicates that $62,000 of supplies are on hand.
5. The company will pay employees $30,000 for wages earned for the thirty-day period ending January 15, 1998. Assume that the $30,000 is earned at a rate of $1,000 per day.
6. On November 1, 1997 the company began renting office space to a small insurance agency. The contract calls for rent receipts of $5,000 per month. No rent has been received as of the end of the year.
7. The $50,000 note payable was issued on August 1, 1997. It matures on January 1, 1998 and has a stated annual interest rate of 12 percent.

REQUIRED:

a. Prepare the adjusting journal entries necessary on December 31, 1997.
b. Prepare closing journal entries.
c. Prepare the 1997 income statement and the balance sheet as of December 31, 1997.

P5-17

(Appendix 5A: Comprehensive problem)

The following balance sheet is presented for J.D.F. Company as of December 31, 1996.

J.D.F. COMPANY
BALANCE SHEET
DECEMBER 31, 1996

ASSETS		
Cash		$ 170,000
Accounts receivable		188,000
Merchandise inventory		200,000
Prepaid insurance		74,000
Supplies inventory		40,000
Long-term investments		160,000
Equipment	$480,000	
Less: Accumulated depreciation	98,000	382,000
Machinery	$950,000	
Less: Accumulated depreciation	230,000	720,000
Patent		75,000
Total assets		$2,009,000
LIABILITIES AND STOCKHOLDERS' EQUITY		
Accounts payable		$ 220,000
Wages payable		73,000
Mortgage payable		300,000
Bonds payable		500,000
Common stock		500,000
Retained earnings		416,000
Total liabilities and stockholders' equity		$2,009,000

During 1997, J.D.F. entered into the following transactions.
1. Made credit sales of $1,350,000 and cash sales of $350,000. The cost of the inventory sold was $700,000.
2. Purchased $820,000 of merchandise inventory on account.
3. Made cash payments of $400,000 to employees for salaries. This amount includes the wages due employees as of December 31, 1996.
4. Purchased $110,000 of supplies inventory by issuing a six-month note that matures on March 12, 1998.
5. Collected $850,000 from customers in payment of open accounts receivable.
6. Paid suppliers $870,000 for payment of open accounts payable.
7. Sold a long-term investment for $37,000. The investment had been purchased for $30,000.
8. Paid $60,000 cash for advertising, $36,000 cash for rent, and $52,000 cash for maintenance. It is company policy to expense all such payments.

9. Issued additional common stock for $120,000 cash.
10. On September 30, 1997 a customer gave the company a note due on May 1, 1998 in pay-
    ment of a $72,000 account receivable.
11. The company declared and paid a cash dividend of $50,000.
12. The company purchased stock in Microsoft as a long-term investment for $50,000.

J.D.F. used the following information to prepare adjusting journal entries on December 31,
1997.

(a) 40 percent of the prepaid insurance on January 1 was still in effect as of December 31,
     1997.
(b) A physical count of the supplies inventory indicated that the company had $40,000 on
     hand as of December 31, 1997.
(c) A review of the company's advertising campaign indicates that of the expenditures made
     during 1997 for advertising, $25,000 applies to promotions to be undertaken during 1998.
(d) The company is charged at a rate of $3,500 per month for its rental contracts. Note that it
     paid $36,000 for rent during the year.
(e) The company owes employees $43,000 for wages as of December 31, 1997.
(f) The $72,000 note receivable accepted in payment of an account receivable (see [10] above)
     specifies an annual interest rate of 9 percent.
(g) Equipment has an estimated useful life of ten years, and machinery has an estimated use-
     ful life of twenty years. The patent originally cost $125,000 and had an estimated useful
     life of ten years. The company uses the straight-line method to depreciate and amortize all
     property, plant, equipment, and intangibles.
(h) The note issued by the company (see [4] above) has a stated rate of 10 percent and was
     issued on September 12, 1997.

REQUIRED:

a. Open T-accounts for all balance sheet accounts as of January 1, 1997. Post beginning bal-
    ances. Leave room for twenty-two additional T-accounts with nine lines per account.
 b. Prepare journal entries for the activity during 1997. Post the entries to the ledger.
c. Prepare a work sheet and an unadjusted trial balance.
d. Prepare adjusting journal entries. Post these entries to the appropriate T-accounts and to
    the work sheet.
e. Prepare closing entries, and complete the work sheet. Post these entries to the appropriate
    T-accounts.
f. Prepare an income statement, a statement of retained earnings, a balance sheet, and a state-
    ment of cash flows using the direct and indirect methods.

P5-18

*(Appendix 5B: T-
accounts analysis)*

Excerpts from the financial statements of Tree Tops Services are provided below.

	1997	1996
Balance Sheet:		
Accounts receivable	$ 2,500	$ 3,100
Unearned revenue	1,300	2,600
Income Statement:		
Revenues from services	54,700	49,800
Statement of Cash Flows:		
Net cash from operations	62,400	58,700

Note: Net cash from operations consist of two components: (1) cash collections from services
rendered, and (2) cash payments due to operating activities.

REQUIRED:

For 1997, compute (1) cash collections from services rendered, and (2) cash payments due to
operating activities.

P5–19

(Appendix 5B: T-accounts analysis)

Mayberry Enterprises has two sources of revenue. It sells advertising displays to retail firms and provides a consulting service on how to mount and use these displays. You represent a large manufacturing company that is considering purchasing Mayberry. You have reviewed Mayberry's most recent financial statements, excerpts of which are provided below, and are concerned about which of the two revenue sources is growing in importance for Mayberry. Mayberry's customers always pay for the consulting services in advance, indicating that the accounts receivable balance is associated only with sales of advertising displays.

	1997	1996	1995
Income Statement:			
Revenues	$89,500	$76,000	$67,000
Balance Sheet:			
Accounts receivable	29,500	32,200	35,000
Statement of Cash Flows:			
Collections from display sales	43,500	41,500	39,500

REQUIRED:

Which of the two revenue sources is growing in importance for Mayberry? Support your conclusion with calculations.

P5–20

(Appendix 5B: T-accounts analysis)

You are a credit analyst for First American Bank, and Badger Business has applied for a loan. The company claims to have more than tripled profits from 1996 to 1997 and believes that it should be given prime credit terms. In addition, you note that Badger has expanded its operations, recently paying $37,000 for new equipment that replaced older equipment, which was sold that same year. No other transactions affected the company's equipment account. Excerpts from the company's 1997 financial statements are provided below.

	1997	1996
Balance Sheet:		
Equipment	$97,400	$84,800
Accumulated Depreciation	(26,400)	(24,300)
Income Statement:		
Net Income	5,200	1,500
Depreciation Expenses	8,700	7,600
Statement of Cash Flows:		
Proceeds form equipment sale	23,400	0

REQUIRED:

Reconstruct the journal entry to record the sale of equipment, and comment on Badger's claim that profits more than tripled in 1997.

CASES

C5–1

(Journalizing a transaction and its effect on the accounting equation and balancè sheet)

Several years ago MCI Communications Corporation purchased Satellite Business Systems (SBS) from International Business Machines Corporation (IBM). In the transaction, MCI issued common stock to IBM valued at $376 million and signed a note payable for $104 million. MCI received miscellaneous assets valued at $52 million and the SBS system.

REQUIRED:

Respond to the following.

a. At what dollar amount was the SBS system recorded on MCI's balance sheet?

b. Describe how this transaction affected the accounting equation from MCI's point of view.

c.   Describe how this transaction affected MCI's balance sheet.

d.   Identify the financial statement accounts affected, the direction of the effect, and the dollar amount of the effect on each account.

e.   Prepare the journal entry MCI recorded when the transaction took place.

C5–2

(The effects of transactions on the accounting equation)

The "Big 3" auto makers (General Motors, Ford, and Chrysler) did not have good years in 1990 and 1991. To bolster cash reserves and raise credit ratings, each of the three had major stock issuances during the period. General Motors raised about $600 million, Ford raised over $750 million, and Chrysler sold more than $350 million in newly issued common stock. While each company used the proceeds a little differently, they all used some of it to reduce debt, update plant and equipment, and increase current assets.

REQUIRED:

a.   Describe how the issuance of stock to reduce debt, update plant and equipment, and increase current assets affects the fundamental accounting equation.

b.   Explain how the issuance of stock could increase a company's credit rating.

C5–3

(Differences between net income and net cash flow due to operating activities)

Several years ago the Boeing Company reported a profit increase over the previous year of about 18 percent. Net cash flows due to operating activities, on the other hand, dropped significantly to a negative $680.1 million.

REQUIRED:

a.   Boeing reported depreciation of approximately $300 million during the year. Would this account for the fact that net cash flows due to operating activities were far below earnings? Why or why not?

b.   What other explanations might account for the difference?

c.   During the same year, the market price of Boeing stock fell from $44 1/8 to $19 3/4, a drop of approximately 55 percent. Provide several reasons why this stock price decline may have occurred.

C5–4

(Cash flows and business failures)

The W. T. Grant Company was the nation's largest retailer when it filed for bankruptcy in 1975, only one year after it had reported profits of over $20 million for more than 10 consecutive years. Yet, cash flow provided by operations started dipping as early as 1969 and remained negative until the company's collapse.

REQUIRED:

a.   What kind of items might account for such a divergence between net income and cash flow provided by operations?

b.   What information on the financial statements could have provided some warning of the company's failure?

C5–5

(Capitalize or expense?)

An article published in *The Wall Street Journal* (October 21, 1992) entitled "Polluted Numbers: Audit Report Shows How Far Chambers Would Go For Profits" describes how Chambers Development Co., a large waste-disposal firm, used inappropriate accounting methods to "report strong profits while actually losing money." From 1985 to 1992 the company overstated profits by a total of $362 million . . . "by grossly understating expenses [via capitalizing the costs of waste disposal improperly] and, in the process, violating generally accepted accounting principles . . . The company also admitted capitalizing, as intangible assets, $43 million of internal costs relating to the acquisition of other companies, $65 million of interest cost that should have been expensed, and $27 million in start-up costs for new business and trash hauling routes . . . Chambers put off recognizing $362 million in costs that other companies typically acknowledge as expenses."

REQUIRED:

a.   Explain how Chambers' accounting methods enabled it to grossly overstate it profits.

b. The article further notes that in March of 1992 "the company disclosed it was abandoning its unorthodox accounting methods and taking a $27 million after-tax charge for 1991. Chambers' stock plummeted. In one day, the stockholdings of [the majority owners] lost $493 million in value." Explain how a $27 million charge could reduce the company's value by as much as $493 million.

c. The accounting fraud at Chambers was not uncovered until 1991 when Grant Thornton, the company's external auditors, brought in a fresh team of auditors. The previous Grant Thornton auditors were recently hired by Chambers into top-level finance and accounting positions. An accounting professor at the University of Pittsburgh reacted to this situation by commenting: "If you're simultaneously auditing a company and looking for a job at that company, you may be less aggressive." Explain what the professor means.

C5–6

(Watch cash flow)

Herbert S. Bailey, Jr. published the following poem in *Publishers Weekly* (Jan. 13, 1975) which was written in the meter of Edgar Allen Poe's famous poem, *The Raven*.

> *Though my bottom line is black, I am flat upon my back.*
> *My cash flows out and customers pay slow.*
> *The growth of my receivables is almost unbelievable;*
> *The result is certain - unremitting woe!*
> *And I hear the banker utter an ominous low mutter,*
> *"Watch cash flow."*

REQUIRED:
Explain Mr. Bailey's message.

C5–7

(Appendix 5B: T-account analysis)

Refer to the financial statements of MCI and compute the book gain or loss recognized during 1994 on the sale of marketable securities. Note that MCI carries marketable securities in both the "Current assets" and "Other assets" sections of the balance sheet, and the "Investing activities" section of the statement of cash flows reports cash flows from marketable security purchases and sales. Note also that MCI adopted SFAS 115 in 1994. Under which account on which financial statement would this gain or loss be included?

C5–8

(Appendix 5B: T-account analysis)

Refer to the financial statements of MCI and compute the book value of Communication System property and equipment (including the "Systems in service" and "Other property and equipment" accounts) sold during 1994. Assume that the depreciation charge recorded by MCI during 1994 was associated with these two accounts only, and that cash outflows for the communication system and customer-specific equipment represent additions to these accounts.

P A R T   3

ASSETS: A CLOSER LOOK

CHAPTER 6

THE CURRENT ASSET CLASSIFICATION, CASH, AND ACCOUNTS RECEIVABLE

LEARNING OBJECTIVES

LO 1 Define current assets, working capital, current ratio, and quick ratio, and explain how these measures can be used to assess the solvency position of a company.

LO 2 Recognize how and why managers use "window dressing" techniques to affect the reporting of current assets, working capital, and the current ratio.

LO 3 Identify the techniques used when accounting for and controlling cash.

LO 4 Define accounts receivable, and explain how they are valued on the balance sheet.

LO 5 Explain how the allowance method accounts for uncollectible receivables.

LO 6 Explain the major concerns of financial statement users in the area of receivables reporting.

Parts 1 and 2 of this textbook (Chapters 1–5) provide an overview of the entire accounting process from a manager's perspective. They cover the economic environment in which financial statements exist, how to read and analyze them, the theory underlying accounting measurement, and the mechanics involved in linking transactions to the statements and the statements back to transactions. Parts 3 and 4 provide more specific and detailed discussions of the accounts that compose the balance sheet, income statement, and statement of retained earnings. This chapter covers the current asset classification, cash, and accounts receivable. Chapters 7–12 are devoted to inventories, investments in equity securities, property, plant, and equipment, current liabilities, long-term liabilities, and stockholders' equity, respectively. While the coverage of the accounts follows the order in which they appear on the balance sheet, do not conclude that the income statement is ignored. Each account on the balance sheet is directly related to one or more accounts on the income statement, which suggests that a thorough discussion of the balance sheet naturally implies coverage of the related income statement accounts. Also note that many of the transactions covered in this section of the textbook involve cash flows which, in turn, will be reflected on the statement of cash flows.

This chapter is divided into three sections. Section 1 covers the current asset classification and the measures of solvency and liquidity that use current assets. The dollar amounts in the Cash and Accounts Receivable accounts make up an important part of current assets and are therefore important components of these measures. Sections 2 and 3 consider the definitions, disclosure rules, and methods of accounting for cash and accounts receivable. Two appendices are included at the end of this chapter: 6A—Short-Term Notes Receivable and 6B—Accounting for Receivables and Payables Expressed in Foreign Currencies.

THE CURRENT ASSET CLASSIFICATION

LO 1 Current assets are so named because they are intended to be converted to cash (*liquidated*) in the near future. The exact definition of the near future is subjective, so the accounting profession has provided guidelines. According to professional standards, a **current asset** is defined as any asset that is intended to be converted into cash within one year or the company's **operating cycle**, whichever is longer.[1] As illustrated in Figure 6–1, a company's operating cycle is the time it takes the company to convert its cash to inventory (to purchase or manufacture inventory), sell the inventory, and collect cash from the sale. In other words, the operating cycle is the time required for a company to go through all the required phases of the production and sales process.

FIGURE 6–1

The Operating Cycle

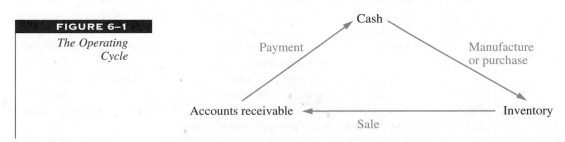

1. "Current Assets and Current Liabilities," *Accounting Research Bulletin No. 43, Restatement and Revision of Accounting Research Bulletin* (New York: American Institute of Accountants, 1953), Chapter 3A.

As the definition of current assets states, if the operating cycle is longer than one year, it serves as the time period for current assets. Companies with different operating cycles therefore use different time periods to define current assets. Compare, for example, the relatively short operating cycles of grocery chains like Safeway, Albertsons, and Lucky Stores, to the operating cycles of companies in the aerospace industry like The Boeing Company and McDonnell Douglas, which require several years to manufacture aircraft. Indeed, the time periods of current assets differ widely from company to company. However, the accounts included in the current asset section on the balance sheets of all companies are virtually the same. They are Cash, Short-Term Investments, Short-Term Accounts and Notes Receivable, Inventories, and Prepaid Expenses. The individual accounts that compose the current asset classification were briefly discussed and illustrated in Chapter 2.

THE RELATIVE SIZE OF CURRENT ASSETS ACROSS INDUSTRIES

The relative size of current assets differs significantly across companies in different industries. Note in Figure 6–2 that current assets as a percentage of total assets varies from an average of 32 percent in the telephone communication industry to over 80 percent for certain retailers and security brokers. Indeed, the current assets of MCI, a member of the telephone communication industry, are only 29% of total assets, while the ratio of current to total assets for Merrill Lynch, a security broker, is approximately 80 percent.

These variations are large because each company's operations are very different. Retailers carry large amounts of inventory and receivables, especially if they provide their own credit cards (e.g., J.C. Penney). Security brokers (e.g., Salomon Brothers) hold large amounts of cash and receivables and invest heavily in short-term securities, while automobile manufacturers (e.g., General Motors) carry significant inventories. On the other hand, the primary investment for eating places (e.g., McDonald's) and telephone communications companies (e.g., AT&T) is in property, plant and equipment. Consequently, accounting for and managing current assets, while important for all industries, is especially important for retailers, financial services, and certain manufacturers.

MEASURES USING CURRENT ASSETS: WORKING CAPITAL, CURRENT RATIO, AND QUICK RATIO

The distinction between current and noncurrent assets is useful because it provides an easy-to-determine, low-cost measure of a company's ability to produce cash in the short run. Current assets are often compared to current liabilities (the liabilities expected to require cash payments within the same time period as current assets) as an indicator of a company's solvency position.[2] Reasoning that current liabilities are a measure of short-run cash outflows, these comparisons appear to be logical. Three such comparisons, which were discussed in Chapter 3, are working capital and two solvency ratios, the current ratio and the quick ratio. **Working capital** is defined as current assets less current liabilities; the **current ratio** is equal to current assets divided by current liabilities; and the **quick ratio** divides cash plus short-term investments plus short-term receivables by current liabilities.[3]

---

2. Current liabilities are introduced and listed in Chapter 2 and discussed extensively in Chapter 10.
3. The quick ratio is sometimes calculated with only cash and short-term investments in the numerator.

FIGURE 6–2	INDUSTRY	SIC CODE	NO. OF COMPANIES	AVERAGE CURRENT ASSETS/TOTAL ASSETS
	MANUFACTURING			
	Motor Vehicles	3711	95	.71
	Petroleum and Gas	1311	872	.41
	RETAILING			
	Department Stores	5311	641	.77
	Hobby, Toy & Games	5945	519	.83
	GENERAL SERVICES			
	Eating Places	5812	2,427	.36
	Telephone Commun.	4813	1,130	.32
	FINANCIAL SERVICES			
	Bank Holding Co.	6719	188	.51
	Security Brokers	6211	1,312	.84

Current assets as a percentage of total assets (industry averages)

Note: Throughout the text these four general industry groupings (Manufacturing, Retailing, General Services, and Financial Services) and sample industries will be used for comparison. In Dun & Bradstreet a different SIC Code is assigned to each of the hundreds of separate industries listed in the publication; for example, SIC Code 3711 is used to identify the motor vehicles manufacturing industry, which consists of 95 companies. The three largest companies in this industry are General Motors, Ford, and Chrysler. The seven remaining industries represented on the table also include a number of well-known companies: Petroleum and Gas (Exxon, Mobil, and Texaco), Department Stores (J.C. Penney, Wal-Mart, and Kmart), Hobby, Toy & Games (Toys "R" Us, Lionel, and Child World), Eating Places (McDonald's, Wendy's, and Ryan's Steak House), Telephone Communications (AT&T, Ameritech, and MCI), Bank Holding Companies (Citicorp, J.P. Morgan, and BankAmerica), and Security Brokers (Merrill Lynch, Morgan Stanley, and Salomon Brothers).

Source: Compiled from data published in *Industry Norms and Key Business Ratios* (Dun & Bradstreet, Inc., 1994)

The magnitude of a typical current ratio can be assessed by referring to Figure 6–3. The average current ratios listed vary from 1.3 for eating places to 3.6 for retail department stores. However, the current ratios of individual companies can vary even more. Ryan's Steak House, a successful fast-food chain, normally reports a current ratio of about .14, which is well below the averages indicated in Figure 6–3.

Average current ratios vary across industries because the relative importance of current assets and the methods used to finance them vary across companies in different industries. A large dollar value of current assets, financed by long-term debt or profitable operations (retained earnings), for example, will give rise to a large current ratio.

For example, a company such as J.C. Penney, a giant in the retail industry, has current assets representing almost 70 percent of total assets. As a retail operation, J.C. Penney must carry large amounts of short-term receivables and inventories, which are financed through long-term borrowings and profitable operations. The company's current ratio is consequently relatively large, ranging between 2.5 and 3.0. The current assets of companies such as Wendy's International and McDonald's Corporation, on the other hand, represent a significantly smaller portion of total assets: approximately 13 percent for Wendy's and 5 percent for McDonald's. The largest assets on these companies' balance sheets are land, buildings, and restaurant equipment. Both

FIGURE 6–3	INDUSTRY	SIC CODE	No. OF COMPANIES	AVERAGE CURRENT ASSETS/AVERAGE CURRENT LIABILITIES
Current ratios: current assets/current liabilities (industry averages)	**MANUFACTURING**			
	Motor Vehicles	3711	95	1.6
	Petroleum and Gas	1311	872	1.6
	RETAILING			
	Department Stores	5311	641	3.6
	Hobby, Toy & Games	5945	519	3.4
	GENERAL SERVICES			
	Eating Places	5812	2,427	1.3
	Telephone Commun.	4813	1,130	2.9
	FINANCIAL SERVICES			
	Bank Holding Co.	6719	188	2.2
	Security Brokers	6211	1,312	2.6

Source: Compiled from data published in *Industry Norms and Key Business Ratios* (Dun & Bradstreet, Inc., 1994)

companies also rely heavily on long-term debt and profitable operations to finance asset acquisitions, but their relatively small current asset accounts cause their current ratios to be well below 1.0.

THE ECONOMIC CONSEQUENCES OF WORKING CAPITAL, THE CURRENT RATIO, AND THE QUICK RATIO

Managers must understand how transactions affect working capital, the current ratio, and the quick ratio because these measures are often used by investors, bankers, and other lenders (e.g., bondholders) to help assess a company's ability to meet current obligations as they come due. For example, Dun & Bradstreet, a widely used service that rates the creditworthiness of a large number of U.S. businesses, includes both the current ratio and the quick ratio as solvency measures in its list of fourteen key business ratios. Another of these key ratios, sales/working capital, is described as indicating whether a company has enough (or too many) current assets to support its sales volume. The formula used by Dun & Bradstreet to determine a company's credit rating, which in turn relates to the company's ability to borrow funds and the terms of its outstanding loans, includes these fourteen ratios.[4]

The measures of working capital and the current ratio also appear in loan contracts and debt covenants, where they specify certain minimum dollar amounts or ratios that a debtor company must maintain. For example, a recent financial report of Cummins Engine Company, a manufacturer of heavy-duty truck engines, indicated that loan agreements entered into by the company require maintenance of a 1.25 current ratio. This means that Cummins must maintain a current ratio of 1.25, or the creditor has the right to call for the immediate payment of the entire loan principal. Similarly, McDonnell Douglas, a giant in the aerospace industry, has revolving credit agreements with a number of banks specifying that the company must maintain a certain level of working capital.

---

4. Many of the 14 ratios were discussed in Chapter 3, but Dun & Bradstreet use others as well.

Working capital, the current ratio, and the quick ratio are also used by auditors. For example, an AICPA list of "red flags" alerting auditors to possible management fraud includes "inadequate working capital." The AICPA reasons that low amounts of working capital may put pressure on management to fraudulently manipulate the financial records in an effort to deceive stockholders, creditors, investors, and others. In addition, examining a company's working capital and current ratio can help an auditor assess whether there is substantial doubt about a company's ability to continue operations in the future. Information that helps to predict business failures is valuable to auditors because such failures lead to investor and creditor losses, which in turn can lead to costly lawsuits against auditors.

LIMITATIONS OF THE CURRENT ASSET CLASSIFICATION

L O 2 While working capital, the current ratio, and the quick ratio are used extensively in business to assess solvency, they have a number of inherent and significant weaknesses. These limitations are related to the fundamental fact that current assets and current liabilities fail to accurately reflect future cash inflows and outflows, the essence of a company's ability to meet its debts as they come due. As noted by Leopold A. Bernstein,

The current ratio is not fully up to the task [of assessing short-term liquidity] because it is a static or "stock" concept of what resources are available at a given moment to meet the obligations at that moment. Moreover, working capital . . . does not have a logical or causative relationship to the future funds which flow through it. The future flows are, of course, the focus of our greatest interest in the assessment of short-term liquidity. And yet, these flows depend importantly on elements not included in the current ratio, such as sales, profits, and changes in business conditions.[5]

In addition, management has incentives to choose accounting methods and make operating decisions for no reason other than to "cosmetically" inflate the balances in the current asset accounts. For example, Datapoint, a computer manufacturer, once was charged by the SEC with materially overstating its receivables and revenues. The company was apparently shipping computers without customer authorization and thereby recording sales and receivables prematurely. Several years ago, General Motors changed its method of accounting for inventory and by doing so increased the dollar amount reported in its inventory account, and therefore its current assets, by $224 million. Such actions can have a significant impact on solvency ratios, which in turn may affect the company's credit rating as well as determine whether a company is in violation of a loan contract or debt covenant.

From these examples, it is clear that managers have discretion over the accounts in the current asset section of the balance sheet and thus have some control over measures like working capital, the current ratio, and the quick ratio. Exercising such discretion to inflate these measures is called **window dressing** and includes choosing accounting methods or making operating decisions that are designed solely to make the financial statements appear more attractive. Keep in mind, however, that while the practice of window dressing is widespread, it may not serve management's long-run interest. Managers who attempt to deceive by manipulating the dollar amounts on the financial statements risk reducing the credibility of the statements, which may actually hinder their abilities to raise debt and equity capital.

---

5. Leopold A. Bernstein, "Working Capital as a Tool," *Journal of Accountancy* (December 1981), pp. 82, 84, 86.

A MOVEMENT TOWARD CASH FLOW ACCOUNTING

In view of these limitations, measures like working capital, the current ratio, and the quick ratio are rarely viewed as the only ways to assess solvency. Cash flow numbers are quickly gaining popularity as indicators of a company's ability to meet its debts as they come due. The statement of cash flows, for example, which discloses the net cash flows from operating, investing, and financing activities, is increasingly being used by investors and creditors to assess solvency. For example, Loyd C. Heath, an accounting professor at the University of Washington, states that "the emphasis in credit analysis has shifted from analysis of working capital position to dynamic analysis of future cash receipts and payments,"[6] and a recent survey of investors published in *Management Accounting* (July, 1992) notes "investors use the statement of cash flows more, and the income statement less, than previously."

Nonetheless, solvency and liquidity measures based on the current asset classification are still important and widely used. Working capital, the current ratio, and the quick ratio are low-cost surrogates for cash flow measures and are still used extensively by investors and creditors and in loan contracts and debt covenants. It is important, therefore, that you as a manager understand how transactions affect these measures and how these measures can be used to assess solvency and earning power. As we move now into discussions of each individual current asset, keep in mind that the accounting methods and operating decisions that affect these assets also affect working capital, the current ratio, and the quick ratio.

CASH

LO 3 The cash account is the first asset listed in the current asset section of the balance sheet. It consists of coin, currency, and checking accounts, as well as money orders, certified checks, cashiers' checks, personal checks, and bank drafts received by a company. Remember also that cash is the standard medium of exchange and thus provides the basis for measuring all financial statement accounts.

Companies use a number of different titles to describe the Cash account on their balance sheets. *Accounting Trends and Techniques* (1994) provided the summary contained in Figure 6–4 of the balance sheet captions of 600 of the largest companies in the United States. Note that the title *Cash* is decreasing in popularity, while *Cash and Equivalents* is becoming much more common.

FIGURE 6–4	1993	1992	1991	1990
Cash: balance sheet captions				
Cash	84	94	96	123
Cash and equivalents	451	439	425	391
Cash, including certificates of deposit or time deposits	9	9	10	10
Cash and marketable securities	53	56	66	73
No amount for cash	3	2	3	3
Total companies	600	600	600	600

Source: *Accounting Trends and Techniques* (1994).

6. Loyd C. Heath, "Is Working Capital Really Working?" *Journal of Accountancy* (August 1980), pp. 55–62.

The relative size of the Cash account on the balance sheet varies across companies in different industries. Figure 6–5 shows that cash is a relatively small asset for large manufacturers (e.g., Ford Motor Co.) and department stores (e.g., Wal-Mart), but somewhat more important for security brokers (e.g., Morgan Stanley) and eating places (e.g., Kentucky Fried Chicken). Companies that transact in cash, such as financial institutions, motion picture theaters, and grocery stores tend to carry larger amounts of cash on hand than companies that sell large ticket items (e.g., automobiles, household appliances) often on credit.

Three issues concerning cash are particularly important to managers: (1) restrictions on the use of cash, (2) proper management of cash, and (3) control of cash.

FIGURE 6–5 *Cash as a percentage of total assets and current assets (industry averages)*	INDUSTRY	SIC CODE	NO. OF COMPANIES	CASH/ TOTAL ASSETS	CASH/ CURRENT ASSETS
	MANUFACTURING				
	Motor Vehicles	3711	95	.09	.13
	Petroleum and Gas	1311	872	.14	.36
	RETAILING				
	Department Stores	5311	641	.11	.14
	Hobby, Toy & Games	5945	519	.16	.19
	GENERAL SERVICES				
	Eating Places	5812	2,427	.17	.48
	Telephone Commun.	4813	1,130	.13	.40
	FINANCIAL SERVICES				
	Bank Holding Co.	6719	188	.16	.31
	Security Brokers	6211	1,312	.33	.39

Source: Compiled from data published in *Industry Norms and Key Business Ratios* (Dun & Bradstreet, Inc., 1994).

RESTRICTIONS ON THE USE OF CASH

In general, cash presents few problems from a reporting standpoint. There are no valuation problems because cash always appears on the balance sheet at face value. The only reporting issue is whether there are restrictions on its use.

Restrictions placed on a company's access to its cash are typically imposed by creditors to help insure future interest and principal payments. As part of a loan agreement, for example, a creditor may require that a certain amount of cash be held in **escrow**; that is, controlled by a trustee until the debtor's existing liability is discharged. In addition, banks sometimes require that minimum cash balances be maintained on deposit in the accounts of customers to whom they lend money or extend credit. These amounts are called **compensating balances**.

Cash held in escrow and compensating balances are examples of cash amounts that a company may own but cannot immediately use. Such restricted cash should be separated from the general Cash account on the balance sheet, and the restrictions should be clearly described either on the balance sheet itself or in the footnotes to the financial statements. If the restricted cash is to be used for payment of obligations maturing within the time period of current assets, the separate cash account is appropriately classified as a current asset. If it is to be held for a longer period of time, it should be classified as noncurrent.

Owens-Corning Fiberglas Corporation, for example, noted in a recent financial report that $85 million, almost 96 percent of its $89 million cash balance, was restricted. Approximately $70 million was held in escrow to be used in the following year for the payment of a long-term debt, and $15 million was temporarily "locked" in a Brazilian bank. That same year, Atlantic Richfield Company's financial report noted that "the company maintains compensating balances for some of its various banking services and products." Both Owens-Corning and Atlantic Richfield included the restricted funds among their current assets. Manville Corporation, in its financial report, indicated that $278 million was placed in escrow in connection with bankruptcy proceedings. These funds were not included as current assets.

PROPER MANAGEMENT OF CASH

Proper cash management requires that enough cash be available to meet the needs of a company's operations, yet too much is undesirable because idle cash provides no return and loses purchasing power during periods of inflation. Maintaining a proper balance is one of management's greatest challenges. On one hand, enough cash must be available so that a company can meet its cash obligations as they come due. Purchases are often made in cash, and payments on accounts payable require cash. Wages, salaries, and currently maturing long-term debts must be honored in cash. Normally the cash needed for such operating activities is kept on the premises in the form of **petty cash** (small amounts of cash to cover day-to-day needs) or deposited in an interest-bearing checking account, where it earns a moderate rate of interest and can be withdrawn immediately as cash needs arise.

Cash in and of itself, however, is not a productive asset. Consider, for example, a recent popular TV game show that left $1 million under a plastic dome sitting out on the stage. The amount of annual interest income that was forgone by leaving that amount of cash idle, assuming a 10 percent interest rate, was $100,000 ($1,000,000 × 10%). Furthermore, during inflationary times, cash continually loses purchasing power. Assuming a 5 percent annual rate of inflation, it would require $1.05 million at the end of a year to buy the same goods and services that could have been purchased with $1 million at the beginning of the year. Consequently, cash over and above the amount needed for operations should be invested in income-producing assets, like short-term investments, inventories, long-term investments, property, plant, and equipment, and intangible assets, or returned to shareholders as dividends.

A company that maintains a cash balance of more than is necessary for its day-to-day needs is not operating at its full potential. It is, of course, a desirable practice to keep a little extra in the checking account to meet unforeseen cash requirements, but in general, cash in excess of the amount necessary to cover day-to-day cash obligations should be invested in assets that produce a higher return. Determining this amount and where to invest the excess is a very important concern of a company's managers.

Cash management decisions often are based on the information provided by the accounting system. One useful tool for cash management, which is an output of the accounting systems, is a **cash budget**, a report that projects future cash inflows and outflows and thereby helps to assess future cash operating needs. This report, however, is generated and used internally and is not available to stockholders, investors, creditors, and other parties outside a company. It contains classified information and future projections that cannot be objectively verified and audited. Consequently, this text does not cover cash budgets; they are normally covered in managerial accounting courses.

CONTROL OF CASH

The control of cash is an important responsibility of a company's accounting system. It is a special concern for businesses such as grocery stores, movie theaters, restaurants, financial institutions, retail stores, department stores, and bars, which process frequent cash transactions. There are two aspects to the control of cash: record control and physical control.

RECORD CONTROL OF CASH

Record control refers to the procedures designed to ensure that the cash account on the balance sheet reflects the actual amount of cash in the company's possession. Problems of record control arise when many different kinds of transactions involve cash, and it is difficult to record them all accurately. Proper control of cash records requires that all cash receipts and disbursements be faithfully recorded and posted. Periodically, the dollar amount of cash indicated in the cash account in the ledger should be checked against and reconciled with the cash balance indicated on the statement provided by a company's bank.

PHYSICAL CONTROL OF CASH

Physical control of cash refers to the procedures designed to safeguard cash from loss or theft. Problems of physical control arise because cash is the standard medium of exchange; it is universally desired and easily concealed and transported. Cash embezzlement by a company's employees is always a threat. Indeed, *U.S. News and World Report* reported that there were 12,600 arrests for embezzlement during 1986 in the United States.[7]

Proper physical control of cash requires that a minimum amount of cash be kept on a company's premises at any one time. Petty cash amounts used to cover day-to-day office expenses and cash receipts from sales or receivable payments should be handled by as few employees as possible and stored in a safe or locked cash drawer. Cash amounts in excess of petty cash requirements should be taken to the bank at frequent intervals.

ACCOUNTS RECEIVABLE

LO 4 **Accounts receivable** arise from selling goods or services to customers who do not immediately pay cash. Often backed by oral rather than written commitments, accounts receivable represent short-term extensions of credit that are normally collectible within thirty to sixty days. These credit trade agreements are often referred to as **open accounts**. Often many such transactions are enacted between a company and its customers, and it is impractical to create a formal contract for each one. Open accounts typically reflect running balances because at the same time customers are paying off previous purchases, new purchases are being made. If an account receivable is paid in full within the specified thirty- or sixty-day period, no interest is charged. Payment after this period, however, is usually subject to a significant financial charge. Credit card arrangements with department stores, like Sears and J.C. Penney, and oil companies, like Exxon and Chevron, are common examples of open accounts.

---

7. Harold R. Kennedy et al. "Resolving Mysterious Credit Charges," *U.S. News and World Report*, March 14, 1988, p. 108.

The following journal entries illustrate the recognition of accounts receivable from (1) the sale of merchandise[8] and (2) the sale of a service.

Accounts Receivable (+A)	500	
Sales (R, +SE)		500

Sold two items of inventory for $250 each on account.

Accounts Receivable (+A)	150	
Fees Earned (or Service Revenue) (R, +SE)		150

Provided consulting services for $150 on account.

Note that the recognition of the account receivable in each case is accompanied by the recognition of a revenue: sales or fees earned (service revenue). Both the balance sheet and the income statement are therefore affected when accounts receivable are established. Note also that the recognition of an account receivable is an application of the accrual system of accounting. Recall from Chapter 4 that revenues are recognized when the four criteria of revenue recognition are met.[9] Accounts receivable, therefore, are established in those cases where these four criteria are met prior to cash collection.

As the following journal entry below illustrates, when cash is ultimately received, the accounts receivable balance is removed from the balance sheet and no revenue is recognized.

Cash (+A)	500	
Accounts Receivable (−A)		500

Collected cash on account.

The Accounts Receivable account therefore appears on the balance sheet during the time period between the recognition of a revenue and the receipt of the related cash payment.

IMPORTANCE OF ACCOUNTS RECEIVABLE

In our heavily credit-oriented economy, transactions that give rise to accounts receivable make up a significant portion of total business transactions. Indeed, *Business Week* notes that "trade credit is a significant part of most companies' balance sheets. The Federal Reserve Board reports trade credit held by U.S. nonfinancial corporations accounts for about 41 percent of their financial assets."[10] Figure 6–6 contains a selected list of industries and indicates the importance of accounts receivable relative to total assets and current assets.

Restaurants and grocery stores carry relatively small levels of receivables because their customers normally pay with cash, personal checks, or bank cards such as MasterCard, VISA, and American Express.[11] Department stores, such as J.C. Penney and Sears, carry larger portions of short-term receivables because they issue their own charge cards, which their customers use extensively. Professional services (e.g., major public accounting firms), which are not represented in Figure 6–6, bill their clients

---

8. The sale of merchandise also involves the outflow of inventory, which must be recognized before financial statements are prepared.

9. The four criteria of revenue recognition are: (1) the earning process is substantially complete, (2) revenue is objectively measurable, (3) post-sale costs can be estimated, and (4) cash collection is reasonably assured.

10. Kathleen Madigan, "Economic Trends," *Business Week*, April 11, 1988, p. 27.

11. When a customer uses a bank card to pay for an item or service (e.g., VISA or MasterCard), the selling company does not carry the receivable on its balance sheet. The receivable is "sold" to the finance company that issued the card. Such an arrangement is called *factoring*.

FIGURE 6–6

Accounts receivable as a percentage of total assets and current assets (industry averages)

INDUSTRY	SIC CODE	No. OF COMPANIES	ACCOUNTS RECEIVABLE/ TOTAL ASSETS	ACCOUNTS RECEIVABLE/ CURRENT ASSETS
MANUFACTURING				
Motor Vehicles	3711	95	.16	.22
Petroleum and Gas	1311	872	.16	.39
RETAILING				
Department Stores	5311	641	.14	.18
Hobby, Toy & Games	5945	519	.03	.03
GENERAL SERVICES				
Eating Places	5812	2,427	.04	.12
Telephone Commun.	4813	1,130	.11	.36
FINANCIAL SERVICES				
Bank Holding Co.	6719	180	.11	.21
Security Brokers	6211	1,312	.10	.12

Source: Compiled from data published in *Industry Norms and Key Business Ratios* (Dun & Bradstreet, Inc., 1994).

and normally receive final payment several months after the billed service is completed. Receivables constitute a large portion of the total assets of such firms because they carry virtually no inventory and relatively few fixed assets. Their professionals are their most important assets.

NET REALIZABLE VALUE: THE VALUATION BASE FOR ACCOUNTS RECEIVABLE

The key factor in valuing accounts receivable on the financial statements is the amount of cash that the receivables are expected to generate. The cash is expected to be received in the future; in theory, therefore, present value should be used as the valuation base. The expected future cash receipt should theoretically be discounted. However, as indicated earlier, the period of time from the initial recognition of an account receivable to cash collection is normally quite short (thirty to sixty days). Consequently, the difference between the amount of cash to be received and the present value of the expected cash flows from the receivable is considered immaterial. For example, the difference between $100 and the present value of $100 to be received in one month, given a 10 percent annual interest rate, is approximately $.76. Therefore, the face value of the receivable, the amount of cash to be collected, is judged to be a reasonable approximation of present value and, accordingly, provides the starting point for balance sheet valuation.

While the face value of the receivable represents a starting point, there are a number of reasons why it may not represent the actual amount of cash ultimately collected. Many companies, for example, offer cash discounts, allowing customers to pay lesser amounts if they pay within specified time periods. Other accounts receivable may produce no cash at all because customers simply refuse to pay (bad debts) or choose to return previously sold merchandise (sales returns). Each of these issues must be considered when placing a value on the Accounts Receivable account on the balance sheet.

Accordingly, the valuation base for the Accounts Receivable account is not the face amount of the receivables but rather the **net realizable value**, an estimate of the cash that is expected to be produced by the receivables.

Net Realizable Value of Accounts Receivable = Face Value − Adjustments for (1) Cash Discounts, (2) Bad Debts, and (3) Sales Returns

CASH DISCOUNTS

When a good or service is sold on credit, creating a receivable, the company making the sale naturally wants to collect the cash as soon as possible. To encourage prompt payment, many companies offer discounts (called **cash discounts**) on the gross sales price. There are benefits associated with offering these discounts because collected cash can be used to earn a return, and eliminating receivables quickly reduces the costs of maintaining records for and collecting outstanding receivables. Presumably, companies that offer cash discounts believe that these benefits exceed the reduction in future cash proceeds that results from the discount.

Cash discounts simply specify that an amount of cash less than the gross sales price is sufficient to satisfy an outstanding receivable, if the cash is received within a certain time period. Certain sales on account, for example, may be subject to a 2 percent (of the gross sales price) cash discount if paid within ten days. Such terms are expressed in the following way: *2/10, n/30*, which reads "two-ten, net thirty." This expression means "a discount in the amount of 2 percent of the gross sales price is available, if payment is received within ten days. To avoid finance charges over and above the gross price, payment must be received within thirty days." Other terms on cash discounts are also common: *3/20, n/30*, for example, means "a discount in the amount of 3 percent of the gross sales price is available, if payment is received within twenty days, and finance charges over and above the gross price can be avoided if payment is received within thirty days." *n/10, EOM* means that the net amount of the sale (gross price less cash discount) is due no later than ten days after the end of the month.

CASH DISCOUNTS VS. QUANTITY DISCOUNTS AND MARKDOWNS

Cash discounts, which can be viewed as incentives for prompt payment of open accounts, should be distinguished from quantity discounts and markdowns, which are simply reductions in sales prices. A **quantity discount** is a reduction in the per-unit price of an item if a certain quantity is purchased. "Cheaper by the dozen" is an example. **Markdowns**, which are quite common in the retail clothing industry, are reductions in sales prices normally due to decreased demand.

This distinction is important because cash discounts are reflected in the financial statements, but quantity discounts and markdowns are not. To illustrate, in conjunction with an end-of-season sale, suppose that Macy's Department Store reduces the price of a certain line of shoes from $40 to $25. This $15 markdown is simply a reduction in the sales price of the shoes and would not be reflected in Macy's books when the shoes are sold. The journal entry to record the sale of a pair of shoes would simply be:

Cash (or Accounts Receivable) (+A)   25
    Sales (R, +SE)   25
Sold merchandise for cash (or on account).

Note that the books give no recognition to the fact that the original sales price was $40. The asset (Cash or Accounts Receivable) and the revenue (Sales) are valued at the exchange price at the time of the transaction. The fact that the shoes were originally priced at $40 is ignored.

ACCOUNTING FOR CASH DISCOUNTS

There are two ways to account for cash discounts: the **gross method** and the net method. The gross method is more straightforward and much more common in practice. Consequently, we cover only the gross method. Figure 6–7 illustrates the entries involved in the gross method.

The gross method initially recognizes the transaction at $1,000, the gross sales price, and thereby is based on the assumption that Buyer Company, the customer, will not receive the cash discount. If Buyer Company pays within the ten-day discount period (Case 1), a Cash Discount account is used to balance the difference between the gross receivable ($1,000) and the cash proceeds ($980). Cash Discount is a temporary account that appears on the income statement of Seller Company. Its debit balance serves as a contra account to the credit balance in the Sales account, giving rise to an income statement number called *net sales*. An example of the form of this disclosure follows.

Sales	**$50,000**
Less: Cash discounts	**1,000**
Net sales	**$49,000**

If Buyer Company misses the ten-day discount (Case 2), the $1,000 cash receipt after the expiration of the discount period exactly matches the gross amount in Seller Company's Accounts Receivable account.

FIGURE 6–7

Accounting for cash discounts

GIVEN INFORMATION:
Assume that Seller Company sells goods on account with a gross sales price of $1,000 to Buyer Company on December 15, 1996 (terms 2/10, n/30). The following journal entries would be recorded on the books of Seller Company using the gross method for two different cases.

Initial sale on December 15.	Accounts Receivable (+A)	1,000	
	Sales (R, +SE)		1,000
	Sold goods on account.		
CASE 1:			
Assume that Seller Company receives full payment on December 20 (within the 10-day discount period).	Cash (+A)	980	
	Cash Discount (−R, −SE)	20	
	Accounts Receivable (−A)		1,000
	Paid on account.		
CASE 2:			
Assume full payment is received by Seller Company on January 3 (beyond the 10-day discount period).	Cash (+A)	1,000	
	Accounts Receivable (−A)		1,000
	Paid on account.		

ACCOUNTING FOR UNCOLLECTIBLES (BAD DEBTS)

In an ideal world all receivables would be satisfied and there would be no need to consider bad debts. However, accounts that are ultimately uncollectible are an unfortunate fact of life, and companies must act both to control them and to estimate their effects on the financial statements. To give you some idea of the magnitude of bad debts, Figure 6–8 shows 1994 uncollectibles as a percentage of outstanding receivables for several major U.S. corporations.

FIGURE 6–8	COMPANY	BAD DEBTS/ OUTSTANDING RECEIVABLES
Bad debts as a percentage of outstanding receivables	**May Department Stores**	3%
	General Electric	3
	Federal Express	3
	American Telephone and Telegraph	4
	PepsiCo	6
	Sprint	8

Source: 1994 Annual Reports

Controlling bad debts is a costly undertaking for many companies. The creditworthiness of potential customers can be checked by subscribing to credit-rating services such as Dun & Bradstreet, Moody's or Standard & Poor's. Companies can create and maintain collection departments, hire collection agencies, and pursue legal proceedings. Certainly, each of these alternatives can improve cash collections, but each does so at a significant cost. In the extreme, management can institute a policy requiring that all sales be paid in cash. Such a policy would certainly eliminate collection costs and drive bad debts to zero, but it could also be extremely costly because it could dramatically reduce sales revenue. For most companies, then, bad debts are an inevitable cost of everyday operations that must be considered in the management of accounts receivable.

From an accounting standpoint, the inevitability of bad debts reduces the cash expected to be collected from accounts receivable. It thereby reduces the value of Accounts Receivable on the balance sheet. Bad debt losses also represent after-the-fact evidence that certain sales should not have been recorded, since the fourth criteria of revenue recognition (i.e., cash collection is assured) was not met for those sales. As a result, both Accounts Receivable and net income are overstated if bad debts are ignored. Proper accounting for bad debts, therefore, involves two basic adjustments: (1) an adjustment to reduce the value of Accounts Receivable on the balance sheet and (2) an adjustment to reduce net income.

THE ALLOWANCE METHOD

LO 5 The **allowance method** is used to account for bad debts. This method involves three basic steps: (1) the dollar amount of bad debts is estimated at the end of the accounting period, (2) an adjusting journal entry, which recognizes a bad debt expense on the income statement and reduces the net balance in Accounts Receivable, is recorded in the books, and (3) a write-off journal entry is recorded when a bad debt actually occurs. The following example illustrates the basic steps of the allowance method.

Suppose that during 1996, its first year of operations, Q-Mart had credit sales of $20,000 and a balance in Accounts Receivable of $6,000 as of December 31.

1. **Estimating bad debts**. After reviewing the relevant information, Q-Mart's accountants estimate that 2.5 percent ($500) of its credit sales will not be collected.

2. **Adjusting journal entry.** The following journal entry would be recorded on December 31.

Bad Debt Charge (−R, −SE)	500	
Allowance for Doubtful Accounts (−A)		500

   Recognized provision for doubtful accounts.

3. **Write-off journal entry.** On January 18, 1997, Q-Mart is notified that ABM Enterprises has declared bankruptcy and will not be able to pay the $200 it owes to Q-Mart. The following journal entry would then be recorded in the books of Q-Mart.

Allowance for Doubtful Accounts (+A)	200	
Accounts Receivable/ABM (−A)		200

   Wrote off uncollectible account/ABM.

STEP 1: ESTIMATING BAD DEBTS. The allowance method requires that the dollar value of bad debts be estimated at the end of each accounting period. The most common method of estimating bad debts for financial reporting purposes is the **percentage-of-credit-sales approach**.[12] This approach simply multiplies a percentage times the credit sales of the period. In the example given, $500 (2.5% × $20,000) of the credit sales of 1996 were estimated to be uncollectible.

The percentage of credit sales used in the calculation of bad debt expense is based primarily on a company's past experience. For a company such as Q-Mart, which is in its first year of operations, the typical bad debt rate of the other companies in its industry may provide a useful benchmark. Nonetheless, the percentage is an estimate, which by definition is inexact and uncertain. These estimates represent an area of potential disagreement between managers, who often want the financial statements to be as attractive as possible, and auditors whose professional ethics and exposure to legal liability encourage them to prefer conservative reporting.

The problem of estimating bad debts is significant for financial institutions, which have a large portion of their assets in outstanding loans. Such problems are discussed in Appendix 6A which covers short-term notes receivable. However, most service, retail, and manufacturing companies, especially those that have been in business for many years, can estimate uncollectibles with reasonable accuracy. The major retail companies, in particular, experience bad debts at a fairly constant percentage of credit sales across time. Bad debt charges for J.C. Penney, for example, were equal to 1 percent of sales in 1992, 1993, and 1994. Thus, while it may be difficult to predict whether an individual account will be uncollectible, for many companies it is relatively easy to predict the percentage of bad debt losses from a large group of credit sales.

STEP 2: ADJUSTING JOURNAL ENTRY. The proper method of accounting for bad debts requires an end-of-period adjusting journal entry that reduces both net income and the balance sheet carrying value of Accounts Receivable.

---

12. Later in the chapter we discuss another method of estimating bad debts, called the *aging method.*

Allowance for Doubtful Accounts. The credit side of the adjusting journal entry recorded by Q-Mart in the previous example, Allowance for Doubtful Accounts, reduces the balance sheet value of accounts receivable by $500, the expected dollar amount of bad debts.[13] Allowance for Doubtful Accounts is a permanent contra asset account with a credit balance. It is listed immediately below, and subtracted from, Accounts Receivable on the balance sheet. The form of this disclosure in the current asset section of the balance sheet follows.

Accounts receivable	**6,000**
Less: Allowance for doubtful accounts	**500**
	5,500

Disclosing the Allowance for Doubtful Accounts account in this way reflects the fact that less cash than is indicated by the face value of the receivables is expected to be collected. In the case above, $5,500 of the outstanding receivables are expected to be received. Such disclosure helps to report Accounts Receivable at net realizable value.[14]

Bad Debt Charge. The debit side of the adjusting journal entry records a contra revenue on the income statement (Bad Debt Charge). Recognizing the $500 contra revenue in 1996 indicates that certain (unidentifiable as of December 31) credit sales should not have been recorded in 1996. It thereby serves to reduce revenues for sales that actually were never made.[15]

STEP 3: THE WRITE-OFF JOURNAL ENTRY. The write-off journal entry recorded by Q-Mart reduces both the allowance account and the Accounts Receivable balance. It is particularly important to note that this entry has no effect on the income statement and only serves to remove from the books the specific account receivable of ABM.

The write-off entry has virtually no effect on the financial statements because it simply identifies a specific bad debt that (on average) was known to be uncollectible and was recognized as such at the end of the previous accounting period. Indeed, the entry does not affect the net Accounts Receivable balance, current assets, working capital, the current ratio, quick assets, or net income.

To illustrate, assume that as of December 31 net Accounts Receivable of Nordstrom appeared as follows:

Accounts receivable	**79,000**
Less: Allowance for doubtful accounts	**3,000**
	76,000

13. The account title "Allowance for Doubtful Accounts" is used in this text. However, in a survey of 600 major U.S. companies, *Accounting Trends and Techniques* (1994) reports that slightly less than half of these companies use this title. The remaining companies use any of eight different descriptions, including Allowance, Allowance for Losses, and Reserve for Doubtful Accounts.

14. Most major U.S. companies do not disclose the dollar amount in the allowance account explicitly on the balance sheet. Instead, they simply report the net amount of receivables, after the dollar amount in the allowance account has been subtracted.

15. The bad debt estimate represents revenues that should never have been recorded because the fourth criteria of revenue recognition (cash collection is reasonably assured) was not met—giving rise to a contra revenue account, which is subtracted from sales on the income statement. However, generally accepted accounting principles do not specifically address how this charge should be disclosed, and some companies record the adjustment as an expense.

On January 12 of the following year, the company receives notice that Intermec Corporation will not be able to pay the $800 it owes to Nordstrom, and the following journal entry is recorded in Nordstrom's books.

Allowance for Doubtful Accounts (+A)	**800**	
Accounts Receivable/Intermec (−A)		**800**

Wrote off uncollectible account/Intermec.

This write-off entry reduces the balance of both Accounts Receivable and Allowance for Doubtful Accounts by $800. Consequently, the net Accounts Receivable balance after the write-off entry appears as follows:

Accounts receivable	**78,200**
Less: Allowance for doubtful accounts	**2,200**
	76,000

Note that the write-off entry had no effect on the net realizable value of Accounts Receivable. The net balance of $76,000 is unchanged because both Accounts Receivable and Allowance for Doubtful Accounts were reduced by the same dollar amount. As a result, current assets, the current ratio, working capital, the quick ratio, and net income are all unaffected. The financial statement effect occurred at the end of the previous period (Step 2) when the adjusting journal entry was recorded.

So far we have implied that bad debts are discovered when a specific event occurs. For example, in the preceding illustrations the bad debt write-offs were recorded when a company received notice that a given customer was bankrupt or could not pay for some other reason. While bad debt write-offs can be recorded in this manner, it is probably more common for companies to write off bad debts when they decide that given receivables have been outstanding too long and are too costly to pursue. The following excerpt, which summarizes a typical write-off policy, was taken from a recent financial report of J.C. Penney Company, Inc.

The Company's policy is to write off accounts when the scheduled minimum payment has not been received for six consecutive months, or if any portion of the balance is more than twelve months past due, or if it is otherwise determined that the customer is unable to pay.

BAD DEBT RECOVERIES. Specific accounts that have been written off the books are occasionally recovered later. When such a receivable is reinstated, the write-off entry is simply reversed. This procedure corrects what was (in retrospect) recorded in error at a previous time. For example, the recovery of a previously written-off $800 account receivable would be recorded as follows:

Accounts Receivable/Intermec (+A)	**800**	
Allowance for Doubtful Accounts (−A)		**800**

Recovered $800 accounts receivable/Intermec.

Cash (+A)	**800**	
Accounts Receivable/Intermec (−A)		**800**

Received $800 cash on account.

INACCURATE BAD DEBT ESTIMATES. Inaccurate bad debt estimates give rise to preadjustment balances in the Allowance for Uncollectibles Account. For example, if a company estimates $4,000 of bad debts on December 31, 1996, and only $3,400 actually occur during 1997, as shown in Figure 6–9, the Allowance for Doubtful Accounts contains a $600 credit balance *before adjusting entries are recorded* at the end of 1997. If, instead of $3,400, $4,400 of bad debts actually occur during 1997, as shown in Figure 6–10, the *preadjustment December 31, 1997 balance* in Allowance for Doubtful Accounts is a $400 debit.

FIGURE 6–9

Overestimated bad debts

Allow. for Dbt. Accts. (+A)	3,400					Bad Debt Exp. (E, −SE)	4,000
Accts. Rec. (−A)		3,400				Allow. for Dbt. Accts. (−A)	4,000
Wrote off accts. rec.—1997						*1996 adjusting entry.*	

ALLOWANCE FOR DOUBTFUL ACCOUNTS

	4,000
3,400	
	Preadj. bal. 600

FIGURE 6–10

Underestimated bad debts

Allow. for Dbt. Accts. (+A)	4,400					Bad Debt Exp. (E, −SE)	4,000
Accts. Rec. (−A)		4,400				Allow. for Dbt. Accts. (−A)	4,000
Wrote off accts. rec.—1997						*1996 adjusting entry.*	

ALLOWANCE FOR DOUBTFUL ACCOUNTS

	4,000
4,400	
Preadj. bal. 400	

Because estimates are rarely correct, preadjustment balances in Allowance for Doubtful Accounts are common, but they are usually ignored because across time under- and overestimates in individual years tend to neutralize each other. However, a significant debit or credit accumulation in the preadjustment balance over several periods may indicate that the estimates are not only inaccurate but also biased. Consistent overestimates give rise to preadjustment credit accumulations (Figure 6–9), while consistent underestimates create preadjustment accumulations on the debit side of Allowance for Doubtful Accounts (Figure 6–10). Such accumulations, which often indicate that a company's estimating formula should be revised, can lead to balance sheet misstatements in the allowance account because they are reflected in the year-end, post-adjustment balance. Users can detect these misstatements by comparing the amount in the allowance account to such numbers as sales and accounts receivable across time. Unusual deviations or well-defined trends may reveal a bad debt estimation problem, which may raise questions about management's competence and/or incentives.

AN AGING SCHEDULE: ANOTHER METHOD OF ESTIMATING BAD DEBTS. Another common method of estimating bad debt losses is to establish an **aging schedule** of outstanding accounts receivable. This method categorizes individual accounts in terms of the length of time each has been outstanding and applies a different bad debt rate to each category. The bad debt rate applied to categories comprising older accounts is greater than that applied to categories comprising younger accounts, on the assumption that the longer an account has been outstanding, the more likely it is to be uncollectible.

AGING ESTIMATES: AN ILLUSTRATION. To illustrate how an aging schedule can be used to estimate bad debts, assume that each of the accounts that make up a $4,000 end-of-year balance in Accounts Receivable is placed into one of three categories that represent the lengths of time the accounts have been outstanding: (1) six to twelve months, (2) three to six months, and (3) less than three months. It is the company's policy to write off accounts when they become one year old. Assume also that the percentage of uncollectibles expected for each of the three categories is 30 percent for Category (1), 10 percent for Category (2), and 2 percent for Category (3). The bad debt estimate for the entire Accounts Receivable balance is computed in Figure 6–11. The $324 estimate is computed by totaling the dollar amount of the bad debts expected from each of the three categories.

FIGURE 6–11	AGE OF ACCOUNTS	AMOUNT	PERCENT UNCOLLECTIBLE	ESTIMATE	
An aging schedule					
	6–12 months	$ 500	30%	$150	(500 × 30%)
	3–6 months	1,300	10	130	(1,300 × 10%)
	Less than 3 months	2,200	2	44	(2,200 × 2%)
	Total	$4,000		$324	

Aging as a Management Tool. Maintaining control over outstanding accounts receivable is an important part of effective management for many companies. Because of the time value of money, receivables should be collected as quickly as possible. Bad debts should also be held to a minimum. Aging schedules help companies control bad debts in a number of significant ways.

An aging schedule, for example, can identify slow-moving accounts, thus directing collection efforts and defining the maximum costs that should be incurred by those efforts. Collection efforts should be directed toward the accounts in the older categories, but the costs associated with these efforts should not exceed the expected loss from the accounts. For example, a company may have $10,000 of accounts receivable that have been outstanding for over six months. Past experience indicates that 20 percent of such accounts are uncollectible. The $2,000 ($10,000 × 20%) expected loss from these accounts determines a maximum dollar amount for the costs incurred to collect them.

An aging schedule can also be helpful in estimating how much money a company is losing in potential interest charges. Such information can be useful in deciding whether to offer cash discounts and in determining the appropriate terms for such discounts.

Although aging schedules can provide useful information, keep in mind that they can be costly to establish and maintain. For companies that rely on credit sales to a wide variety of customers, maintaining the age and balance of each account can be quite time-consuming. Computerized accounting systems are almost a necessity for efficient aging analyses and receivables control. Most large companies, of course, have computerized their receivables accounting, and when small companies change from manual to computerized accounting systems, receivables applications are often used first to improve control over accounts receivable.

ACCOUNTING FOR SALES RETURNS

For many companies it is common that merchandise sold on account is returned by customers at a later date. These returns are important in the retail industry and book publishers, like South-Western—the publisher of this text, are especially affected because customers can often return large amounts of product sixty days or more after the initial sale. When returned items were initially sold, the sale and the associated account receivable were recognized on the books. Because sales returns are usually accompanied by either the removal of the receivable or the granting of future credit, companies with significant returns must adjust both the income statement and Accounts Receivable on the balance sheet. The methods used to account for sales returns are similar to those used to account for bad debts; that is, at the end of each period an estimate of expected sales returns is made which, in turn, determines the dollar value of an adjusting journal entry that reduces income and establishes an Allowance account. This account is disclosed on the balance sheet as a contra to Accounts Receivable. Actual returns are then debited against the allowance and credited against Accounts Receivable.

ACCOUNTS RECEIVABLE FROM A USER'S PERSPECTIVE

LO 6   When accounting for short-term receivables, two general questions are of significant economic importance: (1) When should a receivable be recorded in the books? and (2) At what dollar amount should a receivable be valued on the balance sheet?

WHEN SHOULD A RECEIVABLE BE RECORDED?

Revenues and related receivables are recognized when the four criteria of revenue recognition have been met. Establishing exactly when this occurs, however, is difficult and subjective. A well-known article from *Forbes* indicates that "managers have a good bit of freedom to determine when and how a sale [and the associated receivable] gets put on the books."[16] This freedom gives rise to widely different practices. For example, General Electric recognizes revenues when goods are shipped, while HarperCollins, a large book publisher, recognizes revenues when it invoices customers, sometimes a month before orders are shipped. Revenue-recognition practices even differ among companies in the same industry. A survey of 200 software companies, for example, revealed that 26 (13 percent) companies waited until cash was received before recognizing a sale, while 30 (15 percent) companies recognized a sale as soon as an order was received.[17]

Users of financial statements must realize that, even within the guidelines of generally accepted accounting principles, managers can use discretion to speed up or slow down the recognition of revenue. This concern is particularly important for transactions that occur near the end of an accounting period. Recognizing a receivable and a revenue on December 30 instead of January 2, for example, can significantly

16. Jill Andresky, "Setting the Date," *Forbes*, July 16, 1984, p. 90.
17. Ibid.

affect current assets, working capital, and net income on the December 31 financial statements.

To illustrate, suppose that current assets, current liabilities, and net income for Johnson and Sons as of December 29 are $45,000, $34,000, and $14,000, respectively. Johnson and Sons provides a service to Ace Manufacturing that is billed at $20,000. The service is ordered by Ace on December 30 and completed by Johnson and Sons on January 5. Payment is made by Ace after January 5. The current ratio, working capital position, and net income as of December 31 for Johnson and Sons are computed in Figure 6–12, assuming that (1) the revenue is recognized when the service is completed on January 5, and (2) the revenue is recognized when the service is ordered on December 30.

FIGURE 6–12 *The timing of revenue and receivable recognition*		(1) REVENUE IS RECOGNIZED ON JANUARY 5.	(2) REVENUE IS RECOGNIZED ON DECEMBER 30.
December 31 current ratio **(current asset ÷ current liabilities)**		1.32	1.91
December 31 working capital **(current assets − current liabilities)**		$11,000	$31,000
Net income, year ended December 31		$14,000	$34,000

Note that the timing of revenue recognition can have a significant effect on important financial statement numbers. Recognizing the sale in the earlier period increased the current ratio by 45 percent, and increased working capital and net income each by $20,000. Such effects have economic significance because they may influence a company's credit rating or determine if it violates the terms of debt agreements. Since the timing of revenue and receivable recognition has a direct effect on net income and current assets, financial statement users should pay special attention to it.

Extreme cases of premature revenue and receivable recognition, or the complete fabrication of sales, is often interpreted as management fraud. The SEC, for example, charged three former officers of a California electronic parts manufacturer, called Matrix Science Corp., for "prematurely recognizing revenue by engaging in pre-invoicing and other accounting tricks. The SEC described pre-invoicing as recording revenue from orders for products that haven't been shipped, or in some cases haven't even been assembled. . . The officers prevented [the] outside auditors from discovering the practice by reprinting invoices and moving inventory off the premises."[18] Other famous cases of inappropriate revenue recognition have involved such companies as MiniScribe, a software manufacturer, Regina Corporation, a well-known home appliance maker, and Orion Pictures, a motion picture studio that produced a number of box office hits. In all three cases aggressive management under intense pressure to perform either fabricated sales or used questionable accounting practices to accelerate the recognition of revenues in an effort to increase reported profits and improve solvency measures. While these unethical behaviors may have delayed and

18. Thomas E. Ricks, "Former Officers of Electronics Company Charged by SEC with Inflating Profit," *The Wall Street Journal*, November 2, 1988, p. A14.

obscured the companies' financial problems, they certainly did little to solve them, and in most cases made matters much worse.

BALANCE SHEET VALUATION OF RECEIVABLES

The appropriate dollar amount at which to value receivables on the balance sheet is primarily a question of whether the outstanding receivable will, in fact, be paid. Companies like General Motors and Westinghouse Electric have billions of dollars in outstanding receivables, many of which may never produce any cash. Estimating such uncollectibles, which can significantly affect both the income statement and the balance sheet, can be very subjective and can lead to substantial disagreements between management and its auditors.

Several years ago, for example, a major auditing firm postponed rendering an opinion on Federal Home Loan Bank of Dallas because the bank carried $500 million of questionable receivables on its balance sheet. Furthermore, bad debt write-offs can be enormous. It was reported in the *Wall Street Journal* recently that Westinghouse Electric "took a massive $1.68 billion charge" to cover uncollectible receivables. The action was described by management as "painful."[19] Indeed, as stated in *Forbes*, "since [estimating bad debts] involves judgment, there is a real temptation [for managers] to ignore potential problems and keep net income up."[20]

These examples suggest that (1) bad debts can be significant, (2) estimating bad debts is subjective, and (3) management is often unwilling to establish large bad debt provisions. Users must be aware of these concerns and pay close attention to the size and activity in the Allowance for Uncollectibles account as well as the annual bad debt charge. For example, consider a case where the following information is taken from the financial statements of a company you are currently reviewing as a possible investment.

	1997	1996
BALANCE SHEET		
Accounts receivable	$12,500	$13,200
Allowance for uncollectibles	(1,300)	(1,500)
INCOME STATEMENT		
Sales	$99,000	$82,500
Bad debt charge	(1,700)	(1,650)
Net income	5,000	4,200

At first glance the company's financial performance appears to be strong and improving. Both sales and net income increased by 20 percent during 1997, and accounts receivable decreased, which suggests that receivables collections may have improved. However, a closer look at the activity in the Allowance for Uncollectibles account and Bad Debt Charge raises a concern. Using T-account analysis, as illustrated in Figure 6–13, you can see that the bad debt charge was insufficient, $200 less than the write-offs during 1997. Further review shows that the charge, as a percent of sales, decreased from 2 percent in 1996 to 1.7 percent in 1997. Had 2 percent been used in

19. Gabriella Stern, "Westinghouse Battles to Keep Core Units As Losses Grow from Real Estate Spree," *The Wall Street Journal*, October 24, 1991, p. A3.
20. Laura Sanders, "The SEC Takes on Loan Losses," *Forbes*, June 4, 1984, p. 4.

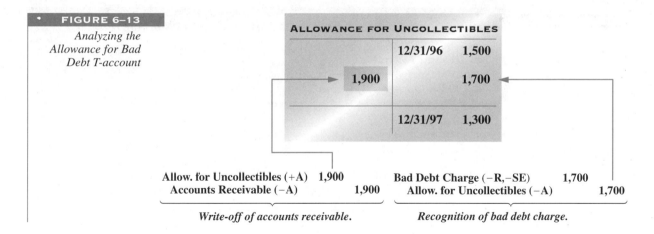

FIGURE 6–13

Analyzing the Allowance for Bad Debt T-account

ALLOWANCE FOR UNCOLLECTIBLES

	12/31/96	1,500
1,900		1,700
	12/31/97	1,300

Allow. for Uncollectibles (+A)   1,900
    Accounts Receivable (−A)   1,900

Write-off of accounts receivable.

Bad Debt Charge (−R,−SE)   1,700
    Allow. for Uncollectibles (−A)   1,700

Recognition of bad debt charge.

1997, the charge would have been $1,980, and net income would have been lower by $280. It seems that management reduced the bad debt charge, which increased reported net income, even though bad debt write-offs did not decrease during 1997.

In summary, the methods used to account for accounts receivable can lead to significant economic consequences, affecting a company's credit rating, determining whether debt covenants are violated, accelerating bankruptcy proceedings, and introducing the potential for sizable lawsuits against managers and auditors. Recall from Chapter 3 that the combination of such economic effects and reporting subjectivity can encourage managers to use reporting strategies, like overstating income and financial condition, "taking a bath," and building "hidden reserves," that can serve their interests at the expense of the stockholders. Recall also that practicing such strategies need not be fraudulent, because generally accepted accounting principles are sufficiently flexible to allow a large amount of management discretion.

THE COLLECTION PERIOD FOR ACCOUNTS RECEIVABLE

We have already explained how the methods used to account for accounts receivables can affect net income, the current ratio, working capital, the quick ratio, and other important financial statement numbers. Another ratio that uses the accounts receivable balance is called the **collection period**. This ratio, which is one of Dun & Bradstreet's fourteen key business ratios, is calculated as follows:

Receivable collection period = (Accounts Receivable/Sales) × 365 days

This calculation indicates how many days, in general, the accounts receivable of a given company are outstanding. Investors and creditors use it to determine how quickly a company's receivables are normally converted into cash; thus it can be helpful in determining whether a company can meet its debts as they come due. To illustrate how this ratio is calculated, consider the financial information in Figure 6–14, which was taken from the 1994 financial report of the Ralston Purina Company.

FIGURE 6–14		1994	1993
The calculation of collection period	**Sales**	$ 5,759.3*	$5,911.4
	Net accounts receivable	730.6	673.2
	Collection period		
	1993 (673.2 ÷ 5,911.4) × 365		42 days
	1994 (730.6 ÷ 5,759.3) × 365	46 days	

*Dollars in millions

The accounts receivable held by Ralston Purina were outstanding, on average, for 42 days in 1993 and 46 in 1994. These calculations indicate that the time period between the company's sales and the collection of cash increased from 1993 to 1994, which may indicate receivables management problems—especially when combined with decreasing sales numbers. As a basis for comparison, the average collection periods in selected industries are contained in Figure 6–15.

FIGURE 6–15	INDUSTRY	SIC CODE	NO. OF COMPANIES	AVERAGE COLLECTION PERIOD (DAYS)
Average accounts receivable collection periods (industry averages)	**MANUFACTURING**			
	Motor Vehicles	3711	95	20
	Petroleum and Gas	1311	872	61
	RETAILING			
	Department Stores	5311	641	24
	Hobby, Toy & Games	5945	519	4
	GENERAL SERVICES			
	Eating Places	5812	2,427	6
	Telephone Commun.	4813	1,130	49
	FINANCIAL SERVICES			
	Bank Holding Co.	6719	180	53
	Security Brokers	6211	1,312	32

Source: Compiled from data published in *Industry Norms and Key Business Ratios* (Dun & Bradstreet, Inc., 1994)

ETHICS IN THE REAL WORLD

Allied Bancshares, a Houston-based group of banks, recently reported a string of 31 quarterly earnings increases. In an interview with three Goldman Sachs security analysts, one of the bank's senior officers explained that the bank intentionally overstates its bad debt expense in good quarters and understates it in poor quarters. In this manner the fluctuations in earnings from one quarter to the next can be smoothed out. The bank's auditors have written clean opinions on the bank's financial statements over this time period, and this strategy maximizes the bonuses paid to the bank's executives. In addition, presumably it is in the best interest of the bank's shareholders, partly because it helps the bank maintain its legal reserve requirements.

ETHICAL ISSUE

Is it ethical for companies like Bancshares to intentionally overstate expenses in some periods and understate them in others to achieve consistent increases in reported net income across time?

REVIEW PROBLEM

This section provides a review problem that covers the methods used to account for bad debts. The facts given are accounted for using the allowance method with a percentage-of-credit-sales estimate.

Assume that Credit Inc. began operations on January 1, 1996. The relevant transactions for 1996 and 1997 are summarized in the accounts receivable T-account provided in Figure 6–16. Sales on account during 1996 totaled $10,000, and cash receipts for those sales equaled $6,000. The Accounts Receivable balance at the end of 1996

FIGURE 6–16	**GENERAL LEDGER**

Bad debt review problem

ACCOUNTS RECEIVABLE

Beginning balance	0		
1996 credit sales	10,000		
		1996 cash receipts	6,000
12/31/96 balance	4,000		
1997 credit sales	12,000		
		1997 cash receipts	11,000
		1997 bad debt	500
12/31/97 balance	4,500		

Allowance Method (percentage of credit sales estimate)

December 31, 1996

$700 (7% × $10,000)

Estimate entry	Bad Debt Charge (−R, −SE)	700	
	Allow. for Doubt. Accts. (−A)		700

June 5, 1997

Write off entry	Allow. for Doubt. Accts. (+A)	500	
	Accts. Rec. (−A)		500

December 31, 1997

$840 (7% × $12,000)

Estimate entry	Bad Debt Charge (−R, −SE)	840	
	Allow. for Doubt. Accts. (−A)		840

ALLOWANCE FOR DOUBTFUL ACCOUNTS

		Beginning balance	0
		12/31/96	700
		12/31/96 balance	700
6/5/97	500	Preadj. balance	200
		12/31/97	840
		12/31/97 balance	1,040

was $4,000 ($10,000 − $6,000). Sales on account during 1997 totaled $12,000, and cash receipts during the same period, from sales made in both 1996 and 1997, were $11,000. On June 5, 1997, Credit Inc. received notice that a $500 account established in 1996 would not be collectible. This account was written off, and the December 31, 1997 balance in accounts receivable is $4,500 ($4,000 + $12,000 − $11,000 − $500). Assume that companies in Credit's industry typically experience bad debt losses of approximately 7 percent of credit sales.

The allowance method gives rise to end-of-period adjusting journal entries that decrease revenues in the appropriate period and reduce the value of Accounts Receivable on the balance sheet to net realizable value, the amount of cash expected to be collected from the receivables. The write-off entry on June 5, 1997, has virtually no effect on the financial statements of Credit Inc.

Note that the preadjustment balance in the Allowance for Doubtful Accounts account as of December 31, 1996 is a $200 credit ($700 estimate − $500 write-off). Either Credit overestimated its bad debt losses for 1996, or certain outstanding accounts created from 1996's credit sales may still be written off. If this preadjustment balance accumulates over a period of several years, Credit should review and possibly revise its estimating formula. Otherwise, it is ignored.

SUMMARY OF LEARNING OBJECTIVES

LO 1 *Define current assets, working capital, current ratio, and quick ratio, and explain how these measures can be used to assess the solvency position of a company.*

Current assets are assets that can be converted into cash within one year or the company's operating cycle, whichever is longer. Working capital is equal to current assets less current liabilities, which are the liabilities expected to be required for payment with the assets listed as current. The current ratio is equal to current assets divided by current liabilities. The quick ratio is equal to cash plus marketable securities plus accounts receivable, divided by current liabilities.

These low-cost measures are useful in assessing a company's solvency position because they compare a measure of short-run cash inflows to a measure of short-run cash outflows. They are often used by banks and other lenders, and they appear in many loan agreements and debt covenants, enabling lenders to protect their investments by requiring that management maintain certain levels of liquidity.

LO 2 *Recognize how and why managers use "window dressing" techniques to affect the reporting of current assets, working capital, and the current ratio.*

Window dressing refers to management's use of discretion in reporting accounting numbers to make the financial statements appear more attractive. Such discretion is used, for example, to make it easier to attract capital, to increase bonus compensation, or to avoid violating the terms of debt contracts. There are three basic ways in which management can window dress: (1) management can choose to use accounting methods that improve the reported numbers, (2) it can bias the estimates required to apply a given accounting method, and (3) it can make operating decisions that directly affect the reported numbers.

 Identify the techniques used when accounting for and controlling cash.

Cash held in escrow or compensating balances are examples of restrictions on a company's use of its cash. Such restrictions should be clearly disclosed on the balance sheet or in the footnotes, and restricted cash should be included in separate accounts.

There are two aspects to the control of cash that are largely the responsibility of the company's accountants: record control and physical control. Problems of record control arise because there are many transactions that involve the Cash account, and it is often difficult to ensure that the Cash account on the balance sheet reflects the actual amount of cash in a company's possession. Problems of physical control arise because cash is universally desired and easily concealed and transported.

 Define accounts receivable, and explain how they are valued on the balance sheet.

Accounts receivable arise from transactions with customers who have purchased goods or services but have not yet paid for them. They are amounts owed by customers for goods and services sold as part of the normal operations of the business. Often backed up by oral rather than written commitments, accounts receivable represent short-term extensions of credit that are normally collectible within thirty to sixty days. Accounts receivable are valued at net realizable value, the gross amount of the receivable less adjustments for cash discounts, uncollectibles, and sales returns.

 Explain how the allowance method accounts for uncollectible receivables.

Under the allowance method, at the end of each accounting period the amount of uncollectibles is estimated. Then an adjusting journal entry is made to reduce revenue via a contra revenue account and a contra account to Accounts Receivable, Allowance for Doubtful Accounts, is credited. Later, when the uncollectible is actually realized, both the value of accounts receivable and the allowance account are reduced.

 Explain the major concerns of financial statement users in the area of receivables reporting.

For many companies, accounts receivable are a significant percentage of total and current assets; accordingly, the methods used to account for them can have direct and often significant effects on such measures as current assets, working capital, the current ratio, the quick ratio, the collection period and net income. Financial statement users must realize that managers can influence these measures by speeding up or slowing down the recognition of revenue and related receivables and that the estimate of uncollectibles is very subjective. Such practices can affect a company's credit rating, determine whether debt terms are violated, accelerate bankruptcy proceedings, and bring about sizable lawsuits against managers and auditors. In this area users must pay close attention to the activity in the sales, accounts receivable, bad debt, and allowance for uncollectible accounts.

APPENDIX 6A

SHORT-TERM NOTES RECEIVABLE

Short-term notes receivable differ from accounts receivable primarily because they involve formal promissory notes, rather than informal promises to pay. Promissory notes usually identify the parties of the transaction and state the principal amount to be paid (the face value, or maturity value, of the note), the date of principal payment (maturity date), and a provision for interest (the stated interest rate). The maturity date of a short-term note receivable is usually more than sixty days from the date it is established but less than the length of time that defines current assets. Ninety-day notes are quite common. Companies often accept notes instead of transacting on open accounts because formal notes are usually easier to enforce, can include security provisions and other management restrictions, and normally enjoy a higher priority for claims on the debtor's assets in case of bankruptcy.

Like accounts receivable, short-term notes receivable can arise from the sale of goods or services to customers. It also happens, as illustrated in the following journal entry, that a short-term note receivable is established in exchange for an account receivable. Such an exchange might occur when a company wishes to contractually obligate a slow-paying customer.

Short-Term Notes Receivable (+A)	300	
Accounts Receivable (−A)		300

Converted an account receivable to a note receivable.

However, short-term notes receivable usually result from cash loans, which are naturally common for banks and other financial institutions. The following journal entry records such a loan, a short-term note receivable in exchange for $1,000 cash.

Short-Term Notes Receivable (+A)	1,000	
Cash (−A)		1,000

Received short-term note for cash.

ACCOUNTING FOR SHORT-TERM NOTES RECEIVABLE

There are two basic methods of accounting for short-term notes receivable that are fundamentally the same. They value the assets related to the note at the same dollar amount, and they recognize the same amount of interest revenue in the same time periods. However, they involve different sets of journal entries, and the resulting disclosures are somewhat different. Method 1 recognizes the note receivable in an amount equal to the principal and accrues interest receivable over the life of the note. Method 2, on the other hand, recognizes the note receivable in the amount of the principal and the interest to be received. This method requires the recognition of a *discount*, which is converted to interest revenue over the life of the note. The following example compares the two methods.

EXAMPLE: HOUSING FINANCE COMPANY

Assume that on December 1, 1996, Housing Finance Company loans Johnson Construction $5,000 in exchange for a ninety-day note with a stated annual interest rate of 12 percent. Housing Finance pays $5,000 to Johnson on December 1 and receives $5,150 ($5,000 principal plus $150 [5,000 × 12% × 3/12] interest) from Johnson on March 1, 1997. The accounting procedures under Methods 1 and 2 are compared in Figure 6A–1.

Under Method 1 the face amount of the note receivable is established at $5,000, the amount of the principal. One-third of the interest ($50) is accrued in 1996, and the remaining amount of the interest revenue ($100) is recognized in 1997.

Under Method 2 the face value of the note is equal to the total principal and interest ($5,000 + $150), the original cash payment by Housing Finance is equal to the principal ($5,000), and a discount is established in the amount of the difference: $150, the total interest to be received. The Discount on Note account is a contra asset account that is disclosed on the balance sheet immediately below, and subtracted

FIGURE 6A–1

Accounting for short-term notes receivable

METHOD 1

December 1, 1996:

Notes Receivable (+A)	5,000	
Cash (−A)		5,000

Issued note.

December 31, 1996 (end-of-period adjusting entry):

Interest Receivable (+A)	50*	
Interest Revenue (R, +SE)		50

Recognized one month of accrued interest.

*(5,000 × 12%) ÷ 12

December 31, 1996 (balance sheet assets related to note):

BALANCE SHEET
DECEMBER 31, 1996

Notes receivable	$5,000
Interest receivable	50
Total	$5,050

March 1, 1997:

Cash (+A)	5,150*	
Notes Receivable (−A)		5,000
Interest Receivable (−A)		50
Interest Revenue (R, +SE)		100

Received principal and interest payment.

*5,000 + (5,000 × 12% × 3/12)

METHOD 2:

December 1, 1996:

Notes Receivable (+A)	5,150	
Cash (−A)		5,000
Discount on Note (−A)		150

Issued note and recognized discount.

December 31, 1996 (end-of-period adjusting entry):

Discount on Note (+A)	50*	
Interest Revenue (R, +SE)		50

Recognized one month of accrued interest.

December 31, 1996 (balance sheet assets related to note):

BALANCE SHEET
DECEMBER 31, 1996

Notes receivable	$5,150	
Less: Discount on note	100	$5,050

March 1, 1997:

Cash (+A)	5,150*	
Discount on Note (+A)	100	
Interest Revenue (R, +SE)		100
Notes Receivable (−A)		5,150

Received principal and interest payment.

from, the Notes Receivable account. In a sense, the discount can be viewed as unearned interest, which is amortized (converted) into interest revenue over the life of the note. The December 31 end-of-period adjusting entry amortizes one-third ($50) of the discount into Interest Revenue.

Note the disclosure under Method 2 on the December 31, 1996 balance sheet. The net balance sheet value of the note receivable is $5,050, the face value ($5,150) less the unamortized discount ($100 = $150 − $50). The journal entry to record the final principal and interest receipt ($5,150) (1) amortizes the remaining discount into Interest Revenue ($100) and (2) writes off the Note Receivable account ($5,150).

METHODS 1 AND 2 COMPARED

Although the journal entries used by Methods 1 and 2 are not the same, there is actually no difference between the resulting balance sheet and income statement values. Both methods value the assets related to the note at the same dollar amount (as of December 31, $5,050), and both methods recognize equivalent dollar amounts of interest revenue in 1996 ($50) and 1997 ($100). The difference between the two methods is only a matter of disclosure. Method 1 treats the Note Receivable and the Interest Receivable related to the note independently, establishing separate accounts for each. Method 2, on the other hand, establishes a Discount on Notes Receivable account and discloses it as a contra asset against Note Receivable on the balance sheet. The discount is treated like unearned interest revenue, in that it is converted to interest revenue as the interest on the note is earned. Under Method 2 a separate Interest Receivable account is not used.

FINANCIAL INSTITUTIONS AND UNCOLLECTIBLE LOANS

The methods used to account for uncollectible notes receivable are similar to those used to account for accounts receivable bad debts. That is, generally accepted accounting principles require that the allowance method be used if uncollectibles can be estimated in a reasonably objective manner. As mentioned in Chapter 6, estimating the dollar value of uncollectible loans is particularly important for financial institutions, because such institutions carry such large amounts of outstanding notes receivable. The 1994 balance sheet of Bank America, for example, indicated that $141 billion in loans (short- and long-term) were outstanding as of the end of the year. This amount represented 66 percent of the company's total assets. Of the $141 billion in loans, the company estimated that $3.7 billion (3 percent) would not be collected.

The banking, savings and loan, and insurance industries have been plagued with a number of outstanding notes on which no interest or principal payments have been received. These nonperforming loans are due primarily to risky foreign investments, decreasing farm and oil prices, and a nationwide real estate slump. For example, *The Wall Street Journal* reported that First Republic Bank Corporation, Texas's largest banking concern, "plans to add still more real estate and foreign loans to its $4 billion mountain of nonperforming loans . . . and will make additional provisions (on their financial statements) for loan losses and write-offs." The article went on to state that "some crucial financial ratios are slipping, and First Bank may default on about $33 million of long-term debt. Such a default could accelerate the calling of that debt and trigger calling of fully half of the corporation's $539.9 million of long-term debt. 'These factors, among others,' said Arthur Andersen & Co., independent auditors of

First Bank, 'indicate that the corporation may be unable to continue in its present form.'"[21]

In another example, Seafirst Bank, the largest bank holding company in the state of Washington, found itself on the brink of bankruptcy several years ago, largely because of loans in the Southwest that were never paid. When Seafirst stock plummeted in value, irate stockholders brought a multimillion-dollar suit against the managers of Seafirst for entering into such loans and also sued the bank's auditors, Arthur Andersen & Co., for failing to ensure that an adequate loan-loss provision was established on the financial statements. Fortunately, BankAmerica Corporation rescued the troubled Washington bank by acquiring it and pumping in needed funds, enabling it to continue operations.

Nonperforming loans (notes receivable) have also caused the major credit rating agencies to lower the ratings of even the nation's largest banks. In 1991, *The Wall Street Journal* reported:

"Standard & Poor's Corp. lowered the debt ratings of Continental Bank Corp., citing . . . the drag from a high level of nonperforming loans. Even with the $150 million third quarter special provision for loan losses, the company may need to supplement the loss reserve in future periods, S&P said."[22]

Economic pressures on the managers of these financially troubled financial institutions have caused them to use accounting techniques to conceal the problems. In 1990, for example, *The Wall Street Journal* reported:

"As banks struggle to clear away bad real estate loans, a growing number are using accounting techniques that often confuse analysts and have the effect of concealing problems in bank loan portfolios, according to federal regulators."[23]

The difficulties in America's financial institutions have brought about several significant changes relevant to accountants. First, the FASB has recently ruled that banks both disclose the market values of their outstanding loans and create larger reserves for bad debts. This rule, which generated much opposition from the banking industry, has reduced the balance sheet value of most U.S. banks. Difficulties in the financial institutions have also imposed additional legal liability on the audit profession. Leading accounting firms have been sued for billions of dollars for their alleged roles in the recent failures of hundreds of savings and loan companies. Such suits were initiated by both savings and loan shareholders and government regulators. Indeed, the accounting issues surrounding notes receivable can lead to significant economic consequences.

APPENDIX 6B

ACCOUNTING FOR RECEIVABLES AND PAYABLES EXPRESSED IN FOREIGN CURRENCIES

As companies expand, they often search for new sources of supply and new markets in other countries. Most major U.S. companies operate in more than one country, and

21. Leonard M. Apcar, "String of Losses Seen by First Republic Bank," *The Wall Street Journal*, March 31, 1988, p. 3.
22. Mark Robichaux, "Continental Bank Ratings Lowered by S&P," *The Wall Street Journal*, October 9, 1991, p. C13.
23. Ron Suskind, "Some Banks Use Accounting Techniques that Conceal Loan Woes, Regulators Say," *The Wall Street Journal*, November 29, 1990, p. A4.

many have operations in countries throughout the world. IBM, for example, has operations in approximately eighty foreign countries. Such companies are called **multinational** or **transnational corporations**.

Consider, for example, Johnson & Johnson which generated almost $16 billion in world-wide revenues in 1994. Fifty percent of the total was generated from operations in countries other than the United States. Figure 6B–1 compares the relative importance of foreign operations in the generation of sales, profits, and total assets for three well-known U.S. companies: Goodyear Tire and Rubber Company, General Electric, and Quaker Oats Company.

FIGURE 6B–1 *The importance of foreign operations in 1994 (dollars in millions)*	GOODYEAR	GENERAL ELECTRIC	QUAKER OATS
Total sales	$12,288	$ 60,109	$5,955
Foreign sales/total	39%	17%	32%
Total operating income (before taxes)	$ 1,193	$ 9,718	$ 231
Foreign operating income/total	50%	13%	26%
Total assets	$ 9,123	$185,871	$3,043
Foreign/total	40%	18%	38%

Source: 1994 financial reports.

The internationalization of business introduces an issue of major concern to accountants: that is, most transactions with foreign entities involve currencies other than the U.S. dollar. For example, when Polaroid makes a sale to a Japanese customer, the receivable is often expressed in Japanese yen. An accounting problem arises because the financial statements of Polaroid, a U.S. company, must be expressed in terms of U.S. dollars, and the exchange rate between the U.S. dollar and the Japanese yen is constantly fluctuating. In this appendix we explain exchange rates and describe how exchange rate changes affect receivables and payables held by U.S. companies expressed in foreign currencies.

EXCHANGE RATES AMONG CURRENCIES

An **exchange rate** is the value of one currency in terms of another currency. For example, as of June 20, 1994, $1.61 could be exchanged for 1 British pound, $.87 could be exchanged for 1 Swiss franc, and $.012 could be exchanged for 1 Japanese yen. Expressed in another way, as of that same date, $1 (U.S.) could have been exchanged for .62 (1/1.61) British pounds, 1.15 (1/.87) Swiss francs, or 84 (1/.012) Japanese yen. Like the prices of all goods and services, the exchange rates among currencies vary from one day to the next. Figure 6B–2 shows the rates at which selected foreign currencies could be exchanged for U.S. dollars on two different dates 1 week apart: June 12, 1995 and June 20, 1995.

Observe the changes on the right side of the table and note that in general the value of the U.S. dollar fell over the time period. Fluctuations in exchange rates of this nature can give rise to economic gains and losses for individuals and entities that transact in these currencies.

To illustrate, suppose that you paid $1,587 to purchase 1,000 British pounds on June 12, and on June 20 you converted the pounds back into dollars. You would have received $1,613 dollars in the exchange and therefore would have incurred an economic gain of $26 ($1,613 − $1,587) on the transactions. In essence, you held 1,000 British pounds during a period in which the value of the pound rose relative to the U.S. dollar. On the other hand, had you paid 1,000 British pounds to purchase $1,587 on June 12 and on June 20 exchanged the dollars back into pounds, you would have collected only 984 pounds and suffered an economic loss of 16 (1,000 − 984) British pounds.

FIGURE 6B-2	JUNE 20, 1995	JUNE 12, 1995	CHANGE
Foreign exchange rates (foreign currency per dollar)			
Australia (dollar) 1.38		1.39	−.007
Britain (pound) .62		.63	−.02
Canada (dollar) 1.37		1.38	−.007
Germany (mark) 1.39		1.40	−.007
Japan (yen) 84		84	.000
Mexico (peso) 6.25		6.19	+.01
Switzerland (franc) 1.15		1.16	−.009

Source: *The Wall Street Journal*; June 20, 1995 and June 12, 1995.

RECEIVABLES AND PAYABLES HELD IN OTHER CURRENCIES

Many U.S. companies engage in transactions with non-U.S. entities that give rise to receivables or payables denominated in foreign currencies. Since the exchange rate between the dollar and the foreign currency fluctuates, the values of the receivables or payables change, giving rise to gains or losses that must be recognized on the financial statements.

HOLDING RECEIVABLES EXPRESSED IN FOREIGN CURRENCIES[24]

Suppose that International Inc., a U.S. company that prepares financial statements expressed in U.S. dollars, sold inventories to Swiss Airlines and accepted a note receivable in return. The note states that Swiss Airlines is to pay International 5,000 Swiss francs. The note was signed on December 1, when 1 U.S. dollar was equivalent to 2 Swiss francs. The value of the transaction in terms of U.S. dollars as of December 1 was $2,500 (5,000/2); accordingly, International recorded a receivable at the time of the transaction in the amount of $2,500. The currency conversion calculation and the journal entry to record the sale are provided in Figure 6B–3.

FIGURE 6B-3	Conversion of Swiss francs to U.S. dollars:
Recording a sale in a non-U.S. currency	$2,500 = 5,000 Swiss francs × (1 dollar ÷ 2 Swiss francs)

Dec. 1   Notes Receivable (+A)   2,500
          Sales (R, +SE)   2,500
         Sold inventory for 5,000 Swiss francs.

24. To make the computations easier, the exchange rates used in these examples are not realistic.

Assume further that on December 31, when International prepares financial statements, the rate of exchange between U.S. dollars and Swiss francs changed to 1 U.S. dollar per 1.8 Swiss francs. The note receivable that was recorded on the books at $2,500 on December 1 is now worth $2,778 (5,000/1.8 or $2,500 × 2.0/1.8). Therefore, International has enjoyed an economic gain of $278 ($2,778 − $2,500) because it held a right to 5,000 Swiss francs during a period of time in which Swiss francs increased in value relative to U.S. dollars. In simple terms, 5,000 Swiss francs can be exchanged for more U.S. dollars on December 31 than they could on December 1. The currency conversion calculation and the journal entry that would restate the note receivable and record the gain, an exchange gain, is provided in Figure 6B–4. The exchange gain would appear on International's income statement.

FIGURE 6B–4	

Recognizing an exchange gain on a receivable	**Conversion of Swiss francs to U.S. dollars:**
	    $2,778 = 5,000 Swiss francs × (1 U.S. dollar ÷ 1.8 Swiss francs)
	
	Adjustment: $2,778 − $2,500 = $278 (gain)
	
	Dec. 31 Notes Receivable (+A) 278
	                 Exchange Gain (Ga, +SE) 278
	                 Recognized exchange gain on a receivable
	                 expressed in Swiss francs.

An exchange loss will be recognized on International's books if, at a later date, the value of the U.S. dollar rises relative to the Swiss franc. Assume that, as of January 31 of the following year, 1 U.S. dollar could be exchanged for 2.2 Swiss francs. In this case the adjustment would be calculated and the adjusting journal entry recorded by International as in Figure 6B–5.

FIGURE 6B–5	

Recognizing an exchange loss on a receivable	**Conversion of Swiss francs to U.S. dollars:**
	    $2,273 = 5,000 Swiss francs × (1 U.S. dollar ÷ 2.2 Swiss francs)
	
	Adjustment: $2,273 − $2,778 = $505 (loss)
	
	Jan. 31 Exchange Loss (Lo, −SE) 505
	                 Notes Receivable (−A) 505
	                 Recognized exchange loss on a receivable
	                 expressed in Swiss francs.

HOLDING PAYABLES EXPRESSED IN FOREIGN CURRENCIES

Exchange gains and losses can also occur from holding payables denominated in non-U.S. (foreign) currencies. Assume that on December 1 Cross Cultural, Inc., purchased inventory from a Japanese company, promising to pay 100,000 yen at a later date. At that time 140 Japanese yen could be exchanged for 1 U.S. dollar. As of December 31 and the following January 31, 125 and 160 yen, respectively, could be exchanged for 1 U.S. dollar. Assuming that Cross Cultural, Inc., held the payable throughout the two-month time period and prepared financial statements on December 31 and January 31, the journal entries and related calculations that are shown in Figure 6B–6 would have been recorded to reflect these changes in the exchange rates.

FIGURE 6B-6	DECEMBER 1: PURCHASE OF INVENTORY

Recognizing exchange losses and gains on payables

DECEMBER 1: PURCHASE OF INVENTORY

Conversion of Japanese yen to U.S. dollars:
$714 = 100,000 \text{ yen} \times (1 \text{ U.S. dollar} \div 140 \text{ yen})$

| Dec. 1 | Inventory (+A) | 714 | |
| | Accounts Payable (+L) | | 714 |

Purchased inventory for 100,000 Japanese yen.

DECEMBER 31: COMPUTATION AND RECOGNITION OF EXCHANGE LOSS

Conversion of Japanese yen to U.S. dollars:
$800 = 100,000 \text{ yen} \times (1 \text{ U.S. dollar} \div 125 \text{ yen})$

Adjustment: $714 - $800 = $86 (loss)

| Dec. 31 | Exchange Loss (Lo, −SE) | 86 | |
| | Accounts Payable (+L) | | 86 |

Recognized exchange loss on holding a payable expressed in Japanese yen.

JANUARY 31: COMPUTATION AND RECOGNITION OF EXCHANGE GAIN

Conversion of Japanese yen to U.S. dollars:
$625 = 100,000 \text{ yen} \times (1 \text{ U.S. dollar} \div 160 \text{ yen})$

Adjustment: $800 - $625 = $175 (gain)

| Jan. 31 | Accounts Payable (−L) | 175 | |
| | Exchange Gain (Ga, +SE) | | 175 |

Recognized exchange gain on holding a payable expressed in Japanese yen.

EXCHANGE GAINS AND LOSSES: FOUR POSSIBLE COMBINATIONS

To summarize, the recognition of an exchange gain or loss depends on the combination of two factors: (1) whether the U.S. company holds a receivable or payable that is denominated in a foreign currency, and (2) whether the foreign currency increases or decreases in value relative to the U.S. dollar. Figure 6B–7 illustrates the four possible combinations.

If a U.S. company holds a receivable denominated in a foreign currency, and the foreign currency rises in value relative to the U.S. dollar, the U.S. company recognizes an exchange gain on its income statement as illustrated in Cell 1. Holding a receivable in a currency that decreases in value relative to the U.S. dollar, on the other hand, gives rise to an exchange loss as illustrated in Cell 3. Holding a payable expressed in terms of a foreign currency produces exactly the opposite effect: that is, as the foreign currency rises in value, exchange losses are recognized as illustrated in Cell 2. As the foreign currency drops in value, exchange gains accrue as illustrated in Cell 4.

HEDGING AND THE ECONOMIC CONSEQUENCES OF FLUCTUATING EXCHANGE RATES

Exchange rate fluctuations are constant and often significant. As illustrated in the previous section, such erratic movement can give rise to exchange gains and losses that cause income and other reported values (e.g., receivables and payables) to vary sub-

Exchange gains and losses

		Item held by U.S. Company	
		Receivable	Payable
Change in the value of the foreign currency relative to the U.S. dollar	Increase	1 Exchange gain	2 Exchange loss
	Decrease	3 Exchange loss	4 Exchange gain

stantially from one period to the next. Variations in exchange rates, as a result, can give rise to economic consequences through their effects on stock prices, credit ratings, management compensation, and debt covenants. Such consequences increase the economic risks associated with engaging in transactions that are denominated in foreign currencies.

While management has very little control over exchange rates, it can reduce some of the risks associated with holding receivables and payables denominated in foreign currencies. Multinational companies commonly use a strategy called hedging to reduce the variation in income due to fluctuating exchange rates. This strategy involves taking a position in a foreign currency in an amount that is equal and opposite to a particular receivable or payable expressed in that currency.

To illustrate, assume that on July 1 General Motors (GM) sells a group of automobiles to British Petroleum (BP), receiving in exchange a note stating that BP will pay GM 100,000 British pounds in one year. If the exchange rate as of July 1 is $1.70 per British pound, GM would record the following journal entry.

Conversion of British pounds to U.S. dollars:
   $170,000 = 100,000 British pounds × ($1.70 ÷ 1 pound)

July 1	Notes Receivable (+A)	170,000	
	Sales (R, +SE)		170,000

Sold automobiles in exchange for a note receivable expressed in British pounds.

If GM chooses not to hedge this receivable, and the exchange rate changes to $1.50 per British pound as of December 31, GM will recognize a $20,000 exchange loss during the period when it records the following adjusting journal entry at the end of the year. This loss would appear on GM's income statement.

Conversion of British pounds to U.S. dollars:
   $150,000 = 100,000 British pounds × ($1.50 ÷ 1 pound)
   Adjustment: $170,000 − $150,000 = $20,000 (loss)

Dec. 31	Exchange Loss (Lo, −SE)	20,000	
	Notes Receivable (−A)		20,000

Recognized exchange loss on a receivable expressed in British pounds.

GM could have negated the effect on income of this $20,000 loss if it had chosen to hedge the receivable. That is, GM could have borrowed 100,000 British pounds on July 1 and agreed to pay it back one year later. By doing so, GM would have taken a position in British pounds that was equal and opposite to the outstanding receivable. It would have entered into a payable (100,000 British pounds) that would have balanced the outstanding receivable (100,000 British pounds). Had GM adopted such a strategy, on December 31 it would have recognized a $20,000 exchange gain on the outstanding payable, which would have negated the effect on income of the $20,000 exchange loss recognized on the receivable. The journal entries to record the borrowing and the recognition of the exchange gain are provided in Figure 6B–8.

Hedging is commonly practiced by U.S. multinationals to reduce the risks associated with holding receivables and payables in foreign currencies, where exchange rates are constantly fluctuating. General Motors, for example, holds long-term debt that is payable in Canadian dollars, Australian dollars, Swiss francs, Japanese yen, German marks, Spanish pesatas, Belgian francs, British pounds, and other currencies. Many of these payables were established by GM to hedge the effects on income and reduce the economic risks associated with holding outstanding receivables denominated in these currencies. The following excerpt from a recent financial report of the Goodyear Tire & Rubber Company describes long-term debts held by the company that are payable in Japanese yen and Swiss francs:

The Swiss franc bonds totaling $341.4 million and $201.8 million of yen bonds and bank term loan are completely hedged by foreign currency exchange agreements with five domestic and international financial institutions whereunder the Company is entitled to purchase 438 million Swiss francs and 27.2 billion Yen for $330.4 million. . . . , $212.8 million associated with these agreements was recorded in long-term accounts and notes receivable on the Consolidated Balance Sheet.

FIGURE 6B–8	**JULY 1:**
Hedging an outstanding receivable	**Conversion of British pounds to U.S. dollars:** $170,000 = 100,000 British pounds × ($1.70 ÷ 1 pound)

July 1	Cash (+A)	170,000	
	Notes Payable (+L)		170,000

Borrowed 100,000 British pounds.

DECEMBER 31:

Conversion of British pounds to U.S. dollars:
$150,000 = 100,000 British pounds × ($1.50 ÷ 1 pound)

Adjustment: $170,000 − $150,000 = $20,000

Dec. 31	Notes Payable (−L)	20,000	
	Exchange Gain (Ga, +SE)		20,000

Recognized exchange gain on a payable expressed in British pounds.

KEY TERMS

Note: Definitions for these terms are provided in the glossary at the end of the text.

Accounts receivable (p. 267)
Aging schedule (p. 276)
Allowance method (p. 272)
Cash budget (p. 266)
Cash discounts (p. 270)
Collection period (p. 281)
Compensating balances (p. 265)
Current asset (p. 259)
Current ratio (p. 260)
Escrow (p. 265)
Exchange rate (p. 290)
Gross method (p. 271)
Markdowns (p. 270)
Multinational (transnational) corporations (p. 290)

Net realizable value (p. 270)
Open accounts (p. 267)
Operating cycle (p. 259)
Percentage-of-credit-sales approach (p. 273)
Petty cash (p. 266)
Physical control (p. 267)
Quantity discount (p. 270)
Quick ratio (p. 260)
Record control (p. 267)
Short-term notes receivable (p. 286)
Window dressing (p. 263)
Working capital (p. 260)

QUESTIONS FOR DISCUSSION AND REVIEW

1. What is the definition of current assets? How is it used? What weaknesses are inherent in the measure of current assets?
2. Would the current assets classification on the balance sheet of a bridge-building company mean the same as the current assets classification on the balance sheet of a small retailer? Why?
3. What is "window dressing?" How and why might managers manipulate the current ratio by choosing certain accounting methods or biasing estimates used in applying these methods? How might managers manipulate the current ratio by making certain operating decisions?
4. Explain why window dressing may not be in the best interest of a company, its stockholders, or its management.
5. Provide two examples of restrictions on a company's use of the cash it owns. How are these restrictions reported on the financial statements? Why should restricted cash be separated from cash that is free and clear?
6. What two issues must managers consider in their efforts to maintain the proper cash balance?
7. What two methods for providing both physical and record control of the cash balance are discussed in the chapter?
8. Explain the link between accounts receivable and the income statement. How is the recognition of an account receivable related to the four criteria of revenue recognition?
9. The Sales account, which appears on the income statement, usually differs from Cash Inflows Due to Operating Activities, which is found on the statement of cash flows. Why? How can accounts receivable be used to reconcile these two numbers?
10. Provide three examples of how a manager may practice window dressing with respect to accounts receivable.
11. Discuss why auditors are concerned that sales on account be recognized in the proper time period and that bad debts be estimated accurately.
12. The valuation base for accounts receivable is called *net realizable value*. What is the definition of net realizable value with respect to accounts receivable?

13. Distinguish cash discounts from quantity discounts and sales discounts (markdowns). Why are quantity discounts and sales discounts not explicitly recognized in financial accounting statements?

14. Why do companies offer cash discounts? State your answer in terms of the trade-offs between the time value of money, collection costs, and the terms of the cash discount.

15. Explain how the account "Cash Discounts" is recognized on the financial statements.

16. What can companies do to reduce uncollectible accounts receivable? How could they reduce them to zero? Why don't they do it?

17. Explain how bad debts are accounted for under the allowance method and estimated by using a percentage of credit sales. What kind of information is used by management when preparing such an estimate?

18. What is an aging of accounts receivable? Describe the computation, and explain how it provides information that is useful to managers. How can aging accounts receivable help managers set the terms of their cash discounts? What effect has the computerization of accounts receivable had on management's inclination to perform aging analyses? Why?

19. Discuss the role of the Allowance for Doubtful Accounts account. What financial statement numbers are affected when a bad debt is written off the books? How are current assets, working capital, the current ratio, and net income affected?

20. Suppose you are an investor attempting to decide whether to invest a substantial sum of money in a small manufacturing company. While examining the financial statements, you note that the company has shown large profits over the past several years and that the balance in the Allowance for Uncollectibles account is decreasing as a percentage of accounts receivable. How and why might this information affect your investment decision?

21. If a company that uses the allowance method to account for bad debts consistently overestimates bad debts, how does this show up in the books? If the same company consistently understates the bad debt estimate, how does this show up in the books?

22. (Appendix 6A) Two basic methods are used to account for notes receivable. Compare the two methods in terms of the net values of the assets related to the note (i.e., Notes Receivable and Interest Receivable) and the amount and timing of interest revenue recognition. One of the methods uses a Discount on Notes Receivable account. Explain the role of this account, where it is disclosed on the balance sheet, and why it is very similar to an Unearned Revenue account, which would appear as a current liability.

23. (Appendix 6A) Briefly explain some of the problems in U.S. financial institutions, and describe how these problems relate to the accounting issues covered in this chapter.

24. (Appendix 6B) What is an exchange rate and how can fluctuating exchange rates give rise to gains and losses recognized on the financial statements?

25. (Appendix 6B) Define hedging, and explain how and why companies enter into hedging transactions.

EXERCISES

E6–1

(Classifying cash on the balance sheet)

Boyer International is currently preparing its financial statements for 1996. The company has several different sources of cash and is trying to decide how to classify them. The sources of cash follow:

a. $30,000 in a checking account with The First National Bank.

b. $3,000 in checks dated December 4, 1996, received from customers.

c. $250,000 in certificates of deposit through The First National Bank that are to mature on November 15, 1999.

d. $40,000 in a savings account with The First National Bank.

e. $1,000 in the petty cash fund. As of December 31, 1996, there are receipts totaling $600 in the petty cash drawer.

f. $50,000 held as a compensating balance for a loan with The First National Bank. The loan agreement requires Boyer International to maintain a compensating balance equal to 10 percent of the loan balance. During 1997, the outstanding principal balance will be reduced to $350,000.

g. $8,000 in a checking account with Interstate Federal Savings.

REQUIRED:
Indicate how each source listed should be classified on the December 31, 1996 balance sheet. Explain each answer.

E6–2

(Classifying cash on the balance sheet)

The following items relate to the financial statements of Melvin Construction Company.
a. $2,000 in a checking account.
b. $8,000 invested in a treasury note due to mature in ninety days.
c. $3,000 in a savings account that cannot be withdrawn until a $10,000 outstanding debt is paid off.
d. $18,000 invested in securities that will be sold in two years to finance an expansion of the plant.
e. $2,500 invested in IBM common shares. Management intends to liquidate this investment in less than six months.
f. $15,000 held in escrow by a bank, serving as earnest money that binds management to a real estate contract.
g. A $3,000 money order received in payment from a customer.

REQUIRED:
Classify each item as either (a) unrestricted cash, (b) restricted cash, or (c) investment.

E6–3

(Accounting for cash discounts)

On December 12, Woodington sold goods on account for a gross price of $40,000. The terms of the sale were 2/10, n/30. As of December 31, when financial statements were prepared, no payment had been received by Woodington. Full payment was received on January 5 of the following year.

REQUIRED:
a. Prepare journal entries for these transactions.
b. Assume that full payment was received on December 20. Prepare journal entries and discuss how the timing of the cash receipt affected the income statement and statement of cash flows.

E6–4

(Accounting for cash discounts)

On May 1, 1997 Crab Cove Fishing Company sold Maine lobster on account for a gross price of $30,000. On May 5 the company also sold cod on account for a gross price of $20,000. The terms of both sales were 3/10, n/30. Crab Cove received payment for the first sale on May 6, 1997 and payment for the second sale on May 31, 1997.

REQUIRED:
Provide all necessary journal entries.

E6–5

(Bad debts under the allowance method)

Arlington Cycle Company began operations on January 1, 1996. The company reported the following selected items in the 1997 financial report.

	1997	1996
Gross sales	$1,400,000	$1,500,000
Accounts receivable	600,000	650,000
Actual bad debt write-offs	22,000	10,000

Arlington estimates bad debts at 2 percent of gross sales.

REQUIRED:
Analyze the activity in the "Allowance for Doubtful Accounts" T-account, and comment on whether the bad debt estimate has been sufficient to cover the write-offs.

E6–6

(Accounting for uncollectibles)

In its 1996 financial report Sound Unlimited reported the following items:
1. A credit balance in Allowance for Doubtful Accounts of $200,000.
2. A debit balance in accounts receivable of $7,500,000.
3. Sales of $3,250,000.

During 1996 the company was involved in the following transactions that affected Allowance for Doubtful Accounts.
(1) Wrote off accounts considered uncollectible totaling $195,000.
(2) Recovered $45,000 that had previously been written off.

Assume that historically 5 percent of sales have proven to be uncollectible.

REQUIRED:

a. Compute the December 31, 1995 balance in Allowance for Doubtful Accounts.
b. Assume that all sales were on credit, and cash collections from customers during 1996 totaled $4,200,000. Compute the 12/31/95 balance in accounts receivable.

E6–7

(Accounting for doubtful accounts: the allowance method)

The following items were extracted from the financial records of Stein Glass Company.

Sales	$ 980,000
Accounts Receivable	1,025,000
Allowance for Doubtful Accounts	50,000 (cr.)

After analyzing individual accounts, the company's accountant wrote off $35,000 of accounts receivable as uncollectible, and then estimated, from historical data, that 4 percent of this year's sales will be uncollectible.

REQUIRED:

a. Prepare the entry to record bad debt charge.
b. Compute the final balance in the Allowance for Doubtful Accounts account.

E6–8

(Inferring bad debt write-offs and reconstructing related journal entries)

The 1997 annual report of Johnson Services reveal the following information. The dollar amounts are end-of-year balances.

	1997	1996
Credit sales	$75,300	$61,500
Accounts receivable	9,400	9,200
Allowance for doubtful accounts	1,300	1,000
Bad debt recoveries	55	70

Johnson estimates bad debts each year at 2 percent of credit sales.

REQUIRED:

a. Compute the actual amount of write-offs during 1997.
b. Infer the journal entries that explain the activity in Accounts Receivable and the related allowance account during 1997.

E6–9

(Preparing an aging schedule)

Potter Stables uses the aging method to estimate its bad debts. Sherman Potter, the company president, has given you the following aging of accounts receivable as of December 31, 1997 along with the historical probabilities that the account balances will not be collected.

ACCOUNT AGE	BALANCE	NONCOLLECTION PROBABILITY
Current	$290,000	2%
1–45 days past due	110,000	5
46–90 days past due	68,000	8
Over 90 days past due	40,000	15

REQUIRED:
Compute total receivables and expected bad debts as of December 31, 1997.

E6-10

(Appendix 6A: Two methods to account for short-term notes receivable)

Peffer Financial loaned $9,000 to Slatten Brothers on December 1, 1996. The ninety-day note (both principal and interest) was due March 1 of the following year and had a stated annual interest rate of 8 percent.

REQUIRED:
a. Prepare the journal entries on Peffer Financial's books related to this note that were recorded on December 1, when the note was issued, on December 31, when financial statements were prepared, and March 1, when the note was paid in full assuming the following:
    (1) The note receivable is recorded at face value, and no discount is recognized.
    (2) The note receivable is recorded at face value plus interest, and a discount is recognized.
b. Does Method 1 affect the December 31 financial statements differently from Method 2? Explain your answer in terms of the effects on net income and current assets as well as in terms of general balance sheet and income statement disclosure.

E6-11

(Appendix 6B: Exchange gains/losses on outstanding receivables)

On January 1, 1997, Outreach Incorporated sold services to a Canadian supply company and accepted a three-year note in the amount of 11,000 Canadian dollars. Exchange rates between the U.S. dollar and the Canadian dollar are provided below.

DATE	U.S. DOLLARS PER CANADIAN DOLLARS
January 1, 1997	$.85
December 31, 1997	.90
December 31, 1998	.80

REQUIRED:
Provide the journal entries (in U.S. dollars) prepared by Outreach to record the receipt of the note and the exchange gains/losses recognized on December 31, 1997, and December 31, 1998. Ignore any interest on the note.

E6-12

(Appendix 6B: Hedging to reduce the risk of currency fluctuations)

This exercise refers to *E6-11*. Assume that Outreach hedged the 11,000 (Canadian dollar) receivable by borrowing 11,000 Canadian dollars from a Canadian bank on January 1, 1997. Demonstrate using journal entries how this transaction removes Outreach's exposure to the risk of fluctuating exchange rates. Explain.

PROBLEMS

P6-1

(Classifying cash on the balance sheet)

On September 30, 1996, Print-O-Matic Inc. entered into an arrangement with its bank to borrow $250,000. The principal is due on October 1, 2001, and the note has a stated annual interest rate of 10 percent. Under the borrowing agreement, Print-O-Matic agreed to maintain a compensating balance of $60,000 in a non-interest-bearing account. As of December 31, 1996, Print-O-Matic has an additional $225,000 in various savings and checking accounts that earn an annual rate of 6 percent. The controller intends to classify the entire $285,000 in cash as a current asset.

REQUIRED:

a. Do you agree with the classification of the $285,000 of cash as a current asset? Explain your answer.

b. Print-O-Matic reported interest expense associated with this note for the year ended December 31, 1996, in the amount of $6,250 ([$250,000 × 10%] × 1/4). Do you agree with this classification? Should any other factors be considered in the interest cost? Explain.

P6–2

(Cash discounts)

During the month of March, QNI Corporation made the following credit sales and had the following related collections. QNI prepares financial statements for the first quarter of operations at the end of March.

March 3 Sold goods to AAA company for a gross price of $1,400. The terms of the sale were 2/10, n/30.

March 8 Sold goods to BBB company for a gross price of $800. The terms of the sale were 2/10, n/30.

March 11 Received full payment from AAA.

March 28 Received full payment from BBB.

March 29 Sold goods to CCC Company for a gross price of $1,800. The terms of sale were 2/10, n/30.

REQUIRED:

a. Prepare the journal entries to record these transactions.

b. Note that BBB missed the discount period by ten days. Compute the annual interest rate BBB paid for the use of the $800 for that ten-day period. Assuming that BBB can borrow money from the bank at 9 percent, what should BBB have done differently?

P6–3

(Bad debts over time)

Financial information for CNG Inc., follows.

	1997	1996	1995
Credit sales	$205,000	$200,000	$180,000
Actual bad debt write-offs	11,000	10,000	6,000

The company estimates bad debts for financial reporting purposes at 3 percent of credit sales. The balance in Allowance for Doubtful Accounts as of January 1, 1995, was $10,000.

REQUIRED:

a. Provide the journal entries related to Allowance for Doubtful Accounts for 1995, 1996, and 1997.

b. Compute the balance in Allowance for Doubtful Accounts as of December 31, 1997.

c. Comment on the sufficiency of the bad debt charge and allowance over the 3-year period. How did you come to your conclusion?

P6–4

(Accounting for uncollectibles over two periods)

Glacier Ice Company uses a percentage-of-net-sales method to account for estimated bad debts. Historically, 3 percent of net sales have proven to be uncollectible. During 1996 and 1997 the company reported the following:

	1997	1996
Gross sales	$1,500,000	$1,800,000
Sales discounts	100,000	130,000
Sales returns	50,000	20,000

REQUIRED:

a. Prepare the necessary adjusting entry on December 31, 1996 to record the estimated bad debt charge for 1996.

b. Assume that the January 1, 1996 balance in Allowance for Doubtful Accounts was $65,000 (credit) and that $70,000 in bad debts were written off the books during 1996. What is the December 31, 1996 balance in this account *after adjustments?*

c. Prepare the necessary adjusting entry on December 31, 1997 to record the estimated bad debt charge for 1997.

d. What is the December 31, 1997 balance in Allowance for Doubtful Accounts? Assume that $85,000 in bad debts were written off the books during 1997.

P6–5

(Ignoring potential bad debts can lead to serious overstatements)

The following financial information represents Hadley Company's first year of operations, 1996.

INCOME STATEMENT		BALANCE SHEET	
Sales	$200,000	Cash	$ 5,000
Cost of goods sold	102,000	Accounts receivable	85,000
Gross profit	$ 98,000	Other assets	40,000
Expenses	65,000	Total assets	$130,000
Net income	$ 33,000	Current liabilities	$ 13,000
		Long-term notes payable	80,000
		Stockholders' equity	37,000
		Total liabilities and stockholders' equity	$130,000

After reading Hadley's financial statements, you conclude that the company had a very successful first year of operations. However, after further examination you note that the sales figure on the income statement was not adjusted for a bad debt charge. You also realize that a large percentage of Hadley's sales were to three customers, one of which, Litzenberger Supply, is in very questionable financial health, although still in business. Litzenberger owes Hadley $50,000 as of the end of 1996.

REQUIRED:

a. Adjust the financial statements of Hadley Company to reflect a more conservative reporting with respect to bad debts. That is, establish a provision for the uncollectibility of Litzenberger's account. Recompute net income. How does this adjustment affect your assessment of Hadley's first year of operations?

b. Why would auditors probably require that Hadley choose the more conservative reporting?

c. Hadley's chief financial officer claims that no bad debt charge should be recorded because Litzenberger is still conducting operations as of the end of 1996. How would you respond to this claim?

P6–6

(Estimating uncollectibles, financial ratios, and loan agreements)

Excerpts from the 1996 financial statements of Finley, Ltd., a service company, follow.

Fees earned	$240,000
Accounts receivable	68,000
Allowance for doubtful accounts	3,400
Total current assets	105,000
Total current liabilities	65,000
Net income	15,000
Dividends declared	5,000
Bad debt charge	3,400

Auditors from Price and Company reviewed the financial records of Finley and found that a credit sale (for services rendered) of $10,000, which was included in the Fees earned amount above, should not have been recognized until January 20, 1997. The auditors also noted that a more reasonable estimate of future bad debts would be 10 percent of the Accounts Receivable balance. The auditors have informed Finley's management that the audit opinion will be qualified if Finley does not adjust the financial statements accordingly.

REQUIRED:

a.   Compute the effect of the auditor's recommended adjustment on the 1996 Fees Earned, Accounts Receivable, Allowance for Doubtful Accounts, current ratio, working capital, and net income reported by Finley.

b.   Assume that Finley has a loan agreement with a bank requiring it to maintain a current ratio of 1.5 and limiting its annual dividend payment to 50 percent of net income. How might these restrictions have influenced the reporting decisions of Finley's managers?

P6–7

(Uncollectibles: Ignoring an allowance)

Fine Linen Service began operations on January 28, 1993. The company does not establish an allowance for bad debts. It simply recognizes a bad debt charge when an account is deemed uncollectible. Over the past five years the company has written off the following items.

July 6, 1993	Wrote off $10,000 as uncollectible from a sale made on March 1, 1993.
Feb. 3, 1994	Wrote off $50,000 as uncollectible from a sale made on October 28, 1993.
Mar. 11, 1995	Wrote off $25,000 as uncollectible from a sale made on December 20, 1993 ($12,000) and a sale made on May 10, 1994 ($13,000).
Mar. 24, 1995	Recovered $5,000 that had been written off on February 3, 1994. It is company policy to credit Bad Debt Charge when an account is recovered.
Aug. 8, 1996	Wrote off $75,000 as uncollectible from sales made in 1993 ($20,000), in 1994 ($25,000), and in 1995 ($30,000).
Dec. 2, 1996	Wrote off $5,000 as uncollectible from a sale made on April 26, 1996.
Sep. 19, 1997	Wrote off $90,000 as uncollectible from sales in 1993 ($5,000), in 1994 ($30,000), in 1995 ($25,000), in 1996 ($20,000), and in 1997 ($10,000).

ADDITIONAL INFORMATION

a.   Over the period 1993 to 1997, Fine Linen Service realized the following sales and reported the following ending balances in accounts receivable.

	SALES	ACCOUNTS RECEIVABLE
1993	$1,000,000	$ 950,000
1994	975,000	900,000
1995	1,025,000	1,200,000
1996	1,032,000	1,175,000
1997	990,000	1,095,000

b.   At the beginning of operations, a consultant had informed Fine Linen Service that the company should expect not to collect 8 percent of total sales.

REQUIRED:

a. List the bad debt charge and the balance sheet value of Accounts Receivable for each year over the five-year period under both Fine Linen's current method and the allowance method. Use the following format.

	1993	1994	1995	1996	1997
Current method:					
Bad debt charge					
Accounts receivable value					
Allowance method:					
Bad debt charge					
Accounts receivable value					

b. Compute the total bad debt charge over the five-year period under the two methods. Why is the allowance method preferred to Fine Linen's current method?

P6–8

(Accounting for uncollectibles and the aging estimate)

In an attempt to include all relevant information for decision-making purposes, Merimore Company estimates bad debts using the aging method. However, for external reporting purposes, the company estimates bad debts as a percentage of credit sales. Merimore prepares monthly adjusting journal entries. From trends over the past five years, the company controller has estimated that 2 percent of monthly credit sales will prove to be uncollectible. Following are the monthly credit sales and bad debt write-offs for Merimore Company for 1996.

MONTH	CASH COLLECTIONS	CREDIT SALES	WRITE-OFFS
January	$ 1,200,000	$ 1,000,000	
February	1,050,000	925,000	
March	910,000	1,010,000	
April	1,000,000	975,000	$ 87,000
May	875,000	950,000	
June	1,080,000	1,200,000	
July	950,000	1,150,000	52,000
August	1,011,000	1,075,000	
September	1,105,000	1,025,000	
October	980,000	980,000	
November	1,100,000	900,000	
December	865,000	750,000	100,000
Total	$12,126,000	$11,940,000	$239,000

On December 31, 1996, the controller prepared the following aging of accounts receivable.

ACCOUNT CLASSIFICATION	BALANCE	PERCENT UNCOLLECTIBLE
Current	$ 700,000	2.0%
1–30 days past due	1,200,000	5.5
31–75 days past due	550,000	10.0
Over 75 days past due	800,000	25.0

The Allowance for Doubtful Accounts balance on Jan. 1, 1996, was a credit of $70,000.

REQUIRED:

a. Prepare the adjusting journal entry necessary on December 31, 1996, so that the statements will be in accordance with the company's external reporting policies. Remember that the company prepares monthly adjusting journal entries.

b. Compute the balance in Allowance for Doubtful Accounts after the entry in (a) has been recorded and posted.
c. Compute the balance in Accounts Receivable as of January 1, 1996.
d. Prepare the December 31 adjusting entry for bad debts using the percentage of sales method and compute the estimated bad debts using the aging method.
e. Why would a company want to estimate bad debts using two different methods? Which of the two methods is more costly and time-consuming to implement? Which provides more useful information?

P6–9

(Inferring reporting strategies)

Excerpts from the financial statements of Ticheley Enterprises are provided below.

	1997	1996	1995
INCOME STATEMENT			
Bad debt charge	$ 1,700	$ 2,900	$ 2,100
Net income	15,800	15,300	14,400
BALANCE SHEET			
Accounts receivable	$27,400	$23,200	$23,100
Allowance for bad debts (cr.)	2,100	3,000	2,300
Stockholders' equity	78,500	75,000	71,400

On December 27, 1996, Ticheley sent merchandise with a sales price of $8,500 to a major customer. The merchandise was in transit as of December 31. The cost of the inventory shipped was $2,900, and the company chose to record the sale and outflow of inventory on January 4, 1997, when the customer received the shipment. Ticheley's management is compensated partially on an annual bonus where all managers share equally in a $10,000 bonus pool if reported net income exceeds 20 percent of shareholders' equity.

REQUIRED:
a. Ticheley's president recently stated in a letter to the shareholders that the company has reported profit increases consistently over the last three years. Comment on this statement.
b. Why would a company establish a management compensation system where a bonus is paid if reported income exceeds a certain percentage of stockholders' equity?
c. Identify any reporting strategy that Ticheley may be using, and support your position with calculations.
d. Explain why Ticheley may be using the strategy you mentioned above, and support your position with calculations.

P6–10

(Appendix 6A: Accounting for short-term notes receivable)

Napier Plumbing Supply entered into the following transactions involving short-term notes receivable during 1996.

Jan. 29 Sold merchandise with a sales value of $80,000 in exchange for a three-month note with a stated annual rate of 8 percent.

Mar. 1 Loaned $14,000 to one of the company employees. The note called for a 10 percent annual interest rate and was to be paid in full at the end of the year.

Apr. 29 Note issued on Jan. 29 is repaid.

May 31 Accepted a five-month note with a stated annual rate of 9 percent in payment of a $25,000 open account receivable.

July 14 Sold merchandise for $45,000. Five thousand dollars was collected in cash, and the remainder was accepted in the form of a six-month note with a stated annual rate of 12 percent.

Oct. 31 Note issued on May 31 is repaid.

Dec. 1 Sold merchandise for $30,000 in exchange for a 45-day note with a stated annual rate of 8 percent.

REQUIRED:

a.   Assuming that the notes are recorded at face value and no discount is recognized, prepare journal entries that would cover the following:
   1. The issuance of the notes
   2. The principal and interest payments
   3. The adjusting entries on December 31

b.   Assume that the notes are recorded at face value plus interest and a discount is recognized. Prepare journal entries to cover the same items as in (a).

P6–11

(Appendix 6B: Exchange gains and losses)

Hughes International is a U.S. company that conducts business throughout the world. Listed below are selected transactions entered into by the company during 1996.

1.   Sold merchandise to Royal Equipment Company (a United Kingdom company) in exchange for an account receivable in the amount of 320,000 pounds. At the time, the exchange rate was .50 British pounds per U.S. dollar.
2.   Sold merchandise to Honda Automobile Company (a Japanese company) in exchange for a note receivable that calls for a payment of 350,000 yen. The exchange rate was 150 yen to the U.S. dollar.
3.   Purchased inventory from Venice Leathers (an Italian company) in exchange for a note payable that calls for a payment of 50 million lira. The exchange rate was 1,500 lira to the U.S. dollar.
4.   Purchased inventory from B. C. Lumber (a Canadian company) in exchange for an account payable in the amount of 200,000 Canadian dollars. The exchange rate was 1.50 Canadian dollars per U.S. dollar.

On December 31, 1996, the exchange rates were as follows.

FOREIGN CURRENCY	CURRENCY PER U.S. DOLLAR
British pound	.60
Japanese yen	140
Italian lira	1,600
Canadian dollar	1.20

REQUIRED:

a.   Convert each transaction above to the equivalent amount in U.S. dollars.
b.   Prepare journal entries to record each transaction.
c.   Assume that the receivables and payables are still outstanding as of December 31, 1996. Compute the amount of exchange gain or loss for each transaction.
d.   Why do fluctuating exchange rates give rise to exchange gains and losses?

P6–12

(Appendix 6B: Fluctuating exchange rates, debt covenants, and hedging)

International Services entered into a debt covenant requiring it to maintain a current ratio of at least 1.5:1. The company's condensed balance sheet as of December 31 follows.

ASSETS		LIABILITIES AND STOCKHOLDERS' EQUITY	
Current assets	$ 80,000	Current liabilities	$ 50,000
Noncurrent assets	200,000	Long-term liabilities	100,000
		Stockholders' equity	130,000
		Total liabilities and	
Total assets	$ 280,000	stockholders' equity	$280,000

International's primary customer is Buckingham, Ltd., a company located in Britain, and as of December 31 Buckingham owed International 40,000 British pounds. The exchange rate as of December 31 between U.S. dollars and British pounds was $1.70 per pound.

REQUIRED:

a. What dollar amount of International's current assets on the balance sheet is associated with the receivable owed by Buckingham?

b. Assume that all account balances remain the same over the next year. Below what exchange rate (U.S. dollars per British pound) would International be in violation of the debt covenant?

c. Assume that $1,600 of Accounts Payable on the balance sheet represents a debt to a British bank of 1,000 British pounds. Below what exchange rate would International be in violation of the debt covenant now? Consider both the receivable and the payable.

d. Describe how International could hedge to reduce the risk of being in violation of the debt covenant.

CASES

C6–1

(Working capital, debt covenants, and restrictions on management decisions)

Excerpts from the June 30, 1994 balance sheet of The Quaker Oats Company are provided below (dollars in millions).

	1994	1993	1992
Current assets:			
Cash and short-term investments	$ 140.4	$ 61.0	$ 95.2
Receivables	509.4	478.9	575.3
Inventories	385.5	354.0	435.3
Other current assets	218.3	173.7	150.4
Current liabilities	1,259.1	1,105.1	1,087.5

REQUIRED:

a. The notes to the company's 1992 financial statements state that "under the most restrictive terms of the various loan agreements . . . minimum working capital of $150 million must be maintained." Compute how close The Quaker Oats Company came to this restriction at the end of 1992, and discuss what has happened since that time.

b. In Quaker Oats' 1994 annual report, it states "under the most restrictive terms of the Revolving Credit Agreements, the company must maintain total shareholders' equity greater than $300 million." Comment on possible explanations for the changing restrictions.

C6–2

(Restricted cash and solvency ratios)

In a recent financial statement, AMAX, Inc., a coal-mining company, reported the following:

Assets (in thousands)
  Cash and cash equivalents (Note 9) $46,700

Note 9:

AMAX had on deposit with commercial banks a total of $42 million of cash and equivalents that is restricted as to use. Of that amount, $15 million was held for the repurchase of common shares from an affiliated company. The remainder represents a time deposit that is restricted to repayment of a short-term loan.

REQUIRED:

a. Why would a potential investor or creditor reading AMAX's financial statements want to know about restrictions on cash?

b. Assume the January 3 repurchase of common shares will result in a long-term investment. Should the restricted cash be disclosed as current or noncurrent? Why?

c. How might disclosure of such a restriction affect the calculation of working capital, the current ratio, and the quick ratio?

d.   A time deposit is like a savings account that matures and becomes available on a particular day. When the cash becomes available and the short-term loan is paid off, will working capital be increased, decreased, or unaffected? Why?

C6–3

(Cash discounts from the company's and the customers' standpoint)

Throughout the late 1980s major U.S. retailers, such as Sears and J.C. Penney, reported only slight gains in sales. An analyst for this industry said that "consumers are stretched with debt," indicating that they were unwilling to increase their current levels of debt. In an effort to increase sales, some of the retailers considered offering cash discounts for customers who pay cash immediately or within a very short period of time (e.g., ten days).

REQUIRED:

a.   Most large retail companies currently assess no finance charge for outstanding accounts of less than thirty days. Suppose that a company, such as Sears, changed its credit policy and began granting cash discounts with terms of 2/10, n/30. Would such a policy necessarily increase sales volume? Why or why not? What would happen, for example, if the cash discount rate were set too high?

b.   Assume that you purchased merchandise from Sears on account with a gross price of $500 under terms of 2/10, n/30. If you paid your account in ten days, how much would you have to pay? If you paid your account in twenty days, how much would you pay, and at what annual rate of interest would you be paying? If you paid your account in thirty days, how much would you pay, and at what annual rate of interest would you be paying?

C6–4

(Bad debt rates over time)

The following information was computed from the 1994 financial report of the merchandising division of Sears, Roebuck and Co. (dollars in millions).

	1994	1993	1992
Merchandise sales	$26,173	$23,811	$21,584
Credit sales as a percentage of total	59%	59%	57%
Bad debt charge	$ 650	$ 795	$ 872
Bad debt write-offs	$ 869	$ 821	$ 770

REQUIRED:

a.   Assume that Sears uses a percentage-of-credit-sales method to estimate bad debts. Compute the percentages used by Sears in 1992, 1993, and 1994.

b.   Assume that the merchandise division of Sears began 1992 with a $200 credit balance in Allowance for Doubtful Accounts. Prepare the journal entries that affected the allowance account for 1992, 1993, and 1994, and compute the balance as of December 31, 1994.

c.   Have the rates used by Sears to estimate bad debts been consistently over or under its bad debt experience? How can you tell? Would you expect Sears' auditor to encourage the company to lower its bad debt estimate? Why or why not?

C6–5

(Uncertain loans, accounting procedures, and audit qualifications)

The Farm Credit System is the nation's largest lender to farmers. In the fourth quarter of 1987 it posted a profit of $179 million, avoiding a loss by using an unusual accounting technique. As reported in *The Wall Street Journal*, "the System would have posted a fourth-quarter loss of about $43 million had it not taken $222 million out of its reserve for loan losses [Allowance for Doubtful Accounts] . . . . The System began that practice in the 1987 second quarter, as federal subsidy payments buoyed the farm economy and problem loans declined. The practice is highly unusual, though not a violation of generally accepted accounting principles."

Source: Jeff Bailey, "Farm Credit Posts 4th-Quarter Profit, Reflecting Unusual Accounting Method," *The Wall Street Journal*, February 19, 1988, p. 40.

REQUIRED:

a.   Prepare the journal entry recorded by the Farm Credit System described above. Explain why such an entry was described as "highly unusual."

b. Explain how subsidy payments from the U.S. government to farmers would allow the Farm Credit System to justify such an accounting practice.

c. The article goes on to report that "The System's auditor, Price Waterhouse, . . . qualified its opinion of the System's financial statements . . . The qualification for the 1987 books is based on uncertainties of parts of the 1987 federal bailout being implemented." Why would Price Waterhouse qualify the System's financial statements due to uncertainties over the federal subsidy payments?

C6–6

(Revenue recognition, ethics, and reputation)

The Wall Street Journal (April 7, 1993) reported that "For more than 10 years, IBM has quietly turned to Merrill Lynch & Co. and others to execute a rare financial maneuver that propped up the results of IBM's big leasing business. The maneuver allowed IBM to book immediately all the revenue from a long-term computer lease—even though the actual dollars would flow in over the life of the lease. That didn't break any rules, but some accountants term it an end-run that many blue-chip companies would avoid. [Price Waterhouse, IBM's audit firm] called the revenue booster troubling . . . and urged IBM to take immediate action to use the maneuver less." Later, the article states, "Questions about IBM's accounting could be awkward for the wounded computer giant [because] IBM long enjoyed a reputation as the epitome of financial conservatism, with triple-A-rated debt and the bluest of blue-chip stocks."

REQUIRED:

a. Discuss how using an aggressive method to recognize revenue, like the one described above, might affect IBM's reputation as "the epitome of financial conservatism."

b. Discuss some of the economic consequences associated with the use of such a method, mentioning some of the benefits and costs affecting IBM and its management.

c. The article mentions later that IBM requires all employees to swear that they have read [the IBM] "Business Conduct Guidelines" manual that warns them against not only reporting information inaccurately, but also organizing it in a way that is intended to mislead or misinform. Comment on whether this policy is consistent with the use of the aggressive revenue recognition method mentioned above.

C6–7

(Appendix 6A: Nonperforming loans, write-offs, and outstanding debt)

This chapter notes that First Republic Bank, the largest banking concern in Texas, experienced serious financial problems in 1988 because many of its outstanding loans were not performing. It also points out that writing off these loans had caused certain financial ratios to drop, which could trigger the calling of approximately $270 million of the company's long-term debt. These problems influenced the bank's auditor to question whether the bank could continue in its present form.

REQUIRED:

a. What does it mean to *call a debt*, and why would this present a problem for First Republic Bank?

b. Explain how loan write-offs could cause financial ratios to drop and trigger the calling of debt.

c. Would the bank's auditors be likely to issue an unqualified opinion on First Republic Bank? Why or why not?

C6–8

(Appendix 6B: Accounting for foreign currencies: an economic consequence)

An article in *Forbes* noted that "accounting rules . . . can often change the way companies do business." Under the accounting rule covering receivables and payables denominated in foreign currencies, for example, "it is very important for companies to monitor their currency dealings." A case in point is R. J. Reynolds Industries, who recently "opened regional treasury offices in London and Hong Kong to keep tabs on world-wide cash flow and direct local borrowings." In that same article a partner from a major accounting firm indicated that "more and more companies are centralizing their treasury-management function. Those that don't may be operating at a disadvantage."

Source: Christopher Power, "RJR's Foreign Coup," *Forbes*, September 12, 1983, p. 226.

REQUIRED:

a. Explain why the methods of accounting for foreign currencies might cause a company to centralize its treasury-management function, and why those that don't may be operating at a disadvantage.

b. What is one of the main strategies used by U.S. companies to reduce the risks of holding receivables or payables denominated in non-U.S. currencies?

c. Explain how the strategy in (b) works—specifically, how it might be used to reduce the possibility of violating a covenant on an outstanding debt.

C6–9

(MCI)

Refer to the annual report of MCI and answer the following questions.

a. What title does MCI use to describe cash on the balance sheet? What does MCI include as "cash equivalents?"

b. What was the dollar amount of the change in MCI's working capital from 1993 to 1994, and to what event was the change primarily attributable?

c. What policy is used by MCI to recognize revenues, and how is the uncollectible charge handled on the income statement?

d. Compute MCI's gross accounts receivable for 1993 and 1994. Are receivables a significant percentage of current assets? Are total assets?

e. What percentage of MCI's receivables are considered to be uncollectible? Did that percentage change from 1993 to 1994, and if so, by how much and in what direction?

CHAPTER 7

MERCHANDISE INVENTORY

LEARNING OBJECTIVES

LO 1 Define inventory, and describe how the methods used to account for it affect the financial statements.

LO 2 Identify the four main issues that must be addressed when accounting for inventory.

LO 3 Describe the general rules for including items in inventory and attaching costs to these items.

LO 4 Explain the differences between the perpetual and periodic methods and the trade-offs involved in choosing between them.

LO 5 Identify the three cost flow assumptions and the measurement and economic trade-offs that concern both managers and users.

LO 6 Explain how the lower-of-cost-or-market rule is applied to ending inventories and why it is often criticized.

LO 1 Inventory refers to items held for sale in the ordinary course of business. It is very important to retail and manufacturing enterprises, whose performance depends significantly on their sales. The demand for a company's products is often the most important determinant of its success. Indeed, the 1994 annual report of Procter & Gamble opened with the following comments from the company's chief executive. "Your company made strong progress in fiscal 1993/94 against its four primary business objectives: increasing the flow of innovative products to the market place; expanding the global presence of P&G brands; offering better value to customers; and increasing the efficiency and productivity of our operations."

Stockholders, creditors, managers, and auditors are all justifiably interested in the amount, condition, and marketability of a company's inventory. Stockholders are interested in future sales, profits, and dividends, all of which are related to the demand for inventory, and in the efficiency with which managers acquire, carry, and sell inventory. Creditors are interested in the ability of inventory sales to produce cash that can be used to meet interest and principal payments. Creditors may also view inventory as potential collateral or security for loans. Management must ensure that inventories are acquired (or manufactured) and carried at reasonable costs. Enough inventory must be carried and available to meet constantly changing consumer demands; yet carrying too much inventory can be very costly.[1] Auditors must ensure that the inventory dollar amount disclosed in the financial statements is determined using generally accepted accounting principles and reflects the value of the inventories actually owned. The value and marketability of a company's inventory can also provide an indication of its ability to continue as a going concern.

THE RELATIVE SIZE OF INVENTORIES

While the relative size of inventories varies across companies in different industries, for many companies inventory is both the largest current asset and the largest of all assets on the balance sheet. Figure 7–1 shows reported inventory amounts as a percentage of total assets and current assets for a selected group of industry classifications.

Note that financial institutions and services rely very little on inventories, while they are very important to retailers and certain manufacturers. Citicorp, one of the largest banks in the United States, carries no inventories on its balance sheet, and likewise for H&R Block, a tax preparation service. On the other hand, Chrysler Corporation, one of the "Big 3" U.S. automakers, and Wal-Mart, the nation's largest department store, carry inventories of over $3 billion and $6 billion, respectively.

ACCOUNTING FOR INVENTORY: FOUR IMPORTANT ISSUES

LO 2 Figure 7–2 summarizes four important issues that must be addressed when accounting for inventory. At the top of the figure, the life cycle of inventory is divided into four segments. Inventory is (1) acquired, through purchase

---

1. In recent years U.S. manufacturers have become especially concerned with the levels of inventory they maintain. This concern is particularly important in the automobile industry, where U.S. automakers, like General Motors, Ford, and Chrysler, compete with Japanese companies, like Honda, Toyota, and Mitsubishi, who are able to save substantial costs by carrying lower levels of inventory.

FIGURE 7-1	INDUSTRY	SIC CODE	NO. OF COMPANIES	INVENTORY/ TOTAL ASSETS	INVENTORY/ CURRENT ASSETS
Inventory as a percentage of total assets and current assets (Industry Averages)	**MANUFACTURING**				
	Motor Vehicles	3711	95	.37	.52
	Petroleum and Gas	1311	872	.02	.04
	RETAILING				
	Department Stores	5311	641	.46	.60
	Hobby, Toy & Games	5945	519	.61	.74
	GENERAL SERVICES				
	Eating Places	5812	2,427	.07	.21
	Telephone Commun.	4813	1,130	.01	.04
	FINANCIAL SERVICES				
	Bank Holding Co.	6719	188	.04	.09
	Security Brokers	6211	1,312	.01	.01

Source: Compiled from data published in *Industry Norms and Key Business Ratios* (Dun & Bradstreet, Inc., 1994)

FIGURE 7–2

Accounting for inventory: four important issues

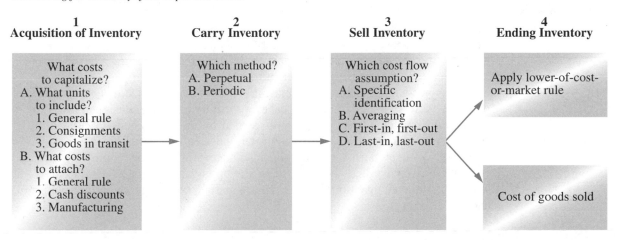

1
Acquisition of Inventory

What costs to capitalize?
A. What units to include?
  1. General rule
  2. Consignments
  3. Goods in transit
B. What costs to attach?
  1. General rule
  2. Cash discounts
  3. Manufacturing

2
Carry Inventory

Which method?
A. Perpetual
B. Periodic

3
Sell Inventory

Which cost flow assumption?
A. Specific identification
B. Averaging
C. First-in, first-out
D. Last-in, last-out

4
Ending Inventory

Apply lower-of-cost-or-market rule

Cost of goods sold

or manufacture, and then (2) carried on the company's balance sheet. It is then either (3) sold, or it remains on the balance sheet as (4) ending inventory. At each of these four points an important issue in financial accounting must be addressed. The remainder of the chapter covers these four points in order.

ACQUIRING INVENTORY: WHAT COSTS TO CAPITALIZE?

Inventory costs are capitalized because inventories are assets that provide future economic benefits. When inventories are sold, these benefits are realized, and according to the matching principle, the capitalized cost should at this time be matched against the revenue recognized from the sale. Determining the amount of capitalized cost involves two steps: the number of items or units that belong in inventory must first be determined, and then costs must be attached to each item.

WHAT ITEMS OR UNITS TO INCLUDE?

 Decisions as to what items or units to include in inventory are governed by a general rule. However, the general rule is not always simple to apply.

GENERAL RULE

Items should be included in a company's inventory if they are being held for sale and the company has complete and unrestricted ownership of them. Such ownership indicates that (1) the company bears the complete loss if the inventory is lost, stolen, or destroyed and (2) the company owns all rights to the benefits produced by the items.

In most cases ownership is accompanied by possession: companies that own inventory are usually in possession of it. Under these circumstances, determining the number of units that belong in inventory is straightforward: the number of inventory units on the company's premises can simply be counted. In some cases, however, ownership is not accompanied by possession and it becomes somewhat more difficult to find and determine the appropriate number of inventory units. Consignments and goods in transit are two common examples.

CONSIGNMENTS

In a **consignment**, a *consignor* (the owner) transfers inventory to a *consignee* (receiver), who takes physical possession and places the inventory up for sale. When it is sold, the consignee collects the sale proceeds, keeps a percentage of the proceeds for the service, and transfers the remainder to the consignor.

When accounting for consignments, it is important to realize that ownership, not physical possession, determines the balance sheet upon which consigned inventory is disclosed. Since consigned inventory is owned by the consignor, it belongs on the consignor's balance sheet, even though it is physically located on the consignee's premises. When preparing or using financial statements, managers must be sure that consigned inventory has been treated in the appropriate manner. Misclassifying it would misstate the inventory balance, current assets, cost of goods sold, gross profit, and net income.

GOODS IN TRANSIT

When inventory is sold, the seller records a sale, and the buyer records a purchase. Theoretically, both parties should record the transaction at exactly the same moment: the point in time when the ownership of the inventory transfers from the seller to the buyer. For practical purposes, however, most sales are recorded when goods are shipped, and most purchases are recorded when goods are received. Since goods are often in transit between the seller and the buyer for as long as several days, sellers and buyers often record the same transaction at two different points in time. This practice is acceptable except in cases where there are **goods in transit** at the end of an accounting period. For example, suppose that Buyer & Co. (located in Seattle, WA) purchased goods on account from Seller Inc. (located in New York, NY) on December 29, 1996. Seller delivered the goods immediately to XYZ Trucking Co., and on December 31, the balance sheet date for both Buyer and Seller, the goods are in transit.

Accounting for this transaction in an appropriate manner involves determining who owns the goods while they are in transit. The most common way of determining ownership is to examine the freight terms associated with the shipment. These terms normally indicate which party bears the responsibility for shipping the goods and thereby owns them while they are in transit. Freight terms are usually expressed in one of two ways: FOB shipping point or FOB destination.

FOB (free on board) shipping point indicates that the seller is responsible for the goods only to the point from which they are shipped. In the example, if the goods were shipped FOB shipping point, Seller Inc. would be responsible to deliver the goods to XYZ Trucking. From that point to Seattle, Buyer would be considered the owner of the goods, and their value would belong on Buyer's December 31 balance sheet. Both an inventory purchase on Buyer's books and a sale on Seller's books should be recorded.

FOB (free on board) destination indicates that the seller is responsible for the goods all the way to their destination. If the goods in the example were shipped FOB destination, Seller Inc. would be considered the owner of the goods until they reached Seattle. In this case, the goods would belong in Seller's inventory, and neither a purchase nor a sale would be recognized as of December 31. Figure 7–3 summarizes the rules of accounting for goods in transit as of the end of an accounting period.

Transactions near the end of an accounting period are often difficult to account for correctly. Managers must examine freight invoices and other related documents to ensure that sales and purchases are placed in the proper accounting periods and that, as of the balance sheet date, the number of inventory units on a company's balance sheet accurately reflects the inventory units actually owned. Similar to consignments, misclassifying goods in transit can misstate important financial statement numbers and ratios.

FIGURE 7–3 *Accounting for goods in transit*	SHIPPING TERMS	OWNER IN TRANSIT	JOURNAL ENTRIES	
	FOB shipping point	**Buyer**	**Buyer**	**(debit Inventory, credit Accounts Payable or Cash)***
			Seller	**(debit Accounts Receivable or Cash, credit Sales)** **(debit Cost of Goods Sold, credit Inventory)***
	FOB destination	**Seller**	**Buyer**	**(no entries)**
			Seller	**(no entries)**

*Assumes that buyer and seller both use the perpetual inventory method, which is discussed later in the chapter.

WHAT COSTS TO ATTACH?

Once the number of items to be included in inventory has been determined, costs must be attached to these items to produce the total capitalized inventory cost. The general rule that guides this process and how it applies to inventory purchases and manufacturing operations are discussed in the following sections.

GENERAL RULE

All costs associated with the manufacture, acquisition, storage, or preparation of inventory items should be capitalized and included in the Inventory account. Included are the cost required to bring inventory items to saleable condition, such as the costs of purchasing, shipping in (called **freight-in** or **transportation-in**), manufacturing, and packaging. This rule is not difficult to apply in most cases, but two relatively common areas require further discussion. They are (1) accounting for cash discounts on inventory purchases and (2) determining the costs of manufacturing inventories.

ACCOUNTING FOR CASH DISCOUNTS

Chapter 6 discusses accounting for cash discounts from the seller's point of view. There we commented that the *gross method* establishes a credit sale and the corresponding account receivable at the gross price and recognizes a discount if payment is received within the discount period. Accounting for cash discounts on inventory purchases is exactly the same, except now from the buyer's point of view. The inventory purchase is booked at the gross price, and if payment is made within the discount period, the carrying value of the inventory is reduced by the discount. If the discount is missed, the inventory is carried at the gross amount.

It is generally not advisable for companies to miss discounts. Under terms 2/10 n/30, for example, a purchasing company that makes a $1,000 payment 20 days after the expiration of the 10-day discount period would be paying a $20 financial charge. This situation is equivalent to borrowing cash at a 36.5 percent ([$20/$1,000] $\times$ [365 days/20 days]) annual rate of interest. Missing cash discounts, therefore, can be very expensive. Indeed, companies that miss discounts because they are short of cash would be better off to borrow from a bank at a rate much lower than 36.5 percent and use the proceeds to pay those suppliers offering cash discounts. Consequently, most purchasing companies attempt to make payment within the discount period. Inability to do so can be a sign of mismanagement and/or serious financial problems.

DETERMINING THE COSTS OF MANUFACTURING INVENTORIES

Retail companies, like Sears, Wal-Mart, Kmart, May Department Stores, and J.C. Penney, simply purchase inventories (usually from manufacturers) and sell them for prices that exceed their costs. Retailers primarily provide a distribution service, rarely changing or improving the inventories they sell. As a result, the capitalized inventory cost for a retail operation consists primarily of only two components: (1) the purchase cost and (2) freight-in, the cost of shipping the goods to the retailer. If Kmart, for example, purchases merchandise for $5,000 cash and pays $500 to have the goods shipped to one of its stores, the following journal entry would be recorded.[2]

Inventory (+A)	5,500	
Cash (−A)		5,500

Purchased inventory including freight-in charges.

The operations of **manufacturing companies**, like IBM, General Electric, General Motors, Procter & Gamble, RJR Nabisco, and Johnson & Johnson, on the other hand, are much more complex. These companies purchase raw materials and use processes involving labor and other costs to manufacture their inventories. The capitalized inventory cost therefore includes the cost of acquiring the raw materials, the cost of the labor used to convert the raw materials to finished goods, and other costs that support the production process. These other costs, called **overhead,** include

---

2. The journal entry assumes that Kmart uses the perpetual method of inventory accounting.

such items as indirect materials (e.g., paint, screws, nails, etc.), indirect labor (e.g., salaries of line managers), depreciation of fixed assets, and utility and insurance costs.

The capitalized inventory costs of manufacturing operations include all costs required to bring the inventory to saleable condition. In this general respect, accounting for manufacturing operations is no different from accounting for retail operations. However, in manufacturing, virtually any cost that can be linked to the production process should be allocated to the Inventory account. Costs like depreciation, wages and salaries, rent and insurance, therefore, are often capitalized as part of the inventory cost and, accordingly, are matched against revenues when the finished inventory is sold.

Financial statement users should be aware that allocating overhead costs to inventory is a very subjective process, requiring expertise, that can have significant effects on important financial numbers and ratios. These allocations give management substantial influence over the financial statements. Several years ago, for example, General Electric reported in the footnotes of its annual report that it "changed its accounting procedures to include certain inventory costs [including depreciation and other product costs] previously charged directly to expense." The change increased reported net income by $281 million.

CARRYING INVENTORY: THE PERPETUAL OR PERIODIC METHOD?

LO 4 Two methods are used to record and carry inventory on the books: the perpetual method, which we have used so far in this chapter, and the periodic method. These methods determine Cost of Goods Sold and Inventory in different ways. The perpetual method keeps an up-to-date record in the Inventory account, allocating inventory costs to the Cost of Goods Sold account each time an item is sold. Under the periodic method, inventory purchases are recorded as they occur, but Inventory and Cost of Goods Sold are not determined until the end of the period after an inventory count is taken. An example that compares the two methods appears in Figure 7–4.

Under the **perpetual method**, the inventory account is increased (debited) when inventory is purchased and decreased (credited) when inventory is sold. As a result, a *perpetual* balance, which should equal the inventory on hand at all times, is maintained in the Inventory account. As Figure 7–5 shows, the balance of the Inventory account on the balance sheet can simply be taken from the ending balance in the Inventory T-account. Cost of Goods Sold is also kept up to date because the cost of sold inventory is transferred from the Inventory account to Cost of Goods Sold at each sale.

Under the **periodic method**, no record is made of inventory outflows when inventory is sold. No inventory costs, therefore, are transferred to Cost of Goods Sold during the period. As a result, the balance in the Inventory T-account at the end of the period is the dollar amount of the beginning balance plus the purchases made during the period, and the balance in Cost of Goods Sold is zero. These amounts must be adjusted to reflect the end-of-period dollar amounts in the two accounts, which is achieved in three steps:

1. An inventory count is taken.
2. Costs are attached to the number of items determined by the count.
3. A journal entry is recorded.

Perpetual and periodic methods

Given Information

Assume that inventory at the beginning of December is $2,500 (125 units at $20 per unit). The following transactions occurred during December.

	PERPETUAL METHOD			PERIODIC METHOD		
December 10: Purchased 100 units of inventory on account for $20 per unit.	Inventory (+A)	2,000ᵃ		Inventory (+A)	2,000ᵃ	
	Accts. Pay. (+L)		2,000	Accts. Pay. (+L)		2,000
	Purchased inventory on account.			*Purchased inventory on account.*		
December 20: Sold 50 units of inventory for cash at $30 per unit.	Cash (+A)	1,500ᵇ		Cash (+A)	1,500ᵇ	
	Sales (R, +SE)		1,500	Sales (R, +SE)		1,500
	Sold inventory.			*Sold inventory.*		
	COGS (E, −SE)	1,000ᶜ		(No entry recorded to reflect outflow of inventory.)		
	Inventory (−A)		1,000			
	Recognized cost of goods sold and outflow of inventory.					
December 31: Books are closed and financial statements are prepared.	(No journal entry required.)			COGS (E, −SE)	1,000ᵈ	
				Inventory (end.) (+A)	3,500ᵉ	
				Inventory (−A)		4,500
				Recognized cost of goods sold and ending inventory.		

ᵃ(100 units × $20)
ᵇ(50 units × $30)
ᶜ(50 units × $20)
ᵈ$2,500 + $2,000 − $3,500
ᵉAn inventory count is required to determine the number of remaining units (175 units × $20)

Inventory T-account: the perpetual method

INVENTORY

Beginning balance	2,500		
12/10 purchase	2,000		
		12/20 sale	1,000
Ending balance	**3,500**		

In the preceding example we assumed that the inventory count determined the following:

1. There were 175 units on hand at the end of the period.
2. A $20 cost was attached to each of the 175 units (175 units × $20 = $3,500).
3. The following journal entry was recorded.

Cost of Goods Sold (E, −SE)   1,000
Inventory (ending) (+A)   3,500
  Inventory (beginning plus purchases) (−A)   4,500
Recognized cost of goods sold and ending inventory.

The end-of-period entry performs two functions: (1) it updates the inventory account, and (2) it recognizes the cost of goods sold for the period. Note that the dollar amount recorded in the Cost of Goods Sold account is the amount necessary to bring the debits and credits of the journal entry into balance. Once the balance in the Inventory account has been determined, the cost of goods sold can also be calculated using the following formula:[3]

$$\text{Cost of Goods Sold} = \text{Beginning Inventory} + \text{Purchases} - \text{Ending Inventory}$$
$$\$1,000 \quad = \quad \$2,500 \quad + \quad \$2,000 \quad - \quad \$3,500$$

PERPETUAL AND PERIODIC METHODS: COSTS AND BENEFITS

The perpetual method requires more bookkeeping procedures than the periodic method because it recognizes the cost of goods sold and the outflow of inventory at each sale. Further, both methods require that an end-of-period inventory count be taken: the perpetual method to check the accuracy of the ending balance in the Inventory T-account, and the periodic method to determine an ending inventory amount. As a result, many companies, especially those that sell large volumes of widely different inventory items (e.g., a department store), use the periodic method because it is less costly for them to implement. Bear in mind, however, that the periodic method provides less useful information for both a company's management and those who use its financial statements. To illustrate, consider the following example.

Suppose that Retail International is a medium-sized retail store that began in 1996 with 45,000 units of inventory. During 1996 the company purchased 42,000 units, sold 27,000 units, and lost (were either broken, misplaced, or stolen) 8,000 units. Assuming that the cost of each unit is $1, the actual ending inventory balance for Retail International would be as follows:

$$\text{End. Inventory} = \text{Beg. Inv.} + \text{Purchases} - \text{Sales (at cost)} - \text{Lost Inventory}$$
$$\$52,000 \quad = \quad \$45,000 + \quad \$42,000 \quad - \quad \$27,000 \quad - \quad \$8,000$$

THE PERIODIC METHOD

Assume that Retail International uses the periodic inventory method. The company would record the purchases as they were made but would not recognize the cost of goods sold as the units were sold. At the end of 1996, an inventory count would indicate that there were 52,000 units of inventory on hand. Each unit has a cost of $1, so the following entry would be recorded during the closing process.

Cost of Goods Sold (E, −SE)	35,000	
Inventory (ending) (+A)	52,000*	
Inventory (beginning plus purchases) (−A)		87,000

Recognized ending inventory and cost of goods sold.
*$1 × 52,000 units

Note that Cost of Goods Sold ($35,000) is not determined independently. Instead, it represents the dollar amount required to bring the journal entry into balance. Consequently, under the periodic method, Retail International and those who read the financial statements can ascertain only that $35,000 of inventory is gone. There is no indication on the financial statements that inventory with a cost of $8,000 was lost: the loss is "buried" in the Cost of Goods Sold account.

---

3. A more complete formula for cost of goods sold, which includes freight-in, purchases discounts, and purchases returns, is provided below.
Cost of Goods Sold = Beg. Inventory + Net Purchases* + Freight-In − End. Inventory
*Net Purchases = Purchases − Purchases Discounts − Purchases Returns

THE PERPETUAL METHOD

Assume instead that Retail International uses the perpetual method. Figure 7–6 includes the journal entry to record the inventory purchases and sale as well as the Inventory T-account.

FIGURE 7–6

Perpetual inventory method: Retail International

GENERAL JOURNAL		
Inventory (+A)	42,000	
Accounts Payable (+L)		42,000
Purchased inventory on account.		
Cost of Goods Sold (E, −SE)	27,000	
Inventory (−A)		27,000
Recognized cost of goods sold and reduction in inventory.		

GENERAL LEDGER

INVENTORY

Beginning inventory	45,000		
Purchase	42,000		
		Sold inventories	27,000
Ending inventory	60,000		

Inventory purchases and sales are recorded directly in the Inventory T-account, and the year-end balances in Inventory and Cost of Goods Sold are $60,000 and $27,000, respectively. At year-end, an inventory count reveals that units with a cost of $52,000 are on hand. By comparing the Inventory T-account balance ($60,000) with the actual goods on hand ($52,000), Retail International is now aware that $8,000 of inventory is unaccounted for, and management is alerted to a control problem (e.g., shoplifting, inaccurate record keeping, breakage) that should be addressed and corrected. The following journal entry would be recorded at the end of 1996:

Inventory Shortage (E, −SE)	8,000	
Inventory (−A)		8,000
Recognized inventory shortage for period.		

The Inventory Shortage account would be treated as a separate expense on the income statement and, if material, would indicate to financial statement users and management that Retail International should review its inventory control procedures.[4]

This illustration represents only one of many ways in which the perpetual method provides more useful information than the periodic method. Although the perpetual method requires additional bookkeeping procedure, computer systems have recently reduced the costs of such procedures significantly. As a result, more and more companies, even those that handle high volumes of widely diversified inventories, are moving toward the perpetual method. The major supermarket chains like Safeway, Giant Foods, and Lucky Stores, Inc., represent a case in point. Many have recently moved to automated bar code sensors, devices that reduce the cost of using the perpetual method for merchandisers who sell a wide variety of relatively low-cost items. Similarly, many of the major retailers, like Kmart, Sears, and J.C. Penney are moving toward perpetual systems. The following excerpt was taken from a recent Kmart annual report.

---

4. The dollar amount in the inventory shortage account can be a key indicator of the extent of inventory control problems. *The Wall Street Journal* (October 5, 1992) reports that in the retail industry billions of dollars in inventory are lost each year. The major reasons for the losses, in order of importance, are employee theft, shoplifting, and booking errors.

A significant factor in improved expense control was the continued expansion of the retail automation program. This year an additional 421 point-of-sale (POS - bar code) systems were installed in domestic Kmart stores, bringing the total number to 1,180. The company plans to install an additional 503 POS systems in existing stores and equip all new Kmart stores with POS systems.

ERRORS IN THE INVENTORY COUNT

Inventory counts are made at the end of each period under both the perpetual and periodic methods. It is often difficult to ensure that such counts are accurate because many companies carry so many different kinds of inventory that each group of items cannot be counted at a reasonable cost. In such cases auditors and managers rely on estimates, and sometimes errors are committed.

An error in an inventory count will misstate both inventory on the balance sheet and net income on the income statement of that period. Such errors also misstate net income in the subsequent period by an equal dollar amount in the opposite direction. For example, an error in the inventory count taken at the end of 1996 that understates inventory by $2,000 will also understate 1996's net income by $2,000. In addition, this error if uncorrected will cause net income of 1997 to be overstated by $2,000. Such effects occur whether a company uses the perpetual method or the periodic method.

To illustrate using the periodic method, assume that Rainier Corporation began operations on January 1, 1996. Figure 7–7 summarizes the transactions entered into by the company during 1996 and 1997 and contains accurate inventory balances and income statements for the two years. Assume that the only expenses incurred by the company were the costs of sold inventories.

Suppose that Rainier Corporation made no accounting errors during 1996 or 1997, except that it failed to include 20 items of inventory, each with a cost of $1, in its inventory count at the end of 1996. Inventory was thus determined incorrectly to be $280 instead of $300. Inventory was correctly counted at the end of 1997. The cost of goods sold and the inventory calculations for 1996 and 1997 appear in Figure 7–8. Income statements assuming accurate information and the miscounting error are shown in Figure 7–9.

FIGURE 7–7		INVENTORY	SALES
Rainier Corporation: transactions for 1996–1997	**1996**		
	(1) Purchased 500 units of inventory for $1 per unit.	$500	
	(2) Sold 200 units of inventory for $3 per unit.	(200)	$ 600
	Ending inventory	$300	
	Sales ($600) − Cost of Goods Sold ($200) = Net Income ($400)		
	1997		
	Beginning inventory	$300	
	(1) Purchased 600 units of inventory for $1 per unit.	600	
	(2) Sold 700 units of inventory for $3 per unit.	(700)	$2,100
	Ending inventory	$200	
	Sales ($2,100) − Cost of Goods Sold ($700) = Net Income ($1,400)		

FIGURE 7–8	Cost of Goods Sold Calculation:

Inventory errors: periodic method

	Cost of Goods Sold	=	Beginning Inventory	+	Purchases	−	Ending Inventory
1996:	$220	=	$0	+	$500	−	$280
1997:	$680	=	$280	+	$600	−	$200

FIGURE 7–9		ACCURATE	ERROR

Comparative income statements: Rainer Corporation

1996		
Sales	$ 600	$ 600
Cost of goods sold	200	220
Net income	$ 400	$ 380
1997		
Sales	$2,100	$2,100
Cost of goods sold	700	680
Net income	$1,400	$1,420

In summary, a single error in the counting of inventory caused net income of 1996 and net income of 1997 to be misstated by equal dollar amounts ($20) in opposite directions. Although both income statements are incorrect, the balance sheet as of the end of 1997 is properly stated. The accurate inventory count at year-end corrected the Inventory balance, and the $20 understatement of retained earnings due to understated net income in 1996 was counterbalanced by a $20 overstatement to net income in 1997.

Inventory errors are not unusual and at times can be quite significant. For example, the auditor for Comnet Corp., a computer software and health-care products company, discovered that management had unintentionally overvalued inventories by $1.6 million on the company's financial statements. Consequently, Comnet's reported net income of $2.6 million was reduced to $1.0 million, and net income the following year was $1.6 larger.

A recent article in *The Wall Street Journal* (December 14, 1992) entitled "Inventory Chicanery Tempts More Firms, Fools More Auditors" reports that "When companies are desperate to stay afloat, inventory fraud is the easiest way to produce instant profits and dress up the balance sheet . . . [and] the recent raise in inventory fraud is one of the biggest single reasons for the proliferation of accounting scandals." The article describes how recent inventory frauds at Comptronix Corp., an Alabama electronics company, Laribee Wire Manufacturing, L.A. Gear, and the discount drugstore, Phar Mor, were perpetrated simply by management creating fictitious inventories— undetected by the external auditor—that instantly increased profits. "Experts say that many companies overvalue obsolete goods and supplies. Others create phantom items in the warehouse to augment the assets needed for loan collateral. Still others count inventory that they pretend they have ordered but that will never arrive . . . [in these cases] the auditor was either taken or missed the obvious."

SELLING INVENTORY: WHICH COST FLOW ASSUMPTION?

Perhaps the most important and difficult question of inventory accounting involves how to allocate the capitalized inventory cost between the cost of goods sold and ending inventory. The examples so far have assumed that the cost of the sold inventory is known, but such situations are relatively unusual. In most cases, companies are unable to determine exactly which items are sold and which items remain in ending inventory. When this occurs, an assumption must be made about the cost flow of the inventory items. The assumption chosen can significantly affect net income, current assets, working capital, and the current ratio because it determines the relative costs allocated to the cost of goods sold and ending inventory.

This section first discusses the specific identification method, which is used when the cost of the sold inventory items can be determined. We then cover three cost flow assumptions that are used extensively in practice: averaging, first-in, first-out (FIFO), and last-in, first-out (LIFO). Each assumption is illustrated under the periodic method in the remainder of the chapter.[5]

SPECIFIC IDENTIFICATION

In some cases, especially with relatively infrequent sales of large-ticket items (e.g., jewelry, furniture, automobiles, land), it is possible to specifically identify which inventory items have been sold and which remain. In such situations, the allocation of inventory cost between the cost of goods sold and ending inventory is relatively straightforward. Suppose, for example, that on March 1, Used Cars & Co. had three 1996 Honda Accords for sale. Cars 1 and 2 were purchased from the same dealer at a cost of $10,000 each. Car 3 was purchased recently at an auction for $12,000. The three cars are in equivalent condition, and the selling price for each is $18,000. The March 1 inventory for Used Cars & Co. follows.

CAR	COST
1	$10,000
2	10,000
3	12,000
Total	$32,000

Assume that on March 15, Sammy Sportsman agrees to purchase any one of the three cars for $18,000. Used Cars gives Sammy Car 3 (cost = $12,000), and the following journal entries (perpetual method) are recorded:

Cash (+A)	18,000	
Sales (R, +SE)		18,000
Sold Honda.		
Cost of Goods Sold (E, −SE)	12,000	
Inventory (−A)		12,000
Recognized cost of goods sold for		
Honda with cost of $12,000.		

It is fairly clear in this situation that $12,000 should have been allocated to Cost of Goods Sold, and $20,000 should remain in ending inventory. An inventory item (Car 3) with a cost of $12,000 was sold. Thus, the specific identification procedure is a relatively straightforward way to determine the cost of goods sold and ending inventory. Nonetheless, it does have limitations.

---

5. Each assumption can be combined with the perpetual method also. However, for reporting purposes most companies use the periodic method even if they use the perpetual method for internal purposes.

First, the **specific identification** procedure is impractical for most companies, which cannot specifically identify which inventory is sold and which inventory remains on hand. Its use is limited primarily to operations that experience infrequent sales of large-ticket items.

A second limitation is that in many cases specific identification allows a manager to manipulate net income and the ending inventory value. Suppose in the example that the manager of Used Cars & Co. chose to give Sammy Sportsman either Car 1 or Car 2, instead of Car 3. Recall that Sammy was indifferent among the three automobiles. In this situation the following journal entries would have been recorded.

Cash (+A)	18,000	
Sales (R, +SE)		18,000
Sold Honda.		

Cost of Goods Sold (E, −SE)	10,000	
Inventory (−A)		10,000
Recognized cost of goods sold for		
Honda with cost of $10,000.		

The decision to give Sammy Car 1 or Car 2 would have produced net income and ending inventory values that were $2,000 ($12,000 − $10,000) greater than the decision to give Sammy Car 3. The specific identification procedure allowed the manager to manipulate income and inventory by choosing which inventory item to deliver to the customer. While manipulating the financial statement in this way is not a misrepresentation, it does allow management to influence the timing of income recognition.

THREE INVENTORY COST FLOW ASSUMPTIONS: AVERAGING, FIFO, AND LIFO

LO 5 The inventories of many companies are acquired at so many different prices that it is impossible to specifically identify the costs of the items sold and the costs of the items in ending inventory. In such cases an assumption must be invoked. To illustrate and compare the three different cost flow assumptions, consider the following example. The chart in Figure 7–10 describes the inventory purchase and sales data for Discount Sales Company during its first year of operations.

FIGURE 7–10

Inventory purchase and sales schedule: Discount Sales Company

DESCRIPTION	(1) No. Units	(2) Cost	(3) Sales Price	Total Costs (1) × (2)	Total Sales Proceeds (1) × (3)
Beginning inventory	20	$4		$ 80	
Purchase 1	30	5		150	
Sale 1	10		$15		$150
Purchase 2	30	6		180	
Sale 2	25		15	____	375
Ending inventory	45				
Capitalized inventory costs				$410	
Units sold	35				
Total sales proceeds					$525

Beginning inventory consisted of 20 units, a total of 60 units were purchased, and 35 units were sold during the year, producing an ending inventory of 45 units. Note that each unit of beginning inventory had a cost of $4, Purchase 1 was at a $5 unit cost, and Purchase 2 was at a $6 unit cost. Inventory costs increased during the period. Total capitalized inventory costs were $410, and $330 ($150 + $180) of those costs represented new purchases. Sold units were priced at $15 each. The following assumptions each allocate the $410 of capitalized inventory cost to Cost of Goods Sold and Inventory in a different way.

AVERAGING ASSUMPTION/PERIODIC METHOD: A WEIGHTED AVERAGE

The **averaging assumption** applied to the periodic method involves the calculation of the per-unit weighted average cost at the end of the period after the inventory count is taken. The total capitalized inventory cost ($410) is divided by the number of available units (80 = 20 + 30 + 30) to compute the per-unit average cost ($5.125 = $410/80 units). Ending inventory is calculated by multiplying the per-unit average cost times the number of units on hand ($231 = $5.125 × 45 units). Once ending inventory is determined, the cost of goods sold can be calculated in the following manner. Note that the total capitalized inventory cost is allocated between Cost of Goods Sold and ending inventory.

Cost of Goods Sold = Beginning Inventory + Purchases − Ending Inventory
$179   = $80   + $330   − $231
(45 units × $5.125)

Cost of goods sold	=	$179
Ending inventory	=	231
Total capitalized inventory cost	=	$410

FIFO ASSUMPTION/PERIODIC METHOD

Under the **first-in, first-out (FIFO)** assumption, the costs of the units sold are assumed to be equal to the costs of the oldest available units in the financial records. The 45 units in ending inventory, therefore, are assumed to consist of those most recently purchased: that is, the 30 units from Purchase 2 and the 15 units from Purchase 1. Ending inventory and Cost of Goods Sold are computed as follows:

FIFO ending inventory = (30 units from Purchase 2 × $6/unit) $180
+ (15 units from Purchase 1 × $5/unit)   75
$255

Cost of Goods Sold = Beginning Inventory + Purchases − Ending Inventory
$155   = $80   + $330   − $255

Cost of goods sold	=	$155
Ending inventory	=	255
Total capitalized inventory cost	=	$410

LIFO ASSUMPTION/PERIODIC METHOD

Under the **last-in, first-out (LIFO)** assumption, the costs of the units sold are assumed to be equal to the costs of those most recently purchased. The 45 units in ending inventory, therefore, are assumed to consist of the oldest available in the financial records:

that is, the 20 units from beginning inventory and 25 units from Purchase 1. Ending inventory and Cost of Goods Sold are computed as below.

$$
\begin{aligned}
\textbf{LIFO ending inventory} = &\textbf{(25 units from Purchase 1} \times \textbf{\$5/unit)} & \textbf{\$125} \\
&+ \textbf{(20 units from beginning inventory} \times \textbf{\$4/unit)} & \underline{\ \ 80} \\
& & \underline{\textbf{\$205}}
\end{aligned}
$$

$$
\begin{array}{ccccccc}
\textbf{Cost of Goods Sold} = & \textbf{Beginning Inventory} & + & \textbf{Purchases} & - & \textbf{Ending Inventory} \\
\textbf{\$205} & = & \textbf{\$80} & + & \textbf{\$330} & - & \textbf{\$205}
\end{array}
$$

Cost of goods sold	=	$205
Ending inventory	=	<u>205</u>
Total capitalized inventory cost	=	<u>$410</u>

INVENTORY COST FLOW ASSUMPTIONS: EFFECTS ON THE FINANCIAL STATEMENTS

Figure 7–11 compares the averaging, FIFO, and LIFO cost flow assumptions with respect to the cost of goods sold, gross profit, net income and ending inventory. Assume further that Discount Sales Company incurred $150 of expenses (excluding the cost of goods sold) during the period.

Several features about the comparisons in Figure 7–11 are noteworthy. First, under all three cost flow assumptions, the entire $410 of capitalized inventory cost is allocated either to ending inventory or Cost of Goods Sold. The three assumptions differ in that they give rise to different allocations.

Second, the relative dollar amounts on the financial statements produced by the three assumptions are driven by the changes in the inventory purchase costs that occurred during the period. In this illustration, for example, per-unit inventory purchase costs increased during the period from $4 for beginning inventory to $5 for Purchase 1 to $6 for Purchase 2. This cost increase caused ending inventory under FIFO ($255) to be greater than ending inventory under averaging ($231), which in turn was greater than ending inventory under LIFO ($205). Inventory cost increases also caused Cost of Goods Sold under FIFO ($155) to be less than Cost of Goods Sold under averaging ($179), which in turn was less than Cost of Goods Sold under LIFO ($205). We chose to illustrate an inflationary trend because, in reality, prices tend to increase over time. However, it is important to realize that if inventory costs had decreased during the period, the orders shown above would have been reversed: the

FIGURE 7–11		FIFO	AVERAGING	LIFO
Financial statement effects of the three inventory cost flow assumptions	Sales (35 units × $15)	$525	$525	$525
	Cost of goods sold	<u>155</u>	<u>179</u>	<u>205</u>
	Gross profit	$370	$346	$320
	Expenses	<u>150</u>	<u>150</u>	<u>150</u>
	Net income before taxes	<u>$220</u>	<u>$196</u>	<u>$170</u>
	Ending inventory	$255	$231	$205
	Cost of goods sold	<u>155</u>	<u>179</u>	<u>205</u>
	Total capitalized inventory cost	<u>$410</u>	<u>$410</u>	<u>$410</u>

LIFO assumption would have resulted in the greatest ending inventory and the least Cost of Goods Sold dollar amounts. In fact, had inventory costs remained stable throughout the period, no differences would have resulted: all three assumptions would have reported the same ending inventory and Cost of Goods Sold amounts.

Finally, in the example, the FIFO assumption gave rise to the highest, and the LIFO assumption gave rise to the lowest, net income and ending inventory dollar amounts. In times of increasing inventory costs, therefore, using the FIFO assumption can boost important financial ratios, such as earnings per share, working capital, and the current ratio. Choosing LIFO, on the other hand, may value inventories at unrealistically low levels. *Forbes* warns that financial statement users should pay close attention to a company's inventory cost flow assumption because it can "significantly distort" important financial ratios.[6]

INVENTORY COST FLOW ASSUMPTIONS: EFFECTS ON FEDERAL INCOME TAXES

As the previous example shows, if inventory costs are increasing, using the LIFO assumption gives rise to the lowest net income amount. During inflationary times, therefore, the LIFO assumption is an attractive alternative for determining a company's federal income tax liability, which is computed as a percentage of taxable income: less taxable income means less federal income tax liability.

Federal income tax law states that if a company uses the LIFO assumption for computing its tax liability, it must also use the LIFO assumption for preparing its financial statements. If a company uses a cost flow assumption other than LIFO for tax purposes, it can use the LIFO, averaging, or FIFO assumption for financial reporting. This regulation is called the **LIFO conformity rule**, and it causes most companies to use the same cost flow assumption for both income tax and financial reporting purposes. Companies that choose LIFO for tax purposes must use it for reporting purposes. Companies that want to use FIFO for reporting purposes may not use LIFO for tax purposes.

Figure 7–12 shows the effects of the different cost flow assumptions on federal income taxes. The comparison uses the numbers from Figure 7–11, except that federal income taxes have been assessed as a percentage (34 percent) of net income before taxes and are listed as an expense on the income statement.

Note in Figure 7–12 that, in times of rising inventory costs, if a company chooses to minimize its federal income taxes by using the LIFO assumption, it must report

FIGURE 7–12		FIFO	AVERAGING	LIFO
Income tax effects of the three inventory cost flow assumptions	Sales (35 units × $15)	$525	$525	$525
	Cost of goods sold	155	179	205
	Gross profit	$370	$346	$320
	Expenses	150	150	150
	Net income before taxes	$220	$196	$170
	Federal income taxes (34%)	75	67	58
	Net income after taxes	$145	$129	$112

6. Karen Cook, "Sacking the Mattress," *Forbes*, July 6, 1981, p. 114.

lower net income and inventory on its financial statements. The effects on the financial statements of using LIFO can be significant. For example, as of December 31, 1994, the inventories of Sears, a LIFO user, were valued at about $692 million less than they would be under FIFO. In another example, DuPont reduced its current assets and reported net income by $612 million when it changed from FIFO to LIFO several years ago.

On the other hand, companies using the FIFO assumption to boost reported net income and ending inventory must pay additional federal income taxes. These additional tax payments can be very significant. For example, in an article in *The Wall Street Journal*, Gary Biddle, an accounting professor, reported that Eastman Kodak saved $204 million in taxes by choosing LIFO instead of FIFO. In a single year Amoco, General Electric, and U.S. Steel together would have paid $3 billion in additional taxes if they had used FIFO.[7]

CHOOSING AN INVENTORY COST FLOW ASSUMPTION: TRADE-OFFS

For most companies it is impractical to specifically identify the inventory items sold during a given period. Management must therefore choose from among the three assumptions discussed above. *Accounting Trends and Techniques* (1994) reports that of 600 major U.S. companies surveyed, 348 (58%) used LIFO, 417 (70%) used FIFO, and 189 (32%) used averaging for at least some of their inventories. Most of these companies used different methods for different kinds of inventory. Of those using LIFO, 191 (55%) used it for 50 percent or more of their inventories. The choice of a cost flow assumption is a difficult problem that depends on the situation faced by a given company.

Before considering the trade-offs involved in choosing an inventory cost flow assumption, remember that the assumption does not necessarily reflect the actual movement of the inventory. In fact, there is often no relationship between the assumption used to value the inventory for reporting purposes and the actual cost of the inventory on hand. Choosing a cost flow assumption is largely independent of the nature of the inventory itself.

It is also difficult to change a cost flow assumption once it has been chosen. As discussed in Chapter 5, the principle of consistency requires that accounting methods be consistent from year to year, and such changes, even when approved by an auditor, must be fully described in the footnotes, mentioned in the audit report, and their effect on income must be separately disclosed on the income statement. Recently, only a few major U.S. companies have changed their inventory cost flow assumptions. In 1994, for example, *Accounting Trends and Techniques* reports that only 2 of the 600 major U.S. companies surveyed chose to make such a change.

The trade-offs involved in choosing an inventory cost flow assumption are divided into two categories: (1) income and asset measurement and (2) economic consequences. *Income and asset measurement* refers to how well each assumption produces measures that reflect the actual performance and financial condition of a company. *Economic consequences* refer to the costs and benefits associated with using a particular assumption.

---

7. Gary Biddle, "Paying FIFO Taxes: Your Favorite Charity," *The Wall Street Journal*, January 19, 1981, p. 18.

INCOME AND ASSET MEASUREMENT

In terms of income and asset measurement, neither LIFO nor FIFO is clearly preferred. The LIFO assumption is a better application of the matching principle than the FIFO assumption. LIFO allocates the most current purchase costs to Cost of Goods Sold, where they are matched against current sales in the determination of net income. FIFO matches relatively old costs against current revenues.

FIFO, on the other hand, is generally viewed as producing a more current measure of inventory on the balance sheet. Ending inventory under FIFO reflects the costs of the most recent purchases; LIFO reports ending inventory in terms of older, less relevant, costs. Using LIFO over a period of time, therefore, can give rise to ending inventory costs that are grossly out of date. An article in *Forbes* stated that using LIFO leads to a "less realistic balance sheet." Union Carbide's net worth (assets − liabilities), for example, was understated by about 18 percent simply because it used LIFO, and the *inventory turnover* (Cost of Goods Sold ÷ Inventory) of Monsanto, another LIFO user, was overstated by approximately 50 percent.[8]

ECONOMIC CONSEQUENCES

Economic consequences refer to the costs and benefits associated with choosing an inventory flow assumption related to such factors as income taxes and liquidity problems, bookkeeping costs, LIFO liquidations and purchasing practices, debt and compensation contracts, and the capital market.

INCOME TAXES AND LIQUIDITY. Often the most important economic consideration when choosing an inventory cost flow assumption is the tax consequence. When inventory costs are rising, LIFO yields a lower net income number than FIFO, resulting in a lower tax liability. Consequently, choosing LIFO can improve a company's liquidity position by minimizing cash payments for income taxes. As mentioned earlier, the magnitudes of such savings can be significant.

Using FIFO can create liquidity problems. In times of rising prices, FIFO produces higher income than LIFO because it matches relatively old costs against current revenues. Because old costs are lower than current costs, FIFO creates **paper profits**, profits that are due to rising inventory costs instead of efficient operations. Paper profits appear on the income statement, but they are not backed by cash inflows. Unfortunately, these inflated profits are also used to determine a company's tax liability, which must be paid in cash. As a result, operating cash inflows may not be sufficient to cover the required cash outflows, and the company's liquidity position suffers.

In the early 1970s, for example, while the United States experienced economic recession and double-digit inflation, many U.S. companies suffered serious liquidity problems. In response over 400 FIFO users adopted LIFO. It has been estimated that the income tax savings enjoyed by these companies averaged approximately $26 million each.[9] Unquestionably, this tax savings did much to ease their cash flow problems.

BOOKKEEPING COSTS. While LIFO usually brings about a lower tax liability than FIFO, it requires more bookkeeping procedures and is generally more costly to implement. For example, accounting professors Michael Granof and Daniel Short conducted a survey of FIFO users and found that many companies did not adopt LIFO

---

8. Richard Greene, "No Free LIFO," *Forbes*, December 6, 1982, pp. 168, 171.
9. Gary Biddle, "Paying FIFO Taxes: Your Favorite Charity," *The Wall Street Journal*, January 19, 1981, p. 18.

because "the record-keeping requirements of LIFO are burdensome and costly."[10] Indeed, short-cut methods for estimating LIFO have been devised to reduce the costs of maintaining LIFO records.

LIFO LIQUIDATION AND INVENTORY PURCHASING PRACTICES. The use of LIFO can give rise to grossly overstated net income amounts when inventory levels are cut back. Consider, for example, Atlantic Richfield, a giant in the oil industry and a long-time LIFO user. In the early 1980s the dollar amount in the company's inventory balance consisted of very old, very low, and very outdated costs. Then an oil glut occurred, and the market price of oil decreased sharply. In response, Atlantic Richfield and a number of other oil companies cut inventory levels significantly. This action caused the low and outdated costs in inventory to be matched against Atlantic Richfield's current revenues. The result was a $105 million increase in the company's profits. That same year the profits of Gulf Oil, Standard Oil of California, and Texaco, other LIFO users, were inflated for the same reasons by $200 million, $165 million, and $315 million, respectively.[11] Unfortunately, these high profits were due to the liquidation of LIFO inventories, not the effective and efficient operations of the oil companies or the condition of the oil industry, which at the time was suffering. Moreover, additional income taxes had to be paid on these profits.

Many LIFO users allow such inventory liquidations to occur, but other companies intentionally avoid them by maintaining their inventory purchases to prevent their inventory levels from diminishing. Such a practice avoids increased taxes, but at the same time, can give rise to other problems. It may not be the appropriate time to purchase inventory. Inventory costs may be at a seasonal high, for example, or significant discounts may not be available. Further, such action does nothing to solve the problem associated with LIFO's understated inventory valuation; it merely postpones a problem that grows worse with each passing year.

DEBT AND COMPENSATION CONTRACTS. FIFO may be attractive to management because, when inventory costs are rising, FIFO produces higher reported net income and higher inventory values than LIFO. Compensation paid to management expressed as a percentage of FIFO income tends to be higher than compensation based on LIFO income. In addition, debt covenants using ratios based on FIFO will impose less restrictive constraints on managers than those based on LIFO.

However, the relative effects of LIFO and FIFO on the financial statements are reversed when prices are decreasing. For example, the 1994 annual report of May Department Stores noted: "We value our department store inventories using the LIFO (last-in, first-out) method. Usually, this decreases earnings . . . [however] in 1994, we experienced deflation, which resulted in a pretax LIFO credit [earnings increase] of $46 million."

THE CAPITAL MARKET. Management may also choose FIFO over LIFO because it believes that FIFO's higher net income and inventory amounts are valued more highly by investors and creditors in the capital market. They reason that using FIFO could improve the company's credit rating, which may lead to better terms on its borrowings and higher prices for its outstanding debt securities. Some believe that FIFO may also bring about higher prices for the company's outstanding equity securities.

---

10. Michael Granof and Daniel Short, "For Some Companies FIFO Accounting Makes Sense," *The Wall Street Journal*, August 30, 1982, p. 12.
11. Laura Sanders and Laura Rohman, "A LIFO Boomerang," *Forbes*, January 17, 1983, pp. 101, 104.

For example, one manager, when asked by Granof and Short in the survey mentioned earlier "why [the company] did not use LIFO," responded that using LIFO "would depress the market price of its stock."[12] If such assertions are correct, using FIFO would make it easier to raise capital as well as increase management's value in the managerial labor market.

The validity of this reasoning is still open to question. A number of research studies in accounting suggest that the stock market "looks through" a company's accounting methods and values the company on the basis of the underlying cash flows. Since using LIFO usually saves taxes, these studies suggest, and some support the conclusion, that companies using LIFO are more highly valued by the stock market than companies using FIFO. However, the evidence is mixed, and all such conclusions are still tentative.[13]

Under generally accepted accounting principles, companies using LIFO are allowed to report in the footnotes to the financial statements what the value of their inventories would be if they used FIFO. Also, they are required to report the income effects of any LIFO liquidations during the year. The excerpt below was taken from the 1994 annual report of Deere and Co.

INVENTORIES
Substantially all inventories owned by Deere & Company and its United States equipment subsidiaries are valued at cost on the "last-in, first-out" (LIFO) method. Remaining inventories are generally valued at the lower of cost, on the "first-in, first-out" (FIFO) basis, or market. The value of gross inventories on the LIFO basis represented 82 percent and 83 percent of worldwide gross inventories at FIFO value on October 31, 1994 and 1993, respectively.

Under the LIFO inventory method, cost of goods sold ordinarily reflects current production costs, thus providing a matching of current costs and current revenues in the income statement. However, when LIFO-valued inventories decline, as they did in 1993 and 1992, lower costs that prevailed in prior years are matched against current year revenues, resulting in higher reported net income. Benefits from the reduction of LIFO inventories totaled $51 million ($33 million or $.43 per share after income taxes) in 1993 and $65 million ($43 million or $.56 per share after income taxes) in 1992. A LIFO benefit was not recognized in 1994.

Raw material, work-in-process and finished goods inventories at October 31, 1994 totaled $698 million on a LIFO value basis compared with $464 million one year ago. If all inventories had been valued on a FIFO basis, estimated inventories by major classification at October 31 in millions of dollars would have been as follows:

	1994	*1993*
Raw materials and supplies	*$ 206*	*$ 192*
Work-in-process	*357*	*295*
Finished machines and parts	*1,079*	*919*
Total FIFO value	*$1,642*	*$1,406*
Adjustment to LIFO basis	*944*	*942*
Inventories	*$ 698**	*$ 464*

*Includes $59 million of Homelite inventories.

12. Granof and Short, "For Some Companies FIFO Accounting Makes Sense," p. 12.
13. See, for example, the section on "Accounting Alternatives and the Capital Market" in *Financial Accounting Theory*, 3d ed., ed. Stephen Zeff and Thomas Keller (New York: McGraw-Hill, 1985, p. 569).

THE LIFO RESERVE: A USER PERSPECTIVE. In addition to disclosing that LIFO liquidations boosted reported net income in 1993 and 1992 by $51 million and $65 million, respectively, the footnote also includes a line item called "Adjustment to the LIFO basis"—$944 million (1994) and $942 million (1993). These dollar amounts are often referred to as **LIFO reserves,** and they provide useful information. For example, they enable users to compute for Deere & Company, a LIFO user: (1) inventory value if the company used FIFO, (2) net income and the additional tax liability if the company switched to FIFO in a given year, and (3) FIFO net income if the company had switched to FIFO in a previous year. Adding the LIFO reserve to the LIFO inventory value produces the FIFO inventory value. Multiplying the reserve by the company's effective tax rate (which can be found in the footnotes) provides an estimate of the additional tax liability associated with a change from LIFO to FIFO, and subtracting this amount from the reserve and adding the remainder to net income provides an estimate of the income Deere & Company would report if it changed from LIFO to FIFO in a given year. Adding the change in the reserve [LIFO reserve (n) − LIFO reserve (n-1)] to the current year's net income, after adjusting for taxes, results in the net income Deere & Company would report if it had switched to FIFO in a previous year. Using the numbers from Deere & Company's 1994 annual report, these calculations are provided in Figure 7–13.

As illustrated in Figure 7–13, the LIFO reserve allows users to more validly compare companies that use LIFO with companies that use FIFO; it indicates to managers the trade-offs involved with changing from LIFO to FIFO—higher reported income at the cost of additional tax liability; and it provides an estimate of the accumulated tax savings enjoyed by companies that use LIFO. Indeed, an understanding of the LIFO reserve can improve the decisions made by both managers and financial statement users.

FIGURE 7–13

Using the LIFO Reserve (dollars in millions)

(1) **Adjusting 1994 LIFO inventory to 1994 FIFO inventory:**

1994 inventory (LIFO) + 1994 LIFO reserve = 1994 inventory (FIFO)
$698   + $944   = $1,642

(2) **If Deere & Co. switched from LIFO to FIFO in 1994:**

Net income (LIFO) + 1994 LIFO reserve × (1 − tax rate) = Net income (FIFO)
$604   + $944   ×   (1 − .35)   = $1,218

Additional 1994 tax liability = 1994 LIFO reserve × tax rate
                                  = $944   ×   .35
                                  = $330

(3) **If Deere & Co. adopted FIFO some time before 1994:**

1994 net income (LIFO) + Increase in LIFO reserve = 1994 net income (FIFO)
$604   + ($944 − $942) × (1 − .35) = $(605.3)

ENDING INVENTORY: APPLYING THE LOWER-OF-COST-OR-MARKET RULE

LO 6 The inventory cost flow assumption determines the capitalized cost allocated to ending inventory. However, inventories on the balance sheet are not necessarily carried at this dollar amount. Based on conservatism, ending inventory is valued at cost or market value, whichever is lower.

Applying the lower-of-cost-or-market rule to ending inventory is accomplished by comparing the cost allocated to ending inventory with the market value of the inventory. If the market value exceeds the cost, no adjustment is made and the inventory remains at cost. If the market value is less than the cost, the inventories are written down to market value with an adjusting journal entry.

Suppose, for example, that ABC Enterprises uses the FIFO assumption, which gives rise to an ending inventory of $100. If the market value of the inventory is $150, no adjusting journal entry need be recorded. The ending inventory remains at cost because cost ($100) is lower than market value ($150). If the market value of the inventories is $80, however, the inventory would have to be written down (reduced) from $100 to $80. The following journal entry represents one way of recording such a write-down.

Loss on Inventory Write-Down (Lo, −SE)	**20**	
Inventory (−A)		**20**

Wrote down inventory to market value ($100 − $80).

Inventory write-downs are fairly common and sometimes quite large. In a recent financial report, for example, Alcoa reported a write-down of approximately $213 million, while that same year Gerber Products Company recorded a $2.9 million charge to write down certain inventories to market value. Neglecting to properly write down inventories can also give rise to serious misstatements, and sometimes fraud. *The Wall Street Journal* (December 14, 1992) reported "Experts say many companies overvalue obsolete goods and supplies . . . [and recently] lawsuits have been filed against Digital Equipment Corporation for failing to set aside reserves for absolute inventory."

In the preceding illustration, applying the lower-of-cost-or-market rule was relatively straightforward. In reality, however, the process is somewhat more complex because inventory market values can be quite subjective and are rarely easy to determine. This issue is covered in Appendix 7A.

THE LOWER-OF-COST-OR-MARKET RULE AND HIDDEN RESERVES

The lower-of-cost-or-market rule is often criticized because it treats inventory price changes inconsistently. Price decreases, based on difficult-to-determine market values, are recognized immediately, while price increases are not recognized until the inventory is sold in an objective and verifiable transaction. This conservative, but inconsistent, treatment can create "hidden reserves" that managers can use to manipulate income.

Consider a company that is just about to complete a very good year. In fact, reported earnings are expected to be so high that management is seeking to reduce income, and perhaps move some of the earnings to future periods that may be less successful. One way to execute this "income smoothing" strategy is to write down inventory in the current year and sell it in a future period. Suppose, for example, that management chooses to write down an inventory item with an original cost of $10 to its subjectively determined market value of $8. A $2 loss is immediately recognized, reducing the current year's net income. Assume further that during the following year the inventory item is sold for $12, giving rise to a book gain that increases that year's net income by $4 ($12 − $8). Note that by writing down the inventory in the first year, management was able to transfer $2 of net income from the first to the second year. A "hidden reserve" was created by the write-down, which was realized in a subsequent period.

Certainly, the conservative and inconsistent nature of the lower-of-cost-or-market rule combined with subjective inventory write-downs can create "hidden reserves" that can be used to manage the reported values on the financial statements. However, it is important to keep in mind that conservative accounting is a response to the liability faced by those who must provide and audit financial statements. The potential costs to these parties associated with understating inventories and profits are typically less than those associated with overstating them. From an economic standpoint, therefore, the lower-of-cost-or-market rule may be justifiable, even though it produces questionable measures on the financial statements. In any event, investors, creditors, managers, auditors, and other interested parties must be aware of these weaknesses.

INTERNATIONAL PERSPECTIVE: JAPANESE BUSINESS AND INVENTORY ACCOUNTING

In this text we have commented several times that the business environment and practices in individual countries determine the accounting methods used in those countries. The situation in Japan with respect to inventories provides an interesting example. Japan has a long history of what might loosely be described in the United States as "corporate groups." Typically, such groups are made up of a number of different entities, many of which perform different functions and hold equity interest in the others. The Board of Directors of each company is normally comprised of representatives from each of the member entities. Mitsubishi, Sanwa, Nippon Steel, Hitachi, Nissan, and Toyota are all organized in such interlocking networks.

This group orientation, which is not evident in the United States, offers a number of significant advantages, most of which relate to planning and coordination among the group members. In most cases, for example, the presidents of the group companies hold meetings periodically to promote coordination, mutual understanding, and eliminate overlap in the activities conducted by the membership. These groups are then better able to share business risks and when a company within a group faces difficulties, various means are pursued by other group members to assist it.

In many situations, such as in the Japanese auto and electronics industries, the group network contains both the manufacturer and its main suppliers. Proper coordination and planning among these parties can help to minimize material and product inventories as well as lead time and delivery items, giving rise to lower inventory carrying cost and better customer service. Just-in-Time (JIT) inventory systems, which are just now becoming popular in the United States because they reduce the costs of carrying large amounts of inventory without jeopardizing customer service, have long been a characteristic of this Japanese system and have given the Japanese a definite advantage when competing against U.S. industry.

The implication for financial reporting is that Japanese manufacturers, in general, carry much lower levels of inventory that turn over at much higher rates than those in the United States. This difference decreases the importance of inventory accounting in Japan, making the effects on the financial statements of choosing among the various cost flow assumptions relatively insignificant. Consequently, unlike U.S. companies who normally choose FIFO or LIFO for some significant economic reason, neither is very popular in Japan, with most companies using the averaging method.

It is well known that inventory fraud is an easy way for a company to produce instant profits and dress up the balance sheet. Indeed, many famous frauds have involved the creation of fictitious inventories. In 1991, for example, Laribee Wire Manufacturing Co. filed for bankruptcy, at which time it was discovered that much of Laribee's reported inventory did not exist. Similar situations occurred with Phar Mor, the Youngstown drugstore chain, Miniscribe, Crazy Eddie's, and Regina Vacuum Cleaners. Even L.A. Gear and Digital Equipment Corporation have been cited in lawsuits filed by investors who lost money relying on financial statements that contained inventory overstatements.

ETHICS IN THE REAL WORLD

The Wall Street Journal (December 14, 1992) reports that "auditors at even the top accounting firms are often fooled [by such shenanigans] . . . outside auditors can fail to catch inventory scams because they either trust management too much or fear they will lose clients by being tougher . . . spotting inventory fraud requires bigger staffs than some accounting firms . . . are willing to send out to do the inventory audits . . . If auditors were more skeptical of management claims, particularly in bad times,

they would look at a far greater portion of the inventory in certain instances and do more surprise audits, which . . . nowadays are unusual."

On the other hand, auditors do face intense competition for clients, and audit fees have been reduced significantly in recent years. Accordingly, there is much pressure to control audit costs by reducing the number of audit hours in an effort to maintain profit levels, and inventory frauds are very difficult to uncover. Alan Winters, the AICPA's director of audit research, stated "it is difficult if not impossible for the outside auditor to spot inventory fraud [especially] if top management is directing it."

ETHICAL ISSUE

Consider an auditor who has a large client in danger of being lost due to fee competition (i.e., a competitor has agreed to provide an audit for a lower fee). Is it ethical for this auditor to cut back on the number of hours devoted to auditing the inventory account so that the client can be charged a lower fee, and a profit can still be made on this audit?

REVIEW PROBLEM

On December 1, Jane Lee contributed $1,000 of her own funds to begin an Oriental grocery store that sells white rice. The rice is kept in a large bin, and customers help themselves by filling plastic bags with a large scoop. During December the transactions described in Figure 7–14 took place. Assume that Jane incurred cash expenses (excluding the cost of goods sold and inventory shortages) of $400 during December, and she pays income taxes at a rate of 30 percent of net income before taxes on December 31.

Jane purchased rice on two occasions at two different prices. By multiplying the number of pounds purchased times the cost per pound, the total capitalized inventory cost for January can be computed ($510). Three hundred pounds of rice were sold for a price of $5/lb., creating total sales of $1,500 (300 lb. × $5).

On December 31, when financial statements are prepared, Jane is able to determine beginning inventory ($0) and total purchase costs ($510) because she recorded the purchases as they were made. Assume that Jane took an inventory at this time (i.e., weighed the rice) and noted that there were 150 pounds of rice on hand. The following figures (7–15 and 7–16) contain the income statements and balance sheets prepared by JL Oriental Foods under the periodic method with the FIFO and LIFO cost flow assumptions. In Figure 7–17 the net income, ending inventory, and cash balance produced under the two cost flow assumptions are compared.

FIGURE 7–14	DATE	DESCRIPTION	TOTAL INVENTORY COST
December transactions for JL Oriental Foods	Dec. 1	Jane Lee, owner, contributed $1,000.	
	7	Purchased 300 pounds of rice for $1.00 per pound.	$300
	25	Sold 250 pounds of rice for $5.00 per pound.	
	27	Purchased 150 pounds of rice for $1.40 per pound.	210
	28	Sold 50 pounds of rice for $5.00 per pound.	
	29	Paid cash expenses of $400.	
	31	Paid income tax liability.	
	Total capitalized inventory cost		$510

FIGURE 7–15

Periodic method: FIFO assumption

JL ORIENTAL FOODS
INCOME STATEMENT
FOR THE MONTH ENDED DECEMBER 31, 1996

Sales (300 lb. × $5)	$1,500
Cost of goods sold	300[a]
Gross profit	$1,200
Expenses	400
Net income before taxes	$ 800
Income tax expense ($800 × .30)	240
Net income after taxes	$ 560

[a]Beginning inventory + Purchases − Ending inventory
$0   +($300 + $210) − (150 lb. × $1.40)

JL ORIENTAL FOODS
BALANCE SHEET
DECEMBER 31, 1996

Cash	$1,350[a]
Inventory	210[b]
Total assets	$1,560
Common stock	$1,000
Retained earnings	560
Total liabilities and stockholders' equity	$1,560

[a]Capital contribution − Purchases + Sales − Expenses − Taxes
$1,000   − ($300 + $210) + $1,500 − $400 − $240
[b]150 lb. × $1.40

Assume that on December 31 the market value of rice drops suddenly to $1.20 per pound. The total market value of Jane's 150 pounds of rice, therefore, is $180 (150 lb. × $1.20). If Jane used the FIFO assumption, she would record the following journal entry to apply the lower-of-cost-or-market rule.

Loss on Inventory Write-Down (Lo, −SE)	30	
Inventory (−A)		30

Wrote down inventory to market value ($210 − $180).

If Jane used the LIFO assumption, she would record no journal entry, because the cost of the ending inventory ($150) is already below the market value ($180).

FIGURE 7–16	JL ORIENTAL FOODS INCOME STATEMENT FOR THE MONTH ENDED DECEMBER 31, 1996

Periodic method:
LIFO assumption

Sales (300 lb. × $5)	$1,500
Cost of goods sold	360[a]
Gross profit	$1,140
Expenses	400
Net income before taxes	$ 740
Income tax expense ($740 × .30)	222
Net income after taxes	$ 518

[a]Beginning inventory + Purchases − Ending inventory
       $0   +($300 + $210) − (150 lb. × $1.00)

JL ORIENTAL FOODS INCOME SHEET DECEMBER 31, 1996

Cash	$1,368[a]
Inventory (150 lb. × $1.00)	150
Total assets	$1,518
Common stock	$1,000
Retained earnings	518
Total liabilities and stockholders' equity	$1,518

[a]Capital contribution − Purchases + Sales − Expenses − Taxes
      $1,000   − ($300 + $210) + $1,500 − $400   − $222

FIGURE 7–17		FIFO/PERIODIC	LIFO/PERIODIC
Inventory	Net income	$ 560	$ 518
assumption:	Ending inventory	210	150
method	Cash balance	1,350	1,368
comparisons			

SUMMARY OF LEARNING OBJECTIVES

 Define inventory, and describe how the methods used to account for it affect the financial statements.

Inventory includes asset items held for sale in the ordinary course of business. The ending inventory balance appears on the balance sheet and, for manufacturing and retail companies, is often the largest current asset. The methods used to account for inventory affect the allocation of the capitalized inventory cost between ending inventory and the Cost of Goods Sold. This allocation, in turn, affects net income and the ending inventory amount reported on the balance sheet. The effects of inventory accounting methods in the current and subsequent periods can be assessed by examining the following formula:

Cost of Goods Sold = Beginning Inventory + Purchases − Ending Inventory

The ending inventory valuation of the current period decreases cost of goods sold and, thereby, increases gross profit and net income. Ending inventory of the current period becomes beginning inventory of the subsequent period. Beginning inventory increases cost of goods sold and decreases gross profit and net income.

 Identify the four main issues that must be addressed when accounting for inventory.

The four main issues that must be addressed when accounting for inventories are (1) what costs to include in the capitalized inventory cost (what items to include and what costs to attach to these items), (2) which method to use to carry the inventory (perpetual or periodic), (3) which cost flow assumption to use (specific identification, averaging, FIFO, or LIFO), and (4) how to apply the lower-of-cost-or-market rule.

 Describe the general rules for including items in inventory and attaching costs to these items.

Items held for sale should be included in a company's inventory if the company has complete and unrestricted ownership of them. In a consignment, even though the inventory is in the possession of the consignee, it should be reported on the consignor's balance sheet. Goods in transit as of the balance sheet date that are sent FOB shipping point should be included in the buyer's inventory. Goods in transit as of the balance sheet date that are sent FOB destination should be included in the seller's inventory.

Any cost required to bring an inventory item to saleable condition should be capitalized and treated as an inventory cost. This includes all costs that can reasonably be associated with the manufacture, acquisition, storage, or preparation of inventory items.

 Explain the differences between the perpetual and periodic methods and the trade-offs involved in choosing between them.

The perpetual method keeps an up-to-date record of all inventory flows. Inventory purchases are recorded in the inventory account at cost, and Cost of Goods Sold is debited for the cost of items when they are sold.

The periodic method updates the inventory account at the end of each accounting period. Inventory purchases are recorded at cost, but cost of goods sold is not recognized when the inventory is sold. Instead, at the end of each accounting period, an inventory count is taken and the inventory and cost of goods sold balances are updated.

The perpetual method requires more bookkeeping procedures than the periodic method and is therefore usually more costly to implement. Nevertheless, the perpetual method provides more up-to-date information. As computer systems have reduced the processing costs of maintaining inventory records, the perpetual method has become more popular.

Identify the three cost flow assumptions and the measurement and economic trade-offs that concern both managers and users.

The three cost flow assumptions are averaging, first-in, first-out (FIFO), and last-in, first-out (LIFO). Under averaging, average costs are allocated to the goods sold and the goods that remain in ending inventory.

Under FIFO, the first items purchased are assumed to be the first items sold. This assumption matches old inventory costs with sales but places relatively up-to-date inventory costs on the balance sheet. In times of rising inventory costs, this assumption tends to inflate net income and increase a company's tax liability.

Under LIFO, the most recent items purchased are assumed to be the first items sold. This assumption matches current inventory costs with sales but tends to place old and outdated inventory costs on the balance sheet. LIFO can also be costly to implement and may encourage managers to purchase inventory items at inappropriate times. However, this assumption provides a reasonable measure of net income, and in times of rising inventory costs, it helps to minimize a company's tax liability. LIFO users also disclose the LIFO reserve, which allows the computation of FIFO inventory and net income as well as the accumulated tax savings associated with using LIFO.

LO 6 *Explain how the lower-of-cost-or-market rule is applied to ending inventories and why it is often criticized.*

Under the lower-of-cost-or-market rule the cost of ending inventory is compared to its market value. If the cost is greater than the market value, the inventory is written down to market and a loss is recognized. If the cost is less than the market value, no write-down is necessary. The lower-of-cost-or-market rule is often criticized because it can be used to create hidden reserves, allowing managers to manipulate income, and it gives rise to reporting inconsistencies.

APPENDIX 7A

DETERMINING MARKET VALUES FOR INVENTORIES AND APPLYING THE LOWER-OF-COST-OR-MARKET RULE

The accounting profession has concluded that there are three possible market values which can be used to compare with historical cost when applying the lower-of-cost-or-market rule: (1) replacement cost, the price a company would have to pay to replace its inventories, (2) net realizable value, the amount a company can expect to receive for its inventories less the costs of completing and selling them, and (3) net realizable value less a normal profit margin, which is equal to (2) less a company's normal markup.

Given these three market values, applying the lower-of-cost-or-market rule to inventories involves four steps.

1. Determine *historical cost.* This is the dollar amount allocated to ending inventory after the cost flow assumption is applied.
2. Choose the *appropriate market value* from replacement cost, net realizable value, and net realizable value less a normal profit margin. Replacement cost is chosen if it is between net realizable value and net realizable value less a normal profit margin. If replacement cost exceeds net realizable value (referred to as the "ceiling"), net realizable value is chosen. If replacement cost is less than net realizable value less a normal profit margin (referred to as the "floor"), net realizable value less a normal profit margin is chosen. It always turns out that the *middle of the three market values* is the appropriate one.

3. *Compare* historical cost (Step 1) to the appropriate market value (Step 2), and choose the lower of the two.
4. If historical cost is less than the appropriate market value, no adjusting journal entry is necessary. If historical cost is greater than the appropriate market value, an *adjusting journal entry* of the following form should be recorded in the books.

Loss on Inventory Write-Down (Lo, −SE)   XX
     Inventory (−A)   XX

Assume, for example, that the information contained in Figure 7A–1 was compiled from the inventory records of four different companies.

FIGURE 7A–1 *The lower of cost or market*	HISTORICAL COST	REPLACEMENT COST	NET REALIZABLE VALUE	NET REALIZABLE VALUE LESS NORMAL PROFIT	LOWER OF COST OR MARKET
Company A	$200	$180	$210	$150	$180
Company B	350	375	360	310	350
Company C	125	100	150	120	120
Company D	480	500	530	490	480

In the case of Company A, replacement cost ($180) is between net realizable value ($210) and net realizable value less a normal profit margin ($150). Replacement cost is the appropriate market value and is therefore compared to historical cost. Replacement cost ($180) is less than historical cost ($200) and serves as the basis for inventory valuation. Since inventories are presently at historical cost, the following journal entry would be recorded in the books.

Loss on Inventory Write-Down (Lo, −SE)   20
     Inventory (−A)   20
Wrote down inventory to market value.

For Company B, net realizable value ($360) is the middle market value and is compared to historical cost ($350). Historical cost is lower, so no journal entry need be prepared. For Company C, replacement cost is below net realizable value less a normal profit margin, and thus net realizable value less a normal profit margin ($120) represents the appropriate market value. It is below historical cost ($125), so the inventory must be written down with the journal entry that appears below.

Loss on Inventory Write-Down (Lo, −SE)   5
     Inventory (−A)   5
Wrote down inventory to market value.

In the case of Company D, replacement cost ($500) is the middle market value and above historical cost ($480). Consequently, no adjusting entry is recorded and the ending inventory remains at historical cost.

KEY TERMS

Note: Definitions for these terms are provided in the glossary at the end of the text.

Averaging assumption (p. 325)
Consignment (p. 314)
First-in, first-out (FIFO) (p. 325)
FOB (free on board) destination (p. 315)
FOB (free on board) shipping point (p. 315)
Freight-in (p. 316)
Goods in transit (p. 314)
Last-in, first-out (LIFO) (p. 325)
LIFO conformity rule (p. 327)

LIFO reserves (p. 332)
Manufacturing companies (p. 316)
Overhead (p. 316)
Paper profits (p. 329)
Periodic method (p. 317)
Perpetual method (p. 317)
Retail companies (p. 316)
Specific identification (p. 324)
Transportation-in (p. 316)

QUESTIONS FOR DISCUSSION AND REVIEW

1. What is inventory? Why are managers, investors, creditors, and auditors interested in the methods used to account for it?

2. How is the Inventory account on the balance sheet linked to the income statement? How does the allocation of the capitalized inventory cost affect the financial statements?

3. Name the four major issues that must be addressed when accounting for inventory. Briefly describe each issue and explain how it is related to the others.

4. What is the general rule for deciding what items to include in inventory? What is a consignment, and how does it relate to inventory accounting? How might consignments be difficult for auditors?

5. Assume that Rawlers Corporation acts as a consignee for Matton Manufacturing. If Matton's inventory is mistakenly included on the balance sheet of Rawlers, how will the financial statements of Rawlers be misstated?

6. What factors must be considered when attempting to determine who owns goods that are in transit at the end of an accounting period? What is the meaning of *FOB shipping point* and *FOB destination*? How might these shipping terms be helpful in determining whether a sale or purchase has been completed as of the end of an accounting period?

7. What is the general rule for deciding what costs to attach to inventory items? Discuss the basic differences between a retailer and a manufacturer and how these differences affect inventory accounting.

8. What is the basic difference between the perpetual and the periodic inventory methods? Which method is easier to implement? Why?

9. The advent of computer systems has caused a number of companies to switch from the periodic method of carrying inventory to the perpetual method. Why would companies do this? What advantages does the perpetual method have over the periodic method? Provide an example.

10. The specific identification method is a procedure for determining which inventory costs are allocated to Cost of Goods Sold and which inventory costs are allocated to ending inventory. What are the advantages and disadvantages of this procedure? How can this procedure be used by a manager to manipulate net income and other financial ratios?

11. What is the basic difference between FIFO and LIFO cost flow assumptions? If inventory costs are stable across time, is there any difference between the cost of goods sold and ending inventory produced under FIFO and LIFO? Why or why not?

12. From a measurement standpoint, which assumption (FIFO or LIFO) is preferred? State your answer in terms of the matching principle and the balance sheet valuation of inventory.

13. State the LIFO conformity rule. How might this rule affect a manager's decision to choose an inventory flow assumption?

14. List the economic advantages and disadvantages of LIFO and FIFO, and explain why companies choose one or the other.

15. Is it advisable simply to choose FIFO because in times of rising inventory costs it provides higher inventory and net income numbers? Might a higher income number increase the value of a company's capital stock? Discuss.

16. What is a *LIFO liquidation*, and how might one inflate net income?

17. In periods of rising inventory costs, why would a manager who uses LIFO want to avoid a year in which sales significantly exceed purchases? How might it be done? What problems may be associated with this strategy?

18. Define the LIFO reserve and explain how it can be used to provide useful information.

19. Describe the lower-of-cost-or-market rule as applied to inventories. Why is it viewed as inconsistent by a number of its critics? From a measurement standpoint, do these arguments have merit? If so, how would the lower-of-cost-or-market rule have to be justified?

20. What is inventory turnover? What problems could be indicated by low inventory turnover? What problems could be indicated by high inventory turnover?

21. Explain how company groups in Japan can lead to lower inventory levels and inventory carrying costs. What are the implications for the use of LIFO and FIFO in Japan?

22. *(Appendix 7A)* Why is applying the lower-of-cost-or-market rule to inventories often difficult? Are inventory market values objectively determined? What three market values are considered in the rule? Which market value is preferred if it does not exceed the "ceiling" or dip below the "floor"? Which market value serves as the "ceiling"? Which market value serves as the "floor"?

EXERCISES

E7–1

(Accounting for inventory purchases)

Nick's Fish Market purchased Maine lobster on account on October 10, 1997, for a gross price of $76,000. Nick also purchased Alaskan king crab on account on October 11, 1997, for a gross price of $36,000. The terms of both sales were 2/15, n/30. Nick paid for the first purchase on October 20, 1997, and for the second purchase on October 30, 1997. He uses the perpetual inventory method.

REQUIRED:
Prepare journal entries for each transaction.

E7–2

(Accounting for inventory purchases)

Baymont Corporation purchased inventory on account on March 3, 1997, for a gross price of $50,000. The company purchased additional inventory on account on March 10, 1997, for a gross price of $140,000. The terms of both sales were 3/12, n/30. Baymont Corporation paid for the first purchase on April 25, 1997, and for the second purchase on March 20, 1997. The company prepares monthly adjusting journal entries and uses the perpetual inventory method.

REQUIRED:
Prepare journal entries for each transaction.

E7–3

(Compute the missing values)

The following information was extracted from the financial records of House Designs.

	12/31/97	12/31/96	12/31/95	12/31/94
Beginning inventory	$110,000	?	$125,000	$ 90,000
Purchases	?	$ 75,000	60,000	50,000
Purchase discounts	(10,000)	?	(5,000)	?
Cost of goods available for sale	155,000	190,000	?	135,000
Ending inventory	75,000	?	130,000	?
Cost of goods sold	?	80,000	50,000	10,000

REQUIRED:

a. Compute the missing information for each year.
b. Assume that House Designs uses the periodic method to account for inventory. Prepare the end-of-period entry to recognize the ending inventory and Cost of Goods Sold at the end of each year.

E7–4

(The financial statement effects of inventory errors)

Pacers Corporation reported the following items in its 1997 financial report.

		1997		1996
Sales		$400,000		$250,000
Cost of goods sold:				
Beginning inventory	$190,000		$175,000	
Purchases	240,000		125,000	
Goods available for sale	$430,000		$300,000	
Less: Ending inventory	235,000		190,000	
Cost of goods sold		195,000		110,000
Gross profit		$205,000		$140,000

ADDITIONAL INFORMATION:

The ending inventory amount was obtained by a physical count of the inventory on hand at the end of the year. Counting errors caused the ending inventory in 1996 to be understated by $9,000 and the ending inventory in 1997 to be overstated by $9,000.

REQUIRED:

a. Compute the impact of these errors on Cost of Goods Sold for the year ended December 31, 1996, and on the inventory balance as of December 31, 1996.
b. Compute the impact of these errors on Cost of Goods Sold for the year ended December 31, 1997, and on the inventory balance as of December 31, 1997.
c. What is the impact of these errors on Cost of Goods Sold over the two-year period ended December 31, 1997?

E7–5

(Goods in transit as of the end of the accounting period)

Dallas Manufacturing engaged in five transactions involving inventory at the end of 1997:

1. Ordered $50,000 of inventory on December 29, 1997. The goods were shipped on December 30, 1997, with the terms FOB shipping point. Dallas received the inventory on January 4, 1998.
2. Received an order to sell inventory with a cost of $40,000. The goods were shipped to the customer on December 31, 1997, and received on January 3, 1998. The terms of the sale were FOB shipping point.
3. Received an order to sell inventory with a cost of $15,000. The goods were shipped to the customer on December 29, 1997, and received on January 2, 1998. The terms of the sale were FOB destination.
4. Ordered $10,000 of inventory on December 27, 1997. The inventory was shipped on December 27, 1997, with the terms FOB destination. Dallas received the inventory on December 31, 1997.
5. Ordered $75,000 of inventory on December 30, 1997. The inventory was shipped on December 31, 1997, with the terms FOB destination. Dallas received the inventory on January 3, 1998.

REQUIRED:

Assume that Dallas included in inventory (12/31/97) all items from the five cases above. Explain how the resulting financial statements would be misstated.

E7-6

(Carrying inventories: perpetual and periodic methods)

The following information comes from the records of Telly's Supply.

Beginning inventory	**$32,000**
Inventory purchases	**85,000**
Transportation-in	**4,300**

An inventory count taken at year end indicates that inventory with a cost of $50,000 is on hand as of December 31, 1997.

REQUIRED:

a. Assume that Telly's uses the periodic inventory method. Compute Cost of Goods Sold and prepare the year-end closing journal entry.

b. Assume that Telly's uses the perpetual method and that inventory purchases and transportation-in are both reflected in the Inventory account, which shows an ending balance of $52,000. Compute Cost of Goods Sold under the perpetual method along with any adjusting entries required at the end of the period.

c. Explain why the periodic method produces a value for Cost of Goods Sold that is different from that produced by the perpetual method. What information does the perpetual method provide that is not provided by the periodic method?

E7-7

(Income manipulation under specific identification)

Marian's Furs specializes in full-length mink coats. As of January 1, Marian had four top-of-the-line coats. Although the four coats are equivalent, they were purchased the previous year at different costs:

	COST
Coat 1	**$8,400**
Coat 2	**7,100**
Coat 3	**7,600**
Coat 4	**6,800**

During January a customer decided to buy any one of the mink coats for $12,000. This was the only sale in January.

REQUIRED:

a. If Marian wished to maximize January's profits and ending inventory, which of the minks would she have sold to the customer? Compute the gross profit on the sale and January's ending inventory. Discuss why Marian might wish to maximize profits and ending inventory.

b. If Marian wished to minimize January's profits and ending inventory, which of the minks would she have sold to the customer? Compute the gross profit on the sale and January's ending inventory. Discuss why Marian might wish to minimize profits and ending inventory.

E7-8

(Inventory assumptions and manipulating income under specific identification)

Vinnie's House of Televisions has 75 identical 27-inch color monitors in stock on January 1, 1997. Vinnie maintains records of the serial numbers of each monitor to track their costs. Vinnie purchased the 75 monitors on December 5, 1996, for $450 each. He also purchased 50 on January 2, 1997, for $500 each, and an additional 65 on January 15, 1997, for $600 each. Each monitor is priced to sell at $1,000. Vinnie sold 130 monitors during the month of January.

REQUIRED:

a. Compute gross profit and ending inventory for the month if the company uses the periodic method and adheres to each of the following:
    (1) FIFO cost flow assumption
    (2) Averaging cost flow assumption

(3) LIFO cost flow assumption
b. Assume that Vinnie uses the specific identification method to compute the cost of goods sold. Explain how Vinnie could manipulate the gross profit number. What are the highest and the lowest gross profit amounts Vinnie could report? What are some possible factors that could motivate Vinnie to report either the highest or the lowest net income amount?

E7–9

(Inventory flow assumptions over several periods and income taxes)

Heller Bottling Company began business in 1993. Inventory units purchased and sold for the first year of operations and each of the following four years follow.

	UNITS PURCHASED	COST PER UNIT	UNITS SOLD
1993	10,000	$12	5,000
1994	12,000	16	16,000
1995	5,000	18	2,000
1996	10,000	21	10,000
1997	2,000	23	6,000

Inadequate cash flows forced the Heller Bottling Company to cease operations at the end of 1997.

REQUIRED:

a. Compute Cost of Goods Sold for each of the five years if the company uses the following:
   (1) LIFO cost flow assumption
   (2) FIFO cost flow assumption
   (3) Averaging cost flow assumption
b. Does the choice of a cost flow assumption affect total net income over the life of a business? Explain your answer.
c. If the choice of a cost flow assumption does not affect net income over the life of a business, how does the choice of a cost flow assumption give rise to a tax benefit?

E7–10

(Using the LIFO reserve)

The following disclosure was included in the footnotes of Microline Company, which uses the LIFO cost flow assumption and reported net income of $38,200 for 1997. The company's effective tax rate is 35%.

	1997	1996
Inventories at current cost	$23,500	$24,300
Less: Adjustment to LIFO basis	(3,200)	(2,800)
Inventories on LIFO basis	$20,300	$21,500

REQUIRED:

a. Compute 1997 reported net income for Microline if it had chosen to change from LIFO to FIFO at the end of 1997.
b. Compute the accumulated income tax savings enjoyed by Microline due to the choice of LIFO as opposed to FIFO.
c. Compute 1997 reported net income for Microline if it had chosen to change from LIFO to FIFO in 1990.
d. Explain how the information generated in (a), (b), and (c) above could be useful.

E7–11

(The lower-of-cost-or-market rule and hidden reserves)

Central Incorporated has two items in inventory as of December 31, 1997. Each item was purchased for $40. Company management chose to write down Item #1 to $28, which at year end was assessed to be its market value. Management did not write down Item #2 because its market value was estimated to be greater than $40. During 1998 each item was sold for $50 cash.

REQUIRED:

a. Assume that the company uses the perpetual inventory method, and prepare journal entries for each activity (i.e., the write-down, the sale of item #1, and the sale of item #2).
b. Compute the profit or loss associated with each item in 1997 and 1998.
c. Explain how management could manipulate reported earnings when applying the lower-of-cost-or-market rule.

E7–12

(Appendix 7A: Applying the lower-of-cost-or-market rule)

The following information concerns the ending inventory of five different companies.

COMPANY	HISTORICAL COST	NET REALIZABLE VALUE	REPLACEMENT COST	NET REALIZABLE VALUE LESS A NORMAL PROFIT MARGIN
Wheaton	$32,300	$40,000	$37,300	$ 34,300
Loners	65,200	63,100	65,800	59,200
Flowe	17,400	18,300	14,500	13,100
Roberts	6,800	8,200	4,300	7,100
Strayling	26,300	26,800	18,900	19,400

REQUIRED:

a. In each case choose the market value which is to be compared to historical cost when applying the lower-of-cost-or-market rule.
b. In each case choose the value at which ending inventory should be carried on the balance sheet.
c. In each case prepare the journal entries that would be required under the lower-of-cost-or-market rule.

PROBLEMS

P7–1

(Purchases and cash discounts)

On November 15 and 26, Brown and Swazey purchased merchandise on account for gross prices of $8,000 and $12,000, respectively. Terms of both purchases were 2/10, n/30. The company uses the perpetual inventory method, none of these items have been sold, and both accounts are paid in full on December 2.

REQUIRED:

Provide all the journal entries that would be recorded for these events.

P7–2.

(The gross method and partial payments)

Stober Corporation made two purchases of inventory on account during the month of March. The first purchase was made on March 5 for $30,000, and the second purchase was made on March 10 for $60,000. The terms of each purchase were 2/10, n/30. The first purchase was settled on March 13, and the second was settled on July 18. The company uses the perpetual inventory method.

REQUIRED:

a. Prepare all the necessary journal entries associated with these transactions.
b. Assume that with respect to the second purchase, the company settled 2/3 of the accounts payable balance on March 19 and settled the remaining balance on August 7. The first purchase was settled on March 13. Prepare all the necessary journal entries associated with the second purchase.

P7–3

(The financial effects of inventory errors)

The information below was taken from the records of Rice Brothers.

	1997	1996	1995
Sales	$100,000	$90,000	$85,000
Cost of goods sold	50,000	42,000	40,000
Gross profit	$ 50,000	$48,000	$45,000
Expenses	37,000	32,000	20,000
Net income	$ 13,000	$16,000	$25,000

You are auditing the Rice Brothers' books in early 1998 and discover that their inventory counting procedures are flawed. Accordingly, ending inventory was overstated by $5,000 in 1995, understated by $1,500 in 1996, and overstated by $3,200 in 1997. Rice uses the periodic inventory method (1994 ending inventory was correctly stated).

REQUIRED:

Compute the corrected cost of goods sold and net income for 1995, 1996, and 1997.

P7–4

(The financial statement effects of inventory in transit and consignments)

The income statement and balance sheet as of December 31, 1996, for Thomas and Sons are provided below. The company uses the FIFO cost flow assumption.

INCOME STATEMENT

Sales	$200,000
Cost of goods sold	130,000
Gross profit	$ 70,000
Selling and admin. expenses	40,000
Net income	$ 30,000

BALANCE SHEET

Cash	$ 35,000	Current liabilities	$ 20,000
Inventory	40,000	Long-term liabilities	50,000
Noncurrent assets	120,000	Stockholders' equity	125,000
		Total liabilities and	
Total assets	$195,000	stockholders' equity	$195,000

While examining the company's financial statements, the auditor noted that the following items were ignored when the financial statements were prepared.

Purchases in transit on December 31, 1996:

AMOUNT	SHIPPING TERMS	
$14,000	FOB shipping point	Cost of inventory out on consignment
8,000	FOB destination	(recorded as a purchase but ignored in
		the physical ending inventory count) $12,000

REQUIRED:

a. Prepare the income statement and balance sheet for Thomas and Sons in light of the additional information discovered by the auditor.

b. Does it make any difference whether Thomas uses the perpetual or the periodic inventory method? Why or why not?

P7–5

(Including goods in transit and consignments in ending inventory)

Yakima Sporting Goods reported the following information as of December 31, 1996:

Inventory (based on a physical count on 12/31/96) $2,345,000
Accounts payable   778,000

ADDITIONAL INFORMATION:

1. Yakima Sporting Goods had ordered $80,000 of merchandise from its suppliers on December 27, 1996, with the terms FOB destination. The goods were shipped on December 31, 1996, and received on January 2, 1997.

2. Included in the physical inventory count was $35,000 in merchandise held on consignment for Power Sunblock Company.

3. Yakima Sporting Goods received a freight bill for items purchased during December 1996 in the amount of $15,000 on January 6, 1997. These freight charges had not been included in either Inventory or Accounts Payable as of December 31, 1996. Two-thirds of the merchandise purchased during December 1996 was still in the inventory as of December 31, 1996.

4. Yakima Sporting Goods shipped a large order to an out-of-city customer in the amount of $95,000 (at retail) on December 30, with the terms FOB destination. The customer received the goods on January 2, 1997. Cost of goods sold is 80 percent of the retail price.

5. Yakima Sporting Goods received a shipment from a vendor on December 30, 1996, which was included in the physical inventory count. The vendor invoice of $20,000 was not included in Accounts Payable as of December 31, 1996, due to a temporary breakdown in the company's internal controls.

6. Yakima Sporting Goods had $50,000 of weightlifting equipment on consignment at a local health club as of December 31, 1996. The equipment was not included in the company's physical inventory count.

REQUIRED:

a. Prepare a schedule in the following format.

	INVENTORY	ACCOUNTS PAYABLE
Reported dollar amounts	$2,345,000	$778,000
Adjustments		
1.		
2.		
3.		
4.		
5.		
6.		
Adjusted dollar amounts		

b. Complete the schedule for each item listed above. If the item requires no adjustment, state "No effect."

P7-6

(The financial statement and income tax effects of averaging, FIFO, and LIFO)

The purchase schedule for Lumbermans and Associates is provided below.

DATE	ITEMS PURCHASED	COST PER ITEM
March 15	6,000	$1.30
July 30	9,000	1.50
December 17	7,000	1.60
Total	22,000	

The inventory balance as of the beginning of the year was $15,000 (15,000 units @ $1), and an inventory count at year-end indicated that 11,000 items were on hand. The company uses the periodic inventory method. Sales and expenses (excluding Cost of Goods Sold) totaled $55,000 and $15,000, respectively. The federal income tax rate is 30 percent of taxable income.

REQUIRED:

a. Prepare three income statements, one under each of the assumptions: FIFO, averaging, and LIFO.
b. How many tax dollars would be saved by using LIFO instead of FIFO?
c. Assume that the market value of an inventory item dropped to $1.35 as of year-end. Apply the lower-of-cost-or-market rule, and provide the appropriate journal entry (if necessary) under the FIFO, averaging, and LIFO assumptions.
d. Repeat (a) above assuming that the costs per item were as follows.

Beginning inventory	$1.60
March 15	1.40
July 30	1.30
December 17	1.20

Which of the three assumptions gives rise to the highest net income and ending inventory amounts now? Why?

P7-7

(Avoiding LIFO liquidations)

IBT has used the LIFO inventory cost flow assumption for five years. As of December 31, 1995, IBT had 700 items in its inventory, and the $9,000 inventory dollar amount reported on the balance sheet consisted of the following costs.

WHEN PURCHASED	NUMBER OF ITEMS	COST PER ITEM	TOTAL
1992	500	$ 12	$6,000
1994	200	15	3,000
Total	700		$9,000

During 1996, IBT sold 900 items for $75 each and purchased 350 items at $30 each. Expenses other than the cost of goods sold totaled $20,000, and the federal income tax rate is 30 percent of taxable income.

REQUIRED:

a. Prepare IBT's income statement for the year ending December 31, 1996.
b. Assume that IBT purchased an additional 550 items on December 20, 1996, for $30 each. Prepare IBT's income statement for the year ending December 31, 1996.
c. Compare the two income statements, and discuss why it might have been wise for IBT to purchase the additional items on December 20. Discuss some of the disadvantages of such a strategy.

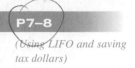

P7–8

(Using LIFO and saving tax dollars)

Financial statements as of December 31, 1996, for Beverly Company are provided below. Beverly used the FIFO inventory cost flow assumption to prepare the following financial statements.

INCOME STATEMENT

Sales		$80,000
Cost of goods sold:		
Beginning inventory	$20,000	
Purchases	40,000	
Goods available for sale	$60,000	
Less: Ending inventory	25,000	
Cost of goods sold		35,000
Gross profit		$45,000
Selling & administrative expenses		20,000
Net income before taxes		$25,000
Federal income tax (30%)		7,500
Net income		$17,500

BALANCE SHEET

Cash	$15,000	Current liabilities	$18,000
Inventory	25,000	Long-term liabilities	20,000
Other noncurrent assets	40,000	Stockholders' equity	42,000
		Total liabilities and	
Total assets	$80,000	stockholders' equity	$80,000

On December 31, 1996, Beverly decided to change from the FIFO to the LIFO inventory cost flow assumption. The ending inventory value under the LIFO assumption is $13,000.

REQUIRED:

a. Compute the change in Beverly's current ratio associated with the change from FIFO to LIFO. Round to two decimal places.
b. Compute the change in Beverly's gross profit and net income associated with the change from FIFO to LIFO. Assume that the dollar amount of the change is reflected in Cost of Goods Sold.
c. How many tax dollars would be saved by the change from FIFO to LIFO?
d. Discuss some of the disadvantages associated with the change to LIFO.

P7–9

(LIFO liquidations, income tax implications, and year-end purchases)

Ruhe Auto Supplies began operations in 1983. The following represents the company's inventory purchases and sales in the first and subsequent years of operations.

YEAR	UNITS PURCHASED	COST PER UNIT	UNITS SOLD	YEAR	UNITS PURCHASED	COST PER UNIT	UNITS SOLD
1983	20,000	$ 5	4,000	1990	8,000	65	9,000
1984	8,000	10	8,000	1991	9,500	70	9,000
1985	7,000	15	9,000	1992	7,000	75	8,000
1986	8,500	20	7,000	1993	8,500	80	8,500
1987	6,000	25	7,500	1994	9,000	85	7,500
1988	7,500	30	7,000	1995	8,500	90	9,500
1989	9,000	50	8,000	1996	9,500	95	20,000

ADDITIONAL INFORMATION:

1. The company's federal income tax rate is 30 percent.
2. For the year ended December 31, 1996, Ruhe Auto Supplies generated $3,000,000 in revenues and incurred $800,000 in expenses (exclusive of Cost of Goods Sold).

3. Ruhe Auto Supplies uses the periodic method and the LIFO cost flow assumption to account for inventory.

REQUIRED:
a. Compute ending inventory as of December 31, 1995. Identify the number of units in ending inventory and the costs attached to each unit.
b. Compute the company's 1996 income tax liability and net income after taxes for the year ended December 31, 1996.
c. Assume that Ruhe Auto Supplies was able to purchase an additional 10,500 units of inventory on December 31, 1996, for $95 per unit. Would you advise the company to purchase these additional units? Explain your answer.

P7–10

(The gross method, the periodic method, and the LIFO and FIFO cost flow assumptions)

The Magic Teddy Bear Toy Company entered into the following transactions during January 1996.

1. January 3:   Purchased 7,000 teddy bears at $20 each with the terms 2/10, n/30.
2. January 3:   Sold 2,000 teddy bears at $50 each for cash.
3. January 9:   Sold 4,000 teddy bears at $50 each on account.
4. January 10:   Settled the purchase made on January 3.
5. January 15:   Purchased 10,000 teddy bears. Three thousand of the bears were purchased for cash at $24.50 each, and the remaining bears were purchased on account for a gross price of $25.00 each (terms 2/10, n/30).
6. January 19:   Purchased 7,000 teddy bears at $26 each with the terms 2/10, n 30.
7. January 23:   Paid for one-half of the teddy bears purchased on account on January 15.
8. January 27:   Purchased 4,000 teddy bears at $28 each for cash.
9. January 28:   Settled the remaining open account from the purchase made on January 15.
10. January 28:   Settled the open account from the purchase made on January 19.
11. January 29:   Sold 6,000 teddy bears at $60 each for cash.
12. January 30:   Sold 5,000 teddy bears at $60 each on account.
13. January 31:   Purchased 2,000 teddy bears at $30 each for cash.
14. January 31:   Received a freight bill covering all purchases made during January 1993 in the amount of $30,000.

The Magic Teddy Bear Toy Company has 5,000 teddy bears at $19 each on hand as of January 1, 1996.

REQUIRED:
Assume that The Magic Teddy Bear Toy Company accounts for purchase cash discounts under the gross method and uses the periodic inventory method. Prepare all necessary entries, including adjusting journal entries, during January 1996 if the company uses the following:
a. LIFO cost flow assumption
b. FIFO cost flow assumption

(*Hint:* Compute the total cost per unit in order to calculate ending inventory and Cost of Goods Sold.)

P7–11

(Using the LIFO reserve)

You are a financial analyst presently reviewing the financial statements of Danner International and Brady Enterprises, two companies of similar size within the same industry. Net income of $39,300 and $42,700 was reported for 1997 by Danner and Brady, respectively. After a thorough comparison of the accounting methods used by the two companies, you find that they are similar except for the inventory cost flow assumption—Danner uses FIFO and Brady uses LIFO. You conduct a further review of Brady's footnotes and discover the following. Inventories declined during 1997, causing a LIFO liquidation, which accounted for $5,100 of the before-tax net income reported in 1997.

	1997	1996
Inventories at current cost	$36,200	$42,400
Less: Adjustment to LIFO	(3,500)	(4,800)
Inventories at LIFO	$32,700	$37,600

REQUIRED:

a. Assume that Brady's effective tax rate is 35%, and restate Brady's 1997 reported net income as if the company had always been a FIFO user. Is Brady's restated reported income higher or lower than Danner's reported net income? Explain.

b. As of the end of 1997, how much accumulated income tax had Brady saved due to its choice of LIFO instead of FIFO. How much as of the end of 1996? Does LIFO save taxes in every year? Explain.

c. Would it be advisable for Brady to change its cost flow assumption from LIFO to FIFO? Discuss.

P7–12

(Appendix 7A: Applying the lower-of-cost-or-market rule)

J. Hartney, controller of Babbit Plumbing, has compiled the following information to aid him in applying the lower-of-cost-or-market rule to the company's inventory.

	REPLACEMENT COST	NET REALIZABLE VALUE	NET REALIZABLE VALUE LESS A NORMAL PROFIT	HISTORICAL COST
Item A	$52	$55	$ 7	$60
Item B	61	57	10	55
Item C	72	75	3	77
Item D	45	50	5	44
Item E	40	47	9	50
Item F	39	40	1	40
Item G	12	17	5	8
Item H	10	8	1	5

REQUIRED:

a. Compute the amount that Babbit Plumbing should report in the account "Inventory" under the lower-of-cost-or-market rule assuming that the company applies this rule to each item individually.

b. Prepare any journal entries necessary to adjust inventory to the lower of cost or market.

CASES

C7–1

(The lower-of-cost-or-market rule and the recognition of loss/income)

TII Industries makes over-voltage protectors, power systems, and electronic products primarily for use in the communications industry. Several years ago, the company reported that it took "a substantial inventory write-down" resulting in a loss for its third quarter, ending June 24. The write-down was estimated to be $12 million and stems from customers' changes in product specifications.

REQUIRED:

a. Provide the journal entry to record the write-down.

b. Assume that the original cost of the inventory was $52 million and that it was written down to its market value of $40 million. If TII Industries sells it for $48 million cash in the following period, what journal entries would be recorded? Assume that TII uses the perpetual inventory method.

c. Applying the lower-of-cost-or-market rule in this case would cause TII to recognize a loss in the period of the write-down and income in the subsequent period. Does such recognition seem appropriate? Why or why not?

C7–2

(LIFO reporting)

In its December 31, 1994, annual report, Amoco Corporation reported the following inventories:

MILLIONS OF DOLLARS	1994	1993
Crude oil and petroleum products	$ 349	$ 415
Chemical products	375	377
Other products and merchandise	24	21
Materials and supplies	294	297
	$1,042	$1,110

During the year ended December 31, 1993, the corporation reduced certain inventory quantities which were valued at lower LIFO costs prevailing in prior years. The effect of this reduction was to increase net income by approximately $50 million. The similar effect in 1994 was not material.

Inventories carried under the LIFO method represented approximately 51 percent of total year-end inventory carrying values in 1994 and 47 percent in 1993. It is estimated that inventories would have been approximately $1,100 million higher than reported on December 31, 1994, and approximately $900 million higher on December 31, 1993, if the quantities valued on the LIFO basis were instead valued on the FIFO basis.

REQUIRED:

a. Why would a potential investor or creditor who is considering investing in Amoco be interested in the difference between LIFO and FIFO inventory values?
b. Explain why reducing certain inventory quantities, valued under LIFO, would increase net income and why an investor would be interested in such a disclosure.
c. Assuming a tax rate of 30 percent, approximately how much more income tax would Amoco have paid if at the end of 1994 it switched to FIFO for all of its inventory? Assume that inventories presently not carried at LIFO are carried at FIFO.

C7–3

(LIFO liquidation and hidden reserves)

In the early 1980s an oil glut caused Texaco, a LIFO user, to delay drilling, which cut its oil inventory levels by 16%. The LIFO cushion (i.e., the difference between LIFO and FIFO inventory values) that was built into those barrels over the year amounted to $454 million and transformed what would have been a drop in net income to a modest gain.

REQUIRED:
Explain how using LIFO could be interpreted as building "hidden reserves."

C7–4

(Choosing FIFO or LIFO)

A partner from a major accounting firm made the following comment when asked about the accounting methods used by companies in the software industry:

"Accounting policies that have adverse short-term effects on financial statements cannot help the industry raise capital."

After reading such a comment, one might conclude that managers who wish to raise capital by borrowing from banks or issuing equity or debt securities should choose the FIFO cost flow assumption instead of LIFO. Yet, others have written that they are "puzzled" about why thousands of U.S. companies use FIFO instead of LIFO.*

*Gary Biddle, "Paying FIFO Taxes: Your Favorite Charity," *The Wall Street Journal*, January 19, 1981, p. 18.

REQUIRED:
Discuss.

C7–5

(Inventory fraud)

The following quote was taken from *The Wall Street Journal* (December 14, 1992):

How an audit can misfire is illustrated by the way Deloitte & Touche, the auditors of Laribee Manufacturing Co., failed to realize that the New York copper wire maker was buoying a sinking ship by creating fictitious inventories.

Laribee was plagued by huge debt—almost seven times its equity—generated by a major acquisition in 1988. Meanwhile, its sales to the troubled construction industry, its major customer for copper wire, were declining. In 1990, Laribee borrowed $130 million from six banks. The banks say that they relied on the clean opinion that Deloitte & Touche gave Laribee's financial statement for 1989, when the company reported $3 million in net income. A major portion of the loan collateral consisted of Laribee's inventories of the copper rod used to draw wire at its six U.S. factories.

But after Laribee filed for bankruptcy court protection in early 1991, a court-ordered investigation by other accountants, attorneys and bank specialists showed that much of Laribee's inventory didn't exist. Some was on the books at bloated values. Certain wire product stocks carried at $2.20 a pound were selling at only $1.70 to $1.75 a pound.

REQUIRED:

a. Identify factors that could have been used in advance by Deloitte & Touche to indicate that Laribee might be a risky audit.
b. What two methods did Laribee use to increase its inventory valuation, and what short-run advantage did the company gain by doing so?
c. What principles of inventory valuation were violated by Laribee?
d. What did the auditors fail to do, and to what parties are they responsible?

C7–6

(Just-in-time inventory)

The Wall Street Journal (January 31, 1991) recently reported that many U.S. manufacturers are following the Japanese and moving toward just-in-time manufacturing methods to cut inventory carrying costs and speed production. The same article also notes, however, that these companies were hurt especially by supply shipment delays caused by the 1991 Gulf War. Representatives from IBM, Dow Chemical, and GE all suggested that the just-in-time system magnified the problems associated with the delivery disruptions.

REQUIRED:

a. Briefly explain what the just-in-time system is and why U.S. manufacturers are adopting it.
b. How does using a just-in-time system affect the importance of the choice between LIFO and FIFO and why?
c. Explain how the just-in-time system could magnify the problems associated with delivery disruptions caused by the Gulf War.

C7–7

(MCI)

Review the MCI annual report and answer the following questions.
a. In what industry would you classify MCI—manufacturer, retail, financial services, or other services? Why?
b. How important is inventory management to MCI? Identify some of the major asset management issues faced by the company.

INVESTMENTS IN EQUITY SECURITIES

LEARNING OBJECTIVES

LO 1 Identify the criteria that must be met before a security can be listed in the current assets section of the balance sheet.

LO 2 Define trading and available-for-sale securities, and explain how the mark-to-market rule is used to account for them.

LO 3 Explain why companies make long-term investments in equity securities.

LO 4 Distinguish among the mark-to-market method, the cost method, and the equity method of accounting for long-term equity investments, and describe the conditions under which each method is used.

LO 5 Define consolidated financial statements, and describe when they are prepared and how they differ from financial statements that account for equity investments using the equity method.

LO 6 Explain why goodwill accounting is controversial.

An **equity investment** occurs when one company purchases another company's outstanding common stock. Recall from Chapter 1 that equity holders have the right to receive dividends, if declared, and to vote for the board of directors at the annual meeting of the stockholders. Companies make investments in equity securities for two basic reasons: (1) to earn investment income in the form of dividends and stock price appreciation and (2) to exert influence or control over the board of directors and management of the investee company. Relatively small equity investments are normally made to earn income over a short period of time, while larger, long-term equity investments often signal an attempt by the investing company to influence the operations of the target company.

To illustrate, as of December 31, 1994, Deere & Company, manufacturer of the well-known John Deere agricultural equipment, disclosed over $1.1 billion in marketable securities. Most of these securities consisted of small-percentage holdings of the equity securities from a wide variety of other companies. At the same time, the company held investments in companies where between 20% and 50% of the equity securities had been purchased. These holdings were carried on the balance sheet at over $150 million. Also, in August of 1994 Deere & Company acquired the Homelite division of Textron, Inc., for approximately $120 million. This acquisition was designed to give Deere & Company a greater presence in the outdoor power equipment market.

The next section covers equity investments classified as current because they are readily marketable and intended to be sold within the time period of current assets. The chapter then discusses long-term equity investments and divides the coverage into three categories, based on the proportion of the common stock holdings: (1) equity holdings of less than 20%, (2) equity holdings from 20%-50%, and (3) equity holdings of greater than 50%. As we note later, these three situations are accounted for differently. Appendix 8A is devoted to consolidated financial statements, which are prepared when a company holds more than 50% of the outstanding common stock in another company.

EQUITY SECURITIES CLASSIFIED AS CURRENT

LO 1 Idle cash held by a company earns no return and during inflation actually declines in purchasing power. Nevertheless, proper cash management must ensure that enough cash is available to meet a company's day-to-day cash needs. Such cash needs tend to fluctuate, sometimes unexpectedly, making it difficult for management to consistently strike an appropriate balance between available cash and return-producing investments. In an effort to both earn a return and be able to produce cash on short notice, companies often purchase readily marketable securities. A recent annual report of Brown and Company, Inc., for example, indicates that it is "company policy to invest cash in excess of operating requirements in income-producing investments." Such investments, which include stocks and bonds traded on public security exchanges, provide income through dividends, interest, or price appreciation, and can be readily converted to cash when needed to meet current cash requirements.[1]

---

1. Short-term investments can also consist of certificates of deposit, money market accounts, and commercial paper. Certificates of deposit are usually purchased from banks in denominations of at least $5,000. They provide a fixed rate of return over a specified period of time. Money market accounts are similar to savings or checking accounts but provide a slightly higher rate of interest, and there are usually restrictions on the withdrawal of funds. Commercial paper is a short-term note issued by corporations with good credit ratings. They are usually issued in denominations of $5,000 and $10,000 and provide returns which exceed those of money market accounts.

The relative size of short-term investments on the balance sheet varies significantly across companies in different industries. Retailers such as hardware, department, clothing, and sporting goods stores typically maintain dollar amounts of less than 3 percent of total assets. Financial institutions, insurance companies, and some services on the other hand, which have greater needs for ready cash, often carry short-term investment portfolios that represent a larger percent of total assets. The 1994 annual reports of May Department Store and Kmart show no holdings of short-term investments. Citibank carries short-term investments of about 5 percent of total assets. H&R Block holds short-term equity investments of almost 20 percent of total assets.

Short-term investments are listed in the current assets section of the balance sheet. It is important to realize that they are distinct from long-term investments in equity and debt securities, which are included in the long-term investments section. Two criteria must be met for an investment in a security to be considered current and thus warrant inclusion as a current asset:

1. The investment must be *readily marketable*.
2. Management must *intend to convert* the investment into cash within the time period of current assets (one year or the operating cycle, whichever is longer).

If either criterion is not met, the investment must be included in the long-term investments section.

THE EXISTENCE OF A READY MARKET

Readily marketable means that the security can be sold and converted into cash on demand. Stocks and bonds traded actively on the public stock exchanges (e.g., New York Stock Exchange, American Stock Exchange) usually meet this criterion. Objective market prices exist for such securities, which ensure that they can be sold on very short notice. In most cases all a company must do is request that its stockbroker sell the security.

Some securities, on the other hand, are not publicly traded, often because there are restrictions on their sale. Common stocks of privately held corporations, for example, may have very limited markets because restrictions exist on who can own them (e.g., ownership is sometimes limited to family members). Objective market prices do not exist for such securities, and they cannot be readily converted into cash. Accordingly, they fail to meet the readily marketable criterion and should be listed in the long-term investments section of the balance sheet.

THE INTENTION TO CONVERT: ANOTHER AREA OF SUBJECTIVITY

The second criterion, **intention to convert** the investment to cash, is much more difficult to determine objectively. Consequently, it can be a very difficult area for the auditor, who must determine whether a company's financial statements conform with generally accepted accounting principles. Simply asking managers whether they intend to sell securities within the time period of current assets does not provide sufficiently objective evidence. Recall that managers have incentives to window dress, which in this case might consist of including what would appropriately be a long-term investment in the current assets section. Such a decision might be made to increase a company's quick ratio, current ratio, or working capital number.

For example, several years ago PepsiCo acquired two Canadian soft drink bottling operations of the Seven-Up Company from Philip Morris Companies for approximately $246 million in cash. PepsiCo's financial report for that year indicated that "as it is management's intention to resell the Canadian bottling operations . . . [this investment] has been accounted for as a temporary investment and included . . . under the caption current assets." The decision to include this investment as current instead of long-term may certainly have been legitimate and, in fact, was allowed by PepsiCo's auditors, but it did serve to increase PepsiCo's current ratio by approximately 12 percent, from 1.01 to 1.13.[2]

Auditors often must deduce management's intention to convert by examining the company's past practices and the nature and size of the investment in question. Has the company in the past been in the habit of selling and buying short-term securities as its cash needs rise and fall? Securities are often purchased in large enough quantities to exert influence or control over another company. If so, conversion to cash in the near future would seem to be unlikely. Is the investee company a supplier or client of the investor company? Does the investor company have members on the board of directors of the investee company? Some securities are purchased as part of a fund for plant expansion or the retirement of long-term debt. Is this management's intention? These and similar kinds of questions must frequently be considered by auditors in their efforts to deduce what motivates management's behavior and, accordingly, how security investments should be classified on the balance sheet.

Auditors must always be aware that management may use its discretion to manipulate the reported dollar amounts on the financial statements. Even so, management needs to keep in mind that it is in the company's long-run best interest to exhibit upright, credible, and consistent reporting behavior. Stockholders, investors, creditors, and other interested parties will place greater value on financial reports they can trust.

TRADING AND AVAILABLE-FOR-SALE SECURITIES

LO 2 Investments in readily marketable equity securities, are classified into one of two categories: (1) trading securities or (2) available-for-sale securities. **Trading securities** are bought and held principally for the purpose of selling them in the near future with the objective of generating profit on short-term price changes. Investments not classified as trading securities are considered **available-for-sale** securities. Trading securities are always listed in the current section of the balance sheet, while available-for-sale securities are listed as current or long-term, depending on management's intention.[3]

Both trading and available-for-sale securities are accounted for using the **mark-to-market rule,** which states that readily marketable securities be carried on the bal-

---

2. The following year, consistent with management's intention, PepsiCo sold one of the bottling operations for approximately $45 million. However, the remaining investments were still disclosed as current assets on that year's balance sheet.

3. This chapter considers investments in equity securities, and this particular section is based on Statement of Financial Accounting Standards No. 115, "Accounting for Certain Investments in Debt and Equity Securities." Investments in debt securities are classified into one of three categories: (1) trading, (2) available-for-sale, or (3) held-to-maturity. The methods used to account for trading and available-for-sale debt securities are the same as those used for trading and available-for-sale equity securities, which are covered later in the chapter. The methods used to account for debt securities intended to be held to maturity are discussed in Appendix 11A.

ance sheet at current market value. The following example considers four separate events: (1) the purchase of the securities, (2) the declaration and receipt of related cash dividends, (3) the sale of the securities (at either a gain or a loss), and (4) changes in the prices of the securities on hand at the end of the accounting period. The first three events use the same methods to account for trading and available-for-sale securities. The fourth event, however, applies the mark-to-market rule differently.

PURCHASING TRADING AND AVAILABLE-FOR-SALE SECURITIES

When trading and available-for-sale securities are purchased, they are capitalized and recorded on the balance sheet at cost. As with other capitalized assets (inventory, long-term investments, fixed assets, and intangible assets), cost includes the purchase price as well as any *incidental acquisition costs*, such as brokerage commissions and taxes.[4] For example, assume that Goodyear Tire and Rubber Company purchased three different kinds of securities (Dow Chemical, Abbott Laboratories, and Eli Lilly) on December 1, 1996. Each security is readily marketable, and the company intends to sell the Dow and Abbott investments in the near future. Thus, the investments in Dow and Abbott are classified as trading securities, and the investment in Lilly is classified as available-for-sale. The following prices were paid.[5]

10 shares of Dow Chemical at $10/share	**$100**
20 shares of Abbott Laboratories at $12/share	**240**
15 shares of Eli Lilly at $20/share	**300**
Total cost	**$640**

Assuming that all prices *include* brokerage commissions, the following journal entry reflects the purchase of the three sets of securities.

Trading Securities (+A)	**340***	
Available-for-Sale Securities (+A)	**300**	
Cash (−A)		**640**
Purchased trading and available-for-sale securities.		

*$100 (Dow) + $240 (Abbott)

DECLARATION AND RECEIPT OF CASH DIVIDENDS

Cash dividends declared on trading and available-for-sale securities, to which Goodyear has a legal right, are initially recognized as a receivable and a revenue. When the cash dividend is received, the receivable is exchanged for cash. Continuing the example, suppose that on December 15, 1996, the board of directors of Abbott declared dividends of $1 per share, to be paid to the holders of its common stock on January 15, 1997. The following journal entries would be recorded in the books of Goodyear.

---

4. Actual brokerage commissions range from 1 percent to 5 percent.
5. For computational ease, the dollar amounts used in this example are unrealistically small. Multiplying the totals by 100 would produce numbers of a more realistic magnitude.

December 15 — at declaration of dividend:

Dividend Receivable (+A)   20*
     Dividend Income (R, +SE)   20
Recognized declaration of dividend.
*($1/share × 20 shares)

January 15—at receipt of dividend:

Cash (+A)   20
     Dividend Receivable (−A)   20
Received cash dividend.

SALE OF SECURITIES

When trading and available-for-sale securities are sold, the balance sheet value is removed from the books, and the difference between the balance sheet value and the proceeds from the sale is recognized as a realized gain or loss. If the proceeds exceed the balance sheet value, a **realized gain** is recognized; if they are less than the balance sheet value, a **realized loss** is recognized.

Continuing the example, assume that on December 4, Goodyear sold all ten shares of Dow Chemical stock for $13/share and ten of the fifteen shares of Eli Lilly stock for $10/share. Assuming that brokerage commissions have already been deducted from the sales price, these sales would give rise to the following journal entries:

Cash (+A)   130
     Trading Securities (Dow) (−A)   100*
     Realized Gain on Sale of Trading Securities (Ga, +SE)   30
Sold Dow Chemical stock.
*($10/share × 10 shares)

Cash (+A)   100
Realized Loss on Sale of Available-for-Sale Sec. (Lo, −SE)   100
     Available-for-Sale Securities (Lilly) (−A)   200**
Sold Lilly stock.
**($20/share × 10 shares)

The realized gain and loss accounts represent the difference between the sale proceeds and the balance sheet value of the sold securities and, therefore, provide a measure of management's performance with respect to the buying and selling of these securities. These accounts appear on the income statement and thus figure in the determination of net income. Chapter 13 points out that these book gains and losses, and others like them, appear in a special section of the income statement, entitled "Other Revenues and Expenses."

PRICE CHANGES OF SECURITIES ON HAND AT THE END OF THE ACCOUNTING PERIOD

At the end of each accounting period the current market values of all trading and available-for-sale securities held by the company are determined. Adjusting journal entries restate the balance sheet values of the securities to reflect their current market values. These adjustments give rise to **unrealized gains and losses**, often called **holding gains or losses.** In the case of trading securities these gains or losses are considered temporary accounts, appear on the income statement, and are reflected in retained earnings. *In the case of available-for-sale securities, the **unrealized price changes** are considered permanent accounts and are carried in the stockholders' equity section of the balance sheet.*

END-OF-PERIOD ADJUSTMENTS: TRADING SECURITIES

Continuing the example, assume that Goodyear held all 20 shares of Abbott on December 31, 1996, the end of the accounting period. The shares were purchased for $12 each and are presently trading for $15 each. To mark the investment to market value, an adjusting journal entry of the following form would be recorded on December 31.

Trading Securities (Abbott) (+A)	**60***	
Unrealized Gain on Trading Securities (Ga, +SE)		**60**

Revalued Abbott securities to market.
*[($15 − $12) × 20 shares]

If instead of $15/share, the Abbott shares were trading for $10 each on December 31, the following adjusting journal entry would have been recorded.

Unrealized Loss on Trading Securities (Lo, −SE)	**40***	
Trading Securities (Abbott) (−A)		**40**

Revalued Abbott securities to market.
*[($12 − $10) × 20 shares]

The unrealized holding gain (loss) represents the extent to which Goodyear's wealth increased (decreased) due to holding Abbott securities from December 1 to December 31. Because the investment in these securities is classified as trading and, therefore, is expected to be sold in the near future, the unrealized holding gain (loss) is considered part of Goodyear's income for the accounting period. Note also that the balance sheet value of the investment in Abbott on December 31, 1996, reflects the current market price of the securities, which is carried into the next period and used in the determination of future realized and unrealized gains and losses.

END-OF-PERIOD ADJUSTMENTS: AVAILABLE-FOR-SALE SECURITIES

Assume that Goodyear held five shares of Eli Lilly stock on December 31, 1996, with a current market value of $22 each. (Recall that fifteen shares were originally purchased on December 1 at $20 each, and ten shares were sold on December 4 for $10 each.) To mark the investment to market value, the following adjusting journal entry would be recorded on December 31.

Available-for-Sale Securities (+A)	**10***	
Unrealized Price Increase on Available-for-Sale Sec. (+SE)		**10**

Revalued Lilly securities to market.
*[($22 − $20) × 5 shares]

If instead of $22/share, the Lilly shares were trading for $14 each on December 31, the following adjusting journal entry would have been recorded.

Unrealized Price Decrease on Available-for-Sale Sec. (−SE)	**30***	
Available-for-Sale Securities (Lilly) (−A)		**30**

Revalued Lilly securities to market.
*[($20 − $14) × 5 shares]

Again, the unrealized price increase (decrease) represents the extent to which Goodyear's wealth increased (decreased) due to holding Lilly securities from December 1 to December 31. However, because the investment in these securities is classified as available-for-sale and, therefore, is not expected to be sold in the near future, the unrealized price change is not considered part of Goodyear's income for the accounting period. Instead, it is *disclosed in the stockholders' equity section of the balance sheet*. Unrealized price increases (credits) increase stockholders' equity, while unrealized price decreases (debits) decrease stockholders' equity. Both the market value of the investment and the dollar amount of the unrealized price change in the stockholders' equity account are carried into the next accounting period, and adjusted if the securities are sold or the market value of the securities change. Below, we illustrate how the balance sheet values of the investment and unrealized price change accounts are adjusted under two separate conditions: (1) if the securities are sold in the next period and (2) if the market value of the securities changes in the next period.

(1) If the Available-for-Sale Securities Are Sold. Assume as in the most recent example above that Eli Lilly shares were trading at $14 each as of December 31, 1996, and a $30 unrealized price decrease (debit) was disclosed in the stockholders' equity section of the December 31 balance sheet. If Goodyear sold all five Lilly shares for $16 each on April 5, 1997, the following journal entry would be recorded.

Cash (+A)	**80***	
Realized Loss on Available-for-Sale Sec. (Lo, −SE)	**20**	
Available-for-Sale Securities (Lilly) (−A)		**70****
Unrealized Price Decrease on Available-for-Sale Sec. (+SE)		**30**

Sold Lilly securities.
*($16/share × 5 shares]
**($14/share × 5 shares]

Note first that Cash is debited for the proceeds of the sale ($16/share × 5 shares). The $30 unrealized price decrease and the balance sheet value of the available-for-sale securities account, which reflects the market value of the securities as of December 31 ($14/share × 5 shares), are both written off the books because Goodyear no longer holds the securities. The realized loss of $20 is the "plug" that brings the entry into balance, but more importantly, it represents the difference between the original cost ($100 = $20/share × 5 shares) of the securities and the proceeds from the sale ($80).

(2) If the Market Value of the Available-for-Sale Securities Changes. Assume once again that Eli Lilly shares were trading at $14 each as of December 31, 1996, and a $30 unrealized price decrease was disclosed in the stockholders' equity section of the December 31 balance sheet. If on December 31, 1997, the securities are still held by Goodyear and the price has changed to $16, the following journal entry would be recorded.

Available-for-Sale Securities (Lilly) (+A)	**10***	
Unrealized Price Decrease on Available-for-Sale Sec. (+SE)		**10**

Revalued Lilly securities to market.
*[($16 − $14) × 5 shares]

In this case the available-for-sale account is adjusted to reflect its current market value and the unrealized price decrease account is reduced because the market price has increased since the previous balance sheet date. The December 31, 1997 balance in the Unrealized Price Decrease account in the stockholders' equity section of Goodyear's balance sheet would be $20 ($30 − $10).

RECLASSIFICATIONS AND PERMANENT MARKET VALUE DECLINES

Companies sometimes choose to change the classifications of security investments from trading to available-for-sale, or vice versa. In such cases unrealized holding gains or losses should be recognized immediately as income. When transferring securities from the trading to the available-for-sale classification, unrealized holding gains and losses that accrued since the most recent financial statement date should be recognized as income on the date of the transfer. When transferring securities from the available-for-sale to the trading classification, unrealized holding gains and losses from two sources should be recognized as income on the date of the transfer: (1) those that accrued since the most recent financial statement date and (2) the unrealized price change disclosed in the stockholders' equity section of the most recent balance sheet.

Investments sometimes suffer a permanent market value decline; the price declines and is not expected to recover. In such cases the security should be written down to its market value, and whether classified as trading or available-for-sale, a *realized loss* that reduces net income should be recognized immediately. Determining a permanent decline is very subjective, and GAAP provides very few guidelines. Perhaps the best way to assess such a decline is to consider the financial condition of the firm that issued the security. We return to this issue in Chapter 9 of this text when we discuss permanent write-downs of fixed assets and how management can use its discretion in this area to manage reported financial numbers.

DISCUSSION OF MARK-TO-MARKET ACCOUNTING

Mark-to-market accounting, which has only recently been adopted by the FASB, is a step in the direction of financial statements being based on market values. Many accounting theorists have argued for years that such statements provide more useful information than those based on historical cost. However, policymakers have been slow to adopt market value accounting because market values are subjective, and in certain cases (e.g., property, plant & equipment) may not be that relevant. Further, if reflected in current income, market value changes can create large fluctuations in earnings from one period to the next. Historically, management has resisted reporting such variation.

The form of mark-to-market accounting described above avoids these criticisms because it only applies to investment securities (securities available for sale), and these securities must have readily determinable and objective market values. In addition, the market value changes of only those securities intended to be sold in the very near future (trading securities) are reflected in current income. Unrealized price changes related to available-for-sale securities are not included on the income statement. This form of mark-to-market accounting, however, can be criticized on the basis of subjectivity because the distinction between trading and available-for-sale investments is unclear, relying heavily on management's intention. Thus, management has some control over net income through the choice of classifying investments as either trading or available-for-sale and, as noted above, in determining a permanent market decline. On balance, though mark-to-market accounting as applied to equity investments represents a move toward more useful financial statements. As the markets for other assets (e.g., inventories and long-term assets) become more like the security markets (i.e., efficiently producing market prices for those assets), possibly other forms of mark-to-market accounting applied to inventories and long-term assets will become generally accepted.

LONG-TERM EQUITY INVESTMENTS

LO 3 As indicated earlier in this chapter, companies make investments in the equity securities of other companies primarily for two reasons: (1) investment income in the form of dividends and stock price appreciation and (2) management influence, where the voting power of the purchased shares allows the investor company to exert some control over the board of directors and management of the investee company. The primary motivation behind the long-term equity investments for most major U.S. companies is reason (2), influence over the investee company's operations and management.

Most large, well-known U.S. companies are constantly involved in acquisitions, whereby they purchase all, or a majority, of the outstanding common stock of another company and then change the investee company's operations and/or management. Several years ago, for example, General Electric (GE) purchased all of the outstanding common stock of RCA Corporation, which at the time owned National Broadcasting Company (NBC), for $6.4 billion. As reported in GE's financial report, "subsequent to the acquisition, GE sold . . . a number of RCA and NBC operations whose activities were not compatible with GE's long-range strategic plans."

In another example, DuPont stated in a recent financial report that in one year alone "the company completed six major acquisitions for a total purchase price of $1.2 billion." These investments included majority interests of the outstanding common stock of Inland Steel Coal Company, Sierra Coal Company, and Tau Laboratories, Inc. In each case DuPont made significant changes to either the operations or the management of the acquired companies.

It is also common to exert influence over the operations and management of a company by purchasing a significant portion, but less than a majority (51 percent), of the company's outstanding common stock. *Accounting Trends and Techniques* (New York: AICPA, 1994) reports that, of the 600 major U.S. companies surveyed, well over half reported such investments. For example, as of January 25, 1995, Kmart held a significant portion, but less than 51 percent, of the outstanding common stock of three companies: Meldisco Footware (49 percent), OfficeMax, Inc. (25 percent), and Sports Authority, Inc. (29 percent).

ACCOUNTING FOR LONG-TERM EQUITY INVESTMENTS

Since long-term investments in equity securities are commonly made to exert influence over the operations and management of the investee company, financial accounting standards define the appropriate accounting method in terms of the potential for such influence—specifically, in terms of the percentage of outstanding voting stock owned by the investor company.

If the investor company owns less than 20 percent of the outstanding voting stock of the investee company, the potential for influence is relatively small, and the two entities can be viewed as independent. The equity investment, therefore, is accounted for using either the mark-to-market method or the cost method. When the percentage of ownership is between 20 percent and 50 percent, the investor company has the potential to exert "significant influence" over the investee company, and the two entities cannot be viewed as completely independent. The investor company uses the equity method to account for the equity investment. When the percentage of ownership is greater than 50 percent, the investor company has "control" over the investee company, and for accounting purposes, the two entities are viewed as one, and consolidated financial statements are prepared. Figure 8–1 summarizes the conditions that define the methods used to account for long-term equity investments.

FIGURE 8–1	PERCENTAGE OF STOCK OWNERSHIP	POTENTIAL TO INFLUENCE	ACCOUNTING METHOD
Accounting for long-term investments in equity securities	Less than 20%	Small	Mark-to-market or cost method
	20%–50%	Significant	Equity method
	Greater than 50%	Control	Consolidated statements

The following discussion presents the mechanics involved in applying the cost and equity methods and the conditions under which each method is used.[6]

THE COST METHOD

LO 4 Some equity securities have no readily determinable market values. Equity securities in corporations whose securities are not publicly traded (i.e., closely held corporations or private companies), for example, may have restrictions on trading and therefore have no public market values. Relatively small investments (less than 20 percent of the outstanding voting stock) in such securities, which by definition cannot easily be liquidated, are accounted for using the **cost method**. It is impossible to apply the mark-to-market method to such securities because their market values cannot be determined.

Applying the cost method is very straightforward. Purchases of equity securities are recorded at cost, including incidental costs of acquisition; dividends are recorded as income when declared; and sales, when they eventually occur, give rise to realized book gains or losses reflected on the income statement.

To illustrate, suppose that on January 15, 1996, Beldon Inc. purchased 100 equity securities in a closely held corporation for $10 per share. On December 15 Beldon received a $50 dividend that had been declared on November 29. No other activity occurred in the account until May 5, 1997, when Beldon sold the securities privately for $7 each. The journal entries contained in Figure 8–2 would reflect these transactions.

---

6. Long-term investments in securities classified as available-for-sale are accounted for under the mark-to-market method, which was covered in the previous section. Also, consolidated statements are only briefly introduced in the text of this chapter. More complete discussions can be found in Appendix 8A as well as in intermediate and advanced financial accounting texts.

FIGURE 8–2	**1996:**			
The cost method of accounting for long-term equity investments	**Jan. 15**	**Long-Term Investment in Equity Securities (+A)**	**1,000**	
		Cash (−A)		**1,000**
		Purchased 100 equity shares at $10 per share.		
	Nov. 29	**Dividend Receivable (+A)**	**50**	
		Dividend Income (R, +SE)		**50**
		Declared a dividend to be received.		
	Dec. 15	**Cash (+A)**	**50**	
		Dividend Receivable (−A)		**50**
		Received previously declared $50 dividend.		
	1997:			
	May 5	**Cash (+A)**	**700**	
		Loss on Sale of Long-Term Equity Securities (Lo, −SE)	**300**	
		Long-Term Investment in Equity Securities (−A)		**1,000**
		Sold 100 equity shares, originally purchased at $10 each, for $7 per share.		

THE EQUITY METHOD

Some companies have the ability to significantly influence the operating decisions and management policies of other companies. Such influence indicates a substantive economic relationship between the two companies and may be evidenced, for example, by representation on the board of directors, the interchange of management personnel between companies, frequent or significant transactions between companies, or the technical dependency of one company on the other. Significant investments in the equity securities (voting stock) of another company may also indicate significant influence and a substantive economic relationship. To achieve a reasonable degree of uniformity, the accounting profession concluded that an investment of 20 percent or more in the voting stock of another company represents a "significant influence" and that equity investments from 20 percent to 50 percent of the voting stock should be accounted for using the **equity method**.

The accounting procedures used to apply the equity method reflect a substantive economic relationship between the investor and the investee companies. The equity investment is originally recorded on the investor's books at cost but is adjusted each subsequent period for changes in the net assets of the investee. As the balance sheet value of the investee increases or decreases, so does the Long-Term Equity Investment account of the investor.

Specifically, the carrying value of the long-term investment on the investor's balance sheet is (1) periodically increased (decreased) by the investor's proportionate share of the net income (loss) of the investee and (2) decreased by all dividends transferred to the investor from the investee.[7] In other words, the equity method of accounting acknowledges a close economic link between the two companies. Investee earnings, which indicate net asset growth, and investee dividends, which represent net asset reductions, are reflected proportionately on the balance sheet of the investor.

---

7. The investor's account is also decreased by an amount that represents the amortization of goodwill recognized on the purchase. Goodwill is discussed later in the chapter, in Appendix 8A, and in a number of other places throughout the remainder of the text. For purposes of illustrating the equity method here, however, we make the simplifying assumption that no goodwill is recognized on the purchase. Intermediate and advanced coverages of the equity method do not make such an assumption.

To illustrate, assume that on January 1, 1996, American Electric Company purchased 40 percent of the outstanding voting stock of Masley Corporation for $40,000. During 1996 Masley recognized net income of $10,000 and declared (Dec. 1) and paid (Dec. 20) dividends of $1,500 to American Electric. During 1997 Masley recognized a net loss of $5,000 and declared (Dec. 1) and paid (Dec. 20) only a $500 dividend to American Electric. Under the equity method, the journal entries contained in Figure 8–3 would be recorded on the books of American Electric.

FIGURE 8–3	**1996:**			
The equity method of accounting for long-term equity investments	**Jan. 1**	Long-Term Investment in Equity Securities (+A)	40,000	
		Cash (−A)		40,000
		Purchased 40% of Masley's outstanding shares.		
	Dec. 1	Dividend Receivable (+A)	1,500	
		Long-Term Investment in Equity Securities (−A)		1,500
		Declared $1,500 dividend by Masley.		
	Dec. 20	Cash (+A)	1,500	
		Dividend Receivable (−A)		1,500
		Received dividend declared on December 1.		
	Dec. 31	Long-Term Investment in Equity Securities (+A)	4,000	
		Income from Long-Term Equity Investments (R, +SE)		4,000
		Recognized 40% of Masley's 1996 net income ($10,000 × 40%).		
	1997:			
	Dec. 1	Dividend Receivable (+A)	500	
		Long-Term Investment in Equity Securities (−A)		500
		Declared dividend by Masley.		
	Dec. 20	Cash (+A)	500	
		Dividend Receivable (−A)		500
		Received dividend declared on December 1.		
	Dec. 31	Loss on Long-Term Equity Investment (Lo, −SE)	2,000	
		Long-Term Investment in Equity Securities (−A)		2,000
		Recognized 40% of Masley's 1997 net loss ($5,000 × 40%).		

It is important to understand how the equity method reflects a significant economic relationship between the investor and investee companies. The net income (loss) of the investee serves to proportionately increase (decrease) the investment account of the investor. Thus the investee's net asset growth or decline is reflected on the investor's balance sheet and income statement. Note also that dividends transferred from the investee to the investor are not treated as revenue on the investor's books. Revenue is recognized when the investor's proportionate share of the investee's net income is recorded, not when the dividends are declared or transferred. Dividends are simply treated as an exchange of assets on the investor's books. The Long-Term Investment account is decreased; Dividends Receivable is increased on the date of declaration; and the receivable is exchanged for cash on the date of payment.

Equity investments in the amount of 20–50 percent of an investee company's voting stock are very common for major U.S. companies. *Accounting Trends and*

Techniques (New York, AICPA, 1994) reports that, of the 600 companies surveyed, over 50 percent reported using the equity method of accounting. Figure 8–4 indicates the importance of investments accounted for under the equity method, relative to total assets, to several major U.S. corporations as of December 31, 1994. Investee companies that are 20-50 percent owned by investor companies are often referred to as **affiliated** or **associated companies**.

FIGURE 8–4	COMPANY	AMOUNT OF INVESTMENT (MILLIONS OF DOLLARS)	PERCENTAGE OF TOTAL ASSETS
The relative importance of investments in affiliate companies (selected U.S. companies)	Time Warner	$ 985	6%
	Scott Paper	227	4
	Kmart	368	2
	Texaco	3,906	2
	Goodyear Tire and Rubber Co.	133	1

Source: 1994 financial reports.

Income from equity investments can also represent a material percentage of net income. In recent annual reports, for example, Alcoa, J.C. Penney, and Dow Chemical reported income from affiliate companies (as a percentage of total net income) of 10 percent, 6 percent, and 3 percent, respectively. The following excerpt, taken from the 1994 financial report of Goodyear Tire and Rubber Co., describes how the company accounts for equity investments in affiliate companies:

The company's investments in 20% to 50% owned companies in which it has the ability to exercise significant influence over operating and financial policies are accounted for in the equity method. Accordingly, the company's share of the earnings of these companies is included in consolidated net income.

SOME CAUTIONS TO FINANCIAL STATEMENT USERS ABOUT THE EQUITY METHOD

Several features about the equity method should cause financial report users to view it carefully. First, the equity method provides another reason why a company's net income (loss) differs from its cash flow from operations. The income recognized from the investee company rarely equals the cash dividends received by the investor. *Forbes* magazine describes the equity method as "misleading" because "the investor company never really sees any nondividend cash from the investee company" on which it often recognizes substantial income.[8] For example, in 1995 Kmart recognized $80 million in income from affiliate companies, which represented 27% of its 1995 earnings. However, Kmart received only $38 million in cash dividends from the affiliates. An astute user can learn how much cash was received from affiliate investments by examining the operating section of the statement of cash flows. In Kmart's case, the $42 million difference between reported equity income ($80 million) and cash received ($38 million) was subtracted from net income in the calculation of net cash from operations and described as "undistributed equity income."

8. Aaron Bernstein, "Reading Between the Lines," *Forbes*, May 10, 1982, p. 78.

In addition, the equity method ignores price (market value) changes in the affiliate's equity securities. For example, price decreases, even if substantial, are not recognized on the investor's books and, in fact, may even be accompanied by the recognition of income and the receipt of dividends if the affiliate reports positive income and declares dividends during the period of the price decline. Astute users should keep track of the price changes of the affiliate's equity shares, if they are publicly available.

Third, the percent of ownership (20%–50%) is not always a valid indication of "significant influence." Influence comes in many different forms. Time Warner, for example, was able to block a bid by Turner Broadcasting Systems (TBS) to acquire CBS even though Time Warner owned less than 20% of TBS stock. Time Warner did, however, have two members on the TBS board of directors. Similarly, it is possible to exert a controlling influence with less than 51% of the stock, especially when the remaining stock is owned by stockholders who represent a wide variety of interests.

Finally, as we discuss later in this chapter, using the equity method can be considered a method of off-balance-sheet financing because it fails to reflect the liabilities of the affiliate on the balance sheet of the investor company. Financial accounting standards require that a summary of the financial statements of all affiliate companies be included in the footnotes of the investor's financial statements. Users should review these summaries to see if including the affiliate's assets and liabilities on the investor's balance sheet would affect solvency and liquidity ratios.

BUSINESS ACQUISITIONS, MERGERS, AND CONSOLIDATED FINANCIAL STATEMENTS

L O 5 A **business acquisition** occurs when an investor company acquires a **controlling interest** (more than 50 percent of the voting stock) in another company. If the two companies continue as separate legal entities, the investor company is referred to as the **parent company**, and the investee company is called the **subsidiary**. In 1994, for example, Procter & Gamble purchased 100% of the stock of Revlon, Inc.'s worldwide Max Factor and Beatrix lines of cosmetics and fragrances for over $1 billion. These companies now operate as Procter & Gamble subsidiaries. In such cases the parent prepares **consolidated financial statements** (including the income statement, balance sheet, statement of retained earnings, statement of cash flows, and statement of stockholders' equity). Consolidated statements ignore the fact that the parent and the subsidiary are actually separate legal entities and, for reporting purposes, treat the two companies as a single operating unit.

Consolidated statements are prepared for financial accounting purposes only. The parent and the subsidiary maintain separate legal status. In many respects they may continue to operate as relatively independent entities, and the subsidiary maintains a separate set of financial statements. Only because the parent has a controlling interest over the subsidiary do professional accounting standards require that the financial condition of the two companies be represented to the public as one.

A **merger**, or **business combination**, occurs when two or more companies combine to form a single legal entity. In most cases the assets and liabilities of the smaller company are merged into those of the larger, surviving company. The stock of at least one company, usually the smaller one, is often retired, and it ceases to exist as a separate entity. When Chemical Bank was merged into Chase Manhattan in 1995, for example, the surviving entity was named Chase Manhattan. Technically speaking, consolidated financial statements are not prepared after a merger because no parent/subsidiary relationship exists. At least one of the companies involved in the combination no longer exists. However, the financial statements of the surviving company do reflect the assets and liabilities of the merged entities.

Most business acquisitions and combinations consummate when cash and/or other assets (often stock) of the parent are paid to the stockholders of the subsidiary in exchange for the assets and liabilities of the subsidiary.[9] Such transactions are commonly accounted for under the **purchase method**, when the assets and liabilities of the subsidiary are recorded on the balance sheet of the parent at fair market value (FMV), and the difference between the purchase price and the net FMV of the subsidiary's assets and liabilities is recorded as goodwill.[10] As noted in Chapter 9 and Appendix 9A, which cover long-lived assets, goodwill (an intangible asset) must be amortized over a period not to exceed forty years.

For example, when Delta Air Lines, Inc., purchased all the outstanding shares of Western Air Lines, Inc., for $787 million, the purchase price consisted of $383 million in cash and Delta common stock valued at $404 million. Delta received the assets and liabilities of Western, which at the time of the transaction had fair market values as described in Figure 8–5.

FIGURE 8–5 Computation of goodwill		FAIR MARKET VALUE (IN MILLIONS)
Current assets		$349
Property, plant, and equipment		748
Other assets		24
Less: Current liabilities	$310	
Long-term debt	431	(741)
Net FMV of Western's assets and liabilities		$380
Less: Purchase price		787
Goodwill (excess of purchase price over FMV of net assets)		$407

In a simplified sense, to record the purchase, Delta made the following journal entry. The assets and liabilities of Western were then included on the balance sheet of Delta.

Current Assets (+A)	349	
Property, Plant, and Equipment (+A)	748	
Other Assets (+A)	24	
Goodwill (+A)	407	
Current Liabilities (+L)		310
Long-Term Liabilities (+L)		431
Cash (−A)		383
Common Stock (+SE)		404

Purchased Western Air Lines.

---

9. In the following discussion we use the terms *parent* and *subsidiary* to denote the investor and investee companies. In the case of business combinations, however, the term *parent* should be interpreted as the survivor company and the term *subsidiary* as the merged company.

10. Another method used to account for a business combination is called the *pooling-of-interests method*. Goodwill is not recognized, and the assets, liabilities, and retained earnings of the subsidiary are recorded on the balance sheet of the parent at cost. This method is discussed in advanced accounting texts.

Accounting for business acquisitions and mergers and preparing consolidated financial statements are actually more complex than we have indicated here. Further discussion can be found in Appendix 8A and in intermediate and advanced financial accounting texts.

THE EQUITY METHOD OR CONSOLIDATED STATEMENTS?

Accounting for an equity investment under the equity method can give rise to financial statements that are much different from those prepared as consolidated statements. The following example describes an equity investment, comparing the balance sheet produced under the equity method to a consolidated balance sheet.

Figure 8–6 shows the December 31, 1996, balance sheets of Megabucks, a large manufacturing company, and Tiny Inc., a smaller distribution outlet. Note initially that the debt/equity ratio of Megabucks is 67 percent ($20,000 ÷ $30,000), and assume further that on that day Megabucks purchased the outstanding stock of Tiny Inc. for $10,000.

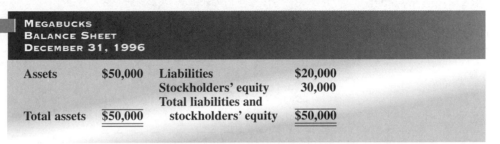

FIGURE 8–6

The balance sheets of Megabucks and Tiny Inc.

MEGABUCKS
BALANCE SHEET
DECEMBER 31, 1996

Assets	$50,000	Liabilities	$20,000
		Stockholders' equity	30,000
		Total liabilities and	
Total assets	$50,000	stockholders' equity	$50,000

TINY INCORPORATED
BALANCE SHEET
DECEMBER 31, 1996

Assets	$20,000	Liabilities	$15,000
		Stockholders' equity	5,000
		Total liabilities and	
Total assets	$20,000	stockholders' equity	$20,000

THE EQUITY METHOD

Under the equity method, Megabucks would record the following journal entry.

Long-Term Investment (+A)	10,000	
Cash (−A)		10,000

Purchased Tiny Inc. for $10,000.

Note that the journal entry to record the investment has no effect on the total assets, total liabilities, total stockholders' equity, or the debt/equity ratio of Megabucks. The transaction is simply recorded as an exchange of two assets, a long-term investment and cash. In future periods under the equity method, Megabucks' total assets will reflect the net incomes (losses) reported by Tiny Inc., less any dividends.

CONSOLIDATED FINANCIAL STATEMENTS

If Megabucks accounts for this acquisition as a purchase and prepares consolidated financial statements, it would record the transaction with the following journal entry. Assume that Tiny's assets and liabilities are reported on its balance sheet at FMV.

Assets (+A)	20,000	
Goodwill (+A)	5,000	
Liabilities (+L)		15,000
Cash (−A)		10,000

Acquired Tiny Inc. for $10,000.

In this case both the assets and the liabilities of Megabucks would be increased by $15,000. The resulting consolidated balance sheet would appear as in Figure 8–7. Note that the debt/equity ratio is now 1.17 ($35,000 ÷ $30,000). Treating the transaction as a purchase and preparing a consolidated balance sheet, as opposed to using the equity method, increases the debt/equity ratio of Megabucks from .67 to 1.17.

FIGURE 8–7	MEGABUCKS BALANCE SHEET DECEMBER 31, 1996

Consolidated balance sheet

Assets	$65,000	Liabilities	$35,000
		Stockholders' equity	30,000
		Total liabilities and	
Total assets	$65,000	stockholders' equity	$65,000

This difference between the equity method and preparing consolidated financial statements has encouraged many companies in the past to choose the equity method when possible, especially when the investee company carries considerable debt. Such a choice may come in the form of purchasing slightly less than 50 percent of the investee company's common stock, purchasing over 50 percent and claiming that "control is temporary or does not rest with the majority owner," or acquiring 100 percent and claiming that preparing consolidated statements would distort the financial statements because the subsidiary is so unlike the parent. In *Forbes* magazine, the national director of accounting and auditing at Seidman & Seidman, a major accounting firm, noted that the equity method can be viewed as a method of off-balance-sheet financing. He pointed out that using the equity method can "present a more favorable impression of debt/equity ratios, working capital ratios, and returns on assets invested in the business."[11] Consequently, financial statement users and auditors should pay special attention to cases where some question arises about whether the equity method should be used or consolidated financial statements should be prepared.

ACCOUNTING FOR EQUITY INVESTMENTS: A SUMMARY

Figure 8–8 provides a framework that summarizes the methods used to account for investments in equity securities. It summarizes the appropriate accounting methods for all (short-term and long-term) investments in equity securities. In general, three

11. Ann McGrath, "The Best of Both Worlds," *Forbes*, September 26, 1983, pp. 102, 106.

FIGURE 8–8

Accounting for equity securities (Common Shares of Other Companies)

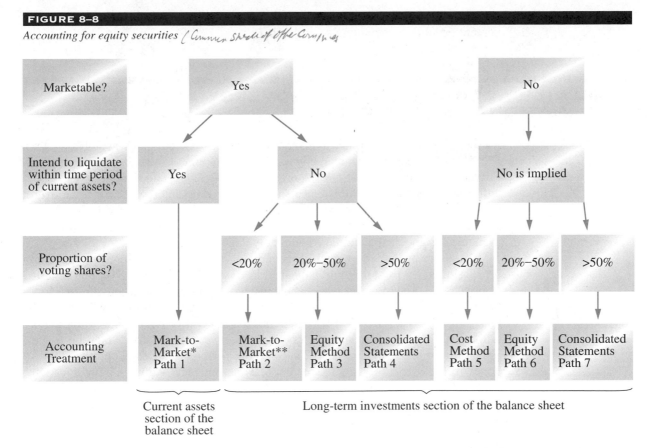

Current assets
section of the
balance sheet

Long-term investments section of the balance sheet

*Trading or available-for-sale securities, depending on expected liquidations.
**Available-for-sale securities.

questions must be answered before the appropriate accounting method and disclosure can be determined: (1) Is the security marketable? (2) Does management intend to liquidate the security within the time period of current assets? and (3) Is the proportion of ownership less than 20 percent, between 20 percent and 50 percent, or greater than 50 percent?

If the purchased equity securities are marketable, and management intends to liquidate them within the time period of current assets, the investment is considered short-term. This is regardless of the proportion of ownership and whether it is considered trading or available-for sale, and it is carried on the balance sheet at market value (Path 1). If the purchased securities are marketable, but management does not intend to liquidate them within the time period of current assets, the investment is considered long-term. Such long-term investments, where less than 20 percent of the voting shares are held, are considered available-for-sale and are carried on the balance sheet at market value (Path 2). Long-term investments of between 20 percent and 50 percent of the voting shares are accounted for using the equity method (Path 3). Long-term investments of 50 percent or more of the voting shares give rise to consolidated statements (Path 4).

Equity investments that are not marketable are accounted for using the cost method if they represent less than 20 percent of the voting shares (Path 5), or the equity method if they represent an investment of between 20 percent and 50 percent

(Path 6). Consolidated statements should be prepared if such investments represent 50 percent or more of the voting stock (Path 7).

GOODWILL ACCOUNTING: CONTROVERSY AND INTERNATIONAL IMPLICATIONS

LO 6 U.S. accounting rules require that when one company acquires another, goodwill must be recognized in the amount of the excess of the acquisition price over the FMV of the acquired company's assets and liabilities. The goodwill account appears on the balance sheet and must be amortized to income over a period of time not to exceed forty years. Further, only recently have U.S. tax rules been changed to allow a tax deduction for amortized goodwill. This deduction is not available for goodwill acquired prior to July 25, 1991.

These two aspects of goodwill accounting have met with much recent opposition in the United States. An article published in *Business Week* (July 31, 1989) entitled "Goodwill Is Making a Lot of People Angry" reported that when Philip Morris Company acquired Kraft, Inc., it recognized over $11 billion of goodwill, which virtually ensured that Philip Morris would not report positive net income for a number of years in the future because the goodwill amortization expense would be at least $275 million per year. Similarly, Time Warner currently carries about $8 billion of goodwill left over from the 1990 merger of Time, Inc., and Warner Communications, Inc., and this $8 billion must also be charged against future income without the benefit of a tax deduction.

ETHICS IN THE REAL WORLD

The methods for recognizing and amortizing goodwill acquired when a company is purchased vary widely across different countries. In the U.S. goodwill must be amortized to earnings over a period of time not to exceed 40 years, while many countries, such as Switzerland and Britain, deduct goodwill directly from the stockholders' equity—avoiding the income statement altogether. Some claim that these differences give Swiss and British companies advantages over U.S. firms when bidding to acquire other companies. The recent takeover battle for Gerber Products Co., for example, included bids by a number of U.S. companies, including Quaker Oats, which entered a bid of $35 per share. Swiss drug giant Sandoz Ltd. won the battle quickly, however, by raising the ante to $53 per share. Some investment bankers claimed that the favorable accounting treatment for goodwill practiced in Switzerland gave Sandoz the advantage it needed to outbid Quaker Oats.

These accounting differences also seem to have discouraged certain large foreign companies from raising capital on the U.S. stock exchanges. For example, *Forbes* (June 20, 1994) reports that Nestle, a Swiss food giant, says it is not willing to redo its financial statements to conform to U.S. GAAP (a requirement of the U.S. stock exchanges). The main reason is that its earnings would look about 10% lower, primarily due to the more conservative goodwill treatment in the U.S.

These accounting differences have elicited complaints from U.S. businesses that certain foreign countries are allowing liberal accounting methods, which provide unfair trade advantages for their local companies and capital markets.

ETHICAL ISSUE

Is it ethical for the government or standard-setting body in a particular country to set accounting standards that are designed to provide international economic advantages enjoyed solely by the companies and capital markets in that country?

Some claim that these accounting and tax rules put U.S. corporations at a distinct disadvantage when bidding against foreign buyers for acquisitions because most foreign countries have less restrictive rules concerning goodwill accounting. In Britain, for example, goodwill must be recognized on an acquisition, but it is amortized directly to stockholders' equity without reducing reported earnings. *Forbes* (January 23, 1989) suggests that this rule enabled Grand Metropolitan, a large British firm, to outbid other U.S. firms for Pillsbury. Peter Berger, a partner at Arthur Andersen, notes that U.S. chief executives are hesitant to get into bidding wars with their British counterparts because "chief executives are compensated based on earnings per share, [which] makes them very wary about taking a big bite of goodwill." In Japan and Germany, two other countries who have established strong ownership positions in the United States, goodwill amortization has been an allowable tax deduction for many years.

Many accountants believe that as business becomes increasingly globalized and transnational, more uniform international accounting standards are needed. This concern put more pressure on the *International Accounting Standards Committee* (see discussion in Chapter 1), a London-based organization, to promulgate rules that reduce imbalances like those associated with goodwill accounting. However, as *Forbes* (November 28, 1988) points out:

[This organization] has been bogged down by international political bickering for years, [which has allowed U.S.] accountants to help foreigners buy pieces of America at bargain prices.

REVIEW PROBLEM I

The following information relates to the marketable security investments of Macon Construction. Securities held on December 31, 1996, are described in the table below. AAA and BBB are classified as trading securities, and CCC is classified as available-for-sale.

SECURITIES	NO. OF SHARES	COST/SHARE	TOTAL COST	VALUE/SHARE	TOTAL MARKET VALUE
AAA	10	$14	$140	$17	$170
BBB	25	15	375	14	350
CCC	15	8	120	10	150
			$635		$670

Early in 1997 Macon sold all of its investment in AAA securities for $18 per share. The company also sold five shares of BBB for $13 per share. During 1997 Macon received dividends of $3 per share on the remaining twenty shares of BBB, and dividends of $2 per share were declared, but not yet received, on the fifteen shares of CCC stock. The per-share market values of BBB and CCC on December 31, 1997, were $12 and $9, respectively. During 1998, Macon sold the remaining twenty shares of BBB stock for $13 per share and the 15 shares of CCC for $11 per share.

REQUIRED:
a. Prepare the appropriate journal entries that would be required for 1996 under the mark-to-market rule.
b. Prepare all appropriate journal entries to reflect 1997 activities involving short-term equity investments.
c. Prepare the journal entries to reflect the sales of short-term equity investments.

SOLUTION:

a. 1. **Trading Securities (AAA) (+A)**   30*
            Unrealized Gain on Trading Securities (R, +SE)   30
        Revalued AAA securities to market.
        *10 sh. × $3 per sh.

    2. **Unrealized Loss on Trading Securities (Lo, −SE)**   25
            Trading Securities (BBB) (−A)   25*
        Revalued BBB securities to market.
        *25 sh. × $1 per sh.

    3. **Available-for-Sale Securities (CCC) (+A)**   30*
            **Unrealized Price Increase on Available-for-Sale
                Securities (+SE)**   30
        Revalued CCC securities to market.
        *15 sh. × $2 per sh.

b. 1. **Cash (+A)**   180*
            Trading Securities (−A)   170**
            Realized Gain on Sale of Trading Sec. (Ga, +SE)   10
        Sold ten shares of AAA stock at $18.
        *10 sh. × $18 per sh.
        **10 sh. × $17 per sh.

    2. **Cash (+A)**   65*
        Realized Loss on Sale of Trading Sec. (Lo, −SE)   5
            Trading Securities (−A)   70**
        Sold five shares of BBB stock at $13 per share.
        *5 sh. × $13 per sh.
        **5 sh. × $14 per sh.

    3. **Cash (+A)**   60*
        Dividend Receivable (+A)   30**
            Dividend Revenue (R, +SE)   90
        *Received BBB dividends and declared
        dividends on CCC stock.*
        *20 sh. × $3 per sh.
        **15 sh. × $2 per sh.

    4. **Unrealized Loss on Trading Securities (Lo, −SE)**   40
            Trading Securities (BBB) (−A)   40*
        Revalued BBB shares to market.
        *20 sh. × $2 per sh.

    5. **Unrealized Price Increase on Available-for-Sale
            Securities (−SE)**   15
            Available-for-Sale Securities (CCC) (−A)   15*
        Revalued CCC shares to market.
        *15 sh. × $1 per sh.

c. 1. **Cash (+A)**   260*
            Trading Securities (BBB) (−A)   240**
            Realized Gain on Trading Securities (R, +SE)   20
        Sold twenty shares of BBB stock at $13 per share.
        *20 sh. × $13 per sh.
        **20 sh. × $12 per sh.

    2. **Cash (+A)**   165*
        **Unrealized Price Increase on Available-for-Sale
            Sec. (−SE)**   15
            Available-for-Sale Securities (CCC) (−A)   135**
            **Realized Gain on Available-for-Sale
                Sec. (Ga, +SE)**   45
        Sold fifteen shares of CCC stock at $11 per share.
        *15 sh. × $11 per sh.
        **15 sh. × $9 per sh.

REVIEW PROBLEM II

Trailor Corporation entered into the three transactions listed below on January 1, 1996. For each transaction, prepare the related journal entries that would be recorded over the subsequent two-year period.

a. On January 1, 1996, Trailor purchased 30 percent of the outstanding common stock of Rowers Company for $50,000. Income reported by Rowers during 1996 and 1997 was $15,000 and $8,000, respectively. Rowers declared and paid dividends to Trailor in the amount of $3,000 during each of the two years.

b. On January 1, 1996, Trailor purchased 100 percent of the outstanding common stock of Kleece Corporation for $20,000. The FMVs of the individual assets and liabilities of Kleece Corporation, as of the time of the acquisition, were $40,000 and $28,000, respectively. Trailor amortizes goodwill over a forty-year period.

SOLUTION:

a. **1996:**

Jan. 1	**Investment in Equity Securities (+A)**	**50,000**	
	Cash (−A)		**50,000**
	Purchased Rowers common stock.		

Dec. 31	**Investment in Equity Securities (+A)**	**4,500***	
	Income from Equity Investments (R, +SE)		**4,500**
	Recognized income from equity securities.		
	*$15,000 × 30%		

	Cash (+A)	**3,000**	
	Investment in Equity Securities (−A)		**3,000**
	*Recognized 30% of Rowers' income and received dividends.**		
	*Assume that dividends were declared and paid on the same day.		

1997:

	Investment in Equity Securities (+A)	**2,400***	
	Income from Equity Invest. (R, +SE)		**2,400**
	*$8,000 × 30%		

	Cash (+A)	**3,000**	
	Investment in Equity Securities (−A)		**3,000**
	*Recognized 30% of Rowers' income and received dividends.**		
	*Assume that dividends were declared and paid on the same day.		

b. **1996:**

Jan. 1	**Assets (+A)**	**40,000**	
	Goodwill (+A)	**8,000**	
	Liabilities (+L)		**28,000**
	Cash (−A)		**20,000**
	Acquired Kleece Corporation.		

Dec. 31	**Amortization Expense (E, −SE)**	**200***	
	Goodwill (−A)		**200**
	Amortized goodwill.		
	*$8,000 ÷ 40 years		

1997:

Dec. 31	**Amortization Expense (E, −SE)**	**200***	
	Goodwill (−A)		**200**
	Amortized goodwill.		
	*$8,000 ÷ 40 years		

SUMMARY OF LEARNING OBJECTIVES

 Identify the criteria that must be met before a security can be listed in the current assets section of the balance sheet.

Two criteria must be met before an investment in a security can be listed in the current assets section of the balance sheet: (1) the security must be able to be converted into cash within the time period that defines current assets (i.e., the current operating cycle or one year, whichever is longer), and (2) management must intend to convert the security into cash within the time period that defines current assets.

LO 2 *Define trading and available-for-sale securities, and explain how the mark-to-market rule is used to account for them.*

Trading securities are bought and held principally for the purpose of selling them in the near future with the objective of generating profit on short-term price changes. Investments not classified as trading securities are considered available-for-sale securities. Trading securities are always listed in the current assets section of the balance sheet, while available-for-sale securities are listed as current or long-term, depending on management's intention. In applying the mark-to-market rule to trading available-for-sale securities, four separate events must be considered.

1. *Purchase of securities.* When the securities are purchased, they are capitalized and recorded on the balance sheet at cost. The cost includes the purchase price as well as any incidental acquisition costs, such as brokerage commissions and taxes.
2. *Declaration and payment of dividends.* Cash dividends declared on these securities are initially recognized as receivables and revenues. When a cash dividend is received, the receivable is exchanged for cash.
3. *Sale of securities.* When these securities are sold, their balance sheet value is removed from the books and the difference between this amount and the proceeds of the sale is recognized on the books as either a realizable gain or a realized loss.
4. *End-of-accounting period adjustment.* Both trading and available-for-sale securities are adjusted to current market value at the end of the accounting period. In the case of trading securities, the related unrealized holding gain or loss is reflected directly in income; in the case of available-for-sale securities, the related unrealized price change is booked to stockholders' equity.

LO 3 *Explain why companies make long-term investments in equity securities.*

Companies make long-term investments in the equity securities of other companies for two primary reasons: (1) investment income in the form of dividends and/or stock price appreciation and (2) management influence, where the voting power of the purchased shares allows the investor company to exert influence or control over the board of directors and management of the investee company. The primary motivation behind the long-term equity investments for most major U.S. companies is reason (2), influence over the investee company's operations and management.

 Distinguish among the mark-to-market method, the cost method, and the equity method of accounting for long-term equity investments, and describe the conditions under which each method is used.

The mark-to-market rule, which is summarized in LO2 above, is used to account for trading securities, which are always considered current, and available-for-sale securities whether they are classified in the current or long-term assets section of the balance sheet.

Under the cost method, purchases of equity securities are recorded at cost, including incidental costs of acquisition, dividends are recorded as income when declared, and sales give rise to book gains or losses in the amount of the difference between the acquisition cost of the securities and the proceeds from the sale. The cost method is used for investments in nonmarketable securities that involve less than 20 percent of the investee company's voting stock.

Under the equity method, the purchase of equity securities is originally recorded at cost, and the carrying value of the long-term investment on the investor's balance sheet is (1) periodically increased (decreased) by the investor's proportionate share of the net income (loss) of the investee and (2) decreased by all dividends transferred to the investor from the investee. The equity method is used for investments in marketable or nonmarketable securities that involve from 20 to 50 percent of the investee company's voting stock.

LO 5 *Define consolidated financial statements, and describe when they are prepared and how they differ from financial statements that account for equity investments using the equity method.*

Consolidated financial statements represent the combined financial statements of a parent company and any companies acquired by the parent. Such acquisitions occur when the parent purchases a controlling interest (51 percent of the outstanding voting stock) in another company, or as the result of a merger, where the merged company ceases to exist. Consolidated statements should be prepared when a parent owns 51 percent or more of a subsidiary's outstanding common stock.

When the parent prepares consolidated financial statements, it includes the assets and liabilities of the subsidiary with its own. If the purchase price exceeds the FMV of the subsidiary's net assets, goodwill, which is subject to amortization, is also recognized on the balance sheet of the parent. Under the equity method, the assets and liabilities of the investee company are not included with those of the parent, and this, in turn, can represent a form of off-balance-sheet financing.

LO 6 *Explain why goodwill accounting is controversial.*

Goodwill accounting is controversial because, in the United States, goodwill must be amortized to earnings, and the amortization of any goodwill acquired prior to 1993 is not an allowable tax deduction. Some contend that these rules have made it difficult for U.S. companies to compete for acquisitions against firms from foreign countries that have less restrictive rules. Such countries include Britain, Japan, and Germany.

APPENDIX 8A

CONSOLIDATED FINANCIAL STATEMENTS

Many companies expand by purchasing other companies and/or extending operations into other countries. For example, as of December 31, 1994, Johnson & Johnson, one of the world's largest consumer products companies, owned 28 different U.S. companies as well as more than 150 companies that operated in 60 different countries throughout the world. In 1994 alone Johnson & Johnson spent $1.9 billion acquiring other domestic and foreign operations. Each of these acquisitions involved acquiring large amounts of the outstanding equity securities of the investee companies. This appendix covers the methods used to account for investments in excess of 50 percent of the investee company's outstanding voting stock.

Such transactions give rise to consolidated financial statements which reflect the combined accounts of both the investor and the investee companies. Virtually all major U.S. corporations prepare financial statements on a consolidated basis. The following excerpt is from the 1994 financial report of IBM and is typical of the disclosures made by other major U.S. companies.

The consolidated financial statements include the accounts of International Business Machines Corporation and its U.S. and non-U.S. subsidiary companies. Investments in . . . other companies, in which IBM has a 20–50 percent ownership, are accounted for by the equity method. Investments of less than 20 percent are accounted for by the cost method.

ACCOUNTING FOR BUSINESS ACQUISITIONS AND MERGERS: THE PURCHASE METHOD

Equity shares in other companies can be acquired by paying cash or other assets, issuing stock, or issuing bonds to the acquired company's shareholders. Often some combination of these forms of payment is used. When Delta Air Lines acquired Western Air Lines, for example, the $787 million payment to Western's shareholders consisted of $383 million in cash and 8.3 million shares of Delta stock, each with a value of $48.75.

For simplicity, in the following examples we assume that cash is paid for the acquired stock. In such cases, and in the overwhelming majority of all cases, the purchase method is used to account for acquisitions and mergers. Several years ago, for example, McGraw-Hill, Inc., a large publishing company, made fourteen acquisitions, all for cash, and all accounted for as purchases. In certain limited situations, however, where a large portion of the payment entails issuing common stock to the subsidiary's shareholders, another method, called pooling-of-interests, can be used. This appendix is devoted almost exclusively to the purchase method. In-depth coverage of the pooling-of-interests method can be found in advanced accounting textbooks.

To illustrate how the purchase method is used to account for business acquisitions and mergers, assume that on December 31, 1996, Multi Corporation acquired a controlling interest in the equity shares of Littleton Company. The December 31 balance sheets for both companies and some additional information for Littleton Company appear in Figure 8A–1.

When a parent company (Multi Corporation) purchases a controlling interest in a subsidiary (Littleton), the parent is essentially purchasing the assets and liabilities of the subsidiary. It is important to realize that the historical costs of the subsidiary's assets, which are included on Littleton's balance sheet in Figure 8A–1, are of little consequence to the purchase decision. The parent is actually purchasing the FMVs, not the historical costs, of the assets and liabilities of the subsidiary. An important rule, therefore, in understanding the purchase method of accounting for consolidated financial statements is the following: Under the purchase method, when a parent purchases a controlling interest in a subsidiary, the assets and liabilities of the subsidiary are recorded on the balance sheet of the parent at their FMVs.

FIGURE 8A–1

Balance sheets for Multi Corporation and Littleton Company (before acquisition)

MULTI CORPORATION
BALANCE SHEET
DECEMBER 31, 1996

ASSETS

Cash	$ 65,000
Accounts receivable	70,000
Notes receivable	35,000
Inventory	120,000
Long-lived assets (net)	230,000
Total assets	$520,000

LIABILITIES AND STOCKHOLDERS' EQUITY

Accounts payable	$ 90,000
Long-term notes payable	130,000
Common stock	200,000
Retained earnings	100,000
Total liabilities and stockholders' equity	$520,000

LITTLETON COMPANY
BALANCE SHEET
DECEMBER 31, 1996

ASSETS

Cash	$ 6,000
Accounts receivable	9,000
Inventory	10,000
Long-lived assets (net)	35,000
Total assets	$60,000

LIABILITIES AND STOCKHOLDERS' EQUITY

Accounts payable	$14,000
Long-term notes payable	16,000
Common stock	22,000
Retained earnings	8,000
Total liabilities and stockholders' equity	$60,000

Additional information:
Common shares
outstanding   8,000

Consequently, from Multi Corporation's standpoint it is more appropriate to view the value of Littleton's net assets as shown in Figure 8A–2, where all assets and liabilities have been valued at their individual FMVs. As of December 31, 1996, 8,000 shares of Littleton common stock are outstanding. The per-share market value of the net assets, therefore, is $5 ($40,000 ÷ 8,000 shares).

FIGURE 8A–2

FMV of Littleton's net assets

LITTLETON COMPANY
SCHEDULE OF FAIR MARKET VALUES OF ASSETS AND LIABILITIES
DECEMBER 31, 1996

Cash	$ 6,000
Accounts Receivable	9,000
Inventory	15,000
Long-Lived Assets	40,000
Accounts Payable	(14,000)
Long-Term Notes Payable	(16,000)
FMV of net assets	$ 40,000

The following sections account for Multi Corporation's purchase of Littleton shares under four independent cases: (1) purchase 100 percent of the common stock for a price equal to the per-share market value of the net assets, (2) purchase between 50 percent and 100 percent of the common stock for a price equal to the per-share market value of the net assets, (3) purchase 100 percent of the common stock for a price greater than the per-share market value of the net assets, and (4) purchase between 50 percent and 100 percent of the common stock for a price greater than the per-share market value of the net assets.[12]

CASE 1: PURCHASE 100 PERCENT OF LITTLETON STOCK
AT THE PER-SHARE MARKET VALUE OF THE NET ASSETS

Assume that Multi Corporation purchased all 8,000 shares of the outstanding stock of Littleton for $5 per share, a total cost of $40,000. To record the initial acquisition, Multi Corporation would make the following journal entry.

Dec. 31	Investment in Subsidiary (+A)	40,000	
	Cash (−A)		40,000
	Purchased 8,000 shares of Littleton common stock at $5.		

When consolidated financial statements are prepared, Multi Corporation must add Littleton's assets and liabilities, at their *fair market values,* to its balance sheet. At the same time, to avoid double counting, Multi must eliminate the $40,000 originally recognized in the Investment in Subsidiary account. One way to think about this procedure is to assume that Multi Corporation records the following journal entry.

Cash (+A)	6,000	
Accounts Receivable (+A)	9,000	
Inventory (+A)	15,000	
Long-Lived Assets (+A)	40,000	
Accounts Payable (+L)		14,000
Long-Term Notes Payable (+L)		16,000
Investment in Subsidiary (−A)		40,000
Added assets and liabilities of Littleton at FMV		
and eliminated investment account.		

This entry simply serves to add the assets and liabilities of Littleton, the subsidiary, to the balance sheet of Multi Corporation, the parent, at their FMV. Note that recording the assets and liabilities of the subsidiary on the parent's balance sheet at FMV does not violate the historical cost principle. From the parent's standpoint, these dollar amounts represent the costs of the assets and liabilities purchased in the acquisition. They can be documented by an objectively verifiable transaction.

Note also that under the purchase method, the stockholders' equity accounts of the subsidiary (e.g., Common Stock, Additional Paid-In Capital, and Retained Earnings) are not reflected on the consolidated financial statements of the parent. These accounts represent the ownership interests of Littleton's original stockholders, which now have been transferred to the stockholders of Multi Corporation in the form of Littleton's assets and liabilities. To include both the assets and liabilities of Littleton as well as its stockholders' equity accounts on the consolidated financial statements would essentially be counting the same items twice.

As stated earlier, one way to think about the preparation of consolidated statements is to assume that Multi Corporation recorded the second entry illustrated above. While this entry captures the economics of the transaction and can be used for illustrative purposes, it would not be recorded in the books of Multi Corporation. Instead, Multi Corporation would prepare a work sheet similar to that illustrated in Figure 8A–3.

To prepare a consolidated balance sheet using a work sheet, the separate balance sheets of Multi Corporation and Littleton, after the acquisition, should initially be placed in the first two columns of the work sheet. The adjusting/eliminating entry serves (1) to adjust the inventory ($5,000) and long-lived assets ($5,000) of Littleton

---

12. It is unusual for a company to be purchased for less than the FMV of its net assets, and we do not cover such cases in this text. These situations are covered in advanced financial accounting texts.

Work sheet for Multi Corporation: Case 1

MULTI CORPORATION
CONSOLIDATED WORK SHEET
DECEMBER 31, 1996

ACCOUNTS	MULTI CORP.	LITTLETON CO.	ADJUSTMENTS AND ELIMINATIONS DR.	CR.	CONSOLIDATED BALANCE SHEET
Cash	25,000	6,000			31,000
Accounts Receivable	70,000	9,000			79,000
Notes Receivable	35,000	—			35,000
Inventory	120,000	10,000	5,000		135,000
Investment in Subsidiary	40,000	—		40,000	—
Long-Lived Assets	230,000	35,000	5,000		270,000
Total Assets	520,000	60,000	10,000	40,000	550,000
Accounts Payable	90,000	14,000			104,000
Long-Term Notes Payable	130,000	16,000			146,000
Common Stock	200,000	22,000	22,000		200,000
Retained Earnings	100,000	8,000	8,000		100,000
Total Liabilities and Stockholders' Equity	520,000	60,000	30,000		550,000

to reflect their FMVs and (2) to eliminate the $40,000 Investment in Subsidiary account as well as Littleton's Common Stock ($22,000) and Retained Earnings ($8,000) accounts from the consolidated balance sheet. After recording the adjusting/eliminating entry on the work sheet, the totals for the consolidated balance sheet accounts are prepared simply by adding (or subtracting) across the rows.

CASE 2: PURCHASE BETWEEN 50 PERCENT AND 100 PERCENT OF STOCK AT THE PER-SHARE MARKET VALUE OF THE NET ASSETS

Assume that Multi Corporation purchased 6,400 shares (80 percent) of Littleton's outstanding stock for $5 per share, a total cost of $32,000. The purchase entry and illustrative adjusting entry are provided in Figure 8A–4.

In this case, as in Case 1, the illustrative adjusting entry serves to add the assets and liabilities of Littleton to the balance sheet of Multi Corporation at their FMVs. However, in this case the purchase price ($32,000) is less than the FMV of Littleton's net assets and liabilities ($40,000) because Multi Corporation purchased only 80 percent of Littleton's stock. As a result, $4,800 is credited to an account called Minority Interest, which represents that portion of the subsidiary's stock owned by individuals or entities other than the parent (minority stockholders). The dollar amount of this credit ($8,000) is computed by multiplying the net value of Littleton's assets and liabilities ($40,000) by the portion of Littleton's stock that is owned by the minority stockholders (20 percent). The Minority Interest account is necessary because Multi Corporation included all of Littleton's assets and liabilities on the consolidated balance sheet, yet it owns only 80 percent of the outstanding stock.

The economic significance of minority interest is somewhat unclear. It can be interpreted as a liability, in that it represents an interest held by outsiders in a portion of the net assets listed on the consolidated balance sheet. On the other hand, it resembles a stockholders' equity item because the interest held by outsiders is an equity interest held by outside stockholders. Consequently, minority interest is normally

FIGURE 8A-4	Dec. 31			
Consolidated journal entries for Multi Corporation: Case 2		Investment in Subsidiary (+A)	32,000	
		Cash (−A)		32,000
		Purchased 6,400 shares (80%) of Littleton common stock.		
		Cash (+A)	6,000	
		Accounts Receivable (+A)	9,000	
		Inventory (+A)	15,000	
		Long-Lived Assets (+A)	40,000	
		Accounts Payable (+L)		14,000
		Long-Term Notes Payable (+L)		16,000
		Minority Interest (+L or +SE)		8,000*
		Investment in Subsidiary (−A)		32,000
		Added assets and liabilities of Littleton at FMV and eliminated investment account.		

*20% × $40,000

disclosed on the consolidated balance sheet between the long-term liability and the stockholders' equity sections.[13]

As in Case 1, the consolidated balance sheet would actually be prepared using a work sheet as illustrated in Figure 8A–5. The work sheet in Figure 8A–5 differs from

FIGURE 8A-5

Work sheet for Multi Corporation: Case 2

MULTI CORPORATION
CONSOLIDATED WORK SHEET
DECEMBER 31, 1996

			ADJUSTMENTS AND ELIMINATIONS		CONSOLIDATED
ACCOUNTS	MULTI CORP.	LITTLETON CO.	DR.	CR.	BALANCE SHEET
Cash	33,000	6,000			39,000
Accounts Receivable	70,000	9,000			79,000
Notes Receivable	35,000	—			35,000
Inventory	120,000	10,000	5,000		135,000
Investment in Subsidiary	32,000	—		32,000	—
Long-Lived Assets	230,000	35,000	5,000		270,000
Total Assets	520,000	60,000	10,000	32,000	558,000
Accounts Payable	90,000	14,000			104,000
Long-Term Notes Payable	130,000	16,000			146,000
Minority Interest	—	—		8,000	8,000
Common Stock	200,000	22,000	22,000		200,000
Retained Earnings	100,000	8,000	8,000		100,000
Total Liabilities and Stockholders' Equity	520,000	60,000	30,000	8,000	558,000

13.   There are several different views on how to account for purchases where a parent acquires between 50 percent and 100 percent of the subsidiary's outstanding stock. As a result, the appropriate computation of minority interest and its classification as a liability or a stockholders' equity item on the consolidated balance sheet are also somewhat controversial. In this text we have adopted primarily what is called an *entity view* because we believe it to be logical, consistent, and understandable. However, other views, which are discussed in advanced accounting texts, are followed by a significant number of U.S. companies.

that in Figure 8A–3 (Case 1) in two basic ways: (1) Multi Corporation's cash position is $8,000 higher, because the investment in the subsidiary is $32,000 instead of $40,000, and (2) Minority Interest in the amount of $8,000 is recognized on the transaction.

In Cases 1 and 2 note that the FMV of the net assets and liabilities exactly equals the purchase price. Such situations, however, are unusual because most companies have accumulated a certain amount of goodwill, which implies that the value of the subsidiary exceeds the FMV of its net assets. The more common case, where the purchase price exceeds the FMV of the net assets, is illustrated next in Cases 3 and 4.

CASE 3: PURCHASE 100 PERCENT OF STOCK AT A PRICE GREATER THAN THE PER-SHARE MARKET VALUE OF THE NET ASSETS

Assume that Multi Corporation purchased all 8,000 shares of the outstanding stock of Littleton for $8 per share, a total cost of $64,000. The purchase entry and illustrative adjusting entry appear in Figure 8A–6.

FIGURE 8A–6	**Dec. 31**	**Investment in Subsidiary (+A)**	**64,000**	
Consolidated.		Cash (−A)		**64,000**
journal entries for		*Purchased 8,000 shares of Littleton common*		
Multi Corporation:		*stock at $8.*		
Case 3				
		Cash (+A)	**6,000**	
		Accounts Receivable (+A)	**9,000**	
		Inventory (+A)	**15,000**	
		Long-Lived Assets (+A)	**40,000**	
		Goodwill (+A)	**24,000***	
		Accounts Payable (+L)		**14,000**
		Long-Term Notes Payable (+L)		**16,000**
		Investment in Subsidiary (−A)		**64,000**
		Added assets and liabilities of Littleton at FMV and		
		eliminated investment account.		

*$3 ($8 price per share − $5 per-share market value of net assets) × 8,000 sh.

The purchase price in this case ($64,000) exceeds the FMV of Littleton's net assets ($40,000) by $24,000; therefore, goodwill of $24,000 is recognized on the acquisition. Multi Corporation apparently believes that Littleton is worth more than the FMV of its net assets. It paid $3 per share over and above the $5 ($40,000 ÷ 8,000 shares) per-share market value of the net assets, resulting in a total payment of $24,000 ($3/sh. × 8,000 shares) for goodwill, which Littleton had accumulated up to the date of the purchase. Goodwill, an intangible asset, appears on the asset side of the consolidated balance sheet, usually below fixed assets, and is amortized over a period of time not to exceed forty years. As in Cases 1 and 2, the consolidated balance sheet would actually be prepared using a work sheet, as illustrated in Figure 8A–7.

Transactions where 100 percent of a subsidiary's stock is purchased at a price that exceeds the per-share market value of the subsidiary's net assets are very common. In a recent year alone, Ralston Purina Company, for example, made four such acquisitions (Eveready Batteries, Drake Bakeries, Continental Baking Company, and Benco Pet Foods, Inc.), each of which was accounted for under the purchase method.

FIGURE 8A–7

Work sheet for Multi Corporation: Case 3

**MULTI CORPORATION
CONSOLIDATED WORK SHEET
DECEMBER 31, 1996**

ACCOUNTS	MULTI CORP.	LITTLETON CO.	ADJUSTMENTS AND ELIMINATIONS DR.	CR.	CONSOLIDATED BALANCE SHEET
Cash	1,000	6,000			7,000
Accounts Receivable	70,000	9,000			79,000
Notes Receivable	35,000	—			35,000
Inventory	120,000	10,000	5,000		135,000
Investment in Subsidiary	64,000	—		64,000	—
Long-Lived Assets	230,000	35,000	5,000		270,000
Goodwill	—	—	24,000		24,000
Total Assets	520,000	60,000	34,000	64,000	550,000
Accounts Payable	90,000	14,000			104,000
Long-Term Notes Payable	130,000	16,000			146,000
Common Stock	200,000	22,000	22,000		200,000
Retained Earnings	100,000	8,000	8,000		100,000
Total Liabilities and Stockholders' Equity	520,000	60,000	30,000		550,000

CASE 4: PURCHASE BETWEEN 50 PERCENT AND 100 PERCENT OF STOCK AT A PRICE GREATER THAN THE PER-SHARE MARKET VALUE OF THE NET ASSETS

Assume that Multi Corporation purchased 6,400 shares (80 percent) of Littleton's outstanding stock for $8 per share, a total cost of $51,200. The purchase entry and illustrative adjusting entry appear in Figure 8A–8.

FIGURE 8A–8

Consolidated journal entries for Multi Corporation: Case 4

Dec. 31			
	Investment in Subsidiary (+A)	51,200	
	Cash (−A)		51,200
	Purchased 6,400 shares (80%) of Littleton common stock at $8.		
	Cash (+A)	6,000	
	Accounts Receivable (+A)	9,000	
	Inventory (+A)	15,000	
	Long-Lived Assets (+A)	40,000	
	Goodwill (+A)	19,200*	
	Accounts Payable (+L)		14,000
	Long-Term Note Payable (+L)		16,000
	Minority Interest (+L or +SE)		8,000**
	Investment in Subsidiary (−A)		51,200
	Added assets and liabilities of Littleton at FMV and eliminated investment account.		

*$3 ($8 price per share − $5 per-share market value of net assets) × 6,400 sh.
**20% × $40,000

In this case both goodwill and minority interest are recognized. Goodwill is recognized because Multi Corporation paid $8 for each share, which is $3 more than the $5 per-share market value of the net assets. The total goodwill recognized by Multi Corporation on the transaction is $19,200 (6,400 shares × $3). Minority interest is recognized because Multi Corporation purchased only 80 percent of Littleton's stock. As in Case 2, the amount of minority interest recognized on the transaction is computed by multiplying the FMV of Littleton's net assets ($40,000) times the percentage of Littleton's shares owned by the minority stockholders (20 percent). As in Cases 1, 2, and 3, the consolidated balance sheet would actually be prepared using a work sheet, as illustrated in Figure 8A–9.

FIGURE 8A–9

Work sheet for Multi Corporation: Case 4

MULTI CORPORATION
CONSOLIDATED WORK SHEET
DECEMBER 31, 1996

ACCOUNTS	MULTI CORP.	LITTLETON CO.	ADJUSTMENTS AND ELIMINATIONS DR.	CR.	CONSOLIDATED BALANCE SHEET
Cash	13,800	6,000			19,800
Accounts Receivable	70,000	9,000			79,000
Notes Receivable	35,000	—			35,000
Inventory	120,000	10,000	5,000		135,000
Investment in Subsidiary	51,200	—		51,200	—
Long-Lived Assets	230,000	35,000	5,000		270,000
Goodwill	—	—	19,200		19,200
Total Assets	520,000	60,000	29,200	51,200	558,000
Accounts Payable	90,000	14,000			104,000
Long-Term Notes Payable	130,000	16,000			146,000
Minority Interest	—	—		8,000	8,000
Common Stock	200,000	22,000	22,000		200,000
Retained Earnings	100,000	8,000	8,000		100,000
Total Liabilities and Stockholders' Equity	520,000	60,000	30,000	8,000	558,000

Acquisitions where both goodwill and minority interest are recognized occur periodically in the United States, but are much less common than those where 100 percent of the subsidiary's stock is purchased. Often such transactions are followed quite closely by the acquisition of the outstanding minority stock. For example, when Alcoa acquired approximately 91 percent of the outstanding stock of TRE Corporation for $326 million, the transaction recognized both goodwill and minority interest, which were included in Alcoa's balance sheet. Shortly after the acquisition, Alcoa acquired the remaining outstanding stock, and TRE became a wholly owned subsidiary of Alcoa.

INTERCOMPANY RECEIVABLES AND PAYABLES

When the parent company prepares a consolidated balance sheet, in addition to the work sheet entries that add the assets and liabilities at FMV and eliminate the investment account, any receivables or payables between the parent and the subsidiary (intercompany receivables and payables) must also be eliminated. Such eliminating entries avoid including receivables and payables that, from the perspective of the consolidated financial statements, do not exist. The following excerpt from the 1994 financial report of J. C. Penney describes how major U.S. companies account for intercompany transactions when preparing consolidated financial statements:

"The consolidated financial statements present the results of J. C. Penney Company, Inc. and all of its wholly-owned and majority-owned subsidiaries. All significant intercompany transactions and balances have been eliminated in consolidation."

Suppose, for example, that prior to the acquisition of Littleton, Multi Corporation loaned Littleton $7,000. After the loan, the $7,000 would appear as a note receivable on Multi Corporation's balance sheet and a note payable on Littleton's. If no eliminating entry is recorded when Multi Corporation acquires Littleton, both the receivable and the payable will appear on Multi Corporation's consolidated financial statement, and it would seem that Multi Corporation owed money to itself. To avoid such a misstatement, Multi Corporation would record the following eliminating entry on the consolidated work sheet.

Dec. 31	Notes Payable (−L)	7,000	
	Notes Receivable (−A)		7,000
	Eliminated $7,000 intercompany receivable and payable.		

To illustrate how such an elimination would appear on the consolidated work sheet, assume the same facts as in Case 4 (Figure 8A–9), except that Littleton owed Multi Corporation $7,000, which gave rise to a receivable and payable that required elimination. The work sheet appears in Figure 8A–10.

FIGURE 8A–10

Work sheet for Case 4 with eliminating entries

MULTI CORPORATION
CONSOLIDATED WORK SHEET
DECEMBER 31, 1996

ACCOUNTS	MULTI CORP.	LITTLETON CO.	ADJUSTMENTS AND ELIMINATIONS DR.	CR.	CONSOLIDATED BALANCE SHEET
Cash	13,800	6,000			19,800
Accounts Receivable	70,000	9,000			79,000
Notes Receivable	35,000	—		7,000	28,000
Inventory	120,000	10,000	5,000		135,000
Investment in Subsidiary	51,200	—		51,200	—
Long-Lived Assets	230,000	35,000	5,000		270,000
Goodwill	—	—	19,200		19,200
Total Assets	520,000	60,000	29,200	58,200	551,000
Accounts Payable	90,000	14,000			104,000
Long-Term Notes Payable	130,000	16,000	7,000		139,000
Minority Interest	—	—		8,000	8,000
Common Stock	200,000	22,000	22,000		200,000
Retained Earnings	100,000	8,000	8,000		100,000
Total Liabilities and Stockholders' Equity	520,000	60,000	37,000	8,000	551,000

CONSOLIDATED INCOME STATEMENT

Each of the four cases discussed in the preceding example illustrate how a consolidated balance sheet is prepared under the purchase method for an acquisition made on December 31, 1996, the last day of the year. The revenues and expenses of the subsidiary that were recognized during 1996 are not combined with those of the parent to form a consolidated income statement for 1996. Under the purchase method, only the revenues and expenses of the subsidiary that are recognized *after the date of the acquisition* are consolidated with those of the parent. In the four cases illustrated earlier, for example, the initial consolidated income statement would be prepared for the year 1997, not 1996. Subsidiary revenues and expenses recognized prior to the acquisition are not consolidated. This is because the price paid for the subsidiary's stock by the parent, which appears on the December 31, 1996, consolidated balance sheet in the form of the FMV of the subsidiary's net assets and goodwill, should already reflect the subsidiary's operating activities during 1996.

Preparing a consolidated income statement for a period subsequent to an acquisition requires that the revenues and expenses recognized by the subsidiary during that period be combined with those of the parent. As in the case of a consolidated balance sheet, intercompany transactions must also be eliminated to prevent double counting. Common intercompany revenues and expenses that must be eliminated when preparing a consolidated income statement include (1) sales and purchases of goods and services between the parent and the subsidiary and (2) interest on receivables and payables between the parent and the subsidiary.[14] The following example illustrates how a consolidated balance sheet and a consolidated income statement can be prepared using a work sheet. Note that the consolidated statements are prepared one year after the date of the acquisition.

Assume that on January 1, 1996, Mammoth Corporation purchased 100 percent of the 10,000 outstanding shares of Small Company for $7 per share, a total price of $70,000. At that time the book value of Small Company was $35,000 ($25,000 in common stock and $10,000 in retained earnings). The book values of Small's inventory and long-lived assets were less than their FMVs by $5,000 and $10,000, respectively, and the remaining assets and liabilities approximately reflected their market values. Thus, the FMV of Small's net assets totaled $50,000 ($35,000 + $5,000 + $10,000), and Mammoth paid $20,000 ($70,000 − $50,000) for goodwill.

During 1996 Mammoth loaned $9,000 to Small Company, the principal of which was outstanding at year end, and accrued interest owed by Small to Mammoth totaled $600. The $9,000 appeared as a note receivable on Mammoth's balance sheet and a note payable on Small's balance sheet. The $600 in accrued interest was recognized as a receivable and a revenue by Mammoth and as a payable and an expense by Small. Also during 1996 Mammoth provided a service for Small Company, receiving $12,000 cash in payment, which was recognized as a revenue by Mammoth and an expense by Small. Figure 8A–11 shows the consolidated financial statements prepared by Mammoth, as of December 31, 1996.

Mammoth Corporation's consolidated statements were prepared in six steps:

1. The following journal entry was recorded on January 1, 1996, to recognize the purchase of Small's common stock for $70,000.

Investment in Subsidiary (+A)	**70,000**	
Cash (−A)		**70,000**
Purchased Small's stock for $70,000.		

---

14. Other intercompany transactions that require elimination are not covered in this text. Such transactions are described in intermediate or advanced texts.

FIGURE 8A–11

Work sheet for consolidated financial statements of Mammoth Corporation

MULTI CORPORATION
CONSOLIDATED WORK SHEET
DECEMBER 31, 1996

ACCOUNTS	MAMMOTH	SMALL CO.	ADJUSTMENTS AND ELIMINATIONS DR.	CR.	CONSOLIDATED FINANCIAL STATEMENTS
BALANCE SHEET					
Cash	11,000	10,000			21,000
Accounts Receivable	69,000	9,000			78,000
Interest Receivable	1,000	—		600[c]	400
Notes Receivable	35,000	—		9,000[b]	26,000
Inventory	120,000	14,000	5,000[a]		139,000
Investment in Subsidiary	70,000	—		70,000[a]	—
Long-Lived Assets	230,000	44,000	10,000[a]		284,000
Goodwill	—	—	20,000[a]		20,000*
Total Assets	536,000	77,000	35,000	79,600	568,400
Accounts Payable	96,000	15,000			111,000
Interest Payable	—	3,000	600[c]		2,400
Long-Term Notes Payable	140,000	16,000	9,000[b]		147,000
Common Stock	200,000	25,000	25,000[a]		200,000
Retained Earnings	100,000	18,000	10,000[a]		108,000
Total Liabilities and Stockholders' Equity	536,000	77,000	44,600		568,400
INCOME STATEMENT					
Sales	215,000	45,000	12,000[e]		248,000
Interest Income	4,500		600[d]		3,900
Cost of Goods Sold	(120,000)	(23,000)			(143,000)
Selling and Administrative Expenses	(45,000)	(9,000)		12,000[e]	(42,000)
Interest Expenses	(15,000)	(2,000)		600[d]	(16,400)
Taxes	(12,000)	(3,000)			(15,000)
Net Income	27,500	8,000	12,600	12,600	35,500

[a] Entry to adjust assets to fair market value, eliminate investment account and Small's stockholders' equity section, and recognize goodwill.
[b] Entry to eliminate intercompany notes receivable/payable of $9,000.
[c] Entry to eliminate intercompany interest receivable/payable of $600.
[d] Entry to eliminate intercompany interest income/expense of $600.
[e] Entry to eliminate intercompany sale/expense of $12,000.
* Note: Although not illustrated in this example, Mammoth should amortize a portion of the dollar amount of goodwill at the end of 1996.

2. The work sheet was prepared and the financial statements of Mammoth and Small, as of December 31, 1996, were placed in the first two columns. Note that the financial statements are dated one year after the acquisition.
3. The assets of Small were adjusted to FMV, the investment account and Small's stockholders' equity section were eliminated, and goodwill was recognized as of the acquisition date (note a).
4. Intercompany receivables and payables and revenues and expenses were eliminated (notes b, c, and d). To avoid double counting, the $9,000 amount owed by Small to Mammoth (note b), the $600 of interest accrued on the loan (notes c and d), and Mammoth's $12,000 sale to Small (note e) were removed from the books of both companies.

5. The dollar amounts for each balance sheet and income statement account were totaled across the rows of the work sheet. Note that the $18,000 retained earnings balance disclosed by Small consists of the $10,000 beginning-of-the-year balance plus the $8,000 net income earned during 1996.

6. A portion of the goodwill that was recognized on the consolidation was amortized.

USERS: A NOTE OF CAUTION

To keep the illustrations simple, we have assumed thus far that the fair market values of the subsidiary's net assets are known. This assumption makes it relatively easy to determine the amount of goodwill that should be recognized when a parent purchases a subsidiary for an amount exceeding the fair market value of the subsidiary's net assets. Goodwill is simply the difference between the purchase price and the fair market value of the net assets. In more realistic settings, however, the fair market values of the subsidiary's net assets are not easy to determine. In these cases, for purposes of consolidation the entire purchase price must be allocated to the assets and liabilities of the subsidiary as well as to goodwill. In Chapter 9, we discuss such situations in a section entitled Lump Sum Purchases and show how these allocations can be very subjective, leaving much to management's discretion.

PREPARING CONSOLIDATED FINANCIAL STATEMENTS FOR MULTINATIONALS

This appendix has covered the preparation of consolidated financial statements. Appendix 6B demonstrated how assets and liabilities expressed in foreign currencies are converted to U.S. dollars and how exchange gains and losses are determined. This section discusses how multinational companies prepare consolidated financial statements in cases where their subsidiaries' financial statements are expressed in foreign currencies. The accounting methods used in this area are complex and controversial, and in this section we cover only the basic ideas. More complete coverage can be found in intermediate or advanced financial accounting texts.

Multinational U.S. companies often own subsidiaries that operate in other countries and have financial statements that are expressed in foreign currencies. General Mills, for example, has major subsidiaries in France, Holland, Belgium, Spain, Canada, and Latin America, all of which publish their own financial statements denominated in their own local currencies. When General Mills prepares consolidated financial statements at year end, the financial statements of these subsidiaries must be translated into U.S. dollars and then combined with the accounts of General Mills.

The process of preparing consolidated financial statements for a U.S. multinational basically consists of three steps: (1) classifying the foreign subsidiaries, (2) expressing each subsidiary's financial statements in terms of U.S. dollars, and (3) following the rules of preparing consolidated statements as described earlier.

CLASSIFYING FOREIGN SUBSIDIARIES

Foreign subsidiaries fall into two general classes: Type I and Type II. Type I foreign subsidiaries operate independently from the parent and are integrated within the country or countries in which they operate. General Electric, for example, owns CGR, a company that manufactures, sells, and services medical equipment in Europe and Latin America. CGR is considered a Type I foreign subsidiary because its operations are largely independent of General Electric.

Type II foreign subsidiaries, on the other hand, are integral parts or extensions of parent companies. Such subsidiaries may act as suppliers for the parents or as channels of marketing and distribution for the parents' products. General Mills, for example, has several Type II foreign subsidiaries in Canada that are involved primarily in the marketing and distribution of food products produced by the parent (e.g., Cheerios breakfast cereal).

All subsidiaries located in countries that experience hyperinflation (i.e., more than 100 percent cumulative inflation over a three-year period) are considered Type II foreign subsidiaries, even if they operate independently from the parent. Brazil, Mexico, and Argentina are examples of hyperinflation economies.

EXPRESSING THE STATEMENTS OF TYPE I AND TYPE II SUBSIDIARIES IN TERMS OF U.S. DOLLARS

When the financial statements of Type I foreign subsidiaries are translated into U.S. dollars, any gain or loss due to the translation is referred to as a *translation adjustment*. Such adjustments are not considered part of income and are disclosed in the stockholders' equity section of the consolidated balance sheet. The dollar values of the translation adjustments each year are cumulated, giving rise to a stockholders' equity account called Cumulative Translation Adjustment.

Figure 8A–12 illustrates the disclosure and relative size of the Cumulative Translation Adjustment account. It contains excerpts of the stockholders' equity section taken from the 1994 financial reports of several major U.S. companies.

Note that the cumulative translation adjustment can be significant and either positive or negative. Positive dollar amounts result when the foreign currency of the subsidiary increases in value relative to the U.S. dollar, and negative amounts result when the currency of the subsidiary decreases in value relative to the U.S. dollar.

FIGURE 8A–12	1994 CUMULATIVE TRANSLATION ADJUSTMENT	TOTAL STOCKHOLDERS' EQUITY
Stockholders' equity and the cumulative translation adjustment (dollars in millions)		
Texaco	$ 87	$ 9,749
Colgate-Palmolive	(439)	1,823
Johnson & Johnson	(35)	7,122
Kmart	(58)	6,032
Quaker Oats	(75)	446
AT&T	145	17,921

Source: 1994 financial reports

When the financial statements of Type II foreign subsidiaries are translated to U.S. dollars, gains or losses resulting from the translation process are considered part of consolidated income. Type II foreign subsidiaries are viewed as integral parts of the parent, and therefore translation gains and losses are included as components of the parent's income. Since subsidiaries located in hyperinflation economies are also included in the Type II category, gains and losses resulting from their restatements are also included in consolidated income.

Exchange gains and losses from the restatement of Type II foreign subsidiaries can also be significant, as shown by the following excerpt from a recent financial report of Johnson & Johnson.

Net currency transaction and translation gains and losses included in other expenses were after tax losses of $124 million . . . incurred principally in Latin America.

PREPARING CONSOLIDATED FINANCIAL STATEMENTS

After foreign subsidiaries have been classified as either Type I or Type II and their statements have been translated to U.S. dollars, consolidated financial statements are prepared by the parent in the manner described earlier. Figure 8A–13 summarizes the general rules covered in this section. Keep in mind that we have discussed only the basic ideas involved in understanding the preparation of consolidated financial statements for multinational companies. The technical rules and the specific procedures can get quite involved.

FIGURE 8A–13	STEP	TYPE I SUBSIDIARY	TYPE II SUBSIDIARY
Preparing consolidated financial statements for multinationals with foreign subsidiaries	1. Classify foreign subsidiaries.	Independent of parent.	Integral part or extension of parent. Hyperinflation countries.
	2. Express financial statements of each subsidiary in U.S. dollars.	Cumulative translation adjustment; stockholders' equity.	Exchange gain or loss; income statement.
	3. Prepare consolidated financial statements.	Follow procedures described earlier.	Follow procedures described earlier.

KEY TERMS

Note: Definitions for these terms are provided in the glossary at the end of the text.

Affiliated (associated) companies (p. 368)
Available-for-sale securities (p. 358)
Business acquisition (p. 369)
Business combination (p. 369)
Consolidated financial statements (p. 369)
Controlling interest (p. 369)
Cost method (p. 365)
Equity investment (p. 356)
Equity method (p. 366)
Holding gains or losses (p. 360)
Intention to convert (p. 357)

Mark-to-market rule (p. 358)
Merger (p. 369)
Parent company (p. 369)
Purchase method (p. 370)
Readily marketable (p. 357)
Realized gains/losses (p. 360)
Subsidiary (p. 369)
Trading securities (p. 358)
Unrealized gains/losses (p. 360)
Unrealized price changes (p. 361)

QUESTIONS FOR DISCUSSION AND REVIEW

1. What role do short-term investments in securities play in managing the cash balance?
2. What two criteria must be met before an investment in a security can be listed as current? Why is the second criterion so difficult to apply? How can managers window dress by structuring their investments in securities?
3. What is the difference between a realized gain/loss and a recognized gain/loss? Are all realized and unrealized gains/losses on short-term security investments recognized?
4. Differentiate a trading security from an available-for-sale security. In what ways are they accounted for differently?

5. Evaluate the mark-to-market rule as applied to investments in equity securities. In what manner does it provide useful information, and how and to what extent can management's subjective judgment influence the reported dollar amounts?

6. Differentiate a short-term equity investment from a long-term equity investment in terms of management's intention.

7. What bearing does the percentage of stock ownership have on the method used to account for a long-term equity investment? Why?

8. Refer to Figure 8–8 and describe the conditions under which the following four methods are used to account for short- and long-term equity investments: (a) mark-to-market, (b) cost, (c) equity, and (d) consolidated statements.

9. Under the equity method, why do dividends declared by the investee company reduce the Long-Term Investment account?

10. Why must users be cautious when analyzing the financial statement of a company that uses the equity method?

11. What is the difference between a business acquisition and a merger?

12. Describe goodwill, and explain why it is never accrued but often appears on the balance sheets of major U.S. companies.

13. Explain why a company might prefer the equity method to consolidated statements when accounting for a long-term equity investment.

14. Why is goodwill accounting controversial and possibly puts U.S. chief executives at a disadvantage when bidding against foreign competition for acquisitions?

15. (Appendix) Under the purchase method, why is it important to consider the net market value of the subsidiary's assets instead of the book value? Is adding the assets and liabilities of the subsidiary to the balance sheet of the parent a violation of the historical cost principle? Why or why not?

16. (Appendix) Under what conditions is goodwill recognized on the balance sheet of the parent? Why does the recognition of goodwill imply lower future net income numbers?

17. (Appendix) Under what conditions is minority interest recognized on the balance sheet of the parent? What is minority interest? Is it considered a liability or an element of stockholders' equity? Why?

18. (Appendix) How are the values of goodwill and minority interest determined when both are recognized in an acquisition?

19. (Appendix) Why are the revenues and expenses of a subsidiary that are recognized prior to an acquisition not included in consolidated income under the purchase method?

20. (Appendix) Define intercompany receivables, payables, revenues, and expenses, and explain how and why they are eliminated when preparing consolidated financial statements.

21. (Appendix) Describe the three basic steps followed by multinationals when they prepare consolidated financial statements.

22. (Appendix) Distinguish between a Type I and a Type II foreign subsidiary. In which category are subsidiaries that operate in hyperinflation countries included? Where on the financial statements are the translation adjustments disclosed for each type of subsidiary?

EXERCISES

E8–1

(Accounting for short-term equity securities)

Monroe Auto Supplies engaged in several transactions involving short-term equity securities during 1997, shown in the following list. The company had never invested in equity securities prior to 1997. All securities were classified as trading securities.

1. Purchased 1,000 shares of IBM for $50 per share.
2. Purchased 500 shares of General Motors for $80 per share.
3. Sold 750 shares of IBM for $60 per share.
4. Received a dividend of $1.50 per share from General Motors. Assume that the dividend was declared in a previous period.
5. Purchased 200 shares of Xerox for $40 per share.
6. Sold the remaining 250 shares of IBM for $30 per share.

7. Sold the 200 shares of Xerox for $58 per share.
8. Sold the 500 shares of General Motors for $60 per share.

REQUIRED:
a. Prepare journal entries for each transaction.
b. What effect did these transactions have on the company's 1997 net income?

E8–2

(Mark-to-market accounting)

The following information was extracted from the December 31, 1996 current asset section of the balance sheets of four different companies.

	WEAREVER FABRICS	FRAMES CORP.	PACIFIC TRANSPORT	VIDEO MAGIC
Trading securities	$800,000	$490,000	$645,000	$210,000
Available-for-sale securities	130,000	40,000	250,000	85,000
Short-term equity invest.	$930,000	$530,000	$895,000	$295,000

There were no transactions in short-term equity securities during 1997, and as of December 31, 1997 the controllers of each company collected the following information.

	WEAREVER FABRICS	FRAMES CORP.	PACIFIC TRANSPORT	VIDEO MAGIC
Trading securities	$820,000	$480,000	$625,000	$220,000
Available-for-sale securities	122,000	52,000	246,000	88,000
Short-term equity invest.	$942,000	$532,000	$871,000	$308,000

REQUIRED:
a. Compute the change in the wealth levels of each of the four companies due to the market value changes in their equity investments.
b. Compute the effect on 1997 reported income for each of the four companies due to the market value changes in their equity investments.
c. Explain why the answers to (a) and (b) are not the same.

E8–3

(Mark-to-market accounting)

The following information relates to the activity in the short-term investment account of Lido International, which held no short-term investments as of January 1.

(1) **January 28**   Purchased ten shares of Able Co. stock at $14 per share.
(2) **February 18** Purchased twenty shares of Baker Co. stock at $26 per share.
(3) **March 15**   Received dividends from Able Co. of $1 per share.
(4) **April 29**   Sold five shares of Able Co. for $15 per share
(5) **May 18**   Received dividends from Baker Co. of $2 per share.
(6) **June 1**   Sold five shares of Baker Co. for $22 per share.
(7) **June 30**   Market value of Able shares is $17 per share.
                     Market value of Baker shares is $20 per share.

REQUIRED:
a. Prepare journal entries for each transaction excluding the June 30 adjusting entry. Use the asset account "Short-Term Investments" and assume that dividends were declared and paid on the same day.
b. Prepare the June 30 adjusting entry, and describe the effect on reported income, assuming: (1) Able and Baker shares are both considered trading securities, (2) Able is considered a trading security, and Baker is considered an available-for-sale security, (3) Able is considered an available-for-sale security, and Baker is considered a trading security, and (4) both Able and Baker are considered available-for-sale securities.
c. Which combination in (b) depicts management as most successful in the current period? Explain.

E8–4

(Activity in the short-term investment account across time periods)

On November 11, 1997, Wadsworth Company purchased 20 shares of ZZZ for $8 per share. Wadsworth held the investment for the remainder of 1997, and as of December 31 the per share market value of ZZZ had risen to $10. During 1998 Wadsworth sold 10 shares of ZZZ for $9 each, and at the end of 1998 the per share market price of the remaining 10 ten shares was $12. During 1999 the remaining shares of ZZZ were sold for $14 each. Assume that Wadsworth held no other equity investments during this time period.

REQUIRED:

a. Complete the following chart. The first column assumes that the investment was classified as trading securities; the second column assumes that the investment was classified as available-for-sale securities.

	TRADING	AVAILABLE-FOR-SALE
1997 income		
12/31/97 balance sheet investment value		
1998 income		
12/31/98 balance sheet investment value		
1999 income		
Total income ('97 + '98 + '99)		

b. Comment on the differences.

E8–5

(Reporting problems with mark-to-market accounting as applied to available-for-sale securities)

Tom Miller and Larry Rogers each started a business on December 1, 1996 by contributing $6,000 of their own funds. Early in December both men purchased 120 shares of Diskette common stock, which was selling at the time for $26 per share, and classified the investment as available-for-sale securities. During December they both also purchased $1,500 of inventory on account.

　　As of December 30, the market price of Diskette common stock had risen to $32 per share. Tom was delighted by the price increase but chose simply to hold the stock, expecting that the price would continue to appreciate for at least another month. Larry, on the other hand, sold his shares, but immediately repurchased them because he too believed that they would continue to appreciate.

REQUIRED:

a. Prepare year-end balance sheets for both Tom and Larry.
b. Compute net income, working capital, and the current ratio for both Tom and Larry.
c. From the financial statements alone, which of the two appears to be in the better financial position? Why?
d. Assume that there are brokerage commissions on all security purchases and sales. Which of the two is actually in the better financial position? Why?

E8–6

(Choosing the appropriate method to account for long-term equity investments)

Indicate the answers that would complete the following chart with the appropriate method of accounting for long-term equity investments: (1) mark-to-market method, (2) cost method, (3) equity method, (4) consolidated financial statements.

	ARE THE SECURITIES MARKETABLE?	
	YES	NO
Percentage of ownership in investee company:		
1. Less than 20%		
2. 20%–50%		
3. Greater than 50%		

E8–7

(Classifying and accounting for equity investments)

Hartney Consulting Services is involved in the following investments as of December 31, 1996.

1. Owns 40 percent of the common stock issued by Doyle Corporation. Doyle Corporation's stock is actively traded, and Hartney Consulting intends to hold this investment for at least five years.

2. Owns 55 percent of the common stock issued by Jacobs Automotive Parts Manufacturing. This stock is actively traded. Hartney Consulting intends to hold this investment indefinitely.
3. Owns 10 percent of the common stock issued by Markert Computers. Markert Computers is a closely held company with just two other stockholders.
4. Owns 45 percent of the common stock issued by Luther Brewery. Luther Brewery has just recently joined the New York Stock Exchange. Hartney intends to sell this investment to raise cash within the next five years.
5. Owns 15 percent of the common stock of Hartney Farms. The stock is publicly traded, but Hartney intends to hold the investment indefinitely.
6. On November 30, 1997, Hartney Consulting owned 18 percent of Whittenbach Industries. During December Hartney Consulting purchased an additional 15 percent of the company. This company's stock is actively traded, and Hartney fully intends to hold this stock for four years.

REQUIRED:

a. Indicate whether each investment should be classified as short-term or long-term on the December 31, 1997, balance sheet. Also indicate the appropriate accounting treatment for each investment. Explain your answer.
b. Explain why the nonmarketable equity securities are disclosed in the long-term investment section of the balance sheet and are not carried at market value.

E8–8

(The cost method)

Mystic Lakes Food Company began investing in equity securities for the first time in 1996. During 1996, the company engaged in the following transactions involving equity securities. Assume that the stock of Thayers International and Bayhe Enterprises is not considered marketable and that ownership is less than 20 percent of the equity. Prepare journal entries to record these transactions.

1. Purchased 10,000 shares of Thayers International for $26 per share.
2. Purchased 25,000 shares of Bayhe Enterprises for $35 per share.
3. Thayers International declared a $2 per share dividend to be paid at a later date.
4. Sold 4,500 shares of Bayhe Enterprises for $30 per share.
5. Sold 8,000 shares of Thayers International for $32 per share.

E8–9

(Applying the mark-to-market rule)

Refer to the data provided in E8–8.

REQUIRED:

a. Assume that the stock of Thayers International and Bayhe Enterprises is considered marketable, and Mystic Lakes Food Company wishes to hold all investments indefinitely. Prepare journal entries to record these transactions.
b. Assume that the market values on December 31, 1996, of Thayers International and Bayhe Enterprises are $25 and $32, respectively. Prepare the entry to adjust the company's long-term investments to market value.

E8–10

(The equity method)

On January 1, 1996, Nover Solar Systems purchased 10,000 shares of Reilly Manufacturing for $190,000. The investment represented 25 percent of Reilly's outstanding common stock. Nover intended to hold the investment indefinitely. During 1996 Reilly earned net income of $75,000, and during 1997 Reilly suffered a net loss of $6,000. Reilly paid dividends both years of $1.50 per share.

REQUIRED:

a. Prepare all relevant journal entries that would be recorded on Nover's books during 1996 and 1997.
b. Compute the book value of Nover's Long-Term Equity Investment account as of December 31, 1996, and December 31, 1997.

E8–11

(Inferring information about the equity method from the financial statements)

Mainmont Industries uses the equity method to account for its long-term equity investments. The following information from the financial statements of Mainmont refers to an investment in the securities of Tumbleweed Construction, a company 30 percent owned by Mainmont.

	1997	1996
Long-term investment in equity securities	$29,000	$25,000
Income from equity securities	12,000	7,000

Mainmont neither purchased nor sold any equity securities during 1997.

REQUIRED:
a. How much net income did Tumbleweed Construction earn during 1997?
b. What was the dollar amount of the total dividend declared by Tumbleweed Construction during 1997?
c. Provide the journal entries recorded by Mainmont during 1997 with respect to its investment in Tumbleweed Construction.

E8–12

(Recording an acquisition under the purchase method)

Multiplex purchased 100 percent of the outstanding common stock of Lipley Company for $900,000. At the time of the acquisition, the fair market values of Lipley's individual assets and liabilities follow.

Cash	$ 90,000
Accounts receivable	60,000
Inventory	160,000
Plant and equipment	560,000
Payables	300,000

REQUIRED:
a. Provide the journal entry recorded by Multiplex at the time of the acquisition.
b. Assume that Multiplex amortizes goodwill over a forty-year period using the straight-line method. Compute the dollar amount of goodwill that was amortized during the year following the acquisition.
c. Assume that the book values of the assets and liabilities on Lipley's balance sheet as of the date of the acquisition were $550,000 and $300,000, respectively. Explain how the net book value of Lipley could be less than the net FMV of Lipley's assets and liabilities, which in turn is less than the price Multiplex paid for Lipley's common stock.

E8–13

(Appendix: 100 percent purchases in excess of the net market value of the assets and liabilities)

The following chart describes six transactions where 100 percent of a subsidiary's voting stock was purchased for cash. Provide the missing values.

	PURCHASE PRICE	NET BOOK VALUE	NET FMV IN EXCESS OF BOOK VALUE	GOODWILL
1.	?	$ 7,000	$ 1,000	$ 1,000
2.	$ 6,000	6,000	?	0
3.	12,000	?	4,000	3,000
4.	15,000	10,000	3,000	?
5.	?	2,000	1,000	3,000
6.	12,000	4,000	8,000	?

E8–14

(Appendix: Per-share book and market value)

The book value of a share of Camden common stock on December 31 is $12. The balance sheet value and the market value of the company's assets and liabilities as of that date follow.

	BALANCE SHEET VALUE	MARKET VALUE
Cash	$ 15,000	$ 15,000
Receivables	26,000	24,000
Inventories	15,000	25,000
Fixed assets	40,000	47,000
Liabilities	(60,000)	(60,000)
Net book value	$ 36,000	
Net market value		$ 51,000

On December 31, Conglomerate, Inc., purchased 100 percent of the outstanding stock of Camden for $22 per share.

REQUIRED:

a. How many shares of common stock did Camden have outstanding as of December 31?
b. Compute the per-share net market value of Camden's common stock.
c. Why would Conglomerate pay more than the per-share market value for a share of Camden common stock?
d. Prepare the entry that reflects the acquisition.

E8–15

(Appendix: Computing goodwill and minority interest)

Maxwell Industries paid $18 per share for 80 percent of the 10,000 outstanding shares of Kendall Hall. The balance sheet of Kendall Hall and additional market value information follow. Compute the amounts of goodwill and minority interest recognized by Maxwell.

	HISTORICAL COST	FMV
Current assets	$125,000	$150,000
Noncurrent assets	65,000	80,000
Liabilities	70,000	70,000
Stockholders' equity	120,000	—

E8–16

(Appendix: Completing a consolidated work sheet)

Glover Chemical purchased 100 percent of the outstanding stock of Ward Supply on December 31 for $100,000 cash. As of that date the FMVs of the inventory and fixed assets of Ward equaled $70,000 and $125,000, respectively. Assume that cash, accounts receivable, and the liabilities are on the books of Ward at FMV. Provide the information to complete the following consolidated work sheet, which already reflects the entry recorded at acquisition.

ACCOUNTS	GLOVER	WARD	ADJUSTMENTS AND ELIMINATIONS DR.	CR.	CONSOLIDATED BALANCE SHEET
Cash	73,000	10,000			
Accounts Receivable	110,000	40,000			
Inventory	220,000	60,000			
Investment in Subsidiary	100,000	—			
Fixed Assets	615,000	120,000			
Goodwill	30,000	—			
Total Assets	1,148,000	230,000			
Accounts Payable	80,000	70,000			
Long-Term Notes	450,000	80,000			
Common Stock	500,000	70,000			
Retained Earnings	118,000	10,000			
Total Liabilities and Stockholders' Equity	1,148,000	230,000			

PROBLEMS

P8–1

(Applying the mark-to-market rule to investments in equity securities)

O'Leary Enterprises began investing in short-term equity securities in 1996. The following information was extracted from its 1996 internal financial records. Houser and Miller were classified as trading securities, while Letter and Nordic were classified as available-for-sale securities.

SECURITY	PURCHASES	SALES	TOTAL DIVIDENDS RECEIVED	12/31/96 MARKET VALUE*
Houser Company	90 shares @ $22	60 shares @ $25	$ 40	$ 25
Miller, Inc.	180 shares @ $40	90 shares @ $30	85	35
Letter Books	75 shares @ $48	5 shares @ $55	30	46
Nordic Equipment	170 shares @ $70	145 shares @ $95	50	90

*Per share

REQUIRED:

Compute the effect on reported 1996 income from all investment transactions and price changes.

P8–2

(Trading securities: purchases, sales, dividends, and end-of-period adjustments)

Anderson Cabinets began operations during 1990. During the initial years of operations, the company invested primarily in fixed assets to promote growth. During 1996 H. Hurst, the company president, decided that the company was sufficiently stable that it could now invest in short-term marketable securities. During 1996 the company entered into the following transactions concerning marketable securities.

(1) March 10   Purchased 1,000 shares of Arctic Oil & Gas for $28 per share.
(2) March 31   Purchased 800 shares of Humphries Manufacturing for $10 per share.
(3) May 26   Received a cash dividend of $1.25 per share from Arctic Oil & Gas.
(4) July 10   Purchased 1,000 shares of Kingsman Game Co. for $18 per share.
(5) September 11   Sold 800 shares of Arctic Oil & Gas for $35 per share.
(6) September 27   Sold 500 shares of Humphries Manufacturing for $8 per share.
(7) October 19   Purchased 1,000 shares of Quimby, Inc., for $25 per share.
(8) November 6   Received a cash dividend of $1.25 per share from Arctic Oil & Gas.
(9) December 8   Sold the remaining shares of Arctic Oil & Gas and Humphries Manufacturing for $30 and $15, respectively.
(10) December 31   According to *The Wall Street Journal*, the market values of these securities at the close of business on December 31 follow.

Arctic Oil & Gas	$32
Humphries Manufacturing	14
Kingsman Game Company	15
Quimby, Inc.	26

REQUIRED:

a. Prepare the necessary journal entries for each of these transactions. Assume that any dividends were declared and paid on the same day.
b. Prepare the short-term equity securities section of the balance sheet as of December 31, 1996.
c. Compute the impact of these transactions on the income statement for the year ended December 31, 1996.

P8–3

(Changing security investment classifications)

On October 18, 1996 Daley, Inc. purchased 100 shares of Orthon @ $32 per share. The investment was classified as available-for-sale securities. The shares were held throughout the remainder of 1996 and 1997, and by December 31, 1996 and 1997 the per share market price had risen to $40 and $50, respectively. On December 31, 1997 Daley decided to change the classification from available-for-sale to trading securities.

REQUIRED:
a. Provide the journal entries recorded at October 18, 1996; December 31, 1996; and December 31, 1997.
b. Assume that the investment was originally classified as trading securities, and then changed to available-for-sale on December 31, 1997. Provide the journal entries recorded at October 18, 1996; December 31, 1996; and December 31, 1997.
c. Compute the 1996 and 1997 income effects under the two assumptions.

(Window dressing and the mark-to-market rule)

Levy Company and Guyer Books made the same equity investment—200 shares of Watson Manufacturing at a cost of $12 per share—on November 18. On December 31, the market value of Watson had risen to $45 per share. Guyer Books held its investment in Watson, while Levy sold the shares and immediately repurchased them at the December 31 market value.

REQUIRED:
a. Compute the balance sheet value and income effect associated with these events recorded by the two companies assuming that the investment was classified as trading and available-for-sale. That is, fill in the following chart with the appropriate dollar values.

	GUYER BOOKS		LEVY CO.	
	BALANCE SHEET VALUE	INCOME EFFECT	BALANCE SHEET VALUE	INCOME EFFECT
Investment classified as:				
Trading securities				
Available-for-sale securities				

b. Discuss the differences.

(Trading vs. available-for-sale classifications)

Rochester Enterprises purchased 500 shares of Newark Corporation for $15 per share on June 15, 1996, when Newark had approximately 10,000 equity shares outstanding. Rochester held the investment throughout 1996, and as of December 31 the per share market price had risen to $18. On January 16, 1997 Rochester sold 300 shares for $19 per share, and on October 20 sold the remaining 200 shares for $13 each. The company held no other security investments during this time period.

REQUIRED:
a. Assume that Rochester classified the investment as trading securities, and provide the journal entries recorded on June 15, 1996; December 31, 1996; January 16, 1997; and October 20, 1997.
b. Assume that Rochester classified the investment as available-for-sale securities, and provide the journal entries recorded on June 15, 1996; December 31, 1996, January 16, 1997; and October 20, 1997.
c. Compute the net cash effect of these transactions across 1996 and 1997.
d. Compute the 1996, 1997, and total income effect assuming that the investment was classified as trading securities.
e. Compute the 1996, 1997, and total income effect assuming that the investment was classified as available-for-sale securities.
f. Comment on the difference between the two assumptions.

(Inferring from balance sheet disclosures)

The following information was taken from the 1996 annual report of Orleans Enterprises.

	1996	1995
Trading securities	$25,440	$27,000

Related Footnote: The 1996 and 1995 balances in the trading securities account consist of 1,600 and 1,800 equity shares of Atwater Company, respectively. During 1996, in the only transaction related to these securities, 200 shares were sold for $15.50 each.

REQUIRED:

a. Compute the 1996 income effect related to the company's investment in Atwater. Divide the effect into its realized and unrealized components.
b. Repeat (a) assuming that the securities were classified as available-for-sale and that Orleans' first investment in these securities occurred on December 31, 1995.

P8-7

(Long-term equity investments: the mark-to-market method versus the equity method)

A summary of the December 31, 1995 balance sheet of Masonite Tires follows.

Assets	$160,000	Liabilities	$ 70,000
		Stockholders' equity	90,000
Total	$160,000	Total	$160,000

On January 1, 1996, Masonite purchased 2,000 (20 percent of the outstanding common shares) shares of Bingo Boots for $40,000 and held the investment throughout 1996 and 1997. During 1996 and 1997 Bingo earned net income of $15,000 and $20,000, respectively. Bingo paid total dividends of $10,000 and $15,000 during 1996 and 1997. The per-share prices of Bingo common stock as of the end of 1996 and 1997 were $18 and $21, respectively. During 1996 and 1997 Masonite generated revenues (excluding revenues related to the investment in Bingo) of $85,000 and $75,000, respectively, and incurred expenses of $50,000 and $70,000, respectively. Assume that all these revenues and expenses involve cash. Masonite pays no dividends.

REQUIRED:

a. Assume that Masonite uses the mark-to-market method and the investment in Bingo was classified as available-for-sale.
    (1) Prepare a balance sheet as of January 1, 1996.
    (2) Prepare a balance sheet as of December 31, 1996 and income statement for the year ended December 31, 1996.
    (3) Prepare a balance sheet as of December 31, 1997 and income statement for the year ended December 31, 1997.
b. Assume that Masonite uses the equity method.
    (1) Prepare a balance sheet as of January 1, 1996.
    (2) Prepare a balance sheet as of December 31, 1996 and income statement for the year ended December 31, 1996.
    (3) Prepare a balance sheet as of December 31, 1997 and income statement for the year ended December 31, 1997.
c. Identify some reasons why the management of Masonite may wish to use the mark-to-market method instead of the equity method. Describe why the equity method might be preferred. Does holding 20 percent of a company's outstanding common stock necessarily mean that the investor company can exert substantial influence over the investee?

P8-8

(The equity method versus consolidated financial statements)

A summary of the 1996 balance sheet of Alsop, Ltd., follows:

Assets	$180,000	Liabilities	$ 90,000
		Stockholders' equity	90,000
Total	$180,000	Total	$180,000

On January 1, 1996, Alsop acquired 100 percent of the outstanding common stock of Martin Monthly for $62,000 cash. At the time of the acquisition, the fair market values of the assets and liabilities of Martin were $86,000 and $64,000, respectively. During 1996 Martin operated as a subsidiary of Alsop; it recognized $15,000 of net income and paid a $10,000 dividend.

REQUIRED:

a. Account for the acquisition as a purchase. Provide the journal entry to record the acquisition, and prepare Alsop's consolidated balance sheet as of January 1, 1996.

b. How much goodwill will Alsop amortize during 1996 if the company amortizes goodwill over forty years using the straight-line method?

c. Account for the acquisition using the equity method. Provide the journal entry to record the acquisition, and prepare Alsop's balance sheet as of January 1, 1996.

d. Compute the debt/equity ratios produced by the two methods of accounting for this investment. Explain why Alsop's management might wish to use the equity method instead of preparing consolidated financial statements.

F8–9

(Inferring information from the financial statements)

Excerpts from the financial statements of Macy Limited are provided below. (Numbers are in thousands.)

	1997	1996
BALANCE SHEET		
Assets:		
Short-term investments	$ 290	$160
Investment in affiliate	530	0
Stockholders' equity:		
Unrealized price decrease on short-term investments	(20)	0
INCOME STATEMENT		
Realized gain on short-term investments	$ 80	
Unrealized gain on short-term investments	30	
Income on equity investment	40	
STATEMENT OF CASH FLOWS		
Operating section (The following amounts were subtracted from net income in the calculation of net cash from operating activities.):		
Gains on short-term investments	$(110)	
Equity income in excess of cash received	(30)	
Investing section:		
Investment in affiliate	(500)	
Investment in short-term investments	(280)	
Sale of short-term investments	240	

Footnotes:

Short-term investments. As of December 31, 1996, trading securities were valued at $130, and during 1997 no available-for-sale securities were acquired or sold.

Investment in affiliate. On January 30, 1997, the company purchased 40% (50,000 shares) of the outstanding equity of Lehmon Financial Services @$10 per share.

REQUIRED: Compute the following dollar amounts.

a. The 12/31/97 market value of the short-term equity investments classified as available-for-sale.

b. The balance sheet carrying value of the trading securities sold during 1997.

c. Compute the earnings per share dollar amount reported by the affiliate.

d. Compute the per share dividend declared by the affiliate.

P8-10

(Appendix: 100 percent purchase and the recognition of goodwill)

The condensed balance sheets as of December 31 for Rice and Associates and Rachel Excavation are provided below.

	RICE	RACHEL
ASSETS		
Cash	$ 196,000	$ 10,000
Accounts receivable	150,000	40,000
Inventory	300,000	40,000
Fixed assets	400,000	130,000
Total assets	$1,046,000	$220,000
LIABILITIES AND STOCKHOLDERS' EQUITY		
Accounts payable	$ 80,000	$ 20,000
Long-term liabilities	300,000	50,000
Common stock	400,000	90,000
Additional paid-in capital	140,000	10,000
Retained earnings	126,000	50,000
Total liabilities and stockholders' equity	$1,046,000	$220,000

As of December 31, the market values of Rachel's inventories and fixed assets were $70,000 and $120,000, respectively. Liabilities are at FMV on the balance sheet.

On December 31 Rice and Associates purchased Rachel Excavation for $180,000 cash. The preceding balance sheets were prepared immediately prior to the acquisition.

REQUIRED:
a. Prepare the journal entry recorded by Rice to recognize the acquisition.
b. Prepare a consolidated work sheet and a consolidated balance sheet.

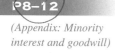

P8-11

(Appendix: Minority interest and no goodwill)

This problem refers to P8–10. Assume that Rice and Associates purchased 80 percent of the outstanding stock of Rachel for $136,000 cash.

REQUIRED:
a. Prepare the journal entry recorded by Rice to recognize the acquisition.
b. Prepare a consolidated work sheet and a consolidated balance sheet.

P8-12

(Appendix: Minority interest and goodwill)

This problem refers to P8–10. Assume that Rice and Associates purchased 80 percent of the 10,000 shares of outstanding stock of Rachel for $140,000 cash.

REQUIRED:
a. Prepare the journal entries recorded by Rice to recognize the acquisition.
b. Prepare a consolidated work sheet and a consolidated balance sheet.

P8-13

(Allocating the excess purchase price among tangible assets and goodwill)

This problem refers to P8–10. Assume the same facts as in P8–10 except that the FMVs for the inventory and fixed assets of Rachel are not as precisely specified. That is, appraisers have indicated that the FMV of the inventory is between $65,000 and $75,000 and that the FMV of the fixed assets is between $115,000 and $125,000. You, as the accountant for Rice and Associates, can use any value within these ranges to record the acquisition.

REQUIRED:

a. Assume that you wish to maximize reported income in the next period. What dollar amounts would you allocate to Rachel's inventory, fixed assets, and goodwill when recording the acquisition? Explain.

b. Assume that you wish to minimize reported income in the next period (e.g., when preparing the transaction for tax purposes). What dollar amounts would you allocate to Rachel's inventory, fixed assets, and goodwill when recording the acquisition? Explain.

P8–14

(Appendix: Eliminating intercompany transactions)

Safeton owns 100 percent of the outstanding stock of Mayliner. When Safeton prepared its consolidated financial statements on December 31, the accountant noticed that Safeton loaned $80,000 to Mayliner on July 1 of that year. Accrued but unpaid interest on the loan as of December 31 totaled $6,800.

REQUIRED:

Provide the journal entry to eliminate the following:

a. The intercompany note receivable/payable
b. The intercompany interest receivable/payable
c. The intercompany revenue/expense

P8–15

(Appendix: Minority interest and goodwill)

Groomer purchased a controlling interest in three companies during 1996. Financial information concerning the three companies follows.

	COMPANY X	COMPANY Y	COMPANY Z
Cash	$ 6,000	$ 4,000	$ 2,000
Accounts receivable	12,000	9,000	7,000
Inventory	30,000	12,000	18,000
Fixed assets	70,000	30,000	15,000
Total assets	$118,000	$55,000	$42,000
Current liabilities	$ 7,000	$12,000	$ 5,000
Long-term liabilities	25,000	20,000	18,000
Common stock	50,000	10,000	15,000
Retained earnings	36,000	13,000	4,000
Total liabilities and stockholders' equity	$118,000	$55,000	$42,000
FMV:			
Inventory	$ 45,000	$18,000	$18,000
Fixed assets	75,000	35,000	15,000

All other assets and liabilities on the balance sheet are at FMV.

Shares of stock outstanding before acquisition   10,000   1,000   2,000

Groomer purchased 8,000, 600, and 1,500 shares of Company X, Company Y, and Company Z, respectively. The share prices and cash payments follow.

Company X   8,000 ×$10.60 = $84,800
Company Y   600 × 40.00 = 24,000
Company Z   1,500 × 11.00 = 16,500

REQUIRED:

For each company prepare the journal entry to record the acquisition by Groomer. Then, for each company prepare a journal entry that could have been recorded to include the individual assets and liabilities on the books of Groomer.

P8–16

*(Appendix:
Consolidated
statements, the equity
method, and debt
covenants)*

Mammoth Enterprises purchased 50 percent of the outstanding stock of Atom, Inc., on December 31 for $60,000 cash. On that date the book value of Atom's net assets was $70,000. The market value of Atom's assets was $180,000, $20,000 above book value. Mammoth's condensed balance sheet, immediately before the acquisition, follows.

ASSETS		LIABILITIES AND STOCKHOLDERS' EQUITY	
Current assets	$150,000	Current liabilities	$ 30,000
Noncurrent assets	350,000	Long-term liabilities	200,000
		Common stock	100,000
		Retained earnings	170,000
		Total liabilities and	
Total assets	$500,000	stockholders' equity	$ 500,000

Mammoth entered into a debt covenant earlier in the year that requires the company to maintain a debt/equity ratio of less than 1:1.

REQUIRED:

a. Assume that Mammoth treats the transaction as a purchase, and compute Mammoth's debt/equity ratio both before and after the acquisition. Consider minority interest a liability.

b. Explain why in this situation Mammoth would probably prefer the equity method instead of treating this transaction as a purchase and preparing consolidated financial statements.

CASES

In 1994 Texaco reported net income of $910 million, $494 million of which was income recognized on investments in affiliate companies accounted for under the equity method. In that same year Texaco received much less than that amount in dividends from these affiliates. Some accountants have argued that the net income amount reported by Texaco from the equity method is distorted because the company received much less cash on its investment.

REQUIRED:

a. Comment on this criticism of the equity method. In your answer, explain the accounting procedures that characterize the equity method and why income is recognized that is not always backed up by cash receipts. Also explain why investors and creditors must be careful when analyzing financial statements that reflect the use of the equity method.

b. Texaco uses the indirect method of presenting the statement of cash flows. Indicate the direction of the adjustment to net income associated with earnings and dividends under the equity method that appears in the operating section of the statement.

C8–2

*(Consolidating a
finance subsidiary's
financial statement:
economic
consequences)*

Several years ago wholly owned finance subsidiaries of major U.S. companies were accounted for by the parent using the equity method. These companies justified the procedure by claiming that the operations of the subsidiaries were so unlike those of the parents that consolidating the subsidiaries' financial statements would distort those of the parents. At the same time, by using the equity method the parents were able to avoid including the subsidiaries' liabilities, which were often quite large, on their consolidated balance sheets. In 1985, for example, adding the liabilities of General Motors Acceptance Company, a finance subsidiary, to those of General Motors (GM), the parent, would have quadrupled GM's debt/equity ratio.

Forbes commented that if the FASB required such companies to consolidate their finance subsidiaries, it "could cause difficulties with bond indenture agreements and loan covenants requiring that certain ratios be maintained."* Others have commented that such problems are of little concern because they can be avoided by writing debt covenants so that all financial ratios are defined in terms of generally accepted accounting principles. Moreover, most financial statement users are reasonably sophisticated and are already aware of the subsidiary's debt. Credit-rating agencies claim, for example, that as long as the debt of the subsidiary is disclosed, it matters little whether it is consolidated or not.

*Jinny St. Goer, "Back to the Balance Sheet," *Forbes*, February 25, 1985, pp. 122–23.

REQUIRED:

a. Briefly explain the difference between using the equity method and preparing consolidated financial statements, and describe how requiring the consolidation of subsidiary financial statements could "cause difficulties with bond indenture agreements."

b. How might the fact that most financial statement users are reasonably sophisticated affect the nature of the accounting standards developed by the FASB?

C8–3

(Accounting practices in different countries: problems and solutions)

Barbara Thomas, in an article published in *Business Law* (August 1983), noted that "The internationalization of capital markets and the dramatic increase in the foreign direct investments of multinational enterprises have increased the need for relevant, timely, and comparable information about the activities of business enterprises having operations in more than one nation." However, this need will be difficult to fulfill "because the various national governments approach accounting measurements and financial disclosure matters differently. The following major items typify these differences."

1. Consolidation practices vary widely. In some countries, for example, it is not customary to present consolidated financial statements at all.
2. In some countries there are practical links between income tax and financial reporting.
3. Foreign currency translations are measured and reported in a variety of ways.
4. In many parts of the world financial statements are required only on an annual basis.
5. A statement of cash flows is not required in some jurisdictions.
6. The standards governing the qualification of auditors and the role of the audit vary widely across countries.

REQUIRED:

a. Explain why differences like those listed exist and why they make it difficult for investors operating in an international environment.

b. Briefly describe what is being done to promote greater uniformity in international accounting practices.

C8–4

(Mergers and the difference between earnings and cash flow)

When Time, Inc., and Warner Communications merged, it represented one of the largest business combinations of all time. Since then the company has reported consistent net losses despite relatively strong operating cash flows. In its 1994 annual report Time Warner often emphasized EBITDA (Earnings before interest, taxes, depreciation, and amortization), noting several times that this number was a better measure of the companies performance than earnings.

REQUIRED:

a. Explain how, after a large merger, the resulting company could report consistent net losses while also reporting strong and positive operating cash flows.

b. Why might the company view EBITDA as the best measure of its performance?

c. Time Warner holds a significant stake (19.6%) in Turner Broadcasting System, Inc. and regularly receives dividends from TBS. How do such dividends affect the reported profits and operating cash flows of Time Warner? Explain.

C8–5

(Accounting rules and foreign investment in the United States)

An article appearing in *Fortune* (February 13, 1989) entitled "What Foreigners Will Buy Next" points out that foreign companies bidding to acquire U.S. companies often pay huge premiums over the market prices of the target companies' outstanding stocks. Examples include Bridgestone's (Japanese tiremaker) $80 per share bid to acquire Firestone, Campeau Corporation's (former Canadian retail empire) purchase of Allied Stores, and Maxwell Publishing's (British publication house) $90 per share bid for Macmillan Publishing. The article notes that "part of the reason foreign companies can afford to pay so much is that they live by different accounting rules."

REQUIRED:

Identify the accounting rules referred to above, explain how the U.S. rules differ from those in other countries, and explain how these differences can enable foreign companies to outbid U.S. companies. Are the foreign companies necessarily better off because they chose to pay these premiums?

C8–6

(MCI annual report)

Refer to the annual report of MCI in Appendix, and answer the questions below.
a. What portion of total assets is comprised of marketable securities? What percentage of these investments are reported as short-term, and how is short-term defined?
b. Describe the kinds of securities (debt or equity) that make up MCI's marketable securities portfolio. Are these securities classified as "trading" securities or "available-for-sale" securities?
c. How much cash did MCI invest in marketable securities in 1994, and how much cash was collected on sales of these securities?
d. MCI's cash and marketable securities accounts grew by approximately $3 billion during 1994. Explain why.
e. What portion of total assets is comprised of investments accounted for under the equity method? How much cash did MCI invest in affiliate companies in 1994?
f. On MCI's balance sheet "investment in affiliates" increased by $169 million during 1994, yet this dollar amount does not match MCI's cash investment in affiliates. Explain why.
g. *(Appendix: Consolidations and goodwill)* Describe MCI's principles of consolidation, and calculate the amount of goodwill amortization recorded by MCI for 1994 (Hint: compare revelant dollar values listed on the income statement and statement of cash flows). Compute how much goodwill was recognized on MCI's 1994 acquisitions.

C8–7

(Appendix: Exchange rates and subsidiaries)

The Wall Street Journal (May 3, 1989) reported that Eastman Kodak was "battered" by unfavorable currency exchange rates in its key imaging subsidiary. The latest earnings for the first quarter of 1989 were far below expectations and Kodak stock fell $3.25 in response to the news. The imaging subsidiary is essential to Kodak's operations, and its earnings alone plunged by 20%, from $201 to $160 million.

REQUIRED:
Explain.

Quality of Earnings Cases: A Comprehensive Review

CASE 1: LIBERTY MANUFACTURING

You have recently been hired by Capital City Bank as a credit analyst. One of the tasks of your new position is to review the financial statements submitted by loan applicants. You have been instructed to assess the solvency and earning power of the applicants as well as the quality and persistence of the reported earnings number. After completing your analysis, you should report your conclusions to your supervisor, recommending whether the applicant should be further considered for the loan, and why.

COMPANY DESCRIPTION

You are now asked to review the file of a loan applicant, Liberty Manufacturing, which has applied for a long-term $500,000 loan. This company is a medium-sized, family-run operation that manufactures a component used in a wide variety of engines. Liberty has been in existence for approximately 20 years and over that time period has grown consistently, reporting profits in each of the last 10 years. The company has recently begun to move into foreign markets and is seeking the loan to finance investments in property, plant, and equipment and to complete the acquisition of a small foreign supplier, Packer Technical.

The demand for Liberty's product seems stable, and the company has made recent technical advancements in product design that may lead to increased sales in the future. At present, the company appears to hold a solid position in its industry. Prices in the industry, both input and output, have been rising at an above average rate, and the industry-wide inflation rate in 1995 was approximately 10 percent.

NOTE FROM YOUR SUPERVISOR

Contained in the file is a note from your supervisor, Anne Mayor, who has made a cursory review of the financial statements. In addition to your task of assessing Liberty's solvency, earning power, and quality and persistence of the reported earnings number, she raises several other points that you should address in your report.

First, Anne would like you to closely examine the investing activities entered into by Liberty in late 1994 and during 1995. It seems that the company both acquired and sold property, plant, and equipment, land, and short-term investments. It also made a large investment in an affiliate company, Packer, which it intends to increase with the proceeds from the loan under consideration. Is Packer a profitable company, and will this be a prudent investment? Perhaps your analysis can shed some light on why the company entered into these transactions and how they affect the financial statements.

Anne also notes that there were large changes in the accounts receivable, inventory, and accounts payable balances, and suggests that you should pay particular attention to these developments. With respect to receivables, for example, she wonders just how much cash was generated from customers and what was the dollar value of the actual bad debt write-offs during the year. Is the allowance for uncollectibles sufficient?

Finally, Anne is curious about the foreign currency translation gain reported by Liberty. Specifically, she wonders whether it can be considered persistent and what exchange rate between German deutsche marks and U.S. dollars as of the balance sheet date gave rise to the $12,500 gain.

FINANCIAL STATEMENTS

The financial statements and selected additional information are provided below and on the following pages. Based upon this information only, prepare a report for your supervisor. The following financial statements have been audited by a major public accounting firm and have received an unqualified opinion. Dollar amounts on the statements are in thousands.

ADDITIONAL INFORMATION

Short-Term Investments. Short-term investments are carried at market value, and consist solely of an investment in a single firm, Fredericks Ltd., which has 500,000 shares outstanding. As of December 31, 1994, Liberty held 40,000 shares, which cost $2 per share when they were acquired in 1994, and all shares are accounted for as available-for-sale securities. On December 16, 1995, Liberty sold all 40,000 shares for $3 per share. The price remained constant for the next few days, and on December 20 Liberty purchased 46,667 Fredericks shares.

Receivables. Uncollectibles on accounts receivable are accounted for under the allowance method. On December 1, 1995, Liberty completed a service for Bundes A.G., a manufacturer located in Germany. Liberty received a note from Bundes promising a payment of 100,000 German deutsche marks within 30 days. On December 1, 1994, two deutsche marks exchanged for one U.S. dollar.

Inventories. The last-in, first-out (LIFO) method is used, and inventories are carried at the lower-of-cost-or-market value. Inventories at December 31, 1994, consisted of 10,000 units @ $6 each, 10,000 units @ $3 each, and 30,000 units @ $1 each. Inventory costs have risen consistently in recent years. During 1995, 50,000 units were sold @ $10 each, and 25,000 units were purchased @ $8 each. For reporting purposes Liberty uses the periodic inventory method.

Investments. On December 20, 1994, Liberty purchased a tract of land for $40,000, and sold the land on December 18, 1995. On January 2, 1995, Liberty purchased 100,000 shares of Packer Technical @ $2.50 per share. Packer has 250,000 shares outstanding (including those held by Liberty). As of December 31, 1995, the share price of Packer shares had fallen to $2 per share.

Property, Plant, & Equipment. Property, plant, and equipment is depreciated using the straight-line method.

Outstanding Debts. Interest rates on outstanding loans range from 9 percent to 12 percent.

LIBERTY MANUFACTURING
BALANCE SHEET
DECEMBER 31, 1995

	1995	1994
ASSETS		
Cash	$ 29.0	$ 10.0
Short-term investments	140.0	84.0
Accounts receivable	275.0	150.0
Less: Allowance for uncollectibles	(5.0)	(10.0)
Notes receivable	62.5	0
Inventory	25.0	120.0
Investment in affiliate	265.0	0
Investment in land	0	40.0
Property, plant, and equipment	550.0	500.0
Less: Accumulated depreciation	(142.0)	(100.0)
Total assets	$1,199.5	$794.0
LIABILITIES AND STOCKHOLDERS' EQUITY		
Accounts payable	$ 110.0	$ 50.0
Other short-term payables	90.0	90.0
Long-term liabilities	600.0	300.0
Common stock	200.0	200.0
Unrealized price increase on available-for-sale investments	0	4.0
Retained earnings	199.5	150.0
Total liabilities and stockholders' equity	$1,199.5	$794.0

LIBERTY MANUFACTURING
INCOME STATEMENT
FOR THE PERIOD ENDED DECEMBER 31, 1995

Revenues:		
Sales	$500.0	
Fees earned	50.0	$550.0
Cost of goods sold		295.0
Gross profit		$255.0
Miscellaneous operating expenses		(120.0)
Interest expense		(45.0)
Depreciation expense		(50.0)
Bad debt expense		(20.0)
Gain on sale of plant		5.0
Realized gain on short-term investments		40.0
Gain on sale of land		2.0
Income on equity investment		20.0
Foreign currency translation gain		12.5
Net income before taxes		$ 99.5
Income taxes		20.0
Net income		$ 79.5

LIBERTY MANUFACTURING
STATEMENT OF CASH FLOWS
FOR THE PERIOD ENDED DECEMBER 31, 1995

Operating activities:		
Net income	$ 79.5	
Depreciation	50.0	
Realized gain on short-term investments	(40.0)	
Gain on sale of plant	(5.0)	
Gain on sale of land	(2.0)	
Income not received in cash on equity investment	(15.0)	
Increase in net accounts receivable	(130.0)	
Decrease in inventory	95.0	
Increase in notes receivable	(62.5)	
Increase in accounts payable	60.0	
Net cash from operating activities		$ 30.0
Investing activities:		
Investment in property, plant, and equipment	$ (60.0)	
Sale of plant	7.0	
Investment in affiliate	(250.0)	
Sale of land	42.0	
Investment in short-term securities	(140.0)	
Sale of short-term securities	120.0	
Net cash from investing activities		(281.0)
Financing activities:		
Issuance of long-term note	$300.0	
Payment of dividend	(30.0)	
Net cash from financing activities		270.0
Increase in cash		$ 19.0
Beginning cash balance		10.0
Ending cash balance		$ 29.0

LIBERTY MANUFACTURING
STATEMENT OF RETAINED EARNINGS
FOR THE PERIOD ENDED DECEMBER 31, 1995

Beginning balance in retained earnings	$150.0
Plus: Net income	79.5
Less: Dividends	(30.0)
Ending balance in retained earnings	$199.5

CASE 2: MICROLINE CORPORATION

You work in the finance and investment department of Mega Industries, which recently purchased several small hi-tech companies. An additional company, Microline Corporation, is presently under consideration. You have been asked to serve on a project team that is preparing a recommendation to the chief financial officer about whether Mega should attempt to acquire Microline. Your duty on this team is to review the company's financial statements and write a memo to the team leader, Sharon Sonneborn. The memo should analyze Microline's solvency position, earning power potential, and the extent to which the reported financial statements reflect the company's "true" financial position and performance. After a brief review of Microline, Sharon believes that in your report you should also address the following important questions:

1. Is there any evidence that management's bonus caused it to enter into any transactions, especially at year-end, that may not have been in the shareholders' interest?
2. Has the debt covenant imposed any restrictions that may have influenced any of management's reporting choices?
3. What was the acquisition price of Littleton when it was purchased by Microline?
4. Is Microline's bad debt allowance sufficient?
5. How much cash was received by Ellery Inc. during 1995, and what percentage of Ellery's total income was paid out in the form of dividends?
6. How much cash was collected from customers during 1995?

Microline's most recent financial statements are as follows (dollars in thousands).

MICROLINE CORPORATION
BALANCE SHEETS
DECEMBER 31, 1995 AND 1994

	1995	1994
ASSETS		
Cash	$ 2,400	$ 2,200
Short-term investments in equity securities	5,000	2,000
Accounts receivable (net)	11,400	7,300
Inventory	13,500	10,500
Prepaid interest expense	700	1,500
Total current assets	$ 33,000	$ 23,500
Investment in affiliate	12,000	10,000
Land	15,000	12,000
Property, plant, & equipment	40,000	35,000
Less: Accumulated depreciation	(8,000)	(6,000)
Goodwill	10,000	10,500
Total assets	$102,000	$85,000
LIABILITIES AND STOCKHOLDERS' EQUITY		
Accounts payable	$ 8,000	$ 6,000
Dividends payable	3,000	2,000
Miscellaneous payables	3,000	3,000
Unearned rent revenue	12,000	14,000
Total current liabilities	$ 26,000	$25,000
Long-term notes payable	29,000	15,000
Common stock	25,000	25,000
Accumulated unrealized revaluations on equity inv.	500	0
Retained earnings	21,500	20,000
Total liabilities & stockholders' equity	$102,000	$85,000

MICROLINE CORPORATION
INCOME STATEMENTS
FOR THE PERIODS ENDING DECEMBER 31, 1995 AND 1994

Sales	$120,000	$105,000
Cost of goods sold	68,000	63,000
Gross profit	$ 52,000	$ 42,000
Selling and administrative expenses	(45,500)	(35,000)
Bad debt expense	(500)	(700)
Depreciation and amortization expense	(5,500)	(4,200)
Interest expense	(2,000)	(1,200)
Other gains (losses)	10,500	2,500
Net income before taxes	$ 9,000	$ 3,400
Income tax expense	3,000	1,600
Net income	$ 6,000	$ 1,800
Earnings per share	$ .24	$ .072

MICROLINE CORPORATION
STATEMENT OF CASH FLOWS
FOR THE PERIOD ENDING DECEMBER 31, 1995

Cash flows from operating activities:		
Net income	$ 6,000	
Depreciation and amortization	5,500	
Loss on sale of machinery	1,800	
Unrealized revaluation of equity investments	500	
Gain on sale of land	(3,000)	
Undistributed affiliate income	(2,000)	
Increase in accounts receivable (net)	(4,100)	
Increase in inventory	(3,000)	
Decrease in prepaid interest expense	800	
Increase in accounts payable	2,000	
Decrease in unearned rent revenue	(2,000)	
Net cash from operating activities		$ 2,500
Cash flows from investing activities:		
Purchases of plant and equipment	$(20,000)	
Purchases of land	(8,000)	
Proceeds from sale of machinery	10,200	
Proceeds from sale of land	8,000	
Net cash from investing activities		(9,800)
Cash flows from financing activities:		
Increases in long-term notes (net)	$ 14,000	
Dividend payments	(3,500)	
Net cash from financing activities		10,500
Increase in cash and short-term equity investments		$ 3,200
Beginning balance in cash and short-term equity investments		4,200
Ending balance in cash and short-term equity investments		$ 7,400

FOOTNOTES (DOLLARS IN THOUSANDS)

Short-Term Equity Investments. Short-term equity investments consist of trading securities and available-for-sale securities. The trading securities were valued at

$4,000 and $1,500 as of December 31, 1995 and 1994, respectively. The available-for-sale securities consists of 50,000 common shares of Acme Inc. that were held throughout 1995. During 1995, equity investments classified as trading securities were actively traded, and related sales generated $2,000 in cash.

Accounts Receivable. The allowance for bad debts was $800 and $700 as of December 31, 1995 and 1994, respectively. Microline estimates bad debts as a percentage of credit sales.

Inventory. Microline carries inventories using the LIFO cost flow assumption and the lower-of-cost-or-market method. The LIFO reserve was $2,800 and $2,500 as of December 31, 1995 and 1994, respectively.

Equity Investments. Microline acquired 40 percent of the outstanding voting stock of Ellery Incorporated, a highly leveraged financial institution, at the beginning of 1994. The corporation paid an amount equal to 40 percent of Ellery's book value at the time of the acquisition and uses the equity method to account for this investment. During 1994 Ellery reported income of $2,000 and declared and paid dividends of $800.

Land. Microline deals in land as an investment. The land is carried on the balance sheet at cost. As of December 31, 1995, the market value of the land was approximately equal to its cost. As of December 31, 1994, the market value of the land was approximately $3,000 in excess of its cost. Land values remained constant throughout 1995, and near the end of the year Microline sold one parcel of land and immediately purchased another similar parcel.

Property, Plant, & Equipment. Microline depreciates its plant and equipment using accelerated rates for both financial reporting and income tax purposes.

Goodwill. Microline has acquired only one company, Littleton Enterprises, since its inception. Goodwill was recognized on the acquisition in the amount by which the purchase price exceeded the fair market value of assets and liabilities of Littleton. At the time of the acquisition the net fair market value of the assets and liabilities of Littleton was $15,000. Microline amortizes goodwill using the straight-line rate over a 40-year period.

Other Gains (Losses). The following chart provides further detail about the other gains (losses) that Microline recognized during 1995 and 1994.

	1995	1994
Rent revenue	$ 4,800	$3,200
Inventory write-down		(1,500)
Realized gains on short-term equity securities	800	
Unrealized gains on short-term equity securities	200	
Gain on sale of land	3,000	
Foreign exchange gain	1,000	
Income from affiliate	2,500	800
Loss on sale of machinery	(1,800)	
Total	$10,500	$2,500

Exchange Gain. On December 3, 1995, Microline sold goods to a customer in Germany and agreed to accept 8,000 deutsche marks in payment. The receivable was still outstanding as of December 31, 1995, at which time the exchange rate of deutsche marks to dollars was 1.6dm/$1. No other transactions were conducted outside U.S. borders during 1994 or 1995.

Short- and Long-Term Debt. On November 15, 1995, Microline signed a 90-day note payable in the amount of $8,000. As of December 31, 1995, this note was classified as long term because Microline intends to refinance it indefinitely. Microline also signed a long-term note in the amount of $6,000. This 10-year note includes an interest rate of 8 percent and requires that Microline maintain a current ratio of greater than 1.0 over the 10-year life.

Income Taxes. Microline's effective income tax rate is 34 percent.

Executive Compensation. At the end of each year Microline's executives share equally in a bonus, which is equal to 25 percent of the dollar amount by which the corporation's net income exceeds 10 percent of the stockholders' equity dollar amount at the beginning of the year.

Revenue Recognition. All sales made by Microline are on credit, and Microline recognizes revenue when goods are shipped.

CASE 3: TECHNIC ENTERPRISES AND SONAR-SUN INC.

You are an investment analyst for Timken Brothers, a small brokerage firm. Recent developments in the medical equipment industry have caused a number of Timken's customers to inquire about two particular companies, Technic Enterprises and Sonar-Sun Incorporated. You have been asked to analyze the financial statements of these two companies and—on that basis only—rate them on a scale from 1 (very weak) to 10 (very strong) with respect to (1) solvency position, (2) earning power and persistence, and (3) earnings quality. In addition to the ratings, you have been asked to provide a memo stating why the ratings on these three dimensions do (or do not) differ between the two companies. The ratings and the memo will comprise part of a report that will be used by Timken's brokers to guide their buy/sell recommendations. The financial statements of Technic Enterprises and Sonar-Sun Inc. follow.

TECHNIC ENTERPRISES

The financial statements of Technic Enterprises and selected additional information are provided on the following pages. Dollar amounts in thousands.

TECHNIC ENTERPRISES
BALANCE SHEETS
DECEMBER 31, 1995 AND 1994

	1995	1994
ASSETS		
Cash	$ 250	$ 200
Short-term investments	2,900	1,600
Accounts receivable	5,500	3,000
Less: Allowance for uncollectibles	(100)	(200)
Notes receivable	1,250	0
Inventory	1,100	2,400
Total current assets	$10,900	$ 7,000
Investment in affiliate	5,300	0
Investment in land	700	800
Property, plant, and equipment	10,900	10,000
Less: Accumulated depreciation	(2,900)	(2,000)
Total assets	$24,900	$15,800
LIABILITIES AND STOCKHOLDERS' EQUITY		
Accounts payable	$ 2,700	$ 1,000
Other short-term payables	2,400	1,800
Total current liabilities	$ 5,100	$ 2,800
Long-term liabilities	12,000	6,000
Common stock	4000	4,000
Unrealized price decrease on short-term investments	(200)	0
Retained earnings	4,000	3,000
Total liabilities and stockholders' equity	$24,900	$15,800

TECHNIC ENTERPRISES
INCOME STATEMENT
FOR THE PERIOD ENDED DECEMBER 31, 1995

Revenues:		
Sales	$10,000	
Fees earned	1,000	
Less: Bad debt charge	(400)	$10,600
Cost of goods sold		(5,900)
Gross profit		$ 4,700
Miscellaneous operating expenses		(2,400)
Interest expense		(900)
Depreciation expense		(1,000)
Income on equity investment		400
Miscellaneous gains and losses (net)		1,480
Net income before taxes and accounting change		$ 2,280
Income tax expense		700
Net income before accounting change		$ 1,580
Income effect of change in inventory costing method		250
Net income		$ 1,830

TECHNIC ENTERPRISES
STATEMENT OF RETAINED EARNINGS
FOR THE PERIOD ENDED DECEMBER 31, 1995

Beginning balance in retained earnings	$3,000
Plus: Net income	1,830
Less: Dividends	(830)
Ending balance in retained earnings	$4,000

TECHNIC ENTERPRISES
STATEMENT OF CASH FLOWS
FOR THE PERIOD ENDED DECEMBER 31, 1995

Operating activities:		
Net income	$ 1,830	
Depreciation	1,000	
Gains on short-term investments	(1,100)	
Gain on sale of building	(80)	
Gain on sale of land	(200)	
Equity income in excess of cash received	(300)	
Increase in net accounts receivable	(2,600)	
Decrease in inventory	1,300	
Increase in notes receivable	(1,250)	
Increase in accounts payable	1,700	
Increase in other short-term payables	600	
Net cash from operating activities		$ 900
Investing activities:		
Investment in property, plant, and equipment	$(1,040)	
Sale of building	120	
Investment in affiliate	(5,000)	
Investment in land	(700)	
Sale of land	1,000	
Investment in short-term investments	(2,800)	
Sale of short-term investments	2,400	
Net cash from investing activities		(6,020)
Financing activities:		
Issuance of long-term note	$6,000	
Payment of dividend	(830)	
Net cash from financing activities		5,170
Increase in cash		$ 50
Beginning cash balance		200
Ending cash balance		$ 250

FOOTNOTES (DOLLARS IN THOUSANDS, EXCEPT PER SHARE AMOUNTS)

Revenue Recognition. All sales of inventory are on credit and are recorded in the sales account when goods are shipped. Services are exchanged for short-term notes and recorded in the fees earned account when the service is substantially complete.

Uncollectibles. The allowance method is used to account for bad debts, and accounts are written off when payment is not made within one year.

Notes receivable. On November 15, 1995, Technic completed a service for Belton A.G., a manufacturer located in Germany. Technic received a note from Belton promising payment of 2,000 German deutsche marks within 30 days, and on that date two deutsche marks exchanged for one U.S. dollar. Technic has no other exposure to foreign currency exchange risk.

Short-Term Investments. Short-term investments are carried on the balance sheet at market value and consist of equity securities classified as either trading or available-for-sale. As of December 31, 1994, trading securities were valued at $1,300. During 1995 no available-for-sale securities were acquired or sold.

Inventory. Technic uses the first-in, first-out (FIFO) cost flow assumption and carries inventories at the lower-of-cost-or-market value. All inventory purchases are made on account and recorded as accounts payable.

In addition, during 1995 Technic changed the method used to allocate labor costs to cost of goods manufactured. To achieve a better matching of revenues and expenses, the company now allocates certain of these costs to inventory that previously were charged directly to operating expenses. The change increased 1995 net income by $250, net of applicable income taxes.

Investment in Affiliate. On January 30, 1994, Technic purchased 40% (50,000 shares) of the outstanding equity of Lehmon Financial Services @ $100.00 per share. No goodwill was recognized on the purchase. The information below refers to Lehmon Financial Services.

	1995	1994
Assets	$9,900.00	$8,300.00
Liabilities	8,300.00	7,500.00
Stockholders' equity	1,600.00	800.00
Stock price per share (Dec. 31)	8.50	10.35

Land Investments. During 1994 Technic invested in ten equivalent parcels of land, paying approximately $80 for each parcel. In November of 1995 the company sold these parcels, but chose to repurchase seven of them in December, when it revised its estimate of future real estate appraisal rates.

Property, Plant, and Equipment. Technic uses the straight-line method of depreciation and depreciates property, plant, and equipment over time periods ranging from 5 to 40 years.

Miscellaneous Gains and Losses. Miscellaneous gains and losses consist of the following items:

Write-down of inventory to market value	$ (150)
Gain on sale of building	80
Realized gain on short-term investments	800
Unrealized gain on short-term investments	300
Gain on sale of land	200
Foreign currency translation gain	250
Total	$1,480

Additional Information. Interest rates on outstanding loans range from 6 percent to 10 percent, and general inflation during 1995 was approximately 5 percent. The company's effective income tax rate is 34 percent.

SONAR-SUN INC.

The financial statements of Sonar-Sun Inc. and selected additional information are provided on the following pages. Dollar amounts in thousands.

FOOTNOTES (DOLLARS IN THOUSANDS)

Revenue Recognition. All sales of inventory are made on account. Sonar-Sun recognizes revenue on such sales when goods are shipped. Revenues on services, where cash is received in advance, are estimated at year end, based on the extent to which the service is completed.

Accounts Receivable. Sonar-Sun uses the allowance method to account for uncollectible accounts. The dollar value in the allowance account as of the end of 1995 was $800. Outstanding receivables are written off when they are deemed uncollectible, and during 1995 $500 of such accounts were removed from the books.

Inventory. Inventory is carried at the lower-of-cost-or-market rule using the last-in, first-out (LIFO) inventory cost flow assumption. Current costs of the inventory as of the end of 1995 and 1994 were $45,000 and $37,000, respectively.

Equity Investments. Equity investments listed as non-current are considered available-for-sale securities. No sales of such securities were made during 1995.

Investment in Affiliate. Sonar-Sun owns 25 percent of the outstanding voting stock of EDM Suppliers, and this investment is carried on the financial statements under the equity method.

Property, Plant, & Equipment. Sonar-Sun uses accelerated methods to depreciate its plant and equipment for both reporting and tax purposes. At the end of 1995 and 1994, accumulated depreciation totaled $12,000 and $8,000, respectively.

Wholly Owned Subsidiaries. Sonar-Sun owns 100 percent of the outstanding voting stock of two companies: Kenworth South and Wallingford Atlantic. The stock of Kenworth South was purchased for cash on January 1, 1992. The stock of Wallingford Atlantic was purchased near the end of 1995. The purchase price consisted of $24,000 in cash and a $5,000 long-term note. Wallingford was comprised of machinery and real estate only. Goodwill acquired in these acquisitions is amortized over a 5-year period using the straight-line rate.

Write-Downs. Sonar-Sun reduced the book value of its inventory by $3,000 to replacement cost in accordance with the lower-of-cost-or-market rule. It also wrote off certain equipment at a book loss of $2,000.

Foreign Currency. Sonar-Sun purchases a considerable portion of its inventory from a French supplier, paying its accounts in French francs. Certain accounts payable owed to this supplier were revalued as of year-end to reflect the advance of the French franc against the dollar from 6 francs per dollar to 5 francs per dollar.

Income Taxes. Sonar-Sun's effective tax rate is 34 percent.

SONAR-SUN INC.
BALANCE SHEET
DECEMBER 31, 1995 AND 1994

	1995	1994
ASSETS		
Cash	$ 8,500	$ 2,600
Accounts receivable (net)	17,200	13,700
Inventory	39,000	33,000
Prepaid insurance	4,000	3,000
Total current assets	$ 68,700	$ 52,300
Equity investments	7,000	4,000
Investments in affiliate	11,300	12,000
Real estate	28,000	25,000
Property, plant, & equipment (net)	44,000	37,000
Goodwill	13,000	8,000
Total assets	$172,000	$138,300
LIABILITIES AND STOCKHOLDERS' EQUITY		
Accounts payable	$ 24,000	$ 13,000
Dividends payable	12,000	13,000
Unearned revenues	15,000	5,000
Other payables	15,000	14,000
Total current liabilities	$ 66,000	$ 45,000
Long-term bank notes	45,000	40,000
Common stock	20,000	15,000
Unrealized price increase on equity investments	1,000	0
Retained earnings	40,000	38,300
Total liabilities and stockholders' equity	$172,000	$138,300

SONAR-SUN INC.
INCOME STATEMENT
FOR THE PERIOD ENDED DECEMBER 31, 1995

Sales	$145,000
Revenues from services	35,000
Income from affiliate	4,000
Cost of goods sold	(63,000)
Operating expenses	(65,000)
Depreciation and amortization expenses	(10,000)
Bad debt expense	(1,000)
Writedowns	(5,000)
Loss on translation of foreign currencies	(1,500)
Interest expense	(5,800)
Net income before taxes	$ 32,700
Income tax expense	(12,000)
Net income	$ 20,700

SONAR-SUN INC.
STATEMENT OF CASH FLOWS
FOR THE PERIOD ENDED DECEMBER 31, 1995

Operating activities:		
Net income	$20,700	
Depreciation and amortization	10,000	
Writedown of equipment	2,000	
Dividends received over income from affiliates	700	
Increase in accounts receivable	(3,500)	
Increase in prepaid insurance	(1,000)	
Increase in inventory	(6,000)	
Increase in accounts payable	11,000	
Increase in unearned revenues	10,000	
Increase in other short-term payables	1,000	
Net cash from operating activities		$44,900
Investing activities:		
Investments in equity securities	$ (2,000)	
Acquisition of Wallingford Atlantic	(24,000)	
Sale of real estate	2,000	
Net cash used in investing activities		(24,000)
Financing activities:		
Issuance of common stock	$ 5,000	
Dividends paid	(20,000)	
Net cash from financing activities		(15,000)
Increase in cash balance		$ 5,900
Beginning cash balance		2,600
Ending cash balance		$ 8,500

CHAPTER 9

LONG-LIVED ASSETS

LEARNING OBJECTIVES

LO 1 Define long-lived assets, and describe how the matching principle underlies the methods used to account for them.

LO 2 Identify the major questions that must be addressed when accounting for long-lived assets and how the answers to these questions can affect the financial statements.

LO 3 Identify the costs that should be included in the capitalized cost of a long-lived asset.

LO 4 Describe the accounting treatment of postacquisition expenditures.

LO 5 Explain how the cost of a long-lived asset is allocated over its useful life, and describe the alternative allocation methods.

LO 6 Identify the major economic consequences associated with the methods used to account for long-lived assets.

LO 7 Specify how to account for the disposition of long-lived assets.

L O   1 This chapter concerns long-lived assets, which are assets used in the operations of a business and that provide benefits that extend beyond the current operating period. Included in this category of assets are land, buildings, machinery, equipment, natural resource costs, intangible assets, and deferred costs.

Land includes the cost of real estate that is used in the operations of the company. **Fixed assets**, such as buildings, machinery, and equipment, are often located on this real estate. **Natural resource costs** include the costs of acquiring the rights to extract natural resources. Such costs are very important in the operations of the extractive industries (e.g., mining, petroleum, and natural gas). **Intangible assets** are characterized by rights, privileges, and benefits of possession rather than physical existence. Examples include the costs of acquiring patents, copyrights, trademarks, and goodwill. **Deferred costs** represent a miscellaneous category of intangible assets, often including prepaid expenses that provide benefits for a length of time that extends beyond the current period, organization costs, and other start-up costs associated with beginning operations (e.g., legal and licensing fees). These definitions are often firm specific. Land, for example, represents the inventory of a real estate firm, but it is a long-lived asset for a retailer. Similarly, Boeing carries aircraft in its inventory that when sold becomes a fixed asset on the balance sheet of United Air Lines, the purchaser. The methods used to account for land, fixed assets, and natural resource costs (often using an account called Property, Plant, and Equipment) are covered in the main text of this chapter. Intangible assets and deferred costs are discussed in Appendix 9A, and a critique of the methods used to account for long-lived assets is provided in Appendix 9B.

Stockholders, investors, creditors, managers, and auditors are interested in the nature and condition of a company's long-lived assets because such assets represent the company's capacity to produce and sell goods and/or services in the future. Planning and executing major capital expenditures in such items as land, buildings, and machinery are some of management's most important concerns. Long-lived asset turnover (Sales/Average long-lived assets) is a financial ratio used to assess how efficiently a company uses its long-lived assets. In general, if the ratio is high the company is generating large amounts of sales with a relatively small investment in long-lived assets. As discussed in the next section, this ratio may be particularly useful when comparing the relative performance of manufacturers and service enterprises.

THE RELATIVE SIZE OF LONG-LIVED ASSETS

The relative size of long-lived assets on the balance sheet of major U.S. companies varies across industries. Figure 9–1 contains the ratio of property, plant, and equipment plus intangibles to total assets for a selected group of industries. Note that the ratio varies considerably from over 60 percent in general services to less than 20 percent in financial services. Eating places like McDonald's, Wendy's, and Ryan's Steak House invest heavily in restaurant buildings. Indeed, each of these companies reports fixed assets of over 70 percent of its total assets. At the other extreme, BankAmerica, Citicorp, and Merrill Lynch hold fixed assets of less than 3 percent of their total assets because financial institutions rely more heavily on receivables and security investments. Retailers, like Kmart and Toys "R" Us, require almost no equipment and often lease their facilities. Their investment in long-lived assets is relatively less than that of manufacturers, like Chrysler and Exxon, who own their facilities and whose oper-

FIGURE 9–1	INDUSTRY	SIC CODE	NO. OF COMPANIES	PP&E + INTANGIBLES/ TOTAL ASSETS
Property, plant, and equipment (PP&E) plus intangibles as a percentage of total assets (industry averages)	**MANUFACTURING**			
	Motor Vehicles	3711	95	.29
	Petroleum and Gas	1311	872	.59
	RETAILING			
	Department Stores	5311	641	.23
	Hobby, Toy & Games	5945	519	.17
	GENERAL SERVICES			
	Eating Places	5812	2,427	.64
	Telephone Commun.	4813	1,130	.68
	FINANCIAL SERVICES			
	Security Brokers	6211	1,312	.16

Source: Compiled from data published in *Industry Norms and Key Business Ratios* (Dun & Bradstreet, Inc., 1994)

ations require heavy machinery and equipment. As a result, the issues discussed in this chapter are generally more important to manufacturers and services, those entities that tend to invest heavily in long-lived assets.

LONG-LIVED ASSET ACCOUNTING: GENERAL ISSUES AND FINANCIAL STATEMENT EFFECTS

LO 2 The matching principle states that efforts (expenses) should be matched against benefits (revenues) in the period when the benefits are recognized. The cost of acquiring a long-lived asset, which is expected to generate revenues in future periods is, therefore, capitalized in the period of acquisition. As the revenues associated with the long-lived asset are recognized, these costs are **amortized** with a periodic adjusting journal entry. Stated another way, since expenses represent the costs of assets consumed in conducting business, at the end of each accounting period an entry is recorded to reflect the expense associated with the portion of the long-lived asset consumed during that period.

The form of journal entries to capitalize and amortize a piece of equipment follows. Assume that the equipment is purchased on January 1 for $10,000, and its cost is amortized evenly over its four-year useful life. Recall that amortization of a fixed asset is called **depreciation** and that the dollar amount of the depreciation expense recognized each year is accumulated in an accumulated depreciation account.

Jan. 1	Equipment (+A)	10,000	
	Cash (−A)		10,000
	Acquired equipment.		
Dec. 31	Depreciation Expense (E, −SE)	2,500	
	Accumulated Depreciation (−A)		2,500
	Recognized depreciation during first year.		

The preceding description and journal entries indicate implicitly that three basic questions must be answered when accounting for long-lived assets:

1. What dollar amount should be included in the capitalized cost of the long-lived asset?
2. Over what time period should this cost be amortized?
3. At what rate should this cost be amortized?

As the following illustration shows, the answers to these questions can have significant effects on the financial statements.

Assume that Rudman Manufacturing acquired equipment for a purchase price of $9,000 and paid an additional $3,000 to have it painted. Figure 9–2 compares the journal entries to record the acquisition and the depreciation charge and the resulting balance sheet value of the equipment in four different cases. In Case 1 Rudman capitalizes the entire $12,000 cost and depreciates it evenly ($4,000 per year) over a three-year period. In Case 2 Rudman capitalizes the $9,000 purchase cost, expenses the $3,000 painting charge, and depreciates the purchase cost evenly ($3,000 per year) over a three-year period. In Case 3 Rudman capitalizes the entire $12,000 cost and depreciates it evenly ($6,000 per year) over a two-year period. In Case 4 Rudman capitalizes the entire $12,000 cost and depreciates it over a three-year period using an accelerated rate, i.e., greater depreciation charges are recognized in the early years of the asset's life.

Comparing Case 1 to Case 2 illustrates the financial statement effects of varying the amount of capitalized cost. Note that increasing the amount of capitalized cost (Case 1) reduces the total expense recognized in Year 1, but this increases the depreciation expense recognized during each year of the asset's useful life.

Comparing Case 1 to Case 3 illustrates the financial statement effects of varying the estimated useful life. As the life estimate gets shorter (Case 3), the amount of depreciation expense recognized in each year increases. In the extreme case, estimating the useful life of an asset at one year is equivalent to expensing its cost.

Comparing Case 1 to Case 4 illustrates the financial statement effects of varying the depreciation rate. Using an accelerated rate (Case 4) increases the amount of depreciation expense recognized in the early years, but it gives rise to smaller amounts of depreciation expense in later years.

The differences among the four cases, with respect to the amount of expense recognized and the balance sheet value of the equipment, are summarized in Figure 9–3. Note that the total amount of expense recognized under the four cases is the same ($12,000). Varying the capitalized cost, estimated life, and depreciation rate affects only the timing of the expense recognition throughout the three-year period.

Choosing to capitalize and amortize or expense the costs associated with acquiring long-lived assets can have significant effects on the financial statements. For example, Owens-Corning Fiberglass increased its 1994 income by $123 million when it chose to capitalize, instead of expense, the costs of rebuilding its glass metal furnaces. The major railroads, including Burlington Northern, CSX Sante Fe, Norfolk & Western, and Union Pacific, increased profits by an average of 25 percent when they chose to capitalize and amortize, instead of expense, the costs of laying track. The net income of Comserv, a Minneapolis-based maker of software systems, was boosted by $6.5 million because the company chose to capitalize and amortize, instead of expense, software development costs. Changing the useful-life estimate or adjusting the rate at which a long-lived asset is amortized can also significantly affect the financial statements and important financial ratios. American Airlines decreased expenses by $14.6 million and increased earnings per share from $0.72 to $1.11 when it decided to depreciate the cost of its aircraft over a longer period of time. Blockbuster

FIGURE 9–2

The effects of depreciation period on the financial statements: Rudman Manufacturing

CASE 1: $12,000 cost is capitalized and depreciated evenly over a three-year period.

YEAR 1			YEAR 2			YEAR 3		
Equipment (+A)	12,000							
Cash (−A)		12,000						
Depr. Exp. (E, −SE)	4,000		Depr. Exp. (E, −SE)	4,000		Depr. Exp. (E, −SE)	4,000	
Accum. Depr. (−A)		4,000	Accum. Depr. (−A)		4,000	Accum. Depr. (−A)		4,000
Balance sheet value:*	$8,000		$4,000			$0		

CASE 2: $9,000 cost is capitalized and depreciated evenly over a three-year period.

YEAR 1			YEAR 2			YEAR 3		
Equipment (+A)	9,000							
Cash (−A)		9,000						
Maint. Exp. (E, −SE)	3,000							
Cash (−A)		3,000						
Depr. Exp. (E, −SE)	3,000		Depr. Exp. (E, −SE)	3,000		Depr. Exp. (E, −SE)	3,000	
Accum. Depr. (−A)		3,000	Accum. Depr. (−A)		3,000	Accum. Depr. (−A)		3,000
Balance sheet value:*	$6,000		$3,000			$0		

CASE 3: $12,000 cost is capitalized and depreciated evenly over a two-year period.

YEAR 1			YEAR 2			YEAR 3		
Equipment (+A)	12,000							
Cash (−A)		12,000						
Depr. Exp. (E, −SE)	6,000		Depr. Exp. (E, −SE)	6,000				
Accum. Depr. (−A)		6,000	Accum. Depr. (−A)		6,000			
Balance sheet value:*	$6,000		$0			$0		

CASE 4: $12,000 cost is capitalized and depreciated over a three-year period at an accelerated rate.

YEAR 1			YEAR 2			YEAR 3		
Equipment (+A)	12,000							
Cash (−A)		12,000						
Depr. Exp. (E, −SE)	6,000		Depr. Exp. (E, −SE)	4,000		Depr. Exp. (E, −SE)	2,000	
Accum. Depr. (−A)		6,000	Accum. Depr. (−A)		4,000	Accum. Depr. (−A)		2,000
Balance sheet value:*	$6,000		$2,000			$0		

*Balance sheet value, also known as *book value*, equals capitalized cost less accumulated depreciation.

FIGURE 9–3

Comparative expense amounts and balance sheet values

	YEAR 1	YEAR 2	YEAR 3	TOTAL
CASE 1:				
Expense	$4,000	$4,000	$4,000	$12,000
Balance sheet value	8,000	4,000	0	
CASE 2:				
Expense	6,000	3,000	3,000	12,000
Balance sheet value	6,000	3,000	0	
CASE 3:				
Expense	6,000	6,000	0	12,000
Balance sheet value	6,000	0	0	
CASE 4:				
Expense	6,000	4,000	2,000	12,000
Balance sheet value	6,000	2,000	0	

Video recently slowed the amortization period for its tapes from 9 to 36 months, a choice that added 20% to its reported income. A recent report of Burlington Northern disclosed that the company's net income was reduced by $336 million when it changed the rate at which it depreciated its railroad assets.

AN OVERVIEW OF LONG-LIVED ASSET ACCOUNTING

Figure 9–4 summarizes and organizes the topics covered in the remainder of the chapter. As shown at the top of the figure, there are three points in time during the life of a long-lived asset when important accounting issues must be addressed: (1) when the long-lived asset is acquired (purchased or manufactured), (2) while the long-lived asset is in use, and (3) when the long-lived asset is disposed of.

FIGURE 9–4

Accounting for long-lived assets

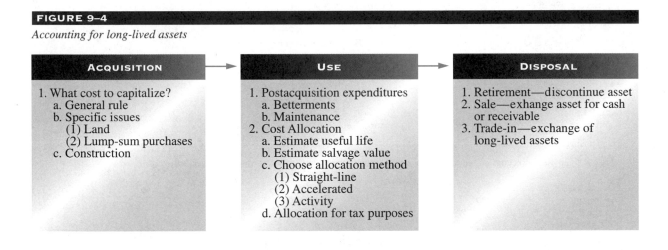

ACQUISITION	USE	DISPOSAL

1. What cost to capitalize?
  a. General rule
  b. Specific issues
    (1) Land
    (2) Lump-sum purchases
  c. Construction
	1. Postacquisition expenditures
	  a. Betterments
	  b. Maintenance
	2. Cost Allocation
	  a. Estimate useful life
	  b. Estimate salvage value
	  c. Choose allocation method
	    (1) Straight-line
	    (2) Accelerated
	    (3) Activity
	  d. Allocation for tax purposes
		1. Retirement—discontinue asset
		2. Sale—exhange asset for cash or receivable
		3. Trade-in—exchange of long-lived assets

ACQUISITION: WHAT COSTS TO CAPITALIZE?

LO 3 The acquisition cost of a long-lived asset is determined by either (1) the fair market value (FMV) of the acquired asset or (2) the FMV of what was given up to acquire the asset, whichever is more readily determinable. In almost all cases, the FMV of what was given up is used because cash, which by definition is at FMV, is normally given up in such exchanges. Further, the capitalized cost (i.e., the FMV of what was given up) should include all costs required to bring the asset into serviceable or usable condition and location. Such costs include not only the actual purchase cost of the asset but also costs like freight, installation, taxes, and title fees. For example, suppose that the purchase cost of a piece of equipment is $25,000, and it costs $2,000 to have it delivered, $1,500 to have it installed, and taxes and title fees total $500 and $300, respectively. The total capitalized cost of the equipment would then be $29,300 ($25,000 + $2,000 + $1,500 + $500 + $300), and the following journal entry would be entered to record the acquisition, assuming that cash is paid for the equipment.

Equipment (+A)   29,300
    Cash (−A)   29,300
Acquired equipment.

THE ACQUISITION OF LAND

All costs incurred to acquire land and make it ready for use should be included in the land account. They include (1) the purchase price of the land; (2) closing costs, such as title, legal, and recording fees; (3) costs incurred to get the land in condition for its intended use, such as razing old buildings, grading, filling, draining and clearing (less any proceeds from the sale of salvaged materials); (4) assumptions of any back taxes, liens, or mortgages; and (5) additional land improvements assumed to be permanent, such as landscaping, street lights, sewers, and drainage systems. While the costs incurred to acquire land and prepare it for use are capitalized, *they are not amortized* over future periods. The process of amortization requires the estimate of a useful life. Because land is considered to have an indefinite life, its cost cannot be amortized.

LUMP-SUM PURCHASES

A special problem arises when more than one asset is purchased at a single (lump-sum) price. In such situations the total purchase cost must be allocated to the individual assets. If the FMVs of the purchased assets can be objectively determined, the total purchase cost can be allocated to each asset on the basis of its relative FMV. This cost allocation scheme is based on the assumption that costs vary in direct proportion to FMV.

To illustrate, assume that ABC Incorporated purchases three assets (inventory, land, and equipment) from Liquidated Limited, a company that is in the process of liquidation. The total price for the assets is $40,000. The individual FMVs of the three assets and the allocation of the $40,000 purchase cost to each asset appear in Figure 9–5.

Note that the cost allocated to each asset is in direct proportion to the asset's portion of the total FMV. The inventory, for example, accounts for 40 percent ($20,000/$50,000) of the total FMV and thereby receives 40 percent ($16,000/$40,000) of the total costs. The equipment is treated similarly. Land accounts for 20 percent ($10,000/$50,000) of the total FMV and receives 20 percent ($8,000/$40,000) of the total cost.

Two features about this cost allocation approach are very important. First, it is based on FMVs, which by nature are very subjective and therefore are often expressed in terms of ranges rather than precise estimates. Second, while all three costs in this example are capitalized, each is treated differently in the future. The $16,000 inventory

FIGURE 9–5	FMVs	ALLOCATION FORMULA	ALLOCATED COST
Cost allocation on the basis of relative FMVs			
Inventory	$20,000	[($20,000 ÷ $50,000) × $40,000]	$16,000
Land	10,000	[($10,000 ÷ $50,000) × $40,000]	8,000
Equipment	20,000	[($20,000 ÷ $50,000) × $40,000]	16,000
Total	$50,000		$40,000

cost will be converted to Cost of Goods Sold when the inventory is sold, the $8,000 land cost is not subject to amortization, and the $16,000 equipment cost will be depreciated over the equipment's useful life. Taken together, these two features indicate that the subjective choice of FMVs can have significant effects on future net income amounts, a fact that management may be able to exploit. For example, if management wishes to maximize income, it can choose from within the FMV ranges values that allocate as much cost as possible to land, which will not be amortized, and as little as possible to inventory, which will be converted to Cost of Goods Sold relatively soon. On the other hand, management can minimize income (e.g., income tax reporting, building hidden reserves, or taking a bath) by allocating as much cost as possible to inventory and as little as possible to land.

To illustrate, assume in the previous example that the FMV of equipment was assessed at $20,000, but the FMVs of inventory and land were expressed as being somewhere within the following ranges: inventory ($15,000−$25,000), land ($5,000−$15,000). Figure 9–6 compares the resulting costs under two allocation schemes: (1) "Maximize future income" where the lowest value for inventory ($15,000) and the highest value for land ($15,000) are used, and (2) "Minimize future income" where the highest value for inventory ($25,000) and the lowest value for land ($5,000) are used.

The procedure of allocating costs on the basis of FMVs is also used when a company acquires the assets and liabilities of another company (i.e., through the purchase of outstanding stock) and must allocate the purchase price to those assets and liabilities (see Appendix 8A). As illustrated in Figure 9–6, such allocations can be very subjective, giving management much reporting discretion in this area.

FIGURE 9–6

Comparing cost allocation methods

(1) MAXIMIZE FUTURE INCOME:

	FMVs	ALLOCATION FORMULA	ALLOCATED COST
Inventory	$15,000	[($15,000 ÷ $50,000) × $40,000]	$12,000
Land	15,000	[($15,000 ÷ $50,000) × $40,000]	12,000
Equipment	20,000	[($20,000 ÷ $50,000) × $40,000]	16,000
Total	$50,000		$40,000

(2) MINIMIZE FUTURE INCOME:

	FMVs	ALLOCATION FORMULA	ALLOCATED COST
Inventory	$25,000	[($25,000 ÷ $50,000) × $40,000]	$20,000
Land	5,000	[($ 5,000 ÷ $50,000) × $40,000]	4,000
Equipment	20,000	[($20,000 ÷ $50,000) × $40,000]	16,000
Total	$50,000		$40,000

CONSTRUCTION OF LONG-LIVED ASSETS

When companies construct their own long-lived assets, all costs required to get the assets into operating condition must be included in the long-lived asset account, including the costs of materials, labor, and overhead used in the construction process.

The costs may also include interest on funds borrowed to finance the construction. For example, note the following excerpts from annual reports of Adolph Coors Company and Standard Oil Company.

*   Adolph Coors Company: "Properties: The Company has engineering and construction staffs responsible for the majority of plant expansion projects and installation of machinery and equipment. Capitalized costs of projects undertaken internally consist of direct materials, labor, and allocated overhead."
*   Standard Oil Company: "Capitalized Interest: Interest costs incurred in connection with significant expenditures for the construction or acquisition of property, plant, and equipment are capitalized."

Although determining the costs of materials and labor is relatively straightforward, allocating overhead and interest to the cost of long-lived assets can be difficult and is often arbitrary. Such issues are normally covered in management or intermediate financial accounting courses.

POSTACQUISITION EXPENDITURES: BETTERMENTS OR MAINTENANCE?

LO 4 Costs are often incurred subsequent to the acquisition or manufacture of a long-lived asset. Such **postacquisition expenditures** serve either to improve the existing asset or merely to maintain it. Costs incurred to improve the asset are called **betterments**, and costs incurred merely to repair it or maintain its current level of productivity are classified as **maintenance**.

The following guidelines are used to distinguish betterments from maintenance expenditures. In order to be considered a betterment, a postacquisition expenditure must improve the long-lived asset in at least one of four ways:

1. Increase the asset's useful life over that which was originally estimated.
2. Improve the quality of the asset's output.
3. Increase the quantity of the asset's output.
4. Reduce the costs associated with operating the asset.

Betterments are usually infrequent and tend to involve large dollar amounts. Maintenance expenditures, on the other hand, fail to meet any of the criteria mentioned above and tend to be periodic. Also, maintenance items are normally small, but certain expenditures (e.g., replacing a building roof every ten years) can be significant.

Postacquisition expenditures classified as betterments should be capitalized, added to the cost of the long-lived asset, and then amortized over its remaining life. Expenditures classified as maintenance should be treated as current expenses. For example, note the following excerpts from annual reports of American Standard, Inc., and Adolph Coors Company.

*   American Standard, Inc.: "Facilities: The company capitalizes in the Facilities account costs, including interest during construction, fixed-asset additions, improvements, and betterments that add to productive capacity or extend the asset life. Maintenance and repair expenditures are charged against income."
*   Adolph Coors Company: "Properties: Expenditures for new facilities and significant betterments of existing properties are capitalized at cost. Maintenance and repairs are expensed as incurred."

Distinguishing between a betterment and a maintenance expenditure, even with the criteria mentioned above, is often difficult in practice, giving management reporting discretion in this area. In many cases, however, materiality plays an important role because postacquisition expenditures are frequently small and in such situations they are expensed, regardless of their nature.

To illustrate the accounting treatment for betterments and maintenance expenditures, assume that Jerry's Delivery Service purchased an automobile on January 1, 1996, for $10,000. The purchase cost was capitalized, and the useful life of the automobile was estimated to be four years from the date of purchase. Each year Jerry had the car tuned up and serviced at a cost of $300. During the second year the muffler was replaced for $80, and during the third year the car was painted at a cost of $450. At the beginning of the fourth year Jerry paid $1,000 to have the engine completely overhauled. The overhaul increased the automobile's expected life beyond the original estimate by an additional year. Figure 9–7 traces the book value, depreciation, and maintenance expenses associated with the automobile over its five-year life.

Note that all postacquisition costs are treated as expenses except for the overhaul, which increased the automobile's life beyond the original 4-year estimate. The $1,000 cost of the overhaul was capitalized at the beginning of the fourth year and, with the book value ($2,500) at that time, was depreciated evenly over the remaining two years of the car's useful life.

FIGURE 9–7	1996	1997	1998	1999	2000
Betterments and maintenance expenditures: Jerry's Delivery Service					
Book value (1/1)	$10,000	$7,500	$5,000	$2,500	$1,750
Overhaul				1,000	
Less: Depreciation	2,500[b]	2,500	2,500	1,750[c]	1,750
Book value[a] (12/31)	$ 7,500	$5,000	$2,500	$1,750	$ 0
Maintenance expenses:					
Tune-up	300	300	300	300	300
Muffler replacement		80			
Paint job			450		

[a]Book value equals cost less accumulated depreciation.
[b]2,500 = ($10,000 ÷ 4 years)
[c]1,750 = ($2,500 + $1,000) ÷ 2 years

COST ALLOCATION: AMORTIZING CAPITALIZED COSTS

Once the cost of a long-lived asset has been determined, it must be allocated over the asset's useful life. Such allocation is necessary if the costs are to be matched against the benefits produced by the asset. The allocation process requires three steps: (1) estimate a useful life, (2) estimate a salvage value, and (3) choose a cost allocation (depreciation) method.

ESTIMATING THE USEFUL LIFE AND SALVAGE VALUE

Accurately estimating the useful life and salvage value of a long-lived asset is extremely difficult. An important consideration is the **physical**

obsolescence of the asset. At what time in the future will the asset deteriorate to the point when repairs are not economically feasible, and what will be the asset's salvage value at that time? It is virtually impossible to predict accurately the condition of an asset very far into the future, let alone predict the **salvage value**, the dollar amount that can be recovered when the asset is sold, traded in, or scrapped.

The problem of predicting useful lives and salvage values is complicated further by technological developments. The usefulness of a long-lived asset is largely determined by technological advancements, which could at any time render certain long-lived assets obsolete. **Technical obsolescence**, in turn, could force the early replacement of a long-lived asset that is still in reasonably good working order.

As a result, generally accepted accounting principles provide no clear guidelines for determining the useful lives and future salvage values of long-lived assets. In practice, many companies assume salvage value to be zero and estimate useful lives by referring to guidelines developed by the Internal Revenue Service. These guidelines, however, were established for use in determining taxable income and need not be followed in the preparation of the financial statements. Consequently, management can use its own discretion when estimating salvage values and useful lives. As long as the estimates seem reasonable and are applied in a systematic and consistent manner, auditors generally allow managers to do what they wish in this area. Sears, Roebuck & Co., for example, depreciates its equipment generally over a 5–10 year period, and its real property over a 40–50 year period. Figure 9–8 shows the range of estimated useful lives for different kinds of fixed assets reported by 600 major U.S. companies.

FIGURE 9–8		
Estimated useful lives of fixed assets	**Buildings and improvements**	**10–40 years**
	Machinery and equipment	**5–10 years**
	Furniture and fixtures	**5–20 years**
	Automotive equipment	**3–4 years**

Source: *Accounting Trends and Techniques* (New York: American Institute of Certified Public Accountants, 1994).

These broad ranges can complicate the decisions of individuals who use financial statements to compare performance across companies. This problem is particularly evident in the airline industry, where the estimated lives used to depreciate aircraft often differ across companies. Delta Airlines depreciates its planes over 15 years; Pan Am estimates a life of 25 years for the same 727s that Delta writes off in 15; and Texas Air writes off its planes over a period *up to* 25 years.

REVISING THE USEFUL-LIFE ESTIMATE

Estimating the useful life of a long-lived asset when it is acquired is a very subjective process. After using such assets for several years, companies often find that their original estimates were inaccurate. For example, Delta Airlines recently increased the estimated useful life of its aircraft from ten to fifteen years. In these situations the portion of the long-lived asset's depreciation base (cost − salvage value) that has not yet been depreciated is depreciated over the remainder of the revised useful life.

To illustrate, suppose that ABC Airlines purchased aircraft for $110,000 on January 1, 1991, and at the time estimated the useful life of the aircraft and the salvage value to be ten years and $10,000, respectively. If the company depreciated equal portions ($10,000) of the amount subject to depreciation ($100,000) each year, it would have recognized $50,000 of accumulated depreciation by the end of 1995, and the aircraft would be reported on the 1995 balance sheet in the following manner:

Aircraft   **$110,000**
Less: Accumulated depreciation   **50,000**   **60,000**

Assume that as of January 1, 1996, the company's accountants believe that the aircraft will actually be in service through 2006, ten years beyond the present time, and fifteen years from the date of acquisition (1991). In other words, the company changed its original useful-life estimate from ten to fifteen years. At that point ABC would not make a correcting journal to restate the financial statements of the previous periods. Instead, it would simply depreciate the remaining depreciation base [$60,000 (book value) − $10,000 (salvage value)] over the remaining life of the aircraft (ten years). The following journal entry would be recorded in the company's books at the end of 1996 and at the end of each year until and including December 31, 2005.

Dec. 31   Depreciation Expense (E, −SE)   **5,000**
                 Accumulated Depreciation (−A)   **5,000**
                 Recognized depreciation on aircraft ($50,000/10 yr.).

Depreciating the book value of the asset over the remaining useful life, as of the date of the estimate revision, is known as treating the revision *prospectively*. That is, no "catch up" adjusting entry is recorded to restate the books. Estimate revisions are not considered errors, and therefore, the financial statements as of the time of the revision are not in need of correction. Instead, the new information that led to the revision affects only the manner in which the aircraft is accounted for in the future. However, if the revision gives rise to a reported net income amount that is materially different from what would have been reported without the revision, the company is required to describe the revision in the footnotes. The excerpt below was taken from the annual report of Delta Airlines.

. . . the Company increased the estimated useful lives of substantially all of its flight equipment . . . The effect of this change was a decrease of approximately $130 million in depreciation expense and a $69 million [after income taxes] increase in net income for the year ended . . .

COST ALLOCATION (DEPRECIATION) METHODS

The useful-life estimate determines the period of time over which a long-lived asset is to be amortized. The salvage-value estimate in conjunction with the capitalized cost determines the **depreciation base**[1] (capitalized cost − salvage value): the dollar amount of cost that is amortized over the asset's useful life. The cost-allocation methods discussed in this section determine the rate of amortization or, in other words, the amount of cost that is to be converted to an expense during each period of a long-lived asset's useful life. Three basic allocation (depreciation) methods are allowed under generally accepted accounting principles: (1) straight-line, (2) accelerated, and (3) activity.

---

1. *Depletion base* and *amortization base* are the terms used for natural resource costs and intangibles, respectively.

THE STRAIGHT-LINE METHOD OF AMORTIZATION (DEPRECIATION)

The discussion and most of the examples so far have assumed that equal dollar amounts of a long-lived asset's cost are amortized during each period of its useful life. This assumption, which is referred to as the **straight-line method**, is used by most companies to depreciate their fixed assets and by almost all companies to amortize their intangible assets.[2] The straight-line method can be chosen for several reasons: (1) management believes that the asset provides equal benefits across each year of its estimated useful life, (2) in comparison to the other methods, it is simple to apply, and (3) it tends to produce higher net income numbers and higher long-lived asset book values in the early years of a long-lived asset's life. The following example illustrates the straight-line method.[3]

Assume that Midland Plastics purchased a Van Wagon for $15,000 on January 1, 1993. The life and salvage value of the wagon are estimated to be five years and $3,000, respectively. Under the straight-line method, the annual depreciation expense would be calculated as shown in Figure 9–9, which also includes the related adjusting journal entry.

FIGURE 9–9	**FORMULA**			
The straight-line method: Midland Plastics	Straight-line depreciation $2,400 per year	= (Cost = ($15,000 | − Salvage Value)* − $3,000)	÷ Estimated Life ÷ 5 years	

GENERAL JOURNAL ENTRY

Depreciation Expense (E, −SE)	2,400	
Accumulated Depreciation (−A)		2,400
Recognized annual depreciation.		

*Depreciation base

Under the straight-line method, the same dollar amount of depreciation is recognized in each year of the asset's useful life. At $2,400 per year for five years, the total amount of depreciation taken would be $12,000, the depreciation base. At the end of the wagon's estimated life, its book value ($15,000 − $12,000) is equal to its estimated salvage value ($3,000).

The next two methods discussed, sum-of-the-years'-digits and double-declining-balance, are *accelerated methods of amortization*. They are called **accelerated methods** because greater amounts of the capitalized cost are allocated to the earlier periods of the asset's life than to the later periods. Accelerated methods are used by some companies to depreciate fixed assets when preparing financial reports. Apple Computer, Inc., and Liz Claiborne, Inc., for example, use double-declining-balance as their primary depreciation method, while General Electric Company uses the sum-of-the-years'-digits method. *Accounting Trends and Techniques (1994)* reports that sum-of-the-years'-digits is the predominant method used to depreciate machinery and office equipment, while the double-declining-balance method is commonly used to depreciate automotive equipment.

---

2. *Accounting Trends and Techniques* (New York: AICPA, 1994) reports that, of the 600 U.S. companies surveyed, 570 (95%) used the straight-line method to depreciate at least some of their fixed assets. The straight-line method is used predominantly to depreciate buildings.

3. The information from this example is also used in the illustrations of the accelerated methods that follow.

SUM-OF-THE-YEARS'-DIGITS METHOD

To illustrate the **sum-of-the-years'-digits method**, assume the same facts as in the previous example: a wagon with an estimated useful life of five years and an estimated salvage value of $3,000 is purchased for $15,000 on January 1, 1993. The general formula and calculations for each year for Midland Plastics Company appear in Figure 9–10.

FIGURE 9–10	**FORMULA**

*Sum-of-the-years'-
digits method:
Midland Plastics*

Sum-of-the-Years'-Digits Depreciation = (Cost − Salvage Value)* × $\dfrac{R}{N(N+1) \div 2}$

where R = **the remaining useful life of the asset as
of the beginning of the current year**
          N = **the entire estimated useful life**

CALCULATIONS

1993: $(\$15,000 - \$3,000) \times \dfrac{5}{5(5+1) \div 2} = \$\ 4,000$

1994: $(\$15,000 - \$3,000) \times \dfrac{4}{5(5+1) \div 2} =\ 3,200$

1995: $(\$15,000 - \$3,000) \times \dfrac{3}{5(5+1) \div 2} =\ 2,400$

1996: $(\$15,000 - \$3,000) \times \dfrac{2}{5(5+1) \div 2} =\ 1,600$

1997: $(\$15,000 - \$3,000) \times \dfrac{1}{5(5+1) \div 2} =\ \underline{800}$

Total depreciation expense recognized $\underline{\underline{\$12,000}}$

*Depreciation base

Under the sum-of-the-years'-digits method, the depreciation amount in a given year is computed by multiplying the depreciation base times the ratio of the remaining years in the asset's life (R) to [N(N + 1) ÷ 2], where N equals the estimated useful life. Note that R decreases by 1 as each year passes and [N(N + 1) ÷ 2] is equal to (5 + 4 + 3 + 2 + 1), the sum of the digits in the estimated useful life. This computation differs from the straight-line method in that it produces a decreasing amount of depreciation in each subsequent year. Yet, similar to the straight-line method, at the end of the asset's estimated useful life the book value ($15,000 − $12,000) is equal to the estimated salvage value ($3,000).

DOUBLE-DECLINING-BALANCE METHOD

To illustrate the **double-declining-balance method**, assume once again the facts of the preceding example. Figure 9–11 shows the general formula and calculations for each year.

Under the double-declining-balance method, each year's depreciation is computed by multiplying 2 times the book value of the asset (cost − accumulated depreciation) and dividing the result by N, the estimated useful life.[4] Note that salvage value is not part of the general formula. However, the book value of the asset cannot

---

4. The formula for the double-declining-balance method can also be expressed as [(Cost − Accumulated depreciation) × (2 × the straight-line rate)]. The straight-line rate is equal to the percentage of the depreciation base charged each year under the straight-line method (1/N). Using the numbers in the example above, this formula appears as follows: ($15,000 − Accumulated depreciation) × 40 percent.

FIGURE 9-11	FORMULA
The double-declining-balance method: Midland Plastics	Double-Declining-Balance Depreciation = (2 × Book Value) ÷ N where Book value* = cost − accumulated depreciation N = the estimated useful life

CALCULATIONS

1993:	(2 × $15,000) ÷ 5 = Accumulated depreciation = $6,000	$ 6,000
1994:	[2 × ($15,000 − $6,000)] ÷ 5 = Accumulated depreciation = $9,600 ($6,000 + $3,600)	3,600
1995:	[2 × ($15,000 − $9,600)] ÷ 5 = Accumulated depreciation = $11,760 ($9,600 + $2,160)	2,160
1996:	Reduce book value ($15,000 − $11,760) to salvage value ($3,000) Accumulated depreciation = $12,000 ($11,760 + $240)	240
1997:	No depreciation recognized because book value cannot be reduced below salvage value	0
	Total depreciation expense recognized	$12,000

be reduced below the asset's estimated salvage value. In 1996, for example, only the amount of depreciation ($240) necessary to bring the asset's book value ($15,000 − $11,760) to its estimated salvage value ($3,000) was recognized. For this same reason, in 1997 no depreciation expense was recognized.

STRAIGHT-LINE, SUM-OF-THE-YEARS'-DIGITS, AND DOUBLE-DECLINING-BALANCE: A COMPARISON

This section compares the financial statement effects of the three cost-allocation methods discussed above. The general formulas, the depreciation expenses, and the related book values for each year of the estimated useful life under each of the three methods appear in Figure 9–12. This comparison uses the same information given in the previous examples.

FIGURE 9-12

Depreciation methods compared

	STRAIGHT-LINE		SUM-OF-THE-YEARS'-DIGITS		DOUBLE-DECLINING-BALANCE	
	$SL = (C − SV) ÷ N$		$SYD = (C − SV) × \dfrac{R}{N(N + 1) ÷ 2}$		$\dfrac{2 × BV}{N}$	
	EXPENSE	BOOK VALUE	EXPENSE	BOOK VALUE	EXPENSE	BOOK VALUE
1993	2,400	15,000 −2,400 12,600	4,000	15,000 −4,000 11,000	6,000	15,000 −6,000 9,000
1994	2,400	15,000 −4,800 10,200	3,200	15,000 −7,200 7,800	3,600	15,000 −9,600 5,400
1995	2,400	15,000 −7,200 7,800	2,400	15,000 −9,600 5,400	2,160	15,000 −11,760 3,240
1996	2,400	15,000 −9,600 5,400	1,600	15,000 −11,200 3,800	240	15,000 −12,000 3,000
1997	2,400	15,000 −12,000 3,000	800	15,000 −12,000 3,000	0	15,000 −12,000 3,000

The straight-line method results in the same amount of depreciation ($2,400) in each of the five years. The two accelerated methods (sum-of-the-years'-digits and double-declining-balance) show greater amounts of depreciation in the early periods of the asset's life (1993 and 1994) and lesser amounts of depreciation in the later periods (1996 and 1997). All three methods recognize total depreciation of $12,000 over the five-year period and thus depreciate the long-lived asset only to its salvage value ($3,000).

Choosing among the three methods can have a significant effect on the timing of reported income. Assume that Midland Plastics, which purchased the wagon in the preceding examples, has revenues of $12,000 and expenses other than depreciation of $5,000 in each of the five years, 1993–97. Figure 9–13 contains the income numbers for each of the three methods for each of the five years.

FIGURE 9–13	METHODS	1993	1994	1995	1996	1997	TOTAL
The comparative effects on net income of different depreciation methods	Straight-line	$4,600	$4,600	$4,600	$4,600	$4,600	$23,000
	Sum-of-the-years'-digits	3,000	3,800	4,600	5,400	6,200	23,000
	Double-declining-balance	1,000	3,400	4,840	6,760	7,000	23,000

Note: The net income numbers appearing in Figure 9–13 were determined in the following manner:

Net income = $12,000 (revenues) − $5,000 (other expenses) − depreciation expense
Straight-line method for all five years: $4,600 = $12,000 − $5,000 − $2,400
Sum-of-the-years'-digits method for 1993: $3,000 = $12,000 − $5,000 − $4,000

Note first that the total income recognized across the five-year periods is the same ($23,000) under each method because each method recognizes $12,000 ($15,000 − $3,000) of depreciation expense over the life of the asset. However, the amount of depreciation recognized in each period differs across the three methods, giving rise to different income patterns over the life of the asset. The graph in Figure 9–14 compares these income patterns.

Two aspects about this graph are important and can be generalized. First, compared to both accelerated methods, net income under the straight-line method is higher in the early periods and lower in the later periods of the asset's estimated useful life. Second, the change in net income from one period to the next is greater under the double-declining-balance method than it is under the sum-of-the-years'-digits method. The double-declining-balance method, therefore, is the most extreme form of accelerated depreciation. Relatively speaking, the double-declining-balance method (and to a lesser extent, the sum-of-the-years'-digits method) produces low levels of net income in the early periods that increase rapidly over the life of the asset. The straight-line method measures net income as relatively higher in the early periods and remaining constant over the asset's life.

THE ACTIVITY (UNITS-OF-PRODUCTION) METHOD AND NATURAL RESOURCE DEPLETION

The **activity method**[5] allocates the cost of a long-lived asset to future periods on the basis of its activity. This method is used primarily in the mining, oil, and gas industries to **deplete** the costs associated with acquiring the rights to and extracting natural

---

5. Referred to as the *units-of-production method* in *Accounting Trends and Techniques* (New York: AICPA, 1994), p. 363.

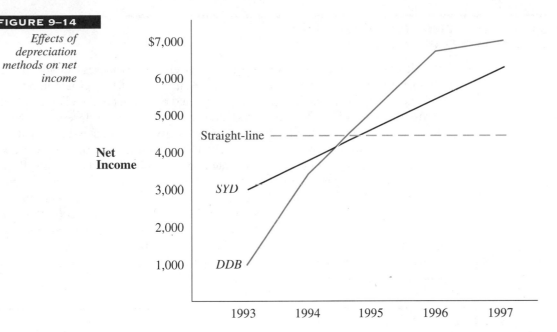

FIGURE 9–14

Effects of depreciation methods on net income

Note: *SYD* = Sum-of-the-years'-digits;   *DDB* = Double-declining-balance.

resources. The following excerpt, for example, was taken from the annual report of Pennzoil, a large oil and gas mining operation.

Provision for depreciation, depletion, and amortization is determined on a field-by-field basis using the units-of-production method.

The estimated life under the activity method is expressed in terms of units of activity (e.g., miles driven, units produced, barrels extracted) instead of years, as is done under the previous methods. In periods when an asset is very active (e.g., production is high), a relatively large amount of the cost is amortized. In periods when the asset is less active, relatively fewer costs are amortized.

To illustrate, assume that a company purchases mining properties for $1 million in cash. It estimates that the properties will yield 500,000 saleable tons of ore, and during the first year of production the company mines 10,000 tons. The computation of the depletion rate and the journal entries that would be made to record this series of events appear in Figure 9–15.

FIGURE 9–15

Depletion rate and related journal entries

DEPLETION RATE

$1,000,000 ÷ 500,000 estimated tons = $2 per ton

GENERAL JOURNAL ENTRIES

Mineral Deposits (+A)	1,000,000	
Cash (−A)		1,000,000
Acquired right to extract ore.		
Depletion Expense (E, −SE)	20,000	
Mineral Deposits (or Accumulated Depletion) (−A)		20,000
Recognized depletion for first year		
(10,000 tons × $2 per ton).		

COST ALLOCATION METHODS AND
THE MATCHING PRINCIPLE

Recall that the matching principle states that efforts (expenses) should be matched against the benefits (revenues) they produce. In terms of this principle, the straight-line method assumes that the revenues generated by the depreciated asset are constant across the asset's life; the accelerated methods assume that such revenues are high in early periods and low in later periods; and the activity method assumes that revenues are generated in proportion to the asset's activity. While each of these methods may represent the best application of the matching principle for certain assets, the activity method is probably the most consistent overall. Presumably, the more active an asset is, the more benefits it should produce. The extent to which a given amortization method is consistent with the matching principle is an important factor that should be considered by management when choosing an allocation method. Such consistency helps to improve the quality and usefulness of the reported financial numbers. However, other economic factors, discussed in the next section, are also considered when making such decisions.

HOW DOES MANAGEMENT CHOOSE AN
ACCEPTABLE COST ALLOCATION METHOD?

LO 6 Management may choose a given cost allocation method for a variety of economic reasons. Perhaps the most obvious is that the method has a significant and desired effect on important financial ratios, such as earnings per share, that are used by stockholders, investors, and creditors to evaluate management performance. When RTE Corporation, an electrical equipment manufacturer, more than doubled earnings per share by changing its depreciation method, its controller justified the action by stating: "We realize that compared to our competitors, our (past) conservative (accelerated) method of depreciation may have hurt us with investors because of its negative impact on net earnings." In a similar context, Inland Steel's controller commented "Why should we put ourselves at a disadvantage by depreciating more conservatively (i.e., accelerated methods) than other steel companies do?"[6]

Note, however, that changing accounting methods, such as switching to the depreciation method, to inflate net income in an effort to positively influence the assessments of investors and creditors may not be an effective strategy. When IBM shifted from the accelerated to the straight-line method several years ago, it increased reported earnings by $375 million. Did its share value increase? Some evidence suggests that stock market prices do not react positively to such changes, and many accountants question whether credit-rating services, like Dun & Bradstreet, adjust their ratings. In fact, knowledgeable stockholders, investors, and creditors may interpret a change to a less conservative depreciation method (e.g., from accelerated to straight-line) as a negative signal, indicating that management may be attempting to hide poor performance that it anticipates in the future. It is also true that the use of accelerated methods can lead to the creation of "hidden reserves," giving management greater ability to manage reported financial numbers in the future.

Management may also consider compensation contracts based on net income and debt covenants when choosing a depreciation method. Compared to accelerated methods, straight-line, for example, would tend to produce greater amounts of net-income-based compensation in the early periods of an asset's useful life. Similarly, the

6. Jill Andresky, "Double Standard," *Forbes,* November 22, 1982, p. 178.

depreciation method chosen may affect whether a company violates a debt covenant. The 1995 annual report of Timberland, a manufacturer of outdoor footware, reports that existing credit agreements require a certain balance in retained earnings. Also, several years ago Nike was required by certain covenants to report positive profits. Since the depreciation method affects net income, which in turn affects the balance in retained earnings, the depreciation method can determine whether such covenants are violated.

DEPRECIATION METHODS FOR INCOME TAX PURPOSES

Management is not required to choose the same depreciation method for income tax purposes that it uses for financial reporting. Indeed, many companies, such as Sundstrand Corporation (aerospace) and Merck and Company, Inc. (pharmaceuticals), use the straight-line method for financial reporting and an accelerated method for tax purposes. *Forbes* reports:

Like most businesses, Anheuser-Busch keeps two sets of books, one for tax purposes and one for its owners. [The company] uses accelerated depreciation for taxes but straight-line for reporting to investors.

Using accelerated depreciation for tax purposes gives rise to significant tax savings for these companies. In a single year, for example, Anheuser-Busch saved $67.8 million in taxes by using accelerated depreciation instead of straight-line for tax purposes.[7]

We have shown that estimating useful lives and salvage values in addition to choosing among alternative depreciation methods gives management considerable flexibility in reporting the amount of depreciation on the financial statements. However, the current rules specified in the **Internal Revenue Code**, which cover depreciation for tax purposes, are much less flexible.

The **Modified Accelerated Cost-Recovery System (MACRS)** defines the maximum amount at which the cost of a fixed asset can be depreciated for the purpose of determining taxable income in a given year. To determine this amount, a fixed asset is placed into one of eight categories, based on its estimated useful life as specified in the **Asset Depreciation Range (ADR)** system. The ADR is a document published by the Internal Revenue Service that defines the minimum allowable useful lives for various kinds of fixed assets. In the MACRS each of the eight categories is then linked with an allowable depreciation method, as indicated in Figure 9–16.

FIGURE 9–16

Depreciation rules for income tax purposes

CATEGORY	ESTIMATED LIFE AS STATED IN ADR	ALLOWABLE DEPRECIATION METHOD AS STATED IN MACRS
1	3 years	Double-declining-balance
2	5 years	Double-declining-balance
3	7 years	Double-declining-balance
4	10 years	Double-declining-balance
5	15 years	150% declining-balance*
6	20 years	150% declining-balance*
7	27.5 years	Straight-line
8	31.5 years	Straight-line

*Formula — [1.5 × (cost − accumulated depreciation)] ÷ life

7. Jane Carmichael, "Rollover," *Forbes,* January 18, 1982, pp. 75, 78.

Automobiles, for example, are placed in Category 2, which allows them to be depreciated over a five-year life using the double-declining-balance method. Equipment and machinery are normally included in Categories 1, 2, 3, or 4 and therefore are depreciated over lives ranging from 3–10 years, using the double-declining-balance method. Apartments, buildings, and warehouses are generally classified in Categories 7 or 8, which are subject to the straight-line method over an estimated life of either 27.5 or 31.5 years.

For purposes of determining taxable income, management should use the depreciation strategy that provides the greatest economic benefit for the company. The appropriate strategy, however, may not be entirely obvious to students, because income tax payments are based on income, and as Figure 9–13 shows, all depreciation strategies give rise to the same total income over the life of an asset. Consequently, all depreciation strategies produce the same total dollar amount of income tax payment over the life of the asset. The key consideration in management's choice of a depreciation strategy for tax purposes is not the amount, but the *timing*, of the income tax payments produced by the strategy. Accelerated methods and shorter estimated lives are preferred for tax purposes because they save tax dollars in the early years of the asset's life and thereby minimize the present value of the stream of income tax payments.

To illustrate, refer back to Figure 9–13 which compares net income numbers produced by the straight-line, sum-of-the-years'-digits, and double declining-balance methods of depreciation. Note that the total income recognized under the three methods is the same ($23,000). Now assume a corporate income tax rate of 30 percent. The income tax payments reported in Figure 9–17 would then be due under each of the three methods for each of the five years. The table also provides the present value of each stream of tax payments, assuming a 10 percent discount rate.[8]

The tax payments included in Figure 9–17 are simply the income numbers in Figure 9–13 multiplied by the 30 percent tax rate. The total tax payments are equal across all three methods ($6,900), but the present values of the tax payments are not. The double-declining-balance method has the lowest present value ($4,896), followed by sum-of-the-years'-digits ($5,058). Thus, the more accelerated the depreciation method, the lower the present value of the tax payments. In general, the depreciation method chosen for tax purposes should be the one that recognizes the greatest amount of depreciation in the early years of the life of an asset's life. The shortest acceptable life and the most accelerated form of depreciation should be chosen for tax purposes.

FIGURE 9–17

Income tax payments (Tax rate equals 30 percent of income)

METHOD	1993	1994	1995	1996	1997	TOTAL	PRESENT VALUE
Straight-line	$1,380	$1,380	$1,380	$1,380	$1,380	$6,900	$5,231
Sum-of-the-years'-digits	900	1,140	1,380	1,620	1,860	6,900	5,058
Double-declining-balance	300	1,020	1,452	2,028	2,100	6,900	4,896

8. Appendix 4A covers the time value of money and the concept of present value.

DISPOSAL: RETIREMENTS, SALES, AND TRADE-INS

LO 7 Long-lived assets are acquired at cost, amortized as they are used in the operation of a business, and eventually disposed of. The disposal can take one of three forms: retirement, sale, or trade-in. The accounting procedures followed in all three cases have much in common. The depreciation is recorded to the date of the disposal, the cost and accumulated depreciation (or *net cost*, as in the case of intangibles and natural resources) of the long-lived asset are removed from the books, and any receipt or payment of cash or other assets is recorded when the asset is disposed of.[9] A gain or loss on the exchange is recognized in the amount of the difference between the book value of the asset and the net value of the receipt. Such gains and losses are usually found in the "other revenues and expenses" section of the income statement. Consider, for example, the following excerpt from the 1994 annual report of General Mills:

When an item is sold or retired, the accounts are relieved of its cost and related accumulated depreciation; the resulting gains and losses, if any, are recognized.

RETIREMENT OF LONG-LIVED ASSETS

It is not unusual for companies to retire, close, or abandon their long-lived assets. **Retirement** of an asset can be due to obsolescence, the lack of a market for the asset in question, or closure by a regulatory body. In the early 1990s, for example, each of the "Big 3" automakers closed a number of plants in an effort to control costs. In such cases the original cost and accumulated depreciation of the long-lived asset are simply written off the books. No gain or loss is recognized if the asset is fully depreciated at the time of the retirement. A loss is recognized if the asset is not yet fully depreciated.

Assume, for example, that Ajax and Brothers retired two pieces of equipment that were purchased ten years ago. Item 1 was purchased for $10,000 and was depreciated over eight years with no expected salvage value. At the time of its retirement, it was fully depreciated (i.e., accumulated depreciation was $10,000). Item 2 was purchased for $13,000 and was expected to have a $1,000 salvage value after its useful life of twelve years. At the time of its retirement, the Accumulated Depreciation account was equal to $10,000. The journal entries accompanying the retirement of the two pieces of equipment are provided below.

Accumulated Depreciation (+A)	**10,000**	
Equipment (−A)		**10,000**
Retired Item 1.		
Loss on Retirement (Lo, −SE)	**3,000**	
Accumulated Depreciation (+A)	**10,000**	
Equipment (−A)		**13,000**
Retired Item 2.		

9. Long-lived assets are rarely acquired or disposed of on the first or last day of the accounting period. In practice, therefore, companies must consider whether they wish to compute depreciation for partial periods. This text does not cover such computations for two reasons. First, many companies follow either of two policies: (1) recognize a full year of depreciation in the year of acquisition and zero depreciation in the year of disposition, or (2) recognize zero depreciation in the year of acquisition and a full year of depreciation in the year of disposition. Such policies eliminate the need to compute depreciation for partial periods. Second, computing depreciation for a partial period can get somewhat involved, especially under the accelerated methods, and we leave such discussion to intermediate accounting textbooks.

No gain or loss is recognized on the retirement of Item 1 because an asset with a book value of zero was simply abandoned. The $3,000 loss on the retirement of Item 2 is recognized because the disposal of an asset with a book value of $3,000 generated no benefit.

Accounting for asset retirements is highly subjective and controversial. Generally accepted accounting principles require that when the value of an asset is "permanently impaired," it should be written down, but the guidelines provided are subject to judgment, leaving management much discretion over the amount and timing of such write-downs. Simply, it is very difficult to determine exactly when an asset has been permanently impaired and by how much. In addition, these write-downs can be huge. General Motors, Chrysler, Ford, Kmart, Westinghouse and MCI have each recorded multi-billion dollar asset write-downs in recent years. Often part of an overall strategy to restructure company operations, management frequently chooses to record such write-downs in particularly poor years, enabling the company to "take the hit" when it does the least harm. This "taking a bath" strategy recognizes losses immediately that would normally be recorded as expenses (e.g., depreciation) in future years which, in turn, can improve future reported profits. The *Wall Street Journal* (November 2, 1994) reported that the FASB has recently "cracked down on corporate America's habit of seizing upon restructurings as an occasion to take a bushel of write-offs all at once, making an earnings turnaround look speedier and more significant when it happens."

Management may also choose to record large "permanent impairment" write-downs in particularly good years. Polaroid, for example, recorded such a write-down in the same year it recognized a multi-billion dollar gain from a well-known legal settlement against Kodak for patent infringement. This reporting decision could be interpreted as "building a hidden reserve" which may enable Polaroid to "smooth" reported income over time. General Electric was recently cited in the *Wall Street Journal* (November 3, 1994) for using such write-offs frequently to "offset one-time gains."

SALE OF LONG-LIVED ASSETS

Accounting for the sale of a long-lived asset is essentially the same as accounting for its retirement, except that cash is received in the exchange. For example, Computer Services purchased office furniture on March 1, 1993, for $24,000. At the time of the purchase the company estimated the useful life of the furniture to be 10 years and the salvage value to be $4,000, and it used the straight-line method of depreciation. On July 1, 1996 (three years and four months later), Computer Services remodeled its office and sold all the original furniture for $13,000. The company policy on recognizing depreciation for partial periods is to recognize no depreciation in the year of acquisition and a full year's depreciation in the year of disposition. The relevant calculations and the related journal entries appear in Figure 9–18.

On the date of sale, the depreciation is updated, and the sale is recorded. The loss on the sale ($5,000) represents the difference between the updated book value ($24,000 − $6,000) and the cash proceeds ($13,000).

TRADE-INS OF LONG-LIVED ASSETS

In a **trade-in,** two or more long-lived assets are exchanged, and cash is often received or paid. The methods used to account for such transactions depend on whether the

FIGURE 9–18	DEPRECIATION COMPUTATIONS	DEPRECIATION EXPENSE	ACCUMULATED DEPRECIATION
The sale of a long-lived asset: Computer Services	1993 (Year of acquisition)	$ 0	$ 0
	1994 ($24,000 − $4,000) ÷ 10 years	2,000	2,000
	1995 ($24,000 − $4,000) ÷ 10 years	2,000	4,000
	1996 (Year of disposition)	2,000	6,000

GENERAL JOURNAL ENTRIES

1996
July 1   Depreciation Expense (E, −SE)   2,000
                Accumulated Depreciation (−A)   2,000
         Recognized depreciation in year of disposition.

     1   Cash (+A)   13,000
         Accumulated Depreciation (+A)   6,000
         Loss on Sale (Lo, −SE)   5,000
                Furniture (−A)   24,000
         Sold long-lived asset.

exchanged assets are similar or dissimilar. This text limits its coverage to exchanges of **dissimilar assets**, those that are of a different general type, perform different functions, and are employed in different lines of business. The methods used to account for exchanges of similar assets are normally covered in intermediate accounting textbooks.

In general, the accounting procedures described in the section on retirements and the section on sales of long-lived assets also apply when dissimilar assets are exchanged.[10] That is, the depreciation of the asset given up is updated, its capitalized cost and accumulated depreciation are written off the books, and the receipt or payment of cash is recorded. However, a problem arises when accounting for exchanges because it is difficult to determine the dollar amount at which the asset received should be valued on the balance sheet. This problem, in turn, makes it equally difficult to measure the gain or loss that is recognized on the exchange.

The asset received in a trade-in should be valued on the balance sheet at either: (1) the FMV of the assets given up or (2) the FMV of the assets received, whichever is clearly more evident and objectively determinable. Applying this rule is often difficult because the list price of an asset does not necessarily reflect its FMV, and determining the FMV of the asset given up is normally very subjective. Often the accountant must consult industry publications or obtain data on recent transactions involving similar assets to determine FMVs.

To illustrate, Mastoon Industries exchanged a delivery truck, which originally cost $17,000 (Accumulated Depreciation = $9,000) for a new printing press. The dealer agreed to accept the truck plus $12,000. Based on a list price of $18,000 for the printing press, the dealer claims to be granting a $6,000 ($18,000 − $12,000) trade-in allowance on the truck. However, the accountant for Mastoon finds that recent sales of comparable printing presses have realized, on average, $16,000, and a publication of used truck prices indicates that the value of the truck is approximately $4,000.

Given these facts, there are two acceptable ways to value the printing press on the balance sheet of Mastoon, each leading to the same result: (1) the FMV of the assets

10. Keep in mind that a sale is simply the exchange of a long-lived asset for cash, a dissimilar asset.

given up ($16,000 = $12,000 cash + $4,000 value of truck) or (2) the FMV of the asset received ($16,000 determined from recent sales). The resulting journal entry follows.

Printing Press (+A)	**16,000**	
Accumulated Depreciation (+A)	**9,000**	
Loss on Trade-In (Lo, −SE)	**4,000**	
Truck (−A)		**17,000**
Cash (−A)		**12,000**

Traded truck and cash for a press.

Note also that the list price ($18,000) was not used as the FMV of the printing press. List prices are nothing more than invitations to negotiate, and astute buyers can often bargain for lower prices. Is it normally economically prudent, for example, to pay the list price for a new automobile? Moreover, since the actual FMV of the printing press seems to be $16,000 instead of $18,000, a better estimate of the trade-in allowance on the truck is $4,000 ($16,000 − $12,000) rather than $6,000 ($18,000 − $12,000). It is not uncommon for dealers, especially in the automobile industry, to lead customers to believe that they are receiving more for their trade-ins than they actually are.

INTERNATIONAL PERSPECTIVE: LONG-LIVED ASSETS AND CURRENT VALUES

In the financial statements of U.S. companies, the Property, Plant, & Equipment account is carried at historical cost less accumulated depreciation. Several years ago a financial accounting standard was passed by the FASB that required certain large companies to disclose in the footnotes the current values of their fixed assets and inventories and to disclose with them depreciation and cost of goods sold amounts based on those values. This standard was so controversial that after a few years it was abandoned, and at present there appears to be no movement to reintroduce it.

In a number of foreign countries, however, fixed asset accounting is not based on historical cost. Instead, property, plant, & equipment revaluations based on current values are allowed and often practiced. In the Netherlands, the United Kingdom, France, and Australia, for example, depreciable fixed assets are often written up to their current values by recording an adjusting entry that debits the fixed asset account and credits stockholders' equity. Future depreciation charges are based on the revalued asset which, in turn, can give rise to an accumulated depreciation balance that exceeds the asset's historical cost. The large and well-known Philips Company, which is based in the Netherlands, has practiced such accounting methods for over 40 years.

Writing up fixed assets often requires considerable judgment that, in turn, can give foreign managers a certain amount of discretion over important financial numbers. To illustrate, *Forbes* (March 10, 1986) reported that Australian-based News Corp., a global media company owned by the famous financial tycoon, Rupert Murdock, was able to reduce its debt/equity ratio from 3.4/1.0 to 0.8/1.0 by writing up certain fixed assets to reflect their market values and thereby increasing stockholders' equity. The article suggested that Murdock may have chosen to record these revaluations to obscure the effect on News Corp.'s balance sheet of the excessive debt he incurred to finance a series of major acquisitions, including a number of magazines and publishing houses, Twentieth Century Fox, and Metromedia Broadcasting. It was further suggested that Murdock's choice may have been motivated by the threat of violating debt covenants.

Such write-ups, however, make it difficult for foreign firms attempting to raise capital in the U.S. capital markets. When their financial statements are restated to U.S. GAAP, which is required by the major U.S. exchanges, their earnings numbers often fall. *Forbes* (June 2, 1994), for example, reported that the restated earnings of Daimler-Benz, a large German company, was almost $1.5 billion less because it was required to value its fixed assets at historical cost. For a similar reason, Nestles, the Swiss chocolate giant, recently decided not to list its shares on the New York Stock Exchange.

ETHICS IN THE REAL WORLD

"With a simple bookkeeping change, companies can turn profits into losses—and vice versa. In many cases, the changes are perfectly justified, but the practice creates big opportunities for abuse." (*Forbes,* June 12, 1989).

So began an article that focused on the difficulty involved with determining the depreciation and/or amortization rates for long-lived assets and the level of discretionary judgment used by management in the area. Major U.S. companies, such as Cineplex Odeon, Blockbuster, General Motors, IBM, and Delta Airlines, are cited in the article for the wide variety of methods they use. Blockbuster changed the amortization period for its video tapes from 9 to 36 months in 1988, adding nearly 20% to its reported income; GM added $2.55 to its earnings per share number by adjusting the way in which it amortizes its tools and dies; IBM increased its "bottom line" by $375 million by changing from accelerated to straight-line; and Delta depreciates its planes over 15 years while most of the rest of the airline industry uses 20–25 year useful life. In each case the policies were disclosed and within the guidelines of GAAP, and the article notes further that "When it comes to amortization and depreciation, GAAP provides only the vaguest of guidelines."

However, the SEC chief accountant suggests that the disclosures are not adequate: "when a company says its depreciating its plant over 3 to 40 years, we don't know the intimate details and there is no practical way we could. I'd like accountants to take more responsibility for it."

ETHICAL ISSUE

Is it ethical for management to use methods to account for long-lived assets that are within the guidelines of GAAP, but fail to provide disclosure that is sufficient for stockholders to understand the financial condition and performance of the company?

REVIEW PROBLEM

Norby Enterprises purchased equipment on January 1, 1994, for $8,000. It cost $1,500 to have the equipment shipped to the plant and $500 to have it installed. The equipment was estimated to have a five-year useful life and a salvage value of $1,000. On January 1, 1997, the equipment was overhauled at a cost of $1,000, and the overhaul extended its estimated useful life by an additional year (from five to six years). On January 1, 1998, the equipment and $13,000 cash were traded in for a dissimilar piece of equipment with a FMV of $15,000. Norby uses the straight-line method of depreciation. The computations and journal entries related to the acquisition, depreciation, overhaul, and disposal of the equipment appear in Figure 9–19.

FIGURE 9–19

Solution to review problem: Norby Enterprises

DESCRIPTION/DATE	JOURNAL ENTRY			ACCUMULATED DEPRECIATION	BOOK VALUE[a]
Acquisition of equipment (1/1/94)	Equipment (+A)	10,000[b]			
	Cash (−A)		10,000	0	10,000
Depreciation[c] (12/31/94)	Depreciation Expense (E, −SE)	1,800			
	Accumulated Depreciation (−A)		1,800	1,800	8,200
Depreciation[c] (12/31/95)	Depreciation Expense (E, −SE)	1,800			
	Accumulated Depreciation (−A)		1,800	3,600	6,400
Depreciation[c] (12/31/96)	Depreciation Expense (E, −SE)	1,800			
	Accumulated Depreciation (−A)		1,800	5,400	4,600
Overhaul (1/1/97)	Equipment (+A)	1,000			
	Cash (−A)		1,000	5,400	5,600
Depreciation[d] (12/31/97)	Depreciation Expense (E, −SE)	1,533			
	Accumulated Depreciation (−A)		1,533	6,933	4,067
Trade-in (1/1/98)	Equipment (new) (+A)	15,000			
	Accumulated Depreciation (+A)	6,933			
	Loss on Trade-In (Lo, −SE)	2,067			
	Equipment (old) (−A)		11,000		
	Cash (−A)		13,000		

[a]Book value = Equipment cost − accumulated depreciation
[b]Equipment cost: $8,000 purchase + $1,500 shipping + $500 installation = $10,000
[c]Depreciation expense before overhaul: ($10,000 cost − $1,000 salvage) ÷ 5-year life = $1,800
[d]Depreciation expense after overhaul: ($4,600 book value + $1,000 overhaul − $1,000 salvage) ÷ 3-year remaining life = $1,533

SUMMARY OF LEARNING OBJECTIVES

 1   *Define long-lived assets, and describe how the matching principle underlies the methods used to account for them.*

Long-lived assets are assets that are used in the operations of the business, providing benefits that extend beyond the current accounting period. Included are land (not held for resale), buildings, machinery, equipment, costs incurred to acquire the right to extract natural resources, intangible assets, and deferred costs.

According to the matching principle, efforts (expenses) should be matched against benefits (revenues) in the period when the benefits are recognized. Since the benefits provided by long-lived assets extend beyond the current period, the cost of acquiring long-lived assets are capitalized in the period of acquisition and then amortized as their useful lives expire.

LO 2   *Identify the major questions that must be addressed when accounting for long-lived assets and how the answers to these questions can affect the financial statements.*

Accounting for most long-lived assets consists primarily of answering three questions: (1) What dollar amount should be included in the capitalized cost of the long-lived asset? (2) Over what time period should this cost be amortized? (3) At what rate should this cost be amortized? These questions are addressed for all long-lived assets except land, which is not subject to amortization.

Answering these questions in various ways can have significant effects on the timing of asset and income recognition. Capitalizing instead of expensing a cost defers expense recognition, giving rise to higher asset values and net income in the period of acquisition. Similarly, allocating the cost of a long-lived asset over a long, instead of a short, period of time defers expense recognition and creates higher asset and income values in the early years of the asset's life. However, these financial statement effects are a matter of timing, not magnitude. That is, a method giving rise to higher asset and income values in the early years of an asset's life will create lower asset and income values in the later years.

 Identify the costs that should be included in the capitalized cost of a long-lived asset.

The acquisition cost of a long-lived asset is determined by either (1) the FMV of the acquired asset or (2) the FMV of what was given up to acquire the asset, whichever is more readily determinable. In almost all cases, the FMV of what was given up is used because cash, which by definition is at FMV, is normally given up in such exchanges. Further, the capitalized cost (i.e., the FMV of what was given up) should include all costs required to bring the asset into serviceable or usable condition and location. This includes not only the cost of purchasing a long-lived asset, but also costs such as freight, installation, taxes, title fees, idle time while the asset is being installed, the costs of preparing land for use in the business, indirect overhead costs incurred while manufacturing a long-lived asset, and interest costs on borrowed funds used to construct long-lived assets. When long-lived assets are purchased as part of a group of assets for a single, lump-sum price, the overall price is allocated to each asset on the basis of its relative FMV.

 Describe the accounting treatment of postacquisition expenditures.

Postacquisition expenditures are costs incurred subsequent to the acquisition or manufacture of a long-lived asset. Costs incurred to improve the asset (as defined by a set of criteria) are called *betterments* and should be capitalized as part of the cost of the asset and amortized over its remaining life. Betterments are usually infrequent and tend to involve relatively large dollar amounts. Costs incurred to repair an asset or maintain its current level of productivity are classified as maintenance and are immediately expensed. Maintenance expenditures tend to be periodic and relatively small. It is often difficult to distinguish between a betterment and a maintenance expenditure, so management has much reporting discretion in this area.

 Explain how the cost of a long-lived asset is allocated over its useful life, and describe the alternative allocation methods.

To allocate the cost of a long-lived asset over its useful life, three issues must be addressed: (1) the useful life must be estimated, (2) the salvage value must be estimated, and (3) a cost-allocation method must be chosen. The useful-life estimate defines the period of time over which the asset's cost is to be amortized. The capitalized cost less the salvage value defines the amortization base, the total amount of cost to be amortized. The cost-allocation method determines the amount of cost to be amortized each period.

Three basic cost-allocation methods are considered systematic and reasonable: (1) straight-line, (2) accelerated, and (3) activity. The straight-line method recognizes equal amounts of depreciation each period throughout the life of the asset. Accelerated methods, including sum-of-the-years'-digits and double-declining-balance, recognize larger amounts of depreciation in the early periods of an asset's life and smaller amounts in the later periods. The activity method bases the amount of amortization each period on the activity of the asset during that period. The life of the asset is expressed in terms of a unit of activity, and as each unit is produced, a portion of the asset's cost is amortized. This method is normally used to deplete the costs associated with mining natural resources.

 Identify the major economic consequences associated with the methods used to account for long-lived assets.

The methods used to account for long-lived assets can have significant economic effects. The amount of cost to capitalize, the estimated useful life, the chosen amortization method, and the timing and amount of permanent write-downs can have significant effects on the timing of net income and important financial ratios. These numbers are used by interested parties to evaluate management and assess earning power, solvency, and determine credit ratings. They are also used in compensation contracts and debt covenants to control and direct management behavior.

 Specify how to account for the disposition of long-lived assets.

Long-lived assets are disposed of through retirement, sale, or trade-in. When a long-lived asset is retired, depreciation is updated, the original cost and accumulated depreciation of the asset is written off the books, and a loss is recognized if the asset is not fully depreciated as of the time of the retirement. Determining when to write down such assets and how is very subjective.

When long-lived assets are sold for cash, depreciation is updated, cash is debited, the original cost and accumulated depreciation are written off the books, and a gain or loss, which represents the difference between the book value of the asset and the proceeds, is recognized on the transaction.

When two dissimilar assets and cash are exchanged, depreciation is updated, the cash receipt or payment is recorded, the original cost and accumulated depreciation of the asset given up are written off the books, the asset received is given a dollar value, and a gain or loss is recognized on the transaction. The general rule for valuing the asset received is to use the FMV of the assets given up (cash and the asset given up) or the FMV of the asset received, whichever is more objectively determinable.

APPENDIX 9A

INTANGIBLE ASSETS AND DEFERRED COSTS

Intangible assets are characterized by the rights, privileges, and benefits of possession rather than by physical existence. Some accountants also suggest that intangible assets have a higher degree of uncertainty than tangible assets. Among other items, intangibles include the costs of acquiring copyrights, patents, trademarks, trade names, licenses, and goodwill. Deferred costs include prepaids, which extend beyond the current accounting period, and the costs incurred prior to the point when a company is fully operational (start-up or organizational costs). Intangible assets and deferred costs are often reported on the balance sheet as "other assets." In general, the costs of acquiring such assets should be capitalized, and professional standards require that they be amortized over their legal or useful lives, whichever is shorter, but not to exceed 40 years. Most companies use the straight-line method to amortize intangibles for both reporting and tax purposes.

The useful life of an intangible asset is often difficult to estimate, and the decline in service potential is often almost impossible to measure. As a result, the allocation of the capitalized cost to future periods is very subjective, and different intangible assets are treated in different ways. Figure 9A–1 shows the amortization periods of more common intangible assets and deferred costs used by a selected group of 600 major U.S. companies during 1994.

FIGURE 9A–1

Amortization periods, 1994 (number of companies)

PERIOD	GOODWILL	PATENT	TRADEMARK	LICENSE	NONCOMPETE
40 years	155	1	6	1	—
"Not exceeding 40 years"	83	3	3	3	—
25–30 years	15	—	2	1	—
20 years	11	—	2	—	—
10–15 years	13	—	—	—	1
Legal/estimated life	43	46	26	9	11
Other	88	19	12	5	13
Total	408	69	51	19	25

Source: *Accounting Trends and Techniques* (New York: American Institute of Certified Public Accountants, 1994).

COPYRIGHTS, PATENTS, AND TRADEMARKS

Copyrights are exclusive rights granted by law to control literary, musical, or artistic works. They are granted for fifty years beyond the life of the creator. Patents are granted by the U.S. Patent Office, and they give the holders exclusive rights to use, manufacture, or sell a product or process for a period of twenty years. A trademark or trade name is a word, phrase, or symbol that distinguishes or identifies a particular enterprise or product. The right to use a trademark is also granted by the U.S. Patent Office exclusively to the holder. The trademark lasts for a period of ten years but can be renewed indefinitely. Kleenex, Pepsi-Cola, Excedrin, and Wheaties are just a few examples of trade names that are so familiar that they are now a part of our culture.

THE COSTS OF DEVELOPING COMPUTER SOFTWARE

SFAS No. 86 specifies that the costs of developing and producing computer software products that will be available for sale or lease should be capitalized and amortized over their economic lives. Prior to this standard all such costs incurred prior to the development of a prototype were expensed, and many small software development companies claimed that this practice understated net income, making it very difficult to attract outside capital. This standard had a significant impact on the financial statements of many companies involved in the development of computer software. For example, consider the excerpt below from a financial report of Wang Laboratories, Inc. Note that the net effect of the change increased net income by $19.3 million.

The Company adopted a change of accounting for costs of computer software. The change was made in accordance with provisions of Statement of Financial Accounting Standards No. 86, which specifies that certain costs incurred in the development of computer software to be sold or leased to customers are to be capitalized and amortized over the economic life of the software product. Total costs capitalized during the year approximated $21.1 million, of which $1.8 million has been amortized and charged to expense.

GOODWILL

When one company purchases another for a dollar amount that is greater than the net FMV of the purchased company's assets and liabilities, goodwill is recognized on the purchasing company's balance sheet. Goodwill is a common asset on the balance sheets of the major U.S. companies. Figure 9A–1 shows that 408 of the 600 companies surveyed disclosed goodwill on their balance sheet. For many companies, such as Chrysler Corporation, Marriott Corporation, and General Electric, goodwill is quite significant. It accounts for 10 percent or more of their total assets. As of December 31, 1994, goodwill represented over 28 percent of the total assets of Time Warner.

To illustrate how goodwill is acquired, consider PepsiCo's acquisition of several major bottling operations from Philip Morris Companies and Kentucky Fried Chicken from RJR Nabisco, Inc., for a total of $1,678.3 million dollars. The FMVs of the physically identifiable assets and liabilities purchased by PepsiCo in these transactions were $1,191.4 million and $458.5 million, respectively. Accordingly, the transaction was accounted for as if the following journal entry had been recorded on PepsiCo's books. Assets in the journal entry include cash, receivables, inventories, investments, and long-lived assets; liabilities include short-term payables and long-term debts. (dollars in thousands)

Assets (+A)	1,191,400	
Goodwill (+A)	945,400	
Liabilities (+L)		458,500
Cash (−A)		1,678,300

Purchased bottling operations and Kentucky Fried Chicken.

Note in the transaction that the amount of goodwill is simply the difference between the purchase price and the net value of the purchased companies' assets and liabilities. It represents PepsiCo's assessment that the purchased companies are worth more as working units than is indicated by the values of their individual assets and liabilities.

Goodwill is a long-lived asset, and for financial reporting purposes, it is amortized over a period of time not to exceed forty years, normally using the straight-line method.[11] Note in Figure 9A–1 that major U.S. companies use a variety of periods

---

11. Professional standards state that goodwill should not be immediately written off unless it can be proven that future earnings is insufficient to cover the annual amount of goodwill amortization.

over which to amortize goodwill. In fact, goodwill acquired before October 31, 1970, need not be amortized at all, and many companies leave it on the balance sheet indefinitely.

It is also important to realize that goodwill acquired prior to 1991 is not subject to amortization for income tax purposes. For many years the Internal Revenue Service took the controversial position that goodwill is fundamentally an investment with an indefinite useful life, similar to land, and as such should not be amortized for purposes of determining taxable income. Only recently was the law changed to allow a tax deduction for amortized goodwill. This change made corporate acquisitions much more attractive from an economic standpoint. Additional discussion about goodwill can be found in Chapter 8.

ORGANIZATIONAL COSTS

Organizational costs represent another subjective area in accounting for intangible assets. These costs are incurred prior to the start of a company's operations, typically including fees for underwriting, legal and accounting services, licenses, titles, and promotional expenditures. It is relatively clear that such costs are incurred to generate future revenues, and therefore, it seems that organizational costs should be capitalized. However, the service potential of such an asset cannot be associated with any future revenue in particular, and thus, it is difficult to determine how it should be amortized. In a sense, organizational costs are of value to the company throughout its entire life. Does that mean that they should be left on the balance sheet indefinitely? Conceptually it may, but as stated earlier, professional pronouncements require that intangible assets be amortized over a period of time not to exceed forty years.

Organizational costs can be amortized in the determination of taxable income. For such purposes, most companies choose to amortize organizational costs over a useful life that is much shorter than that chosen for financial reporting purposes.

RESEARCH AND DEVELOPMENT COSTS

Research and development (R&D) costs are incurred to generate revenue in future periods through the creation of new products or processes. Such costs are significant for many major U.S. manufacturers. In 1994, for example, Johnson & Johnson invested $1.3 billion in research and development.

The matching principle clearly suggests that R&D costs should be capitalized and amortized over future periods. However, it is difficult to match specific research and development expenditures with the creation of specific products or processes. Some R&D expenditures are for basic research, others lead to failures, and still others provide only indirect benefits, or benefits that could not have been foreseen when the expenditure was incurred.

Concerned with the wide variety of practices used by companies to capitalize and amortize R&D expenditures, the FASB published *SFAS No. 2* in 1974. This pronouncement required that expenditures for most types of R&D costs be expensed in the year incurred, rather than capitalized and amortized as intangible assets. While this pronouncement promoted uniformity of accounting practices in the area of R&D, relieved pressures on auditors and managers to subjectively determine which R&D

costs should be capitalized, and reduced some of management's ability to manipulate the financial statements, it is definitely inconsistent with the matching principle. In line with this standard, many R&D costs that will clearly benefit future periods are being immediately expensed. As with organizational costs, accounting for R&D costs represents an example of theoretical measurement principles being compromised in the interest of practical considerations.

The requirement to expense all R&D costs can have significant effects on the financial statements. Had Boeing, for example, been allowed to capitalize half of its R&D expenditures in 1994, its net income would have increased from $856 million to over $2 billion. There is also some evidence suggesting that the negative effects on net income and other important financial ratios of *SFAS No. 2* serve to discourage companies from making R&D expenditures. *The Wall Street Journal* (May 22, 1995) recently noted that R&D expenditures are way down recently. IBM, for example, reduced its R&D expenditures by $2 billion from 1990 to 1994. Some believe that the requirement to expense R&D may be part of the cause.

APPENDIX 9B

ACCOUNTING FOR LONG-LIVED ASSETS—A REVIEW AND CRITIQUE

The introduction to this chapter noted that accounting for long-lived assets basically involves addressing three questions: (1) What dollar amount should be included in the capitalized cost of the long-lived asset? (2) Over what time period should this cost be amortized? (3) At what rate should this cost be amortized? The answers to these questions, though guided by the matching principle, can lead to reporting problems and misunderstandings.

PROBLEMS WITH HISTORICAL COST

Long-lived assets are capitalized at historical cost when they are acquired. This procedure gives rise to problems for two fundamental reasons. First, there is some question about the usefulness of historical cost for decision-making purposes. Investors and creditors, for whom the financial statements are primarily intended, may find that the historical cost of a long-lived asset is not particularly relevant to the decisions they face. The asset's present value, FMV, or replacement cost may represent more relevant and useful information. FMC Corporation, for example, uses replacement cost instead of historical cost in the performance measures used to evaluate internal management decisions. However, such valuation bases do not underlie the dollar amounts at which long-lived assets are carried on the balance sheet. As indicated in the chapter, in a number of foreign countries fixed assets are often carried at market values, which are certainly more subjective than historical costs, but if reliable they are definitely more informative.

The second problem with historical cost is that, although it is generally more objective than the other valuation bases, often it must be determined in a relatively subjective manner. Examples discussed in the text include lump-sum purchases, constructing long-lived assets, postacquisition expenditures, and determining the costs of long-lived assets received through trade-ins. In such cases managers can subjectively influence important financial statement numbers.

PROBLEMS WITH COST ALLOCATION

Accurately predicting the useful life and the salvage value of a long-lived asset is virtually impossible. It is also extremely difficult to choose a method of depreciation that allocates the cost of a fixed asset on the basis of the revenues it generates. Many fixed assets have very little to do with the direct generation of revenues. Instead, they help to support a general process that eventually leads to revenues. There is no way to apply the matching principle in such cases with any degree of confidence. Managers are left to choose from several alternatives and are generally allowed to do what they wish as long as the method chosen is reasonable and systematic. In several areas of the chapter we demonstrated how financial statement numbers are sensitive to the different cost-allocation methods. In addition, writing down the cost of a long-lived asset in cases when it is "permanently impaired" is very subjective and can have huge effects on reported financial numbers.

MISCONCEPTIONS ABOUT COST ALLOCATION

Two aspects about the cost-allocation process are often misunderstood. First, the goal of the cost-allocation process is to achieve a reasonable matching of revenues and expenses. It is not an attempt to carry the long-lived asset on the balance sheet at present value, FMV, or replacement cost. The book value of a long-lived asset cannot be viewed as an approximation of any of these valuation bases. Book value is simply historical cost less accumulated amortization: nothing more, nothing less.

It is often claimed that an objective of cost allocation is to provide funds for the future replacement of long-lived assets as they are sold or retired. In a direct sense this claim is clearly untrue. The basic depreciation entry, for example, which is illustrated below, does not involve cash. Cash is neither received nor transferred to some replacement fund. Cost allocation does not in and of itself provide funds for replacement.

Depreciation Expense (E, −SE)   **100**
    Accumulated Depreciation (−A)   **100**
Recognized depreciation of a fixed asset.

In an indirect way, however, depreciation can provide funds for future replacement of long-lived assets. If dividend payments are based on net income, for example, and depreciation reduces net income, then depreciation indirectly reduces dividend payments and saves cash, which, in turn, can be used to replace long-lived assets. Similarly, to the extent that taxable income is reduced by depreciation, tax dollars can be saved and invested in long-lived assets.

Thus, the depreciation journal entry, which does not reflect a cash inflow in and of itself, can reduce cash outflows due to dividends and taxes, as well as any other expenses that are based on reported income (e.g., management incentive compensation).

In this way it might indirectly be viewed as providing funds for the replacement of long-lived assets. Nevertheless, the cash savings is usually considerably less than the dollar amount of the depreciation entry, and there is certainly no guarantee that either the cash savings will equal the cost of replacing the long-lived asset or that management will choose to use it in that way.

KEY TERMS

Note: Definitions for these terms are provided in the glossary at the end of this text.

Accelerated methods (p. 435)
Activity method (p. 438)
Amortized (p. 425)
Asset Depreciation Range (ADR) (p. 441)
Betterments (p. 431)
Deferred costs (p. 424)
Deplete (p. 438)
Depreciation (p. 425)
Depreciation base (p. 434)
Dissimilar assets (p. 445)
Double-declining-balance method (p. 436)
Fixed assets (p. 424)
Intangible assets (p. 424)
Internal Revenue Code (p. 441)

Land (p. 424)
Maintenance (p. 431)
Modified Accelerated Cost-Recovery
  System (MACRS) (p. 441)
Natural resource costs (p. 424)
Physical obsolescence (p. 432)
Postacquisition expenditures (p. 431)
Retirement (p. 443)
Salvage value (p. 433)
Straight-line method (p. 435)
Sum-of-the-years'-digits method (p. 436)
Technical obsolescence (p. 433)
Trade-in (p. 444)

QUESTIONS FOR DISCUSSION AND REVIEW

1. List and define the different kinds of long-lived assets. Why are long-lived assets of interest to stockholders, investors, creditors, managers, and auditors?
2. This chapter mentions three basic issues that must be addressed when accounting for long-lived assets. What are these issues and how are they related to the matching principle?
3. Differentiate among land, fixed assets, natural resource costs, and intangible assets. In each case how is the capitalized cost allocated to future periods? What accounts are involved?
4. The different methods of accounting for long-lived assets give rise to timing differences in asset and income recognition. Explain what this means and provide an illustration.
5. Long-lived assets are (1) acquired, (2) used, and then (3) disposed of. Briefly describe the accounting issues that are addressed at each of these three stages.
6. What is the general rule for determining the amount of cost that should be capitalized for a long-lived asset? What kind of costs are typically included?
7. Distinguish between the costs included in the Land account and the costs included in the Land Improvements account. How are they accounted for differently?
8. How is the cost of a lump-sum purchase allocated to the component items purchased? If inventory, land, and equipment were all purchased for one lump sum, why would it make a difference on the financial statements how the total cost was allocated to each item? Explain.
9. What are postacquisition expenditures? Differentiate a betterment from a maintenance expenditure, and describe the methods used to account for each. What criteria are used to define a betterment? Describe the role of materiality with respect to accounting for betterments and maintenance expenditures.

10. What three steps are required to allocate the cost of a long-lived asset over its useful life? How do these three steps affect the measurement of assets and net income?

11. The chapter describes and illustrates four cost-allocation methods. Describe each method and compare their effects on the income statement and the balance sheet. Which methods tend to make a company look as if its performance is improving? In those cases where there is a close association between the activity of a long-lived asset and its decline in service potential, which method represents the best application of the matching principle? Why?

12. Provide an example of how the terms of an outstanding loan liability (i.e., debt covenant) might influence a manager to choose a particular depreciation method.

13. Explain why a large, well-established company might not choose to change from an accelerated method of depreciation to straight-line. How might investors and creditors interpret such a move?

14. Describe the activity method and how it is used to deplete the costs of acquiring rights to extract natural resources.

15. Briefly describe the tax law with respect to the depreciation of fixed assets. Why do most companies choose one depreciation method for reporting purposes and another for tax purposes? When managers have a choice, why do they generally depreciate fixed assets for tax purposes using as short a life as possible and the double-declining-balance method? Are fewer tax dollars paid over the life of the asset?

16. List the three ways described in the chapter to dispose of long-lived assets. What do the methods used to account for these three events have in common?

17. Under what conditions should long-lived assets be written down? How can management use the accounting standards in this area to "manage" reported earnings numbers over time?

18. What is the general rule for valuing an asset received in exchange for a dissimilar asset and cash? Prepare the form of a journal entry (i.e., debited and credited accounts but no dollar amounts) used to record such a transaction. Assume that a loss is recognized on the exchange.

19. Name three countries that allow fixed assets to be carried on the balance sheet at current values. Explain how fixed asset revaluations affect the financial statements and why they increase management's ability to influence financial numbers.

20. Has the ability to revalue long-lived assets helped foreign companies raise capital in U.S. markets? Explain.

21. *Appendix 9A.* List and define five different intangible assets. What methods are used to allocate the cost of intangible assets to future periods?

22. *Appendix 9A.* What is goodwill, and how is it recognized on the financial statements? What factors would affect the period over which goodwill is amortized?

23. *Appendix 9A.* How are the methods used to account for research and development costs inconsistent with the matching principle? Why have they not been changed?

24. *Appendix 9B.* What are the two fundamental problems with valuing long-lived assets at historical cost? What problems are there with the cost-allocation process?

25. *Appendix 9B.* Some claim that an objective of allocating the costs of long-lived assets to future periods is to provide funds for the future replacement of those assets. Evaluate this statement, pointing out both how it is inaccurate as well as how, in an indirect way, it might be viewed as correct.

EXERCISES

E9–1

(Different amortization methods achieve different objectives)

The controller of Elton Furniture Store is currently trying to decide what depreciation method to use for a particular fixed asset. The controller has prepared the following list of possible objectives that might be accomplished through a depreciation method. Which method(s):

a. most closely matches the asset's cost with the benefits resulting from the asset's use?

b. allocates the cost of the asset over the asset's useful life?

c. generates the largest net income in the last year of the asset's useful life?
d. does not directly use the asset's salvage value in computing the depreciation expense?
e. is best for tax purposes (i.e., minimizes the present value of future tax payments)?
f. recognizes an equal charge to expense every period?
g. generates the largest depreciation expense in the asset's last year?
h. does not allow the asset's book value to drop below the asset's salvage value?

REQUIRED:

Consider each objective independently, and indicate the depreciation method(s) that achieve each objective.

E9-2

(Determining the capitalized cost and depreciation base)

Lowery, Inc., purchased new plant equipment on January 1, 1996. The company paid $920,000 for the equipment, $62,000 for transportation of the equipment, and $10,000 for insurance on the equipment while it was being transported. The company also estimates that over the equipment's useful life it will require additional power, which will cause utility costs to increase $90,000. The equipment has an estimated salvage value of $50,000.

REQUIRED:

a. What amount should the company capitalize for this equipment on January 1, 1996?
b. What is the depreciation base of this equipment?
c. What amount will be depreciated over the life of this equipment?

E9-3

(Allocating cost on the basis of relative market value)

AJB Real Estate purchased a ten-acre tract of land for $320,000. The company divided the land into four lots of two and one-half acres each. Lot 1 had a beautiful view of the mountains and was valued at $160,000. Lot 2 had a stream running through it and was valued at $120,000. Lots 3 and 4 were each valued at $60,000. Assume that each lot is sold for the values indicated. Compute the profit on each of the four sales.

E9-4

(Betterments or maintenance?)

The following items represent common postacquisition expenditures incurred on machinery. Identify each as a betterment or a maintenance item.
a. Lubrication service
b. Painting costs
c. Cleaning expenditures
d. Rewiring costs to increase operating speed
e. Repairs
f. Replacement of defective parts
g. An overhaul to increase useful life
h. Cost of a muffler to reduce machine noise
i. Costs of redesign to increase output

E9-5

(Depreciation calculations and journal entries)

Stockton Corporation purchased a new computer system on January 1, 1996, for $300,000 cash. The company also incurred $25,000 in installation costs and $10,000 to train its employees on the new system. The computer system has an estimated useful life of five years and an estimated salvage value of $70,000.

REQUIRED:

a. Prepare the entry to record the acquisition of the computer system.
b. Calculate the depreciation expense recognized each year over the life of the system for each of the following assumptions:
    (1) Stockton uses straight-line depreciation.
    (2) Stockton uses sum-of-the-years'-digits depreciation.

(3) Stockton uses double-declining-balance depreciation.
c.   Provide the journal entry recorded by Stockton at the end of 1996 under the double-declining-balance method.

E9–6

(Computing depreciation and choosing a depreciation method)

Benick Industries purchased a new lathe on January 1, 1996, for $300,000. Benick estimates that the lathe will have a useful life of four years and that the company will be able to sell it at the end of the fourth year for $60,000.

REQUIRED:

a.   Compute the depreciation expense that Benick Industries would record for 1996, 1997, 1998, and 1999 under each of the following methods:
(1) Straight-line depreciation
(2) Sum-of-the-years'-digits depreciation
(3) Double-declining-balance depreciation
b.   If you were the president of Benick Industries, what might you consider when choosing a depreciation method for financial reporting purposes? Why?

E9–7

(How the matching principle is applied affects the timing of income recognition)

The condensed balance sheet as of December 31, 1996, for Van Den Boom Enterprises follows.

ASSETS		LIABILITIES AND STOCKHOLDERS' EQUITY	
Current assets	**$40,000**	**Liabilities**	**$35,000**
Land	**50,000**	**Stockholders' equity**	**55,000**
		Total liabilities and	
Total assets	**$90,000**	**stockholders' equity**	**$90,000**

Revenues and expenses (other than amortization) are predicted to be $65,000 and $20,000, respectively, for 1997, 1998, and 1999. All revenues and expenses are received or paid in cash. On January 1, 1997, Van Den Boom pays $40,000 cash for an item.

REQUIRED:

a.   Assume that Van Den Boom Enterprises engaged in operating activities only during 1997, 1998, and 1999. Prepare income statements for 1997, 1998, and 1999 and the balance sheet as of December 31 for 1997, 1998, and 1999, assuming the $40,000 cash payment is treated in each of the following ways:
(1) Immediately expensed.
(2) Capitalized and amortized evenly over two years.
(3) Capitalized and amortized evenly over three years.
b.   Compute the total income recognized over the three-year period under each assumption above.
c.   What is interesting about the 12/31/99 balance sheet prepared under all three assumptions?

E9–8

(Revising the estimated life)

Portland Products purchased a machine on January 1, 1993, for $60,000 and estimated its useful life and salvage value at five years and $12,000, respectively. On January 1, 1996, the company added three years to the original useful-life estimate.

REQUIRED:

a.   Compute the book value of the machine as of January 1, 1996, assuming that Portland uses the straight-line method of depreciation.
b.   Prepare the journal entry entered by the company to record depreciation on December 31, 1996.

E9–9

(The activity method of depreciation)

Apex Trucking purchased a truck for $100,000 on January 1, 1996. The useful life of the truck was estimated to be either five years or 200,000 miles. Salvage value was estimated at $20,000. Over the actual life of the truck it logged the following miles:

Year 1	48,000 miles
Year 2	35,000 miles
Year 3	40,000 miles
Year 4	25,000 miles
Year 5	35,000 miles
Year 6	10,000 miles

At the end of the sixth year, the truck was sold for $12,000.

REQUIRED:
Prepare the journal entries to record depreciation over the life of the truck, and its sale, assuming these methods:

1. Activity method
2. Straight-line method

E9–10

(Which costs are subject to depreciation?)

Firton Brothers purchased a tract of land that included an abandoned warehouse for $90,000. The warehouse was razed and the site was prepared for a new building at a cost of $10,000. Scrap materials from the warehouse were sold for $7,000. A building was then constructed for $140,000, a driveway and parking lot were laid for $32,000, and permanent landscaping was completed for $4,000. Firton Brothers depreciates fixed assets over a 20-year period using the straight-line method.

REQUIRED:
a. Compute the amount of cost to be placed in the Land, Land Improvements, and Building accounts.
b. Assuming a salvage value of zero, compute the depreciation expense associated with the items above for the first year.

E9–11

(The effect of estimated useful life on income and dividends)

Stork Freight Company owns and operates fifteen planes that deliver packages worldwide. The planes were purchased on January 1, 1993, for $1 million each. The company estimates that the planes will be scrapped after twelve years. Stork Freight uses straight-line depreciation.

REQUIRED:
a. Assume that in a typical year the company generates revenues of $50 million and operating expenses (excluding depreciation expense) of $25 million. Prepare an income statement for a typical year.
b. Assume that the company had originally estimated the useful life at six, instead of twelve, years. Prepare an income statement for a typical year. What is the percent change in net income?
c. Assume that the company policy is to pay dividends in the amount of 30 percent of net income. Compute the difference in the dividend payment between the two cases above.

E9–12

(Fixed asset sales)

Savory Enterprises reported the following information regarding the company's fixed assets in the footnotes to the company's 1996 financial statements.

Office furniture	$500,000	
Less: Accumulated depreciation	300,000	200,000

a.   Assume that Savory Enterprises sells all of its office furniture for $235,000 in cash on January 1, 1997. Prepare the entry to record the sale.
b.   Assume that Savory Enterprises sells all of its office furniture for $185,000 in cash on January 1, 1997. Prepare the entry to record the sale.

E9–13

(Retiring, selling, and trading in a fixed asset)

Paris Company purchased equipment on January 1, 1994, for $25,000. The estimated useful life of the equipment is five years, the salvage value is $5,000, and the company uses the double-declining-balance method to depreciate fixed assets.

REQUIRED:

a.   Provide the journal entry if the equipment is scrapped after three years.
b.   Provide the journal entry if the equipment is scrapped after five years.
c.   Provide the journal entry if the equipment is sold for $8,000 after three years.
d.   Provide the journal entry if, at the end of the fifth year, the equipment and $28,000 cash are traded in for a dissimilar asset with an objectively determined FMV of $30,000.

E9–14

(An error in recording the acquisition of a fixed asset)

Lewis Real Estate purchased a new photocopy machine on January 1, 1996, for $120,000. The company's bookkeeper made the following entry to record the acquisition.

Depreciation Expense (E, −SE)   120,000
   Cash (−A)   120,000

The photocopy machine has an estimated useful life of four years and an estimated salvage value of $20,000. Lewis Real Estate did not make any adjusting entry on December 31, 1996, or in any subsequent year associated with the photocopy machine. Furthermore, the company never discovered the error.

REQUIRED:

a.   Assume that Lewis Real Estate uses the straight-line method to depreciate its fixed assets. Compute the values for the following chart.

YEAR	DEPRECIATION EXPENSE PER COMPANY'S BOOKS	CORRECT DEPRECIATION EXPENSE	ANNUAL DIFFERENCE	CUMULATIVE DIFFERENCE
1996				
1997				
1998				
1999				

b.   In what direction and by how much will the account Accumulated Depreciation be misstated as of December 31, 1998?
c.   In what direction and by how much will the account Retained Earnings be misstated *prior* to closing entries on December 31, 1998?
d.   In what direction and by how much will the account Retained Earnings be misstated *after* closing entries on December 31, 1998?

E9–15

(Depletion and matching)

Natural Extraction Industries paid $4 million for the right to drill for oil on a tract of land in western Texas. Engineers estimated that this oil deposit would produce 100,000 barrels of crude oil.

REQUIRED:

a. During the first year of operations Natural Extraction extracted 30,000 barrels of oil. Prepare the entry to record Depletion for the first year.

b. During the second year the company extracted 50,000 barrels. Prepare the entry to record Depletion for the second year.

c. What dollar amount would Natural Extraction report on its balance sheet at the end of the second year for oil deposits?

E9–16

(Reverse T-account analysis)

The financial information below was taken from the records of White Bones, Inc.

	1997	1996
BALANCE SHEET		
Equipment	$37,500	$32,700
Less: Accumulated depreciation	17,600	14,300
Net book value	$19,900	$18,400
INCOME STATEMENT		
Depreciation expense	$ 7,200	$ 6,800
Gain on sale of equipment	2,100	0

Note: The company purchased equipment for $12,000 during 1997.

REQUIRED:

a. How much cash was collected on the sale of equipment during 1997?

b. Reconstruct the entry that recorded the sale of equipment during 1997.

E9–17

(Reverse T-account analysis)

The financial information below was taken from the records of Frederickson and Peffer.

	1997	1996
BALANCE SHEET		
Equipment	$26,900	$23,400
Less: Accumulated depreciation	10,500	9,800
Net book value	$16,400	$13,600
INCOME STATEMENT		
Depreciation expense	$3,800	$3,500
Loss on sale of equipment	900	0
STATEMENT OF CASH FLOWS		
Cash received on sale of equipment	$4,300	$0

REQUIRED:

a. Reconstruct the entry that recorded the sale of equipment during 1997.

b. How much equipment was purchased during 1997?

E9–18

(Appendix 9A: Intangible assets: expense or capitalize and amortize?)

Swift Corporation incorporated on January 1, 1996, and incurred $45,000 in organization costs.

REQUIRED:

a. Should Swift Corporation capitalize or expense these costs? Defend your answer.

b. If these costs are capitalized, over what period of time should they be amortized? Provide the amortization journal entry for a single year if the maximum period of time is chosen.

c. What arguments could be used to justify capitalizing organization costs but not allocating them to future periods?

d. Assume that during 1996, Swift acquired a patent for $65,000. Should this cost be expensed or capitalized? Why one and not the other?

e. Assume that during 1996, Swift invested $220,000 to research and develop new products. Should these costs be expensed or capitalized?

f. What arguments could be used to justify capitalizing research and development costs, and if capitalized, how should these costs be amortized to future periods?

E9–19

(Appendix 9A: The capitalized cost of a patent)

The following information was taken from the internal financial records of Southern Robotics regarding a patent filed in 1996 for a new robotics arm used for manufacturing.

1. Legal and filing fees of $50,000 were paid during 1996 for filing the patent.
2. Legal fees of $200,000 were incurred and paid during 1997 to defend the patent against infringement by another company.

The patent was granted on December 31, 1996. The company estimated that the patent would provide an economic benefit to the company for five years. It is company policy not to amortize intangible assets in the year of acquisition.

REQUIRED:
a. Assume that Southern Robotics successfully defended its patent against the infringement.
   (1) What amount should Southern Robotics report for this patent on the company's December 31, 1996, balance sheet?
   (2) What amount should Southern Robotics report for this patent on the company's December 31, 1997, balance sheet?
   (3) Prepare the entry to amortize the patent on December 31, 1997.
b. Assume that Southern Robotics was unsuccessful in defending its patent against the infringement.
   (1) What amount should Southern Robotics report for this patent on the company's December 31, 1996, balance sheet?
   (2) What amount should Southern Robotics report for this patent on the company's December 31, 1997, balance sheet?
   (3) Prepare the entry to write off the patent.

PROBLEMS

P9–1

(Determining capitalized cost and the depreciation base)

Stonebrecker International recently purchased new manufacturing equipment. The equipment cost $1 million. The company also incurred additional costs related to the acquisition of the equipment. The total cost to transport the equipment to Stonebrecker's plant was $80,000, half of which was paid by Stonebrecker. The company also paid $8,000 to insure the equipment while it was being transported to its plant. The initial installation costs totaled $20,000. After installing the equipment, however, it was discovered that the floor under the equipment would have to be reinforced. Materials and direct labor to reinforce the floor totaled $15,000. While the equipment was being installed and the floor was being reinforced, the plant workers could not perform their normal functions. The cost to Stonebrecker of the employee downtime was $10,000. Stonebrecker estimates that the equipment will have a salvage value in ten years of $100,000.

REQUIRED:
a. What dollar amount should Stonebrecker capitalize on its books for this equipment?
b. Prepare the journal entry to capitalize the equipment.
c. What is the depreciation base of this equipment?

d.   Over the life of this equipment, what dollar amount will be depreciated under the straight-line method? Under the sum-of-the-years'-digits method? Under the double-declining-balance method?

P9–2

(Lump-sum purchases and cost allocation)

The JHP Company purchased a building, some office equipment, two cranes, and some land on January 1, 1996, for a total of $1 million cash. JHP has obtained the following appraisals of these assets.

ASSET	FMV ON 1/1/96	ESTIMATED LIFE	ESTIMATED SALVAGE VALUE
Building	$300,000	20 years	$75,000
Office equipment	150,000	3 years	35,000
Crane	75,000	5 years	15,000
Crane	75,000	5 years	15,000
Land	600,000	Indefinite	15,000

JHP company uses the straight-line method to depreciate fixed assets.

REQUIRED:
a.   Prepare the journal entry to record the purchase.
b.   Prepare the journal entry to record depreciation expense for each type of asset for the year ended December 31, 1996.
c.   Assuming that all of these assets are still held as of December 31, 1999, present these fixed assets as they would be shown on the December 31, 1999, balance sheet.

P9–3

(Determining capitalized cost and depreciation)

Gidley, Inc., purchased a piece of equipment on January 1, 1996. The following information is available for this purchase.

Purchase price	**$950,000**	**Salvage value**	**$50,000**
Transportation	**$100,000**[a]	**Useful life**	**4 years**
Installation	**$130,000**[b]		

[a]Included in the transportation cost is $1,000 for insurance covering the shipment of the equipment to Gidley.
[b]Included in the cost of installation is $80,000 in wages paid to employees who helped install the equipment.

REQUIRED:
a.   Compute the cost of the fixed asset that should be capitalized.
b.   Prepare the entry to record depreciation expense for the year ended December 31, 1996, assuming the company uses each of the following:
     (1) Sum-of-the-years'-digits depreciation method
     (2) Double-declining-balance depreciation method
     (3) Straight-line depreciation method
c.   Assuming that the equipment was sold on January 1, 1997, for $250,000, prepare the entry to record the sale of the equipment, assuming the company uses each of the following methods.
     (1) Sum-of-the-years'-digits depreciation method
     (2) Double-declining-balance depreciation method
     (3) Straight-line depreciation method

P9–4

(Accounting for betterments and maintenance costs)

McCartney Manufacturing purchased a dryer for $100,000 on January 1, 1993. The estimated life of the dryer is five years, and the salvage value is estimated to be $10,000. McCartney uses the straight-line method of depreciation.

On January 1, 1997, McCartney paid $160,000 to have the dryer overhauled, which increased the speed of the dryer and extended its estimated useful life to December 31, 2000. Each year McCartney pays $1,000 to have the dryer serviced. On November 12, 1997, a major repair was required at a cost of $5,000. Salvage value is still estimated to be $10,000.

REQUIRED:

a. Provide the journal entry on January 1, 1993, to record the purchase of the dryer.
b. How should the service and repair costs be treated on the books of McCartney?
c. Compute the depreciation expense that would be recognized during each year of the dryer's eight-year useful life.

P9–5

(Accounting for betterments)

Hulteen Hardware purchased a new building on January 1, 1992, for $1,500,000. The company expects the building to last 25 years and expects to be able to sell it then for $150,000. During 1997 the building was painted at a cost of $5,000. Almost ten years after acquiring the building, the roof was destroyed by a storm. The company had a new roof constructed at a cost of $200,000. The new roof was completed on January 1, 2002, and it extended the estimated life of the building by five years, to a total of thirty years. All other estimates are still accurate. Hulteen Hardware uses the straight-line method to depreciate the cost of all fixed assets.

REQUIRED:

a. Prepare the entry to record the purchase of the building, assuming that the company paid cash.
b. Prepare the entry to record the purchase of the new roof on January 1, 2002.
c. Prepare the entry to record depreciation expense for the year ended December 31, 2002.
d. Prepare the journal entry that would be recorded if the building was sold for $1,200,000 on December 31, 2007.

P9–6

(Revising the estimated useful life)

Burke Copy Center purchased a machine on January 1, 1991, for $180,000 and estimated its useful life and salvage value at ten years and $30,000, respectively. On January 1, 1996, the company added three years to the original useful-life estimate.

REQUIRED:

a. Compute the book value of the machine as of January 1, 1996, assuming Burke recognizes the depreciation using straight-line.
b. Prepare the journal entry to record depreciation entered by the company on December 31, 1996, assuming that Burk uses straight-line.

P9–7

(Why is double-declining-balance preferred for tax purposes?)

Note: Knowledge of the time value of money is necessary for this problem (see Appendix 4A). Kimberly Sisters purchased equipment for $80,000 on January 1, 1996. Kimberly can use the double-declining-balance method for tax purposes but does not understand why it should be preferred over straight-line. Given the following information, what is your advice?

Estimated useful life	**4 years**
Estimated salvage value	**$ 20,000**
Expected revenues over each of the next four years	**$100,000**
Expected expenses (excluding depreciation) over each of the next four years	**$ 60,000**
Tax rate (percent of net income)	**35 percent**

REQUIRED:

a. Which of the two methods will give rise to the greater amount of depreciation over the life of the equipment? Support your answer with computations.
b. Which of the two methods will result in the payment of less taxes over the life of the equipment? Support your answer with computations.

c. Why is the double-declining-balance method preferred for tax purposes?
d. Assume a discount rate of 10 percent. How much money would be saved by using double-declining-balance instead of straight-line?

P9–8

(The effect of depreciation on taxes, bonuses, and dividends)

Bently Poster Company pays income taxes on net income at the rate of 32 percent. The company pays a bonus to its officers of 8 percent of net income after taxes and pays dividends to its stockholders in the amount of 75 percent of net income after taxes. On January 1, 1996, the company purchased a fixed asset for $400,000. Such assets are usually depreciated over a 10-year period. Salvage value is expected to be zero. Assume that the bonus payment is not included as an expense in the calculation of taxable income and reported income.

REQUIRED:

Assume that revenues and expenses (excluding depreciation) for 1996 are $250,000 and $140,000, respectively. Compute the tax, bonus and dividend payment for 1996 if the company uses the following:

a. The straight-line method of depreciation
b. The double-declining-balance method of depreciation
c. The straight-line method of depreciation, assuming a five-year useful life

P9–9

(Expensing what should be capitalized can misstate net income)

Westmiller Construction Company purchased a new truck on December 31, 1994, for $48,000. The truck has an estimated useful life of three years and an estimated salvage value of $12,000. When the truck was purchased, the company's accountant mistakenly made the following entry:

Depreciation Expense—Truck (E, −SE)   48,000
    Cash (−A)   48,000

Over the life of the truck, the company made no other entries associated with it.

REQUIRED:
a. What entry should Westmiller Construction Company have made on December 31, 1994?
b. Assuming that the straight-line method of depreciation should have been used, and the error was not discovered, in what direction and by how much was net income misstated in 1994 and 1995?
c. Assuming that the double-declining-balance method of depreciation should have been used, and the error was not discovered, in what direction and by how much was net income misstated in 1994 and 1995?

P9–10

(Inferring a depreciation method and related journal entries)

Jalen Enterprises reports the following information in its 1996 financial report:

	12/31/96	12/31/95
Plant equipment	$1,000,000	$750,000
Less: Accumulated depreciation	590,000	490,000
	$ 410,000	$260,000

ADDITIONAL INFORMATION:
1. Jalen Enterprises began operations on January 1, 1994, and the entire Plant Equipment balance reported on December 31, 1995, was purchased for cash on the first day of operations. This equipment had an estimated salvage value of $50,000 and an estimated useful life of four years. The company neither bought nor sold any plant equipment during 1994 and 1995.
2. On January 1, 1996, Jalen Enterprises sold for cash some plant equipment that originally cost $200,000, at a book gain of $25,000. When the equipment was acquired on January 1,

1994, it had no estimated salvage value. The original estimates for the salvage value and the useful life are still accurate for the remaining equipment.

3. The company purchased additional plant equipment on January 1, 1996, for cash. This equipment is expected to be scrapped after five years and has an estimated salvage value of $30,000.

REQUIRED:

a. Prepare the entry to record the plant equipment acquired on January 1, 1994.
b. What method does the company use to depreciate plant equipment?
c. Prepare the entry to record the depreciation expense for the year ended December 31, 1994.
d. Prepare the entry to record the depreciation expense for the year ended December 31, 1995.
e. Prepare the entry to record the sale of the plant equipment on January 1, 1996.
f. Prepare the entry to record the purchase of plant equipment on January 1, 1996.
g. Prepare the entry to record the depreciation expense for the year ended December 31, 1996.

P9–11

(Selling and trading in fixed assets)

Webb Net Manufacturing purchased a new net weaving machine on January 1, 1994, for $500,000. The new machine has an estimated life of five years and an estimated salvage value of $100,000. It is company policy to use straight-line depreciation for all of its machines.

REQUIRED:

a. Assume that Webb Net Manufacturing sells this machine on January 1, 1997, for $325,000. Prepare the entry to record this transaction.
b. Assume that Webb Net Manufacturing sells this machine on June 30, 1997, for $320,000. Prepare the entry or entries to record this transaction.
c. Assume that Webb Net Manufacturing trades in this machine for a tract of land on January 1, 1997. The list price of the land is $250,000, and it has an appraised value of $210,000. The company is granted a trade-in allowance on the machine of $75,000 and pays an additional $175,000 in cash for the land. The net weaving machine is appraised at $75,000. Prepare the entry to record the trade-in assuming the land is valued as follows:
   (1) The FMV of the asset received.
   (2) The FMV of the assets given up.

P9–12

(Natural resources: different methods of cost allocation depend on the nature of the asset)

Garmen Oil Company recently discovered an oil field on one of its properties in Texas. In order to extract the oil, the company purchased drilling equipment on January 1, 1996, for $800,000 cash and also purchased a mobile home on the same date for $54,000 cash, to serve as on-site headquarters. The drilling equipment has an estimated useful life of 12 years but will be abandoned when the company shuts down this well. The mobile home has an estimated useful life of 7 years and an estimated salvage value of $5,000. The company expects to use the mobile home on other drilling sites after work on this site is completed.

Company geologists estimated correctly that the well would produce two million barrels of oil. Actual production from the well for 1996, 1997, and 1998 was 600,000 barrels, 750,000 barrels, and 650,000 barrels, respectively. All extracted barrels were immediately sold. This well is now dry and Garmen Oil has shut it down.

REQUIRED:

a. Prepare the entry to record the purchase of the drilling equipment and the mobile home.
b. Prepare the entries to record depletion expense for the drilling equipment using the activity method for 1996, 1997, and 1998.
c. Prepare the entries to record depreciation expenses for 1996, 1997, and 1998 for the mobile home using the straight-line method. Why are different methods used to allocate the costs of the drilling equipment and the mobile home?
d. Assume that Garmen Oil discovered that the well was dry at the end of 1997 (i.e., the well produced only 1,350,000 barrels of oil). Repeat parts (b) and (c).

P9–13

(Appendix 9A: Recognizing and amortizing goodwill)

On January 1, 1996, Diversified Industries purchased Specialists, Inc., for $1,800,000. The balance sheet of Specialists, Inc., at the time of purchase follows.

ASSETS		LIABILITIES AND STOCKHOLDERS' EQUITY	
Current assets	$650,000	Liabilities	$250,000
Long-lived assets	330,000	Stockholders' equity	730,000
		Total liabilities and	
Total assets	$980,000	stockholders' equity	$980,000

The total FMV of the individual assets of Specialists is $1,350,000, and the liabilities are valued on the balance sheet at FMV.

REQUIRED:

a. How can the FMV of Specialists' assets exceed the value of the assets on the balance sheet?
b. Why would Diversified pay more for Specialists than the FMV of the assets less the liabilities?
c. Provide the journal entry to record the purchase.
d. Assume that Diversified chooses accounting methods to maximize reported net income each year. What journal entry would Diversified record on December 31, 1996, with respect to this purchase?
e. Some have argued that goodwill should be written off in the period of acquisition and not amortized to future periods. Provide an argument in support of this position.

CASES

C9–1

(Lump-sum sales and purchase)

MGM Grand, Inc., purchased two Las Vegas casinos and the adjoining land for a total of $167 million. Soon afterwards the company agreed to sell one of the casinos and 58.7 acres of adjacent land for $110 million.

REQUIRED:

a. What issues need to be addressed in order to determine the gain or loss resulting from the sale of one of the casinos? How should the cost of the sold casinos be established?
b. Assume that each casino had a cost of $75 million and the adjacent land originally cost $17 million. Provide the journal entry prepared by MGM Grand to record the sale.
c. Explain how the casino and the land would each be valued on the balance sheet of the purchasing company.
d. Assume that an appraiser assesses the value of the land without the hotel to be $43 million. Compute the annual depreciation charge recognized by the purchasing company if it depreciates buildings using the straight-line rate over a period of 25 years. Assume no salvage value.

C9–2

(Write-downs due to impairments)

The Wall Street Journal (December 12, 1995) reported that the FASB now requires that companies must estimate the future expected value of *individual* assets and take a write-down in each case if the future value is less than the book value. While this requirement is expected to reduce the earnings numbers of many firms, it is expected to hit the oil companies especially hard. Texaco, for example, took a $640 million charge related to the rule, noting that the new rule eliminated their practice of assessing the value of oil fields collectively, requiring them to assess each field individually.

REQUIRED:

a. Explain how applying this rule on an asset-by-asset basis could give rise to a greater write-down than applying the rule collectively.

b. A security analyst, John Tumazos, commented in the article that "the new rule shouldn't cause panic among investors in general . . . for healthy companies the standard merely represents a different way of recognizing losses and profits at a given time." Explain what Mr. Tumazos means, and how this rule could help companies more effectively practice certain reporting strategies.

C9-3

(Recognizing depreciation and economic consequences)

In the past, private colleges, which are subject to the accounting and reporting standards for nonprofit entities, have not been required to recognize depreciation on their financial statements. However, *The Wall Street Journal* reported that "many of the nations 1,500 private colleges are considering ignoring a new accounting rule that would require them to depreciate buildings and equipment. . . . Several colleges received assurances from Standard & Poor's Corp. and Moody's Investors Services, Inc., that the bond-rating agencies wouldn't lower the colleges' bond ratings based on noncompliance with the FASB Statement. . . . The FASB's rules have the informal blessing of the Securities and Exchange Commission and, if not followed, would result in a qualified (audit) opinion. Such qualifications could cloud the status of some college bonds by triggering spending limits in bond covenants."

Source: Lee Berton, "Several Private Colleges May Ignore New Accounting Rule on Depreciation," *The Wall Street Journal*, February 4, 1988, p. 28.

REQUIRED:

a. Explain why colleges might not want to recognize depreciation on their financial statements.

b. Why would such institutions be interested in the assurances described above from companies such as Standard & Poor's and Moody's?

c. Why might an auditor qualify the audit opinion on a college that did not conform to this accounting rule?

d. Why would a spending limit be part of the bond covenant, and how could a qualified audit opinion trigger such a limit?

C9-4

(Betterments or maintenance and subsequent depreciation)

Ford Motor Company said it would spend $200 million to refurbish its Mustang assembly plant in Dearborn, Michigan. The aging factory had been discussed as a candidate for closing, but Ford's current capacity of Mustang production is barely able to keep pace with demand.

REQUIRED:

a. What issues must be considered when deciding whether to capitalize or expense the $200 million expenditures?

b. Under what conditions could the $200 million cost be expensed even if it improved instead of maintained the plant?

c. Assume that the $200 million cost is capitalized and that the refurbishment extends the useful life of the factory. Explain how Ford will compute depreciation on its factory over its remaining useful life.

C9-5

(Property, plant, & equipment investments in the newspaper industry)

J. Kendrick Noble, analyst at Paine Webber, was quoted in *USA Today* (June 19, 1990) as saying in reference to a spending boom in the newspaper industry: "We're seeing more spent on plant and equipment today than at any time since just after World War II." Indeed, during 1990 newspapers like *The New York Times,* the *Los Angeles Times, The Philadelphia Inquirer, The Dallas Morning News,* and *The Seattle Times* spent well in excess of $1 billion to replace worn out equipment, buy presses capable of printing color and customized newspapers, and move operations into suburban plants. Lately, Rockwell International, the largest U.S. printing press maker, has sold more than $1 billion a year of its specialized Goss presses in response to this demand.

REQUIRED:

Discuss the important accounting issues related to this activity. Specifically, what issues will these newspaper companies have to consider when accounting for old equipment? On which financial statements will these activities be reflected? And what issues must be considered when accounting for the new investments?

C9–6

(Fair market value accounting for museums?)

An article published in *The New York Times* (May 1, 1990) entitled "Pricing the Priceless: Museums Resist, Accountants Insist" states that "many museums' most valuable assets, from moon rocks to Michelangelos, are nowhere on their books." In response, the FASB "is drafting tough new accounting rules that would require museums to state the value of their collections on their balance sheet to earn an unqualified opinion from their auditors . . . most museums are concerned because they have long found it useful to have audited financial statements for fund raising and other purposes."

REQUIRED:

a. Do you believe that museums, non-profit institutions, should be required to have their art objects appraised and the values be placed on their balance sheets? Discuss.
b. Why would museums resist such a rule, and be concerned about receiving unqualified opinions from their auditors?

C9–7

(Corporate restructuring)

After being asked how General Electric has maintained such consistent earnings growth over the past decade, Dennis Dammerman, the company's chief financial officer says, "We're the best company in the world." However, *The Wall Street Journal* (November 3, 1994) offers another explanation. It notes that from the period of time, 1983 through 1993, General Electric recorded six discretionary restructuring charges, ranging in magnitude from $147 million to over $1 billion—totaling $3.95 billion. Coincidentally, in each of the years when a restructuring charge was recognized, GE booked a sizable one-time gain. In 1987, for example, the company recognized an $858 million one-time gain due to changes in accounting methods for taxes and inventory while taking a $1,027 million restructuring write-off, and in 1993 GE matched a $1 billion restructuring charge against the $1.4 billion one-time gain it recognized on the sale of an aerospace unit to Martin Marietta. "To smooth out fluctuations, GE frequently offsets one-time gains from big asset sales with restructuring charges; that keeps earnings from rising so high that they can't be topped the following year. GE also times sales of some equity stakes and even acquisitions to produce profit gains when needed."

REQUIRED:

a. What reporting strategy does GE seem to be using, and explain how it works.
b. Explain how discretionary restructuring charges help GE to implement that reporting strategy, and why the company would want to pursue it.
c. *The Wall Street Journal* (November 2, 1994) reports that "investors love restructurings" and that such charges seem to boost stock prices. Yet, the FASB is seriously considering cracking down on this popular corporate practice. Explain why investors might love restructurings, stock prices seem to rise when they are announced, yet the FASB is acting to limit such behavior.

C9–8

(Current values?)

As discussed in this chapter, U.S. accounting standards at one time contained a requirement that certain large companies disclose current values for inventories and fixed assets. Such disclosure included dollar amounts for cost of goods sold and depreciation that were based on current instead of historical cost. This requirement, however, was quickly abandoned in response to heated controversy.

REQUIRED:

a. Consider the case of News Corp. described in this chapter, and build an argument against requiring current values on the balance sheet.

b. Consider the usefulness of historical costs for decision-making purposes, and build a case for requiring current values on the balance sheet.

c. Which of the two arguments do you find most convincing?

C9–9

(MCI annual report)

Refer to the annual report of MCI in Appendix C and answer the following questions.

a. What is the major fixed asset category for MCI? What percent of MCI's total assets come from this category?

b. MCI's annual report mentions SOP (Statement of Position) 93-7 "Reporting on Advertising Costs." What does this statement say about how advertising costs should be accounted for, and how does it affect MCI?

c. How large is MCI's depreciation expense in absolute size and as a percent of total operating costs? How much did it increase during 1994, and why did it increase by so much? What method of depreciation does MCI use for its communication system, and what useful life estimates are used? Why are depreciation and amortization added back to net income in the "reconciliation of net income to cash from operating activities," but not included in the "Operating activities" section of the statement of cash flows?

d. How much cash did MCI invest in its communication system in 1994, and how was this investment funded? How much does MCI intend to spend in 1995 on capital expenditures, and where will the money come from?

e. What does the "Construction in progress" account represent, and what costs are contained in the "Communication systems" accounts? By how much did interest expense decrease in 1994, and why?

f. How does MCI handle maintenance and repair costs?

g. (Appendix) How large is the goodwill account in absolute size and as a percent of total assets? How much amortization was recognized on goodwill in 1994, and how much goodwill was recognized on acquisitions during 1994? Over what period of time does MCI amortize its goodwill?

C9–10

(Appendix 9A: Accounting for intangibles)

Forbes (July 11, 1988) reports that King World Productions Inc., the $285-million-per-year television syndicator of *Jeopardy, Wheel of Fortune,* and *Oprah Winfrey,* reported on its 1987 balance sheet a shareholders' equity amount of a negative $30 million. The article reports further that "this firm and many like it are proof that traditional accounting methods . . . no longer accurately reflect the importance of intangible assets to the service and 'idea' industries. . . . King World's top programs are on the books for only around $3 million—the amortized cost to the company of acquiring the rights to syndicate them—and Wheel of Fortune is on the books for nothing. Yet King World has contracts for these properties in most major U.S. markets through 1991 and beyond, which will bring in some $700 million in licensing fees over the next several years."

REQUIRED:

a. Explain how a company can have negative stockholder's equity and still be a viable entity.

b. What aspect of accounting for intangibles is the *Forbes* article criticizing?

c. Provide several recommendations on how these accounting problems could be addressed, and also point out some of the trade-offs involved in following your recommendations.

C9–11

(Appendix 9A: Goodwill write-offs)

Under current accounting rules, companies can deduct in a single year the goodwill they obtained through acquisitions—provided they can prove that future earnings won't cover the annual deduction for goodwill amortization. Recently, several companies have chosen to exercise this option after recognizing huge dollar amounts of goodwill on large acquisitions financed primarily through borrowings. In 1993 Pathmark Corp. and Fort Howard Corp., for example, recorded immediate goodwill write-offs of $600 million and $2 billion, respectively. Other companies considered similar actions.

The Wall Street Journal (November 16, 1993) reported that the FASB is seriously considering making it more difficult for companies to write off goodwill in the year of acquisition by not allowing an interest deduction in the calculation of projected future earnings. Many of the companies, which would choose to immediately write off goodwill, finance their acquisitions with large amounts of debt. Disallowing interest in the calculation of future earnings would make it more difficult for these companies to "prove that future earnings won't cover the annual deduction for goodwill amortization." The article notes that "The rule could be particularly troublesome for companies that have (financed major acquisitions with debt) and now decide they want to sell stock to the public again."

REQUIRED:

a. Why would a company wish to write off goodwill immediately in the year of the acquisition, and why would the FASB wish to make it more difficult for a company to do so?

b. How would the new rule limit such write-offs, and how might it hurt "companies that have (financed major acquisitions with debt) and now decide they want to sell stock to the public again?"

PART 4

LIABILITIES AND STOCKHOLDERS' EQUITY: A CLOSER LOOK

INTRODUCTION TO LIABILITIES: ECONOMIC CONSEQUENCES, CURRENT LIABILITIES, AND CONTINGENCIES

L E A R N I N G   O B J E C T I V E S

LO 1
Define a liability.

LO 2
Describe the economic consequences associated with reporting liabilities on the financial statements.

LO 3
Distinguish between determinable liabilities and contingent liabilities.

LO 4
Define a current liability, and list and briefly describe the most common current liabilities.

LO 5
Explain why bonus systems and profit-sharing arrangements are used to compensate employees, and describe the reporting incentives they create.

LO 6
Describe the methods used to account for contingencies and how they apply to lawsuits and warranties.

This chapter and Chapter 11 are devoted to liabilities: obligations of a company to disburse assets or provide services in the future. Liabilities are divided on the balance sheet into two categories: current liabilities and long-term liabilities. Current liabilities primarily include short-term payables; long-term liabilities relate to long-term notes, bonds, leases, retirement costs, and deferred income taxes. This chapter introduces liabilities in general and covers the methods used to account for current liabilities and contingent liabilities, which can be either current or long term. Accounting for retirement costs and deferred income taxes are briefly reviewed in Appendix 10A and 10B, respectively. Chapter 11 is devoted to long-term notes, bonds, and leases. These three liabilities are covered in a single chapter because the same basic method, called the *effective interest method,* is used to account for them.

WHAT IS A LIABILITY?

LO 1 The FASB has defined liabilities as "probable future sacrifices of economic benefits arising from present obligations of a particular entity to transfer assets or provide services to other entities in the future as a result of past transactions or events." The Board commented further that all liabilities appearing on the balance sheet should have three characteristics in common: (1) they should be present obligations that entail settlements by probable future transfers or uses of cash, goods, or services; (2) they should be unavoidable obligations; and (3) the transaction or event obligating the enterprise must have already happened.[1]

While the FASB's definition makes the measurement of most liabilities relatively straightforward, the liabilities listed on the balance sheet do entail a wide variety of items, including credit balances with suppliers, debts from borrowings, services yet to be performed, withholdings from employees' wages and salaries, dividend declarations, product warranties, deferred income taxes, and a number of complex financing arrangements. As we discuss later, there is some question whether all these items are liabilities in an economic sense as well as whether all the economic liabilities of a company are included on its balance sheet.

THE RELATIVE SIZE OF LIABILITIES ON THE BALANCE SHEET

Figure 10–1 contains liabilities as a percentage of total assets, often referred to as the **debt ratio**, for selected industries. Note that liabilities are a significant source of financing for all listed industries and that the ratio ranges from approximately 40 percent for security brokers, department stores, and petroleum and gas to almost 60 percent for motor vehicles and eating places. In general, those industries that have relatively large investments in long-lived assets, such as manufacturing and general services, tend to rely more heavily on debt financing. Further, the ratios listed in Figure 10-1 are somewhat less than those of the major firms in each industry classification. For example, Merrill Lynch and Citicorp, giants in the Financial Services area, carry debt ratios in excess of 95 percent, while McDonald's and AT&T, industry

1. Financial Accounting Standards Board (FASB), "Elements of Financial Statements of Business Enterprises," *Statement of Financial Accounting Concepts No. 3* (Stamford, Conn.: FASB, 1980), pars. 28 and 29.

FIGURE 10–1	INDUSTRY	SIC CODE	NO. OF COMPANIES	LIABILITIES/ TOTAL ASSETS
Liabilities as a percentage of total assets (industry averages)	**MANUFACTURING**			
	Motor Vehicles	3711	95	.56
	Petroleum and Gas	1311	872	.41
	RETAILING			
	Department Stores	5311	641	.41
	Hobby, Toy & Games	5945	519	.42
	GENERAL SERVICES			
	Eating Places	5812	2,427	.56
	Telephone Commun.	4813	1,130	.49
	FINANCIAL SERVICES			
	Security Brokers	6211	1,312	.37
	Bank Holding Co.	6719	188	.35

Source: Compiled from data published in *Industry Norms and Key Business Ratios* (Dun & Bradstreet, Inc., 1994)

leaders in General Services, report debt ratios of 60 to 70 percent. The balance sheet of General Motors, which includes the liabilities of GMAC (the company's financing subsidiary), indicates that liabilities are about 80 percent of total assets. These percentages exceed those reported in Figure 10–1 because these industry leaders have financed much of their growth with debt. The main message here is that liabilities are a very important source of financing, especially for large companies, across a wide variety of industries.

REPORTING LIABILITIES ON THE BALANCE SHEET: ECONOMIC CONSEQUENCES

LO 2 The reported values of liabilities affect important financial ratios that stockholders, investors, creditors, and others use to assess management's performance and a company's financial condition. Seven of Dun & Bradstreet's fourteen key business ratios, for example, directly include a measure of liabilities: (1) quick ratio [(cash + marketable securities + receivables)/current liabilities], (2) current ratio (current assets/current liabilities), (3) current liabilities/net worth, (4) current liabilities/inventory, (5) total liabilities/net worth, (6) sales/net working capital, and (7) accounts payable/sales. These ratios and others that include liability measures are used by interested outside parties to determine credit ratings, assess solvency and future cash flows, predict bankruptcy and, in general, assess the financial health of an enterprise. In addition to using liability measures to evaluate the future prospects of a firm, stockholders, investors, creditors, and managers are interested in the reported values of liabilities for other important reasons, several of which are discussed on the next page.

STOCKHOLDERS AND INVESTORS

Stockholders and investors are concerned with liabilities and the contracts that underlie them because interest payments must be met before dividends can be distributed.

Also, in the event of liquidation, outstanding payables must be satisfied before stockholders are paid. Many loan contracts, for example, restrict the amount of dividends that can be paid in any one year to the common stockholders. The Boeing Company, an aircraft manufacturer, operates under certain debt covenants that restrict the payment of dividends and other distributions on the company's stock. As of December 31, 1994, $1.5 billion (19 percent of retained earnings) was available for cash dividends on common stock.

CREDITORS

The creditors of a company have a special interest in the liabilities held by others. These liabilities compete for the resources that must be used to satisfy the obligations owed to them. Creditors often protect their interests by writing terms in loan contracts that require collateral in the case of default or that restrict a company's future borrowings. The 1994 annual report of Owens-Corning Fiberglas contained the following excerpt, which describes the debt covenants imposed by its bank lenders

"As is typical for bank credit, the agreements contain restrictive covenants, including requirements for the maintenance of working capital, interest coverage, and minimum coverage of fixed charges; and limitations on the early retirement of (certain) debt, additional borrowings, certain investments, payment of dividends, and purchase of Company stock. The agreements include a provision which would result in all of the unpaid principal and accrued interest of the facilities becoming due immediately upon a change of control in ownership of the Company. A material adverse change in the Company's business, assets, liabilities, financial condition, or results of operations constitutes a default under the agreements."

MANAGEMENT

Management views short- and long-term borrowings and the related liabilities as important sources of capital for operating, investing, and financing activities. An article in *Forbes* states:

Most companies spend lots of time figuring out when and how to borrow money. That makes sense. Proper timing of debt can save millions in interest payments.[2]

On its 1994 balance sheet The Quaker Oats Company, for example, disclosed about $2.6 billion of outstanding liabilities, representing almost 87 percent of its financing sources. That amount is certainly a significant sum that requires astute and careful management to ensure that sufficient cash is on hand to meet the required payments as they come due. In 1994 alone, Quaker Oats paid approximately $200 million in interest and principal to service its outstanding debt. Effective management of such debt is critical to a company's success and can be used to great advantage. Companies often borrow, using the funds to provide returns that exceed the interest cost associated with the debt. Such a strategy, called financial leverage, is very common as interest payments are deductible in the computation of taxable income.

2. Richard Morris, "None for Me, Thanks," *Forbes,* October 22, 1984, p. 134.

While management often chooses to rely on borrowings for its financial needs, it has incentives to understate liabilities on the balance sheet. Indeed, a well-known article in *Forbes* began:

The basic drives of man are few: to get enough food, to find shelter, and to keep debt off the balance sheet.[3]

Additional debt on the balance sheet, for example, can reduce a company's credit rating, making it increasingly difficult to attract capital in the future. Standard & Poor's Corp., an established credit-rating service, lowered the credit rating of Fleming Company because the company financed an acquisition with borrowings that increased its total debt by $375 million. In reaction to Standard & Poor's announcement, the market price of the company's outstanding stock immediately dropped.

Additional debt on the balance sheet can also decrease the current ratio, increase the debt/asset ratio, and increase the debt/equity ratio. Such changes could cause a company to violate its debt covenants and in general cause it to be viewed as more risky by outside investors and creditors. The national director of accounting and auditing at Seidman & Seidman, for example, points out:

Removing large amounts of debt can present a more favorable impression of debt-to-equity ratios, working capital ratios, and the returns on assets invested in the business.[4]

There are also situations, however, when management may wish to report additional liabilities on the balance sheet. For example, by reporting additional liabilities in the current period, management may be able to report higher net income amounts in future periods. Such a reporting strategy is not unusual for companies that are experiencing exceptionally poor years as well as for those experiencing exceptionally good years.

Several years ago, for example, while in the midst of bankruptcy proceedings, LTV Corporation "took a bath" by accruing a number of significant liabilities, none of which were required at the time by generally accepted accounting principles. A spokesman for LTV was quoted in *The Wall Street Journal* (November, 22, 1988) as saying:

[the company] took the special charges because it believes it should record all its liabilities while in [bankruptcy] proceedings. It's a unique opportunity for us to take it at a time when it does the least harm . . . LTV likely wants a fresh start when it emerges from bankruptcy-law proceedings.

Companies experiencing exceptionally good years may also choose to accrue additional liabilities. The article just cited also pointed out that a number of companies "with strong equity positions" may wish to take early recognition of certain liabilities and, in effect, "bite the bullet early." This reporting strategy, called "building hidden reserves," recognizes losses in a year when they will be overwhelmed by other items of income. It also avoids having to recognize the losses in later years, which may not be so exceptional.

AUDITORS

Auditors must attest that all liabilities are identified and properly reported on the balance sheet. Auditors are particularly careful in this area because significant unreported liabilities may lead to losses incurred in the future by investors and creditors for which auditors may be held liable. For example, a major accounting firm recently

3. Richard Greene, "The Joys of Leasing," *Forbes,* November 24, 1980, p. 59.
4. Anne McGrath, "The Best of Both Worlds," *Forbes,* September 26, 1983, pp. 106,108.

withdrew its opinions on Bombay Palace Restaurants, Inc., accusing the company of supplying false information and invoice documents with respect to certain material liabilities. In a well-known recent case involving Phar Mor drugstores, a major accounting firm was sued for millions of dollars for failing to uncover a fraud that grossly understated the company's liabilities.

CURRENT LIABILITIES

Current liabilities arc obligations expected to require the use of current assets or the creation of other current liabilities. They normally include obligations to suppliers (accounts payable), short-term debts, current maturities on long-term debts, dividends payable to stockholders, deferred revenues (services yet to be performed that are expected to require the use of current assets), third-party collections (e.g., sales tax and payroll deductions), periodic accruals (e.g., wages and interest), and potential obligations related to pending or threatened litigation, product warranties, and guarantees.

Note that current liabilities are defined in terms of obligations "expected to require the use of current assets." Thus, reported obligations that are not expected to require the use of current assets are not disclosed as current. For example, an obligation that is due within a year may not be disclosed in the current liabilities section if it is either (1) expected to be paid from assets that are presently listed as noncurrent or (2) expected to be replaced (refinanced) with a long-term liability or equity issuance. Such obligations would normally be disclosed as long-term.

THE RELATIVE SIZE OF CURRENT LIABILITIES ON THE BALANCE SHEET

The relative size of current liabilities varies across companies from different industries. Figure 10–2 contains the current liability/total liability ratio for selected industries. Note that current liabilities are usually over 50% of total liabilities, and for some

FIGURE 10–2	INDUSTRY	SIC CODE	NO. OF COMPANIES	CURRENT LIABILITIES/ TOTAL LIABILITIES
Current liabilities as a percentage of total liabilities (industry averages)	**MANUFACTURING**			
	Motor Vehicles	3711	95	.76
	Petroleum and Gas	1311	872	.65
	RETAILING			
	Department Stores	5311	641	.61
	Hobby, Toy & Games	5945	519	.71
	GENERAL SERVICES			
	Eating Places	5812	2,427	.54
	Telephone Commun.	4813	1,130	.34
	FINANCIAL SERVICES			
	Security Brokers	6211	1,312	.88
	Bank Holding Co.	6719	188	.58

Source: Compiled from data published in *Industry Norms and Key Business Ratios* (Dun & Bradstreet, Inc., 1994)

industries, like security brokers and motor vehicles, current liabilities represent an extremely important form of financing. Indeed, 89 and 98 percent of the liabilities of Merrill Lynch and General Motors, respectively, are current. The large banks, such as Citicorp, BankAmerica, and J. P. Morgan, who finance operations with short-term deposits, have current liabilities that represent over 90 percent of total liabilities and over 80 percent of total assets.

The importance of current liabilities is relatively small in industries, like telephone communications, where firms invest heavily in long-lived assets. For example, Ameritech, a member of the telephone communications industry, reports only about one-third of its total liabilities as current. It invests heavily in communications equipment, a long-term investment, and tends to finance that equipment with long-term liabilities.

VALUING CURRENT LIABILITIES ON THE BALANCE SHEET

Most liabilities involve future cash outflows that are specified by formal contract or informal agreement. They can therefore be predicted objectively, and present value methods can be used to value liabilities on the balance sheet. In the case of current liabilities, however, the time period until payment is relatively short and the difference between the **face value** (actual cash payment when the liability is due) of the liability and its present value (discounted future cash payment) is considered to be immaterial. Thus, in the interest of materiality, current liabilities are usually recorded on the balance sheet at face value.

REPORTING CURRENT LIABILITIES: AN ECONOMIC CONSEQUENCE

In most cases the face value of a current liability is easy to determine, and balance sheet valuation is straightforward. The primary problem is one of discovery, ensuring that all existing current liabilities are reported on the balance sheet. Failure to discover and report an existing current liability misstates the financial statements and any of the financial measures that include current liabilities. Two particularly important financial measures are the current ratio and working capital, which help investors and creditors to assess a company's solvency position because they match current obligations against the assets on hand to satisfy them. These ratios are frequently found in loan contracts, like those disclosed in an annual report of Cummins Engine Co., a manufacturer of heavy-duty truck engines, requiring Cummins to maintain a current ratio of 1.25:1. Such debt restrictions can discourage management from reporting current liabilities on the balance sheet.

Consider, for example, JFP Company, which borrows $1 million from Thrift Bank. The loan contract states that the loan is in default if JFP's current ratio, as reported on the balance sheet, dips below 2:1. Defaulting on this loan could mean that JFP must immediately pay the outstanding balance; in most cases, however, the company would be forced to renegotiate the terms of the loan with Thrift Bank. Such renegotiations would probably require that JFP make costly concessions, normally in the form of less desirable loan terms (e.g., higher interest rates, additional collateral).

At year end JFP's accountants determine that current assets equal $100,000. If current liabilities are determined to be $50,000 or less, the current ratio will be at least

2:1, and the loan will not be in default. On the other hand, if current liabilities are determined to be greater than $50,000, the current ratio would dip below 2:1 and JFP would be in violation of the loan contract, which could lead to serious financial problems.

If JFP's management fails, either intentionally or unintentionally, to report a given current liability on the balance sheet, it can avoid violating the terms of the loan contract and the related consequences. Management, therefore, has an incentive either to ignore existing current liabilities, postpone them, or to structure transactions so that current liabilities do not have to be recorded. Auditors must make special efforts to ensure that all existing current liabilities are properly reported on the balance sheet, and financial statement users must be aware of these management incentives.

ACCOUNTING FOR CURRENT LIABILITIES

LO 3 Determining the dollar amounts of all current liabilities, because they represent probable future outlays, involves an element of uncertainty. The relative degree of uncertainty gives rise to two current liability categories: (1) determinable and (2) contingent. Determining the dollar amount of a determinable current liability is relatively straightforward; determining the dollar amount of a contingent liability involves an estimate. Figure 10–3 provides an outline of the current liabilities covered in this section.

FIGURE 10–3		
Outline of current liabilities	**Determinable Current Liabilities**	**Contingent Liabilities**
	A. Accounts payable	A. Lawsuits
	B. Short-term debts	B. Warranties
	1. Short-term notes	
	2. Current maturities of long-term debts	
	C. Dividends payable	
	D. Unearned revenues	
	E. Third-party collections	
	F. Accrued liabilities	
	1. Normal	
	2. Conditional	
	a. Income taxes	
	b. Incentive compensation	

DETERMINABLE CURRENT LIABILITIES

LO 4 In general, **determinable current liabilities** can be precisely measured, and the amount of cash needed to satisfy the obligation and the date of payment are reasonably certain. Determinable current liabilities include accounts payable, short-term debts, dividends payable, unearned revenues, third-party collections, and accrued liabilities.

ACCOUNTS PAYABLE

Accounts payable are dollar amounts owed to others for goods, supplies, and services purchased on **open account**.[5] They arise from frequent transactions between a company and its suppliers that are normally not subject to specific, formal contracts. These extensions of credit are the practical result of a time lag between the receipt of a good, supply, or service and the corresponding payment. The time period is usually short (e.g., thirty to sixty days) and is indicated by the terms of the exchange (e.g., 2/10, n/30).

Accounts payable are usually associated with inventory purchases, which are discussed in Chapter 7, and a recent Dun & Bradstreet survey found that accounts payable are the most popular source of financing for small business owners. The size of the balance in accounts payable can be an important indicator of a company's financial condition, especially in the retail industry where suppliers are heavily relied upon to provide merchandise. The 1990 Christmas season for R. H. Macy, for example, did not produce sufficient revenues to cover the outstanding accounts owed to Macy's suppliers, which, in turn, delayed payments and caused the company's accounts payable balance to increase. Many financial analysts used this information to accurately predict that the company would soon declare bankruptcy. Robert Campeau, who built a retail empire in the 1980s, experienced similar problems prior to the empire's collapse in 1990. His companies paid suppliers so slowly that they ceased sending shipments.

SHORT-TERM DEBTS

Short-term debts (or short-term borrowings) typically include short-term bank loans, commercial paper, lines of credit, and current maturities of long-term debt. **Commercial paper**, a fast-growing means of providing short-term financing, represents short-term notes (30 to 270 days) issued for cash by companies with good credit ratings to other companies. A **line of credit** is usually granted to a company by a bank or group of banks, allowing it to borrow up to a certain maximum dollar amount, interest being charged only on the outstanding balance. Issued commercial paper and existing lines of credit are an indication of a company's ability to borrow funds on a short-term basis; thus, they are very important to investors and creditors who are interested in assessing solvency. Consequently, such financing arrangements are extensively described in the footnotes. The excerpt below, for example, is from the 1994 financial report of Sears, Roebuck and Co.

Short-term borrowings consisted of (dollars in millions):

	DECEMBER 31	
	1994	1993
Commercial paper	$5,919	$4,133
Bank loans	98	107
Agreements with bank trust departments	87	140
Other loans (principally foreign)	86	256
Total short-term borrowings	$6,190	$4,636

At December 31, 1994, the company had credit agreements totaling $8.01 billion (almost $2 billion of which was unused).

---

5. Accounts payable are often referred to as *trade accounts payable. Accounting Trends and Techniques* (New York: AICPA, 1994, p. 209) reports that 118 of the 600 major U.S. companies surveyed used that phrase.

SHORT-TERM NOTES. Short-term notes usually arise from cash loans and are generally payable to banks or loan companies. In most cases the life of a note is somewhere between thirty days and one year, and the bank or loan company lends the borrowing company less cash than is indicated on the face of the note. At the **maturity date** (when the loan is due), the borrowing company pays the lending institution the face amount of the note, and the difference between the face amount and the amount of the loan is treated as interest.

For example, suppose that on January 1, Freight Line Industries borrows $9,400 from Commercial Loan Company and signs a six-month note with a face amount of $10,000. The journal entry to record this transaction is provided below.

Cash (+A)	9,400	
Discount on Notes Payable (−L)	600	
Notes Payable (+L)		10,000

Issued short-term note payable.

The Discount on Notes Payable account serves as a contra account to notes payable on the balance sheet and represents interest that is not yet owed but will be recognized in the future. Perhaps it is helpful to think of it as prepaid interest. Assuming that financial statements are prepared monthly, one-sixth of the discount would be converted to interest expense each month by an adjusting journal entry of the following form:

Interest Expense (E, −SE)	100	
Discount on Notes Payable (+L)		100

Recognized accrual of interest on a short-term note ($600/6).

After this entry is recorded at the end of the first month, the balance of the discount would have been reduced to $500, and the balance sheet carrying amount of the note would be as follows. The net balance ($9,500) represents the amount of cash that would be required to pay off the note as of the balance sheet date.

Notes payable	$10,000	
Less: Discount on note payable	500	$9,500

CURRENT MATURITIES OF LONG-TERM DEBTS. Long-term debts are often retired through a series of periodic installments. The installments that are to be paid within the time period that defines current assets (one year or the current operating cycle, whichever is longer) should be included on the balance sheet as current liabilities; the remaining installments should be disclosed as long-term liabilities.

For example, assume that on December 31, 1996, Wright and Sons borrows $50,000, which is to be paid back in annual installments of $7,000 each. The first payment, which is due on December 31, 1997, will consist of $5,000 in interest and $2,000 in principal. On the December 31, 1996, balance sheet the associated payable would be disclosed in the following way. Note that the $50,000 principal amount is divided up into $2,000, which is due in the current period, and $48,000, which is long-term. The $5,000 in interest will be accrued at the end of 1997 after the company has had use of the funds.

Current liabilities:	
Current maturity of long-term debt	2,000
Long-term liabilities:	
Long-term notes payable	48,000

Current maturities on long-term debts can be quite large, but they rarely represent a major portion of current liabilities. In the 1994 financial report of Goodyear Tire & Rubber Company, for example, current maturities in the amount of $14 million were disclosed. Although significant, this amount represented less than 1 percent of the company's current liabilities.

DIVIDENDS PAYABLE

A liability is created when the board of directors of a corporation declares a dividend to be paid to the stockholders. It is listed as current because dividends are usually paid within several weeks of declaration. The methods used to account for dividends are discussed in Chapter 12.

UNEARNED REVENUES

Payments are often received before contracted services are performed. In such cases an *unearned revenue*, *deferred revenue*, or *receipt in advance* liability is created because the companies receiving the payments are under obligations that must be fulfilled. This liability is then converted to revenue as the related services are performed or the relevant goods are delivered. Recall that one of the primary criteria of revenue recognition is that the earning process must be complete before a revenue can be recognized. If providing the related services or relevant goods is expected to require the use of current assets, the unearned revenue liability should be classified as current.

Unearned revenues arise from a number of different transactions: gift certificates sold by retail stores that are redeemable in merchandise, coupons sold by restaurants that can be exchanged for meals, tickets and tokens sold by transportation companies that are good for future fares, advance payments for magazine subscriptions, and returnable deposits. Two particularly interesting examples are common in the airline industry. Passenger tickets are frequently paid several months before they are used, often because special discount fares are available with prepayment. These receipts are not immediately treated as revenues by the airlines but are recorded as Air Traffic Liability and listed in the current liabilities section of the balance sheet. These liabilities are converted to revenue as the tickets are used. Similarly, the frequent-flyer programs offered by a number of the major airlines create obligations, as customers build up mileage credits that must be paid in the form of free airline tickets. While most airlines have neglected to do so, these liabilities should be recognized as the mileage credits are earned.

To illustrate the basic methods used to account for unearned revenues, assume that Seattle Metro Transit sells bus passes that are good for one month for $20.00 each. On December 15 the transit company sells 50 passes for a total of $1,000. The following journal entries would be recorded on December 15 and December 31, after one-half month had expired.

Dec. 15	Cash (+A)	1,000	
	Unearned Revenue (+L)		1,000
	Sold 50 bus passes for future service.		
Dec. 31	Unearned Revenue (−L)	500	
	Fees Earned (R, +SE)		500
	Recognized completion of one-half future service.		

THIRD-PARTY COLLECTIONS

Companies often act as collecting agencies for government or other entities. The price paid for an item at Kmart, for example, includes sales tax, which Kmart must periodically remit to the proper government authority. Companies are also required by law to withhold from employee wages social security taxes as well as an amount approximating the employee's income tax.[6] These withholdings are periodically sent to the federal government. In addition to payroll tax deductions, companies often withhold insurance premiums or union dues, which in turn must be passed on to the appropriate third party. In each of these cases a liability is created; the company receives or holds cash that legally must be paid to a third party. The liability is discharged when the cash payment is made. These liabilities are usually considered current because payment is expected within the time period of current assets.

To illustrate, assume that Sears, Roebuck sells a small tractor for $1,000, which includes $50 in sales tax. The proper journal entry to record the sale follows.

Cash (or Accounts Receivable) (+A)   1,000
  Sales Tax Payable (+L)   50
  Sales (R, +SE)   950
Sold merchandise and collected sales tax.

When Sears pays the sales tax to the proper government authority, the following entry is recorded.

Sales Tax Payable (−L)   50
  Cash (−A)   50
Paid sales tax.

To illustrate the liability associated with payroll deductions, assume that an assembly-line worker for General Motors earns gross wages of $3,000 per month. However, $210 of that amount is withheld for social security taxes, $300 is withheld for income taxes, and $20 is withheld for union dues. In the U.S. employers are also required to pay to the federal government an amount equal to that paid by each employee for social security taxes. The following journal entries would be recorded when the monthly wages are paid.

Wage Expense (E, −SE)   3,000
  Withholding Taxes Payable (+L)   300
  Social Security Taxes Payable (+L)   210
  Union Dues Payable (+L)   20
  Cash (−A)   2,470
Paid payroll at end of month.

Social Security Tax Expense (E, −SE)   210
  Social Security Taxes Payable (+L)   210
Accrued social security taxes.

Assuming General Motors pays all these liabilities at one time, the following journal entry would be recorded when the liabilities are discharged.

Withholding Taxes Payable (−L)   300
Social Security Taxes Payable (−L)   420
Union Dues Payable (−L)   20
  Cash (−A)   740
Paid payroll liabilities.

ACCRUED LIABILITIES

Obligations are often created prior to the payment of cash. The recognition of such an obligation gives rise to an accrued liability. Accrued liabilities can be divided into two

---

6. Companies must not only withhold employee social security taxes; they must also match them. That is, employers must pay to the government a dollar amount equal to that withheld from the employee's wages. Such payments can be quite large. General Motors, for example, pays well over $100 million each year in matched social security taxes.

categories: normal and conditional. *Normal accrued liabilities* are very common, can be measured with reasonable precision, and the amount of cash needed to satisfy the obligation as well as the date of payment are relatively certain. *Conditional accrued liabilities* are based on net income, which cannot be determined until the end of the accounting period.

NORMAL ACCRUED LIABILITIES. The matching principle states that net income in a particular period is the result of matching the revenues realized in that period with the expenses required to produce them. Revenues represent asset inflows (or discharge of liabilities) due in operations, and expenses represent the asset outflows (or the establishment of liabilities) required to generate the revenues. Normal accrued liabilities arise when services or resources are used before payment is made, and they are recognized in the books at the end of the accounting period with an adjusting journal entry. These liabilities are included in the current liabilities section of the balance sheet because they are usually paid early in the following accounting period. Examples of normal accrued liabilities include wages and salaries payable, interest payable, rent payable, insurance payable, and property taxes payable. These payables are often combined into one account on the balance sheet called Accrued Liabilities. Such liabilities were discussed and illustrated in Chapters 4 and 5.

CONDITIONAL ACCRUED LIABILITIES. The dollar amounts of some accrued liabilities cannot be determined until other items (usually some measure of firm performance) have been determined. These are known as **conditional accrued liabilities**; income taxes payable and payables associated with employee incentive compensation plans are two common examples.

INCOME TAX LIABILITY. Income tax liability for a corporation is based on a percentage of taxable income in accordance with the rules stated in the Internal Revenue Code. Presently, the income tax rate paid by corporations is approximately 35 percent of taxable income. Most corporations are required by law at the beginning of each year to estimate their tax liabilities for the entire year and to make quarterly tax payments based on these estimates.

   For example, assume that on January 1, 1997, Raleigh Trucking Company estimates 1997 taxable income and tax liability to be $58,800 and $20,580 ($58,800 × .35), respectively. The company makes payments of $5,145 each quarter (April, June, September, and December) throughout the year. At year-end Raleigh calculates its actual 1997 taxable income and tax to be $80,000 and $28,000 ($80,000 × .35), respectively. Raleigh has therefore underpaid its 1997 taxes by $7,420 ($28,000 − $20,580), and a liability must be recorded on the balance sheet. The following journal entries would be recorded to reflect these events.

Recorded in April, June, September, and December:

Income Tax Expense (E, −SE)	5,145	
Cash (−A)		5,145
Paid quarterly tax.		
Dec. 31 Income Tax Expense (E, −SE)	7,420	
Income Tax Payable (+L)		7,420
Accrued income tax liability at year-end.		

When the income tax liability is paid the following year, the following journal entry is recorded.

Income Tax Payable (−L)   7,420
    Cash (−A)   7,420
Paid income tax liability.

INCENTIVE COMPENSATION. Basing compensation on net income and/or stock prices is a very popular way to pay executives and managers. Such payments comprise a significant portion of the total compensation of virtually all upper-level executives in major U.S. corporations. Profit-sharing arrangements, which are also based on a measure of net income, are frequently used to compensate employees at lower levels of the corporate hierarchy. *Account Trends and Techniques* (AICPA, 1994) reports that over 90 percent of the 600 major U.S. companies selected for study used incentive compensation plans.

Incentive compensation plans can take a number of different forms. AMP Incorporated, for example, has two incentive bonus plans: (1) a stock plus cash plan and (2) a cash plan. Executive compensation under the first plan is related to the market value of the company's stock; compensation under the second is a percentage of the company's net income. The formula for Chrysler's incentive compensation plan includes a provision of 8 percent of consolidated net income. Exxon's incentive program indicates that the total amount distributed cannot exceed 3 percent of net income or 6 percent of capital invested (as defined by the plan). Figure 10–4 describes the incentive compensation formulas for selected large U.S. corporations.

From an accounting standpoint, liabilities associated with incentive compensation plans must be accrued at year-end because they are based on measures of performance (e.g., net income or stock prices) that cannot be determined until that time. They are listed as current on the balance sheet because they are typically distributed to employees early the following period, at which time the liability is discharged.

Suppose, for example, that Tom Turnstile, an executive for Maylein Stoneware, is paid a bonus each year in the amount of 3 percent of net income before income taxes. If net income before income taxes is determined at year-end to be $300,000,

FIGURE 10–4		
Bonus formulas of selected large corporations for executive compensation pools	Aluminum Co. of America	15% of total cash dividends.
	Ashland Oil	6% of after-tax net income.
	Boeing Co.	6% of before-tax net income.
	Bristol-Myers	Lesser of 6% of before-tax net income or 8% of after-tax net income.
	DuPont	20% of after-tax net income in excess of 6% of stockholders' equity.
	Goodyear Tire & Rubber	10% of after-tax net income in excess of consolidated book value of outstanding capital stock.
	ITT Corp.	12% of after-tax net income in excess of 6% of stockholders' equity.
	International Paper	8% of after-tax net income in excess of 6% of stockholders' equity.
	Rockwell International	2% of the first $100 million of before-tax net income plus 3% of the next $50 million of before-tax net income plus 4% of the next $25 million of before-tax net income plus 5% of the balance.
	Unocal Corp.	3% of after-tax net income in excess of 6% of stockholders' equity.

Source: *The Wall Street Journal* (April 18, 1990).

Turnstile's bonus is $9,000 ($300,000 $\times$ .03), and the following journal entry is recorded.

Bonus Expense (E, −SE)   9,000
    Bonus Liability (+L)   9,000
Accrued bonus liability.

When the bonus is paid the following year, the journal entry below is recorded.

Bonus Liability (−L)   9,000
    Cash (−A)   9,000
Paid bonus liability.

LO 5 Incentive compensation plans are popular because they induce managers and employees to act in a manner consistent with the objectives of the stockholders. By basing compensation on net income or stock prices, such plans encourage management to maximize these measures of performance. Keep in mind, however, that managers have incentives to influence the measure of net income through operating decisions, the choice of accounting methods, estimates, assumptions, the timing of accruals, or even intentional misstatements.[7]

To illustrate, suppose in the previous example that Tom Turnstile, who receives a bonus equal to 3 percent of net income each year, is the chief financial officer for Maylein Stoneware. At year-end, rather than reporting net income at $300,000 as stated in the example, he overlooks a $20,000 accrued expense, chooses an accounting method that recognizes $20,000 less of expenses (e.g., FIFO), or postpones $20,000 in research and development expenditures. Any of these acts would cause expenses to be $20,000 less than otherwise and net income to be $320,000 instead of $300,000. Tom's bonus would then be $9,600 ($320,000 $\times$ .03) instead of $9,000 ($300,000 $\times$ .03), an increase of $600.

While executive compensation systems based on net income encourage management to act in the interests of the stockholders, they also encourage management to manipulate the measure of net income. In certain cases such manipulations could be considered unethical, and furthermore, it may not even be in management's economic interest to do so. As illustrated throughout this text, accounting manipulations normally reverse themselves over time, and stockholders, investors, and creditors may discount the values of companies that provide financial statements of questionable credibility. Nonetheless, all interested parties should still be aware that management has incentives to manipulate income to increase compensation and often controls the mechanism to do so.

Executive compensation can be quite large, and much recent controversy has emerged about the amount and form of the compensation paid to the executives of major U.S. companies. For example, an article in *Time* (May 4, 1992), entitled "The Shareholders Strike Back," notes that angry investors and the public are shocked at the high executive compensation rates, and this issue is becoming a major topic of discussion at annual shareholder meetings. The article reported that 1991 pay for the CEO's of H.J. Heinz, Coca-Cola, and U.S. Surgical ranged from $75 million to $118 million. Coke's CEO defended his pay by pointing out that the company's share value has increased 14-fold in the last ten years and that an overwhelming percentage of his pay is tied directly to the companies' stock performance. A recent article in *Fortune* (Octo-

7. A number of research studies in accounting support the conclusion that management's choice of accounting methods (e.g., FIFO vs. LIFO; straight-line vs. accelerated depreciation) is influenced by the existence and nature of executive compensation plans.

ber 3, 1994) supports this point by noting that large compensation levels may be appropriate when there are direct links between executive pay and corporate performance.

The SEC has responded by recently acting to require increased disclosure about executive pay in the annual proxy statement, which notifies stockholders of matters to be voted on at the annual shareholders' meeting. *The Wall Street Journal* (January 29, 1993) reported that "corporations are required to spell out in more detail than ever before just how much they pay their top five executives in salary, stock grants and options (and that) . . . This year's proxy statements must also include a performance graph comparing a company's five-year total return, including changes in the company's stock price and dividend payout, with (indicators like Standard & Poor's 500 stock index that provide measures of the stock market's overall performance)." Experts like Graef S. Crystal, an executive compensation specialist who publishes a monthly newsletter, recommend that investors should use the information reported in the proxy statement to compare executive pay with shareholder return. She notes, "If the stock's performance is heading south but the pay is trending north, the company isn't playing the game fairly."

CONTINGENCIES AND CONTINGENT LIABILITIES

As defined by the FASB, "a contingency is an existing condition, situation, or set of circumstances involving uncertainty as to possible gain or loss to an enterprise that will ultimately be resolved when one or more future events occurs or fails to occur."[8] A common example is an existing lawsuit that will be settled in the future by the decision of a court. If the possible future outcome represents an increase of assets or a decrease of liabilities, the existing condition is considered a **gain contingency**. If the possible outcome represents a decrease in assets or an increase in liabilities, the condition is considered a **loss contingency**.

Before discussing the methods used to account for contingencies, study the following scenario carefully. It is designed to illustrate some of the economic issues involved in reporting contingencies.

CONTINGENT LIABILITIES: A SCENARIO

Suppose that Harry Jones, the accountant for Chemical Enterprises, is preparing the financial statements as of December 31, 1996. Chemical Enterprises is in need of cash and plans to submit the financial statements to First National Bank with an application for a sizable loan. First National has required that the statements Harry prepares be audited by an independent CPA. To conduct the audit, Chemical has hired the firm of Arthur Mitchell & Co.

The preparation of the statements has gone smoothly for Harry, except for one rather significant problem. Several months ago evidence of a small amount of toxic liquid allegedly from one of Chemical's plants was found in the water supply of a small, midwestern town. The extent of Chemical's responsibility and the nature and

---

8. Financial Accounting Standards Board (FASB), "Accounting for Contingencies," *Statement of Financial Accounting Standards No. 5* (Stamford, Conn.: FASB, 1987) par. 1.

extent of any physical harm to the town's residents are still uncertain, but the town has filed suit against Chemical for $1 million, a material amount, and a court case is currently in process. After reviewing the facts of the case, Chemical's lawyers estimate that there is a 70 percent chance that Chemical will successfully defend itself against the lawsuit.

Harry is uncertain how this lawsuit should affect the financial statements of Chemical as of December 31, 1996. As he sees it, the following alternatives represent the three possible ways to account for it.

1. Ignore the lawsuit on the financial statements.
2. Disclose and describe the lawsuit in the footnotes to the financial statements.
3. Recognize a loss on the income statement and a liability on the balance sheet in the amount of $1 million, and disclose and describe the lawsuit in the footnotes.

ALTERNATIVE 1: IGNORE

Under the first alternative, the lawsuit would not be mentioned anywhere in the financial statements. No loss has occurred as of December 31, 1996, and there is a 70 percent chance, according to the lawyers, that no loss will occur at all. Chemical's management might be inclined to favor this alternative over the others because they suspect that disclosing the lawsuit (Alternative 2) or adjusting the financial statements to reflect it (Alternative 3) could endanger the bank loan or at least make the terms (e.g., interest rate) of the loan less favorable. Ignoring the lawsuit would avoid a negative effect on the financial ratios in general as well as on any contracts based on them.

However, the auditor, Arthur Mitchell & Co., is also aware of the lawsuit and is likely to render a qualified opinion on the financial statements unless some recognition is made of the potential loss. If it is not disclosed, and the auditor grants an *unqualified (clean) opinion,* then if the bank makes the loan, the auditor may be liable for any losses the bank incurs if Chemical loses the litigation. Ignoring the lawsuit would not be a conservative choice for either the auditor or management and may expose them both to significant legal liability.

ALTERNATIVE 2: DISCLOSE

The second alternative entails disclosing the nature and amount of the lawsuit as well as the opinions of Chemical's legal counsel. This alternative would describe the situation to the bank as well as other financial report users, but it would have no effect on the dollar amounts in the financial statements. Consequently, financial ratios and contracts written in terms of financial statement numbers would remain unaffected. However, the bank could make any adjustments it saw fit and thereby assess for itself the magnitude of the potential problem.

ALTERNATIVE 3: ACCRUE

The final alternative is to accrue the loss and the related liability on the financial statements. If Harry chooses this action, he would make the following adjusting journal entry on December 31, 1996.

Contingent Loss (Lo, −SE)	**1,000,000**	
Contingent Liability (+L)		**1,000,000**
Accrued contingent liability.		

The Contingent Loss account is a temporary account that would appear on the income statement, reducing net income and, ultimately, stockholders' equity. The Contingent Liability account would appear on the liability side of the balance sheet and be classified as current if payment were expected to require the use of assets listed as current. If Chemical loses the suit and pays the residents of the town, the contingent liability would be written off in the following manner:

Contingent Liability (−L)   1,000,000
    Cash (−A)   1,000,000
Paid contingent liability.

Alternative 3 would probably be very unattractive to the management of Chemical. Having to recognize the contingent loss and the associated liability on the financial statements would not only endanger the bank loan but could make important financial ratios appear much less favorable. It could, therefore, put the company in technical default on existing debt covenants as well as reduce compensation from bonus and profit-sharing plans. Furthermore, the court might interpret accrual of the loss as Chemical's own admission that the suit is lost, reducing Chemical's chances of successful defense.

On the other hand, accruing the contingent loss is the most conservative choice. It would therefore substantially reduce the liability faced by both the auditor and Chemical's management, and possibly increase the credibility of both parties in the view of financial statement users.

ACCOUNTING FOR CONTINGENCIES

Choosing the appropriate accounting treatment for the situation depicted in the preceding scenario is not a simple matter. Each of the three alternatives is attractive in some respects and unattractive in others. The FASB addresses this problem in *Standard No. 5*, "Accounting for Contingencies," which provides guidelines that should be followed when accounting for contingencies.[9] This standard first distinguishes between gain contingencies, which involve possible future gains, and loss contingencies, which involve possible future losses.

Figure 10–5 illustrates the methods used to account for both gain and loss contingencies. Note first that each is preceded by an initial event (e.g., the filing of a lawsuit). The probability of the related gain or loss is then assessed, usually by experts in the area, and classified as either "highly probable," "reasonably probable," or "remote." In all cases except highly probable contingent losses, this classification determines whether the gain or loss should be ignored or disclosed in the footnotes. In those cases where a contingent loss is considered highly probable, the question of

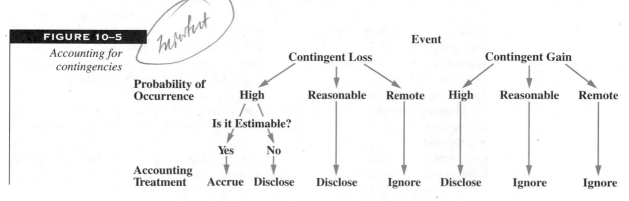

FIGURE 10–5
Accounting for contingencies

9. Ibid.

whether it can be estimated is also addressed. If the loss can be estimated, it is accrued and disclosed. If it cannot, information about the loss is simply disclosed.

GAIN CONTINGENCIES

Gain contingencies are almost never accrued on the financial statements and are rarely disclosed in the footnotes.[10] They are not recognized until they are actually realized, which is consistent with both the principle of objectivity and the concept of conservatism. It avoids any subjective estimates involved in predicting the outcomes of contingent events and ensures that the financial statements do not reflect gains that may not actually occur.

LOSS CONTINGENCIES

Loss contingencies, on the other hand, are often disclosed, and when highly probable and estimable, they are accrued. The resulting liability is considered current if it is expected to require the use of assets that are listed on the balance sheet as current.

Classifying contingent losses as "remote," "reasonably probable," or "highly probable," and estimating the dollar amount of "highly probable" contingent losses is often quite subjective. Managers and auditors normally consult legal counsel or other experts, but in areas like lawsuits it is difficult to predict outcomes accurately. Consequently, relatively few contingent losses stemming from lawsuits are actually accrued on the financial statements. For example, note in the excerpt below, which comes from the 1991 annual report of Quaker Oats, that often companies are hesitant to even accrue what might be considered a "highly probable" contingent loss.

On December 18, 1990, Judge Prentice H. Marshall of the U.S. District Court for the Northern District of Illinois issued a memorandum opinion stating that the court would enter judgment against the Company in favor of Sands, Taylor & Wood Co. The Court found that the use of the words "thirst aid" in advertising GATORADE thirst quencher infringed the Plaintiff's rights in the trademark THIRST-AID. On July 9, 1991, Judge Marshall entered a judgment of $42.6 million . . . The order enjoins use of the phrase THIRST-AID in connection with the advertising or sale of GATORADE thirst quencher in the United States. The Company and its subsidiary, Stokely-Van Camp, Inc., ceased use of the words "thirst aid" in December 1990. The Company, on the advice of inside and outside legal counsel, strongly believes that it will prevail in the appeal of the judgment. Therefore, no provision for loss has been made in the accompanying financial statements.

In those cases when losses are accrued, loss ranges are usually specified in the footnotes, and a "best estimate" within the range typically serves as the dollar amount for the accrual. Owens-Corning, for example, recently accrued a huge liability for outstanding litigation related to asbestos claims dating as far back as 1960. The accompanying footnote described the range of possible settlements, and the amount of the accrual reflected "management's best estimate." If no "best estimate" can be agreed upon, the lowest amount in the range is normally used.

Ignoring potential losses from litigation, even if the probability of loss is low, is also relatively rare. Such a practice is not conservative and can expose management and the auditor to significant levels of legal liability. Therefore, as a practical matter, most contingent losses related to pending litigation are simply disclosed. Opinions of legal counsel, estimates of the dollar amounts of settlements, and other available

---

10. *Accounting Trends and Techniques* reports that, of the 600 major companies examined, only 22 disclosed contingent gains due to lawsuits, and 361 reported contingent losses due to lawsuits.

information concerning potential losses from litigation are usually described in the footnotes to the financial statements. The following excerpt, for example, is from a recent financial report of Amoco Corporation.

Litigation: Suits are pending in various states and federal courts in Illinois against Amoco . . . seeking damages for pollution . . . Amounts originally claimed for pollution damage aggregated about $1.9 billion, but the amount of claims being asserted currently is estimated at approximately $300 million. The suits are not expected to have a material adverse effect on the corporation's consolidated financial position.

While the loss contingencies described in the excerpt above "are not expected to have a material adverse effect" on Amoco's financial position, some loss contingencies can be very significant. In 1988, for example, Rockwood Holding Co. was issued a qualified opinion by its independent auditors, "in connection with litigation related to credit insurance."[11] As reported in *Forbes,* such qualifications are issued by auditors to "protect themselves from future litigation" by alerting investors and "bank credit officers to important footnotes" and material uncertainties about the future of the company.[12]

ENVIRONMENTAL COSTS. Perhaps the major current issue in contingency reporting involves environmental clean-up costs, which some have estimated to be as much as $800 billion. Through "superfund legislation" the U.S. government has established both a fund to clean up pollution and a mandate for companies to clean up existing waste sites. This legislation also empowers the Environmental Protection Agency (EPA) to clean up existing waste sites and then be reimbursed by any party deemed responsible for contaminating the site. Being designated a "potentially responsible party" by the EPA can result in the imposition of a huge liability. By the year 2000 it is expected to cost $65 billion to clean up existing waste sites, and each site is expected to cost an average of $25 million.

Environmental costs are a special concern for heavy manufacturing companies (e.g., petroleum products) and utilities (e.g., power plants) that have been in operation for many years. These companies are finding that they are increasingly being found responsible for environmental clean-up, often due to activities that occurred long before there was much public concern about the environment. While there is often great uncertainty about the actual dollar amount of these liabilities, more and more companies are incurring environmental clean-up costs and, at the same time, are disclosing and accruing contingent environmental liabilities in the annual report. The following excerpt was taken from the 1994 annual report of Goodyear Tire & Rubber Company.

The company expenses environmental expenditures related to existing conditions resulting from past or current operations and from which no current or future benefit is discernible . . . The company determines its liability on a site by site basis and records a liability at a time when it is probable that it can be reasonably estimated. The company's estimated liability is reduced to reflect the anticipated participation of other potentially responsible parties in those instances where it is probable that such parties are legally responsible and financially capable of paying their respective shares of the relevant costs . . . At December 31, 1994, the company had recorded contingent liabilities aggregating $116.4 million for anticipated costs, including legal and consulting fees, site studies, the design and implementation of remediation plans,

---

11. "Qualified Opinion on Rockwood Holding Year End Results Set," *The Wall Street Journal,* April 11, 1988.
12. Jane Carmichael, "The End of the Red Flag," *Forbes,* November 23, 1981, pp. 115–16.

post-remediation monitoring and related activities . . . The Company had recorded $117.3 million for such costs at December 31, 1993. Charges for such costs were $22.8 million, $29.7 million, and $50 million in 1994, 1993, and 1992, respectively.

In addition to litigation and environmental costs, the contingency framework applies to many other important areas of accounting. The allowance method used to account for uncollectibles, for example, treats bad debts as highly probable and therefore accrues estimable loss contingencies. In the next section we consider warranties, another important area of accounting that relies upon the contingency framework.

WARRANTIES: ACCRUED LOSS CONTINGENCIES

L O 6   In a **warranty**, a seller promises to remove deficiencies in the quantity, quality, or performance of a product sold to a buyer. Warranties are usually granted for a specific period, during which time the seller promises to bear all or part of the costs of replacing defective parts, performing necessary repairs, or providing additional services. From the seller's standpoint, warranties entail uncertain future costs. It is unlikely that all buyer's will take advantage of the warranties granted to them, but enough of them do so to consider the future costs probable and reasonably estimable. Thus, warranties are normally accounted for as accrued contingent losses.

For example, suppose that Hauser and Sons sold ten word processors on July 1 for $1,000 each. Each word processor is under warranty for parts and labor for one year, and based on past experience, the company estimates that, on average, warranty costs will be $100 per unit. During the remainder of the year, several machines require servicing, and as of December 31, $350 of warranty costs had been paid. The following entries would be recorded to reflect these events.

Cash or Accounts Receivable (+A)	**10,000**	
Sales (R, +SE)		**10,000**
Sold ten word processors (10 × $1,000).		
Warranty Expense (E, −SE)	**1,000**	
Contingent Warranty Liability (+L)		**1,000**
Recognized contingent liability (10 × $100).		
Contingent Warranty Liability (−L)	**350**	
Cash (−A)		**350**
Paid warranty liability.		

Several features about this accounting treatment are noteworthy. First, the contingent liability is created when the word processors are sold, because at that time Hauser and Sons are responsible for future services. Accordingly, the entire expected warranty expense related to the sale of the ten word processors is recognized in the period of sale, even though only a $350 cost is actually paid. The total warranty expense is thereby matched against sales revenue in the period of sale. Note also that the balance in the Contingent Warranty Liability account at the end of the period is $650 ($1,000 − $350), indicating that costs of $650 are still expected during the following six-month period due to warranties. This amount would be listed as a current liability on the December 31 balance sheet. As the following entry illustrates, the $650 contingent liability is removed from the books when costs are incurred to service the warranties as they are exercised in the second period.

Contingent Warranty Liability (−L)	**650**	
Cash (−A)		**650**
Paid warranty liability.		

The excerpt below is from the 1994 annual report of Ford Motor Company, which has an extensive warranty program. In this disclosure the warranty liability is referred to as "dealer and customer allowances and claims," and note that these accruals are included as current and noncurrent liabilities.

NOTE 7. LIABILITIES—AUTOMOTIVE

CURRENT LIABILITIES

Included in accrued liabilities at December 31 were the following (in millions):

	1994	1993
Dealer and customer allowances and claims	$ 6,716	$ 6,645
Employee benefit plans	1,786	1,415
Postretirement benefits other than pensions	688	674
Salaries, wages, and employer taxes	598	594
Other	1,811	1,487
Total accrued liabilities	$11,599	$10,815

NONCURRENT LIABILITIES

Included in other liabilities at December 31 were the following (in millions):

	1994	1993
Postretirement benefits other than pensions	$14,025	$13,288
Dealer and customer allowances and claims	6,044	5,170
Employee benefit plans	2,232	2,353
Unfunded pension obligation	362	2,873
Minority interests in net assets of subsidiaries	118	161
Other	2,139	2,066
Total other liabilities	$24,920	$25,911

INTERNATIONAL PERSPECTIVE: EXECUTIVE COMPENSATION AND U.S. BUSINESS IN THE GLOBAL MARKETPLACE

Earlier in this chapter we noted that major U.S. corporations compensate their executives on the basis of accounting measures such as net income. These systems are designed to encourage executives to act in the interests of the companies' shareholders, which reflects a basic American business philosophy that the corporation's primary (and perhaps sole) responsibility is to its owners. There are, however, drawbacks associated with this philosophy and accounting-based compensation packages, and many contend that these drawbacks have caused U.S. companies to lose ground to Japan and other countries in the global marketplace.

Compensation based on achieving certain numbers can encourage management to make decisions designed to maximize these numbers in the short run, at the expense of long-run performance. For example, deferring an investment in a research and development activity, to avoid recognizing an expense in the current period, will increase income and compensation in the current period but may reduce performance in future periods. Executive compensation packages, which are viewed by many to be excessive, also contribute to a huge difference between the annual pay of a typical U.S. executive and that of an employee in the same company which, in turn, can alienate executives from employees and discourage worker motivation and productivity.

In their well-known book *Quality or Else: The Revolution of World Business,* Lloyd Dobyns and Clare Crawford-Mason highlight differences between the management philosophies of U.S. and Japanese companies, and they note how such differences have allowed Japan to gain an edge in the global marketplace. The authors note, for example, that the Japanese have never accepted the philosophy that a corporation's sole responsibility is to its shareholders. Instead, the Japanese believe that the needs of the customers, employees, and suppliers must be served before those of the owners. This philosophy removes the emphasis from executive compensation systems to serving the customer by providing high quality products. This can only be accomplished with a system that encourages employees at all levels to innovate and constantly improve by allowing them to share in the successes of the entire business.

To illustrate, Japanese corporate executives, who normally are not compensated with income-based plans, are paid 10 to 20 times the average worker's wage, while in the United States, where such plans prevail, the ratio is close to 90:1. The *New York Times* reported further that in March 1991, despite a recession which resulted in huge layoffs, the top executives in the United States got bigger pay raises in 1990 than any other group of American workers. Indeed, Lee Iacocca received a bonus of over $200,000 in 1990 because the company surpassed certain cost-cutting goals that were stated in Iacocca's compensation package. In that same year, however, Chrysler's earnings plunged 81%, and the company closed several plants and fired thousands of employees. In a trip to Japan to gain trade concessions from the Japanese, then-President Bush and the chief executive officers of the "Big 3" automakers were severely criticized for "bloated" executive pay that "lowers employee morale and reduces corporate savings." Dobyns and Crawford-Mason note further:

When you look at our employee compensation systems [in America] and our reward systems, it is hard to find anything which would engender motivation, or provide incentives or enable the employee to feel a linkage with the organization. In Japan, 93% of the Japanese think that if they work harder and smarter, they'll get something out of it, that the benefits will flow to them. The firm will reward them for their efforts. It's just the reverse in America. Less than 10 percent of American workers think that if they make an extra effort, they're going to get anything out of it. They think it will go to the boss, the stockholders, to somebody, but not to them.

In short, many are convinced that the U.S. presence in the global market place is slipping because U.S. companies are not producing goods of the highest possible quality. This unfortunate situation is partly due to flawed compensation systems that emphasize achieving short-run accounting goals and focus primarily on overcompensated executives. On the brighter side, however, a number of U.S. companies seem to have recognized the problem and are currently doing something about it. *Time* (February 6, 1989) recently carried an article entitled, "They Own the Place," which described a growing trend in American business to adopt employee-stock ownership plans (ESOP), a method of boosting employee morale and productivity by compensating workers in shares of stock and, thus, allowing them to share in the company's successes. Over ten million U.S. workers are currently enrolled in such plans, which is about one quarter of all corporate employees. At Oregon Steel Mills, a Portland-based company, employees have cut the time it takes a worker to make a ton of steel from nine hours to three since the company adopted an ESOP.

REVIEW PROBLEM

Before adjustments and closing on December 31, 1996, the financial records of Martin Brothers indicated the following balances.

Cash	$23,000	Accounts payable		$13,000
Accounts receivable	14,000	Short-term notes	$10,000	
Inventory	32,000	Less: Discount on notes	1,000	9,000
		Unearned revenue		3,000
		Other current liabilities		13,000
Total current assets	$69,000	Total current liabilities		$38,000

The terms of an outstanding long-term note payable state that Martin must maintain a current ratio of 1.5, or the note will be in default. The current ratio computed from the information above is 1.82 ($69,000 ÷ $38,000). However, the following transactions are not reflected in the above balances.

1. Merchandise purchased on account for $5,000 was in-transit as of December 31, 1996. The terms of the purchase were FOB shipping point.
2. One-half of the interest on the $10,000 short-term note payable should be accrued as of December 31.
3. A $4,000 installment on a long-term debt will be due on March 31, 1997. Martin Brothers intends to withdraw $4,000 from a fund, listed on the balance sheet as a long-term investment, to meet the payment.
4. One-third of the unearned revenue has been earned as of December 31.
5. Wages in the amount of $4,000 are owed as of December 31. Federal income and social security taxes withheld on these wages equal $800 and $400, respectively.
6. The total income tax liability for 1996 was estimated at year-end to be $34,000. Income tax payments during the year totaled $32,000.
7. Albinus, Inc., brought suit against Martin Brothers early in 1996. As of December 31, Martin's legal counsel estimates that there is a 50 percent probability that Martin will lose the suit in the amount of $8,000. If Martin loses the suit, payment will be due within the next year.

REQUIRED:
Provide the journal entry, if necessary, for each additional transaction, and compute the current ratio after all adjustments have been recorded. Is Martin in violation of the debt covenant?

SOLUTION:
Refer to Figure 10–6, and note that Martin Brothers will be in default on the long-term liability if the contingent loss is accrued. The current ratio (1.30) will be below the ratio required in the debt covenant (1.5). If the contingent loss is only disclosed, the 1.51 current ratio will meet the requirements of the covenant.

FIGURE 10-6

Solution to review problem: Martin Brothers

TRANS-ACTION	CURRENT ASSETS	JOURNAL ENTRY			CURRENT LIABILITIES
	$69,000				$38,000
1.	+5,000	Inventory (+A)	5,000		
		Accounts Payable (+L)		5,000	+5,000
2.		Interest Expense (E, −SE)	500		
		Discount on Note (+L)		500	+500
3.		No entry—not payable from current assets.			
4.		Unearned Revenue (−L)	1,000		
		Earned Revenue (R, +SE)		1,000	(1,000)
5.		Wage Expense (E, −SE)	4,000		
		Federal Income Tax Payable (+L)		800 ⎫	
		Social Security Tax Payable (+L)		400 ⎬	+4,000
		Wages Payable (+L)		2,800 ⎭	
		Tax Expense (E, −SE)	400		
		Social Security Tax Payable (+L)		400	+400
6.		Income Tax Expense (E, −SE)	2,000		
		Income Tax Payable (+L)		2,000	+2,000
		Recorded income tax liability.			
7.		Depends upon whether a 50 percent probability is considered "reasonably possible" or "probable."			
		If the loss is considered "reasonably possible," it is only disclosed and not included as a current liability.			
		If the loss is considered "probable," the contingent loss is accrued with the following journal entry:			
		Contingent Loss (E, −SE)	8,000		
		Contingent Liability (+L)		8,000	+8,000
	$74,000	Total current assets			
		Total current liabilities:			
		Not including contingent loss			$48,900
		Including contingent loss			$56,900

Current ratio not including contingent loss = 1.51 ($74,000/$48,900)
Current ratio including contingent loss   = 1.30 ($74,000/$56,900)

In 1990 the FASB adopted SFAS No. 106, which requires corporations to recognize post-retirement healthcare and insurance costs as they accrue. When the rule became effective, many large U.S. companies recognized huge expenses on their income statements and liabilities on their balance sheets. IBM, for example, took a charge of $2.6 billion in the first quarter of 1991, and McDonnell Douglas recognized an accrued expense and liability of $700 million. In response to this new rule, many corporations have cut back the amounts they spend on retirement healthcare benefits. *Business Week* (November 23, 1992) relates the story of Clifford Davis, now retired, who worked for 32 years as a maintenance man for Chicago-based truckmaker Navistar International Corp. In response to the new accounting requirement, Navistar, which has paid the medical bills for its 40,000 pensioners for 20 years, now

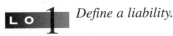

ETHICS IN THE REAL WORLD

wants to cut back its plan—forcing Davis and fellow retirees on fixed incomes to fork over a hefty chunk of money for their coverage. Navistar claims that there never has been a formal contract requiring them to cover such post-retirement costs, and it will go bust if former workers do not cover their own healthcare costs. Davis and many of his fellow retirees, however, contend that they always expected to be covered, and their personal healthcare costs are unaffordable—eating up 25% of their monthly pension check.

ETHICAL ISSUE

Is it ethical for corporations like Navistar to cut back healthcare coverage for retired workers in response to SFAS No. 106, when there is no formal contract requiring these companies to cover such costs?

SUMMARY OF LEARNING OBJECTIVES

 Define a liability.

The FASB recently defined liabilities as "probable future sacrifices of economic benefits arising from present obligations of a particular entity to transfer assets or provide services to other entities in the future as a result of past transactions or events." All liabilities appearing on the balance sheet should have three characteristics in common: (1) they should be present obligations that entail settlements by probable future transfers or uses of cash, goods or services; (2) they should be unavoidable obligations; and (3) the transaction or event obligating the enterprise must have already happened.

LO 2 *Describe the economic consequences associated with reporting liabilities on the financial statements.*

Disclosing a liability on the balance sheet affects important financial ratios (e.g., current ratio, debt/equity, debt/assets) that are used by stockholders, investors, creditors, and others (1) to assess the financial performance and condition of a company and (2) to direct and control the actions of managers through contracts. Each of these parties has an economic interest in the amount of debt that must be paid by a company. Financial ratios, which use balance sheet liabilities, are also found in debt contracts to protect creditors by limiting future borrowings, dividend payments, and other management actions. Such economic consequences create incentives that encourage managers in certain situations to understate, and in other situations to overstate, liabilities.

Distinguish between determinable liabilities and contingent liabilities.

Determinable liabilities can be precisely measured, and the amounts of cash needed to satisfy the obligations and the dates of payment are reasonably certain. Examples include accounts and short-term notes payable, dividends payable, unearned revenues, third-party collections, and accrued liabilities. Determinable liabilities can also be conditional on certain events. Examples include liabilities associated with income tax and employee incentive compensation. Contingent liabilities result from existing conditions that can lead to negative outcomes in the future, depending on the occurrence of given events. Examples include lawsuits, uncollectibles, and warranties.

 Define a current liability, and list and briefly describe the most common current liabilities.

Current liabilities are obligations that are expected to require the use of current assets or the creation of other current liabilities. They include obligations to suppliers, short-term notes payable, current maturities of long-term debts, dividends payable to stockholders, unearned revenues, third-party collections, periodic accruals, certain conditional liabilities, and potential obligations related to pending or threatened litigation, and product warranties.

 Explain why bonus systems and profit-sharing arrangements are used to compensate employees, and describe the reporting incentives they create.

Bonus systems are popular because they provide a means for stockholders to induce management and other employees to act in a manner consistent with the objectives of the stockholders. Such incentives are created by basing compensation on profits. Management has some control, however, over the measure of profits through operating, investing, and financing decisions, the choice of accounting methods, estimates, assumptions, and the timing of accruals, and they can use this control to increase their bonus compensation.

 Describe the methods used to account for contingencies and how they apply to lawsuits and warranties.

Contingencies can be divided into two categories: gain contingencies and loss contingencies. Gain contingencies are rarely accrued and only disclosed in the footnotes when they are highly probable. The probability of a loss contingency should be classified as either remote, reasonably possible, or highly probable. If the probability is remote, the loss need not be disclosed. If the event is reasonably possible, the potential loss and all relevant information about it should be disclosed in the footnotes. If the event is viewed as highly probable and the amount of the loss can be estimated, the potential loss and associated liabilities should be accrued on the financial statements and described in the footnotes. When a sale is made that includes a warranty, the sale is recorded. Because the warranty liability is highly probable and can be estimated with reasonable accuracy, warranty expense and contingent warranty liability should be recognized in the amount of the estimated future warranty costs at the same time. As the warranty costs are paid, the contingent liability is reduced.

APPENDIX 10A

RETIREMENT COSTS: PENSIONS AND POSTRETIREMENT HEALTH CARE AND INSURANCE

This appendix briefly defines and describes how to account for pension and postretirement health care and insurance liabilities.

PENSIONS

A **pension** is a sum of money paid to a retired or disabled employee, the amount of which is usually determined by the employee's years of service. For most large companies, pension plans are an important part of the employees' compensation packages, and they are part of almost all negotiated wage settlements.[13] Pension plans are backed by contractual agreements with the employees and are subject to federal regulation.

Most pension plans are structured so that an employer periodically makes cash payments to a pension fund, which is a legal entity distinct from the sponsoring company. The cash, securities, and other income-earning investments that make up the fund are usually managed by someone outside the company, and the assets in the pension fund do not appear on the company's balance sheet. The employer's cash contributions plus the income generated through the fund's management (i.e., dividends, interest, capital appreciation) provide the cash that is distributed to employees upon retirement. The terms of the pension plan determine the amounts to which individual employees are entitled (benefits).

There are two primary types of pension plans: a defined-contribution plan and a defined benefit plan. The definitions of these plans and the methods used to account for them are discussed below.

DEFINED-CONTRIBUTION PLAN

Under a **defined-contribution plan** an employer agrees only to make a series of contributions of a specified amount to the pension fund. These periodic cash payments are often based on employee wages or salaries, and each employee's percentage interest in the total fund is determined by the proportionate share contributed by the employer on the employee's behalf. Under this type of plan, the employer makes no promises regarding how much the employees will receive upon retirement. The actual benefits depend upon the investment performance of the fund. The employer guarantees only the inputs (contributions), not the outputs (benefits). Most university business school professors are covered by such a plan.

Accounting for a defined-contribution plan is relatively simple, because once the employer makes the contribution, the sponsoring company faces no further liability.

---

13. *Accounting Trends and Techniques* (New York: AICPA, 1994) reports that, of the 600 major U.S. companies surveyed, well over 90 percent disclosed the existence of a pension plan.

The cash payment is simply expensed, as in the following journal entry.

Pension Expense (E, −SE)   1,000
   Cash (−A)   1,000
Paid to a defined-contribution plan.

Defined-contribution plans have gained in popularity over the last several years. An Associated Press article (June 17, 1995) notes that in 1988, 36 percent of U.S. employees were covered by such plans, which rose to 49 percent by 1993. Defined-contribution plans, such as the very common 401(K)s, are considered much less expensive than defined-benefit plans, which are covered in the next section.

DEFINED-BENEFIT PLAN

Under a **defined-benefit plan** the employer promises to provide each employee with a specified amount of benefits upon retirement. Such a guarantee is somewhat more difficult than promising to make specified contributions, because the benefits are received by the employees in the future and therefore are uncertain. The benefits must be predicted, and the employer must contribute enough cash so that the contributions plus the earnings on the assets in the fund will be sufficient to provide the promised benefits as they come due. The employees of most major U.S. companies are covered by defined-benefit plans, but a recent survey conducted by the U.S. Labor Department indicates that the percent of U.S. employees covered by such plans . . . dropped from 63 percent in 1988 to 56 percent in 1995.[14]

In the past many employers under defined-benefit plans either set aside no funds or failed to set aside enough to cover their future pension obligations. They simply paid the obligations as they came due, often out of the company's current operating capital. This practice not only represented poor financial management, but on occasion left retired employees short of their rightful pension benefits. To help assure that retired employees received what was promised them, Congress passed the **Employment Retirement Income Security Act (ERISA)** in 1974, which requires employers to fund their plans at specified minimum levels and provides other safeguards designed to protect employees.

The basic accounting procedures and the theories underlying accounting for defined-benefit pension plans are really quite simple. In accordance with the matching principle, pension expense and the associated liability are accrued each period as employees earn their rights to future benefits (i.e., during the years when the employees provide services and help the company to generate revenues). The periodic adjusting journal entry to record this accrual takes the following form:

Pension Expense (E, −SE)   800
   Pension Liability (+L)   800
Recognized $800 pension liability.

The periodic cash payments made by the employer to the pension fund simply reduce the pension liability as in the following journal entry, and the pension liability that appears on the balance sheet is simply the difference between the accrued liability and the cash payments. A large pension liability indicates that a significant amount of the expected pension costs has yet to be funded.

---

14. The social security system currently operating in the United States is a type of defined-benefit pension plan; the federal government promises U.S. citizens a specified amount of benefits at age 65. Presumably, these benefits are paid out of a fund that contains income-earning securities.

Pension Liability (−L)   **500**
    Cash (−A)   500
Paid $500 to pension fund.

The primary difficulties in accounting for and managing a defined-benefit plan are in (1) determining the appropriate dollar amount of the periodic accrual entry (i.e., Pension Expense debit and Pension Liability credit) and (2) deciding how much cash needs to be contributed to the pension fund to cover the eventual liability. The ultimate pension cost cannot be known for certain until the employees have received all the benefits to which they are entitled. This will not be known until the employees' deaths as well as the deaths of their survivors, who may also be entitled to certain benefits. Unpredictable factors like employee life expectancies, employee turnover rates, future salary and wage rates, and pension-fund growth rates all have a bearing on this determination.

Most companies hire actuaries, statisticians who specialize in such areas as assessing insurance risks and setting premiums, to establish estimates of the future pension costs and to provide methods for allocating those future costs to current periods (called *actuarial cost methods*). Generally accepted accounting principles require that an employer periodically recognize an expense and an associated liability in an amount that is established by one of many acceptable actuarial methods. The amount of this accrual is usually equal to an estimate of the present value of the pension benefits earned by employees during a given period. These amounts are very inexact, depending largely on subjective estimates and assumptions. As a matter of policy, contractual obligation, or law (ERISA), most companies make periodic cash payments to their pension plans in amounts that approximate the accruals they have chosen to record. Thus, the pension liability appearing on most balance sheets is either zero or relatively small.

There are exceptions, however, and astute financial statement users should be aware of them. *U.S.A. Today* (Nov. 23, 1993) recently reported that many well-known companies have significantly underfunded pension plans, including LTV ($2.1 billion), Bethlehem Steel ($2.4 billion), GM ($20.1 billion), Westinghouse Electric ($1.3 billion), and Chrysler ($1.4 billion). While these companies are generally strong and will be able to fund their pension plans, such underfunding can lead to significant balance sheet liabilities and important future obligations.

As specified in Financial Accounting Standards Nos. 87 and 88, the accounting methods and disclosure requirements for pension plans are more comprehensive and complex than indicated in this appendix. The following excerpt from the 1994 financial report of Kmart represents only a small portion of the required disclosures.

Pension Plans

Kmart Corporation and certain domestic subsidiaries have non-contributory pension plans covering most employees who meet certain requirements of age, length of service, and hours worked per year. Benefits paid to retirees are based upon age at retirement, years of credited service, and earnings. Kmart Canada Limited employees are covered by a defined-contribution plan. Kmart Corporation's policy is to fund at least the minimum amounts required by the Employee Retirement Income Security Act of 1974. The plans' assets consist primarily of equity securities, fixed income securities, guaranteed insurance contracts, and real estate. Kmart Corporation contributed $64 to its principal pension plan during fiscal 1994, but was not required to contribute to its principal pension plan in fiscal 1993 or fiscal 1992. Total pension expense was $84 in 1994, $68 in 1993, and $65 in 1992.

Accounting for pension plans is also quite subjective, relying heavily on estimates and assumptions. Further, a small change in an important estimate can have a significant effect on both the amount funded by the company and the pension expense and liability reported on its financial statements. For example, to determine what a company must contribute to the pension plan each year, company accountants must estimate the fund's future annual return.

The Wall Street Journal (September, 1993) recently reported that over the 3-year period 1990–1993, GM predicted an annual return on its pension fund of 11 percent, but only realized an 8.7 percent return. Missing that target understated the company's pension expense by "a couple hundred million" and led to a funding shortfall of similar size.

POSTRETIREMENT HEALTH CARE AND INSURANCE COSTS

Most large companies cover a portion of the health care and insurance costs incurred by employees after retirement. Similar to pensions, such coverage is part of employee compensation and is earned over an employee's years of service. According to the matching principle, therefore, such costs should be accrued over the employee's tenure with the company, and then the associated liability should be written off as the benefits are paid after the employee's retirement. The issues of estimating this liability, providing adequate funds to meet required future payments, and accounting for such transactions are actually very similar to those involved with pensions, and accordingly, the appropriate accounting methods are basically the same.

Until recently, however, most companies neither established funds to pay these future costs nor accrued the related liabilities as the employees earned the coverage. Unlike pensions, currently there is no federal law (like ERISA) requiring employers to establish funds for these liabilities. Standard practice in this area has been to expense these costs simply as they are paid. Such a policy, which is contrary to the matching principle, is referred to as the pay-as-you-go approach.

The FASB, in a very controversial standard passed in 1990, required that companies accrue postretirement health care and insurance costs. Not only did the companies have to accrue a liability in the future as employees earned their benefits, but they also were required to recognize existing liabilities they had failed to accrue in the past. For certain companies these unreported liabilities amounted to well over $1 billion. Indeed, *Barrons* (April 17, 1989) reported:

estimates of the size of this new liability [for the entire economy] range from $400 billion to $1 trillion, depending on whose . . . assumptions you accept.

The FASB, however, did grant the affected companies some latitude. The standard did not have to be implemented until 1993, and the "catch up" entry to recognize the liabilities that had not been accrued in the past could be booked over a period not to exceed 20 years.

This standard, nonetheless, was still very controversial. Some suggest that its adoption is saddling many companies with an annual expense that cuts profits by as much as 130%. *The Wall Street Journal* (March 21, 1989) adds that many corporate executives maintain:

the FASB doesn't seem to care what it does to the U.S economy, and its credibility gap with business is growing . . . Such discontent with the FASB has spurred such powerful lobbying groups as the Business Roundtable to ask for more voice in FASB deliberations.

Fortune (December 19, 1988) pointed out further:

many executives . . . contend that future health costs simply cannot be measured . . . [while] others argue that the rules will prompt companies to seek some way to avoid paying the benefits they have promised.

Indeed, a *Business Week* (November, 1992) article, entitled "Honest Balance Sheets, Broken Promises," points out that "Lots of corporations are axing or curtailing retiree health benefits, hoping to minimize the financial broadside of [the FASB standard] . . . as well as curbing runaway healthcare costs in general."

Companies have implemented this standard in a number of different ways. While most chose to wait until 1993 and to record the "catch up" over several years, some companies actually adopted the standard early and recorded the entire "catch up" at once. Three notable examples include IBM, General Motors, and LTV, all of which experienced very poor years at the time they chose to book the liability, suggesting that in each case management may have been following the "take a bath" strategy mentioned in this chapter.

APPENDIX 10B

DEFERRED INCOME TAXES

We have noted several times that the rules for computing income and expenses for purposes of taxation, as specified by the Internal Revenue Service, are different from generally accepted accounting principles, which specify how financial accounting net income is to be measured. These differences can be divided into two categories: permanent and timing differences. Permanent differences never reverse themselves, while timing differences do. Premiums paid on life insurance policies covering key employees, for example, are not deductible for tax purposes, but they are charged against income for financial reporting purposes. Interest received on municipal bonds is not included in taxable income but is recognized as revenue on a company's income statement. The different treatments for tax and financial accounting purposes in these two examples are considered permanent, because in neither case will the effect on income of the different treatments reverse itself over the life of the asset.

One of many common temporary differences arises when a company depreciates its fixed assets using an accelerated method when computing taxable income and the straight-line method when preparing the financial statements. This strategy causes taxable income to be less than accounting income in the early periods of the asset's life, but as illustrated in Chapter 9, this difference reverses itself in the asset's later years. Many accountants believe that timing differences of this kind create a liability, called deferred income taxes, in the asset's early years, which is discharged in the later years.

THE CONCEPT OF DEFERRED INCOME TAXES

Suppose that Midland Plastics purchased a piece of equipment on January 1, 1994, for $9,000. The equipment is expected to have a three-year useful life and no salvage value. Midland computes depreciation using the double-declining-balance method for income tax purposes and straight-line for reporting purposes. In 1994 Midland's choice to use two different depreciation methods creates an income tax expense on the income statement, which is based on straight-line depreciation, that is greater than its income tax liability, which is based on double-declining-balance depreciation. In 1995 and 1996 the difference reverses itself, and the income tax expense is less than the income tax liability. Figure 10B–1 provides a schedule of these differences and, assuming an income tax rate of 30%, computes the tax effects associated with using double-declining-balance instead of straight-line for tax purposes.

FIGURE 10B–1 Income tax effects due to DDB Depreciation	YEAR	DDB DEPR.[a]		SL DEPR.[b]		EXCESS (UNDER) DEPR.		TAX RATE		TAX BENEFIT (DISBENEFIT)
	1994	$6,000	–	$3,000	=	$ 3,000	×	30%	=	$ 900
	1995	2,000	–	3,000	=	(1,000)	×	30%	=	(300)
	1996	1,000	–	3,000	=	(2,000)	×	30%	=	(600)
	Total	$9,000		$9,000		$ 0				$ 0

[a][$9,000 – accumulated depreciation] × 2 [straight-line rate (33%)]
[b]$9,000/3 yr.

Note that the use of the double-declining-balance method, instead of straight-line, creates a tax savings of $900 in 1994, the first year of the equipment's useful life. In 1995 and 1996, however, this benefit reverses itself, giving rise to additional tax payments of $300 in 1995 and $600 in 1996. As of the end of 1994, Midland can view these additional tax payments as liabilities, because many consider them to be future obligations. Specifically, additional tax payments that total $900 ($300 + $600) are expected in 1995 and 1996. This liability is reported on the balance sheet and referred to as deferred income taxes. Midland Plastics, in other words, would report a deferred income tax liability of $900 in the liability section of its 1994 balance sheet.

During 1995 and 1996, as the tax benefit reverses itself and Midland pays the additional taxes, the deferred income tax liability is reduced by $300 in 1995 and by $600 in 1996. As of the end of 1996, therefore, after the useful life of the equipment has expired, the deferred income tax liability will have been reduced to zero.

ACCOUNTING ENTRIES FOR DEFERRED INCOME TAXES

Preparing the journal entry to record the recognition or discharge of deferred income taxes consists of three steps:

1. Compute the future income tax disbenefit ($900 = $300 + $600) as illustrated in Figure 10B–1. This dollar amount is entered as a credit to the Deferred Income Tax account. The dollar amounts of the reversals (1995: $300, 1996: $600) are entered as debits to the Deferred Income Tax account in future periods.
2. Compute the company's income tax liability (taxable income × corporate income tax rate). This dollar amount is entered as a credit to the Income Tax Payable account.

3. Enter a debit to the Income Tax Expense account in an amount that brings the journal entry into balance.

To illustrate, assume in the preceding example that Midland Plastics recognized taxable income in the amount of $4,000, $8,000, and $9,000 in 1994, 1995, and 1996, respectively. At a 30 percent tax rate, the company's tax liability, therefore, is $1,200 (1994), $2,400 (1995), and $2,700 (1996). Given this information, Figure 10B–2 contains the journal entries and the balance sheet carrying values of the Deferred Income Tax account for the three-year period.

FIGURE 10B–2

Deferred income taxes

1994			1995			1996		
Inc. Tax Exp. (E, −SE)	2,100*		Inc. Tax Exp. (E, −SE)	2,100*		Inc. Tax Exp. (E, −SE)	2,100*	
Deferred Inc. Tax (+L)		900	Deferred Inc. Tax (−L)	300		Deferred Inc. Tax (−L)	600	
Inc. Tax Pay. (+L)		1,200	Inc. Tax Pay. (+L)		$2,400	Inc. Tax Pay. (+L)		$2,700
Balance sheet excerpt:								
Deferred income tax		900	(900 − 300)		600	(600 − 600)		0

*plug

In 1994 a deferred tax liability of $900 is recognized because Midland, which uses the double-declining-balance method for tax purposes, expects to pay additional income taxes of $300 and $600 over the next two years. An income tax liability of $1,200 is also recognized, and Income Tax Expense is debited for an amount ($2,100) that brings the journal entry into balance. In 1995 and 1996, as Midland pays the additional taxes, the Deferred Income Tax account is reduced.

DEFERRED INCOME TAXES: ADDITIONAL ISSUES

The size of the Deferred Income Tax liability account is usually related to the size of a company's investment in fixed assets.[15] Note in Figure 10B–3 that large manufacturing companies, such as Exxon and General Electric, often carry huge balances in their deferred income tax accounts. Such companies normally depreciate their fixed assets using accelerated methods for tax purposes and straight-line for financial reporting purposes, and the resulting differences between their taxable liability and income tax expense can be quite large.[16] On the other hand, financial institutions, which carry limited investments in fixed assets, rarely show balances in the Deferred Income Tax account. Indeed, Chase Manhattan Bank, the American Express Company, and Safeco Insurance report no deferred income taxes on their balance sheets.

15. The Deferred Income Tax account can have a debit balance. When companies recognize expenses (revenues) for reporting purposes more quickly (slowly) than for tax purposes, a deferred tax asset is credited and disclosed on the balance sheet. Companies can carry deferred tax liabilities, deferred tax assets, or both on the balance sheet. Nike, for example, reported a $37.6 million dollar deferred tax asset on the 1994 balance sheet.
16. *Accounting Trends and Techniques* (New York: AICPA, 1994) reports that, of the 600 major U.S. companies surveyed, approximately 80 percent disclosed timing differences due to the use of a different depreciation method for reporting purposes than the method used for tax purposes.

FIGURE 10B–3	COMPANY	DEFERRED TAX LIABILITY (MILLIONS)	PERCENT OF TOTAL ASSETS
Deferred income tax liability (selected U.S. companies)	Exxon	$11,435	13%
	Federated Dept. Stores	993	8
	Scott Paper	345	6
	AT&T	3,913	5
	General Electric	5,205	3
	Ford Motor Co.	948	1

Source: 1994 Annual reports.

As explained earlier, the Deferred Income Tax account can be viewed as a liability, reflecting an obligation for additional income tax that must be paid in the future as certain tax benefits reverse. However, growing companies tend to purchase more fixed assets than they retire which, in turn, causes fixed assets in the early (benefit) periods of their useful lives to exceed those in the later (disbenefit) periods. This phenomenon causes the credit balance in the Deferred Income Tax account to accumulate, and many of the largest companies in the U.S. have amassed huge dollar amounts in deferred income taxes in this manner.[17]

Having observed deferred income taxes accumulating in this manner over the years, many accountants argue that deferred income taxes do not represent liabilities in any economic sense. An article in *Forbes* magazine notes:

These numbers are not valid because most deferred taxes never actually get paid. In the real world . . . companies continually make plant and equipment purchases that create new deductions. The result: treating deferred taxes as a liability presents an inaccurate picture of liquidity and cash flow.[18]

The national director for accounting and auditing for Seidman & Seidman commented further:

The deferred taxes on the balance sheet bear no relationship to what is actually going to be owed. So the current method of income tax accounting makes it impossible for the investors to evaluate a company's liquidity, solvency, or cash flow.[19]

Another interesting aspect about deferred income taxes is that income statement gains and losses can be recognized when income tax rates change. Consider, for example, the General Electric (GE) Company, which had accumulated excess depreciation (i.e., accelerated in excess of straight-line) of approximately $4 billion as of the end of 1986. At the 1986 income tax rate of 48 percent, these benefits translated to a deferred income tax liability of $1.92 billion ($4 billion $\times$ 48%), which GE reported on its 1986 balance sheet. However, in 1987 the corporate income tax rate was reduced to 34 percent, and using the new tax rate, GE recalculated its deferred income tax liability to be $1.36 billion ($4 billion $\times$ 34%). Reducing the liability gave rise to an approximate gain of $560 million ($1.92 billion $-$ $1.36 billion) that was recognized in 1987 and recorded with the following journal entry (dollars in millions).

17. Jane Carmichael, "Rollover," *Forbes,* January 18, 1982, pp. 75, 78.
18. Jill Andresky, "Leaving Well Enough Alone," *Forbes,* May 7, 1984, p. 206.
19. Carmichael, "Rollover," pp. 75, 78.

Deferred Income Tax (−L)   **560**
    Gain on Change in Income Tax Rate (Ga, +SE)   **560**
Recognized gain due to reductions in future
income tax rates.

Similarly, when corporate tax rates went up from 34 percent to 35 percent in 1993, a number of companies were forced to recognize an additional liability and a charge to earnings. Coca-Cola Enterprises, for example, took a $40 million charge in 1993.

The methods used to account for deferred income taxes are controversial and actually much more complicated than indicated in this discussion. More in-depth coverage can be found in intermediate accounting texts. Nonetheless, this issue is important to all interested parties because calculating the amount of deferred income tax and reporting it as a liability or otherwise can have significant economic consequences. For example, should the computation of the debt/equity ratio include or exclude deferred income tax? Considering the size of the deferred income tax liability, how interested parties answer this question can certainly affect their solvency assessments of certain companies.

THE CONSERVATISM RATIO

An important theme in this text is that meaningful financial statement analysis cannot be conducted without assessing the extent to which management has used its discretion when preparing the financial statements. We have noted often that such discretion can be used to understate (report conservatively) or overstate the financial condition and performance of a company. A measure of the extent to which reported income is conservative, called the **conservatism ratio,** can be constructed from information disclosed in the annual report, and is provided below.

Conservatism Ratio: Reported Income Before Taxes/Taxable Income

The intuition underlying this ratio is based on the premise that for tax purposes companies accelerate tax deductible expenses and defer taxable revenues as long as is allowable under income tax laws. Thus, taxable income (taxable revenues − tax deductible expenses), the denominator of the ratio, reflects a very conservative measure of a company's income in a particular year. The extent to which reported income before taxes, the numerator of the ratio, exceeds (or is less than) taxable income indicates how conservative reported income is. Ratio amounts around 1.0 or less indicate relatively conservative levels, while reported income becomes increasingly less conservative as the ratio grows larger than 1.0.

Figure 10B–4 provides 1994 conservatism ratios for selected major U.S. companies. That year income reported to the stockholders of Kmart, AT&T, and Walt Disney was substantially higher than that reported to the IRS. Alcoa, Quaker Oats, and May Department Stores reported slightly more to the tax authorities than they reported to their stockholders. Assuming that all six companies reported conservatively to the IRS, it appears that the financial reporting policies of Kmart, AT&T, and Walt Disney were more aggressive than those of Alcoa, Quaker Oats, and May Department Stores.

The conservatism ratio cannot be computed entirely from the dollar amounts on the financial statements; additional information contained in the footnotes is also required. Reported income before taxes, the numerator, can be taken directly from the income statement. Taxable income, the denominator, must be computed indirectly.

Taxable Income = Annual Tax Liability/The Effective Income Tax Rate

FIGURE 10B–4	MANUFACTURERS	
Conservatism *ratios*	Alcoa	.96
	Quaker Oats	.95
	SERVICES	
	Walt Disney	1.8
	AT&T	2.5
	RETAILERS	
	May Department Stores	.97
	Kmart	2.7

Source: 1994 annual reports

The effective income tax rate is a required disclosure in the footnotes. The annual tax liability can be computed by reconstructing the journal entry to record tax expense, the change in the deferred income tax account, and tax liability. Examples of such entries are provided in Figure 10B–2. To reconstruct the entry—income tax expense can be taken directly from the income statement; the credit or debit to the deferred income tax account can be derived by computing the change in the deferred income tax account over the most recent year; and the amount of income tax payable brings the entry into balance.

To illustrate, the 1994 conservatism ratio for Campbell Soup Company is computed in Figure 10B–5 based on information taken from its 1994 annual report.

FIGURE 10B–5		1994	1993
The conservatism ratio of Campbell Soup Company (dollars in millions)	**BALANCE SHEET**		
	Deferred income tax liability	$211	$164
	INCOME STATEMENT		
	Income before taxes	$963	
	Income tax expense	(333)	
	Net income	$630	
	Effective income tax rate: 34.6%		
	Conservatism ratio: 1.16 ($963/$827*)		
	JOURNAL ENTRY		
	Income Tax Expense (income statement)	333	
	Deferred Income Tax ($211 − $164)		47
	Income Tax Liability (plug)		286

*286/34.6%

The conservatism ratio provides a quick way to assess how conservative management's reporting choices have been in a particular year. Much more important, however, are the reasons and activities that explain the difference between reported income and taxable income, and these can only be identified through a close study of the footnotes.

KEY TERMS

Note: Definitions for these terms are provided in the glossary at the end of this text.

Commercial paper (p. 482)
Conditional accrued liabilities (p. 486)
Conservatism ratio (p. 509)
Debt ratio (p. 475)
Defined-benefit plan (p. 502)
Defined-contribution plan (p. 501)
Determinable current liabilities (p. 481)
Employment Retirement Income Security
   Act (ERISA) (p. 502)

Face value (p. 480)
Gain contingency (p. 489)
Line of credit (p. 482)
Loss contingency (p. 489)
Maturity date (p. 483)
Open account (p. 482)
Pension (p. 501)
Warranty (p. 494)

QUESTIONS FOR DISCUSSION AND REVIEW

1. Define a liability, and identify the three characteristics all balance sheet liabilities have in common.
2. Why is it important to disclose and value all liabilities appropriately on the balance sheet? Why is it important to stockholders, investors, creditors, management, and auditors?
3. How can management benefit from understating liabilities? Why is such a practice often not effective?
4. In what situations might a manager wish to overstate liabilities?
5. When a manager manipulates liabilities, what important financial statement numbers are affected? Is it necessarily in management's best interest to perform such manipulations? Why?
6. What is the definition of a current liability? Why are current liabilities defined in terms of current assets?
7. Explain why financial statement ratios like the current ratio are found in debt covenants. How might such covenants affect the reporting and operating decisions of management?
8. Define and differentiate determinable, conditional, and contingent liabilities. Provide several examples of each.
9. Define accounts payable. Why does the auditor pay special attention to the inventory purchases occurring near the end of an accounting period?
10. Under what conditions should the current installment payment on a long-term debt be disclosed as a current liability on the balance sheet?
11. Are short-term unearned revenues, such as returnable deposits and advance sales, expected to be discharged with current assets in the near future? Discuss.
12. Provide two examples of third-party collections. Do they require cash payments from the company's standpoint? Discuss.
13. Certain liabilities cannot be determined until the end of the accounting period. Two examples are the liabilities associated with income taxes and bonus agreements. What term is used to describe these liabilities, and why can they not be determined until the end of the accounting period?
14. Why do companies compensate their employees through bonus agreements and profit-sharing plans? What role do financial statement numbers play in these compensation schemes, and how might this method of compensation influence the reporting and operating decisions of management?
15. What has the SEC done recently in the area of executive compensation to help stockholders better assess the quality of a firm's management? How will this help stockholders?

16. What is a contingent loss, and under what conditions must it be accrued? Under what conditions are contingent losses ignored or simply disclosed? The guidelines that specify the methods of accounting for contingent liabilities are very subjective. Discuss some of the factors that might influence managers and auditors to want to account for the same contingent liability in different ways.

17. How are gain contingencies accounted for? Why are gain contingencies accounted for in a different manner than loss contingencies?

18. What major contingent loss are many large manufacturing and utility companies presently facing? Explain.

19. Explain why product warranties are classified as contingent liabilities. Under what conditions are the costs associated with product warranties accrued? Briefly explain the procedures involved when accounting for product warranties.

20. Briefly explain why executive compensation in Japan is generally lower than that in the United States.

21. Identify three problems with the executive incentive compensation packages normally used in U.S. corporations.

22. (Appendix 10A) Briefly explain what a pension plan is and why the assets in the pension fund do not appear on a company's balance sheet. Why does a pension liability sometimes appear on the balance sheet?

23. (Appendix 10A) What is the difference between a defined-contribution pension plan and a defined-benefit pension plan? Which of the two is becoming more popular, and why? What are the major difficulties involved with accounting for a defined-benefit pension plan?

24. (Appendix 10A) What is ERISA, and why was it instituted? What role do actuarial estimates play in accounting for defined-benefit pension plans?

25. (Appendix 10A) Define postretirement health care and insurance costs and explain how the FASB requires that they be accounted for. Why has the proposal been so controversial?

26. (Appendix 10B) Why do companies use accelerated methods to depreciate their fixed assets for tax purposes? How does this practice lead to the recognition of a liability?

27. (Appendix 10B) Do deferred income taxes actually represent liabilities? Will they require the future payment of assets? Why are deferred liabilities so large for many major U.S. corporations? Discuss.

28. (Appendix 10B) In 1986 the income tax rate for U.S. corporations was reduced, and several years later it was raised. How did these changes influence the financial statements of U.S. corporations through the deferred income tax account?

29. (Appendix 10B) What is the conservatism ratio, how is it calculated, and what does it measure?

EXERCISES

E10–1

(Reporting current liabilities and the current ratio)

Gemini Incorporated reported current assets of $15,000 and current liabilities of $12,000 on its December 31, 1996, balance sheet. After examining the financial records, the auditor discovered that the following items had either been ignored or were mistakenly recorded in the books.

1. An inventory purchase of $1,600, which was in transit as of December 31 and shipped FOB shipping point, was not recorded. The purchase was made on account.
2. An inventory purchase of $1,700, which was in transit as of December 31 and shipped FOB destination, was recorded. The purchase was made on account.
3. An $800 installment payment on a long-term note payable, due on March 15, 1997, was not included as current. The entire liability was included as long-term.
4. Short-term payables in the amount of $2,100 were listed as current even though they were part of a line of credit that will allow them to be immediately refinanced with long-term liabilities, which management intended to do, when they become due.

REQUIRED:

Compute the amounts needed in the following chart by indicating the effect of each listed item on current assets and current liabilities. Compute Gemini's current ratio after the adjustments.

	CURRENT ASSETS	CURRENT LIABILITIES
	$15,000	$12,000
1.		
2.		
3.		
4.	_____	_____
Total		

E10–2

(Why are current liabilities carried at face value instead of present value?)

Winslow Enterprises reports $40,000 in Accounts Payable on the balance sheet as of December 31, 1996. These payables, on average, will be paid in ten days. Note: Knowledge of present value is required to do this exercise (see Appendix 4A).

REQUIRED:

a. Assuming a 12 percent annual discount rate, approximate the present value of the cash out-flows associated with the accounts payable.

b. Why are accounts payable carried on the balance sheet at face value instead of present value?

E10–3

(Financing with long-term debt, contract terms, and the current ratio)

Darrington and Darling borrowed $100,000 from Commercial Financing to finance the purchase of fixed assets. The loan contract provides for a 12 percent annual interest rate and states that the principal must be paid in full in ten years. The contract also requires that Darrington and Darling maintain a current ratio of 1.5:1. Before Darrington and Darling borrowed the $100,000, the company's current assets and current liabilities were $130,000 and $80,000, respectively.

REQUIRED:

a. Compute the company's current ratio if it invests $50,000 of the borrowed funds in fixed assets and keeps the rest as cash or short-term investments. To what dollar amount can current liabilities grow before the company violates the debt contract?

b. Compute the company's current ratio if it invests $80,000 of the borrowed funds in fixed assets and keeps the rest as cash or short-term investments. To what dollar amount can current liabilities grow before the company violates the debt contract?

c. Compute the company's current ratio if it invests the entire $100,000 of the borrowed funds in fixed assets. To what dollar amount can current liabilities grow before the company violates the debt contract?

E10–4

(Accruals, the current ratio, and net income)

Lily May Electronics recognizes expenses for wages, interest, and rent when cash payments are made. The following related cash payments were made during December 1996.

1. December 1 — Paid $1,100 for rent to cover the subsequent twelve months.
2. December 5 and 20 — Paid wages in the amount of $7,500. Wages in the amount of $7,500 are paid on the fifth and the twentieth of each month for the fifteen days just ended. The next payment will be on January 5, 1997.
3. December 15 — Paid $600 interest on an outstanding note payable. The note has face value of $10,000 and a twelve percent annual interest rate. Interest payments in the amount of $600 are made every six months.

As of December 31 the current assets and current liabilities reported on Lily May's balance sheet were $24,000 and $15,000, respectively. Lily May's income statement reported net income of $7,500.

REQUIRED:

Compute Lily May's current ratio and net income if the company were to account for wages, interest, and rent on an accrual basis.

E10–5

(Short-term notes payable and the actual rate of interest)

On December 1 Spencer Department Store borrowed $19,250 from First Bank and Trust. Spencer signed a ninety-day note with a face amount of $20,000. The interest rate stated on the face of the note is 15 percent per year.

REQUIRED:

a. Provide the journal entry recorded by Spencer on December 1.
b. Provide the adjusting entry recorded by Spencer on December 31 before financial statements are prepared. Show how the note payable would be disclosed on the December 31 balance sheet.
c. Compute the actual annual interest rate on the note.

(Hint: Note that Spencer had the use of $19,250 only over the period of the loan.)

d. Why is the actual interest rate different from the rate stated on the face of the note?

E10–6

(Current maturities and debt covenants)

On January 1, 1992, Lacey Treetoppers borrowed $300,000, which is to be paid back in annual installments of $20,000 on December 30 of each year.

REQUIRED:

a. Assuming that Lacey has met all payments on a timely basis, how should this liability be reported on the December 31, 1996, balance sheet?
b. Assume that during December of 1996 the management of Lacey realizes that including the upcoming $20,000 installment as a current liability reduces the company's current ratio below 2:1, the ratio required in a long-term note payable signed by the company. Discuss how management might be able to avoid classifying the current maturity as a current liability.

E10–7

(Gift certificates and unearned revenue)

Norsums Department Store sells gift certificates that are redeemable in merchandise. During 1996 Norsums sold gift certificates for $88,000. Merchandise with the total price of $52,000 was redeemed during the year. The cost of the sold merchandise to Norsums was $32,000. Norsums sold gift certificates for the first time in 1996.

REQUIRED:

a. Record the sale of the gift certificates.
b. Record the redemption during 1996. Assume that Norsums uses the perpetual inventory method.
c. Compute the balance in the Unearned Revenue account as of December 31, 1997, assuming that gift certificates were sold for $60,000 in 1997 and merchandise with a total price of $80,000 was redeemed.

E10–8

(Third-party collection and payroll accounting)

On November 25 Nate Stober received his monthly paycheck from Linson Motor Services. The employee earnings statement that accompanied the check indicated the following:

Gross monthly earnings	**$6,126**
Social security taxes withheld	**460**
Federal taxes withheld	**1,046**
Contribution to United Way	**50**
Contribution to savings account	**100**
Net pay	**$4,470**

REQUIRED:

a. Briefly describe why Nate earned $6,126 but was paid only $4,470.

b. Prepare the journal entry recorded by Linson Motor Services when Nate is paid.

c. Prepare the journal entries recorded by Linson when the social security taxes, federal income taxes, United Way contribution, and savings plan payment are made.

E10–9

(Quarterly tax payments and federal tax liability)

Laurant Landscaping pays federal income taxes at a rate of 35 percent of taxable income. On January 1, 1996, Laurant estimated that taxable income would be $400,000 for 1996 and based its quarterly tax payments on that amount. Quarterly tax payments of $34,000 were made on April 15, June 15, September 15, and December 15. As of December 31, 1996, actual taxable income was determined to be $415,000.

REQUIRED:

a. Provide the journal entries that Laurant recorded when the quarterly tax payments were made on April 15, June 15, September 15, and December 15.

b. Provide the journal entry to accrue the federal tax liability as of December 31, 1996.

E10–10

(Gain and loss contingencies)

Zeus Power has brought suit against Regional Supply in the amount of $825,000 for patent infringement. As of December 31 the suit is in process, and the attorneys have determined that there is a greater than 50 percent chance that Zeus Power will win the entire $825,000.

REQUIRED:

a. How should Zeus Power account for the situation described above?

b. How should Regional Supply account for the situation described above? Briefly describe some of the factors that might affect how Regional Supply chooses to account for this situation.

c. Why would the two companies account for the same facts in different ways?

E10–11

(Bonus plans and contingent losses)

Jordan Brothers recently instituted a bonus plan to pay its executives. The plan specifies that net income must exceed $200,000 before any bonus payments are made. Cash in the amount of 10 percent of net income in excess of $200,000 is placed in a bonus pool, which is to be shared evenly by each of the executives. Ignore income taxes, and assume that the bonus payment is not included as an expense in the calculation of net income.

REQUIRED:

a. Briefly describe why a company would institute a bonus plan, and compute the amount in the bonus pool if Jordan Brothers shows net income of $300,000. Prepare the journal entry that would be recorded to reflect the bonus liability at the end of the year.

b. How much is in the bonus pool if Jordan Brothers shows net income of $180,000? Assume that as of the end of the year Jordan Brothers is being sued for $60,000. The company's legal counsel believes that there is an 80 percent chance that Jordan will lose the suit and the entire $60,000 will have to be paid. Assume also that the suit was ignored when the $180,000 net income was computed. Why might Jordan's management wish to accrue the loss from the suit in the current year instead of simply disclosing it?

E10–12

(Warranty costs: contingent losses or expense as incurred?)

During 1996 Seagul Outboards sold 200 outboard engines for $250 each. The engines are under a one-year warranty for parts and labor, and from past experience, the company estimates that, on average, warranty costs will equal $20 per engine. As of December 31, 1996, 50 engines had been serviced at a total cost of $1,400. During 1997 engines were serviced at a total cost of $2,600. Assume that all repairs used cash.

REQUIRED:

a. Prepare the journal entries that would be recorded at the following times:

(1) During 1996 to record the sale of the engines.

(2) During 1996 to accrue the contingent loss on warranties.

(3) During 1996 and 1997 to record the actual warranty cost incurred.

b. Assume that Seagul chose not to treat the warranty costs as contingent losses. Instead, they chose to expense warranty costs as they were paid. Compute the total net income for 1996 and 1997 for each of the two accounting treatments.

E10–13

(Appendix 10A: Pension contributions and unfunded pension liability)

Seasaw Seasons instituted a defined-benefit pension plan for its employees three years ago. Each year since the adoption of the plan, Seasaw has contributed $16,000 to the pension fund, which is managed by Fiduciary Trust Associates. As of the end of the current year, it was estimated that contributions of $58,000 would have been necessary to maintain a fund large enough to provide the benefits promised to the employees when they retire.

REQUIRED:

a. Prepare the journal entries that were recorded by Seasaw as it contributed cash to the pension fund.

b. How much pension liability should be recorded on Seasaw's balance sheet as of the end of the current year?

E10–14

(Appendix 10B: Deferred taxes and the tax rate)

Swingley Company uses an accelerated method to depreciate its fixed assets for tax purposes and the straight-line method for financial reporting purposes. In 1996 the accelerated method recognized depreciation of $35,000, while the straight-line method recognized depreciation of $20,000. Taxable income and net income before taxes for that year were $65,000 and $80,000, respectively.

REQUIRED:

a. If the federal income tax rate is 35 percent, prepare the journal entry recorded by Swingley to accrue its 1996 tax liability.

b. If the federal income tax rate is 30 percent, prepare the journal entry recorded by Swingley to accrue its 1996 tax liability.

c. Briefly explain why the Deferred Income Tax account is considered a liability on the balance sheet and why it is less when the tax rate is 35 percent than when the rate is 40 percent.

E10–15

(Appendix 10B: conservatism ratio)

The information below was taken from the annual report of Busytown Industries.

	1996	1995
BALANCE SHEET		
Deferred income tax liability	$ 9,700	$8,300
INCOME STATEMENT		
Income before taxes	$ 68,000	
Income tax expense	(20,400)	
Net income	$ 47,600	
Effective income tax rate: 38%		

REQUIRED:

a. Compute Busytown's conservatism ratio, and comment on how conservative the company's reporting methods are.

b. Explain why the conservatism ratio provides a measure of the extent to which a company's financial accounting methods are conservative, and provide examples of accounting treatments that may increase or decrease the ratio.

E10–16

(Appendix 10B: conservatism ratio)

The information below was taken from the annual report of Sega-Venus Enterprises.

	1996	1995
BALANCE SHEET		
Deferred income tax liability	$ 18,300	$19,400
INCOME STATEMENT		
Income before taxes	$145,500	
Income tax expense	(54,000)	
Net income	$ 91,500	
Effective income tax rate: 34%		

REQUIRED:

a. Compute Sega-Venus's conservatism ratio, and comment on how conservative the company's reporting methods are.
b. Explain why the conservatism ratio provides a measure of the extent to which a company's financial accounting methods are conservative, and provide examples of accounting treatments that may increase or decrease the ratio.

PROBLEMS

P10–1

(Distinguishing current from long-term liabilities)

Beth Morgan, controller of Boulder Corporation, is currently preparing the 1996 financial report. She is trying to decide how to classify the following items.

1. Account payable of $170,000 owed to suppliers for inventory.
2. A $60,000 note payable that matures in three months. The company is planning to acquire a five-year loan from its bank to pay off the note. The bank has agreed to finance the note.
3. A $500,000 mortgage; $75,000 payable within twelve months, and the remaining $425,000 to be paid over the next six years.
4. The sum of $8,000 owed to the phone company for service during December.
5. Advances of $25,000 received from a customer. The contract between the customer and Boulder Corporation states that if the company does not deliver the goods within six months, the $25,000 is to be returned to the customer.
6. The sum of $15,000 due the federal government for income tax withheld from employees during the last quarter of 1996. The government requires that withholdings be submitted by the end of the next quarter to the Internal Revenue Service.
7. A $125,000 note payable; $30,000 is payable within twelve months, and the remaining $95,000 is to be paid over the next two years. Boulder Corporation plans to issue common stock to the creditor for the portion due during the next twelve months.
8. The company declared a cash dividend of $50,000 on December 29, 1996. The dividend is to be paid on January 21, 1997.

REQUIRED:

a. Classify each of the items as a current liability or as a long-term liability. (*Note:* some items may be partially classified as current and as long-term.)
b. Compute the total amount that should be classified as current liabilities.
c. Compute the total amount that should be classified as long-term liabilities.

P10–2

(Recognizing current liabilities can restrict dividend payments)

Linton Industries borrowed $500,000 from Security Bankers to finance the purchase of equipment costing $360,000 and to provide $140,000 in cash. The note states that the loan matures in twenty years, and the principal is to be paid in annual installments of $25,000. The terms of the loan also indicate that Linton must maintain a current ratio of 2:1 and cannot pay dividends that will reduce retained earnings below $200,000. The balance sheet of Linton, immediately prior to the bank loan and the purchase of equipment, follows.

Current assets	$ 120,000	Current liabilities	$ 100,000
Noncurrent assets	1,500,000	Long-term liabilities	300,000
		Capital stock	1,000,000
		Retained earnings	220,000
		Total liabilities and	
Total assets	$1,620,000	stockholders' equity	$1,620,000

REQUIRED:

The board of directors of Linton is about to declare a dividend to be paid to the shareholders early next year. After accepting the loan and purchasing the equipment, how large a dividend can the board pay and not violate the terms of the debt covenant?

P10–3

(Recognizing current liabilities and violating debt covenants)

Before adjustments and closing on December 31, 1996, the current accounts of Seymour and Associates indicated the following balances.

	DEBIT	CREDIT
Cash	$40,000	
Accounts receivable	50,000	
Allowance for doubtful accounts		$ 2,000
Inventory	52,000	
Accounts payable		30,000
Unearned revenues		25,000
Warranty liabilities		5,000
Other current liabilities		10,000

The terms of an outstanding long-term note payable state that Seymour must maintain a current ratio of 2:1 or the note will become due immediately. The following items are not reflected in the balances above.

1. Bad debt losses in the amount of 6 percent of the outstanding accounts receivable balance are expected.
2. The warranty liability on outstanding warranties is estimated to be $12,000.
3. Forty percent of the unearned revenue had been earned as of December 31.
4. Five thousand dollars, listed above under "Other current liabilities," is part of a line of credit and is expected to be immediately refinanced on a long-term basis when due.
5. The total income tax liability for 1996 was estimated at year end to be $23,000. Estimated tax payments during the year totaled $20,000.
6. Trademans, Inc. brought suit against Seymour early in 1996. As of December 31, Seymour's legal counsel estimates that there is a 60 percent probability that the suit will be lost in the amount of $10,000. If the suit is lost, payment will most likely be due in the next year.

REQUIRED:

a. Prepare the journal entries that would be recorded (if necessary) for each of the six items listed.
b. After preparing the journal entries, compute the company's current ratio assuming that the contingent liability described in (6) is not accrued.
c. After preparing the journal entries, compute the company's current ratio assuming that the contingent liability described in (6) is accrued.
d. If you were Seymour's auditor, would you require that the contingent liability be accrued? Discuss.

P10–4

(Computing sales tax liability when sales tax is included in the price of the item sold)

On April 12, General Home Appliances sold a toaster for $48.15 cash. The total sales price included a 7 percent sales tax, which must be remitted to the state government at the end of the month.

REQUIRED:

a. Prepare the journal entry to record the sale. General Home Appliances uses the periodic inventory method. (*Hint:* The sales tax is computed as a percentage of the price of the item sold.)

b. Provide the journal entry to record the payment of the sales tax to the government at the end of April.

P10–5

(Payroll tax withholdings)

Makert Marketing Services pays its employees on the 25th of every month for the first fifteen days of the month. The following information is available for the pay period June 1–June 15.

Gross wages	$2,000,000
Health and life insurance withholding	$38,000
FICA (social security) withholding percentage	7.5%
Federal income tax withholding percentage	15%

REQUIRED:

a. Compute the amount of money withheld from the employees for the following:
   (1) FICA (social security)
   (2) Federal income taxes
b. Compute the employees' total take-home pay.
c. Prepare the entries necessary on June 15 associated with these wages.
d. Prepare the entries necessary on June 25 associated with these wages.

P10–6

(Estimated income tax payments and accrued tax liability)

Trailor Homes showed a federal income tax liability of $15,000 on its 1996 balance sheet. At the beginning of 1997, for purposes of estimated tax payments, the company estimated its taxable income to be $250,000 during 1997. Trailor pays a federal income tax rate of 35 percent of taxable income. The company made the following tax payments during 1997.

April	$36,875
June	21,875
September	21,875
December	21,875

Actual taxable income for the year, determined at the end of 1997, was $280,000.

REQUIRED:

a. Prepare the journal entries to record the tax payments during 1997.
b. Provide the journal entry to accrue Trailor's income tax liability as of December 31, 1997.

P10–7

(Issues surrounding the recognition of a contingent liability)

While shopping on October 13, 1996, at the Floor Wax Shop, Tom Jacobs slipped and seriously injured his back. Mr. Jacobs believed that the Floor Wax Shop should have warned him that the floors were slick; hence, he sued the company for damages. As of December 31, 1996, the lawsuit was still in progress. According to the company's lawyers, it was probable that the company would lose the lawsuit. The lawyers also believed that the company could lose somewhere between $250,000 and $1,500,000, with a best guess of the loss of $742,000. The lawsuit was eventually settled in favor of Mr. Jacobs on August 12, 1997, for $690,000.

REQUIRED:
a. Discuss the issues that the Floor Wax Shop must address in deciding how to report this lawsuit in the 1996 financial report.
b. If you were auditing the Floor Wax Shop, how would you recommend that this lawsuit be reported in the 1996 financial report? Why?
c. Assume that a contingent liability of $742,000 is accrued on December 31, 1996. What journal entry would the company record on August 12, 1997, the date of the settlement?

P10–8

(Accruing warranty costs before they are incurred)

Arden's Used Cars offers a one-year warranty from date of sale on all cars. From historical data, Mr. Arden estimates that, on average, each car will require the company to incur warranty costs of $760. The following is the activity related to the cars during 1996.

1. February 2   Sold five cars.
2. March 23   Sold ten cars.
3. May 30   Incurred warranty costs of $3,000 on four cars sold in 1995.
4. July 5   Sold eight cars.
5. September 2   Incurred warranty costs of $5,000 on five cars sold in 1996.
6. November 15   Incurred warranty costs of $6,000 on one car sold in 1996.
7. December 20   Sold twelve cars.

REQUIRED:
a. Assume that the cars were sold for cash for an average of $9,500. Prepare the entry to record the car sales during 1996 (combine all the sales and make one entry).
b. Prepare the individual entries to record the warranty costs incurred. Assume that the breakdown of warranty costs is 40 percent wages (paid in cash) and 60 percent parts.
c. Arden accrues its warranty liability with a single adjusting journal entry at year end. Prepare that entry.
d. Compute the year-end warranty liability. The beginning balance in the warranty liability account was $3,500.
e. Explain why accountants estimate the warranty expense in the year of sale instead of recording the expenses as the costs are incurred.

P10–9

(Advertising campaigns can give rise to contingent liabilities)

To kick off its 1996 advertising campaign, Rachel's Breakfast Cereal is offering a $1 refund in exchange for five cereal box tops. The company estimates that the tops of 10 percent of the cereal boxes sold will be returned for the refund. The cereal boxes are sold for $2.00 each. During 1996 and 1997, 20,000 and 28,000 cereal boxes are sold, respectively, and 1,500 and 2,000 box tops are received for refunds during 1996 and 1997, respectively.

REQUIRED:
a. Prepare the journal entries to record the sale of the cereal boxes, the recognition of the contingent liability associated with the potential refunds, and the actual refund payments for 1996 and 1997.
b. Compute the liabilities associated with the potential refunds as of the end of 1996 and 1997.

P10–10

(Appendix 10A: Accruing and funding pension liabilities)

Shelby Company instituted a defined-benefit pension plan for its employees at the beginning of 1992. An actuarial method that is acceptable under generally accepted accounting principles indicates that the company should contribute $40,000 each year to the pension fund to cover the benefits that will be paid to the employees. Shelby funded 80 percent of the liability in 1992 and 1993, 90 percent in 1994 and 1995, and 100 percent in 1996.

REQUIRED:
a. Prepare the journal entries to accrue the pension liability and fund it for 1992, 1993, 1994, 1995, and 1996.
b. Compute the balance in the Pension Liability account as of December 31, 1996.

P10–11

(Appendix 10B: Deferred income taxes, changes in tax rates, and investment in long-lived assets)

Acme, Inc., purchased machinery at the beginning of 1992 for $50,000. Management used the straight-line method to depreciate the cost for financial reporting purposes and the double-declining-balance method to depreciate the cost for tax purposes. The life of the machinery was estimated to be four years, and the salvage value was estimated as zero. Revenue less expenses other than depreciation (for financial reporting and tax purposes) equaled $100,000 in 1992, 1993, 1994, and 1995. Acme pays income taxes at the rate of 35 percent of taxable income.

REQUIRED:

a. Prepare the journal entries to accrue income tax expense and income tax liability for 1992, 1993, 1994, and 1995. Indicate the balance in the Deferred Income Tax account as of the end of each of the four years.

b. Assume that the tax rate was changed by the federal government to 20 percent at the beginning of 1994. Repeat the exercise in (a). Would it be appropriate to recognize a gain at the end of 1994 to reflect the tax rate decrease? Why or why not, and if so, how much of a gain?

c. Assume that Acme purchased additional machinery at the beginning of 1993 and 1995. Each purchase was for $50,000, and each machine had a four-year estimated life and no salvage value. Once again, straight-line depreciation method was used for reporting purposes, and double-declining-balance for tax purposes. Repeat the exercise in (a). Why is the Deferred Income Tax account one of the largest liabilities on the balance sheets of many major U.S. companies?

P10–12

(Appendix 10B: conservatism ratio)

You are a security analyst for Magneto Investments, and have chosen to invest in one firm from the semi-conductor manufacturing industry. You have narrowed your choice to either Owen-Foley Company or Amerton Industries, firms of similar size and direct competitors in the industry. The information below was taken from their 1996 annual reports.

OWEN-FOLEY COMPANY	1996	1995
BALANCE SHEET		
Deferred income tax liability	$ 18,400	$16,600
INCOME STATEMENT		
Income before taxes	$163,000	
Income tax expense	(52,000)	
Net income	$111,000	
Effective income tax rate: 36%		

AMERTON INDUSTRIES	1996	1995
BALANCE SHEET		
Deferred income tax liability	$ 18,800	$19,800
INCOME STATEMENT		
Income before taxes	$158,500	
Income tax expense	(53,500)	
Net income	$105,000	
Effective income tax rate: 36%		

REQUIRED:

On the basis of this information explain which of the two firms seems to have the stronger earning power.

CASES

C10-1

(Debt covenants and reporting current liabilities)

Federal Express Corporation, a world leader in express mail services, reported the following in its 1994 financial statements (dollars in millions).

	1994
Current assets	$1,762
Current liabilities	1,536

The company's long-term debt contains restrictive covenants that require the maintenance of certain financial ratios. Assume that these covenants require that the company's current ratio be at least 1.10:1.00.

REQUIRED:

a. What additional dollar value of current liabilities could have been reported as of December 31, 1994, without violating the debt covenant?
b. List several current liabilities that management may have been able to control to ensure at year-end that the covenant was not violated, and explain how these liabilities could have been controlled.
c. Explain what could happen if the company violated the covenant.
d. Assume that at the end of 1994, Federal Express considered a $600 million inventory purchase. Assume also that the company has the necessary cash. Should the company pay cash or purchase the inventory on account, and why? Support your answer with calculations.

C10-2

(Receipts in advance: measurement theory and financial statement effects)

Ingersoll-Rand manufactures specialized heavy-duty construction equipment. Included in a set of recent financial statements is the account "Customers' Advance Payments" with a balance of over $15 million. The notes to the financial statements indicate that, although payments are collected in advance from customers, revenues are recognized when products are shipped. Products are normally shipped within six months of the advance payments.

REQUIRED:

a. On what financial statement and in which section of that statement would the account "Customers' Advance Payments" be found?
b. Explain the accounting treatment associated with this account in terms of the principles of revenue recognition and matching.
c. Under this accounting treatment, how are important financial ratios, such as earnings per share, the current ratio, and the debt/equity ratio, affected when (1) the advance payments are received and (2) when the related goods are shipped?

C10-3

(Lawsuits and contingent liabilities)

The following excerpt was taken from the 1990 annual report of Exxon Corporation.

15. LITIGATION

On March 24, 1989, the Exxon Valdez, a tanker owned by Exxon Shipping Company, a subsidiary of Exxon Corporation, ran aground on Bligh Reef in Prince William Sound off the port of Valdez, Alaska, and released approximately 260,000 barrels of crude oil. More than 215 lawsuits, including class actions, have been brought in various courts against Exxon Corporation and certain of its consolidated subsidiaries. Most of these lawsuits seek unspecified compensatory and punitive damages; several lawsuits seek damages in varying specified amounts. Certain of the lawsuits seek injunctive relief. Of these lawsuits, more than 40 have been dismissed or settled.

The State of Alaska has filed a suit in Superior Court in Alaska against Exxon Shipping Company, Exxon Corporation and others seeking substantial civil penalties and unspecified damages arising from the oil spill. On February 27, 1990, an indictment was returned in the

United States District Court in Anchorage, Alaska, charging Exxon Shipping Company and Exxon Corporation with violation of the Refuse Act, the Migratory Bird Treaty Act, the Clean Water Act, the Waterways Safety Act and the Dangerous Cargo Act.

The potential total costs relating to the matters described above are difficult to predict and may not be resolved for a number of years. It is believed that the ultimate outcome, net of reserves already provided, will not have a materially adverse effect upon the corporation's operations or financial condition.

REQUIRED:

Discuss Exxon's disclosure in terms of (1) the methods used to account for loss contingencies and (2) the potential economic consequences associated with Exxon's disclosure and method of accounting treatment.

C10–4

(Unreported assets)

In early 1991 Lifschultz Industries, a small gas meter company, reported a book value of less than zero (i.e., reported liabilities exceed reported assets). Yet, in late March the company's stock price skyrocketed on news that it was pursuing a massive antitrust and racketeering lawsuit against three of the country's biggest truckers: Consolidated Freightways, Roadway Services, and Yellow Freight Systems. Lifschultz alleged that these truckers conspired to engage in anti-competitive activity, driving it out of the trucking business. The suit, filed in U.S. district court in South Carolina, seeks $1.8 billion. The three truckers have said nothing about the suit publicly other than to footnote it as a "contingency" in their annual reports.

REQUIRED:

a. Explain how Lifschultz can report negative book value and, at the same time, have its stock so highly valued in the stock market.
b. Explain the differences between how Lifschultz should account for the suit and how the three trucking companies should account for it.
c. Provide economic reasons why the plaintiff and defendants account for the same dispute differently.

C10–5

(The economic consequences of a technical default)

The following quote appeared in *The Wall Street Journal* (December 26, 1989). It refers to the problems of Campeau Corporation, a Canadian-based retail empire that declared bankruptcy in early 1990. At the time, Campeau's department store chains included Bloomingdales, Rich's, Burdines, Abraham & Strauss, and Lazarus.

Campeau Corp.'s announcement Friday that its bankers believe it has technically defaulted on $2.34 billion in debt probably will freeze new spring shipments, apparel makers say. Citibank, leader of the bank syndicate providing much of Campeau's debt financing, informed Campeau by letter last week that Campeau had violated certain covenants on debt . . . and unless Campeau can remedy the default by December 31, Citibank stated it may demand full repayment of the loans.

REQUIRED:

a. What is a "technical default," and how is Citibank reacting to it?
b. Explain why apparel makers may "freeze new shipments" and why this could present great problems for the Campeau organization.

C10–6

(Reclassifying short-term notes as long-term debt)

The 1994 annual report of General Mills reported the following (dollars in millions).

	1994	1993
Current assets	$1,129.2	$1,076.9
Current liabilities	1,832.1	1,558.8

Included in current liabilities are notes payable in the amount of $433.3 million and $339.6 million for 1994 and 1993, respectively. In the footnotes the company discloses that the dollar amounts of short-term notes payable listed on the balance sheet are net of $250 million and $200 million in 1994 and 1993, respectively. Because the credit agreement covering these notes "provides us with the ability to refinance short-term borrowings on a long-term basis, we therefore have reclassified a portion of our notes payable to long-term debt."

REQUIRED:
a. Explain what is meant by the footnote disclosure.
b. What effect did the reclassification have on the company's 1994 and 1993 current ratios?
c. Explain why one might claim that a short-term note may appropriately be classified in the long-term debt section of the balance sheet, and discuss how managers may use discretion in this area to serve their own interests.

C10–7

(Using executive compensation disclosures)

The SEC recently required additional information in the proxy statements that describe the compensation packages of the company's top executives. A *Wall Street Journal* article published soon after the requirement (January 29, 1993) offered a list of recommendations about how shareholders might use the additional information. Included in the list: compare executive pay with shareholder returns, check to see if executive compensation is linked to stock market performance, find out how much company stock is owned by the executives, and beware of changes in the auditor.

REQUIRED:
Explain what a proxy statement is, and discuss how each of the recommendations listed above may provide useful information to the shareholders.

C10–8

("Taking a bath" during bankruptcy proceedings)

A major defense contractor, LTV, faced with huge liabilities, sought Chapter 11 protection several years ago. Under Chapter 11, a company continues to operate but is protected from creditors while it tries to work out a reorganization plan. At that time the company's management chose to accrue a $2.26 billion liability to reflect the potential cost of medical and life insurance benefits for its 118,000 current and retired employees. At the time, this charge was not required by generally accepted accounting principles. *The Wall Street Journal* reported that the company chose to recognize the charge because "if the company waited until after it negotiated new credit agreements and emerged from bankruptcy-law proceedings before taking the $2 billion charge, the additional liability could trigger violations of its debt covenants."[20]

REQUIRED:
a. Provide the journal entry to record the $2.26 billion charge recognized by LTV.
b. Explain how taking the charge before negotiating new credit agreements could avoid violating debt covenants.
c. It was also reported that LTV took several other significant charges while it was under bankruptcy proceedings. In addition to its concern about debt covenants, in general, why might management have chosen to take these charges at this time?

C10–9

(Replacing currently maturing debt with a short-term note)

General Cinema Corporation operates the leading movie theater circuits in the United States, is an independent bottler of Pepsi-Cola and related products, and also owns several "high-end" retail stores, including Neiman-Marcus. In a recent set of financial statements, the company reported the following in the current liabilities section.

Long-term liabilities—due within one year	**$ 7,014,000**
Total current liabilities	**339,304,000**

In the notes to the financial statements, the company profiles all the components of its long-term debt.

20. Karen Blumenthal, "LTV To Reserve $2.26 Billion for Retirees," *The Wall Street Journal,* November 22, 1988, pp. A3, A4.

REQUIRED:

a. What kind of assets must General Cinema use to repay the long-term liabilities in order for the portion due within one year to be classified as a current liability?

b. If General Cinema plans in the foreseeable future to refinance the amount of currently maturing long-term debt by issuing long-term notes, how should the debt be classified, as current or long-term? Why?

c. Why might management consider such a refinancing strategy? State your answer in terms of important financial ratios and debt covenants.

C10–10

(The annual report of MCI)

Refer to the annual report of MCI and answer the following questions.

a. Compute the current ratio, working capital, and current liabilities as a percentage of total assets for the company, and comment on any trends that may have developed over the last several years.

b. What are the principle components of telecommunications expense? Explain what the account "Accrued telecommunications expense" represents.

c. What plans have the company adopted that are designed primarily to encourage the employees to act in the interests of the shareholders?

d. Briefly describe the litigation facing MCI as of December 31, 1994.

e. *(Appendix 10A)* What kind of pension plans does MCI provide for its employees, and is the defined-benefit plan underfunded as of the end of 1994? How do you know?

f. *(Appendix 10A)* What effect did the adoption of SFAS 112 "Employers' Accounting for Postemployment Benefits" have on the company's financial statements? Why?

g. (Appendix 10B) How large are deferred income taxes relative to the company's long-term debt, total liabilities, and total assets? Has this account increased or decreased over the last three years? Briefly explain why. What accounting practice by MCI has been the primary reason why its deferred income tax liability is relatively large? Compute MCI's conservatism ratio, and comment on whether the company uses conservative accounting practices.

C10–11

(Appendix 10A: Economic consequences and accounting for postretirement healthcare and insurance costs)

The Chicago Tribune (June 24, 1990) reported that AMR Corporation, in response to the new accounting rule requiring that postretirement healthcare costs be accrued, now requires employees to contribute to their retirement healthcare plan. In the past, AMR provided all the benefits for the plan. The article also noted that "some [companies] have simply ended retiree health benefits for active and future workers. Others have terminated the plan but offered increased pension benefits or created employee stock ownership plans to soften the blow."

REQUIRED:
Briefly describe the FASB's new ruling, and discuss whether it makes economic sense for a company to discontinue its postretirement healthcare plan in response to it.

C10–12

(Appendix 10A: Post-retirement Costs)

At the beginning of 1993 Chrysler had $3.6 billion in unfunded pension liabilities. During the first three quarters of that year the company contributed $2.6 billion to its pension fund as part of an effort to reduce the unfunded liability. But the automaker said "its liability is expected to rise by year-end as a result of low interest rates." (*Wall Street Journal,* November 1993).

REQUIRED:

a. What kind of pension plan does Chrysler have, how do you know, and basically how does it work?

b. How could the liability rise "as a result of low interest rates"?

c. In that same article it was reported that "Because of accounting changes related to retiree expenses, Chrysler reported that its noncurrent postretirement benefits jumped to $7.5 billion from $116 million a year earlier." To what accounting change is this quote referring, and did Chrysler's postretirement benefits really jump that much? Explain.

C10–13

(Appendix 10B: Changes in expected tax rates and net income)

In the third quarter of 1994 General Motors posted net income of $552 million, compared with a loss of $112.9 million a year earlier. Over $200 million of the profit was due to an accounting adjustment in its North American operations because its expected taxes turned out to be lower than it had anticipated in earlier periods. David Healy, an analyst with S.G. Warburg & Co., was quoted in the *Wall Street Journal* (October 21, 1994) as saying "Cynics would say that since they couldn't do it in the auto department, they did it in the accounting department."

REQUIRED:

a. Explain what Mr. Healy means.
b. Explain how a change in expected tax rates can lead to a positive effect on reported earnings.
c. Do you believe that the $200 million gain represents an increase in the overall wealth of GM?

CHAPTER 11

LONG-TERM LIABILITIES: NOTES, BONDS, AND LEASES

LEARNING OBJECTIVES

LO 1 Define long-term notes payable, bonds payable, and leasehold obligations, and explain how companies use these instruments as important sources of financing.

LO 2 Identify important economic consequences created by the excessive borrowing brought on by merger mania during the 1980s.

LO 3 List and define the different forms of contractual obligations.

LO 4 Define the effective interest rate, and describe how it is determined for contractual obligations.

LO 5 Describe the basic rule of the effective interest method, and explain what it ensures about the book value of a long-term obligation.

LO 6 Describe how the effective interest method underlies the accounting for notes, bonds, and leases.

LO 7 Explain how changes in market interest rates can lead to misstated balance sheet values for long-term liabilities.

LO 8 Differentiate operating leases from capital leases, explain the methods used to account for capital leases, and describe how operating lease accounting can create off-balance-sheet financing.

LO 1 This chapter is devoted to long-term notes payable, bonds payable, and leasehold obligations. **Notes payable** are obligations evidenced by formal notes that normally involve direct borrowings from financial institutions or arrangements to finance the purchase of assets. **Bonds payable** are obligations that arise from notes (bonds) that have been issued for cash to a large number of creditors, called *bondholders*. **Leasehold obligations** refer to future cash payments (e.g., rent) that are required for the use or occupation of property during a specified period of time. Each of these liabilities represents an obligation to disburse assets (usually cash) for a time that extends beyond the period that defines current assets. The formal contracts underlying such arrangements contain a number of terms including, for example, the principal amount of the debt, the periodic interest payments, the time period over which the interest and principal are to be paid, and security (e.g., collateral) and other provisions, many of which are designed to protect the interests of the lenders.

Long-term borrowing arrangements, such as notes, bonds and leases, are a common and major source of capital and financing for companies throughout the world. Funds used to acquire other companies, purchase machinery and equipment, finance plant expansion, pay off debts, repurchase outstanding stock, and support operations are often generated by issuing long-term notes and bonds, or entering into lease agreements. The Walt Disney Company, for example, increased long-term borrowing by over $500 million during 1994, primarily to finance theme parks, network television and broadcast programming. In a typical year, U.S. companies will raise as much as $300 billion by issuing bonds.

Accounting Trends and Techniques (New York: AICPA, 1994) reports that, of the 600 major U.S. companies surveyed, 509 (85 percent) disclosed long-term notes payable, 278 (46 percent) disclosed bonds payable, and 320 (53 percent) disclosed leasehold liabilities. In 1994, Kmart Corporation reported long-term liabilities of over $5 billion, consisting primarily of notes, bonds, and leasehold obligations.

THE RELATIVE SIZE OF LONG-TERM LIABILITIES

Figure 11–1 indicates the relative size of long-term liabilities on the balance sheets of U.S. companies for the industries we have followed throughout the text. For each industry the table indicates: (1) long-term liabilities as a percentage of total assets, (2) long-term liabilities as a percentage of total liabilities, and (3) long-term liabilities as a percentage of stockholders' equity.[1] Companies generate assets in three different ways: borrowings, equity issuances, and profitable operations. Long-term liabilities/total assets indicates the relative importance of long-term borrowings in generating a company's assets. Long-term liabilities/total liabilities indicates the importance of long-term borrowings relative to current borrowings. Long-term liabilities/stockholders' equity indicates the importance of long-term borrowings relative to equity issuances and profitable operations as sources of financing.

For the industries listed on the table, the importance of long-term liabilities as a source of financing (ratio column 1) ranges from 5 percent for securities brokers to

---

1. Long-term liabilities on Figure 11–1 include deferred income taxes, but many accountants believe that deferred income taxes do not represent a liability in an economic sense. See Appendix 10B for further discussion on deferred income taxes.

FIGURE 11–1

Relative size of long-term liabilities (LTL) (industry averages)

INDUSTRY	SIC CODE	NO. OF COMPANIES ASSETS	LTL/ TOTAL LIABILITIES	LTL/ TOTAL	LTL/ STOCKHOLDERS' EQUITY
MANUFACTURING					
Motor Vehicles	3711	95	.14	.24	.31
Petroleum and Gas	1311	872	.14	.35	.25
RETAILING					
Department Stores	5311	641	.16	.39	.27
Hobby, Toy & Games	5945	519	.12	.29	.21
GENERAL SERVICE					
Eating places	5812	2,427	.26	.46	.59
Telephone Commun.	4813	1,130	.32	.66	.67
FINANCIAL SERVICES					
Bank Holding Co.	6719	188	.15	.42	.23
Security Brokers	6211	1,312	.05	.12	.07

Source: Compiled from data published in *Industry Norms and Key Business Ratios* (Dun & Bradstreet, Inc., 1994).

32 percent for telephone communication companies. The magnitude of this percentage depends, in general, on the importance of long-term assets (primarily property, plant, and equipment) held by a company, because such assets are normally financed with long-term liabilities. Financial institutions, like Merrill Lynch and Morgan Stanley, do not invest heavily in property, plant, and equipment, while capital intensive companies, like MCI and Ameritech, make significant investments in such assets. Merrill Lynch carries approximately $6 billion in long-term debt with assets of over $70 billion, only $2 billion of which are in the form of property, plant, and equipment. The long-term debt of MCI, on the other hand, represents over 25 percent of its $16 billion in assets, over half of which are in the form of property, plant, and equipment.

The amount of long-term liabilities as a percentage of total liabilities (ratio column 2) is less than 50 percent for most industries. Thus, current liabilities generally represent a more important source of financing than long-term liabilities. As of December 31, 1994, the dollar value of Goodyear Tire & Rubber Co.'s current liabilities, for example, was over twice as large as the dollar value of its long-term liabilities. Indeed, some major U.S. companies, such as Polaroid Corporation, carry no long-term debt on their balance sheets.

Similarly, the long-term liabilities/stockholders' equity ratios indicate that equity issuances and profitable operations are generally more important sources of financing than long-term liabilities. As of December 31, 1994, the balance in the stockholders' equity accounts for Boeing, for example, was 2 times greater than the balance sheet value of its long-term liabilities. However, for certain companies the value of long-term liabilities exceeds stockholders' equity. On its December 31, 1994, balance sheet, the Marriott International reported long-term liabilities of over $1 billion and stockholders' equity of only $767 million.

THE ECONOMIC CONSEQUENCES OF
REPORTING LONG-TERM LIABILITIES

LO 2 Chapter 10 describes the economic consequences of disclosing liabilities on the balance sheet, and that discussion will not be repeated here. It is important, however, to realize that during the 1980s the importance of long-term debt grew to unprecedented amounts in the United States, brought on primarily by numerous takeovers, mergers, and acquisitions that involved billions of dollars (referred to in the financial press as "merger mania"). Individuals like Henry Kravis, Robert Campeau, Michael Milken, Rupert Murdock, Merv Griffin, and Donald Trump engineered mega-mergers that were financed by gigantic amounts of long-term debt. When the 1990s arrived, the surviving companies were left with the challenge of generating enough cash to meet the staggering debt payment schedules created by such borrowings.

In many cases this situation has increased the pressure on companies to more carefully manage their debt payments and to pay special attention to how this debt is reported on the balance sheet. During the first quarter of 1991, for example, defaults on bond payments climbed to a record $8.2 billion, and corporate credit ratings, in general, sunk to new lows. Many firms, including almost the entire auto and retail industries, experienced credit-rating downgrades, and well-known companies, like R. H. Macy, Circle K, Pan Am Airlines, Eastern Airlines, and Campeau's retail empire (including Bloomingdales, Abraham & Straus, and Lazarus), filed for bankruptcy protection.

Merger mania has extended into the 1990s. Indeed, the *Wall Street Journal* (August 1, 1995) reported: "Merger activity in the 1995 first half totaled $164.4 billion, the biggest first half on record." When Disney purchased Capital Cities/ABC in August 1995, for example, it added $10 billion to its balance sheet.

In such a debt-laden environment, measures of solvency, like the debt/equity ratio, and debt covenant provisions take on a particularly important role, and as such, management has strong incentives to manage financial statement numbers by employing reporting strategies like "off-balance-sheet financing."[2] For example, an article in *Business Week* (October 2, 1989) which examined how Rupert Murdock built his global media colossus, News Corp., through debt-financed takeovers, noted that "Murdock has used several ways (referred to later in the article as 'maneuvers and ploys') to raise off-balance-sheet debt." Indeed, at no time in history has the following quote from *Forbes* (November 24, 1980) been more appropriate:

"The basic drives of man are few: to get enough food, to find shelter and to keep debt off the balance sheet."

In response to this debt explosion and the threat of off-balance-sheet financing, the FASB recently passed a standard requiring companies to describe the risks associated with financing arrangements not disclosed on the balance sheet. While this standard falls far short of providing all the information necessary to assess this risk, users can now better assess a company's potential obligations whether or not they appear on the balance sheet.

---

2. Recall that "off balance financing" involves the existence of debt obligations that are not listed in the liability section of the balance sheet.

BASIC DEFINITIONS AND DIFFERENT CONTRACTUAL FORMS

LO 3 Long-term obligations normally represent contractual agreements to make cash payments over a period of time. In addition to other terms, these contracts specify the period of time over which the payments are to be made as well as the dollar amount of each payment. Different contracts express these terms in different ways, giving rise to long-term obligations—and their associated cash flows—that take various forms.

Some contracts, called **interest-bearing obligations**, require periodic (annual or semiannual) cash payments (called **interest**) that are determined as a percentage of the **face, principal, or maturity value**, which must be paid at the end of the contract period. For example, a company may enter into an exchange in which it receives some benefit (e.g., cash, asset, or service) and, in return, promises to pay $1,000 per year for two years and $10,000 at the end of the second year. Such an obligation would have a life of two years, a **stated interest rate** of 10% ($1,000/$10,000), and a maturity, principal, or face value of $10,000. The cash flows associated with this contract are illustrated below.

Period:	0	⟶	1	⟶	2
Payment:	+Receipt		−$1,000		−$1,000
					−$10,000

Non-interest-bearing obligations, on the other hand, require no periodic payments, but only a single cash payment at the end of the contract period. For example, a company may enter into another exchange in which it receives a benefit and, in return, promise to pay $12,000 at the end of two years. This obligation, which is illustrated below, would have a life of two years, a stated interest rate of 0%, and a maturity, principal, or face value of $12,000.

Period:	0	⟶	1	⟶	2
Payment:	+Receipt		−$0		−$0
					−$12,000

In an **installment obligation** periodic payments, covering both interest and principal are made throughout the life of the contract. For example, a company may enter into an exchange in which it receives a benefit and, in return, promises to pay $6,000 at the end of each of two years. The cash flows associated with this obligation are illustrated below.

Period:	0	⟶	1	⟶	2
Payment:	+Receipt		−$6,000		−$6,000

The contractual forms illustrated above represent three common ways to schedule the cash payments associated with long-term obligations. Further, each of these contractual forms may contain additional terms that specify assets pledged as security or **collateral** in case the required cash payments are not met (**default**), as well as additional provisions (**restrictive covenants**) designed to protect the interests of the lenders.

It is also useful to consider the nature of that which is received in exchange for the contractual obligation. In the examples above we have simply referred to it as the "receipt." Often this "receipt" takes the form of cash, as in cases where companies borrow cash from financial institutions, promising to make payments in accordance with the terms of a loan contract. However, contractual obligations also can be exchanged for noncash items, such as long-lived assets, services, or other liabilities. Figure 11–2 illustrates the six combinations that can be obtained by matching each of the three contractual forms with cash and noncash "receipts."

<table>
<tr><td>

FIGURE 11–2

Six possible combinations

</td><td>

1. **Installment**
   A. **Cash received (e.g., bank loan)**
   B. **Noncash received (e.g., lease or real estate purchase)**
2. **Non-interest-bearing**
   A. **Cash received (e.g., zero coupon bond)**
   B. **Noncash received (e.g., equipment purchase)**
3. **Interest-bearing notes**
   A. **Cash received (e.g., bond)**
   B. **Noncash received (e.g., equipment purchase)**

</td></tr>
</table>

In the next section we introduce the very important concept of the effective interest rate in the context of each of the six combinations illustrated in Figure 11–2. We then discuss notes payable, which can be related to all six combinations; bonds payable, which typically relates to 3A; and capital leases, which relate to 1B.

EFFECTIVE INTEREST RATE

LO 4 The **effective interest rate** is the actual interest rate paid by the issuer of the obligation. It may or may not equal the interest rate stated on the contract (for interest-bearing notes), and it is determined by finding the discount rate that sets the present value of the obligation's cash outflows equal to the fair market value (FMV) of that which is received in the exchange.[3] When contractual obligations are exchanged for cash (1A, 2A, and 3A in Figure 11–2), the cash amount received represents the FMV of the receipt. When contractual obligations are exchanged for noncash items (1B, 2B, and 3B), the FMV of the noncash items must be determined through appraisals or some other means.[4] The following examples show how the effective interest rate is determined for the three contractual obligations illustrated earlier: installment, non-interest-bearing, and interest-bearing.

INSTALLMENT AND NON-INTEREST-BEARING OBLIGATIONS

Assume that Able Company entered into an installment obligation requiring the payment of $10,000 at the end of each of two years. In return, the company received a benefit (cash or noncash) with a FMV of $16,900. The cash flows associated with this exchange follow.

Period:	0	1	2
Payment:	+16,900	−$10,000	−$10,000

---

3. The material in this chapter requires an understanding of present value, which is covered in Appendix 4A.
4. If the FMV of the noncash item received in the exchange cannot be determined, the effective interest rate must be estimated by considering the effective interest rates of other similar contractual obligations.

In this case the company has received a benefit of $16,900, promising to pay a $10,000, 2-year, ordinary annuity. The effective (actual) interest rate on the obligation is calculated by finding that interest rate which, when used to discount the two $10,000 payments, results in a present value (PV) of $16,900. The calculation can be set up in the following way.

PV = Annuity Cash Payment × (PV Table Factor Ordinary Annuity: n = 2, i = ?)
$16,900 = $10,000 × ?

Rearranging,

Table 5

PV table factor = $16,900 ÷ $10,000 = 1.69
Since n = 2, i = 12% (effective interest rate)

The effective interest rate is equal to 12% because a $10,000, 2-year, ordinary annuity discounted at 12% is equal to $16,900, the FMV of the benefit received by Able in the exchange.

The method used to compute the effective interest rate for a non-interest-bearing obligation is the same as that used for an installment obligation except that the table *Table 4* factor is taken from the Present Value of a Single Sum table instead of the Present Value of an Ordinary Annuity table. For example, if Baker Company entered into a non-interest-bearing obligation requiring a single $5,000 payment at the end of three years, receiving a benefit (cash or noncash) with a FMV of $3,969, the effective interest rate would be computed as follows.

PV = single sum cash payment × (PV table factor single sum: n = 3, i = ?)
$3,969 = $5,000 × ?

Rearranging,

PV table factor = $3,969 ÷ $5,000 = .7938
Since n = 3, i = 8% (effective interest rate)

It is important to note in both cases that the effective interest rate of a given contractual obligation is determined by the FMV of the benefit received in the exchange. If, for example, the FMV of the benefit received in the non-interest-bearing case was $4,198 instead of $3,969, the effective rate would have been 6% instead of 8%. Similarly, in the installment case if the FMV received was $17,355 instead of $16,900, the effective rate would have been 10% instead of 12%.

INTEREST-BEARING OBLIGATIONS

Assume that Clyde Company entered into an interest-bearing obligation requiring interest payments of $1,000 at the end of each of two years and a principal payment of $10,000 at the end of the second year. In return, the company received a benefit (cash or noncash) with a FMV of $10,000. This obligation has a life of 2 years, a stated interest rate of 10% ($1,000/$10,000), and a maturity, face, or principal value of $10,000. The cash flows associated with this exchange follow.

Period:	0	→	1	→	2
Payment:	+10,000		−$1,000		−$1,000
					−$10,000

In this case the company has received a benefit of $10,000, promising to pay a $1,000, 2-year, ordinary annuity in addition to a $10,000 single sum payment at the end of two years. The effective (actual) interest rate on this obligation is calculated by finding that interest rate which, when used to discount all three payments, results in a present value of $10,000. It is computed as in the previous cases, except here it is more difficult because it requires the use of the trial-and-error method. The calculations are shown below.

PV	= PV of periodic interest payments	+ PV of maturity payment	
PV	= Interest $\times$ (PV ord. annuity: n = 2, i = ?)	+ Maturity $\times$ (PV single sum: n = 2, i = ?)	
$10,000	= $ 1,000 $\times$?	+ $10,000 $\times$?	

Try 12%

PV	= $ 1,000 $\times$	(1.690)	+ $10,000 $\times$	(.7972)
PV	= $ 9,662			

Try 8%

PV	= $ 1,000 $\times$	(1.783)	+ $10,000 $\times$	(.8573)
PV	= $10,356			

Try 10%

PV	= $ 1,000 $\times$	(1.735)	+ $10,000 $\times$	(.8264)
PV	= $10,000			

After setting up the basic equation, different interest rates were simply plugged into the formula until the solution was found. Using a 12 percent interest rate, for example, produced a present value (PV) of $9,662, which was less than $10,000, so a 12 percent discount rate was too high. An 8 percent interest rate was then used, producing a present value of $10,356, which is greater than $10,000, meaning that 8 percent was too low. At this point it was clear that the solution was between 8 percent and 12 percent. Ten percent was then found to be the correct rate. That is, discounting the future cash flows of the obligation at 10 percent produced a present value equal to the FMV of the benefit received ($10,000).

Note in this case that the effective rate of interest (10%) equaled the interest rate stated on the obligation (10%). This equality occurred only because the FMV of the benefit received ($10,000) was equal to the maturity value of the obligation ($10,000). Had the FMV of the benefit received not equaled the maturity value, the effective rate of interest would not have equaled the stated rate. For example, had the FMV of the receipt equaled $9,662, the effective rate would have been 12%.

ACCOUNTING FOR LONG-TERM OBLIGATIONS: THE EFFECTIVE INTEREST METHOD

LO 5   Understanding the effective rate of interest is important because it represents the actual rate of interest associated with an obligation. It is the foundation for the **effective interest method**, which is used to account for long-term contractual obligations—notes, bonds, and capital leases. This method consists of one basic rule:

The interest expense reported during each period of a long-term obligation's contractual life is computed by multiplying the effective interest rate times the balance sheet value of the obligation as of the beginning of the period.

From a user's perspective, the key benefit of this rule is that it guarantees that the long-term liability on the balance sheet (note payable, bond payable, or lease liability) is reported throughout its life at the present value of its future cash flows, discounted at the effective interest rate. Recall from the discussion in Chapter 4 that present value is the theoretical goal of financial measurement.

ACCOUNTING FOR LONG-TERM NOTES PAYABLE

L O 6 Issuing long-term notes is a popular way for major U.S. companies to raise capital. Both **secured** (backed by collateral) and **unsecured notes** are widely used. *Accounting Trends and Techniques* (AICPA, 1994) reports that, of the 600 major U.S. companies surveyed, 429 (72 percent) disclosed unsecured notes and 80 (13 percent) disclosed notes that were backed by collateral.

The issuance of notes normally involves only one or a small group of lenders (usually financial institutions) and can take a number of different contractual forms. Interest-bearing, non-interest-bearing, and installment notes are all quite common, and they can be exchanged for cash and/or noncash items. A **mortgage**, for example, is a cash loan, exchanged for an installment note that is secured by real estate. Machinery and equipment purchases are often received in exchange for (financed with) installment notes. When a note payable is issued to satisfy another outstanding note payable, a **refinancing** has occurred.

The following example illustrates the methods used to account for a non-interest-bearing note exchanged for equipment (2B in Figure 11–2), which is almost identical to such a note being exchanged for cash (2A). Bonds are normally interest-bearing notes exchanged for cash, so that discussion will cover 3A in Figure 11–2. Capital leases are a form of financing the purchase of long-term assets with installment notes, so that discussion will cover 1B in Figure 11–2.

EQUIPMENT EXCHANGED FOR A NON-INTEREST-BEARING NOTE

Assume that on January 1, 1996, Seabell Inc. acquired a piece of equipment with a FMV of $10,288 and, in return, signed a non-interest-bearing note payable with a maturity date of December 31, 1997, and a maturity value of $12,000. The transaction and the associated accounting entries are described in Figure 11–3.

When Seabell acquires the equipment and issues the note, the equipment is recorded at its FMV, the Notes Payable account is recorded at its maturity value, and a Discount on Notes Payable account is debited for the difference. The discount is listed on the balance sheet directly under Notes Payable and subtracted from it in determining the balance sheet value of the note payable, as illustrated in Figure 11–3. The discount can be viewed as a form of "unaccrued interest" because Seabell agreed to pay $12,000 for a piece of equipment that at present is only worth $10,288. Accordingly, the discount is amortized into interest expense over the 2-year life of the note.

The effective interest method is then used to account for the note over its 2-year life. First, the effective interest rate must be determined, which is equal to 8%, the interest rate that equates the present value of the note's future cash flows with the FMV of the equipment ($10,288). Then, the effective interest rate (8%) is multiplied by the book value of the note at the beginning of 1996 ($10,288) to determine the interest expense for 1996 ($823). The adjusting journal entry at the end of 1996 serves to recognize interest expense and amortize a portion of the discount. The remaining amount of the discount ($889) is then subtracted from the Notes Payable account to determine the book value of the liability as of the end of 1996 ($11,111). The same procedure is then followed at the end of 1997 to recognize interest expense and amortize the remainder of the discount ($889), and the maturity value ($12,000) is paid off at the end of the second year.

FIGURE 11–3

Accounting for a non-interest-bearing note exchanged for equipment

Period:	1/1/96 ⟶	12/31/96 ⟶	12/31/97
Payment:	+Equipment	−$0	−$0
	(FMV = $10,288)		−$12,000

JOURNAL

Equipment (+A)	10,288	Interest Exp. (E, −SE)	823*	Interest Exp. (E, −SE)	889**
Disc. on Notes Pay. (−L)	1,712	Disc. on Notes Pay. (+L)	823	Disc. on Notes Pay. (+L)	889
Notes Pay. (+L)	12,000				
				Notes Pay. (−L)	12,000
				Cash (−A)	12,000

BALANCE SHEET VALUE

Notes payable	$12,000		Notes payable	$12,000		
Less: Discount	1,712	$10,288	Less: Discount	889	$11,111	

GENERAL LEDGER

DISCOUNT ON NOTES PAYABLE

(1/1/96)	1,712		
		(12/31/96 adj.)	823
(12/31/96)	889		
		(12/31/97 adj.)	889
	0		

*$10,288 × 8%
**$11,111 × 8%

IMPORTANT POINTS ABOUT THE EXAMPLE

Several features about this example are important. First, the accounting treatment would have been virtually the same had a cash amount of $10,288 been received instead of equipment with a FMV of $10,288. Only the initial entry would have differed, reflecting a cash receipt instead of equipment.

Second, even though the note payable has no stated interest rate, it has an effective (actual) interest rate of 8%, which must be recognized over the life of the note. In line with the effective interest method, the interest expense in each period is simply the effective rate multiplied by the balance sheet value of the note at the beginning of that period. The interest expense recognized in the second period ($889) is greater than that in the first ($823) because the balance sheet value of the note increased from $10,288 to $11,111. The company was one year closer to the ultimate $12,000 payment. Finally, the effective interest method ensured that the balance sheet value of the note throughout its life was equal to the present value of the note's future cash flows, discounted at the effective interest rate. For example, the present value of $12,000 discounted back 1 year at 8% is equal to $11,111 ($12,000 × .92593) and discounted back 2 years is equal to $10,288 ($12,000 × .85734).[5] These fundamental features are very important because they apply to other forms of notes as well as bonds and capital leases.

5. Instead of the effective interest method, some companies amortize Discounts on Long-Term Obligations (e.g., notes and bonds) using the straight-line method. That is, they amortize equal amounts of the discount into interest expense during each period of the note's life. According to generally accepted accounting principles, the straight-line method is acceptable only if it results in numbers (i.e., interest expense and book value of the note payable) that are not materially different from those produced by the effective interest method. The straight-line method misstates periodic interest expense and the balance sheet value of the note because it fails to reflect the actual interest rate paid by the borrower.

BONDS PAYABLE

Companies issue bonds to raise large amounts of capital, usually to finance expensive, long-term projects. Several years ago, for example, DuPont borrowed well over $3 billion, much of it through bond issuances. As stated in the annual report, the proceeds were "primarily used to finance the repurchase of common shares, higher capital expenditures, and higher levels of working capital." Recently, Colgate-Palmolive issued $150 million in thirty-year bonds, which received A1 and A+ ratings from the Moody's and Standard & Poor's rating agencies. The additional cash was used to finance "acquisitions in the United States and internationally to complement core business activity."

Bonds are normally sold to the public through a third party (called an underwriter), such as an investment banker or a financial institution.[6] They are usually interest-bearing notes that involve formal commitments requiring the issuing company to make cash interest payments to the bondholder and a principal payment (usually in the amount of $1,000 per bond) when the bond matures, which is usually between five and thirty years from the date of issuance. After bonds are initially issued, they are generally freely negotiable; that is, they can be purchased and sold in the open market. Both the New York and the American Security Exchanges maintain active bond markets. In the first half of 1991, for example, U.S. companies issued bonds with a total market value of over $200 billion.[7]

BOND TERMINOLOGY

Figure 11–4 summarizes the important components of a bond. The **life** of the bond is the time period extending from the date of its issuance to its maturity date. At the **maturity date,** the end of the bond's life, an amount of cash equal to the face value (*principal, par value, or maturity value*) is paid to the bondholder. The *face value*, the amount written on the face of the bond, is usually $1,000. The **interest payment**, which is paid to the bondholders on each semiannual interest payment date, is computed by multiplying the annual interest rate stated on the bond (the stated or coupon rate) times the face value of the issuance. This amount is then divided by 2 because the stated rate is an annual rate, and the interest payments are made every six months. The **proceeds**, the amount collected by the issuing company when the bonds are issued, are equal to the price paid by the purchasers of the bonds multiplied by the number of bonds issued. This amount is usually net of the issuance costs incurred by the issuing company.[8]

To illustrate, on July 1, 1995, Northern States Power Company issued 250,000 bonds, each with a face value of $1,000 and a stated interest rate of 7.125 percent, due to mature 30 years later, on July 1, 2025. The company collected $990.68 on each bond, which totaled approximately $248 million for the entire bond issuance. In terms similar to those in Figure 11–4, the cash flows associated with this bond issuance and

---

6. Major underwriters include Merrill Lynch, Goldman Sachs, First Boston, Salomon Brothers, Shearson Lehman Hutton, Morgan Stanley, Prudential Bache, Kidder Peabody, Dean Witter, and Paine Webber.
7. *The Wall Street Journal,* July 1, 1991, p. C1.
8. To simplify the discussion, these issuance costs are assumed to be zero in the remainder of the chapter.

FIGURE 11–4

Bond terminology

Issuance Date		Time to Maturity				Maturity Date
0	6 months	1 year	6 months	2 years	(etc.) . . .	
Proceeds at Issuance	Interest Payment	Interest Payment	Interest Payment	Interest Payment	. . .	Interest Payment
						Face Value Payment

TERMS OF BOND CONTRACT

Life: Time period from date of issuance to the maturity date, usually from five to thirty years.

Maturity date: Date when the dollar amount written on face of bond (face value) and final interest payment are paid to the bondholder.

Face value: Dollar amount written on the bond certificate. Sometimes referred to as the *principal*, *par value*, or *maturity value*, the face value is usually $1,000.

Interest payment: The interest rate stated on the bond multiplied by the face value. This rate is called the *stated rated*, or *coupon rate*, and it is usually fixed for the entire life of the bond.

Proceeds at issuance: Dollar amount collected when the bonds are issued, equal to the price the buyers paid for each bond multiplied by the number of bonds issued. This amount is usually net of issuance fees.

Effective interest rate: The actual interest rate paid on the bond. The rate, when used to discount the future interest and principal cash payments, results in a present value that is equal to the amount received by the issuer.

OTHER PROVISIONS OF THE BOND CONTRACT

Restrictions: The bond contract may restrict the issuing company in certain ways to ensure that the interest and principal payments will be made. For example, a certain current ratio or level of working capital may be required, dividends may be restricted, or additional debt may be limited.

Security: The bond contract may specify that collateral be paid in case of default (i.e., interest or principal payments are not made). Unsecured bonds are called *debentures*.

Call provision: The bond contract may specify that the issuing company can buy back (retire) the bonds at a specified price after a certain date during the life of the bond. The specified price is usually greater than the face value.

---

the calculations of the proceeds, the semiannual interest payment, and entire maturity value are shown in Figure 11–5.

In addition to the face value, maturity date, and stated interest rate, the bond contract may include a number of other important provisions. Three such provisions are described in Figure 11–4: restrictive covenants, security, and call provisions.

Restrictive **covenants** are imposed by bondholders to protect their interests and may restrict management in a number of significant ways. Nordstrom, a large specialty store operating throughout the United States, states in its annual report that the company has entered into long-term debt agreements that (1) limit additional long-term debt and lease obligations, (2) require that working capital must be at least $50 million or 25 percent of current liabilities, whichever is greater, (3) limit short-term borrowings, and (4) restrict dividends to shareholders.

FIGURE 11–5

Example of bond issuance: Northern States Power Company (dollars in thousands)

Issuance Date (7/1/95)	Time to Maturity: Thirty Years				Maturity Date (7/1/25)
0 ⟶	6 months ⟶	1 year ⟶	6 months ⟶	2 years ⟶	30 years
Proceeds	Interest	Interest	Interest	Interest ...	Interest and face value
+$247,670[a]	−$8,906[b]	−$8,906	−$8,906	−$8,906	−$8,906 −$250,000

[a] 250,000 bonds × $990.68 = $247,670
[b] (250,000 bonds × $1,000 × 7.125%) ÷ 2 = $8,906

Security provisions also protect the interests of bondholders by ensuring that assets are pledged in case of default. As of December 31, 1994, for example, Ford Motor Company had outstanding bonds with a balance sheet value of 98 million, which were secured by land, buildings, and equipment. Bonds with no assets backing them are called **unsecured bonds** or **debentures**. At December 31, 1994, Ford had outstanding debentures valued on the balance sheet at $560 million.[9]

A **call provision** grants to the issuing company the right to retire (repurchase) outstanding bonds after a designated date for a specified price. This provision serves to protect the interests of the issuing company, enabling it to remove the debt if economic conditions are appropriate. If interest rates and the economy fall, for example, a company may wish to repurchase outstanding bonds that require relatively high interest payments. The following excerpt from a financial report of CBS, a major television network, refers to a call provision on certain of the company's outstanding bonds.

"The . . . debentures are due June 1, 2022 and may not be redeemed prior to June 1, 2002. On and after that date they may be redeemed, at the option of the Company, as a whole at any time, or in part from time to time, at specified redemption prices."

THE PRICE OF A BOND

Bond prices are basically determined by what potential bondholders are willing to pay for the right to receive the semiannual interest payments and cash in the amount of the face value at maturity.[10] The credit rating of the issuing company as well as the stated interest rate, covenants, security arrangements, call provisions, and many other terms of the bond contract directly influence the price at which bonds are issued. Bonds issued by companies with high credit ratings, offering high stated interest rates, and backed by collateral tend to sell for higher prices than unsecured bonds issued by companies with low credit ratings, offering low stated interest rates.

9. Debentures with a very low priority for the issuing company's assets in case of liquidation are referred to as *junk bonds;* bonds rated by credit-rating agencies at lower than investment grade. Many of the mergers in the 1980s were financed with junk bonds. *The Wall Street Journal* (March 1991) reported that 32 U.S. companies defaulted on their junk bond payments in the first quarter of 1991. Such defaults had been rising due to the inability of debt-laden companies to repay, restructure, or refinance their debt.

10. A discussion of how bond prices are determined is contained in Appendix 11B.

Bond prices are usually expressed as a percentage of the face value ($1,000), and may be less than, equal to, or greater than the face value. Bonds issued for less than $1,000 are issued at a *discount*. Bonds issued for $1,000 are issued at *face (or par) value*. Bonds issued for greater than $1,000 are issued at a *premium*.

Late in October of 1995, Mohegan Tribal Gaming Authority, Trizec Finance Ltd., and Hollywood Casino Corporation each announced a major bond issuance in *The Wall Street Journal*. Mohegan offered 175,000 bonds with a time to maturity of seven years and a stated interest rate of 13.5% at a price of 100 (percent) of face value ($1,000 per bond). Trizec offered 250,000 bonds with a time to maturity of ten years and a stated interest rate of 10.875% at a discount price of 99.251 (percent) of face value ($992.51 per bond). Hollywood Casino offered 210,000 bonds with a time to maturity of eight years and a stated rate of 12.75% at a discount price of 95.209 (percent) of face value ($952.09 per bond). Ford Motor Company recently issued bonds with a time to maturity of three years and a stated interest rate of 13 percent at a premium price of 100.6 (percent) of the face value ($1,006 per bond).

THE EFFECTIVE RATE AND THE STATED RATE

As with other interest-bearing obligations, the effective (actual) rate of interest paid on a bond is not necessarily equal to the stated rate. Recall that the effective rate is that rate which, when used to discount the future contractual cash payments, results in a present value that is equal to the FMV of the receipt (i.e., issuance price). Depending on the relationship between the issuance price and the face value, the effective rate of interest on a bond may be lower than, equal to, or higher than the stated interest rate. Figure 11–6 illustrates these three relationships.

The effective interest rates of three different bonds are compared. Each bond has a $1,000 face value, a five-year life, and a 6 percent stated annual interest rate (paid semiannually). They differ in that (1) is issued at an $81 discount (91.9), (2) is issued at a $90 premium (109.0), and (3) is issued at par (100.0). In each case the effective interest rate is determined by finding that rate which, when used to discount the interest and face value payments, results in a present value that equals the issue price.[11] The

FIGURE 11–6

Bond prices and the relationship between the effective rate and the stated rate (bond terms: $1,000 face value, a 6% stated rate, and a 5-year life)

EFFECTIVE RATE		STATED RATE	FACE VALUE	PRICE (PRESENT VALUE)	TYPE OF ISSUE
1. 8%	>	6%	$1,000	$ 919 = 30(8.1109) + $1,000(.6756)	Discount
2. 4%	<	6%	$1,000	$1,090 = 30(8.9826) + $1,000(.8203)	Premium
3. 6%	=	6%	$1,000	$1,000 = 30(8.5302) + $1,000(.7441)	Par

11. When using present value tables to infer an effective interest rate or to compute the price of a bond, keep in mind that interest payments are made on a semiannual basis. Accordingly, when finding the table factors for the interest payment annuity and the lump sum payment, the number of periods must be doubled and the discount rate must be halved. For example, the present value (PV) of a bond with a ten-year life, a $1,000 face value, and a 10 percent stated interest rate, discounted at 8 percent, would be computed as below. Note that the table factors are based on an N of 20 (10 × 2) and an i of 4 percent (8%/2).

$$PV = \text{Semiannual interest (PV of annuity: N = 20, i = 4\%)} + \text{Face value (PV lump sum: N = 20, i = 4\%)}$$

=	$50	(13.59)	+	$1,000	(.456)
=		$679.50	+		$456
= $1,135.50					

relationship among the price, the effective interest rate, and the stated interest rate is summarized below.

1. When the issuance price of a bond is greater that its face value (*premium*), the effective rate is less than the stated rate.
2. When the issuance price of a bond is less than its face value (*discount*), the effective rate is greater than the stated rate.
3. When the issuance price of a bond is equal to its face value (*par*), the effective rate is equal to the stated rate.

ACCOUNTING FOR BONDS PAYABLE

The effective interest method is used to account for bonds payable. The following examples use the effective interest method to account for three different bonds: one issued at face (par) value, one issued at a discount, and one issued at a premium. The following information is used in all three cases.

Assume that Webster International issues ten bonds, each with a face value of $1,000, a stated interest rate of 10 percent, and time to maturity of two years.[12] Interest payments of $500 [($10,000 × 10 percent)/2] are to be made semiannually. In Case 1, the bonds are issued at face (par), so that the effective rate (10 percent) equals the stated rate (10 percent). In Case 2, the bonds are issued at a discount, so that the effective rate (12 percent) is greater than the stated rate (10 percent). In Case 3, the bonds are issued at a premium, so the effective rate (8 percent) is less than the stated rate (10 percent). Figure 11–7 shows the cash flows associated with the three bond issuances. Note that the cash flows are identical for all three bond issuances except for the issuance price.

FIGURE 11–7

Cash flows for bonds payable: three cases compared

Face value: 10 bonds × $1,000 per bond   = $10,000
Semiannual interest payment: ($10,000 × 10%) ÷ 2 = $ 500

Issuance Date	6 months	1 year	6 months	Maturity Date
Case 1: Issued at $10,000 (face) +$10,000	−$500	−$500	−$500	−$ 500 −$10,000
Case 2: Issued at $9,654 (discount) + $9,654	−$500	−$500	−$500	−$ 500 −$10,000
Case 3: Issued at $10,363 (premium) +$10,363	−$500	−$500	−$500	−$ 500 −$10,000

---

12. Bonds are normally issued in much greater amounts, and their lives are usually considerably longer than two years. We have chosen a two-year life and a relatively small issuance to make the example manageable within the structure of this text. The shortened example, however, is sufficient to illustrate the important concepts.

CASE 1: BONDS ISSUED AT PAR

In Case 1 the bonds are issued at par ($10,000) and the effective rate (10 percent) is equal to the stated rate (10 percent). The journal entries, balance sheet values of bonds payable, and present value of the future cash flows discounted at the effective interest rate are shown in Figure 11–8.

FIGURE 11–8

Bonds issued at face value: Case 1

DATE	JOURNAL ENTRY			BALANCE SHEET VALUE	PRESENT VALUE
Issue	Cash (+A)	10,000			
	Bonds Payable (+L)		10,000	$10,000	$10,000
	Issued bond.				
6 months	Interest Expense (E, −SE)	500			
	Cash (−A)		500	10,000	10,000
	Paid interest.				
1 year	Interest Expense (E, −SE)	500			
	Cash (−A)		500	10,000	10,000
	Paid interest.				
6 months	Interest Expense (E, −SE)	500			
	Cash (−A)		500	10,000	10,000
	Paid interest.				
Maturity	Interest Expense (E, −SE)	500			
	Cash (−A)		500	10,000	10,000
	Paid interest.				
	Bonds Payable (−L)	10,000			
	Cash (−A)		10,000	0	0
	Paid principal.				

Interest expense = Balance sheet value at beginning of period × [effective interest rate (10%) ÷ 2]
Cash interest payment = ($10,000 × 10%) ÷ 2
Balance sheet value = Face value ($10,000)
Present value = Remaining cash outflows discounted at effective interest rate (10%)

When bonds are issued at par, the journal entries are very straightforward because neither a discount nor a premium need be considered. The Bonds Payable account is simply carried on the balance sheet at $10,000 until maturity. Note that the present value of the remaining cash flows, discounted at 10 percent, is also equal to $10,000 throughout the life of the bond. The interest expense recognized in each six-month period ($500), which appears on the income statement, is calculated by multiplying the effective interest rate (5 percent = 10 percent/2) times the balance sheet value of the bonds payable at the beginning of the period ($10,000). This calculation is the essence of the effective interest method and in this case gives rise to an amount equal to the $500 cash payment. These two dollar amounts are equal because the effective rate, which determines the interest expense, is equal to the stated rate, which determines the interest payment.

CASE 2: BONDS ISSUED AT A DISCOUNT

In Case 2 the bonds are issued at a $346 discount, and the effective rate of interest (12 percent) is greater than the stated rate (10 percent). Figure 11–9 shows the journal entries, balance sheet value of bonds payable, and present value of the future cash flows discounted at the effective interest rate.

FIGURE 11–9

Bonds issued at a discount: Case 2

DATE	JOURNAL ENTRY			BALANCE SHEET VALUE	PRESENT VALUE
Issue	Cash (+A)	9,654			
	Discount on Bonds (−L)	346			
	Bonds Payable (+L)		10,000	$ 9,654	$ 9,654
	Issued bond.				
6 months	Interest Expense (E, −SE)	579			
	Discount on Bonds (+L)		79	+79	
	Cash (−A)		500	9,733	9,733
	Paid interest and amortized discount.				
1 Year	Interest Expense (E, −SE)	584			
	Discount on Bonds (+L)		84	+84	
	Cash (−A)		500	9,817	9,817
	Paid interest and amortized discount.				
6 months	Interest Expense (E, −SE)	589			
	Discount on Bonds (+L)		89	+89	
	Cash (−A)		500	9,906	9,906
	Paid interest and amortized discount.				
Maturity	Interest Expense (E, −SE)	594			
	Discount on Bonds (+L)		94	+94	
	Cash (−A)		500	10,000	10,000
	Paid interest and amortized discount.				
	Bonds Payable (−L)	10,000			
	Cash (−A)		10,000	0	0
	Paid principal.				

Interest expense = Balance sheet value at beginning of period × [effective interest rate (12%) ÷ 2]
Cash interest payment = ($10,000 × 10%) ÷ 2
Balance sheet value = Face value ($10,000) less unamortized discount

or

Balance sheet value at beginning of period + discount amortized during period
Present value = Remaining cash outflows discounted at effective interest rate (12%)

The bond payable is initially recorded at $10,000, which is greater than the $9,654 cash proceeds; consequently, a $346 **Discount on Bonds Payable** is recognized. This discount is disclosed on the balance sheet as a contra liability and is subtracted from the Bonds Payable account. It can be viewed as unaccrued interest waiting to be expensed over the life of the bond. The balance sheet disclosure of the Bonds Payable account and the discount at issuance appears as follows:

Bonds payable	**$10,000**	
Less: Discount on bonds payable	**346**	**$9,654**

In applying the effective interest method, interest expense is calculated each period by multiplying the effective interest rate (6 percent = 12 percent/2) by the balance sheet value of the bond liability at the beginning of the period. For example, at the end of the first six-month period, the $579 interest expense is computed thus: 6 percent × $9,654. The cash interest payment is only $500, so $79 is credited to the Discount account. The $79 of amortized discount represents the interest cost, recognized in the first period, associated with receiving only $9,654 for a bond that requires a payment of $10,000 at maturity. The remaining (unamortized) portion of the discount ($267 = $346 − $79) is subtracted from Bonds Payable on the balance sheet to bring its balance sheet value to present value ($9,733).[13] This process is repeated every six months throughout the life of the bond, and eventually the entire discount is amortized into interest expense. Note also that the effective interest method ensures that the balance sheet value of the bond liability is equal to the present value of the remaining cash flows, discounted at 12 percent, throughout the life of the bond.

CASE 3: BONDS ISSUED AT A PREMIUM

In Case 3 the bonds are issued at a $363 premium, and the effective rate of interest (8 percent) is less than the stated rate (10 percent). The journal entries, balance sheet value of bonds payable, and present value of the future cash flows discounted at the effective interest rate appear in Figure 11–10.

The bond payable is initially recorded at $10,000, which is less than the $10,363 cash proceeds, so a $363 **Premium on Bonds Payable** is recognized. This premium is disclosed on the balance sheet as an addition to the Bonds Payable account. It can be viewed as a reduction in interest expense (or a deferred revenue) waiting to be recognized over the life of the bond. The balance sheet disclosure of the Bonds Payable account and the premium at issuance appear as follows:

Bonds payable	**$10,000**	
Plus: Premium on bonds payable	**363**	**$10,363**

In applying the effective interest method, interest expense is calculated each period by multiplying the effective interest rate (4 percent = 8 percent ÷ 2) by the balance sheet value of the bond liability at the beginning of the period. For example, at the end of the first six-month period, the $415 interest expense is equal to 4 percent × $10,363. The cash interest payment is $500, so $85 is debited to the Premium on Bonds Payable account. The $85 of amortized premium represents reduced interest cost, recognized in the first period, associated with receiving $10,363 for a bond that requires a payment of only $10,000 at maturity. The remaining (unamortized) portion of the premium ($278 = $363 − $85) is added to Bonds Payable on the balance sheet to bring its balance sheet value to the present value ($10,278).[14] This process is repeated every six months throughout the life of the bond, and eventually the entire premium is amortized

---

13. Subtracting the unamortized portion of the discount from Bonds Payable is equivalent to adding the amortized amount of the discount to the balance sheet value, which is shown in Figure 11–9.
14. Adding the unamortized portion of the premium to Bonds Payable is equivalent to subtracting the amortized amount of the premium from the balance sheet value, which is shown in Figure 11–10.

FIGURE 11–10

Bonds issued at a premium: Case 3

DATE	JOURNAL ENTRY			BALANCE SHEET VALUE	PRESENT VALUE
Issue	Cash (+A)	10,363			
	Premium on Bonds Payable (+L)		363		
	Bonds Payable (+L)		10,000	$10,363	$10,363
	Issued bond.				
6 months	Interest Expense (E, −SE)	415			
	Premium on Bonds Payable (−L)	85		−85	
	Cash (−A)		500	10,278	10,278
	Paid interest and amortized premium.				
1 Year	Interest Expense (E, −SE)	411			
	Premium on Bonds Payable (−L)	89		−89	
	Cash (−A)		500	10,189	10,189
	Paid interest and amortized premium.				
6 months	Interest Expense (E, −SE)	407			
	Premium on Bonds Payable (−L)	93		−93	
	Cash (−A)		500	10,096	10,096
	Paid interest and amortized premium.				
Maturity	Interest Expense (E, −SE)	404			
	Premium on Bonds Payable (−L)	96		−96	
	Cash (−A)		500	10,000	10,000
	Paid interest and amortized premium.				
	Bonds Payable (−L)	10,000			
	Cash (−A)		10,000	0	0
	Paid principal.				

Interest expense = Balance sheet value at beginning of period × [effective interest rate (8%) ÷ 2]
Cash interest payment = ($10,000 × 10%) ÷ 2
Balance sheet value = Face value ($10,000) plus unamortized premium

or

Balance sheet value at beginning of period − premium amortized during period
Present value = Remaining cash outflows discounted at effective interest rate (8%)

into interest expense. Note, once again, that the effective interest method keeps the balance sheet value of the bond liability equal to the present value of the remaining cash flows, discounted at 8 percent, throughout the life of the bond.

ISSUING BONDS AT PAR, DISCOUNT, OR PREMIUM: A COMPARISON

Bond amortization tables for Case 1 (par), Case 2 (discount), and Case 3 (premium) are contained in Figure 11–11. Recall that the effective (semi-annual) interest rates for Case 1, 2, and 3 are 5%, 6%, and 4%.

The effective interest method ensures that the actual interest rate on a bond issuance is constant throughout its life. Note, however, that interest expense is constant when bonds are issued at par, increasing when bonds are issued at a discount, and decreasing when bonds are issued at a premium. This occurs because the effective rate is multiplied by the balance sheet value of the Bonds Payable, which is constant when bonds are issued at par, increasing when they are issued at a discount, and

FIGURE 11–11

Bond amortization tables

DATE	INTEREST PAYMENT	INTEREST EXPENSE	AMORTIZATION DISCOUNT/ PREMIUM	UNAMORTIZED DISCOUNT/ PREMIUM	NET BOOK VALUE
ISSUED AT PAR					
Issue					$10,000
6 months	$500	$500	0	0	10,000
1 year	500	500	0	0	10,000
6 months	500	500	0	0	10,000
Maturity	500	500	0	0	10,000
ISSUED AT DISCOUNT					
Issue				346	$ 9,654
6 months	$500	$579	79	267	9,733
1 year	500	584	84	183	9,817
6 months	500	589	89	94	9,906
Maturity	500	594	94	0	10,000
ISSUED AT PREMIUM					
Issue				363	$10,363
6 months	$500	$415	85	278	10,278
1 year	500	411	89	189	10,189
6 months	500	407	93	96	10,096
Maturity	500	404	96	0	10,000

KEY:

Interest payment = Stated (semiannual) interest rate (5%) × maturity value ($10,000)
Interest expense = Effective interest rate × net book value at beginning of period
Amortized discount/premium = Difference between interest payment and interest expense
Unamortized discount/premium = Discount/premium of prior period minus amortized discount/premium
Net book value = Maturity value ($10,000) minus unamortized discount or plus unamortized premium

decreasing when they are issued at a premium. In all cases the balance sheet value is equal to the face value ($10,000) when the bonds are paid off at maturity.

THE EFFECTIVE INTEREST METHOD AND CHANGING INTEREST RATES

LO 7 We have stated on several occasions that the effective interest method ensures that long-term liabilities on the balance sheet are valued at the present value of the liability's future (remaining) cash flows, discounted at the effective interest rate *as of the date of issuance*. Under this method the same effective interest rate is used throughout the life of the liability, even though interest rates in the financial markets may vary substantially. By ignoring changes in market interest rates, the effective interest method causes the balance sheet amount of the liability to equal something other than its actual present value. It fails to recognize economic gains and losses that affect the issuing company's financial condition.

To illustrate, assume that Olsen Foods issued ten bonds with $1,000 face value for $1,000 each. The stated annual interest rate is 8 percent, and the bonds mature at the end of five years. Because the bonds were issued at face value, the effective interest rate is also 8 percent, and under the effective interest method, the following journal entry would be recorded at issuance.

Cash (+A)   **10,000**
    Bonds Payable (+L)   **10,000**
Issued bond (10 × $1,000).

Throughout its five-year life the bond payable would be carried on the balance sheet at $10,000, the present value (PV) of the remaining cash flows, discounted at 8 percent, the effective interest rate as of the issue date. If market interest rates fall by 2 percent during the first year of the bond's life, however, the economic value of the bond liability becomes $10,702, the present value of the remaining cash flows discounted at 6 percent (8% − 2%).[15] As a result, Olsen would incur an economic loss of approximately $702 ($10,702 − $10,000). The intuition underlying such a loss is that Olsen is paying an effective rate of 8 percent on its outstanding bonds while market rates are somewhat lower. In addition, the liability on Olsen's balance sheet is understated by $702.

If market interest rates rise by 2 percent during the first year, the economic value of the bond liability becomes $9,354, the present value of the remaining cash flows discounted at 10 percent (8% + 2%).[16] Olsen, therefore, would enjoy an economic gain of approximately $646 ($10,000 − $9,354). In this case Olsen is paying only 8 percent on its outstanding bonds while market interest rates are somewhat higher, and the liability on Olsen's balance sheet is overstated by $646.

The fact that fluctuating interest rates are not recognized is an important limitation of the effective interest method. Both net income and the balance sheet value of the outstanding liability are misstated. Astute financial statement users should be aware of this limitation and be able to improve the usefulness of the financial statements by adjusting reported income and liabilities to reflect such fluctuations. As discussed later, certain required disclosures may help users make such adjustments.

BOND REDEMPTIONS

Bonds can be **redeemed** (repurchased or retired) on or before the maturity date. When this occurs, amortization of any discount or premium is updated, the dollar amount in the Bonds Payable account and any unamortized discount or premium are written off the books, a cash payment is recorded, and a gain or loss is recognized on the redemption, if the cash payment differs from the net book value of the liability.

BOND REDEMPTIONS AT MATURITY

When bonds are redeemed at the maturity date, the issuing company simply pays cash to the bondholders in the amount of the face value and removes the bond payable from the balance sheet. At maturity, the bond payable is equal to the face value because,

---

15. The economic value of the liability is equal to the liability's future cash flows discounted at the market rate.
$10,702 = $400 (PV annual: n = 8, i = 3%) + $10,000 (PV single sum: n = 8, i = 3%)
    = $400   (7.01969)   + $10,000   (.78941)
16.
$ 9,354 = $400 (PV annuity: n = 8, i = 5%) + $10,000 (PV single sum: n = 8, i = 5%)
    = $400   (6.46321)   + $10,000   (.67684)

after the final entry to record interest expense, any discount or premium on the bonds will have been completely amortized. Journal entries to record bond redemptions at the maturity dates for bonds issued at face (Case 1), at a discount (Case 2), and at a premium (Case 3) appear in Figures 11–8, 11–9, and 11–10, respectively. Note that in all three cases the journal entry to record the redemption takes the following form.

Bonds Payable (−L)	**10,000**	
Cash (−A)		**10,000**

Redeemed bonds with a $10,000 face value at maturity.

BOND REDEMPTIONS BEFORE MATURITY

Many companies exercise call provisions or purchase their outstanding bonds on the open market before the maturity date. As indicated earlier, as economic conditions (especially interest rates) change, companies may wish to retire long-term debts.

To illustrate, consider companies that issued bonds in the mid-1980's when interest rates, compared to recent rates, were relatively high. Many of these companies recently redeemed these bonds prior to maturity, recognizing losses because the market value of the debt exceeded its book value. Often new bonds were then issued at considerably lower rates. In 1993, for example, Scott Paper Company retired $72.1 million of unsecured bonds (with an effective rate of 11.5%) prior to maturity, and it recognized a $9.6 million loss on the transaction. That same year Scott issued additional debt with effective rates that averaged 8%–9%.

To illustrate the redemption of a bond issuance prior to maturity at a loss, assume that bonds with a $100,000 face value and a $5,000 unamortized discount are redeemed for $102,000. The $7,000 loss on redemption would decrease net income and appear in a separate section of the income statement, referred to as *extraordinary items.*[17]

Bonds Payable (−L)	**100,000**	
Loss on Redemption (Lo, −SE)	**7,000**	
Discount on Bonds Payable (+L)		**5,000**
Cash (−A)		**102,000**

Redeemed bonds prior to maturity.

If bonds with a $100,000 face value and a $3,000 unamortized premium are redeemed for $102,000, the following journal entry is recorded, and a gain on the redemption is recognized on the income statement as an extraordinary item.

Bonds Payable (−L)	**100,000**	
Premium on Bonds Payable (−L)	**3,000**	
Cash (−A)		**102,000**
Gain on Redemption (Ga, +SE)		**1,000**

Redeemed bonds prior to maturity.

FINANCIAL INSTRUMENTS AND OFF-BALANCE-SHEET RISKS

The FASB recently passed a standard requiring that companies disclose the market values of certain financial instruments, whether or not they are recognized on the balance sheet. Financial instruments listed on the balance sheet include (1) short-term

---

17. Extraordinary items are discussed in Chapter 13.

investments in equity securities, (2) notes receivable and investments in debt securities, and (3) long-term debts. The accounting methods used to ensure that (1) and (2) are carried at market value are discussed in Chapter 8 and Appendix 11A, respectively. Considering long-term debts, the market value is usually disclosed in a separate footnote and approximates the present value of the future cash outflows associated with the debt, discounted at the current market rate of interest for similar obligations. The excerpt below, which was taken from the 1994 annual report of Federal Express, illustrates this disclosure.

"At May 31, 1994, the Company's long-term debt . . . had a carrying value of approximately $1,630,000,000 and fair value of approximately $1,740,000,000. The estimated fair value was determined based on quoted market prices or on the current rates offered for debt with similar terms and maturities."

In this case the market (fair) value of the debt ($1.74 billion) exceeds its balance sheet value ($1.63 billion), suggesting that market interest rates have fallen since Federal Express issued the obligations. One could argue that Federal Express experienced a loss in the amount by which the market value exceeds the balance sheet value, even though no such loss appears on the income statement. Users may wish to reduce reported net income accordingly. Similarly, if the balance sheet value exceeded the market value, users may wish to increase the net income reported by Federal Express to reflect the gain.

Many companies also carry financial instruments not listed on the balance sheet, many of which involve significant risks. Examples include commitments to guarantee the credit of third parties (e.g., subsidiaries) and commitments to provide financing to customers who purchase certain inventory items. Another example is financing arrangements often designed to reduce the risks associated with fluctuations in interest rates and the value of foreign currencies relative to the U.S. dollar. While these arrangements are normally covered in advanced texts, users should know that the public disclosures of most major U.S. companies contain extensive descriptions of these instruments and that such instruments often reflect risks borne by the company that are captured nowhere on the balance sheet.

LEASES

L O 8 A **lease** is a contract granting use or occupation of property during a specified period of time in exchange for rent payments. Such contracts are a very popular way to finance business activities. Companies often lease, rather than purchase, land, buildings, machinery, equipment, and other holdings, primarily to avoid the risks and associated costs of ownership. *Accounting Trends and Techniques* (New York: AICPA, 1994) reports that, of the 600 major U.S. companies surveyed, 544 (91 percent) disclosed some form of material lease arrangement. Many of the major retailers, for example, lease most of the facilities in which they conduct operations. Kmart stores are almost always leased for terms of 25 years with multiple five-year renewal options. The company's annual lease payments approximate $1 billion.

A number of commercial airlines have recently moved toward leasing as a means of financing new aircraft. *The Wall Street Journal* reported that "International carriers such as Lufthansa, British Airways, Singapore Airlines, and Malaysian Airlines have viewed (leasing) as more attractive than issuing public debt or arranging bank financing to purchase planes outright. Small airlines, such as Seattle-based Alaska Air

Group, have been leasing companies' principal customers." America West Airlines, based in Phoenix, Ariz., says "its launch would not have been possible if it had had to purchase outright its $70 million of aircraft."[18]

For purposes of financial accounting, lease arrangements are divided into two categories: operating leases and capital leases.

OPERATING LEASES

In a pure leasing arrangement an individual or entity (*lessor*), who owns land, buildings, equipment, or other property, transfers the right to use this property to another individual or entity (*lessee*) in exchange for periodic cash payments over a specified period of time. Normally, the terms of the lease are defined by contract, and over the period of the lease, the owner is responsible for the property's normal maintenance and upkeep. The lessee assumes none of the risks of ownership, and at the end of the lease, the right to use the property reverts to the owner.

These types of agreements are called **operating leases**, and accounting for them is straightforward. The property is reported as an asset on the owner's balance sheet, and the periodic rental payments are recorded as rent revenue on the owner's income statement. If applicable, as in the case of a fixed asset, the capitalized cost of the property is depreciated by the owner. The lessee, on the other hand, recognizes no asset or liability, but simply reports rent expense on the income statement as the periodic rent payments are accrued.

CAPITAL LEASES

Many contractual arrangements, which appear on the surface to be leases, are actually installment purchases, where the risks and benefits of ownership have been transferred to the lessee. The present value of the periodic lease payments, for example, may approximate the FMV of the property. It is also possible that the property may revert, or be sold at a bargain price, to the lessee at the end of the lease period. Further, the period of the lease may be equivalent to the asset's useful life. In such situations the lessee has actually purchased the property from the lessor and is paying it off in installments, i.e., an asset has been received in exchange for an installment note payable. Such leases are referred to as **capital leases**, and they should be treated on the financial statements as purchases. That is, the leased property should be included as an asset on the balance sheet of the lessee, and the obligation associated with the future lease payments should be reported as a liability.

Suppose that on January 1, 1997, Hitzelberger Supply (lessee) signs an agreement to lease a bulldozer from Jones and Sons (lessor) for a period of two years. The contract specifies that Hitzelberger must pay $10,000 on December 31 of 1997 and 1998, and the bulldozer can be purchased by Hitzelberger at the end of the lease for a nominal sum. The market price of the bulldozer at the time of the agreement is $17,355, resulting in an effective interest rate of 10 percent, which is equivalent to the interest rate that would be charged if Hitzelberger borrowed funds to purchase the bulldozer.[19]

18. Eileen White Rerd, "For Airplane Lessors Business Is Greater," *The Wall Street Journal,* May 20, 1988, p. 12.
19. The effective rate of interest is determined by finding that rate which, when used to discount the future cash flows of the lease, results in a present value that is equal to the market price of the bulldozer. Refer to the discussion earlier in this chapter on the effective interest rate.

Hitzelberger should account for this arrangement as a capital lease because the present value of the lease payments discounted at the market rate of interest approximates the FMV of the bulldozer, and the company can purchase the bulldozer at the end of the lease period for a nominal sum. Although the transaction is described as a lease, in economic terms it is actually an installment purchase; stated another way, if Hitzelberger borrowed $17,355 from a bank to purchase the bulldozer and signed a two-year note with a 10% interest rate, the loan payment would be $10,000 per year for two years, the same payments required by the lease. Assuming that the bulldozer is depreciated on a straight-line basis over a five-year useful life, the entries shown in Figure 11–12 would be recorded by Hitzelberger over the life of the lease.

FIGURE 11–12	GENERAL JOURNAL		
Accounting for a capital lease: Hitzelberger Supply	**1997 Jan. 1** Machinery (+A) Lease Liability (+L) *Recognized capital lease ($10,000 × 1.7355*).*	17,355	17,355
	Dec. 31 Depr. Expense (E, −SE) Accumulated Depr. (−A) *Recognized depreciation (17,355 ÷ 5).*	3,471	3,471
	Interest Expense (E, −SE) Lease Liability (−L) (plug) Cash (−A) (annual payment) *Made first lease payment.*	1,736** 8,264	10,000
	1998 Dec. 31 Depr. Expense (E, −SE) Accumulated Depr. (−A) *Recognized depreciation (17,355 ÷ 5).*	3,471	3,471
	Interest Expense (E, −SE) Lease Liability (−L) (plug) Cash (−A) (annual payment) *Made second lease payment.*	909*** 9,091	10,000

*Present value of annuity table n = 2, i = 10%
**10% × $17,355
***10% × $9,091 [Unamortized lease liability ($17,355 − $8,264)]

As with long-term notes payable and bonds payable, the effective interest method is used to compute the interest expense and amortize the lease liability. Specifically, the annual interest expense associated with the installment purchase is computed by multiplying the effective interest rate (10 percent) times the balance sheet value of the liability, and the dollar amount of the liability amortized each period is equal to the difference between the cash payment and the interest expense. This procedure ensures that the lease liability is carried on the balance sheet at present value throughout the life of the lease, assuming that market interest rates remain constant over that time period. Note also that Hitzelberger depreciates the cost of the machinery, reflecting that, for purposes of financial accounting, Hitzelberger is considered the owner of the bulldozer.

OPERATING LEASES, CAPITAL LEASES, AND OFF-BALANCE-SHEET FINANCING

Both operating leases and capital leases are commonly reported on the financial statements of U.S. companies. *Accounting Trends and Techniques* (New York: AICPA, 1994) reports that, of the 600 companies surveyed, 292 (49 percent) disclosed both operating and capital leases, 224 (37 percent) disclosed operating leases only, and 28 (5 percent) disclosed capital leases only.

Recall that from the lessee's standpoint, an operating lease simply gives rise to a periodic rent expense, while a capital lease involves the recognition of an asset, a leasehold liability, and an additional depreciation expense. Because accounting for capital leases increases liabilities and recognizes depreciation expense, which can negatively affect important financial ratios, companies have incentives to account for leases as operating. In 1977, the Financial Accounting Standards Board issued an accounting standard that identified a set of criteria for distinguishing capital from operating leases. In general, these criteria attempt to identify when a leasing arrangement actually represents an installment purchase and therefore should be treated as such (i.e., a capital lease) on the financial statements. Specifically, if any of the four criteria listed in Figure 11–13 are met, the lease should be treated as a capital lease.

FIGURE 11–13	1. The lease transfers ownership of the property to the lessee.
Capital lease criteria	2. The lease contains a bargain purchase option. 3. The lease term is 75% or more of the useful life of the property. 4. The present value of the lease payments equals or exceeds 90% of the FMV of the property.

While these criteria are useful, they have not removed the effects of management's discretion on classifying leases. Indeed, a study sponsored by the Financial Accounting Standards Board, conducted four years after the FASB established the criteria, found that "a majority of the companies surveyed were structuring the terms of new lease contracts to avoid capitalization."[20] Such attempts to finance asset acquisitions without having to report liabilities on the balance sheet may be economically sound in view of the importance of financial ratios in debt covenants and investor and creditor decisions. In one particular case, *Forbes* magazine reported that Dierckx Equipment Corporation, a small privately owned company, could "endanger its credit rating" by capitalizing its leases.[21] Consequently, financial statement users should closely review the lease terms disclosed in the footnotes to financial statements and ascertain for themselves whether a leasing arrangement is in fact a rental agreement or an installment purchase. Furthermore, generally accepted accounting principles require that companies disclose in the footnotes the future cash payments associated with both their operating and their capital leases. Astute financial statement readers can use this information to ascertain the extent to which the financial statements are affected by the lease accounting method. For example, one could reconstruct the

---

20. FASB, "FASB-Sponsored Research Finds Majority of Leases Structured to Avoid Capitalization," *Status Report*, September 1, 1981 (Stamford, Conn.: FASB).
21. Jay Gissen, "The World According to GAAP," *Forbes*, June 8, 1981, pp. 148, 150.

financial statements as if all leases had been accounted for as capital leases by computing the present value of the cash flow payments associated with the company's operating leases, and including that dollar amount as both a liability and an asset on the balance sheet.

The disclosure below was taken from the 1994 annual report of May Department Stores, which includes a wide variety of well-know retailers including Lord & Taylor and Payless ShoeSource. It describes the company's leasing activities.

Lease Obligations. The company owns approximately 76% of its department stores and leases substantially all of its Payless ShoeSource stores.

Rental expense for the company's operating leases consisted of:

(millions)	1994	1993	1992
Minimum rentals	$224	$200	$182
Contingent rentals based on sales	18	18	19
Real property rentals	242	218	201
Equipment rentals	5	7	8
Total	$247	$225	$209

Future minimum lease payments at January 28, 1995 were as follows:

(millions)	Capital Leases	Operating Leases	Total
1995	$ 10	$ 241	$ 251
1996	10	225	235
1997	10	203	213
1998	10	182	192
1999	10	162	172
After 1999	138	620	758
Minimum lease payments	188	$1,633	$1,821
Less inputed interest component	(115)		
Present value of net minimum lease payments of which $2 million is included in current liabilities	$ 73		

The present value of operating leases was $1.1 billion at January 28, 1995. Property under capital leases is summarized as follows:

(millions)	January 28, 1995	January 29, 1994
Cost	$ 78	$ 83
Accumulated amortization	(32)	(30)
Total	$ 46	$ 53

This disclosure explains the rent expense recognized on May's operating leases ($247 million), the balance sheet liability recognized on its capital leases ($73 million), the present value of the future payments on operating leases ($1.1 billion), and the net book value of the capital lease assets ($46 million). Approximately 90 percent of the lease payments are made on leases judged by May to be operating instead of capital. Had these leases been accounted for as capital leases, May would have recognized an additional $1.1 billion in the long-term liability and asset sections of its balance sheet, which in turn would have increased the company's liabilities/total assets ratio from .53 to .63. Indeed, how management accounts for its leases can have significant effects on important financial ratios.

INTERNATIONAL PERSPECTIVE: THE IMPORTANCE OF DEBT FINANCING IN OTHER COUNTRIES

The nature of capital market plays an important role in the determination of the accounting standards and practices in a given country. U.S. companies, for example, rely heavily on both debt and equity capital which, in turn, influences the accounting systems to provide information for both equity and debt investors. Indeed, the importance of both earning power and solvency in the assessment of a company's financial health has been emphasized throughout the text.

In certain other countries, however, the sources of capital are not as balanced between equity and debt. In Japan, Germany, and Switzerland, for example, the environment is characterized by a few, very large banks that satisfy the capital needs of most businesses. The local stock and bond markets, while increasingly becoming more active, are not as heavily relied upon as they are in the United States. The dependence on borrowing in Japan has caused the normal debt/equity ratio for a Japanese company to be well in excess of 75 percent, with most of the debt being in the form of long-term notes from one or more of the large banks.

This situation has had two significant effects on the accounting systems in such countries. First, the accounting disclosure requirements are not nearly as comprehensive as those in the United States, primarily because the information needs of the major capital providers (i.e., banks) are satisfied in a relatively straightforward way—through personal contact and direct visits. In these countries, for example, it is not unusual for the banks to have members on the boards of directors of the companies for which they provide debt capital. Such direct access is an efficient and practical way to monitor a company's financial health, and it precludes the need for extensive accounting disclosures for external parties.

A review of the financial statements of Kmart and Wal-Mart show that both companies lease a large portion of their facilities. Indeed, leasing is common in the retail industry.

A closer examination of the lease arrangements reveals that, while the contractual terms of the leases held by the two companies are quite similar, in the financial statements Kmart classifies a much larger percentage of its leases as "operating" leases, while Wal-Mart considers a larger percentage as "capital" leases. According to GAAP, "capital" leases must be represented as balance sheet liabilities, while "operating" leases do not.

It is well known that classifying leases as "capital" or "operating" is very subjective. While the FASB has provided criteria that should be followed when making such a classification, applying these criteria requires much judgment, and many companies structure their lease contracts in ways that give them the flexibility to classify them as "operating." Such a strategy can be construed as a form of "off-balance-sheet financing," enabling a company to raise debt capital without having to include it on the balance sheet as a liability. In this way the company can avoid violating debt covenants, protect their credit ratings, and generally encourage stockholders and others to believe that the company is carrying less debt than it really is.

ETHICS IN THE REAL WORLD

ETHICAL ISSUE

Is it ethical for a company to structure its leasing contracts in a manner that allows it to avoid reporting debt, when some might consider the lease to be debt?

The second way in which the heavy reliance on debt affects the accounting system is that the disclosures and regulations that are required tend to be designed either to protect the creditor or to help in the assessment of solvency. For example, the Japanese Commercial Code, which determines the accounting rules, also sets a ceiling on the profits available for dividends to the stockholders. Such a regulation helps creditors by ensuring that there will be adequate cash available to meet debt payments on the company's outstanding loans.

REVIEW PROBLEM

Assume that Southern Carbide issues 500 bonds, each with a $1,000 face value on January 1, 1997. The five-year bonds have an annual stated interest rate of 6 percent, to be paid semiannually on December 31 and June 30. The bonds are issued at 91.89, providing an effective annual interest rate of 8 percent. A call provision in the bond contract states that the bonds can be redeemed by Union Carbide after December 31, 1997, for 96.0. Assume that Union Carbide exercises this provision on July 1, 1998.

Figure 11–14 provides the cash flows, journal entries, discount balance, and net book value of the bonds from the time of the bond issuance to the redemption. An explanation of each calculation follows.

CASH FLOW CALCULATIONS:

PROCEEDS. The proceeds of the bond issuance ($459,450) were calculated by multiplying the number of bonds issued (500) by the price per bond ($918.90).

INTEREST PAYMENTS. The semiannual interest payment ($15,000) was calculated by multiplying the number of bonds issued (500) by the face value of each bond ($1,000) by half the stated annual interest rate (3 percent).

REDEMPTION PAYMENT (7/1/98). The payment required to redeem the bonds on July 1, 1998 ($480,000) was calculated by multiplying the number of bonds issued (500) by the redemption price per bond ($960).

JOURNAL ENTRY CALCULATIONS:

AT ISSUANCE. Cash ($459,450) was equal to the cash proceeds. Bonds Payable ($500,000) was calculated by multiplying the number of bonds issued (500) by the face value of each bond ($1,000). The discount ($40,550) represents an interest cost ("unaccrued interest") waiting to be recognized over the life of the bond. It arises because the bond issuance, which will require a $500,000 cash payment at maturity, generated only $459,450 at issuance.

INTEREST PAYMENTS AND DISCOUNT AMORTIZATION. The calculation of the cash interest payments is described above. The effective interest rate (8 percent) was computed by finding the rate that produced a present value equal to the price ($459,450). The amount of interest expense recognized each period was calculated by multiplying half the effective interest rate (4 percent) by the net book value of the bond payable ($500,000 − unamortized discount) at the beginning of the period. The

FIGURE 11–14

Review problem

Terms: Number of bonds issued: 500   **Interest payment dates: Dec. 31, June 30**
Face value: $1,000   **Issue date: January 1, 1997**
Stated interest rate: 6%   **Price: .9189 ($459,450)**
Time to maturity: 5 years   **Effective interest rate: 8%**

Call Provision: Redeemable after 12/31/97 for .9600

CASH FLOWS

12/31/96 ⟶ 1/1/97 ⟶ 6/30/97 ⟶ 12/31/97 ⟶ 6/30/98
                                                        7/1/98

+$459,450   −$15,000   −$15,000   −$15,000
(proceeds)   (interest)   (interest)   (interest)
                                                          −$480,000
                                                           (redemption)

GENERAL JOURNAL

Cash	459,450	
Disc.	40,550	
Bonds Pay.		500,000
Issued bond.		

Int. Exp.	18,378	
Cash		15,000
Discount		3,378
Paid interest and amortized discount.		

Int. Exp.	18,513	
Cash		15,000
Discount		3,513
Paid interest and amortized discount.		

Int. Exp.	18,653	
Cash		15,000
Discount		3,653
Paid interest and amortized discount.		

Bonds Pay.	500,000	
Loss on R.	10,006	
Discount		30,006
Cash		480,000
Redeemed bond.		

DISCOUNT BALANCE

$40,550 $40,550 − $3,378 = $37,172 $37,172 − $3,513 = $33,659 $33,659−$3,653 = $30,006 (before redemption)

NET BOOK VALUE

$500,000 − $40,550 = $459,450 $500,000 − $37,172 = $462,828 $500,000 − $33,659 = $466,341 $500,000 − $30,006 = $469,994 (before redemption)

Bonds Pay. = Bonds Payable
Int. Exp. = Interest Expense
Loss on R. = Loss on Redemption

credit to the discount represents the additional interest expense recognized each period because the bonds were issued at a discount.

REDEMPTION (7/1/98). The calculation of the cash payment at redemption ($480,000) was described earlier. The balance sheet value of the bonds at the time of the redemption (Bonds Payable: $500,000, Discount: $30,006) is removed from the books. The Loss on Redemption ($10,006) represents the difference between the cash paid to redeem the bonds and the balance sheet value of the bonds as of July 1, 1998.

DISCOUNT BALANCE AND BALANCE SHEET VALUE OF BONDS PAYABLE

The ending discount balance each period was calculated by subtracting the amount of the discount amortized during the period from the balance at the beginning of the period. The balance sheet value of the bonds payable at the end of each period was calculated by subtracting the unamortized discount from the face value of the bond issuance ($500,000).

SUMMARY OF LEARNING OBJECTIVES

LO 1 *Define long-term notes payable, bonds payable, and leasehold obligations, and explain how companies use these instruments as important sources of financing.*

Long-term liabilities include notes payable, bonds payable, and leasehold obligations. They represent obligations that require the disbursement of assets (usually cash) at the future time beyond the period that defines current assets. Notes payable refer to obligations evidenced by formal notes. They normally involve direct borrowings from financial institutions or an arrangement to finance the purchase of assets. Bonds payable are notes issued for cash to a large number of creditors called *bondholders*. Leasehold obligations refer to future cash payments (i.e., rent) that are required for the use or occupation of property during a specified period of time.

Long-term notes, bonds, and leases are common and major sources of capital for companies throughout the world. Funds used to acquire other companies, purchase machinery and equipment, finance plant expansion, pay off debts, repurchase outstanding stock, and support operations are often generated by issuing long-term notes, bonds, or entering into lease agreements.

LO 2 *Identify important economic consequences created by the excessive borrowing brought on by merger mania during the 1980s.*

The excessive borrowing in the U.S. during the 1980s forced managers to pay special attention to both their cash flow management policies and how the debt is reported in their financial statements. They entered into creative ways to generate sufficient cash to meet their debt obligations, and they managed the financial statement numbers by practicing strategies like "building hidden reserves," "taking a bath," and especially "off-balance-sheet financing."

List and define the different forms of contractual obligations.

There are three basic forms of contractual obligations: interest-bearing, non-interest-bearing, and installment. Interest-bearing obligations require periodic (annual or semi-annual) cash payments (called interest) that are determined as a percentage of the face, principal, or maturity value, which must be paid at the end of the contract period. Non-interest-bearing obligations require no periodic payments but only a single cash payment at the end of the contract period. In an installment obligation, periodic payments covering both interest and principal are made throughout the life of the contract.

 Define the effective interest rate, and describe how it is determined for contractual obligations.

The effective interest rate is the actual interest rate paid by the issuer of the obligation. It is determined by finding the discount rate that sets the present value of the obligation's cash outflows equal to the fair market value (FMV) of that which is received in the exchange. When contractual obligations are exchanged for cash, the cash amount received represents the FMV of the receipt. When contractual obligations are exchanged for noncash items, the FMV of the noncash items must be determined through appraisals or some other means.

 Describe the basic rule of the effective interest method, and explain what it ensures about the book value of a long-term obligation.

The effective interest method states that the interest expense reported during each period of a long-term obligation's contractual life is computed by multiplying the effective interest rate times the balance sheet value of the obligation as of the beginning of the period. It ensures that the long-term liability on the balance sheet is reported throughout its life at the present value of its future cash flows, discounted at the effective interest rate as of the issue date.

 Describe how the effective interest method underlies the accounting for notes, bonds, and leases.

Notes, bonds, and leases are all forms of contractual obligations. Notes can be interest-bearing, non-interest-bearing, or installment obligations, and can be exchanged for cash or noncash items; bonds are normally interest-bearing obligations exchanged for cash; and leases (capital) are installment obligations exchanged for assets. When accounting for these obligations, the effective interest rate is first computed. This rate is then used to compute the interest expense for each period by multiplying it times the book value of the obligation at the beginning of that period. If the periodic cash payments (interest or principal) differ from the interest expense recognized during the period, the difference serves to adjust the net book value of the obligation which, in turn, is the basis upon which interest expense is computed in the next period.

 Explain how changes in market interest rates can lead to misstated balance sheet values for long-term liabilities.

The effective interest method ensures that over the life of an obligation its balance sheet value is equal to the present value of the obligation's future cash flows, discounted at the effective interest rate as of the date the obligation was issued. If the market rate of interest remains constant over the life of the obligation, then the obligation's balance sheet value will equal its present value. When market interest rates fluctuate, however, the actual present value of the obligation, discounted at the market rate, differs from the balance sheet value of the obligation, which is discounted at the original effective interest rate. In such cases the balance sheet value of the liability is no longer an accurate measure of its present value, and economic gains and losses are experienced by the issuing company but not recognized on the financial statements.

L O 8 *Differentiate operating leases from capital leases, explain the methods used to account for capital leases, and describe how operating lease accounting can create off-balance-sheet financing.*

Operating and capital leases are categories created by generally accepted accounting principles that define the methods used to account for lease contracts. Four criteria, which determine whether the lessor or lessee bears the risks and rewards of owning the leased asset, are listed, and if any one of the criteria are met, the lease is considered a capital lease. Capital leases are treated as installment purchases for financial reporting purposes, requiring that the lessee record both an asset and a liability in the amount of the present value of the future lease payments, discounted at the effective interest rate. The asset is subject to depreciation, and the liability is amortized using the effective interest method. Operating lease payments are simply accounted for as rental expense by the lessee. Companies can practice off-balance-sheet financing by structuring lease contracts so that none of the four criteria are met, which, in turn, allows them to account for leases as operating that may in economic substance be capital. Such treatment keeps the liability associated with the lease off the balance sheet.

APPENDIX 11A

ACCOUNTING FOR LONG-TERM INVESTMENTS IN DEBT SECURITIES

This appendix covers the methods used to account for long-term investments in debt securities: long-term notes receivable and investments in bonds. Note that these methods are very similar to those used to account for long-term notes payable and bonds payable because such investments simply represent the asset side of the same transaction.

A recent financial accounting standard requires that investments in debt securities be placed into one of three categories: trading, available-for-sale, and held-to-maturity. The definitions of and methods used to account for trading and available-for-sale investments are covered in Chapter 8. This appendix is devoted to debt investments that are intended to be held to maturity.

LONG-TERM NOTES RECEIVABLE

Long-term notes receivable normally arise when companies loan money, provide goods, or provide services in exchange for formal promissory notes, designating cash payments that extend beyond the time period that defines current assets. Such notes can be interest-bearing, non-interest-bearing, or installment contracts, and they are held by many major U.S. companies. Their relative size, compared to total assets, ranges from immaterial to very significant. For example, *Accounting Trends and Techniques* (New York: AICPA, 1994) reports that, of the 600 major U.S. companies surveyed, 129 (22 percent) reported some kind of long-term note receivable.[22] For many companies, such as Coca-Cola Enterprises and RJR Nabisco, there was no indication in their 1994 financial reports that they held any long-term notes receivable. Other companies, such as Dow Chemical, McDonald's Corporation, and Alcoa, either disclosed Long-Term Notes Receivable as a separate account on the balance sheet or included them with other assets, disclosing the actual dollar amount in the footnotes to the financial statements. For these three companies the dollar amounts of long-term notes receivable represented only a small percentage of total assets. Companies such as McDonnell Douglas, Chrysler Corporation, General Motors, and financial institutions in general hold substantial investments in long-term notes receivable because these companies provide financing for their customers.

ACCOUNTING FOR LONG-TERM NOTES RECEIVABLE

The effective interest method is used to account for long-term notes receivable, and it ensures that the notes are carried on the balance sheet at the present value of the note's future cash flows, discounted at the effective interest rate as of the date of issuance. It consists of the following rule.

The interest revenue recognized during each period of the receivable's life is equal to the effective interest rate multiplied by the balance sheet value of the receivable as of the beginning of that period.

While notes receivable can take on a number of contractual forms, the following example covers a situation where an interest-bearing note is received at a discount in exchange for cash. Assume that on January 1, 1997, Eastern Bank lends $7,028 to Rockley International. The terms of the loan specify that Eastern will receive $8,000 on December 31, 1998, and $240 in interest at the end of each year for two years. In other words, the amount lent is $7,028, and the note has a principal of $8,000, a time to mature of two years, and a stated annual interest rate of 3 percent ($240 ÷ $8,000). Discounting the future cash inflows (interest and principal payments) at 10 percent results in a present value of $7,028, so the effective interest rate on this note is 10 percent. Figure 11A–1 illustrates the cash flows and the methods Eastern would use to account for this note over its two-year life. Note that the method used to account for this note receivable is exactly the same as that used to account for the long-term obligations discussed in this chapter.

Long-term notes receivable are usually carried on the balance sheet at the principal amount, less both unamortized discounts and an allowance for uncollectibles.[23] To illustrate how companies disclose the methods used to account for long-term notes

22. Descriptions such as *noncurrent receivables* and *other receivables* were often used. Balance sheet classifications also varied. *Long-term investments, other assets, sundry assets*, and other similar descriptions were used to identify the asset category under which long-term receivables were disclosed.
23. The methods used to account for uncollectibles on long-term notes receivable are essentially the same as those used to account for uncollectibles on short-term receivables. See Chapter 6 for a discussion of accounting for bad debts. Accounting for uncollectible notes can pose major problems for banks and other financial institutions.

issued at a discount, consider the following excerpt from a recent annual report of Bank of America.

Loans are generally carried at the principal amount outstanding [less unamortized discounts]. Interest income on discounted loans is generally accrued based on methods that approximate the [effective] interest method . . . A provision for credit losses, which is a charge against earnings, is added to bring the allowance to a level which, in management's judgment, is adequate to absorb future losses inherent in the credit portfolio.

FIGURE 11A–1

Accounting for long-term notes receivable; effective rate (10%) is greater than stated rate (3%)

CASH FLOWS

1/1/97	12/31/97	12/31/98
−$7,028	+$240[a]	+$ 240[a]
		+$8,000

GENERAL JOURNAL

Notes Rec. (+A)	8,000		Cash (+A)	240		Cash (+A)	240	
Disc. on Notes Rec. (−A)		972	Disc. on Notes Rec. (+A)	463		Disc. on Notes Rec. (+A)	509	
Cash (−A)		7,028	Int. Rev. (R, +SE)		703[b]	Int. Rev. (R, +SE)		749[c]
Received note.			*Received interest revenue*			*Received interest revenue*		
			and amortized discount.			*and amortized discount.*		
						Cash (+A)	8,000	
						Notes Rec. (−A)		8,000
						Received principal.		

BALANCE SHEET VALUE

Notes receivable	$8,000		Notes receivable	$8,000	
Less: Discount			Less: Discount		
on notes	972	7,028	on notes	509	7,491

GENERAL LEDGER

DISCOUNT ON NOTES RECEIVABLE

(12/31/97 adjustment)	463	(1/1/97)	972
(12/31/98 adjustment)	509	(12/31/97)	509
			0

[a]$8,000 × 3%
[b]$7,028 × 10%
[c]$7,491 × 10%

INVESTMENTS IN CORPORATE BONDS

Bonds are typically purchased by companies on the open market to provide a relatively low-risk return, primarily in the form of interest receipts and sometimes in the form of price appreciation. Such investments should be classified as long-term if management intends to hold them for longer than the time period of current assets.

The relative size of long-term debt investments (including corporate bonds, government bonds, and in some cases redeemable preferred stocks), compared to total assets, varies significantly across the balance sheets of major U.S. companies.[24] *Accounting Trends and Techniques* (New York: AICPA, 1994) reports that, of the 600 companies surveyed, approximately 25 percent disclosed material long-term investments in debt securities. Most companies, such as IBM and J.C. Penney, include no description of bond investments in their financial reports. Others, such as Abbott Laboratories and H&R Block, describe their debt investments in the footnotes; the relative dollar amounts are normally included in some general asset category (e.g., investments or other assets) on the balance sheet. The dollar amounts of debt investments held by insurance companies, on the other hand, are often well over 50 percent of total assets. Safeco, for example, recently reported debt investments that accounted for 61 percent of total assets.

ACCOUNTING FOR INVESTMENTS IN CORPORATE BONDS

This section consists of three parts. The first covers the purchase of bonds, the second describes the methods used to account for bond investments from purchase to maturity, and the third describes how to account for bonds that are sold prior to maturity.

PURCHASING BOND INVESTMENTS

Bond purchases are recorded in the Bond Investment account at cost, which includes the purchase price and any incidental costs of acquisition, such as brokerage commissions and taxes.[25] To illustrate, assume that Jones and Company purchased 10 bonds, each with a face value of $1,000, a stated interest rate of 10 percent, and a remaining life of two years. These bonds were purchased as a long-term investment for a total cost (including brokerage commissions) of $10,363. At the time of the purchase, Jones recorded the following journal entry.

Bond Investment (+A)   **10,363***
    Cash (−A)   **10,363**
Purchased 10 bonds for $10,363.
*The bond investment account contains a $363 premium.

Premiums and discounts on bond investments are normally included in the bond investment account. These bonds were purchased at a premium: the price of the bonds ($10,363) exceeded the face value ($10,000). Consequently, the effective rate of return provided by the bond investment (8 percent) was less than the stated interest rate (10 percent).

ACCOUNTING FOR BOND INVESTMENTS
FROM PURCHASE TO MATURITY

As in the case of long-term notes receivable, the effective interest method is used to account for bond investments from the date of purchase to the date of maturity. Note in the example contained in Figure 11A–2 how the journal entries and calculations used to account for bond investments are very similar to those used to account for long-term notes receivable. Keep in mind, however, that this example involved bonds purchased at a premium, while the example covered earlier (Figure 11A–1) involved a note receivable issued at a discount.

---

24. See Chapter 12 for a discussion of preferred stocks.
25. Normally, a portion of the amount invested in bonds is for interest accrued since the last interest payment date. In the following examples we make the simplifying assumption that the bonds are purchased immediately after the interest payment date and there is no accrued interest.

FIGURE 11A–2

Accounting for bonds

Annual stated interest rate (10%), annual effective rate of return (8%)

Face value = 10 bonds × $1,000 per bond = $10,000

Semiannual interest payment = ($10,000 × 10%) ÷ 2 = $500

CASH FLOWS

Purchase date	6 mo.	1 year	6 mo.	Maturity date
−$10,363	+$500	+$500	+$500	+$ 500
				+$10,000

PRESENT VALUE OF FUTURE CASH FLOWS DISCOUNTED AT 4% SEMIANNUAL RATE

$10,363	$10,278	$10,189	$10,097	$10,000

GENERAL JOURNAL

Bond Inv. 10,363	Cash	500	Cash	500	Cash	500	Cash	500
Cash	10,363	Int. Rev.	415*	Int. Rev.	411*	Int. Rev.	408*	Int. Rev.	403*
Purchased bonds.		Bond Inv.	85	Bond Inv.	89	Bond Inv.	92	Bond Inv.	97
		Received interest.		*Received interest.*		*Received interest.*		*Received interest.*

				Cash	10,000
				Bond Inv.	10,000
				Sold bonds at maturity.

Bond Inv. = Bond Investment

Int. Rev. = Interest Revenue

*4% × balance sheet value at beginning of period

BALANCE SHEET VALUE

$10,363	$10,278	$10,189	$10,097	$10,000
	($10,363 − $85)	($10,278 − $89)	($10,189 − $92)	($10,097 − $97)

SELLING A BOND INVESTMENT BEFORE MATURITY

When bonds are sold prior to maturity, cash is debited for the proceeds, the Bond Investment account is written off the balance sheet, and a gain or loss is recognized on the transaction.[26] As described in Chapter 13, the gain or loss would normally appear in a special section of the income statement that includes non-operating revenues and expenses. To illustrate, assume that on June 30 Atlantic Company sold a bond investment for a total cash price of $52,000 with a book value of $49,000. The following journal entry would be entered to reflect this transaction.

June 30	Cash (+A)	52,000	
	Bond Investment (−A)		49,000
	Gain on Sale of Bonds (Ga, +SE)		3,000
	Sold bond investment prior to maturity.		

In the example, a $3,000 gain was recognized. Had the bonds been sold for $48,000 instead of $52,000, a loss in the amount of $1,000 would have been recognized with the following entry.

June 30	Cash (+A)	48,000	
	Loss on Sale of Bonds (Lo, −SE)	1,000	
	Bond Investment (−A)		49,000
	Sold bond investment prior to maturity.		

APPENDIX 11B

THE DETERMINATION OF BOND PRICES

The chapter states that bond prices are determined by the dollar amount investors are willing to pay for them. That is, what will investors pay for the right to receive the semiannual interest payments and a cash payment in the amount of the face value at maturity? This appendix identifies and discusses factors considered by debt investors when deciding whether to purchase bonds. These factors have a direct bearing on bond prices.

Suppose, for example, that on June 9, 1997, you were reading *The Wall Street Journal* looking to purchase a bond. You note that on that day Treetley Enterprises lists bonds with the following terms.

Face value	$1,000
Time to maturity	18 years
Stated annual interest rate (paid every 6 months)	8%
Current price	85 1/4 or $853

The decision to buy the bond involves three steps: (1) determine the effective rate of return, (2) determine your required rate of return, and (3) compare the effective rate to the required rate.

---

26. Note again that the example does not consider accrued interest.

DETERMINE THE EFFECTIVE (ACTUAL) RATE OF RETURN

The procedure used to determine the effective rate of return is discussed in this chapter. Recall that the effective rate is that rate which, when used to discount the bond's future cash flows, results in a present value equal to the bond price. The effective rate of the Treetley bond is approximately 10%.

DETERMINE THE REQUIRED RATE OF RETURN

Now that you have determined the effective rate you must decide whether it is large enough to satisfy you. In other words, what rate of return do you require on a bond with these terms issued by Treetley Enterprises?

Your required rate of return is determined by adding the return you could receive from investing your money in a risk-free security (i.e., risk-free return) to the risk premium you would attach to the Treetley bonds. The expression follows.

Required Rate of Return = Risk-Free Return + Risk Premium

DETERMINE THE RISK-FREE RETURN

The **risk-free (or riskless) return** is the annual return you could receive by investing in a riskless security, a security where there is virtually no doubt that the interest and principal payments will be honored. They are often backed by the federal government. The bank interest rate on savings accounts probably represents the lowest estimate of the risk-free return. The annual return on **certificates of deposit**, where a given amount of money is lent to a financial institution for a specified period of time, represents another, perhaps more relevant, example. The annual returns on **treasury notes**, which can be purchased from the federal government and mature up to six months from the date of issue, provide another approximation of the risk-free rate.

Keep in mind that the actual risk-free return can only be approximated and that it fluctuates from day to day, based on such factors as changes in the **prime interest rate** (the interest rate charged by banks to their best customers), changes in the **discount rate** (the lending rate charged to banks by the Federal Reserve Board), and the inflation rate expected in the future. Assume that on June 9, 1997, when you considered purchasing Treetley bonds, a reasonable approximation of the risk-free return was 7%.

DETERMINE THE RISK PREMIUM

The **risk premium** is expressed as a percentage and reflects the probability that Treetley will default on the periodic interest payments or face value payment at maturity. If this probability is high, these bonds would be considered "high risk" and the risk premium would be relatively large, say 5–10 percent. If the probability is low, the risk premium would be considerably less, say 1–3 percent.

The risk premium is associated specifically with the company issuing the bonds. It is determined by a number of factors, including the credit rating of the company and the bond issuance, the solvency and earning power of the company, future movements in the economy and how these movements may affect the operations of the company, and the terms of the bond issuance. For example, covenant restrictions on future debt and dividend payments as well as collateral and call provisions can affect the risk premium by changing the risk levels faced by the holder of the bonds. Analyzing financial statements is an important part of assessing the risk premium associated with investing in a particular company.

Assume that you have assessed the factors described above and have determined that the risk premium associated with the Treetley bonds is 2 percent.

COMPARE THE EFFECTIVE RATE TO THE REQUIRED RATE

The effective rate of return on the Treetley bond is 10 percent. You have determined that your required rate of return is 9 percent (7 percent risk-free rate + 2 percent risk premium). Since the effective rate exceeds the required rate, you will purchase the bond. The bond is selling for $853, and in fact, you would be willing to pay $920 for it, the present value of the bond's future cash flows discounted at 9 percent, your required rate of return. Had your required return been greater than 10 percent, either due to a higher risk-free rate or higher risk premium, you would not have purchased the bond and would not do so until the price decreased to the point where the effective rate exceeded your required rate.

FACTORS DETERMINING BOND PRICES

Bond prices, therefore, are determined by a market of investors, each assessing the economy-wide, risk-free rate as well as the risk premium associated specifically with the issuing company. Any factor affecting either of these two items affects bond prices. Factors that decrease either the risk-free rate or the risk premium tend to increase bond prices, while factors increasing either rate tend to decrease bond prices.

For example, *The Wall Street Journal* often reports on how the actions of the Federal Reserve Board affect economy-wide interest rates. Almost without exception, when the Board acts to reduce interest rates, the bond market rallies, and when the Board acts to increase rates, bond prices fall. This relationship occurs because the Board's behavior has a direct effect on the risk-free rate of return. Indeed, several years ago the *New York Times* reported that Merrill Lynch and Company, which holds a huge portfolio of bond investments, "lost $250 million in a given month because its bond investments plummeted in value when interest rates surged."

The close relationship between the risk premium and bond prices illustrates clearly why companies are so interested in their credit ratings. A decrease in a company's credit rating ordinarily leads to an increase in the market's assessment of the company's risk premium and, accordingly, a decrease in the value of the company's outstanding debt. For example, when Standard & Poor's downgraded $310 million of long-term debt issued by American Stores, the value of American's outstanding debt decreased substantially, making it more difficult for the company to raise debt capital in the future. Standard & Poor's justified the downgrade by claiming that American's "financial risk will increase sharply" as a result of its recent acquisition of Lucky Stores, Inc.

KEY TERMS

Note: Definitions for these terms are provided in the glossary at the end of the text.

Bonds payable (p. 528)	Covenants (p. 538)
Call provision (p. 539)	Debentures (p. 539)
Capital leases (p. 550)	Default (p. 531)
Certificates of deposit (p. 565)	Discount on bonds payable (p. 543)
Collateral (p. 531)	Discount rate (p. 565)

Effective interest method (p. 534)
Effective interest rate (p. 532)
Face, principal, or maturity value (p. 531)
Installment obligation (p. 531)
Interest (p. 531)
Interest-bearing obligations (p. 531)
Interest payment (p. 537)
Lease (p. 549)
Leasehold obligations (p. 528)
Life (p. 537)
Maturity date (p. 537)
Mortgage (p. 535)
Non-interest-bearing obligations (p. 531)
Notes payable (p. 528)

Operating leases (p. 550)
Premium on bonds payable (p. 544)
Prime interest rate (p. 565)
Proceeds (p. 537)
Redeemed (p. 547)
Refinancing (p. 535)
Restrictive covenants (p. 531)
Risk-free (or riskless) return (p. 565)
Risk premium (p. 565)
Secured notes (p. 535)
Stated interest rate (p. 531)
Treasury notes (p. 565)
Unsecured bonds (p. 539)
Unsecured notes (p. 535)

QUESTIONS FOR DISCUSSION AND REVIEW

1. Define long-term notes payable, bonds payable, and leasehold obligations, and explain to what extent companies use such instruments to finance operations. What kinds of projects are long-term liabilities usually used to finance?

2. Explain how a debt covenant can have an important economic consequence on a company's financial condition.

3. Why might management wish to avoid reporting debt on the balance sheet?

4. Identify circumstances in which management might wish to accelerate the recognition of debt and related losses on the financial statement.

5. List and define the three forms of contractual obligations discussed in this chapter.

6. Briefly explain how the effective interest rate on an obligation is computed. Why is it more difficult to compute the effective interest rate for an interest-bearing note than for a non-interest-bearing note? What role does the benefit received in exchange for the long-term obligation play in the determination of the effective interest rate?

7. Why are long-term liabilities carried on the balance sheet at an estimate of present value, while long-lived assets are not?

8. What is the stated interest rate, and how does it differ from the effective interest rate? If you were a manager deciding to borrow money, explain how both the stated rate and the effective rate would affect your decision.

9. State the basic rule of the effective interest method. Give several examples using the effective interest method to value balance sheet liabilities, and explain why it is used to account for long-term notes, bonds, and leases.

10. Why might a company decide to borrow money by issuing a note with a stated interest rate of zero?

11. Explain the process used to amortize a discount on a long-term note or bond payable.

12. Why is issuing bonds such a popular way to raise large amounts of capital?

13. List and briefly explain the important features of a bond contract.

14. What is a debenture? Why might DuPont be able to issue debentures frequently, while Jones Airlines, Inc., a less dependable business, might not?

15. Why might the issuing company allow a debt covenant to be written into a bond contract? How would adding such a provision tend to affect the issue price of the bonds?

16. When a bond is issued at a discount, what is the relationship between the stated interest rate and the effective interest rate? When a bond is issued at a premium, what is the relationship between the stated rate and the effective rate?

17. Does the effective interest method ensure that bond liability is carried on the balance sheet at present value throughout its life? Upon what assumption does the answer to this question depend?

18. Explain how a user could adjust reported earnings in view of the difference between the balance sheet value of outstanding long-term debt and its market value.

19. Why would a company choose to redeem its outstanding bonds prior to maturity, sometimes even at a premium price? Why is a gain or loss usually recognized when a company redeems outstanding bonds prior to maturity?

20. Describe several examples of financing risks that may not be reflected on the balance sheet, and briefly explain how users can assess such risks.

21. Why is leasing such a popular form of financing for many companies? Distinguish a capital lease from an operating lease.

22. Explain the methods used to account for capital leases. How is the lease obligation amortized over the life of the lease?

23. What is off-balance-sheet financing? Why might a company structure a lease so that it is considered an operating lease instead of a capital lease?

24. Describe how a user can use footnote disclosures to make more comparable firms that have different policies concerning the accounting for operating and capital leases.

25. Relative to the United States, how important is debt financing in other countries? How has this affected the financial reporting systems in those countries?

26. *(Appendix 11A)* Explain how the effective interest rate on a note receivable or bond investment is determined. What method is used to account for both?

27. *(Appendix 11A)* When accounting for a bond investment, how is interest revenue computed each period? Under what conditions will the interest revenue be constant from period to period? Under what conditions will it increase? Under what conditions will it decrease?

28. *(Appendix 11A)* To account for a bond investment, the effective interest rate, determined at purchase, is used throughout the life of the bond investment to compute periodic interest revenue even though market interest rates may change over that time period. What bearing will changes in the market rate have on the economic value of the bond? Is this captured on the financial statements?

29. *(Appendix 11B)* Describe the three steps involved when deciding whether to purchase a bond. Define the effective rate of return, the required rate of return, the risk-free rate, and the risk premium, and explain how they are related.

30. *(Appendix 11B)* Explain how a reduction in a company's credit rating would affect the prices at which the company could issue bonds. Would it affect the risk-free rate or the risk premium?

31. (Appendix 11B) If you were holding a portfolio of bonds, would you want future interest rates to increase or decrease? Why?

EXERCISES

E11–1

(Disclosing debt and debt covenants)

The balance sheet as of December 31, 1996, for Melrose Enterprises follows.

ASSETS		LIABILITIES AND STOCKHOLDERS' EQUITY	
Current assets	$200,000	Current liabilities	$200,000
Noncurrent assets	700,000	Long-term liabilities	300,000
		Stockholders' equity	400,000
		Total liabilities and	
Total assets	$900,000	stockholders' equity	$900,000

During 1996 Melrose entered into a loan agreement that required the company to maintain a debt/equity ratio of less than 2:1.

REQUIRED:

a. How much additional debt can Melrose take on before it violates the terms of the loan agreement?
b. Assume that during 1997 Melrose had revenues of $950,000 and expenses of $800,000. Assume that all revenues and expenses were in cash. How much additional debt can Melrose take on before it violates the terms of the loan agreement?
c. Assume again that during 1997 Melrose has cash revenues of $950,000 and cash expenses of $800,000. If Melrose pays a cash dividend of $100,000, how much additional debt can it take on before violating the terms of the loan agreement? If Melrose declares, but does not pay, the dividend during 1997, does it make a difference in the amount of additional debt the company can take on?

E11–2

(Annual or semiannual interest payments?)

Hathaway Manufacturing issued long-term debt on January 1, 1996. The debt has a face value of $300,000 and an annual stated interest rate of 10 percent. The debt matures on January 1, 2001.

REQUIRED:

a. Assume that the debt agreement requires Hathaway Manufacturing to make annual interest payments every January 1. Set up a time line that indicates the timing and magnitude of the future cash outflows of this long-term debt.
b. Assume that the debt agreement requires Hathaway Manufacturing to make semiannual interest payments every July 1 and January 1. Set up a time line that indicates the timing and magnitude of the future cash outflows for this long-term debt.
c. Under the conditions of (a) and (b), compute the present value of these two debt agreements assuming that the effective rate of interest is equal to the stated rate of interest.

E11–3

(The relationship among the stated rate, effective rate, and issuance price of a liability)

The stated and effective interest rates for several notes and bonds follow. Indicate whether each note/bond would be issued at a discount, par value, or a premium.

NOTE/BOND	STATED INTEREST RATE	EFFECTIVE INTEREST RATE
1	10%	10%
2	7	8
3	9	8
4	11.5	9

E11–4

(Computing the proceeds from various notes)

Compute the proceeds from the following notes payable. Interest payments are made annually.

PROCEEDS	STATED INTEREST RATE	EFFECTIVE INTEREST RATE	FACE VALUE	LIFE
?	0%	8%	$ 1,000	4 years
?	0	6	5,000	6 years
?	4	12	8,000	6 years
?	8	8	3,000	7 years
?	10	6	10,000	10 years

E11–5

(Notes issued at a discount and the movement of interest expense)

Tradewell Rentals purchased a piece of equipment with a FMV of $11,348 in exchange for a five-year, non-interest-bearing note with a face value of $20,000.

REQUIRED:

a. Compute the effective interest rate on the note payable.
b. Prepare the journal entry to record the purchase.
c. How much interest expense should Tradewell recognize on the note payable during the first year?

d. What is the balance sheet value of the note at the end of the first year?

e. Will the interest expense recognized by Tradewell in the second year be greater than, equal to, or less than the interest expense recognized in the first year? Why?

f. Will the interest expense recognized in the third year be greater than, equal to, or less than the interest expense recognized in the second year?

E11–6

(Accounting for notes payable with various stated interest rates)

Candleton signed a two-year, interest-bearing note payable with a face value of $8,000 and an effective interest rate of 8 percent. Interest payments on the note are made annually.

REQUIRED:

Provide the journal entries that would be recorded over the life of the note assuming the following stated interest rates.

a. 8 percent

b. 0 percent

c. 6 percent

E11–7

(Determining the effective interest rate)

On January 1, 1997, Wilmes Floral Supplies borrowed $2,413 from Bower Financial Services. Wilmes Floral Supplies gave Bower a $2,500 note with a maturity date of December 31, 1998. The note specified an annual stated interest rate of 8 percent.

REQUIRED:

a. Compute the present value of the note's future cash flows at the following discount rates.
 (1) 8 percent
 (2) 10 percent
 (3) 12 percent

b. What is the effective interest rate of the note?

c. Determine the effective interest rate on the note if Floral Supplies originally borrowed $2,500.

E11–8

(Financing asset purchases with notes payable)

Morrow Enterprises purchased a building on January 1, 1997, in exchange for a three-year, non-interest-bearing note with a face value of $693,000. Independent appraisers valued the building at $550,125.

REQUIRED:

a. At what amount should this building be capitalized?

b. Compute the present value of the note's future cash flows using the following discount rates.
 (1) 6 percent
 (2) 8 percent
 (3) 10 percent

c. What is the effective interest rate of this note?

d. Explain how one could more quickly compute the effective interest rate on the note.

E11–9

(Inferring an effective interest rate from the financial statements)

The following information was extracted from the financial records of Leong Cosmetics.

	1998	1997
BALANCE SHEET		
Notes payable	$200,000	$200,000
Less: Discount on notes payable	12,000	14,400
INCOME STATEMENT		
Interest expense	$ 16,400	$ 16,200

REQUIRED:

a. What is the effective interest rate on the notes payable?

b. Prepare the journal entry to record interest expense during 1998.

E11–10

(Computing bond issuance proceeds and the movement of balance sheet value and interest expense over the bond's life)

Three different bond issuances are listed here with interest payments made semiannually.

BOND ISSUANCE	FACE VALUE	STATED INTEREST RATE	EFFECTIVE INTEREST RATE	LIFE
A	100,000	6%	6%	10 years
B	400,000	8	6	10 years
C	600,000	6	8	5 years

REQUIRED:

a. Compute the proceeds of each bond issuance.
b. For each bond issuance, indicate whether the balance sheet value of the bond liability will increase, decrease, or remain constant over the life of the bond.
c. For each bond issuance, indicate whether the interest expense recognized each period will increase, decrease, or remain constant over the life of the bond.

E11–11

(Accounting for bonds issued at face value)

On January 1, 1996, Collins Copy Machine Company issued thirty $1,000 face-value bonds with a stated annual rate of 10 percent that mature in ten years. Interest is paid semiannually on June 30 and December 31. The bonds were issued at face value.

REQUIRED:

a. Prepare the entry to record the issuance of these bonds on January 1, 1996.
b. Prepare all the entries associated with these bonds during 1996 (excluding the entry to record the issuance).
c. Compute the balance sheet value of the bond liability as of December 31, 1996.
d. Compute the present value of the bond's remaining cash flows as of December 31, 1996, using the effective rate at issuance.
e. Repeat c. and d. as of December 31, 1997 and explain the relationship between the balance sheet value and the present value.

E11–12

(Accounting for bonds issued at a discount)

Tingham Village issued 500 five-year bonds on July 1, 1997. The interest payments are due semiannually (January 1 and July 1) at an annual rate of 6 percent. The effective interest rate on the bonds is 8 percent. The face value of each bond is $1,000.

REQUIRED:

a. Prepare the journal entry that would be recorded on July 1, 1997, when the bonds are issued.
b. Prepare the journal entry that would be recorded on December 31, 1997.
c. Compute the balance sheet value of the bond liability as of December 31, 1997.
d. Compute the present value of the bond's remaining cash flows as of December 31, 1997, using an effective interest rate of 8 percent. Explain the relationship between the balance sheet value and the present value.

E11–13

(Changing market interest rates and economic gains and losses)

Treadway Company issued bonds with a face value of $20,000 on January 1, 1996. The bonds were due to mature in five years and had a stated annual interest rate of 8 percent. The bonds were issued at face value. Interest is paid semiannually.

REQUIRED:

a. As of December 31, 1996, market interest rates had decreased by 2 percent, and the market price of Treadway bonds reflected the entire change. Compute the present value of Treadway's bond liability as of that date using the new effective interest rate (6 percent), and determine the economic gain or loss experienced by the company.
b. Assume instead that as of December 31, 1996, market interest rates had increased by 2 percent, and the market price of Treadway's bonds reflected the entire change. Compute the present value of Treadway's bond liability as of that date, using the new effective interest rate (10 percent), and determine the economic gain or loss experienced by the company.

c. What is the intuition underlying such gains and losses, and why are they not reflected on the financial statements? If you were analyzing the financial statements of Treadway, what could you do to improve the reported numbers?

E11–14

(Redeeming bonds not originally issued at par)

On September 10, 1994, Mooney Plastic Products issued bonds with a face value of $500,000 for a price of 96. During 1997 Mooney exercised a call provision and redeemed the bonds for 101. At the time of the redemption, the bonds had a balance sheet value of $490,000.

REQUIRED:
a. Prepare the journal entry to record the redemption.
b. Assume that the bonds were issued in 1994 for 102, and at the time of redemption they had a balance sheet value of $507,000. Prepare the journal entry to record the bond redemption.

E11–15

(Updating amortization and retiring a bond issuance)

Marker Musical Products issued bonds with a face value of $100,000 and an annual stated interest rate of 8 percent on January 1, 1994. The effective interest rate on the bonds was 10 percent. Interest is paid semiannually on July 1 and January 1. As of December 31, 1996, the company reported the following dollar amounts for these bonds:

Bonds payable   **$100,000**
Less: Discount on bonds payable   **3,546**   **$96,454**

Marker Musical Products retired the bonds on July 2, 1997, by repurchasing them for $91,700 in cash.

REQUIRED:
a. Provide the journal entry recorded on July 1, 1997, when the interest payment is made.
b. Prepare the journal entry to record the retirement of the bonds.

E11–16

(Analyzing bond disclosures)

The information below was taken from the balance sheet of Beasley Brothers as of December 31, 1996.

Bond payable   **$100,000**
Less: Unamortized discount   **5,350**   **$94,650**

FOOTNOTES:
The bonds have a stated interest rate of 5 percent and will mature on December 31, 1998. The market value of the bonds as of December 31, 1996, is $98,167.

REQUIRED:
a. Compute the effective interest rate in effect when the bonds were issued.
b. What effective rate would an investor be earning by purchasing the bonds on December 31, 1996, at the market price and holding the bonds until maturity?
c. Assume that Beasley reported net income of $27,000 for the period ending December 31, 1996. Adjust net income for the gain or loss experienced by the company on these outstanding bonds due to the change in market interest rates. Ignore income taxes. Do you believe that the gain or loss represents an increase or decrease in the wealth of the company? Why?
d. Assume that Beasley retired the bonds by purchasing them on the open market. Record the journal entry, and compare the gain or loss recognized on the retirement with the gain or loss computed in (c) above. Discuss.

E11–17

(Analyzing bond disclosures)

The information below was taken from the balance sheet of Cohort Enterprises as of December 31, 1997.

Bond payable	$200,000	
Less: Unamortized discount	6,941	$193,059

FOOTNOTES:

The bonds have a stated interest rate of 5 percent and will mature on December 31, 1999. The market value of the bonds as of December 31, 1997, is $186,479.

REQUIRED:

a. Compute the effective interest rate in effect when the bonds were issued.
b. What effective rate would an investor be earning by purchasing the bonds on December 31, 1997, at the market price and holding the bonds until maturity?
c. Assume that Cohort reported net income of $38,500 for the period ending December 31, 1997. Adjust net income for the gain or loss experienced by the company on these outstanding bonds due to the change in market interest rates. Ignore income taxes. Do you believe that the gain or loss represents an increase or decrease in the wealth of the company? Why?
d. Assume that Cohort retired the bonds by purchasing them on the open market. Record the journal entry, and compare the gain or loss recognized on the retirement with the gain or loss computed in (c) above. Discuss.

E11–18

(Accounting for leases and the financial statements)

Tradcall, Inc., leases automobiles for its salesforce. On January 1, 1996, the company leased 100 automobiles and agreed to make lease payments of $10,000 per automobile each year. The lease agreement expires on December 31, 2000, at which time the automobiles can be purchased by Tradeall for a nominal price. Assume an effective rate of 10 percent.

REQUIRED:

a. Compute the annual rental expense if the lease is treated as an operating lease.
b. Prepare the journal entry on January 1, 1996, if the lease is treated as a capital lease. What dollar amount represents an approximation of the fair market value of the automobiles?
c. Assume that the automobiles are depreciated over a five-year life, using the straight-line method with no salvage value. Compute the total rental expense (interest and depreciation) associated with the lease during the first year, if the lease is treated as a capital lease.
d. Which of the two methods of treatment (operating or capital) would give rise to a higher net income in the first year? Which method would give rise to a lower debt/equity ratio?
e. Define off-balance-sheet financing, and explain how leases can be arranged to practice it.

E11–19

(Financing asset purchases)

Watts Motors plans to acquire a building and can either borrow cash from a bank to finance the purchase or lease the building from the current owner. The sales price of the building is $149,388. If the company wishes to finance the purchase with a bank loan, it must sign a ten-year note with a face value of $149,388 and a stated interest rate of 12 percent. If the company leases the building, it must make an annual lease payment of a constant-dollar amount for ten years, at which time the building can be purchased for a nominal fee.

REQUIRED:

a. Compute the annual lease payment that would make the two alternatives equivalent. Ignore the nominal purchase fee at the end of year 10.
b. Describe how the timing of the cash flows would differ between the two alternatives.
c. Provide the journal entries that would be recorded when the building is acquired if the company (1) finances the purchase with a bank loan, (2) leases the building and accounts for it as a capital lease, or (3) leases the building and accounts for it as an operating lease.

d. If the company leases the building and accounts for its as a capital lease, compute the balance sheet value of the lease liability after the second lease payment.

e. Compute the present value of the remaining lease payments as of the end of the second year.

E11–20

(Inferring the effective rate of interest)

Compute the effective rate of interest on the following long-term debts. Interest payments on the notes are made annually and interest payments on the bonds are made semiannually.

DEBT	FAIR MARKET VALUE OF RECEIPT	FACE VALUE	LIFE	STATED INTEREST RATE
Note	$10,000	$ 10,000	6 years	8%
Note	35,056	100,000	8 years	0
Note	922	1,000	5 years	7
Bond	11,635	10,000	10 years	6
Bond	54,323	50,000	15 years	9

E11–21

(Appendix 11A: The effective interest method values a note receivable at present value over the note's life)

On January 1, 1996, Bondinger Financial Services lent $9,652 to Weyton Industries. In exchange, Bondinger received a note with a maturity date of December 31, 1997, a face value of $10,000, and a stated annual interest rate of 8 percent, to be paid each December 31 throughout the life of the note.

REQUIRED:

a. Compute the present value of the note's future cash outflows at discount rates of 8 percent, 10 percent, and 12 percent.

b. What is the effective rate of interest on the note?

c. Using the effective rate of interest calculated in (b), compute the present value of the note's future cash inflows as of January 1, 1997.

d. Prepare the journal entries for Bondinger Financial Services to record the transactions on January 1, 1996, December 31, 1996, and December 31, 1997.

e. Compute the net book value of the note receivable as of January 1, 1997. Is this amount greater than, equal to, or less than the present value of the note's future cash inflows calculated in (c)? Why?

E11–22

(Appendix 11A: Accounting for bond investments)

On January 1, 1996, Christie Sohn Company purchased ten bonds ($1,000 face value) with a stated annual interest rate of 10 percent. The bonds mature in five years, and over that time interest is paid semiannually on June 30 and December 31. The bonds were purchased to yield an annual rate of 10 percent.

REQUIRED:

a. Without computing the present value of the bonds, state whether Christie Sohn purchased the bonds at face value, at a premium, or at a discount.

b. Prepare the entry to record the purchase of the bonds.

c. Prepare the entries associated with the bond investment on June 30 and December 31, 1996.

d. Compute the book value of the bond investment as of December 31, 1996.

e. Repeat (a)-(d), assuming that the bonds were purchased to yield 8 percent.

f. Repeat (a)-(d), assuming that the bonds were purchased to yield 12 percent.

E11–23

(Appendix 11B: The decision to purchase a bond)

Dylander bonds are selling on the open market at 89.16. The bonds have a stated interest rate of 8 percent and mature in 8 years. Interest payments are made semiannually.

REQUIRED:

a. Assume that your required rate of return is 12 percent. Would you buy the bonds? Why or why not?

b. At what required rate of return would you be indifferent to purchasing the bonds?

PROBLEMS

P11–1

(Computing the face value of a note payable)

On December 31, 1996, East Race Kayak Club decided to borrow $20,000 for two years. The Bend Bank currently is charging a 10 percent effective annual interest rate on similar loans.

REQUIRED:

a. Assume that the club borrows $20,000 and signs a two-year note with a 10 percent stated annual interest rate. What would be the face amount of the note payable?

b. Assume that the club borrows $20,000 and signs a two-year note with a stated annual interest rate of zero. What would be the face amount of the note payable?

c. Prepare the journal entry to record the note payable, assuming that the club signs
    (1) the note in (a).
    (2) the note in (b).

d. Prepare the entries necessary on December 31, 1998, assuming that the club signs
    (1) the note in (a) (interest payable on December 31).
    (2) the note in (b).

P11–2

(Accounting for bonds with an effective rate greater than the stated rate)

Hartl Enterprises issued ten $1,000 bonds on September 30, 1996, with a stated annual interest rate of 8 percent. These bonds will mature on October 1, 2006, and have an effective rate of 10 percent. Interest is paid semiannually on October 1 and April 1. The first interest payment will be made on April 1, 1997.

REQUIRED:

a. Without computing the present value of the bonds, will they be issued at par value, at a discount, or at a premium? Explain your answer.

b. Prepare the entry to record the issuance of the bonds on September 30, 1996.

c. Prepare any adjusting journal entries necessary on December 31, 1996.

d. Prepare the entry to record the interest payment on April 1, 1997.

P11–3

(The balance sheet value of debt and the long-term debt/equity ratio)

The balance sheet as of December 31, 1996, for Manheim Corporation follows.

ASSETS		LIABILITIES AND STOCKHOLDERS' EQUITY	
Current assets	$ 85,000	Current liabilities	$ 70,000
Noncurrent assets	125,000	Long-term liabilities	40,000
		Stockholders' equity	100,000
		Total liabilities and	
Total assets	$210,000	stockholders' equity	$210,000

REQUIRED:

a. Compute Manheim Corporation's long-term debt/equity ratio.

b. Assume that Manheim Corporation is considering borrowing money and signing a five-year note with the following terms.

Face value	**$40,000**
Stated interest rate	**0%**
Effective interest rate	**11%**

Compute the proceeds of the note, and compute the company's long-term debt/equity ratio if it decides to borrow the money.

c. Assume that the Manheim Corporation is considering issuing bonds that mature on December 31, 2016. The bonds have a face value of $40,000, a stated interest rate of 10 percent, and an effective interest rate of 8 percent. Compute the proceeds from the bond issuance, and compute the company's long-term debt/equity ratio if it issues the bonds. The bonds pay interest semiannually.

P11–4

(Accounting for notes issued at a discount and at face value)

Patnon Plastics needs some cash to finance expansion. Patnon issued the following debt to acquire the cash.

1. A five-year note with a stated interest rate of zero, a face value of $20,000, and an effective interest rate of 10 percent.
2. An eight-year note with an annual stated rate of 8 percent and a face value of $35,000. Interest is paid annually on December 31. The effective interest rate is 10 percent.
3. A ten-year note with an annual stated rate of 8 percent and a face value of $50,000. Interest is paid semiannually on June 30 and December 31. The effective interest rate is 8 percent.

All three notes were issued on January 1, 1997.

REQUIRED:

a. Compute the proceeds from each of the three notes.
b. Prepare the entries to record the issuance of each note.
c. Prepare the entry to record the interest paid on June 30, 1997, on the ten year note.
d. Prepare the entries to record the interest paid on December 31, 1997, on the eight-year note and the ten-year note.
e. Prepare the adjusting entry required on December 31, 1997, to recognize accrued interest on the five-year note.

P11–5

(The effects of various notes payable on the financial statements)

The balance sheet as of December 31, 1997, for Boyton Sons follows.

ASSETS		LIABILITIES AND STOCKHOLDERS' EQUITY	
Current assets	$ 40,000	Current liabilities	$ 30,000
Noncurrent assets	80,000	Long-term liabilities	60,000
		Stockholders' equity	30,000
		Total liabilities and	
Total assets	$120,000	stockholders' equity	$120,000

The company needs capital to finance operations and purchase new equipment. Boyton is not certain how much money it will need and is considering one of the following three-year notes payable. Each note would mature on January 1, 2001.

(A) Face value = $50,000   Stated interest rate = 0%   Proceeds = $37,566
(B) Face value = $50,000   Stated interest rate = 10%*   Proceeds = $50,000
(C) Face value = $50,000   Stated interest rate = 6%*   Proceeds = $45,027

*Interest paid annually.

REQUIRED:

a. Determine the effective interest rate of each note.
b. Compute the amounts that would complete the following table.

	INTEREST EXPENSE (A)	INTEREST EXPENSE (B)	INTEREST EXPENSE (C)
Year 1			
Year 2			
Year 3			

c. Assume that Boyton can earn a 12% return on the borrowed money and that it reinvests all interest that it earns. Compute the annual income (return − interest expense) generated from each of the three notes.
d. Compute the amounts that would complete the following chart. (Hint: Consider the effect of annual income from (c) on stockholders' equity as well as the new debt.)

	DEBT/EQUITY (A)	DEBT/EQUITY (B)	DEBT/EQUITY (C)
12/31/98			
12/31/99			
12/31/2000			

e. Discuss some of the trade-offs involved in choosing among the three notes.

P11–6

(The difference between cash interest payments and interest expense)

Earl Rix, president of Rix Driving Range and Health Club, has provided you with the following information:

	1998	1997
BALANCE SHEET		
Notes payable	$800,000	$800,000
Less: Discount on notes payable	55,000	70,000
INCOME STATEMENT		
Interest expense	$ 95,000	

The stated annual interest rate on the notes is 10 percent, and interest is paid annually on December 31. The $95,000 in interest expense is due solely on these notes. While reviewing the company's 1998 financial statements, Mr. Rix is having difficulty understanding why the amount charged to interest expense does not equal the amount of cash actually disbursed during 1998 in payment of the interest on these notes.

REQUIRED:

a. Assuming that Rix Driving Range and Health Club makes all of its interest payments on time, how much cash was actually disbursed during 1998 for interest payments on these notes?

b. Explain to Mr. Rix why interest expense does not equal the amount of cash disbursed for interest. What does the difference between the cash disbursed and the amount charged as interest expense represent?

c. What was the effective interest rate at the time the notes were issued?

d. Provide the journal entry to record the payment of interest on December 31, 1998.

P11–7

(The effective interest method, interest expense, and present value)

Hartney Enterprises issued twenty $1,000 bonds on June 30, 1997, with a stated annual interest rate of 6 percent that mature in six years. Interest is paid semiannually on December 31 and June 30. The effective interest rate as of June 30, 1997, the date of issuance, was 8 percent.

REQUIRED:

a. Compute the present value of the cash flows associated with these bonds on June 30, 1997, using the following format:

Face value		XX
Present value of cash payments at maturity	XX	
Present value of cash interest payments	+XX	
Less: Total present value		XX
Discount (premium) on bonds		XX

b. Compute the present value of the remaining cash flows associated with these bonds on December 31, 1997. What does the present value on December 31, 1997, represent?

c. What does the difference between the present value of the remaining cash flows associated with these bonds on June 30, 1997, and December 31, 1997, represent?

d. Prepare the entry to record the interest payment on December 31, 1997, using the effective interest method. Is the amount of Discount on Bonds Payable amortized in this entry the same as the amount found in (c)? Why or why not?

P11–8

(The effective interest method and the straight-line method: effects on the financial statements)

Ross Running Shoes issued ten $1,000 bonds with a stated annual rate of 10 percent on June 30, 1997. These bonds mature on June 30, 2000. The bonds have an effective interest rate of 8 percent, and interest is paid semiannually on December 31 and June 30.

REQUIRED:

a. How much must Ross Running Shoes invest in a bank on June 30, 1997, at an annual rate of 8 percent, compounded semiannually, to meet all the future cash flow requirements of these bonds and have no money left after repaying the principal on June 30, 2000?

b. Prepare the entry to record the interest payment on December 31, 1997. Assume that the company uses the effective interest method.

c. Prepare the entry to record the interest payment on December 31, 1997. Assume that the company amortizes an equal amount of premium each year (i.e., straight-line method).

d. Which method (effective interest or straight-line) of amortizing the premium will allow Ross Running Shoes to recognize the higher amount of net income in 1997?

e. Which method (effective interest or straight-line) of amortizing the premium will allow Ross Running Shoes to recognize the higher amount of net income in 2000?

P11-9

(Why the effective interest method is preferred to the straight-line method)

Consider the three notes payable listed here. Each was issued on January 1, 1997, and matures on December 31, 1999. Interest payments are made annually on December 31.

NOTE	FACE VALUE	STATED INTEREST RATE	EFFECTIVE INTEREST RATE
A	$1,000	10%	6%
B	$1,000	10	10
C	$1,000	6	10

REQUIRED:

a. Compute the present value of the remaining cash outflows for each note at each date.

NOTE	1/1/97	12/31/97	12/31/98
A			
B			
C			

b. Compute the balance sheet value of each note payable at each of the above dates using the effective interest method.

c. Compute the balance sheet values of each note payable at each of the above dates using the straight-line method (i.e., amortize an equal amount of the discount or premium each year).

d. Why is the effective interest method preferred to the straight-line method for financial reporting purposes?

P11-10

(Redemption and updating amortization)

Ginny & Rick Eateries reported the following account balances in the December 31, 1996, financial report.

Bonds payable $500,000
Premium on bonds payable   12,600

The bonds have a stated annual interest rate of 8 percent and an effective interest rate of 6 percent. Interest is paid on June 30 and December 31.

REQUIRED:

a. Compute the gain or loss recorded on January 1, 1997, if the bonds are called at 104.
b. Compute the gain or loss recorded on January 1, 1997, if the bonds are called at 108.
c. Compute the gain or loss recorded on July 1, 1997, if the bonds are called at 110.

P11-11

(Call provisions and bond market prices)

Ficus Tree Farm issued five $1,000 bonds with a stated annual interest rate of 12 percent on January 1, 1997, that mature on January 1, 2002. Interest is paid semiannually on June 30 and December 31. The bonds were sold at a price that resulted in an effective interest rate of 14 percent. The bonds can be called for 103.5 beginning June 30, 1999.

REQUIRED:

a. Prepare the entry on January 1, 1997, to record the issuance of these bonds.
b. Prepare the entry on June 30, 1997, to record the interest payment.

c. Assume that Ficus wishes to retire the bonds on June 30, 1999. If the bonds are selling on the open market on that date at a price that would result in a return of 10 percent, should Ficus exercise the call provision or simply attempt to buy the bonds at the market price?

d. Is it likely that Ficus would be able to buy back all outstanding bonds on the bond market at market price?

e. Prepare the entries necessary on June 30, 1999, if Ficus chooses to exercise the call provision.

P11–12

(Tax deductible bond interest and the present value of cash outflows)

Taylor Corporation is contemplating issuing bonds to raise cash to finance an expansion. Before issuing the debt, the controller of the company wants to prepare an analysis of the cash flows and the interest expense associated with the issuance. Taylor Corporation is considering issuing one hundred $1,000 bonds on June 30, 1997, that mature on June 30, 2001. The bonds will have a stated annual interest rate of 6 percent, and interest is to be paid semiannually on December 31 and June 30. The bonds will have an effective interest rate of 10 percent.

REQUIRED:

a. Compute the amounts that would complete the following table with respect to the bond issuance being considered by Taylor.

DATE	INTEREST EXPENSE	CASH PAYMENT	UNAMORTIZED DISCOUNT	BALANCE SHEET VALUE
6/30/97				
12/31/97				
6/30/98				
12/31/98				
6/30/99				
12/31/99				
6/30/2000				
12/31/2000				
6/30/2001				

b. Find the difference between the total cash inflow from issuing the bonds and the total cash outflows from interest and principal payments.

c. Recognizing that cash interest payments are tax deductible and assuming a tax rate of 34 percent, recompute the difference you found in (b).

d. Repeat (c), but now consider the time value of money by using the effective rate of these bonds to compute the present value of the net future cash outflows due to interest and principal payments.

P11–13

(Accounting for a capital lease)

Mackey Company acquired equipment on January 1, 1996, through a leasing agreement that required an annual payment of $30,000. Assume that the lease has a term of five years and that the life of the equipment is also five years. The lease is treated as a capital lease, and the FMV ∈ PV of the equipment is $119,781.30. Mackey uses the straight-line method to depreciate its fixed assets. The effective annual interest rate on the lease is 8 percent.

REQUIRED:

a. Compute the amounts that would complete the table.

DATE	BALANCE SHEET VALUE OF EQUIPMENT	LEASEHOLD OBLIGATION	INTEREST EXPENSE	DEPRECIATION EXPENSE	TOTAL EXPENSE
1/1/96					
12/31/96					
12/31/97					
12/31/98					
12/31/99					
12/31/2000					

b.   Compute rent expense for 1996–2000 if the lease is treated as an operating lease.

c.   Compute total expense over the five-year period under the two methods and comment.

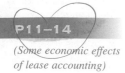

P11–14

(Some economic effects of lease accounting)

The balance sheet as of December 31, 1996, for Thompkins Laundry follows.

ASSETS		LIABILITIES AND STOCKHOLDERS' EQUITY	
Current assets	$10,000	Current liabilities	$10,000
Noncurrent assets	60,000	Long-term liabilities	20,000
		Stockholders' equity	40,000
		Total liabilities and	
Total assets	$70,000	stockholders' equity	$70,000

The $20,000 of long-term debt on the balance sheet represents a long-term note that requires Thompkins to maintain a debt/equity ratio of less than 1:1. If the covenant is violated, the company will be required to pay the entire principal of the note immediately. On January 1, 1997, Thompkins entered into a lease agreement. The agreement provides the company with laundry equipment for five years, for an annual rental fee of $5,000.

REQUIRED:

a.   Compute Thompkins' debt/equity ratio as of January 1, 1997, if the company treats the lease as an operating lease.

b.   Compute Thompkins' debt/equity ratio as of January 1, 1997, if the company treats the lease as a capital lease. Assume an effective interest rate of 12 percent.

c.   Compare the expenses recognized during 1997 if the lease is treated as operating to the expenses recognized during 1997 if the lease is treated as capital. Assume that the leased equipment has a five-year useful life and is depreciated using the straight-line method.

d.   Discuss some of the reasons why Thompkins would want to treat the lease as an operating lease. How might the company arrange the terms of the lease so that it will be considered an operating lease?

P11–15

(Financing asset purchases with notes and inferring the effective rate of interest)

Memminger Corporation purchased equipment on January 1, 1997. The terms of the purchase required that the company pay $1,000 in interest at the end of each year for five years and $20,000 at the end of the fifth year. The FMV of the equipment on January 1, 1997, was $17,604.

REQUIRED:

a.   Prepare the journal entry that would be recorded on January 1, 1997.

b.   Compute the effective interest rate on the note payable.

c.   Prepare the journal entry that would be recorded when the first interest payment is made on December 31, 1997.

d.   Compute the net book value of the note payable as of December 31, 1997.

P11–16

(Appendix 11A: Inferring information about a note receivable from the financial statements)

An excerpt from the financial statement of Lombardy Services follows. The information refers to a single note receivable.

	1997	1996
BALANCE SHEET		
Note receivable	$20,000	$20,000
Less: Discount on note receivable	1,200	1,600
INCOME STATEMENT		
Interest revenue	$ 1,656	$ 1,622

REQUIRED:

a.   What is the effective interest rate on the note receivable?

b.   What is the stated interest rate on the note receivable?

c. Provide the journal entry to record interest revenue during 1997.
d. What is the present value of the note's future cash inflows as of December 31, 1997, using the effective interest rate on the date when the note was issued?

P11–17

(Appendix 11A: Accounting for bond investments purchased at a discount and a premium)

On July 1, 1997, Lawton Corporation purchased bonds as a long-term investment with a total face value of $400,000. The bonds have an annual stated interest rate of 10 percent, and they pay interest semiannually on December 31 and June 30. The bonds mature on June 30, 2007.

REQUIRED:

a. Assume that Lawton Corporation purchased these bonds for $354,118.
   (1) Without computing the effective interest rate on these bonds, state whether the annual effective interest rate would be less than, equal to, or greater than the annual coupon (stated) rate. Explain your answer.
   (2) Compute the present value of the bond's future cash flows using discount rates of 8 percent, 10 percent, and 12 percent. What is the effective rate of return on these bonds?
   (3) Prepare the entry to record the acquisition of these bonds.
   (4) Prepare any entries associated with these bonds necessary on December 31, 1997.
b. Assume that these bonds were purchased at a price that produced an effective annual interest rate of 8 percent.
   (1) Compute the price of these bonds.
   (2) Record the acquisition of these bonds.
   (3) Prepare any entries associated with these bonds necessary on December 31, 1997.

P11–18

(Appendix 11B: Determinants of bond market prices)

Hodge Sports bonds are selling on the open market at par value. The bonds have a stated interest rate of 9 percent and mature in 5 years. You have determined that the risk-free rate is 7 percent.

REQUIRED:

a. What is the maximum risk premium you could attach to these bonds and still be willing to purchase them?
b. Assume that Standard & Poor's lowers the credit rating of Hodge Sports bonds, and this action causes you to increase your risk premium to 5 percent. The bonds have a face value of $1,000 and pay interest semiannually. What price would you be willing to pay for the bonds?
c. (Independent of b.) Assume that you read in *The Wall Street Journal* that the prime rate has been cut by 1 percent. All other factors being equal, would this news tend to increase or decrease the market price of Hodge Sports bonds? Why? Assume that reducing the prime rate by 1 percent reflects a reduction in the risk-free rate of 1 percent, and estimate the magnitude of this effect on the price of Hodge Sports bonds.

CASES

C11–1

(Repurchasing outstanding debt)

Sun Company, an oil-refining concern, purchased all of its outstanding 8 1/2 percent (stated rate) debentures due November 15, 2000, as part of a restructuring plan. The balance sheet value of each outstanding debenture at the time of the repurchase was $875, and the company paid $957.50 for each $1,000 face value bond.

REQUIRED:

a. What is a debenture? Would such bonds tend to be issued at higher or lower prices than secured bonds? Why?
b. Briefly discuss why a company would repurchase its outstanding debt.

c. Explain how this repurchase would affect (increase, decrease, or no effect) the components of the accounting equation: assets, liabilities, stockholders' equity. Would a gain or loss be recognized on the transaction?

d. Would the gain or loss be recognized if Sun Company had not repurchased the bonds? Why or why not?

C11–2

(Bonds with a stated interest rate of zero)

Several years ago, J.C. Penney Company issued bonds with a face value of $200 million and a stated interest rate of zero, which matured eight years later, for 33.24. That same year Martin Marietta, Northwest Industries, and Alcoa also issued bonds with stated interest rates of zero.

REQUIRED:

a. Why would an investor purchase a bond with a stated interest rate of zero?

b. Compute the effective interest rate on the bond issuance.

c. In terms of its cash flows, explain why a company might wish to issue bonds with a stated interest rate of zero.

d. At what price would the bonds have been issued if the stated interest rate had been 5 percent? 18 percent? Assume that interest payments would be made annually.

C11–3

(Buy or lease: financial statement effects)

Assume that United Airlines is planning to purchase a jet passenger plane, with a price of $45,636,480, from the Boeing Company. United is considering structuring the transaction in one of two ways. In Alternative 1, United would borrow the necessary cash from Federal City Bank and sign a note requiring payments of $6 million at the end of each year for fifteen years. The proceeds from the loan would then be used to purchase the airplane. In Alternative 2, United would lease the airplane from Boeing and make annual lease payments of $6 million for fifteen years, at which time it could purchase the airplane from Boeing for a nominal sum. United depreciates its aircraft over a useful life of fifteen years using the straight-line method.

REQUIRED:

a. Determine the effective interest rate on the note and the lease arrangement.

b. Provide the journal entries that would be recorded under Alternative 1 to reflect the borrowing and the purchase of the airplane.

c. Provide the journal entry that would be recorded under Alternative 2 when the lease agreement is signed, if the lease is treated as a capital lease.

d. Compare the effects on the financial statements caused by (b) and (c).

e. Provide the journal entry that would be recorded under Alternative 2 when the lease agreement is signed, if the lease is treated as an operating lease.

f. Which of the three alternative treatments (borrowing, capital lease, operating lease) could be considered off-balance-sheet financing? Explain why United might want to structure the transaction in this way.

C11–4

(Financing acquisition with debt)

"'Out on a limb, over his head'—that's the typical reaction every time Rupert Murdock adds another debt-financed chunk to his global media colossus, News Corp. In the past five years, its reported assets have more than quadrupled [but Murdock is stepping] up to the plate again, with a $1.4 billion offer for MGA/UA Communications Co. . . Murdock is rapidly approaching limits on his ability to borrow. News Corp.'s ratio of debt to equity [is] .98, up from .70, and not far below the 1.1 ceiling imposed by the large group of banks that make up News Corp.'s chief source of borrowing. A News Corp. insider estimates the company has only about $1 billion in additional borrowing power under the bank covenants" (*Business Week,* October 2, 1989).

REQUIRED:

a. Explain why Murdock's financing needs are handled by a large group of banks, rather than a single bank, and why these banks would impose a ceiling on News Corp.'s debt/equity ratio.

b. The article states further that the company's "leverage may well be greater than [what is indicated by News Corp.'s debt/equity ratio]." Explain how this could be and how such a situation would affect the risk incurred by the banks who provide Murdock's financing.

c. The article also states that "in evaluating properties [to acquire], Murdock considers their ability to generate cash . . . as a far more important variable than their asset value." Provide a plausible reason why Murdock would consider the investment's ability to generate cash as so important.

C11–5

(Holding debt in times of recession)

A recent article in *The Wall Street Journal* (October 2, 1990) noted that as the country slid deeper into a recession in the early 1990s, companies with high amounts of cash relative to their debt are likely to be coveted by the stock market, while companies with high levels of debt will be slashing dividends, payrolls, and capital expenditures to stay afloat. High debt, combined with slower sales and increasing energy and labor costs, will prove to be a deadly combination for a number of companies, and Standard and Poor's found that both dividend decreases and omissions were up in 1990. *The Wall Street Journal* reported the following year that defaults on corporate notes and bonds payable rose to a record level as companies missed payments of $8.2 billion of debt. Moody's Investor Service notes further that in the past 15 years an average of only 41 percent of the face value of defaulted debt was recovered by investors; secured bondholders recovered an average of 67 percent of the face value, while holders of debentures recovered an average of only 23 percent.

REQUIRED:

a. U.S. corporations have dramatically increased their debt levels since 1980. Discuss how high levels of debt may influence the way in which a company is managed. That is, how might management concerns and decisions be different because a company is carrying a large amount of debt?

b. Describe the financial statement effects of this borrowing activity, and explain how these effects could have helped investors and creditors to avoid the losses incurred during the recession in the early 1990s. How and why might the reported levels of debt on the balance sheet be less than the actual levels of debt carried by the company?

c. Define a debenture and explain why defaults on debentures would lead to a lower recovery rate for investors than defaults on secured bonds.

C11–6

(Adjusting ratios for lease accounting)

Albertson's and Safeway are leading retail food chains in the United States. As of the end of 1994, Albertson's reported $3.6 billion in total assets and $1.9 billion in total liabilities, while Safeway reported $5 billion in total assets and $4.4 billion in total liabilities. Both companies, as is the case with most large retailers, lease most of their stores. Albertson's incurs about $75 million per year in lease payments, treating about 70 percent of its leases as operating leases for financial reporting purposes. Safeway incurs about $170 million per year in lease payments and treats about 75 percent of its leases as operating leases. The approximate present value of the future cash flows associated with the operating leases of Albertson's and Safeway are $465 million and $820 million, respectively.

REQUIRED:

a. Compute the liabilities/total assets ratio for both companies.

b. Assume that both companies account for all their leases as capital leases, and recompute their liabilities/total assets ratios.

c. By how much does Safeway's adjusted ratio exceed that of Albertson's? Does the adjustment make much of a difference? Why or why not?

d. Explain why an analyst may wish to make the adjustments required above.

C11–7

(Bond prices and economic news)

The Wall Street Journal (June 5, 1995) recently reported:

Alan Greenspan may not see a recession on the horizon, but it sure looks as if a few people in the bond market do. After a fierce month-long price rally, the bond market had another big day

Friday, with the price of 30-year bonds at one point equaling their largest one-day gain in a decade . . . Fueling the buying spree was a Labor Department report showing that nonfarm payrolls in May shrank by 101,000, a startling drop . . . The signs of economic weakness did not stop there . . . April's previously reported employment figure—a decline of 9,000 jobs—was revised upward only slightly, by 2,000 jobs rather than the upward revision of 50,000 or more Wall Street envisioned.

REQUIRED:
Explain why weak economic news would cause a rally in the bond market.

C11–8

(MCI annual report)

Refer to the 1994 annual report of MCI and answer the following questions.
a. Compute MCI's long-term debt-to-equity ratio over the last five years. In general, is it increasing or decreasing, and why did it change significantly during 1993 and 1994?
b. As of December 31, 1994, what portion of MCI's long-term debt was due in the current period?
c. Did MCI issue any long-term debt in 1994, and if so, how much and what were the terms of the issuances?
d. As of December 31, 1994, what is the estimated fair market value of MCI's outstanding long-term debt, and how does this amount compare to the book value? Explain why the market value differs from the book value and whether this difference has any impact on MCI's financial wealth.
e. In 1993 MCI redeemed a sizable amount of its outstanding long-term debt. How much did the company redeem? Where did it get the funds to finance the redemptions? How large a gain or a loss was recognized on the transactions?
f. To what extent does MCI lease its facilities? Estimate the company's annual lease payments and the portion of leases treated as operating leases for financial reporting purposes. What portion of MCI's long-term debt is comprised of capital leases, and what portion of MCI's long-lived assets are comprised of capital lease facilities?

CHAPTER 12

STOCKHOLDERS' EQUITY

LEARNING OBJECTIVES

LO 1 Identify the three forms of financing, and describe the relative importance of each to major U.S. corporations.

LO 2 Distinguish debt from equity, and explain why such a distinction is important to investors and creditors, managers, and accountants.

LO 3 Explain the economic consequences associated with the methods used to account for stockholders' equity.

LO 4 Describe the rights associated with preferred and common stock and the methods used to account for stock issuances.

LO 5 Distinguish among the market value, book value, and par (stated) value of a share of common stock.

LO 6 Define treasury stock, explain why corporations acquire it, and summarize the methods used to account for it.

LO 7 Define a cash dividend, and describe some of the dividend strategies followed by corporations.

LO 8 Distinguish between a stock dividend and a stock split, and briefly explain why corporations declare them.

LO 9 Explain how retained earnings are appropriated and why corporations follow such a practice.

LO 1 Companies generate assets from three sources: (1) borrowings, (2) issuing equity securities, and (3) retaining funds generated through profitable operations. Each of these sources is represented on the right side of the basic accounting equation (balance sheet), which is depicted in Figure 12–1.

FIGURE 12–1

The basic accounting equation

STOCKHOLDERS' EQUITY

Assets = (1) Liabilities + (2) Contributed capital + (3) Earned capital

Preferred stock   Retained earnings
Common stock
Additional paid-in

Chapters 10 and 11 were devoted to current and long-term liabilities, which represent the first of the three financing sources illustrated in Figure 12–1. This chapter is devoted to stockholders' equity, which comprises the other two financing sources: (2) contributed capital and (3) earned capital. **Contributed capital**, which reflects contributions from a company's owners, consists of three components: preferred stock, common stock, and additional paid-in capital. The major component of **earned capital** is retained earnings, a measure of the assets that have been generated through a company's profitable operations and not paid to the owners in the form of dividends. The total dollar amount of stockholders' equity is also referred to as a company's **net assets**, **book value**, or **net worth**.

Contributed and earned capital are important financing sources for many major U.S. companies. Funds used to acquire other companies, purchase machinery and equipment, finance plant expansion, pay off debts, and support operations are often generated by issuing preferred stock, issuing common stock, and retaining funds provided by profitable operations.

An article in *The Wall Street Journal* (November 12, 1992) commented that U.S. companies have recently raised record amounts of capital to pay off high-cost debt piled up in the 1980s. Ford Motor Company, for example, slashed its debt/equity ratio from 42% to 35% through two huge stock offerings that together raised more than $3 billion. "That money has allowed Ford, despite a record $2.3 billion loss in 1991, to continue to launch new vehicles, including the Ford Ranger and Mercury Voyager Minivan." Other companies, like York International and International Paper Company, used money from equity issuances to finance acquisitions, and RJR Nabisco used $3.3 billion in stock offerings "to chop its total debt by one third."

THE RELATIVE IMPORTANCE OF LIABILITIES, CONTRIBUTED CAPITAL, AND EARNED CAPITAL

Figure 12–2 indicates the relative importance of liabilities, contributed capital, and earned capital (retained earnings) on the balance sheets of a selected group of nine major U.S. companies. While these companies are not representative of all U.S. companies, the group does include a wide variety of operations and represents nine different industries.

The relative size of stockholders' equity on the balance sheets of these companies can be computed by summing the percentages of assets provided by contributed cap-

FIGURE 12–2

The relative importance of liabilities, contributed capital, and retained earnings (percentage of total assets)

COMPANY (DESCRIPTION)	LIABILITIES	CONTRIBUTED CAPITAL	RETAINED EARNINGS
Albertsons (grocery chain)	53%	8%	39%
Boeing (aircraft manufacturer)	55	9	36
Citicorp (financial services)	93	3	4
Federal Express (mail delivery)	68	13	19
Ford Motor Company (auto manufacturer)	90	3	7
Goodyear (tire manufacturer)	69	7	24
May Department Stores (retail)	56	2	42
Sears (retail, insurance, real estate)	88	3	9
Sprint (telecommunications)	70	12	18
Average	71%	7%	22%

Source: 1994 annual reports.

ital and retained earnings. On average, stockholders' equity accounts for 29 percent (7% + 22%) of the companies' assets. Current and long-term liabilities account for 71 percent. Thus, these major U.S. companies tend to rely more heavily on debt as a source of financing than on contributed and earned capital.

Within stockholders' equity, retained earnings (21 percent) appears to be a more important source of financing than contributed capital (7 percent). The relative importance of retained earnings is partially because Figure 12–2 consists only of successful, established companies, which have generated profits over many years. In addition, these companies have repurchased much of their outstanding stock, leaving very little contributed capital on the balance sheet. Younger, less-established companies often have not been either profitable enough or in existence long enough to rely heavily on internally generated funds as a source of financing.

Note, however, that there is some variation across the different companies. Citicorp, for example, relies almost exclusively on debt financing. Such reliance is typical of banks and other financial institutions. The heavy reliance of Ford Motor Company on debt (90 percent) is due to the inclusion of Financial Services Group, the subsidiary used to finance customer automobile purchases, in the company's balance sheet.

DEBT AND EQUITY DISTINGUISHED

LO 2 Chapters 10 and 11 presented the basic characteristics of the debt contracts between a company and its creditors. This section describes how the nature of this relationship differs from that between a company and its stockholders. As will be discussed later, such a distinction is important to investors, creditors, management, and auditors.

CHARACTERISTICS OF DEBT

When a company borrows money, it establishes a relationship with an outside party, a *creditor* or *debtholder*, whose influence on the company's operations is defined by a formal legal contract, containing a number of specific provisions. These provisions were discussed in Chapters 10 and 11, and they are summarized in Figure 12–3 along with characteristics of equity.

FIGURE 12–3	DEBT	EQUITY
Characteristics of debt and equity	1. **Formal legal contract** 2. **Fixed maturity date** 3. **Fixed periodic interest payments** 4. **Security in case of default** 5. **No direct voice in management; influence through debt covenants** 6. **Interest is an expense.**	1. **No legal contract** 2. **No fixed maturity date** 3. **Discretionary dividend payments** 4. **Residual asset interest** 5. **Vote for board of directors** 6. **Dividends are not an expense, but a distribution of retained earnings.**

CHARACTERISTICS OF EQUITY

When a corporation raises capital by issuing stock, it establishes a relationship with an owner, often referred to as an *equityholder*, or *stockholder*. Unlike debt, an equity relationship is not evidenced by a precisely specified contract. There is no maturity date, because a stockholder is an owner of a company until it ceases operations or until the equity interest is transferred to another party. Dividend payments are at the discretion of the board of directors, and stockholders have no legal right to receive dividends until they are declared. In case of bankruptcy, the rights of the stockholders to the available assets are subordinate (secondary) to the rights of the creditors, who are paid in an order which can usually be determined by examining the terms in the debt contracts. The stockholders receive the assets that remain. That is, a corporation's owners have a **residual interest** to the corporation's assets in case of bankruptcy.

Stockholders, however, can exert significant influence over corporate management. Each ownership share carries a vote that is cast in the election of the board of directors at the annual stockholder's meeting. The board, whose function is to represent the interests of the stockholders, declares dividends, determines executive compensation, has the power to hire and fire management, and sets the general policies of the corporation. In addition, certain significant transactions, such as the issuance of additional stock, often must be approved by vote of the stockholders.

Finally, distributions by a corporation to the stockholders (dividends) are not considered operating expenses by either generally accepted accounting principles or the Internal Revenue Service. They are considered a return on the owners' original investments. Consequently, dividends are neither included as expenses on the income statement, nor are they considered deductible expenses in the computation of taxable income. On the financial statements, dividends serve to reduce retained earnings without passing through the income statement.

WHY IS IT IMPORTANT TO DISTINGUISH DEBT FROM EQUITY?

It is important to distinguish debt from equity for a number of different reasons, depending primarily on the perspective of the interested party: capital providers (investors or creditors), management, and accountants and external auditors.

DEBT VS. EQUITY: THE CAPITAL PROVIDER'S PERSPECTIVE

Capital providers include individuals and entities who hold debt and equity securities. Debt securities primarily include notes receivable and bonds, and equity securities include stocks. Active markets (e.g., the New York Stock Exchange) exist where such securities are purchased and sold.

EQUITY: HIGHER RISK.

Owning an equity security is usually riskier than owning a debt security. The interest and principal payments associated with debt investments are backed by legal contracts and, in general, are more predictable and dependable than discretionary dividend payments. Debt contracts often include security provisions, and in case of bankruptcy, debtholders have higher priority claims to the existing assets than equityholders, who are often left with nothing. As evidence of the riskier nature of equity securities, stock prices tend to be more volatile than bond prices on the major security exchanges.

EQUITY: HIGHER RETURNS.

A characteristic of the additional risk associated with equity investments is that they can produce higher returns than debt investments. When companies perform exceptionally well, equity holders often receive exceedingly large returns, either in the form of dividends or price appreciation of their securities. Debtholders, on the other hand, are limited only to the interest and principal payments specified by the debt contract. Several years ago, for example, Microsoft, a fast-growing computer software manufacturer, had an exceptional year. During that time the price of its stock increased from $25/share to over $78/share, an annual return for the stockholders of 312 percent. In contrast, during that same year the company paid less than a 9 percent return to its debtholders (i.e., interest rate on outstanding loans).

DEBT VS. EQUITY: MANAGEMENT'S PERSPECTIVE

The decision by management to raise capital by issuing debt or equity is complex. Factors like present and future interest rates, the company's credit rating, the relative amount of debt and equity in the company's capital structure and balance sheet, the condition of the economy, and the nature of the company's operations are usually relevant.

DEBT: CONTRACTUAL RESTRICTIONS.

Issuing debt limits a company in a number of important ways. Contractual interest and principal payments must be met in the future, and assets often must be pledged as security (collateral) during the period of the debt. At the end of 1994, for example, Kmart Corporation reported that capital lease obligations were expected to require cash payments in the future of approximately $5.1 billion. Additional debt may also lower a company's credit rating and reduce its ability to borrow in the future. Recently, Standard & Poor's and Moody's Investor Service lowered the credit rating of McDonnell Douglas Corporation, citing the extensive additional debt recently incurred by the company. Finally, the debt contract itself may restrict a company's future borrowing power, limit dividends, or require that certain accounting ratios be maintained at or above specified levels.

DEBT: LESS EXPENSIVE.

On the other hand, raising capital by issuing debt is attractive because interest payments are *tax deductible*. Texaco Corporation, for example, saved almost $200 million in federal income taxes during 1994 because it was able to deduct the interest on its outstanding debts for tax purposes. Issuing debt, therefore, is generally considered less expensive than issuing equity, as dividend payments are not tax deductible. In general, if management can use debt capital to earn revenues that exceed the after-tax cost of the debt, it is using a concept called **leverage** to provide a return for the stockholders. As indicated in Figure 12–2, such a practice appears to be common, in that these large U.S. corporations tend to rely more heavily on debt than on equity. The tax deductibility of interest, which significantly reduces the cost of issuing debt, is definitely one of the main reasons.

EQUITY: DILUTION OF OWNERSHIP. Another advantage of raising capital by issuing debt instead of equity is that issuing equity can dilute the ownership interests of the existing stockholders. Suppose, for example, that Mr. Jones owns 10 percent of XYZ Corporation, 1,000 of the 10,000 outstanding shares. If XYZ issues an additional 10,000 shares, and Mr. Jones purchases none, his ownership interest decreases from 10 percent to 5 percent (1,000/20,000).[1] Such **dilution**, if not accompanied by higher profits, can reduce both the future dividends paid to Mr. Jones and the market price of his shares. A recent 40 million share stock issuance by Chrysler Corporation, for example, surprised some analysts because it did not depress the company's stock price. Others commented that the dilutive effect would be negated by increased auto sales.

Dilution also reduces the proportionate control of the existing shareholders and, accordingly, can increase the likelihood of a **takeover** by an outsider. In a takeover, another company, an investor, or group of investors (sometimes called a *raider*) purchases enough of the outstanding shares to gain a controlling interest in the purchased company. If the takeover is "hostile," the voting power attached to the acquired shares is often used by the "raider" to elect a new board of directors. Such action can be followed by the replacement of existing management and substantial changes in the nature of the purchased company.

Takeover activity in the United States peaked in the late 1980's, subsided for several years, and recently has re-emerged. The end of merger mania in the 1980s occurred when Kohlberg Kravis Roberts, a firm that specialized in large takeovers, acquired the stock of RJR Nabisco for $25 billion. More recent notable takeovers include Walt Disney's acquisition of Capital Cities/ABC, Westinghouse's takeover of CBS, Time Warner's purchase of Turner Broadcasting, and the merger between Chase Manhattan and Chemical Bank. In each case substantial changes were made in the management and nature of the acquired company.

Corporate managers, whose jobs are threatened by takeovers, are understandably concerned with the dilutive effects of equity issuances. In fact, many companies, like Compac Computer, have recently entered into programs of buying back their own previously issued shares. Such transactions, called **treasury stock** purchases because the acquired shares are often held in the corporation's treasury for reissuance at a later date, make a company less attractive as a takeover target by reducing its cash balance and increasing the proportionate control of the remaining stockholders. Several years ago, for example, the management of Safeway Stores, Inc., purchased all of its publicly traded outstanding stock to elude a takeover attempt by Dart Group Corporation. In other words, the company *went private*—the only shares left outstanding were those held by stockholder-managers who withdrew them from the public markets.

---

1. Some stock certificates carry with them a preemptive right, which allows existing shareholders to share proportionately in any new issue of stock. Also, additional stock issuances sometimes require the approval of the existing stockholders.

DEBT VS. EQUITY: THE ACCOUNTANT'S AND AUDITOR'S PERSPECTIVE

The substantive differences between debt and equity give rise to different accounting treatments: (1) debt and equity issuances are disclosed in different sections of the balance sheet, and (2) debt transactions affect the income statement, while equity transactions do not.

Debt issuances are disclosed in the liabilities section of the balance sheet, while equity issuances are included in the stockholders' equity section. Proper classification is important because the debt/equity distinction affects a number of financial ratios, which are used by investors and creditors and in debt covenants and executive compensation agreements.

Interest payments on outstanding debts and book gains and losses, recognized when debt is redeemed, appear on the income statement and affect the computation of net income. In contrast, transactions involving equity securities, like dividends and the reissuance of treasury stock, do not enter into the computations of net income. Figure 12–4 summarizes why distinctions between debt and equity are important to investors and creditors, management, and accountants and auditors. These distinctions give rise to economic consequences that are discussed in the following section.

FIGURE 12–4	INTERESTED PARTY	DEBT	EQUITY
Distinctions between debt and equity from different perspectives	Investors and Creditors	Lower investment risk Fixed cash receipts (contractual interest and principal)	Higher investment risk Variable cash receipts (discretionary dividends and stock appreciation)
	Management	Contractual future cash payments Effects on credit rating Interest is tax deductible	Dividends are discretionary Effects of dilution/takeover Dividends are not tax deductible
	Accountants and Auditors	Liabilities section of balance sheet Income statement effects from debt transactions	Stockholders' equity section of balance sheet No income statement effects from equity transactions

THE ECONOMIC CONSEQUENCES ASSOCIATED WITH ACCOUNTING FOR STOCKHOLDERS' EQUITY

LO 3 The economic consequences associated with accounting for stockholders' equity arise in part from the effects of financial ratios (e.g., debt/equity) that include the dollar amount of stockholders' equity or its components. Such ratios affect a company's stock prices, credit rating, and any debt covenants that restrict additional borrowings, the payment of dividends, or the repurchase of outstanding equity shares (i.e., treasury stock purchases). Four of Dun & Bradstreet's fourteen key business ratios explicitly use the dollar value of stockholders' equity (net worth) in their calculations: (1) current liabilities/net worth, (2) total liabilities/net worth, (3) fixed assets/net worth, and (4) return on net worth. Dun & Bradstreet uses the values of these ratios to determine a company's credit rating, which in turn can affect the terms (e.g., market price, interest rate, security, restrictive covenants) of the company's debt issuances.

Many companies "manage" their debt/equity ratios to maintain or improve their credit ratings. In general, as a company's debt/equity ratio increases, its credit ratings fall. For example, American Stores, a supermarket and drugstore chain, recently acquired Lucky Stores, Inc. To finance the acquisition, American Stores raised additional capital, which it reported as debt on its balance sheet, increasing the company's debt/equity ratio. Moody's Investor Service responded by lowering the credit rating on American Stores' outstanding bonds, which was followed by a decrease in the market price of the company's stock.

On the other hand, as companies reduce their reliance on debt and increase their reliance on equity issuances and especially retained earnings as sources of financing, their credit ratings tend to rise. Indeed, General Motors recently announced plans to sell as much as $1 billion in stock to "strengthen its balance sheet" (*The Wall Street Journal,* November 12, 1992). In a recent annual report, General Electric commented that during the year its debts were "substantially reduced," leading the major debt-rating agencies to evaluate the company's credit rating as being of the highest standing, *AAA*. Such a rating enabled General Electric to get the best possible terms on its debt issuances as well as maintain or increase the value of the company's outstanding debt securities. In its 1994 annual report, May Department Stores commented: "Our strong capitalization ratios, primarily due to growth in retained earnings and the elimination of certain loans, are consistent with our capital structure objectives and provide us with substantial financial flexibility."

Another important economic consequence associated with the stockholder equity section of the balance sheet relates to restrictions on dividend payments and the repurchase of previously issued, outstanding stock imposed by certain debt covenants. Such restrictions can be very significant. Under the terms of covenants with its debtholders, Turner Broadcasting System, Inc., for example, has been prohibited from paying cash dividends altogether. Similar restrictions may be less binding.

The 1994 annual report of Owens-Corning Fiberglas states "As is typical for bank credit facilities, the agreements . . . contain restrictive covenants, including . . . limitations on . . . the payment of dividends, and purchase of company stock."

Such restrictions protect the interest of creditors by keeping a company from paying all of its available cash to the shareholders through excessive dividends or stock repurchases. Note also that the methods used to account for stock issuances, dividends, treasury stock purchases, and retained earnings, which are covered later in the chapter, can determine whether such restrictions have been violated. The remainder of the chapter describes the methods used to account for the stockholders' equity section of a corporation. Appendix 12A discusses the three forms of business organization: corporations, partnerships, and proprietorships.

ACCOUNTING FOR STOCKHOLDERS' EQUITY

LO 4   The stockholders' equity section of a corporate balance sheet consists of two major components: (1) contributed capital, which primarily reflects contributions of capital from shareholders and includes the Preferred Stock, Common Stock, and Additional Paid-In Capital[2] accounts, and (2) earned capital, which reflects

---

2. While the title *Additional Paid-In Capital* is the most common, there is some variation across companies. For example, The New York Times Company uses *Additional Capital,* Goodyear Tire and Rubber uses *Capital Surplus,* and Chevron Corporation uses *Capital in Excess of Par Value.*

the amount of assets earned and retained by the corporation and consists essentially of the Retained Earnings account. An example of the stockholders' equity sections of a corporate balance sheet appears in Figure 12–5. Spend a moment to review it because it provides an outline of the remaining discussion in this chapter.

FIGURE 12–5

Stockholders' equity section of balance sheet

Contributed capital:		
Preferred stock (authorized, issued and outstanding shares, asset preference, dividend preference, par value, cumulative, nonparticipating)	$ 3,000	
Common stock (authorized, issued and outstanding shares, par value/stated value/no par)	15,000	
Additional paid-in capital (preferred stock, common stock, treasury stock, stock dividends)	86,000	
Total contributed capital		$104,000
Earned capital:		
Retained earnings	$125,000	
Total earned capital		125,000
Less: Treasury stock (cost method)		20,000
Total stockholders' equity		$209,000

PREFERRED STOCK

Preferred stock is so called because preferred stockholders have certain rights that are not shared by common stockholders. These special rights relate to the receipt of dividends and/or to claims on assets in case of liquidation. **Preferred stock as to dividends** confers the right, if dividends are declared by the corporation's board of directors, to receive dividends. **Preferred stock as to assets** carries a claim to the corporation's assets, in case of liquidation, with a higher priority than the claim carried by common stock. The exact characteristics and terms of preferred stock vary from one issue to the next. The following sections describe some of the more important features of preferred stock.

AUTHORIZED, ISSUED, AND OUTSTANDING PREFERRED SHARES

Authorized preferred shares are the number of shares a corporation is entitled to issue by its corporate charter. Additional authorizations must be approved by the board of directors and are often subject to shareholder vote.

Issued preferred shares have been issued previously by a corporation and may or may not be currently outstanding. Some issued shares may have been repurchased by the corporation and held as treasury stock. **Outstanding** preferred shares are the shares presently held by the stockholders. Issued shares less repurchased shares equal outstanding shares. *Accounting Trends and Techniques* (New York: AICPA, 1994) reports that, of the 600 major U.S. corporations surveyed, approximately 25 percent had outstanding preferred issuances.

The number of authorized, issued, and outstanding preferred shares should be disclosed in the annual report. Sears, Roebuck and Company, for example, disclosed in its 1994 annual report that the shareholders had authorized 50 million shares of preferred stock, of which over 10 million had been issued and were presently outstanding.

Many major U.S. corporations have authorized preferred stock issuances but have chosen not to issue them. In such cases, the number of authorized shares should still be disclosed in the financial report. As of the end of 1994, for example, Goodyear Tire and Rubber Company (50 million shares), Ralston Purina Company (6 million shares), and Johnson & Johnson (2 million shares) disclosed authorized preferred shares, none of which had been issued.

PREFERRED DIVIDEND PAYMENTS

The terms of preferred stocks usually include a specific annual dividend that is paid to the preferred stockholders before any payments are made to the common stockholders, assuming a dividend is declared by the Board. The remaining amount of the dividend is then paid to the common stockholders. The amount of the preferred annual dividend payment is normally expressed as either an absolute dollar amount or as a percentage of a dollar amount referred to as the **par value** of the preferred stock.[3]

For example, if dividends are declared in a given year, the holder of 1 share of $5 preferred stock would receive a $5 dividend. The holder of 1 share of 4 percent preferred stock with a par value of $100 would receive a $4 (4% × $100) dividend. As of December 31, 1994, Sears, Roebuck had two kinds of preferred shares outstanding, differentiated by the per-share amount of the annual dividend payment: a $3.75 series and a series that paid an annual dividend of 8.88% of the $25 par value ($2.22).

To illustrate the allocation of a dividend between preferred and common stock, several years ago the board of directors of DuPont declared and paid a total dividend of $802 million. During the year, approximately 1.68 million shares of $4.50 preferred stock, 0.7 million shares of $3.50 preferred stock, and 240 million shares of common stock were outstanding. The dividend allocation to the preferred and common stockholder is shown in Figure 12–6.

FIGURE 12–6

Allocation of a dividend between preferred and common stock

Preferred dividend:		
$4.50 preferred stock × 1.68 million shares	$7.55 million	
$3.50 preferred stock × 0.7 million shares	2.45 million	$ 10 million
Common dividend ($3.30 × 240 million shares)		792 million
Total dividend		$802 million

CUMULATIVE PREFERRED STOCK

With **cumulative preferred stock**, when a corporation misses a dividend, **dividends in arrears** are created in the amount of the missed preferred dividend. In future periods, as dividends are declared, dividends in arrears are first paid to the preferred stockholders, who then receive their normal, annual dividend. Finally, the common stockholders are paid from what remains. If the preferred stock is *noncumulative*, no dividends in arrears are created for missed dividends, and the preferred stockholders receive only their normal, annual dividend in future periods as dividends are declared.

It is important to realize that dividends in arrears are not liabilities to the corporation and therefore are not listed on the balance sheet. They do not represent legal obligations to the preferred stockholders, because dividends are at the discretion of

3. The concept of par value is discussed more completely later in the chapter when we cover common stock. At that time we point out that par value has little or no economic meaning. In the case of preferred stock, however, par value is meaningful in that it is sometimes used to determine the annual dividend payment to the preferred stockholders.

the board of directors. The liability is created at the time the dividends are declared and only in the amount of the dividends. However, the corporation must keep track of dividends in arrears because they must be clearly disclosed in the financial report. Such information is particularly interesting to creditors as well as potential and existing stockholders because it may signal a shortage of cash in the corporation. The amount of dividends in arrears may also affect the dividends that common stockholders can expect to receive in the future.

The excerpt below, which was taken from the 1994 annual report of Sears, Roebuck, illustrates the potential significance of dividends in arrears.

"In the event that dividends payable on preferred stock are in arrears for six quarterly periods, holders of such stock shall have the right to elect two additional directors of the Company until all cumulative dividends have been paid or set apart for payment. Additionally, dividends cannot be paid on the Company's common shares if dividends on preferred shares are in arrears."

Almost all preferred stock issuances are cumulative, and among major U.S. companies, dividends in arrears are relatively rare. Several years ago, however, Stelco (Canada's second largest steelmaker) omitted dividends on its cumulative preferred stocks as it attempted to turn around its money-losing operations. Accordingly, the company disclosed dividends in arrears in its financial report. The company had not missed a dividend payment in 75 years.

PARTICIPATING PREFERRED STOCK

If preferred stock carries a **participating** feature, the preferred stockholders not only have a right to the annual dividend payment, but they also share in the remaining amount of the dividend with the common stockholders. The extent to which the preferred stockholders participate in the remaining dividend is often expressed as a percentage of the par value of the preferred stock. Nonparticipating preferred stock, which is much more common, carries no rights to share in the remaining dividend.

PREFERRED STOCKS: DEBT OR EQUITY?

We have described how most preferred stocks (1) carry higher priority than common stocks in the event of liquidation, (2) specify annual dividend payments of a fixed amount, (3) are cumulative, and (4) do not contain a participation feature. In addition, preferred stocks normally do not carry a right to vote in the election of the board of directors, and many contain a call provision that allows the corporation to redeem the stock for a specified price after a specified date.

Recall the discussion earlier in the chapter on the characteristics of debt and equity (see Figure 12–3), and note how the features listed above closely resemble debt. In fact, in some cases the Internal Revenue Service has allowed corporations to deduct from taxable income the dividends paid on securities classified on the balance sheet as preferred stocks because such dividends were construed as interest. Preferred stocks are definitely hybrid securities, which have characteristics of both debt and equity. They are therefore difficult to classify on the balance sheet. In most cases, the Preferred Stock account is disclosed at the top of the stockholders' equity section, where it is located immediately below long-term liabilities. In some cases, however, preferred stocks are disclosed as debt. On its 1994 balance sheet, for example, Nike, Inc. reported $300 million in preferred stock in the long-term liabilities section of the balance sheet. Financial statement users interested in computing ratios that involve distinctions between debt and equity (e.g., debt/equity) may find it more useful to treat the Preferred Stock account as a long-term liability.

Classifying hybrid securities, like preferred stocks, is indeed a difficult area for accountants and auditors, primarily because the distinction between debt and equity is not always clear-cut, and the guidelines specified by generally accepted accounting principles are not very specific. In an article in *Forbes*, the national director of accounting and auditing at a major accounting firm noted: "the distinction between debt and equity has become so muddied that the accounting rules seem more arbitrary than ever . . . preferred stocks are clever ways to raise cash . . . simply [a form of] off-balance-sheet financing masquerading as equity."[4]

Consequently, by issuing certain kinds of preferred stock, management can raise what is essentially debt capital without increasing the liabilities reported on the balance sheet. Because preferred stock carries no voting power, such a strategy also avoids the problems of dilution and possible takeover associated with issuing common stock. As noted in *Forbes*:

Companies anxious to protect their credit ratings, and unwilling to issue more [common] stock for fear of diluting earnings per share or inviting takeover bids, have turned to these ingenious instruments [preferred stocks] to lower the cost of raising money. But pity the poor accountant who must categorize these hothouse hybrids.[5]

COMMON STOCK

Unlike preferred stock, common stock is typically not characterized by a wide variety of features that differ from issuance to issuance. Moreover, common stock is not designed to provide a fixed return over a specified period of time. Rather, as a true equity security, common stock is characterized by three fundamental rights: (1) the right to receive dividends if they are declared by the board of directors, (2) a residual right to the corporation's assets in case of liquidation, and (3) the right to exert control over management, which includes the right to vote in the annual election of the board of directors and the right to vote on certain significant transactions proposed by management (e.g., the authorization of additional shares, large purchases of outstanding shares, major acquisitions).

MARKET VALUE, BOOK VALUE, AND PAR VALUE

LO 5 The value of the common stock issued by a corporation can be described in a number of different and often confusing ways. This section clarifies some of this confusion by differentiating among the market value, book value, and par value of a share of common stock.

MARKET VALUE. The **market value** of a share of stock, common or preferred, at a particular point in time is the price at which the stock can be exchanged on the open market. This amount varies from day to day, based primarily on changes in investor expectations about the financial condition of the issuing company, interest rates, and other factors. The market prices of the common stocks of publicly traded companies must be disclosed in their financial reports. The 1994 annual report of Walt Disney, for example, disclosed that the market price of the company's common stock fluctuated from a low of approximately $33 per share to a high of slightly over $45 during the year ending December 31, 1994.

---

4. Richard Greene, "What, and Whose, Bottom Line?" *Forbes*, October 7, 1985, p. 101.
5. Jinny St. Goar, "Creative Paper," *Forbes*, June 3, 1985, pp. 178, 180.

BOOK VALUE. The **book value** of a share of common stock is determined by the following formula.

$$\text{Book Value of Common Stock} = \frac{\text{Stockholders' Equity} - \text{Preferred Capital}}{\text{Number of Common Shares Held by the Shareholders}}$$

It is simply the book value of the corporation (less preferred capital), as indicated on the balance sheet, divided by the number of common shares presently held by the shareholders. This value rarely approximates the market value of a common share, because the balance sheet, in general, does not represent an accurate measure of the market value of the company. As of December 31, 1994, the book value of Walt Disney common stock was $10 per share, considerably below the range of market value ($33–$45) indicated in the previous paragraph.

MARKET-TO-BOOK RATIO. Dividing the market value of a company's common stock by its book value (**market-to-book ratio**) provides a ratio that indicates the extent to which the market believes that the balance sheet reflects the company's true value. Ratios equal to 1 indicate that a company's net book value (as measured by the balance sheet) is perceived by the market to be a fair reflection of the company's true value. More commonly, market-to-book ratios are somewhat larger than 1, indicating that the balance sheet is perceived to be a conservative measure of the company's true value. Large ratios can be attributed to a number of reasons: balance sheet assets are at cost, not fair market value; goodwill is ignored on the balance sheet; or accounting methods are conservative. Market-to-book ratios also vary substantially across and within companies. As of the end of 1994, for example, Walt Disney's market-to-book ratio was approximately 4:1, Kmart's was 1.3 to 1; and the ratio for General Mills ranged from 6:1 to almost 9:1 during 1994.

PAR VALUE. The **par value** (sometimes called stated value) of a share of common stock has no relationship to its market value or book value and, for the most part, has little economic significance. At one time it represented a legal concept, instituted by some states, that was intended to protect creditors, but over time the concept proved to be largely ineffective.[6] It is not uncommon for corporations to issue either no-par common stock, or common stock with extremely low par values. For example, the par value of Walt Disney Company common stock as of December 31, 1994, is only $0.25 per share.

While the par (stated) value of a share of common stock has limited legal or economic significance, these values do have financial accounting significance. As the next section demonstrates, under generally accepted accounting principles, these values are used in the journal entries to record certain common stock transactions. Many believe that attributing any significance, accounting or otherwise, to the par or stated value of common stock is unwarranted.

ACCOUNTING FOR COMMON AND PREFERRED STOCK ISSUANCES

As for preferred stock, common stock issuances must be authorized in the corporate charter and approved by the board of directors and sometimes the stockholders. Similarly, the number of shares of common stock outstanding may differ from the

---

6. In some states the concept of stated value was substituted for par value, but like par value, this concept has limited economic meaning. Note, however, that state laws differ in this area.

number of common shares originally issued. As of December 31, 1994, for example, the corporate charter and stockholders of Johnson & Johnson had authorized over 1 billion shares of common stock, 767 million had been issued, and 643 million were currently outstanding—124 million had been repurchased by the company and were held in the form of treasury stock.

The methods used to account for common stock issuances are essentially the same as those used for preferred stock. When no-par common or preferred stock is issued for cash, the Cash account is debited for the proceeds and the Common (or Preferred) Stock account is credited for the entire dollar amount. For example, when Apple Computer, Inc., issued 4.98 million shares of no-par common stock for an average price of $17.592 per share (total cash proceeds of $87.61 million), the company recorded the following journal entry (dollars in millions).

Cash (+A)	**87.61**	
Common Stock (+SE)		**87.61**
Issued no-par common stock.		

When common or preferred stock with a par value is issued for cash, the Cash account is debited for the total proceeds, the Common (or Preferred) Stock account is credited for the number of shares issued times the par value per share, and the Additional Paid-In Capital (Common or Preferred Stock) account is credited for the remainder. The dollar amount credited to the Additional Paid-In Capital account represents the difference between the total issuance price of the stock and the par value of the issuance. For example, when Coca-Cola Enterprises issued 71.4 million shares of $1 par value common stock for $15.62 per share, the company recorded the following journal entry (dollars in millions).

Cash (+A)	**1,115.27**	
Common Stock (+SE)		**71.40***
Additional Paid-In Capital, C/S (+SE)		**1,043.87**
Issued $1 par value common stock.		

*71.4 million sh. × $1

When Weyerhaeuser Company issued 147,000 shares of $1.00 par value preferred stock for $11 per share, it recorded the following journal entry.

Cash (+A)	**1,617,000***	
Preferred Stock (+SE)		**147,000****
Additional Paid-In Capital, P/S (+SE)		**1,470,000**
Issued $1 par value common stock.		

*147,000 sh. × $11
**147,000 sh. × $1

TREASURY STOCK

LO 6   Outstanding common stock is often repurchased and either (1) held *in treasury*, awaiting to be reissued at a later date, or (2) retired.[7] Repurchases of this nature normally must be authorized and approved by a company's stockholders and board of directors. Treasury stock carries none of the usual rights of common stock ownership. That is, while common shares are held in treasury, they lose their voting power and their right to receive dividends.

---

7. Repurchased preferred shares are normally retired and are not held as treasury stock. Most repurchased common shares, on the other hand, are held in treasury. Treasury shares have the status of authorized and unissued shares.

WHY COMPANIES PURCHASE TREASURY STOCK

There are many reasons why corporations purchase outstanding common shares and hold them in treasury. Perhaps the most common is to support employee compensation plans. Johnson & Johnson, for example, purchased over 15 million of its own common shares in both 1993 and 1992, bringing the total number of shares in treasury to over 124 million. During that time period, over 7 million shares, many of which had been held in treasury, were issued to employees as compensation for services.

Other companies, such as Walt Disney, Avco, Gillette, and Safeway, have entered into common stock buy-back programs to fend off possible takeover attempts. We mentioned earlier that by purchasing its own outstanding common stock a company can discourage takeovers by reducing its cash balance and increasing the proportionate control of the remaining shareholders. Gillette, for example, entered into a plan to purchase 11 million of its outstanding common shares. In doing so, the company blocked a takeover attempt by purchasing the 13.9 percent interest held at that time by the Revlon Group, Inc. Columbia Broadcasting Systems (CBS) blocked a takeover attempt by Ted Turner (Turner Broadcasting Systems) by repurchasing a substantial portion of its outstanding common stock.

Purchasing treasury stock can also increase the market price of a company's outstanding stock. Indeed, *The Wall Street Journal* (September 1, 1994) reported:

"Philip Morris Co., in an aggressive move to boost its stock price, announced a $6 billion stock-buyback plan . . . The announcement raised the company's stock to a 52-week high."

Treasury stock purchases are often viewed as a sign of financial strength. During a recent recession, for example, companies with strong cash positions took advantage of the reduced prices on the stock market by purchasing large quantities of their own shares. Many of these shares were reissued later at much higher prices.

A treasury stock purchase can serve to increase a company's earnings per share (net income/outstanding common shares). An article in *Forbes* reported that treasury stock purchases "reduce shares outstanding and hype [i.e., inflate] per-share earnings."[8] For example, by repurchasing 12.2 million common shares, Gulf Oil Company significantly lessened a decrease in its earnings per share. This strategy made Gulf's financial performance appear relatively better than that of many companies in the oil industry, which at the time was experiencing a slump in the price of oil.

Finally, treasury stock purchases are often made to return cash to shareholders. In this sense, it is much like a dividend, especially if the treasury stock purchase is proportionate across the shareholders. Consider, for example, a company that has 6,000 common shares outstanding, held in equal amounts of 2,000 shares by three shareholders. Each shareholder owns one third of the company. If 1,000 common shares are repurchased from each shareholder for $2 per share, each receives $2,000 and still maintains a one-third interest in the company—the exact result that would have occurred had the company paid a $1 per share dividend.

ACCOUNTING FOR TREASURY STOCK: THE COST METHOD

There are two methods of accounting for treasury stock: (1) the cost method and (2) the par value method. While either method is acceptable under GAAP, the cost method is covered below because it is simpler and more widely used.[9]

---

8. Christopher Power, "The Gimmicks of '82," *Forbes,* March 14, 1983, pp. 96, 98.
9. *Accounting Trends and Techniques* (1994) indicates that almost 90 percent of the companies disclosing treasury use the cost method.

PURCHASING TREASURY STOCK. Under the cost method, when a company purchases its own outstanding common stock and holds it in treasury, a permanent account, called Treasury Stock, is debited for the cost of the purchase.[10] This account is disclosed below retained earnings in the stockholders' equity section of the balance sheet (see Figure 12–5). For example, when H&R Block purchased 1.8 million shares of treasury stock for a total cost of $69 million, it recorded the following journal entry (dollars in millions).

Treasury Stock (−SE)	69	
Cash (−A)		69

Purchased 1.8 million shares of treasury stock.

This transaction brought the total number of treasury shares held by H&R Block to 2.8 million, and the stockholders' equity section of H&R Block's 1994 balance sheet appeared as in Figure 12–7.

FIGURE 12–7	H&R BLOCK, INC. BALANCE SHEET STOCKHOLDERS' EQUITY SECTION DECEMBER 31, 1994 (IN THOUSANDS OF DOLLARS)

Disclosure of treasury stock

Common stock (no par, stated value $.01 per share, authorized 200,000,000 shares)	$ 1,089
Additional paid-in capital	90,552
Retained earnings	719,724
Less: Cost of common stock in treasury	103,490
Total stockholders' equity	$707,875

Some accountants have argued that treasury stock, similar to marketable securities, represents an asset that should be disclosed as such on the balance sheet. This argument rests on the premise that treasury stock can be sold and will eventually produce cash. It is also true that corporations can produce cash by issuing authorized and unissued shares. Are such shares assets? In H&R Block's case 200 million common shares have been authorized while only 109 million have been issued. Few would argue that the 91 (200 − 109) million authorized and unissued shares should be listed as balance sheet assets. In practice, treasury stock is listed on the balance sheet as a reduction to stockholders' equity primarily because it is illogical to view a corporation as owning part of itself. Unlike purchasing securities issued by another company (marketable securities), purchasing treasury stock reduces the scale of the purchasing company's operations as well as the equity interest of the stockholders.

The Treasury Stock account is disclosed immediately below retained earnings because in many states dividends cannot legally exceed retained earnings less the cost of all shares held in treasury. Such laws are designed to protect creditors by keeping a corporation from distributing all of its cash to the shareholders in the form of dividends or stock repurchases. By subtracting the dollar amount in the Treasury Stock

---

10. If outstanding stock, preferred or common, is repurchased and then retired, the stock account is debited and the cash payment is credited. If the payment exceeds the stock account, which is frequently the case, additional paid-in capital and/or retained earnings is debited to balance the entry.

account from retained earnings, financial statement readers can determine the maximum amount of cash that legally can be paid to the shareholders as of the balance sheet date.[11]

REISSUING TREASURY STOCK FOR MORE THAN ACQUISITION COST. Common stock held in treasury is often reissued at a later date. If it is reissued at a price greater than its acquisition cost, the Cash account is debited for the proceeds, the Treasury Stock account is credited for the cost, and the difference is credited to the Additional Paid-In Capital (Treasury Stock) account. For example, when PepsiCo, Inc. reissued 139,000 shares of treasury stock, which had an acquisition cost of $2.7 million, for a total of $5.3 million, the company recorded the following journal entry (dollars in millions).

Cash (+A)	5.3	
Treasury Stock (+SE)		2.7
Additional Paid-In Capital, T/S (+SE)		2.6
Reissued treasury stock.		

Note that the treasury shares were reissued for a dollar amount that exceeded the acquisition cost, and Additional Paid-In Capital (Treasury Stock) was credited for the difference. Additional Paid-In Capital is credited instead of a *gain*, which would appear on the income statement and be closed to Retained Earnings, because this transaction represents an exchange with the stockholders of the corporation. It is not an operating transaction, and it is illogical for a corporation to recognize a gain at the expense of its stockholders. Consequently, the amount of the proceeds from the issuance of treasury stock in excess of its acquisition cost is added to the contributed capital portion of stockholders' equity, rather than to earned capital.

REISSUING TREASURY STOCK FOR LESS THAN ACQUISITION COST. If treasury stock is reissued for less than the acquisition cost, the Cash account is debited for the proceeds, the Treasury Stock account is credited for the acquisition cost, and Additional Paid-In Capital (Treasury Stock) is debited for the difference, *if there is a sufficient balance in the account to cover this difference.* If the difference between the acquisition cost and the proceeds exceeds the balance in the Additional Paid-In Capital (Treasury Stock) account, Retained Earnings is debited.

For example, several years ago Eli Lilly and Company reissued 1,271,036 treasury shares, with an acquisition cost of $68.5 million, for $44.5 million. At the time of the transaction, the balance in the Additional Paid-In Capital (Treasury Stock) account exceeded $24 million, the difference between the cost and the proceeds. The following journal entry, therefore, was recorded to reflect the transaction (dollars in millions).

Cash (+A)	44.5	
Additional Paid-In Capital, T/S (−SE)	24.0	
Treasury Stock (+SE)		68.5
Reissued treasury stock.		

The Pillsbury Company reissued 300,000 shares of treasury stock, which had an acquisition cost of $12.9 million, for a total of $11.7 million. The balance in the

---

11. Recall that debt covenants may further restrict the payment of dividends.

Additional Paid-In Capital (Treasury Stock) account at the time of the reissuance was zero. Accordingly, the following journal entry was recorded (dollars in millions).

Cash (+A)	11.7	
Retained Earnings (−SE)	1.2	
Treasury Stock (+SE)		12.9

Reissued treasury stock.

Note that in both preceding examples, an income statement loss is not recognized when treasury stock is reissued for an amount less than the acquisition cost. Reissuing treasury stock is a capital transaction and as such should not affect the income statement. However, debiting Retained Earnings, when the dollar amount in the Additional Paid-In Capital (Treasury Stock) account is insufficient, is a questionable practice—it treats the transaction as a reduction of earned capital when, in fact, it represents a reduction of contributed capital.

THE MAGNITUDE OF THE TREASURY STOCK ACCOUNT

The dollar values of the Treasury Stock account on the balance sheets of major U.S. corporations are often quite significant. As indicated in Figure 12–8, it is not unusual for it to exceed the dollar value of the corporation's total contributed capital (preferred stock, common stock, and additional paid-in capital). This phenomenon can occur because treasury stock is often acquired at prices that are considerably higher than the original issuance prices of the shares.

FIGURE 12–8	COMPANY	TREASURY STOCK/ CONTRIBUTED CAPITAL
The dollar value of treasury stock/total contributed capital (dollars in millions)	**Colgate-Palmolive**	$1,462/1,611 = .91
	Federal Express	2,273/764,818 = .003
	H&R Block	103/92 = 1.12
	Kmart	82/2,699 = .03
	Scott Paper	11/506 = .02
	Walt Disney	1,286/945 = 1.36

Source: 1994 annual reports.

STOCK OPTIONS

Recently **stock options** have become a very popular way to compensate executives in the United States. In addition to cash or other assets, many companies compensate their executives by giving them the option to purchase equity securities at a fixed price over a specified time period. To illustrate, assume that on December 31, 1996, AAA Company stock is trading at $10 per share, and at that time the company grants each of its executives the option to purchase up to 100 shares at $10 per share (the current market price) any time within the next ten years. If within the ten-year period AAA's stock price increases to $15 per share, the executives can exercise the option by purchasing stock from AAA at $10 per share, which can then be sold for $15, creating an immediate $5 gain per share. If AAA's stock decreases to $5 per share, the executives need not exercise their options.

Compensating executives with stock options is attractive to companies because it requires no cash payment and motivates executives to act in a manner that maximizes the company's share price—stock price increases create gains for the executive. These arrangements are attractive to executives because, despite the great upside potential, there is no risk of loss—stock price decreases do not create losses for the executive. *Business Week* (April 24, 1995) reports that for these reasons "many companies are shifting more and more of the chief executive's pay into stock options." To illustrate the upside potential of stock options, the article notes that the options held—but not yet exercised—by Michael Eisner, CEO of Walt Disney, had a value of $172 million as of December 31, 1994.

The methods used to account for stock options are relatively straightforward. No compensation expense is recorded by the company when the options are granted, and an issuance of common stock is recorded when the options are exercised.[12] However, many believe that companies should recognize compensation expense on the income statement when options are granted because options do have value and companies are giving up something by promising to issue shares at prices that in the future may be below market value. Issuing stock at below-market prices dilutes the value of the stockholders' interests without providing comparable assets.

In 1994 the FASB formulated a proposal to require companies to recognize compensation expense when granting options. Industry, however, raised strong objections, arguing that such recognition would make it more difficult to raise capital and determining the dollar amount of compensation expense would be extremely subjective, because options are very difficult to value. The FASB compromised, requiring that companies simply disclose in a footnote how much profit they would have recognized had compensation expense been recorded on options granted during the year. Such disclosure enables users to better assess the compensation costs incurred by companies, producing what *The Wall Street Journal* (July 6, 1995) calls "a small revolution in the information investors get about that most favored of perks, the employee stock option."

RETAINED EARNINGS

Retained earnings is a measure of previously recognized profits that have not been paid to the shareholders in the form of dividends. As indicated in Figure 12–2, major U.S. corporations rely heavily on internally generated funds as a source of capital. This section discusses two factors that affect the Retained Earnings balance: (1) dividends and (2) appropriations.

DIVIDENDS

L O 7 Dividends are distributions of cash, property, or stock to the stockholders of a corporation. They are declared by a formal resolution of the corporation's board of directors (usually quarterly), and the amount is usually announced on a per-share basis. Cash dividends represent distributions of cash to the stockholders. Property dividends (dividends in kind) are distributions of property, usually debt or equity securities in other companies.[13] **Stock dividends** are distributions of a corporation's own shares. Cash dividends are by far the most common. *Accounting Trends and Techniques* (New York: AICPA, 1994) reports that, of the 600 major U.S. companies surveyed, 452 (75 percent) paid cash dividends, during 1993, 10 (2 percent) paid property dividends, and 12 (2 percent) paid dividends in the form of stock.[14]

---

12. Compensation expense is recorded on options granted at prices below the current market price.
13. Accounting for property dividends is normally covered in intermediate financial accounting.
14. Some companies distributed more than one kind of dividend, and others distributed no dividends of any kind.

FIGURE 12-9

Important dividend dates

Date of Declaration	Date of Record	Date of Payment
Board of directors declares dividend and liability is established.	Shareholders holding stock at this date receive the dividend when paid.	Dividend is paid to shareholders of record.

As Figure 12–9 shows, three dates are relevant when dividends are declared: (1) the **date of declaration**, when the dividends are declared by the board, (2) the **date of record**, which determines who is to receive the dividend, and (3) the **date of payment**, when the distribution is actually made. A typical dividend announcement reads as follows:

The Board of Directors of Bennet Corporation, at its regular meeting of March 10, 1996, declared a quarterly dividend of $5 per share, payable on April 20, 1996, to stockholders of record on April 2, 1996.

In this announcement, March 10 is the date of declaration, April 2, the date of record, and April 20, the date of payment.

DIVIDEND STRATEGY. When and how much of a dividend to declare depends on a number of factors, such as the nature, financial condition, and desired image of the company, as well as legal constraints. If dividends are to be paid in cash, the board of directors must first be certain that the corporation has sufficient cash to meet the payment. Such a determination requires a projection of the operating cash flows of the company, including for example, analyses of the company's current cash position, future sales, receivables, inventory purchases, and fixed-asset replacements. It is usually wise to make sure that the company's operating cash needs can be met before cash dividends are paid.

The goals of a corporation and the nature of its activities may also have a bearing on dividend policy. Some companies, like Toys "R" Us, Inc., and Microsoft Corporation, are relatively young, fast-growing companies that have adopted policies of paying no dividends. Such companies, often called growth companies, reinvest their earnings primarily to support growth without having to rely too heavily on debt and dilutive equity issuances. The shareholders receive their investment returns in the form of stock price appreciation. The following excerpt is from an annual report of Toys "R" Us, Inc.

The Company has followed the policy of reinvesting earnings in the business and, consequently, has not paid any cash dividends. At the present time, no change in this policy is under consideration by the Board of Directors. The payment of cash dividends in the future will be determined by the Board of Directors in light of conditions then existing, including the Company's earnings, financial requirements and condition, opportunities for reinvesting earnings, business conditions, and other factors.

More established companies, such as General Electric and Johnson & Johnson, normally pay quarterly dividends in the amount of 30–40 percent of net income and also attempt to consistently increase their dividend payments from year to year. This policy, which provides a consistent dividend while retaining some funds to finance available growth opportunities, tends to reflect an image of stability, strength, and permanence. The following excerpt is from an annual report of General Electric.

Dividends paid totaled $1.777 billion [$1.29 per share]. At the same time, the Company retained sufficient earnings to support enhanced productive capability and to provide adequate financial resources for internal and external growth opportunities. [This increase] in dividends declared . . . marked the twelfth consecutive year of dividend growth.

Some companies consistently increase dividends from year to year, but the distributions do not represent a consistent percentage of net income. Eastman Kodak Company, for example, has increased its dividends each year since 1977. However, as a percentage of net income, dividend payments over that time period varied from around 40 percent to over 100 percent. Apparently, the boards of such companies believe that dividend payments should show consistent growth regardless of how well the company does from one year to the next.

State laws and debt covenants can also limit the payment of dividends. In most states the dollar amount of retained earnings less the cost of treasury stock sets a limitation on the payment of dividends. In addition, the terms of debt contracts may further limit dividend payments to an even smaller portion of retained earnings. As of December 31, 1994, for example, Sears, Roebuck & Company had a balance of retained earnings of almost $9 billion. Yet certain indenture agreements existing at the time limited dividend payments to a maximum amount of $8 billion.

ACCOUNTING FOR CASH DIVIDENDS. When the board of directors of a corporation declares a cash dividend, a liability in the amount of the fair market value of the dividend is created on the date of declaration. At this time a Cash Dividend account is debited, and a current liability account, Dividends Payable, is credited for a dollar value equal to the per-share amount times the number of outstanding shares. Cash Dividend is a temporary account that is closed directly to Retained Earnings at the end of the accounting period. The Dividends Payable account is removed from the balance sheet when the dividend is paid on the date of payment. No entry is recorded on the date of record. The shareholders as of the date of record are simply the recipients of the dividend.

To illustrate, when the board of directors of Marriott Corporation declared a fourth-quarter cash dividend of $0.20 per share on 118.8 million common shares outstanding, the following journal entry was recorded (dollars in millions).

Cash Dividend (−SE)   23.76
    Dividends Payable (+L)   23.76
Declared a cash dividend (118.8 million sh. × $0.20/sh.).

Marriott recorded the following entry on the date of payment (dollars in millions).

Dividends Payable (−L)   23.76
    Cash (−A)   23.76
Paid a cash dividend.

L O 8   **STOCK SPLITS AND STOCK DIVIDENDS.** Corporations can distribute additional shares to existing stockholders by declaring either a stock split or a stock dividend. For practical purposes, there is very little difference between these two actions. In both cases the existing shareholders receive additional shares, and in neither case are the assets or liabilities of the corporation increased or decreased.

In a **stock split** the number of outstanding shares is simply "split" into smaller units, which requires the corporation to distribute additional shares. A 2:1 stock split, for example, serves to double the number of outstanding shares, which requires that the company distribute an additional share for each common share outstanding. A 3:1 stock split effectively triples the number of outstanding shares, which the company executes by distributing two additional shares for each one outstanding. In a 3:2 stock split, one additional share is issued for every two outstanding.

In a **stock dividend** additional shares, usually expressed as a percentage of the outstanding shares, are issued to the stockholders. Large stock dividends have essentially the same effect as stock splits. Both a 100 percent stock dividend and a 2:1 stock split, for example, double the number of outstanding shares. Similarly, both a 50 percent stock dividend and a 3:2 stock split increase outstanding shares by 50 percent. Professional accounting standards recommend that relatively large stock dividends (over 25 percent) be referred to as **stock splits in the form of dividends**. Stock splits and stock splits in the form of dividends are relatively common. *Accounting Trends and Techniques* (New York: AICPA, 1994) reports that, of the 600 major U.S. companies surveyed, 67 (11 percent) reported a stock split or a large stock dividend during 1993. Of those 67 issuances, 1 was less than 3:2, 21 were 3:2, 39 were 2:1, and 6 were greater than 2:1. Relatively small stock dividends (less than 25 percent), which are somewhat less common than either stock splits or stock splits in the form of dividends, are referred to as **ordinary stock dividends**.

ACCOUNTING FOR STOCK DIVIDENDS AND STOCK SPLITS. Stock dividends and splits can be divided into three categories: (1) stock dividends (<25 percent), (2) stock splits in the form of dividends (>25 percent) and (3) stock splits. While each category is accounted for in a slightly different manner, it is important to realize that such actions affect neither the corporation's assets nor its liabilities. Only the accounts within the stockholders' equity section (i.e., Common Stock, Additional Paid-In Capital, or Retained Earnings) are adjusted. Below we cover ordinary stock dividends and stock splits.[15]

ORDINARY STOCK DIVIDENDS. When the board of directors of a corporation declares an ordinary stock dividend, a Dividend account is debited for the number of shares to be issued times the fair market value of the shares, the Common Stock account is credited for the number of shares issued times the par value, and Additional Paid-In Capital is credited for the remainder.[16]

To illustrate, assume that ATP International has 100,000 shares of $1 par value common stock outstanding, each with a fair market value of $25. The company would record the following journal entry if the board of directors decided to distribute 5,000 additional shares by declaring a 5 percent stock dividend.

Stock Dividend (−SE)	125,000*	
Common Stock (+SE)		5,000**
Additional Paid-In Capital, Stock Dividend (+SE)		120,000

Declared five percent stock dividend.

*(100,000 × .05) × $25/sh.
**5,000 sh. × $1/sh.

Note that no assets or liabilities are involved in the transaction; all of the activity takes place in the stockholders' equity section. Retained Earnings is reduced after the Stock Dividend account is closed at the end of the accounting period, and the Common Stock and Additional Paid-In Capital (Stock Dividend) accounts are both

---

15. We do not cover stock splits in the form of dividends because we believe, as many others do, that they are effectively stock splits and should be accounted for as such.
16. We assume here that the stock dividend is declared and issued on the same day.

increased. In other words, Retained Earnings have been *capitalized*. Earned capital has been transferred to contributed capital. Note also that if the issued stock has a par value of zero, the entire amount of the stock dividend is credited to the Additional Paid-In Capital account.

STOCK SPLITS. Under generally accepted accounting principles, no entry is recorded in the books when stock splits are declared. The corporation should simply record the fact that the par value of the issued stock has been reduced in proportion to the size of the split. A 3:1 split, for example, triples the number of outstanding shares and reduces the par value of each share to one-third of its original value. If the stock has no par value, the par value need not be adjusted.

To illustrate, when the board of directors of Walt Disney approved a 4:1 stock split on February 18, 1992, the company recorded no journal entry to reflect the action. The 137 million outstanding shares, each with a par value of $0.10, were simply replaced by 548 (137 × 4) million outstanding shares, each with a par value of $0.025 ($0.10/4). In other words, three additional shares with a par value of $0.025 were distributed for each share outstanding.

WHY DO COMPANIES DECLARE STOCK DIVIDENDS AND STOCK SPLITS?

To understand the reasons behind stock dividends and stock splits, it is important to realize that (1) such actions do not distribute additional assets to the shareholders and (2) their proportionate ownership of the company after the dividend or split is the same as it was before the dividend or split. For example, a shareholder who owns 10 of a company's 100 outstanding shares, each with a market value of $6, owns 10 percent of the company that has a theoretical value of $600 (100 shares × $6). After a 2:1 stock split, the shareholder will own 20 shares of stock, but each share should drop in value to $3 and the 20 shares will still represent only 10 percent of the 200 outstanding shares. Consequently, unlike cash or property dividends, corporations do not declare stock dividends or stock splits to distribute assets to the shareholders.

Perhaps the most popular reason for declaring a stock split or a large stock dividend is to reduce the per-share price of the outstanding shares so that investors can more easily purchase them. When IBM, for example, declared a 4:1 stock split, which quadrupled the number of outstanding shares, the per-share price of IBM stock immediately decreased from $300 to $75 ($300/4). The managements of many corporations believe that such an action encourages better public relations and wider stock ownership. It is also true that a company's stock price often increases after a stock split is announced. In an article entitled "Investors Jump for Joy Over Major Stock Splits," *USA Today* (February 24, 1992) reported:

. . . investors are euphoric over stock splits announced last week at two favorite consumer companies: Coca Cola jumped 2 1/8 . . . on news of a two-for-one split [and] Walt Disney rose 3 1/2 . . . on news of a four-for-one split.

While it is unclear why stock prices jump when stock splits are announced, many believe that such announcements signal to investors that company management believes that it can maintain the value of the stock in the future. Perhaps this signal provides investors with positive information about the company's prospects that was unavailable prior to the announcement.

The reasons for stock dividends are even less clear. Such distributions have a relatively small effect on the number of outstanding shares and thus do little to reduce per-share prices and broaden stock ownership. They do not place assets in the hands of shareholders, which is supported by the IRS position of not considering stock dividends received as taxable income. It is possible that cash-poor corporations distribute stock dividends instead of cash dividends, so that shareholders are at least receiving something, but this strategy could be interpreted simply as a publicity gesture. It may satisfy stockholders, especially if they believe that they have received additional assets, but more likely, it may signal financial problems. Finally, corporations may issue stock dividends to capitalize a portion of Retained Earnings. By reducing Retained Earnings, a stock dividend places a more restrictive limitation on future dividend payments.

APPROPRIATIONS OF RETAINED EARNINGS

LO 9 An **appropriation of retained earnings** is a book entry that serves to restrict a portion of retained earnings from the payment of future dividends. It involves no asset or liability accounts, and no stockholders' equity accounts other than Retained Earnings. Such entries are executed either at the discretion of the board of directors or in conformance with the terms of contracts (e.g., debt covenants).

Suppose, for example, that the board of directors of Rosebud Corporation plans to expand the company's main manufacturing plant. To save cash so that the expansion can be funded internally, the board has decided to place a restriction on the payment of future dividends. Accordingly, a resolution is passed stating that the company cannot pay dividends that reduce retained earnings below $300,000. The following journal entry could accompany this resolution.

Retained Earnings (−SE)	300,000	
Restricted Retained Earnings (+SE)		300,000
Restricted retained earnings.		

Assuming that the balance in the company's Retained Earnings account before the appropriation was $500,000, the stockholders' equity section of Rosebud's balance sheet after the resolution would appear as in Figure 12–10.

Appropriations of retained earnings that result from contractual restrictions are accounted for in a similar manner. If a long-term debt covenant requires that a company maintain a Retained Earnings balance of at least $650,000, that dollar amount would be transferred from Retained Earnings to Restricted Retained Earnings in the following manner.

Retained Earnings (−SE)	650,000	
Restricted Retained Earnings (+SE)		650,000
Restricted retained earnings.		

In practice, most companies simply disclose the existence, nature, and dollar amount of restricted retained earnings instead of recording the journal entries illustrated. Nordstrom, for example, disclosed the following information about restricted

FIGURE 12–10

Disclosing an appropriation of retained earnings

ROSEBUD CORPORATION
BALANCE SHEET
DECEMBER 31, 1996

STOCKHOLDERS' EQUITY

Common stock		$1,200,000
Additional paid-in capital		2,500,000
Retained earnings:		
Restricted	$300,000	
Unrestricted	200,000	500,000
Total stockholders' equity		$4,200,000

retained earnings in a recent annual report and chose not to adjust the balance of Retained Earnings:

Senior Note Agreements contain restrictive covenants which . . . restrict dividends to shareholders to a formula amount (under the most restrictive formula, approximately $247,342 of retained earnings was not restricted).

THE STATEMENT OF STOCKHOLDERS' EQUITY

Generally accepted accounting principles require that the changes during the period in the dollar balances of the separate accounts composing the stockholders' equity section be disclosed in the financial report. A company can either disclose such changes in the footnotes or in a separate financial statement called the **statement of stockholders' equity**. An example of such a statement appears in Figure 12–11.

FIGURE 12–11

Statement of stockholders' equity

COLGATE-PALMOLIVE COMPANY
STATEMENT OF STOCKHOLDERS' EQUITY
FOR THE YEARS ENDED DEC. 31, 1994, 1993, AND 1992 (DOLLARS IN MILLIONS)

RETAINED EARNINGS:	1994	1993	1992
Balance, January 1	$2,163.4	$2,204.9	$1,928.6
Add:			
Net income	580.2	189.9	477.0
	2,743.6	2,394.8	2,405.6
Deduct:			
Dividends declared:			
Series B Convertible Preference Stock, net of income taxes	21.1	21.1	20.2
Preferred stock	.5	.5	.5
Common stock	225.3	209.8	180.0
	246.9	231.4	200.7
Balance, December 31	$2,496.7	$2,163.4	$2,204.9

CAPITAL STOCK:

	COMMON STOCK		ADDITIONAL PAID-IN CAPITAL	TREASURY STOCK	
	SHARES	AMOUNT		SHARES	AMOUNT
Balance, January 1, 1992	147,343,336	$171.5	$ 411.4	24,215,296	$ 447.7
Shares issued in connection with acquisition	11,648,693	11.7	532.4	—	—
Shares issued for stock options	2,441,044	—	9.5	(2,441,044)	(46.6)
Treasury stock acquired	(976,983)	—	—	976,983	54.0
Other	(215,686)	—	32.0	221,656	12.2
Balance, December 31, 1992	160,240,404	183.2	985.3	22,972,891	467.3
Shares issued for stock options	1,408,105	—	9.6	(1,408,105)	(34.7)
Treasury stock acquired	(12,610,423)	—	—	12,610,423	698.1
Other	218,517	—	6.0	(218,517)	(6.7)
Balance, December 31, 1993	149,256,603	183.2	1,000.9	33,956,692	1,124.0
Shares issued for stock options	1,803,574	—	1.6	(1,803,574)	(63.4)
Treasury stock acquired	(6,923,325)	—	—	6,923,325	411.1
Other	267,385	—	17.9	(267,385)	(9.3)
Balance, December 31, 1994	144,404,237	$183.2	$1,020.4	38,809,058	$1,462.4

INTERNATIONAL PERSPECTIVE: THE RISE OF INTERNATIONAL EQUITY MARKETS

We have referred many times in this text to the New York and American Stock Exchanges and the important roles they play in the buying and selling of equity securities in the United States. As the world of business has become internationalized, however, stock exchanges outside the United States have become increasingly important. The stock of J.C. Penney, for example, is traded not only on the New York Exchange, but also on exchanges in Antwerp and Brussels; General Electric is traded in New York, London, and Tokyo; Coca Cola is traded in Frankfurt in addition to five different exchanges in Switzerland; and American Express stock is listed on no less than fifteen stock exchanges, eleven of which are outside the United States. It is also true that many companies outside the United States list their equity securities on U.S. exchanges. Approximately fifty percent of Sony's equity is held in New York, and each year billions of dollars are raised through equity issuances on U.S. stock exchanges by non-U.S. companies. Indeed, a "world stock exchange" seems to be emerging. In the words of Neil Osborn, author of "The Rise of the International Equity" (*Euromoney*, May 1984):

It is quite possible to trade in a Japanese stock with a buyer in Saudi Arabia, a seller in London, and a U.S. broker without the transaction going near Tokyo.

The increasing level of international equity trading has important implications for accountants, who must provide the financial reports necessary to support this investment activity. Each stock exchange, for example, has different reporting requirements, and issuing companies must prepare their financial statements and supporting disclosures in a manner that conforms to those requirements. To date, the requirements of the U.S. exchanges have been the most difficult to meet, which, in turn, has discouraged many companies from listing their securities on the U.S. exchanges. *The Wall Street Journal* (August 29, 1995) noted that "the major roadblock to foreign companies listing their overseas stock on U.S. exchanges has long been the big difference between accounting standards in the U.S. and abroad." International equity trading will also force equity-issuing companies to translate their financial reports into a variety of languages as well as a variety of accounting and reporting standards.

Growth in international equity markets also raises questions about the jurisdictions of the various regulatory commissions operating in each country. The jurisdiction of the Securities and Exchange Commission, for example, presently includes the listed companies on the U.S. public exchanges. Will this jurisdiction change as the stocks of these companies are increasingly traded on other exchanges, where other regulatory commissions have jurisdiction? Finally, the simultaneous use of a company's financial reports in different countries will certainly advance the cause for a single set of international accounting and auditing standards. Perhaps in the not-too-distant future we will see a single report format that can be better understood and compared across different countries, or maybe a two-tiered system where each company prepares two reports: one that meets the requirements of its own country and a second that meets international reporting requirements.

Executive pay has been a controversial issue in American business for many years. *Time* (May 4, 1992) reported that "Angry investors and public have long been shocked by the millions that some corporate bosses make . . . [and that] . . . Shareholders at 43 companies have submitted proposals to curb executive pay." Much of the controversy has focused on the practice of paying executives in the form of stock options—the right to buy shares of a company's stock at a predetermined price. When executives exercise these rights after stock prices have increased, they often reap huge profits. For example, if an executive has the right to purchase 1,000 shares of stock for $10 per share, and the current value of the stock is $50 per share, the executive can purchase the 100 shares and immediately sell them for a profit of $40,000 [1,000 shares × ($50 − $10)]. Recently, Leon Hirsch, CEO of U.S. Surgical, reported personal income of $118 million, $109 million of which came from exercising stock options.

One particularly controversial aspect of paying executives in the form of stock options is that no compensation expense is recognized on the income statement when the options are issued or exercised.

ETHICS IN THE REAL WORLD

Some believe, therefore, that using stock options to pay executives not only leads to grossly overpaid executives, but also creates overstatements of reported net income. In 1994 the Financial Accounting Standards Board introduced an exposure draft designed to require companies to recognize compensation expense on stock options issued to executives. *Business Week* (April 24, 1995) reports that many boards of directors handed out hefty stock option awards [to their executives], hoping to squeeze them in before the new rules went into effect. The proposal, which was ultimately rescinded by the FASB, may have made matters worse. As executive pay consultant Pearl Meyer said, "The threat of FASB intervention led a large number of companies to make unusually large grants of stock options to their top executives . . . [which] will raise the overall tide of executive pay in years to come."

ETHICAL ISSUE

Were these boards of directors acting ethically when they intentionally handed out hefty stock option awards in an attempt to squeeze them in before the FASB rule was expected to take effect?

REVIEW PROBLEM

The following data pertain to the stockholders' equity transactions of Pike Place Corporation over its first three years of operations: 1995, 1996, and 1997. Transactions are described and followed by the appropriate journal entries. The stockholders' equity section of the balance sheet is shown for each of the three years.

1995

(1) The company issues 1,000 shares of $1 par value stock for $70 per share.

Cash (+A)	**70,000***	
Common Stock (+SE)		**1,000****
Additional Paid-In Capital, C/S (+SE)	**69,000**	

Issued common stock.

*1,000 sh. × $70/sh.
**1,000 sh. × $1 par value/sh.

(2) The company issued 500 shares of no par value, $5, cumulative preferred stock for $50 per share.

Cash (+A)	25,000	
Preferred Stock (+SE)		25,000

Issued preferred stock (500 sh. × $50/sh.).

(3) Net income during the year = $2,000
    Dividends = $0

PIKE PLACE CORPORATION
BALANCE SHEET
DECEMBER 31, 1995

STOCKHOLDERS' EQUITY

Preferred stock (500 sh., no par value)	$25,000
Common stock (1,000 sh. @ $1 par value)	1,000
Additional paid-in capital (C/S)	69,000
Retained earnings	2,000
Total stockholders' equity	$97,000

Note: Dividends in arrears on cumulative preferred stock = $2,500 (500 sh. × $5/sh.)

1996

(1) The company purchases 200 treasury (common) shares for $60 per share.

Treasury Stock (−SE)	12,000	
Cash (−A)		12,000

Acquired treasury stock (200 sh. × $60/sh.).

(2) Net income for the year = $20,000
    Dividends = $6,600: $5,000 for preferred stockholders [$2,500 dividends in arrears and $2,500 (500 sh. × $5/sh.)] for 1993, and $1,600 for the common stockholders (800 outstanding sh. × $2/sh.). The dividends were declared and paid.

Preferred Dividends (−SE)	5,000	
Common Dividends (−SE)	1,600	
Dividends Payable (+L)		6,600

Declared dividends.

Dividends Payable (−L)	6,600	
Cash (−A)		6,600

Paid dividends.

PIKE PLACE CORPORATION
BALANCE SHEET
DECEMBER 31, 1996

STOCKHOLDERS' EQUITY

Preferred stock (500 sh., no par value)	$25,000
Common stock (1,000 sh. @ $1 par value)	1,000
Additional paid-in capital (C/S)	69,000
Retained earnings	15,400*
Less: Treasury stock (200 sh. × $60/sh.)	12,000
Total stockholders' equity	$98,400

*$2,000 + $20,000 − $6,600

1997

(1) The company reissued 100 treasury shares for $65 each.

Cash (+A)	6,500*	
Treasury Stock (+SE)		6,000**
Additional Paid-In Capital, T/S (+SE)		500

Reissued treasury stock.

*100 sh. × $65/sh.
**100 sh. × $60/sh.

(2) The company reissued 50 treasury shares for $40 each.

Cash (+A)	2,000*	
Additional Paid-In Capital, T/S (−SE)	500	
Retained Earnings (−SE)	500	
Treasury Stock (+SE)		3,000**

Reissued treasury stock.

*50 sh. × $40/sh.
**50 sh. × $60/sh.

(3) The company declared a 10 percent stock dividend. There were 950 common shares outstanding at the time of the split, each with a fair market value of $5.

Stock Dividend (−SE)	475*	
Common Stock (+SE)		95**
Additional Paid-In Capital (+SE)		380

Declared stock dividend.

*Closed to Retained Earnings
**95 sh. × $1 par value/sh.

(4) The company entered into a debt covenant that required a minimum retained earnings balance of $30,000. The board of directors voted to restrict retained earnings of $30,000.

Retained Earnings (−SE)	30,000	
Restricted Retained Earnings (+SE)		30,000

Restricted retained earnings.

(5) Net income at the end of the year = $35,000

Dividends = $4,590: $2,500 to preferred stockholders and $2,090 to common stockholders [1,045 sh. outstanding × $2/sh.]. The dividends were declared but unpaid at year-end.

Preferred Dividends (−SE)	2,500	
Common Dividends (−SE)	2,090	
Dividends Payable (+L)		4,590

PIKE PLACE CORPORATION
BALANCE SHEET
DECEMBER 31, 1997

STOCKHOLDERS' EQUITY

Preferred stock (500 sh., no par value)		$ 25,000
Common stock (1,045 sh. @ $1 par value)		1,045[a]
Additional paid-in capital		69,380[b]
Retained earnings:		
Restricted	$30,000	
Unrestricted	14,835	44,835[c]
Less: Treasury stock		3,000[d]
Total stockholders' equity		$137,260

[a]$1,000 + $45
[b]$69,000 + $500 − $500 + 380

[c]$15,400 − $500 − $475 + $35,000 − $4,590
[d]50 sh. × $60/sh or $12,000 − $6,000 − $3,000

SUMMARY OF LEARNING OBJECTIVES

 Identify the three forms of financing, and describe the relative importance of each to major U.S. corporations.

Companies can generate assets from three sources: (1) borrowings, (2) issuing equity securities, and (3) retaining funds generated through profitable operations. Borrowings are represented by liabilities on the balance sheet, equity issuances are represented by contributed capital (preferred stock, common stock, and additional paid-in capital), and retaining funds is represented by earned capital (retained earnings). Major U.S. corporations generally rely more heavily on liabilities as a form of financing than on the combined total of contributed and earned capital. Earned capital is typically more important than contributed capital. The relative importance of each form of financing, however, varies across companies, depending upon a number of factors.

 Distinguish debt from equity, and explain why such a distinction is important to investors and creditors, managers, and accountants.

Debt involves a contractual relationship with an outsider. The contract usually states a fixed maturity date, interest charges, security in case of default, and additional provisions designed to protect the interests of the debtholders. Interest is an expense on the income statement and is deductible for tax purposes. In case of liquidation, creditors have rights to the company's assets before owners. Creditors do not vote in the annual election of the board of directors.

Equity involves a relationship with an owner. There is no legal contract, no fixed maturity date, and no periodic interest payment. Dividends are at the discretion of the board of directors. They are not considered an expense on the income statement and are not tax deductible. Equity holders have lower asset priority than debtholders in case of liquidation, but they have a direct voice in the operation of the company, primarily through voting power over the board of directors.

Distinguishing debt from equity is important to investors and creditors because equity investments are generally riskier than debt investments but offer the potential for higher returns. From the company's perspective, issuing debt involves the commitment of future cash outflows, but interest is tax deductible. Issuing equity, while avoiding fixed contractual cash outflows, dilutes the ownership of the existing shareholders and makes it easier for outside investors to gain significant control. From the accountant's perspective, debt and equity are classified in different sections of the balance sheet, and unlike interest payments and debt redemptions, exchanges of equity are never reflected on the income statement.

LO 3 *Explain the economic consequences associated with the methods used to account for stockholders' equity.*

The economic consequences associated with accounting for stockholders' equity arise from the effects of financial ratios that include the dollar amount of stockholders' equity or its components on a company's stock prices, credit rating, or any debt covenants that restrict additional borrowings, the payment of dividends, or the repurchase of outstanding equity shares. Such ratios are also commonly used to define restrictions in debt covenants imposed on management. The use of financial ratios in these ways can encourage management, for example, to structure debt financing in a way that resembles equity so that additional debt need not be reported on the balance sheet. Issuing certain forms of preferred stock and other hybrid securities may represent such a strategy.

 Describe the rights associated with preferred and common stock and the methods used to account for stock issuances.

Stock that is preferred as to dividends carries the right, if dividends are declared by the board, to receive a certain specified dividend payment before the common stockholders receive a dividend. If the preferred stock is cumulative, when the corporation misses a dividend, dividends in arrears are created in the amount of the missed preferred dividend. In future periods, as dividends are declared, dividends in arrears are paid first to the preferred stockholders, the preferred stockholders are then paid their normal, annual dividend, and finally, the common stockholders are paid from what remains. If the preferred stock carries a participating feature, the preferred stockholders not only receive their initial specified amount but they also share in the remaining dividends with the common stockholders. Stock that is preferred as to assets carries a claim to the corporation's assets, in case of liquidation, that has higher priority than the claim carried by common stock. In many ways preferred stock resembles debt.

Common stock is characterized by three fundamental rights: (1) the right to receive dividends if they are declared by the board, (2) a residual right to the corporation's assets in case of liquidation, and (3) the right to exert control over corporate management, which is exercised primarily by voting in the election of the board at the annual stockholders' meeting.

When preferred or common stock with no par value is issued for cash, the Cash account is debited for the proceeds, and the Stock account is credited for the entire dollar amount. When stock with a par (or stated) value is issued for cash, the Cash account is debited for the total proceeds, the Stock account is credited for the number of shares issued times the par value per share, and the Additional Paid-In Capital account is credited for the remainder.

 Distinguish among the market value, book value, and par (stated) value of a share of common stock.

The market value of a share of stock is the price at which the stock can be purchased and sold on the open market. The book value of a share of stock is equal to the book value of the corporation, as indicated on the balance sheet (stockholders' equity or net assets), less preferred capital divided by the number of common shares outstanding. The par (stated) value of a share of stock has no relationship to its market value or book value and, for the most part, has limited economic significance.

 Define treasury stock, explain why corporations acquire it, and summarize the methods used to account for it.

Outstanding common stock is often repurchased by companies. Such stocks are either (1) held in treasury, to be reissued at a later date, or (2) retired. Treasury stock purchases normally must be authorized and approved by the company's board of directors and stockholders. While held in treasury, stock shares carry none of the usual rights of ownership.

Companies purchase treasury stock to support employee compensation plans, to fend off possible takeover attempts, to prepare for merger activity, to increase the market price of the company's outstanding stock, to increase the company's earnings per share (net income/outstanding common shares), and to distribute cash to the shareholders. In general, treasury stock purchases reduce the scale of a company's operations.

Under the cost method, when a company purchases its own outstanding common stock, a permanent account, called Treasury Stock, is debited for the cost of the purchase. This account is disclosed below retained earnings in the stockholders' equity section of the balance sheet. If treasury stock is reissued at a price greater than its original cost, the Cash account is debited for the proceeds, the Treasury Stock account is credited for the cost, and the difference is credited to the Additional Paid-In Capital (Treasury Stock) account. If treasury stock is reissued at an amount less than the original cost, the Cash account is debited for the proceeds, the Treasury Stock account is credited for the original cost, and Additional Paid-In Capital (Treasury Stock) is debited for the difference, if there is a sufficient balance in the account to cover the difference. If the difference between the cost and the proceeds exceeds the balance in the Additional Paid-In Capital account, Retained Earnings is debited.

 Define a cash dividend, and describe some of the dividend strategies followed by corporations.

Cash dividends represent distributions of cash to the stockholders. When a cash dividend is declared, a Cash Dividend account is debited and a current liability account, Dividends Payable, is credited on the date of declaration. The dollar amount is equal to the cash dividend per share multiplied by the number of outstanding shares. The dividend account is a temporary account that is closed directly to Retained Earnings at the end of the accounting period. On the date of record, no entry is made in the books of the corporation. The shareholders as of this date are the recipients of the dividends. On the date of payment, the cash dividend is paid, and the Dividends Payable liability is removed from the balance sheet.

When to declare a dividend and how much to declare depend on the nature, financial condition, and desired image of the company, as well as legal constraints. If dividends are to be paid in cash, the board of directors must first be certain that the corporation has sufficient cash to meet the payment. Some companies have adopted policies of paying no dividends. Such companies reinvest their earnings primarily to support growth without having to rely too heavily on debt and equity financing. Other companies pay quarterly dividends at the rate of a relatively fixed percentage of net income and also attempt to increase their dividend payments consistently from year to year. Some companies consistently increase dividends from year to year, but the distributions do not represent a consistent percentage of net income.

 Distinguish between a stock dividend and a stock split, and briefly explain why corporations declare them.

In a stock split the number of outstanding shares is simply split into smaller units, which requires the corporation to distribute additional shares. In a stock dividend, additional shares, usually expressed as a percentage of the outstanding shares, are issued to the stockholders. Professional accounting standards recommend that relatively large stock dividends (over 25 percent) be referred to as stock splits in the form of dividends and that relatively small stock dividends (less than 25 percent) be referred to as ordinary stock dividends.

Stock splits or stock dividends in the form of splits are often declared to reduce the per-share price of the outstanding shares, so that investors can more easily purchase them. The reasons for small stock dividends are less clear. Such distributions have a relatively small effect on the number of outstanding shares and do little to reduce per-share prices and broaden stock ownership. Corporations that are short of cash may distribute stock, instead of cash, dividends so that the shareholders are at least receiving something. Corporations may also issue stock dividends to capitalize a portion of retained earnings, rendering them unavailable for future dividends. In any case, the issuance of a stock split or stock dividend does not involve a distribution of assets to the shareholders.

 Explain how retained earnings are appropriated and why corporations follow such a practice.

An appropriation of retained earnings is a book entry, involving only the Retained Earnings account, that serves to restrict a portion of retained earnings from the payment of future dividends. It involves no asset or liability accounts. Such entries are executed either at the discretion of the board of directors or in conformance with the terms of contracts (e.g., debt covenants). In practice, most companies simply disclose the existence, nature, and dollar amount of Restricted Retained Earnings instead of recording a journal entry to appropriate retained earnings.

APPENDIX 12A

FORMS OF BUSINESS

There are three major types of business enterprises: corporations, partnerships, and individual proprietorships. Corporations by far control the greatest amount of capital, but partnerships and proprietorships are much more common. Approximately 13 percent of business enterprises in the United States are corporations; 17 percent are partnerships; and 70 percent are proprietorships.

THE CORPORATE FORM OF ORGANIZATION

A **corporation** is a legal entity, separate and distinct from its owners (stockholders). A corporation must be chartered by the state in which its corporate headquarters is located. The chartering process requires the submission of certificates of incorporation and supplementary application forms as well as the payment of the necessary fees. The certificate of incorporation specifies the corporation's purpose, the number of shares it is authorized to issue, and the individuals composing the board of directors. Formal bylaws must be adopted that cover such matters as the issuance and transfer of stock and the meetings of the directors and the stockholders. A corporation has an indefinite life, which continues regardless of changes in ownership. Stockholders of a corporation are usually free to transfer their ownership interests to anyone they wish.

Corporations are usually formed by one or more individuals, known as promoters, who organize the corporation, apply for a charter, and establish the corporate bylaws. The promoters contribute cash and other assets or services in exchange for proportionate amounts of the equity. If additional equity financing is necessary, the promoters arrange for shares of stock to be sold either to the general public (public placement), which can be extremely expensive and involve extensive audits and much paperwork, or to other specific parties (private placement). Corporations can be new businesses, or they are often formed from existing proprietorships or partnerships.

Corporations are owned by stockholders who annually elect a board of directors. The board represents the stockholders' interests in the management of the business and has the power to declare dividends, hire and fire management, determine executive compensation, and in general, set long-term corporate goals and all policy. Typically, the Board meets four times per year to review the progress and future plans of the management and to decide whether to declare dividends. Often a number of the board members and managers are also stockholders.

LIMITED LIABILITY

In a corporation, the liability of the stockholders is limited to the dollar amount of their investments. In other words, the maximum loss a shareholder can sustain is equal to the shareholder's investment. Shareholders' personal assets are not at risk, which means that they cannot be legally required to use personal assets to satisfy the obligations of the corporation. Only in rare cases (e.g., shareholder fraud) can action be taken directly against shareholders, and even in these cases, shareholders are not liable for the negligent or fraudulent action of one another. As a legal entity, a corporation provides a shield that protects the personal assets of the shareholders from the corporate creditors. An individual who chooses to take legal action against a corporation must sue the corporation as an entity, not the individual stockholders.

The **limited liability** feature of the corporate form makes it well suited to raise large amounts of capital through large equity issuances. Many investors are willing to purchase ownership interests in corporations, knowing that their potential gains are unlimited but their losses can be no greater than their initial investments. While corporate shareholders are understandably concerned with the effectiveness of management, such concern is lessened by the fact that even the worst mismanagement at no time places their personal assets at risk. Limited liability is one important reason why most large businesses tend to be corporations.

CORPORATE INCOME TAXES

Corporations, as legal entities, are subject to both federal and state income taxes. The corporate income tax rate, which is approximately 35 percent, is assessed against a corporation's taxable income, and the corporation itself is liable for the tax payment. The amount of income tax paid by the corporation is neither determined nor affected by the amount of dividends declared by the board of directors. However, dividends received by a shareholder must be included in the shareholder's taxable income. In a sense, therefore, corporate profits are taxed twice: once at the corporate level and again when a shareholder received dividends. Such **double taxation** is a disadvantage of the corporate form of organization.

STOCKHOLDER RETURNS: CAPITAL APPRECIATION AND DIVIDENDS

Returns to shareholders of large corporations that are listed on the public security exchanges come in either of two forms: (1) price appreciation of their shares or (2) dividends. Publicly traded stocks are easily transferable, and objective market prices are readily available. Thus, shareholders can cash in their investments at any time they choose. Many publicly traded corporations also pay quarterly dividends. On the other hand, shareholders of small corporations, whose stock is not traded on public security exchanges, find it more difficult to sell their shares. Their returns come primarily in the form of dividends.

PROPRIETORSHIPS AND PARTNERSHIPS

Individual proprietorships and partnerships are organized in much the same way and differ only in terms of the number of owners. Proprietorships are owned by single parties, while partnerships are owned by two or more parties. In general, proprietorships and partnerships are simply extensions of their owners; unlike corporations, they are not legal entities in and of themselves. In the following discussion a proprietorship is viewed as a simplified partnership, that is, a "partnership" consisting of a single partner. You will note that the essence of a partnership is the agreement signed among the partners, but of course such an agreement is not necessary in a proprietorship.

A partnership is not a separate legal entity. No formal charter or state certificate is required to form a partnership, and the government does not generally recognize a partnership as such. One or more individuals simply establish a business by purchasing or renting equipment or space, acquiring inventory, and obtaining any local operating licenses that might be required. It is usually necessary to have an attorney draw up a partnership agreement, which specifies the rights and obligations of the partners (e.g., capital contributions, duties, distributions of profits, and limitations on selling partnership interests), but a partnership agreement is solely for the protection of the partners. It is not required by law. Legally, a partnership is nothing more than an agreement drawn up among the partners. Partnerships are not sued, nor are they taxed. The relevant legal entities are the partners themselves.

While proprietorships and partnerships tend to be relatively small, a number of large enterprises use the partnership form. Professional firms, for example, such as brokerage houses and public accounting and law firms, which generate hundreds of millions of dollars annually, are normally organized as partnerships.

LEGAL LIABILITY OF PARTNERS: UNLIMITED

In a partnership the individual partners, not the partnership itself, are legally responsible for all obligations of the business. If the enterprise incurs debts, suffers losses, or becomes bankrupt, the partners are jointly and severally responsible for all debts incurred. That is, the partners are not only responsible for their own portions of the enterprise's debts, but are also liable for the portions of the other partners, if they are unable to meet their respective responsibilities. Consequently, a partner's personal assets (e.g., home and automobile) are at risk and might be required to satisfy creditor claims. Unlike a corporation, where the liability faced by shareholders is limited to their investment, the liability faced by a partner is unlimited—extending well beyond the amount originally contributed to the business.

INCOME TAXES: PERSONAL RATES AND UNAFFECTED BY WITHDRAWALS

Partnerships are not subject to federal or state income taxes. Instead, the partners must include their portions of the total partnership profit, which are usually specified in the partnership agreement, on their individual income tax returns. Partnership profits, therefore, are taxed at the personal income tax rates of the individual partners, which range from approximately 15 percent to as much as 39 percent in some cases. Recall that corporations, as legal entities, are taxed at the corporate income tax rate (approximately 35 percent).

The amount of taxable partnership profit for each partner is not determined by, or even affected by, the assets (usually cash) each partner withdraws from the partnership. This feature differs from a corporation in that corporate dividends are taxed separately in the hands of the shareholders. While it tends to reduce the total income tax liability of partners, this feature can create a problem for partnerships, especially those that finance expansion with internally generated funds.

For example, assume that Bob and Tom form a partnership and agree to share the rights to the profits equally and to limit their cash withdrawals in the early years, so that cash will be available to the partnership for expansion. In the first year of operations, assume that the partnership recognized net income of $50,000, giving Bob and Tom the right to $25,000 each. However, neither partner could withdraw $25,000 in cash because the partnership's cash was used to purchase productive assets during the year. Nonetheless, Bob and Tom are both required to report $25,000 as taxable income on their federal income tax returns which, in turn, increases the income tax they must pay as individuals. A problem arises in this case because the partnership provided the partners no additional cash with which to pay the additional taxes.

RETURNS TO PARTNERS: LIMITED MARKETS BUT RELATIVELY FREE WITHDRAWALS

Partnership interests are not always easily transferable, and there are only limited markets where such interests are readily purchased and sold. It is often difficult, therefore, to place a market value on a given partner's interest, and it is equally difficult to assess a partner's return in terms of capital appreciation. Instead, the return for most partners comes in the form of cash withdrawals.

Cash withdrawals from a partnership are limited only by agreement among the partners. They may be limited, for example, to a percentage of a partner's interest in the partnership, or they may be restricted in some way to provide working capital for operations or funds for expansion. Certainly, operating a partnership efficiently would be difficult if cash withdrawals by the partners were totally unrestricted. However, the partnership itself is not a legal entity, and within the constraints specified by the partnership agreement, withdrawals are relatively unencumbered.

CHOOSING A FORM OF BUSINESS: A SUMMARY

Figure 12A–1 summarizes the trade-offs involved in choosing between the partnership (proprietorship) or corporate form of business.[17] Relative freedom to create the terms of the partnership contract and lower overall tax rates generally favor the partnership form of business, while limited liability is a distinct advantage of corporations. Some companies, which are owned and operated by relatively few individuals and are not in need of large amounts of capital, are generally not organized as corporations. In such situations the owners and managers often work closely together, mon-

17. There are other forms of business that represent combinations of the characteristics of corporations and partnerships (proprietorships). A Subchapter S corporation, for example, is essentially a corporation that is taxed like a partnership. This form was created to encourage the formation of small businesses by granting them the benefits of the corporate form (e.g., limited liability) without the costs associated with the double taxation of dividends. Another hybrid form, the limited partnership, is essentially a partnership with limited liability. It is used primarily to finance projects with capital from investors, who wish to share in the gains and losses of the project without having to put their personal assets at risk.

itoring each other's activities, which in turn reduces the need for limited liability. Companies in need of large amounts of capital, on the other hand, have difficulty collecting such funds without offering limited liability to investors. Consequently, such enterprises are usually organized as corporations.

FIGURE 12A–1

Trade-offs among the partnership and corporate forms of business

	PARTNERSHIP (INCLUDING PROPRIETORSHIP)	CORPORATION
Owners' liability	Unlimited (personal assets at risk)	Limited to investment
Federal income tax	Personal tax rates of owners, income tax payments unaffected by withdrawals	Corporation is taxed at corporate tax rate and dividends are taxed to shareholders (double taxation)
Owners' returns	Limited markets, relatively free withdrawals	Capital appreciation and dividends declared by the board of directors

KEY TERMS

Note: Definitions for these terms are provided in the glossary at the end of the text.

Appropriation of retained earnings (p. 608)
Authorized (shares) (p. 593)
Book value (of company/shares) (pp. 586, 597)
Contributed capital (p. 586)
Corporation (p. 617)
Cumulative preferred stock (p. 594)
Date of declaration (p. 604)
Date of payment (p. 604)
Date of record (p. 604)
Dilution (p. 590)
Dividends in arrears (p. 594)
Double taxation (p. 618)
Earned capital (p. 586)
Issued (shares) (p. 593)
Leverage (p. 590)
Limited liability (p. 618)

Market-to-book ratio (p. 597)
Market value (of stock) (p. 596)
Net assets (p. 586)
Net worth (p. 586)
Ordinary stock dividends (p. 606)
Outstanding (shares) (p. 593)
Par value (pp. 594, 597)
Participating (preferred stock) (p. 595)
Preferred stock as to assets (p. 593)
Preferred stock as to dividends (p. 593)
Residual interest (p. 588)
Statement of stockholders' equity (p. 609)
Stock dividends (pp. 603, 606)
Stock options (p. 602)
Stock split (p. 605)
Stock splits in the form of dividends (p. 606)
Takeover (p. 590)
Treasury stock (p. 590)

QUESTIONS FOR DISCUSSION AND REVIEW

1. Distinguish between borrowed capital, contributed capital, and earned capital, and explain why such a distinction is important to creditors and investors, managers, and auditors. How is this distinction depicted on the financial statements?

2. Why might a manager wish to structure a financing transaction so that it can be reported as equity instead of debt? What are hybrid securities, and what kinds of problems do they present for accountants?

3. Name and briefly describe the accounts that compose the stockholders' equity section of the balance sheet.

4. Provide several reasons why major U.S. corporations tend to rely on debt more heavily than contributed capital or earned capital as a source of financing.

5. Explain how a debt covenant might impose restrictions on management that are expressed in terms of stockholders' equity accounts.

6. Differentiate debt from equity, and describe why such a differentiation is important to investors and creditors, managers, and accountants.

7. What basic trade-offs does a manager face when deciding to raise capital by issuing either debt or equity?

8. What is a corporate takeover? Explain why managers are concerned by them. What is dilution, and how does it relate to corporate takeovers? How might purchasing outstanding stock help to block a takeover attempt?

9. Distinguish preferred stock from common stock. How do the rights of preferred stockholders differ from those of common stockholders? Why is preferred stock listed at the top of the stockholders' equity section? Should preferred stock always be considered contributed capital?

10. Why would the authorization of new shares be a concern of the existing stockholders? Why does the number of outstanding shares often differ from the number of issued shares?

11. What are dividends in arrears? Are they considered liabilities? Why or why not?

12. Explain how common stockholders have control over management. What is the role of the board of directors?

13. Define and differentiate among the market value, book value, and par value of a share of common stock.

14. Why is the book value of a share of stock often below its market value and how is the market-to-book ratio useful?

15. What is treasury stock, and why do major U.S. corporations purchase so much of it? Explain how the purchase of treasury stock can increase the earnings-per-share ratio.

16. How can the purchase of treasury stock be equivalent to a dividend?

17. When treasury stock is reissued for a dollar amount less than its original cost, what two accounts can be debited for the difference between the cost and the proceeds? How does this method of accounting often confuse the distinction between contributed capital and earned capital?

18. What is a stock option, and why do corporations use them to compensate executives? Explain the controversy surrounding the methods used to account for stock options.

19. What is a dividend, and what three dates are relevant when accounting for dividends?

20. Briefly explain some of the different dividend strategies followed by major U.S. companies. Why would an investor ever wish to invest in a company that paid no dividends?

21. What is the difference between a stock dividend, a stock split in the form of a dividend, and a stock split? Why do companies split their stock? Why do companies issue stock dividends?

22. What is an appropriation of retained earnings? Explain how a debt covenant might underlie an appropriation of retained earnings. Are any assets or liabilities affected when retained earnings are appropriated? If not, what purpose does such an action serve?

23. Briefly describe the statement of stockholders' equity, and describe the kind of information that can be found on it that is not found elsewhere in the financial report.

24. Discuss some of the implications that the increasing level of international equity trading has on accountants.

25. *(Appendix 12A)* Identify and describe the essential features of a corporation. What are some of the important advantages and disadvantages of the corporate form of business?

26. *(Appendix 12A)* Describe the trade-offs between organizing a business as a partnership instead of as a corporation.

EXERCISES

(Debt, contributed, and earned capital, and the classification of preferred stock)

The balance sheet of Lamont Bros. follows.

ASSETS		LIABILITIES AND STOCKHOLDERS' EQUITY	
Current assets	$ 85,000	Current liabilities	$ 52,000
Noncurrent assets	315,000	Long-term note payable	35,000
		Preferred stock	50,000
		Common stock	80,000
		Additional paid-in capital:	
		Preferred stock	50,000
		Common stock	100,000
		Retained earnings	113,000
		Less: Treasury stock	80,000
		Total liabilities and	
Total assets	$400,000	stockholders' equity	$400,000

REQUIRED:

a. What portions of Lamont's assets were provided by debt, contributed capital, and earned capital? Reduce contributed capital by the cost of the treasury stock.

b. Compute the company's debt/equity ratio. Compute the debt/equity ratio if the preferred stock issuance was classified as a long-term debt.

c. In most states, to what dollar amount of dividends would the company be limited?

(The effects of transactions on stockholders' equity)

The following are possible transactions that affect stockholders' equity.
1. A company issues common stock above par value for cash.
2. A company declares a 3-for-1 stock split.
3. A company repurchases 10,000 shares of its own common stock in exchange for cash.
4. A company declares and issues a stock dividend. Assume that the fair market value of the stock is greater than the par value.
5. A company reissues 1,000 shares of treasury stock for $75 per share. The stock was acquired for $60 per share.
6. A company pays a cash dividend that had been declared fifteen days earlier.
7. A company generates net income of $250,000.

REQUIRED:

For each transaction above indicate the following:
a. The accounts within the stockholders' equity section that would be affected.
b. Whether these accounts would be increased or decreased.
c. The effect (increase, decrease, or no effect) of the transaction on total stockholders' equity.

(Authorizing and issuing preferred and common stock)

Deming Contractors was involved in the following events involving stock during 1997. Prepare entries, if appropriate, for each event, describe how each event affects the basic accounting equation, and explain the economic significance of par value.
1. Authorized to issue: (a) 100,000 shares of $100 par value, 8 percent preferred stock; (b) 150,000 shares of no par, $5 preferred stock; and (c) 250,000 shares of $5 par value, common stock.
2. Issued 10,000 shares of $5 par value common stock for $30 per share.
3. Issued 25,000 shares of the $100 par value preferred stock for $150 per share.
4. Issued 50,000 shares of no par preferred stock for $50 each.

E12–4

(The effects of treasury stock purchases on important financial ratios)

On December 30, 1996, Washington and Associates purchased 500 of its 5,000 outstanding common shares at a price of $50 per share. Before the treasury stock purchase, the company's financial statements appeared as below.

INCOME STATEMENT

Revenues	$800,000
Expenses	560,000
Net income	$240,000

BALANCE SHEET

Assets	$1,760,000
Liabilities	900,000
Stockholders' equity	860,000

REQUIRED:

a. Provide the journal entry for the treasury stock purchase.
b. Compute the debt/equity ratio before and after the treasury stock purchase.
c. Compute earnings per share before and after the treasury stock purchase.

E12–5

(Reissuing treasury stock)

Twin Lakes incorporated on April 1, 1997, and was authorized to issue 100,000 shares of $5 par value common stock and 10,000 shares of $8, no par preferred stock. During the remainder of 1997 the company entered into the following transactions.

1. Issued 25,000 shares of common stock in exchange for $500,000 in cash.
2. Issued 5,000 shares of preferred stock in exchange for $60,000 in cash.
3. Purchased 3,000 common shares for $15 per share and held them in the form of treasury stock.
4. Sold 1,000 treasury shares for $18 per share on the open market.
5. Issued 1,000 treasury shares to executives who exercised stock options for a reduced price of $5 per share.

The company entered into no other transactions that affected stockholders' equity during 1997.

REQUIRED:

a. Prepare entries for each of the transactions.
b. Assume that Twin Lakes generated $500,000 in net income in 1997 and did not declare any dividends during 1997. Prepare the stockholders' equity section of the balance sheet as of December 31, 1997.

E12–6

(Reissuing treasury stock)

The stockholders' equity section of Rodman Corporation as of December 31, 1996, follows.

Common stock	$ 80,000
Additional paid-in capital (C/S)	10,000
Retained earnings	60,000
Total stockholders' equity	$150,000

During 1997 the company entered into the following transactions.

1. Purchased 1,000 shares of treasury stock for $60 per share.
2. As part of a compensation package, reissued half of the treasury shares to executives who exercised stock options for $20 per share.
3. Reissued the remainder of the treasury stock on the open market for $66 per share.

REQUIRED:

a. Provide the journal entries for each transaction, and prepare the stockholders' equity section of the balance sheet as of December 31, 1997. Rodman Corporation generated $20,000 in net income during 1997 and did not declare any dividends.

b. What portion of the Additional Paid-In Capital account is attributed to treasury stock transactions?

E12–7

(Treasury stock exceeds contributed capital)

In 1987 Stuart Corporation began operations issuing 100,000 shares of $1 par value common stock for $25 per share. Since that time the company has been very profitable. The stockholders' equity section as of December 31, 1996, follows.

Common stock	$ 100,000
Additional paid-in capital (C/S)	2,400,000
Retained earnings	4,500,000
Total stockholders' equity	$7,000,000

In 1997 the company entered into a program of buying back some of the outstanding shares. During the year the company purchased 30,000 outstanding shares at a price of $95 per share.

REQUIRED:

a. Prepare the journal entry to record the purchase of the treasury shares.

b. Assuming that net income of $350,000 was earned and dividends of $50,000 were declared during the year, prepare the stockholders' equity section of the balance sheet as of the end of 1997.

c. Explain how the dollar value of the treasury stock account can be larger than the dollar amount of contributed capital.

E12–8

(Book value per share, stock issuances, and treasury stock purchases)

The condensed balance sheet of Hemmer, Inc., follows.

Assets	$400,000	Liabilities	$140,000
		Stockholders' equity	260,000
		Total liabilities and	
Total assets	$400,000	stockholders' equity	$400,000

Ten thousand shares of common stock and no preferred stock are presently outstanding.

REQUIRED:

The following requirements are independent.

a. Compute the book value per common share.

b. Compute the book value per common share if the company issues 5,000 shares of common stock at $32 per share.

c. Compute the book value per common share if the company issues 5,000 shares of common stock at $20 per share.

d. Compute the book value per outstanding share of common stock if the company purchases 5,000 shares of treasury stock at $32 per share.

c. Compute the book value per outstanding share of common stock if the company purchases 5,000 shares of treasury stock at $20 per share.

f. What effect does issuing stock have on the book value of the outstanding shares? Upon what does this effect depend?

g. What effect does purchasing treasury stock have on the book value of the outstanding shares? Upon what does this effect depend?

E12–9

(Inferring equity transactions from the statement of stockholders' equity)

The information below was taken from the statement of stockholders' equity of Chinook Furs.

	1997	1996
Preferred stock (no par)	$ 700	$400
Common stock ($1 par value)	1,000	900
Additional paid-in capital:		
Common stock	40	20
Treasury stock	10	—
Less: Treasury stock	130	150

REQUIRED:

Provide the journal entries for the following.
a. The issuance of preferred stock during 1997.
b. The issuance of common stock during 1997.
c. The sale of treasury stock during 1997.

E12–10

(Inferring equity transactions from the statement of stockholders' equity)

The information below was taken from the statement of stockholders' equity of Zielow Siding as of December 31, 1997. The par value of the Zielow stock is $5, and as of the beginning of 1997 the company held 400 shares in treasury.

	COMMON STOCK	ADDITIONAL PAID-IN CAPITAL	RETAINED EARNINGS	TREASURY STOCK
Beginning balances	$10,000	$25,000	$34,000	$ 8,000
Acquisition of Timeco	5,000	23,000		
Treasury share purchases				4,000
Exercised stock options	1,000	800		
Net income			5,600	
Cash dividends			3,520	
Ending balances	$16,000	$48,800	$ 36,080	$12,000

REQUIRED:

a. Zielow issued common stock at one time prior to 1997. How many shares were issued and at what price per share?
b. Zielow purchased treasury stock at one time prior to 1997. How many shares were purchased and at what price?
c. During 1997 Zielow acquired Timeco and issued its own shares as payment in the transaction. How many shares were issued and what was the market value of Timeco at the time of the acquisition?
d. At what price were the stock options exercised, and how did that price compare to the market value of Zielow stock at the time?
e. Compute the per share dividend rate paid by Zielow during 1997. Assume treasury shares acquired in 1997 were purchased at the same price per share prior to 1997.

E12–11

(Inferring equity transactions from the statement of stockholders' equity)

The information below was taken from the statement of stockholders' equity of Kidd Sports as of December 31, 1997. The par value of Kidd stock is $1, and as of the beginning of 1997 the company held 1,500 shares in treasury.

	COMMON STOCK	ADDITIONAL PAID-IN CAPITAL	RETAINED EARNINGS	TREASURY STOCK
Beginning balances	$8,000	$32,000	$27,000	$18,000
Exercised stock options			(2,750)	(3,000)
Net income			5,600	
Cash dividends			(3,500)	
Stock dividend	700	9,800	(10,500)	
Ending balances	$8,700	$41,800	$15,850	$15,000

REQUIRED:

a. Kidd issued common stock at one time prior to 1997. How many shares were issued and at what price per share?

b. Kidd purchased treasury stock at one time prior to 1997. How many shares were purchased and at what price?

c. At what price were the stock options exercised, and how did that price compare to the market value of Kidd stock at the time? Assume that the stock options were exercised immediately prior to the issuance of the stock dividend, which was recorded at market value.

d. Compute the per share dividend rate paid by Kidd during 1997, assuming that the cash dividends were declared prior to the stock dividend but after the stock options were exercised.

E12–12

(Issuing cash dividends on outstanding common stock)

The board of directors of Enerson Manufacturing is in the process of declaring a dividend. The company is considering paying a cash dividend of $12 per share. Enerson Manufacturing is authorized to issue 800,000 shares of common stock. The company has issued 375,000 shares to date and has reacquired 50,000 shares. These 50,000 shares are held in treasury.

REQUIRED:

a. How many shares of common stock are eligible to receive a dividend?

b. Assume that the board declares the dividend. Prepare the appropriate journal entries on the
   (1) Date of declaration
   (2) Date of record
   (3) Date of payment

E12–13

(Cumulative preferred stock and dividends in arrears)

The stockholders' equity section of Mayberry Corporation, as of the end of 1997, follows. Mayberry began operations in 1993. The 5,000 shares of preferred stock have been outstanding since 1993.

Preferred stock (10,000 sh. authorized, 5,000 issued,	
cumulative, nonparticipating, $5 dividends, $10 par value)	**$ 50,000**
Common stock (500,000 sh. authorized, 200,000 sh. issued,	
50,000 held in treasury, no par value)	**1,600,000**
Additional paid-in capital (P/S)	**140,000**
Retained earnings	**110,000**
Less: Treasury stock	**80,000**
Total stockholders' equity	**$1,820,000**

Since 1993 the company has paid the following total cash dividends:

1993	**$ 0**
1994	**30,000**
1995	**80,000**
1996	**15,000**
1997	**40,000**

REQUIRED:

a. Compute the dividends paid to the preferred and common stockholders for each of the years since 1993.

b. Compute the balance of dividends in arrears as of the end of each year.

c. Should dividends in arrears be considered a liability? Why or why not?

E12–14

(Stock dividends and stock splits)

The stockholders' equity section of Pioneer Enterprises as of December 31, 1997, follows.

Common stock (10,000 shares issued @ $6 par)	**$ 60,000**
Additional paid-in capital (C/S)	**100,000**
Retained earnings	**60,000**
Less: Treasury stock (2,000 shares @ $12)	**24,000**
Total stockholders' equity	**$196,000**

REQUIRED:

Prepare journal entries for the following *independent* transactions.

a. The company declares and distributes a 2 percent stock dividend on the outstanding shares. The market price of the stock is $70 per share.
b. The company declares a 3:2 stock split on the outstanding shares.
c. The company declares a 10 percent stock dividend on the outstanding shares. The market price of the stock is $80 per share.
d. The company declares a 2:1 stock split on the outstanding shares.
e. Compute the ratio of contributed capital to earned capital after independently considering each of the four actions listed above. Reduce contributed capital by the cost of the treasury stock. Comment on the difference between a stock dividend and a stock split.

E12–15

(Why do companies declare stock dividends?)

The December 31, 1994, balances in Retained Earnings and Additional Paid-In Capital for Railway Shippers Company are $135,000 and $50,000, respectively. Five thousand, $10 par value common shares are outstanding with a market value of $85 each. The company's cash position at year-end is lower than usual, so the board of directors is considering issuing a stock dividend instead of the normal cash dividend. They are considering the three options listed below.

Option 1: A 10 percent stock dividend: 500 new shares would be issued.
Option 2: A 20 percent stock dividend: 1,000 new shares would be issued.
Option 3: A 2:1 stock split: 5,000 new shares would be issued.

REQUIRED:

a. Prepare the journal entry for Options 1 and 2 above, and comment on why these alternatives may not be attractive. Why do companies issue stock dividends?
b. What effect would Option 3 have on the financial statements?
c. Why do companies split their stock?

E12–16

(Appropriating retained earnings)

Taylor Manufacturing entered into a borrowing arrangement that requires the company to maintain a Retained Earnings balance of $500,000. The company also wishes to finance internally a major plant addition in the not-too-distant future. Accordingly, the board of directors has decided to appropriate $350,000 of the Retained Earnings balance. Prior to the board's action, the balance in the Retained Earnings account was $800,000.

REQUIRED:

a. Why would the board of directors appropriate retained earnings in the situation described above, and why might an auditor insist that it be done?
b. Prepare the journal entry that would accompany the board's decision.
c. Show how retained earnings would be disclosed on the balance sheet after the appropriation.
d. Discuss the constraints with respect to dividend payments that have been imposed on the board by the debt covenant and the appropriation.

PROBLEMS

P12–1

(Hybrid securities and debt covenants)

Lambert Corporation issued 1,000 shares of $100 par value, 8 percent, cumulative, nonparticipating preferred stock for $100 each. The stock is preferred to assets, redeemable after five years at a prespecified price, and the preferred stockholders do not vote at the annual stockholders' meeting. The condensed balance sheet of Lambert prior to the issuance follows.

Assets	$580,000	Liabilities	$250,000
		Stockholders' equity	330,000
		Total liabilities and	
Total assets	$580,000	stockholders' equity	$580,000

Lambert has entered into a debt agreement that requires the company to maintain a debt equity ratio of less than 1:1.

REQUIRED:

a. Provide the journal entry to record the preferred stock issuance, and compute the resulting debt/equity ratio, assuming that the preferred stock is considered an equity security.

b. Compute the debt/equity ratio, assuming that the preferred stock is considered a debt security.

c. What incentives might the management of Lambert have to classify the issuance as equity instead of debt? Do you think that the issuance should be classified as debt or equity? What might Lambert's external auditors think?

P12–2

(The effects of treasury stock transactions on important financial ratios)

The balance sheet of Alex Bros. follows.

Assets	$840,000	Liabilities	$300,000
		Preferred stock	50,000
		Common stock	300,000
		Additional paid-in capital (C/S)	100,000
		Retained earnings	130,000
		Less: Treasury stock	40,000
		Total liabilities and	
Total assets	$840,000	stockholders' equity	$840,000

Of the 200,000 common shares authorized, 50,000 shares were issued for $8 each when the company began operations. There have been no common stock issuances since; 45,000 shares are currently outstanding and 5,000 shares are held in treasury. Net income for the year just ended was $45,000.

REQUIRED:

a. Compute the par value of the issued common shares.

b. Compute the book value of each common share.

c. At what average price were the treasury shares purchased?

d. Alex is considering reissuing the 5,000 treasury shares at the present market price of $10 per share. What effect would this action have on the company's debt/equity ratio, book value per outstanding share, and earnings-per-share ratio?

P12–3

(The significance of par value)

Several independent transactions are listed below. Prepare journal entries for each transaction.

1. 10,000 shares of no-par common stock are issued for $50 per share.
2. 10,000 shares of $1 par value common stock are issued for $40 per share.
3. 10,000 shares of $10 par value common stock are issued for $30 per share.
4. 5,000 shares of no-par preferred stock are issued for $80 per share.
5. What is the significance of par value from a financial accounting standpoint? Is par value significant in any economic sense?

P12–4

(Cash and stock dividends)

Royal Company is currently considering declaring a dividend to its common shareholders, according to one of the following plans:

1. Declare a cash dividend of $15 per share.
2. Declare a 10 percent stock dividend. Royal Company would distribute 1 share of common stock for every 10 shares of common stock currently held. The company's common stock is currently selling for $50 per share.

Royal Company is authorized to issue 100,000 shares of $10 par value common stock. To date, the company has issued 55,000 shares and is currently holding 8,000 shares in treasury stock.

REQUIRED:

a. How many shares of common stock are eligible to receive a dividend?
b. Prepare the entries necessary on the date of declaration, date of record, and the date of payment for the cash dividend.
c. Prepare the entry to record the stock dividend, assuming that the dividend is declared and issued on the same date.
d. Describe how each dividend would affect Royal's debt/equity ratio.
e. Which of the two dividends would you as a shareholder prefer to receive? Why?

P12–5

(Dividend payments and preferred stock)

The following information was extracted from the financial records of Maverick Corporation.

Preferred stock: 15,000 shares outstanding, 10 percent, $50 par value
Common stock: 50,000 shares outstanding, $15 par value

Maverick began operations on January 1, 1991. The company has paid the following amounts in cash dividends over the past 7 years.

1991	$ 65,000
1992	100,000
1993	70,000
1994	50,000
1995	125,000
1996	110,000
1997	99,000

REQUIRED:
Prepare a sheet to contain the following schedule.

YEAR	TOTAL DIVIDENDS DECLARED	DIVIDENDS TO PREFERRED	DIVIDENDS TO COMMON	DIVIDEND PER SHARE (PREFERRED)	DIVIDEND PER SHARE (COMMON)

a. Complete this schedule for each year from 1991 through 1997, assuming that the preferred stock is noncumulative and nonparticipating.
b. Complete this schedule for each year from 1991 through 1997, assuming that the preferred stock is cumulative and nonparticipating.
c. Complete this schedule for each year from 1991 through 1997, assuming that the preferred stock is cumulative and participates at the rate of 1 percent of the par value.

P12–6

(The maximum dividend)

The following selected financial information was extracted from the December 31, 1996, financial records of Cotter Company:

	DEBIT	CREDIT
Cash	25,000	
Short-term investments (2,500 shares of Oreton Corporation)	80,000	
Common stock ($10 par value, 100,000 shares authorized, 50,000 issued)		500,000
Additional paid-in capital (C/S)		100,000
Retained earnings (before closing)		245,000
Net income for 1996		43,000

The company's board of directors is currently contemplating declaring a dividend. The company's common stock is presently selling for $40 per share.

REQUIRED:

a. Given the present financial position of Cotter Company, how large a cash dividend can the board of directors declare?

b. How large a stock dividend can the board legally declare?

c. Assume that the dividends are declared and issued on the same day. Prepare the journal entry to record the maximum dividend in each case above.

d. If the company sold its short-term investments, how large a cash dividend could it declare and pay? The current selling price of Oreton Corp. is $50 per share.

P12–7

(Stock splits and stock dividends)

Stevenson Enterprises is considering the following items:

1. The company may declare a 10 percent stock dividend, issuing an additional share of common stock for every 10 shares outstanding; the common stock is currently selling for $25 per share.

2. The company may issue a 2:1 stock split.

Prior to these events, Stevenson Enterprises reports the following:

Common stock ($6 par value, 650,000 shares authorized, 70,000 issued, 60,000 outstanding, and 10,000 held as treasury stock)	$ 420,000
Additional paid-in capital (C/S)	525,000
Retained earnings	695,000
Less: Treasury stock	100,000
Total stockholders' equity	$1,540,000

REQUIRED:

a. Assume that Stevenson Enterprises declares the stock dividend but not the stock split. Prepare the necessary journal entry. Prepare the stockholders' equity section of the balance sheet to reflect the stock dividend.

b. Assume that Stevenson Enterprises declares the stock split but not the stock dividend. Prepare the stockholders' equity section of the balance sheet to reflect the stock split.

c. Assume that Stevenson Enterprises declares the stock dividend and then the stock split. Prepare the necessary journal entries. Prepare the stockholders' equity section of the balance sheet to reflect both actions.

d. Assume that Stevenson Enterprises declares the stock split and then the stock dividend. Prepare the necessary journal entries. Prepare the stockholders' equity section of the balance sheet to reflect both actions. Assume that the market price of Stevenson's stock drops to $12.50 per share following the stock split.

P12–8

(Miscellaneous stockholders' equity transactions)

The stockholders' equity section of Rudnicki Corp. contained the following balances as of December 31, 1996.

Preferred stock (10%, $10 par value, cumulative)	$1,000
Preferred stock (12%, $10 par value, noncumulative)	1,500
Common stock ($1 par value, 5,000 shares authorized, 3,500 issued and 400 held in treasury)	3,500
Additional paid-in capital:	
Preferred stock (10%)	1,050
Preferred stock (12%)	1,275
Common stock	2,345
Retained earnings	4,256
Less: Treasury stock	5,750
Total stockholders' equity	$9,176

During 1997, Rudnicki Corp. entered into the following transactions affecting stockholders' equity.

1. On May 13, the company repurchased 50 shares of its common stock in the open market at $20 per share.

2. On September 26, the company issued 200 shares of its 10 percent preferred stock at $19 per share.

3. On October 19, the company reissued 30 shares of the stock held in treasury. They sold for $22 per share: all of the shares reissued were purchased prior to May 13 for $12 per share.

4. On December 2, the company declared a cash dividend of $750, which was paid on December 27. The company has not declared a dividend since 1995. (Rudnicki Corp. uses a separate dividend account for each type of stock.)

5. On December 27, the company pays the dividend declared on December 2.

6. On December 29, the company declares a 2:1 stock split on the company's common stock.

REQUIRED:

a. Prepare the necessary entries for each transaction.

b. Assume that Rudnicki Corp. earned net income of $899 during 1997. Prepare the stockholders' equity section as of December 31, 1997.

P12–9

(Inferring transactions from the balance sheet)

The stockholders' equity section of Buzytown Industries balance sheet reports the following:

	1997	1996
Preferred stock (9%, $100 par value)	$ 200,000	$ 110,000
Common stock ($10 par value, 750,000 shares authorized, 90,000 issued and 5,000 held in treasury)	900,000	750,000
Additional paid-in capital:		
Preferred stock	150,000	35,000
Common stock	465,000	298,000
Retained earnings	575,000	495,000
Less: Treasury stock	110,000	—
Total stockholders' equity	$2,180,000	$1,688,000

REQUIRED:

a. How many shares of preferred stock were issued during 1997? What was the average issue price?

b. How many shares of common stock were issued during 1997? What was the average issue price?

c. Prepare the entry to record the repurchase of the company's own stock during 1997. What was the average repurchase price?

d. Assume that the treasury shares were purchased on the last day of 1997. Did the purchase increase or decrease the book value of the outstanding shares? By how much?

P12–10

(Inferring stockholders' equity transactions from information on the balance sheet)

Tracey Corporation reports the following in its December 31, 1996, financial report.

	1996	1995
Cumulative preferred stock (10%, $100 par value)	$ 400,000	$ 400,000
Common stock ($10 par value, 11,000 shares authorized, issued, and outstanding)	110,000	70,000
Additional paid-in capital:		
Common stock	625,000	500,000
Treasury stock	124,000	55,000
Retained earnings	975,000	250,000
Less: Treasury stock	84,000	105,000
Total stockholders' equity	$2,150,000	$1,170,000

The total balance in Treasury Stock on December 31, 1995, represents the acquisition of 1,500 shares of common stock on March 3, 1994.

REQUIRED:

a. Compute the number of shares of common stock issued during 1996.
b. Compute the average market price of the common shares issued during 1996.
c. Assume that Tracey Corporation earned net income of $2,000,000 during 1996. Compute the amount of dividends that were declared during 1996.
d. If Tracey Corporation did not declare or pay any dividends during 1995, and again assuming a net income during 1996 of $2,000,000, compute the amount declared as dividends to common stockholders during 1996.
e. Prepare the entry that would have been necessary on March 3, 1994, to record the purchase of the treasury stock.
f. Assume that all shares of treasury stock reissued during 1996 were reissued at the same time and at the same price. Prepare the entry to record the reissuance of the treasury stock.
g. At what per-share price was the treasury stock reissued?

P12–11

(Stockholders' equity over a four-year period)

Aspen Industries incorporated in the state of Colorado on March 23, 1994. The company was authorized to issue 1,000,000 shares of $6 par value common stock. Since the date of incorporation, Aspen Industries has entered into the following transactions that affected contributed and earned capital.

1. On March 23, 1994, the company issued 50,000 shares of common stock in exchange for $15 per share.
2. On December 5, 1994, the company issued a 10 percent stock dividend. The market value of the stock is $18 per share.
3. On May 6, 1995, the company issued 60,000 shares of common stock in exchange for $22 per share.
4. On September 24, 1995, the company repurchased 15,000 shares of its own stock for $25 per share.
5. On December 1, 1995, the company reissued 5,000 shares held in treasury for $27 per share.
6. On February 14, 1996, the company declared a 3:1 stock split and adjusted the par value of the stock. (Hint: Consider the effect of the stock split on treasury stock.)
7. On August 19, 1996, the company reissued 8,000 shares held in treasury for $10 per share.
8. On December 27, 1996, the company declared a cash dividend of $50,000.
9. On January 3, 1997, the company paid the dividend declared on December 27, 1996.
10. On October 31, 1997, the company reissued 2,000 shares held in treasury for $15 per share.

REQUIRED:

a. Prepare the necessary journal entries to record these transactions.
b. Prepare the stockholders' equity section of Aspen's balance sheet as of December 31, 1997. Assume that net income for 1994, 1995, 1996, and 1997 was $400,000, $100,000, $100,000 and $20,000, respectively.

P12–12

(Blocking takeovers and treasury stock purchases)

Five shareholders together own 35 percent of the outstanding stock of Edmonds Industries. The remaining 65% is divided among several thousand stockholders. There are 400,000 shares of Edmonds stock currently outstanding. A condensed balance sheet follows.

ASSETS		LIABILITIES AND STOCKHOLDERS' EQUITY	
Cash	$ 3,150,000	Liabilities	$ 1,250,000
Other current assets	4,200,000	Common stock	8,000,000
Noncurrent assets	8,220,000	Retained earnings	6,320,000
		Total liabilities and	
Total assets	$15,570,000	stockholders' equity	$15,570,000

It has become known that Vadar, Inc., is planning to take over Edmonds by purchasing a controlling interest of the outstanding stock. Vadar hopes to gain enough control to elect a new board of directors and replace Edmonds' current management. The current board of directors, on which the five major stockholders serve, is considering how to block the apparent takeover attempt.

REQUIRED:

a. Describe how the company might be able to block the takeover attempt through a program of treasury stock purchases. How many shares would the company need to purchase to concentrate ownership enough to keep Vadar from acquiring a controlling interest? Assume that the other members of the board own no stock.

b. The current market price of the outstanding stock is $45, but the board feels that any major buy-back would have to be at a premium—approximately $50 per share. How much cash would Edmonds need to purchase enough shares to block the takeover attempt?

c. Assume that Edmonds was able to borrow $4,000,000 and used the cash to buy back the necessary number of shares. Prepare the balance sheet of Edmonds after stock had been purchased.

d. Compute the debt/equity ratio for Edmonds both before and after the treasury stock purchase. Comment on the effect of the purchase on the company's financial position.

P12–13

(Bankruptcy and protecting the interests of the creditors)

The balance sheet of Natathon International is provided below.

ASSETS		LIABILITIES AND STOCKHOLDERS' EQUITY	
Current assets	$200,000	Liabilities	$400,000
Fixed assets	500,000	Common stock	150,000
		Additional paid-in capital	50,000
		Retained earnings	100,000
		Total liabilities and	
Total assets	$700,000	stockholders' equity	$700,000

Although the balance sheet appears reasonably healthy, Natathon is on the verge of ceasing operations. Appraisers have estimated that, while current assets are worth $200,000, the fixed assets of the company can be sold for only $450,000. There are 1,000 outstanding shares of common stock owned by ten stockholders, each with a 10 percent interest (i.e., 100 shares). Before ceasing operations, the board of directors, which is comprised primarily of the major stockholders, is considering several alternative courses of action.

1. Liquidate the assets, declare a $250 per-share dividend, and distribute the remaining assets to the creditors.

2. Liquidate the assets, declare a $400 per-share dividend, and distribute the remaining assets to the creditors.

3. Liquidate the assets, purchase the outstanding shares for $250 each, and distribute the remaining assets to the creditors.

4. Liquidate the assets, and purchase the outstanding shares for $650 each.

REQUIRED:

a. Prepare the journal entry to reflect the write-down of the fixed assets.

b. Prepare the journal entry to accompany each of the alternative courses of action.

c. Comment on the legality of each of the board's proposals, and explain how the assets should be distributed after liquidation.

CASES

Egghead, Inc., is a software chain with over 120 stores nationwide. Until recently, all the common shares of the company were held by its founders and employees. Several years ago the company filed for an initial public offering of 3.6 million common shares. The shares were priced at $15 each. After the offering, Egghead had 15.6 million shares outstanding. Assume that the company holds no treasury stock.

REQUIRED:

a. Assume that Egghead's common stock has a $1 par value. Provide the journal entry to record the issuance of the new shares.
b. Assume all the shares originally outstanding were sold for $10 per share. Provide the contributed capital section of Egghead's balance sheet both before and after the sale of the new stock.
c. Do you think that the company's board of directors and existing shareholders had to approve the public issuance before it occurred? Why or why not?
d. Provide several reasons that may have caused the company to raise the $54 million with an equity, instead of a debt, issuance.

F.W. Woolworth Co, a major retailer, recently increased its quarterly dividend by 24 percent, from 33 cents to 41 cents per share. The new dividend was declared on April 10, payable June 1 to the shareholders of record on May 2. The company cited strong earnings as the reason for the increase.

REQUIRED:

a. Assume that Woolworth had 10 million shares of stock outstanding. Provide the journal entries that would be recorded on April 10, May 2, and June 1.
b. Would each entry increase, decrease, or have no effect on the company's current ratio, working capital position, and debt/equity ratio? Assume that the dividend is immediately reflected in Retained Earnings.
c. Like Woolworth, many companies base their dividend payments on earnings. Are dividends actually paid out of profits? Are all profitable companies in a position to pay large dividends? Why or why not?
d. Briefly explain some of the major factors considered by the boards of directors of companies deciding whether or not to pay dividends and how much to pay.

Between 1957 and 1977 Westinghouse Electric Corp. used PCBs in the manufacture of electrical capacitors at its plant in Bloomington, Indiana. A federal consent-decree has ordered the company to be prepared to build an incinerator in the future to destroy the PCB-contaminated materials. The decree, with which Westinghouse agrees, contains a clause stating that if Westinghouse's net worth (balance sheet assets less balance sheet liabilities) drops to $1.9 billion, the company is required to place in escrow (set aside) $325 million to ensure that funds will be available if and when the incinerator is built.

A recent pronouncement from the FASB requires that Westinghouse as well as other companies change the way in which they account for certain employee retirement costs. After adopting this mandated change, Westinghouse's net worth plunged to $1.85 billion, which is below the dollar amount indicated in the consent-decree. According to the agreement, therefore, Westinghouse should transfer $325 million to an escrow account. Westinghouse has refused to make the payment, however, claiming that the reduction in net worth was due to a new accounting standard not in effect at the time the agreement was signed.

REQUIRED:

Discuss this issue from the perspective of the following:

a. An executive of Westinghouse.
b. A representative of the federal government.
c. A resident of Bloomington, Indiana.

C12–4

(Do stock dividends represent economic exchanges between a corporation and its shareholders?)

On April 26, 1990, Quantum Chemical Corporation declared a 2 percent stock dividend. After the stock dividend, the number of shares outstanding increased to approximately 27.54 million. Assume that the stock dividend was declared and paid on the same day.

REQUIRED:

a. How many shares of stock were outstanding prior to the dividend?
b. The market price of the stock was $20 per share and the par value was $2.50 per share on the day the dividend was declared and paid. Provide the journal entry to record the distribution.
c. Compute the value of Quantum Chemical if all outstanding shares, prior to the stock dividend, could have been sold for $20 each. Using this value, compute the per-share value of the company's outstanding share after the stock dividend.
d. Assume that Mr. Jones owned 0.9 million shares prior to the stock dividend. How many shares did Mr. Jones own after the stock dividend? What percent of the company did Mr. Jones own before and after the stock dividend? What was the value of Mr. Jones' total shareholdings before and after the stock dividend based on the amounts from part (c)?
e. Does a stock dividend actually represent an economic exchange between a corporation and its shareholders? Why or why not?
f. Provide several reasons why a company would issue a stock dividend.

C12–5

(Economic consequences of treasury stock purchases and cash dividends)

The Wall Street Journal (September 1, 1994) reported that "Philip Morris Cos., in an aggressive move to boost its stock price, announced a $6 billion stock buy-back plan and raised its quarterly dividend nearly 20% . . . The announcement, which came after a regularly scheduled board meeting, raised the company's stock to a 52-week high . . . Separately, rating agencies Standard & Poor's Rating Group and Moody's Investors Service Inc. confirmed their ratings on Philip Morris's debt. While both agencies said Philip Morris is continuing to generate strong cash flow, Moody's . . . placed Philip Morris at the low end of its current rating level.

REQUIRED:

Explain how this announcement can increase Philip Morris's stock price while at the same time reduce its credit rating.

C12–6

(Economic issues involving treasury stock purchases)

The following quotes are from *The Wall Street Journal.*

RJR Nabisco Inc. said it plans to buy back as much as 8 percent of its outstanding stock for $52 to $58 dollars per share, or up to $1.2 billion. Analysts said the move probably signals that the tobacco and food giant has decided not to acquire another company. It also is an apparent effort to bolster the price of RJR shares, which like other tobacco stocks, have lagged the market . . . Earnings [per share] will go up . . . and the fear of dilutive acquisition will be down.

John Hegler, *The Wall Street Journal*, March 29, 1988, p. 8.

Georgia-Pacific Corp.'s Board authorized an ambitious buy-back program that could result in the purchase of as much as 19 percent of the company's stock. The action will boost the forest products giant's debt but is meant to bolster its stock price . . . To accommodate the buy-back, Georgia-Pacific's Board approved raising the company's debt/equity target ratio of 40 percent to 45 percent from its current 30 percent to 35 percent.

John Hegler, *The Wall Street Journal*, March 30, 1988, p. 25.

Gillette Co. . . . said it will accelerate a stock buy-back program and purchase as many as 11 million of its shares on the open market during the next few months . . . Moody's Investors Service said it placed Gillette's . . . long-term debt ratings . . . under review for possible downgrade because of Gillette's stock buy-back acceleration.

David Stuff, *The Wall Street Journal*, April 20, 1988, p. 32.

REQUIRED:

Explain how a treasury stock purchase could accomplish the following:

a. Bolster a company's stock price per share and its earnings per share.
b. Reduce the threat of a dilutive acquisition.
c. Cause a company to boost its debt and result in an increase in its debt/equity ratio.
d. Cause a credit-rating service to downgrade a company's credit rating.

C12–7

(Issuing hybrid securities: economic consequences)

Forbes (June 3, 1985) points out that companies wishing to protect their credit ratings and unwilling to issue more stock are raising capital by issuing hybrid securities. The article specifically mentions certain kinds of preferred stock issuances.

REQUIRED:

a. What is a hybrid security? Explain why certain kinds of preferred stocks are considered to be hybrid securities.
b. How can a company protect its credit rating by issuing hybrid securities instead of bonds?
c. How can a company avoid violating a debt covenant by issuing hybrid securities instead of bonds?
d. How can a company avoid diluting its stock and inviting a takeover by issuing hybrid securities instead of common stocks?

C12–8

(Exchanging equity for debt)

The two quotes below were taken from *The Wall Street Journal*.

A month after he staved off financial ruin by getting his bankers to lend him $65 million, Donald Trump is about to ask his casino bondholders for a similar financial favor. Mr. Trump and his advisers have tentatively decided to propose to holders of all or part of the $1.3 billion in debt to accept equity in his casinos in exchange for letting him cancel some interest payments . . . What ails Mr. Trump's casinos is . . . his properties are not earning enough cash to pay interest on the debt." (July 26, 1990)

RJR Nabisco Holding Corp. said it raised $1.13 billion by selling 100 million shares at $11.25 each, in the largest equity offering by a U.S. corporation since 1987. The stock offering marks a further step in RJR's year-long campaign to reduce its debt and increase its equity. The tobacco and food company has said that proceeds from the offering will be used primarily to retire some of its high-yield junk bonds, which [were used to finance a leverage buyout several years earlier and] carry 17 percent interest rates. (April 12, 1991)

REQUIRED:

a. These quotes describe equity issuances by Trump Atlantic City Associates and RJR Nabisco. Provide a plausible explanation for why these two entities issued equity and comment on the situations faced by the two companies.
b. Describe the effects of these transactions on the financial statements of the two entities.
c. Discuss the trade-offs considered by RJR Nabisco's management when they decided to issue equity and use the proceeds to retire outstanding junk bonds.

C12–9

(Off-balance-sheet financing and preferred stock)

Business Week (October 2, 1989) notes that Rupert Murdoch's company, News Corp., is rapidly approaching limits on its ability to borrow, as indicated by covenants imposed by the large group of banks that have provided most of the company's financing. An executive close to News Corp. commented that "Murdoch has several ways he can raise off-balance-sheet debt or reduce News Corp.'s debt. One favorite ploy: News Corp. has often raised cash by selling "preference," or preferred shares. Fully $1.4 billion worth of such shares were outstanding on June 30 . . ."

REQUIRED:

Describe the nature of preferred shares and explain how raising cash by selling them can be interpreted as off-balance-sheet financing. Why would Murdoch pursue such an activity, and how might a creditor adjust the reported financial statements to make them more representative of News Corp.'s financial position?

C12–10

(Corporate dividend policies)

In 1991 the Big 3 automakers all slashed dividends in response to weak earnings reports: Ford by 47% (from 75 cents to 40 cents), and both General Motors and Chrysler cut their dividends in half. *USA Today* (April 21, 1991) noted that "some analysts were predicting a bigger Ford dividend cut [but] the Ford family [who have a controlling interest] played a role in keeping the dividend from being chopped further. There is a general feeling that 'widows and orphans' live off the Ford dividend, including some 'widows and orphans' named Ford."

REQUIRED:
a. What is meant by the phrase "widows and orphans?"
b. Describe several dividend strategies used by major U.S. corporations, and explain how "widows and orphans" fit into Ford's strategy.
c. The market value of Ford's outstanding stock remained unchanged at $31 7/8 after the company announced the 47 percent dividend cut. Provide a plausible explanation for how this could be.

C12–11

(Stock split and stock prices)

On February 19, 1992, Walt Disney Co. declared a 4:1 split of its common stock, an announcement that boosted the entertainment company's shares up $3.50 to close at a record price of $146.50.

REQUIRED:
a. What is a 4:1 stock split, and how did it affect the financial statements of Walt Disney Co.?
b. Why should the market value of Disney's stock rise?
c. *The Wall Street Journal* (February 19, 1992) reported that the stock split was "a psychological boost and an indication that management has confidence in their performance and that the stock price can be sustained." Explain how this explanation could account for the stock price increase.

C12–12

(International accounting standards)

The major roadblock to foreign companies listing their overseas stock on U.S. exchanges has long been the big difference between accounting standards in the United States and abroad. Recently, several of the major accounting policymaking boards, including the FASB, have shown an interest in developing a separate set of accounting standards for companies that wish to raise equity capital outside of their home countries. The New York Stock Exchange (NYSE) appears to favor this proposal because it would encourage a number of foreign companies to have their securities listed in the United States, which *The Wall Street Journal* (August 29, 1995) reports would "almost double" the NYSE's volume. However, some analysts fear that such a proposal would not be worth the price. That same article notes that "Pat McConnell, Bear, Sterns & Co.'s accounting guru, maintains that this gap would create the potential for big lies in financial statements of companies in foreign countries with weak accounting rules. Indeed, she frets that it would prevent U.S. investors from making meaningful comparisons of U.S. and foreign stocks."

REQUIRED:
Discuss this issue from the perspective of the following:
a. A foreign company wishing to raise capital in the U.S.
b. A U.S. company that has equity securities already listed in the NYSE.

c. An executive of the NYSE.

d. An investment analyst who makes recommendations to buy and sell equity securities.

C12–13

(International financing)

Although Japanese investments in large, high technology U.S. businesses have won increasing attention recently, a number of small U.S. manufacturing firms are attracting Japanese capital as well. MASI Limited, an investment banking firm, recently raised over $75 million in equity financing from Japanese investors for an Illinois-based rubber goods maker and an Iowa-based machine tools company. Such companies often have a difficult time obtaining financing from U.S. sources, but Japanese investors like them because their shares are lower priced than shares in comparable Japanese firms. In addition, the reporting requirements in Japan are not as burdensome as those in the major U.S. exchanges.

REQUIRED:

a. Provide several plausible reasons why a small U.S. firm may wish to raise equity capital only in a non-U.S. market.

b. A partner at Grant Thornton, a large U.S. public accounting firm, commented that "European investors are looking to [provide equity capital for] some mature manufacturing companies in the United States. Many of these investors are risk-averse and looking for the stability that these companies provide" *The Wall Street Journal* (July 16, 1990). Explain how this and the case above represent examples of an expanding global capital market, and comment on the implications of such a market for financial accounting and reporting standards.

C12–14

(The annual report of MCI)

Review the annual report of MCI and answer the following questions.

a. As of December 31, 1994, how many preferred and common shares was MCI authorized to issue? How was this established?

b. MCI had a major preferred stock issuance during 1993. How many shares were issued, how much cash was collected, and why were the shares issued?

c. MCI had a major common stock issuance during 1994. How many shares were issued, how much cash was collected, and explain why the shares were issued?

d. How many treasury shares did MCI purchase in 1992, 1993, and 1994? Compute the average price at which the shares were purchased in each of the three years. How many treasury shares were reissued during each of the three years, and for what purpose?

e. Does MCI maintain a dividend rate that is a constant percent of reported net income each year? Would you consider MCI a company that pays high or low dividends? Provide a plausible explanation for why they have chosen such a strategy.

f. How did MCI account for the stock dividend (split) it recorded in 1992? What effect did this event have on the company's debt/equity ratio?

INCOME AND CASH FLOWS

CHAPTER 13

THE COMPLETE INCOME STATEMENT

LEARNING OBJECTIVES

LO 1
Describe the economic consequences associated with reporting net income.

LO 2
Describe the difference between an operating transaction and a capital transaction, and indicate how capital transactions are categorized on the capital/operating continuum.

LO 3
List the five categories that constitute a complete income statement and explain how they provide measures of income that address the objectives of financial reporting.

LO 4
Describe how earnings per share is disclosed on the income statement.

LO 5
Define intraperiod tax allocation, and explain how it relates to the income statement.

Chapters 6 through 12 consider the accounts that appear on the balance sheet. It is clear from the discussion in these chapters that virtually all balance sheet accounts are linked to at least one account on the income statement. By covering the balance sheet, therefore, we have already implicitly covered much of the income statement, but we have not yet discussed that statement as a coordinated whole by considering such issues as income measurement, the difference between operating and capital transactions, and the disclosure and classification rules specified by generally accepted accounting principles. The objective of this chapter is to bring together into one coordinated discussion the concepts underlying income measurement and the categories that compose the income statement.

This chapter is divided into four sections. The first three sections consider (1) the economic consequences associated with income measurement and disclosure, (2) conceptual issues of income measurement, and (3) the disclosure rules that must be followed when preparing an income statement. The fourth section covers the statement of retained earnings.

THE ECONOMIC CONSEQUENCES ASSOCIATED WITH INCOME MEASUREMENT AND DISCLOSURE

LO 1 Income is the most common measure of a company's performance. It has been related to stock prices, suggesting that equity investors use income in their decisions to buy and sell equity securities. *The Journal of Accountancy* has stated that "[accounting] research . . . has provided some well-established conclusions. Perhaps the most conclusive finding is the importance of accounting income to investors."[1] *The Wall Street Journal* (Nov. 1, 1995), for example, reported that "some Wall Street analysts trimmed fourth-quarter earnings estimates for U.S. car makers, sending stocks of the Big 3 (GM, Ford, and Chrysler) lower."

Income has also been related to bond prices, which indicates that debt investors use income in their decisions to buy and sell corporate bonds. Credit-rating agencies, such as Standard & Poor's, Moody's, and Dun & Bradstreet, use income numbers to establish credit ratings. In response to "problematic profitability," Standard & Poor's Co. recently lowered the credit rating on McDonnell Douglas bonds from BBB+ to BBB which, in turn, lowered the market value of the outstanding debt. In addition, three of Dun & Bradstreet's fourteen key business ratios (return on sales, return on assets, and return on net worth) explicitly use a measure of income in the formula, and most of the numbers used in the remaining eleven ratios are indirectly affected by the dollar amount of reported income.

Due to the importance attached to income, periodic public earnings announcements, which appear in newspapers such as *The Wall Street Journal* and in corporate annual reports, are also considered important news items, having important effects on the economy. For example, an article in *USA Today* (October 10, 1990) entitled "Do Profits Matter?" noted:

Profit is the compass of the free enterprise system. When it dries up, the repercussions echo at every level of society. . . . Profits keep a free-market economy humming. They help pay for the development of new plants, products, and jobs. A sizable chunk of

1. James W. Deitrick and Walter T. Harrison, Jr., "EMH, CMR, and the Accounting Profession," *Journal of Accountancy* (February 1984) pp. 88–94.

profits helps finance government in the form of taxes. Another chunk goes as dividends to shareholders—often the pension funds that pay for your retirement. Says an economist from the University of Chicago: "Economies . . . won't grow without corporate profit."

Various measures of income are also found in contracts written among stockholders, creditors, and managers. Such contracts are normally designed either to protect the interests of creditors or to control managers and encourage them to act in the interests of the stockholders. Loan agreements relating to the outstanding debts of Marriott Corporation, for example, limit the company's annual dividends to a portion of net income. Such covenants serve to protect the investments of corporate creditors by limiting the amount of cash that can be paid to stockholders in the form of dividends. The board of directors of May Department Stores Company encourages company employees to act in the stockholders' interests by providing incentive compensation in the form of a profit sharing plan. As reported in the 1994 financial report, the payment of this compensation is based on changes in the company's annual earnings per share.

Indeed, the measurement, definition, and disclosure of income is important to investors, creditors, managers, auditors, and the general public in a number of different ways. Students of accounting, therefore, must understand how it is measured and presented.

THE MEASUREMENT OF INCOME: DIFFERENT MEASURES FOR DIFFERENT OBJECTIVES

As stated in the *Statement of Financial Accounting Concepts No. 1*,[2] the objectives of financial reporting are to provide information that is: (1) useful to those making investment and credit decisions who have a reasonable understanding of business and economic activities; (2) helpful to present and potential investors, creditors, and others in assessing the amounts, timing, and uncertainty of future cash flows; and (3) about economic resources, the claims to those resources, and changes in them. There are three important features about this objective that are directly related to the income statement and the measure of income. It focuses on providing useful information to those who provide debt and equity capital to the firm; the information should help to predict future cash flows; and the information should reflect changes (increases or decreases) in the company's resources. No single measure of income can achieve this set of broad objectives, and income statements prepared under GAAP are designed to provide a variety of different measures of income. It is important that financial statement users understand how they differ and the situations under which each should be used.

To achieve this understanding one must be familiar with several important definitions that appear in the *Statement of Financial Accounting Concepts No. 6*.[3] Figure 13–1 contains the definitions of ten key concepts, referred to as the elements of financial statements.

While we have covered these definitions at various times in this text, two points are particularly important. First, the term **comprehensive income** represents a very broad definition of income—any change in the company's equity due to nonowner

2. "Objectives of Financial Reporting by Business Enterprises," *Statement of Financial Accounting Concepts No. 1* (Stanford, Conn.: FASB, November 1978), pars. 5–8.
3. "Elements of Financial Statements," *Statement of Financial Accounting Concepts No. 6* (Stanford, Conn.: FASB, December 1985), pp. ix and x.

FIGURE 13–1

Elements of the Financial Statements

Assets. Probable future economic benefits obtained or controlled by a particular entity as a result of past transactions or events.

Liabilities. Probable future sacrifices of economic benefits arising from present obligations of a particular entity to transfer assets or provide services to other entities in the future as a result of past transactions or events.

Equity. Residual interest in the assets of an entity that remains after deducting its liabilities. In a business enterprise, the equity is the ownership interest.

Investments by Owners. Increases in net assets of a particular enterprise resulting from transfers to it from other entities of something of value to obtain or increase ownership interests (or equity) in it. Assets are most commonly received as investments by owners, but that which is received may also include services or satisfaction or conversion of liabilities of the enterprise.

Distributions to Owners. Decreases in net assets of a particular enterprise resulting from transferring assets, rendering services, or incurring liabilities by the enterprise to owners. Distributions to owners decrease ownership interests (or equity) in an enterprise.

Comprehensive Income. Change in equity (net assets) of an entity during a period from transactions and other events and circumstances from nonowner sources. It includes all changes in equity during a period except those resulting from investments by owners and distributions to owners.

Revenues. Inflows or other enhancements of assets of an entity or settlement of its liabilities (or a combination of both) during a period from delivering or producing goods, rendering services, or other activities that constitute the entity's ongoing major or central operations.

Expenses. Outflows or other using up of assets or incurrences of liabilities (or a combination of both) during a period from delivering or producing goods, rendering services, or carrying out other activities that constitute the entity's ongoing major or central operations.

Gains. Increases in equity (net assets) from peripheral or incidental transactions of an entity and from all other transactions and other events and circumstances affecting the entity during a period except those that result from revenues or investments by owners.

Losses. Decreases in equity (net assets) from peripheral or incidental transactions of an entity and from all other transactions and other events and circumstances affecting the entity during a period except those that result from expenses or distributions to owners.

transactions. While this notion reflects changes in a company's resources, which is one of the objectives stated above, it is not clear that all such changes reflect future cash flows, which is another important objective stated above. Comprehensive income can be viewed as the broadest possible way to define income, but certainly there are other ways to measure income that may better reflect future cash flows. In addition, the concept of comprehensive income is not yet being applied in practice.

A second important point is that these definitions distinguish revenues and expenses, which are ongoing and central to the company's operations, from gains and losses, which are peripheral or incidental to operations. Revenues and expenses occur frequently and are part of a company's core activities and, therefore, are related to the company's future cash flows. Gains and losses, on the other hand, tend to be infrequent and/or tangential to the company's core activities. Such items would not be expected to reflect future cash flows, yet they would be part of a company's comprehensive income and reflect changes in a company's resources.

To illustrate, consider two transactions entered into by a company: (1) sale of inventory with a cost of $50 million for $75 million, and (2) winning a settlement of $25 million in a one-time lawsuit. Both transactions increased the company's net assets by $25 million, making the company wealthier. Should they be included in income and reflected on the income statement? Transaction (1) involved the sale of inventory, a transaction that occurs frequently and is part of the company's core activities. It is likely to occur again, so it both reflects future cash flows and increases the company's resources. It seems that including this transaction on the income statement helps it to meet the objectives of financial reporting under almost any definition of income. Transaction (2) is a different story. The lawsuit was one-time, so it is not expected to occur again, and winning lawsuits is not part of the company's core activities. Consequently, this transaction would not be a good indicator of future cash flows, but it did increase the company's resources. It could be included, therefore, under a broad definition of income—comprehensive income.

This illustration demonstrates that there are different ways to measure income, and different measures of income address different objectives of financial reporting. It also shows that the nature of individual transaction must be considered to determine if and how they should be reflected in income. The following section develops a framework that describes different kinds of transactions and relates them to the different measures of income used in present-day financial statements.

CAPITAL AND OPERATING TRANSACTIONS: A FRAMEWORK

LO 2 **Capital transactions** basically involve setting up a company so that it can conduct operations, while **operating transactions** entail the actual conduct of the operations. In Chapter 2 of this text we referred to a company as a fruit tree: capital transactions affect the size and structure of the tree (represented by the balance sheet), and operating transactions reflect the harvest and sale of the fruit (represented by the income statement). While these definitions are useful, some transactions are difficult to classify because they reflect some characterisitics of each.

Figure 13–2 represents a continuum for classifying capital and operating transactions. Note that five categories of transactions are described, and each is placed at a point along the continuum. Category 1 at the extreme left contains purely capital transactions, and Category 5 contains operating transactions. Categories 2, 3, and 4 include events considered to be capital transactions under generally accepted accounting principles, but the categories toward the middle (e.g., Category 4) contain transactions that increasingly resemble operating activities. Later we point out that operating transactions can also be subdivided into categories, based primarily on how germane they are to the normal, everyday operating activities of a company. Review the figure closely as we will be discussing it in detail in the following paragraphs.

(1) EXCHANGES WITH STOCKHOLDERS

Exchanges with owners include (1) issuances of preferred or common stock, (2) purchases, retirements, and reissuances of treasury stock, and (3) cash, property, and stock dividends. This group of financing transactions is located on the far left side of the continuum, because these are purely capital transactions involved exclusively with the formation and dissolution of the company's equity capital and the returns (i.e., dividends) to the company's owners. The most distinctive and important feature about the transactions in this category is that they never affect the income statement. Even when treasury stock is reissued for an amount different from its cost, the dollar amount of the difference is not recognized as a gain or a loss on the income statement.

FIGURE 13–2

Classifying capital and operating transactions

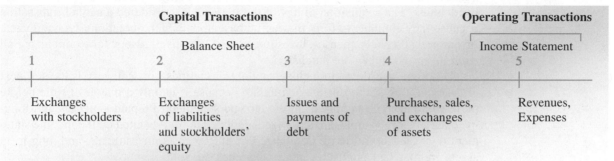

1. Exchanges with stockholders: Stock issuances, stock redemptions, and dividend payments.
2. Exchanges of liabilities and stockholders' equity: Debt refinancing and conversion of convertible bonds and stocks.
3. Issues and payments of debt: Cash borrowings evidenced by notes payable, issuing bonds, and payments on debts, including the redemption of debt.
4. Purchases, sales, and exchanges of assets: Purchases, sales, and exchanges of all assets.
5. Revenues: Inflows of assets (or outflows of liabilities) due to operations.
   Expenses: Outflows of assets (or inflows of liabilities) due to the generation of revenues.

(2) EXCHANGES OF LIABILITIES AND STOCKHOLDERS' EQUITY

Exchanges of liabilities and stockholders' equity refer to transactions in which liabilities are exchanged for other liabilities (debt refinancing arrangements) or converted into stockholders' equity (conversion of convertible bonds or preferred stocks to common stock). Such financing exchanges are considered capital transactions because they deal only with a company's capital structure. Accordingly, they generally do not affect the income statement. However, these transactions are located to the right of exchanges with stockholders because in certain limited circumstances they can give rise to gains or losses that appear on the income statement.[4]

(3) ISSUES AND PAYMENTS OF DEBT

Issues and payments of debt include cash borrowings associated with the issuance of notes or bonds payable as well as the cash payments required to service or retire such liabilities. These transactions involve exchanges with a company's creditors and thus are reflected in the liability section of the balance sheet. They are considered capital transactions because they involve how a company finances its operations through debt. However, these transactions are not completely separate from a company's operations. Interest payments on debt are directly reflected on the income statement through interest expense; book gains and losses are recognized when debt is retired; and premiums and discounts on notes and bonds are amortized to the income statement over the life of the debt. Consequently, this category of transactions is located to the right of exchanges of liabilities and stockholders' equity.

---

4. The methods used to account for refinancing arrangements and the conversion of convertible bonds and stocks are complex and controversial, and we do not discuss them in this textbook. For our purposes it is sufficient to note that, according to current generally accepted accounting principles, such transactions rarely give rise to income statement gains and losses.

(4) PURCHASES, SALES, AND EXCHANGES OF ASSETS

Category 4 includes the purchase, sale, or exchange of all assets. Such assets include marketable securities, inventories, prepaid expenses, long-term investments, and long-lived assets. The acquisition of any of these assets is considered a capital transaction because they combine to form the capital base upon which operations are conducted. Inventories, prepaid expenses, investments, and long-lived assets, for example, are all *capitalized* when they are purchased.

Although considered to include capital transactions, this category is located next to the operating section of the continuum because it is only a matter of time before these capitalized costs appear on the income statement. Prepaid expenses and long-lived assets, for example, are amortized, depleted, or depreciated on the income statement over their useful lives. Capitalized inventory costs, investments, and long-lived assets are matched against revenues when they are sold.[5]

(5) REVENUES AND EXPENSES

The right side of the continuum includes exchanges that are considered operating transactions. Revenues represent inflows of assets (or outflows of liabilities) due to a company's operating activities, and in line with the matching principle, expenses represent outflows of assets (or inflows of liabilities) associated with the generation of the revenues.

CLASSIFYING OPERATING TRANSACTIONS

Present-day income statements include transactions ranging from those that are fundamental and necessary to a company's operations to those that are only marginally related to operations. Figure 13–3 shows three groups of operating transactions, based primarily on how germane the transactions are to the normal operations of a company and how frequently they occur.

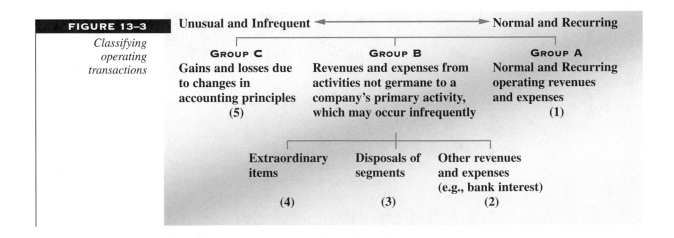

FIGURE 13–3

Classifying operating transactions

Unusual and Infrequent ← → Normal and Recurring

GROUP C
Gains and losses due to changes in accounting principles
(5)

GROUP B
Revenues and expenses from activities not germane to a company's primary activity, which may occur infrequently

GROUP A
Normal and Recurring operating revenues and expenses
(1)

Extraordinary items
(4)

Disposals of segments
(3)

Other revenues and expenses (e.g., bank interest)
(2)

---

5. Many companies also sell outstanding accounts receivable to financial institutions for immediate cash, and an income statement gain or loss is recognized in the amount of the difference between the book value of the receivable and the cash proceeds. These transfers accelerate cash collections from sales on account as well as pass on the risks and costs associated with uncollectible accounts to the financial institution. Such exchanges are called *factoring* arrangements. Sales made on credit using major credit cards, such as VISA, American Express, and MasterCard represent factoring arrangements.

Group A contains revenues and expenses that result from transactions that are normal to company operations and occur frequently. Examples include the sale of the company's inventories or services and the payment and recognition of expenses due to such items as wages, utilities, rent, insurance, depreciation, and other administrative and selling activities.

Group B contains items that are much less germane to the normal activities of a company and/or may occur infrequently. Examples include interest earned on bank savings accounts held by manufacturing, retail, and service companies; rent earned from temporarily leasing company property planned to be used later for other purposes; gains and losses recognized on sales of long-lived assets and debt retirements; and gains and losses related to such items as litigation, employee strikes, and infrequent natural disasters.

Group C contains gains and losses recognized from such activities as changes in accounting principles (e.g., from LIFO to FIFO, or from double declining-balance to straight-line depreciation), which reflect very little about the operations occurring during the periods in which such changes were made. They are simply bookkeeping entries that do not reflect an economic event.

In the past there was considerable controversy over the proper classification and disclosure of the transactions contained in Groups B and C. Some accountants argued that transactions from Group C should not enter into the computation of net income. Others took an even more extreme view and suggested that transactions in both Groups B and C were not germane to operations and, accordingly, should not appear on the income statement, which should be limited to operating revenues and expenses in the strictest sense.

In 1966 the accounting profession adopted the position that nonoperating items (Groups B and C) should be included on the income statement, but they must be separately and clearly disclosed in specific categories. Specifically, it was recommended that the income statement consist of five categories: (1) operating revenues and expenses, (2) other revenues and expenses, (3) disposals of business segments, (4) extraordinary items, and (5) changes in accounting principles. In terms of Figure 13–3, Category 1 corresponds to Group A, Categories 2, 3, and 4 come from Group B, and Category 5 corresponds to Group C.

The different categories on the income statement allow users to assess the significance of the items in each category and choose to include or exclude them in the computation of net income as the situation dictates. The next section defines and illustrates the five categories of a complete income statement.

A COMPLETE INCOME STATEMENT: DISCLOSURE AND PRESENTATION

LO 3 Figure 13–4 provides an income statement that contains each of the five categories introduced in the previous section. Review the statement carefully. The following discussion considers first the income statement in general and then covers each category individually.

The computation of net income on the income statement involves five major components, each representing one of the five categories. In general, as one moves from the top to the bottom of the income statement, the events become increasingly less important to the operations of the business. Net operating income (operating revenues less operating expenses) reflects financial performance resulting from transactions

FIGURE 13–4

A complete income statement[6]

XYZ COMPANY
INCOME STATEMENT
FOR THE PERIOD ENDING DECEMBER 31, 1997

Gross sales		$325	⎫
Less: Sales discounts and returns		25	⎬ **1. Operating revenues**
Net sales		$300	⎭
Less: Cost of goods sold:			
Beginning inventory	$ 75		
+ Gross purchases	150		
− Purchase discounts and returns	(5)		
+ Freight-in	20		
− Ending inventory	(80)	160	
Gross profit		$140	
Operating expenses:			⎫
Wages and salaries	$ 30		⎪ **1. Operating expenses**
Advertising	10		⎪
Insurance	8		⎬
State and local taxes	7		⎪
Depreciation	25		⎪
Utilities	20		⎪
Miscellaneous	15	115	⎭
Net operating income		$ 25	
Other revenues		10	⎫
Less: Other expenses		(13)	⎬ **2. Other revenues and expenses**
Net income from continuing operations before tax		$ 22	
Less: Federal income tax		7	
Net income from continuing operations		$ 15	
Income (loss) on segment up to disposal (net of tax)		(3)	⎫ **3. Disposal of business segment**
Gain (loss) on disposal of segment (net of tax)		5	⎭
Net income before extraordinary items		$ 17	
Extraordinary gain (loss) (net of tax)		(5)	⎬ **4. Extraordinary item**
Net income before changes in accounting principle		$ 12	
Income effect due to change in accounting principle			
(net of tax)		7	⎬ **5. Changes in accounting principles**
Net income		$ 19	
Earnings per share (100 shares outstanding):			
Net income from continuing operations			
(after tax)		$ .15	
Disposal of business segment		.02	
Extraordinary items		(.05)	
Change in accounting principle		.07	
Total earnings per share		$ .19	

that are both fundamental to a company's normal activities and occur frequently. Other revenues and expenses and disposals of business segments reflect the financial effects of events that are either not part of a company's normal operations or do not

6. Most real-world income statements are variations of two basic formats: (1) Single-step or (2) multi-step. This income statement uses the multi-step format. Under the single-step format all revenues and expenses above "Net income from continuing operations" are grouped into two separate categories. Below "net income from continuing operations" the two formats are identical.

occur frequently. Extraordinary gains and losses result from events that are both highly unusual and infrequent, and gains and losses due to changes in accounting principles result simply from book entries.

The income statement is divided into these categories to enable users to distinguish transactions that are due to operations from those due to unusual, infrequent, and sometimes uncontrollable events (e.g., extraordinary items), or simply to changes in accounting principles (e.g., LIFO to FIFO). Presumably, measures of profit disclosed near the top of the income statement (e.g., net operating income) better reflect management's performance and are more indicative of the future than are those disclosed near the bottom of the statement (e.g., net income). The boards of directors of many companies, for example, express their management compensation agreements in terms of net operating income instead of net income. The boards apparently believe that if management acts to increase net operating income, it will increase the long-run earnings of the company and thus further the interests of the stockholders. Consider the following excerpt from the 1994 financial report of The Pillsbury Company:

Certain employees of the Company participate in compensation programs which include a base salary plus incentive payments based on the level of operating earnings.

(1) OPERATING REVENUES AND EXPENSES: USUAL AND FREQUENT

Operating revenues and expenses refer to asset and liability inflows and outflows related to the acquisition and delivery of the goods or services provided by a company. They are considered usual and frequent. The term **usual** refers to the normal operations of the business. If a company is in business to sell furniture, for example, *usual* revenues come from furniture sales. Automobile dealerships, on the other hand, are in business to sell and service automobiles; for them, revenues generated from selling office furniture would not be considered usual.

The term **frequent** refers to how often the revenue is generated or the expense incurred. Revenues and expenses are considered frequent if they are expected to recur in the foreseeable future. They are not "one-shot," unpredictable events. For many companies the sale of a fixed asset or a long-term investment, for example, which can generate either a gain or a loss, is a transaction that tends to occur infrequently.

(2) OTHER REVENUES AND EXPENSES: UNUSUAL OR INFREQUENT

The section of the income statement headed "Other revenues and expenses" contains revenues and expenses related to a company's secondary or auxiliary activities. The most common examples are interest income and interest expense, which relate to the company's investments and debt financing, respectively. While interest is certainly important and recurring, with the exception of financial institutions, it is not directly a part of the acquisition and selling of a company's goods and services. IBM Corporation and Coca-Cola Enterprises, like many other large U.S. companies, include both interest income and interest expense in this category. Another item commonly disclosed in this section is income (or loss) from long-term investments accounted for under the equity method. Both Scott Paper Company and Kmart, for example, disclosed equity earnings from associated companies in this manner on their 1994 income statements.

Other examples include dividend income from investments, gains and losses from sales of investments and long-lived assets, receivable and inventory write-downs, gains and losses on foreign currency transactions, losses due to employee strikes, income from the rental of excess warehouse space, and gains and losses due to litigation.[7] Many companies, like Kmart, Quaker Oats, Deere and Company, and the Big 3 automakers, have recently restructured their operations and reported the associated costs in this section of the income statement. In 1989 Exxon recorded a $2.5 billion charge for the Valdez incident in this way, and Johnson & Johnson reported a $140 million loss due to the write-down of inventory in the same manner. From 1992–1994 Goodyear Tire and Rubber Company recorded gains and losses from asset sales and write-downs, workforce reductions, and lawsuits in this section of the income statement.

The key feature about the items in this section of the income statement is that they are "unusual or infrequent, but not both." Interest and dividend income, for example, are considered unusual because they are not germane to the normal operations of the business. They are secondary to the major activities of most companies. At the same time, however, interest and dividend revenue may be recognized every year and are therefore considered to occur frequently. Receivables and inventory write-downs and losses from employee layoffs, on the other hand, while part of the normal business risks faced by virtually all companies, occur infrequently. They are, therefore, considered to be infrequent but not unusual.

The nature of a particular business and the environment in which it operates must be considered when deciding what is unusual and/or infrequent. Dividend and interest income, for example, are secondary to the operations of manufacturing, retailing, and service companies, yet they represent the primary revenues for financial institutions. Interest income for BankAmerica Corporation, for example, normally represents 80–85 percent of total revenues generated by the company. Consequently, for BankAmerica interest income is an operating item, both usual and frequent.

(3) DISPOSAL OF A BUSINESS SEGMENT

A **business segment** is defined as a separate line of business, product line, or class of customer involving an operation that is independent from a company's other operations. Highly diversified companies consist of many independent segments. DuPont, for example, consists of nine different segments: agriculture, biomedical products, coal, fibers, industrial and consumer products, petroleum exploration, petroleum refining, marketing and transportation, and polymer products. Each of DuPont's segments generates well over $1 billion in revenue each year. The sale or discontinuance of any one of these segments would be referred to as a disposal of a business segment, and the related financial effects would be disclosed separately on the income statement.

In the late 1980s and early 1990s a number of major U.S. companies sold or discontinued independent segments, often to raise cash that was needed to meet debt obligations. In 1994, Ford Motor Company sold First Nationwide Bank, a wholly-owned subsidiary, recognizing a $475 million loss on the transaction; that same year Texaco, Inc. sold its worldwide chemical operations to Huntsman Corporation for $850 million; Eli Lilly sold its cosmetic segment, Elizabeth Arden, to Faberge for $557 million; and Westinghouse recently sold off its huge financial subsidiary. In each

7. Book gains and losses due to foreign currency translations were discussed in Appendix 6B.

case the income or loss attributed to the segment's operations up to the time of the disposal, and the gain or loss from the disposal itself was reported on the income statement under the caption "disposal of business segments."

The disposal of a business segment is a significant and complex transaction that is subject to a number of detailed rules under generally accepted accounting principles. We do not cover these detailed rules here. For our purposes, it is sufficient to view the disposal of a segment as similar to the sale or retirement of a long-lived asset: more specifically, the sale or retirement of a large piece of equipment that generates revenues and incurs expenses that are independent of the company's other operations.

Note in the complete income statement in Figure 13–4 that two separate disclosures are associated with a disposed business segment.[8] The first reflects the income or loss associated with the segment's operations for the time period extending from the previous balance sheet date to the point when the segment is actually disposed of. Since the segment is an independent entity, the expenses associated with it can be matched against its revenues to provide a net income or loss for that time period. The second disclosure reflects the gain or loss recognized when the segment is actually disposed of. At that time, the assets and liabilities of the segment are written off the books, the proceeds (if the segment is sold) are recorded, and a gain or loss on the disposal is recognized in the dollar amount of the difference between the book value of the segment and the proceeds. This duel disclosure allows users to ascertain both the profitability of the segment and the book gain or loss on the disposal.

To illustrate, in 1994 H&R Block completed the sale of its wholly owned subsidiary, Interim Services Inc., collecting $218 million and recognizing a $27.265 million gain (net of taxes) on the sale. Figure 13–5 shows how this transaction was reflected on the 1994 income statement.

FIGURE 13–5

Accounting for disposal of a business segment

H&R BLOCK
EXCERPT FROM INCOME STATEMENT
FOR THE YEAR ENDED DECEMBER 31, 1994
(IN THOUSANDS)

	1994	1993	1992
Earnings from continuing operations before taxes	**$283,184**	$275,894	$246,787
Taxes on earnings	**119,189**	104,877	93,043
Net earnings from continuing operations	**$163,995**	$171,017	$153,744
Net earnings from discontinued operations			
(less applicable taxes of $8,706, $9,688 and $8,964)	**9,268**	9,688	8,509
Net gain on sale of discontinued operations			
(less applicable taxes of $16,711)	**27,265**	—	—
Net earnings	**$200,528**	$180,705	$162,253
Earnings per share from continuing operations	**$1.54**	$1.59	$1.41
Earnings per share	**$1.88**	$1.68	$1.49

8. The following discussion somewhat oversimplifies the two separate disclosures associated with a disposed business segment. More detailed coverage can be found in intermediate or advanced financial accounting texts.

(4) EXTRAORDINARY ITEMS: UNUSUAL AND INFREQUENT

Extraordinary items are defined as material events of a character significantly different from the typical, customary business activities of an entity, which are not expected to recur frequently in the ordinary operating activities of a business. In other words, extraordinary items are both unusual and infrequent.

The most common extraordinary items reported by major U.S. companies are gains and losses resulting from early retirements of long-term debts.[9] *Accounting Trends and Techniques* (New York: AICPA, 1994) reports that, of the 600 major U.S. companies surveyed, 95 (16 percent) disclosed at least one extraordinary item on the income statement, and 79 (83 percent) of these resulted from gains or losses recognized on early debt retirements. Sprint, Sears, and Scott Paper Company, for example, all recognized gains or losses from early debt retirements in 1994. Each reported the gain or loss as an extraordinary item on their 1994 income statement.

Other examples of extraordinary items include income tax benefits from operating loss carryforwards;[10] gains and losses from terminating pension plans; gains and losses from litigation settlements; losses resulting from casualties like floods, earthquakes, tornadoes, hurricanes, droughts and volcanoes; and gains and losses resulting from expropriations (forced government takeovers or purchases of company property) and prohibitions under new law. Note, however, that losses due to employee layoffs, inventory write-downs due to obsolescence, receivables write-downs, and foreign currency translation gains and losses should never be classified as extraordinary according to generally accepted accounting principles. Such items are considered to arise from normal operating business risks.

As in the case of "Other revenues and expenses," the nature of the company in question and the environment in which it operates are critical in determining what is, and is not, considered extraordinary. A company that operates in a low-land area where floods are common, for example, would not report a flood loss as extraordinary because it would not be infrequent. Similarly, gains and losses from lawsuits may or may not be considered extraordinary. Most large U.S. companies are constantly involved in various forms of litigation, so that gains and losses from lawsuits are considered unusual, but not infrequent. Many smaller companies, on the other hand, are infrequently involved in litigation, so resulting gains or losses would be considered extraordinary. However, the size of the settlement may also determine whether it is disclosed as extraordinary. Pennzoil, for example, reported as extraordinary a $1.66 billion gain which resulted from winning a legal claim against Texaco. As you can see, determining whether an item is extraordinary is often a judgment call and management has much discretion in this area.

(5) CHANGES IN ACCOUNTING PRINCIPLES

Chapter 4 defines the concept of consistency and mentions that once a company chooses an acceptable principle or method of accounting (e.g., straight-line deprecia-

9. The early retirement of long-term debt is a fairly common transaction for many major U.S. companies. Consequently, it does not always meet the infrequent criterion for an extraordinary item. A number of years ago, many corporations appeared to be manipulating income from continuing operations by timing their long-term debt retirements. Accounting policymakers combatted this manipulation by requiring that the associated gains and losses be disclosed as extraordinary.

10. When a company incurs a loss for tax purposes in a given year, it may match that loss against revenues earned in subsequent periods. This procedure serves to reduce the tax liability in those periods. The dollar amount of the tax benefit in each future period is called an *operating loss carryforward* and is disclosed on the income statement of that period as an extraordinary item. Operating loss carryforwards are relatively common and, except for early debt retirements, are the most frequently reported extraordinary item.

tion, FIFO inventory valuation, etc.), it must continue to use that method consistently from one year to the next. Consistency helps to maintain the credibility of accounting reports, enabling investors, creditors, and other interested parties to make more meaningful comparisons and to identify more easily the trends in a company's performance across time.

If a company can convince its auditors, however, that the environment in which it operates has changed and another accounting method is now more appropriate than the one currently in place, it can change the accounting method and still be in conformance with generally accepted accounting principles. Such changes can have significant effects on reported income and must be disclosed in three prominent places in the financial report: (1) the auditor's report to the shareholders must mention the change, (2) the footnotes to the financial statement must clearly describe the change, and (3) the cumulative effects of the change on net income must be disclosed (net of tax) separately on the income statement, immediately below extraordinary items. Figure 13–6 shows how Owens-Corning Fiberglas disclosed an accounting change in its 1994 annual report.

FIGURE 13–6	OWENS-CORNING FIBERGLAS CORPORATION
Accounting change disclosures	EXCERPTS FROM THE ANNUAL REPORT FOR THE YEAR ENDED DECEMBER 31, 1994

NOTES TO THE FINANCIAL STATEMENTS

Note 6. Effective January 1, 1994, the Company adopted the capital method of accounting for the cost of rebuilding glass melting furnaces. Under this method, costs are capitalized when incurred and depreciated over the estimated useful lives of the rebuilt furnaces . . . . The change to the capital methods provides a more appropriate measure of the Company's capital investment and is consistent with industry practice.

AUDITOR'S REPORT TO THE SHAREHOLDERS

As discussed in Note 6 . . . the Company changed its methods of accounting for furnace rebuilds . . .

1994 INCOME STATEMENT (IN MILLIONS OF DOLLARS)

Income before cumulative effect of accounting change	$ 74
Cumulative effect of accounting change (net of taxes of $54)	123
Net Income	$197

The cumulative effects on net income due to changes in accounting methods are common and can be very significant. For example, AT&T and Burlington Northern decreased net income by $175 million and $336 million (net of tax), respectively, when they changed to the units-of-production method of depreciation. General Electric increased net income by $858 million by changing its methods of accounting for deferred income taxes and inventories. In each case the change was clearly described in the footnotes, the auditors concurred with and mentioned the change in the opinion letter, and the cumulative effect of the change on net income was separately disclosed on the income statement.

Nonetheless, financial statement users must still be careful not to overlook or be confused by such changes. As reported in *Forbes*: "When a company changes its accounting practices from one year to the next, all but the most diligent readers of annual reports can get lost."[11] General Motors Corporation, for example, changed accounting methods five different times between 1986 and 1988. In each case the changes served to increase net income. A GM spokesman commented: "each change brings us more in line with the industry," [and that] "we're not trying to hide anything at all." An industry analyst, on the other hand, noted: "[GM's] management is under pressure to show a good financial performance, and these changes serve to make it harder to compare the company's financial results over time."[12]

So far this discussion has focused on discretionary accounting changes. That is, companies often voluntarily choose to change from one method to another. It happens frequently, however, that companies are forced by FASB mandate to change accounting methods. The FASB recently issued new standards covering the methods of accounting for post-retirement healthcare and insurance costs, income taxes, and pensions. In each case a number of companies were required to change their accounting methods to conform with these new standards, and these changes were accompanied by prominent disclosure in the footnotes, on the income statement, and in the audit opinion. Sprint, for example, disclosed a $384 million loss due to adopting the FASB standard on post-retirement healthcare costs in 1993, and in 1992 booked a $23 million gain due to adopting the new standard on income tax accounting. The disclosure requirements and methods of accounting for these mandatory changes are generally the same as those required for voluntary changes. However, users should be aware that management's incentives drive voluntary changes, but not those of a mandatory nature. Consequently, voluntary changes should be interpreted much more cautiously because they may be the result of strategies designed to manage the reported numbers.

Regardless of their nature, changes in accounting principles can make it more difficult to compare a company's financial performance across time because in the annual report the financial statements from periods prior to the change are prepared using the previous accounting methods. However, generally accepted accounting principles require that net income on a **pro forma (as if) basis** be disclosed on the face of the income statement for all periods presented, as if the newly adopted principle had been applied to those periods. This disclosure enables users to make more meaningful comparisons, at least across the periods presented on the face of the income statement.

One final point: it is important to realize that an accounting method differs from an accounting estimate, which is used to implement an accounting method. Straight-line depreciation, for example, is an accounting method, which is implemented by estimating the useful life and salvage value of a long-lived asset. The allowance method of accounting for bad debts is implemented by estimating the amount of bad debts at the end of each year. This section has discussed how to account for a change in an accounting method. How to account for revisions in accounting estimates is described in Chapter 9.

EARNINGS-PER-SHARE DISCLOSURE

LO 4 Generally accepted accounting principles also require that earnings per share be disclosed on the face of the income statement and that the specific dollar amounts associated with (1) net income from continuing operations (after tax), (2) disposals of business segments, (3) extraordinary items, and (4) changes

11. Laura Rohmann, "Add a Dash of Cumulative Catch-up," *Forbes*, June 6, 1983, p. 98.
12. Jacob M. Schlesinger, "GM Net Rose 18% in Quarter on Special Item," *The Wall Street Journal*, April 22, 1988, p. 18.

in accounting principles be disclosed separately. Note the form of this disclosure in Figure 13–4. The earnings-per-share amount for each category is calculated by dividing the dollar amount of the gain or loss associated with that category by the number of common shares outstanding. The income statement in Figure 13–7 was taken from

FIGURE 13–7

Disclosing earnings per share

SCOTT PAPER COMPANY
INCOME STATEMENT (PARTIAL)
FOR THE YEARS ENDED DECEMBER 31, 1994, 1993, AND 1992

(IN MILLIONS, EXCEPT ON A PER SHARE BASIS)	1994	1993	1992
Sales	**$3,581.1**	**$3,584.9**	**$3,856.0**
Costs and expenses:			
Product costs	$2,510.8	$2,576.4	$2,745.7
Marketing and distribution	479.9	536.7	572.0
Research, administration and general	189.0	208.3	218.3
Restructuring and divestments	—	401.1	—
Other	(100.2)	8.5	(2.9)
	$3,079.5	$3,731.0	$3,533.1
Income (Loss) from continuing operations	$ 501.6	$ (146.1)	$ 322.9
Interest expense	131.2	123.8	141.4
Other income and (expense)	9.6	4.1	11.1
Income (Loss) from continuing operations before taxes	$ 380.0	$ (265.8)	$ 192.6
Income taxes	139.8	(49.7)	50.5
Income (Loss) from continuing operations before share of earnings (loss) of international equity affiliates, extraordinary loss and cumulative effects of accounting change	$ 240.2	$ (216.1)	$ 142.1
Share of earnings (loss) of international equity affiliates	23.9	(21.7)	5.4
Income (Loss) from continuing operations before extraordinary loss and cumulative effect of accounting change	$ 264.1	$ (237.8)	$ 147.5
Discontinued operation—printing and publishing papers:			
Income (Loss) from operations through December 20, 1994, net of income tax expense (benefit) of $4.0 $(14.3) and $8.0 for 1994, 1993 and 1992, respectively	6.8	(51.3)	19.7
Gain (Loss) on disposal	—	—	—
Income (Loss) before extraordinary loss and cumulative effect of accounting change	$ 270.9	$ (289.1)	$ 167.2
Extraordinary loss on early extinguishment of debt, net of income tax benefit of $35.8 and $5.2 for 1994 and 1993, respectively	(61.1)	(9.6)	—
Cumulative effect of change in accounting for income taxes	—	21.7	—
Net Income (Loss)	**$ 209.8**	**$ (277.0)**	**$ 167.2**
Per share:			
Income (Loss) from continuing operations before extraordinary loss and cumulative effect of accounting change	**$3.54**	**$(3.22)**	**$1.99**
Income (Loss) from discontinued printing and publishing papers operation	**.09**	**(.69)**	**.27**
Extraordinary loss on early extinguishment of debt	**(.82)**	**(.13)**	**—**
Cumulative effect of change in accounting for income taxes	**—**	**.29**	**—**
Earnings (Loss) per share	**$2.81**	**$(3.75)**	**$2.26**
Dividends per share	$.80	$.80	$.80
Average common shares outstanding	74.7	74.0	73.9

the 1994 annual report of Scott Paper Company. Note, in particular, the earnings-per-share disclosure near the bottom. These breakdowns allow users to focus on the earnings-per-share numbers that best meet their needs.

Generally accepted accounting principles require an additional disclosure, called **fully diluted earnings per share**, for companies that have the potential for significant dilution. Many companies, for example, have issued and presently have outstanding options to purchase their common stocks or bonds that can be converted to common stocks in the future. If and when these options and conversion privileges are exercised, the number of outstanding common shares will increase, which, in turn, will dilute the ownership interests of the existing common stockholders. The calculation of fully diluted earnings per share, which is described in intermediate and advanced financial accounting textbooks, reflects these possibilities by essentially increasing the denominator of the earnings-per-share ratio and thereby reducing its dollar value. The extent of potential dilution, as measured by the difference between fully diluted and unadjusted (primary) earnings per share, can be useful information to existing or potential stockholders, who are concerned with maintaining the value of their investments.

INTRAPERIOD TAX ALLOCATION

L O 5   Federal income taxes, which do not include state and local taxes, are disclosed in two different ways on the income statement. The first income tax disclosure immediately follows net income from continuing operations (before tax). It represents the tax expense resulting from all taxable revenues and deductible expenses except for those listed below it on the income statement.[13]

The dollar amounts associated with the remaining items (disposal of business segments, extraordinary items, and changes in accounting principles) are all disclosed *net of tax*. Such presentation means that each of these revenue and expense items is disclosed on the income statement after the related income tax effect has been removed. The practice of including the income tax effect of a particular transaction with the transaction itself on the income statement is known as **intraperiod tax allocation**. It enables users to assess the total financial impact of these special transactions as well as the tax benefit or cost associated with them.

For example, when CBS Inc. retired long-term debt with a book value of $28.6 million for $29.1 million dollars, a loss of $.5 million was recognized on the transaction with the following journal entry (dollars in millions).

Long-Term Debt (−L)	**28.6**	
Extraordinary Loss on Early Retirement of Debt (Lo, −SE)	**.5**	
Cash (−A)		**29.1**
Retired long-term debt.		

The loss, however, was tax deductible and served to decrease CBS's tax liability by $.2 million. This tax benefit was recorded in the books with the following journal entry, and a loss on early retirement (net of tax) of $.3 million ($.5 million − $.2 million) was disclosed on CBS's income statement. This loss was disclosed on the income statement under extraordinary items.

---

13. Appendix 10B, which covers deferred income taxes, provides a more complete description of tax expense listed in the income statement.

Income Tax Liability (−L)   .2
    Extraordinary Loss on Early Retirement of Debt (−Lo, +SE)   .2
Recognized tax benefit.

In another example, Ralston Purina Company sold its Van Camp Seafood division several years ago for $260 million. The book value of Van Camp was $147.3 million, and a gain of $112.7 million was recognized on the transaction with the following journal entry (dollars in millions).

Cash (+A)   260
    Net Assets of Van Camp Seafood (−A)   147.3
    Gain on Disposal of Segment (Ga, +SE)   112.7
Sold business segment.

The gain, however, was included in Ralston Purina's taxable income and increased the company's tax liability by $42.5 million. The increase in tax liability was recorded with the following journal entry (dollars in millions), and Ralston Purina disclosed a $70.2 million ($112.7 − $42.5) gain on its income statement. The gain appeared under disposals of business segments.

Gain on Disposal of Segment (−Ga, −SE)   42.5
    Income Tax Liability (+L)   42.5
Recorded increase in tax liability.

The general formula for computing the net-of-tax dollar amount for a revenue or expense item is provided below.

Net-of-Tax Dollar Amount = (Gross Revenue or Expense) × (1 − Tax Rate)

If, for example, an accounting change leads to a book and tax gain or loss of $10,000, and the company's federal income tax rate is 35 percent, the net-of-tax dollar amount disclosed on the income statement would be calculated as follows:

Net of Tax Dollar Amount = $10,000 × (1 − 35%)
    = $6,500

INCOME STATEMENT CATEGORIES: USEFUL FOR DECISIONS BUT SUBJECTIVE

The income statement classifications discussed in this chapter introduce a very important concept to those who use financial accounting information to predict the future cash flows of an enterprise. The concept is called **earnings persistence**, and it reflects the extent to which a particular earnings dollar amount can be expected to continue in the future and, thus, generate future cash flows. Earnings amounts with high levels of persistence are expected to continue in the future, while those with low levels of persistence are not. The income statement classifications are useful because, for the most part, they are defined in terms of their persistence. Net operating income is the result of usual and frequent activities that can be expected to continue in the future; "other revenues and expenses" are considered to have somewhat less persistence; and disposals of segments, extraordinary items, and accounting changes are all considered to be "one shot" events that should not be counted on in the future. Astute financial statement users cannot ignore these classifications, since they contain valuable information about a company's future prospects.

In terms of the objectives of financial accounting, earnings numbers with high persistence are considered to reflect future cash flows, while low persistence earnings are not. Both kinds of earnings, however, reflect changes in the company's resources and in that respect are considered useful.

It is also important to realize, however, that income statement classifications can be quite subjective, and management has incentives to use its discretion to disclose the financial results of certain events in categories that serve its interests. For example, management may use its reporting discretion to include certain "gains" in the operating section and certain "losses" in the nonoperating sections of the income statement. By using such a strategy, management might influence users to believe that the "gains" are persistent while the "losses" are not. As noted in *Forbes* magazine: "clever accountants can find all sorts of different meanings in those simple sounding words [usual and frequent]. . . . It all comes down to a judgement."[14]

Consider Primerica Corporation, a large financial service supplier. In its preliminary *unaudited* financial statements the company disclosed $183 million in income from continuing operations, and a $61 million extraordinary loss. The loss, which the company treated as extraordinary because management considered it both unusual and infrequent, came from investments that decreased in value during the period. However, the company's auditors took the position that investment losses are not an infrequent occurrence for a financial service supplier, and on its audited financial statements Primerica Corp. included the $61 million loss in "other revenues and expenses." The accounting treatment required by the auditors reduced income from continuing operations by 33 percent, to $122 million.

In another case, Western Savings of Phoenix, a savings and loan company, reported $49 million in *operating* income, almost half of which ($24 million) was due to the sale of one large investment. Many accountants agreed that this particular sale was nonrecurring and that similar gains could not be expected in the future. Consequently, the gain on this transaction should not have been included in the operating section of the income statement. *Forbes* pointed out that this and other accounting practices followed by the company suggested: "Western is a classic case of how reported profits can misrepresent economic reality."[15]

Very recently, *The Wall Street Journal* (January 30, 1996) noted that many companies use subjective restructuring charges to manage earnings. Often, they prematurely recognize expenses within a charge that is disclosed on the income statement outside of the operating section. This activity reduces future operating expenses and increases net income from operations. The article went on to say: "The most obvious way restructuring charges make companies' earnings look better is if the company can convince investors that operating earnings—before the charges—provide a more meaningful indication of trends."

The subjectivity associated with classifying gains and losses in different sections of the income statement can give rise to other significant economic consequences. We noted earlier in the chapter, for example, that The Pillsbury Company has instituted a compensation plan that rewards management on the basis of operating income. An important question is whether interest expense is considered to be an operating or a nonoperating expense in the measurement of operating income as defined by the plan. Including interest as an operating expense could discourage management from borrowing needed funds; including it as a nonoperating expense, on the other hand, could encourage managers to borrow too much. Classifying interest as operating or nonop-

14. Penelope Wang, "Dictionary Please," *Forbes*, March 7, 1988, p. 88.
15. Allan Sloan, "Phoenix' Wild West Show," *Forbes*, May 31, 1988, pp. 37–38.

erating is a subjective decision; yet it can influence the manner in which a company functions.

RETAINED EARNINGS AND PRIOR PERIOD ADJUSTMENTS

In Chapter 12 we discussed and illustrated the statement of stockholders' equity, which describes the activity during a given period in each of the stockholders' equity accounts: common stock, preferred stock, additional paid-in capital, and retained earnings. All items on the income statement are eventually transferred (closed) to Retained Earnings, so net income (loss) appears as an adjustment to Retained Earnings on the statement of stockholders' equity. We have noted in the text that the financial effects of other events, such as the declaration of dividends, the appropriation of retained earnings, and the sale of treasury stock for an amount less than its acquisition cost are also booked directly to the Retained Earnings account.

In addition to these items, generally accepted accounting principles require that the financial effects of several rather unusual events be booked directly to Retained Earnings. The most common such event is the correction in the current period of an accounting error made in a previous period. When such a correction is made, a journal entry is recorded to correct the misstated asset or liability and the other half of the entry serves to increase or decrease Retained Earnings directly. The entry is called a **prior period adjustment**, and similar to disposals of business segments, extraordinary items, and changes in accounting methods, the financial effect is disclosed net of tax on the financial statements. The dollar amount of the net adjustment appears on the statement of stockholders' equity.

INTERNATIONAL PERSPECTIVE: INVESTMENTS AND INCOME STATEMENT DISCLOSURE

Many times in this textbook we have commented that U.S. businesses are increasingly investing in foreign markets and operations. Such investments introduce certain risks and opportunities that are different from those characterizing domestic business activities. The following quote from Coca-Cola's annual report provides an illustration.

The Company distributes its products in nearly 170 countries and [transacts in approximately 40 different currencies]. Approximately 80 percent of total operating income is generated outside the United States. International operations are subject to certain risks and opportunities, including currency fluctuation and government actions. The Company closely monitors its methods of operating in each country and adopts strategies responsive to changing economic and political environments.

Such a strong international presence increases the number of transactions that require special disclosure on the income statement. Owens-Corning Fiberglas, for example, has significant investments in six different non-U.S. affiliated companies (two in Saudi Arabia, and one each in Canada, Japan, Brazil, and Mexico). A portion of the income reported by these affiliates is disclosed, under the equity method, as a special item on the company's income statement. Merck & Co., Inc., which has investments in foreign assets that total $2.5 billion, has sold and restructured foreign subsidiaries frequently the last several years. For example, the company sold subsidiaries in South Africa, Lebanon, and Nigeria and restructured operations in

Argentina, Brazil, and Venezuela. These activities led to special disclosures in its income statement.

The unique risks associated with investments in countries with high inflation and volatile economies also often give rise to special income statement disclosures. Several years ago Johnson & Johnson disclosed two special charges on the income statement: (1) a $104 million write-off for permanently impaired assets and operations in Latin America, which was disclosed in the operating section of the income statement, and (2) a $36 million loss from the liquidation of Argentine debt. The company's 1994 annual report also mentions the risks of foreign currency fluctuations and describes how the company hedges these risks, reporting only a $19 million loss on currency fluctuations in 1994.

In such an international investment environment, financial statement users must be particularly aware of, and carefully interpret, the special gains and losses that are reported on the income statement. They should attempt to completely understand the underlying transaction and appreciate the context in which it occurred. An article in *The Wall Street Journal* (September 18, 1990) cautions investors about gains that arise from foreign currency translations in particular.

Foreign exchange gains resulting from the dollar's [recent] tumble . . . raise questions about the quality of soon-to-be released earnings reports for those U.S. firms with big foreign operations. For example, American Family Corp., Gillette Co., American Brands Inc., and Colgate-Palmolive Co. all derive more than 60 percent of their sales from foreign operations . . . Investors should [not overemphasize the importance of] currency-related earnings . . . because they're really a one-time gain that could easily reverse itself.

These issues underline the importance of carefully reading the footnotes in an annual report. Most of the information required to make the assessments discussed in

---

The boards of directors of most major U.S. companies have established executive compensation plans that base executive pay on some measure of company performance. While these plans differ widely across companies, a large percentage use some form of reported earnings as the measure of performance. Recognizing that there are many different ways to measure earnings, these compensation contracts must be very specific about which earnings measure is used. Pillsbury, for example, bases its formula on operating earnings, the result of subtracting operating expenses from operating revenues, excluding such items as interest expense, interest income, gains and losses on asset sales, extraordinary gains and losses, and the effects of accounting changes. Other companies, such as DuPont and Ashland Oil, base their formulas on net income after such items—the "bottom line."

ETHICS IN THE REAL WORLD

Consider a company that has a compensation plan like that of DuPont, where compensation is a function of earnings after interest expense, and assume that management is analyzing how to finance a particular capital investment—that is, should it be financed with debt or equity? Management knows that if debt is chosen, net income and its compensation will be reduced by the interest expense recognized on the debt. On the other hand, if management chooses equity there will be no interest expense to reduce its compensation amount.

ETHICAL ISSUE

Is it ethical for management to consider the impact of the financing decision on its compensation amount, or should such impact be completely ignored when choosing between debt and equity?

this section is not disclosed on the face of the financial statements but is normally buried somewhere in the footnotes. The breakdown of domestic and foreign sales, for example, can often be found in the footnote section of the annual report. As businesses become more international and operations become more complex, financial statement users will be forced to rely more heavily on the footnotes.

REVIEW PROBLEM

The operating revenues and expenses of Panawin Enterprises for 1997 follow, along with descriptions of several additional transactions, events, and pieces of information. Review the information provided, including the related journal entries. Assume that income taxes on income from continuing operations are $7,000, the effective income tax rate on other items is 34 percent, the balance in Retained Earnings as of December 31, 1996, is $106,000, and that dividends declared during 1997 total $16,000.

Operating revenues	**$85,000**
Operating expenses	**62,000**
Net operating income	**$23,000**

ADDITIONAL INFORMATION

1. Machinery with an original cost of $14,000 and a book value of $11,000 was sold for $9,000. The transaction was considered unusual but not infrequent.

Cash (+A)	**9,000**	
Accumulated Depreciation (+A)	**3,000**	
Loss on Sale of Machinery (Lo, −SE)	**2,000**	
Machinery (−A)		**14,000**
Sold machinery.		

2. A separate line of business (segment) was sold on March 14, 1997, for $18,000 cash. The book values of the assets and liabilities of the segment as of the date of the sale were $10,000 and $4,000, respectively. The business segment recognized revenues of $18,500 and expenses of $14,000 from January 1, 1997, to March 14, 1997.

Revenues of the Segment	**18,500**	
Expense of the Segment		**14,000**
Income Summary		**4,500**
Recognized business segment income		
(closing entry recorded at time of sale).		
Income Summary (E, −SE)	**1,530**	
Income Tax Liability (+L)		**1,530**
Recognized income tax liability related to		
1997 operations ($4,500 × 34%).		
Cash (+A)	**18,000**	
Liabilities (−L)	**4,000**	
Assets (−A)		**10,000**
Gain on Sale (Ga, +SE)		**12,000**
Sold business segment.		
Gain on Sale (−Ga, −SE)	**4,080**	
Income Tax Liability (+L)		**4,080**
Recognized additional tax liability ($12,000 × 34%).		

3. On September 12, 1997, Panawin retired outstanding bonds with a face value of $120,000 before maturity for a cash payment of $130,000. The bonds were originally issued at a premium, and the unamortized premium as of the date of retirement was $3,000. The loss on the retirement is considered extraordinary.

Bonds Payable (−L)	120,000	
Unamortized Premium (−L)	3,000	
Loss on Retirement (Lo, −SE)	7,000	
Cash (−A)		130,000
Retired outstanding bonds.		
Income Tax Liability (−L)	2,380	
Loss on Retirement (−Lo, +SE)		2,380
Recognized tax benefit ($7,000 × 34%).		

4. The company changed its inventory flow assumption from last-in, first-out (LIFO) to first-in, first-out (FIFO). This change increased the ending inventory balance for 1997 by $8,000.

Inventory (+A)	8,000	
Income from Accounting Change (Ga, +SE)		8,000
Recognized change from LIFO to FIFO.		
Income from Accounting Change (−Ga, −SE)	2,720	
Income Tax Liability (+L)		2,720
Recognized additional tax liability ($8,000 × 34%).		

Now note how the income statement (Figure 13–8) and reconciliation of retained earnings (Figure 13–9) have been prepared.

FIGURE 13–8

Income statement for review problem

PANAWIN ENTERPRISES
INCOME STATEMENT
FOR THE YEAR ENDED DECEMBER 31, 1997

Operating revenues	$85,000	(given)
Operating expenses	62,000	(given)
Net operating income	$23,000	
Loss on sale of machinery	(2,000)	
Net income from continuing operations before tax	$21,000	
Less: Federal income tax	7,000	(given)
Net income from continuing operations	$14,000	
Income from disposed segment (net of tax)	2,970	($4,500 − $1,530)
Gain on sale of segment (net of tax)	7,920	($12,000 − $4,080)
Net income before extraordinary items	$24,890	
Extraordinary loss on retirement of debt (net of tax)	(4,620)	(−$7,000 + $2,380)
Net income before change in accounting principle	$20,270	
Income effect from change from LIFO to FIFO (net of tax)	5,280	($8,000 − $2,720)
Net income	$25,550	
Earnings per share (10,000 shares outstanding):		
Net income from continuing operations	$ 1.40	(14,000 ÷ 10,000)
Disposal of business segment	1.09	[($2,970 + $7,920) ÷ 10,000]
Extraordinary item	(.46)	($4,620 ÷ 10,000)
Change in accounting principle	.53	($5,280 ÷ 10,000)
Total earnings per share	$ 2.56	($25,550 ÷ 10,000)

FIGURE 13-9	PANAWIN ENTERPRISES
Reconciliation of retained earnings for review problem	STATEMENT OF RETAINED EARNINGS FOR THE YEAR ENDED DECEMBER 31, 1997

Beginning retained earnings balance	$106,000
Plus: Net income	25,550
Less: Dividends	(16,000)
Ending retained earnings balance	$115,550

SUMMARY OF LEARNING OBJECTIVES

 Describe the economic consequences associated with reporting net income.

Income is the most common measure of a company's performance. It has been related to stock prices, suggesting that equity investors use income in their decisions to buy and sell equity securities. It has been related to bond prices, indicating that debt investors use income in their decisions to buy and sell corporate bonds. Income is also used by credit-rating agencies to establish credit ratings. Various income measures are also found in contracts written among stockholders, creditors, and managers. Such contracts are normally designed either to protect the interests of creditors or to encourage managers to act in the interests of the stockholders.

L O 2 *Describe the difference between an operating transaction and a capital transaction, and indicate how capital transactions are categorized on the capital/operating continuum.*

Capital transactions involve setting up a company so that it can conduct operations. Operating transactions entail the actual conduct of the operations. The text identifies five categories of transactions, each of which falls in a different place on the capital/operating continuum. The categories are (1) exchanges with stockholders, (2) exchanges of liabilities and stockholders' equity, (3) issues and payments of debt, (4) purchases, sales, and exchanges of assets and (5) operating transactions (revenues and expenses). Generally accepted accounting principles consider Categories 1–4 as capital transactions.

Exchanges with stockholders are considered purely capital because they are involved exclusively with the formation and dissolution of the company's equity capital and the returns to the company's stockholders. Exchanges of liabilities and stockholders' equity are considered capital transactions because they deal only with a company's capital structure. Issues and payments of debt involve exchanges with a company's creditors and are reflected in the liability section of the balance sheet. Purchases, sales, or exchanges of assets are considered capital transactions because assets represent the capital base upon which operations are conducted.

L O 3 *List the five categories that constitute a complete income statement and explain how they provide measures of income that address the objectives of financial reporting.*

The financial effects of five types of events warrant special disclosure and presentation on the income statement: (1) operating revenues and expenses, (2) other revenues and expenses, (3) disposals of business segments, (4) extraordinary items, and (5) changes in accounting principles.

These classifications highlight income numbers that vary in persistence. In terms of the objectives of financial accounting, earnings numbers with high persistence (e.g. operating earnings) are considered to reflect future cash flows, while low persistence earnings are not. Both kinds of earnings, however, reflect changes in a company's resources, and in that respect are considered useful.

 Describe how earnings per share is disclosed on the income statement.

Generally accepted accounting principles require that earnings per share be disclosed on the face of the income statement and that the specific amounts associated with (1) net income from continuing operations (after tax), (2) disposals of business segments, (3) extraordinary items, and (4) changes in accounting principles be disclosed separately. The calculation involves dividing the dollar amounts of each of the four items listed by the average number of shares outstanding during the accounting period.

LO 5 *Define intraperiod tax allocation, and explain how it relates to the income statement.*

Federal income taxes are disclosed in two different ways on the income statement. The first income tax disclosure immediately follows net income from continuing operations (before tax). It represents the tax expense recognized by the company due to taxable revenues and deductible expenses not related to the items listed below net income from continuing operations on the income statement.

The dollar amounts associated with the remaining items (disposal of business segments, extraordinary items, and changes in accounting principles) are all disclosed *net of tax.* Such presentation means that each of these revenue and expense items is disclosed on the income statement after the related income tax effect has been removed. The practice of including the income tax effect of a particular transaction with the transaction itself on the income statement is known as *intraperiod tax allocation.*

KEY TERMS

Note: Definitions for these terms are provided in the glossary at the end of the text.

Business segment (p. 652)   Fully diluted earnings per share (p. 658)
Capital transactions (p. 646)   Intraperiod tax allocation (p. 658)
Comprehensive income (p. 644)   Operating transactions (p. 646)
Earnings persistence (p. 659)   Prior period adjustment (p. 661)
Extraordinary items (p. 654)   Pro forma (as if) basis (p. 656)
Frequent transaction (p. 651)   Usual transaction (p. 651)

QUESTIONS FOR DISCUSSION AND REVIEW

1. Why is the amount of income such an important number? Briefly explain how it is used by investors, creditors, and other interested parties.

2. What is comprehensive income, and in terms of the objectives of financial accounting, how is it useful?

3. What is a capital transaction, and how does it differ from an operating transaction?

4. The text states that all transactions can be placed on the capital/operating continuum. List the five categories of transactions discussed in the chapter, and briefly explain why each is placed where it is on the capital/operating continuum.

5. Define the terms *usual* and *frequent* as they are used in the chapter. Provide an example of (a) a transaction that is both usual and frequent, (b) a transaction that is usual and infrequent, (c) a transaction that is unusual and frequent, and (d) a transaction that is unusual and infrequent.

6. Describe how transactions that fall into each of the four categories identified in (5) are presented on the income statement, and explain how these categories are useful in terms of the objectives of financial accounting.

7. Define a business segment. What two items are disclosed on the income statement when a business segment is sold or discontinued?

8. What is an extraordinary item? Explain how a certain transaction entered into by one company might be considered extraordinary, while the same transaction entered into by another company might be considered a part of normal operations.

9. Is a change in an accounting principle/method inconsistent with the notion of consistency? If management wishes to change an accounting principle, of what must the auditors be convinced?

10. Differentiate between a voluntary and a mandated accounting method change. Why should users be aware of the difference?

11. In what three places in the financial report can you find evidence that a company changed a major accounting principle?

12. How are earnings per share disclosed on the face of the income statement? Why is it done in this manner? What is fully diluted earnings per share, and why should potential or existing shareholders be concerned about it?

13. Explain the idea of intraperiod tax allocation. List the items that are disclosed net of tax on the income statement and statement of stockholders' equity.

14. Define the concept of earnings persistence, and explain how the income statement classifications provide information about it. How is this concept useful?

15. How can dividing income into its components (i.e., income from operations, income from continuing operations, discontinued operations, extraordinary items, and changes in accounting methods) give rise to economic consequences? State your answers in terms of the prices of a company's equity securities, its credit ratings, the contracts it has with its creditors, and management compensation systems.

16. Explain why users must be careful when relying on classification on the income statement provided by management.

17. List the items that are normally disclosed on the reconciliation of retained earnings. Where is this reconciliation found in the financial reports of many major U.S. companies?

18. What are prior period adjustments, and how are they disclosed in the financial statements?

19. Why must investors and creditors be particularly cautious about investing in companies that have significant international operations? What effect can such operations have on the income statement?

EXERCISES

E13–1

(Which statement is affected?)

Listed below are transactions or items that are frequently reported in financial statements.

1. Income effect due to changing from the double-declining-balance method to the straight-line method of depreciation.

2. Collection of accounts receivable.

3. Purchase an insurance policy on December 31 that provides coverage for the following year.

4. Accrue wages earned by the employees.
5. Estimate uncollectible accounts receivable using the aging method.
6. Recognize a gain on the sale of plant equipment.
7. Recognize a loss when the government expropriates land for a highway.
8. Declare a dividend valued at $100,000.
9. Under the requirements of a debt covenant, appropriate a portion of retained earnings.
10. Receive dividends on stocks held as a short-term investment. The dividends were declared and paid on the same day.
11. Recognize the cost of inventory sold during the year under the periodic method.
12. Pay rent for the current year.

REQUIRED:

a. Indicate whether each item would be included on the company's income statement, statement of stockholders' equity, or neither, using the following codes:

   IS   Income statement
   SE   Statement of stockholders' equity
   N   Neither

b. Indicate whether the items you coded IS would be considered
   (1) usual and frequent,
   (2) unusual or infrequent,
   (3) unusual and infrequent, or
   (4) other.

c. Provide a brief explanation of your choice in (b) of (1), (2), (3), or (4).

E13–2

(Capital or operating transactions?)

A number of transactions are described below.
  1. Declaration of a stock dividend.
  2. Purchase of 50 percent of the outstanding stock of another company.
  3. Payment of previously accrued interest payable.
  4. Accrual of interest expense.
  5. Purchase of machinery.
  6. Recognition of depreciation on machinery.
  7. Purchase of treasury stock.
  8. Sale of treasury stock at a price less than its original cost.
  9. Conversion of debt to common stock.
 10. Receipt of cash on an outstanding receivable.
 11. Sale of inventory on account.
 12. Purchase of inventory on account.
 13. Declaration of dividends.
 14. Receipt of dividends on short-term marketable securities.
 15. Early retirement of outstanding long-term debt.

REQUIRED:

a. Refer to Figure 13–2 in the text, and classify each transaction in one of the following categories.
   (1) Exchanges with stockholders
   (2) Exchanges of liabilities and stockholders' equity
   (3) Issues and payments of debt
   (4) Purchases, sales, and exchanges of assets
   (5) Operating transactions

b. Briefly explain why the transactions are considered increasingly operating (or decreasingly capital) as the categories move from 1 to 5.

E13–3

(Debt covenants expressed in terms of income)

Morton Manufacturing maintains a credit line with First Bank that allows the company to borrow up to $1 million. A covenant associated with the loan contract limits the company's dividends in any one year to 20 percent of net income. The 1997 income statement data of Morton Manufacturing is provided below.

Net sales	$840,000
Less: Cost of goods sold	570,000
Gross profit	$270,000
Selling and administrative expenses	120,000
Net operating income	$150,000
Gain on sale of securities	14,000
Interest expense	(4,000)
Net income from continuing operations before tax	$160,000
Less: Income tax	51,200
Net income from continuing operations	$108,800
Extraordinary gain (net of tax)	22,000
Net income before change in accounting principle	$130,800
Income effect due to change in accounting principle	52,000
Net income	$182,800

REQUIRED:

a. Compute the maximum amount of dividends Morton can pay if the debt covenant is expressed as 20 percent of each of the following:
   (1) Net income
   (2) Income before change in accounting principle
   (3) Income before extraordinary items (from continuing operations)
   (4) Net operating income

b. Explain why the bank may wish to state the contractual limitation on dividends in terms of income from operations instead of net income.

E13–4

(Comprehensive income)

The December 31, 1997, balance sheet of Smedley Company is provided below.

Assets	$70,000	Liabilities	$15,000
		Stockholders' equity	55,000
		Total liabilities and	
Total assets	$70,000	stockholders equity	$70,000

During 1998 the company entered into the following transactions.
1. Common stock was issued for $35,000 cash.
2. Services were performed for $50,000 cash.
3. Cash expenses of $24,000 were incurred.
4. Long-term liabilities of $15,000 were paid.
5. Dividends of $7,000 were declared and paid.

REQUIRED:

a. Classify each transaction as operating or capital and then prepare an income statement.
b. Compute comprehensive income, and compare it to the income amount calculated in (a).
c. Explain why the two dollar amounts are equal.

E13–5

(Comprehensive income)

The income statement data for the year ended December 31, 1997, of Bentley Brothers follows.

Operating revenues	$35,000
Operating expenses	20,000
Net operating income	$15,000
Loss on sale of short-term investments	3,000
Net income from continuing operations before tax	$12,000
Less: Income tax	3,840
Net income from continuing operations	$ 8,160
Extraordinary gain (net of tax)	6,000
Net income before change in accounting principle	$14,160
Income effect due to change in accounting principle (net of tax)	8,000
Net income	$22,160

During 1997 Bentley issued common stock for $25,000. The company also declared and paid a $9,000 dividend. The book value of the company on January 1, 1997, was $35,000.

REQUIRED:
a. Compute the book value of Bentley Brothers as of December 31, 1997 and calculate comprehensive income.
b. Which of the income measures on the income statement is equal to comprehensive income? Discuss how that and the other measures may be useful.

E13–6

(Disposal of a business segment)

LTB Enterprises consists of four separate divisions: building products, chemicals, mining, and plastics. On March 15, 1996, LTB sold the chemicals division for $625,000 cash. Financial information related to the chemicals division follows.

(1/1–3/15/96)		(3/15/96)	
Sales	$175,000	Assets	$1,850,000
Operating expenses	160,000	Liabilities	1,400,000
Net operating income (loss)	$ 15,000		

REQUIRED:
a. Provide the journal entry (or entries) to record the sale of the chemicals division. Assume an income tax rate of 35 percent.
b. Prepare the section of LTB's 1996 income statement that relates to the disposal of the business segment.

E13–7

(Management choices and earnings persistence)

It is December, 1997, and Sharon Sowers, the CEO of Mallory Services, has decided to sell the clerical division. She has received an offer for $105,000, but is undecided about whether she wishes to complete the sale in 1997 or 1998. She is currently evaluating the effects of the sale on 1997 reported net income. Income from continuing operations for 1997 is estimated to be $950,000 (excluding the activities of the clerical division), and information about the clerical division is provided below. The company's tax rate is 35 percent.

YEAR ENDED 1997		DECEMBER 1997	
Revenues	$35,000	Assets	$93,000
Expenses	23,000	Liabilities	26,000

REQUIRED:
a. Prepare the 1997 income statement beginning with net income from continuing operations assuming that Sharon accepts the offer, and explain how a user might interpret the items on the income statement in terms of earnings persistence.
b. Prepare the 1997 income statement beginning with net income from continuing operations assuming that Sharon chooses not to sell the division in 1997, and explain how a user might interpret the items on the income statement in terms of earnings persistence.
c. Describe some of the important trade-offs faced by Sharon as she decides whether to complete the sale in 1997 or 1998.

E13–8

(Management choices and earnings persistence)

It is December, 1997, and Rob Blandig, the CEO of Carmich Industries, has decided to sell the chemical division. He has received an offer for $350,000, but is undecided about whether he wishes to complete the sale in 1997 or 1998. He is currently evaluating the effects of the sale on 1997 reported net income. Income from continuing operations for 1997 is estimated to be $1,930,000 (excluding the activities of the chemical division and management's bonus), and the company anticipates a weak year in 1998. Information about the division is provided below. The company's tax rate is 35 percent, and company management is paid a bonus each year in the amount of 20% × net income from continuing operations. For purposes of the bonus calculation, net income from continuing operations is not reduced by the bonus.

YEAR ENDED 1997		DECEMBER 1997	
Revenues	$145,000	Assets	$437,000
Expenses	120,000	Liabilities	218,000

REQUIRED:

a. Prepare the 1997 income statement beginning with net income from continuing operations assuming that Rob accepts the offer, and explain how a user might interpret the items on the income statement in terms of earnings persistence.
b. Prepare the 1997 income statement beginning with net income from continuing operations assuming that Rob chooses not to sell the division in 1997, and explain how a user might interpret the items on the income statement in terms of earnings persistence.
c. Describe some of the important trade-offs faced by Rob as he decides whether to complete the sale in 1997 or 1998.

E13–9

(Accounting for unusual losses)

You are currently auditing the financial records of Paxson Corporation, which is located in San Francisco, California. During the current year, inventories with an original cost of $2,325,000 were destroyed by an earthquake. The company was unsure how to record this loss and is seeking your advice. The loss is deductible for tax purposes, and the company's tax rate is 35 percent.

REQUIRED:

a. Prepare the journal entry (or entries) to record the loss of the inventory if the loss is not considered extraordinary.
b. Prepare the journal entry (or entries) to record the loss of the inventory if the loss is considered extraordinary.
c. Should the loss be classified as an extraordinary loss or as an ordinary loss? Explain.
d. Would your answer to (c) change if the plant had been located in Miami, Florida? Explain.

E13–10

(Earnings-per-share disclosure)

The following income statement was reported by Battery Builders for the year ending December 31, 1997.

Sales	$85,000	
Rent revenue	23,000	
Interest income	7,000	
Total revenues		$115,000
Cost of goods sold	$52,000	
Operating expenses	24,000	
Interest expense	12,000	
Loss on sale of fixed asset	6,000	
Total expenses		94,000
Income from continuing operations (before tax)		$ 21,000
Less: Income tax		10,000
Income from continuing operations		$ 11,000
Income from disposed segment (net of tax)		3,000
Gain on sale of disposed segment (net of tax)		2,000
Income before extraordinary items		$ 16,000
Extraordinary loss (net of tax)		7,000
Income before change in accounting principle		$ 9,000
Income due to change in accounting principle (net of tax)		6,000
Net income		$ 15,000

REQUIRED:

Show how Battery Builders would report earnings per share on the face of the income statement assuming the following:
a. An average of 15,000 shares of common stock was outstanding during 1997.
b. An average of 25,000 shares of common stock was outstanding during 1997.
c. An average of 30,000 shares of common stock was outstanding during 1997.

E13–11

(Considering an item as extraordinary can have significant economic consequences)

The management of Sting Enterprises share in a bonus that is determined and paid at the end of each year. The amount of the bonus is defined by multiplying net income from continuing operations (after tax) by 12 percent. The bonus is not used in the calculation of income from continuing operations. During 1997 Sting was a defendant in a lawsuit and was required to pay $480,000 over and above the amount covered by insurance. The loss is tax deductible, and the company's tax rate is 35 percent. The company was last involved in a lawsuit five years ago. Net income from continuing operations (before tax), excluding the loss from the lawsuit, for 1997 was $800,000.

REQUIRED:

a. Compute management's 1997 bonus, assuming that the lawsuit is considered unusual but not infrequent.
b. Compute management's 1997 bonus, assuming that the lawsuit is considered extraordinary.
c. Repeat (a) and (b) above, assuming that Sting was awarded the $480,000 settlement instead of having to pay it.
d. Explain how the decision to include or not to include an item as extraordinary can have significant economic consequences.

E13–12

(Intraperiod tax allocation and the financial statements)

The following information was taken from the 1997 financial records of Rothrock Consolidated. All items below are pretax.

	DEBIT	CREDIT
Operating Revenues		87,000
Operating Expenses	32,500	
Gain on Sale of Short-Term Investments		5,200
Loss on Sale of Business Segment	21,000	
Income Earned on Disposed Business Segment		3,000
Extraordinary Loss	5,000	
Income Due to Change in Accounting Principle		12,500
Retained Earnings (beginning balance)		72,000
Dividends Declared	18,000	

The company's income tax rate is 35 percent, and the items above are treated identically for financial reporting and tax purposes.

REQUIRED:

Prepare the following:

a. An income statement.
b. A reconciliation of retained earnings.

E13–13

(Intraperiod tax allocation)

The following pretax amounts were obtained from the financial records of Watson Company for 1997.

	DEBIT	CREDIT
Retained Earnings (1/1/97)		847,000
Sales Revenues		1,385,000
Rent Revenue		360,000
Cost of Goods Sold	475,000	
Administrative Expenses	100,000	
Depreciation Expense	250,000	
Selling Expenses	189,000	
Extraordinary Loss	202,000	
Loss on Sale of Fixed Assets	105,000	
Dividends Declared	460,000	

The company's tax rate is 35 percent.

REQUIRED:

a. Prepare an income statement for the year ended December 31, 1997, using the multistep format.

b. Prepare a statement of retained earnings for the year ended December 31, 1997.

c. What is the income tax effect associated with each item that is reported net of tax? Assuming that no taxes were owed at the beginning of 1997 and no tax payments were made during 1997, what is the total income tax liability at the end of 1997?

E13–14

(Covenant restrictions and income reporting)

Kennington Company has outstanding debt that contains restrictive covenants limiting dividends to 15 percent of net income from continuing operations. During 1997 the company reported net income from operations after taxes of $235,000, excluding the following items— all of which ignore tax effects.

1. A $25,000 gain was recognized on the sale of an investment.
2. A $62,000 loss was recognized on lawsuit.
3. A $38,000 loss was recognized on the early retirement of debt.

REQUIRED:

Assume that the gain in (1) is taxable, the losses in (2) and (3) are tax deductible, and the company's tax rate is 35 percent.

a. Provide the income statement, beginning at net income from operations, and compute the maximum amount of dividends that the company can declare, assuming that (1) the investment in (1) is a business segment that broke even during 1997 and (2) lawsuits are common for Kennington.

b. Provide the income statement, beginning at net income from operations, and compute the maximum amount of dividends that the company can declare, assuming that (1) the investment in (1) is a short-term equity security and (2) lawsuits are very rare for Kennington.

E13–15

(Stock market reactions to income reporting)

Madigan International is planning a major stock issuance in early 1998. During 1997 the company reported net income from operations before taxes of $865,000. The four items below describe major events that occurred during 1997. The company's accountants chose to include items (1) and (4) in the computation of net income from continuing operations and chose to disclose items (2) and (3) as extraordinary items.

1. A $42,000 gain was recognized on the sale of a subsidiary.
2. Inventory was written down by $53,000 due to earthquake damage.
3. An outstanding accounts receivable of $38,000 was written off when a major customer declared bankruptcy.
4. A $25,000 gain was recognized due to the change of an accounting principle.

REQUIRED:

Assume that items (1) and (4) are taxable, items (2) and (3) are tax deductible, and that the company's tax rate is 35 percent.

a. Present the income statement, beginning with net income from operations.

b. Critique the accounting treatment chosen by Madigan's accountants, and provide an income statement that is consistent with generally accepted accounting principles.

c. Discuss how Madigan's accounting treatment could influence the price at which the company's stock is sold in 1998, and provide a rationale for why Madigan may have made such choices.

PROBLEMS

P13–1

(Classifying transactions as capital or operating)

Lundy Manufacturing produces and sells football equipment. The company was involved in the following transactions or events during 1997.

1. The company purchased $250,000 worth of materials to be used during 1998 to manufacture helmets and shoulder pads.

2. The company sold football equipment for a price of $500,000. The inventory associated with the sale cost the company $375,000.
3. One of the company's plants in San Francisco was damaged by a minor earthquake. The total amount of the damage was $100,000.
4. The company issued 10 ($1,000 face value) bonds at a discount (.98).
5. The company incurred $143,000 in wage expenses.
6. The company was sued by a high school football player who was injured while using some of the company's equipment. The football player will probably win the suit, and the amount of the settlement has been estimated at $10,000. This is the sixth lawsuit filed against the company in the past three years.
7. The company switched from the double-declining-balance depreciation method to the straight-line depreciation method.
8. The company declared and paid $50,000 in dividends.
9. The company incurred a loss when it sold some securities it was holding as an investment.

REQUIRED:
a. Classify each of these transactions as capital or operating.
b. Refer to Figures 13–2 and 13–3 in the text, and identify the category in which each of the items listed should be placed.
c. Which of these items should be included on the company's income statement? Briefly describe how they should be disclosed.

P13–2

(Bonus contracts based on income can affect management's business decisions)

The managers of Martin House are paid a salary and share in a bonus that is determined at the end of each year. The total bonus is determined by multiplying the company's income from operations by 25 percent. The bonus is not considered an operating expense. Interest on borrowed funds is considered an operating expense when computing the bonus.

During 1997 the company decided to expand its plant facility. The estimated cost of the expansion was $1 million. To raise the necessary funds, the company could either borrow $1 million at an annual interest rate of 8 percent or issue 50,000 shares of common stock at $20 each. The company raised the funds using one of these two methods, and income from operations (excluding any interest charges) for 1997 was reported as follows.

Operating revenues	**$6,800,000**
Operating expenses (excluding interest)	**5,600,000**
Income from operations	**$1,200,000**

REQUIRED:
a. Assume that on January 1, 1997, Martin House borrowed the $1 million. Compute the total bonus shared by the company's managers.
b. Assume that on January 1, 1997, Martin House issued common stock to raise the $1 million. Compute the total bonus shared by the company's managers.
c. Why might management choose to issue equity instead of borrow the $1 million? Is such a decision necessarily in the best interest of the company's stockholders?
d. Repeat (a) and (b) above, assuming the interest expense is not considered an operating expense when computing the bonus.

P13–3

(Capital-maintenance and transaction views of income)

Raleigh Corporation began operations on February 10, 1997. During 1997 the company entered into the following transactions.
1. Issued $110,000 of common stock and $25,000 of preferred stock.
2. Performed services for $580,000.
3. Issued $475,000 in long-term debt for cash.
4. Incurred expenses: $125,000 for wages, $35,000 for supplies, $80,000 for depreciation, and $75,000 for miscellaneous expenses.
5. Purchased fixed assets for $250,000 cash.
6. Declared, but did not pay, cash dividends of $10,000.
7. Purchased fixed assets in exchange for a long-term note valued at $85,000.

REQUIRED:

a. Classify each transaction as either an operating transaction or a capital transaction.
b. Prepare an income statement.
c. Compute comprehensive income and compare it to the income reported on the income statement. Discuss.

P13–4

(Preparing an income statement)

Excerpts from Crozier Industries' financial records as of December 31, 1997, follow:

	DEBIT	CREDIT
Sales		977,000
Sales Returns	9,000	
Costs of Goods Sold	496,000	
Dividends	50,000	
Rent Expense	90,000	
Wages Payable		175,000
Loss on Sale of Food Services Division	2,000	
Loss Incurred by Food Services Division	10,000	
Depreciation Expense	100,000	
Cumulative Effect on Income of Change in Depreciation Methods	130,000	
Gain on Land Appropriated by the Government		92,000
Insurance Expense	12,000	
Inventory	576,000	
Administrative Expenses	109,000	
Prepaid Insurance	48,000	
Gain on Sale of Short-Term Investments		142,000

The amounts shown do not include any tax effects. Crozier's tax rate is 35 percent. Assume that all items are treated the same for accounting and income tax purposes.

REQUIRED:

a. Indicate which items should be included on the company's income statement. Classify each item to be included on the income statement as one of the following.
   (1) Usual and frequent
   (2) Unusual or infrequent
   (3) Disposal of business segment
   (4) Unusual and infrequent
   (5) Change in accounting method
b. Prepare an income statement using the single-step format, and assess the persistence of each item on the income statement.

P13–5

(Disclosing extraordinary items)

In its 1997 financial report Meeks Company reported $850,000 under the line item "Extraordinary losses" on the income statement. The company's tax rate is 35 percent. The footnote pertaining to extraordinary losses indicates that the $850,000 loss, before tax, is comprised of the following items.

1. A loss of $260,000 incurred on a warehouse in Florida damaged in a hurricane.
2. A loss of $150,000 incurred when Meeks sold the assets of a business segment.
3. A loss of $225,000 incurred when a warehouse in Iowa was blown up by a disgruntled employee.
4. Accounts receivable written off in the amount of $125,000.
5. A loss of $90,000 incurred when one of the company's distribution centers in Arizona was damaged by a flood.

REQUIRED:

a. Discuss how each of these items should be disclosed in the financial statements, including whether or not they should be disclosed net of tax.
b. Show how the "extraordinary items" section of the income statement should have been reported.

P13–6

(Disclosing net of tax, and the earnings-per-share calculation)

Woodland Farm Corporation has the following items to include in its financial statements.

	DEBIT	CREDIT
Extraordinary Loss from a Flood	250,000	
Extraordinary Gain from Bond Retirement		55,000
Sale of Inventory		250,000
Loss on Disposal of Business Segment	100,000	
Income Effect Due to Change in Accounting Method		80,000
Advertising Expense	50,000	
Income Earned by Disposed Business Segment		150,000

None of the listed amounts include any income tax effects. The company's tax rate is 35 percent.

REQUIRED:

a.   Describe how each item above would be disclosed on the income statement or statement of retained earnings.
b.   Compute the tax effect of each of the items that should be disclosed net of tax. What dollar amount would be shown on the financial statements for each of these items?
c.   Assume that income from continuing operations (after tax) was $600,000, and 200,000 shares of common stock were outstanding during the year. Provide the earnings-per-share calculation.

P13–7

(Intraperiod tax allocation, income tax expense, and income tax liability)

The following information has been obtained from the internal financial records of MTM Company.

Retained earnings, December 31, 1996	$1,259,000
Dividends declared and paid during 1997	100,000
Dividends declared during 1997 but not paid	75,000
Dividends declared during 1996 and paid in 1997	90,000
1997 income from continuing operations (before taxes)	850,000
Extraordinary losses in 1997 (before tax effect)	135,000

The company's tax rate is 35 percent. Assume that financial accounting income equals income for tax purposes.

REQUIRED:

a.   What is the company's net income for the year ended December 31, 1997?
b.   Compute income tax expense reported in MTM's 1997 income statement.
c.   Prepare a reconciliation of retained earnings for the year ended December 31, 1997.
d.   Assume that the Income Tax Liability account had a balance of $70,000 on January 1, 1997, and that tax payments of $200,000 were made during 1997. What should be the balance in this account on December 31, 1997?

P13–8

(Income effect due to a change in depreciation methods)

On January 1, 1992, Boxer Corporation purchased some manufacturing equipment for $3,000,000. The equipment was estimated to have a salvage value of $500,000 and a useful life of ten years. The company used the straight-line method of depreciation for both book and tax purposes. On December 31, 1996, Boxer Corporation decided that it should use the double-declining-balance method for both book and tax purposes. The company's tax rate is 35 percent.

REQUIRED:

a.   Compute depreciation expense and accumulated depreciation for 1992, 1993, 1994, and 1995 using both the straight-line method and the double-declining-balance method.
b.   Prepare the journal entry (or entries) that would be recorded on December 31, 1996, to record the change from the straight-line method to the double-declining-balance method for both book and tax purposes.
c.   How and where on the financial statements would the income effect of this change be disclosed?

P13–9

(Preparing an income statement)

Tom Brown, controller of Microbiology Labs, informs you that the company has sold a segment of its business. Mr. Brown also provides you with the following information for 1997.

	CONTINUING OPERATIONS	DISCONTINUED SEGMENT
Sales	$10,000,000	$850,000
Cost of goods sold	2,500,000	600,000
Operating expenses	750,000	100,000
Loss on sale of office equipment	60,000	—
Gain on disposal of discontinued segment		250,000

ADDITIONAL INFORMATION

The following information is not reflected in any of the above amounts.
1. Microbiology Labs is subject to a 35 percent tax rate.
2. Microbiology Labs switched from the straight-line to the double-declining-balance method of depreciation for financial reporting purposes. The company already uses double-declining-balance for tax purposes, and the cumulative effect of this change on income is a decrease of $230,000.
3. During 1997, Microbiology Labs retired outstanding bonds that were to mature in 1999. The company incurred a loss of $80,000, prior to taxes, on the retirement of the bonds.
4. Microbiology Labs owns several apple orchards as part of its operations. During 1997 the company's apple crop was destroyed by an infestation of a rare insect. This unusual and infrequent loss, prior to taxes, totaled $800,000.
5. Two million shares of common stock were outstanding throughout 1997.

REQUIRED:

Prepare an income statement for the year ended December 31, 1997, including the recommended earnings-per-share disclosures. In terms of the objectives of financial accounting, comment on the usefulness of each of the different measures of income.

P13–10

(Comprehensive problem)

Laidig Industries has prepared the following unadjusted trial balance as of December 31, 1997.

	DEBIT	CREDIT
Cash	$110,000	
Accounts Receivable	340,000	
Allowance for Doubtful Accounts		$ 50,000
Inventory (balance 1/1/97)	467,000	
Prepaid Insurance	60,000	
Fixed Assets	850,000	
Accumulated Depreciation		287,000
Accounts Payable		200,000
Dividends Payable		45,000
Bonds Payable		500,000
Common Stock		100,000
Retained Earnings		673,000
Sales		1,256,000
Gain on Sale of Land		76,000
Extraordinary Loss	35,000	
Income Effect Due to Change in Accounting Principle	60,000	
Purchases	750,000	
Administrative Expenses	100,000	
Selling Expenses	255,000	
Interest Expense	25,000	
Dividends	135,000	

ADDITIONAL INFORMATION

1. A physical count of inventory on December 31, 1997, indicated that the company had $480,000 of inventory on hand.
2. An aging of accounts receivable indicates that $75,000 is uncollectible.
3. The company uses straight-line depreciation. The assets have a ten-year life and zero salvage value.
4. The company used a third of the remaining insurance policy during 1997.
5. The company pays interest for its bond payable on December 31 of every year. The coupon rate and the effective rate are both 10 percent per year.
6. The company's tax rate is 35 percent. All income tax charges are recorded at the end of the year.
7. 200,000 shares of common stock were outstanding during 1997.

REQUIRED:

Prepare the following:

a. The necessary adjusting and closing entries on December 31, 1997.
b. An income statement including recommended earnings per share disclosures.
c. A statement of retained earnings.
d. In terms of the objectives of financial accounting, discuss the usefulness of the various measures of income included on the statement.

CASES

C13–1

(Public earnings announcements)

On November 17, 1995 *The Wall Street Journal* reported:

"Kmart Corp., hurt by the cost of getting rid of discontinued merchandise and closing stores, posted a $69 million third quarter loss on a 2.5% sales increase. The discount retailer's loss would have been greater except for a $48 million gain from the sale of its equity interest in Sports Authority, Inc. . . . [However] . . . Wall Street did not punish Kmart's stock price."

REQUIRED:

a. Discuss the relevant issues involved in deciding where on the income statement to disclose the gain on the sale of the equity interest in Sports Authority, Inc.
b. The same week that Kmart announced its loss, DuPont posted a 19% increase in third quarter net income, which led to a 6 percent drop in its stock price. Explain how Wall Street could have viewed Kmart's announcement favorably and DuPont's unfavorably.

C13–2

(Changing accounting principles/methods)

In 1994 Owens-Corning Fiberglas changed its method of accounting for the cost of rebuilding its glass melting furnaces, which increased that year's income by $177 million before recognizing the tax effect. In 1994, the company's effective tax rate was 31 percent.

REQUIRED:

a. What dollar amount of gain due to the accounting change was reported on the income statement by the company?
b. Where on the income statement was this amount disclosed, and in what other places in the financial report could additional information about the change be found?
c. Owens-Corning reported net income in 1994, 1993, and 1992 of $159 million, $131 million, and $73 million, respectively. Do you believe that this accounting change was voluntary? If so, identify a reporting strategy that the company may be following.
d. How should investors react to earnings increases due solely to accounting changes?

C13–3

(Extraordinary losses)

Weyerhaeuser Company is principally engaged in the growing and harvesting of timber and the manufacture, distribution, and sale of forest products. When Mount St. Helens, a volcano located in Washington State, erupted, 68,000 acres of the company's standing timber, logs, buildings, and equipment were destroyed. As a result, the company recognized a $36 million (net of tax) extraordinary loss on its income statement.

REQUIRED:
a. What must have been true for Weyerhaeuser to classify this event as *extraordinary*?
b. If Mount St. Helens continues to erupt periodically, would future related losses necessarily be classified by Weyerhaeuser as extraordinary? Why or why not?
c. At the same time of the eruption, Weyerhaeuser's income tax rate was approximately 48 percent. Compute the entire loss (ignoring the tax effect) incurred by the company and provide the journal entries prepared by the company's accountants to record the loss and the related income tax effect.

C13–4

(Disclosing nonoperating items on the income statement)

Several years ago PepsiCo's earnings either rose or fell, depending upon the source of the information. Standard & Poor's reported that PepsiCo experienced a 25 percent earnings gain while Value Line, another investor service, reported that PepsiCo experienced a 7 percent loss. The discrepancy involved a "normal but nonrecurring charge" taken by PepsiCo to write down foreign bottling assets. Standard & Poor's ignored the charge in its earning calculation, while Value Line included the charge.

REQUIRED:
a. Provide reasonable arguments that could have been used by Standard & Poor's and Value Line to support the decision either to ignore or include the charge in the calculation of PepsiCo's income.
b. Briefly describe the categories comprising a complete income statement and explain how such categories are usually disclosed.
c. *Forbes* (May 21, 1984) reports that "most financial analysts [are not concerned about] the geographic location of such items on the income statement." It is only important that they be disclosed. Explain why financial analysts might take such a position; at the same time, however, provide an argument suggesting that the specific location of an item on the income statement is important in an economic sense. State your argument in terms of earnings persistence and how income numbers are used on contracts.

C13–5

(Profits and stock prices)

A recent Associated Press release (June 13, 1992) noted:

Many Wall Street analysts have been raising their estimates of corporate profits lately, but the projections of the stock market outlook aren't all going up at the same time. In fact, while they are raising their sights on what businesses can earn for their shareholders, some observers have lowered their expectations for the market.

One particular analyst explains this apparent inconsistency by noting:

An impending rise in profits may mean little to stocks if the market has already anticipated those gains.

REQUIRED:
Discuss the relationship between reported profits and the stock prices of publicly traded companies.

C13–6

(Reporting strategies and unusual items)

The 1994, 1993, and 1992 income statements of Scott Paper Company were provided in Figure 13–7.

REQUIRED:
Review the statements and answer the following questions.
a. Identify a reporting strategy that Scott appeared to use in 1993, and support your choice with specific examples.
b. Note that in 1993 the company disclosed a gain on the adoption of an accounting standard on income taxes that was recently mandated by the FASB. Explain why the recognition of this gain is not inconsistent with the strategy you identified in (a).

C13–7

(Litigation, reported income, and stock prices)

In 1990 Eastman Kodak recorded a third quarter net loss of $206 million, but at the same time posted a 22 percent rise in operating earnings to $835 million. Much of the loss was due to a $909.5 million charge taken to cover the costs associated with a patent infringement ruling, where Kodak was ordered to pay almost $1 billion to Polaroid for infringing on Polaroid's instant photography patents. The dollar amount awarded Polaroid was far below the company's multi-billion dollar claim. Kodak's shares jumped $1.25 to $29.75 in response to the news.

REQUIRED:

a. Where on Kodak's income statement should the charge be disclosed, and should the amount be reported net of tax? If so, assume a 34 percent tax rate and compute the net amount.
b. The patent infringement case between Kodak and Polariod was well publicized and extended over several years. How do you think this situation was reported in Kodak's 1989 annual report? In Polaroid's 1989 annual report?
c. Explain why Kodak's stock could have increased in value in response to news that the company reported a $206 net loss for the quarter.

C13–8

(Management's discretionary reporting and investing decisions)

In 1988 Pennzoil Company was awarded $3 billion cash in settlement of all litigation between Pennzoil and Texaco arising out of Texaco's interference with Pennzoil's contractual rights to purchase a minority interest in Getty Oil Company. A $1.67 billion gain was reported as an extraordinary item on Pennzoil's 1988 income statement. That same year Pennzoil's management and board of directors completed a strategic review of the company, concluding that certain charges should be recorded. These charges included write-downs for asset impairments and abandonments of $387 million, write-downs of refinery assets of $115 million, and miscellaneous other write-downs in the amount of $46 million. These charges were disclosed in the operating section of the income statement.

REQUIRED:

a. Why was the dollar amount recorded on the income statement for the $3 billion litigation award considerably less than $3 billion?
b. Provide a plausible explanation for why Pennzoil decided to record several significant write-downs in 1988, the same year when they received such a large litigation settlement.
c. In 1989 Pennzoil's income from continuing operations was an astounding $235 million, far above the levels of any previous year. Late that same year the company decided to divest itself of a wholly-owned subsidiary, Purolator Products Company, and recognized a loss of almost $132 million on the sale. Provide a plausible explanation for why Pennzoil would decide to sell Purolator Products in 1989 instead of 1990.
d. Consider Pennzoil's decisions discussed in (b) and (c) above and comment on any similarities you might notice.

C13–9

(Foreign currency fluctuations)

The 1994 annual report of Hasbro, a world leader in toy manufacturing, reported:

"The Company's growth in the international marketplace approximated 10% in 1994 following a marginal decrease experienced in 1993. European growth was led by the U.K., France, Italy, and Spain while elsewhere Mexico was the most significant, in local currency up more than 60%. During 1994, changes in foreign currency rates had a positive impact of approximately $19 million while in 1993 they negatively affected revenues by approximately $107 million."

REQUIRED:

a. What aspect about foreign exchange gains and losses is very evident in this quote?
b. Hasbro reported net income of $175 million and $200 million in 1994 and 1993, respectively. Would you consider foreign currency gains and losses to be an important part of the company's reported earnings? Discuss how your answer influenced your assessment of the company's earnings persistence.

C13–10

(The annual report of MCI)

Review the annual report of MCI and answer the following questions.

a. What is the trend in MCI's earnings from 1992–1994? Which definition of earnings did you use and why?

b. What dollar amounts on MCI's 1994, 1993, and 1992 income statements correspond to net income from continuing operations?

c. Compute the total loss (ignoring the income tax benefit) recognized by MCI on the early debt redemptions in 1993.

d. Provide the numerator and denominator for the earnings per share dollar amounts disclosed for 1994 ($1.32), 1993 ($1.04), and 1992 ($1.11).

THE STATEMENT OF CASH FLOWS

LEARNING OBJECTIVES

LO 1 Describe the basic structure and format of the statement of cash flows.

LO 2 Define cash flows from operating, investing, and financing activities.

LO 3 Explain how the statement of cash flows complements the other financial statements and how it can be used by those interested in the financial condition of a company.

LO 4 Identify the important investing and financing transactions that do not appear on the statement of cash flows, and describe how they are reported.

LO 5 Describe the economic consequences associated with the statement of cash flows.

LO 6 Express the statement of cash flows in terms of the basic accounting equation, and understand how to prepare a statement of cash flows from the information contained in two balance sheets, an income statement, and a statement of retained earnings.

L O   1 The statement of cash flows contains a summary of the transactions entered into by a company over a period of time that involve the Cash account. It is designed to highlight the cash flows associated with three aspects of the company's economic activities: (1) operations, (2) investments, and (3) financing. The basic structure of the statement of cash flows is provided in Figure 14–1. The reported numbers were taken from the 1994 annual report of The Walt Disney Company.

FIGURE 14–1	THE WALT DISNEY COMPANY
Sample statement of cash flows	STATEMENT OF CASH FLOWS FOR THE YEAR ENDED DECEMBER 31, 1994 (IN MILLIONS)

Cash provided (used) by operating activities	$ 2,807.3
Cash provided (used) by investing activities	(2,886.7)
Cash provided (used) by financing activities	(96.7)
Increase (decrease) in cash	$ (176.1)
Cash—beginning of year	363.0
Cash—end of year	$ 186.9

Recall that the statement of cash flows has already been presented and briefly discussed. Chapter 1 introduced the statement and provided an example. Chapter 2 discussed the basic nature of the statement and related it to the income statement, balance sheet, and statement of retained earnings. Chapter 3 described how it can be interpreted to assess solvency, and Chapter 5 briefly explained how a statement of cash flows can be prepared from the cash T-account. Thus, you have already been exposed to the fundamentals of the statement of cash flows. This chapter provides a more complete discussion of the nature of the statement, how it can be used, and how it is prepared.

The statement of cash flows is a relatively new addition to the set of financial accounting statements required under generally accepted accounting principles. It was established as a standard of financial reporting in 1987 when the Financial Accounting Standards Board decided (in FASB Statement No. 95, *Statement of Cash Flows*) to modify the statement of changes in financial position, which had been required since 1971.[1]

THE DEFINITION OF CASH

Chapter 6 of this text defines cash for purposes of balance sheet disclosure and points out that it consists of coin, currency, and available funds on deposit at the bank. Negotiable instruments like money orders, certified checks, cashiers' checks, personal checks, and bank drafts are also considered cash. The total of these items as of the balance sheet date is the cash amount that appears on the balance sheet.

When preparing the statement of cash flows, companies commonly consider as cash the items already mentioned as well as certain **cash equivalents**, which include

---

1. Financial Accounting Standards Board, Statement of Financial Accounting Standard No. 95, *The Statement of Cash Flows*, (Stamford, Conn.: FASB, 1987).

commercial paper and other debt investments with maturities of less than three months.[2] They do so because these items can be converted to cash immediately; for all intents and purposes, therefore, they are virtually the same as cash. In the remainder of this chapter, where we illustrate the statement of cash flows, we will also treat cash equivalents as cash. The following excerpt, which represents a typical description of these cash equivalents, is from the 1994 annual report of Procter & Gamble Company.

Highly liquid investments with maturities of three months or less when purchased are considered to be cash equivalents.

A GENERAL DESCRIPTION OF THE STATEMENT OF CASH FLOWS

LO 2 Take a moment now and refer back to Chapter 2. It describes the statement of cash flows in terms of the other financial statements, explaining the change in the cash balance from one balance sheet date to the next. Figure 14–2 illustrates the statement of cash flows more completely. This statement is divided into three sections (operating activities, investing activities, and financing activities) and shows the cash inflow and outflow categories that normally comprise each section.

FIGURE 14–2	XYZ CORPORATION STATEMENT OF CASH FLOWS FOR THE YEAR ENDED DECEMBER 31, 1996

Standard statement of cash flows

Operating activities:		
Cash received from customers	$ 7,000	
Cash paid for operations (to suppliers, employees, and others)	(5,200)	
Cash provided (used) by other operating items	(870)	
Net cash provided (used) by operating activities		$ 930
Investing activities:		
Cash outflows for the purchase of noncurrent assets	$(3,000)	
Cash inflows from sale of noncurrent assets	400	
Net cash provided (used) by investing activities		(2,600)
Financing activities:		
Cash inflows from borrowings	$ 3,000	
Cash inflows from stock issuances	2,000	
Cash outflows for debt retirements	(1,460)	
Cash outflows for treasury stock purchases	(1,550)	
Cash outflows for dividend payments	(200)	
Net cash provided (used) by financing activities		1,790
Net increase (decrease) in cash and cash equivalents		$ 120
Cash and cash equivalents at the beginning of the year		100
Cash and cash equivalents at the end of the year		$ 220

2. Commercial paper and short-term debt instruments are discussed in Chapter 10. Also, some corporations, like McDonnell Douglas, Eli Lilly, and Walt Disney, also include short-term investments, such as marketable securities, in the definition of cash for purposes of the statement of cash flows. Such a practice is acceptable under generally accepted accounting principles because marketable securities, by definition, are highly liquid.

CASH PROVIDED (USED) BY OPERATING ACTIVITIES

Cash provided (used) by **operating activities** includes those cash inflows and outflows associated directly with the acquisition and sale of the company's inventories and services. This category includes the cash receipts from sales and accounts receivable as well as cash payments for the purchase of inventories, payments on accounts payable, selling and administrative activities, and interest and taxes. In general, the items appearing in this section also appear on the income statement. Keep in mind, however, that the dollar amounts associated with these items on the statement of cash flows usually differ from those on the income statement, which is prepared on an accrual basis.

THE DIRECT METHOD

The statement of cash flows illustrated in Figure 14–2 was prepared using the **direct method**. It is so called because the computation of cash provided (used) by operating activities ($930) consists of cash inflows and outflows that can be traced *directly* to the Cash T-account. For example, the $7,000 collected from customers, the $5,200 paid for operations, and the $870 used for other operating items all represent aggregate totals of journal entries that were initially recorded in the journal and posted to the Cash account in the ledger.

THE INDIRECT METHOD

Another method of computing and disclosing cash provided (used) by operating activities that is acceptable under GAAP is called the **indirect method**. Under this method, cash provided (used) by operating activities is computed *indirectly*, by beginning with the net income figure, which appears on the income statement, and adjusting it for the differences between cash flows and accruals. The indirect method of computing cash from operating activities is illustrated in Figure 14–3.

FIGURE 14–3	**Operating activities:**	
Cash from operating activities: Indirect method	Net income	**$1,085**
	Noncash charges to noncurrent accounts:	
	Depreciation, amortization, and other noncash	
	charges on noncurrent items	$ 400	
	Book losses	50	
	Book gains	(450)	0
	Changes in current accounts other than cash:	
	Net decreases (increases) in current assets	$ 105	
	Net increases (decreases) in current liabilities	(260)	(155)
	Net cash provided (used) by operating activities		$ 930

In general, items added back to net income in the computation of Cash provided (used) by operating activities (e.g., depreciation, amortization, book losses, and decreases in current assets) decrease net income on the income statement but involve no cash outflows. Items subtracted from net income in this computation (e.g., book gains, decreases in current liabilities) increase net income on the income statement but involve no cash inflows. Note also that these adjustments are separated into two categories: (1) noncash charges to the noncurrent accounts and (2) changes in current accounts. The first category includes depreciation and amortization charges as well as book gains and losses recognized on the transfer of long-term assets and liabilities. The second category includes the changes during the period in the current asset and current liability accounts other than cash.

Both the direct and the indirect methods result in the same dollar amount ($930) for cash provided (used) by operating activities; in that respect, they simply represent two different forms of presentation. In fact, when the FASB made the statement of cash flows a requirement, it allowed either the direct or the indirect method. If the direct method is chosen, however, the FASB requires that it be accompanied by a schedule of the adjustments that reconcile net income to cash provided (used) by operating activities. This schedule can appear either in the footnotes to the financial statements or on the face of the statement itself. Also, generally accepted accounting principles require that under either method cash amounts paid for taxes and interest must be separately disclosed.

Since the adjustments on this schedule are the same as those disclosed under the indirect method, the direct method (including the accompanying schedule) discloses more about the changes in the Cash account than the indirect method. To encourage increased disclosure and what the FASB believes to be a more straightforward presentation, it has recommended that companies use the direct method. However, the vast majority of major U.S. companies choose not to follow this recommendation; they use the indirect method probably because it requires fewer disclosures.[3]

CASH PROVIDED (USED) BY INVESTING ACTIVITIES

Cash provided (used) by **investing activities** includes the cash inflows and outflows associated with the purchase and sale of a company's noncurrent assets.[4] This section includes the cash effects from purchases and sales of long-term investments, long-lived assets, and intangible assets. The statement of cash flows in Figure 14–2, for example, shows that $3,000 was used to purchase such items, and $400 was collected from selling noncurrent assets. These cash inflows and outflows can all be traced to entries in the Cash account in the company's ledger.

CASH PROVIDED (USED) BY FINANCING ACTIVITIES

Cash provided (used) by **financing activities** includes cash inflows and outflows associated with a company's two sources of outside capital: liabilities and contributed capital. This category primarily includes the cash inflows associated with borrowings and equity issuances as well as the cash outflows related to debt repayments, treasury stock purchases, and dividend payments. The statement of cash flows in Figure 14–2 shows that the company borrowed $3,000, raised $2,000 by issuing stock, made principal payments on debt in the amount of $1,460, used $1,550 to purchase treasury stock, and paid cash dividends of $200. These cash flows can also be traced to the Cash account in the company's ledger.

Note also that cash interest payments are not included in this section, even though they represent a cost of financing. Instead, such payments are included in the operating section of the statement of cash flows. This practice might be questioned because it confuses the distinction between financing and operating activities. Perhaps the FASB chose to classify interest payments as operating activities to preserve the correspondence between the items on the income statement and those comprising the

---

3. *Accounting Trends and Techniques* (1994) reports that, of the 600 major U.S. companies surveyed, only fifteen used the direct form of presentation. The remaining 585 all used the indirect form. The statement of cash flows reported by MCI, which is included at the end of this text, is based on the direct form of presentation.

4. Investing activities can include the purchase and/or sale of securities listed as short-term, but frequently these investments are included as cash equivalents, and in many cases they are not material.

operating section of the statement of cash flows. Figure 14–4 provides an example of a recently published statement of cash flows prepared under the indirect form of presentation. It was taken from the 1994 annual report of Sprint.

FIGURE 14–4

Example of statement of cash flows: Indirect method

SPRINT
CONSOLIDATED STATEMENTS OF CASH FLOWS

For the Years Ended December 31, (in millions)	1994	1993	1992
Operating Activities			
Net income	$ 890.7	$ 54.9	$ 502.8
Adjustments to reconcile net income to net cash provided by operating activities			
Depreciation and amortization	1,478.4	1,358.7	1,391.5
Deferred income taxes and investment tax credits	74.6	(34.5)	3.0
Gain on sale of investment in equity securities	(34.7)	—	—
Gain on divestiture of telephone properties	—	—	(81.1)
Extraordinary losses on early extinguishments of debt	—	20.4	14.2
Cumulative effect of changes in accounting principles	—	384.2	(22.7)
Changes in operating assets and liabilities			
Accounts receivable, net	(239.2)	(185.8)	257.8
Inventories and other current assets	(84.5)	(42.7)	(13.9)
Accounts payable, accrued expenses and other current liabilities	197.8	362.0	126.8
Noncurrent assets and liabilities, net	134.3	135.1	152.3
Other, net	54.6	60.1	(80.1)
Net cash provided by operating activities	2,472.0	2,112.4	2,250.6
Investing Activities			
Capital expenditures	(2,015.9)	(1,594.7)	(1,466.2)
Proceeds from sale of investment in equity securities	117.7	—	—
Equity investments	(49.2)	9.0	(1.7)
Acquisition of Limited Partnership minority interest	—	—	(250.0)
Proceeds from divestiture of telephone properties	—	—	114.0
Other, net	(34.5)	17.3	26.0
Net cash used by investing activities	(1,981.9)	(1,568.4)	(1,577.9)
Financing Activities			
Proceeds from long-term debt	107.9	840.4	951.2
Retirements from long-term debt	(597.0)	(1,589.0)	(1,257.4)
Net increase in notes payable and commercial paper	321.5	393.5	147.0
Payment of note payable to minority partner	—	—	(280.0)
Proceeds from common stock issued	42.7	70.8	51.6
Proceeds from employees stock purchase installments	33.1	28.3	13.2
Dividends paid	(349.4)	(347.1)	(300.1)
Other, net	(2.4)	7.1	4.7
Net cash used by financing activities	(443.6)	(596.0)	(669.8)
Increase (Decrease) in Cash and Equivalents	46.5	(52.0)	2.9
Cash and Equivalents at Beginning of Year	76.8	128.8	125.9
Cash and Equivalents at End of Year	$ 123.3	$ 76.8	$ 128.8
Supplemental Cash Flows Information			
Cash paid for interest	$ 418.1	$ 453.6	$ 507.5
Cash paid for income taxes	$ 435.1	$ 292.4	$ 269.0
Noncash Financing Activities			
Common stock contributed to employee savings plans, at market	$ 31.0	$ 39.0	$ 28.0

HOW THE STATEMENT OF CASH FLOWS COMPLEMENTS THE INCOME STATEMENT AND BALANCE SHEET

LO 3 On several occasions we have discussed the important distinction between operating and capital (investing and financing) transactions and how information about these two activities is useful to investors, creditors, and other interested parties. We have also pointed out the usefulness of information prepared on both the accrual and cash basis. As Figure 14–5 illustrates, combining the three types of transactions (operating, investing, and financing) with the two measurement bases (accrual and cash) gives rise to six kinds of potentially useful information.

FIGURE 14–5	MEASUREMENT BASIS	TYPE OF TRANSACTION		
Six kinds of useful information		OPERATING	INVESTING	FINANCING
	Cash	1 (SCF)	2 (SCF)	3 (SCF)
	Accrual	4 (IS/BS)	5 (BS)	6 (BS)

SCF = Statement of cash flows   IS = Income statement   BS = Balance sheet

The income statement provides a summary of a company's operating transactions on an accrual basis (cell 4). The balance sheet represents the accumulated accruals of the company's operating, investing, and financing transactions as of a particular point in time (cells 4, 5, and 6). Comparing two balance sheets at different points of time can provide an indication of the company's investing and financing activities during the intervening time period (cells 5 and 6).

Note that the income statement and balance sheet do not appear in cells 1, 2, or 3 because these statements indicate little about the cash effects of the company's operating, investing, and financing activities. The statement of cash flows is designed to fill this void. Professor Loyd Heath, whose writings did much to motivate the development of the statement of cash flows, describes it as being *complementary* to the income statement and balance sheet, "reporting a different type of information."[5]

The FASB's move to require the statement of cash flows was primarily a response to a perceived lack of what many considered to be important and useful cash flow information. Diana Kahn, project manager for the FASB, said, "Cash flow is one of the best measures of corporate liquidity," and Pat McConnell, associate director of a major securities firm, commented that the FASB's decision to require the statement of cash flows "will generally be a boon for financial analysts who want to know more about the current cash position of the companies they cover."[6] An article published in *The Wall Street Journal* (October 2, 1990) entitled "Why Cash Is King in the Current Climate" notes that during a recession:

companies with high amounts of cash relative to debt are likely to be coveted by investors as economic growth turns increasingly sluggish. Cash may be a new gauge of value in the stock market.

---

5. Loyd Heath, "Let's Scrap the Funds Statement," *The Journal of Accountancy* (October 1978), pp. 94–103.
6. Lee Burton, "FASB Rule Requires Public Companies to Issue Annual Cash-Flow Statements," *The Wall Street Journal*, November 23, 1987, p. 10.

HOW THE STATEMENT OF CASH FLOWS CAN BE USED

The statement of cash flows is used primarily to assess performance in two basic areas: (1) a company's ability to generate cash and (2) the effectiveness of a company's cash management. The ability to generate cash is determined by the strength of the company's operating activities as well as its **financial flexibility**, which reflects the company's capacity to borrow, issue equity, and sell nonoperating assets (e.g., investments). During 1994, for example, Alcoa generated $1.39 billion through its operating activities, which was sufficient to finance $300 million of additional investments, reduce $600 million of its outstanding debts, pay a $300 dividend, and increase its cash balance by $200 million. L.A. Gear, on the other hand, generated negative cash flow from operations several years ago, but had enough financial flexibility to finance over $6 million in capital expenditures, primarily through common stock issuance.

Effective cash management requires that two competing objectives be balanced. On one hand, cash must be available to meet debts as they come due. That is, **solvency** must be maintained. On the other hand, cash must be invested in productive assets that provide returns. Sources of cash include the sale of inventories and services, borrowings, equity issuances, and the selling of long-term assets. Uses of cash include purchasing and manufacturing inventories, covering selling and administrative costs, making debt interest and principal payments, purchasing long-term assets, purchasing treasury stock, and paying dividends. Effective cash management involves managing these cash sources and uses in a way that provides a high return without bearing too great a risk of insolvency.

ANALYZING THE STATEMENT OF CASH FLOWS

The statement of cash flows provides information about a company's ability to generate cash and the effectiveness of its cash management by explaining the change in the cash balance over a period of time, in terms of the operating, investing, and financing activities that occurred during that time. Questions like the following can be answered by referring to the statement of cash flows: Is the company's cash balance increasing or decreasing? What portion of the company's cash is generated through operations, the sale of investments, or the issuance of debt and equity securities? What portions of the company's cash payments go toward supporting operations, capital investments, repayments of debt, purchasing treasury stock, and dividends? To gain a general understanding of how the statement of cash flows helps to answer such questions, refer to Figure 14–6, which summarizes the 1994 statements of cash flows for ten different companies, from each of the three major industry groups.

Note first that nine of the ten companies use the indirect form of presentation. Also, in all cases except Kmart, cash from operations exceeds net income, and in several cases by quite a large amount. Most of this difference is due to depreciation, which reduces net income but does not represent an operating cash outflow. AT&T, for example, reported over $4 billion of depreciation. In the case of Kmart, a substantial increase in inventories is the primary reason why cash from operations is less than net income.

Again, all companies except Kmart report negative cash from investments. These companies are expanding their operations by investing in productive assets and other companies. Large negative dollar amounts in this area of the statement often indicate an aggressive growth strategy. Citicorp, for example, increased its loan portfolio by

FIGURE 14–6

The statement of cash flows (ten major U.S. corporations)

(DOLLARS IN MILLIONS) COMPANY	NET INCOME	CASH FROM OPERATIONS	CASH FROM INVESTMENTS	CASH FROM FINANCING	NET CASH CHANGE	METHOD (DIRECT/ INDIRECT)
MANUFACTURING						
Goodyear	$ 567	$ 765	$ (496)	$ (196)	$ 62	I
Colgate-Palmolive	580	829	(458)	(343)	26	I
Texaco	910	2,859	(1,105)	(1,845)	(84)	I
RETAIL						
May Depart.	782	999	(815)	(175)	9	I
Kmart	260	76	1,160	(1,205)	31	I
Sears, Roebuck	1,454	1,930	(3,458)	1,133	(398)	I
SERVICES						
AT&T	4,710	8,956	(9,755)	1,314	537	I
Citicorp	3,366	3,538	(16,838)	14,905	1,634	I
FedEx	204	767	(394)	(136)	238	I
MCI	795	2,355	(4,917)	3,826	1,264	D

$18 billion; Sears made a substantial investment in available-for-sale securities; and AT&T invested primarily in capital expenditures and long-term receivables. Kmart, which was experiencing cash flow problems, generated cash by selling equity investments held in other companies.

Cash from financing activities is almost evenly split across the ten companies—four are positive and six are negative. Citicorp financed its aggressive growth by issuing long-term debt and increasing deposits; MCI issued common stock and long-term notes. On the other hand, Texaco and Kmart reported net financing cash outflows. Texaco reduced its long-term debt and paid large dividends, while Kmart reduced its debts and capital leases and still managed to pay a reasonable dividend.

Overall, cash from operations generated by Goodyear, Colgate-Polmolive, Texaco, May Department Stores, and Federal Express was sufficient to finance their growth, reduce debts, and pay dividends—an indication that the solvency positions of these companies are strong. AT&T, Citicorp, MCI, and Sears show aggressive growth, but financing this growth required sources other than cash from operations. While these companies appear to be financially strong, their aggressive growth does introduce additional risks that should be evaluated by users. Kmart is involved in substantial restructuring. It made dividend payments and reduced outstanding debts, but it sold productive assets to finance these activities because it did not generate a large amount of cash from operations. These signs identify a company going through a period of transition.

THE IMPORTANCE OF CASH FROM OPERATING ACTIVITIES

The amount of cash generated through operating activities is especially important to financial statement users because the successful sale of a company's services or inventories is a prerequisite for a successful business. Also, while cash flows from investing and financing activities tend to vary from one year to the next, operating activities, by definition, are normal and expected to recur. Consequently, positive net cash flows from operations, especially across several periods of time, can indicate financial strength. As Figure 14–6 shows, operations are an important source of cash for major U.S. companies.

It is generally desirable to finance asset purchases and debt payments with cash generated from operations. Companies able to follow such a strategy consistently tend to have higher credit ratings and are generally viewed as financially more stable than those unable to do so. DuPont, for example, one of the ten largest companies in the world with a AAA credit rating, commented in a recent annual report:

Cash provided by operations was sufficient to finance the company's capital expenditures, repurchase 1,968,000 shares of the company's common stock, reduce borrowings, and pay dividends.

The management of AT&T, the largest communications company in the world, stated that same year:

Strong cash flow from operations permitted us to continue efforts toward increased financial flexibility. We redeemed $830 million of preferred stock and retired $147 million of long-term debt. Our external financing was limited to $343 million. Consequently, for the second consecutive year, we have reduced our utilization of external sources of financing.

THE IMPORTANCE OF SIGNIFICANT NONCASH TRANSACTIONS

LO 4 The statement of cash flows includes only those transactions that directly affect cash or cash equivalents. Many important transactions, however, neither increase nor decrease Cash and, as a result, are excluded from the face of the statement. For example, the purchase of a long-lived asset in exchange for a long-term note payable can be a significant capital transaction, yet as illustrated by the journal entry below, it has no effect on the Cash account.

Equipment (+A)	20,000	
Notes Payable (+L)		20,000

Purchased equipment financed with a long-term note.

Similarly, the acquisition of land in exchange for a note payable, the acquisition of a subsidiary by issuing stock, the payment of a debt with common stock, and the declaration of a dividend are capital transactions that are not found on the statement of cash flows.

These kinds of capital transactions can be very important to a company's financial condition, and the FASB requires in its standard on cash flows that they be described clearly in the footnotes to the financial statements. It is important that such information be accessible to readers who are interested in examining the financing and investing activities of a company.

For example, several years ago, MCI acquired Satellite Business Systems (SBS) and selected other assets from IBM. In exchange, MCI issued common stock and signed a note payable. No cash was exchanged in the transaction, and accordingly, neither the acquired assets nor the increases in the Common Stock and Notes Payable accounts appeared on MCI's statement of cash flows. However, the transaction was important enough to warrant disclosure, and MCI reported it directly below the statement of cash flows in the following manner.

Acquisition of SBS (in millions):

Common stock issued to acquire SBS	*$ 376*
Communications systems acquired	*(428)*
Other assets acquired	*(52)*
Current obligations assumed	*104*
Cash outflow to acquire SBS	*$ 0*

Important operating transactions that do not affect cash, like the sale or purchase of inventory on account, also do not appear directly on the statement of cash flows. However, the existence of such transactions can be determined by analyzing the adjustments that reconcile net income with cash flows provided (used) by operating activities. Such adjustments are discussed and illustrated later in the chapter.

THE STATEMENT OF CASH FLOWS: ECONOMIC CONSEQUENCES

LO 5 The economic consequences associated with the statement of cash flows result primarily from investors, creditors, and other interested parties using it to assess the investment potential and creditworthiness of companies and the equity and debt securities they issue. *Forbes* magazine reports: "a number of stock advisers are basing their work in part on cash flow . . . an investor who ignores cash flow in picking stocks is being deprived of one of the most valuable tools in an arsenal." Furthermore, many writers have claimed that had investors relied more heavily on cash flow numbers, instead of working capital and the current ratio, famous bankruptcies, like W.T. Grant, Penn Central, Sambo's Restaurants, AM Internationals, and Wickes might have been foreseen earlier.[7] A recent survey found: "The evidence could not be clearer. Investors use the statement of cash flows more, and the income statements less, than previously."[8]

The increasing importance of cash flow information to investors and creditors creates incentives for management to **window dress** the statement of cash flows. Such incentives can be troublesome because in the short run it is relatively easy for management to present a favorable cash position. Delaying payments on short-term payables, for example, can significantly boost the amount of cash provided (used) by operating activities. Selling investments, even if it is not in the stockholders' long-run interests, can increase cash inflows from investing activities, while delaying debt payments, and dividends can inflate cash from financing activities. Accounting Professors Edward Swanson and Richard Vangermeersch, for example, have stated: "the possibilities for manipulating the cash provided by operations figure, as well as other sources and uses of cash, are endless."[9]

Consequently, those who use the statement of cash flows must be careful not to place too much importance on the cash flows of a particular period, which can be manipulated. However, such manipulation is much less effective when statements are

7. Richard Greene and Paul Bornstein, "A Better Yardstick," *Forbes*, September 27, 1982, pp. 66, 69.

8. Marc J. Epstein and Moses L. Paun, "How Useful is the Statement of Cash Flows?," *Management Accounting*, July 1992, p. 52.

9. Edward P. Swanson and Richard Vangermeersch, "Correspondence Relating to 'Let's Scrap the Funds Statement'," *Journal of Accountancy* (December 1979), pp. 88–97.

viewed across several periods because payments that are delayed in one period must normally be paid in the next. For this reason the FASB requires that cash flow statements from at least the previous three years be disclosed in the report.

From management's standpoint, it is also important to realize that decisions designed to manipulate the disclosures on the statement of cash flows can be counterproductive. While such decisions may improve the appearance of a company's cash position in the current period, they can (1) represent poor business decisions, (2) make the cash position of the company look worse in the future, (3) reduce the credibility of the company and its financial reports in the eyes of investors, creditors, and other interested parties, and if fraudulent, (4) can expose management to future lawsuits. In addition, such manipulations may simply be unethical.

THE MECHANICS OF PREPARING THE STATEMENT OF CASH FLOWS

LO 6   In Chapter 5 of this text, we prepared a simple statement of cash flows by focusing on the cash effects of the individual transactions of the period. That is, we prepared the statement from the entries to the cash T-account. This section demonstrates how the statement of cash flows can be prepared when the analysis of individual transactions is either impractical or, in some cases, impossible. We show that the statement can be prepared primarily from the information contained in two balance sheets, the intervening income statement, and the statement of retained earnings. This method is followed by most companies, and the resulting statement of cash flows is the same as that prepared from analyzing the entries to the cash T-account. In most cases, however, the method we illustrate here is far more practical.

We explain this method by first showing that the change in the Cash account during a given period can be explained in terms of changes in the balances of the other accounts on the balance sheet. We then illustrate the procedure using the information contained in a set of financial statements.

A CONCEPTUAL DESCRIPTION OF THE STATEMENT OF CASH FLOWS

The statement of cash flows can be viewed as one way of explaining how the balance sheet at the beginning of a particular period became the balance sheet at the end of that period. It focuses on Cash, a specific balance sheet account, and consists of a series of line items that summarize how changes in the Cash account can be explained in terms of changes in the other balance sheet accounts.

Recall the basic accounting equation (assets = liabilities + stockholders' equity), which can be stated as follows.

$$A = L + SE$$

Total assets can be divided into cash and noncash assets, and stockholders' equity consists of contributed capital and retained earnings. The accounting equation, therefore, can also be expressed as follows. That is, cash (C) plus noncash assets (NA) is equal to liabilities (L) plus contributed capital (CC) plus retained earnings (RE).

$$C + NA = L + CC + RE$$

Liabilities (L) can be separated into current liabilities (CL) and long-term liabilities (LTL), and noncash assets (NA) can be separated into current noncash assets (CNA) and long-term noncash assets ($LTNA$). Thus the equation becomes:

$$C + CNA + LTNA = CL + LTL + CC + RE$$

This equation can be rearranged and expressed in terms of cash by adding $-CNA$ and $-LTNA$ to both sides. As a result, cash (C) equals current liabilities (CL) plus long-term liabilities (LTL) plus contributed capital (CC) plus retained earnings (RE) minus current noncash assets (CNA) minus long-term noncash assets ($LTNA$).

$$C = CL + LTL + CC + RE - CNA - LTNA$$

Changes in cash, therefore, can be expressed in terms of changes in the noncash balance sheet accounts.

$$\Delta C = \Delta CL + \Delta LTL + \Delta CC + \Delta RE - \Delta CNA - \Delta LTNA$$

The change in retained earnings (ΔRE) for a period is equal to revenues (R) less expenses (E) less dividends (D). In addition, changes in long-term liabilities (ΔLTL) can be separated into those affecting cash (ΔLTL_c) and those not affecting cash (ΔLTL_{nc}). In a similar manner, changes in long-term assets ($\Delta LTNA$) can be separated into those affecting cash ($\Delta LTNA_c$) and those not affecting cash ($\Delta LTNA_{nc}$). Inserting these substitutes in the preceding equation and rearranging the terms produces the equation contained in Figure 14–7, which represents a conceptual description of the statement of cash flows, expressed in terms of the changes in the noncash balance sheet accounts.

FIGURE 14–7

A conceptual description of the statement of cash flows

	Operating Activities		Investing Activities	Financing Activities
$\Delta C = \underbrace{R - E}$	$\underbrace{+ \Delta LTL_{nc} - \Delta LTNA_{nc}}$	$\underbrace{+ \Delta CL - \Delta CNA}$	$\underbrace{- \Delta LTNA_c}$	$\underbrace{+ \Delta LTL_c + \Delta CC - D}$
Net income	Noncash charges to noncurrent accounts (e.g., depreciation, amortization, gains and losses)	Changes in current accounts	Purchases and sales of long-term assets	Long-term borrowings and repayments, stock issuances and repurchases, and dividends

---

To illustrate how Figure 14–7 can be interpreted, review the statement of cash flows of Sprint contained in Figure 14–4. Note first that the indirect method of presentation is used, which means that the operating section begins with net earnings ($R - E$). The depreciation and amortization charges are then added to net earnings, each representing a decrease to a long-term noncash asset that did not affect Cash ($\Delta LTNA_{nc}$). For the same reason, book gains and losses, respectively, are subtracted from and added to net earnings. The changes in the current accounts other than Cash represent changes in noncash current assets (ΔCNA) and current liabilities (ΔCL).

In the computation of cash used in investing activities, the acquisition of property and purchase of investment securities represent changes in long-term assets accounts that affect Cash ($\Delta LTNA_c$). In the computation of cash used in financing activities, the borrowing transactions represent changes in long-term liabilities (ΔLTL_c). The treasury stock purchase and exercise of stock options represent changes in contributed capital (ΔCC). Dividends (D) were paid.

The algebraic description contained in Figure 14–7 shows that the statement of cash flows can be prepared from the information contained in two balance sheets, the income statement, and the statement of retained earnings. In the next section we illustrate how it is done.

DERIVING CASH FLOW FROM ACCRUAL FINANCIAL STATEMENTS

Figure 14–8 contains the December 31, 1996 and 1997 balance sheets of ABC Enterprises and the related income statement and statement of retained earnings. Additional information is disclosed in the section that appears below the statements.

In the sections that follow Figure 14–8, we prepare a statement of cash flows under both the direct and indirect methods from the information contained in Figure 14–8. Cash provided (used) by operating activities is derived first, followed by the

FIGURE 14–8	ABC ENTERPRISES, INC. BALANCE SHEETS FOR DECEMBER 31, 1996 AND 1997		
The financial statements of ABC Enterprises			

		1997	1996
ASSETS			
Cash		$ 5,900	$ 8,000
Accounts receivable		23,200	12,000
Less: Allowance for bad debts		(1,300)	(1,000)
Inventory		4,000	3,000
Prepaid Insurance		1,000	2,000
Land		30,000	20,000
Machinery		6,000	8,000
Less: Accumulated depreciation		(2,500)	(2,000)
Building		30,000	—
Less: Accumulated depreciation		(1,500)	—
Patent		6,000	8,000
Total assets		$100,800	$58,000
LIABILITIES AND STOCKHOLDERS' EQUITY			
Accounts payable		$ 9,000	$12,000
Accrued payables		3,000	1,500
Income taxes payable		200	500
Payments in advance		—	3,000
Dividends payable		3,000	1,000
Notes payable		24,000	25,000
Less: Discount on notes payable		(1,800)	(2,000)
Common stock		42,000	10,000
Additional paid-in capital		19,300	2,000
Retained earnings		2,100	6,000
Less: Treasury stock		—	(1,000)
Total liabilities and stockholders' equity		$100,800	$58,000

FIGURE 14-8
(Concluded)

ABC ENTERPRISES, INC.
INCOME STATEMENT
FOR THE YEAR ENDED DECEMBER 31, 1997

Sales		$ 32,000
Fees earned		3,000
Cost of goods sold		(11,000)
Gross profit		$ 24,000
Operating expenses:		
Miscellaneous expenses	$11,000	
Insurance expense	1,000	
Bad debt expense	1,100	
Depreciation expense (machinery)	1,000	
Depreciation expense (building)	1,500	
Amortization of patent	2,000	17,600
Net operating income		$ 6,400
Nonoperating revenues and expenses:		
Loss on sale of machinery	$ 100	
Interest expense	2,000	2,100
Net income from continuing operations		
before taxes		$ 4,300
Less: Income tax expense		1,200
Net income		$ 3,100

ABC ENTERPRISES, INC.
STATEMENT OF RETAINED EARNINGS
FOR PERIOD ENDING DECEMBER 31, 1997

Beginning retained earnings balance		$ 6,000
Plus: Net income		3,100
Less: Cash dividends	$ 3,000	
Stock dividends	4,000	(7,000)
Ending retained earnings balance		$ 2,100

Additional Information:
1. Two thousand shares of common stock ($10 par; $15 fair market value) were issued for a building early in 1997.
2. A 5% stock dividend on 4,000 outstanding shares was distributed late in 1997 when the fair market value of the $10 par value stock was $20 per share.
3. Treasury stock that was originally purchased for $1,000 was reissued for $1,300.

cash provided (used) by investing activities, and cash provided (used) by financing activities. In the figures that appear throughout these sections, italics are used to indicate dollar amounts taken directly from the information in Figure 14–8.

CASH PROVIDED (USED) BY OPERATING ACTIVITIES

This section analyzes the cash flows associated with each income statement account: Sales and Bad Debt Expense, Fees Earned, Cost of Goods Sold, Miscellaneous

Expenses, Insurance Expense, Depreciation of Machinery and of Building, Amortization of Patent, Loss on Sale of Machinery, Interest Expense, and Income Tax Expense.

SALES AND BAD DEBT EXPENSE

The cash inflow from sales can be determined by analyzing the changes in Accounts Receivable and Allowance for Bad Debts. Refer to the T-accounts and related journal entries in Figure 14–9.

FIGURE 14–9

Determining cash inflow from sales

TRANSACTIONS	ACCOUNTS	DEBIT (NET)	CREDIT (NET)
(1)	Accounts Receivable	32,000	
	Sales		32,000
(2)	Bad Debt Expense	1,100	
	Allowance for Bad Debts		1,100
(3)	Allowance for Bad Debts	800	
	Accounts Receivable		800
(4)	Cash	20,000	
	Accounts Receivable		20,000

Cash collections from sales: $20,000

The beginning and ending balances in Accounts Receivable and the Allowance for Bad Debts appear on the balance sheets in Figure 14–8. We assume that all sales were made on account, and therefore, $32,000 (see income statement) was debited to Accounts Receivable during the year. The $1,100 bad debt expense (see income statement) was credited to the Allowance for Bad Debts at year-end, which (when the beginning and ending balances in the allowance account are considered) implies that uncollectibles in the amount of $800 must have been written off and credited to Accounts Receivable. Therefore, an additional credit of Accounts Receivable of $20,000 must have been entered during the year. The corresponding debit represents cash receipts on outstanding accounts during the year.

FEES EARNED

The cash inflow related to Fees Earned can be determined by analyzing the change in the Payments in Advance account. Refer to Figure 14–10.

FIGURE 14–10

FIGURE 14–10

Determining cash inflow from fees earned

FEES EARNED		PAYMENTS IN ADVANCE	
(1) 3,000		(1) 3,000	3,000
			0

EFFECT ON ACCOUNTS

TRANSACTIONS	ACCOUNTS	DEBIT (NET)	CREDIT (NET)
(1)	Payments in Advance	3,000	
	Fees Earned		3,000

Cash collections from fees earned: $0

The beginning ($3,000) and ending ($0) balances in the Payments in Advance account appear on the balance sheets in Figure 14–8. The recognition of $3,000 in Fees Earned (see income statement) involved a $3,000 debit to Payments in Advance. This entry accounts for the entire change in the Payments in Advance account, indicating that no cash inflow was associated with fees earned.

COST OF GOODS SOLD

The cash outflow associated with Cost of Goods Sold can be determined by analyzing the changes in the Inventory and Accounts Payable accounts. Refer to Figure 14–11.

FIGURE 14–11

Determining cash outflow from inventory purchases

COST OF GOODS SOLD		INVENTORY		ACCOUNTS PAYABLE	
(1) 11,000		3,000			12,000
		(2) 12,000	(1) 11,000	(3) 15,000	(2) 12,000
		4,000			9,000

EFFECT ON ACCOUNTS

TRANSACTIONS	ACCOUNTS	DEBIT (NET)	CREDIT (NET)
(1)	Cost of Goods Sold	11,000	
	Inventory		11,000
(2)	Inventory	12,000	
	Accounts Payable		12,000
(3)	Accounts Payable	15,000	
	Cash		15,000

Cash paid to suppliers: $15,000

The beginning and ending balances in Inventory and Accounts Payable appear on the balance sheets in Figure 14–8. The $11,000 debit to Cost of Goods Sold (see income statement) was credited to Inventory, which (when the beginning and ending balances in the inventory account are considered) implies that inventory purchases of $12,000 must have been made during the year. Assuming that all inventory purchases were made on account, $12,000 must have been credited to Accounts Payable. Considering the beginning and ending balances in Accounts Payable, an additional debit of $15,000 must have been recognized during the year. The corresponding credit represents cash payments of $15,000 on accounts payable during the year.

MISCELLANEOUS EXPENSES

The cash outflow related to Miscellaneous Expenses can be determined by analyzing the change in the Accrued Payables account. Refer to Figure 14–12.

FIGURE 14–12

Determining cash outflow from miscellaneous expenses

MISCELLANEOUS EXPENSES		ACCRUED PAYABLES	
(1) *11,000*			*1,500*
			(1) *11,000*
		(2) *9,500*	
			3,000

EFFECT ON ACCOUNTS

TRANSACTIONS	ACCOUNTS	DEBIT (NET)	CREDIT (NET)
(1)	Miscellaneous Expenses	11,000	
	Accrued Payables		11,000
(2)	Accrued Payables	9,500	
	Cash		9,500

Cash paid for miscellaneous expenses: $9,500

The beginning ($1,500) and ending ($3,000) balances in Accrued Payables appear on the balance sheets in Figure 14–8. Assuming that all miscellaneous expenses were accrued, the debit of $11,000 to Miscellaneous Expenses (see income statement) must have involved an $11,000 credit to Accrued Payables. Considering the beginning and ending balances in accrued payables, a $9,500 debit must have been entered in the account. The corresponding credit represents cash payments on accrued payables.

INSURANCE EXPENSE

The cash outflow related to Insurance Expense can be determined by analyzing the change in the Prepaid Insurance account. Refer to Figure 14–13.

FIGURE 14–13

Determining cash outflow related to insurance expense

INSURANCE EXPENSE		PREPAID INSURANCE	
(1) *1,000*		*2,000*	
			(1) *1,000*
		1,000	

EFFECT ON ACCOUNTS

TRANSACTIONS	ACCOUNTS	DEBIT (NET)	CREDIT (NET)
(1)	Insurance Expense	1,000	
	Prepaid Insurance		1,000

Cash paid for insurance: $0

The beginning ($2,000) and ending ($1,000) balances in Prepaid Insurance appear on the balance sheets in Figure 14–8. The debit of $1,000 to Insurance Expense (see income statement) involved a $1,000 credit to Prepaid Insurance. This entry accounts for the entire change in the Prepaid Insurance account, indicating that no cash was paid for insurance during the year.

DEPRECIATION OF MACHINERY, DEPRECIATION OF BUILDING, AMORTIZATION OF PATENT, AND LOSS ON SALE OF MACHINERY

There are no cash effects associated with depreciation, amortization, or book gains and losses.

INTEREST EXPENSE

The cash outflow related to Interest Expense can be determined by analyzing the change in the Discount on Notes Payable account. Refer to Figure 14–14.

FIGURE 14–14
Determining cash outflow related to interest expense

INTEREST EXPENSE

(1) 2,000

DISCOUNT ON NOTES PAYABLE

2,000
                  (1)   200
1,800

EFFECT ON ACCOUNTS

TRANSACTIONS	ACCOUNTS	DEBIT (NET)	CREDIT (NET)
(1)	Interest Expense	2,000	
	Discount on Notes Payable		200
	Cash		1,800

Cash paid for interest: $1,800

The beginning ($2,000) and ending ($1,800) balances in the Discount on Notes Payable account appear on the balance sheets in Figure 14–8. The $200 difference between the beginning and ending balances indicates that the discount was amortized in the amount of $200 during the year. Discounts are amortized into Interest Expense as illustrated in Figure 14–14. Thus, $1,800 cash must have been paid for interest during the year.

INCOME TAX EXPENSE

The cash outflow related to Income Tax Expense can be determined by analyzing the changes in the Income Tax Payable account. Refer to Figure 14–15.

Cash paid for income taxes: $1,500

The beginning ($500) and ending ($200) balances in the Income Tax Payable account appears on the balance sheets in Figure 14–8. The debit of $1,200 to Income Tax Expense (see income statement), assuming that income taxes were accrued, involved a $1,200 credit to income tax payable. Considering the beginning and ending balances in Income Tax Payable, $1,500 must have been debited to the account during the year. The corresponding credit represents cash payments for income taxes.

FIGURE 14–15

Determining cash outflow related to income taxes

INCOME TAX EXPENSE	INCOME TAX PAYABLE
(1) 1,200	500
	(1) 1,200
	(2) 1,500
	200

EFFECT ON ACCOUNTS

TRANSACTIONS	ACCOUNTS	DEBIT (NET)	CREDIT (NET)
(1)	Income Tax Expense	1,200	
	Income Tax Payable		1,200
(2)	Income Tax Payable	1,500	
	Cash		1,500

CASH PROVIDED (USED) BY INVESTING ACTIVITIES

In this section we determine the cash inflows and outflows associated with investing activities by analyzing changes in the long-lived asset accounts. Specifically, we analyze the $10,000 increase in the Land account and the $2,000 decrease in the Machinery account. The building was acquired in exchange for stock and involved no cash exchange, while the $2,000 decrease in the Patent account reflects amortization, which also involved no cash receipt or payment.

PURCHASE OF LAND

The $10,000 increase in the Land account (see Figure 14–8) indicates that land was acquired during the period. Since there is no indication that noncash assets were exchanged for the land or a liability was credited, we assume that the land was purchased for a $10,000 cash payment. Refer to Figure 14–16.

FIGURE 14–16

Determining cash outflow for land purchases

LAND	
20,000	
(1) 10,000	
30,000	

EFFECT ON ACCOUNTS

TRANSACTIONS	ACCOUNTS	DEBIT (NET)	CREDIT (NET)
(1)	Land	10,000	
	Cash		10,000

Cash payment for land: $10,000

SALE OF MACHINERY

The cash inflow from the sale of machinery can be determined by using the available information to reconstruct the journal entry that recorded the transaction. Refer to Figure 14–17.

FIGURE 14–17

Determining cash inflow from sale of machinery

MACHINERY		ACCUMULATED DEPRECIATION		LOSS ON SALE OF MACHINERY		DEPRECIATION EXPENSE	
8,000			2,000	(2) 100		(1) *1,000*	
	(2) 2,000	(1) 1,000					
		(2) 500					
6,000			2,500				

EFFECT ON ACCOUNTS

TRANSACTIONS	ACCOUNTS	DEBIT (NET)	CREDIT (NET)
(1)	Depreciation Expense	1,000	
	Accumulated Depreciation		1,000
(2)	Cash	1,400	
	Accumulated Depreciation	500	
	Loss on Sale of Machinery	100	
	Machinery		2,000

Cash receipt for sale of machinery: $1,400

The beginning and ending balances in the Machinery and Accumulated Depreciation accounts can be found on the balance sheets in Figure 14–8. Depreciation expense on the machinery in the amount of $1,000 (see income statement) was recognized during the period; accordingly, $1,000 must have been credited to Accumulated Depreciation. The Accumulated Depreciation account, therefore, must have been debited for $500 when the machine was sold. Given the $100 loss on the sale (see income statement), the $2,000 reduction in the Machinery account, and the $500 debit to Accumulated Depreciation, the journal entry to record the sale can be reconstructed and the amount of cash received ($1,400) can be determined.

CASH PROVIDED (USED) BY FINANCING ACTIVITIES

In this section we determine the cash inflows and outflows associated with financing activities by analyzing changes in the long-term liability and stockholders' equity accounts. Specifically, we analyze the $1,000 decrease in the Notes Payable account, the increase in the Common Stock and Additional Paid-in Capital accounts, the issuance of treasury stock for $1,300, and the declaration of a $3,000 cash dividend.

PRINCIPAL PAYMENT ON NOTES PAYABLE

We have no indication that the $1,000 decrease in the Notes Payable account (see Figure 14–8) was due to anything other than the payment of cash. Refer to Figure 14–18.

Cash payment of notes payable: $1,000

ISSUANCE OF COMMON STOCK AND TREASURY STOCK

The cash inflows from the issuance of common stock and treasury stock can be determined by analyzing the changes in the Common Stock, Additional Paid-in Capital, and Treasury Stock accounts. Note that the "Additional Information" section of Figure 14–8 indicates that a building was acquired for common stock, a stock dividend was distributed, and treasury stock was sold for $1,300. Refer to Figure 14–19.

FIGURE 14–18

Determining cash outflow from payments on notes

NOTES PAYABLE

	25,000
(1) 1,000	
	24,000

EFFECT ON ACCOUNTS

TRANSACTIONS	ACCOUNTS	DEBIT (NET)	CREDIT (NET)
(1)	Notes Payable	1,000	
	Cash		1,000

FIGURE 14–19

Determining cash inflow from stock issuances

BUILDING

0	
(1) 30,000	
30,000	

TREASURY STOCK

1,000	
	(3) 1,000
0	

STOCK DIVIDEND

(2) 4,000	

COMMON STOCK

	10,000
	(1) 20,000
	(2) 2,000
	(4) 10,000
	42,000

ADDITIONAL PAID-IN CAPITAL

	2,000
	(1) 10,000
	(2) 2,000
	(3) 300
	(4) 5,000
	19,300

EFFECT ON ACCOUNTS

TRANSACTIONS	ACCOUNTS	DEBIT (NET)	CREDIT (NET)
(1)	**Building**	**30,000**	
	Common Stock		**20,000**
	Additional Paid-In Capital		**10,000**
(2)	**Stock Dividend**	**4,000**	
	Common Stock		**2,000**
	Additional Paid-In Capital		**2,000**
(3)	Cash	1,300	
	Treasury Stock		1,000
	Additional Paid-In Capital		300
(4)	Cash	15,000	
	Common Stock		10,000
	Additional Paid-In Capital		5,000

Cash receipts from issuance of treasury stock: $1,300

Cash receipts from issuance of common stock: $15,000

The beginning and ending balances in Common Stock, Additional Paid-In Capital, and Treasury Stock appear on the balance sheets in Figure 14–8. The purchase of the $30,000 building increased Common Stock and Additional Paid-In

Capital by $20,000 and $10,000, respectively. Common Stock and Additional Paid-In Capital each increased by $2,000 when the $4,000 stock dividend was distributed. Additional Paid-In Capital increased by $300 when the treasury stock was issued for $1,300 cash, which was greater than its $1,000 cost. The additional information that follows the financial statement in Figure 14–8 describes these three transactions. Given the ending balances in Common Stock and Additional Paid-In Capital, there must have been a stock issuance for cash in the amount of $15,000 during the year.

CASH DIVIDENDS

The cash dividend payment can be determined by analyzing the changes in the Dividends Payable account. Refer to Figure 14–20.

FIGURE 14–20

Determining cash outflow from dividend payments

CASH DIVIDENDS

| (1) | 3,000 | |

DIVIDENDS PAYABLE

			1,000
(2)	1,000	(1)	3,000
			3,000

EFFECT ON ACCOUNTS

TRANSACTIONS	ACCOUNTS	DEBIT (NET)	CREDIT (NET)
(1)	Cash Dividends	3,000	
	Dividends Payable		3,000
(2)	Dividends Payable	1,000	
	Cash		1,000

Cash payment for dividends: $1,000

The beginning ($1,000) and ending ($3,000) balances in the Dividends Payable account appear on the balance sheets in Figure 14–8. The declaration of the $3,000 cash dividend (see statement of retained earnings) created a $3,000 dividend payable liability. Therefore, $1,000 must have been debited to Dividends Payable during the year, which represents cash payments to the stockholders.

THE COMPLETE STATEMENT OF CASH FLOWS

We have now derived the cash flows of the period and can prepare the statement of cash flows. The next section covers the direct method, which is followed by the indirect method. Another section reconciles the two methods.

THE DIRECT METHOD

A statement of cash flows prepared under the direct method is provided in Figure 14–21. Note that the dollar amounts are identical to the cash flows derived in the previous section.

THE INDIRECT METHOD

Figure 14–22 contains a statement of cash flows prepared under the indirect method. In many ways it is exactly the same as the statement of cash flows (direct method) in

FIGURE 14–21	ABC ENTERPRISES, INC.

STATEMENT OF CASH FLOWS
FOR THE YEAR ENDED DECEMBER 31, 1997

Statement of cash flows for ABC Enterprises: Direct method

Operating activities:		
Cash collections from sales and accounts receivable	$ 20,000	
Cash paid to suppliers	(15,000)	
Cash paid on miscellaneous expenses	(9,500)	
Cash paid for interest	(1,800)	
Cash paid for income taxes	(1,500)	
Net cash provided (used) by operating activities		$ (7,800)
Investing activities:		
Purchase of land	$(10,000)	
Sale of machinery	1,400	
Net cash provided (used) by investing activities		(8,600)
Financing activities:		
Proceeds from issuing common stock	$ 15,000	
Proceeds from sale of treasury stock	1,300	
Cash dividends	(1,000)	
Principal payment on outstanding note payable	(1,000)	
Net cash provided (used) by financing activities		14,300
Net increase (decrease) in cash balance		$ (2,100)
Beginning cash balance		8,000
Ending cash balance		$ 5,900

FIGURE 14–22	ABC ENTERPRISES, INC.

STATEMENT OF CASH FLOWS
FOR THE YEAR ENDED DECEMBER 31, 1997

Statement of cash flows: Indirect method

Operating activities:		
Net income	$ 3,100	
Noncash charges to noncurrent accounts		
Depreciation of machinery	1,000	
Depreciation of building	1,500	
Amortization of patent	2,000	
Loss on sale of machinery	100	
Decrease in discount on notes payable	200	
Changes in current accounts other than cash		
Increase in net accounts receivable	(10,900)	
Increase in inventory	(1,000)	
Decrease in accounts payable	(3,000)	
Increase in miscellaneous expenses and taxes payable	1,200	
Decrease in payments in advance	(3,000)	
Decrease in prepaid insurance	1,000	
Net cash provided (used) by operating activities		$(7,800)
Investing activities:		
Purchase of land	$(10,000)	
Sale of machinery	1,400	
Net cash provided (used) by investing activities		(8,600)

Continued

FIGURE 14–22		
(Concluded)		

Financing activities:

Proceeds from issuing equity	$ 15,000	
Proceeds from the sale of treasury stock	1,300	
Cash dividends to stockholders	(1,000)	
Principal payments on outstanding note payable	(1,000)	
Net cash provided (used) by financing activities		14,300
Net increase (decrease) in cash balance		$(2,100)
Beginning cash balance		8,000
Ending cash balance		$ 5,900

Figure 14–21. The dollar amount of cash provided (used) by operating activities is the same (−$7,800), and the sections devoted to investing and financing activities are identical. The only difference between the two methods involves the way in which cash provided (used) by operating activities is computed.

Under the indirect method, cash provided (used) by operating activities (−$7,800) is computed by adjusting net income ($3,100), which appears on the income statement, for the timing differences between operating accruals and cash flows. As indicated earlier in the chapter, these adjustments are classified into two categories: (1) noncash charges to noncurrent accounts (e.g., depreciation, amortization, book losses and gains) and (2) changes in current accounts other than Cash (e.g., Accounts Receivable, Inventory, Accounts Payable, Income Tax and Miscellaneous Accruals, Payments in Advance, and Prepaid Insurance). Note also how the conceptual description of the statement of cash flows (Figure 14–7) conforms to the format used in Figure 14–22.

THE DIRECT AND INDIRECT METHODS: A RECONCILIATION

The adjustments to reconcile net income with cash provided (used) by operating activities can be viewed as the adjustments necessary to convert an accrual-based income statement to the operating section of the statement of cash flows prepared under the direct method. Such a reconciliation is provided in Figure 14–23. The column on the left represents the income statement (Figure 14–8). The adjustments in the middle can be found on the statement of cash flows prepared under the indirect method (Figure 14–22). The column on the right represents operating cash flows presented under the direct method (Figure 14–21).

Note that the adjustments required to convert the revenues and expenses on the income statement to operating cash inflows and outflows are expressed in terms of changes in the related balance sheet accounts. The adjustment to sales, for example, is related to the change during the period in the net balance of Accounts Receivable. The adjustment to Fees Earned is expressed in terms of the change in the Payments in Advance account, while the adjustment to Cost of Goods Sold is related to the change in both Inventory and Accounts Payable. Although not indicated in Figure 14–23, the adjustments to depreciation, amortization, and the book loss can all be expressed in terms of changes in such accounts as Accumulated Depreciation, Machinery, and Patent. The main point is that every revenue and expense account is related to one or more accounts on the balance sheet and that the changes in these balance sheet accounts during a period can be used to determine the corresponding cash inflows and outflows.

FIGURE 14–23

Converting an income statement to a statement of operating cash flows

INCOME STATEMENT		ADJUSTMENTS		OPERATING CASH FLOWS: DIRECT METHOD
Sales	$ 32,000			
Bad debt expense	(1,100)			
	$ 30,900	Increase in net accounts receivable	$(10,900)	$ 20,000
Fees earned	3,000	Decrease in payments in advance	(3,000)	0
Cost of goods sold	(11,000)	Increase in inventory	(1,000)	
		Decrease in accounts payable	(3,000)	(15,000)
Misc. expenses		Net increase in misc. expenses and		
and tax expense	(12,200)	taxes payable	1,200	(11,000)
Insurance expense	(1,000)	Decrease in prepaid insurance	1,000	0
Depreciation:				
Machinery	(1,000)			
Building	(1,500)	Add back (no cash effect)	2,500	0
Amortization:				
Patent	(2,000)	Add back (no cash effect)	2,000	0
Loss on sale of				
machinery	(100)	Add back (no cash effect)	100	0
Interest expense	(2,000)	Amortization of discount	200	(1,800)
Net income	$ 3,100	Cash provided (used) by operating activities		$ (7,800)

ANALYZING THE STATEMENT OF CASH FLOWS: AN APPLICATION

Now that the statement of cash flows has been prepared, we can use it to assess ABC Enterprises' cash management policies.

EXPLAINING THE CHANGES IN THE CASH BALANCE

ABC's cash position decreased (from $8,000 to $5,900) during 1997. For the most part, this decrease was caused by investing and operating activities, which required $8,600 and $7,800, respectively. Financing activities, which provided $14,300, almost made up for these cash deficits. While the exact sources and uses of cash in each of these three areas should be examined, the $7,800 cash deficit due to operating activities appears to be the most troublesome and definitely deserves special attention.

SUMMARIZING THE CASH EFFECTS OF OPERATING TRANSACTIONS

ABC's income statement shows that net income for 1997 totaled $3,100. At the same time, the operations that produced net income reduced the cash balance by $7,800. Interestingly, these two measures produce significantly different numbers that are used to evaluate the same (operating) activities.

The statement of cash flows under the indirect method (Figure 14–22) explains the difference between net income and cash provided (used) by operations. Four items appear to be the most important: (1) the $10,900 buildup in net accounts receivable, (2) the $3,000 decrease in accounts payable, (3) the $3,000 decrease in payments in advance, and (4) the depreciation and amortization of the long-lived assets.

The net accounts receivable buildup increased net income but not cash. Coupled with the decrease in accounts payable, it indicates that ABC paid its suppliers more quickly than it received payments from its customers. Such a strategy can give rise to cash flow problems. The $3,000 decrease in payments in advance was reflected in revenues (and thus net income) but produced no cash. Presumably, the $3,000 was received some time before December 31, 1996. The depreciation and amortization of long-lived assets reduced net income by a total dollar amount of $4,500 ($1,000 + $1,500 + $2,000) but required no cash.

Keep in mind also that the management of ABC could have manipulated cash provided (used) by operating activities. For example, had management chosen to defer cash payment on accounts payable, cash provided (used) by operating activities would have been considerably higher. This particular decision would have had no effect on net income.

SUMMARIZING THE CASH EFFECT OF INVESTING AND FINANCING TRANSACTIONS

ABC Enterprises relied heavily on stock issuances for its cash needs during 1997. The statement of cash flows shows that common stock was issued for cash in the amount of $15,000 and that the sale of treasury stock produced $1,300. Both issuances diluted ABC's outstanding stock. The sale of a piece of machinery produced $1,400.

The cash produced by the financing and investing sources was used primarily to cover the cash deficit from operating activities (−$7,800) and to purchase land ($10,000). Dividend and principal payments on outstanding loans amounted to $1,000 each.

Note that ABC Enterprises issued 2,000 shares of common stock, valued at $15 each, for a building (see Figure 14–8). While this transaction does not affect ABC's Cash balance and does not appear on the statement of cash flows, it is nonetheless very important and should be reported in the footnotes to the financial statements. Apparently, ABC relied even more heavily on equity issuances and purchased more long-term assets than the statement of cash flows indicates.

INTERNATIONAL PERSPECTIVE: THE STATEMENT OF CASH FLOWS

The recent rise in international investing and other activities has introduced a number of important issues relevant to the statement of cash flows. In this section we briefly discuss two such issues: (1) the disclosure requirements in other countries with respect to the statement of cash flows and (2) reporting foreign currency gains and losses on the statement of cash flows.

As mentioned earlier in the chapter, the statement of cash flows is a relatively recent addition to the required financial statements for U.S. corporations. It is not surprising, therefore, that the statement is not required in most other countries. Some countries, like Britain, require a "statement of sources and applications of funds." Other countries, like France, recommend a "sources and uses of funds statement," and still other countries, like Japan, are considering requiring a "statement of changes in financial position." While all of these statements resemble the statement of cash flows, they are different in many ways, and as you can see above, they normally are not mandatory. In fact, in most countries no statement even resembling the statement of cash flows is required.

In the near future, however, it is likely that this situation will change. The importance of credit capital in many foreign countries places a premium on cash flow information, which is important for credit analysis, and the growing influence of U.S. accounting standards on international accounting practices will increasingly encourage companies in other countries to provide statements of cash flow.

We have also mentioned in this text that U.S. corporations are increasingly conducting operations in foreign countries. These activities often involve transactions that are expressed in foreign currencies. A U.S. corporation, for example, may sell goods or services to a customer in a foreign country, giving rise to a receivable that is expressed in a foreign currency. When the value of the foreign currency changes relative to the U.S. dollar, the value of the receivable on the U.S. company's balance sheet must be restated, which, in turn, gives rise to a gain or loss that is reported on the income statement.[10]

Foreign currency exchange gains and losses, however, involve no cash flow. Consequently, when the statement of cash flows is prepared under the indirect method, an adjustment must be made to net income. Partly because these adjustments are becoming more and more significant, recent accounting pronouncements require that they be disclosed separately at the bottom of the statement, immediately before "net increase (decrease) in cash and cash equivalents." General Motors, for example, reported a $131 million adjustment for foreign exchange rate gains as a separate line item on a recent statement of cash flows, and Toys "R" Us routinely discloses such adjustments on its statement of cash flows.

A survey reported in *Management Accounting* (July 1992) found that investors are increasingly using the statement of cash flows, and currently it is considered to be almost as useful as the balance sheet and income statement. Over the last 15 years the perceived usefulness of the cash flow statement increased significantly, while the perceived usefulness of the income statement fell. It seems that in many ways net cash from operations is replacing net income as a key measure of a company's operating performance, especially in terms of debt-paying ability. For example, in an aggressive move that boosted its stock price, Philip Morris recently bought back approximately $6 billion of its own stock, and raised its quarterly dividend by 20%. A spokesperson for the company said, "the company's strong cash position made these moves possible" (*The Wall Street Journal*, September 1, 1994). Both Standard & Poor's Rating Group and Moody's Investors Service confirmed their high ratings on

ETHICS IN THE REAL WORLD

Philip Morris' debt, noting the company's continuing ability to generate strong cash flows.

One problem with relying on the statement of cash flows, and net income from operations in particular, is that reported cash flows are very easy to manipulate. By judiciously timing its cash receipts and payments, management can influence the dollar amounts reported on the statement of cash flows, rendering them somewhat less useful for determining the company's solvency position. For example, by delaying payments to suppliers by as little as a few days, a company can increase net cash from operations substantially, which in turn may delay a credit rating reduction.

ETHICAL ISSUE

Is it ethical for a company in weak financial condition to manage the timing of its cash receipts and payments in an effort to delay signaling that weakness to the public?

---

10. The methods used to account for such transactions are covered in Appendix 6B.

REVIEW PROBLEM

Figure 14–24 contains balance sheets (December 31, 1996 and 1997) for XYZ Enterprises and the intervening income statement and statement of retained earnings. Following these statements are several selected pieces of information that more completely describe the activity of XYZ during 1997. The two forms of the statement of cash flows are contained in Figures 14–25 (direct method) and 14–26 (indirect method). We have included relevant calculations on the statements to explain how the numbers were derived. Examine each cash flow statement closely, and trace the calculations back to the original financial statements and given information in Figure 14–24.

FIGURE 14–24

Financial statements for XYZ Enterprises

XYZ ENTERPRISES
BALANCE SHEETS
FOR DECEMBER 31, 1996 AND 1997

	1997	1996
ASSETS		
Cash	$ 3,000	$ 2,500
Accounts receivable	4,500	4,000
Inventory	10,500	8,000
Prepaid rent	3,000	2,000
Fixed assets	40,000	35,000
Less: Accumulated depreciation	(12,000)	(10,000)
Patent	8,000	9,000
Total assets	$57,000	$50,500
LIABILITIES AND STOCKHOLDERS' EQUITY		
Accounts payable	$ 6,500	$ 3,000
Other current payables	7,000	10,000
Bonds payable	19,000	19,000
Plus: Premium on bonds payable	2,500	3,000
Common stock	15,000	10,000
Additional paid-in capital	4,000	3,000
Retained earnings	3,000	2,500
Total liabilities and stockholders' equity	$57,000	$50,500

XYZ ENTERPRISES
INCOME STATEMENT
FOR THE YEAR ENDED DEC. 31, 1997

Sales	$55,000
Less: Cost of goods sold	35,000
Gross profit	$20,000
Rent expense	(2,000)
Interest expense	(2,000)
Miscellaneous expense	(9,000)
Depreciation of fixed assets	(5,000)
Amortization of patent	(1,000)
Gain on sale of machinery	1,000
Net income	$ 2,000

XYZ ENTERPRISES
STATEMENT OF RETAINED EARNINGS
FOR THE YEAR ENDED DEC. 31, 1997

Beginning balance	$2,500
Plus: Net income	2,000
Less: Cash dividends	(1,500)
Ending balance	$3,000

Additional information:
1. Purchased $3,000 of prepaid rent.
2. Sold a piece of machinery (cost: $5,000; accumulated depreciation: $3,000) for $3,000 cash. Purchased additional machinery for $10,000 cash.
3. Paid annual interest of $2,500 on note payable.
4. Issued 500 shares of $10 par value common stock for $12 per share.

FIGURE 14–25

Statement of cash flows for XYZ Enterprises: Direct method

XYZ ENTERPRISES
STATEMENT OF CASH FLOWS
FOR THE YEAR ENDED DECEMBER 31, 1997

OPERATING ACTIVITIES:

INCOME STATEMENT		ADJUSTMENT/EXPLANATION	OPERATING CASH FLOWS	
Sales	$ 55,000	(500) [increase in accounts receivable]	$ 54,500	
COGS	(35,000)	(2,500) [increase in inventory]		
		+3,500 [increase in accounts payable]	(34,000)	
Rent	(2,000)	(1,000) [increase in prepaid rent]	(3,000)	
Interest	(2,000)	(500) [decrease in premium]	(2,500)	
Misc.	(9,000)	(3,000) [decrease in other current payables]	(12,000)	
Depreciation	(5,000)	[no cash effect]	0	
Amortization	(1,000)	[no cash effect]	0	
Gain	1,000	[no cash effect]	0	
Net income	$ 2,000	Net cash from operations		$ 3,000

INVESTING ACTIVITIES:

Sale of machinery	[see note below]		$ 3,000	
Purchase of machinery	[see note below]		(10,000)	
Net cash provided (used) by investing activities				(7,000)

FINANCING ACTIVITIES:

Issue of common stock	[increase in common stock and APIC]		$ 6,000	
Cash dividends	[see statement of retained earnings and no increase in dividend payable]		(1,500)	
Net cash provided (used) by financing activities				4,500
Increase (decrease) in cash balance				$ 500
Beginning cash balance				2,500
Ending cash balance				$ 3,000

NOTE:

		COST OF FIXED ASSETS	ACCUMULATED DEPRECIATION	
Beginning balance		$35,000		$10,000
Plus: Increases	(purchases)	10,000	(depreciation expense)	5,000
Less: Decreases	(sales)	(5,000)	(sold machinery)	(3,000)
Ending balance		$40,000		$12,000

Cash (+A)	3,000	
Accumulated Depreciation (+A)	3,000	
Machinery (−A)		5,000
Gain on Sale of Machinery (Ga, +SE)		1,000

XYZ ENTERPRISES
STATEMENT OF CASH FLOWS
FOR THE YEAR ENDED DECEMBER 31, 1997

OPERATING ACTIVITIES:		
Net income	$ 2,000	
Noncash charges to noncurrent accounts		
Depreciation of fixed assets	5,000	
Amortization of patent	1,000	
Gain on sale of machinery	(1,000)	
Decreases in premium	(500)	
Changes in current accounts other than cash		
Increase in accounts receivable	(500)	
Increase in inventory	(2,500)	
Increase in prepaid rent	(1,000)	
Decrease in other payables	(3,000)	
Increase in accounts payable	3,500	
Cash provided (used) by operating activities		$ 3,000
INVESTING ACTIVITIES:		
Sale of machinery	$ 3,000	
Purchase of machinery	(10,000)	
Cash provided (used) by investing activities		(7,000)
FINANCING ACTIVITIES:		
Issue of common stock	$ 6,000	
Cash dividends	(1,500)	
Net cash provided (used) by financing activities		4,500
Net increase (decrease) in cash balance		$ 500
Beginning cash balance		2,500
Ending cash balance		$ 3,000

SUMMARY OF LEARNING OBJECTIVES

 Describe the basic structure and format of the statement of cash flows.

The statement of cash flows explains the change in a company's cash account from one accounting period to the next. It is divided into three sections: (1) cash provided (used) by operating activities, (2) cash provided (used) by investing activities, and (3) cash provided (used) by financing activities. Each of these sections contains the cash inflows and outflows of the period that were associated with the indicated activity.

 Define cash flows from operating, investing, and financing activities.

Cash flows from operating activities include those cash inflows and outflows associated directly with the acquisition and sale of a company's inventories and services. Such activities include the cash receipts from sales and accounts receivable, as well as cash payments from the purchase of inventories, payments on accounts payable, selling and administrative expenses, and interest and taxes. The sale or purchase of inventory on account are operating transactions that do not appear on the statement of cash flows.

Cash flows from investing activities include the cash inflows and outflows associated with the purchase and sale of a company's noncurrent assets. Cash activities include the cash effects from the purchase and sale of long-term investments, long-lived assets, and intangible assets.

Cash flows from financing activities include cash inflows and outflows associated with a company's two sources of outside capital: liabilities and contributed capital. Such activities include the cash inflows associated with borrowings and equity issuances as well as the cash outflows associated with debt repayment, treasury stock purchases, and dividends.

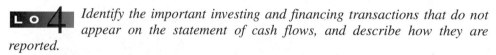

L O 3 *Explain how the statement of cash flows complements the other financial statements and how it can be used by those interested in the financial condition of a company.*

While the income statement provides a summary of a company's operating transactions on an accrual basis, and the balance sheet represents the accumulated accruals of the company's operating, investing, and financing transactions as of a particular point in time, neither statement indicates much about the cash effects of the company's operating, investing, and financing activities. The statement of cash flows is designed to fill this void by summarizing the cash effects of the company's operating, investing, and financing transactions.

The statement of cash flows is used primarily to evaluate a company's ability to generate cash (i.e., financial flexibility) as well as the effectiveness of its cash management policies. Financial flexibility reflects a company's ability to generate cash through operations, borrowings, issuing equity, or selling noncurrent assets. Effective cash management involves investing cash to provide a high rate of return while maintaining enough cash to meet debts as they come due (i.e., solvency). The statement of cash flows is helpful to this evaluation in three interrelated ways: (1) it explains the change in the cash balance, (2) it summarizes the cash effects of operating transactions, and (3) it summarizes the cash effects of capital (investing and financing) transactions.

L O 4 *Identify the important investing and financing transactions that do not appear on the statement of cash flows, and describe how they are reported.*

The statement of cash flows includes only those transactions that either increase or decrease the Cash account. Many important operating and capital transactions do not affect the Cash account and are therefore excluded from the statement. For example, the purchase of machinery in exchange for a long-term note payable, the acquisition of land or the payment of a debt with capital stock, and the declaration of a dividend are all capital transactions that have no effect on the Cash account and are therefore excluded from the statement.

The FASB requires that capital transactions that do not affect the Cash account be described clearly in the footnotes to the financial statements. No special disclosures are required for operating transactions that do not affect the Cash account, because the effects of such transactions can be inferred from the reconciliation of net income to net cash provided (used) by operating activities.

L O 5 *Describe the economic consequences associated with the statement of cash flows.*

The economic consequences associated with the statement of cash flows occur when investors, creditors, and other interested parties use it to assess the investment potential and creditworthiness of companies and the equity and debt securities they issue. The rising importance of cash flow information to report users creates incentives for managers to window dress the statement of cash flows. Such incentives can present problems, because in the short run, it is relatively easy for management to present a favorable cash position. Such manipulation is much less effective, however, when statements are viewed across several periods, because payments delayed in one period must normally be paid in the next. For this reason the FASB requires that cash flow statements from at least the previous three years be disclosed in the financial report.

LO 6 *Express the statement of cash flows in terms of the basic accounting equation, and understand how to prepare a statement of cash flows from the information contained in two balance sheets, an income statement, and a statement of retained earnings.*

The equation that appears in Figure 14–7 represents an algebraic statement of the statement of cash flows, illustrating how the change in the Cash balance can be explained in terms of changes in the balance sheet accounts. One can prepare the statement of cash flows, under either the direct or indirect method, by reconstructing the T-account for each balance sheet account, posting the transactions that are reflected on the income statement and statement of retained earnings, and deriving the related cash flows.

KEY TERMS

Note: Definitions for these terms are provided in the glossary at the end of this text.

Cash equivalents (p. 683)   Investing activities (p. 686)
Direct method (p. 685)   Operating activities (p. 685)
Financial flexibility (p. 689)   Solvency (p. 689)
Financing activities (p. 686)   Window dress (p. 692)
Indirect method (p. 685)

QUESTIONS FOR DISCUSSION AND REVIEW

1. The statement of cash flows is divided into three sections. Name these sections, and explain how such a division is useful.
2. How is cash defined with respect to the statement of cash flows? Why is this definition used?
3. Define cash provided (used) by operating activities, and differentiate this dollar amount from net income, which appears on the income statement.
4. Cash can be generated by selling inventory or services, selling long-term assets like investments and equipment, and borrowing or issuing equity. How are these various forms of generating cash treated on the statement of cash flows, and why are they treated differently?
5. Of what use is the statement of cash flows to investors, creditors, and others interested in the financial situation of a company?
6. How does the statement of cash flows complement the other financial statements? What kind of information does it provide that the others do not?
7. What is a capital transaction, and how can it be differentiated from an operating transaction? What are investing and financing transactions, and how do they relate to capital transactions?

8. What is financial flexibility, and how does the statement of cash flows provide information about it?

9. What is involved in cash management, and why is it important that a company manage its cash correctly?

10. What is solvency, and of what use is the statement of cash flows in evaluating the solvency position of a company?

11. In what ways can the statement of cash flows be used to evaluate a company's ability to generate cash and its cash management policies?

12. Why do managers have incentives to manipulate the dollar amounts on the statement of cash flows? Provide several examples of how managers might window dress the statement of cash flows. What has the FASB done to mitigate this problem?

13. Why is manipulating information on the statement of cash flows often not in the best interest of management?

14. Describe the differences between the income statement and the operating section of the statement of cash flows. Do both operating statements provide the same kind of information? If not, how do they differ? Is it possible for a profitable company to go bankrupt? How?

15. Provide several examples of important financing and investment transactions that would not appear on the statement of cash flows. What does the FASB require with respect to such transactions?

16. Explain how one could infer the existence of operating transactions that do not affect the Cash account. For example, how could a reader of a company's financial statements be able to determine if the company made a large inventory purchase on account?

17. Differentiate the direct method from the indirect method in preparing the statement of cash flows. Which method is more straightforward, and why? Which method provides more disclosure?

18. Converting an income statement to a statement of operating cash inflows and outflows (and vice-versa) is very important in understanding the statement of cash flows and how it relates to the income statement. In general, how does one make such conversions, and why might they be useful to financial statement users?

19. When preparing a reconciliation between net income and cash provided (used) by operating activities for purposes of a statement of cash flows under either the direct or indirect method, into what two categories are the required adjustments separated? Provide several examples of the adjustments included in each category.

20. Name an asset account and a liability account that are directly related to the revenue accounts, Sales and Fees Earned. Name asset and/or liability accounts that are directly related to the income statement accounts, Interest Expense, Depreciation Expense, Insurance Expense, Wage Expense, and Cost of Goods Sold.

21. How are book gains and losses, depreciation, and amortization treated when converting accrual numbers to cash-basis numbers? Why?

22. Express the change in the Cash balance during a period in terms of changes in the other balance sheet accounts. Begin with the basic accounting equation, and explain how this expression can be used to prepare a statement of cash flows from the information contained in two balance sheets, an income statement, and a statement of retained earnings.

23. Are you likely to find a statement of cash flows in the set of financial statements provided by companies in foreign countries? Explain.

24. Why are foreign currency exchange gains and losses disclosed on the statement of cash flows prepared under the indirect method?

EXERCISES

E14–1

(Classifying transactions)

Classify each of the following transactions as an operating, investing, or financing activity, even those that would not appear explicitly on the statement of cash flows. Some transactions may be classified in more than one category.

1. Purchase of machinery for cash

2. Issuance of common stock for cash
3. Sale of inventory on account
4. Purchase of outstanding stock (treasury stock) for cash
5. Sale of land held as a long-term investment
6. Purchase of a building for cash and a mortgage payable
7. Cash payment for principal and interest on an outstanding debt
8. Cash payment on accounts payable
9. Payment of a cash dividend
10. Payment of wages to employees

E14–2

(Operating, investing, or financing activity?)

The following are several activities that Wallingford, Inc., engaged in during 1997.
1. Wrote off an open receivable as uncollected.
2. Purchased a piece of plant equipment.
3. Reacquired 5,000 shares of its common stock.
4. Sold a building in exchange for a five-year note.
5. Declared, but did not pay, a cash dividend.
6. Retired bonds payable by issuing common stock.
7. Collected on a long-term note receivable.
8. Issued a stock dividend.
9. Recorded depreciation on fixed assets.
10. Paid interest on long-term debt.
11. Purchased inventory on account.
12. Collected open accounts receivable.
13. Exchanged a building for land.
14. Issued 75,000 shares of preferred stock.
15. Purchased a two-year fire insurance policy.

REQUIRED:

Assume that each of these transactions involved cash unless otherwise indicated. Indicate in which section of the statement of cash flows each transaction would be classified. Classify each transaction as one of the following:
a. An operating activity
b. An investing activity
c. A financing activity
d. Not included on the statement of cash flows

E14–3

(Cash management policies across companies)

Summaries of the 1997 statements of cash flows for five different companies follow. For each company compute the missing dollar amount, and briefly describe the company's cash management policy for 1997.

| COMPANY | CASH PROVIDED (USED) BY | | | NET INCREASE (DECREASE) |
	OPERATIONS	INVESTMENTS	FINANCING	
AAA	320	?	$(180)	$ (38)
BBB	219	(450)	190	?
CCC	?	(414)	80	(137)
DDD	120	(130)	?	420
EEE	?	(120)	(100)	70

E14–4

(Journalizing and classifying transactions)

Presented below is a list of transactions entered into by Kaitland Manufacturing during 1997.
1. Recorded depreciation expense of $170,000.
2. Sold 10,000 shares of common stock ($10 par value) for $18 per share.
3. Purchased 5,000 shares of IBM for $75 per share.
4. Purchased a three-year insurance policy for $27,000.
5. Purchased a building with a fair market value of $200,000 in exchange for a twenty-five year mortgage. The agreement called for a down payment of $40,000.

REQUIRED:

Assume that each transaction is independent. Provide the journal entry for each transaction, and indicate how the cash effect, if any, would be disclosed on the company's statement of cash flows. That is, provide

a.   the dollar amount of the cash effect,

b.   whether it increases or decreases cash, and

c.   the section of the statement of cash flows in which it would appear.

E14–5

(Converting accrual to cash numbers)

The following are several account titles that could appear on an income statement.

1. Cost of Goods Sold	6. Wage Expense
2. Insurance Expense	7. Supplies Expense
3. Sales Revenue	8. Interest Expense
4. Rent Expense	9. Rent Revenue
5. Dividend Revenue	10. Depreciation Expense

Several possible balance sheet accounts follow.

a. Cash	m. Deferred Income Taxes
b. Merchandise Inventory	
c. Retained Earnings	n. Prepaid Rent
d. Unearned Sales Revenue	o. Wages Payable
e. Interest Payable	p. Common Stock
f. Dividends Receivable	q. Supplies Inventory
g. Fixed Assets	r. Discount on Bonds Payable
h. Rent Payable	s. Unearned Rent
i. Accounts Payable	t. Marketable Securities
j. Accounts Receivable	u. Prepaid Interest
k. Premium on Bonds Payable	v. Bonds Payable
l. Allowance for Doubtful Accounts	w. Accumulated Depreciation
	x. Prepaid Insurance

REQUIRED:

a.   Assume that you wish to compute the cash inflow or outflow associated with each income statement account. Match each income statement account with the related balance sheet account (or accounts) you would analyze in this computation.

b.   For Sales Revenue, Cost of Goods Sold, and Interest Expense, indicate whether an increase in the related balance sheet accounts [identified in (a)] would be added to or deducted from the income statement item when computing the cash effect.

E14–6

(Depreciation: a source of cash?)

Your boss asks you to examine the following income statements of Hamilton Hardware, Crozier Crafts Supplies, and Watson Glass.

	HAMILTON HARDWARE	CROZIER CRAFTS SUPPLIES	WATSON GLASS
Sales	$900,000	$900,000	$900,000
Cost of goods sold	400,000	400,000	400,000
Depreciation expense	50,000	70,000	100,000
Other expenses	200,000	200,000	200,000
Net income	$250,000	$230,000	$200,000

In the notes to the financial statements you notice that Hamilton Hardware uses the straight-line method of depreciation, that Crozier Crafts Supplies uses the sum-of-the-years'-digits method, and that Watson Glass uses the double-declining-balance method.

REQUIRED:

a.   Assume that the dollar amounts for sales, cost of goods sold, and other expenses reflect total cash collections from customers, total cash paid for inventory, and total cash paid for

other expenses, respectively. Compute cash provided (used) by operating activities for each company using each of the following:
1. The direct method format
2. The indirect method format
b. Why is the cash provided (used) by operations different from net income? Which of the two methods shows this more clearly?
c. Would you agree or disagree with the following statement? *"Depreciation is an important source of cash for most companies."* Explain your answer.

E14–7

(Preparing a statement of cash flows from original transactions)

Tony began a small retailing operation on January 1, 1997. During 1997 the following transactions occurred.
1. Tony contributed $20,000 of his own money to the business.
2. $60,000 was borrowed from the bank.
3. Long-lived assets were purchased for $25,000 cash.
4. Inventory was purchased: $25,000 cash and $15,000 on account.
5. Inventory with a cost of $25,000 was sold for $80,000: $20,000 cash and $60,000 on account.
6. Cash payments included $18,000 for operating expenses, $5,000 for loan principal, and a $2,000 dividend.
7. $15,000 in expenses were accrued at the end of the year.

REQUIRED:
a. Prepare journal entries for each economic event.
b. Prepare a balance sheet as of the end of 1997 and an income statement and statement of retained earnings for 1997 for Tony's business.
c. Prepare a Cash T-account and a statement of cash flows using the direct method.
d. Prepare a statement of cash flows using the indirect method, but this time prepare it from the company's two balance sheets, the income statement, and the statement of retained earnings. Tony's first balance sheet contains all zero balances.

E14–8

(Preparing a statement of cash flows from the cash account in the ledger)

Driftwood Shipbuilders entered into the following transactions during 1997.
1. Sold $6,000 of no-par common stock.
2. Purchased $6,000 of inventory on account.
3. Purchased new equipment for $5,000 in cash.
4. Collections on accounts receivable totaled $10,000.
5. Made payments to suppliers of $5,000.
6. Declared and paid dividends of $2,000.
7. Paid rent of $6,000 for the last six months of 1997 and $6,000 for the first six months of 1998.
8. Made sales totaling $100,000: $35,000 on account and the remainder for cash.
9. Paid $40,000 in cash for miscellaneous expenses.
10. Sold investments with a cost of $20,000 for $25,000.

REQUIRED:
a. Prepare journal entries for each transaction.
b. Prepare a Cash T-account and post all transactions affecting cash to the account. Assume a beginning cash balance of $25,000.
c. Prepare a statement of cash flows (direct method) from the Cash T-account.

E14–9

(Computing cash outflows from accrual information)

The following year-end totals were taken from the records of Landau's Supply House. Compute the cash outflows associated with insurance and wages during 1997.

	1997	1996
Prepaid insurance	$7,000	$4,200
Wages payable	6,000	0
Insurance expense	3,000	4,700
Wage expense	8,500	3,000

E14–10

(Reconstructing a transaction and its cash effect)

The following information was taken from the records of Dylan's Toys.

	1997	1996
Machinery	$ 45,000	$ 20,000
Accumulated depreciation	(15,000)	(10,000)
Depreciation expense	7,000	6,000
Gain on sale of machinery	2,000	500

ADDITIONAL INFORMATION:
Machinery with a cost of $8,000 was sold during 1997.

REQUIRED:
a. How much machinery was purchased during 1997?
b. How much cash was collected on the sale of the machinery during 1997?
c. Provide the journal entry to record the sale of the machinery.

E14–11

(Computing cash provided by operations from accrual information)

Income statement and balance sheet excerpts of Shevlin and Shores for the period ending December 31, 1997, follow. Compute cash provided (used) by operating activities for the period ending December 31, 1997. Use both the direct and indirect forms of presentation.

INCOME STATEMENT EXCERPTS

Sales		$48,000
Cost of goods sold		30,000
Gross profit		$18,000
Wage expense	$4,000	
Advertising expense	1,000	
Depreciation expense	2,000	7,000
Net income		$11,000

BALANCE SHEET EXCERPTS	1997	1996
Accounts receivable	$4,000	$ 5,000
Deferred revenues	0	3,000
Inventory	9,000	11,000
Accounts payable	3,000	4,000
Wages payable	1,800	900
Prepaid advertising	3,000	1,200
Accumulated depreciation	5,000	3,000

E14–12

(Preparing a statement of cash flows from information contained in two balance sheets, an income statement, and a statement of retained earnings)

The following information was taken from the records of Grimes Pools. Prepare a statement of cash flows (direct method) for the period ending December 31, 1997. Assume that all transactions involve cash.

	1997	1996
Cash	$ 4,000	$ 6,000
Noncash operating assets	15,000	15,000
Nonoperating assets	20,000	28,000
Operating liabilities	2,000	8,000
Nonoperating liabilities	6,000	4,000
Contributed capital	26,000	30,000
Retained earnings	5,000	7,000
Revenues	35,000	
Expenses	34,000	
Dividends	3,000	

E14-13

(Preparing a statement of cash flows from information contained in two balance sheets, an income statement, and a statement of retained earnings)

The following information was taken from the records of Romora Supply House. Prepare a statement of cash flows (direct method) for the period ending December 31, 1997. Assume that all transactions involve cash.

	1997	1996
Cash	$12,000	$ 5,000
Noncash operating assets	18,000	23,000
Nonoperating assets	27,000	23,000
Operating liabilities	7,000	2,000
Nonoperating liabilities	6,000	8,000
Contributed capital	35,000	32,000
Retained earnings	9,000	9,000
Revenues	64,000	
Expenses	61,000	
Dividends	3,000	

E14-14

(Computing net income from cash provided by operating activities)

The operating cash flows and balance sheet excerpts of Schlee and Associates for the period ending December 31, 1997, follow. Compute net income for the period ending December 31, 1997.

OPERATING ACTIVITIES

Cash inflows from sales	$ 65,000
Cash payments for inventories	(40,000)
Cash payments for wages	(6,000)
Cash payments for advertising	(1,000)
Cash provided (used) by operating activities	$ 18,000

BALANCE SHEET EXCERPTS	1997	1996
Accounts receivable	$ 3,000	$ 9,000
Deferred revenues	4,000	1,000
Inventory	18,000	10,000
Accounts payable	7,000	3,000
Salaries payable	2,100	1,300
Prepaid advertising	5,000	8,000
Accumulated depreciation	8,000	5,000

PROBLEMS

P14-1

(Placing transactions on the statement of cash flows)

The following events occurred during 1997 for Frames Unlimited.
1. Purchased inventory for $60,000 in cash.
2. Recorded $40,000 in insurance expense for the portion of an insurance policy acquired in 1991 that expired during 1997.
3. Paid $40,000 for rental space that the company will not use until 1998.
4. Sold land with a cost of $80,000 for $94,000 cash.
5. Paid $90,000 on a long-term note. Included in the $90,000 is $15,000 in interest, $9,000 of which was accrued in 1996.
6. Recorded bad debt expense in the amount of $30,000 (allowance method).
7. Reissued 5,000 shares of treasury stock for $30 per share. The stock was acquired at $18 per share.
8. Declared and issued a stock dividend. 10,000 shares of common stock ($10 par value) were issued with a fair market value at the time of $25 per share.

9. Issued $500,000 face value bonds for cash at a total discount of $25,000.
10. Purchased a building for $100,000 in cash, $50,000 in common stock, and a note with a present value of $217,000.
11. Recorded $35,000 in sales to customers on account.

Frames Unlimited is in the process of preparing a statement of cash flows under the direct method.

REQUIRED:
Use a chart like the one below to indicate the following.
a. The section of the statement of cash flows in which each transaction should be listed. Use the following terms:
    (1) Operating—for operating activities
    (2) Investing—for investing activities
    (3) Financing—for financing activities
    (4) N/A—for items that would not be included on the statement of cash flows
b. Whether the transaction would involve an inflow or an outflow of cash.
c. The dollar amount, if appropriate, that the company would report on the statement of cash flows.

The first transaction is done for you as an example.

TRANSACTION	SECTION	INFLOW	OUTFLOW	AMOUNT
1.	Operating		X	$60,000

P14–2

(Placing transactions on the statement of cash flows)

Endnote Enterprises entered into the following transactions during 1997.
1. Sold merchandise for $52,000 in cash.
2. Purchased a parcel of land. The company paid $12,000 in cash and issued a $30,000 note payable for the remainder.
3. Purchased a three-year insurance policy for $30,000.
4. Purchased a building in exchange for a long-term note with a face value and present value of $115,000.
5. Collected $100,000 on a long-term note receivable. Included in the $100,000 is $6,000 in interest earned and accrued in the previous period and $4,000 in interest earned in the current period.
6. Collected $45,000 from customers that will not be earned until 1998.
7. Reacquired 5,000 shares of its common stock for $10 per share.
8. Declared and paid a cash dividend of $40,000.
9. Paid $25,000 for wages accrued in a prior year.
10. Retired $500,000 in bonds payable. The company gave the creditor $300,000 in cash and $200,000 in common stock.
11. Purchased $60,000 of inventory on account.
12. Wrote off an open account ($5,000) as uncollectible (allowance method).
13. Recorded $84,000 in depreciation expense for the year.

Endnote Enterprises is in the process of preparing its statement of cash flows under the direct method.

REQUIRED:
Use the following chart format to indicate the following.
a. The section of the statement of cash flows in which each transaction would be listed. Use the following terms:
    (1) Operating—for operating activities
    (2) Investing—for investing activities
    (3) Financing—for financing activities
    (4) N/A—for items that would not be included on the statement of cash flows.

b.   Whether the transaction would involve an inflow or an outflow of cash.
c.   The dollar amount, if appropriate, that the company would report on the statement of cash flows.

The first transaction is done for you as an example.

TRANSACTION	SECTION	INFLOW	OUTFLOW	AMOUNT
1.	**Operating**	**X**		**$52,000**

P14–3

(Classifying transactions and their cash effects)

MHT Enterprises entered into the following transactions during 1997.
 1. Sold a piece of equipment with a book value of $8,000 for $1,200.
 2. Purchased a parcel of land for $13,000.
 3. Purchased a three-year insurance policy for $9,000.
 4. Issued 1,000 shares of common stock at $7 per share.
 5. Collected a short-term note, including interest, in the amount of $2,500.
 6. Collected $3,000 from customers that will not be earned until 1998.
 7. Purchased a building in exchange for a long-term note with a face value of $15,000 (the present value of the note is $12,000).
 8. Declared and paid a cash dividend of $7,000.
 9. Paid $5,000 in wages.
10. Converted an outstanding receivable into a short-term note receivable that matures in February 1998.
11. Purchased $4,500 of inventory on account.
12. Wrote off an account ($500) as uncollectible (allowance method).
13. Recorded $9,000 in depreciation expense for the year.

REQUIRED:

a.   The controller of MHT Enterprises is trying to explain the change in the company's cash balance from January 1, 1997, to December 31, 1997. The controller has asked you to analyze each of the transactions. You are to indicate whether cash was provided, used, or not affected by each transaction. If the cash balance is affected by the transaction, indicate the dollar amount of the increase or decrease. Unless otherwise indicated, assume that all transactions involve cash.
b.   Classify each transaction identified in (a) as affecting cash as one of the following:
     (1) An operating activity
     (2) An investing activity
     (3) A financing activity

P14–4

(Classifying transactions and their cash effects)

Several transactions entered into by Travis Retail during 1997 follow.
 1. Received $50,000 for wine previously sold on account.
 2. Paid $55,000 in wages.
 3. Sold a building for $100,000. The building had cost $170,000, and the related accumulated depreciation at the time of sale was $55,000.
 4. Declared and paid a cash dividend of $70,000.
 5. Repurchased 10,000 shares of outstanding common stock at $50 per share.
 6. Purchased a two-year $100,000 fire and storm insurance policy on June 30.
 7. Purchased some equipment in exchange for 1,000 shares of common stock. The stock was currently selling for $75 per share.
 8. Purchased $500,000 in equity securities considered to be long-term.
 9. Issued $200,000 face value in bonds. The bonds were sold at 101.
10. Owed $30,000 in rent as of December 31.

REQUIRED:

Record each transaction on a chart like the following. Classify the sections of the statement of cash flows as a cash flow from operating, investing, or financing activities. Transaction (1) is done as an example.

TRANSACTION	EFFECT ON CASH	SECTION OF STATEMENT	EXPLANATION
1.	+50,000	Operating	Operations is defined in terms of inventory activity.

Ruttman Enterprises began operations in early 1995. Summaries of the statement of cash flows for the years 1995, 1996, and 1997 follow.

	1997	1996	1995
Cash provided (used) by operating activities	?	$(202)	?
Cash provided (used) by investing activities	$ 160	?	$(500)
Cash provided (used) by financing activities	(150)	280	900
Increase (decrease) in cash	$?	$ (2)	$ 110
Cash balance at beginning of year	86	?	0
Cash balance at end of year	$ 176	$ 86	$?

REQUIRED:
a. Compute the missing dollar amounts.
b. Briefly comment on the company's cash management policy over the three-year period.

Webb Industries reported the following information concerning the company's property, plant, and equipment in the 1997 financial report.

	1997	1996
Buildings	$ 750,000	$820,000
Accumulated depreciation	(100,000)	(80,000)
Equipment	500,000	380,000
Accumulated depreciation	(75,000)	(85,000)
Land	250,000	250,000
Depreciation expense—buildings	40,000	25,000
Depreciation expense—equipment	15,000	12,000

Listed below are four independent cases involving buildings, equipment, and land during 1997.
1. The company purchased a building for $60,000.
2. The company sold equipment in December 1997 that was purchased for $50,000. It recorded a gain of $5,000 on the sale.
3. The company sold a piece of land for $300,000 at a gain of $75,000.
4. The company acquired a building in exchange for land. The land had a book value of $150,000 and a market value of $600,000.

REQUIRED:
a. For each case explain the change from 1996 to 1997 in the affected Buildings, Equipment, and Land accounts. [For example, in case (1) explain the change in the Building account, the related Accumulated Depreciation account, and the balance in the related Depreciation Expense account.]
b. For each case compute the effect on the cash balance and indicate the appropriate disclosure on the statement of cash flows.

The stockholders' equity section of Mountvale's Associates is provided below.

	1997	1996
Common stock ($1 par value)	$128,000	$100,000
Additional paid-in capital (C/S)	95,000	12,000
Retained earnings	41,000	35,000
Total stockholders' equity	$264,000	$147,000

ADDITIONAL INFORMATION:

1. 1/1/97: A 20 percent stock dividend was issued. The fair market value of the stock at the time was $3.00 per share.
2. 8/25/97: Land was purchased in exchange for 6,000 shares of common stock. The fair market value of the stock was $3.00 per share.
3. 12/31/97: Common stock was issued for cash.

REQUIRED:

How many shares of common stock did Mountvale issue on December 31, 1997, and how much cash did the issuance generate? Show all calculations clearly. *(Hint:* Calculate the number of shares of common stock issued for cash.)

P14–8

(Converting cash flow numbers to accrual numbers, and vice versa)

Taylor Brothers began operations in 1996. The following selected information was extracted from its financial records.

	1997	1996
Sales returns	$ 25,000	$ 20,000
Cost of goods sold	375,000	250,000
Inventory	110,000	130,000
Accounts receivable	150,000	95,000
Insurance expense	50,000	35,000
Cash collected on sales	500,000	350,000
Accounts payable	115,000	105,000
Cash paid for insurance	90,000	65,000

REQUIRED:

a. Compute gross sales (accrual basis) for 1996 and 1997.
b. Calculate the amount of cash paid to suppliers during 1997 for inventory.
c. Compute the balance in the Prepaid Insurance account as of December 31, 1996, and December 31, 1997.

P14–9

(Reconciling the income statement, the direct method, and the indirect method)

Battery Builders, Inc., prepared statements of cash flows under both the direct and the indirect methods. The operating sections of each statement under the two methods follow. Prepare an income statement from the information provided.

DIRECT METHOD

Collections from customers	$ 26,000
Payments to suppliers	(13,000)
Payments for operating expenses	(10,000)
Cash provided (used) by operating activities	$ 3,000

INDIRECT METHOD

Net income	$ 9,000
Depreciation	3,000
Gain on sale of equipment	(2,000)
Increase in inventory	(3,000)
Increase in accounts receivable	(3,000)
Increase in accounts payable	1,000
Decrease in accrued payables	(2,000)
Cash provided (used) by operating activities	$ 3,000

P14–10

(Manipulating dollar amounts on the statement of cash flows)

Pendleton Enterprises began operations on January 1, 1995. Balance sheet and income statement information for 1995, 1996, and 1997 follow.

	1997	1996	1995
Cash	$ 6,000	$ 9,000	$7,000
Accounts receivable	8,000	5,000	4,000
Accounts payable	5,000	3,000	2,000
Revenues	12,000	14,000	8,000
Expenses	14,000	9,000	6,000

REQUIRED:

a. Prepare the operating sections of the statement of cash flows for 1995, 1996, and 1997 under the direct method.

b. Assume that the $4,000 of outstanding accounts receivable on December 31, 1995, was actually collected before the end of 1995, but that the accounts receivable balances for 1996 and 1997 are unchanged. Prepare the statements of cash flows under the direct method for all three years.

c. Ignore the assumption in (b), and assume alternatively that the company deferred an additional $3,000 on the payment of accounts payable as of December 31, 1995 (i.e., accounts payable equal $5,000, and cash equals $10,000 on December 31, 1995). The accounts receivable balances for 1996 and 1997 are unchanged. Prepare the operating section of the statements of cash flows for all three periods.

d. How can managers manipulate cash provided (used) by operations, and what usually happens in the subsequent period?

P14–11

(Preparing the statement of cash flows from two balance sheets and an income statement)

The 1996 and 1997 balance sheets and related income statement of Watson and Holmes Detective Agency follow. Prepare a statement of cash flows under both the direct and the indirect methods for 1997.

	1997	1996
BALANCE SHEET		
ASSETS		
Cash	$10,000	$ 6,000
Accounts receivable	7,000	2,000
Less: Allowance for doubtful accounts	(1,000)	(500)
Inventory	8,000	10,000
Long-lived assets	12,000	11,000
Less: Accumulated depreciation	(4,000)	(2,000)
Total assets	$32,000	$26,500
LIABILITIES AND STOCKHOLDERS' EQUITY		
Accounts payable	$ 5,000	$ 6,000
Deferred revenues	1,000	2,000
Long-term note payable	10,000	10,000
Less: Discount on note payable	(800)	(1,000)
Common stock	12,000	6,000
Retained earnings	4,800	3,500
Total liabilities and stockholders' equity	$32,000	$26,500

	1997
INCOME STATEMENT	
Revenues	$42,000
Cost of goods sold	(24,000)
Depreciation expense	(2,000)
Interest expense	(3,000)
Bad debt expense	(2,000)
Other expense	(9,000)
Net income	$ 2,000

P14–12

(Paying short-term debts: effects on working capital, the current ratio, and the statement of cash flows)

ISS Inc. began operations on January 1, 1997. They engaged in the following economic events during 1997.

1. Issued 6,000 shares of no-par common stock for $10 per share.
2. Purchased on account 20,000 units of inventory for $1 per unit.
3. Paid and capitalized $7,000 for rent covering 1997 and 1998.
4. Purchased furniture for $30,000, paying $20,000 in cash and signing a long-term note for the remaining balance.
5. Sold on account 8,800 units of inventory for $4.00 per unit.
6. Paid one-half of the outstanding accounts payable.
7. Received $12,000 from customers on open accounts.
8. Paid miscellaneous expenses of $10,000 for the year.
9. Depreciation recorded on the furniture totaled $5,000.
10. Accrued interest on the long-term note payable amounted to $1,000.
11. Declared dividends of $3,000 at year end to be paid in January 1998.
12. Recorded entry for $3,000 of rent expired during 1997.

REQUIRED:

a. Prepare journal entries for these events.
b. Prepare an income statement, statement of retained earnings, balance sheet, and statement of cash flows (indirect method).
c. Compute working capital and the current ratio.
d. Assume that the company pays the outstanding accounts payable on the final day of 1997. Recompute working capital, the current ratio, and cash provided (used) by operating activities.

P14–13

(Preparing the statement of cash flows and reconciling the operating section with the income statement)

Sunshine Enterprises included the following statements in its 1997 financial report.

INCOME STATEMENT	1997
Marketing revenue	$1,000,000
Salary expense	(250,000)
Office supplies used	(175,000)
Depreciation expense	(100,000)
Insurance expense	(60,000)
Rent expense	(120,000)
Net income	$ 295,000

BALANCE SHEET	1997	1996
Cash	$ 100,000	$120,000
Accounts receivable	150,000	105,000
Office supply inventory	75,000	85,000
Prepaid insurance	50,000	10,000
Office furniture	500,000	465,000
Less: Accumulated depreciation	(325,000)	(225,000)
Total assets	$ 550,000	$560,000
Rent payable	$ 20,000	$ 8,000
Common stock ($10 par value)	100,000	100,000
Additional paid-in capital	125,000	125,000
Retained earnings	305,000	327,000
Total liabilities and stockholders' equity	$ 550,000	$560,000

REQUIRED:

a. Convert each of the accrual-basis income statement accounts to a cash basis. Would you classify this method as directly or indirectly computing cash provided (used) by operating activities?

b. Prepare a proof of results. That is, begin with net income and adjust net income to arrive at cash provided (used) by operating activities. Would you classify this method as directly or indirectly computing cash provided (used) by operating activities?

c. Refer to Figure 14–23 in the chapter, and use the same format to reconcile the income statement with operating cash flows.

P14–14

(Preparing the statement of cash flows from two balance sheets and an income statement: book losses and amortized discounts)

The following information was extracted from the financial records of Bower Manufacturing Industries.

INCOME STATEMENT	1997
Sales	$190,000
Cost of goods sold	(80,000)
Depreciation expense	(30,000)
Interest expense	(10,000)
Salary expense	(12,000)
Supplies expense	(7,000)
Loss on sale of marketable sec.	(4,000)
Loss on sale of fixed assets	(10,000)
Net income	$ 37,000

BALANCE SHEETS	1997	1996
Cash	$ 747,000	$ 593,000
Marketable securities	85,000	140,000
Accounts receivable	450,000	400,000
Supplies inventory	10,000	12,000
Inventory	150,000	175,000
Short-term notes receivable	100,000	50,000
Machinery and equipment	550,000	500,000
Less: Accumulated depreciation	(90,000)	(75,000)
Total assets	$2,002,000	$1,795,000
Accounts payable	$ 60,000	$ 95,000
Salaries payable	10,000	10,000
Bonds payable	500,000	500,000
Discount on bonds payable	(5,000)	(10,000)
Common stock ($10 par value)	200,000	100,000
Additional paid-in capital	900,000	800,000
Retained earnings	337,000	300,000
Total liabilities and stockholders' equity	$2,002,000	$1,795,000

ADDITIONAL INFORMATION:

1. The company purchased machinery in exchange for 10,000 shares of common stock. The stock was selling for $20 per share at that time.

2. The short-term receivable was received from a customer in exchange for the sale of merchandise inventory.

REQUIRED:

Prepare a statement of cash flows for the year ended December 31, 1997, using both the direct and the indirect methods.

P14-15

(Preparing the statement of cash flows from two balance sheets and an income statement: book gains and amortized premiums)

The following information was extracted from the 1997 financial records of Price Restaurant Supply Company.

INCOME STATEMENT

Sales	$160,000
Cost of goods sold	(100,000)
Depreciation expense	(12,000)
Insurance expense	(10,000)
Interest expense	(11,000)
Gain on sale of plant equipment	10,000
Net income	$ 37,000

BALANCE SHEETS	1997	1996
Cash	$173,000	$120,000
Accounts receivable	60,000	65,000
Inventory	210,000	110,000
Prepaid insurance	14,000	24,000
Plant equipment	275,000	350,000
Less: Accumulated depreciation	(67,000)	(75,000)
Total assets	$665,000	$594,000
Accounts payable	$ 51,000	$ 50,000
Bonds payable	200,000	200,000
Premium on bonds payable	3,000	5,000
Common stock ($10 par value)	75,000	40,000
Additional paid-in capital	125,000	95,000
Retained earnings	211,000	204,000
Total liabilities and stockholders' equity	$665,000	$594,000

ADDITIONAL INFORMATION:

The company sold a piece of plant equipment for cash that had originally cost $100,000. The accumulated depreciation associated with the equipment at the time of sale was $20,000.

REQUIRED:

Prepare a statement of cash flows for the year ended December 31, 1997, using both the direct and the indirect methods.

P14-16

(Preparing the statement of cash flows and using it to set dividend policy)

Lynch Engineering Firm provided the following income statement for 1997 in its annual financial report.

	1997		1996	
Sales		$5,967,000		$5,590,000
Salary expense	$2,025,000		$1,794,000	
Advertising expense	755,000		710,000	
Bad debt expense	275,000		260,000	
Administrative expenses	898,000		832,000	
Janitorial expense	132,000		120,000	
Supplies expense	281,000		299,000	
Depreciation expense	963,000	5,329,000	978,000	4,993,000
Net income		$ 638,000		$ 597,000

ADDITIONAL INFORMATION:

1. The company declared and paid a dividend of $550,000 in 1996 but did not declare any dividends in 1997.
2. 1996:
   (a) 35 percent of the sales were on account.
   (b) The accounts receivable balance decreased by $2,980,000 from January 1 to December 31.
   (c) As of December 31, the company still owed $145,000 in wages and $67,000 on the supplies used during the year.
3. 1997:
   (a) 75 percent of the sales were on account.
   (b) The Accounts Receivable balance increased by $1,671,750 from January 1 to December 31.
   (c) As of December 31, the company still owed $25,000 in wages and $50,000 in advertising.
   (d) On January 1, 1996, the company had a balance of $13,245 in cash.
4. The company had no write-offs on recoveries of accounts receivable during 1996 or 1997.

REQUIRED:

a. Prepare the operating section of the statement of cash flows for 1996 and 1997, using the direct method.
b. Assume that you are a member of the board of directors of the Lynch Engineering Firm. Several influential stockholders have called you and complained that the company generated more net income in 1997 than in 1996, yet chose not to declare a dividend in 1997. How would you explain the board's position on dividends in 1996 versus 1997?

P14–17

(Preparing a complete set of financial statements from a set of original transactions)

Mick's Photographic Equipment began operations on January 1, 1996. During 1996 the company entered into the following transactions.

1. Issued 50,000 shares of $15 par value common stock for $30 per share in exchange for cash. Also issued, for cash, 1,000 shares of 10 percent, $100 par value preferred stock for $102 per share.
2. Purchased $750,000 of fixed assets in exchange for cash.
3. Issued twenty bonds, each with a face value of $1,000, at 146 (annual coupon rate = 16 percent and annual yield rate = 10 percent). The bonds pay interest semiannually on December 31 and June 30.
4. Purchased land in exchange for 1,000 shares of $15 par value common stock. The shares were selling for $40 per share at the time.
5. Purchased $2,000,000 of inventory on account. $1,075,000 was subsequently paid during 1996.
6. Sold $2,050,000 of merchandise in exchange for cash. The related inventory had cost $875,000.
7. Purchased a two-year insurance policy for $80,000.
8. Purchased short-term marketable securities for $250,000.
9. Sold $880,000 of merchandise on account. The related inventory had a cost of $490,000. $500,000 of the sales made on account were collected during the year.
10. Paid $500,000 in miscellaneous expenses (rent, utilities, and wages).
11. Declared, but did not pay, a $100,000 dividend.
12. Made the first interest payment on the bonds on December 31.

ADJUSTING ENTRIES:

(a) The fixed assets were purchased on January 1 and had an estimated useful life and salvage value of five years and $50,000, respectively. The company uses the straight-line depreciation method.
(b) The company used one-fourth of the insurance policy during 1996.

(c) The market value of the marketable securities on December 31 was $225,000.

(d) As of December 31, the company had incurred, but had not yet paid, $75,000 in miscellaneous expenses.

(e) The company estimates that 8 percent of credit sales will prove uncollectible.

(f) The market value of the inventory was $5,000 less than the cost.

REQUIRED:

a. Prepare journal entries for each of the original and adjusting transactions. Establish T-accounts for each account. Post the entries to the T-accounts.

b. Prepare the necessary closing entries. Post these entries.

c. Prepare the income statement and balance sheet for Mick's Photographic Equipment for the year ended December 31, 1996.

d. Prepare the statement of cash flows for Mick's Photographic Equipment for the year ended December 31, 1996, using both the direct and the indirect methods.

CASES

C14–1

(Using the cash flow statement to spot earnings quality problems)

An article in *Business Week* (October 30, 1995) describes how Bob Olstein, a successful stock analyst, predicts that the prices of stocks issued by firms who "engage in aggressive accounting practices" will go down, stating that other "investors have unrealistic expectations of the earnings potential." He cites Mattel as an example by noting that big changes in net receivables, inventories, and deferred income taxes as well as foreign currency translation gains that produced no cash accounted for most of Mattel's earnings growth in the first half of 1995. The company's debt also jumped "from $440 million to $630 million in about two years."

REQUIRED:

a. Explain how the statement of cash flows, especially if prepared under the indirect format, can be used to identify "quality of earnings" and "earnings persistence" problems.

b. Specifically describe how the information mentioned above about Mattel was used to indicate these kinds of problems.

c. Do you think that it is possible to identify over- and under-valued stocks by identifying firms that use aggressive accounting practices?

C14–2

(Equity in unconsolidated affiliates)

As of December 31, 1994, Safeway Inc., one of the world's largest food retailers, held a 35% equity interest in Vons, which operated 336 grocery stores located mostly in southern California, and a 49% equity interest in Casa Ley, which operated 70 stores in western Mexico. These investments totaled $329 million on the company's 1994 balance sheet. In its 1994 annual report Safeway reported that the income recognized on these investments fell from $39.1 million in 1992, to $33.5 million in 1993, to $27.3 million in 1994. These same dollar amounts were subtracted from net income in the operating section of the statements of cash flows for 1992, 1993, and 1994 in the calculation of net cash flow from operations in those three years.

REQUIRED:

a. Explain why these three dollar amounts were subtracted from net income in the calculation of net cash from operations for 1992, 1993, and 1994.

b. Compute the net income and dividends declared by Vons and Casa Ley in 1992, 1993, and 1994.

c. These dollar amounts were reported on Safeway's income statements for 1992, 1993, and 1994. In 1992 the $39.1 million of equity income represented almost 90% of the company's earnings. Discuss the "quality" of these earnings amounts from a financial statement user's perspective.

C14–3

(Accrual and cash flow accounting)

In *Forbes*, Loan Officer, Han Blackford, commented that cash flow analysis has risen in importance due to a "trend over the past twenty years toward capitalizing and deferring more and more expenses. Although the practice may match revenues and expenses more closely, a laudable intent, it has also made it harder to find the available cash in a company—and easier for lenders to wind up with a loss." The article further stated that "During [a recent recession] a wave of bankruptcies drew attention to the need for better warning signals of the sort cash flow analysis could provide."*

*Jinny St. Goar, "Where's 4th Quarter Profits Reflecting Unusual Accounting Method?" *Forbes*, April 8, 1985, p. 120.

REQUIRED:
a. Why would the process of capitalizing match revenues and expenses more closely, yet make it harder to find the cash available in a company?
b. Discuss the difference between earning power and solvency, why both are essential for a successful business, and how present-day financial accounting statements provide measures of each.
c. Explain why a wave of bankruptcies would draw attention to cash flow analysis.

C14–4

(Classifying cash flows, especially interest and dividends)

King's Table operates buffet-style restaurants throughout the United States. The company recently pursued a strategy of remodeling and expansion, using cash from operating activities and bank borrowings.

REQUIRED:
a. In which section of the statement of cash flows (operating, investing, or financing) would the following items appear? (1) Cash borrowed from a bank, (2) Cash paid for remodeling, (3) Cash paid to build a new restaurant
b. If the company had issued stock specifically to raise cash for expansion projects, in which section of the statement of cash flows would the cash proceeds from the sale of stock appear?
c. In which sections of the statement of cash flows would interest paid on the bank borrowings and dividends paid to the stockholders appear? Since interest represents a return to debt capital providers, why is it not disclosed in the same section as dividends, which represents a return to equity capital providers?

C14–5

(Analyzing the operating section of the statement of cash flows)

Federal Express provides door-to-door delivery service of small packages and documents throughout the United States. Its December 31, 1994, statement of cash flows included the following:

YEARS ENDED MAY 31 (IN THOUSANDS)	1994	1993	1992
OPERATING ACTIVITIES			
Net income (loss)	$ 204,370	$ 53,866	$(113,782)
Adjustments to reconcile income (loss) to net cash provided by operating activities:			
Depreciation and amortization	599,357	579,896	577,157
Provision for uncollectible accounts	45,763	33,552	31,670
Provision (credit) for deferred income taxes and other	3,810	19,910	(75,219)
(Gain) loss from disposals of property and equipment	(11,897)	(5,648)	1,810
Cumulative effect of accounting change	—	55,943	—
Changes in assets and liabilities, net of effects from purchases and dispositions of businesses:			
(Increase) in receivables	(173,902)	(41,535)	(727)
(Increase) decrease in other current assets	(7,826)	(5,813)	61,749
Increase in accounts payable, accrued expenses and other liabilities	110,508	13,651	33,620
Other, net	(2,905)	21,259	4,543
Net cash provided by operating activities	$ 767,278	$725,081	$ 520,821

REQUIRED:

a. Depreciation and amortization are added to net income in the computation of net cash provided by operating activities. Does this mean that depreciation and amortization are sources of cash? Explain.

b. What method does Federal Express use to account for uncollectible accounts? Explain why a provision for uncollectible accounts is added to net income in the computation of net cash provided by operating activities.

c. What can one infer about how Federal Express is managing its current assets and liabilities from the operating section of the statement of cash flows?

C14–6

(Misunderstandings in the financial press)

USA Today (February 12, 1991), in an article about how financial analysts follow cable TV companies, commented: "Analysts look at cable companies' cash flow—earnings plus cash set aside for depreciation—rather than just earnings."

REQUIRED:

Critique the statement published in *USA Today*.

C14–7

(Analyzing the statement of cash flows)

Refer to the statements of cash flows for the years ending 1994, 1993, and 1992 at the top of the next page. The statements were taken from the 1994 annual report of The Quaker Oats Company (dollars in millions).

REQUIRED:

a. The company has expanded considerably over the past three years. Describe the nature of the expansion, and describe the primary sources of funding for the expansion. What else has this financing source enabled the company to do?

b. What earnings amounts would have been reported in 1993 and 1994 without the accounting change and the restructuring charge? What were the cash flow effects of these two events?

c. What major financing activity has the company participated in over the last three years?

d. Comment in general on the solvency position of Quaker Oats.

C14–8

(Analyzing the statement of cash flows)

Refer to the statements of cash flows for the years ended 1994, 1993, and 1992 for Sprint, which can be found in Figure 14–4 in the text, and answer the following questions.

a. In what general ways has cash provided by operating activities been used in 1992, 1993, and 1994?

b. Comment on Sprint's dividend payment strategy during 1992, 1993, and 1994.

c. Describe the change in borrowing strategy evident over the past three years.

d. What has happened to the company's current assets and liabilities during 1992 through 1994?

C14–9

(Mergers and the statement of cash flows)

During the 1980s many huge mergers were financed with large amounts of debt. On December 1, 1988, for example, RJR Nabisco agreed to be purchased for $25 billion by takeover artists Kohlberg Kravis Roberts in a deal that depended heavily on junk bonds, and in late 1989 Time, Inc., merged with Warner Communications in a $14 billion deal, which was financed with $8.3 billion of long-term debt and approximately $5.6 billion of preferred stock.

REQUIRED:

a. Explain why it is difficult for the companies that result from such mergers to report profits in the years immediately following the mergers, yet in those same years report positive cash flow for operations.

b. In the year of the merger what special items would you expect to see on the resulting company's statement of cash flows, and where would they be reported on the statement?

c. Immediately after the merger, RJR Nabisco went on a rampage of asset sales, selling more than $5.4 billion in assets, including Del Monte foods, Chun King oriental foods, and Nabisco's international brands unit. Why do you think the company sold these assets, and where would such transactions be reported on the statement of cash flows?

CONSOLIDATED STATEMENTS OF CASH FLOWS YEAR ENDED JUNE 30	DOLLARS IN MILLIONS		
	1994	1993	1992
Cash Flows from Operating Activities:			
Net income	$ 231.5	$ 171.3	$ 247.6
Adjustments to reconcile net income to net cash provided by operating activities:			
Cumulative effect of accounting changes	—	115.5	—
Depreciation and amortization	171.2	156.9	155.9
Deferred income taxes	(7.7)	(46.4)	—
Restructuring charges and gains on divestitures—net	108.6	20.5	(1.0)
Loss on disposition of property and equipment	15.0	23.8	23.1
(Increase) decrease in trade accounts receivable	(77.7)	59.1	84.7
(Increase) decrease in inventories	(67.6)	41.9	(14.3)
(Increase) in other current assets	(56.3)	(25.8)	(10.1)
Increase (decrease) in trade accounts payable	44.1	(7.6)	24.0
Increase (decrease) in other current liabilities	6.6	(6.4)	132.5
Change in deferred compensation	15.6	11.0	11.6
Other items	67.5	44.4	(43.1)
Change in payable to Fisher-Price	—	—	(29.6)
Net Cash Provided by Operating Activities	450.8	558.2	581.3
Cash Flows from Investing Activities:			
Additions to property, plant and equipment	(175.1)	(172.3)	(176.4)
Change in other receivables and investments	(6.4)	(25.6)	(20.0)
Purchase and sale of property and business—net	(82.1)	1.2	16.5
Net Cash Used in Investing Activities	(263.6)	(196.7)	(179.9)
Cash Flows from Financing Activities:			
Cash dividends	(144.6)	(140.3)	(132.8)
Change in short-term debt	83.3	67.0	(19.6)
Proceeds from long-term debt	222.2	0.5	1.1
Reduction of long-term debt	(100.6)	(59.0)	(46.2)
Proceeds from short-term debt to be refinanced	—	—	50.0
Issuance of common treasury stock	11.8	23.3	20.3
Repurchases of common stock	(214.9)	(323.1)	(235.1)
Repurchases of preferred stock	(1.2)	(1.1)	(0.9)
Net Cash Used in Financing Activities	(144.0)	(432.7)	(363.2)
Effect of Exchange Rate Changes on Cash and Cash Equivalents	36.2	37.0	(17.6)
Net Increase (Decrease) in Cash and Cash Equivalents	79.4	(34.2)	20.6
Cash and Cash Equivalents—Beginning of Year	61.0	95.2	74.6
Cash and Cash Equivalents—End of Year	$ 140.4	$ 61.0	$95.2

C14–10

(The annual report of MCI)

Refer to the annual report of MCI and answer the questions below.

a. What major reasons explain the large increase in MCI's cash position from 1993 to 1994?

b. Cash from operating activities ($2,355) is calculated in two different ways on the statement of cash flows. Discuss the differences and the relative usefulness to the reader of the two methods.

c. What were MCI's main investing activities in 1994 and how were they financed?

d. Describe the major preferred stock transactions entered into by MCI in 1992 and 1993.

e. Does MCI pay large amounts in dividends? Explain.

f. How much cash was collected over the three-year period on stock issuances associated with employee compensation plans, and where is MCI getting the stock issued for this purpose?

Quality of Earnings Cases: A Comprehensive Review

CASE 1: AVERY CORPORATION

Tracey Sellers, a retired musical artist, and his two brothers own a substantial amount of the outstanding common stock of Avery Corporation, a young and fast-growing manufacturer of cartons, containers, and a wide variety of packaging materials. The company's home office is in Cleveland, Ohio, and regional sales offices are operating at several locations across the United States.

Tracy and his brothers, who recently inherited the stock from their aunt, know very little about the business. Just a few days ago, each received the company's 1995 annual report, and Tracy plans to attend the annual stockholders' meeting in Cleveland, scheduled next month. He would also like to take an active part at the meeting—representing both his own and his brothers' interests—especially because doubts about the quality of the company's board of directors and management have recently been raised. However, he knows very little about analyzing annual report information and has hired you to help him prepare for the meeting.

Tracy begins by showing you Avery's 1995 annual report, which includes a letter from Avery's chief executive officer, Arnold Tennenden, a set of consolidated financial statements, and the related footnotes. He cautions you that he wonders whether the CEO's letter accurately characterizes the company's performance and financial position, and he is asking you to ascertain whether this letter reasonably represents Avery's financial situation. Tracy suspects that many of the comments made by Arnold at the upcoming stockholders' meeting will be similar to those contained in the annual report letter, and he hopes to be able to accurately evaluate and respond to them. The CEO's letter is provided below.

LETTER FROM THE CHIEF EXECUTIVE OFFICER

To the Shareholders:

Avery has just completed another successful year, demonstrating strong earning power. Total revenues increased by almost 8 percent, and profits increased by a whopping 30 percent. The profit rise would have been even greater had management chosen not to record a highly unusual $5 million write-off due to the obsolescence of certain inventory items.

The company used the cash generated from these earnings to make an important acquisition, to increase its investment in property, plant, and equipment, and to increase common shareholder dividends. Indeed, Avery has grown substantially in this recent year and the shareholders have prospered. It is particularly impressive that Avery has been able to maintain its rate of growth without relying heavily on debt financing. The company's debt/equity ratio as of the end of 1995 is only 0.65, and profits are more than adequate to cover debt interest payments.

In sum, I am proud to report to you that Avery is an extremely solvent company with great earning power potential. Management plans to keep it that way far into the future.

Arnold Tennenden
Chief Executive Officer

Tracy has also attempted to review the statements himself, and in addition to evaluating the CEO's letter, he would like you to answer the questions listed below.

1. Why did the company's 1995 earnings-per-share number decrease even though net income seems to have increased?
2. How many shares of stock were issued in the 1995 stock dividend, and how did this issuance affect the assets and liabilities of the company?
3. Is it likely that the company will exercise its option to call its outstanding bonds in the near future? Why?
4. The company's debt/equity ratio as of December 31, 1995, is only 0.65. Is that ratio an accurate measure of the company's actual debt position?
5. Is the 1995 sales number disclosed in the footnotes a measure of the cash collected from customers during 1995? If not, how much cash was actually collected from customers in that year? How much cash was paid in 1995 to Avery's suppliers for inventory purchases?
6. Inventory and accounts receivable levels have increased dramatically over the past two years. Is that a positive sign?
7. Are the elements that make up the increase in profits from 1994 to 1995 likely to persist in future years?
8. What was the value of Buckeye's property, plant, and equipment when Buckeye was acquired by Avery in 1995?
9. What was the book value of the equipment that was sold by Avery in December of 1995?
10. How much cash did Avery contribute to its pension fund during 1994?

FOOTNOTES TO THE FINANCIAL STATEMENTS

1. Revenue recognition. The company recognizes revenue when goods are shipped and all sales are made on credit. The dollar amounts for operating revenues reported on the consolidated statement of income include the following items (dollars in thousands):

ITEM	1995	1994
Sales	$115,000	$120,000
Income from affiliate	1,800	1,500
Gain on sale of equipment	6,000	—
Special services	8,000	—
Total	$130,800	$121,500

2. Inventory. Inventory is carried at lower of cost or market under the first-in, first-out cost flow assumption. Inventory purchase costs have risen consistently over the past several years. The Company wrote off certain inventories during 1995 due to obsolescence.

AVERY CORPORATION
CONSOLIDATED BALANCE SHEET
(IN THOUSANDS OF DOLLARS)
DECEMBER 31, 1995, 1994, AND 1993

	1995	1994	1993
ASSETS			
Cash plus marketable securities	$ 14,235	$ 58,676	$ 3,500
Accounts receivable	45,000	35,000	25,000
Less: Allowance for uncollectibles	(600)	(550)	(500)
Inventory	55,000	45,000	30,000
Investment in affiliate	11,950	10,900	10,000
Property, plant, and equipment	94,000	50,000	50,000
Less: Accumulated depreciation	(19,000)	(20,000)	(15,000)
Goodwill	15,000	—	—
Total assets	$215,585	$179,026	$103,000
LIABILITIES AND STOCKHOLDERS' EQUITY			
Accounts payable	$ 16,000	$ 8,200	$ 6,000
Accrued payables	14,000	6,000	7,700
Unearned revenues	—	8,000	—
Unfunded pension liability	7,339	5,339	2,339
Bonds payable	50,000	50,000	50,000
Less: Unamortized discount	(4,868)	(5,335)	(5,759)
Deferred income taxes	3,155	3,196	2,720
Preferred stock	50,000	50,000	—
Common stock	5,350	5,000	5,000
Additional paid-in capital	64,900	55,000	25,000
Retained earnings	27,709	31,626	30,000
Less: Treasury stock	(18,000)	(38,000)	(20,000)
Total liabilities and stockholders' equity	$215,585	$179,026	$103,000

3. Property, plant, and equipment. Property, plant, and equipment are carried at cost less accumulated depreciation. Depreciation is calculated on a straight-line basis, assuming no salvage value and a 10-year useful life. In December of 1995 the Company sold equipment with a cost of $20 million and soon thereafter purchased additional equipment for $14 million.

4. Acquisitions. In December of 1993 the Company acquired 30 percent of the outstanding common stock of Spartan Savings, a highly leveraged financial institution, for $10 million. The Company has held this interest through December of 1995.

In early December of 1995 the Company acquired 100 percent of the outstanding common stock of Buckeye Corporation, which consisted primarily of property, plant, and equipment and goodwill. The purchase price included $50 million cash and 1,000,000 shares of the Company's common stock, which had been held in treasury. The stock had a market value at the time of the acquisition of $15 per share.

5. Employee pension. The amount of pension expense accrued each year is based on a number of actuarial assumptions regarding the life expectancy of the current

AVERY CORPORATION
CONSOLIDATED INCOME STATEMENT
(IN THOUSANDS OF DOLLARS, EXCEPT PER-SHARE NUMBERS)
FOR THE YEARS ENDED DECEMBER 31, 1995 AND 1994

	1995	1994
Operating revenues	$130,800	$121,500
Less: Cost of goods sold	(60,500)	(60,000)
Selling and administrative expenses	(23,000)	(25,000)
Depreciation expense	(5,000)	(5,000)
Accrued pension expense	(10,000)	(8,000)
Bad debt expense	(500)	(450)
Operating lease expense	(10,000)	(10,000)
Net income from operations	$ 21,800	$ 13,050
Loss due to Inventory write-down	(5,000)	—
Interest expense	(4,467)	(4,424)
Pretax income from continuing operations	$ 12,333	$ 8,626
Income tax expense	5,000	3,000
Net income	$ 7,333	$ 5,626
Earnings per share:		
From continuing operations	$ 3.20	$ 3.75
Due to extraordinary loss	(1.30)	—
Total $	1.90	$ 3.75

workforce and other factors. Payments to the pension fund have met all regulatory requirements.

6. Bond issuance. In January of 1993 the Company issued 5,000 bonds, each with a face value of $1,000, a stated interest rate of 8 percent, and a maturity date of January 2000. The bonds sold for $877.10 each, producing an effective interest rate of 10 percent. The terms of the issuance state that beginning in 1996 and thereafter the Company can call the bonds for 2 percent above the face value. Current market interest rates are 8 percent.

7. Deferred income taxes. The deferred income tax account arises solely from the Company's choice to use straight-line depreciation for financial reporting purposes and double-declining-balance for income tax reporting purposes. For both purposes property, plant, & equipment are assumed to have a 10-year life and no salvage value. The Company's effective tax rate is 0.38.

8. Leases. The Company leases certain facilities in which operations are conducted. Under the lease contract the Company is responsible for maintenance and can acquire the leased properties at the end of the lease term for an amount that is equal to 50 percent of the market value at that time. The current lease was entered into in January of 1992 and will expire in January of 2002. Lease payments are set at $10 million per year over the period of the lease.

9. Stock transactions. In 1993 the Company was authorized to issue 10,000,000 shares of $1 par value common stock, and it chose to issue 5,000,000 shares for a

AVERY CORPORATION
CONSOLIDATED STATEMENT OF CASH FLOWS
(IN THOUSANDS OF DOLLARS)
FOR THE YEARS ENDED DECEMBER 31, 1995 AND 1994

	1995	1994
Operating activities:		
Net income	$ 7,333	$ 5,626
Depreciation	5,000	5,000
Inventory write-down	5,000	—
Income in excess of cash from affiliate	(1,050)	(900)
Amortization of bond discount	467	424
Gain from sale of property, plant, & equipment	(6,000)	—
Deferred income taxes	(41)	476
Increase (decrease) in unfunded pension liability	2,000	3,000
(Increase) decrease in net accounts receivable	(9,950)	(9,950)
(Increase) decrease in inventory	(15,000)	(15,000)
Increase (decrease) in accounts payable	7,800	2,200
Increase (decrease) in accrued payables	8,000	(1,700)
Increase (decrease) in unearned revenues	(8,000)	8,000
Net cash from operating activities	$ (4,441)	$ (2,824)
Investing activities:		
Cash payments for acquisitions	$(50,000)	$ —
Cash payments for equipment purchases	(14,000)	—
Cash from equipment sales	20,000	—
Net cash from investing activities	$(44,000)	$ 0
Financing activities:		
Cash from preferred stock issuance	$ —	$ 80,000
Cash from exercise of executive stock options	10,000	—
Cash payments for treasury stock purchases	—	(18,000)
Cash payments for dividends	(6,000)	(4,000)
Net cash from financing activities	$ 4,000	$ 58,000
Increase (decrease) in cash balance	$(44,441)	$ 55,176
Beginning cash balance	58,676	3,500
Ending cash balance	$ 14,235	$ 58,676

AVERY CORPORATION
CONSOLIDATED STATEMENT OF STOCKHOLDERS' EQUITY
(IN THOUSANDS OF DOLLARS)
FOR THE YEARS ENDED DECEMBER 31, 1995 AND 1994

TRANSACTION	PREFERRED STOCK	COMMON STOCK	ADDITIONAL PAID-IN CAPITAL	RETAINED EARNINGS	TREASURY STOCK
Beginning balance (12/31/93)	$ 0	$5,000	$25,000	$30,000	$(20,000)
Net income				5,626	
Cash dividends				(4,000)	
Issue of preferred stock	50,000		30,000		
Purchase of treasury stock					(18,000)
Ending balance (12/31/94)	$50,000	$5,000	$55,000	$31,626	$(38,000)
Net income				7,333	
Preferred stock dividend				(6,000)	
Exercise of stock options					10,000
Issue for acquisition			5,000		10,000
Stock dividend		350	4,900	(5,250)	
Ending balance (12/31/95)	$50,000	$5,350	$64,900	$27,709	$(18,000)

price of $6 per share. Later that year, the Company repurchased 2,000,000 of these shares for $10 per share and held them in treasury. Additional treasury shares were purchased in 1994 for $12 per share.

In December of 1994 the Company issued 1,000,000 shares of $50 par value preferred stock for $80 per share. Annual dividend payments are set at 12 percent of par value and the shares are callable at par value by the Company in 1999. There are 1,000,000 authorized but unissued shares of preferred stock.

Company executives are paid bonuses in the form of options to purchase common stock. In 1995, 1,000,000 options were exercised. Five million options are outstanding as of December 31, 1995.

10. Stock dividend. At the end of 1995 the Company declared and issued a 10 percent stock dividend on all outstanding common shares. At the time of the issuance the common stock had a market value of $15 per share.

CASE 2: ZENITH SERVICES

It is early in January 1996. You have just been hired by Zenith Services and have been assigned to the accounting department. The company specializes in creative sales displays used to market point-of-purchase goods, and it has several large customers that annually hire Zenith to design and manufacture displays for retail outlets. The company has grown quickly and recently has moved from a pure manufacturing firm to one that provides both manufacturing and creative services. In fact, the company's name was just changed from Zenith Manufacturing to Zenith Creations.

Recently, two giant companies in the industry have shown a serious interest in acquiring Zenith, which has caused Zenith's management to be particularly concerned with how the financial statements are interpreted by outside parties—especially the potential buyers, who will likely base their offers on assessments of Zenith's financial condition and performance. At the same time, management is considering several actions and wants to know in advance how these actions will affect the financial statements, financial ratios, and outsider evaluations of Zenith's financial condition and performance. The actions are listed below.

- Purchase treasury stock at the current market price.
- Write off a relatively large uncollectible accounts receivable.
- Issue a 20 percent stock dividend.
- Redeem the remaining notes payable for $23,200,000.
- Sell the real estate received in the acquisition of Lyon Real Estate for $12,000,000.
- Change the amortization period for the goodwill acquired in the acquisition of Lyon Real Estate to 10 years.
- Change the inventory cost flow assumption from LIFO to FIFO.

Your supervisor has asked you to prepare a memo that will be part of a report presented to Zenith's board of directors concerning the possible acquisition. Your memo should consist of two parts: (1) an objective evaluation of Zenith's financial condition and performance, and (2) an assessment of how each of the actions listed above will affect that evaluation. Zenith's financial statements and related footnotes are contained on the following pages.

ZENITH CREATIONS
CONSOLIDATED BALANCE SHEET
(IN THOUSANDS OF DOLLARS)
DECEMBER 31, 1995, 1994, AND 1993

	1995	1994	1993
ASSETS			
Cash plus marketable securities	$ 43,933	$ 30,260	$ 3,500
Accounts receivable	15,900	16,800	28,000
Less: Allowance for uncollectibles	(1,400)	(800)	(1,000)
Inventory	22,500	23,500	30,500
Investment in affiliate	4,900	5,600	6,000
Property, plant, and equipment	82,000	85,000	60,000
Less: Accumulated depreciation	(14,000)	(20,000)	(15,000)
Goodwill	16,000	20,000	—
Total assets	$169,833	$160,360	$112,000
LIABILITIES AND STOCKHOLDERS' EQUITY			
Accounts payable	$ 19,000	$ 6,000	$ 3,000
Accrued payables	14,700	9,700	7,700
Unearned revenues	4,000	8,000	5,000
Restructuring reserve	14,000	—	—
Unfunded pension liability	5,900	3,900	2,400
Notes payable	25,000	50,000	50,000
Less: Unamortized discount	(5,335)	(11,518)	(12,289)
Deferred income taxes	4,920	6,420	5,220
Preferred stock	12,500	—	—
Common stock ($1 par value)	13,555	12,500	10,000
Additional paid-in capital	61,605	47,500	25,000
Retained earnings	19,488	47,658	35,969
Less: Treasury stock	(19,500)	(19,800)	(20,000)
Total liabilities and stockholders' equity	$169,833	$160,360	$112,000

FOOTNOTES TO THE FINANCIAL STATEMENTS (DOLLAR AMOUNTS, EXCEPT PER SHARE, IN THOUSANDS):

1. Revenue recognition. The company recognizes revenue when goods are shipped or services are provided, and all sales are made on credit. The dollar amounts for operating revenues reported on the consolidated statement of income include the following items:

ITEM	1995	1994
Sales	$110,000	$120,000
Income (loss) from affiliate	(200)	800
Loss on sale of equipment	(4,000)	—
Special services	4,000	5,000
Total	$109,800	$125,800

2. Inventory. Inventory is carried at lower of cost or market under the LIFO cost flow assumption. LIFO reserves for 1993, 1994, and 1995 are $1,400, $1,250, and $1,100, respectively. The company has experienced LIFO liquidations in each of the three

ZENITH CREATIONS
CONSOLIDATED INCOME STATEMENT
(IN THOUSANDS OF DOLLARS, EXCEPT PER-SHARE NUMBERS)
FOR THE YEARS ENDED DECEMBER 31, 1995 AND 1994

	1995	1994
Operating revenues	$109,800	$125,800
Less: Cost of goods sold	(47,000)	(52,000)
Selling and administrative expenses	(27,000)	(23,000)
Depreciation and amortization expenses	(10,000)	(5,000)
Accrued pension expense	(8,000)	(7,500)
Bad debt expense	(1,500)	(1,000)
Operating lease expense	(8,000)	(8,000)
Net income from operations	$ 8,300	$ 29,300
Interest expense	(3,848)	(3,771)
Loss on inventory write-down	(2,000)	—
Restructuring charge	(15,000)	—
Pretax income (loss) from continuing operations	$(12,548)	$ 25,529
Income tax expense	500	6,000
Net income (loss) from continuing operations	$(13,048)	$ 19,529
Extraordinary loss due to debt retirement	2,462	—
Net income (loss)	$(15,510)	$ 19,529
Earnings per share:		
From continuing operations	$ (1.24)	$ 1.86
Due to extraordinary loss	(.23)	—
Total (excludes stock dividend)	$ (1.47)	$ 1.86

years, but the effects on income due to the liquidations have been immaterial. The company wrote off certain inventories at the end of 1995 due to obsolescence.

3. Property, plant, and equipment. Property, plant, and equipment are carried at cost less accumulated depreciation. Depreciation is calculated on a straight-line basis, assuming no salvage value and a 10-year useful life. During 1995 the company sold equipment with an original cost of $18,000.

4. Acquisitions. In January of 1993 the company acquired 40 percent of the outstanding common stock of University Services for $5,000. The company has held this equity interest through December of 1995.

In December of 1994 the company acquired 100 percent of the outstanding common stock of Lyon Real Estate, which consisted of land and goodwill. The purchase price included $10,000 cash, and the company issued 2,500,000 shares of common stock. The stock had a market value at the time of the acquisition of $10 per share. The company uses the straight-line method to amortize goodwill.

5. Employee pension. The amount of pension expense accrued each year is based on a number of actuarial assumptions regarding the life expectancy of the current workforce and other factors. Payments to the pension fund have met all regulatory requirements.

6. Note payable. In December of 1993 the company signed a note with a face value of $50,000, a stated interest rate of 6 percent, and a maturity date of December 2003.

ZENITH CREATIONS
CONSOLIDATED STATEMENT OF CASH FLOWS
(IN THOUSANDS OF DOLLARS)
FOR THE YEARS ENDED DECEMBER 31, 1995 AND 1994

	1995	1994
Operating activities:		
Net income (loss)	$(15,510)	$ 19,529
Depreciation and amortization	10,000	5,000
Affiliate distributions over earnings	700	400
Amortization of bond discount	848	771
Loss from sale of property, plant, & equipment	4,000	—
Loss on debt retirement	2,462	
Noncash restructuring charge	14,000	
Deferred income taxes	(1,500)	1,200
Increase (decrease) in unfunded pension liability	2,000	1,500
(Increase) decrease in net accounts receivable	1,500	11,000
(Increase) decrease in inventory	1,000	7,000
Increase (decrease) in accounts payable	13,000	3,000
Increase (decrease) in accrued payables	5,000	2,000
Increase (decrease) in unearned revenues	(4,000)	3,000
Net cash from operating activities	$ 33,500	$ 54,400
Investing activities:		
Cash payments for acquisitions	$ —	$(10,000)
Cash payments for equipment purchases	(15,000)	(10,000)
Cash from equipment sales	2,000	—
Net cash from investing activities	$(13,000)	$(20,000)
Financing activities:		
Cash from preferred stock issuance	$ 15,000	$ —
Cash from exercise of executive stock options	300	160
Cash payment to retire debt	(22,127)	—
Cash payments for dividends	—	(7,800)
Net cash from financing activities	$ (6,827)	$ (7,640)
Increase (decrease) in cash balance	$ 13,673	$ 26,760
Beginning cash balance	30,260	3,500
Ending cash balance	$ 43,933	$ 30,260

ZENITH CREATIONS
CONSOLIDATED STATEMENT OF STOCKHOLDERS' EQUITY
(IN THOUSANDS OF DOLLARS)
FOR THE YEARS ENDED DECEMBER 31, 1995 AND 1994

TRANSACTION	PREFERRED STOCK	COMMON STOCK	ADDITIONAL PAID-IN CAPITAL	RETAINED EARNINGS	TREASURY STOCK
Beginning balances (12/31/93)	$ 0	$10,000	$25,000	$35,969	$(20,000)
Net income				19,529	
Cash dividends				(7,800)	
Issue for acquisition		2,500	22,500		
Exercise of stock options				(40)	200
Ending balance (12/31/94)	$ 0	$12,500	$47,500	$47,658	$(19,800)
Net loss				(15,510)	
Exercise of stock options					300
Issue of preferred stock	12,500		2,500		
Stock dividend		1,055	11,605	(12,660)	
Ending balance (12/31/95)	$12,500	$13,555	$61,605	$19,488	$(19,500)

The annual effective interest rate is 10 percent, and the proceeds at issuance were $37,711. Half of the notes were redeemed in December 1995, and a loss of $2,462 was recognized on the redemption.

7. Deferred income taxes. The deferred income taxes are recognized on timing differences between taxable income and reported net income. The company's effective income tax rate is 35 percent.

8. Leases. The company leases certain facilities in which operations are conducted. Under the lease contract the company is responsible for maintenance and can acquire the leased properties at the end of the lease term for an amount equal to 90 percent of the market value at that time. The current lease was entered into in January of 1989 and will expire in January of 2009. Lease payments are set at $8 million per year over the period of the lease.

9. Stock transactions. The company is authorized to issue 25 million, $1 par value, common shares. During 1993, in its only treasury stock purchase, the company acquired 2 million shares at $10 each.

In December of 1995 the company issued 500,000 shares of $25 par value preferred stock for $30 per share. Annual dividend payments are set at 10 percent of par value and the shares are callable at par value by the company after 1999. There are 500,000 authorized but unissued shares of preferred stock.

10. Executive compensation. Company executives are paid bonuses in the form of options to purchase common stock. The option price is equal to the per share market price at the time options are issued to the executives. Certain of these options were exercised in 1994 and 1995.

11. Stock dividend. At the end of 1995 the company declared and issued a 10 percent stock dividend on all outstanding common shares.

12. Restructuring. During 1995 the company began a major restructuring and chose to accrue certain future costs associated with employee layoffs, plant closings, and equipment replacement. A $15,000 charge was taken against 1995 income, and a restructuring reserve was established for the future costs. The portion of the reserve due to expected layoffs is considered a current liability.

CASE 3: PIERCE AND SNOWDEN

Pierce and Snowden is an established manufacturer of a wide variety of household items that are sold through retailers all over the United States. Wellington Mart and Wagner Stores, two retailers, have recently expressed an interest in carrying a number of Pierce and Snowden products. While these two potential customers could generate considerable volume for the company, both retailers would require the extension of a significant amount of credit, and in general, retail sales throughout the United States have been somewhat slow for several years.

You work in the finance department of Pierce and Snowden and have been asked to serve on a team whose task is to make a recommendation to management about whether, or how much, credit should be extended to Wellington Mart and Wagner

Stores. The recommendation in part will be based on the solvency position and earning power of these two companies.

Your assignment is to analyze the financial statements of these two companies and—on that basis only—rate them on a scale from 1–10 (weak to strong) with respect to solvency position, earning power and persistence, and earnings quality. In addition to the ratings, provide a memo to the team captain stating why the ratings on these three dimensions do (or do not) differ between the two companies. The financial statements of Wellington Mart and Wagner Stores follow.

WELLINGTON MART
CONSOLIDATED BALANCE SHEET
(IN THOUSANDS OF DOLLARS)
DECEMBER 31, 1994 AND 1993

	1994	1993
ASSETS		
Cash	$ 1,870	$ 2,650
Trading securities	2,000	3,500
Net accounts receivable	18,450	12,000
Inventory	4,200	15,800
Investment in affiliate	28,700	34,200
Investment in real estate	45,500	10,500
Buildings, machinery, and equipment	122,500	119,500
Less: Accumulated depreciation	(7,900)	(12,400)
Goodwill	36,000	—
Total assets	$251,320	$185,750
LIABILITIES AND STOCKHOLDERS' EQUITY		
Accounts payable	$ 22,400	$ 8,900
Accrued payables	25,200	11,200
Current maturities of long-term debts	6,100	6,100
Income tax liability	3,050	5,050
Long-term notes payable	26,100	12,200
Bonds payable	16,788	16,540
Postretirement healthcare liability	6,200	—
Deferred income tax	9,500	11,300
Preferred stock	50,000	50,000
Common stock	28,100	20,000
Additional paid-in capital	72,160	35,860
Retained earnings	14,302	44,680
Less: Treasury stock	(28,580)	(36,080)
Total liabilities and stockholders' equity	$251,320	$185,750

FOOTNOTES TO THE FINANCIAL STATEMENTS OF WELLINGTON MART (DOLLAR VALUES, EXCEPT PER-SHARE AMOUNTS, ARE IN THOUSANDS)

1. Revenue recognition. The company recognizes revenue when goods are shipped, and all sales are made on credit.

WELLINGTON MART
INCOME STATEMENT
(IN THOUSANDS OF DOLLARS, EXCEPT PER-SHARE NUMBERS)
FOR THE YEAR ENDED DECEMBER 31, 1994

	1994
Sales	$150,000
Cost of goods sold	(90,000)
Gross profit	$ 60,000
Selling and administrative expenses	(45,000)
Depreciation and amortization expenses	(16,500)
Bad debt expense	(1,550)
Interest expense	(2,328)
Net loss from operations	$ (5,378)
Other revenues and expenses	(4,100)
Net loss before taxes	$ (9,478)
Income tax expense	(4,200)
Net loss before change in accounting principle	$ (13,678)
Charge for postretirement healthcare expenses	(6,200)
Net loss	$ (19,878)
Loss per outstanding common share:	
Before charge for postretirement healthcare	$ (5.49)
Due to charge for postretirement healthcare	(2.68)
Total	$ (8.17)

2. Other revenues and expenses. Other revenues and expenses consist of the following items (dollars in thousands):

Gain on sale of trading securities	$ 2,000
Unrealized gain on trading securities	500
Translation gain on outstanding accounts payable	1,500
Income from affiliate	2,500
Inventory write-down to market	(1,600)
Restructuring charge	(9,000)
Total	$(4,100)

3. Trading securities. In the only transaction involving trading securities during 1994, 50 common stock shares of Mammoth Corporation were sold in April.

4. Accounts receivable. Further breakdown of the net accounts receivable balances is provided below.

	GROSS ACCOUNTS RECEIVABLE	ALLOWANCE	NET
12/31/93	$12,300	$300	$12,000
12/31/94	19,400	950	18,450

5. Inventory. Inventory is carried at lower of cost or market under the LIFO cost flow assumption. Inventory purchase costs have remained relatively constant over the past several years. The LIFO reserve was $730 and $750 as of December 31, 1994 and 1993, respectively. The company wrote off certain inventories during 1994 due to obsolescence.

WELLINGTON MART
CONSOLIDATED STATEMENT OF CASH FLOWS
FOR THE YEAR ENDED DECEMBER 31, 1994

	1994
Operating activities:	
Net loss	$(19,878)
Depreciation and amortization	16,500
Noncash restructuring charge	8,000
Charge for postretirement healthcare	6,200
Amortization of discount on bonds payable	248
Dividends from affiliate (net of income recognized)	5,500
Decrease in deferred income taxes	(1,800)
Increase in net accounts receivable	(6,450)
Decrease in inventory	11,600
Increase in accounts payable	13,500
Increase in accrued payables	14,000
Decrease in income tax liability	(2,000)
Net cash flow from operating activities	$ 45,420
Investing activities:	
Investment in buildings	$ (8,000)
Investment in machinery and equipment	(15,000)
Acquisition of Marilyn Real Estate	(50,000)
Net cash flow from investing activities	(73,000)
Financing activities:	
Increase in long-term notes payable	$ 13,900
Stock issuances for exercised options	11,400
Net cash flow from financing activities	25,300
Decrease in cash and trading securities	$ (2,280)
Beginning balance in cash and trading securities	6,150
Ending balance in cash and trading securities	$ 3,870

WELLINGTON MART
CONSOLIDATED STATEMENT OF STOCKHOLDERS' EQUITY
(IN THOUSANDS OF DOLLARS)
FOR THE YEAR ENDED DECEMBER 31, 1994

TRANSACTION	PREFERRED STOCK	COMMON STOCK	ADDITIONAL PAID-IN CAPITAL	RETAINED EARNINGS	TREASURY STOCK
Beginning balance (12/31/93)	$50,000	$20,000	$35,860	$ 44,680	$(36,080)
Net income				(19,878)	
Stock dividend		2,100	8,400	(10,500)	
Stock issue for options			3,900		7,500
Stock issue for acquisition		6,000	24,000		
Ending balance (12/31/94)	$50,000	$28,100	$72,160	$ 14,302	$(28,580)

6. Affiliate. The company owns 49 percent of the outstanding voting stock of Ellery, Inc. A condensed balance sheet for Ellery as of December 31, 1994, is provided below (dollar amounts in thousands).

Current assets	$24,000	Current liabilities	$21,000
Noncurrent assets	46,000	Long-term liabilities	35,000
		Stockholders' equity	14,000
Total assets	$70,000	Total liabilities and stockholders' equity	$70,000

7. Buildings, machinery, and equipment. Buildings, machinery, and equipment are carried at cost less accumulated depreciation. Depreciation is calculated on a straight-line basis over estimated useful lives ranging from 5 years for machinery and equipment to 20 years for buildings. The cost and related accumulated depreciation for buildings and for machinery and equipment are provided below.

	12/31/93	INCREASES	DECREASES	12/31/94
Buildings:				
Cost	$65,000	$ 8,000	$20,000	$53,000
Accumulated depreciation	10,400	3,000	12,000	1,400
Machinery and equipment:				
Cost	54,500	15,000	—	69,500
Accumulated depreciation	2,000	4,500	—	6,500

In December of 1994 the company closed a plant with an original cost of $20,000. A loss, which included cash payments required to complete the closure, was recognized in 1994 as a restructuring charge.

8. Acquisitions. In January of 1994 the company acquired 100 percent of the outstanding common stock of Marilyn Real Estate. The Company paid cash and issued 600,000 common shares to the shareholders of Marilyn in the acquisition, and the $80,000,000 purchase price was allocated between real estate and goodwill. The goodwill is being amortized over a 5-year period using the straight-line rate.

9. Long-term debt. Long-term notes outstanding as of December 31, 1993, are being paid off in equal installments of $6,100, of which the current portion is listed as a current liability. The interest rate on these notes is approximately 5.5 percent, and the book value of the notes is approximately equal to the market value. An additional note payable was issued during 1994.

The outstanding bond liabilities listed on the balance sheet were issued on January 1, 1989. The bond issuance has a face value of $18,000, an annual stated interest rate (payable semiannually) of six percent, and a maturity date of December 31, 1998. The bonds were issued to yield an annual effective rate of return of eight percent. As of December 31, 1994, the annual market rate of interest on similar bond issuances was ten percent, and the Company has the right to call the bonds any time after December 31, 1994, at face value. A covenant in the bond indenture requires that the Company's ratio of total liabilities to total assets cannot exceed 0.60 during the term of the bonds.

10. Accounting changes. The Company adopted SFAS No. 106, Accounting for Postretirement Healthcare Benefits, at the end of 1994. The present value of the future liability associated with these costs was estimated, and the entire dollar amount of the liability was charged against income. The discount factor used to compute the present value of the future estimated costs was 12 percent. The charge was not deductible for income tax purposes. Previously, the Company accounted for these costs on the cash basis.

11. Deferred income taxes. Deferred income taxes are recognized on timing differences between income recognized for tax purposes and income for financial reporting purposes. Increases to the deferred tax liability arise primarily because the Company uses straight-line depreciation for financial reporting purposes and accelerated depreciation for income tax reporting purposes. Decreases to the deferred income tax liability arose from charges to reported income for restructuring, postretirement healthcare, inventory write-downs, and certain bad debt expenses. The Company's effective tax rate for 1994 was 34 percent.

12. Stockholders' equity transactions. In December of 1992 the Company issued 500,000 shares of eight percent preferred stock, each with a par value of $100. The shares are callable, cumulative, and nonparticipating. As of December 31, 1994, dividends in arrears on these shares total $4,000.

As of December 31, 1994, the Company was authorized to issue 3,000,000 shares of $10 par value common stock; 2,810,000 have been issued; 2,310,000 were outstanding; and 500,000 were held in treasury. During 1994 the Company issued 600,000 common shares in the acquisition of Marilyn Real Estate, issued 300,000 treasury shares to executives who exercised stock options, and on December 20, 1994, declared a ten percent common stock dividend.

13. Employee pension. The Company has a defined contribution pension plan that covers all employees, and the payments associated with this plan are expensed as incurred.

14. Leases. The Company leases certain facilities in which operations are conducted. Under the lease contract the Company is responsible for maintenance, and at the end of the lease term it can either acquire the leased properties for an amount equal to 25 percent of the market value or renew the contract. The current lease was entered into in January of 1991 and will expire in January of 2001. Required lease payments, included in selling and administrative expenses, are equal to $12,000,000 per year over the period of the lease, and are paid at the beginning of each period.

15. Contingencies. The Company is currently under investigation by the Environmental Protection Agency for toxic waste management violations. In several cases the Company has been identified by the agency as a "potentially responsible party," and it is likely that the Company will be required to clean up certain waste sites in the future. It is also possible that the Company will be subject to certain fines and punitive damages. At this time there is no way to reliably estimate these possible costs, which management believes to be somewhere between $1,000,000 and $25,000,000.

WAGNER STORES
CONSOLIDATED BALANCE SHEET
(IN THOUSANDS OF DOLLARS)
DECEMBER 31, 1994 AND 1993

	1994	1993
ASSETS		
Cash	$ 4,920	$ 6,200
Trading securities	1,050	800
Accounts receivable (net)	7,250	9,400
Inventory	16,700	12,300
Prepaid insurance	1,800	2,500
Notes receivable	2,586	3,320
Investment in affiliate	10,600	8,000
Property, plant, & equipment (net)	42,200	12,400
Goodwill	800	900
Total assets	$87,906	$55,820
LIABILITIES AND STOCKHOLDERS' EQUITY		
Accounts payable	$ 9,700	$ 4,700
Accrued payables	4,000	3,300
Income tax payable	1,700	600
Dividend payable	700	500
Bonds payable (net)	28,502	13,242
Capital lease obligations	4,771	5,228
Deferred income taxes	7,200	6,000
Preferred stock	5,000	5,000
Common stock	11,900	6,400
Additional paid-in capital	4,100	4,200
Retained earnings	14,233	9,850
Less: Treasury stock	(3,900)	(3,200)
Total liabilities and stockholders' equity	$87,906	$55,820

WAGNER STORES
INCOME STATEMENT
(IN THOUSANDS OF DOLLARS, EXCEPT PER-SHARE NUMBERS)
FOR THE YEAR ENDED DECEMBER 31, 1994

	1994
Sales	$ 72,000
Cost of goods sold	(28,000)
General operating expenses	(14,000)
Operating leases	(6,200)
Insurance expense	(2,800)
Depreciation and amortization	(1,300)
Bad debt expense	(150)
Income tax expense	(6,300)
Operating income	$ 13,250
Other income (losses)	(5,267)
Net income	$ 7,983
Earnings per share*	$16

* Net income divided by the weighted average of the common shares outstanding during 1994.

WAGNER STORES
STATEMENT OF CASH FLOWS
(IN THOUSANDS OF DOLLARS)
FOR THE YEAR ENDED DECEMBER 31, 1994

	1994	
Operating activities:		
Net income	$ 7,983	
Noncurrent adjustments:		
Depreciation and goodwill amortization	1,300	
Loss on write-down of equipment lines	3,200	
Increase in deferred income taxes	1,200	
Amortization of discount on long-term debt	260	
Equity income not received in cash	(300)	
Realized and unrealized gains on trading securities	(150)	
Gain on sale of vehicles	(200)	
Current adjustments:		
Decrease in net accounts receivable	2,150	
Increase in inventory	(4,400)	
Decrease in prepaid insurance	700	
Increase in accounts payable	5,000	
Increase in accrued payables	700	
Increase in income tax payable	1,100	
Net cash from operating activities		$ 18,543
Investing activities:		
Investments in trading securities	$ (400)	
Proceeds from sales of trading securities	300	
Investment in affiliate	(2,300)	
Receipts of principal on notes receivable	734	
Investments in property, plant, & equipment	(34,500)	
Proceeds from sales of vehicles	500	
Net cash used in investing activities		(35,666)
Financing activities:		
Proceeds from bond issuance	$ 15,000	
Principal payments on capital leases	(457)	
Proceeds from common stock issuance	5,800	
Treasury stock purchases	(2,500)	
Proceeds from treasury stock issuances	800	
Dividend payments	(2,800)	
Net cash from financing activities		15,843
Decrease in cash balance		$ (1,280)
Beginning cash balance (12/31/93)		6,200
Ending cash balance (12/31/94)		$ 4,920

FOOTNOTES TO THE FINANCIAL STATEMENTS OF WAGNER STORES

1. Trading securities. Trading securities are carried at fair market value as of the balance sheet date. During 1994 trading securities with a total book value of $250 were sold.

2. Revenue recognition and accounts receivable. Sales are recorded when goods are shipped, and all sales to customers are on account. Accounts receivable are carried at net realizable value with an allowance for uncollectibles. The dollar amounts in the allowance account were $100 and $120 at the end of 1994 and 1993, respectively.

WAGNER STORES
STATEMENT OF STOCKHOLDERS' EQUITY
(IN THOUSANDS OF DOLLARS)
FOR THE YEAR ENDED DECEMBER 31, 1994

TRANSACTION	PREFERRED STOCK	COMMON STOCK	ADDITIONAL PAID-IN CAPITAL	RETAINED EARNINGS	TREASURY STOCK
Beginning balance (12/31/93)	$5,000	$ 6,400	$ 4,200	$ 9,850	$(3,200)
Net income				7,983	
Cash dividends				(3,000)	
Stock dividend issued		500	100	(600)	
Common stock issuance		5,000	800		
Exercise of stock options			(1,000)		1,800
Treasury stock purchases					(2,500)
Ending balance (12/31/94)	$5,000	$11,900	$ 4,100	$14,233	$(3,900)

3. **Inventory.** Inventory is carried at lower of cost or market value under the first-in, first-out assumption. All inventory purchases are made on account.

4. **Note receivable.** On January 1, 1993, the Company received an installment note in exchange for services. The note is accounted for under the effective interest method and specifies that the Company receive a fixed amount of cash at the end of 1993, 1994, 1995, 1996, and 1997.

5. **Investment in affiliate.** For several years the Company has held a 45 percent interest in Truax Incorporated, a financial holding company, which in turn holds interests in a wide variety of financial institutions. At the end of 1994 the Company acquired a 25 percent interest in Billingsly Financial. The Company uses the equity method to account for these investments.

6. **Property, plant, & equipment.** This category includes all properties used in the operations of the business, including assets acquired through capitalized leases. Straight line methods are used to depreciate the assets in this category. Accumulated depreciation totaled $2,700 and $3,000 as of the end of 1994 and 1993, respectively. During 1994 one of the Company's lines of equipment was discontinued, and the book value of this line was written off the books. In addition, the Company sold a small fleet of vehicles with an original cost of $800.

7. **Goodwill.** The Company acquired 100 percent of the outstanding stock of Machen Suppliers at the beginning of 1993, accounting for the acquisition as a purchase and recognizing goodwill. Goodwill is amortized over 10 years using the straight-line method.

8. **Accounts payable.** Accounts payable includes only outstanding account balances with the Company's inventory suppliers.

9. **Accrued payables.** Accrued payables refer to the Company's general operating expenses.

10. **Bonds payable.** On January 1, 1992, the Company issued 10-year bonds with a face value of $16,000 and a stated interest rate of 5 percent. Interest payments are made at the end of each year, and the bonds were issued at a discount to yield an 8 percent effective interest rate. The Company has the option to call these bonds at a premium of 2 percent above the face value. The market value of these bonds as of

December 31, 1994, is $14,350. At the end of 1994 the Company issued additional 10-year bonds at face value. These bonds have a stated interest rate of 9 percent.

11. Lease obligations. The Company leases most of its facilities and machinery. Lease payments during 1994 totaled $7,180. Projected future lease payments under capitalized leases are $980 per year until December 31, 2000. Projected future lease payments under operating leases are $6,200 at the end of each year for the next 20 years. Both projections exclude executory costs.

12. Deferred income taxes. Deferred income taxes arise due to timing differences between financial reporting and tax reporting. In general, the Company attempts to minimize its income tax liability by accelerating expense recognition and deferring revenue recognition within the rules of the Internal Revenue Service. For example, the Company uses straight-line depreciation for financial reporting purposes and accelerated methods for income tax reporting purposes. Such practices have accumulated a deferred income tax obligation, which is reported on the balance sheet. The Company's effective income tax rate is 35 percent, which is expected to be constant in the foreseeable future.

13. Pension obligation. The Company carries a defined contribution pension plan on all its employees. During 1994 the Company contributed $1,500 to the plan, which is reflected in the general operating section of the income statement.

14. Stock option plan. The Company maintains a stock option plan, which compensates certain executives with 10-year options to purchase the Company's stock at a price that equals the stock's market value as of the date of the issuance. Certain options were exercised during 1994.

15. Stockholders' equity. At December 31, 1993, the Company had issued 640 shares of $10 par value stock, 400 of which were held in treasury. During 1994 the Company issued 500 shares of $10 par value common stock; 150 shares were issued when executive stock options were exercised; and 224 additional treasury shares were acquired. At the end of 1994 the Company issued a 7.5 percent stock dividend on all outstanding shares.

   In addition, the Company has 500 shares of preferred stock outstanding, which pays annual dividends at a rate of 10 percent of the par value. The nonvoting preferred shares are cumulative and nonparticipating, and the preferred stockholders have an option to require redemption at par value beginning in 1996.

16. Other income (losses). The Other Income (Losses) Account consists of the following items:

Interest revenue earned on note receivable	$ 266
Realized and unrealized gains on trading securities	150
Equity income	1,500
Gain on sale of vehicles	200
Interest expense	(1,583)
Loss on write-down of inventory to market	(2,600)
Loss on discontinued equipment	(3,200)
Net loss	$(5,267)

CONVERTING ACCRUAL NUMBERS TO CASH FLOWS: THE DIRECT AND INDIRECT FORMS OF PRESENTATION

This appendix covers how the dollar values on an income statement can be converted to the cash flow numbers reported in the operating section of the statement of cash flows. It also examines how the operating section of the statement of cash flows can be presented under either the direct or indirect method. Take a moment to examine the review problem at the end of Chapter 5 (Kelly Supply) because the dollar values in this problem are used to illustrate the procedure.

1. Identify Related Balance Sheet Accounts

An accrual-based income statement can be converted to a cash basis by recognizing first that each income statement account is related to one or more balance sheet accounts. For example, when a revenue is recognized, any of three balance sheet accounts could be affected: (1) cash is increased, (2) receivables are increased, or (3) unearned revenues are decreased. The chart in Figure A–1 summarizes these relationships for the income statement accounts of Kelly Supply. It includes each account appearing on the income statement, the related balance sheet accounts, and the reference numbers of the related entries recorded by Kelly Supply. Note that for any given income statement account, the related balance sheet accounts are those that typically appear in the entry recorded when the revenue or expense is recognized.

FIGURE A-1	INCOME STATEMENT ACCOUNTS	BALANCE SHEET ACCOUNTS	JOURNAL ENTRY
Related income statement and balance sheet accounts	Sales	Cash, accounts receivable, unearned revenue	(1) (2) (13)
	Interest revenue	Cash, interest receivable	(14)
	Cost of goods sold	Cash, inventory, accounts payable	(3) (4) (12)
	Wage expense	Cash, wages payable	(5) (17)
	Rent expense	Cash, prepaid rent	(19)
	Interest expense	Cash, interest payable	(6) (18)
	Depreciation expense	Accumulated depreciation	(15)
	Amortization expense	Patent	(16)

2. Adjust Accrual Numbers for Changes in Related Balance Sheet Accounts

The second step involves adjusting the accrual-based numbers for the changes in the related, noncash balance sheet accounts. For example, Sales Revenue is adjusted for changes in accounts receivable and unearned revenues, while Cost of Goods Sold is adjusted for changes in inventory and accounts payable. These adjustments are summarized in Figure A–2, which expresses them in terms of the fundamental accounting equation.

FIGURE A-2		Assets	=	Liabilities + Stockholders' Equity
Converting accrual numbers to cash flow numbers	Increase	Subtract from Accrual Numbers		Add to Accrual Numbers
	Decrease	Add to Accrual Numbers		Subtract from Accrual Numbers

As indicated, increases in related asset accounts and decreases in related liability and stockholders' equity accounts are subtracted from accrual-based numbers in the computation of cash flows. Decreases in related asset accounts and increases in related liability and stockholders' equity accounts are added to accrual-based numbers in the computation of cash flows.

To compute cash receipts from sales revenues in a given period, for example, first identify whether the related, noncash balance sheet accounts, Accounts Receivable and Unearned Revenues, increased or decreased during the period. Following Figure A–2, if Accounts Receivable increased and/or Unearned Revenues decreased, subtract these amounts from the sales revenue number. If Accounts Receivable decreased and/or Unearned Revenue increased, add these amounts to the sales revenue number.

3. Prepare the Operating Section of the Statement of Cash Flows

Figure A–3 illustrates how the income statement of Kelly Supply can be converted to the operating section of the statement of cash flows. Note how each income statement account is adjusted for changes in the related, noncash balance sheet accounts in accordance with Figure A–2. Note also that the cash flow statement in Figure A–3 is

FIGURE A–3

Accrual: Cash reconciliation

INCOME STATEMENT		ACTIVITY IN RELATED BALANCE SHEET ACCOUNT	STATEMENT OF CASH FLOWS: OPERATING SECTION	
Sales revenue	$27,000	Less: Increase in accounts receivable (22,000 − 15,000 = 7,000) Less: Decrease in unearned revenue (3,000 − 1,000 = 2,000)	$18,000	Cash inflow from sales
Interest revenue	50	Less: Increase in interest receivable (50 − 0 = 50)	0	Cash inflow from interest
Cost of goods sold	(9,000)	Less: Increase in merchandise inventory (13,000 − 12,000 = 1,000) Less: Decrease in accounts payable (8,000 − 5,000 = 3,000)	(13,000)	Cash outflow from inventory
Wage expense	(8,000)	Less: Decrease in wages payable (3,000 − 1,000 = 2,000)	(10,000)	Cash outflow from wages
Rent expense	(1,000)	Plus: Decrease in prepaid rent (3,000 − 2,000 = 1,000)	0	Cash outflow from rent
Interest expense	(3,000)	Plus: Increase in interest payable (2,000 − 1,000 = 1,000)	(2,000)	Cash outflow from interest
Depreciation expense	(3,000)	Plus: Increase in accumulated depreciation (8,000 − 5,000 = 3,000)	0	Cash outflow from depreciation
Amortization expense	(500)	Plus: Decrease in patent (5,000 − 4,500 = 500)	0	Cash outflow from amortization
Net income	$ 2,550		$(7,000)	Net cash increase (decrease) from operating activities

virtually identical to the operating section of the statement of cash flows prepared from the cash T-account in the Kelly Supply example (Figure 5–22).

T-ACCOUNT ANALYSIS: ANOTHER METHOD TO CONVERT ACCRUAL NUMBERS TO CASH FLOWS

Another method of converting accrual-based dollar amounts to cash flows involves analyzing the T-accounts of the related balance sheet items and deriving the journal entries that originally recorded the cash flows. Assume, for example, that you wish to compute the cash outflow associated with wage expense, which is disclosed in the amount of $8,000 on the 1997 income statement (Figure 5–21). Figure A–4 illustrates the approach. Note first that Wages Payable, the related balance sheet account, had a balance of $3,000 on the 1996 balance sheet (Figure 5–18) and a balance of $1,000 on the 1997 balance sheet (Figure 5–21). Since wages are accrued, the dollar amount for wage expense on the income statement indicates that during 1997 the Wages Payable account must have been increased by $8,000. The entry to the left side of the T-account, therefore, must have been $10,000, the amount of cash paid for wages during 1997. Thus, the $10,000 cash outflow associated with wages can be derived in either of the two ways illustrated in Figures A–3 and A–4. The T-account approach can also be used to derive the cash flows associated with the other income statement accounts, and it is more fully described and illustrated in Appendix 5B and Chapter 14.

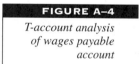

FIGURE A–4

T-account analysis of wages payable account

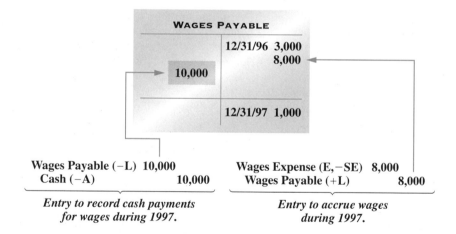

	WAGES PAYABLE
	12/31/96 3,000
	8,000
10,000	
	12/31/97 1,000

Wages Payable (−L)	10,000	
Cash (−A)		10,000

Entry to record cash payments for wages during 1997.

Wages Expense (E,−SE)	8,000	
Wages Payable (+L)		8,000

Entry to accrue wages during 1997.

PRESENTING THE OPERATING SECTION OF THE STATEMENT OF CASH FLOWS: DIRECT AND INDIRECT METHODS

The operating section of the statement of cash flows can be presented in either of two ways: direct method or indirect method. Under the direct method the cash inflow or outflow associated with each income statement account is disclosed in the operating section of the statement of cash flows. The direct method is illustrated in Figure 5–22 for Kelly Supply and is also used by MCI (see Appendix C). The **indirect method**, however, is much more common. It begins with net income and, using the adjustments to the related, noncash balance sheet accounts discussed earlier, derives net cash flow from operating activities. In Figure A–5 the direct and indirect methods of presentation are compared.

Note how the direct method of presentation is prepared by *directly* adjusting each of the income statement accounts for the differences between accruals and cash flows. The indirect method of presentation uses the same adjustments to reconcile net income with net cash used from operating activities. The two methods of presentation are actually quite similar in that both rely on the accrual-to-cash adjustments illustrated in Figure A–2. Also, the relatively few companies that use the direct method of presentation are required under generally accepted accounting principles to disclose the reconciliation between net income and net cash flows from operations.[1]

FIGURE A–5

Direct and indirect presentation of the operating section of the statement of cash flows

INCOME STATEMENT			DIRECT PRESENTATION	
Sales	$27,000	$(7,000)		
		(2,000)	$18,000	Cash receipts from sales
Interest revenue	50	(50)	0	Cash receipts from interest
Cost of goods sold	(9,000)	(1,000)		
		(3,000)	(13,000)	Cash payments for inventory
Wage expense	(8,000)	(2,000)	(10,000)	Cash payments for wages
Rent expense	(1,000)	1,000	0	Cash payments for rent
Interest expense	(3,000)	1,000	(2,000)	Cash payments for interest
Depreciation expense	(3,000)	3,000	0	Cash payments for depreciation
Amortization expense	(500)	500	0	Cash payments for amortization
Net income	$ 2,550		$(7,000)	Net cash from operations
Inc. in accounts rec.	(7,000)			
Dec. in unearned rev.	(2,000)			
Inc. in interest rec.	(50)			
Inc. in inventory	(1,000)			
Dec. in accounts pay.	(3,000)	← Adjustments		
Dec. in wages pay.	(2,000)			
Dec. in prepaid rent	1,000			
Inc. in interest pay.	1,000			
Inc. in accumulated dep.	3,000			
Dec. in patent	500			
Net cash from operations	$ (7,000)			

INDIRECT PRESENTATION

1. Note in the MCI annual report (Appendix C) that, although the direct method is used to present the statement of cash flows, a reconciliation of net income to cash from operating activities is also provided.

We have now covered the mechanics of converting an accrual-based income statement to the operating section of the statement of cash flows, but a word of caution is in order. Memorizing or blindly applying Figure A–2 in an effort to learn how accrual numbers are converted to cash flows may not be a very productive strategy. It is important that you understand the relationships among the accounts and how they affect the financial statements. In this appendix we have only introduced the basics involved in preparing a statement of cash flows. We return to this topic in Chapter 14 and at that time cover it in much greater depth.

EXERCISES

EA-1

The following balance sheet and income statement data were taken from the records of L. L. Beeno for the year ended December 31, 1996.

	1996	1995
BALANCE SHEET		
Cash	$ 3,000	$ 2,800
Accounts receivable	5,600	4,500
Inventory	7,500	7,800
Prepaid insurance	600	900
Total current assets	$16,700	$16,000
Machinery (net)	29,000	26,000
Total	$45,700	$42,000
Accounts payable	$ 5,600	$ 7,300
Wages payable	4,500	3,400
Total current liabilities	$10,100	$10,700
Bonds payable (net)	14,000	14,800
Capital stock	5,000	5,000
Retained earnings	16,600	11,500
Total	$45,700	$42,000

INCOME STATEMENT	
Revenues	$47,000
Cost of goods sold	25,000
Gross profit	$22,000
Wage expense	(6,200)
Insurance expense	(4,200)
Interest expense	(1,600)
Depreciation expense	(3,300)
Net income before taxes	$ 6,700
Tax expense	1,200
Net income	$ 5,500

REQUIRED:

Prepare the operating section of the statement of cash flows, and present it under both the direct and the indirect methods.

The following balance sheet and income statement data were taken from the records of Martland Stores for the year ended December 31, 1996.

	1996	1995
BALANCE SHEET		
Cash	$ 6,000	$ 1,400
Accounts receivable	12,000	13,500
Inventory	4,500	9,800
Prepaid insurance	900	1,200
Total current assets	$23,400	$25,900
Machinery (net)	38,000	37,500
Total	$61,400	$63,400
Accounts payable	$12,600	$13,100
Wages payable	9,500	7,400
Total current liabilities	$22,100	$20,500
Bonds payable (net)	17,000	17,000
Capital stock	15,000	15,000
Retained earnings	7,300	10,900
Total	$61,400	$63,400

INCOME STATEMENT	
Revenues	$96,000
Cost of goods sold	64,000
Gross profit	$32,000
Wage expense	(18,600)
Insurance expense	(9,200)
Interest expense	(2,100)
Depreciation expense	(5,700)
Net loss	$ 3,600

REQUIRED:
Prepare the operating section of the statement of cash flows, and present it under both the direct and the indirect methods.

The following balance sheet and income statement data were taken from the records of Mako Retail Supply for the year ended December 31, 1996.

	1996	1995
BALANCE SHEET		
Cash	$ 6,000	$ 5,400
Accounts receivable	11,200	9,000
Inventory	15,000	15,600
Prepaid rent	1,200	1,800
Total current assets	$ 33,400	$31,800
Equipment (net)	58,000	52,000
Total	$ 91,400	$83,800

(continued)

	1996	1995
BALANCE SHEET		
Accounts payable	$ 11,200	$14,600
Wages payable	9,000	6,800
Interest payable	1,500	2,200
Unearned revenue	6,500	4,700
Total current liabilities	$ 28,200	$28,300
Bonds payable (net)	28,000	28,400
Capital stock	10,000	10,000
Retained earnings	25,200	17,100
Total	$ 91,400	$83,800

INCOME STATEMENT	
Revenues	$109,100
Cost of goods sold	56,000
Gross profit	$ 53,100
Wage expense	(15,200)
Rent expense	(9,000)
Interest expense	(2,900)
Depreciation expense	(6,200)
Loss on sale of equipment	(4,200)
Net income before taxes	$ 15,600
Tax expense	4,400
Net income	$ 11,200

REQUIRED:

Prepare the operating section of the statement of cash flows, and present it under both the direct and the indirect methods.

EA-4

The following balance sheet and income statement data were taken from the records of Steeler and Jones for the year ended December 31, 1996.

	1996	1995
BALANCE SHEET		
Cash	$ 6,400	$ 7,400
Accounts receivable	11,900	13,000
Inventory	14,100	15,600
Prepaid rent	1,300	900
Total current assets	$33,700	$ 36,900
Equipment (net)	52,000	66,000
Total	$85,700	$102,900
Accounts payable	$ 9,200	$ 14,600
Wages payable	4,500	6,800
Interest payable	1,500	1,300
Unearned revenue	6,500	8,700
Total current liabilities	$21,700	$ 31,400
Bonds payable (net)	16,500	24,300
Capital stock	20,000	25,000
Retained earnings	27,500	22,200
Total	$85,700	$102,900

INCOME STATEMENT

Revenues	$87,400
Cost of goods sold	46,700
Gross profit	$40,700
Wage expense	(13,200)
Rent expense	(11,000)
Interest expense	(1,900)
Depreciation expense	(5,700)
Plus: Gain on sale of equipment	5,200
Net income before taxes	$14,100
Tax expense	4,800
Net income	$ 9,300

REQUIRED:

Prepare the operating section of the statement of cash flows, and present it under both the direct and the indirect methods.

EA–5

The following balance sheet and income statement data were taken from the records of Harbaugh Auto Supply for the year ended December 31, 1996.

	1996	1995
BALANCE SHEET		
Cash	$ 10,100	$ 8,400
Accounts receivable	14,400	13,900
Inventory	21,600	18,700
Interest receivable	1,200	1,500
Prepaid rent	2,600	1,400
Total current assets	$ 49,900	$ 43,900
Investments	35,400	32,100
Equipment (net)	98,000	91,700
Total	$183,300	$167,700
Accounts payable	$ 18,700	$ 21,300
Wages payable	9,800	11,200
Interest payable	2,300	1,700
Dividend payable	1,700	1,200
Taxes payable	3,100	4,300
Unearned revenue	12,300	15,100
Total current liabilities	$ 47,900	$ 54,800
Long-term notes payable (net)	68,300	62,800
Capital stock	42,000	42,000
Retained earnings	25,100	8,100
Total	$183,300	$167,700
INCOME STATEMENT		
Sales revenues	$ 47,500	
Service revenue	35,200	
Interest revenue	9,300	$ 92,000
Cost of goods sold		(21,200)
Wage expense		(17,600)
Rent expense		(15,300)
Interest expense		(6,200)
Depreciation expense		(11,500)
Add: Gain on sale of investments		13,200
Net income before taxes		$ 33,400
Tax expense		9,100
Net income		$ 24,300

ADDITIONAL INFORMATION:

The Company sells goods and provides services. All sales are made on account, and cash is received in advance on services with service revenues being recognized after services are performed.

REQUIRED:

Prepare the operating section of the statement of cash flows, and present it under both the direct and the indirect methods.

EA–6

The following balance sheet and income statement data were taken from the records of Standard Center Manufacturing for the year ended December 31, 1996.

	1996	1995
BALANCE SHEET		
Cash	$ 20,200	$ 22,800
Accounts receivable	28,800	34,800
Inventory	42,900	43,900
Interest receivable	4,100	6,300
Prepaid rent	3,900	1,200
Total current assets	$ 99,900	$109,000
Investments	18,200	23,500
Equipment (net)	43,900	62,500
Total	$162,000	$195,000
Accounts payable	$ 12,500	$ 8,600
Wages payable	11,100	11,500
Interest payable	1,800	2,100
Dividend payable	900	1,700
Taxes payable	1,200	3,200
Unearned revenue	7,200	9,600
Total current liabilities	$ 34,700	$ 36,700
Long-term notes payable (net)	75,400	97,300
Capital stock	25,000	25,000
Retained earnings	26,900	36,000
Total	$162,000	$195,000

INCOME STATEMENT		
Sales revenues	$ 67,500	
Service revenue	28,200	
Interest revenue	7,300	$103,000
Cost of goods sold		(19,500)
Wage expense		(28,400)
Rent expense		(21,500)
Interest expense		(7,200)
Depreciation expense		(4,300)
Loss on sale of investments		(17,900)
Net income before taxes		$ 4,200
Tax expense		1,400
Net income		$ 2,800

ADDITIONAL INFORMATION:

The Company sells goods and provides services. All sales are made on account, and cash is received in advance on services with service revenues being recognized after services are performed.

REQUIRED:

Prepare the operating section of the statement of cash flows, and present it under both the direct and the indirect methods.

EA–7

Review the statement of cash flows in the annual report of MCI, and answer the following questions.

a.   What method does MCI use to present the operating section of the statement of cash flows?

b.   Explain how MCI used two methods to compute the $2,355 cash from operating activities amount. What kind of different information is provided by the two methods?

c.   In the reconciliation of net income to cash from operating activities, why are depreciation and amortization added back to net income in the computation of cash from operating activities?

d.   What is EBITDA, and what is it used to measure? Discuss how it differs from cash from operating activities.

FINANCIAL ACCOUNTING SIMULATION PROJECT

OVERVIEW

This project requires you to design and use a financial accounting simulation for EXTUS company. In the simulation, which uses a spreadsheet (e.g., EXCEL, LOTUS), inputs provided by you must be connected through formulas to a set of financial statements (income statement, statement of retained earnings, balance sheet, and statement of cash flows) and important financial ratios (return on equity, return on assets, earnings per share, return on sales, times interest earned, current ratio, quick ratio, receivables turnover, inventory turnover, financial leverage, and total liabilities/stockholders' equity) over a two-year period. This project contains 10 separate assignments. The first three involve setting up the basic spreadsheet, and subsequent assignments require you to build upon it and use it to analyze questions faced by the management of EXTUS. The assignments are described in detail below.

Figure B–1 provides the format for the entire spreadsheet, including the inputs to the spreadsheet program, as well as the financial statements and ratios that result from those inputs. The inputs are primarily management decisions—divided into financing activities, investing activities, operating activities, and accounting methods. Read through the descriptors in the first column (column A) under the heading MANAGEMENT INPUTS. The open cells that follow these descriptors indicate where management decisions will be entered. Note, for example, that on January 1, 1997 (column B), open cells are available for inputs concerning the issuance of stock and long-term debt, investments in property, plant, & equipment, and accounting choices. During 1997 and 1998 (columns C and D), open cells are available for inputs concerning the purchase of outstanding shares (i.e., treasury stock), cash dividends, purchases of land and inventory, inventory selling prices, inventory sales, and the timing of certain receivables and payables. The values entered into these open cells must be linked to the values in the FINANCIAL STATEMENTS and Financial Ratio sections of the spreadsheet.

HINT FOR STUDENTS: *Review the FINANCIAL STATEMENTS and Financial Ratios that follow MANAGEMENT INPUTS, and keep in mind that designing the spreadsheet involves writing formulas that link the amounts entered in the open cells located in the MANAGEMENT INPUTS section to the open cells located in the FINANCIAL STATEMENTS and Financial Ratios sections.*

FIGURE B–1

Basic Spreadsheet EXTUS Company

	A	B	C	D	E
1	MANAGEMENT INPUTS	1/1/97	12/31/97	12/31/98	
2					
3	**Financing activities:**				
4	Number of common shares issued				
5	Issue price per common share ($)				
6	Treasury shares purchased				
7	Treasury share purchase price ($)				
8	Number of shares outstanding (calc.)				
9	Long-term debt—face value ($)				
10	Life of long-term debt (years)				
11	Annual stated interest rate (%)				
12	Annual effective interest rate (%)				
13	Present value of debt payments (calc.)				
14	Cash dividends (% net income)				
15					
16					
17					
18	**Investing activities:**				
19	Investment in property, plant, & equip. ($)				
20	Number of land parcels purchased				
21	Market value/parcel ($)				
22	Number of parcels sold				
23	Ending number of land parcels held (calc.)				
24	Units of inventory purchased				
25	Cost per unit of inventory purchased ($)				
26					
27					
28					
29	**Operating activities:**				
30	Price per unit of inventory sold ($)				
31	Units of inventory sold (calc.)				
32	Accounts receivable (% sales)				
33	Actual bad debts (% previous year sales)				
34	Ending inventory in units (calc.)				
35	Accounts payable (% purchase cost)				
36	Selling & admin. expenses (% sales)				
37	Accrued payables (% sell. & adm. exp.)				
38	Income tax rate (% net income before tax)				
39	Income tax payable (% of tax expense)				
40					
41					
42					
43	**Accounting methods:**				
44	Bad Debts				
45	Direct write-off (1) or Allowance (2)?				
46	If allowance, bad debt estimate (% sales)				
47	Inventory				
48	FIFO (1) or LIFO (2)?				
49	Book and Tax Depreciation				
50	Estimated useful life (years)				
51	Salvage value ($)				
52	Straight-line (1) or Double-declining-bal. (2)?				
53					
54					
55					
56					

FIGURE B-1 (CONTINUED)

Basic Spreadsheet EXTUS Company

	A	B	C	D	E
57	**FINANCIAL STATEMENTS**				
58					
59	**Income Statement**		12/31/97	12/31/98	
60	Sales				
61	Cost of goods sold:				
62	Beginning inventory				
63	Purchases				
64	Less: Ending inventory				
65	Total cost of goods sold				
66	Gross profit				
67	Selling & administrative expenses				
68	Depreciation expense				
69	Bad debt expense				
70	Net income from operations				
71	Interest expense				
72	Gain (loss) on sale of land				
73	Net income (loss) before taxes				
74	Income tax expense				
75	Net income (loss)				
76					
77	**Statement of Retained Earnings**		12/31/97	12/31/98	
78	Beginning balance in retained earnings				
79	Net income (loss)				
80	Less: Cash dividends				
81	Ending balance in retained earnings				
82					
83	**Balance Sheet**		12/31/97	12/31/98	
84	Cash				
85	Accounts receivable				
86	Less: Allowance for bad debts				
87	Net accounts receivable				
88	Inventory				
89	Total current assets				
90					
91	Land				
92	Property, plant, & equipment				
93	Less: Accumulated depreciation				
94	Net property, plant, & equipment				
95	Total assets				
96					
97			12/31/97	12/31/98	
98	Accounts payable				
99	Accrued payables				
100	Income tax payable				
101	Total current liabilities				
102					
103	Long-term debt				
104	Less: Discount on long-term debt				
105	Net long-term debt				
106					
107	Capital stock				
108	Retained earnings				
109	Less: Treasury stock				
110	Total liabilities and stockholders' equity				
111					
112					

FIGURE B–1 (CONCLUDED)

Basic Spreadsheet EXTUS Company

	A	B	C	D	E
113	**Statement of Cash Flows**		12/31/97	12/31/98	
114	Net income				
115	Noncash charges:				
116	Depreciation				
117	Loss (gain) on sale of land				
118	Reduction in discount on long-term debt				
119	Change in current noncash accounts:				
120	Decrease (increase) in net accts rec.				
121	Decrease (increase) in inventory				
122	Increase (decrease) in accounts payable				
123	Increase (decrease) in accrued payables				
124	Increase (decrease) in taxes payable				
125	Net cash from operating activities				
126					
127	Receipts from selling land				
128	Payments for land purchases				
129	Payments for PP&E purchases				
130	Net cash from investing activities				
131					
132	Receipts from common stock issuances				
133	Receipts from debt issuances				
134	Payments for treasury stock purchases				
135	Payments of dividends				
136	Net cash from financing activities				
137					
138	Net increase (decrease) in cash				
139	Beginning balance in cash				
140	Ending balance in cash				
141					
142					
143					
144	**Financial Ratios**		12/31/97	12/31/98	
145					
146	Profitability ratios:				
147	Return on equity				
148	Return on assets				
149	Earnings per share ($)				
150	Return on sales				
151	Times interest earned				
152					
153	Solvency ratios:				
154	Current ratio				
155	Quick ratio				
156					
157	Activity ratios:				
158	Receivables turnover (times/year)				
159	Inventory turnover (times/year)				
160					
161	Capitalization ratios:				
162	Financial leverage				
163	Total liabilities/stockholders' equity				
164					
165					
166					
167					
168					

ASSIGNMENT 1. COPY SPREADSHEET FORMAT.

Copy Figure B–1 on to your own spreadsheet. You can use any spreadsheet program you wish, but you should copy the descriptors in column A exactly as they are in the figure, leaving open the appropriate cells in columns B (1/1/97), C (12/31/97), and D (12/31/98).

HINT FOR STUDENTS: *As you copy the spreadsheet, pay close attention to the names and locations of the MANAGEMENT INPUTS, accounts on the FINANCIAL STATE- MENTS, and the Financial Ratios. The more familiar you are with these items, the easier and more meaningful this exercise will be.*

When designing the spreadsheet in the next assignment, it will be helpful to note that many of the descriptors in column A under MANAGEMENT INPUTS contain brief parenthetical explanations, indicating what is to be placed in the open cells following the descriptor. Some indicate the measuring unit (e.g., $, years) of the input; others indicate that a percentage (e.g., %) or decimal is to be entered into the cell, still others indicate that a formula (e.g., % sales and calc.) is to be placed in the open cells. For example, "Accounts receivable (% sales)"—row 32—indicates that the open cells in columns C and D will contain formulas that compute the accounts receivable balance as a percentage of sales in 1997 and 1998, respectively. Similarly, "units of inventory sold (calc.)"—row 31—indicates that the open cells in columns C and D will contain formulas that compute the number of inventory units sold (i.e., beginning units + purchased units − ending unit) in 1997 and 1998, respectively. The descriptors in the FINANCIAL STATEMENTS and Financial Ratios sections of the spreadsheet do not contain such indicators because they are always followed by cells containing formulas.

ASSIGNMENT 2. PROGRAM THE FINANCIAL STATEMENTS AND RATIOS.

Input the amounts or formulas required to derive values for the financial statement accounts and financial ratios listed below. This activity deals only with the FINAN- CIAL STATEMENTS and Financial Ratios sections of the spreadsheet.[1] Assume that EXTUS is in its first year of operations. The spreadsheet resulting from these inputs should closely resemble Figure B–2.

HINT FOR STUDENTS: *Account balances as of 1/1/97, such as the beginning bal- ances of inventory, retained earnings, and cash, are zero.*

Income Statement (rows 59–75): Beginning inventory, Total cost of goods sold, Gross profit, Net income from operations, Net income (loss) before taxes, and Net income (loss).

Statement of Retained Earnings (rows 77–81): Beginning balance in retained earnings, Net income (loss), and Ending balance in retained earnings.

Balance Sheet (rows 83–110): Cash, Net accounts receivable, Total current assets, Net property, plant, & equipment, Total assets, Total current liabilities, Net long-term debt, Retained earnings, and Total liabilities and stockholders' equity.

---

1. The formula for earnings per share is an exception in that it contains a reference to a cell in the MANAGEMENT INPUTS section.

FIGURE B–2

Assignment 2 Spreadsheet EXTUS Company

	A	B	C	D	E
57	**FINANCIAL STATEMENTS**				
58					
59	**Income Statement**		12/31/97	12/31/98	
60	Sales				
61	Cost of goods sold:				
62	Beginning inventory		0	0	
63	Purchases				
64	Less: Ending inventory				
65	Total cost of goods sold		0	0	
66	Gross profit		$0	$0	
67	Selling & administrative expenses				
68	Depreciation expense				
69	Bad debt expense				
70	Net income from operations		$0	$0	
71	Interest expense				
72	Gain (loss) on sale of land				
73	Net income (loss) before taxes		$0	$0	
74	Income tax expense				
75	Net income (loss)		$0	$0	
76					
77	**Statement of Retained Earnings**		12/31/97	12/31/98	
78	Beginning balance in retained earnings		$0	$0	
79	Net income (loss)		0	0	
80	Less: Cash dividends				
81	Ending balance in retained earnings		$0	$0	
82					
83	**Balance Sheet**		12/31/97	12/31/98	
84	Cash		$0	$0	
85	Accounts receivable				
86	Less: Allowance for bad debts				
87	Net accounts receivable		0	0	
88	Inventory				
89	Total current assets		0	0	
90					
91	Land				
92	Property, plant, & equipment				
93	Less: Accumulated depreciation				
94	Net property, plant, & equipment		0	0	
95	Total assets		$0	$0	
96					
97			12/31/97	12/31/98	
98	Accounts payable				
99	Accrued payables				
100	Income tax payable				
101	Total current liabilities		0	0	
102					
103	Long-term debt				
104	Less: Discount on long-term debt				
105	Net long-term debt		0	0	
106					
107	Capital stock				
108	Retained earnings		0	0	
109	Less: Treasury stock				
110	Total liabilities and stockholders' equity		$0	$0	
111					
112					

FIGURE B–2 (CONCLUDED)

Assignment 2 Spreadsheet EXTUS Company

	A	B	C	D	E
113	**Statement of Cash Flows**		**12/31/97**	**12/31/98**	
114	Net income		$0	$0	
115	Noncash charges:				
116	Depreciation				
117	Loss (gain) on sale of land				
118	Reduction in discount on long-term debt				
119	Change in current noncash accounts:				
120	Decrease (increase) in net accts. rec.				
121	Decrease (increase) in inventory				
122	Increase (decrease) in accounts payable				
123	Increase (decrease) in accrued payables				
124	Increase (decrease) in taxes payable				
125	Net cash from operating activities		$0	$0	
126					
127	Receipts from selling land				
128	Payments for land purchases				
129	Payments for PP&E purchases				
130	Net cash from investing activities		$0	$0	
131					
132	Receipts from common stock issuances				
133	Receipts from debt issuances				
134	Payments for treasury stock purchases				
135	Payments of dividends				
136	Net cash from financing activities		$0	$0	
137					
138	Net increase (decrease) in cash		$0	$0	
139	Beginning balance in cash		0	0	
140	Ending balance in cash		$0	$0	
141					
142					
143					
144	**Financial Ratios**		**12/31/97**	**12/31/98**	
145					
146	Profitability ratios:				
147	Return on equity		#DIV/0!	#DIV/0!	
148	Return on assets		#DIV/0!	#DIV/0!	
149	Earnings per share ($)		#DIV/0!	#DIV/0!	
150	Return on sales		#VALUE!	#VALUE!	
151	Times interest earned		#DIV/0!	#DIV/0!	
152					
153	Solvency ratios:				
154	Current ratio		#DIV/0!	#DIV/0!	
155	Quick ratio		#DIV/0!	#DIV/0!	
156					
157	Activity ratios:				
158	Receivables turnover (times/year)		#DIV/0!	#DIV/0!	
159	Inventory turnover (times/year)		#DIV/0!	#DIV/0!	
160					
161	Capitalization ratios:				
162	Financial leverage		#DIV/0!	#DIV/0!	
163	Total liabilities/stockholders' equity		#DIV/0!	#DIV/0!	
164					
165					
166					
167					
168					

HINT FOR STUDENTS: *For the cash account on the balance sheet use the ending cash balance from the statement of cash flows.*

Statement of Cash Flows (rows 113–140): Net income, Net cash from operating activities, Net cash from investing activities, Net cash from financing activities, Net increase (decrease) in cash, Beginning balance in cash, and Ending balance in cash.

Financial Ratios (rows 144–163): Use the formulas provided in this text (see Chapter 3, Figure 3–16) with the following exception. In all cases where the formula calls for using an "average" amount (e.g., return on equity = net income / average stockholders' equity), use the ending balance instead of the "average" when inputting the formula for 12/31/97. Since 1997 is the first year of operations, using "average" amounts can distort the ratios because the beginning balances are zero. However, this problem does not arise for 1998, so use the "average" amounts, as indicated in the text, when inputting the formulas for 12/31/98.

ASSIGNMENT 3. LINK MANAGEMENT INPUTS TO THE FINANCIAL STATEMENTS.

Input the following formulas, most of which provide links between MANAGEMENT INPUTS and the FINANCIAL STATEMENTS and Financial Ratios. Note that only certain basic formulas are required here. Other formulas are required later for subsequent assignments.

a. Input the formulas that link "Number of common shares issued"—row 4—and "Issue price per common share ($)"—row 5—to the Balance Sheet (Capital stock)—row 107—and the Statement of Cash Flows (Receipts from common stock issuances)—row 132.
b. Input the formulas for "Number of shares outstanding (calc.)"—row 8.
c. Input formulas that link "Long-term debt—face value"—row 9—to the Balance Sheet (Long-term debt)—row 105—and the Statement of Cash Flows (Receipts from debt issuances)—row 133.
d. Input formulas that link the "annual effective interest rate (%)"—row 12—to the Income Statement (Interest expense)—row 71.

HINT FOR STUDENTS: *For purposes of Assignment 3, assume that the "annual effective interest rate (%)"—row 12—is the same as the "annual stated interest rate (%)"—row 11—and that the "Long-term debt—face value ($)"—row 9—is equal to the "Present value of the debt payments (calc.)"—row 13—as of 1/1/97, 12/31/97, and 12/31/98.*

e. Input the formulas that link "Cash dividends (% of net income)"—row 14—to the Statement of Retained Earnings (Less: Cash dividends)—row 80—and the Statement of Cash Flows (Payment of dividends)—row 135.
f. Input the formulas that link "Investment in property, plant, & equip. ($)"—row 19—to the Balance Sheet (Property, plant, & equipment)—row 92—and the Statement of Cash Flows (Payments for PP&E purchases)—row 129.
g. Input the formulas that link "Units of inventory purchased"—row 24—and "Cost per unit of inventory purchased ($)"—row 25—to the Income Statement (Purchases)—row 63.

h. Input the formula for "Units of inventory sold (calc.)"—row 31—which is provided below.

> HINT FOR STUDENTS: *Inputting these formulas requires the use of "IF" statements and nested "IF" statements, which are described in your spreadsheet's documentation.*

The number of units sold in each year is a positive function of the initial investment in property, plant, & equipment, and a negative function of the sales price in that year. That is, as the investment in property, plant, & equipment increases, the number of units sold increases, and as the sales price increases, the number of units sold decreases. Specifically, the number of units sold—the demand function—is defined in the following way:

If investment in PP&E is:	Units sold is defined by the following formula:
$0	0
> $0 and ≤ $20,000	$(5{,}000 \times 100) / (\text{sales price})^2$
> $20,000 and ≤ $40,000	$(12{,}000 \times 100) / (\text{sales price})^2$
> $40,000	$(15{,}000 \times 100) / (\text{sales price})^2$

i. Input the formulas that link "Price per unit of inventory sold ($)"—row 30—and "Units of inventory sold (calc.)"—row 31—to the Income Statement (Sales)—row 60.

j. Input the formulas for "Ending inventory in units (calc.)"—row 34.

k. Input the formulas that link "Ending inventory in units (calc.)"—row 34—and "Cost per unit of inventory purchased ($)"—row 25—to the Income Statement (Ending inventory)—row 64, the Balance Sheet (Inventory)—row 88, and the Statement of Cash Flows (Decrease [increase] in inventory)—row 121.

> HINT FOR STUDENTS: *Assume a first-in, first-out (FIFO) inventory cost flow, and that total unit sales in 1997 and 1998 together always exceeds the number of inventory units purchased in 1997. Place a "1" in the cell following the inventory cost flow assumption—row 48. (Note: The "1" plays no role in the spreadsheet at this time, but will be necessary for Assignment 7.)*

l. Input the formulas that link "Selling & admin. expenses (% sales)"—row 36—to the Income Statement (Selling & administrative expenses)—row 67.

m. Input the formulas that link "Income tax rate (% net income before tax)"—row 38—to the Income Statement (Income tax expense)—row 74.

n. Input the formulas that link "Estimated useful life (years)"—row 50—and "Salvage value ($)"—row 51—to the Income Statement (Depreciation expense)—row 68, the Balance Sheet (Less: Accumulated depreciation)—row 93, and the Statement of Cash Flows (Depreciation)—row 116.

> HINT FOR STUDENTS: *Recall that these accounting estimates refer to the "Investment in property, plant, & equip."—row 19—and assume the straight line method. Place a "1" in the cell following depreciation method—row 52. (Note: The "1" plays no role in the spreadsheet at this time, but will be necessary for Assignment 7.)*

The spreadsheet should now be ready to analyze the transactions described in Assignments 4–10.

ASSIGNMENT 4. BASIC ANALYSIS—NET INCOME, SALES PRICES, AND ESTIMATED USEFUL LIVES.

Input the amounts contained in Figure B–3. These entries indicate that the company issued 1,000 common shares at a price per share of $20; issued debt with a face value of $30,000 and a 10-year life with annual and effective rates of interest of 6% ($30,000 was collected from the issuance); paid dividends of 40% of net income in 1997 and 1998; invested $35,000 in property, plant, & equipment; purchased inventory units of 27,000 @ $4.00/unit and 25,000 @ $4.50/unit in 1997 and 1998, respectively; established sales prices of $7.00/unit and $7.25/unit in 1997 and 1998, respectively; experienced selling and administrative expenses of 30% of sales in 1997 and 1998; paid income taxes at a rate of 34% of net income in 1997 and 1998; used the FIFO inventory flow assumption; and used the straight-line method of depreciation, estimating a useful life of 10 years and a salvage value of $5,000.

After inputting this information, use the spreadsheet to answer the following questions. Treat each question as independent, returning input values to their original states before answering the next question.

a. What amount of net income did the company report in 1997 and 1998? Explain why net income decreased.

b. What net income would have been reported in 1998 if the company had not increased its sales price in 1998? What sales price in 1998 would have generated the largest 1998 net income, and at that price how many units are sold?

> **HINT FOR STUDENTS:** *Use the trial-and-error method, inputting different sales prices (in increments of $.25) to find the sales price that maximizes net income.*

c. What amount of net income would have been reported if the company used a 5-year estimated useful life instead of a 10-year life for purposes of depreciating its property, plant, & equipment? How would this change have affected the company's net cash from operations in 1997 and 1998? Explain why.

d. Compute the change in financial leverage from 1997 to 1998, and explain why financial leverage either increased or decreased.

ASSIGNMENT 5. PROGRAM LAND TRANSACTIONS, ACCRUALS, THE METHOD OF ACCOUNTING FOR BAD DEBTS.

a. Input the formulas for "Ending number of land parcels held (calc.)"—row 23.

b. Input the formulas that link "Number of land parcels purchased"—row 20, "Market value per parcel ($)"—row 21, and "Number of parcels sold"—row 22 to the Income Statement ("Gain [loss] on sale of land")—row 72, the Balance Sheet ("Land")—row 91, the Statement of Cash Flows ("Receipts from selling land," "Payments for land purchases," and "Loss [gain] on sale of land")—rows 127, 128, 117.

c. Input the formulas that link "Accounts receivable (% sales)—row 32" to the Balance Sheet ("Accounts receivable")—row 85, and the Statement of Cash Flows ("Decrease [increase] in net accts. rec.")—row 120.

d. Input the formulas that link "Accounts payable [% purchase cost]"—row 35, "Accrued payables [% sell. & adm. exp.]"—row 37, and "Income tax payable [% tax expense]"—row 39 to the Balance Sheet ("Accounts payable," "Accrued

FIGURE B–3

Assignment 4 Inputs EXTUS Company

	A	B	C	D	E
1	**MANAGEMENT INPUTS**	**1/1/97**	**12/31/97**	**12/31/98**	
2					
3	**Financing activities:**				
4	Number of common shares issued	1,000			
5	Issue price per common share ($)	$20.00			
6	Treasury shares purchased				
7	Treasury share purchase price ($)				
8	Number of shares outstanding (calc.)		1,000	1,000	
9	Long-term debt—face value ($)	$30,000			
10	Life of long-term debt (years)	10			
11	Annual stated interest rate (%)	0.06			
12	Annual effective interest rate (%)	0.06			
13	Present value of debt payments (calc.)	$30,000	$30,000	$30,000	
14	Cash dividends (% net income)		0.40	0.40	
15					
16					
17					
18	**Investing activities:**				
19	Investment in property, plant, & equip. ($)	$35,000			
20	Number of land parcels purchased				
21	Market value/parcel ($)				
22	Number of parcels sold				
23	Ending number of land parcels held (calc.)				
24	Units of inventory purchased		27,000	27,000	
25	Cost per unit of inventory purchased ($)		$4.00	$4.50	
26					
27					
28					
29	**Operating activities:**				
30	Price per unit of inventory sold ($)		$7.00	$7.25	
31	Unites of inventory sold (calc.)		concealed	concealed	
32	Accounts receivable (% sales)				
33	Actual bad debts (% previous year sales)				
34	Ending inventory in units (calc.)		concealed	concealed	
35	Accounts payable (% purchase cost)				
36	Selling & admin. expenses (% sales)		0.30	0.30	
37	Accrued payables (% sell. & adm. exp.)				
38	Income tax rate (% net income before tax)		0.34	0.34	
39	Income tax payable (% of tax expense)				
40					
41					
42					
43	**Accounting methods:**				
44	Bad Debts				
45	Direct write-off (1) or Allowance (2)?				
46	If allowance, bad debt estimate (% sales)				
47	Inventory				
48	FIFO (1) or LIFO (2)?	1			
49	Book and Tax Depreciation				
50	Estimated useful life (years)	10			
51	Salvage value ($)	$5,000			
52	Straight-line (1) or Double-declining-bal. (2)?	1			
53					
54					
55					
56					

payables," and "Income tax payable"—rows 98, 99, 100) and the Statement of Cash Flows ("Increase [decrease] in accounts payable," "Increase [decrease] in accrued payables," and "Increase [decrease] in taxes payable"—rows 122, 123, and 124).

e. Input the formulas that link "Actual bad debts [% previous year sales]"—row 33, the choice of the "Direct write-off (1)" or "Allowance (2)"—row 45, and "If allowance, bad debt estimate (% sales)"—row 46 to the Income Statement ("Bad debt expense")—row 69 and the Balance Sheet ("Less: Allowance for bad debts")—row 86.

HINT FOR STUDENTS: *The formula for row 45 requires the use of an "IF" statement, which is described in your spreadsheet's documentation. If a "1" is placed in the cell following the bad debt write-off method, the financial statements should reflect the use of the direct write-off method. If a "2" is placed in the cell, the financial statements should reflect the use of the allowance method, which requires that a bad debt estimate (% of sales) be provided.* ***Also, under the allowance method, assume that the 12/31/98 balance in Accounts receivable (row 85), which is expressed as a percentage of sales, already reflects write-offs of actual bad debts determined in 1998. In other words, do not reduce the balance for the write-offs recorded in 1998.***

ASSIGNMENT 6. ANALYSIS—LAND TRANSACTIONS, CASH FLOW MANAGEMENT, AND ACCOUNTING FOR BAD DEBTS.

Input the amounts contained in Figure B–4. This assignment builds upon Assignment 4, so that the inputs required in Assignment 4 are also required here. In addition, the company purchased 2 parcels of land in 1997 at a market value of $5,000/parcel; sold 1 parcel of land in 1998 at a price of $7,000; set credit terms so that outstanding receivables equaled 8% of sales in 1997 and 1998; experienced actual bad debts in 1998 of 1% of 1997 sales; delayed payments to suppliers so that outstanding accounts payable equaled 8% of purchases in 1997 and 1998; delayed payments on selling and administrative expenses so that accrued payables equaled 4% of selling and administrative expenses in 1997 and 1998; delayed payments on income taxes so that income tax payable equaled 25% of income tax expense in 1997 and 1998; and used the allowance method to account for bad debts, estimating bad debts at 1% of sales.

After inputting this information, use the spreadsheet to answer the following questions. Treat each question as independent, returning input values to their original states before answering the next question.

a. By how much and in what direction was 1998 net income changed by the sale of the parcel of land? By how much and in what direction was 1998 net cash flow from operations changed by the sale of land? Explain why the changes are different.

HINT FOR STUDENTS: Use the following format.

	NO LAND SALE	LAND SALE	CHANGE
1998 Net income			
1998 Net cash from operations			

b. Compute the change in receivables turnover (times) from 1997 to 1998, and explain why the ratio increased or decreased.

FIGURE B–4

Assignment 6 Inputs EXTUS Company

	A	B	C	D	E
1	**MANAGEMENT INPUTS**	**1/1/97**	**12/31/97**	**12/31/98**	
2					
3	**Financing activities:**				
4	Number of common shares issued	1,000			
5	Issue price per common share ($)	$20.00			
6	Treasury shares purchased				
7	Treasury share purchase price ($)				
8	Number of shares outstanding (calc.)		1,000	1,000	
9	Long-term debt—face value ($)	$30,000			
10	Life of long-term debt (years)	10			
11	Annual stated interest rate (%)	0.06			
12	Annual effective interest rate (%)	0.06			
13	Present value of debt payments (calc.)	$30,000	$30,000	$30,000	
14	Cash dividends (% net income)		0.40	0.40	
15					
16					
17					
18	**Investing activities:**				
19	Investment in property, plant, & equip. ($)	$35,000			
20	Number of land parcels purchased		2		
21	Market value/parcel ($)		$5,000	$7,000	
22	Number of parcels sold			1	
23	Ending number of land parcels held (calc.)		2	1	
24	Units of inventory purchased		27,000	25,000	
25	Cost per unit of inventory purchased ($)		$4.00	$4.50	
26					
27					
28					
29	**Operating activities:**				
30	Price per unit of inventory sold ($)		$7.00	$7.25	
31	Units of inventory sold (calc.)		concealed	concealed	
32	Accounts receivable (% sales)		0.08	0.08	
33	Actual bad debts (% previous year sales)			0.01	
34	Ending inventory in units (calc.)		concealed	concealed	
35	Accounts payable (% purchase cost)		0.08	0.08	
36	Selling & admin. expenses (% sales)		0.30	0.30	
37	Accrued payables (% sell. & adm. exp.)		0.04	0.04	
38	Income tax rate (% net income before tax)		0.34	0.34	
39	Income tax payable (% of tax expense)		0.25	0.25	
40					
41					
42					
43	**Accounting methods:**				
44	Bad Debts				
45	Direct write-off (1) or Allowance (2)?	2			
46	If allowance, bad debt estimate (% sales)	0.010			
47	Inventory				
48	FIFO (1) or LIFO (2)?	1			
49	Book and Tax Depreciation				
50	Estimated useful life (years)	10			
51	Salvage value ($)	$5,000			
52	Straight-line (1) or Double-declining-bal. (2)?	1			
53					
54					
55					
56					

c. By what amount and in what direction does the current ratio change in 1997 and 1998 if the company carries an accounts payable balance equal to 12% (instead of 8%) of purchases? How is the net cash flow from operations effected?

HINT FOR STUDENTS: *Use the following format.*

	A/P (8%)	A/P (12%)	CHANGE
1997 Current ratio			
1998 Current ratio			
1997 Net cash from operating activities			
1998 Net cash from operating activities			

d. By what amount and in what direction does net income in 1997 and 1998 change if the direct write-off method is used instead of the allowance method?

HINT FOR STUDENTS: Use the following format.

	ALLOWANCE	DIRECT WRITE-OFF	CHANGE
1997 Net income			
1998 Net income			

e. If the allowance method is used, by what amount and in what direction does net income in 1997 and 1998 change if the bad debt estimate is 1.5% instead of 1%? How does the Allowance for Bad Debts account change?

HINT FOR STUDENTS: Use the following format.

	ALLOWANCE (1%)	ALLOWANCE (1.5%)	CHANGE
1997 Net income			
1998 Net income			
1997 Allowance			
1998 Allowance			

ASSIGNMENT 7. PROGRAM INVENTORY FLOW ASSUMPTIONS AND DEPRECIATION METHODS.

a. Input formulas that link the inventory cost flow assumptions "FIFO (1) or LIFO (2)"—row 48 to the Income Statement ("Less: Ending inventory")—row 64, the Balance Sheet ("Inventory")—row 88, and the Statement of Cash Flows ("Decrease [increase] in inventory")—row 121.

HINT FOR STUDENTS: *Inputting these formulas requires the use of "IF" statements, which are described in your spreadsheet's documentation. If a "1" is placed in the cell following the inventory cost flow assumption, the financial statements should reflect the use of FIFO. If a "2" is placed in the cell, the financial statements should reflect the use of LIFO.*

b. Input formulas that link the methods of depreciation "Straight-line (1)" or "Double-declining-bal. (2)"—row 52 to the Income Statement ("Depreciation expense")—row 68, the Balance Sheet ("Less: Accumulated depreciation")—row 93, and the Statement of Cash Flows ("Depreciation")—row 116.

HINT FOR STUDENTS: Inputting these formulas requires the use of "IF" statements, which are described in your spreadsheet's documentation. If a "1" is placed in the cell following the method of depreciation, the financial statements should reflect the use of straight-line. If a "2" is placed in the cell, the financial statements should reflect the use of the double-declining-balance method. You may wish to use the DDB function described in your spreadsheet's documentation.

ASSIGNMENT 8. ANALYSIS—INVENTORY COST FLOW ASSUMPTIONS AND DEPRECIATION METHODS.

Input the amounts contained in Figure B–5. This assignment builds upon Assignment 6, so that the inputs required in Assignment 6 are also required here with the following exceptions: the company uses (1) the LIFO inventory cost flow assumption and (2) the double-declining-balance method of depreciation.

After inputting this information, use the spreadsheet to answer the following questions.

a. Complete the following charts. In chart 1 fill in the net income amounts reported for 1998 under the four different combinations, and in chart 2 fill in the 1998 amounts for net cash from operating activities under the same four combinations. Discuss the important tradeoffs involved in choosing an inventory cost flow assumption and a depreciation method, and indicate which of the two choices (cost flow assumption or depreciation) makes a larger difference in this case.

CHART 1. 1998 NET INCOME

	INVENTORY COST FLOW	
	LIFO	FIFO
Depreciation method:		
Straight-line		
Double-declining-balance		

CHART 2. 1998 NET CASH FROM OPERATING ACTIVITIES

	INVENTORY COST FLOW	
	LIFO	FIFO
Depreciation method:		
Straight-line		
Double-declining-balance		

b. Repeat the analysis above assuming that the cost per unit of inventories purchased dropped from $4.00 in 1997 to $3.50 in 1998 (instead of increasing to $4.50). Briefly discuss.

ASSIGNMENT 9. PROGRAM TREASURY STOCK PURCHASES AND THE EFFECTIVE INTEREST RATE.

a. Input formulas that link "Treasury shares purchased"—row 6 and the "Treasury share purchase price ($)"—row 7 to the Balance Sheet ("Less: treasury stock")—row 109, the Statement of Cash Flows ("Payments for treasury stock purchases")—row 134, and the ("Earnings-per-share ratio")—row 149.

FIGURE B–5

Assignment 8 Inputs EXTUS Company

	A	B	C	D	E
1	**MANAGEMENT INPUTS**	**1/1/97**	**12/31/97**	**12/31/98**	
2					
3	**Financing activities:**				
4	Number of common shares issued	1,000			
5	Issue price per common share ($)	$20.00			
6	Treasury shares purchased				
7	Treasury share purchase price ($)				
8	Number of shares outstanding (calc.)		1,000	1,000	
9	Long-term debt—face value ($)	$30,000			
10	Life of long-term debt (years)	10			
11	Annual stated interest rate (%)	0.06			
12	Annual effective interest rate (%)	0.06			
13	Present value of debt payments (calc.)	$30,000	$30,000	$30,000	
14	Cash dividends (% net income)		0.40	0.40	
15					
16					
17					
18	**Investing activities:**				
19	Investment in property, plant, & equip. ($)	$35,000			
20	Number of land parcels purchased		2		
21	Market value/parcel ($)		$5,000	$7,000	
22	Number of parcels sold			1	
23	Ending number of land parcels held (calc.)		2	1	
24	Units of inventory purchased		27,000	25,000	
25	Cost per unit of inventory purchased ($)		$4.00	$3.50	
26					
27					
28					
29	**Operating activities:**				
30	Price per unit of inventory sold ($)		$7.00	$7.25	
31	Units of inventory sold (calc.)		concealed	concealed	
32	Accounts receivable (% sales)		0.08	0.08	
33	Actual bad debts (% previous year sales)			0.01	
34	Ending inventory in units (calc.)		concealed	concealed	
35	Accounts payable (% purchase cost)		0.08	0.08	
36	Selling & admin. expenses (% sales)		0.30	0.30	
37	Accrued payables (% sell. & adm. exp.)		0.04	0.04	
38	Income tax rate (% net income before tax)		0.34	0.34	
39	Income tax payable (% of tax expense)		0.25	0.25	
40					
41					
42					
43	**Accounting methods:**				
44	Bad Debts				
45	Direct write-off (1) or Allowance (2)?	2			
46	If allowance, bad debt estimate (% sales)	0.010			
47	Inventory				
48	FIFO (1) or LIFO (2)?	2			
49	Book and Tax Depreciation				
50	Estimated useful life (years)	10			
51	Salvage value ($)	$5,000			
52	Straight-line (1) or Double-declining-bal. (2)?	2			
53					
54					
55					
56					

b. Input formulas that link the "Long-term debt—face value ($)"—row 9, "Life of long-term debt (years)"—row 10, "Annual stated interest rate (%)"—row 11, and "Annual effective interest rate (%)"—row 12 to the "Present value of the debt payments (calc.)"—row 13.

HINT FOR STUDENTS: *You may wish to use one of the Present Value functions described in your spreadsheet's documentation.*

c. Input the formulas that link the "Present value of the debt payments (calc.)"— row 13 to the Balance Sheet ("Less: Discount on long-term debt")—row 104 and the Statement of Cash Flows ("Reduction in discount on long-term debt")—row 118. Assume that all debt is issued either at face or at a discount.

ASSIGNMENT 10. ANALYSIS—TREASURY STOCK PURCHASES AND CHANGES IN THE EFFECTIVE RATE OF INTEREST.

Input the amounts contained in Figure B–6. This assignment builds upon Assignment 8, so that the inputs required in Assignment 8 are also required here. In addition, the company purchased 25 treasury shares @ $25/share and 50 treasury shares @ $26/share in 1997 and 1998, respectively; and the effective rate of interest was 8%.

After inputting this information, use the spreadsheet to answer the following questions. Treat each question as independent, returning input values to their original states before answering the next question.

a. By how much and in what direction did the purchase of treasury shares in 1998 affect 1998 earnings per share, the 1998 current ratio, and 1998 total liabilities to stockholders' equity? Explain why each ratio changed.

HINT FOR STUDENTS: Use the following format.

	NO TREASURY SHARES PURCHASED	TREASURY SHARES PURCHASED	CHANGE
Earnings per share			
Current ratio			
Total liabilities/ **stockholders' equity**			

b. Assume that the management of EXTUS needs $30,000 on 1/1/97. At an annual effective interest rate of 8%, how large a note (face value) must the company sign (round to the nearest thousand dollars), given a 10-year life and a 6% annual stated interest rate? If the annual effective rate goes up to 10%, how large a note must the company sign to collect $30,000 on 1/1/97? Comparing these two scenarios, briefly describe and explain the effects of the rising annual effective interest rate (from 8% to 10%) on the financial ratios of the company.

HINT FOR STUDENTS: *Given the terms of each note (i.e., life, stated rate, effective rate), use the trial-and-error approach to find that face value that produces a "Present value of debt payments (calc.)"—row 13 of $30,000, which should also be the dollar amount produced for "Receipts from debt issuances"—row 133 on the Statement of Cash Flows.*

FIGURE B–6

Assignment 10 Inputs EXTUS Company

	A	B	C	D	E
1	**MANAGEMENT INPUTS**	**1/1/97**	**12/31/97**	**12/31/98**	
2					
3	**Financing activities:**				
4	Number of common shares issued	1,000			
5	Issue price per common share ($)	$20.00			
6	Treasury shares purchased		25	50	
7	Treasury share purchase price ($)		$25.00	$26.00	
8	Number of shares outstanding (calc.)		975	925	
9	Long-term debt—face value ($)	$30,000			
10	Life of long-term debt (years)	10			
11	Annual stated interest rate (%)	0.06			
12	Annual effective interest rate (%)	0.08			
13	Present value of debt payments (calc.)	$25,974	$26,252	$26,552	
14	Cash dividends (% net income)		0.40	0.40	
15					
16					
17					
18	**Investing activities:**				
19	Investment in property, plant, & equip. ($)	$35,000			
20	Number of land parcels purchased		2		
21	Market value/parcel ($)		$5,000	$7,000	
22	Number of parcels sold			1	
23	Ending number of land parcels held (calc.)		2	1	
24	Units of inventory purchased		27,000	25,000	
25	Cost per unit of inventory purchased ($)		$4.00	$4.50	
26					
27					
28					
29	**Operating activities:**				
30	Price per unit of inventory sold ($)		$7.00	$7.25	
31	Units of inventory sold (calc.)		concealed	concealed	
32	Accounts receivable (% sales)		0.08	0.08	
33	Actual bad debts (% previous year sales)			0.01	
34	Ending inventory in units (calc.)		concealed	concealed	
35	Accounts payable (% purchase cost)		0.08	0.08	
36	Selling & admin. expenses (% sales)		0.30	0.30	
37	Accrued payables (% sell. & adm. exp.)		0.04	0.04	
38	Income tax rate (% net income before tax)		0.34	0.34	
39	Income tax payable (% of tax expense)		0.25	0.25	
40					
41					
42					
43	**Accounting methods:**				
44	Bad Debts				
45	Direct write-off (1) or Allowance (2)?	2			
46	If allowance, bad debt estimate (% sales)	0.010			
47	Inventory				
48	FIFO (1) or LIFO (2)?	2			
49	Book and Tax Depreciation				
50	Estimated useful life (years)	10			
51	Salvage value ($)	$5,000			
52	Straight-line (1) or Double-declining-bal. (2)?	2			
53					
54					
55					
56					

MCI COMMUNICATIONS CORPORATION ANNUAL REPORT

Contents

In addition to being the second-largest provider of long distance communications in the U.S. and the third-largest carrier of international calling, MCI offers consumers and businesses a wide array of voice, data and video communications, local telecommunications services, on-line information, electronic mail, network management services and communications software.

This year's annual report reflects a more concise, cost-effective approach to reporting MCI's financial performance. Stockholders who want information in addition to financial reporting can contact MCI's Investor Relations Department at 1-800-765-2115 (Internet: 640-5834@mcimail.com).

For information on MCI® products and services contact MCI's national sales centers at the numbers below.

Teleconsumers: 1-800-444-3333

Business Customers: 1-800-937-6000

networkMCI BUSINESS: 1-800-955-5195

Integrated Client Services: Division 1-800-813-4491

To MCI's Stockholders:

MCI has become a major player in worldwide telecommunications by pursuing a clear, consistent strategy over the years: 1) grow market share profitably, 2) expand globally, and 3) leverage our core skills into new markets.

We delivered another strong performance in 1994 in line with that long-term strategy. MCI achieved 20 percent revenue market share, while net income increased more than 30 percent. We formed joint ventures with British Telecommunications plc (BT) and Mexico's Grupo Financiero Banamex-Accival (Banacci). And we continued to build a portfolio of iniatives that position MCI to compete in new businesses.

Nineteen ninety-four was a pivotal year for MCI in terms of strategic progress, and 1995 will be even more so.

Grow Market Share Profitably

The core business continues to be a strong source of rapidly growing profits for MCI. Our focus in 1994 was to direct greater resources into higher-value products and services.

Revenue for the year was $13.3 billion, an increase of nearly 12 percent over 1993 revenue of $11.9 billion. MCI's $1.4 billion revenue increase represents 38 percent of the $3.8 billion growth in the overall long distance market.

Operating cash flow was a record $2.7 billion. Net income, as reported was $795 million, or $1.32 per share. Excluding unusual items, net income was $887 million, or $1.47 per share. Measured either way net income increased more than 30 percent in 1994.

In the business market, revenue and minutes grew more than twice the overall industry rate, driven by double-digit increases in each major customer segment. Notably, MCI has gained six points of share in the 800 market since portability.

In the consumer market, MCI had strong revenue gains for the full year, although competitive pressures were intense late in the year. The full-year gains were driven by successful products like 1-800-COLLECT®, international calling and Personal 800®.

MCI's position as a technology leader was strengthened in 1994 with a $2.9 billion capital investment. The majority of that was used to increase network capacity by more than one billion circuit miles. MCI also deployed technologies such as SONET and ATM that provide the bandwidth capacity and switching speed necessary for multimedia applications.

Expand Globally

MCI is now the world's third-largest carrier of international calling Globally, our priorities are to continue serving consumers and businesses wherever they want to send or receive information, and to participate in key markets in the Americas.

On September 30, MCI and BT completed an historic $4.3 billion alliance, together providing the resources, scale and talent to become the premier global competitive force.

Concert, our joint venture company with BT, was launched July 1 and has begun providing global voice and data network services to multinational businesses. Other carriers have now only announced their global alliances. Concert was the first to market with a virtual network product (Concert VNS, introduced in November) for connecting corporate locations in the U.S., Europe and the Asia-Pacific region.

MCI moved closer to its goal of completing a seamless North American network by forming AVANTEL, S.A., a joint venture with Banacci. AVANTEL will compete in Mexico's booming communications market, thus complementing our 1992 strategic alliance with Stentor (in Canada) and providing a gateway to potential opportunities in Latin America.

Pending governmental decisions regarding licensing and rights-of-way, AVANTEL will build a fiber-optic network linking the country's leading financial centers: Mexico City, Monterrey and Guadalajara.

Leverage Core Skills Into New Markets

MCI continued to increase its focus in 1994 on emerging markets, driven by the exciting convergence of communications, computing and content.

Foremost among our new ventures is our MCImetro^{SM} subsidiary. As competitive barriers fall in the $90 billion local telephone market, MCImetro will provide a full range of local wireline and enhanced services.

MCImetro has fiber-optic facilities up and running in Atlanta, Washington, DC., Dallas, Boston, and Los Angeles. These facilities are used to connect business customers directly to their long distance company, lowering access costs. MCImetro is also moving ahead to install the switching equipment that will make it a full-service local telephone company—going beyond access services to actually providing dial tone.

MCI also acquired an interest in In Flight Phone Corporation, which provides digital, air-to-ground communications, information and entertainment services to airline travelers.

In September 1994, MCI delivered a breakthrough product to the business market: networkMCI BUSINESS™. This is the first software package MCI has ever marketed. The ensemble provides single-source access to information banks, electronic mail, fax messaging, videoconferencing and, soon on-line merchandising in an inexpensive, PC-based package.

One element of the ensemble is internetMCI^{SM}, a comprehensive set of Internet services from local access to on-line shopping. It will also offer the critical link in bringing commerce to the Internet: a secure environment for on-line transactions.

In the wireless market, MCI had announced in February 1994 a strategic alliance with Nextel communications and Comcast Corporation to provide nationwide wireless communications. While that agreement was terminated in August, our wireless strategy has not changed: we plan to offer a nationwide branded MCI wireless service. MCI chose not to participate in the Personal Communications Services (PCS) auctions. As a result, MCI is in the advantageous position of being able to associate with any of the companies providing the underlying facilities in major markets.

Why have we chosen this path? Because for MCI, wireless is a product, not a specific technology Ownership control of wireless networks is not a necessary ingredient to a successful wireless strategy. We intend to offer nationwide wireless services that are bundled with current services; access wireless platforms to design products that are uniquely MCI'S; and plug in our intelligent network and service centers to create unified service and billing environments.

Looking Ahead at 1995

MCI is well-positioned to take advantage of future opportunities because it has some of the rarest resources in telecommunications: powerful brands, global reach, an intelligent network capable of delivering the products and services customers demand, and a nationwide sales and service force. The first days of 1995 provided good evidence of these capabilities.

In January, we unveiled Friends & Family Connections^{SM}, the latest extension of the top brand in this industry. It is the first consumer communications service that integrates all the ways Americans stay in touch—paging, electronic mail, personal 800 services, calling cards and more.

MCI's paging services, Friends & Family Paging^{SM} and networkMCI PAGING^{SM}, were introduced and integrated into our branded consumer and business products. These services are the result of agreements announced January 6 with Paging Network, Inc. (PageNet) and SkyTel Corporation.

Also in January, we achieved our largest commercial contract win ever—a multi-year agreement with the General Electric Company. GE will use a variety of MCI voice and data services to enhance customer service and information transmission among its hundreds of locations worldwide.

We will make significant progress this year positioning MCI in the local telephone market. By year-end, MCImetro will have fiber-optic networks operational in 20 major cities. These cities represent 40 percent of the business access market. How aggressively we can expand in the local market will depend on how quickly regulatory barriers fall. So MCI will be deeply involved, as always, in the legislative and regulatory arenas.

Telecommunications reform is on the agenda of the Congress and many states. MCI has long maintained that the top priority of telecommunications public policy should be enabling real,

effective competition in the local telephone market. Until the Bell Operating Companies lose their local monopoly control, which carries with it both the ability and incentive to impair competition in long distance, they should not be allowed to compete in long distance. If local competition is not mandated through federal legislation, then MCI will continue working state by state toward that goal.

MCI is evolving from a company focused solely on delivering voice and data to a company delivering applications that integrate the worlds of communications, computing and content. We will continue in 1995 doing what we started in 1994: using our strong financial position to make strategic investments, adding vitality to our core business while establishing MCI in emerging opportunities across multiple industries.

We believe that this strategic direction requires using a portfolio approach to measure our performance and value. While we view traditional earnings per share measurements as important, operating cash flow and other indicators also may be appropriate gauges for our strategic initiatives and investments, and even our core business in the future. These alternative measurements are consistent with those being applied to other companies in the emerging markets that MCI is addressing.

To help investors more clearly assess and focus upon our strategic direction, MCI will provide additional financial information about its new business initiatives starting this year.

The Future

Telecommunications is no longer just about sending sound, text or images along copper wires, optical fibers or even in the air. It is also about computer-telephony integration and the distribution of digitized content.

So while we continue to nourish and grow profitably our core long distance business, MCI will also be acquiring electronic gateways and developing the technological infrastructure to ensure we provide the global voice, data, information and entertainment services our customers demand. We will preserve and enhance our entrepreneurial culture so that MCI will always respond to customers through product leadership and premier customer service.

Bringing competition to the long distance market was the experience of a lifetime for MCI employees, and it continues to create significant value for customers and investors. But compared to where we are headed, it will be just a footnote.

Bert C. Roberts

Bert C. Roberts, Jr.
Chairman and Chief Executive Officer

February 24, 1995

Selected Financial Information

MCI Communications
Corporation and Subsidiaries

Year ended December 31,	1994	1993	1992	1991	1990
(In millions, except per share amounts and employees)					
Summary of Operations					
Revenue	$13,338	$11,921	$10,562	$ 9,491	$ 8,454
Total operating expenses	(11,882)	(10,653)	(9,351)	(8,400)	(7,834)
Income from Operations	1,456	1,268	1,211	1,091	620
Interest expense	(153)	(178)	(218)	(212)	(213)
Interest income	50	8	3	6	21
Income before extraordinary item	795	627	609	551	299
Net income	795	582	609	551	299
Earnings Applicable to Common Stockholders	794	581	589	522	270
Earnings per common and					
common equivalent shares:					
Income before extraordinary item	1.32	1.12	1.11	1.00	.53
Loss on early debt retirements	—	(.08)	—	—	—
Total	1.32	1.04	1.11	1.00	.53
Cash dividends per share	.05	.05	.05	.05	.05
Balance Sheet					
Cash and cash equivalents and marketable securities	$ 3,092	$ 165	$ 235	$ 51	$ 231
Gross investment in communications system	13,408	11,618	10,316	9,684	8,708
Annual investment in communications system	2,885	2,095	1,371	1,381	1,283
Total assets	16,366	11,276	9,678	8,834	8,249
Long-term debt	2,997	2,366	3,432	3,104	3,147
Stockholders' equity	9,004	4,713	3,150	2,959	2,340
Operations					
Capacity circuit miles	4,767	3,556	2,107	1,888	1,477
Billable calls	19,411	16,484	14,245	12,189	9,914
Number of full-time employees	40,667	36,235	30,964	27,857	24,509

In 1994, British Telecommunications plc (BT) completed the purchase of 136 million shares of the company's recently authorized Class A common stock for $4.3 billion, resulting in a 20 percent voting interest in the company. This was achieved by the issuance of 108.5 million shares of Class A common stock to BT for $3.5 billion on September 30, 1994 and BT's conversion of 13,736 shares of Series D convertible preferred stock, purchased for $830 million in June 1993, into 27.5 million shares of Class A common stock. This investment is reflected in stockholders' equity.

All per share amounts prior to and including 1993 have been retroactively restated as a result of a two-for-one stock split in the form of a 100% stock dividend issued on July 9, 1993.

In August 1990, the company acquired all the outstanding shares of common stock of Telecom*USA. The acquisition was accounted for as a purchase; accordingly, the net assets and results of operations of Telecom*USA are included in the information above since the acquisition date.

Management's Discussion and Analysis — Overview

MCI Communications
Corporation and Subsidiaries

The following discussion and analysis provides information which management believes is relevant to an assessment and understanding of the company's consolidated results of operations and financial condition. The discussion should be read in conjunction with the consolidated financial statements and notes thereto.

In 1994, the company continued to operate in a single industry segment, the long distance telecommunications industry. More than 90% of its operating revenue and assets relate to activities in this industry.

Financial Summary

Revenue grew $1.4 billion or 12% to $13.3 billion in 1994 versus 13% and $1.4 billion in 1993. The company's revenue growth was 38% of the total industry revenue growth estimated at $3.8 billion in 1994. Also in 1994, the company's revenue and traffic grew at the same rate, marking an improvement in the variance between revenue and traffic growth experienced during 1993.

	1994 vs 1993	1993 vs 1992
% increase in revenue	12%	13%
% increase in traffic	12%	14%
Revenue to traffic variance		(l)%

The positive movement resulted primarily from growth in international and data revenue in 1994. Although international and data revenues are expected to continue to provide a positive impact on this variance in 1995, competitive pressures in the consumer marketplace may have an unfavorable impact. The revenue to traffic variance in 1993 generally reflected the impact of various product promotions and discounts, changes in the mix of products sold and migration of some business customers to lower-priced products.

Income from operations increased 15% to $1,456 million in 1994 from $1,268 million in 1993, following a 5% increase in 1993. Operating margins increased to 10.9% in 1994 from 10.6% in 1993. The 1994 increase was primarily attributable to cost savings realized in telecommunications expense. In 1994 and 1993, operating income was affected by unusual items of $133 million and $150 million respectively. Excluding these items, which are discussed below, operating income and margins would have been $1,589 million or 11.9%, and $1,418 million or 11.9%, in 1994 and 1993, respectively.

Earnings were $794 million or $1.32 per share, $581 million or $1.04 per share and $589 million or $1.11 per share, for 1994, 1993 and 1992, respectively. The investment in the company by British Telecommunications plc (BT), completed on September 30, 1994, had a dilutive impact on earnings per share in 1994 and 1993, and will have a full year dilutive impact on earnings per share in 1995. All earnings per share amounts have been restated as a result of a two-for-one stock split in the form of a 100% stock dividend issued on July 9, 1993.

Excluding unusual items and an extraordinary loss on early debt retirements in 1993, earnings per share in 1994 and 1993 would have been $1.47 and $1.28, respectively. The 1994 unusual pre-tax items of $148 million consisted of $70 million incremental advertising and sales expense related to the launch of networkMCI BUSINESS, a $63 million additional depreciation charge to recognize the reduced utility of older

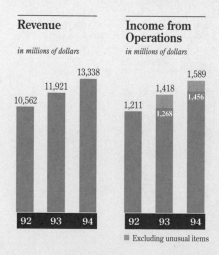

Revenue
in millions of dollars

10,562   11,921   13,338

92   93   94

Income from Operations
in millions of dollars

1,211   1,418   1,589
1,268   1,456

92   93   94

■ Excluding unusual items

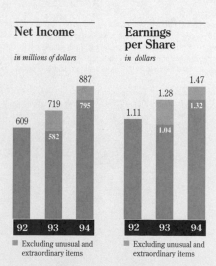

Net Income
in millions of dollars

609   719   887
582   795

92   93   94

■ Excluding unusual and extraordinary items

Earnings per Share
in dollars

1.11   1.28   1.47
1.04   1.32

92   93   94

■ Excluding unusual and extraordinary items

asynchronous fiber-optic transmission and other equipment, a $25 million charge in connection with the settlement of two 900 service class action lawsuits and a $10 million gain on the sale of the company's interest in AAP Telecommunications Pty. Ltd. (AAPT). The 1993 pre-tax charge of $150 million was primarily to recognize costs associated with the company's strategic realignment, streamlining of engineering and network operations facilities and relocation of certain operations to lower cost areas, virtually all of which were completed in 1994. In addition, 1993 included an extraordinary loss of $45 million, net of tax benefit, for the early retirement of debt.

British Telecommunications Investment

On September 30, 1994, the company and BT completed their global alliance. This alliance enables both companies to draw upon their combined technical, financial and marketing strengths to provide enhanced and value-added global telecommunications services. This alliance included several financial transactions. First, BT purchased a 20% voting interest in the company for approximately $4.3 billion at a blended purchase price of $32 per share. This amount included $830 million paid in June 1993. Second, the company invested approximately $79 million for a 24.9% interest in Concert Communications Company (Concert), a business venture launched by BT in July 1994 to provide global telecommunications services for business customers. The company intends to continue making contributions to Concert in order to maintain its proportionate interest. Third, reflecting the geographic world marketing segmentation as envisioned in the alliance, the company purchased from BT both substantially all of the operations of BT North America Inc. (BTNA) in January 1994 for $108 million and a 23.5% interest in Belize Telecommunications Ltd. in February 1995 for approximately $19 million. The company also divested its interest in AAPT of Australia in October 1994.

Alliances, Investments and Initiatives

In January 1994, the company announced the formation of MCImetro, a wholly-owned subsidiary, which will provide a full range of basic and enhanced local telecommunications services through fiber-optic networks and local switching centers throughout the U.S., as regulatory authorities permit. The company's goals, with respect to MCImetro, are to reduce the fees it pays to local phone companies to access its customers and to prepare for the provision of local telecommunications services as the local market becomes competitive. MCImetro has applications with utility regulators pending in 6 states to provide local phone service and is authorized to provide local service in the following five states: Maryland, Washington, New York, Massachusetts and Wisconsin. MCImetro is engineering and constructing networks in a number of U.S. cities and currently owns or operates conduit and fiber cable facilities in more than 200 U.S. cities. The company is planning capital expenditures of approximately $500 million for MCImetro during 1995 and expects to make significant additional investments in MCImetro over the next several years.

In June 1994, the company made an investment in In-Flight Phone Corporation (In-Flight). In-Flight provides airline passengers digital air-to-ground communications services.

In September 1994, the company launched networkMCI BUSINESS, an integrated software application which provides e-mail, fax messaging, information services/automated news monitoring, document sharing, and videoconferencing capability and which will soon provide access to online multimedia business catalogs and the Internet.

In October 1994, the company formed a Mexican alliance, AVANTEL, S.A. (AVANTEL), which along with the company's alliance with Stentor in Canada, will complete its seamless North American network. AVANTEL is a business venture formed by the company and Grupo Financiero Banamex-Accival (Banacci) to provide competitive domestic and international long distance telecommunications services in Mexico. The company's cash investment in the business venture is expected to be $450 million over the next several years. The transaction with Banacci is subject to the grant of a concession from the government of Mexico and the satisfaction of various other conditions.

In January 1995, the company formalized agreements with two of the nation's largest wireless messaging companies, SkyTel Corporation and Paging Network, Inc., that will enable the company to integrate paging and wireless messaging services with certain of the company's residential and business products. Following the execution of these agreements, the company introduced networkMCI PAGING and Friends & Family Paging, which is a component of Friends & Family Connections. Friends & Family Connections is a new offering for the residential consumer which combines paging and electronic mail along with the company's voice offerings. The company is exploring other alternatives to enable it to compete successfully in the nationwide wireless markets.

As most of the aforementioned alliances and investments are in the early stages of development, the company anticipates net losses on them in 1995.

Recent Accounting Pronouncements

The American Institute of Certified Public Accountants (AICPA) has issued Statement of Position (SOP) 93-7, "Reporting on Advertising Costs." SOP 93-7 provides guidance on accounting and reporting of advertising costs. In general, SOP 93-7 requires reporting the costs of all advertising as expenses in the periods in which the costs are incurred, or the first time the advertising takes place. One exception is for direct-response advertising, the primary purpose of which is to elicit sales to customers who could be shown to have responded specifically to the advertising, and which results in probable future benefits. Such direct-response advertising costs should be recorded as assets and amortized over the estimated period of the benefits. SOP 93-7 is effective for financial

statements for years beginning after June 15, 1994. The company anticipates that SOP 93-7 will not have a material impact on the company's results of operations in 1995.

The Financial Accounting Standards Board (FASB) issued Statement of Financial Accounting Standards (SFAS) No. 119, "Disclosure About Derivative Financial Instruments and Fair Value of Financial Instruments." SFAS No. 119 requires disclosures about amounts, nature, terms of derivative financial instruments and whether financial instruments are held or issued for trading purposes. SFAS No. 119 is effective for financial statements issued for fiscal years ending after December 15, 1994. The company uses derivatives to manage interest rate risk and foreign currency rate fluctuations. It does not engage in speculation. As of December 31, 1994, the amount of derivative financial instruments held by the company was not material.

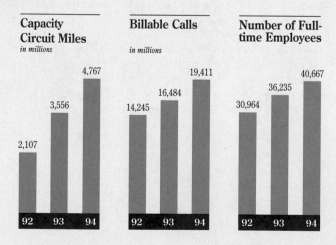

Capacity Circuit Miles
in millions

2,107 (92)   3,556 (93)   4,767 (94)

Billable Calls
in millions

14,245 (92)   16,484 (93)   19,411 (94)

Number of Full-time Employees

30,964 (92)   36,235 (93)   40,667 (94)

Income Statements

MCI Communications
Corporation and Subsidiaries

Year ended December 31,	1994	1993	1992
(In millions, except per share amounts)			
Revenue	$13,338	$11,921	$10,562
Operating expenses			
Telecommunications	6,916	6,373	5,684
Sales, operations and general	3,790	3,310	2,794
Depreciation	1,176	970	873
Total operating expenses	11,882	10,653	9,351
Income from operations	1,456	1,268	1,211
Interest expense	(153)	(178)	(218)
Interest income	50	8	3
Other expense, net	(73)	(53)	(33)
Income before income taxes and extraordinary item	1,280	1,045	963
Income tax provision	485	418	354
Income before extraordinary item	795	627	609
Extraordinary loss on early debt retirements, less applicable tax benefit of $26 million	—	45	—
Net income	$ 795	$ 582	$ 609
Dividends on preferred stock	1	1	20
Earnings applicable to common stockholders	$ 794	$ 581	$ 589
Earnings per common and common equivalent shares			
Income before extraordinary item	$ 1.32	$ 1.12	$ 1.11
Loss on early debt retirements	—	(.08)	—
Total	1.32	$ 1.04	$ 1.11
Weighted average number of common shares	$ 604	562	532

See accompanying Notes to Consolidated Financial Statements

Management's Discussion and Analysis of Results of Operations

MCI Communications
Corporation and Subsidiaries

Revenue

Business Markets

Revenue and traffic volume in the business market grew in 1994 and 1993 primarily as a result of the continued success of the company's virtual private network product (Vnet®), its Vision® and Preferred® products, particularly the 800 service components of these products, and international traffic. A portion of this growth was attributable to the FCC's 800 service number portability ruling which took effect in May 1993. Traffic and revenue growth in these periods were also enhanced by the company's introduction of its Proof Positive® service in 1993, which continued to be a success in 1994. The company's various data products also experienced revenue growth during 1994, attributable in part to the company's purchase of BTNA, and are expected to continue to grow due to the anticipated increases in demand.

Consumer Markets

Increased competitive pressure in the consumer market caused residential traffic and revenue to grow at a slower rate in 1994 than 1993. Revenue and traffic growth in both 1994 and 1993 was derived primarily from the company's Friends & Family® brand of products, 1-800-COLLECT, and the international and multilingual markets.

Although the company anticipates continued revenue growth in the consumer market, the previously mentioned decline in the rate of revenue growth could continue into 1995. In response to these competitive pressures, in January 1995, the company announced an extension to the Friends & Family brand of products, NEW Friends & Family®. NEW Friends & Family, a part of Friends & Family Connections, is a more flexible discount program designed to reestablish the company's savings position and benefit a wider range of consumers. While the company expects this product to be well-received, it is too early to evaluate its impact on the company's results of operations.

Telecommunications Expense

The principal components of telecommunications expense are the cost of access facilities provided by local exchange carriers and other domestic service providers, and payments made to foreign telephone companies (international settlements) to complete calls made from the U.S. by the company's customers. Telecommunications expense as a percentage of revenue decreased to 51.9% in 1994 from 53.5% in 1993 and 53.8% in 1992. These decreases were due to reductions in domestic access and international settlement rates, and to efficiencies resulting from operator services automation. The company expects access and international settlement charges to continue to trend downward in 1995.

Sales, Operations and General

Sales, operations and general expenses increased as a percentage of revenue to 28.4% in 1994 from 27.8% in 1993 and 26.5% in 1992. Excluding incremental expenses of $70 million for the launch of networkMCI BUSINESS in 1994 and the $150 million realignment charge in 1993, sales, operations and general expenses would have been 27.9% and 26.5% of revenue in 1994 and 1993, respectively. The 1994 increase as a percentage of revenue was primarily due to higher personnel costs, higher levels of advertising, and related sales and marketing expenses.

Depreciation

Depreciation expense was $1,176 million in 1994 and $970 million in 1993, an increase of 21% and 11%, respectively, over the prior year. These increases correspond with the company's continuing expansion of its communications network. Included in the 21% increase in 1994 was an additional $63 million depreciation charge to recognize the reduced utility of older asynchronous fiber-optic transmission equipment and to reflect the results of an asset utilization review. The company expects depreciation expense to continue to increase with the expansion of the communications system network.

Other

Interest expense decreased in 1994 and 1993 from the prior years. These decreases resulted from lower average debt balances combined with increases in capitalized interest, which is consistent with the company's increased investment in its communications system during 1994 and 1993. The decrease in 1993 interest expense compared to 1992 was also a result of interest savings from the early retirement of debt and a decline in interest rates during 1993.

Interest income increased significantly in 1994 from 1993 and 1992 due to investment of the BT proceeds. The amount of interest income to be recognized in 1995 will depend upon the timing and investment of existing cash balances currently invested in short and medium-term marketable securities.

Other expense, net increased by $20 million in 1994 primarily due to a $25 million charge in connection with the settlement of two class action suits relating to the provision of 900 services and to a $16 million loss related to the company's share of the newly formed business venture, Concert, offset by a $10 million gain on the sale of the company's equity investment in AAPT. Due to the start-up nature of Concert, losses of $10 to $15 million per quarter are expected to continue in 1995.

Balance Sheets

MCI Communications
Corporation and Subsidiaries

December 31,	1994	1993
(In millions)		
Assets		
Current assets		
Cash and cash equivalents	$ 1,429	$ 165
Marketable securities	839	—
Receivables, net of allowance for uncollectibles of $226 and $211 million	2,266	2,131
Other current assets	354	305
Total current assets	4,888	2,601
Communications system		
System in service	9,766	8,563
Other property and equipment	2,452	2,172
Total communications system in service	12,218	10,735
Accumulated depreciation	(4,349)	(4,297)
Construction in progress	1,190	883
Total communications system, net	9,059	7,321
Other assets		
Goodwill, net	1,103	1,093
Noncurrent marketable securities	824	—
Investment in affiliates	199	30
Other assets and deferred charges, net	293	231
Total other assets	2,419	1,354
Total assets	$16,366	$11,276
Liabilities and stockholders' equity		
Current liabilities		
Accrued telecommunications expense	$ 1,505	$ 1,507
Accounts payable	609	742
Other accrued liabilities	893	737
Long-term debt due within one year	130	215
Total current liabilities	3,137	3,201
Noncurrent liabilities		
Long-term debt	2,997	2,366
Deferred taxes and other	1,228	996
Total noncurrent liabilities	4,225	3,362
Stockholders' equity		
Preferred stock, $.10 par value, authorized 50 million shares and 20 million shares: Series D convertible, outstanding 0 and 13,736 shares	—	1
Class A common stock, $.10 par value, authorized 500 million and 0 shares, issued and outstanding 136 million and 0 shares	14	—
Common stock, $.10 par value, authorized 2 billion and 800 million shares, issued 592 million shares	60	60
Additional paid in capital	6,227	2,493
Retained earnings	3,548	2,785
Treasury stock at cost, 48 and 51 million shares	(845)	(626)
Total stockholders' equity	9,004	4,713
Total liabilities and stockholders' equity	$16,366	$11,276

See accompanying Notes to Consolidated Financial Statements

Management's Discussion and Analysis of Financial Condition, Liquidity and Capital Resources

MCI Communications
Corporation and Subsidiaries

The Balance Sheet shows the company's financial condition at 1994 year end compared with the previous year end. This section provides information to assist in assessing factors such as the company's liquidity and financial resources.

Working Capital

The company had positive working capital (current assets less current liabilities) of $1.8 billion as of December 31, 1994, while it had a working capital deficit of $600 million as of December 31, 1993. The significant increase is primarily attributable to the $3.5 billion received by the company in September 1994 from BT. Approximately $2.2 billion of these proceeds were invested in short-term marketable securities. The remaining funds were invested in high-grade medium-term marketable securities which primarily have maturities of less than three years, as of December 31, 1994. In addition, during 1994 the company repaid $93 million principal amount of maturing Senior Notes.

Communications System

In 1994, the company continued to increase its investment in its communications system to increase network capacity and capability and to enhance network intelligence to meet customers' increasing demands for new products and services and to improve redundancy. Synchronous Optical Network (SONET) technology, which enables the provision of high-speed multimedia applications and information services, is now being deployed throughout the company's domestic network and is expected to be operational on international routes by year end 1995. Cash outflows for the communications system and customer-specific equipment were approximately $2.9 billion and $1.7 billion in 1994 and 1993, respectively. The company's investment during 1994 was funded with cash generated from operating activities, debt issuances and the BT proceeds. Retirements were $1.1 billion and $792 million in 1994 and 1993, respectively.

Funding of Alliances, Investments and Initiatives

In 1995, the company plans to spend approximately $3 billion on capital expenditures. This includes $2.3 billion for the network, $500 million for MCImetro and $200 million for new service initiatives. In addition, the company expects to invest approximately $450 million on strategic investments. This funding will be achieved with the company's existing cash and cash equivalents, marketable securities and cash flows from operating activities. Cash and cash equivalents and marketable securities as of December 31, 1994 totaled approximately $3.1 billion. The company also has available a $2 billion bank credit facility which expires in July 1999 and is available to support the company's commercial paper program. In addition, on December 30, 1994, the company filed a $1 billion shelf registration which will enable the company to issue debt securities with a range of maturities at either fixed or variable rates. There were no amounts outstanding under such registration statement, the commercial paper program or the credit facility at December 31, 1994.

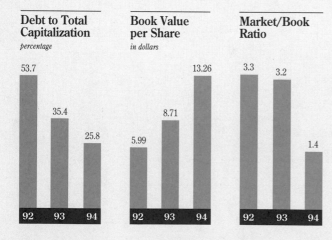

Debt to Total Capitalization
percentage

53.7 (92) 35.4 (93) 25.8 (94)

Book Value per Share
in dollars

5.99 (92) 8.71 (93) 13.26 (94)

Market/Book Ratio

3.3 (92) 3.2 (93) 1.4 (94)

Statements of Cash Flows

MCI Communications
Corporation and Subsidiaries

Year ended December 31, *(In millions)*	1994	1993	1992
Operating activities			
Receipts from customers	$13,298	$11,546	$10,328
Payments to suppliers and employees	(10,472)	(9,106)	(8,156)
Taxes paid	(393)	(321)	(292)
Interest paid	(100)	(150)	(156)
Interest received	22	9	2
Cash from operating activities	2,355	1,978	1,726
Investing activities			
Cash outflow for communications system	(2,790)	(1,635)	(1,251)
Cash outflow for customer-specific equipment	(107)	(98)	(21)
Purchases of marketable securities	(4,096)	—	—
Proceeds from sales of marketable securities	2,424	3	7
Investment in affiliates	(284)	(8)	22
Other, net	(64)	(21)	(18)
Cash used for investing activities	(4,917)	(1,759)	(1,261)
Net cash flow before financing activities	(2,562)	219	465
Financing activities			
Issuance of Senior Notes and other debt	939	756	481
Retirement of Senior Notes and other debt	(246)	(1,468)	(218)
Commercial paper and bank credit facility activity, net	(239)	(497)	(69)
Issuance of preferred stock	—	830	—
Redemption of preferred stock	—	—	(400)
Issuance of Class A common stock	3,510	—	—
Issuance of common stock for employee plans	248	319	168
Payment of dividends on common and preferred stock	(32)	(28)	(56)
Purchase of treasury stock	(354)	(198)	(180)
Cash from (used for) financing activities	3,826	(286)	(274)
Net increase (decrease) in cash and cash equivalents	1,264	(67)	191
Cash and cash equivalents at beginning of year	165	232	41
Cash and cash equivalents at end of year	$ 1,429	$ 165	$ 232
Reconciliation of net income to cash from operating activities:			
Net income	$ 795	$ 582	$ 609
Adjustments to earnings:			
Depreciation and amortization	1,230	1,019	955
Deferred income tax provision	269	253	213
Net change in operating activity accounts:			
Receivables	(135)	(370)	(155)
Payables	36	(68)	(120)
Other operating activity accounts	160	562	224
Cash from operating activities.	$ 2,355	$ 1,978	$ 1,726

See accompanying Notes to Consolidated Financial Statements

Management's Discussion and Analysis of Cash Flows

MCI Communications
Corporation and Subsidiaries

Changes in cash and cash equivalents result from changes in cash flows from operating, financing and investing activities which are explained below. Earnings before interest, taxes, depreciation and amortization (EBITDA) is another measure of the company's ability to generate cash flows.

EBITDA

EBITDA, excluding unusual items, increased 13% to $2,702 million in 1994 from $2,388 million in 1993. Many investment professionals consider EBITDA, also known as operating cash flow, to be a useful indicator of the company's ability to generate cash flow. EBITDA should be considered in addition to, but not as a substitute for, or superior to, operating income, net income, cash flow, and other measures of financial performance reported in accordance with generally accepted accounting principles.

Cash From Operating Activities

Cash from operating activities increased 19% and 15% in 1994 and 1993, respectively, paralleling the growth in the company's income from operations in such periods. In general, cash from operating activities has been the company's primary source of cash to finance capital expenditures and other investments. In 1994, financing activities were also a significant source of cash as a result of the BT transaction and debt issuances.

Cash Used for Investing Activities

Cash used for investing activities grew in 1994 and 1993, mainly because of increases in year-over-year expenditures for the company's communications system of $1,155 million and $384 million in 1994 and 1993, respectively. The continued investment in the company's transmission network, switching facilities and SONET technology was required to meet customers' demands for new services, redundancy and enhanced network intelligence. Additionally, during 1994, the company invested most of the BT proceeds in short and medium-term marketable securities, purchased substantially all the operations of BTNA for $108 million, made an investment in Concert of $79 million and completed several other strategic investments totaling $97 million.

Cash From Financing Activities

Cash from financing activities increased significantly in 1994 as a result of the issuance of 108.5 million shares of Class A common stock to BT for a cash payment of $3.5 billion on September 30, 1994. As a result of this equity infusion from BT, the company's ratio of debt to total capitalization, defined as total debt to total debt plus equity, has declined to 26% at December 31, 1994 from 35% at December 31, 1993. In March 1994, the company issued an aggregate principal amount of $950 million of Senior Notes and Debentures and from these issuances repaid commercial paper borrowings with a substantial portion of the proceeds. The remaining proceeds were used for general corporate purposes. During 1994, the company also repaid $93 million of maturing Senior Notes.

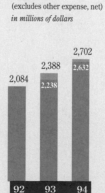

Statements of Stockholders' Equity

MCI Communications
Corporation and Subsidiaries

	Preferred Stock	Class A Common Stock	Common Stock	Additional Paid in Capital	Retained Earnings	Treasury Stock, at Cost	Stock-holders' Equity
(In *millions*)							
Balance at December 31, 1991	$1	—	$ 30	$1,788	$1,669	$(529)	$2,959
Preferred stock redeemed	(1)	—	—	(399)	—	—	(400)
Common stock issued for employee stock and benefit plans (10 million shares). . . .	—	—	—	72	—	129	201
Tax benefit of common stock transactions related to employee benefit plans	—	—	—	18	—	—	18
Net income.	—	—	—	—	609	—	609
Common and preferred dividends	—	—	—	—	(47)	—	(47)
Treasury stock purchased (6 million shares)	—	—	—	—	—	(190)	(190)
Balance at December 31, 1992	—	—	30	1,479	2,231	(590)	3,150
Common stock issued for employee stock and benefit plans (23 million shares). . . .	—	—	—	179	—	160	339
Tax benefit of common stock transactions . . . . . . related to employee benefit plans	—	—	—	36	—	—	36
Net income.	—	—	—	—	582	—	582
Common and preferred dividends.	—	—	—	—	(28)	—	(28)
Convertible preferred stock issued	1	—	—	829	—	—	830
Stock split effected in the form of a 100% stock dividend	—	—	30	(30)	—	—	—
Treasury stock purchased (8 million shares)	—	—	—	—	—	(196)	(196)
Balance at December 31, 1993	1	—	60	2,493	2,785	(626)	4,713
Class A common stock issued (136 million shares) and preferred stock converted	(1)	$14	—	3,496	—	—	3,509
Common stock issued for employee stock and benefit plans (18 million shares). . . .	—	—	—	180	—	124	304
Tax benefit of common stock transactions related to employee benefit plans	—	—	—	63	—	—	63
Unrealized loss on marketable securities	—	—	—	(5)	—	—	(5)
Net income.	—	—	—	—	795	—	795
Common and preferred dividends.	—	—	—	—	(32)	—	(32)
Treasury stock purchased (15 million shares)	—	—	—	—	—	(343)	(343)
Balance at December 31, 1994.	$—	$14	$60	$6,227	$3,548	$(845)	$9,004

See accompanying Notes to Consolidated Financial Statements

Notes to Consolidated Financial Statements

Note 1. Significant Accounting Policies

Principles of Consolidation

The financial statements include the consolidated accounts of MCI Communications Corporation and its majority-owned subsidiaries (collectively, the company) with all significant intercompany transactions eliminated. The company uses the equity method to account for entities in which it has less than a majority interest but can exercise significant influence. Other investments are recorded at cost.

Revenue

The company records as revenue the amount of communications services rendered, as measured primarily by the minutes of traffic processed, after deducting an estimate of the traffic which will be neither billed nor collected.

Communications System

The investment in communications system is recorded at cost and includes material, interest, labor and overhead. The costs of construction and equipment are transferred to communications system in service as construction projects are completed and/or equipment is placed in service. Depreciation is recorded commencing with the first full month that the assets are in service and is provided using the straight-line method over their estimated useful lives. Most of the company's communications system assets are grouped in like pools for depreciation purposes. For these asset groups, the cost of equipment retired in the ordinary course of business, less proceeds, is charged to accumulated depreciation. The company periodically reviews and adjusts the useful lives assigned to fixed assets to ensure that depreciation charges provide appropriate recovery of capital costs over the estimated physical and technological lives of the assets. The weighted average depreciable life of the assets comprising the communications system in service approximates 10 years. Other property and equipment includes buildings and administrative assets that are depreciated using lives of up to 35 years. Maintenance and repairs are charged to expense as incurred.

Goodwill

Goodwill represents the excess of the cost to acquire subsidiaries over the estimated fair market value of the net assets acquired. These amounts are amortized using the straight-line method over lives ranging from 10 to 40 years. Accumulated amortization at December 31, 1994 and 1993 was $131 million and $101 million, respectively.

Other Assets and Deferred Charges

Included in other assets and deferred charges are rights-of-way agreements with third parties, debt issuance costs and unamortized customer discounts and service incentives. Rights-of-way costs are amortized as the assets are placed in service, over the lesser of the remaining term of the agreements or 25 years. Debt issuance costs are amortized over the life of the applicable debt. Deferred customer discounts and service incentives are amortized over the life of the specific contract to which they relate.

Capital Leases

Certain of the company's lease obligations meet the criteria of a capital lease. These obligations are recorded for financial reporting purposes at the present value of the future lease payments, including estimated bargain purchase options, discounted at the approximate interest rate implicit in each lease. Corresponding amounts are capitalized and depreciated over the estimated useful lives of the equipment, which are generally longer than the terms of the leases.

Income Taxes

The company files a consolidated federal income tax return on a March 31 fiscal year end. Deferred income taxes are provided on transactions which are reported in the financial statements in different periods than for income tax purposes. Effective January 1, 1993, the company adopted Statement of Financial Accounting Standards No. 109 (SFAS 109), Accounting for Income Taxes. The adoption of SFAS 109 had no impact on the company's results of operations for the year ended December 31, 1993. Income tax benefits of tax deductions related to common stock transactions with the company's employee benefit plans are recorded directly to additional paid in capital.

Earnings Per Common and Common Equivalent Share

Earnings per common and common equivalent share amounts are based on the weighted average number of shares of common stock outstanding during each year adjusted for the effect of common stock equivalents arising from the assumed exercise of stock options, if dilutive, and the assumed conversion of the Series D convertible preferred stock in 1993 and the subordinated convertible debt in 1992. Fully diluted earnings per share are not materially different from primary earnings per share.

Cash and Cash Equivalents

Cash equivalents consist primarily of certificates of deposit, securities of the U.S. Government and its agencies and corporate debt securities all having maturities of ninety days or less when purchased. The carrying amount reported in the accompanying balance sheet for cash equivalents approximates fair value due to the short-term maturity of these instruments.

At December 31, 1994 and 1993, checks not yet presented for payment of $192 million and $193 million in excess of cash balances, respectively, were included in current liabilities. The company had sufficient funds available to cover these outstanding checks when they were presented for payment.

Marketable Securities

The company adopted Statement of Financial Accounting Standards No. 115 (SFAS 115), Accounting for Certain Investments in Debt and Equity Securities, on January 1, 1994. SFAS 115 established new accounting and reporting requirements for certain debt and equity securities. Since the company does not intend to hold its securities for trading purposes or until maturity, SFAS 115 requires the company to classify and record its securities as available-for-sale. In accordance with the provisions of SFAS 115, investments classified as available-for-sale are recorded at fair value and any holding gains and losses are excluded from earnings and reported as a net amount in additional paid in capital until realized. The fair values are based on quoted market prices. Realized gains and losses are recorded in the income statement and the cost assigned to securities sold is based on the specific identification method.

Foreign Exchange Contracts and Interest Rate Swaps

The company enters into foreign exchange contracts and interest rate swap agreements to hedge its foreign currency risks and reduce its interest rate exposure (see Note 5). While the company does not engage in speculation, it is exposed to credit loss in the event of nonperformance by the other parties to the agreements. The company manages this credit risk by regularly monitoring and evaluating the counterparties. As of December 31, 1994, the fair values of and potential risk of loss on these agreements were not material.

Reclassification

Certain prior year information has been reclassified to conform to the current year presentation.

Note 2. British Telecommunications Investment

On September 30, 1994, British Telecommunications plc (BT) completed the purchase of 136 million shares of the company's recently authorized Class A common stock for $4.3 billion in cash, resulting in its ownership of a 20% voting interest in the company. This purchase was achieved by the company's issuance of 108.5 million shares of Class A common stock to BT for $3.5 billion in cash on September 30, 1994 and BT's conversion of 13,736 shares of Series D convertible preferred stock, purchased for $830 million in June 1993, into 27.5 million shares of Class A common stock (see Note 7 for further discussion).

In conjunction with the above investment, the company purchased for approximately $79 million, a 24.9% equity interest in Concert Communications Company (Concert), a business venture launched by BT in July 1994 which provides global telecommunications services for business customers. The company intends to continue making contributions to Concert in order to maintain its proportionate interest. In addition, the company purchased from BT substantially all of the operations of BT North America Inc. (BTNA) in January 1994 for $108 million and divested its interest in AAP Telecommunications Pty. Ltd. (Australia) in October 1994.

The company and BT lease each others' access lines at prevailing market rates in the ordinary course of business to process traffic in the United States and the United Kingdom. The company also conducts business with Concert through the provision and receipt of communications services at prevailing market rates. During 1994 and 1993, the amounts associated with those transactions were immaterial to the company.

Note 3. Marketable Securities

As discussed in Note 1, effective January 1, 1994, the company adopted SFAS 115 which requires accounting for debt and equity securities based upon the company's intent to hold or sell the securities. As of December 31, 1994, all of the company's marketable securities were classified as available-for-sale and consisted of the following

(In millions)	Amortized Cost	Gross Unrealized Gains	Gross Unrealized Losses	Fair Value
Marketable securities included in cash equivalents:				
Certificates of deposit....	$ 602	–	–	$ 602
U.S. Government agency securities	265	–	–	265
Corporate debt securities ..	449	–	–	449
	1,316	–	–	1,316
Marketable securities maturing within one year:				
Certificates of deposit....	146	–	–	146
U.S. Government agency securities	444	–	$(2)	442
Corporate debt securities ..	252	–	(1)	251
	842	–	(3)	839
Marketable securities maturing between one year and five years:				
U.S. Government agency securities	166	–	(1)	165
Corporate debt securities ..	358	–	(1)	357
U.S. Treasury securities...	230	–	(3)	227
Asset-backed securities ...	76	–	(1)	75
	830	–	(6)	824
Total marketable securities ..	$2,988	–	$(9)	$2,979

At December 31, 1994, an unrealized loss of $9 million, net of estimated tax benefit, reduced additional paid in capital by $5 million. Sales of available-for-sale marketable securities during 1994 resulted in a net realized loss of $3 million included in interest income.

Note 4. Supplementary Balance Sheet Information

December 31,	1994	1993
(In millions)		
Other current assets:		
Deferred income taxes	$ 115	$116
Other receivables. net	110	119
Other	129	70
Total other current assets	$ 354	$305
Other accrued liabilities:		
Taxes. other than income	$ 263	$183
Payroll and employee benefits	156	182
Other	474	372
Total other accrued liabilities	$ 893	$737
Deferred taxes and other:		
Deferred taxes.......................	$1,192	$927
Other	36	69
Total deferred taxes and other..............	$1,228	$996

Note 5. Debt

Company debt consists of:

December 31,	1994	1993
(In millions)		
Senior Notes, with maturities ranging from August 1995 to August 2004, at a weighted average interest rate of 6.9%, net of unamortized discount of $1 million......	$1,501	$1,095
Senior Debentures, with maturities ranging from January 2023 to March 2025, at a weighted average interest rate of 7.9%, net of unamortized discount of $6 million	884	437
Capital lease obligations at a weighted average interest rate of 8.7%	596	689
Commercial paper and bank credit facility borrowings	–	239
Other debt at a weighted average interest rate of 5.4%	146	121
Total debt	3,127	2,581
Debt due within one year	(130)	(215)
Total long-term debt	$2,997	$2,366

Annual maturities of long-term debt for the five years after December 31, 1994 are as follows: $130 million in 1995; $424 million in 1996; $122 million in 1997; $89 million in 1998 and $558 million in 1999.

Total interest costs were $231 million in 1994, $239 million in 1993 and $270 million in 1992, of which $78 million, $61 million and $52 million, respectively, were capitalized.

At December 31, 1994 and 1993, the estimated fair value of the company's long-term debt, excluding capital lease obligations, is listed below. This valuation represents either quoted market values, where available, or the company's estimate based upon market prices of comparable debt instruments.

December 31,	1994		1993	
	Carrying Amount	Estimated Fair Value	Carrying Amount	Estimated Fair Value
(In millions)				
Senior Notes	$1,501	$1,438	$1,095	$1,159
Senior Debentures	884	793	437	462
Commercial paper and bank credit facility borrowings	—	—	239	239
Other debt	146	146	121	121
Total long-term debt, excluding capital leases . .	$2,531	$2,377	$1,892	$1,981

The favorable change in the fair value of debt reflects that a majority of the company's debt was at fixed rates that were below the prevailing market rates as of December 31, 1994.

Senior Notes and Debentures

In March 1994, the company issued $450 million principal amount of 7 3/4% Senior Debentures due March 23, 2025, $300 million principal amount of 6 1/4% Senior Notes due March 23, 1999 and $200 million principal amount of Senior Floating Rate Notes due March 16, 1999 (Senior Floating Rate Notes). In conjunction with the issuance of the Senior Floating Rate Notes, the company entered into an interest rate swap agreement for a notional principal amount of $200 million which resulted in an effective fixed interest cost of 6.37%. A substantial portion of the net proceeds from these issuances was used to repay commercial paper borrowings while the remaining proceeds were used for general corporate purposes. During 1994, the company also repaid $93 million of maturing Senior Notes, leaving $2,385 million of debt securities outstanding at a weighted average annual interest rate of 7.25% as of December 31, 1994.

On December 30, 1994, the company filed a $1 billion shelf registration which will enable the company to issue debt securities with a range of maturities at either fixed or variable rates. The company had no amounts outstanding under the shelf registration as of December 31, 1994.

Commercial Paper and Bank Credit Facility Borrowings

On July 8, 1994, the company executed a $2 billion bank credit facility agreement (Credit Facility) which replaced its previous $1.25 billion bank credit facility. The Credit Facility expires in July 1999. This Credit Facility supports the company's commercial paper program and, in conjunction with this program, will be used to fund fluctuations in working capital and other general corporate requirements.

During 1994, the company issued commercial paper and borrowed under the credit facilities an aggregate of $6,637 million and repaid an aggregate of $6,876 million of credit facility and commercial paper borrowings, leaving no amounts outstanding under the Credit Facility and commercial paper program at December 31, 1994. Borrowings under the commercial paper program and Credit Facility are classified as noncurrent if the remaining term of the Credit Facility agreement exceeds one year and the unused commitment thereunder equals or exceeds the amount of commercial paper then outstanding.

Retirements and Redemptions

In 1993, the company redeemed all $616 million, net of the unamortized discount, of its Zero-Coupon Subordinated Convertible Notes due December 11, 2004. The funds for this redemption came from the issuance of Senior Notes, Senior Debentures, commercial paper and credit facility borrowings. Also in 1993, the company redeemed all $575 million principal amount of its 10% Subordinated Debentures due April 1, 2011. These redemptions were funded from segregated cash generated by the company's operations and earnings, as well as a portion of the proceeds from the sale of preferred stock to BT (see Note 2). An extraordinary loss of $45 million, net of current income tax benefit of $26 million, was recorded for the 1993 redemptions.

Note 6. Lease Transactions

The gross and net book values of communications system financed by capital leases was $604 million and $271 million, respectively, as of December 31, 1994 and $799 million and $359 million, respectively, as of December 31, 1993. Leases not capitalized are primarily for land on which communications equipment is located and for administrative facilities, including office buildings, vehicles, certain data processing equipment and office equipment. Total rental expense for all operating leases was $262 million, $227 million and $229 million for the years ended December 31, 1994, 1993 and 1992, respectively.

Future minimum rental commitments for capital leases are as follows: $120 million in 1995; $112 million in 1996; $105 million in 1997; $52 million in 1998; $48 million in 1999 and $636 million thereafter. At December 31, 1994, aggregate future minimum capital lease payments were $1,073 million including interest of $477 million. The present value of future capital lease payments at December 31, 1994 was $596 million.

Future minimum rental commitments for noncancellable operating leases are as follows: $174 million in 1995; $146 million in 1996; $110 million in 1997; $85 million in 1998; $69 million in 1999 and $203 million thereafter. At December 31, 1994, aggregate future minimum payments for noncancellable operating leases were $787 million.

Note 7. Stockholders' Equity

On September 30, 1994, the company amended its certificate of incorporation to increase the number of authorized shares of preferred stock from 20 million to 50 million and of common stock from 800 million to 2 billion and authorized 500 million shares of Class A common stock. These changes, which became effective September 30, 1994, had been previously approved by the company's stockholders at a special meeting held on March 11, 1994.

Preferred Stock Rights Plan

On September 7, 1994, the company's board of directors adopted a stockholders' rights plan (Rights Plan), effective September 30, 1994, and declared a dividend, payable to the holders of record on October 11, 1994, of one preferred share purchase right (Right) for each outstanding share of common stock and Class A common stock (collectively, Common Shares) to the stockholders of record on that date. The Rights will also be attached to certain future issuances of Common Shares. Each Right entitles the registered holder to purchase from the company one one-hundredth of a share of the company's Series E Junior Participating Preferred Stock, par value $.10 per share, (Series E Preferred Stock) for an initial purchase price of $100, subject to adjustment.

The Rights will become exercisable upon the occurrence of certain specified events, including a public announcement that a person or group of affiliated or associated persons (Acquiring Person) have acquired beneficial ownership of 10% or more of the outstanding Common Shares (more than 20.1% in the case of share acquisitions by BT). In the event that any person or group of affiliated or associated persons becomes an Acquiring Person, each holder of a Right (other than Rights beneficially owned by the Acquiring Person, which will become void), will thereafter have the right, subject to certain restrictions, to receive upon exercise in lieu of Series E Preferred Stock that number of shares of the company's common stock (or, at the option of the company, that number of one one-hundredth of Series E Preferred Stock) determined as set forth in the Rights Plan.

For purposes of the Rights Plan, the company's board of directors has designated 10 million shares of Series E Preferred Stock which amount may be increased or decreased by the board of directors. All Rights expire on September 30, 2004, unless this date is extended or the Rights are earlier redeemed or exchanged by the company in accordance with the Rights Plan.

Series D Convertible Preferred Stock

In June 1993, the company issued 13,736 shares of preferred stock, designated as Series D convertible preferred stock (Series D), to BT for $830 million. On September 30, 1994, all of the Series D was converted into 27.5 million shares of Class A common stock. The company paid dividends of $50 and $100 per share on the Series D in 1994 and 1993, respectively.

Class A Common Stock

On September 30, 1994, BT completed the purchase of 136 million shares of the company's recently authorized Class A common stock for $4.3 billion, resulting in a 20% voting interest in the company. This purchase was achieved by the company's issuance of 108.5 million shares of Class A common stock to BT for a cash payment of $3.5 billion on September 30, 1994, and BT's conversion of 13,736 shares of Series D purchased for $830 million in June 1993, into 27.5 million shares of Class A common stock.

As of December 31, 1994, all of the Class A common stock was held by BT. The Class A common stock is equivalent on a per share basis to the existing common stock, except with respect to certain voting rights. BT is entitled to proportionate representation on the company's board of directors, which currently equates to three seats. In addition to board representation, BT is entitled to preemptive rights with respect to the issuance of additional shares of common stock and to investor protections with respect to certain corporate actions of the company. Shares of Class A common stock automatically convert into common stock upon transfer and in certain other events.

Due to the timing of the issuance of the Class A common stock, the company paid one of its semiannual dividends of $.025 per share on its Class A common stock in 1994.

Common Stock

On May 24, 1993, the company's board of directors declared a two-for-one stock split in the form of a 100% stock dividend, which was issued on July 9, 1993 to stockholders of record as of the close of business on June 11, 1993. The following have been adjusted for the effect of the common stock dividend: all per share amounts, 1994 and 1993 treasury stock transactions, the December 31, 1994 and 1993 treasury stock share balances and data as to common stock options and the employee stock purchase plan.

In 1994, 1993 and 1992, the company paid semiannual dividends in the aggregate of $.05 per share on its common stock.

Note 8. Stock Option and Employee Stock Purchase Plans

Employee and Directors' Stock Option Plans

The current Employee Stock Option Plan (the Plan) provides for the issuance of up to 102 million shares of common stock. On an annual basis, pursuant to the Plan, the board of directors may increase the maximum number of shares available for issuance under the Plan as of each January 1, by up to 5% of the number of shares of common stock outstanding at each such date. Options granted under the Plan are exercisable at such times and in such installments as determined by the compensation committee of the board of directors. Options granted under the Plan may not have an option price less than the fair market value of the common stock on the date of the grant.

Stock appreciation rights may be granted in combination with a stock option either at the time of the grant or anytime thereafter. No stock appreciation rights had been granted as of December 31, 1994.

The compensation committee may also grant restricted stock awards and performance share awards, subject to such conditions, restrictions and requirements as the committee may determine in its sole discretion. During the year ended December 31, 1994, there were 330,000 restricted shares granted. As of December 31, 1994, there were approximately 1,062,000 restricted shares outstanding. No performance share awards had been issued as of December 31, 1994.

The compensation committee may grant both incentive stock options and non-qualified options under the Plan. All options granted in the last three years have been non-qualified options. These non-qualified options expire after ten years and are exercisable to the extent of 33% of the option shares after one year, 66% after two years and 100% after three years. Incentive stock options expire between five and ten years after issuance and are exercisable to the extent of 33% of the option shares after one year, 66% after two years and 100% after three years.

The Plan permits the holder of an option to pay the purchase price for stock option exercises by surrendering shares of the company's common stock having a fair market value equal to, or greater than, the purchase price.

The company also has a stock option plan for non-employee directors (the Directors' Plan) which provides for the issuance of up to 1,000,000 shares of common stock. Under the Directors' Plan, each non-employee director has been granted a five-year option to purchase up to 40,000 shares of common stock at the closing price of the common stock on the date of grant. The options are exercisable after the first anniversary of the date of grant, in cumulative installments of 25% per year. Similar options will be granted automatically to all new board members who are not employees, including the nominee directors from BT. Upon the fifth anniversary of the date of grant of options, the unexercised portion of the grant shall be canceled and a new option for 40,000 shares shall be granted automatically.

Additional information with respect to stock options under these plans is:

	Number of Shares	Option Amount Per Common Share	Total
(In millions, except per common share amounts)			
Shares under option,			
December 31, 1991	44.8	$2.69-22.44	$ 546.3
Options granted	17.0	15.82-17.38	269.7
Options exercised	(9.0)	2.69-19.57	(85.2)
Options terminated	(2.8)	2.69-22.44	(39.9)
Shares under option,			
December 31, 1992	50.0	3.25-22.44	690.9
Options granted	18.6	20.56-28.75	394.5
Options exercised	(15.0)	3.25-22.44	(202.4)
Options terminated	(2.3)	9.38-28.75	(40.6)
Shares under option,			
December 31, 1993	51.3	3.44-28.75	842.4
Options granted	22.3	18.88-26.88	587.1
Options exercised	(8.1)	3.44-22.44	(110.2)
Options terminated	(3.2)	3.81-28.75	(74.9)
Shares under option,			
December 31, 1994	62.3	$3.44-28.75	$1,244.4
Options exercisable,			
December 31, 1994	26.6	$3.44-28.75	$ 406.8
Shares available for future grant, December 31, 1994	19.3		

Employee Stock Purchase Plan

Under the company's Employee Stock Purchase Plan (the ESPP Plan), 45 million shares of common stock are available for purchase by eligible employees of the company through payroll deductions of up to 15% of their eligible compensation. The purchase price is equal to the lesser of (a) 85% of the fair market value of the stock on the date it is purchased or (b) 85% of the fair market value of the stock on certain specified valuation dates.

Common Stock Reserved for Future Issuance

At December 31, 1994, 100.9 million shares of the company's authorized common stock were reserved for future issuance under the Employee and Directors' Stock Option Plans and the ESPP Plan. The company has opted to use treasury shares to fulfill the purchases made under these plans during the three-year period ended December 31, 1994.

Note 9. Employee Benefit Plans

Pension Plans

The company maintains a noncontributory defined benefit pension plan (MCI Plan) and a supplemental pension plan (Supplemental Plan). Western Union International, Inc. (WUI), a subsidiary of the company, also has a defined benefit pension plan (WUI Plan). Collectively, these plans cover substantially all full-time employees.

The MCI Plan and the Supplemental Plan provide pension benefits that are based on the employee's compensation for each year of service prior to retirement. The WUI Plan provides pension benefits based on the employee's compensation for each year of service after 1990 and prior to retirement.

The company's policy is to fund the MCI Plan and the WUI Plan in accordance with the funding requirements of the Employee Retirement Income Security Act of 1974 and within the limits of allowable tax deductions. The assets of the plans are primarily invested in corporate equities, government securities and corporate debt securities.

Net periodic pension cost includes:

Year ended December 31,	1994	1993	1992
(In millions)			
Service cost during the period	$37	$18	$15
Interest cost on projected benefit obligation	21	14	12
Actual return on plan assets	3	(21)	(11)
Net amortization and deferral	(20)	7	(2)
Net pension cost	$41	$18	$14

Pension cost increased in 1994 primarily due to a plan amendment which increased MCI Plan benefits effective January 1, 1994.

The company's pension asset (obligation) consists of:

December 31,	1994	1993
(In millions)		
Plan assets at fair value	$254	$188
Accumulated benefit obligation including vested benefits of $173 in 1994 and $168 in 1993	(194)	(186)
Plan assets in excess of accumulated benefit obligation	60	2
Plan assets at fair value	254	188
Projected benefit obligation for service rendered to date	(271)	(224)
Projected benefit obligation in excess of plan assets	(17)	(36)
Unrecognized net (gain) loss from past experience different from that assumed	(16)	5
Prior service cost not yet recognized in net periodic pension cost	64	18
Unrecognized net asset at January 1, 1986 being recognized over 16 years	(5)	(6)
Total pension asset (obligation)	$ 26	$ (19)

The discount rate and rate of increase in future compensation levels used in determining the actuarial present value of the projected benefit obligation at December 31, 1994 were 8.75% and 5%, respectively, for both the MCI and WUI plans. At December 31, 1993, the discount rate used was 7.75% for the MCI Plan and 7.25% for the WUI Plan and the rate of increase in future compensation levels was 5% for both plans. The expected long-term rate of return on assets in both 1994 and 1993 was 9% for the MCI Plan and 8.5% for the WUI Plan.

Annual service cost is determined using the Projected Unit Credit actuarial method and prior service cost is amortized on a straight-line basis over the average remaining service period of employees.

Employee Stock Ownership Plan and 401 (k) Plans
The company has combined employee stock ownership (ESOP) and 401(k) retirement savings plans (RSP) covering substantially all of its employees. The savings plans allow employees to defer pre-tax income in accordance with the requirements of Internal Revenue Code Section 401(k). The company matches employee contributions up to a certain limit. Participants vest in the company's matching contributions at a rate of 20% per year of service and are immediately 100% vested in their elective deferrals.

During 1994, the company made a one time supplemental contribution of 874,317 shares of common stock to the 401(k) sections of its plans in place of a contribution to the ESOP for the plan year ended December 31, 1993. At this time, future contributions to the ESOP have been suspended. The company contributed 1,015,414 shares of its common stock to the ESOP for the plan year ended December 31, 1992. Effective January 1, 1994 the company increased the matching contribution on 401(k) contributions to encourage employee savings. The company contributed 1,454,600 shares, 791,447 shares and 904,796 shares of its common stock as the company's matching contribution to the RSP for the plan years ended December 31, 1994, 1993 and 1992, respectively.

WUI sponsors a 401(k) savings plan for its collectively bargained employees (WUI 401(k)). The savings plan is intended to meet requirements of Internal Revenue Code Section 401(k). WUI 401(k) participants vest in the company's matching contributions at a rate of 20% per year of service and are immediately 100% vested in their elective deferrals. The company contributed 21,870 shares, 18,974 shares and 27,486 shares of its common stock to the WUI 401(k) for the plan years ended December 31, 1994, 1993 and 1992, respectively.

Postemployment Benefits
Effective January 1, 1994, the company adopted statement of Financial Accounting Standards No. 112 (SFAS 112), Employers' Accounting for Postemployment Benefits. SFAS 112 requires that if defined conditions are met, postemployment benefits be estimated and accrued rather than recognized as an expense when paid. Adoption of this new standard did not have a material impact on the company's financial position or results of operations as of and for the year ended December 31, 1994.

Note 10. Income Taxes

The components of the total income tax provision are:

Year ended December 31, (In millions)	1994	1993	1992
Current			
Federal	$190	$148	$121
State and local	26	17	20
Current income tax provision	216	165	141
Deferred			
Federal	243	227	193
State and local	26	26	20
Deferred income tax provision	269	253	213
Total income tax provision	$485	$418	$354

A reconciliation of the statutory federal income tax rate to the company's effective income tax rate is:

Year ended December 31,	1994	1993	1992
Statutory federal income tax rate	35%	35%	34%
State and local income taxes, net of federal income tax effect	3	3	3
Nondeductible amortization	1	1	1
Changes in federal tax laws	—	1	—
Other	(1)	—	(1)
Effective income tax rate	38%	40%	37%

In 1994, 1993 and 1992 the company recorded a tax benefit of $63 million, $36 million and $18 million, respectively, to additional paid in capital for tax deductions related to common stock transactions with its employee benefit plans.

At December 31, 1994, 1993 and 1992, the company's net deferred income tax liability is comprised of the following:

(In millions)	1994	1993	1992
Deferred income tax asset	$ 321	$ 338	$ 292
Deferred income tax liability	(1,398)	(1,149)	(850)
Net deferred income tax liability	$(1,077)	$ (811)	$(558)
The components of these amounts are:			
Communications system	$(1,312)	$(1,097)	$(831)
Allowance for uncollectibles	46	20	50
Realignment expenses	4	56	—
License fees	10	29	35
Customer discounts	(61)	(43)	(5)
Alternative minimum and general business tax credits	102	116	83
Other, net	134	108	110
Net deferred income tax liability	$(1,077)	$ (811)	$(558)

The company has not recorded any valuation allowances against its deferred income tax assets, either upon adoption of SFAS 109 or during the years ended December 31, 1994 and 1993.

At December 31, 1994, for federal income tax purposes, the company has available $22 million of general business tax credit carryforwards expiring after the year 2000 and $196 million of Alternative Minimum Tax (AMT) credit carryforwards which have no expiration date. In addition, the company has available $60 million of acquired net operating loss carryforwards and $62 million of acquired AMT net operating loss carryforwards expiring through 2006.

Note 11. Contingencies

The company, in the normal course of business, is a party to a number of lawsuits and regulatory and other proceedings. The company's management does not expect that the results in these lawsuits and proceedings will have a material adverse effect on the consolidated financial position or results of operations of the company.

In December 1992, the company petitioned the United States District Court for the District of Columbia for a declaratory ruling that certain patents being asserted by AT&T Corp. (AT&T) were invalid and that AT&T should be otherwise barred from enforcing them against the company. AT&T counterclaimed that the company was violating certain additional patents. In May 1993, AT&T and Unitel Communications Inc., a Canadian corporation in which AT&T has an equity interest, filed a companion suit in Canada, alleging that the company and the Stentor Group of Canadian telephone companies (with which the company has an alliance) are infringing in Canada four of the patents at issue in the U.S. litigation. Although these actions are still in their early stages, the company does not expect that either of these matters will have a material adverse effect on the consolidated financial position or results of operations of the company.

Note 12. Selected Quarterly Information (Unaudited)

Three months ended	Dec. 31, 1994	Sept. 30, 1994	June 30, 1994	Mar. 31, 1994
(In millions, except per share amounts)				
Revenue	$3,401	$3,407	$3,309	$3,221
Operating expenses:				
Telecommunications	1,764	1,765	1,715	1,672
Sales, operations, and general	999	952	933	906
Depreciation	358	282	272	264
Income from operations	280	408	389	379
Net income	151	220	215	209
Earnings applicable to common stockholders	151	220	214	209
Earnings per common and common equivalent shares	.22	.38	.37	.36
Weighted average number of shares of common stock and common stock equivalents outstanding	685	579	575	580

Three months ended	Dec. 31, 1993	Sept. 30, 1993	June 30, 1993	Mar. 31, 1993
(In millions, except per shure amounts)				
Revenue	$3,128	$3,054	$2,929	$2,810
Operating expenses:				
Telecommunications	1,659	1,636	1,573	1,505
Sales, operations, and general	992	814	772	732
Depreciation	256	245	236	233
Income from operations	221	359	348	340
Income before extraordinary item	107	174	178	168
Net income	107	174	150	151
Earnings applicable to common stockholders	107	174	149	151
Earnings per common and common equivalent shares:				
Income before extraordinary item	.18	.30	.32	.31
Loss on early debt retirements	—	—	(.05)	(.03)
Total	.18	.30	.27	.28
Weighted average number of shares of common stock and common stock equivalents outstanding	581	580	554	538

The three months ended December 31, 1994 includes incremental expenses of $70 million associated with the launch of networkMCI BUSINESS, an additional $63 million depreciation charge, a $25 million charge for the settlement of two class action suits relating to the provision of 900 services and a $10 million gain on the sale of AAP Telecommunications Pty. Ltd.

The three months ended December 31, 1993 includes a $150 million charge primarily associated with the company's strategic realignment, streamlining of engineering and network operations facilities and relocation of certain operations to lower cost areas.

Since there are changes in the weighted average number of shares outstanding each quarter, the sum of earnings per share by quarter does not equal the earnings per share for the year.

Reports of Management and Independent Accountants

Report of Management

The management of the company is responsible for the financial information and representations contained in the financial statements, notes and all other sections of the annual report. The financial statements have been prepared in conformity with generally accepted accounting principles appropriate under the circumstances to reflect, in all material respects, the substance of events and transactions which have occurred. In preparing the financial statements, it is necessary that management make informed estimates and judgments based on currently available information in order to record the results of certain events and transactions.

The company maintains a system of internal controls designed to enable management to meet its responsibility for reporting reliable financial information. The system is designed to provide reasonable assurance that assets are safeguarded and transactions are recorded and executed with management's authorization. Internal control systems are subject to inherent limitations due to the necessity to balance costs incurred with benefits provided. The company believes that the existing system of internal controls provides reasonable assurance that errors or irregularities that could be material to the financial statements are prevented or would be detected in a timely manner.

The board of directors pursues its oversight role for the financial statements through its audit committee, which is comprised solely of directors who are not officers or employees of the company. They are responsible for engaging, subject to stockholder approval, the independent accountants. The audit committee meets periodically with management and the independent accountants to review their activities in connection with financial reporting matters. The independent accountants have full and free access to meet with the audit committee, without management representatives present, to discuss the results of their examination and the adequacy and quality of internal controls and financial reporting.

The report of our independent accountants, Price Waterhouse LLP, appears herewith. Their audit of the financial statements includes a review of the company's system of internal controls and testing of records as required by generally accepted auditing standards.

B C Spat

Bradley E. Sparks
Vice President and Controller
January 25, 1995

Report of Independent Accountants
Price Waterhouse LLP

To the Board of Directors and Stockholders of
MCI Communications Corporation

In our opinion, the consolidated balance sheets and the related consolidated income statements, statements of cash flows and stockholders' equity appearing on pages 8, 10, 12 and 14 through 24 present fairly, in all material respects, the financial position of MCI Communications Corporation and its subsidiaries at December 31, 1994 and 1993, and the results of their operations and their cash flows for each of the three years in the period ended December 31, 1994, in conformity with generally accepted accounting principles. These financial statements are the responsibility of the company's management our responsibility is to express an opinion on these financial statements based on our audits. We conducted our audits of these statements in accordance with generally

accepted auditing standards which require that we plan and perform the audit to obtain reasonable assurance about whether the financial statements are free of material misstatement. An audit includes examining, on a test basis, evidence supporting the amounts and disclosures in the financial statements, assessing the accounting principles used and significant estimates made by management, and evaluating the overall financial statement presentation. We believe that our audits provide a reasonable basis for the opinion expressed above.

Price Waterhouse LLP

Price Waterhouse LLP
January 25, 1995
Washington, D.C.

Board of Directors

Bert C. Roberts, Jr.
Chairman and Chief Executive Officer

Clifford L. Alexander, Jr.
President
Alexander and Associates, Inc.
Washington, DC

Judith Areen
Executive Vice President of
Law Center Affairs
and Dean of the Law Center
Georgetown University
Washington, DC

Michael H. Bader
Partner
Haley, Bader & Potts
Arlington, Virginia

Michael L. Hepher
Group Managing Director
British Telecommunications plc.

Richard M. Jones
Former Chairman and
Chief Executive Officer
Guaranty Federal Savings Bank
Chicago, Illinois

Gordon S. Macklin
Corporate Financial Advisor
Washington, DC

Alfred T. Mockett
Managing Director of Global
Communications Division
British Telecommunications plc.

Richard B. Sayford
President and Chief Executive Officer
Strategic Enterprises, Inc.
Edwards, Colorado

Gerald H. Taylor
President and Chief Operating Officer

Judith Whittaker
Vice President-Legal
Hallmark Cards
Kansas City, Missouri

John R. Worthington
General Counsel

Officers

Corporate

Bert C. Roberts, Jr.
Chairman and Chief Executive Officer

Gerald H. Taylor
President and Chief Operating Officer

Douglas L. Maine
Chief Financial Officer

John R. Worthington
General Counsel

John H. Zimmerman
Chief Human Resources Officer

C. Bolton-Smith, Jr.
Secretary

Bradley E. Sparks
Controller

Jonelle St. John
Treasurer

networkMCI Services

John W. Gerdelman
President

Lawrence J. Bouman
Senior Vice President, networkMCI Operations

Frank J. Kozel, Jr.
Senior Vice President, networkMCI Implementation

Sherry R. Morehouse
Senior Vice President, networkMCI Planning & Engineering

MCI Communications Services

Timothy F. Price
Group President and Executive Vice President

Kevin J. Bennis
President Integrated Client Services Division

James E. Hoffman
Chief Information Officer

Vinton G. Cerf
Senior Vice President, Data Architecture

William D. Wooten
Senior Vice President, Human Resources

Business Markets

Scott B. Ross
President

Daniel M. Dennis
President, Carrier Sales

Richard G. Ellenberger
Senior Vice President, Worldwide Sales

Consumer Markets

Angela O. Dunlap
President

James M. Schneider
Senior Vice President, Finance

Ventures and Alliances

Michael J. Rowny
Executive Vice President

Daniel E. Crawford
Chief Operating Officer AVANTEL, S.A.

Gary M. Parsons
Chief Executive Officer MCImetro

Nathaniel A. Davis
Chief Operating Officer MCImetro

Susan Mayer
Senior Vice President, Corporate Development

Public Policy

Laurence E. Harris
Senior Vice President

Gerald J. Kovach
Senior Vice President, External Affairs

James L. Lewis
Senior Vice President, Regulatory Affairs

MCI International, Inc.

Seth D. Blumenfeld
Group Executive

Jerry A. DeMartino
President

Engineering

Fred M. Briggs
Chief Engineering Officer

Corporate Information

Annual Stockholders Meeting
April 17, 1995 – 12 noon
North Carolina Bar Center
Cary, NC

Common Stock Transfer Agent and Registrar
Mellon Securities Trust Company
120 Broadway
New York, NY 10271
1-800-934-6242
412-236-8000
Mellon's TDD number for the speech and
hearing-impaired is 1-800-231-5469

**Common Stock traded on the
NASDAQ Stock Market**
NASDAQ Symbol: MCIC. There is no trading market
for the Class A Common Stock.

Trustee—Senior Debt
Citibank, N.A.
Corporate Trust Department
120 Wall Street, 13th Floor
New York, NY 10043
1-800-422-2066
201-262-8644

Trustee—Subordinated Debt
Bankers Trust Company
Corporate Trust & Agency Company
4 Albany Street, 8th Floor
New York, NY 10015
212-250-2500

Independent Accountants
Price Waterhouse LLP
1301 K Street, N.W., 800 W
Washington, DC 20005

Dividend Record
In 1993 and 1994, MCI paid a dividend on its Common Stock
of $.025 per share in both July and December.

Street-Name Accounts
Stockholders whose stock is held by banks and brokerage
firms who wish to receive MCI Annual Reports directly from
the company should contact Mellon Securities Trust
Company, c/o Corporate Investor Communications, Inc.,
111 Commerce Road, Carlstadt, NJ 07072
Telephone: 201-896-5680.

Stock Price Range

Quarter Ended	Sale Price	
	High	Low
March 31, 1993	$23	$18 13/16
June 30, 1993	28 15/16	21 7/16
September 30, 1993	29 7/8	26 1/4
December 31, 1993	29 5/8	24 1/8
March 31, 1994	29	22 5/8
June 30, 1994	24 15/16	21 3/8
September 30, 1994	25 7/8	21 1/2
December 31, 1994	25 1/2	17 1/4

Record Holders of Common Stock at
December 31, 1994: 52,512.

Stockholder Services
■ Change of address
■ Lost stock certificates
■ Dividend payments
■ Transfer of stock to another person
■ Other administrative concerns

Please direct these inquiries directly to the Common Stock
Transfer Agent.

Corporate Information/Investor Services
The following information is available without charge to stockholders and interested parties:

■ Annual report
■ Form 10K, annual report to the
  Securities and Exchange Commission
■ Form 10Q, quarterly report to the
  Securities and Exchange Commission
■ Corporate Capabilities Brochure

To request these publications or for additional
information on the company, its finances, operations and
services, contact:

Constance K. Weaver
Vice President, Investor Relations
MCI Communications Corporation
1801 Pennsylvania Avenue, N. W.
Washington, DC 20006
Telephone 1-800-765-2115
202-887-2028
Fax 202-887-2967
MCI Mail: MCI Investor Relations
Internet address: 640-5834@mcimail.com

MCI Worldwide Locations

United States

MCI Communications Corporation
1801 Pennsylvania Avenue, N.W.
Washington, DC, 20006
202-872-1600

MCI Business Markets
MCI Center
Three Ravinia Drive
Atlanta, GA 30346
404-668-6000

MCI Consumer Markets
1200 S. Hayes Street
Arlington, VA 22202
703-415-6000

MCI International, Inc.
Two International Drive
Rye Brook, NY 10573
914-937-3444

MCImetro
1650 Tysons Boulevard
McLean, VA 22102
703-506-6002

networkMCI Services
2400 North Glenville Drive
Richardson, TX 75082
214-918-3000

MCI Software Development
2424 Garden of the Gods Road
Colorado Springs, CO 80919
719-535-1300

International

Argentina
Australia
Belgium
Bangladesh
Bolivia
Brazil
Canada
Chile
China
Colombia
Costa Rica
Ecuador
Egypt
El Salvador
Ethiopia
France
Germany
Greece
Guam
Guatemala
Haiti
Hong Kong
India
Indonesia
Ireland
Israel
Italy
Japan
Jordan
Korea
Kuwait
Lebanon
Malaysia
Mexico
Morocco
Netherlands
Nigeria
Pakistan
Panama
Peru
Philippines
Puerto Rico
Qatar
Russia
Saudi Arabia
Singapore
Spain
Sweden
Switzerland
Syria
Taiwan
Thailand
Trinidad/Tobago
Tunisia
Turkey
United Kingdom
Uruguay
Venezuela

Ventures, Alliances and Investments

Concert – British Telecommunications plc (BT)

AVANTEL, S.A. – Grupo Financiero Banamex-Accival (Banacci)

Stentor – alliance of Canada's major telecommunications companies

In-Flight Phone Corporation, Inc.

Interactive Cable Systems, Inc.

Belize Telecommunications, Ltd.

CLEAR Communications, Ltd.

Geneval Communication, Inc.

Design: Arnold Saks Associates, New York, NY

Printed on recycled paper. © 1995 MCI Communications Corporation

A

accelerated methods (p. 435) Methods used to depreciate fixed assets under which greater costs are allocated to earlier periods than are allocated to later periods.

accounting cycle (p. 215) The procedures leading from an exchange transaction to the preparation of the financial statements, including journal entries, posting to the ledger, and preparing the work sheet.

accounting equation (p. 184) Assets equal liabilities plus stockholders' equity; the equation upon which the balance sheet and all other financial statements are based.

accounting period (p. 218) The period of time between the preparation of the financial statements. Statements are often prepared monthly, quarterly, semiannually, or annually.

accounts payable (p. 46) A balance sheet account indicating the dollar amount owed to suppliers from purchases (usually of inventory) made on open account.

accounts receivable (pp. 43, 267) A balance sheet account indicating the dollar amount due from customers from sales made on open account.

accrual accounting (p. 197) A system of accounting that recognizes revenues and expenses when assets and liabilities are created or discharged because of operating activities. The revenues and expenses are not necessarily recognized when cash is received or paid. The income statement is prepared on an accrual basis.

accruals (p. 197) Adjusting journal entries designed to ensure that assets and liabilities that are created or discharged because of operating activities of the current period are recognized as revenues and expenses in that period. Examples include accrued wages and accrued interest.

activity method (p. 438) A method of amortizing the cost of long-lived assets that allocates costs to accounting periods on the basis of the asset's activity during that period. This method is used primarily to amortize natural resource costs.

activity ratios (p. 89) Ratios that measure the speed with which assets move through operations.

adjusted trial balance (p. 220) The trial balance which is listed on the work sheet after the adjusting entries are added to the unadjusted trial balance.

adjusting journal entries (p. 197) Journal entries recorded at the end of the accounting period to ensure that all assets and liabilities created or discharged during that period are recognized in that period. The three kinds of adjusting journal entries are accruals, cost expirations, and revaluation adjustments.

affiliated (associated) companies (p. 368) Investee companies that are 20–50 percent owned by investor companies.

aging schedule (p. 276) A method of estimating bad debts and analyzing outstanding accounts receivable that categorizes individual accounts on the basis of the amount of time each has been outstanding. Each category is then multiplied by a different uncollectible percentage, under the assumption that older accounts are more likely than new accounts to be uncollectible.

allowance method (p. 272) A method used to account for bad debts that estimates the dollar amount of bad debts at the end of each accounting period; records an adjusting journal entry to recognize bad debt expense and reduce the net accounts receivable balance; and writes off actual bad debts into an allowance account when they occur.

American Institute of Certified Public Accountants (AICPA) (p. 20) The official organization of certified public accountants in the United States. This organization sets the standards of performance and ethics for practicing certified public accountants.

amortization (p. 425) The systematic allocation of a deferred charge over its life. It is often used with specific reference to intangible assets, but prepaid expenses are amortized, and so are discounts and premiums on long-term receivables and payables. Depreciation is the amortization of a fixed asset.

annual interest (p. 12) A periodic charge on a borrowing or debt investment, usually determined by multiplying the annual interest rate times the principal of the debt.

annual report (p. 15) A document that a company publishes each year, containing the financial statements, a description of the company and its operations, an audit report, a management letter, footnotes to the financial statements, and other financial and nonfinancial information.

appropriation of retained earnings (p. 608) A book entry involving only the Retained Earnings account that serves to restrict a portion of retained earnings from the payment of dividends. Such restrictions can be imposed contractually or voluntarily.

asset (p. 10) An item listed on the left side of the balance sheet that has been acquired by the company in an objectively measurable transaction and has future economic benefit. Assets include cash, securities, receivables, inventory, prepaid expenses, long-term investments, property, plant, equipment, and intangibles.

asset depreciation range (ADR) (p. 441) Guidelines published by the Internal Revenue Service that define the minimum allowable useful lives and maximum depreciation rates for various kinds of long-lived assets. These lives are used in the depreciation of long-lived assets for purposes of computing taxable income.

audit committee (p. 18) A subcommittee of the board of directors that works with management to choose the external auditor and monitor the audit so that it is conducted in a thorough, objective, and independent manner.

auditor's report (p. 6) A letter written and signed by a CPA that indicates the extent of the audit and whether or not the financial statements fairly reflect the financial position and operations of a company and have been prepared in conformance with generally accepted accounting principles.

authorized (shares) (p. 593) The number of shares a company is entitled to issue, as stated in the corporate charter.

available-for-sale securities (p. 358) Investments not classified as trading securities.

averaging assumption (p. 325) A method of determining cost of goods sold and the ending inventory by computing a weighted average cost of the items sold and the items remaining.

B

balance sheet (p. 10) A financial statement that indicates the financial condition of a business as of a given point in time. It includes assets, liabilities, and stockholders' equity, and it represents a statement of the basic accounting equation.

betterment (p. 431) A postacquisition expenditure that improves a fixed asset by increasing its life, increasing the quality or quantity of its output, or decreasing the cost of operating it. The cost of a betterment is included in the capitalized cost of the asset and amortized over its remaining life.

Big 6 (p. 17) The six public accounting firms that audit most of the large companies. The Big 6 is made up of Arthur Anderson & Co., Coopers & Lybrand, Deloitte & Touche, Ernst & Young, KPMG Peat Marwick, and Price Waterhouse.

board of directors (p. 13) A group of individuals who are elected by the stockholders of a corporation and have the power to declare dividends, set executive compensation, hire and fire management, and set corporate policy. The board also appoints the audit committee.

bond (p. 528) A debt security usually issued by a corporation to a large number of investors to raise a large amount of cash. A bond involves a formal commitment that requires the issuing company to make cash interest payments to the bondholder and a principal payment when the bond matures, usually between five and thirty years after the bond is issued.

bonds payable (pp. 47, 528) A balance sheet long-term liability account indicating the total face amount of outstanding bonds.

book value (of company/shares) (pp. 586, 597) The book value of a company is equal to the balance sheet value of stockholders' equity, which is sometimes referred to as *net assets* or *net worth*. The book value of a share of outstanding stock is the book value of the company divided by the number of outstanding shares.

British-American-Dutch Model (p. 25) The system of financial accounting in North America, the United Kingdom, Australia, India, and Holland. It is based primarily on the generally accepted accounting principles of the United States.

business acquisition (p. 369) An event by which an investor company acquires a controlling interest (51 percent or more of the voting stock) in another (investee) company. The investor company is called the *parent* and the investee company is called the *subsidiary*.

business combination (p. 369) *See* **merger**.

business segment (p. 652) A separate line of business, production line, or class of customer representing an operation that is independent of a company's other operations.

business transaction (p. 185) Asset and liability exchanges that are entered into by a company in the course of conducting business.

C

call provision (p. 539) A provision in a debt contract that allows the issuing company to repurchase outstanding bonds after a specified date for a specified price.

capital lease (p. 550) A lease that is treated as a purchase for the purposes of financial accounting. In a capital lease the lessee is considered to have purchased the leased asset and financed it through the periodic lease payments. Capital leases give rise to the recognition of both balance sheet assets and liabilities.

capital transaction (p. 646) A business transaction that involves building or financing the productive capacity of the company. These transactions are not reflected on the income statement and are represented on the statement of cash flows under the sections that list the company's investing and financing activities.

capitalization ratios (p. 90) Ratios that help users to evaluate the capital structure of a company or, in general, the composition of the liability and stockholders' equity side of the balance sheet.

capitalize (p. 200) To place the cost of an expenditure on the balance sheet.

cash budget (p. 266) An accounting report, prepared and used internally, that projects future cash inflows and outflows and thereby helps to assess a company's future cash needs.

cash discount (p. 270) Usually attached to a sale or purchase on open account, a cash discount is an offer to receive or pay less than the gross price if payment is made within a designated discount period.

cash equivalent (p. 683) Commercial paper and other debt instruments with maturities of less than three months. Such items are often included in the definition of cash for purposes of the balance sheet and the statement of cash flows.

certificate of deposit (p. 565) A short-term obligation of a bank that pays a specified rate of interest for a specified period of time. Often interest penalties are assessed in the case of early withdrawal.

certified public accountants (CPAs) (p. 6) Those individuals, designated on a state-by-state basis, who have passed the certification exam developed by the American Institute of Certified Public Accountants and who have the requisite amount of public accounting experience. Individuals who render opinions on financial statements must be certified public accountants.

class-action lawsuit (p. 148) A legal action taken against a defendant by a group of individuals who have suffered damages. Class-action suits are often filed by stockholders and creditors who have incurred losses against a company's management and auditors.

classified balance sheet (p. 40) A balance sheet divided into classifications, including current assets, long-term investments, fixed assets, intangible assets, current liabilities, long-term liabilities, and stockholders' equity.

closing entries (p. 222) The entries to the work sheet, journal, and ledger that transfer the end-of-period balances in the temporary (Revenue, Expense, and Dividend) accounts to Retained Earnings. Revenue and Expense accounts are first closed into the Income Summary.

collateral (p. 531) Assets designated to be paid to a creditor in case of default on a loan by a debtor. Often referred to as *security* on the loan.

collection period (p. 281) A financial ratio indicating how many days, on average, the short-term receivables of a given company are outstanding: (Accounts Receivable ÷ Sales) × 365 days.

commercial paper (p. 482) Short-term notes issued by companies with high credit ratings in exchange for cash from other companies.

common stock (p. 10) An ownership interest in a corporation. Holding a common stock certificate usually carries with it the right to receive dividends if they are declared and the right to vote for the corporation's board of directors.

Common-size financial statements (p. 84) Statements showing financial statement numbers expressed as percentages of other numbers on the same statements.

Communist model (p. 26) The system of financial accounting used in countries in the Communist bloc. This system produces information required and primarily oriented toward government planners.

compensating balance (p. 265) Minimum cash balances that must be maintained in savings or checking accounts until certain loan obligations are satisfied.

compensation contracts (p. 17) Contracts that specify the form and amount of compensation paid to the managers or employees of the firm. Accounting numbers, such as net income, are often used in such contracts to motivate management to act in the interests of the firm's owners.

compound journal entry (p. 190) A journal entry involving more than two accounts.

comprehensive income (p. 644) A very broad definition of income, including any change in the company's equity due to nonowner transactions.

conceptual framework (p. 23) An ongoing project conducted by accounting standard setters that is designed to guide policymakers as they set accounting standards. It includes a statement of objectives, the desirable characteristics of accounting information, and the definitions of important accounting terms.

conditional accrued liabilities (p. 486) Accrued liabilities having dollar amounts that cannot be determined until other items (usually some measure of firm performance) have been determined. Income taxes payable is a common example.

conservatism (p. 147) An exception to the principles of financial accounting; it holds the following: "When in doubt, understate rather than overstate an entity's value."

conservatism ratio (p. 509) A measure of the extent to which reported income is conservative.

consignment (p. 314) An agreement by which a consignor (owner) transfers inventory to a consignee (receiver) who takes physical possession and places the items up for sale. When the inventory is sold, the consignee collects the sales proceeds, keeps a percentage, and returns the remainder to the consignor.

consistency (p. 145) A principle of financial accounting holding that business entities should use the same accounting methods from one period to the next.

consolidated financial statements (pp. 17, 369) Financial statements of a company that include its assets and liabilities as well as the assets and liabilities of its majority-owned subsidiaries.

Continental model (p. 26) The system of financial accounting used in Japan and most of the Western European countries. This system is not oriented toward the needs of investors; it provides information primarily to meet government requirements.

contra account (p. 205) A balance sheet account that offsets another balance sheet account. Examples include Accumulated Depreciation, Allowance for Uncollectibles, and Bond Discounts and Premiums.

contributed capital (pp. 47, 586) That portion of the stockholders' equity section of the balance sheet of a corporation that indicates contributions from stockholders.

controlling interest (p. 369) Ownership of 51 percent or more of outstanding voting stock of a company.

corporation (p. 617) A legal entity separate and distinct from its owners. Corporations are taxed and can be sued and provide legal liability protection for their owners. The owners of a corporation are referred to as stockholders or shareholders.

cost expiration (p. 200) The process of converting a capitalized cost to an expense. Adjusting journal entries are often used to expire previously capitalized costs. Depreciation of fixed assets and amortization of intangible assets are examples.

cost method (p. 365) A method used to account for equity investments with no ready market. Under this method, the balance sheet value of the investment is carried at its historical cost.

cost of goods sold (p. 50) An account on the income statement that indicates the cost of the inventory sold during the period.

covenant (p. 538) An agreement between a company's creditors and its managers that often restricts the managers' behavior in some way. These restrictions are usually designed to protect the creditor's investment, and they are often written in terms of accounting numbers and ratios.

creating hidden reserves (p. 99) A strategy that recognizes accounting losses in the current period to ensure that reported earnings is not too high and to guarantee that the loss will not have to be recognized in future periods when reported earnings may be less than impressive.

credit (p. 190) The right side of a journal entry, indicating a decrease in an asset account or an increase in a liability or stockholders' equity account.

creditor (p. 10) An individual or entity to which a company has an outstanding debt.

cumulative preferred stock (p. 594) When a company misses a dividend on preferred stock with a cumulative feature, the missed dividend becomes a *dividend in arrears*, which must be paid if and when the company issues a dividend in the future.

current assets (pp. 42, 259) Assets on the balance sheet that are expected to be converted to cash or expired in one year or the operating cycle, whichever is longer.

current liabilities (p. 46) Obligations on the balance sheet that are expected to be paid with the use of assets presently listed as current on the balance sheet.

current maturity of long-term debt (p. 46) A balance sheet current liability account representing that portion of a long-term liability that is due in the current period.

current ratio (p. 260) Current assets divided by current liabilities. This ratio is often used to assess the solvency position of a company.

D

date of declaration (p. 604) The date that a board of directors declares a dividend, thereby establishing a liability.

date of payment (p. 604) The date that a dividend is paid to shareholders of record.

date of record (p. 604) The date that the shareholders holding stock on that date will receive the dividend when paid.

debentures (p. 539) Unsecured bonds.

debit (p. 190) The left side of the journal entry, indicating an increase in an asset account or a decrease in a liability or stockholders' equity account.

debt investment (p. 12) The purchase of a debt security by a company or a loan of goods or services to another entity.

debt ratio (p. 475) Total debt divided by total assets; a measure of the proportion of assets generated through borrowings.

debt restriction (p. 12) A term written into a debt contract or covenant that restricts the behavior of the company's managers. Such restrictions are often written in terms of accounting numbers. *See* **covenant**.

default (p. 531) To fail to make a contractual payment on a debt.

deferred cost (p. 424) A miscellaneous category of assets that often includes prepaid expenses extending beyond the current accounting period and intangible assets such as organizational costs and other start-up costs.

defined-benefit plan (p. 502) A pension plan in which the employer promises to provide each employee with a specified benefit at retirement.

defined-contribution plan (p. 501) A pension plan where the employer promises only to make a series of contributions of a specified amount to a pension fund.

deplete (p. 438) To amortize the costs of acquiring and extracting natural resources.

depreciation (pp. 142, 425) The periodic allocation of the cost of a fixed asset to the income statement over the asset's useful life. It loosely approximates the reduction in the asset's usefulness.

depreciation base (p. 434) The portion of the cost of a long-lived asset that is subject to depreciation: capitalized cost less estimated salvage value.

determinable current liability (p. 481) A current liability that can be precisely measured, for which the amount of cash required to satisfy the obligation and the date of payment are reasonably certain.

dilution (p. 590) A reduction in a stockholder's relative ownership due to the issuance of additional stock to other stockholders.

discount on bonds payable (p. 543) A contra liability account representing the amount by which the face value of a bond exceeds the cash proceeds.

discount rate (p. 565) The lending rate charged to banks by the Federal Reserve Board. Also used to describe the rate used in present-value computations.

direct method (p. 685) A method of presenting the statement of cash flows where the cash inflows and outflows can be traced directly to the Cash account in the ledger. Under the direct method, net cash flow from operating activities is computed by adjusting each income statement item for its cash effect.

dissimilar assets (p. 445) Long-lived assets of different general types that perform different functions and are employed in different lines of business. The methods used to account for exchanges of similar assets are different from those used to account for exchanges of dissimilar assets.

dividends (p. 11) Payments made to the stockholders of a corporation as returns on their equity investments. Dividends are declared by the board of directors.

dividends in arrears (p. 594) Missed dividends on preferred stock with a cumulative feature. Dividends in arrears are not liabilities, but they must be paid when and if the company declares a dividend.

double-declining-balance method (p. 436) The most extreme form of accelerated depreciation. Each period the book value of the fixed asset is multiplied by two times the straight-line rate. This method is very popular for tax purposes.

double entry system (p. 190) The cornerstone of financial accounting, which specifies that all transactions involve exchanges where something is received and something is given up. Transactions are recorded with journal entries, consisting of at least one debit and one credit, which measure the increase and decrease in the affected accounts in a way that maintains the equality of the accounting equation.

double taxation (p. 618) A phenomenon that occurs in a corporation where both corporate profits and dividends received by the shareholders are separately subject to federal income taxes.

E

earned capital (p. 586) A measure of a company's assets that have been generated through profitable operations and not paid out in the form of dividends. On the balance sheet, earned capital is represented by the Retained Earnings balance.

earning power (pp. 10, 78) The ability of a company to generate profits and net assets in the long-run future. Net income is considered an indication of earning power.

earnings persistence (pp. 78, 659) An income statement concept reflecting the extent to which a particular earnings dollar amount can be expected to continue in the future and thus generate future cash flows.

economic consequence perspective (p. 4) Considering and understanding how economic events affect the financial statements, and how reported numbers bring about economic effects.

economic consequences (p. 24) The costs and benefits to investors, managers, auditors, and consumers associated with establishing, changing, or implementing accounting standards.

economic entity assumption (p. 132) An assumption of financial accounting holding that a company is a separate economic entity that can be identified and that its performance can be measured.

economic event (p. 183) Any occurrence that involves a transfer of resources from one party to another.

effective interest method (p. 534) The accounting method used to value long-term liabilities and long-term notes receivable, and the related interest charges, so that the book value of such a note represents an estimate of the present value of the note's future cash flows, assuming that the discount rate is constant over the life of the note.

effective interest rate (p. 532) The actual rate of interest on an obligation or receivable. It is that rate which, when used to discount the future cash payments associated with the obligation or receivable, results in a present value that is equal to the initial proceeds provided by the obligation or receivable.

Employment Retirement Income Security Act (ERISA) (p. 502) The Act passed by Congress in 1974 which requires employers to fund their pension plans at specified minimum levels and provides other safeguards designed to protect employees.

entrepreneur (p. 39) A person who starts and operates a business.

equity (p. 12) An ownership interest.

equity investment (p. 356) The purchase of an ownership interest (e.g., common stock) in a company.

equity method (p. 366) A method used to account for equity investments in the amount of 20 percent to 50 percent of the investee company's outstanding voting stock. The accounting procedures of this method reflect a substantial economic relationship between investee and investor companies.

error of overstatement (p. 148) An error that leads financial statement users to believe that an entity is in better financial condition than it actually is.

error of understatement (p. 148) An error which leads financial statement users to believe that an entity is in worse financial condition than it actually is.

escrow (p. 265) The state of an item (e.g., cash) that has been put into the custody of a third party until certain conditions are fulfilled.

ethics (p. 20) The standards of conduct and behavior.

exchange rate (p. 290) The value of one currency expressed in terms of another currency.

expense (p. 11) Asset outflows or liabilities that are created in an effort to generate revenues for a company. Examples include cost of goods sold, salaries, interest, advertising, taxes, utilities, depreciation, and others. Revenues less expenses is equal to net income.

expensed (p. 200) Treated an expenditure as an expense by running the account through the income statement and closing it to retained earnings.

extraordinary item (p. 654) An event significantly different from the typical, customary business activities of an entity, which is not expected to recur frequently in the ordinary activities of the business. Book gains or losses resulting from extraordinary items are disclosed separately in the income statement.

F

face value (pp. 138, 480, 531) The value printed on the face of an item (e.g., cash). The face value of an account receiv-

able is the total dollar amount of the outstanding account. When used in the context of notes or bonds, the face value is the amount that is written on the face of the note or bond certificate and paid to the holder at maturity.

fair market value (FMV) (p. 137) The sales price of an item in the output market.

fees earned (p. 49) Revenues earned by a company for services to its clients.

final trial balance (p. 223) The trial balance that results from the completion of the work sheet. It contains the end-of-period balances of the permanent accounts: assets, liabilities, and stockholders' equity.

financial accounting (p. 3) A process through which managers report financial information about an economic entity to a variety of individuals who use this information for various decision-making purposes.

Financial Accounting Standards Board (FASB) (p. 23) The professional body that is currently responsible for establishing financial accounting standards.

financial flexibility (pp. 95, 689) A company's capacity to raise cash through methods other than operations. Examples include borrowings, issuing equity, or selling assets.

financing activities (pp. 11, 39, 689) The activities of a company by which it generates capital to pay for its operations. The financial effects of the financing activities of a given period are summarized on the statement of cash flows and typically involve the management of borrowings and equity issuances.

first-in, first-out (FIFO) (p. 325) A method for valuing cost of goods sold and ending inventory; it assumes that the first items purchased are the first items sold.

fiscal period assumption (p. 133) An assumption of financial accounting holding that an entity's life can be divided into individual fiscal periods.

fiscal year (p. 134) A year ending on a date other than December 31. Many U.S. companies have accounting periods that are fiscal years.

fixed assets (p. 424) A category of long-lived assets including buildings, machinery, and equipment.

FOB (free on board) destination (p. 315) Freight terms indicating that the seller is responsible for the freight until it is received by the buyer.

FOB (free on board) shipping point (p. 315) Freight terms indicating that the seller is responsible for the freight only to the point from which it is shipped.

footnotes (to the financial statements) (p. 9) Descriptions and schedules included in the financial report that further explain the numbers on the balance sheet, income statement, statement of retained earnings or statement of stockholders' equity, and statement of cash flows.

freight-in (p. 316) An income statement account indicating the freight costs of purchased inventory. Also called *transportation-in*.

frequent transactions (p. 651) Operating transactions that are expected to recur repeatedly in the foreseeable future.

fully diluted earnings per share (p. 666) A disclosure required by GAAP for companies that have the potential for significant dilution. The calculation for it essentially increases the denominator of the earnings-per-share ratio and reduces its dollar value.

G

gain contingency (p. 489) A contingency where the possible future outcome is an increase in assets or a decrease in liabilities. Gain contingencies are rarely disclosed on the financial statements.

general journal (p. 216) The journal containing all journal entries except those recorded in the special-purpose journals. In the absence of special-purpose journals, the general journal contains all the journal entries.

general ledger (p. 217) The ledger that contains an account and a dollar balance for each account appearing on the financial statements. The general ledger contains the control accounts for those accounts with related subsidiary ledgers.

generally accepted accounting principles (GAAP) (p. 22) The standards that guide the preparation of financial accounting statements in the United States. They include the principles established by the Committee on Accounting Procedures, the Accounting Principles Board, and the Financial Accounting Standards Board, those bodies that have been given authoritative support by the Securities and Exchange Commission. The auditor states in the auditor's report whether or not the company's financial statements are prepared in conformance with these standards.

going concern assumption (p. 134) An assumption of financial accounting holding that the life of an economic entity is indefinite, i.e., the entity will not be discontinued in the current period.

goods in transit (p. 314) Goods that are in transit between the buyer and the seller as of the end of an accounting period.

gross method (p. 271) A method of accounting for cash discounts that recognizes the initial sale or purchase at the gross sales price and recognizes a cash discount only if payment is received within the discount period.

H

historical cost (pp. 12, 138) The dollar amount paid for an asset when it was acquired. Many assets on the balance sheet are carried at historical cost.

holding gains or losses (p. 360) *See* **unrealized gains and losses**.

human capital (p. 100) The value of a company's human resources. Such valuations do not fall within the scope of generally accepted accounting principles and, accordingly, are not reflected on the financial statements.

I

income statement (p. 11) A financial statement, prepared on an accrual basis, that indicates the performance of a company during a particular period. The income statement contains revenues and expenses and highlights the net income number.

income summary (p. 222) A ledger account created specifically for the purpose of closing the Revenue and Expense accounts. In the closing process, the Revenue and Expense accounts are closed into the Income Summary account, which in turn is closed into the Retained Earnings account. The dollar amount of the difference between revenues and expenses is equal to the net income of the period, which is highlighted in the Income Summary account during this process.

independent audit (p. 6) The examination conducted by an individual or entity, having no financial interest in the company, which determines whether the financial statements of the company fairly reflect its financial condition and whether the statements have been prepared in conformance with generally accepted accounting principles.

indirect method (p. 685) A method of preparing the statement of cash flows that computes cash flows from operating activities by adjusting net income for the differences between cash flows and accruals.

industries (p. 16) A classification of a group of companies based on the nature of their operations. Three basic categories are manufacturing, retailing, and services.

input market (p. 136) The market where an entity purchases the inputs for its operations.

installment obligation (p. 531) Long-term obligations requiring periodic payments covering both interest and principal.

intangible asset (pp. 45, 424) Balance sheet assets that have no physical substance. They usually represent legal rights to the use or sale of valuable names, items, processes, or information. Patents, trademarks, and goodwill on acquired companies are examples.

intention to convert (p. 357) A phrase that describes one of the criteria by which an investment in a security is classified in the current assets section of the balance sheet. Management must intend to convert the investment into cash within the time period for current assets.

interest (p. 531) The price, usually expressed as an annual rate, associated with transferring (borrowing or lending) money for a period of time.

interest-bearing obligation (p. 531) Long-term obligations requiring periodic interest payments that are determined as a percentage of the face value.

interest payment (on a bond) (p. 537) The periodic cash interest payment made by the issuing company to the bondholders. It is equal to the stated interest rate times the face value. Bond interest payments are usually made semiannually.

internal control system (p. 8) Procedures and records designed to ensure that (1) a company's assets are adequately protected from loss or misappropriation, and that (2) all relevant and measurable economic events are accurately reflected in the company's financial statements.

internal revenue code (p. 441) The document prepared by the Internal Revenue Service that contains the official federal income tax laws.

International Accounting Standards Committee (IASC) (p. 26) A private-sector body founded in 1973 that works to develop and encourage uniform worldwide accounting practices.

intraperiod tax allocation (p. 658) The practice of disclosing the income tax effect of a particular income statement or statement of retained earnings item with the item itself. Such items (e.g., disposals of segments, extraordinary items, changes in accounting principles, and prior-period adjustments) are disclosed net of their income tax effects.

investing activities (pp. 11, 39, 686) The activities of a company by which it manages its long-term assets. The investment activities of a given period are summarized on the statement of cash flows and typically involve the purchases and sales of long-term assets.

issued (shares of stock) (p. 593) Shares of stock which have been issued to the stockholders and may or may not be currently outstanding. Some previously issued shares, for example, may have been repurchased by the company and held in the form of treasury stock.

J

journal (p. 216) The original book of record that contains a chronological list of the transactions entered into by a company, usually in journal entry form. The journal consists of the general journal and all special-purpose journals.

journal entry (p. 190) The form in which transactions are initially recorded in the financial records. Such an entry consists of three components: (1) the accounts affected (asset, liability, stockholders' equity, revenue, expense, or dividend), (2) the direction of the effect (debit or credit), and (3) the dollar amount of the effect. The left side of the journal entry is referred to as the debit, and the right side is referred to as the credit.

journalizing (p. 216) The process of recording a journal entry in the journal.

L

land (p. 424) Real estate held for investment purposes, usually appearing in the long-term investments section of the balance sheet. Land used in the operations of a business is considered a long-lived asset and is normally referred to as *property*.

last-in, first-out (LIFO) (p. 325) A method of valuing cost of goods sold and ending inventory, which assumes that the most recent items purchased are the first items sold.

lease (p. 549) A contract granting use or occupation of property during a specified period of time in exchange for specified rent payments.

leasehold obligation (p. 528) The present value of the future payments associated with a capital lease; a long-term liability on the balance sheet.

ledger (p. 217) The book of record where a running balance for each asset, liability, stockholders' equity, revenue, expense, and dividend account is maintained. It consists of both the general ledger and all subsidiary ledgers.

legal liability (p. 18) The responsibility of a person, e.g., an auditor or a manager, to conduct work in a diligent and ethical manner.

leverage (p. 590) A strategy that involves borrowing funds and investing them in assets that produce returns exceeding the after-tax cost of the borrowing.

liabilities (p. 10) Financial obligations that must be met in the future by a company, listed on the right side of the balance sheet.

life of a bond (p. 537) The period of time from the issuance of a bond to the maturity date, when the face value is paid to the bondholders.

LIFO conformity rule (p. 327) A federal income tax requirement that if a company uses the LIFO assumption for computing its tax liability, it must also use the LIFO assumption for preparing its financial statements.

LIFO reserves (p. 332) Dollar amounts that represent the difference between LIFO and FIFO inventory. It helps users to validly compare companies that use LIFO with companies that use FIFO; they indicate trade-offs involved with changing from LIFO to FIFO.

limited liability (p. 618) A characteristic of a corporation stating that the liability of the stockholders is limited to the dollar amount of their investments.

line of credit (p. 482) The credit granted to a company by a bank or group of banks, allowing it to borrow up to a certain maximum dollar amount, with interest being charged only on the outstanding balance.

liquidity (pp. 42, 96) The speed with which an asset can be converted into a cash inflow or a liability becomes a cash outflow. Highly liquid assets can be converted to cash almost immediately.

loan contracts (p. 12) The contracts that underlie the borrowings of a company. Loan contracts typically contain a provision for interest, a maturity date, security arrangements in case of default, and restrictions on the behavior of management.

long-term investments (p. 44) A section on the asset side of the balance sheet that includes investments in equity securities, debt securities, real estate, life insurance, and other special funds. These investments are intended to be held, and they provide benefits for a period of time beyond that of current assets.

loss contingency (p. 489) A contingency where the possible future outcome leads to a reduction in assets or an increase in liabilities.

lower-of-cost-or-market rule (p. 138) The rule underlying accounting for security investments and inventories stating that the balance sheet value of such items will be the item's historical cost or its market value, whichever is lower.

M

maintenance (expenditure) (p. 431) A postacquisition cost that serves to repair or maintain a long-lived asset in its present operating condition. Maintenance expenditures are immediately expensed.

management letter (p. 6) A letter in the financial report stating primarily that management is responsible for the preparation and integrity of the financial statements. Management letters differ from one company to the next and often contain a number of statements referring to management's responsibilities.

managers (p. 16) Individuals, supplied with capital by a company's equity owners (stockholders), who are compensated through wages, salaries, and bonuses to earn returns for the owners. *Manager* is also used to describe an individual who has a management position in a public accounting firm.

manufacturing company (p. 316) A company that acquires raw materials and, through a process, combines labor and overhead to manufacture inventory.

markdown (p. 270) A reduction in sales price normally due to decreased demand for an item.

market ratios (p. 92) Ratios that measure returns to common stockholders that are due to changes in the market price of the common stock and the receipt of dividends.

market-to-book ratio (p. 597) The ratio from dividing the market value of a company's common stock by its book value; indicates the extent to which the market believes that the balance sheet reflects the company's true value.

market value (of stock) (p. 596) The price at which a share of stock can be exchanged in the open market as of a particular point in time.

mark-to-market rule (p. 358) The rule that certain investments be carried on the balance sheet at market value.

matching principle (pp. 142, 200) The principle stating that performance is measured by matching efforts against benefits in the time period in which the benefits are realized. Net income is the result of matching expenses against revenues in the time period in which the revenues are realized.

materiality (p. 146) An exception to the principles of financial accounting stating that only those transactions dealing with dollar amounts large enough to make a difference to financial statement users need be accounted for in a manner consistent with the principles of financial accounting.

maturity date (pp. 483, 537) The date when a loan agreement ends. As of the maturity date, if the payments are made on the loan, the associated debt is satisfied. Normally, the face value of the note is paid to the holder on the maturity date.

maturity value (p. 531) *See* **face value**.

merchandise inventory (p. 43) Items or products on hand that a company intends to sell to its customers.

merger (p. 369) A business combination whereby two or more companies combine to form a single legal entity. In most cases the assets and liabilities of the smaller company are merged into those of the larger company, and the stock of the smaller, merged company is retired.

modified accelerated cost-recovery system (MACRS) (p. 441) The tax law covering the acceptable methods of depreciating fixed assets.

mortgage (p. 535) A cash loan exchanged for an installment note that is secured by real estate.

mortgage payable (p. 47) A balance sheet account which refers to long-term obligations secured by real estate.

multinationals (p. 208) Corporations that have their home in one country but operate and have subsidiaries operating under the laws of other countries.

multinational (transnational) corporation (p. 290) A corporation with operations or subsidiaries in foreign countries.

N

natural resource costs (p. 424) The costs of acquiring the rights to and extracting natural resources.

net assets (p. 586) Total balance sheet assets less liabilities, equal to stockholders' equity. Often referred to as *net worth*.

net book value (pp. 45, 205) The dollar value assigned to an item on the balance sheet. The net book value of a company (i.e., stockholders' equity) is equal to total assets less total liabilities.

net income (profit) (p. 11) The difference between the revenues generated by a company in a particular time period and the expenses required to generate those revenues.

net realizable value (pp. 138, 270) The net cash amount expected from the sale of an item, usually equal to the selling price of an item less the cost to complete the item and the cost to sell the item.

net worth (p. 586) *See* **stockholders' equity** or **net assets**.

non-interest-bearing obligations (p. 531) A note receivable or payable with a stated interest rate of zero.

nonprofit entity (p. 17) An organization that is not designed to make a profit. Rather, most nonprofit entities generate funds through contributions, user fees, or taxes and use these funds to achieve some organizational or social purpose.

notes payable (pp. 47, 528) Obligations evidenced by formal notes. They normally involve direct borrowings from financial institutions or arrangements to finance the purchase of assets.

O

objectivity (p. 140) A principle of financial accounting stating that the values of transactions and the assets and liabilities created by them must be objectively determined.

open accounts (pp. 267, 482) Informal credit trade agreements; the term is usually used to describe accounts receivable or accounts payable.

operating activities (pp. 11, 39, 685) The activities of a company that involve the provision of a service to its clients or the buying and selling of its product to its customers. The financial effects of the operating activities of a given period are summarized on both the income statement and the statement of cash flows.

operating cycle (p. 259) The time it takes, in general, for a company to begin with cash, convert the cash to inventory, sell the inventory, and receive cash payment. Operating cycles vary greatly across different companies.

operating expenses (p. 51) A section on the income statement that includes the periodic and usual expenses a company incurs to generate revenues.

operating lease (p. 550) A rental arrangement in which an owner (lessor) transfers property to a lessee for a specified period of time for a specified price. After the lease expires, the property reverts to the lessor. For financial accounting purposes, operating leases are treated as simple rentals.

operating performance (p. 95) A company's ability to increase its net assets through operating activities.

operating transactions (p. 646) Business exchanges directly involving the acquisition and sale of a company's inventories or services.

ordinary stock dividend (p. 606) A relatively small stock dividend; the number of shares issued represents less than 25 percent of the number of shares outstanding before the issuance.

original cost (p. 137) The input price paid when originally purchased.

output market (p. 136) The market where an entity sells the outputs that result from its operations.

outstanding (shares of stock) (p. 593) Issued shares that are presently held by shareholders.

overhead (p. 316) Manufacturing costs that cannot be directly linked to particular products. Overhead costs include indirect materials, indirect labor, utility, taxes, insurance costs, and depreciation charges.

overstating the financial condition (p. 98) A strategy to devise a more favorable picture of financial condition and operating performance, achieved by accelerating the recognition of revenues or deferring the recognition of expenses.

owners' equity (p. 48) The section of the right side of the balance sheet that measures the portion of a company's assets that has either been contributed by the company's owners or generated through profitable operations and not distributed to or withdrawn by the owners. Owners' equity is usually used in the context of partnerships or proprietorships.

P

paper profits (p. 329) Profits that appear on the income statement but are not backed by increases in the firm's wealth.

par value (pp. 594, 597) In the context of preferred stock, par value is often used in the determination of the amount of the annual preferred dividend payment. It also determines the dollar amount disclosed in the Preferred Stock account on the balance sheet. In the context of common stock, par value has little economic significance, but it is used to determine the dollar amount disclosed in the Common Stock account on the balance sheet.

parent company (p. 369) A company that owns a controlling interest (more than 50 percent of the voting stock) in another (subsidiary) company.

participating (preferred stock) (p. 595) Stocks preferred as to dividends, which have the right, if dividends are declared, not only to an annual dividend amount (determined by the dividend percentage) but also a right to a portion of the additional dividend paid to the common stockholders.

pension (p. 501) A sum of money paid to a retired or disabled employee, the amount of which is usually determined by the employee's years of service.

percentage-of-credit-sales approach (p. 273) A method of estimating bad debts that multiplies a given percentage by the credit sales of a given accounting period.

periodic method (p. 317) A method of carrying inventory on the books that records each purchase as it occurs and takes an inventory count to determine ending inventory at the end of the accounting period.

permanent accounts (p. 222) Financial statement accounts that accumulate from one accounting period to the next. Included are asset, liability, and stockholders' equity accounts.

perpetual method (p. 317) A method of carrying inventory on the books that maintains an up-to-date record, recording each purchase as it occurs, and recording an inventory outflow at each sale.

petty cash (p. 266) Small amounts of cash kept on a company's premises to cover the day-to-day cash needs of office operations.

physical control (p. 267) The procedures and records designed to safeguard assets from loss or theft.

physical obsolescence (p. 432) The state of an asset when repairs are not economically feasible.

plant and equipment (p. 45) The physical structures owned by a company and involved in its operations. The plant account is a long-lived asset account that includes such items as factories, office buildings, and warehouses.

Equipment includes such items as machinery, vehicles, and office equipment.

postacquisition expenditures (p. 431) Costs incurred to improve or maintain long-lived assets after they have been acquired.

preferred stock as to assets (p. 593) Stock preferred as to assets carries a claim to corporate assets in the case of liquidation that has a higher priority than the residual claim held by the common stockholders.

preferred stock as to dividends (p. 593) Stock preferred as to dividends carries a right to receive dividends of a specified amount before dividends are distributed to the common stockholders.

premium on bonds payable (p. 544) A financial statement account representing the amount by which the proceeds of a bond issuance exceed the face value. Bond premiums are amortized over the life of the bonds into interest expense.

prepaid expenses (p. 44) A balance sheet account representing expenses that have been paid before the corresponding service or right is actually used.

present value (p. 137) The current monetary amount that is equivalent in value to a future cash payment.

prime interest rate (p. 565) The interest rate charged by a bank to its best (lowest risk) customers.

principal (p. 531) The sum of money owed as a debt, upon which interest is calculated.

prior period adjustment (p. 661) The financial effects of certain transactions (usually error corrections) that result in direct adjustments to the Retained Earnings account. All prior period adjustments occurred prior to the beginning of the current accounting period and are disclosed on the statement of retained earnings.

proceeds (p. 537) The amount of cash collected on a sale, a borrowing, a bond issuance, or a stock issuance.

profit (p. 11) The difference between the revenues generated by a firm in a particular time period and the expenses required to generate those revenues. Often referred to as *net income* or *earnings*.

profitability ratios (p. 85) Ratios designed to measure earning power by comparing net income (profit) to other measures of financial activity or condition.

pro forma (as if) basis (p. 656) A form of disclosure that requires information for all periods presented to appear as if the newly adopted principle had been applied to those periods.

property (p. 45) A long-lived asset account representing the real estate upon which a company conducts its operations.

purchase method (p. 370) A method of accounting for a business acquisition by which the assets and liabilities of the subsidiary are added to those of the parent at fair market value, and the difference between the purchase price and the fair market value of the subsidiary's net assets is recorded as goodwill.

purchasing power (p. 135) The amount of goods and services a monetary amount can buy at a given point in time.

Q

quality of earnings (p. 98) A concept measuring how much the profits companies publicly report diverge from true operating earnings.

quantity discount (p. 270) A reduction in the per-unit price of an item if a certain number of items are purchased.

quick ratio (p. 260) Cash plus marketable securities plus short-term receivables, divided by current liabilities; often used as an indication of a company's solvency position.

R

ratio analysis (p. 85) Computing additional ratios using two or more financial statement numbers.

readily marketable (p. 357) Able to be sold immediately. This expression is usually used to describe marketable securities listed as current assets.

realized gains/losses (p. 360) The difference between the balance sheet value of and the proceeds from the sale of trading and available-for-sale securities.

record control (p. 267) The procedures and records designed to ensure that all relevant and measurable economic events are accurately reflected in a company's financial statements.

redeemed (p. 547) Repurchased outstanding debt (e.g., bonds) either before or at the maturity date.

refinancing (p. 535) Issuing a note payable to satisfy another outstanding note payable.

relevant events (p. 183) Any event having economic significance to a company. Events that affect a company's future cash flows are considered to be economically significant.

replacement cost (p. 137) The current price that an entity would pay in the input market to replace an existing asset.

residual interest (p. 588) The right of common stockholders to receive corporate assets in the case of liquidation, after the creditors and preferred stockholders have received their shares.

restrictive covenants (p. 531) Additional provisions of a contractual obligation which are designed to protect the interests of the lenders.

retail company (p. 316) A company that simply purchases inventory and sells it for a price greater than its cost. Retailers provide primarily a distribution service, doing little to change or improve the product.

retained earnings (pp. 11, 48) The account on the right side of the balance sheet that represents the amount of the company's assets that have been generated through profitable operations and not paid out in the form of dividends.

retirement (p. 443) To discontinue the use of an asset or to buy back outstanding bonds.

revaluation adjustments (p. 206) Adjusting journal entries designed to bring the dollar amounts of certain accounts in line with the existing facts. Examples include bad debt estimates, adjustments due to bank reconciliations, revaluations of marketable securities and inventories to apply the lower-of-cost-or-market rule, and the accrual of contingent liabilities.

revenue recognition (p. 142) A principle of financial accounting stating that revenue cannot be recognized until the following four criteria have been met: (1) the earning process must be substantially complete, (2) the revenue must be objectively measurable, (3) the future cost associated with the sale must be estimatible, and (4) the cash collection must be assured.

revenues (p. 11) Asset inflows or liability reductions associated with the operating activities of a company. Examples include sales, fees earned, service revenues, interest income, and various book gains.

risk premium (p. 565) The return over and above the risk-free rate that reflects the level of risk associated with a debtor company. The risk-free rate plus the risk premium equals the required rate of return.

risk-free return (p. 565) The return associated with a riskless security (e.g., certificates of deposit and treasury notes).

S

sales (p. 49) A revenue associated with the sale of a good or product.

salvage value (p. 433) The value of a long-lived asset at retirement.

secured notes (p. 535) Formal promissory notes backed by assets (collateral) that are distributed to creditors in the event of default.

Securities and Exchange Commission (p. 22) The government body responsible for the information available on the public security markets. The Securities and Exchange Commission delegated the authority to set accounting standards to the accounting profession but still takes a very active role.

service revenue (p. 49) Revenues earned on services provided. *See* **fees earned**.

short-term investments (p. 43) Securities that are readily marketable and intended by management to be sold within a short period of time, usually less than one year.

short-term notes receivable (p. 286) Balance sheet assets that are backed by formal contracts and expected to provide assets in the current period.

solvency (pp. 11, 78, 689) The ability of a company to meet its cash obligations as they come due. The statement of cash flows and other solvency ratios are used to assess a company's solvency position.

South American model (p. 26) A system of financial accounting used primarily in South America. This system is oriented toward the needs of government planners, and its rules are imposed on virtually all entities.

specific identification (p. 324) A procedure used to value cost of goods sold and ending inventory that allocates actual costs to items sold and items remaining.

stable dollar assumption (p. 135) An assumption of financial accounting stating that the value of the monetary unit used to measure an entity's performance is stable across time and across entities.

standard audit report (p. 79) A report an auditor renders stating that the financial statements fairly reflect the financial position and operations of the company.

stated interest rate (p. 531) The annual rate of interest stated on the face of a formal promissory note or bond certificate. The stated interest rate times the face value determines the periodic interest payments.

statement of cash flows (p. 11) This financial statement traces the cash inflows and outflows of a company during a given period. It is divided into three areas of cash flow: operating activities, investment activities, and financing activities.

statement of retained earnings (p. 11) This financial statement reconciles the balance in the Retained Earnings account from one period to the next. The beginning balance in Retained Earnings, plus net income, less dividends is usually equal to the ending balance in Retained Earnings.

statement of stockholders' equity (p. 609) A financial statement normally included in the annual reports of major U.S. companies that explains the changes in the Stockholders' Equity accounts during an accounting period. Generally accepted accounting principles require that these changes be described somewhere in the annual report.

statements of financial accounting standards (p. 23) The official statements of the Financial Accounting Standards Board that govern external financial reporting.

stock dividend (pp. 603, 606) A dividend paid to a corporation's stockholders in the form of the corporation's stock.

stock market (p. 16) The markets where equity securities are publicly traded.

stock options (p. 602) Options to purchase equity securities at a fixed price over a specified time period.

stock split (p. 605) An action taken by a corporation's board of directors to divide the number of outstanding shares into a larger number of less valuable units.

stock split in the form of dividends (p. 606) A relatively large stock dividend; the number of outstanding shares are increased by 25 percent or more.

stockholders (p. 12) Individuals or entities that hold ownership interests (common stocks) in a corporation; often referred to as *shareholders*.

stockholders' equity (pp. 10, 47) The section of a corporate balance sheet that represents the stockholders' interests in the corporation. It consists primarily of contributed capital and retained earnings.

straight-line depreciation method (pp. 206, 435) A procedure for depreciating long-lived assets (or amortizing intangibles) that recognizes equal amounts of depreciation (or amortization) in each year of the asset's useful life. Straight-line is also used to amortize premiums and discounts on notes or bonds, if the results do not differ materially from those produced by the effective-interest method.

subsidiary (p. 369) A company with the majority of its outstanding stock owned by another company, called the *parent*.

subsidiary ledgers (p. 218) Ledgers that tie directly to control accounts and provide further breakdowns of the balances in those control accounts.

sum-of-the-years'-digits method (p. 436) A method of accelerated depreciation that is less extreme than the double-declining-balance method. Each period the depreciation base is multiplied by a ratio relating the remaining life to the sum of the life's digits.

T

T-account (p. 193) A useful way to think about the accounts contained in the ledger. Each account is in the form of a "T." The left side of the "T" represents the debit, while the right side represents the credit.

T-account analysis (p. 230) A mechanical process that involves examining the activity in a given T-account to acquire information that is not directly disclosed on the financial statements or footnotes.

take a bath (p. 98) An expression used to describe a company that chooses to record a large write-off in an unsuccessful year to improve reported net income in future years.

takeover (p. 590) A situation where another company, investor, or group of investors purchases enough of the outstanding stock to gain a controlling interest (50 percent or more of the voting stock) in the purchased company.

technical obsolescence (p. 433) The state of an asset when technical advances have rendered the asset's services no longer useful.

temporary accounts (p. 222) Financial statement accounts that are set to zero through the closing process at the end of each accounting period. Included are revenue, expense, and dividend accounts.

trade-in (p. 444) A transaction in which an old asset and usually cash are exchanged for a new asset.

trading securities (p. 358) Investments in readily marketable securities bought and held principally for the purpose of selling them in the near future to generate profit on short-term price changes.

transportation-in (p. 316) An income statement account indicating the freight costs of purchased inventory, also called *freight-in*.

treasury notes (p. 565) Obligations of the federal government that pay interest at a specified rate for a specified period of time, usually less than 6 months.

treasury stock (p. 590) Previously issued stock that has been repurchased by the issuing company and held in treasury. Treasury stock is often reissued at a later date.

U

unadjusted trial balance (p. 219) The list of accounts and end-of-period account balances copied from the ledger to the work sheet. Preparing the unadjusted trial balance represents the first step in completing the work sheet.

unearned revenues (p. 203) A liability account that reflects the receipt of an asset before the associated service has been performed. Also referred to as *Payments in Advance or Deferred Revenues*.

uniformity (p. 145) The extent to which all business entities use the same accounting methods.

unrealized gains and losses (p. 360) Gains and losses represented by price changes of held securities. These gains and losses have not been cashed in.

unrealized price changes (p. 361) Changes in the prices of securities that have not yet been sold. Unrealized price changes in trading securities are recognized in income; unrealized price changes in available-for-sale securities are recognized in the stockholders' equity section of the balance sheet.

unsecured bonds (p. 539) Bonds with no assets backing them.

unsecured notes (p. 535) Formal promissory notes that are not backed by collateral, also called *debentures*.

user orientation (p. 4) The perspective of managers that they need to know how to read, evaluate, and analyze financial statements.

usual transaction (p. 651) An operating transaction that reflects the normal and customary activities of a company.

V

valuation bases (p. 137) The values (e.g., historical cost, replacement cost, fair market value, present value) used to determine the dollar amount of an entity's assets and liabilities on the balance sheet.

W

warranty (p. 494) An agreement by which a seller promises to remove deficiencies in the quantity, quality, or performance of a product sold to a buyer.

window dress (pp. 263, 692) A phrase used to describe the activity of managers who use accounting methods or make operating decisions purely to make the financial statements appear more attractive to financial statement users.

work sheet (p. 218) A document used at the end of an accounting period to systematically transfer the balances in the ledger to the financial statements.

working capital (p. 260) Current assets less current liabilities.

COMPANY INDEX

TABLE 1

Future value of $1 (future amount of single sum)

Periods (n)	2%	3%	4%	5%	6%	7%	8%
1	1.02000	1.03000	1.04000	1.05000	1.06000	1.07000	1.08000
2	1.04040	1.06090	1.08160	1.10250	1.12360	1.14490	1.16640
3	1.06121	1.09273	1.12486	1.15763	1.19102	1.22504	1.25971
4	1.08243	1.12551	1.16986	1.21551	1.26248	1.31080	1.36049
5	1.10408	1.15927	1.21665	1.27628	1.33823	1.40255	1.46933
6	1.12616	1.19405	1.26532	1.34010	1.41852	1.50073	1.58687
7	1.14869	1.22987	1.31593	1.40710	1.50363	1.60578	1.71382
8	1.17166	1.26677	1.36857	1.47746	1.59385	1.71819	1.85093
9	1.19509	1.30477	1.42331	1.55133	1.68948	1.83846	1.99900
10	1.21899	1.34392	1.48024	1.62889	1.79085	1.96715	2.15892
11	1.24337	1.38423	1.53945	1.71034	1.89830	2.10485	2.33164
12	1.26824	1.42576	1.60103	1.79586	2.01220	2.25219	2.51817
15	1.34587	1.55797	1.80094	2.07893	2.39656	2.75903	3.17217
20	1.48595	1.80611	2.19112	2.65330	3.20714	3.86968	4.66096
30	1.81136	2.42726	3.24340	4.32194	5.74349	7.61226	10.06266
40	2.20804	3.26204	4.80102	7.03999	10.28572	14.97446	21.72452

Periods (n)	9%	10%	11%	12%	14%	15%
1	1.09000	1.10000	1.11000	1.12000	1.14000	1.15000
2	1.18810	1.21000	1.23210	1.25440	1.29960	1.32250
3	1.29503	1.33100	1.36763	1.40493	1.48154	1.52088
4	1.41158	1.46410	1.51807	1.57352	1.68896	1.74901
5	1.53862	1.61051	1.68506	1.76234	1.92541	2.01136
6	1.67710	1.77156	1.87041	1.97382	2.19497	2.31306
7	1.82804	1.94872	2.07616	2.21068	2.50227	2.66002
8	1.99256	2.14359	2.30454	2.47596	2.85259	3.05902
9	2.17189	2.35795	2.55804	2.77308	3.25195	3.51788
10	2.36736	2.59374	2.83942	3.10585	3.70722	4.04556
11	2.58043	2.85312	3.15176	3.47855	4.22623	4.65239
12	2.81266	3.13843	3.49845	3.89598	4.81790	5.35025
15	3.64248	4.17725	4.78459	5.47357	7.13794	8.13706
20	5.60441	6.72750	8.06231	9.64629	13.74349	16.36654
30	13.26768	17.44940	22.89230	29.95992	50.95016	66.21177
40	31.40942	45.25926	65.00087	93.05097	188.88351	267.86355

TABLE 2

Future value of an ordinary annuity of $1

Periods (n)	2%	3%	4%	5%	6%	7%	8%
1	1.00000	1.00000	1.00000	1.00000	1.00000	1.00000	1.00000
2	2.02000	2.03000	2.04000	2.05000	2.06000	2.07000	2.08000
3	3.06040	3.09090	3.12160	3.15250	3.18360	3.21490	3.24640
4	4.12161	4.18363	4.24646	4.31013	4.37462	4.43994	4.50611
5	5.20404	5.30914	5.41632	5.52563	5.63709	5.75074	5.86660
6	6.30812	6.46841	6.63298	6.80191	6.97532	7.15329	7.33593
7	7.43428	7.66246	7.89829	8.14201	8.39384	8.65402	8.92280
8	8.58297	8.89234	9.21423	9.54911	9.89747	10.25980	10.63663
9	9.75463	10.15911	10.58280	11.02656	11.49132	11.97799	12.48756
10	10.94972	11.46388	12.00611	12.57789	13.18079	13.81645	14.48656
11	12.16872	12.80780	13.48635	14.20679	14.97164	15.78360	16.64549
12	13.41209	14.19203	15.02581	15.91713	16.86994	17.88845	18.97713
15	17.29342	18.59891	20.02359	21.57856	23.27597	25.12902	27.15211
20	24.29737	26.87037	29.77808	33.06595	36.78559	40.99549	45.76196
30	40.56808	47.57542	56.08494	66.43885	79.05819	94.46079	113.28321
40	60.40198	75.40126	95.02552	120.79977	154.76197	199.63511	259.05652

Periods (n)	9%	10%	11%	12%	14%	15%
1	1.00000	1.00000	1.00000	1.00000	1.00000	1.00000
2	2.09000	2.10000	2.11000	2.12000	2.14000	2.15000
3	3.27810	3.31000	3.34210	3.37440	3.43960	3.47250
4	4.57313	4.64100	4.70973	4.77933	4.92114	4.99338
5	5.98471	6.10510	6.22780	6.35285	6.61010	6.74238
6	7.52333	7.71561	7.91286	8.11519	8.53552	8.75374
7	9.20043	9.48717	9.78327	10.08901	10.73049	11.06680
8	11.02847	11.43589	11.85943	12.29969	13.23276	13.72682
9	13.02104	13.57948	14.16397	14.77566	16.08535	16.78584
10	15.19293	15.93742	16.72201	17.54874	19.33730	20.30372
11	17.56029	18.53117	19.56143	20.65458	23.04452	24.34928
12	20.14072	21.38428	22.71319	24.13313	27.27075	29.00167
15	29.36092	31.77248	34.40536	37.27971	43.84241	47.58041
20	51.16012	57.27500	64.20283	72.05244	91.02493	102.44358
30	136.30754	164.49402	199.02088	241.33268	356.78685	434.74515
40	337.88245	442.59256	581.82607	767.09142	1342.02510	1779.09031

TABLE 3
Future value of an annuity due of $1

Periods (n)	2%	3%	4%	5%	6%	7%	8%
1	1.02000	1.03000	1.04000	1.05000	1.06000	1.07000	1.08000
2	2.06040	2.09090	2.12160	2.15250	2.18360	2.21490	2.24640
3	3.12161	3.18363	3.24646	3.31013	3.37462	3.43994	3.50611
4	4.20404	4.30914	4.41632	4.52563	4.63709	4.75074	4.86660
5	5.30812	5.46841	5.63298	5.80191	5.97532	6.15329	6.33593
6	6.43428	6.66246	6.89829	7.14201	7.39384	7.65402	7.92280
7	7.58297	7.89234	8.21423	8.54911	8.89747	9.25980	9.63663
8	8.75463	9.15911	9.58280	10.02656	10.49132	10.97799	11.48756
9	9.94972	10.46388	11.00611	11.57789	12.18079	12.81645	13.48656
10	11.16872	11.80780	12.48635	13.20679	13.97164	14.78360	15.64549
11	12.41209	13.19203	14.02581	14.91713	15.86994	16.88845	17.97713
12	13.68033	14.61779	15.62684	16.71298	17.88214	19.14064	20.49530
15	17.63929	19.15688	20.82453	22.65749	24.67253	26.88805	29.32428
20	24.78332	27.67649	30.96920	34.71925	38.99273	43.86518	49.42292
30	41.37944	49.00268	58.32834	69.76079	83.80168	101.07304	122.34587
40	61.61002	77.66330	98.82654	126.83976	164.04768	213.60957	279.78104

Periods (n)	9%	10%	11%	12%	14%	15%
1	1.09000	1.10000	1.11000	1.12000	1.14000	1.15000
2	2.27810	2.31000	2.34210	2.37440	2.43960	2.47250
3	3.57313	3.64100	3.70973	3.77933	3.92114	3.99338
4	4.98471	5.10510	5.22780	5.35285	5.61010	5.74238
5	6.52333	6.71561	6.91286	7.11519	7.53552	7.75374
6	8.20043	8.48717	8.78327	9.08901	9.73049	10.06680
7	10.02847	10.43589	10.85943	11.29969	12.23276	12.72682
8	12.02104	12.57948	13.16397	13.77566	15.08535	15.78584
9	14.19293	14.93742	15.72201	16.54874	18.33730	19.30372
10	16.56029	17.53117	18.56143	19.65458	22.04452	23.34928
11	19.14072	20.38428	21.71319	23.13313	26.27075	28.00167
12	21.95338	23.52271	25.21164	27.02911	31.08865	33.35192
15	32.00340	34.94973	38.18995	41.75328	49.98035	54.71747
20	55.76453	63.00250	71.26514	80.69874	103.76842	117.81012
30	148.57522	180.94342	220.91317	270.29261	406.73701	499.95692
40	368.29187	486.85181	645.82693	859.14239	1529.90861	2045.95385

*always me Hrs.s Table
Now-intest*

TABLE 4

Present value of $1 (present value of a single sum)   *pery acfs.*

Periods (n)	2%	3%	4%	5%	6%	7%	8%
1	0.98039	0.97087	0.96154	0.95238	0.94340	0.93458	0.92593
2	0.96177	0.94260	0.92456	0.90703	0.89000	0.87344	0.85734
3	0.94232	0.91514	0.88900	0.86384	0.83962	0.81630	0.79383
4	0.92385	0.88849	0.85480	0.82270	0.79209	0.76290	0.73503
5	0.90573	0.86261	0.82193	0.78353	0.74726	0.71299	0.68058
6	0.88797	0.83748	0.79031	0.74622	0.70496	0.66634	0.63017
7	0.87056	0.81309	0.75992	0.71068	0.66506	0.62275	0.58349
8	0.85349	0.78941	0.73069	0.67684	0.62741	0.58201	0.54027
9	0.83676	0.76642	0.70259	0.64461	0.59190	0.54393	0.50025
10	0.82035	0.74409	0.67556	0.61391	0.55839	0.50835	0.46319
11	0.80426	0.72242	0.64958	0.58468	0.52679	0.47509	0.42888
12	0.78849	0.70138	0.62460	0.55684	0.49697	0.44401	0.39711
15	0.74301	0.64186	0.55526	0.48102	0.41727	0.36245	0.31524
20	0.67297	0.55368	0.45639	0.37689	0.31180	0.25842	0.21455
30	0.55207	0.41199	0.30832	0.23138	0.17411	0.13137	0.09938
40	0.45289	0.30656	0.20829	0.14205	0.09722	0.06678	0.04603
50	0.37153	0.22811	0.14071	0.08720	0.05429	0.03395	0.02132
60	0.30478	0.16973	0.09506	0.05354	0.03031	0.01726	0.00988

Periods (n)	9%	10%	11%	12%	14%	15%
1	0.91743	0.90909	0.90090	0.89286	0.87719	0.86957
2	0.84168	0.82645	0.81162	0.79719	0.76947	0.75614
3	0.77218	0.75131	0.73119	0.71178	0.67497	0.65752
4	0.70843	0.68301	0.65873	0.63552	0.59208	0.57175
5	0.64993	0.62092	0.59345	0.56743	0.51937	0.49718
6	0.59627	0.56447	0.53464	0.50663	0.45559	0.43233
7	0.54703	0.51316	0.48166	0.45235	0.39964	0.37594
8	0.50187	0.46651	0.43393	0.40388	0.35056	0.32690
9	0.46043	0.42410	0.39092	0.36061	0.30751	0.28426
10	0.42241	0.38554	0.35218	0.32197	0.26974	0.24718
11	0.38753	0.35049	0.31728	0.28748	0.23662	0.21494
12	0.35553	0.31863	0.28584	0.25668	0.20756	0.18691
15	0.27454	0.23939	0.20900	0.18270	0.14010	0.12289
20	0.17843	0.14864	0.12403	0.10367	0.07276	0.06110
30	0.07537	0.05731	0.04368	0.03338	0.01963	0.01510
40	0.03184	0.02209	0.01538	0.01075	0.00529	0.00373
50	0.01345	0.00852	0.00542	0.00346	0.00143	0.00092
60	0.00568	0.00328	0.00191	0.00111	0.00039	0.00023

end Period

alway use This table for bonds

TABLE 5

Present value of an ordinary annuity of $1

Periods (n)	2%	3%	4%	5%	6%	7%	8%
1	0.98039	0.97087	0.96154	0.95238	0.94340	0.93458	0.92593
2	1.94156	1.91347	1.88609	1.85941	1.83339	1.80802	1.78326
3	2.88388	2.82861	2.77509	2.72325	2.67301	2.62432	2.57710
4	3.80773	3.71710	3.62990	3.54595	3.46511	3.38721	3.31213
5	4.71346	4.57971	4.45182	4.32948	4.21236	4.10020	3.99271
6	5.60143	5.41719	5.24214	5.07569	4.91732	4.76654	4.62288
7	6.47199	6.23028	6.00205	5.78637	5.58238	5.38929	5.20637
8	7.32548	7.01969	6.73274	6.46321	6.20979	5.97130	5.74664
9	8.16224	7.78611	7.43533	7.10782	6.80169	6.51523	6.24689
10	8.98259	8.53020	8.11090	7.72173	7.36009	7.02358	6.71008
11	9.78685	9.25262	8.76048	8.30641	7.88687	7.49867	7.13896
12	10.57534	9.95400	9.38507	8.86325	8.38384	7.94269	7.53608
15	12.84926	11.93794	11.11839	10.37966	9.71225	9.10791	8.55948
20	16.35143	14.87747	13.59033	12.46221	11.46992	10.59401	9.81815
30	22.39646	19.60044	17.29203	15.37245	13.76483	12.40904	11.25778
40	27.35548	23.11477	19.79277	17.15909	15.04630	13.33171	11.92461
50	31.42361	25.72976	21.48218	18.25593	15.76186	13.80075	12.23348
60	34.76089	27.67556	22.62349	18.92929	16.16143	14.03918	12.37655

Periods (n)	9%	10%	11%	12%	14%	15%
1	0.91743	0.90909	0.90090	0.89286	0.87719	0.86957
2	1.75911	1.73554	1.71252	1.69005	1.64666	1.62571
3	2.53129	2.48685	2.44371	2.40183	2.32163	2.28323
4	3.23972	3.16987	3.10245	3.03735	2.91371	2.85498
5	3.88965	3.79079	3.69590	3.60478	3.43308	3.35216
6	4.48592	4.35526	4.23054	4.11141	3.88867	3.78448
7	5.03295	4.86842	4.71220	4.56376	4.28830	4.16042
8	5.53482	5.33493	5.14612	4.96764	4.63886	4.48732
9	5.99525	5.75902	5.53705	5.32825	4.94637	4.77158
10	6.41766	6.14457	5.88923	5.65022	5.21612	5.01877
11	6.80519	6.49506	6.20652	5.93770	5.45273	5.23371
12	7.16073	6.81369	6.49236	6.19437	5.66029	5.42062
15	8.06069	7.60608	7.19087	6.81086	6.14217	5.84737
20	9.12855	8.51356	7.96333	7.46944	6.62313	6.25933
30	10.27365	9.42691	8.69379	8.05518	7.00266	6.56598
40	10.75736	9.77905	8.95105	8.24378	7.10504	6.64178
50	10.96168	9.91481	9.04165	8.30450	7.13266	6.66051
60	11.04799	9.96716	9.07356	8.32405	7.14011	6.66515

beg'n period

TABLE 6

Present value of an annuity due of $1

Periods (n)	2%	3%	4%	5%	6%	7%	8%
1	1.00000	1.00000	1.00000	1.00000	1.00000	1.00000	1.00000
2	1.98039	1.97087	1.96154	1.95238	1.94340	1.93458	1.92593
3	2.94156	2.91347	2.88609	2.85941	2.83339	2.80802	2.78326
4	3.88388	3.82861	3.77509	3.72325	3.67301	3.62432	3.57710
5	4.80773	4.71710	4.62990	4.54595	4.46511	4.38721	4.31213
6	5.71346	5.57971	5.45182	5.32948	5.21236	5.10020	4.99271
7	6.60143	6.41719	6.24214	6.07569	5.91732	5.76654	5.62288
8	7.47199	7.23028	7.00205	6.78637	6.58238	6.38929	6.20637
9	8.32548	8.01969	7.73274	7.46321	7.20979	6.97130	6.74664
10	9.16224	8.78611	8.43533	8.10782	7.80169	7.51523	7.24689
11	9.98259	9.53020	9.11090	8.72173	8.36009	8.02358	7.71008
12	10.78685	10.25262	9.76048	9.30641	8.88687	8.49867	8.13896
15	13.10625	12.29607	11.56312	10.89864	10.29498	9.74547	9.24424
20	16.67846	15.32380	14.13394	13.08532	12.15812	11.33560	10.60360
30	22.84438	20.18845	17.98371	16.14107	14.59072	13.27767	12.15841
40	27.90259	23.80822	20.58448	18.01704	19.94907	14.26493	12.87858
50	32.05208	26.50166	22.34147	19.16872	16.70757	14.76680	13.21216
60	35.45610	28.50583	23.52843	19.87575	17.13111	15.02192	13.36668

Periods (n)	9%	10%	11%	12%	14%	15%
1	1.00000	1.00000	1.00000	1.00000	1.00000	1.00000
2	1.91743	1.90909	1.90090	1.89286	1.87719	1.86957
3	2.75911	2.73554	2.71252	2.69005	2.64666	2.62571
4	3.53129	3.48685	3.44371	3.40183	3.32163	3.28323
5	4.23972	4.16987	4.10245	4.03735	3.91371	3.85498
6	4.88965	4.79079	4.69590	4.60478	4.43308	4.35216
7	5.48592	5.35526	5.23054	5.11141	4.88867	4.78448
8	6.03295	5.86842	5.71220	5.56376	5.28830	5.16042
9	6.53482	6.33493	6.14612	5.96764	5.63886	5.48732
10	6.99525	6.75902	6.53705	6.32825	5.94637	5.77158
11	7.41766	7.14457	6.88923	6.65022	6.21612	6.01877
12	7.80519	7.49506	7.20652	6.93770	6.45273	6.23371
15	8.78615	8.36669	7.98187	7.62817	7.00207	6.72448
20	9.95011	9.36492	8.83929	8.36578	7.55037	7.19823
30	11.19828	10.36961	9.65011	9.02181	7.98304	7.55088
40	11.72552	10.75696	9.93567	9.23303	8.09975	7.63805
50	11.94823	10.90630	10.03624	0.30104	8.13123	7.65959
60	12.04231	10.96387	10.07165	9.32294	8.13972	7.66492